BRITISH HIT SINGLES

10th EDITION

Paul Gambaccini

Tim Rice

Jonathan Rice

Editorial Associate:

Tony Brown

GUINNESS PUBLISHING

acknowledgments

The three authors would like to thank **Alan Jones**, **Graham Walker**, **Simon Harper**, **Anne Forey**, **John Kutner, Alex Rice** and **Mathew Bedford** for their contributions to this edition.

Special thanks, too, to **Eileen Heinink** and **Jan Rice**. We also want to thank **New Musical Express** and **CIN** for their charts, **Redferns**, **LFI**, **Popperfoto** and **Pictorial Press** for their photographs, and the many record company press offices for their patient help.

© GRR PUBLICATIONS LTD 1995

First edition 1977. Second edition 1979. Third edition 1981. Fourth edition 1983. Fifth edition 1985. Sixth edition 1987. Seventh edition 1989. Eighth edition 1991. Ninth edition 1993.
Reprint 10 9 8 7 6 5 4 3 2 1

Published in Great Britain by Guinness Publishing Ltd., 33 London Road, Enfield, Middlesex.

Printed and bound in Great Britain by The Bath Press.

'Guinness' is a registered trade mark of Guinness Publishing Ltd.

The right of Paul Gambaccini, Tim Rice and Jonathan Rice to be identified as Authors of this Work has been asserted in accordance with the Copyright, Designs & Patents Act 1989.

EDITOR: **David Roberts**

DEPUTY EDITOR: **Hal Norman**

PAGE MAKE-UP AND TYPESETTING: **Alex Reid, Sallie Collins and Helen Rodger.**

DESIGN: **Ad Vantage**, London

COVER DESIGN: **Electric Echo**

A catalogue record for this book is available from The British Library.
ISBN 0-85112-633-2

C o n t e n t s

All statistics and information cover the period 14 November 1952 to
31 December 1994, and are as follows:

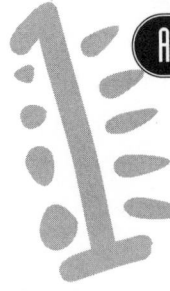

ALPHABETICALLY BY ARTIST

Chart acts listed alphabetically with chronological title list showing date
disc first hit the chart, title, label, catalogue number, highest position
reached and number of weeks on chart. Top Ten placings and number
ones are highlighted.

ALPHABETICALLY BY TITLE

Hits listed alphabetically by title, with artists' names and year of initial
chart entry. Different versions of the same song and different songs
with the same title are indicated.

FACTS AND FEATS

All you need to know and more about the record charts record
breakers including

Most Weeks On Chart

Most Top Ten Hits

Longest Gap Between Chart Hits

Top Twenty Acts Of All Time

A League Table Of Football Hits

Least Successful Chart Acts

The Number One Hits

Eurovision Statistics

Song Title Geography

Tom Sawyer, Mark Twain's immortal Mississippi River rascal, had the unique pleasure of attending his own funeral while still alive and hearing loved ones who believed him deceased deliver eulogies. Twain himself was prematurely said to have passed on, leading him to utter his famous words 'The reports of my death have been greatly exaggerated'.

So it has proved with the single record in Britain, declared dead or dying in the early 1990s but rising from its sick bed by mid-decade. Annual sales which had slid from 59 million in 1990 to 56 million the following year fell a further three million in 1992. It was all over bar the burial: the format was declared dead on TV and in the pages of publications from Wapping and Fleet Street. We heard how we had loved the Beatles in the 1960s, got down to disco in the 1970s, rode a new wave of British talent in the 1980s, and then suddenly decided en masse to chuck it all in for albums and computer games.

In 1993 something unexpected happened. The corpse quivered. Sales actually went up three million. The following year, the single got up and walked, with figures rising an additional eight per cent. It turned out it wasn't dead at all. It was just pining for the fjords. The single as a form of delivering music hadn't died. It was seven-inch vinyl that had passed into history. The media confused the two.

In 1993-94, one inevitable thing and two unpredictable developments coincided to the benefit of the single. The first was that the British public continued to adapt to new technology. This specifically meant proceeding with the transition from vinyl record players to compact disk systems. By the end of 1994 it was estimated that 40% of the nation had CD players. Considering that the music industry had recently been promoting discs that could be played by less than half the population, it was no wonder sales had fallen.

What could not have been predicted was that there would be both a period of economic recovery and the emergence of a new generation of hit-makers. Although the "feel good" factor failed to appear in the general public, retail sales rose, and singles shared in the action. A few years ago, we complained when the record business on both sides of the Atlantic dropped the sales requirement for gold and platinum certification. The industry felt that since sales were dropping, standards had to be lowered to create the illusion of achievement. We opined that the business was mistaking changes in musical styles and a shift in delivery, from vinyl to compact disc and cassette, for a reduction in public interest. We predicted that a rash of metallic awards would follow, many to discs that would have qualified under the old rules. The prophecy became reality in 1994. Two singles sailed past the old platinum standard of a million sales for the first time since 1984 and a third approached it.

Many of the artists who benefited from the upsurge in buying were new to the charts. Among the hundreds of acts who appear for the first time in our pages are several who have already accumulated a few sizable hits, ranging from Eternal to Oasis.

Take That and East 17, who made their first visits to the top ten in 1992, consolidated their success in 1993 and 1994, as our summaries of those two years (see pages **8** and **9**) indicate. They were the leading acts in a proliferation of boy bands. By the end of 1994, this type of group was the one most frequently achieving multiple hits. Dance was still the genre of music that produced more substantial hits than any other, but none of the many popular styles of dance music overwhelmed the others.

Since Dance is the variety of music with the quickest turnover of hits, with popular titles rotating at the head of its chart with dizzying speed, it should come as no surprise to hear that the British singles list itself is in a phase of rapid movement. In no two-year period has there been as high a number of entries in the top 75 as in 1993-94.

Conversely, since the American charts contain an airplay factor that effectively discriminates against dance discs, this type of music is not dominating the US lists, and chart movement is at its slowest since the late 1970s. Indeed, during this past two-year period Boyz II Men rewrote the history books again. In 1992 they had passed the record 11 weeks at number

one by Elvis Presley's double-sided 'Don't Be Cruel/Hound Dog' with their 13-week winner 'End Of The Road', only to be almost immediately overtaken themselves by Whitney Houston's 14-week wonder 'I Will Always Love You'. The Motown quartet equalled Whitney's mark in 1994 with 'I'll Make Love To You' and then became the first act since the Beatles to succeed themselves at the top with 'On Bended Knee', in so doing tying Presley's record of 16 weeks with consecutive number ones.

These records of longevity merely show that the

BLUR won the BRIT award for Best Single of 1994, 'Parklife'.

American pop chart is now a logjam. When major forms of best-selling music are excluded because they are not getting airplay the songs that do get played will linger on the list. In the introduction to our previous edition, we reported on the pressure building up within the British music industry to include an airplay factor in the UK chart. This interest collapsed almost completely with the calamitous dive in the listening figures of BBC Radio 1 FM. However, activity on the fringes shows that the concept was not dead, just set back by the slaughter in Broadcasting House. The Network Chart, set up for a group of local commercial radio stations, included an airplay factor in numbers 11 to 40, maintaining only the top ten in strict sales terms. In January 1995 the *Billboard* group launched a new publication, *Music Monitor*, that included a Hot 100 amalgamating airplay information from Broadcast Data Systems and retail sales from Gallup. With the emergence of newly-established acts mentioned above, and the presence of several mass-appeal big sellers, the official chart slowed down in 1994 in comparison to 1993. The mooted airplay factor, legendary before it even arrives, would inhibit movement even more.

It is wonderful to be able to report that each of America's top ten singles of 1994 was a top ten hit at some point in the year in Britain. It is not so wonderful to report that the reverse is not true. Because the airplay factor required the very biggest US hits to be true mass-audience favourites, they travelled the Atlantic safely. With no such screening process needed to score in the sales-based UK chart, many top titles sank off Land's End. 1994 was the worst year for British music in the US singles chart in memory. Only one and two-third British hits featured in the year-end American top 50, and they were both film songs by veteran stars, 'All For Love' by Bryan Adams (of Canada), Rod Stewart and Sting from *The Three Musketeers* and 'Can You Feel The Love Tonight' by Elton John from *The Lion King*. The Swedish group Ace Of Base did better than the entire British nation. Even more shockingly, only one British artist achieved a debut entry in the US top 20 in the entire year. The lone pioneer was Des'ree.

This does not merely go to prove that new native talent is not exporting to America. After all, with maturation, at least a few of the mid-1990s British stars will inevitably become late-

Left: 'All That She Wants' from **Ace Of Base** and, below: **Des'ree**'s lone British debut success in the USA.

1990s American favourites. But the above paragraph does say a great deal about the localising of success. Entire forms of US music are not making it in the UK. Gangsta rap and country appeal only to greatly-reduced segments of the population. So do the anatomically graphic r&b and dance hits that have recently been enormous American successes.

One consequence of this is that the music industry has started to measure export success in terms of achievement in European or Australasian countries. But even here there are more local hit-makers than one might have predicted ten years ago. America and Britain, which so dominated the international pop scene after the historic breakthroughs of Elvis Presley and the Beatles, were complacent in assuming that they would automatically not only maintain but also build on their world market share. In fact, the growth of the record business made it financially viable for other countries to develop their own industries, and the burgeoning electronic media allowed local talent to get exposure. The staggering consequence is that, using traditional criteria, there has been no world pop star to emerge since the mid-1980s. Mariah Carey has come close, but by the end of 1994 she was still primarily a disc-seller and had not yet become a major live attraction or show business personality. Since there can never be ten years of nothing - something, after all, must have happened - we must conclude that the old model of stardom has gone the way of vinyl. It may return one day in an evolved form, but for now the likes of Take That and East 17 must be content with tremendous success in their home country and only considerable popularity in several other nations, rather than world domination. After all, few readers of this book are aware of the feats of Luis Miguel, Mr. Children or Eric Moo, but this has not stopped these artists from becoming major stars in other parts of the globe. At the end of 1994, Marco Borsato, Cabballero and Ice MC were number one in certain European countries, though they mean little here. Nothing unites these artists except the fact that they are all stars somewhere in the increasingly fragmented world of popular music.

As we proudly publish our tenth edition, ever grateful for your continued support, we contemplate the changes that have occurred since our first book. Although mass-appeal ballads are always popular, from 'Mull Of Kintyre' to 'Love Is All Around', fashions come and go. Yesterday's punk is today's raver, and tomorrow he or she will be following another fad. The format of preference has changed from seven-inch vinyl to compact disc. Major stars release singles not on a regular basis but as promotions for their occasional albums, leaving a large percentage of the singles chart open for fresh artists producing new music. Technological innovation has made it possible to make records not only in a studio but in a bedroom. New generations of independent labels thriving on the music of the moment have emerged to annoy the majors. More countries have become credible sources of hit music. Stardom is ever more fleeting and localised.

All these factors conspire to make unprecedented demands on our time. We must now stop writing and resume listening. More hits by more artists from more countries leaves little time to loaf. Reports of the death of the single were greatly exaggerated.

Paul Gambaccini • Tim Rice • Jonathan Rice

New constellations of stars formed in 1993. After 1992, in which no artist had more than one of the top 30 hits of the year nor as many as 40 weeks on the chart, chartologists who believe that major acts help make a strong scene were relieved to see one group with three in the 30 best-sellers and a trio of names with at least 40 weeks on chart.

Take That were the darlings of the year, whether measured in space occupied on bedroom walls or at the heights of the chart. Three consecutive releases came straight in at number one, shattering Slade's 20-year record of two in a row. These hits, 'Pray', 'Relight My Fire' and 'Babe', all figured in the top 30 of the year. Two further top ten titles were included in the annual top 100 to give the quintet the most entries in both lists. The Manchester band was unquestionably the group of the year.

The female vocalist of 1993 was Whitney Houston, whose 'I Will Always Love You' spent the first six weeks of the year at number one to complete a run of ten, surpassing Doris Day's nine-week wonder from 1954, 'Secret Love', to become the longest running chart-topper by a woman. Indeed, the smash from the film *The Bodyguard* now ranked joint fifth in the all-time longest running number ones. Whitney added two more top ten hits from the movie to total 50 weeks on chart, leading that list as well. Other female stars of note during the year included Gabrielle, who had a mighty number one

I'D DO ANYTHING FOR LOVE
(BUT I WON'T DO THAT)

in 'Dreams', Dina Carroll, who achieved two top five singles, Lisa Stansfield and Sybil. The last three appeared in the ten acts with most weeks on chart.

Michael Jackson, who had been top of that table in 1992, was one of only two artists to reappear in the 1993 equivalent, Take That being the other. Jackson notched up 30 weeks as he concluded his sequence of singles from *Dangerous*. The male vocalist of the year, however, had to be Meat Loaf, who biked back from chart oblivion to score the number one of the year, 'I'd Do Anything For Love (But I Won't Do That)'. On the album side, Loaf had long been legend, but he had only previously achieved one top ten single, and even that had been a duet with an uncredited Cher. During the last weeks of 1993 his new Jim Steinman song and production motored past the year's other top sellers: '(I Can't Help) Falling In Love With You' by UB40, 'All That She Wants' by Ace Of Base and 'No Limit' by 2 Unlimited.

Each of these major hits was of significance. UB40 were enjoying their third number one, but this otherwise self-contained group again required a cover version to go all the way. The Ace Of Base debut began a string of successes that quickly established them as the third major act to emerge from Sweden, following Abba and Roxette. The number one by 2 Unlimited, who had lived up to their name by peaking at two with their first two hits, helped them to amass 40 weeks on chart during the year and marked a major advance for Continental dance music.

Several unusual distinctions deserved notice. Freddie Mercury achieved a posthumous number one with 'Living On My Own' while George Michael and Queen outpaced the pack with the 'Five Live' EP, spotlighting Mercury's composition 'Somebody To Love'. Adding the re-issued 'Bohemian Rhapsody' from 1991-92 gave Freddie posthumous number ones as a soloist, group member and songwriter, an unprecedented after life tribute. Chaka Demus and Pliers had three top five hits, their 'Twist And Shout' becoming the first version of that standard to reach number one. Elton John and Kiki Dee released their first hit duet in 17 years, the Bluebells had a number one long after they had split, and Mr. Blobby became the first non-human to have a Christmas number one.

DINA CARROLL
DON'T BE A STRANGER

The chart was all Wet in 1994. 'Love Is All Around' by Wet Wet Wet came, saw, conquered, and stayed, drenching the chart for 15 weeks at number one. This was the second longest consecutive stay at number one, missing by one week the mark set by Bryan Adams' 1991 smash '(Everything I Do) I Do It For You'. As with that song from *Robin Hood: Prince Of Thieves*, 'Love Is All Around' was from a hit film, in this case *Four Weddings And A Funeral*, and was not available on one of the artist's own albums. Just as with the Bryan Adams, many buyers confronted with the option of purchasing the soundtrack album or the single made the less expensive choice. There can hardly be better evidence that the current record company vogue for taking singles by major artists from already-released albums is restraining sales on these discs. Given a fine fresh single, the public responds with enthusiasm.

This was dramatically proven by the best-sellers of 1994. The top two both passed the one million mark, the first time a brace of singles had done so since 1984. The number two was 'Saturday Night' by the Continental songstress Whigfield. This favourite of summer holiday-makers was given a delayed release, building demand to such an extent that in its first week out it soared to number one. This was extremely inconvenient for Wet Wet Wet, who had gone through an elaborate public relations job convincing the nation that 'Love Is All Around' would soon be deleted, presumably to encourage people to buy the disc at once and keep it on top for a record-tying 16th straight week. Sales did increase, but 'Saturday Night' leapfrogged over it to become the first debut hit by any artist to enter the chart at number one. Deleted though it may have been, sales of back stock kept 'Love Is All Around' on the chart until the end of

the year. It had a final 1994 total of 33 weeks and was still in the top 75 in early 1995.

The year's third best-seller was the Christmas number one, 'Stay Another Day' by East 17, which overtook 'Baby Come Back' by Pato Banton and 'I Swear' by All-4-One in cumulative sales in 1994's final week. The massive seller by the Walthamstow lads came from the LP *Steam*, which had underperformed until the holiday hit propelled it to new heights on the album side. Both 'Stay Another Day' and 'I Swear' were

examples of the genre that most often produces major hits, the mass-appeal ballad. 'I Swear' had in fact originally been a country chart-topper for John Michael Montgomery. All-4-One found themselves soaked by Wet Wet Wet, held at number two for a record-breaking seven weeks.

The Pato Banton success was a cover of the 1968 number one by the Equals and featured Robin and Ali Campbell of UB40. As such it shared the latter group's unbroken string of only getting to number one with revivals. Unlikely cover hits typified the year. 'Baby Come Back' and 'I Swear' were joined in the year end top thirty by Boyzone's version of the Osmonds' 1974 number one 'Love Me For A Reason', the B-52's recording of the television-cum-movie theme '(Meet) The Flintstones' as the BC-52s, and Big Mountain giving Peter Frampton's 'Baby I Love Your Way' a reggae treatment. In addition, Mariah Carey and Luther Vandross, who had never previously shown 'Endless Love' for each other, enjoyed a substantial hit with their recreation of the 1981 Diana Ross and Lionel Richie duet. With two solo hits in the 1994 top 30, including her revival of Nilsson's 1972 number one 'Without You', and with more weeks on chart than any other artist, 45, Carey was the year's top female vocalist. It would be difficult to identify a top male artist, since unusually few of the year's noteworthy titles were by solo men. Pato Banton did have the best-selling disc by an individual male, but one should also mention that Bruce Springsteen had his biggest hit single with the Oscar-winning 'Streets Of Philadelphia' and Elton John had the most weeks on chart by a male artist.

'Things Can Only Get Better', sang D:Ream in one of the year's number ones, and they also got stranger. Three number ones that had grown ever less likely with the passage of time finally occurred. A football team that was not a World Cup Squad finally got to number one in the form of Manchester United's 'Come On You Reds'. The charleston, a popular dance of the 1920s, finally had a number one evocation in Doop's eponymous hit, the first basically instrumental chart-topper in 21 years. Prince, who had registered over three dozen hits without heading the class, finally got a number one, but not as Prince. By the time 'The Most Beautiful Girl In The World' was issued he wished to be known as ⚥.

It had taken him 14 years to get his number one, but this time period was but a moment for Louis Armstrong, who posthumously enjoyed a top three hit with his re-issued James Bond theme 'We Have All The Time In The World'. Satchmo was the only artist on the chart in its first year, 1952, to be there again in 1994, but this staggering hit-making career of 42 years is further extended if one considers his first American hit in 1926.

THE CHARTS

n compiling this book, we have used the charts published by the *New Musical Express* from the date of their first chart, which was the first UK record sales chart, for the week ending 14 November 1952. We continue to use the *NME* chart, as the longest established and most complete chart available, until the appearance of the first UK top 50 in what was then called the *Record Retailer* (now *Music Week*), on 10 March 1960.

It is possible to argue that the *Record Retailer* chart in the first few years of its existence was not the most widely accepted chart, and we often receive angry letters from people wondering why, for example 'Please Please Me' by the Beatles or 'Are You Sure' by the Allisons are not listed as number ones, because they were on other charts. However, the *Record Retailer* was always the fullest chart, and it was always the one compiled and supported by the industry, and was certainly no less accurate than any other available chart. By the mid-1960s, it was accepted as the national chart of record, something which no other chart since the earliest days of the *NME* chart could claim.

The size of the chart has varied over the years:

1 4   N O V   5 2
First ever chart, a 'Top 12' containing 15 hits!

1   O C T   5 4
Chart becomes a Top 20

3 0   D E C   5 5
Top 25 published, for this week only

1 3   A P R   5 6
Chart becomes a Top 30

2 6   F E B   6 0
Last *NME* Top 30 used by *British Hit Singles*

1 0   M A R   6 0
Record Retailer chart inaugurated. This is a publication date, the chart date being week ending 5 March

3   J A N   6 3
Top 50 now independently audited

1 3   F E B   6 9
Top 50 now 'compiled for Record Retailer and the BBC by British Market Research Bureau'

6   F E B   7 1
Top 40 only, for seven weeks as postal strikes limit the collection of chart sales information

2 7   M A R   7 1
Top 50 resumes

6   J A N   7 3
Top 30 only, for one week

2 2   D E C   7 3
Top 30 only, for one week

6   M A Y   7 8
Top 75 begins

8   J A N   8 3
Chart compilation taken over by Gallup

1 2   F E B   9 4
Chart compilation taken over by Millward Brown. Charts are now '© CIN, produced in co-operation with the BPI and BARD, based on a sample of more than 1,000 record outlets, incorporating 7 inch, 12 inch, cassette and CD single sales'

Occasionally a week went by with no chart being compiled (this often happened at Christmas in the early years of the chart). In these cases, the previous week's charts has been used again. If ever a chart was compiled but not published, or if a chart was published incorrectly, the correct chart has been found and used in the compilation of *British Hit Singles*.

I n this first section of *The Guinness Book of British Hit Singles,* we list every record that has hit the UK singles chart from 14 November 1952 to the final chart of 1994. The information is presented alphabetically by artist, and then chronologically for each artist. Each hit single is catalogued with the following information: *date disc first hit the chart, title of hit, label and catalogue number, highest position the hit reached on the chart, total number of weeks spent on the chart.*

Records which were not hits are not listed. A record is a hit if it appears in the charts, even for just one week at number 75, the lowest position listed.

It should be noted that the date given for the entry of a disc into the chart is the week ending date, which is the way charts have historically been dated. In other words, Abba's 'Waterloo' entered the chart in the week ending 20 April 1974, which means that their first day of chart action was actually 14 April 1974.

Number one records are highlighted with a star, other top ten records by a dot. A dagger indicates hits still on the chart at the end of 1994, as follows:

★ **NUMBER ONE SINGLE**

● **TOP TEN SINGLE**

† **SINGLE STILL ON CHART AT 31 DECEMBER 1994**

For the purposes of this book, a record is considered a re-issue if it hits the chart for a second time with a new catalogue number. Otherwise, the reappearance of any record is considered a mere re-entry.

MARIAH CAREY

In this edition once again we have credited hits in combination with other chart acts to both artists' lists. So, for example, you will find George Michael and Elton John's number one hit 'Don't Let The Sun Go Down On Me' listed twice, once under Elton John and once under George Michael. There is no separate entry for them as a duo, and the weeks that record spent on the chart are credited to both singers. A box after the catalogue number of any hit will indicate that the credit on the record label is not just that of the artist in whose list of hits the boxes appear. At the foot of each act's list there is an explanation of the details of each of these alternative label credits.

Describing a record act in one sentence is often fraught with danger, but we have attempted to do so above each act's list of hits. Although we are aware that many of the 'vocalists' thus described also play an instrument, we have only mentioned this fact where the artist's instrumental skills were an important factor in their chart success.

Once more we have calculated the total weeks spent on the chart by every single act, and this total appears at the top right of each act's entry.

Alert readers will note that some acts (e.g. Elvis Presley and Cliff Richard) have a weeks on chart grand total that is slightly less than the figure obtained by adding up the weeks totals of each of their hit titles. This is because in the early days of the charts (the *NME* charts of 1952 to 1960) both sides of the same record were sometimes listed simultaneously in different positions (e.g. Elvis Presley's 'Party' and 'Got A Lot O'Livin' To Do'). In these instances the two sides score only one week towards the act's total, not two.

Catalogue numbers are generally those of the 7-inch version of the single, but where there is a good reason for using an alternative (if, for example, the record was not issued on a 7-inch single), then the best-selling alternative format catalogue number is used.

This tenth edition of the Guinness Book Of British Hit Singles includes photos of each of the top 50 acts of all time, as listed in the Most Weeks On Chart table in Part Three. These 50 artists are indicated by a special symbol accompanying their photo containing their ranking in the top 50. For example, our photo of Shirley Bassey is accompanied by **TOP 25 50**.

AALIYAH *US, female vocalist* **7 wks**

2 Jul 94	**BACK AND FORTH** *Jive JIVECD 357* **16**	5 wks
15 Oct 94	**(AT YOUR BEST) YOU ARE LOVE** *Jive JIVECD 359*....**27**	2 wks

ABBA
Sweden/Norway, male/female vocal/instrumental group **252 wks**

20 Apr 74	★ **WATERLOO** *Epic EPC 2240* **1**	9 wks
13 Jul 74	**RING RING** *Epic EPC 2452* **32**	5 wks
12 Jul 75	**I DO I DO I DO I DO I DO** *Epic EPC 3229*...........**38**	6 wks
20 Sep 75	● **S. O. S.** *Epic EPC 3576* **6**	10 wks
13 Dec 75	★ **MAMMA MIA** *Epic EPC 3790* **1**	14 wks
27 Mar 76	★ **FERNANDO** *Epic EPC 4036* **1**	15 wks
21 Aug 76	★ **DANCING QUEEN** *Epic EPC 4499* **1**	15 wks
20 Nov 76	● **MONEY MONEY MONEY** *Epic EPC 4713*...........**3**	12 wks
26 Feb 77	★ **KNOWING ME KNOWING YOU** *Epic EPC 4955* **1**	13 wks
22 Oct 77	★ **THE NAME OF THE GAME** *Epic EPC 5750*...........**1**	12 wks
4 Feb 78	★ **TAKE A CHANCE ON ME** *Epic EPC 5950* **1**	10 wks
16 Sep 78	● **SUMMER NIGHT CITY** *Epic EPC 6595* **5**	9 wks
3 Feb 79	● **CHIQUITITA** *Epic EPC 7030* **2**	9 wks
5 May 79	● **DOES YOUR MOTHER KNOW** *Epic EPC 7316* **4**	9 wks
14 Jul 79	● **ANGELEYES / VOULEZ-VOUS** *Epic EPC 7499* **3**	11 wks
20 Oct 79	● **GIMME GIMME GIMME (A MAN AFTER MIDNIGHT)** *Epic EPC 7914* **3**	12 wks
15 Dec 79	● **I HAVE A DREAM** *Epic EPC 8088* **2**	10 wks
2 Aug 80	★ **THE WINNER TAKES IT ALL** *Epic EPC 8835*...........**1**	10 wks
15 Nov 80	★ **SUPER TROUPER** *Epic EPC 9089* **1**	12 wks
18 Jul 81	● **LAY ALL YOUR LOVE ON ME** *Epic EPC A 1314* **7**	7 wks
12 Dec 81	● **ONE OF US** *Epic EPC A 1740* **3**	10 wks
20 Feb 82	**HEAD OVER HEELS** *Epic EPC A 2037* **25**	7 wks
23 Oct 82	**THE DAY BEFORE YOU CAME** *Epic EPC A 2847*...........**32**	6 wks
11 Dec 82	**UNDER ATTACK** *Epic EPC A 2971* **26**	8 wks
12 Nov 83	**THANK YOU FOR THE MUSIC** *CBS A 3894* **33**	6 wks
5 Sep 92	**DANCING QUEEN (re-issue)** *Polydor PO 231* **16**	5 wks

ABBACADABRA
UK, male/female, vocal/instrumental group **1 wk**

5 Sep 92	**DANCING QUEEN** *PWL International PWL 246* **57**	1 wk

Russ ABBOT *UK, male vocalist* **22 wks**

6 Feb 82	**A DAY IN THE LIFE OF VINCE PRINCE** *EMI 5249* **61**	1 wk
20 Feb 82	**A DAY IN THE LIFE OF VINCE PRINCE (re-entry)** *EMI 5249* **75**	1 wk
29 Dec 84	● **ATMOSPHERE** *Spirit FIRE 4* **7**	13 wks
13 Jul 85	**ALL NIGHT HOLIDAY** *Spirit FIRE 6* **20**	7 wks

Gregory ABBOTT *US, male vocalist* **13 wks**

22 Nov 86	● **SHAKE YOU DOWN** *CBS A 7326* **6**	13 wks

ABC *UK, male vocal/instrumental duo* **92 wks**

31 Oct 81	**TEARS ARE NOT ENOUGH** *Neutron NT 101* **19**	8 wks
20 Feb 82	● **POISON ARROW** *Neutron NT 102* **6**	11 wks
15 May 82	● **THE LOOK OF LOVE** *Neutron NT 103* **4**	10 wks
4 Sep 82	● **ALL OF MY HEART** *Neutron NT 104* **5**	8 wks
15 Jan 83	**THE LOOK OF LOVE (re-entry)** *Neutron NT 103* **71**	1 wk
5 Nov 83	**THAT WAS THEN BUT THIS IS NOW** *Neutron NT 105* **18**	4 wks

21 Jan 84	**S.O.S.** *Neutron NT 106* **39**	5 wks
10 Nov 84	**HOW TO BE A MILLIONAIRE** *Neutron NT 107* **49**	4 wks
6 Apr 85	**BE NEAR ME** *Neutron NT 108* **26**	4 wks
15 Jun 85	**VANITY KILLS** *Neutron NT 109* **70**	1 wk
18 Jun 86	**OCEAN BLUE** *Neutron NT 110* **51**	3 wks
6 Jun 87	**WHEN SMOKEY SINGS** *Neutron NT 111* **11**	10 wks
5 Sep 87	**THE NIGHT YOU MURDERED LOVE** *Neutron NT 112* **31**	8 wks
28 Nov 87	**KING WITHOUT A CROWN** *Neutron NT 113*...........**44**	3 wks
27 May 89	**ONE BETTER WORLD** *Neutron NT 114* **32**	4 wks
23 Sep 89	**THE REAL THING** *Neutron NT 115* **68**	1 wk
14 Apr 90	**THE LOOK OF LOVE (re-mix)** *Neutron NT 116* **68**	1 wk
27 Jul 91	**LOVE CONQUERS ALL** *Parlophone R 6292* **47**	2 wks
11 Jan 92	**SAY IT** *Parlophone R 6298* **42**	3 wks

The act were a UK, male vocal/instrumental group for first six hits, and a UK/US, male/female vocal/instrumental group for the next four.

Paula ABDUL *US, female vocalist* **64 wks**

4 Mar 89	● **STRAIGHT UP** *Siren SRN 111* **3**	13 wks
3 Jun 89	**FOREVER YOUR GIRL** *Siren SRN 112* **24**	6 wks
19 Aug 89	**KNOCKED OUT** *Siren SRN 92* **45**	3 wks
2 Dec 89	**(IT'S JUST) THE WAY THAT YOU LOVE ME** *Siren SRN 101* **74**	1 wk
7 Apr 90	● **OPPOSITES ATTRACT** *Siren SRN 124* **1** **2**	13 wks
21 Jul 90	**KNOCKED OUT (re-mix)** *Virgin America VUS 23* **21**	5 wks
29 Sep 90	**COLD HEARTED** *Virgin America VUS 27* **46**	3 wks
22 Jun 91	● **RUSH RUSH** *Virgin America VUS 38* **6**	11 wks
31 Aug 91	**THE PROMISE OF A NEW DAY** *Virgin America VUS 44* **52**	2 wks
18 Jan 92	**VIBEOLOGY** *Virgin America VUS 53* **19**	6 wks
8 Aug 92	**WILL YOU MARRY ME** *Virgin America VUS 58* **73**	1 wk

1 Paula Abdul with the Wild Pair

ABIGAIL *UK, female vocalist* **4 wks**

16 Jul 94	**SMELLS LIKE TEEN SPIRIT** *Klone CDKLONE 25* **29**	4 wks

Colonel ABRAMS *US, male vocalist* **35 wks**

17 Aug 85	● **TRAPPED** *MCA MCA 997*...........**3**	23 wks
7 Dec 85	**THE TRUTH** *MCA MCA 1022* **53**	3 wks
8 Feb 86	**I'M NOT GONNA LET YOU (GET THE BEST OF ME)** *MCA MCA 1031* **24**	7 wks
15 Aug 87	**HOW SOON WE FORGET** *MCA MCA 1179* **75**	2 wks

ABSOLUTELY FABULOUS - *See PET SHOP BOYS*

AC/DC *Australia/UK, male vocal/instrumental group* **122 wks**

10 Jun 78	**ROCK 'N' ROLL DAMNATION** *Atlantic K 11142*........**24**	9 wks
1 Sep 79	**HIGHWAY TO HELL** *Atlantic K 11321* **56**	4 wks
2 Feb 80	**TOUCH TOO MUCH** *Atlantic K 11435* **29**	9 wks
28 Jun 80	**DIRTY DEEDS DONE DIRT CHEAP** *Atlantic HM 2* **47**	3 wks
28 Jun 80	**HIGH VOLTAGE (LIVE VERSION)** *Atlantic HM 1* **48**	3 wks
28 Jun 80	**IT'S A LONG WAY TO THE TOP (IF YOU WANNA ROCK 'N' ROLL)** *Atlantic HM 3* ..**55**	3 wks
28 Jun 80	**WHOLE LOTTA ROSIE** *Atlantic HM 4* **36**	8 wks
13 Sep 80	**YOU SHOOK ME ALL NIGHT LONG** *Atlantic K 11600* **38**	6 wks
29 Nov 80	**ROCK 'N' ROLL AIN'T NOISE POLLUTION** *Atlantic K 11630* **15**	8 wks
6 Feb 82	**LET'S GET IT UP** *Atlantic K 11706* **13**	6 wks
3 Jul 82	**FOR THOSE ABOUT TO ROCK (WE SALUTE YOU)** *Atlantic K 11721* **15**	6 wks
29 Oct 83	**GUNS FOR HIRE** *Atlantic A 9774* **37**	4 wks
4 Aug 84	**NERVOUS SHAKEDOWN** *Atlantic A 9651*...........**35**	5 wks
6 Jul 85	**DANGER** *Atlantic A 9532* **48**	4 wks
18 Jan 86	**SHAKE YOUR FOUNDATIONS** *Atlantic A 9474* **24**	5 wks
24 May 86	**WHO MADE WHO** *Atlantic A 9425* **16**	5 wks
30 Aug 86	**YOU SHOOK ME ALL NIGHT LONG (re-issue)** *Atlantic A 9377* **46**	4 wks
16 Jan 88	**HEATSEEKER** *Atlantic A 9136*...........**12**	6 wks

2 Apr 88	THAT'S THE WAY I WANNA ROCK 'N' ROLL		
	Atlantic A 9098	22	5 wks
22 Sep 90	THUNDERSTRUCK Atco B 8907	13	5 wks
24 Nov 90	MONEYTALKS Atco B 8886	36	3 wks
27 Apr 91	ARE YOU READY Atco B 8830	34	3 wks
17 Oct 92	HIGHWAY TO HELL (LIVE) Atco B 8479	14	4 wks
6 Mar 93	DIRTY DEEDS DONE DIRT CHEAP (LIVE)		
	Atco B 6073CD	68	1 wk
10 Jul 93	BIG GUN Atco B 8396CD	23	3 wks

ACE UK, male vocal / instrumental group — 10 wks

9 Nov 74	HOW LONG Anchor ANC 1002	20	10 wks

Richard ACE Jamaica, male vocalist — 2 wks

2 Dec 78	STAYIN' ALIVE Blue Inc. INC 2	66	2 wks

ACE OF BASE
Sweden, male / female vocal / instrumental group — 55 wks

8 May 93	★ ALL THAT SHE WANTS London 8612702	1	16 wks
28 Aug 93	WHEEL OF FORTUNE London 8615452	20	6 wks
13 Nov 93	HAPPY NATION London 8619272	42	3 wks
26 Feb 94	● THE SIGN London ACECD 1	2	16 wks
11 Jun 94	● DON'T TURN AROUND London ACECD 2	5	11 wks
15 Oct 94	HAPPY NATION (re-issue) London 8610972	40	3 wks

ACEN UK, male producer — 4 wks

8 Aug 92	TRIP II THE MOON Production House PNT 042	38	3 wks
10 Oct 92	TRIP II THE MOON (re-mix)		
	Production House PNT 042RX	71	1 wk

ACES - See Desmond DEKKER and the ACES

Tracy ACKERMAN - See Q

ACT UK / Germany, male / female vocal / instrumental group — 2 wks

23 May 87	SNOBBERY AND DECAY ZTT ZTAS 28	60	2 wks

ACT ONE US, male / female vocal / instrumental group — 6 wks

18 May 74	TOM THE PEEPER Mercury 6008 005	40	6 wks

Arthur ADAMS US, male vocalist — 5 wks

24 Oct 81	YOU GOT THE FLOOR RCA 146	38	5 wks

Bryan ADAMS
Canada, male vocalist / instrumentalist - guitar — 134 wks

12 Jan 85	RUN TO YOU A & M AM 224	11	12 wks
16 Mar 85	SOMEBODY A & M AM 236	35	7 wks
25 May 85	HEAVEN A & M AM 256	38	5 wks
10 Aug 85	SUMMER OF '69 A & M AM 267	42	7 wks
2 Nov 85	IT'S ONLY LOVE A & M AM 285 [1]	29	6 wks
21 Dec 85	CHRISTMAS TIME A & M AM 297	55	7 wks
22 Feb 86	THIS TIME A & M AM 295	41	7 wks
12 Jul 86	STRAIGHT FROM THE HEART A & M AM 322	51	3 wks
28 Mar 87	HEAT OF THE NIGHT A & M ADAM 2	50	2 wks
20 Jun 87	HEARTS ON FIRE A & M ADAM 3	57	3 wks
17 Oct 87	VICTIM OF LOVE A & M AM 407	68	2 wks
29 Jun 91	★ (EVERYTHING I DO) I DO IT FOR YOU		
	A & M AM 789	1	24 wks
14 Sep 91	CAN'T STOP THIS THING WE STARTED		
	A & M AM 612	12	6 wks
23 Nov 91	THERE WILL NEVER BE ANOTHER TONIGHT		
	A & M AM 838	32	3 wks
28 Dec 91	(EVERYTHING I DO) I DO IT FOR YOU (re-entry)		
	A & M AM 789	73	1 wk
22 Feb 92	● THOUGHT I'D DIED AND GONE TO HEAVEN		
	A & M AM 848	8	7 wks
18 Jul 92	ALL I WANT IS YOU A & M AM 879	22	5 wks
26 Sep 92	DO I HAVE TO SAY THE WORDS A & M AM 0068	30	3 wks
30 Oct 93	● PLEASE FORGIVE ME A & M 5804232	2	16 wks
15 Jan 94	● ALL FOR LOVE A & M 5804772 [2]	2	13 wks

[1] Bryan Adams and Tina Turner [2] Bryan Adams, Rod Stewart and Sting

Cliff ADAMS UK, orchestra — 2 wks

28 Apr 60	LONELY MAN THEME Pye International 7N 25056	39	2 wks

Gayle ADAMS US, female vocalist — 1 wk

26 Jul 80	STRETCHIN' OUT Epic EPC 8791	64	1 wk

Marie ADAMS - See Johnny OTIS SHOW

Oleta ADAMS US, female vocalist — 30 wks

24 Mar 90	RHYTHM OF LIFE Fontana OLETA 1	52	2 wks
3 Nov 90	RHYTHM OF LIFE (re-entry) Fontana OLETA 1	56	3 wks
12 Jan 91	● GET HERE Fontana OLETA 3	4	12 wks
13 Apr 91	YOU'VE GOT TO GIVE ME ROOM /		
	RHYTHM OF LIFE (re-issue) Fontana OLETA 4	49	3 wks
29 Jun 91	CIRCLE OF ONE Fontana OLETA 5	73	1 wk
28 Sep 91	DON'T LET THE SUN GO DOWN ON ME		
	Fontana TRIBO 1	33	5 wks
25 Apr 92	WOMAN IN CHAINS (re-issue)		
	Fontana IDEA 16 [1]	57	1 wk
10 Jul 93	I JUST HAD TO HEAR YOUR VOICE		
	Fontana OLECD 6	42	3 wks

[1] Tears For Fears featuring Oleta Adams

The original release of Woman In Chains credited Tears For Fears only.

ADAMSKI UK, male instrumentalist / producer — 38 wks

20 Jan 90	N-R-G MCA MCA 1386	12	6 wks
7 Apr 90	★ KILLER MCA MCA 1400	1	18 wks
8 Sep 90	● THE SPACE JUNGLE MCA MCA 1435	7	8 wks
17 Nov 90	FLASHBACK JACK MCA MCA 1459	46	2 wks
9 Nov 91	NEVER GOIN' DOWN / BORN TO BE ALIVE		
	MCA MCS 1578 [1]	51	2 wks
4 Apr 92	GET YOUR BODY MCA MCS 1613 [2]	68	1 wk
4 Jul 92	BACK TO FRONT MCA MCS 1644	63	1 wk

[1] Adamski featuring Jimi Polo/Adamski featuring Soho [2] Adamski featuring Nina Hagen

Featured vocalist on Killer was Seal.

ADDAMS and GEE UK, male instrumental duo — 1 wk

20 Apr 91	CHUNG KUO (REVISITED) Debut DEBT 3108	72	1 wk

ADDRISI BROTHERS US, male vocal duo — 3 wks

6 Oct 79	GHOST DANCER Scotti Brothers K 11361	57	3 wks

ADEVA US, female vocalist — 57 wks

14 Jan 89	RESPECT Cooltempo COOL 179	17	9 wks
25 Mar 89	MUSICAL FREEDOM (MOVING ON UP)		
	Cooltempo COOL 182 [1]	22	8 wks
12 Aug 89	WARNING Cooltempo COOL 185	17	8 wks
21 Oct 89	I THANK YOU Cooltempo COOL 192	17	7 wks
16 Dec 89	BEAUTIFUL LOVE Cooltempo COOL 195	57	5 wks
28 Apr 90	TREAT ME RIGHT Cooltempo COOL 200	62	2 wks
6 Apr 91	RING MY BELL Cooltempo COOL 224 [2]	20	5 wks
19 Oct 91	IT SHOULD'VE BEEN ME Cooltempo COOL 236	48	3 wks
29 Feb 92	DON'T LET IT SHOW ON YOUR FACE		
	Cooltempo COOL 248	34	4 wks

ABBA enjoyed yet another international revival in the mid-1990s courtesy of the Australian films *Priscilla: Queen Of The Desert* and *Muriel's Wedding*. (Ted Hawes/LFI)

Jenny, Linn and Jonas Berggren were joined by singer/ songwriter/ producer Ulf Ekberg to form **ACE OF BASE**. (Gregg De Guire/LFI)

6 Jun 92	**UNTIL YOU COME BACK TO ME**		
	Cooltempo COOL 254 ....**45**	3 wks
17 Oct 92	**I'M THE ONE FOR YOU** Cooltempo COOL 264 ....**51**	2 wks
11 Dec 93	**RESPECT (re-mix)** Network NWKCD 79 ....**65**	1 wk

1 Paul Simpson featuring Adeva 2 Monie Love vs Adeva

ADICTS UK, male vocal/instrumental group   **1 wk**

| 14 May 83 | **BAD BOY** Razor RZS 104 ....**75** | 1 wk |

Larry ADLER - See Kate BUSH

ADONIS featuring 2 PUERTO RICANS, A BLACK MAN AND A DOMINICAN
US, male vocal/instrumental group   **4 wks**

| 13 Jun 87 | **DO IT PROPERLY ('NO WAY BACK')/** | |
| | **NO WAY BACK** London LON 136 ....**47** | 4 wks |

ADRENALIN M.O.D. US, male vocal/instrumental group **5 wks**

| 8 Oct 88 | **O-O-O** MCA RAGAT 2 ....**49** | 5 wks |

ADULT NET
UK/US, male/female vocal/instrumental group   **2 wks**

| 10 Jun 89 | **WHERE WERE YOU** Fontana BRX 2 ....**66** | 2 wks |

ADVENTURES UK, male vocal/instrumental group   **24 wks**

15 Sep 84	**ANOTHER SILENT DAY** Chrysalis CHS 2000...............**71**	2 wks
1 Dec 84	**SEND MY HEART** Chrysalis CHS 2001 ....**62**	4 wks
13 Jul 85	**FEEL THE RAINDROPS** Chrysalis AD 1 ....**58**	3 wks
9 Apr 88	**BROKEN LAND** Elektra EKR 69 ....**20**	10 wks
2 Jul 88	**DROWNING IN THE SEA OF LOVE** Elektra EKR 76 ..**44**	4 wks
13 Jun 92	**RAINING ALL OVER THE WORLD** Polydor PO 211 ..**68**	1 wk

ADVENTURES OF STEVIE V
US, male producer and vocalist   **21 wks**

21 Apr 90	● **DIRTY CASH** Mercury MER 311 ....**2**	13 wks
29 Sep 90	**BODY LANGUAGE** Mercury MER 331 ....**29**	5 wks
2 Mar 91	**JEALOUSY** Mercury MER 337 ....**58**	3 wks

ADVERTS UK, male/female vocal/instrumental group   **11 wks**

| 27 Aug 77 | **GARY GILMORE'S EYES** Anchor ANC 1043 ....**18** | 7 wks |
| 4 Feb 78 | **NO TIME TO BE 21** Bright BR1 ....**38** | 4 wks |

AEROSMITH US, male vocal/instrumental group   **51 wks**

17 Oct 87	**DUDE (LOOKS LIKE A LADY)** Geffen GEF 29............**45**	5 wks
16 Apr 88	**ANGEL** Geffen GEF 34 ....**69**	2 wks
9 Sep 89	**LOVE IN AN ELEVATOR** Geffen GEF 63...............**13**	8 wks
24 Feb 90	**DUDE (LOOKS LIKE A LADY) (re-issue)**	
	Geffen GEF 72 ....**20**	5 wks
14 Apr 90	**RAG DOLL** Geffen GEF 76 ....**42**	4 wks
1 Sep 90	**THE OTHER SIDE** Geffen GEF 79 ....**46**	2 wks
10 Apr 93	**LIVIN' ON THE EDGE** Geffen GFSTD 35...............**19**	4 wks
3 Jul 93	**EAT THE RICH** Geffen GFSTD 46 ....**34**	3 wks
30 Oct 93	**CRYIN'** Geffen GFSTD 56 ....**17**	6 wks
18 Dec 93	**AMAZING** Geffen GFSTD 63 ....**57**	3 wks
2 Jul 94	**SHUT UP AND DANCE** Geffen GFSTD 75 ....**24**	4 wks
20 Aug 94	**SWEET EMOTION** Columbia 6604492 ....**74**	1 wk
5 Nov 94	**CRAZY / BLIND MAN** Geffen GFSTD 80...............**23**	4 wks

AFRICAN BUSINESS
Italy, male vocal/instrumental group   **1 wk**

| 17 Nov 90 | **IN ZAIRE** Urban URB 64 ....**73** | 1 wk |

AFTER 7 US, male vocal group   **3 wks**

| 3 Nov 90 | **CAN'T STOP** Virgin America VUS 31 ....**54** | 3 wks |

AFTER THE FIRE UK, male vocal/instrumental group   **12 wks**

9 Jun 79	**ONE RULE FOR YOU** CBS 7025 ....**40**	6 wks
8 Sep 79	**LASER LOVE** CBS 7769 ....**62**	2 wks
9 Apr 83	**DER KOMMISSAR** CBS A 2399...............**47**	4 wks

AFTERNOON BOYS - See Steve WRIGHT

AFTERSHOCK US, male vocal/instrumental duo   **8 wks**

| 21 Aug 93 | **SLAVE TO THE VIBE** Virgin America VUSCD 75 ....**11** | 8 wks |

AGE OF CHANCE
UK, male/female vocal/instrumental group   **13 wks**

17 Jan 87	**KISS** Fon AGE 5 ....**50**	6 wks
30 May 87	**WHO'S AFRAID OF THE BIG BAD NOISE!**	
	Fon VS 962 ....**65**	2 wks
20 Jan 90	**HIGHER THAN HEAVEN** Virgin VS 1228 ....**53**	5 wks

A-HA Norway, male vocal/instrumental group   **131 wks**

28 Sep 85	● **TAKE ON ME** Warner Bros. W 9006 ....**2**	19 wks
28 Dec 85	★ **THE SUN ALWAYS SHINES ON TV**	
	Warner Bros. W 8846 ....**1**	12 wks
5 Apr 86	● **TRAIN OF THOUGHT** Warner Bros. W 8736...............**8**	8 wks
14 Jun 86	● **HUNTING HIGH AND LOW** Warner Bros. W 6663 ....**5**	10 wks
4 Oct 86	● **I'VE BEEN LOSING YOU** Warner Bros. W 8594...............**8**	7 wks
6 Dec 86	● **CRY WOLF** Warner Bros. W 8500 ....**5**	9 wks
28 Feb 87	**MANHATTAN SKYLINE** Warner Bros. W 8405 ....**13**	6 wks
4 Jul 87	● **THE LIVING DAYLIGHTS** Warner Bros. W 8305 ....**5**	9 wks
26 Mar 88	● **STAY ON THESE ROADS** Warner Bros. W 7936 ....**5**	6 wks
18 Jun 88	**THE BLOOD THAT MOVES THE BODY**	
	Warner Bros. W 7840 ....**25**	4 wks
27 Aug 88	**TOUCHY!** Warner Bros. W 7749 ....**11**	7 wks
3 Dec 88	**YOU ARE THE ONE** Warner Bros. W 7636...............**13**	10 wks
13 Oct 90	**CRYING IN THE RAIN** Warner Bros. W 9547...............**13**	7 wks
15 Dec 90	**I CALL YOUR NAME** Warner Bros. W 9462...............**44**	5 wks
26 Oct 91	**MOVE TO MEMPHIS** Warner Bros. W 0070 ....**47**	2 wks
5 Jun 93	**DARK IS THE NIGHT** Warner Bros. W 0175CD **19**	4 wks
18 Sep 93	**ANGEL** Warner Bros. W 0195CD **41**	3 wks
26 Mar 94	**SHAPES THAT GO TOGETHER**	
	Warner Bros. W 0236CD **27**	3 wks

AHMED US, male rapper   **2 wks**

| 9 Jul 94 | **BACK IN THE DAY** Giant 74321212042 ....**64** | 2 wks |

AIR SUPPLY
UK/Australia, male vocal/instrumental group   **17 wks**

27 Sep 80	**ALL OUT OF LOVE** Arista ARIST 362 ....**11**	11 wks
2 Oct 82	**EVEN THE NIGHTS ARE BETTER** Arista ARIST 474....**44**	4 wks
20 Nov 93	**GOODBYE** Giant 74321153462 ....**66**	2 wks

AIRHEAD UK, male vocal/instrumental group   **10 wks**

5 Oct 91	**FUNNY HOW** Korova KOW 47 ....**57**	3 wks
21 Dec 91	**COUNTING SHEEP** Korova KOW 48...............**35**	5 wks
7 Mar 92	**RIGHT NOW** Korova KOW 49 ....**50**	2 wks

Laurel AITKEN and the UNITONE
Jamaica/Cuba, male vocal/instrumental group   **3 wks**

| 17 May 80 | **RUDI GOT MARRIED** I-Spy SEE 6 ....**60** | 3 wks |

Jewel AKENS US, male/vocalist — 8 wks

| 25 Mar 65 | THE BIRDS AND THE BEES *London HLN 9954* | ...**29** | 8 wks |

ALARM UK, male vocal/instrumental group — 64 wks

24 Sep 83	68 GUNS *IRS PFP 1023*	...**17**	7 wks
21 Jan 84	WHERE WERE YOU HIDING WHEN THE STORM BROKE *IRS IRS 101*	...**22**	6 wks
31 Mar 84	THE DECEIVER *IRS IRS 103*	...**51**	4 wks
3 Nov 84	THE CHANT HAS JUST BEGUN *IRS IRS 104*	...**48**	4 wks
2 Mar 85	ABSOLUTE REALITY *IRS ALARM 1*	...**35**	6 wks
28 Sep 85	STRENGTH *IRS IRM 104*	...**40**	4 wks
18 Jan 86	SPIRIT OF '76 *IRS IRM 109*	...**22**	5 wks
26 Apr 86	KNIFE EDGE *IRS IRM 112*	...**43**	3 wks
17 Oct 87	RAIN IN THE SUMMERTIME *IRS IRM 144*	...**18**	5 wks
12 Dec 87	RESCUE ME *IRS IRM 150*	...**48**	2 wks
20 Feb 88	PRESENCE OF LOVE (LAUGHERNE) *IRS IRM 155*	...**44**	3 wks
16 Sep 89	SOLD ME DOWN THE RIVER *IRS EIRS 123*	...**43**	4 wks
4 Nov 89	A NEW SOUTH WALES/THE ROCK *IRS EIRS 129*	...**31**	5 wks
3 Feb 90	LOVE DON'T COME EASY *IRS EIRS 134*	...**48**	3 wks
27 Oct 90	UNSAFE BUILDING 1990 *IRS ALARME 2*	...**54**	2 wks
13 Apr 91	RAW *IRS ALARM 3*	...**51**	2 wks

A New South Wales features Morriston Orpheus Male Voice Choir.

Morris ALBERT Brazil, male vocalist — 10 wks

| 27 Sep 75 | ● FEELINGS *Decca F 13591* | ...**4** | 10 wks |

ALBERTO Y LOST TRIOS PARANOIAS
UK, male vocal/instrumental group — 5 wks

| 23 Sep 78 | HEADS DOWN NO NONSENSE MINDLESS BOOGIE *Logo GO 323* | ...**47** | 5 wks |

ALESSI US, male vocal duo — 11 wks

| 11 Jun 77 | ● OH LORI *A & M AMS 7289* | ...**8** | 11 wks |

ALEX PARTY Italy/UK, male/female instrumental group — 10 wks

| 18 Dec 93 | SATURDAY NIGHT PARTY *Cleveland City Imports CCICD 17000* | ...**49** | 6 wks |
| 28 May 94 | SATURDAY NIGHT PARTY (READ MY LIPS) (re-entry) *Cleveland City Imports CCICD 17000* | ...**29** | 4 wks |

ALFI and HARRY
US, male vocalist, David Seville under two false names — 5 wks

| 23 Mar 56 | THE TROUBLE WITH HARRY *London HLU 8242* | ...**15** | 5 wks |

See also David Seville.

ALI and FRAZIER UK, female vocal duo — 4 wks

| 7 Aug 93 | UPTOWN TOP RANKING *Arista 74321158842* | ...**33** | 4 wks |

ALICE IN CHAINS US, male vocal/instrumental group — 10 wks

23 Jan 93	WOULD *Columbia 6588882*	...**19**	3 wks
20 Mar 93	THEM BONES *Columbia 6590902*	...**26**	3 wks
5 Jun 93	ANGRY CHAIR *Columbia 6593652*	...**33**	2 wks
23 Oct 93	DOWN IN A HOLE *Columbia 6597512*	...**36**	2 wks

ALISHA US, female vocalist — 2 wks

| 25 Jan 86 | BABY TALK *Total Control TOCO 6* | ...**67** | 2 wks |

ALL ABOUT EVE
UK, female/male vocal/instrumental group — 47 wks

31 Oct 87	IN THE CLOUDS *Mercury EVEN 5*	...**47**	5 wks
23 Jan 88	WILD HEARTED WOMAN *Mercury EVEN 6*	...**33**	4 wks
9 Apr 88	EVERY ANGEL *Mercury EVEN 7*	...**30**	5 wks
30 Jul 88	● MARTHA'S HARBOUR *Mercury EVEN 8*	...**10**	8 wks
12 Nov 88	WHAT KIND OF FOOL *Mercury EVEN 9*	...**29**	4 wks
30 Sep 89	ROAD TO YOUR SOUL *Mercury EVEN 10*	...**37**	4 wks
16 Dec 89	DECEMBER *Mercury EVEN 11*	...**34**	5 wks
28 Apr 90	SCARLET *Mercury EVEN 12*	...**34**	2 wks
15 Jun 91	FAREWELL MR SORROW *Mercury EVEN 14*	...**36**	2 wks
10 Aug 91	STRANGE WAY *Vertigo EVEN 15*	...**50**	3 wks
19 Oct 91	THE DREAMER *Vertigo EVEN 16*	...**41**	2 wks
10 Oct 92	PHASED (EP) *MCA MCS 1688*	...**38**	2 wks
28 Nov 92	SOME FINER DAY *MCA MCS 1706*	...**57**	1 wk

Tracks on Phased (EP): Phased/Mine/Infra Red/Ascent-Descent.

ALL-4-ONE US, male vocal group — 21 wks

2 Apr 94	SO MUCH IN LOVE *Atlantic A 7261CD*	...**60**	1 wk
18 Jun 94	● I SWEAR *Atlantic A 7255CD*	...**2**	18 wks
19 Nov 94	SO MUCH IN LOVE (re-mix) *Atlantic A 7216CD*	...**49**	2 wks

ALL STARS - *See Louis ARMSTRONG*

ALL-STARS - *See Junior WALKER and the ALL-STARS*

ALL SYSTEMS GO UK, male vocal/instrumental group — 2 wks

| 18 Jun 88 | POP MUZIK *Unique NIQ 03* | ...**63** | 2 wks |

Richard ALLAN UK, male vocalist — 1 wk

| 24 Mar 60 | AS TIME GOES BY *Parlophone R 4634* | ...**44** | 1 wk |

Steve ALLAN UK, male vocalist — 2 wks

| 27 Jan 79 | TOGETHER WE ARE BEAUTIFUL *Creole CR 164* | ...**67** | 1 wk |
| 10 Feb 79 | TOGETHER WE ARE BEAUTIFUL (re-entry) *Creole CR 164* | ...**70** | 1 wk |

Donna ALLEN US, female vocalist — 22 wks

| 18 Apr 87 | ● SERIOUS *Portrait PRT 650744 7* | ...**8** | 12 wks |
| 3 Jun 89 | ● JOY AND PAIN *BCM BCM 257* | ...**10** | 10 wks |

ALLISONS UK, male vocal duo — 27 wks

23 Feb 61	● ARE YOU SURE *Fontana H 294*	...**2**	16 wks
18 May 61	WORDS *Fontana H 304*	...**34**	5 wks
15 Feb 62	LESSONS IN LOVE *Fontana H 362*	...**30**	6 wks

ALLNIGHT BAND UK, male instrumental group — 3 wks

| 3 Feb 79 | THE JOKER (THE WIGAN JOKER) *Casino Classics CC 6* | ...**50** | 3 wks |

ALMIGHTY UK, male vocal/instrumental group — 16 wks

30 Jun 90	WILD AND WONDERFUL *Polydor PO 75*	...**50**	2 wks
2 Mar 91	FREE 'N' EASY *Polydor PO 127*	...**35**	2 wks
11 May 91	DEVIL'S TOY *Polydor PO 144*	...**36**	2 wks
29 Jun 91	LITTLE LOST SOMETIMES *Polydor PO 151*	...**42**	2 wks
3 Apr 93	ADDICTION *Polydor PZCD 261*	...**38**	2 wks
29 May 93	OUT OF SEASON *Polydor PZCD 266*	...**41**	2 wks
30 Oct 93	OVER THE EDGE *Polydor PZCD 298*	...**38**	2 wks
24 Sep 94	WRENCH *Chrysalis CDCHS 5014*	...**26**	2 wks

Marc ALMOND UK, male vocalist — 104 wks

2 Jun 83	BLACK HEART *Some Bizzare BZS 19* [1]	...**49**	3 wks
2 Jun 84	THE BOY WHO CAME BACK *Some Bizzare BZS 23*	...**52**	5 wks
1 Sep 84	YOU HAVE *Some Bizzare BZS 24*	...**57**	3 wks
20 Apr 85	● I FEEL LOVE (MEDLEY) *Forbidden Fruit BITE 4* [2]	...**3**	12 wks
24 Aug 85	STORIES OF JOHNNY *Some Bizzare BONK 1*	...**23**	5 wks

26 Oct 85		LOVE LETTER Some Bizzare BONK 2 68	3 wks
4 Jan 86		THE HOUSE IS HAUNTED (BY THE ECHO OF YOUR LAST GOODBYE) Some Bizzare GLOW 1 55	3 wks
7 Jun 86		A WOMAN'S STORY Some Bizzare GLOW 2 [3] 41	5 wks
18 Oct 86		RUBY RED Some Bizzare GLOW 3 47	3 wks
14 Feb 87		MELANCHOLY ROSE Some Bizzare GLOW 4 71	1 wk
3 Sep 88		TEARS RUN RINGS Parlophone R 6186 26	7 wks
5 Nov 88		BITTER SWEET Some Bizzare R 6194 40	3 wks
14 Jan 89	★	SOMETHING'S GOTTEN HOLD OF MY HEART Parlophone R 6201 [4] 1	12 wks
8 Apr 89		ONLY THE MOMENT Parlophone R 6210 45	2 wks
3 Mar 90		A LOVER SPURNED Some Bizzare R 6229 29	4 wks
19 May 90		THE DESPERATE HOURS Some Bizzare R 6252 45	2 wks
23 Mar 91		SAY HELLO WAVE GOODBYE '91 Mercury SOFT 1 [5] 38	3 wks
18 May 91	●	TAINTED LOVE Mercury SOFT 2 [5] 5	8 wks
28 Sep 91		JACKY Some Bizzare YZ 610 17	6 wks
11 Jan 92		MY HAND OVER MY HEART Some Bizzare YZ 633 ..33	5 wks
25 Apr 92	●	THE DAYS OF PEARLY SPENCER Some Bizzare YZ 638 4	7 wks
27 Mar 93		WHAT MAKES A MAN A MAN (LIVE) Some Bizzare YZ 720CD 60	2 wks

[1] Marc and the Mambas [2] Bronski Beat and Marc Almond [3] Marc Almond and the Willing Sinners [4] Marc Almond featuring special guest star Gene Pitney [5] Soft Cell/Marc Almond

I Feel Love medley comprises I Feel Love / Love To Love You Baby / Johnny Remember Me. Say Hello Wave Goodbye '91 is a re-recording of the Soft Cell hit.

ALOOF UK, male vocal / instrumental group   **1 wk**

| 19 Sep 92 | | ON A MISSION Cowboy RODEO 5 ....64 | 1 wk |

Herb ALPERT US, male instrumentalist - trumpet   **106 wks**

3 Jan 63		THE LONELY BULL Stateside SS 138 [1] 22	9 wks
9 Dec 65	●	SPANISH FLEA Pye International 7 N 25335 [2] 3	20 wks
24 Mar 66		TIJUANA TAXI Pye International 7 N 25352 [2] 37	4 wks
27 Apr 67		CASINO ROYALE A & M AMS 700 [2] 27	14 wks
3 Jul 68		THIS GUY'S IN LOVE WITH YOU A & M AMS 727 3	16 wks
26 Mar 69		THIS GUY'S IN LOVE WITH YOU (re-entry) A & M AMS 727 47	1 wk
9 Apr 69		THIS GUY'S IN LOVE WITH YOU (2nd re-entry) A & M AMS 727 49	1 wk
7 May 69		THIS GUY'S IN LOVE WITH YOU (3rd re-entry) A & M AMS 727 50	1 wk
18 Jun 69		WITHOUT HER A & M AMS 755 [2] 36	5 wks
12 Dec 70		JERUSALEM A & M AMS 810 [2] 47	1 wk
2 Jan 71		JERUSALEM (re-entry) A & M AMS 810 [2] 42	2 wks
13 Oct 79		RISE A & M AMS 7465 13	13 wks
19 Jan 80		ROTATION A & M AMS 7500 46	3 wks
21 Mar 87		KEEP YOUR EYE ON ME Breakout USA 602 19	9 wks
6 Jun 87		DIAMONDS Breakout USA 605 27	7 wks

[1] Tijuana Brass [2] Herb Alpert and the Tijuana Brass

Alpert vocalises on This Guy's In Love With You and Without Her. Janet Jackson provides uncredited vocals on Diamonds.

ALPHABETA - See Izhar COHEN and ALPHABETA

ALPHAVILLE Germany, male vocal / instrumental group   **13 wks**

| 18 Aug 84 | ● | BIG IN JAPAN WEA Int. X9505 ....8 | 13 wks |

Gerald ALSTON US, male vocalist   **1 wk**

| 15 Apr 89 | | ACTIVATED RCA ZB 42681 ....73 | 1 wk |

ALTERED IMAGES
UK, male / female vocal / instrumental group   **60 wks**

28 Mar 81		DEAD POP STARS Epic EPC A 1023 67	2 wks
26 Sep 81	●	HAPPY BIRTHDAY Epic EPC A 1522 2	17 wks
12 Dec 81	●	I COULD BE HAPPY Epic EPC A 1834 7	12 wks

27 Mar 82		SEE THOSE EYES Epic EPC A 2198 11	7 wks
22 May 82		PINKY BLUE Epic EPC A 2426 35	6 wks
19 Mar 83	●	DON'T TALK TO ME ABOUT LOVE Epic EPC A 3083 ..7	7 wks
28 May 83		BRING ME CLOSER Epic EPC A 3398 29	6 wks
16 Jul 83		LOVE TO STAY Epic EPC A 3582 46	3 wks

ALTERN 8 UK, male instrumental / production duo   **34 wks**

13 Jul 91		INFILTRATE 202 Network NWK 24 28	7 wks
16 Nov 91	●	ACTIV 8 (COME WITH ME) Network NWK 34 3	9 wks
8 Feb 92		FREQUENCY Network NWKT 37 41	1 wk
11 Apr 92	●	EVAPOR 8 Network NWK 38 6	6 wks
4 Jul 92		HYPNOTIC ST-8 Network NWK 49 16	4 wks
10 Oct 92		SHAME Network NWKTEN 56 [1] 74	1 wk
12 Dec 92		BRUTAL-8-E Network NWK 59 43	5 wks
3 Jul 93		EVERYBODY Network NWKCD 73 58	1 wk

[1] Altern 8 vs Evelyn King.

ALTHIA and DONNA Jamaica, female vocal duo   **11 wks**

| 24 Dec 77 | ★ | UP TOWN TOP RANKING Lightning LIG 506 ....1 | 11 wks |

ALVIN and the CHIPMUNKS - See CHIPMUNKS

ALY-US US, male vocal / insrumental group   **2 wks**

| 21 Nov 92 | | FOLLOW ME Cooltempo COOL 266 ....43 | 2 wks |

AMAZULU UK, female / male vocal / instrumental group   **57 wks**

6 Jul 85		EXCITABLE Island IS 201 12	13 wks
23 Nov 85		DON'T YOU JUST KNOW IT Island IS 233 15	11 wks
15 Mar 86		THE THINGS THE LONELY DO Island IS 267 43	6 wks
31 May 86	●	TOO GOOD TO BE FORGOTTEN Island IS 284 5	13 wks
13 Sep 86		MONTEGO BAY Island IS 293 16	9 wks
10 Oct 87		MONY MONY EMI EM 32 38	5 wks

AMBASSADORS OF FUNK featuring MC
MARIO UK, male DJ and rapper - Simon Harris and Einstein   **8 wks**

| 31 Oct 92 | ● | SUPERMARIOLAND Living Beat SMASH 23 ....8 | 8 wks |

AMEN CORNER UK, male vocal / instrumental group   **67 wks**

26 Jul 67		GIN HOUSE BLUES Deram DM 136 12	10 wks
11 Oct 67		WORLD OF BROKEN HEARTS Deram DM 151 26	6 wks
17 Jan 68	●	BEND ME SHAPE ME Deram DM 172 3	12 wks
31 Jul 68	●	HIGH IN THE SKY Deram DM 197 6	13 wks
29 Jan 69	★	(IF PARADISE IS) HALF AS NICE Immediate IM 073 ..1	11 wks
25 Jun 69		HELLO SUZIE Immediate IM 081 4	10 wks
14 Feb 76		(IF PARADISE IS) HALF AS NICE (re-issue) Immediate IMS 103 34	5 wks

AMERICA US, male vocal / instrumental group   **20 wks**

18 Dec 71		HORSE WITH NO NAME Warner Bros. K 16128 49	2 wks
8 Jan 72	●	HORSE WITH NO NAME (re-entry) Warner Bros. K 16128 3	11 wks
25 Nov 72		VENTURA HIGHWAY Warner Bros. K 16219 43	4 wks
6 Nov 82		YOU CAN DO MAGIC Capitol CL 264 59	3 wks

AMERICAN BREED US, male vocal / instrumental group   **6 wks**

| 7 Feb 68 | | BEND ME SHAPE ME Stateside SS 2078 ....24 | 6 wks |

AMERICAN MUSIC CLUB
US, male vocal / instrumental group   **4 wks**

| 24 Apr 93 | | JOHNNY MATHIS' FEET Virgin VSCDG 1445 ....58 | 2 wks |
| 10 Sep 94 | | WISH THE WORLD AWAY Virgin VSCDX 1512 ....46 | 2 wks |

AMES BROTHERS US, male vocal group — **6 wks**

4 Feb 55	● **NAUGHTY LADY OF SHADY LANE** HMV B 10800	**6**	6 wks

AMOS UK, male vocalist — **2 wks**

3 Sep 94	**ONLY SAW TODAY–INSTANT KARMA** Positiva CDTIV 16	**48**	2 wks

Tori AMOS US, female vocalist — **34 wks**

23 Nov 91	**SILENT ALL THESE YEARS** East West YZ 618	**51**	3 wks
1 Feb 92	**CHINA** East West YZ 7531	**51**	2 wks
21 Mar 92	**WINTER** East West A 7504	**25**	4 wks
20 Jun 92	**CRUCIFY** East West A 7479	**15**	6 wks
22 Aug 92	**SILENT ALL THESE YEARS** (re-issue) East West A 7433	**26**	4 wks
22 Jan 94	● **CORNFLAKE GIRL** East West A 7281CD	**4**	6 wks
19 Mar 94	● **PRETTY GOOD YEAR** East West A 7263CD	**7**	4 wks
28 May 94	**PAST THE MISSION** East West YZ 7257CD	**31**	3 wks
15 Oct 94	**GOD** East West A 7251CD	**44**	2 wks

AND WHY NOT? UK, male vocal/instrumental group — **18 wks**

14 Oct 89	**RESTLESS DAYS (SHE CRIES OUT LOUD)** Island IS 426	**38**	7 wks
13 Jan 90	**THE FACE** Island IS 444	**13**	8 wks
21 Apr 90	**SOMETHING YOU GOT** Island IS 452	**39**	3 wks

Angry ANDERSON Australia, male vocalist — **13 wks**

19 Nov 88	● **SUDDENLY** Food For Thought YUM 113	**3**	13 wks

John ANDERSON BIG BAND UK, big band — **5 wks**

21 Dec 85	**GLENN MILLER MEDLEY** Modern GLEN 1	**63**	2 wks
11 Jan 86	**GLENN MILLER MEDLEY** (re-entry) Modern GLEN 1	**61**	3 wks

Glenn Miller Medley comprises the following tracks: In The Mood/ American Patrol/Little Brown Jug/Pennsylvania 65000.

ANDERSON BRUFORD WAKEMAN HOWE
UK, male vocal/instrumental group — **2 wks**

24 Jun 89	**BROTHER OF MINE** Arista 112379	**63**	2 wks

Carl ANDERSON US, male vocalist — **4 wks**

8 Jun 85	**BUTTERCUP** Streetwave KHAN 45	**49**	4 wks

Carleen ANDERSON US, female vocalist — **11 wks**

12 Feb 94	**NERVOUS BREAKDOWN** Circa YRCDG 112	**27**	4 wks
28 May 94	**MAMA SAID** Circa YRCD 114	**26**	4 wks
13 Aug 94	**TRUE SPIRIT** Circa YRCD 118	**24**	3 wks

Laurie ANDERSON
US, female vocalist/multi-instrumentalist — **6 wks**

17 Oct 81	● **O SUPERMAN** Warner Bros. K 17870	**2**	6 wks

Leroy ANDERSON and his POPS CONCERT ORCHESTRA US, orchestra — **4 wks**

28 Jun 57	**FORGOTTEN DREAMS** Brunswick 05485	**28**	1 wk
12 Jul 57	**FORGOTTEN DREAMS** (re-entry) Brunswick 05485	**30**	1 wk
6 Sep 57	**FORGOTTEN DREAMS** (2nd re-entry) Brunswick 05485	**24**	2 wks

Lynn ANDERSON US, female vocalist — **20 wks**

20 Feb 71	● **ROSE GARDEN** CBS 5360	**3**	20 wks

Moira ANDERSON UK, female vocalist — **2 wks**

27 Dec 69	**HOLY CITY** Decca F 12989	**43**	2 wks

Chris ANDREWS UK, male vocalist — **36 wks**

7 Oct 65	● **YESTERDAY MAN** Decca F 12236	**3**	15 wks
2 Dec 65	**TO WHOM IT CONCERNS** Decca F 22285	**13**	10 wks
14 Apr 66	**SOMETHING ON MY MIND** Decca F 22365	**45**	1 wk
28 Apr 66	**SOMETHING ON MY MIND** (re-entry) Decca F 22365	**41**	2 wks
2 Jun 66	**WHATCHA GONNA DO NOW** Decca F 22404	**40**	4 wks
25 Aug 66	**STOP THAT GIRL** Decca F 22472	**36**	4 wks

Eamonn ANDREWS Ireland, male vocalist — **3 wks**

20 Jan 56	**SHIFTING WHISPERING SANDS (PARTS 1 & 2)** Parlophone R 4106	**18**	3 wks

Hit is 'with Ron Goodwin and his Orchestra and Chorus'.

ANEKA UK, female vocalist — **16 wks**

8 Aug 81	★ **JAPANESE BOY** Hansa HANSA 5	**1**	12 wks
7 Nov 81	**LITTLE LADY** Hansa HANSA 8	**50**	4 wks

Simone ANGEL Holland, female vocalist — **1 wk**

13 Nov 93	**LET THIS FEELING** A & M 5803652	**60**	1 wk

ANGELETTES UK, female vocal group — **5 wks**

13 May 72	**DON'T LET HIM TOUCH YOU** Decca F 13284	**35**	5 wks

ANGELIC UPSTARTS
UK, male vocal/instrumental group — **30 wks**

21 Apr 79	**I'M AN UPSTART** Warner Bros. K 17354	**31**	8 wks
11 Aug 79	**TEENAGE WARNING** Warner Bros. K 17426	**29**	6 wks
3 Nov 79	**NEVER 'AD NOTHIN'** Warner Bros. K 17476	**52**	4 wks
9 Feb 80	**OUT OF CONTROL** Warner Bros. K 17558	**58**	3 wks
22 Mar 80	**WE GOTTA GET OUT OF THIS PLACE** Warner Bros. K 17576	**65**	2 wks
2 Aug 80	**LAST NIGHT ANOTHER SOLDIER** Angelic Upstarts Z 7	**51**	4 wks
7 Feb 81	**KIDS ON THE STREET** Angelic Upstarts Z 16	**57**	3 wks

Bobby ANGELO and the TUXEDOS
UK, male vocal/instrumental group — **6 wks**

10 Aug 61	**BABY SITTIN'** HMV POP 892	**30**	6 wks

ANGELS US, female vocal group — **1 wk**

3 Oct 63	**MY BOYFRIEND'S BACK** Mercury AMT 1211	**50**	1 wk

ANGELS OF LIGHT - See PSYCHIC TV

ANGELWITCH UK, male vocal/instrumental group — **1 wk**

7 Jun 80	**SWEET DANGER** EMI 5064	**75**	1 wk

ANIMAL US, Puppet — **3 wks**

23 Jul 94	**WIPE OUT** BMG Kidz 74321219532	**38**	3 wks

ANIMAL NIGHTLIFE
UK, male / female vocal / instrumental group **22 wks**

13 Aug 83	**NATIVE BOY (UPTOWN)** *Innervision A3584*	60	3 wks
18 Aug 84	**MR. SOLITAIRE** *Island IS 193*	25	12 wks
6 Jul 85	**LOVE IS JUST THE GREAT PRETENDER** *Island IS 200*	28	6 wks
5 Oct 85	**PREACHER, PREACHER** *Island IS 245*	67	1 wk

ANIMALS *UK, male vocal / instrumental group* **147 wks**

16 Apr 64	**BABY LET ME TAKE YOU HOME** *Columbia DB 7247*	21	8 wks
25 Jun 64	★ **HOUSE OF THE RISING SUN** *Columbia DB 7301*	1	12 wks
17 Sep 64	**I'M CRYING** *Columbia DB 7354*	8	10 wks
4 Feb 65	● **DON'T LET ME BE MISUNDERSTOOD** *Columbia DB 7445*	3	9 wks
8 Apr 65	● **BRING IT ON HOME TO ME** *Columbia DB 7539*	7	11 wks
15 Jul 65	● **WE GOTTA GET OUT OF THIS PLACE** *Columbia DB 7639*	2	12 wks
28 Oct 65	● **IT'S MY LIFE** *Columbia DB 7741*	7	11 wks
17 Feb 66	**INSIDE - LOOKING OUT** *Decca F 12332*	12	8 wks
2 Jun 66	● **DON'T BRING ME DOWN** *Decca F 12407*	6	8 wks
27 Oct 66	**HELP ME GIRL** *Decca F 12502* [1]	14	10 wks
15 Jun 67	**WHEN I WAS YOUNG** *MGM 1340* [1]	45	3 wks
6 Sep 67	**GOOD TIMES** *MGM 1344* [1]	20	11 wks
18 Oct 67	● **SAN FRANCISCAN NIGHTS** *MGM 1359* [1]	7	10 wks
14 Feb 68	**SKY PILOT** *MGM 1373* [1]	40	3 wks
15 Jan 69	**RING OF FIRE** *MGM 1461* [1]	35	5 wks
7 Oct 72	**HOUSE OF THE RISING SUN (re-issue)** *RAK RR 1*	25	6 wks
18 Sep 82	**HOUSE OF THE RISING SUN (re-entry of re-issue)** *RAK RR 1*	11	10 wks

[1] Eric Burdon and the Animals

ANIMOTION
US / UK, male / female vocal / instrumental group **12 wks**

11 May 85	● **OBSESSION** *Mercury PH 34*	5	12 wks

Paul ANKA *Canada, male vocalist* **132 wks**

9 Aug 57	★ **DIANA** *Columbia DB 3980*	1	25 wks
8 Nov 57	● **I LOVE YOU BABY** *Columbia DB 4022*	3	15 wks
8 Nov 57	**TELL ME THAT YOU LOVE ME** *Columbia DB 4022*	25	2 wks
31 Jan 58	● **YOU ARE MY DESTINY** *Columbia DB 4063*	6	13 wks
30 May 58	**CRAZY LOVE** *Columbia DB 4110*	26	1 wk
26 Sep 58	**MIDNIGHT** *Columbia DB 4172*	26	1 wk
30 Jan 59	● **(ALL OF A SUDDEN) MY HEART SINGS** *Columbia DB 4241*	10	13 wks
10 Jul 59	● **LONELY BOY** *Columbia DB 4324*	3	17 wks
30 Oct 59	● **PUT YOUR HEAD ON MY SHOULDER** *Columbia DB 4355*	7	12 wks
26 Feb 60	**IT'S TIME TO CRY** *Columbia DB 4390*	28	1 wk
31 Mar 60	**PUPPY LOVE** *Columbia DB 4434*	33	4 wks
14 Apr 60	**IT'S TIME TO CRY (re-entry)** *Columbia DB 4390*	47	1 wk
5 May 60	**PUPPY LOVE (re-entry)** *Columbia DB 4434*	37	3 wks
15 Sep 60	**HELLO YOUNG LOVERS** *Columbia DB 4504*	44	1 wk
15 Mar 62	**LOVE ME WARM AND TENDER** *RCA 1276*	19	11 wks
26 Jul 62	**A STEEL GUITAR AND A GLASS OF WINE** *RCA 1292*	41	4 wks
28 Sep 74	● **(YOU'RE) HAVING MY BABY** *United Artists UP 35713* [1]	6	10 wks

[1] Paul Anka featuring Odia Coates

ANNETTE - See *VARIOUS ARTISTS (EPs & LPs)* - Further Adventures Of North EP

ANOUCHKA - See *Terry HALL*

Adam ANT *UK, male vocalist* **194 wks**

2 Aug 80	**KINGS OF THE WILD FRONTIER** *CBS 8877* [1]	48	5 wks
11 Oct 80	● **DOG EAT DOG** *CBS 9039* [1]	4	16 wks
6 Dec 80	● **ANTMUSIC** *CBS 9352* [1]	2	18 wks
27 Dec 80	● **YOUNG PARISIANS** *Decca F13803* [1]	9	13 wks
24 Jan 81	**CARTROUBLE** *Do It DUN 10* [1]	33	9 wks
24 Jan 81	**ZEROX** *Do It DUN 8* [1]	45	9 wks
21 Feb 81	● **KINGS OF THE WILD FRONTIER (re-entry)** *CBS 8877* [1]	2	13 wks
9 May 81	★ **STAND AND DELIVER** *CBS A 1065* [1]	1	15 wks
12 Sep 81	★ **PRINCE CHARMING** *CBS A 1408* [1]	1	12 wks
12 Dec 81	● **ANT RAP** *CBS A 1738* [1]	3	10 wks
27 Feb 82	**DEUTSCHER GIRLS** *Ego 5* [1]	13	6 wks
13 Mar 82	**THE ANTMUSIC EP (THE B-SIDES)** *Do It DUN 20* [1]	46	4 wks
22 May 82	★ **GOODY TWO SHOES** *CBS A 2367*	1	11 wks
18 Sep 82	● **FRIEND OR FOE** *CBS A 2736*	9	8 wks
27 Nov 82	**DESPERATE BUT NOT SERIOUS** *CBS A 2892*	33	7 wks
29 Oct 83	● **PUSS 'N BOOTS** *CBS A 3614*	5	11 wks
10 Dec 83	**STRIP** *CBS A 3589*	41	6 wks
22 Sep 84	**APOLLO 9** *CBS A 4719*	13	8 wks
13 Jul 85	**VIVE LE ROCK** *CBS A 6367*	50	4 wks
17 Feb 90	**ROOM AT THE TOP** *MCA MCA 1387*	13	7 wks
28 Apr 90	**CAN'T SET RULES ABOUT LOVE** *MCA MCA 1404*	47	2 wks

[1] Adam and the Ants

Tracks on The Antmusic EP (The B-Sides): Friends / Kick / Physical.

Billie ANTHONY *UK, female vocalist* **16 wks**

15 Oct 54	● **THIS OLE HOUSE** *Columbia DB 3519*	4	16 wks

Marc ANTHONY - See *Louie VEGA and Marc ANTHONY*

Miki ANTHONY *UK, male vocalist* **7 wks**

3 Feb 73	**IF IT WASN'T FOR THE REASON THAT I LOVE YOU** *Bell 1275*	27	7 wks

Ray ANTHONY *US, orchestra* **2 wks**

4 Dec 53	● **DRAGNET** *Capitol CL 13983*	7	1 wk
8 Jan 54	**DRAGNET (re-entry)** *Capitol CL 13983*	11	1 wk

Richard ANTHONY *France, male vocalist* **15 wks**

12 Dec 63	**WALKING ALONE** *Columbia DB 7133*	37	5 wks
2 Apr 64	**IF I LOVED YOU** *Columbia DB 7235*	48	1 wk
23 Apr 64	**IF I LOVED YOU (re-entry)** *Columbia DB 7235*	18	9 wks

ANTHRAX *US, male vocal / instrumental group* **37 wks**

28 Feb 87	**I AM THE LAW** *Island IS LAW 1*	32	5 wks
27 Jun 87	**INDIANS** *Island IS 325*	44	4 wks
5 Dec 87	**I'M THE MAN** *Island IS 338*	20	6 wks
10 Sep 88	**MAKE ME LAUGH** *Island IS 379*	26	3 wks
18 Mar 89	**ANTI-SOCIAL** *Island IS 409*	44	3 wks
1 Sep 90	**IN MY WORLD** *Island IS 470*	29	2 wks
5 Jan 91	**GOT THE TIME** *Island IS 476*	16	4 wks
6 Jul 91	**BRING THE NOISE** *Island IS 490* [1]	14	5 wks
8 May 93	**ONLY** *Elektra EKR 166CD*	36	3 wks
11 Sep 93	**BLACK LODGE** *Elektra EKR 171CD*	53	2 wks

[1] Anthrax featuring Chuck D

ANTI-NOWHERE LEAGUE
UK, male vocal / instrumental group **10 wks**

23 Jan 82	**STREETS OF LONDON** *WXYZ ABCD 1*	48	5 wks
20 Mar 82	**I HATE ... PEOPLE** *WXYZ ABCD 2*	46	3 wks
3 Jul 82	**WOMAN** *WXYZ ABCD 4*	72	2 wks

ANTI-PASTI - See *EXPLOITED*

ANTICAPPELLA
Italy / UK, male / female vocal / instrumental group **9 wks**

16 Nov 91	**2√231** *PWL Continental PWL 205*	24	4 wks

| 18 Apr 92 | **EVERY DAY** PWL Continental PWL 220 | **45** | 2 wks |
| 25 Jun 94 | **MOVE YOUR BODY** Media MCSTD 1980 [1] | **21** | 3 wks |

[1] Anticappella featuring MC Fixx It

ANTONIA - See BOMB THE BASS

ANTS - See Adam ANT

ANUNA - See Bill WHELAN featuring ANUNA and the RTE CONCERT ORCHESTRA

APACHE INDIAN UK, male vocalist — 25 wks

28 Nov 92	**FE' REAL** Ten TEN 416 [1]	**33**	3 wks
2 Jan 93	**ARRANGED MARRIAGE** Island CID 544	**16**	6 wks
27 Mar 93	**CHOK THERE** Island CID 555	**30**	4 wks
14 Aug 93	● **NUFF VIBES EP** Island CID 560	**5**	10 wks
22 Oct 93	**MOVIN' ON** Island CID 580	**48**	2 wks

[1] Maxi Priest featuring Apache Indian

The listed flip side of Fe' Real was Just Wanna Know by Maxi Priest. Tracks on Nuff Vibes EP: Boom Shack A Lak / Fun / Caste System / Warning.

APHEX TWIN UK, male producer - Richard James — 5 wks

| 9 May 92 | **DIGERIDOO** R&S RSUK 12 | **55** | 2 wks |
| 27 Nov 93 | **ON** Warp WAP 39CD | **32** | 3 wks |

See also Polygon Window.

APHRODITE'S CHILD Greece, male vocal / instrumental group — 7 wks

| 6 Nov 68 | **RAIN AND TEARS** Mercury MF 1039 | **30** | 7 wks |

APOLLO 440 UK, male instrumental / production group — 4 wks

| 22 Jan 94 | **ASTRAL AMERICA** Stealth Sonic SSXCD 2 | **36** | 2 wks |
| 5 Nov 94 | **LIQUID COOL** Stealth Sonic SSXCD 3 | **35** | 2 wks |

Kim APPLEBY UK, female vocalist — 31 wks

3 Nov 90	● **DON'T WORRY** Parlophone R 6272	**2**	10 wks
9 Feb 91	● **G.L.A.D.** Parlophone R 6281	**10**	6 wks
29 Jun 91	**MAMA** Parlophone R 6291	**19**	8 wks
19 Oct 91	**IF YOU CARED** Parlophone R 6297	**44**	3 wks
31 Jul 93	**LIGHT OF THE WORLD** Parlophone CDR 6352	**41**	2 wks
13 Nov 93	**BREAKAWAY** Parlophone CDR 6362	**56**	1 wk
12 Nov 94	**FREE SPIRIT** Parlophone CDR 6397	**51**	1 wk

See also Mel and Kim.

APPLEJACKS UK, male / female vocal / instrumental group — 29 wks

5 Mar 64	● **TELL ME WHEN** Decca F 11833	**7**	13 wks
11 Jun 64	**LIKE DREAMERS DO** Decca F 11916	**20**	11 wks
15 Oct 64	**THREE LITTLE WORDS** Decca F 11981	**23**	5 wks

APPLES UK, male vocal / instrumental group — 1 wk

| 23 Mar 91 | **EYE WONDER** Epic 6566717 | **75** | 1 wk |

Charlie APPLEWHITE US, male vocalist — 1 wk

| 23 Sep 55 | **BLUE STAR (THE MEDIC THEME)** Brunswick 05416 | **20** | 1 wk |

Helen APRIL - See John DUMMER and Helen APRIL

APRIL WINE Canada, male vocal / instrumental group — 9 wks

| 15 Mar 80 | **I LIKE TO ROCK** Capitol CL 16121 | **41** | 5 wks |
| 11 Apr 81 | **JUST BETWEEN YOU AND ME** Capitol CL 16184 | **52** | 4 wks |

AQUARIAN DREAM US, male / female vocal / instrumental group — 1 wk

| 24 Feb 79 | **YOU'RE A STAR** Elektra LV 7 | **67** | 1 wk |

ARCADIA UK, male vocal / instrumental group — 13 wks

26 Oct 85	● **ELECTION DAY** Odeon NSR 1	**7**	7 wks
25 Jan 86	**THE PROMISE** Odeon NSR 2	**37**	4 wks
26 Jul 86	**THE FLAME** Odeon NSR 3	**58**	2 wks

Tasmin ARCHER UK, female vocalist — 35 wks

12 Sep 92	★ **SLEEPING SATELLITE** EMI EM 233	**1**	15 wks
2 Jan 93	**SLEEPING SATELLITE (re-entry)** EMI EM 233	**67**	2 wks
20 Feb 93	**IN YOUR CARE** EMI CDEMS 260	**16**	6 wks
29 May 93	**LORDS OF THE NEW CHURCH** EMI CDEM 266	**26**	4 wks
21 Aug 93	**ARIENNE** EMI CDEM 275	**30**	4 wks
8 Jan 94	**SHIPBUILDING** EMI CDEM 302	**40**	4 wks

ARCHIES US, male / female vocal group — 26 wks

| 11 Oct 69 | ★ **SUGAR SUGAR** RCA 1872 | **1** | 26 wks |

ARGENT UK, male vocal / instrumental group — 27 wks

4 Mar 72	● **HOLD YOUR HEAD UP** Epic EPC 7786	**5**	12 wks
10 Jun 72	**TRAGEDY** Epic EPC 8115	**34**	7 wks
24 Mar 73	**GOD GAVE ROCK AND ROLL TO YOU** Epic EPC 1243	**18**	8 wks

ARIEL UK, male / female vocal / instrumental group — 2 wks

| 27 Mar 93 | **LET IT SLIDE** Deconstruction 74321134512 | **57** | 2 wks |

ARIZONA - See Zeitia MASSIAH

Ship's Company and Royal Marine Band of H.M.S. ARK ROYAL UK, male choir and Marine band — 6 wks

| 23 Dec 78 | **THE LAST FAREWELL** BBC RESL 61 | **46** | 6 wks |

Joan ARMATRADING UK, female vocalist — 53 wks

16 Oct 76	● **LOVE AND AFFECTION** A & M AMS 7249	**10**	9 wks
23 Feb 80	**ROSIE** A & M AMS 7506	**49**	5 wks
14 Jun 80	**ME MYSELF I** A & M AMS 7527	**21**	11 wks
6 Sep 80	**ALL THE WAY FROM AMERICA** A & M AMS 7552	**54**	3 wks
12 Sep 81	**I'M LUCKY** A & M AMS 8163	**46**	5 wks
16 Jan 82	**NO LOVE** A & M AMS 8179	**50**	5 wks
19 Feb 83	**DROP THE PILOT** A & M AMS 8306	**11**	10 wks
16 Mar 85	**TEMPTATION** A & M AM 238	**65**	2 wks
26 May 90	**MORE THAN ONE KIND OF LOVE** A & M AM 561	**75**	1 wk
23 May 92	**WRAPPED AROUND HER** A & M AM 877	**56**	2 wks

ARMOURY SHOW UK, male vocal / instrumental group — 6 wks

25 Aug 84	**CASTLES IN SPAIN** Parlophone R 6079	**69**	2 wks
26 Jan 85	**WE CAN BE BRAVE AGAIN** Parlophone R 6087	**66**	1 wk
17 Jan 87	**LOVE IN ANGER** Parlophone R 6149	**63**	3 wks

Louis ARMSTRONG US, male jazz band leader, vocalist / instrumentalist - trumpet — 87 wks

19 Dec 52	● **TAKES TWO TO TANGO** Brunswick 04995	**6**	10 wks
13 Apr 56	● **THEME FROM THE THREEPENNY OPERA** Philips PB 574 [1]	**8**	11 wks
15 Jun 56	**TAKE IT SATCH EP** Philips BBE 12035 [1]	**29**	1 wk
13 Jul 56	**THE FAITHFUL HUSSAR** Philips PB 604 [1]	**27**	2 wks

6 Nov 59	**MACK THE KNIFE** Philips PB 967 [1]	**24**	1 wk	
4 Jun 64	● **HELLO DOLLY** London HLR 9878	**4**	14 wks	
7 Feb 68	★ **WHAT A WONDERFUL WORLD / CABARET** HMV POP 1615	**1**	29 wks	
26 Jun 68	**SUNSHINE OF LOVE** Stateside SS 2116	**41**	7 wks	
16 Apr 88	**WHAT A WONDERFUL WORLD (re-issue)** A & M AM 435	**53**	5 wks	
19 Nov 94	● **WE HAVE ALL THE TIME IN THE WORLD** EMI CDEM 357	**3†**	7 wks	

[1] Louis Armstrong with his All-Stars

Tracks on Take It Satch *(EP): Tiger Rag/Mack The Knife/The Faithful Hussar/Back O'Town Blues. Mack The Knife is a re-issue of* Theme From Threepenny Opera *under a different title. Cabaret was not listed with* What A Wonderful World *until 14 Feb 68.*

ARMY OF LOVERS
Sweden/France, male/female vocal/group   **12 wks**

17 Aug 91	**CRUCIFIED** Ton Son Ton WOK 2007	**47**	5 wks
28 Dec 91	**OBSESSION** Ton Son Ton WOK 2009	**67**	1 wk
15 Feb 92	**CRUCIFIED (re-issue)** Ton Son Ton WOK 2017	**31**	5 wks
18 Apr 92	**RIDE THE BULLET** Ton Son Ton WOK 2018	**67**	1 wk

ARNEE and the TERMINATERS
UK, male vocal/instrumental group   **7 wks**

24 Aug 91	● **I'LL BE BACK** Epic 6574177	**5**	7 wks

ARNIE'S LOVE
US, male/female vocal/instrumental group   **3 wks**

26 Nov 83	**I'M OUT OF YOUR LIFE** Streetwave WAVE 9	**67**	3 wks

David ARNOLD - *See BJORK*

Eddy ARNOLD *US, male vocalist*   **21 wks**

17 Feb 66	● **MAKE THE WORLD GO AWAY** RCA 1496	**8**	17 wks
26 May 66	**I WANT TO GO WITH YOU** RCA 1519	**49**	1 wk
9 Jun 66	**I WANT TO GO WITH YOU (re-entry)** RCA 1519	**46**	2 wks
28 Jul 66	**IF YOU WERE MINE MARY** RCA 1529	**49**	1 wk

P. P. ARNOLD *US, female vocalist*   **37 wks**

4 May 67	**FIRST CUT IS THE DEEPEST** Immediate IM 047	**18**	10 wks
2 Aug 67	**THE TIME HAS COME** Immediate IM 055	**47**	2 wks
24 Jan 68	**(IF YOU THINK) YOU'RE GROOVY** Immediate IM 061	**41**	4 wks
10 Jul 68	**ANGEL OF THE MORNING** Immediate IM 067	**29**	11 wks
24 Sep 88	**BURN IT UP** Rhythm King LEFT 27 [1]	**14**	10 wks

[1] Beatmasters with P.P. Arnold

ARPEGGIO *US, male/female vocal group*   **3 wks**

31 Mar 79	**LOVE AND DESIRE (PART 1)** Polydor POSP 40	**63**	3 wks

ARRESTED DEVELOPMENT
US, male/female vocal/instrumental group   **39 wks**

16 May 92	**TENNESSEE** Cooltempo COOL 253	**46**	4 wks
11 Jul 92	**TENNESSEE (re-entry)** Cooltempo COOL 253	**54**	3 wks
24 Oct 92	● **PEOPLE EVERYDAY** Cooltempo COOL 265	**2**	14 wks
9 Jan 93	● **MR. WENDAL / REVOLUTION** Cooltempo CDCOOL 268	**4**	9 wks
3 Apr 93	**TENNESSEE (re-issue)** Cooltempo CDCOOL 270	**18**	6 wks
28 May 94	**EASE MY MIND** Cooltempo CDCOOL 293	**33**	3 wks

Steve ARRINGTON *US, male vocalist*   **19 wks**

27 Apr 85	● **FEEL SO REAL** Atlantic A 9576	**5**	10 wks

6 Jul 85	**DANCIN' IN THE KEY OF LIFE** Atlantic A 9534	**21**	8 wks
7 Sep 85	**DANCIN' IN THE KEY OF LIFE (re-entry)** Atlantic A 9534	**75**	1 wk

ARRIVAL *UK, male/female vocal/instrumental group*   **20 wks**

10 Jan 70	● **FRIENDS** Decca F 12986	**8**	9 wks
6 Jun 70	**I WILL SURVIVE** Decca F 13026	**16**	11 wks

ARROW *Montserrat, male vocalist*   **15 wks**

28 Jul 84	**HOT HOT HOT** Cooltempo ARROW 1	**59**	5 wks
13 Jul 85	**LONG TIME** London LON 70	**30**	7 wks
3 Sep 94	**HOT HOT HOT (re-issue)** The Hit Label HLC 7	**38**	3 wks

ARROWS *US/UK, male vocal/instrumental group*   **16 wks**

25 May 74	● **A TOUCH TOO MUCH** RAK 171	**8**	9 wks
1 Feb 75	**MY LAST NIGHT WITH YOU** RAK 189	**25**	7 wks

ARSENAL F.C. FIRST TEAM SQUAD
UK, male football team vocalists   **10 wks**

8 May 71	**GOOD OLD ARSENAL** Pye 7N 45067	**16**	7 wks
15 May 93	**SHOUTING FOR THE GUNNERS** London LONCD 342 [1]	**34**	3 wks

[1] Arsenal FA Cup Squad featuring Tippa Irie and Peter Hunnigale

ART COMPANY
Holland, male vocal/instrumental group   **11 wks**

26 May 84	**SUSANNA** Epic A 4174	**12**	11 wks

ART OF NOISE
UK, male/female instrumental/production group   **64 wks**

24 Nov 84	● **CLOSE (TO THE EDIT)** ZTT ZTPS 01	**8**	19 wks
13 Apr 85	**MOMENTS IN LOVE / BEAT BOX** ZTT ZTPS 02	**51**	4 wks
9 Nov 85	**LEGS** China WOK 5	**69**	1 wk
22 Mar 86	● **PETER GUNN** China WOK 6 [1]	**8**	9 wks
21 Jun 86	**PARANOIMIA** China WOK 9 [2]	**12**	9 wks
18 Jul 87	**DRAGNET** China WOK 14	**60**	4 wks
29 Oct 88	● **KISS** China CHINA 11 [3]	**5**	7 wks
12 Aug 89	**YEBO** China CHINA 18 [4]	**63**	3 wks
16 Jun 90	**ART OF LOVE** China CHINA 23	**67**	1 wk
11 Jan 92	**INSTRUMENTS OF DARKNESS (ALL OF US ARE ONE PEOPLE)** China WOK 2012	**45**	5 wks
29 Feb 92	**SHADES OF PARANOIMIA** China WOK 2014	**53**	2 wks

[1] Art Of Noise featuring Duane Eddy [2] Art Of Noise featuring Max Headroom [3] Art Of Noise featuring Tom Jones [4] Art Of Noise featuring Mahlathini and the Mahotella Queens

Neil ARTHUR *UK, male vocalist*   **2 wks**

5 Feb 94	**I LOVE I HATE** Chrysalis CDCHSS 5005	**50**	2 wks

ARTISTS UNITED AGAINST APARTHEID *Multi-national, male/female vocal/instrumental charity assembly*   **8 wks**

23 Nov 85	**SUN CITY** Manhattan MT 7	**21**	8 wks

ASAP *UK, male vocal/instrumental group*   **4 wks**

14 Oct 89	**SILVER AND GOLD** EMI EM 107	**60**	2 wks
3 Feb 90	**DOWN THE WIRE** EMI EM 131	**67**	2 wks

ASHAYE *UK, male vocalist*   **3 wks**

15 Oct 83	**MICHAEL JACKSON MEDLEY** Record Shack SOHO 10	**45**	3 wks

Tracks on medley: Don't Stop Til You Get Enough/Wanna Be Startin' Something/Shake Your Body Down To The Ground/Blame It On The Boogie.

John ASHER UK, male vocalist · **6 wks**

15 Nov 75	**LET'S TWIST AGAIN** Creole CR 112	**14**	6 wks

ASHFORD and SIMPSON
US, male / female vocal duo · **22 wks**

18 Nov 78	**IT SEEMS TO HANG ON** Warner Bros. K 17237	**48**	4 wks
5 Jan 85	● **SOLID** Capitol CL 345	**3**	15 wks
20 Apr 85	**BABIES** Capitol CL 355	**56**	3 wks

ASHTON, GARDNER AND DYKE
UK, male vocal / instrumental group · **14 wks**

16 Jan 71	● **RESURRECTION SHUFFLE** Capitol CL 15665	**3**	14 wks

ASIA UK, male vocal / instrumental group · **13 wks**

3 Jul 82	**HEAT OF THE MOMENT** Geffen GEF A2494	**46**	5 wks
18 Sep 82	**ONLY TIME WILL TELL** Geffen GEF A2228	**54**	3 wks
13 Aug 83	**DON'T CRY** Geffen A 3580	**33**	5 wks

ASIA BLUE UK, female vocal group · **2 wks**

27 Jun 92	**ESCAPING** Atomic WNR 882	**50**	2 wks

ASSEMBLY UK, male vocal / instrumental group · **10 wks**

12 Nov 83	● **NEVER NEVER** Mute TINY 1	**4**	10 wks

ASSOCIATES UK, male vocal / instrumental group · **47 wks**

20 Feb 82	● **PARTY FEARS TWO** Associates ASC 1	**9**	10 wks
8 May 82	**CLUB COUNTRY** Associates ASC 2	**13**	10 wks
7 Aug 82	**LOVE HANGOVER / 18 CARAT LOVE AFFAIR** Associates ASC 3	**21**	8 wks
16 Jun 84	**THOSE FIRST IMPRESSIONS** WEA YZ 6	**43**	6 wks
1 Sep 84	**WAITING FOR THE LOVEBOAT** WEA YZ 16	**53**	4 wks
19 Jan 85	**BREAKFAST** WEA YZ 28	**49**	6 wks
17 Sep 88	**HEART OF GLASS** WEA YZ 310	**56**	3 wks

18 Carat Love Affair listed until 28 Aug only. Act was duo on 1982 hits.

ASSOCIATION US, male vocal / instrumental group · **8 wks**

22 May 68	**TIME FOR LIVING** Warner Bros. WB 7195	**23**	8 wks

Rick ASTLEY UK, male vocalist · **91 wks**

8 Aug 87	★ **NEVER GONNA GIVE YOU UP** RCA PB 41447	**1**	18 wks
31 Oct 87	● **WHENEVER YOU NEED SOMEBODY** RCA PB 41567	**3**	12 wks
12 Dec 87	● **WHEN I FALL IN LOVE / MY ARMS KEEP MISSING YOU** RCA PB 41683	**2**	10 wks
27 Feb 88	● **TOGETHER FOREVER** RCA PB 41817	**2**	9 wks
24 Sep 88	● **SHE WANTS TO DANCE WITH ME** RCA PB 42189	**6**	10 wks
26 Nov 88	● **TAKE ME TO YOUR HEART** RCA PB 42573	**8**	10 wks
11 Feb 89	● **HOLD ME IN YOUR ARMS** RCA PB 42615	**10**	8 wks
26 Jan 91	● **CRY FOR HELP** RCA PB 44247	**7**	7 wks
30 Mar 91	**MOVE RIGHT OUT** RCA PB 44407	**58**	2 wks
29 Jun 91	**NEVER KNEW LOVE** RCA PB 44737	**70**	1 wk
4 Sep 93	**THE ONES YOU LOVE** RCA 74321160142	**48**	2 wks
13 Nov 93	**HOPELESSLY** RCA 74321175642	**33**	2 wks

Before 9 Jan 88 When I Fall In Love was listed by itself. After that date My Arms Keep Missing You was the side listed.

ASWAD UK, male vocal / instrumental group · **76 wks**

3 Mar 84	**CHASING FOR THE BREEZE** Island IS 160	**51**	3 wks
6 Oct 84	**54-46 (WAS MY NUMBER)** Island IS 170	**70**	3 wks
27 Feb 88	★ **DON'T TURN AROUND** Mango IS 341	**1**	12 wks
21 May 88	**GIVE A LITTLE LOVE** Mango IS 358	**11**	8 wks
24 Sep 88	**SET THEM FREE** Mango IS 383	**70**	2 wks
1 Apr 89	**BEAUTY'S ONLY SKIN DEEP** Mango MNG 105	**31**	6 wks
22 Jul 89	**ON AND ON** Mango MNG 708	**25**	8 wks
18 Aug 90	**NEXT TO YOU** Mango MNG 753	**24**	6 wks
17 Nov 90	**SMILE** Mango MNG 767 [1]	**53**	2 wks
30 Mar 91	**TOO WICKED EP** Mango MNG 771	**61**	2 wks
31 Jul 93	**HOW LONG** Polydor PZCD 252 [2]	**31**	5 wks
9 Oct 93	**DANCE HALL MOOD** Bubblin' CDBUBB 1	**48**	2 wks
18 Jun 94	● **SHINE** Bubblin' CDBUBB 3	**5**	14 wks
17 Sep 94	**WARRIORS** Bubblin' CDBUBB 4	**33**	3 wks

[1] Aswad featuring Sweetie Irie [2] Yazz and Aswad

Tracks on Too Wicked EP: *Best of My Love / Warrior Re-Charge / Fire / I Shot The Sheriff.*

Gali ATARI - *See MILK AND HONEY featuring Gali ATARI*

Chet ATKINS US, male instrumentalist - guitar · **2 wks**

17 Mar 60	**TEENSVILLE** RCA 1174	**46**	1 wk
5 May 60	**TEENSVILLE (re-entry)** RCA 1174	**49**	1 wk

ATLANTA RHYTHM SECTION
US, male vocal / instrumental group · **4 wks**

27 Oct 79	**SPOOKY** Polydor POSP 74	**48**	4 wks

ATLANTIC OCEAN Holland, male instrumental duo · **11 wks**

19 Feb 94	**WATERFALL** Eastern Bloc BLOCCD 001	**22**	6 wks
2 Jul 94	**BODY IN MOTION** Eastern Bloc BLOCCD 009	**15**	4 wks
26 Nov 94	**MUSIC IS A PASSION** Eastern Bloc BLOCCDX 017	**59**	1 wk

ATLANTIC STARR
US, male / female vocal / instrumental group · **48 wks**

9 Sep 78	**GIMME YOUR LOVIN'** A & M AMS 7380	**66**	3 wks
29 Jun 85	**SILVER SHADOW** A & M AM 260	**41**	6 wks
7 Sep 85	**ONE LOVE** A & M AM 273	**58**	4 wks
15 Mar 86	**SECRET LOVERS** A & M AM 307	**10**	12 wks
24 May 86	**IF YOUR HEART ISN'T IN IT** A & M AM 319	**48**	4 wks
13 Jun 87	● **ALWAYS** Warner Bros. W 8455	**3**	14 wks
12 Sep 87	**ONE LOVER AT A TIME** Warner Bros. W 8327	**57**	3 wks
27 Aug 94	**EVERYBODY'S GOT SUMMER** Arista 74321228072	**36**	2 wks

ATMOSFEAR UK, male vocal / instrumental group · **7 wks**

17 Nov 79	**DANCING IN OUTER SPACE** MCA 543	**46**	7 wks

ATOMIC ROOSTER
UK, male vocal / instrumental group · **25 wks**

6 Feb 71	**TOMORROW NIGHT** B & C CB 131	**11**	12 wks
10 Jul 71	● **THE DEVIL'S ANSWER** B & C CB 157	**4**	13 wks

ATTRACTIONS - *See Elvis COSTELLO and the ATTRACTIONS*

Winifred ATWELL UK, female instrumentalist - piano · **117 wks**

12 Dec 52	**BRITANNIA RAG** Decca F 10015	**11**	1 wk
9 Jan 53	● **BRITANNIA RAG (re-entry)** Decca F 10015	**5**	5 wks
15 May 53	**CORONATION RAG** Decca F 10110	**12**	1 wk
29 May 53	● **CORONATION RAG (re-entry)** Decca F 10110	**5**	5 wks
25 Sep 53	**FLIRTATION WALTZ** Decca F 10161	**12**	1 wk
9 Oct 53	● **FLIRTATION WALTZ (re-entry)** Decca F 10161	**10**	1 wk
6 Nov 53	**FLIRTATION WALTZ (2nd re-entry)** Decca F10161	**12**	1 wk
4 Dec 53	● **LET'S HAVE A PARTY** Philips PB 213	**2**	9 wks
23 Jul 54	● **RACHMANINOFF'S 18TH VARIATION ON A THEME BY PAGANINI (THE STORY OF THREE LOVES)** Philips PB 234	**9**	7 wks
1 Oct 54	**RACHMANINOFF'S 18TH VARIATION ON A THEME BY PAGANINI (THE STORY OF THREE LOVES) (re-entry)** Philips PB 234	**19**	2 wks

26 Nov 54	★ LET'S HAVE ANOTHER PARTY *Philips PB 268*............1	8 wks
26 Nov 54	LET'S HAVE A PARTY (re-entry) *Philips PB 213* 14	6 wks
4 Nov 55	● LET'S HAVE A DING DONG *Decca F 10634*............3	10 wks
16 Mar 56	★ POOR PEOPLE OF PARIS *Decca F 10681* 1	16 wks
18 May 56	PORT AU PRINCE *Decca F 10727* [1] 18	6 wks
20 Jul 56	LEFT BANK *Decca F 10762* 14	7 wks
26 Oct 56	● MAKE IT A PARTY *Decca F 10796* 7	12 wks
22 Feb 57	LET'S ROCK 'N ROLL *Decca F 10852* 28	2 wks
15 Mar 57	LET'S ROCK 'N ROLL (re-entry) *Decca F 10852*.......24	2 wks
6 Dec 57	● LET'S HAVE A BALL *Decca F 10956* 4	6 wks
7 Aug 59	SUMMER OF THE SEVENTEENTH DOLL *Decca F 11143* 24	2 wks
27 Nov 59	● PIANO PARTY *Decca F 11183* 10	7 wks

[1] Winifred Atwell and Frank Chacksfield

Various hits listed above were medleys as follows: Let's Have a Party: *Boomps A Daisy / Daisy Bell / If You Knew Suzie / Knees Up Mother Brown / The More We Are Together / She Was One Of The Early Birds / That's My Weakness Now / Three O'Clock In The Morning.* Let's Have Another Party: *Another Little Drink / Broken Doll / Bye Bye Blackbird / Honeysuckle And The Bee / I Wonder Where My Baby Is Tonight / Lily of Laguna / Nellie Dean / Sheik of Araby / Somebody Stole My Gal / When The Red Red Robin.* Let's Have a Ding Dong: *Happy Days Are Here Again / Oh Johnny Oh Johnny Oh / Oh You Beautiful Doll / Ain't She Sweet / Yes We Have No Bananas / I'm Forever Blowing Bubbles / I'll Be Your Sweetheart / If These Lips Could Only Speak / Who's Taking You Home Tonight.* Make It a Party: *Who Were You With Last Night / Hello Hello Who's Your Lady Friend / Yes Sir That's My Baby / Don't Dilly Dally On The Way / Beer Barrel Polka / After The Ball / Peggy O'Neil / Meet Me Tonight In Dreamland / I Belong To Glasgow / Down At The Old Bull And Bush.* Let's Rock 'n Roll: *Singin' The Blues / Green Door / See You Later Alligator / Shake Rattle And Roll / Rock Around The Clock / Razzle Dazzle.* Let's Have a Ball: *Music Music Music / This Ole House / Heartbreaker / Woody Woodpecker / Last Train To San Fernando / Bring A Little Water Sylvie / Puttin' On The Style / Don't You Rock Me Daddy-O.* Piano Party: *Baby Face / Comin' Thru' The Rye / Annie Laurie / Little Brown Jug / Let Him Go Let Him Tarry / Put Your Arms Around Me Honey / I'll Be With You In Apple Blossom Time / Shine On Harvest Moon / Blue Skies / I'll Never Say 'Never Again' Again / I'll See You In My Dreams. See Various Artists (EPs & LPs) - All Star Hit Parade.*

Brian AUGER - *See Julie DRISCOLL, Brian AUGER and the TRINITY*

AURRA *US, male / female vocal duo* **18 wks**

4 May 85	LIKE I LIKE IT *10 TEN 45* 51	5 wks
19 Apr 86	YOU AND ME TONIGHT *10 TEN 71* 12	8 wks
21 Jun 86	LIKE I LIKE IT (re-issue) *10 TEN 126* 43	5 wks

David AUSTIN *UK, male vocalist* **3 wks**

21 Jul 84	TURN TO GOLD *Parlophone R 6068*.............68	3 wks

Patti AUSTIN *US, female vocalist* **20 wks**

20 Jun 81	RAZZAMATAZZ *A & M AMS 8140* [1] 11	9 wks
12 Feb 83	BABY COME TO ME *Qwest K 15005* [2] 11	10 wks
5 Sep 92	I'LL KEEP YOUR DREAMS ALIVE *Ammi AMM 101* [3] 68	1 wk

[1] Quincy Jones featuring Patti Austin [2] Patti Austin and James Ingram [3] George Benson and Patti Austin

AUTECHRE *UK, male instrumental duo* **1 wk**

7 May 94	BASSCAD *Warp WAP 44CD* 56	1 wk

AUTEURS *UK, male / female vocal / instrumental group* **4 wks**

27 Nov 93	LENNY VALENTINO *Hut HUTCD 36*............41	2 wks
23 Apr 94	CHINESE BAKERY *Hut HUTDX 41* 42	2 wks

AUTUMN *UK, male vocal / instrumental group* **6 wks**

16 Oct 71	MY LITTLE GIRL *Pye 7N 45090* 37	6 wks

Peter AUTY and the SINFONIA OF LONDON
UK, male vocalist with UK orchestra **9 wks**

14 Dec 85	WALKING IN THE AIR *Stiff LAD 1* 42	5 wks
19 Dec 87	WALKING IN THE AIR (re-issue) *CBS GA 3950* 37	4 wks

Label credits the Snowman featuring Peter Auty. See also Digital Dream Baby.

AVALON BOYS - *See LAUREL and HARDY with the AVALON BOYS*

Frankie AVALON *US, male vocalist* **15 wks**

10 Oct 58	GINGERBREAD *HMV POP 517* 30	1 wk
24 Apr 59	VENUS *HMV POP 603* 16	6 wks
22 Jan 60	WHY *HMV POP 688* 20	4 wks
28 Apr 60	DON'T THROW AWAY ALL THOSE TEARDROPS *HMV POP 727* 37	4 wks

AVERAGE WHITE BAND
UK, male vocal / instrumental vocal group **47 wks**

22 Feb 75	● PICK UP THE PIECES *Atlantic K 10489* 6	9 wks
26 Apr 75	CUT THE CAKE *Atlantic K 10605* 31	4 wks
9 Oct 76	QUEEN OF MY SOUL *Atlantic K 10825* 23	7 wks
28 Apr 79	WALK ON BY *RCA XC 1087* 46	5 wks
25 Aug 79	WHEN WILL YOU BE MINE *RCA XB 1096* 49	5 wks
26 Apr 80	LET'S GO ROUND AGAIN PT.1 *RCA AWB 1* 12	11 wks
26 Jul 80	FOR YOUR LOVE *RCA AWB 2* 46	4 wks
26 Mar 94	LET'S GO ROUND AGAIN (re-mix) *The Hit Label HLC 5* 56	2 wks

AVONS *UK, male / female vocal group* **22 wks**

13 Nov 59	● SEVEN LITTLE GIRLS SITTING IN THE BACK SEAT *Columbia DB 4363* 3	13 wks
7 Jul 60	WE'RE ONLY YOUNG ONCE *Columbia DB 4461* 49	1 wk
21 Jul 60	WE'RE ONLY YOUNG ONCE (re-entry) *Columbia DB 4461* 45	1 wk
27 Oct 60	FOUR LITTLE HEELS *Columbia DB 4522* 45	2 wks
1 Dec 60	FOUR LITTLE HEELS (re-entry) *Columbia DB 4522* ..49	1 wk
26 Jan 61	RUBBER BALL *Columbia DB 4569* 30	4 wks

AWESOME 3 *UK, male / female vocal / instrumental group* **6 wks**

8 Sep 90	HARD UP *A & M AM 591* 55	3 wks
3 Oct 92	DON'T GO *Citybeat CBE 1271* 75	1 wk
4 Jun 94	DON'T GO (re-mix) *Citybeat CBX 771CD* 45	2 wks

Hoyt AXTON *US, male vocalist* **4 wks**

7 Jun 80	DELLA AND THE DEALER *Young Blood YB 82*.......48	4 wks

Roy AYERS
US, male vocalist / instrumentalist - vibraphone **12 wks**

21 Oct 78	GET ON UP, GET ON DOWN *Polydor AYERS 7* 41	4 wks
13 Jan 79	HEAT OF THE BEAT *Polydor POSP 16* [1] 43	5 wks
2 Feb 80	DON'T STOP THE FEELING *Polydor STEP 6* 56	3 wks

[1] Roy Ayers and Wayne Henderson

Charles AZNAVOUR *France, male vocalist* **29 wks**

22 Sep 73	THE OLD FASHIONED WAY *Barclay BAR 20* 58	1 wk
20 Oct 73	THE OLD FASHIONED WAY (re-entry) *Barclay BAR 20* 38	12 wks
22 Jun 74	★ SHE *Barclay BAR 26* 1	14 wks

27 Jul 74	THE OLD FASHIONED WAY (2nd re-entry)		
	Barclay BAR 20	47	2 wks

AZTEC CAMERA UK, male vocal / instrumental group — 74 wks

19 Feb 83	OBLIVIOUS Rough Trade RT 122	47	6 wks
4 Jun 83	WALK OUT TO WINTER Rough Trade RT 132	64	4 wks
5 Nov 83	OBLIVIOUS (re-issue) WEA AZTEC 1	18	11 wks
1 Sep 84	ALL I NEED IS EVERYTHING WEA AC 1	34	6 wks
13 Feb 88	HOW MEN ARE WEA YZ 168	25	9 wks
23 Apr 88	● SOMEWHERE IN MY HEART WEA YZ 181	3	14 wks
6 Aug 88	WORKING IN A GOLDMINE WEA YZ 199	31	5 wks
8 Oct 88	DEEP AND WIDE AND TALL WEA YZ 154	55	3 wks
7 Jul 90	THE CRYING SCENE WEA YZ 492	70	3 wks
6 Oct 90	GOOD MORNING BRITAIN WEA YZ 521 [1]	19	8 wks
18 Jul 92	SPANISH HORSES WEA YZ 688	52	3 wks
1 May 93	DREAM SWEET DREAMS WEA YZ 740CD1	67	2 wks

[1] Aztec Camera and Mick Jones

AZYMUTH Brazil, male instrumental group — 8 wks

12 Jan 80	JAZZ CARNIVAL Milestone MRC 101	19	8 wks

Bob AZZAM Egypt, singing orchestra — 14 wks

26 May 60	MUSTAPHA Decca F 21235	23	14 wks

B

Derek B UK, male rapper — 15 wks

27 Feb 88	GOODGROOVE Music Of Life 7NOTE 12	16	6 wks
7 May 88	BAD YOUNG BROTHER Tuff Audio DRKB 1	16	6 wks
2 Jul 88	WE'VE GOT THE JUICE Tuff Audio DRKB 2	56	3 wks

Eric B and RAKIM
US, male vocal / instrumental duo — 26 wks

7 Nov 87	PAID IN FULL Fourth & Broadway BRW 78	15	6 wks
20 Feb 88	MOVE THE CROWD Fourth & Broadway BRW 88	53	2 wks
12 Mar 88	I KNOW YOU GOT SOUL Cooltempo COOL 146	13	6 wks
2 Jul 88	FOLLOW THE LEADER MCA MCA 1256	21	5 wks
19 Nov 88	THE MICROPHONE FIEND MCA MCA 1300	74	1 wk
12 Aug 89	FRIENDS MCA MCA 1352 [1]	21	6 wks

[1] Jody Watley with Eric B and Rakim

JAZZIE B - See Maxi PRIEST: SOUL II SOUL

Lisa B US, female vocalist — 9 wks

12 Jun 93	GLAM ffrr FCD 210	49	2 wks
25 Sep 93	FASCINATED ffrr FCD 218	35	3 wks
8 Jan 94	YOU AND ME ffrr FCD 226	39	4 wks

Sandy B US, female vocalist — 1 wk

20 Feb 93	FEEL LIKE SINGIN' Nervous SANCD 1	60	1 wk

Stevie B US, male vocalist — 9 wks

23 Feb 91	● BECAUSE I LOVE YOU (THE POSTMAN SONG)		
	Polydor PO 126	6	9 wks

Tairrie B US, female rapper — 2 wks

1 Dec 90	MURDER SHE WROTE MCA MCA 1455	71	2 wks

B B and Q BAND US, male vocal / instrumental group — 15 wks

18 Jul 81	ON THE BEAT Capitol CL 202	41	5 wks
6 Jul 85	GENIE Cooltempo COOL 110 [1]	40	4 wks
20 Sep 86	(I'M A) DREAMER Cooltempo COOL 132	35	5 wks
17 Oct 87	RICOCHET Cooltempo COOL 154	71	1 wk

[1] Brooklyn Bronx and Queens

Alice BABS Sweden, female vocalist — 1 wk

15 Aug 63	AFTER YOU'VE GONE Fontana TF 409	43	1 wk

BABY D UK, male / female vocal / instrumental group — 9 wks

18 Dec 93	DESTINY Production House PNC 057	69	1 wk
23 Jul 94	CASANOVA Production House PNC 065	67	1 wk
19 Nov 94	★ LET ME BE YOUR FANTASY Systematic SYSCD 4	1†	7 wks

BABY JUNE UK, male vocalist - Tim Hegarty — 1 wk

15 Aug 92	HEY! WHAT'S YOUR NAME Arista 115271	75	1 wk

BABY O US, male / female vocal / instrumental group — 5 wks

26 Jul 80	IN THE FOREST Calibre CAB 505	46	5 wks

BABY ROOTS UK, male vocalist — 1 wk

1 Aug 92	ROCK ME BABY ZYX ZYX 68027	71	1 wk

BABYFACE US, male vocalist — 7 wks

9 Jul 94	ROCK BOTTOM Epic 6601832	50	4 wks
1 Oct 94	WHEN CAN I SEE YOU Epic 6606592	35	3 wks

BABYS US / UK, male vocal / instrumental group — 3 wks

21 Jan 78	ISN'T IT TIME Chrysalis CHS 2173	45	3 wks

BACCARA Spain, female vocal duo — 25 wks

17 Sep 77	★ YES SIR I CAN BOOGIE RCA PB 5526	1	16 wks
14 Jan 78	● SORRY I'M A LADY RCA PB 5555	8	9 wks

Burt BACHARACH US, orchestra and chorus — 11 wks

20 May 65	● TRAINS AND BOATS AND PLANES		
	London HL 9968	4	11 wks

BACHELORS Ireland, male vocal group — 187 wks

24 Jan 63	● CHARMAINE Decca F 11559	6	19 wks
4 Jul 63	FARAWAY PLACES Decca F 11666	36	3 wks
29 Aug 63	WHISPERING Decca F 11712	18	10 wks
23 Jan 64	★ DIANE Decca F 11799	1	19 wks
19 Mar 64	● I BELIEVE Decca F 11857	2	17 wks
4 Jun 64	● RAMONA Decca F 11910	4	13 wks
13 Aug 64	● I WOULDN'T TRADE YOU FOR THE WORLD		
	Decca F 11949	4	16 wks
3 Dec 64	● NO ARMS CAN EVER HOLD YOU Decca F 12034	7	12 wks
1 Apr 65	TRUE LOVE FOR EVER MORE Decca F 12108	34	6 wks
20 May 65	● MARIE Decca F 12156	9	12 wks
28 Oct 65	IN THE CHAPEL IN THE MOONLIGHT		
	Decca F 12256	27	10 wks
6 Jan 66	HELLO DOLLY Decca F 12309	38	4 wks
17 Mar 66	● THE SOUND OF SILENCE Decca F 12351	3	13 wks
7 Jul 66	CAN I TRUST YOU Decca F 12417	26	7 wks
1 Dec 66	WALK WITH FAITH IN YOUR HEART		
	Decca F 22523	22	9 wks

| 6 Apr 67 | **OH HOW I MISS YOU** Decca F 22592 | **30** | 8 wks |
| 5 Jul 67 | **MARTA** Decca F 22634 | **20** | 9 wks |

BACHMAN-TURNER OVERDRIVE
Canada, male vocal / instrumental group   **18 wks**

| 16 Nov 74 | ● **YOU AIN'T SEEN NOTHIN' YET** Mercury 6167 025 | **2** | 12 wks |
| 1 Feb 75 | **ROLL ON DOWN THE HIGHWAY** Mercury 6167 071 | **22** | 6 wks |

BACK TO THE PLANET
UK, male / female vocal / instrumental group   **2 wks**

| 10 Apr 93 | **TEENAGE TURTLES** Parallel LLLCD 3 | **52** | 1 wk |
| 4 Sep 93 | **DAYDREAM** Parallel LLLCD 8 | **52** | 1 wk |

BACKBEAT BAND
US, male vocal / instrumental group   **5 wks**

26 Mar 94	**MONEY** Virgin VSCDX 1489	**48**	3 wks
23 Apr 94	**MONEY (re-entry)** Virgin VSCDX 1489	**73**	1 wk
14 May 94	**PLEASE MR. POSTMAN** Virgin VSCDX 1502	**69**	1 wk

BACKBEAT DISCIPLES - *See Arthur BAKER*

BACKROOM BOYS - *See Frank IFIELD*

BAD BOYS INC
UK, male vocal group   **31 wks**

14 Aug 93	**DON'T TALK ABOUT LOVE** A & M 5803412	**19**	5 wks
2 Oct 93	**WHENEVER YOU NEED SOMEONE** A & M 5804032	**26**	3 wks
11 Dec 93	**WALKING ON AIR** A & M 5804692	**24**	6 wks
21 May 94	● **MORE TO THIS WORLD** A & M 5806072	**8**	7 wks
23 Jul 94	**TAKE ME AWAY (I'LL FOLLOW YOU)** A & M 5806912	**15**	6 wks
17 Sep 94	**LOVE HERE I COME** A & M 5807752	**26**	4 wks

BAD COMPANY
UK, male vocal / instrumental group   **23 wks**

1 Jun 74	**CAN'T GET ENOUGH** Island WIP 6191	**15**	8 wks
22 Mar 75	**GOOD LOVIN' GONE BAD** Island WIP 6223	**31**	6 wks
30 Aug 75	**FEEL LIKE MAKIN' LOVE** Island WIP 6242	**20**	9 wks

BAD ENGLISH
UK / US, male vocal / instrumental group   **3 wks**

| 25 Nov 89 | **WHEN I SEE YOU SMILE** Epic 6553471 | **61** | 3 wks |

BAD MANNERS
UK, male vocal / instrumental group   **111 wks**

1 Mar 80	**NE-NE NA-NA NA-NA NU-NU** Magnet MAG 164	**28**	14 wks
14 Jun 80	**LIP UP FATTY** Magnet MAG 175	**15**	14 wks
27 Sep 80	● **SPECIAL BREW** Magnet MAG 180	**3**	13 wks
6 Dec 80	**LORRAINE** Magnet MAG 181	**21**	12 wks
28 Mar 81	**JUST A FEELING** Magnet MAG 187	**13**	9 wks
27 Jun 81	● **CAN CAN** Magnet MAG 190	**3**	13 wks
26 Sep 81	● **WALKING IN THE SUNSHINE** Magnet MAG 197	**10**	9 wks
21 Nov 81	**BUONA SERA** Magnet MAG 211	**34**	9 wks
1 May 82	**GOT NO BRAINS** Magnet MAG 216	**44**	5 wks
31 Jul 82	● **MY GIRL LOLLIPOP (MY BOY LOLLIPOP)** Magnet MAG 232	**9**	7 wks
30 Oct 82	**SAMSON AND DELILAH** Magnet MAG 236	**58**	3 wks
14 May 83	**THAT'LL DO NICELY** Magnet MAG 243	**49**	3 wks

BAD NEWS
UK, male vocal group   **5 wks**

| 12 Sep 87 | **BOHEMIAN RHAPSODY** EMI EM 24 | **44** | 5 wks |

BAD SEEDS - *See Nick CAVE*

BAD YARD CLUB - *See David MORALES and the BAD YARD CLUB*

Wally BADAROU
France, male instrumentalist - keyboards   **6 wks**

| 19 Oct 85 | **CHIEF INSPECTOR** Fourth & Broadway BRW 37 | **46** | 6 wks |

BADFINGER
UK, male vocal / instrumental group   **34 wks**

10 Jan 70	● **COME AND GET IT** Apple 20	**4**	11 wks
9 Jan 71	● **NO MATTER WHAT** Apple 31	**5**	12 wks
29 Jan 72	● **DAY AFTER DAY** Apple 40	**10**	11 wks

See also Various Artists (EPs & LPs) - The Apple EP.

BADMAN
UK, male producer – Julian Brettle   **3 wks**

| 2 Feb 91 | **MAGIC STYLE** Citybeat CBE 759 | **61** | 3 wks |

Joan BAEZ
US, female vocalist   **47 wks**

6 May 65	**WE SHALL OVERCOME** Fontana TF 564	**26**	10 wks
8 Jul 65	● **THERE BUT FOR FORTUNE** Fontana TF 587	**8**	12 wks
2 Sep 65	**IT'S ALL OVER NOW BABY BLUE** Fontana TF 604	**22**	8 wks
23 Dec 65	**FAREWELL ANGELINA** Fontana TF 639	**35**	3 wks
20 Jan 66	**FAREWELL ANGELINA (re-entry)** Fontana TF 639	**49**	1 wk
28 Jul 66	**PACK UP YOUR SORROWS** Fontana TF 727	**50**	1 wk
9 Oct 71	● **THE NIGHT THEY DROVE OLD DIXIE DOWN** Vanguard VS 35138	**6**	12 wks

Philip BAILEY
US, male vocalist   **20 wks**

| 9 Mar 85 | ★ **EASY LOVER** CBS A 4915 [1] | **1** | 12 wks |
| 18 May 85 | **WALKING ON THE CHINESE WALL** CBS A 6202 | **34** | 8 wks |

[1] Philip Bailey (duet with Phil Collins)

Adrian BAKER
UK, male vocalist   **8 wks**

| 19 Jul 75 | ● **SHERRY** Magnet MAG 34 | **10** | 8 wks |

See also Gidea Park.

Anita BAKER
US, female vocalist   **22 wks**

15 Nov 86	**SWEET LOVE** Elektra EKR 44	**13**	10 wks
31 Jan 87	**CAUGHT UP IN THE RAPTURE** Elektra EKR 49	**51**	5 wks
8 Oct 88	**GIVING YOU THE BEST THAT I GOT** Elektra EKR 79	**55**	3 wks
30 Jun 90	**TALK TO ME** Elektra EKR 111	**68**	2 wks
17 Sep 94	**BODY & SOUL** Elektra EKR 190CD	**48**	2 wks

Arthur BAKER
US, male producer / multi-instrumentalist   **7 wks**

| 20 May 89 | **IT'S YOUR TIME** Breakout USA 654 [1] | **64** | 2 wks |
| 21 Oct 89 | **THE MESSAGE IS LOVE** Breakout USA 668 [2] | **38** | 5 wks |

[1] Arthur Baker featuring Shirley Lewis [2] Arthur Baker and the Backbeat Disciples featuring Al Green.

See also Wally Jump Jr. and the Criminal Element.

Hylda BAKER and Arthur MULLARD
UK, female / male vocal duo   **6 wks**

| 9 Sep 78 | **YOU'RE THE ONE THAT I WANT** Pye 7N 46121 | **22** | 6 wks |

George BAKER SELECTION
Holland, male / female vocal / instrumental group   **10 wks**

| 6 Sep 75 | ● **PALOMA BLANCA** Warner Bros. K 16541 | **10** | 10 wks |

BALAAM AND THE ANGEL
UK, male vocal / instrumental group   **2 wks**

| 29 Mar 86 | **SHE KNOWS** Virgin VS 842 | **70** | 2 wks |

Long John BALDRY
UK, male vocalist   **36 wks**

| 8 Nov 67 | ★ **LET THE HEARTACHES BEGIN** Pye 7N 17385 | **1** | 13 wks |
| 28 Aug 68 | **WHEN THE SUN COMES SHININ' THRU** Pye 7N 17593 | **29** | 7 wks |

23 Oct 68	**MEXICO** *Pye 7N 17563*	**15** 8 wks
29 Jan 69	**IT'S TOO LATE NOW** *Pye 7N 17664*	**21** 8 wks

Kenny BALL and his JAZZMEN
UK, male jazz band, Kenny Ball vocals and trumpet **136 wks**

23 Feb 61	**SAMANTHA** *Pye Jazz Today 7NJ 2040*	**13** 15 wks
11 May 61	**I STILL LOVE YOU ALL** *Pye Jazz 7NJ 2042*	**24** 6 wks
31 Aug 61	**SOMEDAY** *Pye Jazz 7NJ 2047*	**28** 6 wks
9 Nov 61	● **MIDNIGHT IN MOSCOW** *Pye Jazz 7NJ 2049* ...	**2** 21 wks
15 Feb 62	● **MARCH OF THE SIAMESE CHILDREN** *Pye Jazz 7NJ 2051*	**4** 13 wks
17 May 62	● **THE GREEN LEAVES OF SUMMER** *Pye Jazz 7NJ 2054*	**7** 14 wks
23 Aug 62	**SO DO I** *Pye Jazz 7NJ 2056*	**14** 8 wks
18 Oct 62	**THE PAY OFF** *Pye Jazz 7NJ 2061*	**23** 6 wks
17 Jan 63	● **SUKIYAKI** *Pye Jazz 7NJ 2062*	**10** 13 wks
25 Apr 63	**CASABLANCA** *Pye Jazz 7NJ 2064*	**21** 11 wks
13 Jun 63	**RONDO** *Pye Jazz 7NJ 2065*	**24** 8 wks
22 Aug 63	**ACAPULCO 1922** *Pye Jazz 7NJ 2067*	**27** 6 wks
11 Jun 64	**HELLO DOLLY** *Pye Jazz 7NJ 2071*	**30** 7 wks
19 Jul 67	**WHEN I'M 64** *Pye 7N 17348*	**43** 2 wks

Michael BALL *UK, male vocalist* **33 wks**

28 Jan 89	● **LOVE CHANGES EVERYTHING** *Really Useful RUR 3* ..	**2** 14 wks
28 Oct 89	**THE FIRST MAN YOU REMEMBER** *Really Useful RUR 6* [1]	**68** 2 wks
10 Aug 91	**IT'S STILL YOU** *Polydor PO 160*	**58** 2 wks
25 Apr 92	**ONE STEP OUT OF TIME** *Polydor PO 206*	**20** 7 wks
12 Dec 92	**IF I CAN DREAM (EP)** *Polydor PO 248*	**51** 1 wk
26 Dec 92	**IF I CAN DREAM (EP) (re-entry)** *Polydor PO 248*	**68** 1 wk
11 Sep 93	**SUNSET BOULEVARD** *Polydor PZCD 293*	**72** 1 wk
30 Jul 94	**FROM HERE TO ETERNITY** *Columbia 6606905*	**36** 3 wks
17 Sep 94	**THE LOVERS WE WERE** *Columbia 6607972*	**63** 2 wks

[1] Michael Ball and Diana Morrison

Tracks on If I Can Dream (EP): If I Can Dream / You Don't Have To Say You Love Me / Always On My Mind / Tell Me There's A Heaven.

BALTIMORA *Ireland, male vocalist* **12 wks**

10 Aug 85	● **TARZAN BOY** *Columbia DB 9102*	**3** 12 wks

BAM BAM *US, male vocalist / multi-instrumentalist* **2 wks**

19 Mar 88	**GIVE IT TO ME** *Serious 7OUS 10*	**65** 2 wks

Afrika BAMBAATAA *US, male vocalist* **23 wks**

28 Aug 82	**PLANET ROCK** *Polydor POSP 497* [1]	**53** 3 wks
10 Mar 84	**RENEGADES OF FUNK** *Tommy Boy AFR 1* [1]	**30** 4 wks
1 Sep 84	**UNITY (PART 1 - THE THIRD COMING)** *Tommy Boy AFR 2* [2]	**49** 5 wks
27 Feb 88	**RECKLESS** *EMI EM 41* [3]	**17** 8 wks
12 Oct 91	**JUST GET UP AND DANCE** *EMI USA MT 100*	**45** 3 wks

[1] Afrika Bambaataa and the Soul Sonic Force [2] Afrika Bambaataa and James Brown [3] Afrika Bambaataa featuring UB40 and Family

BANANARAMA *UK, female vocal group* **202 wks**

13 Feb 82	● **IT AIN'T WHAT YOU DO IT'S THE WAY THAT YOU DO IT** *Chrysalis CHS 2570* [1]	**4** 10 wks
10 Apr 82	● **REALLY SAYING SOMETHING** *Deram NANA 1* [2]	**5** 10 wks
3 Jul 82	● **SHY BOY** *London NANA 2*	**4** 11 wks
4 Dec 82	**CHEERS THEN** *London NANA 3*	**45** 7 wks
26 Feb 83	● **NA NA HEY HEY KISS HIM GOODBYE** *London NANA 4*	**5** 10 wks
9 Jul 83	● **CRUEL SUMMER** *London NANA 5*	**8** 10 wks
3 Mar 84	● **ROBERT DE NIRO'S WAITING** *London NANA 6*	**3** 11 wks
26 May 84	**ROUGH JUSTICE** *London NANA 7*	**23** 7 wks
24 Nov 84	**HOTLINE TO HEAVEN** *London NANA 8*	**58** 2 wks
24 Aug 85	**DO NOT DISTURB** *London NANA 9*	**31** 6 wks
31 May 86	● **VENUS** *London NANA 10*	**8** 13 wks
16 Aug 86	**MORE THAN PHYSICAL** *London NANA 11*	**41** 5 wks
14 Feb 87	**TRICK OF THE NIGHT** *London NANA 12*	**32** 5 wks
11 Jul 87	**I HEARD A RUMOUR** *London NANA 13*	**14** 9 wks
10 Oct 87	● **LOVE IN THE FIRST DEGREE** *London NANA 14*	**3** 12 wks
9 Jan 88	**I CAN'T HELP IT** *London NANA 15*	**20** 6 wks
9 Apr 88	● **I WANT YOU BACK** *London NANA 16*	**5** 10 wks
24 Sep 88	**LOVE, TRUTH AND HONESTY** *London NANA 17*	**23** 8 wks
19 Nov 88	**NATHAN JONES** *London NANA 18*	**15** 9 wks
25 Feb 89	● **HELP** *London LON 222* [3]	**3** 9 wks
10 Jun 89	**CRUEL SUMMER (re-mix)** *London NANA 19*	**19** 6 wks
28 Jul 90	**ONLY YOUR LOVE** *London NANA 21*	**27** 4 wks
5 Jan 91	**PREACHER MAN** *London NANA 23*	**20** 6 wks
20 Apr 91	**LONG TRAIN RUNNING** *London NANA 24*	**30** 5 wks
29 Aug 92	**MOVIN' ON** *London NANA 25*	**24** 5 wks
28 Nov 92	**LAST THING ON MY MIND** *London NANA 26*	**71** 2 wks
20 Mar 93	**MORE MORE MORE** *London NACPD 27*	**24** 4 wks

[1] Fun Boy Three and Bananarama [2] Bananarama with Fun Boy Three [3] Bananarama/La Na Nee Nee Noo Noo

The listed flip side of Love In The First Degree was Mr Sleaze by Stock Aitken Waterman. Act were a duo for last two hits.

BAND *Canada / US, male vocal / instrumental group* **18 wks**

18 Sep 68	**THE WEIGHT** *Capitol CL 15559*	**21** 9 wks
4 Apr 70	**RAG MAMA RAG** *Capitol CL 15629*	**16** 9 wks

BAND AID
International, male / female vocal / instrumental group **26 wks**

15 Dec 84	★ **DO THEY KNOW IT'S CHRISTMAS?** *Mercury FEED 1* [1]	**1** 13 wks
7 Dec 85	● **DO THEY KNOW IT'S CHRISTMAS? (re-entry)** *Mercury FEED 1*	**3** 7 wks
23 Dec 89	★ **DO THEY KNOW IT'S CHRISTMAS?** *PWL/Polydor FEED 2* [1]	**1** 6 wks

[1] Band Aid II

BAND AKA *US, male vocal / instrumental group* **12 wks**

15 May 82	**GRACE** *Epic EPC A 2376*	**41** 5 wks
5 Mar 83	**JOY** *Epic EPC A 3145*	**24** 7 wks

BAND OF GOLD
Holland, male / female vocal / instrumental group **11 wks**

14 Jul 84	**LOVE SONGS ARE BACK AGAIN (MEDLEY)** *RCA 428*	**24** 11 wks

BAND OF THIEVES - *See Luke GOSS and the BAND OF THIEVES*

BANDERAS *UK, female vocal / instrumental duo* **16 wks**

23 Feb 91	**THIS IS YOUR LIFE** *London LON 290*	**16** 10 wks
15 Jun 91	**SHE SELLS** *London LON 298*	**41** 6 wks

BANDWAGON - *See Johnny JOHNSON and the BANDWAGON*

Honey BANE *UK, female vocalist* **8 wks**

24 Jan 81	**TURN ME ON TURN ME OFF** *Zonophone Z 15*	**37** 5 wks
18 Apr 81	**BABY LOVE** *Zonophone Z 19*	**58** 3 wks

BANG *UK, male vocal duo* **2 wks**

6 May 89	**YOU'RE THE ONE** *RCA PB 42715*	**74** 2 wks

BANGLES *US, female vocal / instrumental group* **94 wks**

15 Feb 86	● **MANIC MONDAY** *CBS A 6796*	**2** 12 wks
26 Apr 86	**IF SHE KNEW WHAT SHE WANTS** *CBS A 7062*	**31** 7 wks

SHIRLEY BASSEY performs in 1959, the year of her first number one. (LFI)

PATO BANTON reached number one with 'Baby Come Back' 26 years after the Equals, the longest gap between different number one versions of the same song except for those of 'Living Doll', 'This Ole House' and 'Unchained Melody'. (Mark Allan)

Tony of **BAD BOYS INC.** reveals the way to win the *TV Hits* pop quiz. (Tim Roney/TV HITS)

5 Jul 86		GOING DOWN TO LIVERPOOL *CBS A 7255*	56	3 wks
13 Sep 86	●	WALK LIKE AN EGYPTIAN *CBS 650071 7*	3	19 wks
10 Jan 87		WALKING DOWN YOUR STREET *CBS BANGS 1*	16	6 wks
18 Apr 87		FOLLOWING *CBS BANGS 2*	55	3 wks
6 Feb 88		HAZY SHADE OF WINTER *Def Jam BANGS 3*	11	10 wks
5 Nov 88		IN YOUR ROOM *CBS BANGS 4*	35	6 wks
18 Feb 89	★	ETERNAL FLAME *CBS BANGS 5*	1	18 wks
10 Jun 89		BE WITH YOU *CBS BANGS 6*	23	8 wks
14 Oct 89		I'LL SET YOU FREE *CBS BANGS 7*	74	1 wk
9 Jun 90		WALK LIKE AN EGYPTIAN (re-issue) *CBS BANGS 873*	1	1 wk

Tony BANKS - See FISH

BANNED UK, male vocal / instrumental group   6 wks

17 Dec 77	LITTLE GIRL *Harvest HAR 5145*	36	6 wks

BANSHEES - See SIOUXSIE and the BANSHEES

Buju BANTON Jamaica, male vocalist   1 wk

7 Aug 93	MAKE MY DAY *Mercury BUJCD 2*	72	1 wk

Pato BANTON UK, male vocalist   14 wks

1 Oct 94	★ BABY COME BACK *Virgin VSCDT 1522*	1†	14 wks

Sleeve credits Ali and Robin Campbell.

BAR CODES featuring Alison BROWN
UK, male / female vocal group   1 wk

17 Dec 94	SUPERMARKET SWEEP *Blanca Casa BC 101CD*	72	1 wk

BAR-KAYS US, male vocal / instrumental group   15 wks

23 Aug 67	SOUL FINGER *Stax 601 014*	33	7 wks
22 Jan 77	SHAKE YOUR RUMP TO THE FUNK *Mercury 6167 417*	41	4 wks
12 Jan 85	SEXOMATIC *Club JAB 10*	51	4 wks

Chris BARBER'S JAZZ BAND
UK, male jazz band, Chris Barber - trombone   30 wks

13 Feb 59	●	PETITE FLEUR *Pye Nixa NJ 2026*	3	22 wks
31 Jul 59		PETITE FLEUR (re-entry) *Pye Nixa NJ 2026*	22	2 wks
9 Oct 59		LONESOME *Columbia DB 4333*	27	2 wks
4 Jan 62		REVIVAL *Columbia SCD 2166*	50	2 wks
1 Feb 62		REVIVAL (re-entry) *Columbia SCD 2166*	43	2 wks

BARBRA and NEIL - See Barbra STREISAND; Neil DIAMOND

BARCLAY JAMES HARVEST
UK, male vocal / instrumental group   9 wks

2 Apr 77	LIVE EP *Polydor 2229 198*	49	1 wk
16 Apr 77	LIVE EP (re-entry) *Polydor 2229 198*	49	1 wk
26 Jan 80	LOVE ON THE LINE *Polydor POSP 97*	63	2 wks
22 Nov 80	LIFE IS FOR LIVING *Polydor POSP 195*	61	3 wks
21 May 83	JUST A DAY AWAY *Polydor POSP 585*	68	2 wks

Tracks on Live EP: Rock 'n' Roll Star / Medicine Man (Parts 1 & 2).

BARDO UK, male / female vocal duo   8 wks

10 Apr 82	● ONE STEP FURTHER *Epic EPC A2265*	2	8 wks

BARNBRACK UK, male vocal / instrumental group   7 wks

16 Mar 85	BELFAST *Homespun HS 092*	45	7 wks

Jimmy BARNES - See INXS

Richard BARNES UK, male vocalist   10 wks

23 May 70	TAKE TO THE MOUNTAINS *Philips BF 1840*	35	6 wks
24 Oct 70	GO NORTH *Philips 6006 039*	49	1 wk
7 Nov 70	GO NORTH (re-entry) *Philips 6006 039*	38	3 wks

BARRACUDAS UK / US, male vocal / instrumental group   6 wks

16 Aug 80	SUMMER FUN *EMI-Wipe Out Z 5*	37	6 wks

Wild Willy BARRETT - See John OTWAY and Wild Willy BARRETT

J.J. BARRIE Canada, male vocalist   11 wks

24 Apr 76	★ NO CHARGE *Power Exchange PX 209*	1	11 wks

Featured vocalist is Vicki Brown.

Ken BARRIE UK, male vocalist   15 wks

10 Jul 82	POSTMAN PAT *Post Music PP 001*	44	8 wks
25 Dec 82	POSTMAN PAT (re-entry) *Post Music PP 001*	54	3 wks
24 Dec 83	POSTMAN PAT (2nd re-entry) *Post Music PP 001*	59	4 wks

BARRON KNIGHTS
UK, male vocal / instrumental group   94 wks

9 Jul 64	●	CALL UP THE GROUPS *Columbia DB 7317*	3	13 wks
22 Oct 64		COME TO THE DANCE *Columbia DB 7375*	42	2 wks
25 Mar 65	●	POP GO THE WORKERS *Columbia DB 7525*	5	13 wks
16 Dec 65	●	MERRY GENTLE POPS *Columbia DB 7780*	9	7 wks
1 Dec 66		UNDER NEW MANAGEMENT *Columbia DB 8071*	15	9 wks
23 Oct 68		AN OLYMPIC RECORD *Columbia DB 8485*	35	4 wks
29 Oct 77	●	LIVE IN TROUBLE *Epic EPC 5752*	7	10 wks
2 Dec 78	●	A TASTE OF AGGRO *Epic EPC 6829*	3	10 wks
8 Dec 79		FOOD FOR THOUGHT *Epic EPC 8011*	46	6 wks
4 Oct 80		THE SIT SONG *Epic EPC 8994*	44	4 wks
6 Dec 80		NEVER MIND THE PRESENTS *Epic EPC 9070*	17	8 wks
5 Dec 81		BLACKBOARD JUMBLE *CBS A 1795*	52	5 wks
19 Mar 83		BUFFALO BILL'S LAST SCRATCH *Epic EPC A 3208*	49	3 wks

Joe BARRY US, male vocalist   1 wk

24 Aug 61	I'M A FOOL TO CARE *Mercury AMT 1149*	49	1 wk

John BARRY ORCHESTRA
UK, male instrumental group / orchestra   78 wks

10 Mar 60	●	HIT AND MISS *Columbia DB 4414* [1]	10	12 wks
28 Apr 60		BEAT FOR BEATNIKS *Columbia DB 4446*	40	2 wks
9 Jun 60		HIT AND MISS (re-entry) *Columbia DB 4414* [1]	45	1 wk
14 Jul 60		NEVER LET GO *Columbia DB 4480*	49	1 wk
18 Aug 60		BLUEBERRY HILL *Columbia DB 4480*	34	3 wks
8 Sep 60		WALK DON'T RUN *Columbia DB 4505* [1]	49	1 wk
22 Sep 60		WALK DON'T RUN (re-entry) *Columbia DB 4505* [1]	11	13 wks
8 Dec 60		BLACK STOCKINGS *Columbia DB 4554* [1]	27	9 wks
2 Mar 61		THE MAGNIFICENT SEVEN *Columbia DB 4598* [1]	48	1 wk
16 Mar 61		THE MAGNIFICENT SEVEN (re-entry) *Columbia DB 4598* [1]	45	2 wks
6 Apr 61		THE MAGNIFICENT SEVEN (2nd re-entry) *Columbia DB 4598* [1]	50	1 wk
8 Jun 61		THE MAGNIFICENT SEVEN (3rd re-entry) *Columbia DB 4598* [1]	47	1 wk
26 Apr 62		CUTTY SARK *Columbia DB 4806* [1]	35	2 wks
1 Nov 62		JAMES BOND THEME *Columbia DB 4898*	13	11 wks
21 Nov 63		FROM RUSSIA WITH LOVE *Ember S 181*	44	1 wk
19 Dec 63		FROM RUSSIA WITH LOVE (re-entry) *Ember S 181*	39	2 wks
11 Dec 71		THE PERSUADERS *CBS 7469*	13	15 wks

[1] John Barry Seven

Len BARRY US, male vocalist | 24 wks

4 Nov 65 ● 1-2-3 Brunswick 05942 ....**3** 14 wks	
13 Jan 66 ● LIKE A BABY Brunswick 05949 ....**10** 10 wks	

Lionel BART UK, male vocalist | 3 wks

25 Nov 89 HAPPY ENDINGS (GIVE YOURSELF A PINCH) EMI EM 121 ....**68** 1 wk	
23 Dec 89 HAPPY ENDINGS (GIVE YOUSELF A PINCH) (re-entry) EMI EM 121 ....**71** 2 wks	

BAS NOIR US, female vocal duo | 1 wk

11 Feb 89 MY LOVE IS MAGIC 10 TEN 257 ....**73** 1 wk

Rob BASE and DJ E-Z ROCK
US, male vocal duo | 19 wks

16 Apr 88 IT TAKES TWO Citybeat CBE 724 ....**24** 6 wks	
14 Jan 89 GET ON THE DANCE FLOOR Supreme SUPE 139 ...**14** 7 wks	
4 Mar 89 IT TAKES TWO (re-entry) Citybeat CBE 724 ....**49** 3 wks	
22 Apr 89 JOY AND PAIN Supreme SUPE 143 ....**47** 3 wks	

BASEMENT BOYS - See Ultra NATÉ

BASIA Poland, female vocalist | 7 wks

23 Jan 88 PROMISES Epic BASH 4 ....**48** 4 wks	
28 May 88 TIME AND TIDE Epic BASH 5 ....**61** 3 wks	

Count BASIE - See Frank SINATRA

Toni BASIL US, female vocalist | 16 wks

6 Feb 82 ● MICKEY Radialchoice TIC 4 ....**2** 12 wks	
1 May 82 NOBODY Radialchoice TIC 2 ....**52** 4 wks	

Alfie BASS - See Michael MEDWIN, Bernard BRESSLAW, Alfie BASS and Leslie FYSON

BASS BUMPERS
Germany / UK, male / female vocal / instrumental group | 4 wks

25 Sep 93 RUNNIN' Vertigo VERCD 78 ....**68** 1 wk	
5 Feb 94 THE MUSIC'S GOT ME Vertigo VERCD 84 ....**25** 3 wks	

Fontella BASS US, female vocalist | 15 wks

2 Dec 65 RESCUE ME Chess CRS 8023 ....**11** 10 wks	
20 Jan 66 RECOVERY Chess CRS 8027 ....**32** 5 wks	

BASS-O-MATIC UK, male multi-instrumentalist | 19 wks

12 May 90 IN THE REALM OF THE SENSES Virgin VS 1265 ....**66** 3 wks	
1 Sep 90 ● FASCINATING RHYTHM Virgin VS 1274 ....**9** 11 wks	
22 Dec 90 EASE ON BY Virgin VS 1295 ....**61** 4 wks	
3 Aug 91 FUNKY LOVE VIBRATIONS Virgin VS 1355 ....**71** 1 wk	

Shirley BASSEY UK, female vocalist | 315 wks

15 Feb 57 ● BANANA BOAT SONG Philips PB 668 ....**8** 10 wks	
23 Aug 57 FIRE DOWN BELOW Philips PB 723 ....**30** 1 wk	
6 Sep 57 YOU YOU ROMEO Philips PB 723 ....**29** 2 wks	
19 Dec 58 AS I LOVE YOU Philips PB 845 ....**27** 2 wks	
26 Dec 58 ● KISS ME HONEY HONEY KISS ME Philips PB 860 ......**3** 17 wks	
9 Jan 59 ★ AS I LOVE YOU (re-entry) Philips PB 845 ....**1** 17 wks	
31 Mar 60 WITH THESE HANDS Columbia DB 4421 ....**38** 2 wks	

21 Apr 60 WITH THESE HANDS (re-entry) Columbia DB 4421 **31** 2 wks	
12 May 60 WITH THESE HANDS (2nd re-entry) Columbia DB 4421 ....**41** 2 wks	
4 Aug 60 ● AS LONG AS HE NEEDS ME Columbia DB 4490 ....**2** 30 wks	
11 May 61 ● YOU'LL NEVER KNOW Columbia DB 4643 ....**6** 17 wks	
27 Jul 61 ★ REACH FOR THE STARS / CLIMB EV'RY MOUNTAIN Columbia DB 4685 ....**1** 16 wks	
23 Nov 61 ● I'LL GET BY Columbia DB 4737 ....**10** 8 wks	
23 Nov 61 REACH FOR THE STARS / CLIMB EV'RY MOUNTAIN (re-entry) Columbia DB 4685 ....**40** 2 wks	
15 Feb 62 TONIGHT Columbia DB 4777 ....**21** 8 wks	
26 Apr 62 AVE MARIA Columbia DB 4816 ....**34** 4 wks	
31 May 62 FAR AWAY Columbia DB 4836 ....**24** 13 wks	
30 Aug 62 ● WHAT NOW MY LOVE Columbia DB 4882 ....**5** 17 wks	
28 Feb 63 WHAT KIND OF FOOL AM I? Columbia DB 4974 ......**47** 2 wks	
26 Sep 63 ● I (WHO HAVE NOTHING) Columbia DB 7113 ....**6** 20 wks	
23 Jan 64 MY SPECIAL DREAM Columbia DB 7185 ....**32** 7 wks	
9 Apr 64 GONE Columbia DB 7248 ....**36** 5 wks	
15 Oct 64 GOLDFINGER Columbia DB 7360 ....**21** 9 wks	
20 May 65 NO REGRETS Columbia DB 7535 ....**39** 4 wks	
11 Oct 67 BIG SPENDER United Artists UP 1192 ....**21** 15 wks	
20 Jun 70 ● SOMETHING United Artists UP 35125 ....**4** 21 wks	
2 Jan 71 THE FOOL ON THE HILL United Artists UP 35156 ......**48** 1 wk	
23 Jan 71 SOMETHING (re-entry) United Artists UP 35125 ......**50** 1 wk	
27 Mar 71 (WHERE DO I BEGIN) LOVE STORY United Artists UP 35194 ....**34** 9 wks	
7 Aug 71 FOR ALL WE KNOW United Artists UP 35267 ....**46** 1 wk	
21 Aug 71 ● FOR ALL WE KNOW (re-entry) United Artists UP 35267 ....**6** 23 wks	
15 Jan 72 DIAMONDS ARE FOREVER United Artists UP 35293 ....**38** 6 wks	
3 Mar 73 ● NEVER NEVER NEVER United Artists UP 35490 ....**8** 18 wks	
14 Jul 73 NEVER NEVER NEVER (re-entry) United Artists UP 35490 ....**48** 1 wk	
22 Aug 87 THE RHYTHM DIVINE Mercury MER 253 [1] ....**54** 2 wks	

[1] Yello featuring Shirley Bassey

BASSHEADS UK, male / female vocal / instrumental group | 16 wks

16 Nov 91 ● IS THERE ANYBODY OUT THERE Deconstruction R 6303 ....**5** 8 wks	
30 May 92 BACK TO THE OLD SCHOOL Deconstruction R 6310 ....**12** 4 wks	
28 Nov 92 WHO CAN MAKE ME FEEL GOOD Deconstruction R 6326 ....**38** 2 wks	
28 Aug 93 START A BRAND NEW LIFE (SAVE ME) Deconstruction CDR 6353 ....**49** 2 wks	

Mike BATT with the NEW EDITION
UK, male vocalist with male / female vocal group | 8 wks

16 Aug 75 ● SUMMERTIME CITY Epic EPC 3460 ....**4** 8 wks

BAUHAUS UK, male vocal / instrumental group | 35 wks

18 Apr 81 KICK IN THE EYE Beggars Banquet BEG 54 ....**59** 3 wks	
4 Jul 81 THE PASSIONS OF LOVERS Beggars Banquet BEG 59 ....**56** 2 wks	
6 Mar 82 KICK IN THE EYE EP Beggars Banquet BEG 74 ....**45** 4 wks	
19 Jun 82 SPIRIT Beggars Banquet BEG 79 ....**42** 5 wks	
9 Oct 82 ZIGGY STARDUST Beggars Banquet BEG 83 ....**15** 7 wks	
22 Jan 83 LAGARTIJA NICK Beggars Banquet BEG 88 ....**44** 4 wks	
9 Apr 83 SHE'S IN PARTIES Beggars Banquet BEG 91 ....**26** 6 wks	
29 Oct 83 THE SINGLES 1981-83 Beggars Banquet BEG 100E ..**52** 4 wks	

Tracks on Kick In The Eye EP: Kick In The Eye (Searching For Satori) / Harry / Earwax.

Les BAXTER US, orchestra and chorus | 9 wks

13 May 55 ● UNCHAINED MELODY Capitol CL 14257 ....**10** 9 wks

An incredible new sound from the BB5—the kind of gutsy production that makes a No. 1 single!

Capitol RECORDS
5676

THE BEACH BOYS
GOOD VIBRATIONS

The chart prediction for the **BEACH BOYS** was correct, but they were never again referred to as 'The BB5'.

On 15 August 1965, the **BEATLES** took rock music out of indoor venues and into stadia by opening their American tour at a sold out Shea Stadium in New York.
(Michael Ochs/LFI)

BAY CITY ROLLERS
UK, male vocal / instrumental group **113 wks**

18 Sep 71	● KEEP ON DANCING *Bell 1164*	9	13 wks
9 Feb 74	● REMEMBER (SHA-LA-LA) *Bell 1338*	6	12 wks
27 Apr 74	● SHANG-A-LANG *Bell 1355*	2	10 wks
27 Jul 74	● SUMMERLOVE SENSATION *Bell 1369*	3	10 wks
12 Oct 74	● ALL OF ME LOVES ALL OF YOU *Bell 1382*	4	10 wks
8 Mar 75	★ BYE BYE BABY *Bell 1409*	1	16 wks
12 Jul 75	★ GIVE A LITTLE LOVE *Bell 1425*	1	9 wks
22 Nov 75	● MONEY HONEY *Bell 1461*	3	9 wks
10 Apr 76	● LOVE ME LIKE I LOVE YOU *Bell 1477*	4	6 wks
11 Sep 76	● I ONLY WANNA BE WITH YOU *Bell 1493*	4	9 wks
7 May 77	IT'S A GAME *Arista 108*	16	6 wks
30 Jul 77	YOU MADE ME BELIEVE IN MAGIC *Arista 127*	34	3 wks

BBG
UK, male vocal / instrumental group **7 wks**

28 Apr 90	SNAPPINESS [1] *Urban URB 54*	28	5 wks
11 Aug 90	SOME KIND OF HEAVEN *Urban URB 59*	65	2 wks

[1] BBG featuring Dina Taylor

BBM
UK, male vocal / instrumental group **2 wks**

6 Aug 94	WHERE IN THE WORLD *Virgin VSCDG 1495*	57	2 wks

BC-52s - *See B-52s*

BE BOP DELUXE
UK, male vocal / instrumental group **13 wks**

21 Feb 76	SHIPS IN THE NIGHT *Harvest HAR 5104*	23	8 wks
13 Nov 76	HOT VALVES EP *Harvest HAR 5117*	36	5 wks

Tracks on Hot Valves EP: *Maid In Heaven / Blazing Apostles / Jet Silver And The Dolls Of Venus / Bring Back The Spark.*

BEACH BOYS
US, male vocal / instrumental group **277 wks**

1 Aug 63	SURFIN' USA *Capitol CL 15305*	34	7 wks
9 Jul 64	● I GET AROUND *Capitol CL 15350*	7	13 wks
29 Oct 64	WHEN I GROW UP (TO BE A MAN) *Capitol CL 15361*	44	2 wks
19 Nov 64	WHEN I GROW UP (TO BE A MAN) (re-entry) *Capitol CL 15361*	27	5 wks
21 Jan 65	DANCE DANCE DANCE *Capitol CL 15370*	24	6 wks
3 Jun 65	HELP ME RHONDA *Capitol CL 15392*	27	10 wks
2 Sep 65	CALIFORNIA GIRLS *Capitol CL 15409*	26	8 wks
17 Feb 66	● BARBARA ANN *Capitol CL 15432*	3	10 wks
21 Apr 66	● SLOOP JOHN B *Capitol CL 15441*	2	15 wks
28 Jul 66	● GOD ONLY KNOWS *Capitol CL 15459*	2	14 wks
3 Nov 66	★ GOOD VIBRATIONS *Capitol CL 15475*	1	13 wks
4 May 67	● THEN I KISSED HER *Capitol CL 15502*	4	11 wks
23 Aug 67	● HEROES AND VILLAINS *Capitol CL 15510*	8	9 wks
22 Nov 67	WILD HONEY *Capitol CL 15521*	29	6 wks
17 Jan 68	DARLIN' *Capitol CL 15527*	11	14 wks
8 May 68	FRIENDS *Capitol CL 15545*	25	7 wks
24 Jul 68	★ DO IT AGAIN *Capitol CL 15554*	1	14 wks
25 Dec 68	BLUEBIRDS OVER THE MOUNTAIN *Capitol CL 15572*	33	5 wks
26 Feb 69	● I CAN HEAR MUSIC *Capitol CL 15584*	10	13 wks
11 Jun 69	● BREAK AWAY *Capitol CL 15598*	6	11 wks
16 May 70	● COTTONFIELDS *Capitol CL 15640*	5	17 wks
3 Mar 73	CALIFORNIA SAGA - CALIFORNIA *Reprise K 14232*	37	5 wks
3 Jul 76	GOOD VIBRATIONS (re-issue) *Capitol CL 15875*	18	7 wks
10 Jul 76	ROCK AND ROLL MUSIC *Reprise K 14440*	36	4 wks
31 Mar 79	HERE COMES THE NIGHT *Caribou CRB 7204*	37	8 wks
16 Jun 79	● LADY LYNDA *Caribou CRB 7427*	6	11 wks
29 Sep 79	SUMAHAMA *Caribou CRB 7846*	45	4 wks
29 Aug 81	BEACH BOYS MEDLEY *Capitol CL 213*	47	4 wks

22 Aug 87	● WIPEOUT *Urban URB 5* [1]	2	12 wks
19 Nov 88	KOKOMO *Elektra EKR 85*	25	9 wks
2 Jun 90	WOULDN'T IT BE NICE *Capitol CL 579*	58	1 wk
29 Jun 91	DO IT AGAIN (re-issue) *Capitol EMCT 1*	61	2 wks

[1] Fat Boys and the Beach Boys

Walter BEASLEY
US, male vocalist **3 wks**

23 Jan 88	I'M SO HAPPY *Urban URB 14*	70	3 wks

BEASTIE BOYS
US, male rap group **40 wks**

28 Feb 87	(YOU GOTTA) FIGHT FOR YOUR RIGHT (TO PARTY) *Def Jam 650418 7*	11	11 wks
30 May 87	NO SLEEP TILL BROOKLYN *Def Jam BEAST 1*	14	7 wks
18 Jul 87	● SHE'S ON IT *Def Jam BEAST 2*	10	8 wks
3 Oct 87	GIRLS / SHE'S CRAFTY *Def Jam BEAST 3*	34	4 wks
11 Apr 92	PASS THE MIC *Capitol 12CL 653*	47	2 wks
4 Jul 92	FROZEN METAL HEAD EP *Capitol 12CL 665*	55	1 wk
9 Jul 94	GET IT TOGETHER / SABOTAGE *Capitol CDCL 716*	19	4 wks
26 Nov 94	SURE SHOT *Capitol CDCLS 726*	27	3 wks

Tracks on Frozen Metal Head EP: *Jimmy James / Jimmy James (Original) / Drinkin' Wine / The Blue Nun.*

BEAT
UK, male vocal / instrumental group **90 wks**

8 Dec 79	● TEARS OF A CLOWN / RANKING FULL STOP *2 Tone CHS TT 6*	6	11 wks
23 Feb 80	● HANDS OFF - SHE'S MINE *Go Feet FEET 1*	9	9 wks
3 May 80	● MIRROR IN THE BATHROOM *Go Feet FEET 2*	4	9 wks
16 Aug 80	BEST FRIEND / STAND DOWN MARGARET (DUB) *Go Feet FEET 3*	22	9 wks
13 Dec 80	● TOO NICE TO TALK TO *Go Feet FEET 4*	7	11 wks
18 Apr 81	DROWNING / ALL OUT TO GET YOU *Go Feet FEET 6*	22	8 wks
20 Jun 81	DOORS OF YOUR HEART *Go Feet FEET 9*	33	6 wks
5 Dec 81	HIT IT *Go Feet FEET 11*	70	2 wks
17 Apr 82	SAVE IT FOR LATER *Go Feet FEET 333*	47	4 wks
18 Sep 82	JEANETTE *Go Feet FEET 15*	45	3 wks
4 Dec 82	I CONFESS *Go Feet FEET 16*	54	3 wks
30 Apr 83	● CAN'T GET USED TO LOSING YOU *Go Feet FEET 17*	3	11 wks
2 Jul 83	ACKEE 1-2-3 *Go Feet FEET 18*	54	4 wks

See also Various Artists (EPs & LPs) - The Two Tone EP.

BEAT SYSTEM
UK, male vocal / instrumental group **3 wks**

3 Mar 90	WALK ON THE WILD SIDE *Fourth & Broadway BRW 163*	63	2 wks
18 Sep 93	TO A BRIGHTER DAY (O' HAPPY DAY) *ffrr FCD 217*	70	1 wk

BEATLES
UK, male vocal / instrumental group **434 wks**

11 Oct 62	LOVE ME DO *Parlophone R 4949*	17	18 wks
17 Jan 63	● PLEASE PLEASE ME *Parlophone R 4983*	2	18 wks
18 Apr 63	★ FROM ME TO YOU *Parlophone R 5015*	1	21 wks
6 Jun 63	MY BONNIE *Polydor NH 66833* [1]	48	1 wk
29 Aug 63	★ SHE LOVES YOU *Parlophone R 5055*	1	31 wks
5 Dec 63	★ I WANT TO HOLD YOUR HAND *Parlophone R 5084*	1	21 wks
26 Mar 64	★ CAN'T BUY ME LOVE *Parlophone R 5114*	1	14 wks
9 Apr 64	SHE LOVES YOU (re-entry) *Parlophone R 5055*	42	2 wks
14 May 64	I WANT TO HOLD YOUR HAND (re-entry) *Parlophone R 5084*	48	1 wk
11 Jun 64	AIN'T SHE SWEET *Polydor 52 317*	29	6 wks
9 Jul 64	CAN'T BUY ME LOVE (re-entry) *Parlophone R 5114*	47	1 wk
16 Jul 64	★ A HARD DAY'S NIGHT *Parlophone R 5160*	1	13 wks
3 Dec 64	★ I FEEL FINE *Parlophone R 5200*	1	13 wks
15 Apr 65	★ TICKET TO RIDE *Parlophone R 5265*	1	12 wks
29 Jul 65	★ HELP! *Parlophone R 5305*	1	14 wks

9 Dec 65	★ DAY TRIPPER / WE CAN WORK IT OUT		
	Parlophone R 5389 1	12 wks
16 Jun 66	★ PAPERBACK WRITER Parlophone R 5452 1	11 wks
11 Aug 66	★ YELLOW SUBMARINE / ELEANOR RIGBY		
	Parlophone R 5493 1	13 wks
23 Feb 67	● PENNY LANE / STRAWBERRY FIELDS FOREVER		
	Parlophone R 5570 2	11 wks
12 Jul 67	★ ALL YOU NEED IS LOVE Parlophone R 5620 1	13 wks
29 Nov 67	● HELLO GOODBYE Parlophone R 5655 1	12 wks
13 Dec 67	● MAGICAL MYSTERY TOUR (DOUBLE EP)		
	Parlophone SMMT/MMT 1 2	12 wks
20 Mar 68	★ LADY MADONNA Parlophone R 5675 1	8 wks
4 Sep 68	★ HEY JUDE Apple R 5722 1	16 wks
23 Apr 69	★ GET BACK Apple R 5777 [2] 1	17 wks
4 Jun 69	★ BALLAD OF JOHN AND YOKO Apple R 5786.............1	14 wks
8 Nov 69	● SOMETHING / COME TOGETHER Apple R 5814 4	12 wks
14 Mar 70	● LET IT BE Apple R 5833 2	9 wks
24 Oct 70	LET IT BE (re-entry) Apple R 5833 43	1 wk
13 Mar 76	● YESTERDAY Apple R 6013 8	7 wks
27 Mar 76	HEY JUDE (re-entry) Apple R 5722 12	7 wks
27 Mar 76	PAPERBACK WRITER (re-entry) Parlophone R 5452 23	5 wks
3 Apr 76	GET BACK (re-entry) Apple R 5777 [2] 28	5 wks
3 Apr 76	STRAWBERRY FIELDS FOREVER (re-entry)		
	Parlophone R 5570 32	3 wks
10 Apr 76	HELP! (re-entry) Parlophone R 5305 37	3 wks
10 Jul 76	BACK IN THE U.S.S.R. Parlophone R 6016 19	6 wks
7 Oct 78	SGT. PEPPER'S LONELY HEARTS CLUB BAND -		
	WITH A LITTLE HELP FROM MY FRIENDS		
	Parlophone R 6022 63	3 wks
5 Jun 82	● BEATLES MOVIE MEDLEY Parlophone R 6055 10	9 wks
16 Oct 82	● LOVE ME DO (re-entry) Parlophone R 4949 4	7 wks
22 Jan 83	PLEASE PLEASE ME (re-entry) Parlophone R 4983 29	4 wks
23 Apr 83	FROM ME TO YOU (re-entry) Parlophone R 5015 ..40	4 wks
3 Sep 83	SHE LOVES YOU (2nd re-entry)		
	Parlophone R 5055 45	3 wks
26 Nov 83	I WANT TO HOLD YOUR HAND (2nd re-entry)		
	Parlophone R 5084 62	2 wks
31 Mar 84	CAN'T BUY ME LOVE (2nd re-entry)		
	Parlophone R 5114 53	2 wks
21 Jul 84	A HARD DAY'S NIGHT (re-entry)		
	Parlophone R 5160 52	2 wks
8 Dec 84	I FEEL FINE (re-entry) Parlophone R 5200 65	1 wk
20 Apr 85	TICKET TO RIDE (re-entry) Parlophone R 5265 70	2 wks
30 Aug 86	ELEANOR RIGBY / YELLOW SUBMARINE		
	(re-entry) Parlophone R 5493 63	1 wk
28 Feb 87	PENNY LANE / STRAWBERRY FIELDS FOREVER		
	(2nd re-entry)Parlophone R 5570 65	2 wks
18 Jul 87	ALL YOU NEED IS LOVE (re-entry)		
	Parlophone R 5620 47	3 wks
5 Dec 87	HELLO GOODBYE (re-entry) Parlophone R 5655 ...63	1 wk
26 Mar 88	LADY MADONNA (re-entry) Parlophone R 5675 ...67	1 wk
10 Sep 88	HEY JUDE (2nd re-entry) Apple 5722 52	2 wks
22 Apr 89	GET BACK (2nd re-entry) Apple R 5777 [2] 74	1 wk
17 Oct 92	LOVE ME DO (2nd re-entry) Parlophone R 4949 ...53	1 wk

[1] Tony Sheridan and the Beatles [2] Beatles with Billy Preston

Tracks on Magical Mystery Tour (EP): Magical Mystery Tour / Your Mother Should Know / I Am The Walrus / Fool On The Hill / Flying / Blue Jay Way.

BEATMASTERS UK, male/female instrumental group   47 wks

9 Jan 88	● ROK DA HOUSE Rhythm King LEFT 11 [1] 5	11 wks
24 Sep 88	BURN IT UP Rhythm King LEFT 27 [2] 14	10 wks
22 Apr 89	● WHO'S IN THE HOUSE Rhythm King LEFT 31 [3] 8	9 wks
12 Aug 89	● HEY DJ I CAN'T DANCE TO THAT MUSIC YOU'RE		
	PLAYING / SKA TRAIN Rhythm King LEFT 34 [4] 7	11 wks
2 Dec 89	WARM LOVE Rhythm King LEFT 37 [5] 51	2 wks
21 Sep 91	BOULEVARD OF BROKEN DREAMS		
	Rhythm King 6573617 62	1 wk
16 May 92	DUNNO WHAT IT IS (ABOUT YOU)		
	Rhythm King 6580017 [6] 43	3 wks

[1] Beatmasters featuring the Cookie Crew [2] Beatmasters with P.P. Arnold [3] Beatmasters featuring Merlin [4] Beatmasters featuring Betty Boo [5] Beatmasters featuring Claudia Fontaine [6] Beatmasters featuring Elaine Vassell

BEATS INTERNATIONAL
UK, male/female vocal/instrumental group   **30 wks**

10 Feb 90	★ DUB BE GOOD TO ME Go Beat GOD 39 [1] 1	13 wks
12 May 90	● WON'T TALK ABOUT IT Go Beat GOD 43 9	7 wks
15 Sep 90	BURUNDI BLUES Go Beat GOD 45 51	3 wks
2 Mar 91	ECHO CHAMBER Go Beat GOD 51 60	2 wks
21 Sep 91	THE SUN DOESN'T SHINE Go Beat GOD 59 66	2 wks
23 Nov 91	IN THE GHETTO Go Beat GOD 64..................44	3 wks

[1] Beats International featuring Lindy Layton

BEAUTIFUL PEOPLE
UK, male instrumental/sampling group   **1 wk**

28 May 94	IF 60S WERE 90S Essential ESSX 2037 74	1 wk

BEAUTIFUL SOUTH
UK, male/female vocal/instrumental group   **86 wks**

3 Jun 89	● SONG FOR WHOEVER Go! Discs GOD 32 2	11 wks
23 Sep 89	● YOU KEEP IT ALL IN Go! Discs GOD 35 8	8 wks
2 Dec 89	I'LL SAIL THIS SHIP ALONE Go! Discs GOD 38.........31	8 wks
6 Oct 90	★ A LITTLE TIME Go! Discs GOD 47 1	14 wks
8 Dec 90	MY BOOK Go! Discs GOD 48 43	6 wks
16 Mar 91	LET LOVE SPEAK UP ITSELF Go! Discs GOD 53 51	2 wks
11 Jan 92	OLD RED EYES IS BACK Go! Discs GOD 66 22	6 wks
14 Mar 92	WE ARE EACH OTHER Go! Discs GOD 71 30	3 wks
13 Jun 92	BELL BOTTOMED TEAR Go! Discs GOD 78 16	5 wks
26 Sep 92	36D Go! Discs GOD 88 46	2 wks
12 Mar 94	GOOD AS GOLD Go! Discs GODCD 110 23	5 wks
4 Jun 94	EVERYBODY'S TALKIN' Go! Discs GODCD 113 12	8 wks
3 Sep 94	PRETTIEST EYES Go! Discs GODCD 119 37	3 wks
12 Nov 94	ONE LAST LOVE SONG Go! Discs GODCD 122 14	5 wks

BEAVIS and BUTT-HEAD - *See CHER*

Gilbert BECAUD *France, male vocalist*   **12 wks**

29 Mar 75	● A LITTLE LOVE AND UNDERSTANDING		
	Decca F 13537 10	12 wks

BECK *US, male vocalist*   **6 wks**

5 Mar 94	LOSER Geffen GFSTD 67 15	6 wks

Jeff BECK *UK, male vocalist/instrumentalist - guitar*   **57 wks**

23 Mar 67	HI-HO SILVER LINING Columbia DB 8151 14	14 wks
2 Aug 67	TALLYMAN Columbia DB 8227 30	3 wks
28 Feb 68	LOVE IS BLUE Columbia DB 8359 23	7 wks
9 Jul 69	GOO GOO BARABAJAGAL (LOVE IS HOT)		
	Pye 7N 17778 [1] 12	9 wks
4 Nov 72	HI-HO SILVER LINING (re-issue) RAK RR 3 17	11 wks
5 May 73	I'VE BEEN DRINKING RAK RR 4 [2] 27	6 wks
9 Oct 82	HI-HO SILVER LINING (re-entry of re-issue)		
	RAK RR 3 62	4 wks
7 Mar 92	PEOPLE GET READY Epic 6577567 [2] 49	3 wks

[1] Donovan with the Jeff Beck Group [2] Jeff Beck and Rod Stewart

Robin BECK *US, female vocalist*   **13 wks**

22 Oct 88	★ FIRST TIME Mercury MER 270 1	13 wks

Peter BECKETT - *See Barry GRAY ORCHESTRA*

BEDAZZLED *UK, male vocal/instrumental group*   **1 wk**

4 Jul 92	SUMMER SONG Columbia 6581627 73	1 wk

BEDROCKS UK, male vocal/instrumental group — 7 wks

18 Dec 68	OB-LA-DI OB-LA-DA Columbia DB 8516	20	7 wks

Celi BEE and the BUZZY BUNCH
US, male/female vocal/instrumental group — 1 wk

17 Jun 78	HOLD YOUR HORSES BABE TK TKR 6032	72	1 wk

BEE GEES UK, male vocal/instrumental group — 322 wks

27 Apr 67	NEW YORK MINING DISASTER 1941 Polydor 56 161	12	10 wks
12 Jul 67	TO LOVE SOMEBODY Polydor 56 178	50	1 wk
26 Jul 67	TO LOVE SOMEBODY (re-entry) Polydor 56 178	41	4 wks
20 Sep 67	★ MASSACHUSETTS Polydor 56 192	1	17 wks
22 Nov 67	● WORLD Polydor 56 220	9	16 wks
31 Jan 68	● WORDS Polydor 56 229	8	10 wks
27 Mar 68	JUMBO/THE SINGER SANG HIS SONG Polydor 56 242	25	7 wks
7 Aug 68	★ I'VE GOTTA GET A MESSAGE TO YOU Polydor 56 273	1	15 wks
19 Feb 69	● FIRST OF MAY Polydor 56 304	6	11 wks
4 Jun 69	TOMORROW TOMORROW Polydor 56 331	23	8 wks
16 Aug 69	● DON'T FORGET TO REMEMBER Polydor 56 343	2	15 wks
28 Mar 70	I.O.I.O. Polydor 56 377	49	1 wk
5 Dec 70	LONELY DAYS Polydor 2001 104	33	9 wks
29 Jan 72	MY WORLD Polydor 2058 185	16	9 wks
22 Jul 72	● RUN TO ME Polydor 2058 255	9	10 wks
28 Jun 75	● JIVE TALKIN' RSO 2090 160	5	11 wks
31 Jul 76	● YOU SHOULD BE DANCING RSO 2090 195	5	10 wks
13 Nov 76	LOVE SO RIGHT RSO 2090 207	41	4 wks
29 Oct 77	● HOW DEEP IS YOUR LOVE RSO 2090 259	3	15 wks
4 Feb 78	● STAYIN' ALIVE RSO 2090 267	4	12 wks
15 Apr 78	★ NIGHT FEVER RSO 002	1	20 wks
13 May 78	STAYIN' ALIVE (re-entry) RSO 2090 267	63	6 wks
25 Nov 78	● TOO MUCH HEAVEN RSO 25	3	13 wks
17 Feb 79	★ TRAGEDY RSO 27	1	10 wks
14 Apr 79	LOVE YOU INSIDE OUT RSO 31	13	9 wks
5 Jan 80	SPIRITS (HAVING FLOWN) RSO 52	16	7 wks
17 Sep 83	SOMEONE BELONGING TO SOMEONE RSO 96	49	4 wks
26 Sep 87	★ YOU WIN AGAIN Warner Bros. W 8351	1	15 wks
12 Dec 87	E.S.P. Warner Bros. W 8139	51	5 wks
15 Apr 89	ORDINARY LIVES Warner Bros. W 7523	54	3 wks
24 Jun 89	ONE Warner Bros. W 2916	71	1 wk
2 Mar 91	● SECRET LOVE Warner Bros. W 0014	5	11 wks
21 Aug 93	PAYING THE PRICE OF LOVE Polydor PZCD 284	23	5 wks
27 Nov 93	● FOR WHOM THE BELL TOLLS Polydor PZCD 299	4	14 wks
16 Apr 94	HOW TO FALL IN LOVE PART 1 Polydor PZDD 311	30	4 wks

Act was UK/Australia up to and including Tomorrow Tomorrow.

B.E.F. - See Lalah HATHAWAY

BEGGAR and CO UK, male vocal/instrumental group — 15 wks

7 Feb 81	(SOMEBODY) HELP ME OUT Ensign ENY 201	15	10 wks
12 Sep 81	MULE (CHANT NO. 2) RCA 130	37	5 wks

BEGINNING OF THE END
US, male vocal/instrumental group — 6 wks

23 Feb 74	FUNKY NASSAU Atlantic K 10021	31	6 wks

BEIJING SPRING UK, female vocal duo — 5 wks

23 Jan 93	I WANNA BE IN LOVE AGAIN MCA MCSTD 1709	43	3 wks
8 May 93	SUMMERLANDS MCA MCSTD 1761	53	2 wks

Harry BELAFONTE US, male vocalist — 87 wks

1 Mar 57	● BANANA BOAT SONG HMV POP 308	2	18 wks
14 Jun 57	● ISLAND IN THE SUN RCA 1007	3	25 wks
6 Sep 57	SCARLET RIBBONS HMV POP 360	18	6 wks
1 Nov 57	★ MARY'S BOY CHILD RCA 1022	1	12 wks
22 Aug 58	LITTLE BERNADETTE RCA 1072	16	7 wks
28 Nov 58	● MARY'S BOY CHILD (re-entry) RCA 1022	10	6 wks
12 Dec 58	SON OF MARY RCA 1084	18	4 wks
11 Dec 59	MARY'S BOY CHILD (2nd re-entry) RCA 1022	30	1 wk
21 Sep 61	HOLE IN THE BUCKET RCA 1247 [1]	32	2 wks
12 Oct 61	HOLE IN THE BUCKET (re-entry) RCA 1247 [1]	34	6 wks

[1] Harry Belafonte and Odetta

Archie BELL and the DRELLS
US, male vocal/instrumental group — 33 wks

7 Oct 72	HERE I GO AGAIN Atlantic K 10210	11	10 wks
27 Jan 73	THERE'S GONNA BE A SHOWDOWN Atlantic K 10263	36	5 wks
8 May 76	SOUL CITY WALK Philadelphia International PIR 4250	13	10 wks
11 Jun 77	EVERYBODY HAVE A GOOD TIME Philadelphia International PIR 5179	43	4 wks
28 Jun 86	DON'T LET LOVE GET YOU DOWN Portrait A 7254	49	4 wks

Freddie BELL and the BELLBOYS
US, male vocal/instrumental group — 10 wks

28 Sep 56	● GIDDY-UP-A-DING-DONG Mercury MT 122	4	10 wks

Maggie BELL UK, female vocalist — 12 wks

15 Apr 78	HAZELL Swansong SSK 19412	37	3 wks
13 May 78	HAZELL (re-entry) Swansong SSK 19412	74	1 wk
17 Oct 81	HOLD ME Swansong BAM 1 [1]	11	8 wks

[1] B.A. Robertson and Maggie Bell

William BELL US, male vocalist — 22 wks

29 May 68	TRIBUTE TO A KING Stax 601 038	31	7 wks
20 Nov 68	● PRIVATE NUMBER Stax 101 [1]	8	14 wks
26 Apr 86	HEADLINE NEWS Absolute LUTE 1	70	1 wk

[1] Judy Clay and William Bell

BELL and JAMES US, male vocal duo — 3 wks

31 Mar 79	LIVIN' IT UP (FRIDAY NIGHT) A & M AMS 7424	68	1 wk
14 Apr 79	LIVIN' IT UP (FRIDAY NIGHT) (re-entry) A & M AMS 7424	59	2 wks

BELL BIV DEVOE US, male vocal group — 29 wks

30 Jun 90	POISON MCA MCA 1414	19	11 wks
22 Sep 90	DO ME MCA MCA 1440	56	3 wks
15 Aug 92	● THE BEST THINGS IN LIFE ARE FREE PERSS 7400 [1]	2	13 wks
9 Oct 93	SOMETHING IN YOUR EYES MCA MCSTD 1934	60	2 wks

[1] Luther Vandross and Janet Jackson with special guests BBD and Ralph Tresvant

BELLAMY BROTHERS US, male vocal duo — 29 wks

17 Apr 76	● LET YOUR LOVE FLOW Warner Bros. K 16690	7	12 wks
21 Aug 76	SATIN SHEETS Warner Bros. K 16775	43	3 wks
11 Aug 79	● IF I SAID YOU HAVE A BEAUTIFUL BODY WOULD YOU HOLD IT AGAINST ME Warner Bros. K 17405	3	14 wks

BELLBOYS - See Freddie BELL and the BELLBOYS

Regina BELLE US, female vocalist — 13 wks

21 Oct 89	GOOD LOVIN' CBS 655230	73	1 wk
11 Dec 93	A WHOLE NEW WORLD (ALADDIN'S THEME) Columbia 6599002 [1]	12	12 wks

[1] Peabo Bryson and Regina Belle

BELLE and the DEVOTIONS
UK, female vocal group   **8 wks**

| 21 Apr 84 | **LOVE GAMES** *CBS A 4332* .... | **11** | 8 wks |

La BELLE EPOQUE *France, female vocal duo*   **14 wks**

| 27 Aug 77 | **BLACK IS BLACK** *Harvest HAR 5133* .... | **48** | 1 wk |
| 10 Sep 77 | ● **BLACK IS BLACK (re-entry)** *Harvest HAR 5133* .... | **2** | 13 wks |

BELLE STARS *UK, female vocal / instrumental group*   **42 wks**

5 Jun 82	**IKO IKO** *Stiff BUY 150*	**35**	6 wks
17 Jul 82	**THE CLAPPING SONG** *Stiff BUY 155*	**11**	9 wks
16 Oct 82	**MOCKINGBIRD** *Stiff BUY 159*	**51**	3 wks
15 Jan 83	● **SIGN OF THE TIMES** *Stiff BUY 167*..........................	**3**	11 wks
16 Apr 83	**SWEET MEMORY** *Stiff BUY 174*	**22**	9 wks
13 Aug 83	**INDIAN SUMMER** *Stiff BUY 185*	**52**	3 wks
14 Jul 84	**80'S ROMANCE** *Stiff BUY 200*	**71**	1 wk

BELLY *US, male / female vocal / instrumental group*   **5 wks**

| 23 Jan 93 | **FEED THE TREE** *4AD BAD 3001CD* .... | **32** | 3 wks |
| 10 Apr 93 | **GEPETTO** *4AD BADD 2018CD* .... | **49** | 2 wks |

BELMONTS - *See DION*

BELOVED *UK, male / female vocal / instrumental duo*   **40 wks**

21 Oct 89	**THE SUN RISING** *WEA YZ 414*	**26**	7 wks
27 Jan 90	**HELLO** *WEA YZ 426*	**19**	7 wks
24 Mar 90	**YOUR LOVE TAKES ME HIGHER** *East West YZ 463* ..	**39**	3 wks
9 Jun 90	**TIME AFTER TIME** *East West YZ 482*	**46**	4 wks
10 Nov 90	**IT'S ALRIGHT NOW** *East West YZ 541*	**48**	3 wks
23 Jan 93	● **SWEET HARMONY** *East West YZ 709CD*	**8**	10 wks
10 Apr 93	**YOU'VE GOT ME THINKING** *East West YZ 738CD*	**23**	4 wks
14 Aug 93	**OUTERSPACE GIRL** *East West YZ 726CD*	**38**	2 wks

Act were male only before '93.

BELTRAM *US, male producer - Joey Beltram*   **4 wks**

| 28 Sep 91 | **ENERGY FLASH (EP)** *R&S RSUK 3* .... | **52** | 2 wks |
| 7 Dec 91 | **THE OMEN** *R&S RSUK 7* [1] .... | **53** | 2 wks |

[1] Program 2 Beltram

Tracks on Energy Flash (EP): *Energy Flash / Psycho Bass / My Sound / Sub-Base Experience.*

Pat BENATAR *US, female vocalist*   **53 wks**

21 Jan 84	**LOVE IS A BATTLEFIELD** *Chrysalis CHS 2747*	**49**	5 wks
12 Jan 85	**WE BELONG** *Chrysalis CHS 2821*	**22**	9 wks
23 Mar 85	**LOVE IS A BATTLEFIELD (re-issue)** *Chrysalis PAT 1*	**17**	10 wks
15 Jun 85	**SHADOWS OF THE NIGHT** *Chrysalis PAT 2*	**50**	4 wks
19 Oct 85	**INVINCIBLE (THEME FROM 'THE LEGEND OF BILLIE JEAN')** *Chrysalis PAT 3*	**53**	3 wks
15 Feb 86	**SEX AS A WEAPON** *Chrysalis PAT 4*	**67**	3 wks
2 Jul 88	**ALL FIRED UP** *Chrysalis PAT 5*..........................	**19**	10 wks
1 Oct 88	**DON'T WALK AWAY** *Chrysalis PAT 6*	**42**	5 wks
14 Jan 89	**ONE LOVE** *Chrysalis PAT 7*	**59**	3 wks
30 Oct 93	**SOMEBODY'S BABY** *Chrysalis CDCHS 5001*	**48**	1 wk

David BENDETH
Canada, male vocalist and multi-instrumentalist   **5 wks**

| 8 Sep 79 | **FEEL THE REAL** *Sidewalk SID 113* .... | **44** | 5 wks |

BENELUX and Nancy DEE
Belgium / Holland / Luxembourg, female vocal group   **4 wks**

| 25 Aug 79 | **SWITCH** *Scope SC 4* .... | **52** | 4 wks |

Nigel BENN - *See PACK featuring Nigel BENN*

Boyd BENNETT and his Rockets
US, male vocalist and male vocal / instrumental group   **2 wks**

| 23 Dec 55 | **SEVENTEEN** *Parlophone R 4063*.................. | **16** | 2 wks |

Chris BENNETT - *See MUNICH MACHINE*

Cliff BENNETT and the REBEL ROUSERS
UK, male vocal / instrumental group   **23 wks**

1 Oct 64	● **ONE WAY LOVE** *Parlophone R 5173*	**9**	9 wks
4 Feb 65	**I'LL TAKE YOU HOME** *Parlophone R 5229*	**42**	3 wks
11 Aug 66	● **GOT TO GET YOU INTO MY LIFE** *Parlophone R 5489*	**6**	11 wks

Peter E. BENNETT *UK, male vocalist*   **1 wk**

| 7 Nov 70 | **THE SEAGULL'S NAME WAS NELSON** *RCA 1991* .... | **45** | 1 wk |

Tony BENNETT *US, male vocalist*   **61 wks**

15 Apr 55	★ **STRANGER IN PARADISE** *Philips PB 420*..................	**1**	16 wks
16 Sep 55	**CLOSE YOUR EYES** *Philips PB 445*	**18**	1 wk
13 Apr 56	**COME NEXT SPRING** *Philips PB 537*	**29**	1 wk
5 Jan 61	**TILL** *Philips PB 1079*	**35**	2 wks
18 Jul 63	**THE GOOD LIFE** *CBS AAG 153*	**27**	13 wks
6 May 65	**IF I RULED THE WORLD** *CBS 201735*	**40**	5 wks
27 May 65	**I LEFT MY HEART IN SAN FRANCISCO** *CBS 201730*	**46**	2 wks
30 Sep 65	**I LEFT MY HEART IN SAN FRANCISCO (re-entry)** *CBS 201730*	**40**	5 wks
9 Dec 65	**I LEFT MY HEART IN SAN FRANCISCO (2nd re-entry)** *CBS 201730*	**25**	7 wks
23 Dec 65	**THE VERY THOUGHT OF YOU** *CBS 202021*	**21**	9 wks

Gary BENSON *UK, male vocalist*   **8 wks**

| 9 Aug 75 | **DON'T THROW IT ALL AWAY** *State STAT 10* .... | **20** | 8 wks |

George BENSON
US, male vocalist / instrumentalist - guitar   **140 wks**

25 Oct 75	**SUPERSHIP** *CTI CTSP 002* [1]	**30**	6 wks
4 Jun 77	**NATURE BOY** *Warner Bros. K 16921*	**26**	6 wks
24 Sep 77	**THE GREATEST LOVE OF ALL** *Arista 133*	**27**	7 wks
31 Mar 79	**LOVE BALLAD** *Warner Bros. K 17333*	**29**	9 wks
26 Jul 80	● **GIVE ME THE NIGHT** *Warner Bros. K 17673*	**7**	10 wks
4 Oct 80	● **LOVE X LOVE** *Warner Bros. K 17699*	**10**	8 wks
7 Feb 81	**WHAT'S ON YOUR MIND** *Warner Bros. K 17748*	**45**	5 wks
19 Sep 81	**LOVE ALL THE HURT AWAY** *Arista ARIST 428* [2]	**49**	3 wks
14 Nov 81	**TURN YOUR LOVE AROUND** *Warner Bros. K 17877*	**29**	11 wks
23 Jan 82	**NEVER GIVE UP ON A GOOD THING** *Warner Bros. K 17902*	**14**	10 wks
21 May 83	**LADY LOVE ME (ONE MORE TIME)** *Warner Bros. W 9614*	**11**	10 wks
16 Jul 83	**FEEL LIKE MAKIN' LOVE** *Warner Bros. W 9551*.......	**28**	7 wks
24 Sep 83	● **IN YOUR EYES** *Warner Bros. W 9487*..........	**7**	10 wks
17 Dec 83	**INSIDE LOVE (SO PERSONAL)** *WEA Int. W 9427*.....	**57**	5 wks
19 Jan 85	**20/20** *Warner Bros. W 9120*	**29**	9 wks
20 Apr 85	**BEYOND THE SEA (LA MER)** *Warner Bros. W 9014*	**60**	3 wks
16 Aug 86	**KISSES IN THE MOONLIGHT** *Warner Bros. W 8640*..	**60**	4 wks
29 Nov 86	**SHIVER** *Warner Bros. W 8523*	**19**	6 wks
14 Feb 87	**TEASER** *Warner Bros. W 8437*	**45**	4 wks
27 Aug 88	**LET'S DO IT AGAIN** *Warner Bros. W 7780*	**56**	3 wks
5 Sep 92	**I'LL KEEP YOUR DREAMS ALIVE** *Ammi AMMI 101* [3]	**68**	1 wk

[1] George 'Bad' Benson [2] Aretha Franklin and George Benson [3] George Benson and Patti Austin

Brook BENTON US, male vocalist   **18 wks**

10 Jul 59	ENDLESSLY Mercury AMT 1043	**28**	2 wks
6 Oct 60	KIDDIO Mercury AMT 1109	**42**	3 wks
3 Nov 60	KIDDIO (re-entry) Mercury AMT 1109	**41**	3 wks
16 Feb 61	FOOLS RUSH IN Mercury AMT 1121	**50**	1 wk
13 Jul 61	BOLL WEEVIL SONG Mercury AMT 1148	**30**	9 wks

Ingrid BERGMAN - See Dooley WILSON

BERLIN US, male/female vocal/instrumental group   **39 wks**

25 Oct 86	★ TAKE MY BREATH AWAY (LOVE THEME FROM 'TOP GUN') CBS A 7320	**1**	15 wks
17 Jan 87	YOU DON'T KNOW Mercury MER 237	**39**	6 wks
14 Mar 87	LIKE FLAMES Mercury MER 240	**47**	3 wks
20 Feb 88	TAKE MY BREATH AWAY (LOVE THEME FROM 'TOP GUN') (re-entry) CBS A 7320	**52**	3 wks
13 Oct 90	● TAKE MY BREATH AWAY (re-issue) CBS 656361 7	**3**	12 wks

Elmer BERNSTEIN US, orchestra   **11 wks**

| 18 Dec 59 | ● STACCATO'S THEME Capitol CL 15101 | **4** | 10 wks |
| 10 Mar 60 | STACCATO'S THEME (re-entry) Capitol CL 15101 | **40** | 1 wk |

Leonard BERNSTEIN, ORCHESTRA and CHORUS US, male conductor, orchestra and chorus   **4 wks**

| 2 Jul 94 | AMERICA – WORLD CUP THEME 1994 Deutsche Grammophon USACD 1 | **44** | 4 wks |

Chuck BERRY US, male vocalist/instrumentalist - guitar   **91 wks**

21 Jun 57	SCHOOL DAY Columbia DB 3951	**24**	2 wks
12 Jul 57	SCHOOL DAY (re-entry) Columbia DB 3951	**24**	2 wks
25 Apr 58	SWEET LITTLE SIXTEEN London HLM 8585	**16**	5 wks
11 Jul 63	GO GO GO Pye International 7N 25209	**38**	6 wks
10 Oct 63	● LET IT ROCK / MEMPHIS TENNESSEE Pye International 7N 25218	**6**	13 wks
19 Dec 63	RUN RUDOLPH RUN Pye International 7N 25228	**36**	6 wks
13 Feb 64	NADINE (IS IT YOU) Pye International 7N 25236	**27**	6 wks
2 Apr 64	NADINE (IS IT YOU) (re-entry) Pye International 7N 25236	**43**	1 wk
7 May 64	● NO PARTICULAR PLACE TO GO Pye International 7N 25242	**3**	12 wks
20 Aug 64	YOU NEVER CAN TELL Pye International 7N 25257	**23**	8 wks
14 Jan 65	PROMISED LAND Pye International 7N 25285	**26**	6 wks
28 Oct 72	★ MY DING-A-LING Chess 6145 019	**1**	17 wks
3 Feb 73	REELIN' AND ROCKIN' Chess 6145 020	**18**	7 wks

Dave BERRY UK, male vocalist   **76 wks**

19 Sep 63	MEMPHIS TENNESSEE Decca F 11734 [1]	**19**	13 wks
9 Jan 64	MY BABY LEFT ME Decca F 11803 [1]	**41**	1 wk
23 Jan 64	MY BABY LEFT ME (re-entry) Decca F 11803 [1]	**37**	8 wks
30 Apr 64	BABY IT'S YOU Decca F 11876	**24**	6 wks
6 Aug 64	● THE CRYING GAME Decca F 11937	**5**	12 wks
26 Nov 64	ONE HEART BETWEEN TWO Decca F 12020	**41**	2 wks
25 Mar 65	● LITTLE THINGS Decca F 12103	**5**	12 wks
22 Jul 65	THIS STRANGE EFFECT Decca F 12188	**37**	6 wks
30 Jun 66	● MAMA Decca F 12435	**5**	16 wks

[1] Dave Berry and the Cruisers

Mike BERRY UK, male vocalist   **51 wks**

12 Oct 61	TRIBUTE TO BUDDY HOLLY HMV POP 912 [1]	**24**	6 wks
3 Jan 63	● DON'T YOU THINK IT'S TIME HMV POP 1105 [1]	**6**	12 wks
11 Apr 63	MY LITTLE BABY HMV POP 1142 [1]	**34**	7 wks
2 Aug 80	● THE SUNSHINE OF YOUR SMILE Polydor 2059 261	**9**	12 wks
29 Nov 80	IF I COULD ONLY MAKE YOU CARE Polydor POSP 202	**37**	9 wks

| 5 Sep 81 | MEMORIES Polydor POSP 287 | **55** | 5 wks |

[1] Mike Berry with the Outlaws

Nick BERRY UK, male vocalist   **24 wks**

4 Oct 86	★ EVERY LOSER WINS BBC RESL 204	**1**	11 wks
27 Dec 86	EVERY LOSER WINS (re-entry) BBC RESL 204	**72**	2 wks
13 Jun 92	● HEARTBEAT Columbia 6581517	**2**	8 wks
31 Oct 92	LONG LIVE LOVE Columbia 6587597	**47**	3 wks

Adele BERTEI - See JELLYBEAN

BEST COMPANY UK, male vocal duo   **1 wk**

| 27 Mar 93 | DON'T YOU FORGET ABOUT ME ZYX ZYX 69468 | **65** | 1 wk |

BEST SHOT UK, male rap group   **2 wks**

| 5 Feb 94 | UNITED COLOURS East West YZ 795CD | **64** | 2 wks |

BEVERLEY SISTERS UK, female vocal group   **34 wks**

27 Nov 53	I SAW MOMMY KISSING SANTA CLAUS Philips PB 188	**11**	1 wk
11 Dec 53	● I SAW MOMMY KISSING SANTA CLAUS (re-entry) Philips PB 188	**6**	4 wks
13 Apr 56	WILLIE CAN Decca F 10705	**23**	4 wks
1 Feb 57	I DREAMED Decca F 10832	**24**	2 wks
13 Feb 59	● LITTLE DRUMMER BOY Decca F 11107	**6**	13 wks
20 Nov 59	LITTLE DONKEY Decca F 11172	**14**	7 wks
23 Jun 60	GREEN FIELDS Columbia DB 4444	**48**	1 wk
7 Jul 60	GREEN FIELDS (re-entry) Columbia DB 4444	**29**	2 wks

See also Various Artists (EPs & LPs) - All Star Hit Parade No.2.

Frankie BEVERLY - See MAZE featuring Frankie BEVERLY

BEYOND UK, male vocal/instrumental group   **1 wk**

| 21 Sep 91 | RAGING EP Harvest HARS 530 | **68** | 1 wk |

Tracks on Raging EP: Great Indifference / Nail / Eve Of My Release.

B-52s US, male/female vocal/instrumental group   **60 wks**

11 Aug 79	ROCK LOBSTER Island WIP 6506	**37**	5 wks
9 Aug 80	GIVE ME BACK MY MAN Island WIP 6579	**61**	3 wks
7 May 83	FUTURE GENERATION Island IS 107	**63**	2 wks
10 May 86	ROCK LOBSTER (re-issue)/PLANET CLAIRE Island BFT 1	**12**	7 wks
3 Mar 90	● LOVE SHACK Reprise W 9917	**2**	13 wks
19 May 90	ROAM Reprise W 9827	**17**	7 wks
18 Aug 90	CHANNEL Z Reprise W 9737	**61**	2 wks
20 Jun 92	GOOD STUFF Reprise W 0109	**21**	6 wks
12 Sep 92	TELL IT LIKE T-I-IS Reprise W 0130	**61**	3 wks
9 Jul 94	● (MEET) THE FLINTSTONES MCA MCSTD 1986 [1]	**3**	12 wks

[1] BC-52s

Planet Claire only listed from 17 May 86.

BG THE PRINCE OF RAP Germany, male rapper   **2 wks**

| 18 Jan 92 | TAKE CONTROL OF THE PARTY Columbia 6576330 | 71 | 2 wks |

BIBLE UK, male vocal/instrumental group   **8 wks**

| 20 May 89 | GRACELAND Chrysalis BIB 4 | **51** | 4 wks |
| 26 Aug 89 | HONEY BE GOOD Ensign BIB 5 | **54** | 4 wks |

BIBLE OF DREAMS - See Johnny PANIC and the BIBLE OF DREAMS

NICK BERRY has had two major hits, one from each of his popular television series, *EastEnders* and *Heartbeat*. Nick is shown as PC Nick Rowan on *Heartbeat* (Yorkshire Television)

When the **BEE GEES** swept the Grammy Awards for 1978, Barry Gibb (centre) enthused 'We're the happiest three brothers in the world.' (LFI)

TONY BENNETT, shown in the 1960s singing into a WNEW radio microphone, has recently become a cult favourite on MTV in America.

BIDDU UK, orchestra   13 wks

2 Aug 75	**SUMMER OF '42** Epic EPC 3318	**14**	8 wks
17 Apr 76	**RAIN FOREST** Epic EPC 4084	**39**	4 wks
11 Feb 78	**JOURNEY TO THE MOON** Epic EPC 5910	**41**	1 wk

BIG APPLE BAND - See Walter MURPHY and the BIG APPLE BAND

BIG AUDIO DYNAMITE
UK / US, male vocal / instrumental group   27 wks

22 Mar 86	**E = MC^2** CBS A 6963	**11**	9 wks
7 Jun 86	**MEDICINE SHOW** CBS A 7181	**29**	5 wks
18 Oct 86	**C'MON EVERY BEATBOX** CBS 650147	**51**	3 wks
21 Feb 87	**V THIRTEEN** CBS BAAD 2	**49**	5 wks
28 May 88	**JUST PLAY MUSIC** CBS BAAD 4	**51**	3 wks
12 Nov 94	**LOOKING FOR A SONG** Columbia 6610182 [1]	**68**	2 wks

[1] Big Audio

BIG BAD HORNS - See LITTLE ANGELS

BIG BAM BOO UK / Canada, male vocal / instrumental duo 2 wks

| 28 Jan 89 | **SHOOTING FROM MY HEART** MCA MCA 1281 | **61** | 2 wks |

BIG BEN BANJO BAND UK, instrumental group   6 wks

10 Dec 54	● **LET'S GET TOGETHER NO. 1** Columbia DB 3549	**6**	4 wks
9 Dec 55	**LET'S GET TOGETHER AGAIN** Columbia DB 3676	**19**	1 wk
30 Dec 55	**LET'S GET TOGETHER AGAIN (re-entry)** Columbia DB 3676	**18**	1 wk

These hits were both medleys as follows: Let's Get Together No.1: *I'm Just Wild About Harry / April Showers / Rock-a-Bye Your Baby / Swanee / Darktown Strutters Ball / For Me And My Gal / Oh You Beautiful Doll / Yes Sir That's My Baby*. Let's Get Together Again: *I'm Looking Over A Four-leafed Clover / By The Light Of The Silvery Moon / Oh Susannah / Baby Face / I'm Sitting On Top Of The World / My Mammy / Dixie's Land / Margie.*

BIG BOPPER US, male vocalist   8 wks

| 26 Dec 58 | **CHANTILLY LACE** Mercury AMT 1002 | **30** | 1 wk |
| 9 Jan 59 | **CHANTILLY LACE (re-entry)** Mercury AMT 1002 | **12** | 7 wks |

BIG COUNTRY UK, male vocal / instrumental group   100 wks

26 Feb 83	● **FIELDS OF FIRE (400 MILES)** Mercury COUNT 2	**10**	12 wks
28 May 83	**IN A BIG COUNTRY** Mercury COUNT 3	**17**	7 wks
3 Sep 83	● **CHANCE** Mercury COUNT 4	**9**	9 wks
21 Jan 84	● **WONDERLAND** Mercury COUNT 5	**8**	8 wks
29 Sep 84	**EAST OF EDEN** Mercury MER 175	**17**	6 wks
1 Dec 84	**WHERE THE ROSE IS SOWN** Mercury MER 185	**29**	7 wks
19 Jan 85	**JUST A SHADOW** Mercury BCO 8	**26**	4 wks
12 Apr 86	● **LOOK AWAY** Mercury BIGC 1	**7**	8 wks
21 Jun 86	**THE TEACHER** Mercury BIGC 2	**28**	4 wks
20 Sep 86	**ONE GREAT THING** Mercury BIGC 3	**19**	6 wks
29 Nov 86	**HOLD THE HEART** Mercury BIGC 4	**55**	2 wks
20 Aug 88	**KING OF EMOTION** Mercury BIGC 5	**16**	5 wks
1 Oct 88	**KING OF EMOTION (re-entry)** Mercury BIGC 5	**74**	1 wk
5 Nov 88	**BROKEN HEART (THIRTEEN VALLEYS)** Mercury BIGC 6	**47**	4 wks
4 Feb 89	**PEACE IN OUR TIME** Mercury BIGC 7	**39**	3 wks
12 May 90	**SAVE ME** Mercury BIGC 8	**41**	3 wks
21 Jul 90	**HEART OF THE WORLD** Mercury BIGC 9	**50**	2 wks
31 Aug 91	**REPUBLICAN PARTY REPTILE (EP)** Vertigo BIC 1	**37**	2 wks
19 Oct 91	**BEAUTIFUL PEOPLE** Vertigo BIC 2	**72**	1 wk
13 Mar 93	**ALONE** Compulsion CDPULSS 4	**24**	3 wks
1 May 93	**SHIPS (WHERE WERE YOU)** Compulsion CDPULSS 6	**29**	3 wks

Tracks on Republican Party Reptile (EP): *Republican Party Reptile / Comes A Time / You And Me And The Truth.*

BIG DADDY US, male vocal / instrumental group   8 wks

| 9 Mar 85 | **DANCING IN THE DARK** Making Waves SURF 1033 | **21** | 8 wks |

BIG DADDY KANE US, male vocalist   6 wks

13 May 89	**RAP SUMMARY / WRATH OF KANE** Cold Chillin' W 2973	**52**	2 wks
26 Aug 89	**SMOOTH OPERATOR** Cold Chillin' W 2804	**65**	1 wk
13 Jan 90	**AIN'T NO STOPPIN' US NOW** Cold Chillin' W 2635	**44**	3 wks

BIG DISH UK, male vocal / instrumental group   5 wks

| 12 Jan 91 | **MISS AMERICA** East West YZ 529 | **37** | 5 wks |

BIG FAMILY - See JT and the BIG FAMILY

BIG FUN UK, male vocal group   33 wks

12 Aug 89	● **BLAME IT ON THE BOOGIE** Jive JIVE 217	**4**	11 wks
25 Nov 89	● **CAN'T SHAKE THE FEELING** Jive JIVE 234	**8**	9 wks
17 Mar 90	**HANDFUL OF PROMISES** Jive JIVE 243	**21**	6 wks
23 Jun 90	**YOU'VE GOT A FRIEND** Jive CHILD 90 [1]	**14**	6 wks
4 Aug 90	**HEY THERE LONELY GIRL** Jive JIVE 251	**62**	1 wk

[1] Big Fun and Sonia

BIG MOUNTAIN
US, male / female vocal / instrumental group   15 wks

| 4 Jun 94 | ● **BABY I LOVE YOUR WAY** RCA 74321198062 | **2** | 14 wks |
| 24 Sep 94 | **SWEET SENSUAL LOVE** Giant 74321234642 | **51** | 1 wk |

BIG ROLL BAND - See Zoot MONEY and the BIG ROLL BAND

BIG SOUND - See Simon DUPREE and the BIG SOUND

BIG SOUND AUTHORITY
UK, male / female vocal / instrumental group   12 wks

| 19 Jan 85 | **THIS HOUSE (IS WHERE YOUR LOVE STANDS)** Source BSA 1 | **21** | 9 wks |
| 8 Jun 85 | **A BAD TOWN** Source BSA 2 | **54** | 3 wks |

BIG SUPREME UK, male vocal group   5 wks

| 20 Sep 86 | **DON'T WALK** Polydor POSP 809 | **58** | 3 wks |
| 14 Mar 87 | **PLEASE YOURSELF** Polydor POSP 840 | **64** | 2 wks |

BIG THREE UK, vocal / instrumental group   17 wks

| 11 Apr 63 | **SOME OTHER GUY** Decca F 11614 | **37** | 7 wks |
| 11 Jul 63 | **BY THE WAY** Decca F 11689 | **22** | 10 wks |

Barry BIGGS Jamaica, male vocalist   46 wks

28 Aug 76	**WORK ALL DAY** Dynamic DYN 101	**38**	5 wks
4 Dec 76	● **SIDESHOW** Dynamic DYN 118	**3**	16 wks
23 Apr 77	**YOU'RE MY LIFE** Dynamic DYN 127	**36**	4 wks
9 Jul 77	**THREE RING CIRCUS** Dynamic DYN 128	**22**	8 wks
15 Dec 79	**WHAT'S YOUR SIGN GIRL** Dynamic DYN 150	**55**	7 wks
20 Jun 81	**WIDE AWAKE IN A DREAM** Dynamic DYN 10	**44**	6 wks

Ronald BIGGS - See SEX PISTOLS

Ivor BIGGUN UK, male vocalist   15 wks

| 2 Sep 78 | **WINKER'S SONG (MISPRINT)** Beggars Banquet BOP 1 [1] | **22** | 12 wks |

12 Sep 81　**BRAS ON 45 (FAMILY VERSION)**
Dead Badger BOP 6 [2] ....**50**　3 wks

[1] Ivor Biggun and the Red Nosed Burglars [2] Ivor Biggun and the D Cups

BILBO　UK, male vocal / instrumental group　**7 wks**

26 Aug 78　**SHE'S GONNA WIN** *Lightning LIG 548* ....**42**　7 wks

Mr. Acker BILK and his PARAMOUNT JAZZ BAND

UK, male jazz band leader, vocalist / instrumentalist - clarinet　**171 wks**

22 Jan 60 ●	**SUMMER SET** *Columbia DB 4382*	**5**	19 wks
9 Jun 60	**GOODNIGHT SWEET PRINCE** *Melodisc MEL 1547*	**50**	1 wk
18 Aug 60	**WHITE CLIFFS OF DOVER** *Columbia DB 4492*	**30**	9 wks
8 Dec 60 ●	**BUONA SERA** *Columbia DB 4544*	**7**	18 wks
13 Jul 61 ●	**THAT'S MY HOME** *Columbia DB 4673*	**7**	17 wks
2 Nov 61	**STARS AND STRIPES FOREVER / CREOLE JAZZ** *Columbia SCD 2155*	**22**	10 wks
30 Nov 61 ●	**STRANGER ON THE SHORE** *Columbia DB 4750* [1]	**2**	55 wks
15 Mar 62	**FRANKIE AND JOHNNY** *Columbia DB 4795*	**42**	2 wks
26 Jul 62	**GOTTA SEE BABY TONIGHT** *Columbia SCD 2176*......	**24**	9 wks
27 Sep 62	**LONELY** *Columbia DB 4897* [1]	**14**	11 wks
24 Jan 63	**A TASTE OF HONEY** *Columbia DB 4949* [1]	**16**	9 wks
21 Aug 76 ●	**ARIA** *Pye 7N 45607* [2]	**5**	11 wks

[1] Mr. Acker Bilk with the Leon Young String Chorale [2] Acker Bilk, his Clarinet and Strings

BILL　UK, male vocalist　**1 wk**

23 Oct 93　**CAR BOOT SALE** *Mercury MINCD 1* ....**73**　1 wk

BIMBO JET
France, male / female vocal / instrumental group　**10 wks**

26 Jul 75　**EL BIMBO** *EMI 2317* ....**12**　10 wks

Umberto BINDI　*Italy, male vocalist*　**1 wk**

10 Nov 60　**IL NOSTRO CONCERTO** *Oriole CB 1577*.............**47**　1 wk

BIOHAZARD　US, male vocal / instrumental group　**4 wks**

9 Jul 94	**TALES FROM THE HARD SIDE** *Warner Bros. W 0254CD*	**47**	2 wks
20 Aug 94	**HOW IT IS** *Warner Bros. W 0259CD*	**62**	2 wks

La BIONDA　*Italy, male / female vocal group*　**4 wks**

7 Oct 78　**ONE FOR YOU ONE FOR ME** *Philips 6198 227* ...**54**　4 wks

BIRDLAND　UK, male vocal / instrumental group　**7 wks**

1 Apr 89	**HOLLOW HEART** *Lazy LAZY 13*	**70**	1 wk
8 Jul 89	**PARADISE** *Lazy LAZY 14*	**70**	1 wk
3 Feb 90	**SLEEP WITH ME** *Lazy LAZY 17*	**32**	3 wks
22 Sep 90	**ROCK AND ROLL NIGGER** *Lazy LAZY 20*	**47**	1 wk
2 Feb 91	**EVERYBODY NEEDS SOMEBODY** *Lazy LAZY 24*	**44**	1 wk

BIRDS　UK, male vocal / instrumental group　**1 wk**

27 May 65　**LEAVING HERE** *Decca F 12140* ....**45**　1 wk

Jane BIRKIN and Serge GAINSBOURG
UK / France, female / male vocal duo　**34 wks**

30 Jul 69 ●　**JE T'AIME. . . MOI NON PLUS** *Fontana TF 1042* ....**2**　11 wks

4 Oct 69 ★	**JE T'AIME. . . MOI NON PLUS (re-issue)** *Major Minor MM 645*	**1**	14 wks
7 Dec 74	**JE T'AIME. . . MOI NON PLUS (2nd re-issue)** *Antic K 11511*	**31**	9 wks

Elvin BISHOP　US, male instrumentalist - guitar　**4 wks**

15 May 76　**FOOLED AROUND AND FELL IN LOVE** *Capricorn 2089 024* ....**34**　4 wks

Hit has vocal (uncredited) by Mickey Thomas.

BITI - *See DEGREES OF MOTION featuring BITI*

BIZARRE INC　UK, male instrumental / production group　**40 wks**

16 Mar 91	**PLAYING WITH KNIVES** *Vinyl Solution STORM 25R*..	**43**	5 wks
14 Sep 91	**SUCH A FEELING** *Vinyl Solution STORM 32S*	**13**	9 wks
23 Nov 91 ●	**PLAYING WITH KNIVES (re-issue)** *Vinyl Solution STORM 38S*	**4**	8 wks
3 Oct 92	**I'M GONNA GET YOU** *Vinyl Solution STORM 46S* [1] ..	**3**	12 wks
2 Jan 93	**I'M GONNA GET YOU (re-entry)** *Vinyl Solution STORM 46S* [1]	**72**	1 wk
27 Feb 93	**TOOK MY LOVE** *Vinyl Solution STORM 60CD* [1]	**19**	5 wks

[1] Bizarre Inc featuring Angie Brown

BIZZ NIZZ
US / Belgium, male / female vocal / instrumental group　**11 wks**

31 Mar 90 ●　**DON'T MISS THE PARTY LINE** *Cooltempo COOL 203*.............................**7**　11 wks

BJORK　*Iceland, female vocalist*　**27 wks**

27 Apr 91	**OOOPS** *ZTT ZANG 19* [1]	**42**	3 wks
19 Jun 93	**HUMAN BEHAVIOUR** *One Little Indian 112 TP7CD*	**36**	2 wks
4 Sep 93	**VENUS AS A BOY** *One Little Indian 122 TP7CD*	**29**	4 wks
23 Oct 93	**PLAY DEAD** *Island CID 573* [2]	**12**	6 wks
4 Dec 93	**BIG TIME SENSUALITY** *One Little Indian 132 TP7CD*	**17**	8 wks
19 Mar 94	**VIOLENTLY HAPPY** *One Little Indian 142 TP7CD*	**13**	4 wks

[1] 808 State featuring Bjork [2] Bjork and David Arnold

BJORN AGAIN
Australia, male / female vocal / instrumental group　**8 wks**

24 Oct 92	**ERASURE-ISH (A LITTLE RESPECT / STOP!)** *M & G MAGS 32*	**25**	3 wks
12 Dec 92	**SANTA CLAUS IS COMING TO TOWN** *M & G MAGS 35*	**55**	4 wks
27 Nov 93	**FLASHDANCE** *M & G MAGCD 50*	**65**	1 wk

BLACK　UK, male vocalist - Colin Vearncombe　**35 wks**

27 Sep 86	**WONDERFUL LIFE** *Ugly Man JACK 71*	**72**	1 wk
27 Jun 87 ●	**SWEETEST SMILE** *A & M AM 394*	**8**	10 wks
22 Aug 87 ●	**WONDERFUL LIFE** *A & M AM 402*	**8**	9 wks
16 Jan 88	**PARADISE** *A & M AM 422*	**38**	3 wks
24 Sep 88	**THE BIG ONE** *A & M AM 468*	**54**	4 wks
21 Jan 89	**NOW YOU'RE GONE** *A & M AM 491*	**66**	2 wks
4 May 91	**FEEL LIKE CHANGE** *A & M AM 780*	**56**	2 wks
15 Jun 91	**HERE IT COMES AGAIN** *A & M AM 753*	**70**	1 wk
5 Mar 94	**WONDERFUL LIFE (re-issue)** *PolyGram TV 5805552*	**42**	3 wks

Wonderful Life on A & M is a re-recording. It was re-issued on PolyGram TV in '94.

Cilla BLACK　UK, female vocalist　**194 wks**

17 Oct 63	**LOVE OF THE LOVED** *Parlophone R 5065*	**35**	6 wks
6 Feb 64 ★	**ANYONE WHO HAD A HEART** *Parlophone R 5101*	**1**	17 wks
7 May 64 ★	**YOU'RE MY WORLD** *Parlophone R 5133*	**1**	17 wks
6 Aug 64 ●	**IT'S FOR YOU** *Parlophone R 5162*	**7**	10 wks

14 Jan 65	● YOU'VE LOST THAT LOVIN' FEELIN' *Parlophone R 5225*	**2**	9 wks
22 Apr 65	I'VE BEEN WRONG BEFORE *Parlophone R 5269*	**17**	8 wks
13 Jan 66	● LOVE'S JUST A BROKEN HEART *Parlophone R 5395*	**5**	11 wks
31 Mar 66	● ALFIE *(Parlophone R 5427)*	**9**	12 wks
9 Jun 66	● DON'T ANSWER ME *Parlophone R 5463*	**6**	10 wks
20 Oct 66	A FOOL AM I *Parlophone R 5515*	**13**	9 wks
8 Jun 67	WHAT GOOD AM I *Parlophone R 5608*	**24**	7 wks
29 Nov 67	I ONLY LIVE TO LOVE YOU *Parlophone R 5652*	**26**	11 wks
13 Mar 68	● STEP INSIDE LOVE *Parlophone R 5674*	**8**	9 wks
12 Jun 68	WHERE IS TOMORROW *Parlophone R 5706*	**39**	3 wks
12 Feb 69	● SURROUND YOURSELF WITH SORROW *Parlophone R 5759*	**3**	12 wks
9 Jul 69	● CONVERSATIONS *Parlophone R 5785*	**7**	12 wks
13 Dec 69	IF I THOUGHT YOU'D EVER CHANGE YOUR MIND *Parlophone R 5820*	**20**	9 wks
20 Nov 71	● SOMETHING TELLS ME (SOMETHING IS GONNA HAPPEN TONIGHT) *Parlophone R 5924*	**3**	14 wks
2 Feb 74	BABY WE CAN'T GO WRONG *EMI 2107*	**36**	6 wks
18 Sep 93	THROUGH THE YEARS *Columbia 6596982*	**54**	1 wk
30 Oct 93	HEART AND SOUL *Columbia 6598562* [1]	**75**	1 wk

[1] Cilla Black with Dusty Springfield

Frank BLACK *US, male vocalist* **1 wk**

21 May 94	HEADACHE *4AD BADD 4007CD*	**53**	1 wk

Jeanne BLACK *US, female vocalist* **4 wks**

23 Jun 60	HE'LL HAVE TO STAY *Capitol CL 15131*	**41**	4 wks

BLACK BOX
Italy, male/female vocal/instrumental group **68 wks**

12 Aug 89	★ RIDE ON TIME *Deconstruction PB 43055*	**1**	22 wks
17 Feb 90	● I DON'T KNOW ANYBODY ELSE *Deconstruction PB 43479*	**4**	8 wks
2 Jun 90	EVERYBODY EVERYBODY *Deconstruction PB 43715*	**16**	5 wks
3 Nov 90	● FANTASY *Deconstruction PB 43895*	**5**	11 wks
15 Dec 90	THE TOTAL MIX *Deconstruction PB 44235*	**12**	8 wks
6 Apr 91	STRIKE IT UP / RIDE ON TIME (re-mix) *Deconstruction PB 44459*	**16**	8 wks
14 Dec 91	OPEN YOUR EYES *Deconstruction PB 45053*	**48**	4 wks
14 Aug 93	ROCKIN' TO THE MUSIC *Deconstruction 74321158122*	**39**	2 wks

BLACK CROWES *US, male vocal/instrumental group* **22 wks**

1 Sep 90	HARD TO HANDLE *Def American DEFA 6*	**45**	5 wks
12 Jan 91	TWICE AS HARD *Def American DEFA 7*	**47**	3 wks
22 Jun 91	JEALOUS AGAIN / SHE TALKS TO ANGELS *Def American DEFA 8*	**70**	1 wk
24 Aug 91	HARD TO HANDLE (re-issue) *Def American DEFA 10*	**39**	4 wks
26 Oct 91	SEEING THINGS *Def American DEFA 13*	**72**	1 wk
2 May 92	REMEDY *Def American DEFA 16*	**24**	3 wks
26 Sep 92	STING ME *Def American DEFA 21*	**42**	2 wks
28 Nov 92	HOTEL ILLNESS *Def American DEFA 23*	**47**	3 wks

BLACK DIAMOND *US, male vocalist* **1 wk**

17 Sep 94	LET ME BE *Systematic SYSCD 1*	**56**	1 wk

BLACK DUCK *UK, male rapper* **3 wks**

17 Dec 94	WHIGGLE IN LINE *Flying South CDDUCK 1*	**33†**	3 wks

BLACK GORILLA
UK, male/female vocal/instrumental group **6 wks**

27 Aug 77	GIMME DAT BANANA *Response SR 502*	**29**	6 wks

BLACK LACE *UK, male vocal/instrumental group* **82 wks**

31 Mar 79	MARY ANN *EMI 2919*	**42**	4 wks
24 Sep 83	● SUPERMAN (GIOCA JOUER) *Flair FLA 105*	**9**	18 wks
30 Jun 84	● AGADOO *Flair FLA 107*	**2**	30 wks
24 Nov 84	● DO THE CONGA *Flair FLA 108*	**10**	9 wks
1 Jun 85	EL VINO COLLAPSO *Flair LACE 1*	**42**	5 wks
7 Sep 85	I SPEAKA DA LINGO *Flair LACE 2*	**49**	4 wks
7 Dec 85	HOKEY COKEY *Flair LACE 3*	**31**	6 wks
20 Sep 86	WIG WAM BAM *Flair LACE 5*	**63**	3 wks
26 Aug 89	I AM THE MUSIC MAN *Flair LACE 10*	**52**	3 wks

BLACK MACHINE
France/Nigeria, male vocal/instrumental duo **5 wks**

9 Apr 94	HOW GEE *London LONCD 348*	**17**	5 wks

BLACK RIOT *US, male producer* **3 wks**

3 Dec 88	WARLOCK / A DAY IN THE LIFE *Champion CHAMP 75*	**68**	3 wks

A Day In The Life only listed from 17 Dec 88.

BLACK SABBATH
UK/US, male vocal/instrumental group **70 wks**

29 Aug 70	● PARANOID *Vertigo 6059 010*	**4**	18 wks
3 Jun 78	NEVER SAY DIE *Vertigo SAB 001*	**21**	8 wks
14 Oct 78	HARD ROAD *Vertigo SAB 002*	**33**	4 wks
5 Jul 80	NEON KNIGHTS *Vertigo SAB 3*	**22**	9 wks
16 Aug 80	PARANOID (re-issue) *Nems BSS 101*	**14**	12 wks
6 Dec 80	DIE YOUNG *Vertigo SAB 4*	**41**	7 wks
7 Nov 81	MOB RULES *Vertigo SAB 5*	**46**	4 wks
13 Feb 82	TURN UP THE NIGHT *Vertigo SAB 6*	**37**	5 wks
15 Apr 89	HEADLESS CROSS *IRS EIRS 107*	**62**	1 wk
13 Jun 92	TV CRIMES *IRS EIRSP 178*	**33**	2 wks

Group UK only for first three hits and re-issue of Paranoid.

BLACK SHEEP *US, male rap duo* **1 wk**

19 Nov 94	WITHOUT A DOUBT *Mercury MERCD 417*	**60**	1 wk

BLACK SLATE
UK/Jamaica, male vocal/instrumental group **15 wks**

20 Sep 80	● AMIGO *Ensign ENY 42*	**9**	9 wks
6 Dec 80	BOOM BOOM *Ensign ENY 47*	**51**	6 wks

BLACK UHURU *Jamaica, male vocal/instrumental group* **9 wks**

8 Sep 84	WHAT IS LIFE? *Island IS 150*	**56**	6 wks
31 May 86	THE GREAT TRAIN ROBBERY *Real Authentic Sound RAS 7018*	**62**	3 wks

Band of the BLACK WATCH *UK, military band* **22 wks**

30 Aug 75	● SCOTCH ON THE ROCKS *Spark SRL 1128*	**8**	14 wks
13 Dec 75	DANCE OF THE CUCKOOS *Spark SRL 1135*	**37**	8 wks

Bill BLACK'S COMBO
US, male instrument, Bill Black, bass **8 wks**

8 Sep 60	WHITE SILVER SANDS *London HLU 9090*	**50**	1 wk
3 Nov 60	DON'T BE CRUEL *London HLU 9212*	**32**	7 wks

Tony BLACKBURN *UK, male vocalist* **7 wks**

24 Jan 68	SO MUCH LOVE *MGM 1375*	**31**	4 wks
26 Mar 69	IT'S ONLY LOVE *MGM 1467*	**42**	3 wks

BLACKBYRDS US, male vocal/instrumental group — **6 wks**

31 May 75	**WALKING IN RHYTHM** Fantasy FTC 114	**23**	6 wks

BLACKFOOT US, male vocal/instrumental group — **5 wks**

6 Mar 82	**DRY COUNTY** Atco K 11686	**43**	4 wks
18 Jun 83	**SEND ME AN ANGEL** Atco B 9880	**66**	1 wk

J. BLACKFOOT US, male vocalist — **4 wks**

17 Mar 84	**TAXI** Allegiance ALES 2	**48**	4 wks

BLACKFOOT SUE UK, male vocal/instrumental group — **15 wks**

12 Aug 72	● **STANDING IN THE ROAD** Jam 13	**4**	10 wks
16 Dec 72	**SING DON'T SPEAK** Jam 29	**36**	5 wks

BLACKGIRL US, female vocal group — **3 wks**

16 Jul 94	**90S GIRL** RCA 74321217882	**23**	3 wks

BLACKHEARTS - See Joan JETT and the BLACKHEARTS

Honor BLACKMAN - See Patrick MACNEE and Honor BLACKMAN

BLACKSTREET US, male vocal group — **4 wks**

19 Jun 93	**BABY BE MINE** MCA MCSTD 1772 [1]	**37**	3 wks
13 Aug 94	**BOOTI CALL** Interscope A 8250CD	**56**	1 wk

[1] Blackstreet featuring Teddy Riley

BLACKWELLS US, male vocal group — **2 wks**

18 May 61	**LOVE OR MONEY** London HLW 9334	**46**	2 wks

Blaggers I.T.A. UK, male vocal/instrumental group — **7 wks**

12 Jun 93	**STRESSS** Parlophone CDITA 1	**56**	2 wks
9 Oct 93	**OXYGEN** Parlophone CDITA 2	**51**	2 wks
8 Jan 94	**ABANDON SHIP** Parlophone CDITA 3	**48**	3 wks

Vivian BLAINE US, female vocalist — **1 wk**

10 Jul 53	**BUSHEL AND A PECK** Brunswick 05100	**12**	1 wk

BLAIR - See Terry HALL

Peter BLAKE UK, male vocalist — **4 wks**

8 Oct 77	**LIPSMACKIN' ROCK 'N' ROLLIN'** Pepper UP 36295	**40**	4 wks

BLAME UK, male instrumental/production duo — **2 wks**

11 Apr 92	**MUSIC TAKES YOU** Moving Shadow SHADOW 11	**48**	2 wks

BLANCMANGE UK, male vocal/instrumental group — **71 wks**

17 Apr 82	**GOD'S KITCHEN/I'VE SEEN THE WORD** London BLANC 1	**65**	2 wks
31 Jul 82	**FEEL ME** London BLANC 2	**46**	5 wks
30 Oct 82	● **LIVING ON THE CEILING** London BLANC 3	**7**	14 wks
19 Feb 83	**WAVES** London BLANC 4	**19**	9 wks
7 May 83	● **BLIND VISION** London BLANC 5	**10**	8 wks
26 Nov 83	**THAT'S LOVE, THAT IT IS** London BLANC 6	**33**	8 wks
14 Apr 84	● **DON'T TELL ME** London BLANC 7	**8**	10 wks
21 Jul 84	**THE DAY BEFORE YOU CAME** London BLANC 8	**22**	8 wks
7 Sep 85	**WHAT'S YOUR PROBLEM?** London BLANC 9	**40**	5 wks
10 May 86	**I CAN SEE IT** London BLANC 11	**71**	2 wks

Billy BLAND US, male vocalist — **10 wks**

19 May 60	**LET THE LITTLE GIRL DANCE** London HL 9096	**15**	10 wks

BLAST featuring VDC
Italy, male/female vocal/instrumental group — **5 wks**

18 Jun 94	**CRAYZY MAN** UMM MCSTD 1982	**22**	3 wks
12 Nov 94	**PRINCES OF THE NIGHT** UMM MCSTD 2011	**40**	2 wks

BLESSING UK, male vocal/instrumental group — **13 wks**

11 May 91	**HIGHWAY 5** MCA MCS 1509	**42**	6 wks
18 Jan 92	**HIGHWAY 5 (re-mix)** MCA MCS 1603	**30**	6 wks
19 Feb 94	**SOUL LOVE** MCA MCSTD 1940	**73**	1 wk

Mary J BLIGE US, female vocalist — **22 wks**

28 Nov 92	**REAL LOVE** Uptown MCS 1721	**68**	2 wks
27 Feb 93	**REMINISCE** Uptown MCSTD 1731	**31**	4 wks
12 Jun 93	**YOU REMIND ME** Uptown MCSTD 1770	**48**	3 wks
28 Aug 93	**REAL LOVE (re-mix)** Uptown MCSTD 1922	**26**	4 wks
4 Dec 93	**YOU DON'T HAVE TO WORRY** Uptown MCSTD 1948	**36**	2 wks
14 May 94	**MY LOVE** Uptown MCSTD 1972	**29**	3 wks
10 Dec 94	**BE HAPPY** Uptown MCSTD 2033	**30†**	4 wks

BLIND MELON US, male vocal/instrumental group — **11 wks**

12 Jun 93	**TONES OF HOME** Capitol CDCL 687	**62**	2 wks
11 Dec 93	**NO RAIN** Capitol CDCL 699	**17**	6 wks
9 Jul 94	**CHANGE** Capitol CDCL 717	**35**	3 wks

BLINK Ireland, male vocal/instrumental group — **1 wk**

16 Jul 94	**HAPPY DAY** Lime CDR 6385	**57**	1 wk

BLOCKHEADS - See Ian DURY and the BLOCKHEADS

BLONDIE
US/UK, female/male vocal/instrumental group — **149 wks**

18 Feb 78	● **DENIS** Chrysalis CHS 2204	**2**	14 wks
6 May 78	● **(I'M ALWAYS TOUCHED BY YOUR) PRESENCE DEAR** Chrysalis CHS 2217	**10**	9 wks
26 Aug 78	**PICTURE THIS** Chrysalis CHS 2242	**12**	11 wks
11 Nov 78	● **HANGING ON THE TELEPHONE** Chrysalis CHS 2266	**5**	12 wks
27 Jan 79	★ **HEART OF GLASS** Chrysalis CHS 2275	**1**	12 wks
19 May 79	★ **SUNDAY GIRL** Chrysalis CHS 2320	**1**	13 wks
29 Sep 79	● **DREAMING** Chrysalis CHS 2350	**2**	8 wks
24 Nov 79	**UNION CITY BLUE** Chrysalis CHS 2400	**13**	10 wks
23 Feb 80	★ **ATOMIC** Chrysalis CHS 2410	**1**	9 wks
12 Apr 80	★ **CALL ME** Chrysalis CHS 2414	**1**	9 wks
8 Nov 80	★ **THE TIDE IS HIGH** Chrysalis CHS 2465	**1**	12 wks
24 Jan 81	● **RAPTURE** Chrysalis CHS 2485	**5**	8 wks
8 May 82	**ISLAND OF LOST SOULS** Chrysalis CHS 2608	**11**	9 wks
24 Jul 82	**WAR CHILD** Chrysalis CHS 2624	**39**	4 wks
3 Dec 88	**DENIS (re-mix)** Chrysalis CHS 3328	**50**	3 wks
11 Feb 89	**CALL ME (re-mix)** Chrysalis CHS 3342	**61**	2 wks
10 Sep 94	**ATOMIC (re-mix)** Chrysalis CDCHS 5013	**19**	4 wks

BLOOD SWEAT AND TEARS
US/Canada, male vocal/instrumental group — **6 wks**

30 Apr 69	**YOU'VE MADE ME SO VERY HAPPY** CBS 4116	**35**	6 wks

BLOODSTONE US, male vocal/instrumental group — **4 wks**

18 Aug 73	**NATURAL HIGH** Decca F 13382	**40**	4 wks

Bobby BLOOM US, male vocalist   24 wks

29 Aug 70	● MONTEGO BAY Polydor 2058 051	3	14 wks
12 Dec 70	MONTEGO BAY (re-entry) Polydor 2058 051	42	3 wks
9 Jan 71	HEAVY MAKES YOU HAPPY Polydor 2001 122	31	5 wks
9 Jan 71	MONTEGO BAY (2nd re-entry) Polydor 2058 051	47	2 wks

BLOOMSBURY SET
UK, male vocal / instrumental group   3 wks

25 Jun 83	HANGING AROUND WITH THE BIG BOYS Stiletto STL 13	56	3 wks

Tanya BLOUNT US, female vocalist   1 wk

11 Jun 94	I'M GONNA MAKE YOU MINE Polydor PZCD 315	69	1 wk

Kurtis BLOW US, male vocalist   23 wks

15 Dec 79	CHRISTMAS RAPPIN' Mercury BLOW 7	30	6 wks
11 Oct 80	THE BREAKS Mercury BLOW 8	47	4 wks
16 Mar 85	PARTY TIME (THE GO-GO EDIT) Club JAB 12	67	1 wk
15 Jun 85	SAVE YOUR LOVE (FOR NUMBER 1) Club JAB 14 [1]	66	2 wks
18 Jan 86	IF I RULED THE WORLD Club JAB 26	24	8 wks
8 Nov 86	I'M CHILLIN' Club JAB 42	64	2 wks

[1] René and Angela featuring Kurtis Blow

BLOW MONKEYS UK, male vocal / instrumental group   46 wks

1 Mar 86	DIGGING YOUR SCENE RCA PB 40599	12	10 wks
17 May 86	WICKED WAYS RCA MONK 2	60	2 wks
31 Jan 87	● IT DOESN'T HAVE TO BE THIS WAY RCA MONK 4	5	8 wks
28 Mar 87	OUT WITH HER RCA MONK 5	30	6 wks
30 May 87	(CELEBRATE) THE DAY AFTER YOU RCA MONK 6 [1]	52	2 wks
15 Aug 87	SOME KIND OF WONDERFUL RCA MONK 7	67	1 wk
6 Aug 88	THIS IS YOUR LIFE RCA PB 42149	70	2 wks
8 Apr 89	THIS IS YOUR LIFE (re-mix) RCA PB 42695	32	5 wks
15 Jul 89	CHOICE? RCA PB 42885 [2]	22	6 wks
14 Oct 89	SLAVES NO MORE RCA PB 43201 [2]	73	2 wks
26 May 90	SPRINGTIME FOR THE WORLD RCA PB 43623	69	2 wks

[1] Blow Monkeys with Curtis Mayfield [2] Blow Monkeys featuring Sylvia Tella

BLUE UK, male vocal / instrumental group   8 wks

30 Apr 77	GONNA CAPTURE YOUR HEART Rocket ROKN 522	18	8 wks

Babbity BLUE UK, female vocalist   2 wks

11 Feb 65	DON'T MAKE ME Decca F 12053	48	2 wks

Barry BLUE UK, male vocalist   48 wks

28 Jul 73	● (DANCING) ON A SATURDAY NIGHT Bell 1295	2	15 wks
3 Nov 73	● DO YOU WANNA DANCE Bell 1336	7	12 wks
2 Mar 74	SCHOOL LOVE Bell 1345	11	9 wks
3 Aug 74	MISS HIT AND RUN Bell 1364	26	7 wks
26 Oct 74	HOT SHOT Bell 1379	23	5 wks

See also Cry Sisco!

BLUE AEROPLANES
UK, male / female vocal / instrumental group   3 wks

17 Feb 90	JACKET HANGS Ensign ENY 628	72	1 wk
26 May 90	... AND STONES Ensign ENY 632	63	2 wks

BLUE BAMBOO Belgium, male producer - Johan Gielen   4 wks

3 Dec 94	ABC AND D... Escapade CDJAPE 6	23	4 wks

BLUE FEATHER Holland, male vocal / instrumental group   4 wks

3 Jul 82	LET'S FUNK TONIGHT Mercury MER 109	50	4 wks

BLUE FLAMES - See Georgie FAME

BLUE GRASS BOYS - See Johnny DUNCAN and the BLUE GRASS BOYS

BLUE HAZE UK, male vocal / instrumental group   6 wks

18 Mar 72	SMOKE GETS IN YOUR EYES A & M AMS 891	32	6 wks

BLUE JEANS - See Bob B. SOXX and the BLUE JEANS

BLUE MERCEDES UK, male vocal / instrumental duo   18 wks

10 Oct 87	I WANT TO BE YOUR PROPERTY MCA BONA 1	23	11 wks
13 Feb 88	SEE WANT MUST HAVE MCA BONA 2	57	2 wks
23 Jul 88	LOVE IS THE GUN MCA BONA 3	46	5 wks

BLUE MINK
UK / US, male / female vocal / instrumental group   83 wks

15 Nov 69	● MELTING POT Philips BF 1818	3	15 wks
28 Mar 70	● GOOD MORNING FREEDOM Philips BF 1838	10	10 wks
19 Sep 70	OUR WORLD Philips 6006 042	17	9 wks
29 May 71	● BANNER MAN Regal Zonophone RZ 3034	3	14 wks
11 Nov 72	STAY WITH ME Regal Zonophone RZ 3064	11	13 wks
17 Feb 73	STAY WITH ME (re-entry) Regal Zonophone RZ 3064	43	2 wks
3 Mar 73	BY THE DEVIL EMI 2007	26	9 wks
23 Jun 73	● RANDY EMI 2028	9	11 wks

BLUE NILE UK, male vocal / instrumental group   4 wks

30 Sep 89	THE DOWNTOWN LIGHTS Linn LKS 3	67	1 wk
29 Sep 90	HEADLIGHTS ON THE PARADE Linn LKS 4	72	1 wk
19 Jan 91	SATURDAY NIGHT Linn LKS 5	50	2 wks

BLUE OYSTER CULT US, male vocal / instrumental group   14 wks

20 May 78	(DON'T FEAR) THE REAPER CBS 6333	16	14 wks

BLUE PEARL UK / US, male / female vocal / instrumental group   27 wks

7 Jul 90	● NAKED IN THE RAIN Big Life BLR 23	4	13 wks
3 Nov 90	LITTLE BROTHER Big Life BLR 32	31	5 wks
11 Jan 92	(CAN YOU) FEEL THE PASSION Big Life BLR 67	14	6 wks
25 Jul 92	MOTHER DAWN Big Life BLR 73	50	2 wks
27 Nov 93	FIRE OF LOVE Logic 74321170292 [1]	71	1 wk

[1] Jungle High with Blue Pearl

See also Various Artists (EPs & LPs) – Gimme Shelter (EP).

BLUE RONDO A LA TURK
UK, male vocal / instrumental group   9 wks

14 Nov 81	ME AND MR SANCHEZ Virgin VS 463	40	4 wks
13 Mar 82	KLACTOVEESEDSTEIN Diable Noir VS 476	50	5 wks

BLUE ZOO UK, male vocal / instrumental group   17 wks

12 Jun 82	I'M YOUR MAN Magnet MAG 224	55	3 wks
16 Oct 82	CRY BOY CRY Magnet MAG 234	13	10 wks
28 May 83	I JUST CAN'T (FORGIVE AND FORGET) Magnet MAG 241	60	4 wks

BLUEBELLS UK, male vocal / instrumental group   49 wks

12 Mar 83	CATH London LON 20	62	2 wks
9 Jul 83	SUGAR BRIDGE (IT WILL STAND) London LON 27	72	1 wk

24 Mar 84	I'M FALLING London LON 45	11	12 wks
23 Jun 84 ●	YOUNG AT HEART London LON 49	8	12 wks
1 Sep 84	CATH (re-issue) London LON 54	38	7 wks
9 Feb 85	ALL I AM (IS LOVING YOU) London LON 58	58	3 wks
27 Mar 93 ★	YOUNG AT HEART (re-issue) London LONCD 338	1	12 wks

BLUENOTES - See Harold MELVIN and the BLUENOTES

BLUES BAND UK, male vocal/instrumental group   2 wks

| 12 Jul 80 | BLUES BAND EP Arista BOOT 2 | 68 | 2 wks |

Tracks on Blues Band EP: Maggie's Farm / Ain't it Tuff / Diddy Wah Diddy / Back Door Man.

BLUES BROTHERS US, male vocal duo   8 wks

| 7 Apr 90 | EVERYBODY NEEDS SOMEBODY TO LOVE East West A7591 | 12 | 8 wks |

For the first two weeks, the flip side of Everybody Needs Somebody To Love, Think by Aretha Franklin, was listed.

Colin BLUNSTONE UK, male vocalist   29 wks

12 Feb 72	SAY YOU DON'T MIND Epic EPC 7765	15	9 wks
11 Nov 72	I DON'T BELIEVE IN MIRACLES Epic EPC 8434	31	6 wks
17 Feb 73	HOW COULD WE DARE TO BE WRONG Epic EPC 1197	45	2 wks
14 Mar 81	WHAT BECOMES OF THE BROKEN HEARTED Stiff BROKEN 1 [1]	13	10 wks
29 May 82	TRACKS OF MY TEARS PRT 7P 236	60	2 wks

[1] Dave Stewart. Guest vocals: Colin Blunstone

See also Neil MacArthur.

BLUR UK, male vocal/instrumental group   50 wks

27 Oct 90	SHE'S SO HIGH Food FOOD 26	48	3 wks
27 Apr 91 ●	THERE'S NO OTHER WAY Food FOOD 29	8	8 wks
10 Aug 91	BANG Food FOOD 31	24	4 wks
11 Apr 92	POPSCENE Food FOOD 37	32	2 wks
1 May 93	FOR TOMORROW Food CDFOODS 40	28	4 wks
10 Jul 93	CHEMICAL WORLD Food CDFOODS 45	28	4 wks
16 Oct 93	SUNDAY SUNDAY Food CDFOOD 46	26	3 wks
19 Mar 94 ●	GIRLS AND BOYS Food CDFOODS 47	5	7 wks
11 Jun 94	TO THE END Food CDFOODS 50	16	5 wks
3 Sep 94 ●	PARKLIFE Food CDFOOD 53	10	7 wks
19 Nov 94	END OF A CENTURY Food CDFOOD 56	19	3 wks

B-MOVIE UK, male vocal/instrumental group   7 wks

| 18 Apr 81 | REMEMBRANCE DAY Deram DM 437 | 61 | 3 wks |
| 27 Mar 82 | NOWHERE GIRL Some Bizzare BZZ 8 | 67 | 4 wks |

BOB and EARL US, male vocal duo   13 wks

| 12 Mar 69 ● | HARLEM SHUFFLE Island WIP 6053 | 7 | 13 wks |

BOB and MARCIA Jamaica, male/female vocal duo   25 wks

| 14 Mar 70 ● | YOUNG GIFTED AND BLACK Harry J HJ 6605 | 5 | 12 wks |
| 5 Jun 71 | PIED PIPER Trojan TR 7818 | 11 | 13 wks |

BOBBYSOCKS Norway/Sweden, female vocal duo   4 wks

| 25 May 85 | LET IT SWING RCA PB 40127 | 44 | 4 wks |

Karen BODDINGTON and Mark WILLIAMS
Australia, female/male vocal duo   **1 wk**

| 2 Sep 89 | HOME AND AWAY First Night SCORE 19 | 73 | 1 wk |

BODY COUNT US, male vocal/instrumental group   4 wks

| 8 Oct 94 | BORN DEAD Rhyme Syndicate SYNDG 4 | 28 | 2 wks |
| 17 Dec 94 | NECESSARY EVIL Virgin VSCDX 1529 | 45 | 2 wks |

BODYSNATCHERS
UK, female vocal/instrumental group   **12 wks**

| 15 Mar 80 | LET'S DO ROCK STEADY 2 Tone CHS TT 9 | 22 | 9 wks |
| 19 Jul 80 | EASY LIFE 2 Tone CHS TT 12 | 50 | 3 wks |

Humphrey BOGART - See Dooley WILSON

Hamilton BOHANNON
US, male vocalist/instrumentalist - drums   **38 wks**

15 Feb 75	SOUTH AFRICAN MAN Brunswick BR 16	22	8 wks
24 May 75 ●	DISCO STOMP Brunswick BR 19	6	12 wks
5 Jul 75	FOOT STOMPIN' MUSIC Brunswick BR 21	23	6 wks
6 Sep 75	HAPPY FEELING Brunswick BR 24	49	3 wks
26 Aug 78	LET'S START THE DANCE Mercury 6167 700	56	4 wks
13 Feb 82	LET'S START TO DANCE AGAIN London HL 10582	49	5 wks

BOILING POINT US, male vocal/instrumental group   6 wks

| 27 May 78 | LET'S GET FUNKTIFIED Bang BANG 1312 | 41 | 6 wks |

Marc BOLAN - See T. REX

Michael BOLTON US, male vocalist   92 wks

17 Feb 90 ●	HOW AM I SUPPOSED TO LIVE WITHOUT YOU CBS 655397 7	3	10 wks
28 Apr 90 ●	HOW CAN WE BE LOVERS CBS 655918 7	10	10 wks
21 Jul 90	WHEN I'M BACK ON MY FEET AGAIN CBS 656077 7	44	5 wks
20 Apr 91	LOVE IS A WONDERFUL THING Columbia 6567717	23	8 wks
27 Jul 91	TIME LOVE AND TENDERNESS Columbia 6569897	28	7 wks
9 Nov 91 ●	WHEN A MAN LOVES A WOMAN Columbia 6574887	8	9 wks
8 Feb 92	STEEL BARS Columbia 6577257	17	6 wks
9 May 92	MISSING YOU NOW Columbia 6579917 [1]	28	4 wks
31 Oct 92	TO LOVE SOMEBODY Columbia 6584557	16	6 wks
26 Dec 92	DRIFT AWAY Columbia 6588657	18	5 wks
13 Mar 93	REACH OUT I'LL BE THERE Columbia 6588972	37	4 wks
13 Nov 93	SAID I LOVED YOU BUT I LIED Columbia 6598762	15	8 wks
26 Feb 94	SOUL OF MY SOUL Columbia 6601772	32	3 wks
14 May 94	LEAN ON ME Columbia 6604132	14	7 wks

[1] Michael Bolton featuring Kenny G

BOMB THE BASS UK, male producer - Tim Simenon   48 wks

20 Feb 88 ●	BEAT DIS Mister-ron DOOD 1	2	9 wks
27 Aug 88 ●	MEGABLAST / DON'T MAKE ME WAIT Mister-ron DOOD 2 [1]	6	9 wks
26 Nov 88 ●	SAY A LITTLE PRAYER Rhythm King DOOD 3 [2]	10	10 wks
27 Jul 91 ●	WINTER IN JULY Rhythm King 6572757	7	9 wks
9 Nov 91	THE AIR YOU BREATHE Rhythm King 6575387	52	3 wks
2 May 92	KEEP GIVING ME LOVE Rhythm King 6579887	62	2 wks
1 Oct 94	BUG POWDER DUST Stoned Heights BRCD 300 [3]	24	3 wks
17 Dec 94	DARKHEART Stoned Heights BRCD 305 [4]	35†	3 wks

[1] Bomb The Bass featuring Merlin and Antonia/Bomb The Bass featuring Lorraine [2] Bomb The Bass featuring Maureen [3] Bomb The Bass featuring Justin Warfield [4] Bomb The Bass featuring Spikey Tee

BOMBALURINA UK, male/female vocal group   20 wks

| 28 Jul 90 ★ | ITSY BITSY TEENY WEENY YELLOW POLKA DOT BIKINI Carpet CRPT 1 | 1 | 13 wks |

24 Nov 90 **SEVEN LITTLE GIRLS SITTING IN THE BACKSEAT**
Carpet CRPT 2 [1] ....**18** 7 wks

[1] Bombalurina featuring Timmy Mallett

BOMBERS
Canada, male / female vocal / instrumental group **10 wks**

5 May 79 **(EVERYBODY) GET DANCIN'** *Flamingo FM 1* ....**37** 7 wks
18 Aug 79 **LET'S DANCE** *Flamingo FM 4* ....**58** 3 wks

BON JOVI *US, male vocal / instrumental group* **125 wks**

31 Aug 85 **HARDEST PART IS THE NIGHT** *Vertigo VER 22* .....**68** 1 wk
9 Aug 86 **YOU GIVE LOVE A BAD NAME** *Vertigo VER 26* ......**14** 10 wks
25 Oct 86 ● **LIVIN' ON A PRAYER** *Vertigo VER 28* ....**4** 15 wks
11 Apr 87 **WANTED DEAD OR ALIVE** *Vertigo VER 1* ....**13** 6 wks
15 Aug 87 **NEVER SAY GOODBYE** *Vertigo JOV 2* ....**21** 5 wks
24 Sep 88 **BAD MEDICINE** *Vertigo JOV 3* ....**17** 7 wks
10 Dec 88 **BORN TO BE MY BABY** *Vertigo JOV 4* ....**22** 7 wks
29 Apr 89 **I'LL BE THERE FOR YOU** *Vertigo JOV 5* ....**18** 7 wks
26 Aug 89 **LAY YOUR HANDS ON ME** *Vertigo JOV 6* ....**18** 6 wks
9 Dec 89 **LIVING IN SIN** *Vertigo JOV 7* ....**35** 6 wks
24 Oct 92 ● **KEEP THE FAITH** *Jambco JOV 8* ....**5** 6 wks
23 Jan 93 **BED OF ROSES** *Jambco JOVCD 9* ....**13** 6 wks
15 May 93 ● **IN THESE ARMS** *Jambco JOVCD 10* ....**9** 7 wks
7 Aug 93 **I'LL SLEEP WHEN I'M DEAD** *Jambco JOVCD 11* ......**17** 5 wks
2 Oct 93 **I BELIEVE** *Jambco JOVCD 12* ....**11** 6 wks
26 Mar 94 ● **DRY COUNTY** *Jambco JOVCD 13* ....**9** 6 wks
24 Sep 94 ● **ALWAYS** *Jambco JOVCD 14* ....**2†** 15 wks
17 Dec 94 ● **PLEASE COME HOME FOR CHRISTMAS**
Jambco JOVCD 16 ....**7†** 3 wks

Jon BON JOVI *US, male vocalist* **13 wks**

4 Aug 90 **BLAZE OF GLORY** *Vertigo JBJ 1* ....**13** 8 wks
10 Nov 90 **MIRACLE** *Vertigo JBVJ 2* ....**29** 5 wks
See also Bon Jovi.

Ronnie BOND *UK, male vocalist* **5 wks**

31 May 80 **IT'S WRITTEN ON YOUR BODY** *Mercury MER 13* ....**52** 5 wks

Gary 'U.S.' BONDS *US, male vocalist* **39 wks**

19 Jan 61 **NEW ORLEANS** *Top Rank JAR 527* [1] ....**16** 11 wks
20 Jul 61 ● **QUARTER TO THREE** *Top Rank JAR 575* [1] ....**7** 13 wks
30 May 81 **THIS LITTLE GIRL** *EMI America EA 122* ....**43** 6 wks
22 Aug 81 **JOLE BLON** *EMI America EA 127* ....**51** 3 wks
31 Oct 81 **IT'S ONLY LOVE** *EMI America EA 128* ....**43** 3 wks
17 Jul 82 **SOUL DEEP** *EMI America EA 140* ....**59** 3 wks

[1] U.S. Bonds

BONE *UK, male vocal / instrumental duo* **1 wk**

2 Apr 94 **WINGS OF LOVE** *deConstruction 74321176282* ....**55** 1 wk

Elbow BONES and the RACKETEERS
US, male group leader and female backing group **9 wks**

14 Jan 84 **A NIGHT IN NEW YORK** *EMI America EA 165* ....**33** 9 wks

BONEY M
Jamaica / Antilles / Montserrat, male / female vocal group **167 wks**

18 Dec 76 ● **DADDY COOL** *Atlantic K 10827* ....**6** 13 wks
12 Mar 77 ● **SUNNY** *Atlantic K 10892* ....**3** 10 wks
25 Jun 77 ● **MA BAKER** *Atlantic K 10965* ....**2** 13 wks
29 Oct 77 ● **BELFAST** *Atlantic K 11020* ....**8** 13 wks
29 Apr 78 ★ **RIVERS OF BABYLON / BROWN GIRL IN THE RING**
Atlantic/Hansa K 11120 ....**1** 40 wks
7 Oct 78 ● **RASPUTIN** *Atlantic/Hansa K 11192* ....**2** 10 wks
2 Dec 78 ★ **MARY'S BOY CHILD - OH MY LORD**
Atlantic/Hansa K 11221 ....**1** 8 wks
3 Mar 79 ● **PAINTER MAN** *Atlantic/Hansa K 11255* ....**10** 6 wks
28 Apr 79 ● **HOORAY HOORAY IT'S A HOLI-HOLIDAY**
Atlantic/Hansa K 11279 ....**3** 9 wks
11 Aug 79 **GOTTA GO HOME / EL LUTE** *Atlantic/Hansa K 11351* **12** 11 wks
15 Dec 79 **I'M BORN AGAIN** *Atlantic/Hansa K 11410* ....**35** 7 wks
26 Apr 80 **MY FRIEND JACK** *Atlantic/Hansa K 11463* ....**57** 5 wks
14 Feb 81 **CHILDREN OF PARADISE** *Atlantic/Hansa K 11637* ....**66** 2 wks
21 Nov 81 **WE KILL THE WORLD (DON'T KILL THE WORLD)**
Atlantic/Hansa K 11689 ....**39** 5 wks
24 Dec 88 **MEGAMIX / MARY'S BOY CHILD (re-mix)**
Ariola 111947 ....**52** 3 wks
5 Dec 92 ● **BONEY M MEGAMIX** *Arista 74321125127* ....**7** 9 wks
17 Apr 93 **BROWN GIRL IN THE RING (re-mix)**
Arista 74321137052 ....**38** 3 wks

Brown Girl in The Ring *only listed with* Rivers of Babylon *from 5 Aug 78, peaking at position 10. El Lute only listed with Gotta Go Home from 29 Sep 79. The megamixes are different.*

Graham BONNET *UK, male vocalist* **15 wks**

21 Mar 81 ● **NIGHT GAMES** *Vertigo VER 1* ....**6** 11 wks
13 Jun 81 **LIAR** *Vertigo VER 2* ....**51** 4 wks

Graham BONNEY *UK, male vocalist* **8 wks**

24 Mar 66 **SUPERGIRL** *Columbia DB 7843* ....**19** 8 wks

BONO *Ireland, male vocalist* **23 wks**

25 Jan 86 **IN A LIFETIME** *RCA PB 40535* [1] ....**20** 5 wks
10 Jun 89 **IN A LIFETIME (re-issue)** *RCA PB 42873* [1] ....**17** 7 wks
4 Dec 93 ● **I'VE GOT YOU UNDER MY SKIN** *Island CID 578* [2] ....**4** 9 wks
9 Apr 94 **IN THE NAME OF THE FATHER** *Island CID 593* [3] ....**46** 2 wks

[1] Clannad featuring Bono [2] Frank Sinatra with Bono [3] Bono and Gavin Friday

I've Got You Under My Skin *is the listed B-side of* Stay (Faraway So Close) *by U2.*

See also U2.

BONZO DOG DOO-DAH BAND
UK, male vocal / instrumental group **14 wks**

6 Nov 68 ● **I'M THE URBAN SPACEMAN** *Liberty LBF 15144* ....**5** 14 wks

Betty BOO *UK, female rapper* **55 wks**

12 Aug 89 ● **HEY DJ I CAN'T DANCE TO THAT MUSIC
YOU'RE PLAYING** *Rhythm King LEFT 34* [1] ....**7** 11 wks
19 May 90 ● **DOIN' THE DO** *Rhythm King LEFT 39* ....**7** 12 wks
11 Aug 90 ● **WHERE ARE YOU BABY** *Rhythm King LEFT 43* ....**3** 10 wks
1 Dec 90 **24 HOURS** *Rhythm King LEFT 45* ....**25** 8 wks
8 Aug 92 **LET ME TAKE YOU THERE** *WEA YZ 677* ....**12** 8 wks
3 Oct 92 **I'M ON MY WAY** *WEA YZ 693* ....**44** 3 wks
10 Apr 93 **HANGOVER** *WEA YZ 719CD* ....**50** 3 wks

[1] Beatmasters featuring Betty Boo

BOO RADLEYS *UK, male vocal / instrumental group* **6 wks**

20 Jun 92 **DOES THIS HURT / BOO! FOREVER**
Creation CRE 128 ....**67** 1 wk
23 Oct 93 **WISH I WAS SKINNY** *Creation CRESCD 169* ....**75** 1 wk
12 Feb 94 **BARNEY (...& ME)** *Creation CRESCD 178* ....**48** 2 wks
11 Jun 94 **LAZARUS** *Creation CRESCD 187* ....**50** 2 wks

BOO-YAA T.R.I.B.E. *US, male rap group* **6 wks**

30 Jun 90 **PSYKO FUNK** *Fourth & Broadway BRW 179* ....**43** 3 wks
6 Nov 93 **ANOTHER BODY MURDERED** *Epic 6597942* [1] ....**26** 3 wks

[1] Faith No More & Boo-Yaa T.R.I.B.E.

BOOGIE BOX HIGH UK, male vocal / instrumental duo **11 wks**

| 4 Jul 87 | ● JIVE TALKIN' Hardback 7BOSS 4 | **7** | 11 wks |

BOOGIE DOWN PRODUCTIONS
US, male rap / scratch duo   **2 wks**

| 4 Jun 88 | MY PHILOSOPHY / STOP THE VIOLENCE Jive JIVEX 170 | **69** | 2 wks |

BOOKER T. and the M.G.'s
US, male instrumental group   **43 wks**

11 Dec 68	SOUL LIMBO Stax 102	**30**	9 wks
7 May 69	● TIME IS TIGHT Stax 119	**4**	18 wks
30 Aug 69	SOUL CLAP '69 Stax 127	**35**	4 wks
15 Dec 79	● GREEN ONIONS Atlantic K 10109	**7**	12 wks

BOOM BOOM ROOM
UK, male vocal / instrumental group   **1 wk**

| 8 Mar 86 | HERE COMES THE MAN Fun After All FUN 101 | **74** | 1 wk |

BOOMTOWN RATS
Ireland, male vocal / instrumental group   **123 wks**

27 Aug 77	LOOKING AFTER NO. 1 Ensign ENY 4	**11**	9 wks
19 Nov 77	MARY OF THE FOURTH FORM Ensign ENY 9	**15**	9 wks
15 Apr 78	SHE'S SO MODERN Ensign ENY 13	**12**	11 wks
17 Jun 78	● LIKE CLOCKWORK Ensign ENY 14	**6**	13 wks
14 Oct 78	★ RAT TRAP Ensign ENY 16	**1**	15 wks
21 Jul 79	★ I DON'T LIKE MONDAYS Ensign ENY 30	**1**	12 wks
17 Nov 79	DIAMOND SMILES Ensign ENY 33	**13**	10 wks
26 Jan 80	● SOMEONE'S LOOKING AT YOU Ensign ENY 34	**4**	9 wks
22 Nov 80	● BANANA REPUBLIC Ensign BONGO 1	**3**	11 wks
31 Jan 81	THE ELEPHANT'S GRAVEYARD (GUILTY) Ensign BONGO 2	**26**	6 wks
12 Dec 81	NEVER IN A MILLION YEARS Mercury MER 87	**62**	4 wks
20 Mar 82	HOUSE ON FIRE Mercury MER 91	**24**	8 wks
18 Feb 84	TONIGHT Mercury MER 154	**73**	1 wk
19 May 84	DRAG ME DOWN Mercury MER 163	**50**	3 wks
2 Jul 94	I DON'T LIKE MONDAYS (re-issue) Vertigo VERCD 87	**38**	2 wks

Daniel BOONE UK, male vocalist   **25 wks**

14 Aug 71	DADDY DON'T YOU WALK SO FAST Penny Farthing PEN 764	**17**	15 wks
1 Apr 72	BEAUTIFUL SUNDAY Penny Farthing PEN 781	**48**	1 wk
15 Apr 72	BEAUTIFUL SUNDAY (re-entry) Penny Farthing PEN 781	**21**	9 wks

Debby BOONE US, female vocalist   **2 wks**

| 24 Dec 77 | YOU LIGHT UP MY LIFE Warner Bros. K 17043 | **48** | 2 wks |

Pat BOONE US, male vocalist   **296 wks**

18 Nov 55	● AIN'T THAT A SHAME London HLD 8173	**7**	9 wks
27 Apr 56	★ I'LL BE HOME London HLD 8253	**1**	22 wks
27 Jul 56	LONG TALL SALLY London HLD 8291	**27**	3 wks
17 Aug 56	I ALMOST LOST MY MIND London HLD 8303	**14**	7 wks
24 Aug 56	LONG TALL SALLY (re-entry) London HLD 8291	**18**	4 wks
7 Dec 56	● FRIENDLY PERSUASION London HLD 8346	**3**	21 wks
11 Jan 57	AIN'T THAT A SHAME (re-entry) London HLD 8173	**22**	2 wks
11 Jan 57	I'LL BE HOME (re-entry) London HLD 8253	**19**	2 wks
1 Feb 57	● DON'T FORBID ME London HLD 8370	**2**	16 wks
26 Apr 57	WHY BABY WHY London HLD 8404	**17**	7 wks
5 Jul 57	● LOVE LETTERS IN THE SAND London HLD 8445	**2**	21 wks
27 Sep 57	● REMEMBER YOU'RE MINE / THERE'S A GOLDMINE IN THE SKY London HLD 8479	**5**	18 wks
6 Dec 57	● APRIL LOVE London HLD 8512	**7**	23 wks
13 Dec 57	WHITE CHRISTMAS London HLD 8520	**29**	1 wk
4 Apr 58	● A WONDERFUL TIME UP THERE London HLD 8574	**2**	17 wks
11 Apr 58	● IT'S TOO SOON TO KNOW London HLD 8574	**7**	12 wks
27 Jun 58	● SUGAR MOON London HLD 8640	**6**	12 wks
29 Aug 58	IF DREAMS CAME TRUE London HLD 8675	**16**	11 wks
5 Dec 58	GEE BUT IT'S LONELY London HLD 8739	**30**	1 wk
16 Jan 59	I'LL REMEMBER TONIGHT London HLD 8775	**28**	1 wk
6 Feb 59	I'LL REMEMBER TONIGHT (re-entry) London HLD 8775	**21**	1 wk
20 Feb 59	I'LL REMEMBER TONIGHT (2nd re-entry) London HLD 8775	**18**	7 wks
10 Apr 59	WITH THE WIND AND THE RAIN IN YOUR HAIR London HLD 8824	**21**	3 wks
22 May 59	FOR A PENNY London HLD 8855	**28**	3 wks
26 Jun 59	FOR A PENNY (re-entry) London HLD 8855	**19**	6 wks
31 Jul 59	'TWIXT TWELVE AND TWENTY London HLD 8910	**18**	6 wks
18 Sep 59	'TWIXT TWELVE AND TWENTY (re-entry) London HLD 8910	**26**	1 wk
23 Jun 60	WALKING THE FLOOR OVER YOU London HLD 9138	**40**	2 wks
14 Jul 60	WALKING THE FLOOR OVER YOU (re-entry) London HLD 9138	**46**	1 wk
4 Aug 60	WALKING THE FLOOR OVER YOU (2nd re-entry) London HLD 9138	**39**	2 wks
6 Jul 61	MOODY RIVER London HLD 9350	**18**	10 wks
7 Dec 61	● JOHNNY WILL London HLD 9461	**4**	13 wks
15 Feb 62	I'LL SEE YOU IN MY DREAMS London HLD 9504	**27**	9 wks
24 May 62	QUANDO QUANDO QUANDO London HLD 9543	**41**	4 wks
12 Jul 62	● SPEEDY GONZALES London HLD 9573	**2**	19 wks
15 Nov 62	THE MAIN ATTRACTION London HLD 9620	**12**	11 wks

There's A Goldmine In The Sky was only listed for the week of 27 Sep 57, at position 23.

Duke BOOTEE - See GRANDMASTER FLASH, Melle MEL and the FURIOUS FIVE

Ken BOOTHE Jamaica, male vocalist   **22 wks**

| 21 Sep 74 | ★ EVERYTHING I OWN Trojan TR 7920 | **1** | 12 wks |
| 14 Dec 74 | CRYING OVER YOU Trojan TR 7944 | **11** | 10 wks |

BOOTHILL FOOTAPPERS
UK, male / female vocal / instrumental group   **3 wks**

| 14 Jul 84 | GET YOUR FEET OUT OF MY SHOES Go! Discs TAP 1 | **64** | 3 wks |

BOOTSY'S RUBBER BAND
US, male vocal / instrumental group   **3 wks**

| 8 Jul 78 | BOOTZILLA Warner Bros. K 17196 | **43** | 3 wks |

BOOTZILLA ORCHESTRA - See Malcolm McLAREN

BOSS US, male producer - David Morales   **1 wk**

| 27 Aug 94 | CONGO Cooltempo CDCOOL 296 | **54** | 1 wk |

See also David Morales and the Bad Yard Club.

BOSTON US, male vocal / instrumental group   **13 wks**

| 29 Jan 77 | MORE THAN A FEELING Epic EPC 4658 | **22** | 8 wks |
| 7 Oct 78 | DON'T LOOK BACK Epic EPC 6653 | **43** | 5 wks |

Eve BOSWELL Hungary, female vocalist   **13 wks**

30 Dec 55	● PICKIN' A CHICKEN Parlophone R 4082	**9**	7 wks
2 Mar 56	PICKIN' A CHICKEN (re-entry) Parlophone R 4082	**16**	3 wks
6 Apr 56	PICKIN' A CHICKEN (2nd re-entry) Parlophone R 4082	**20**	3 wks

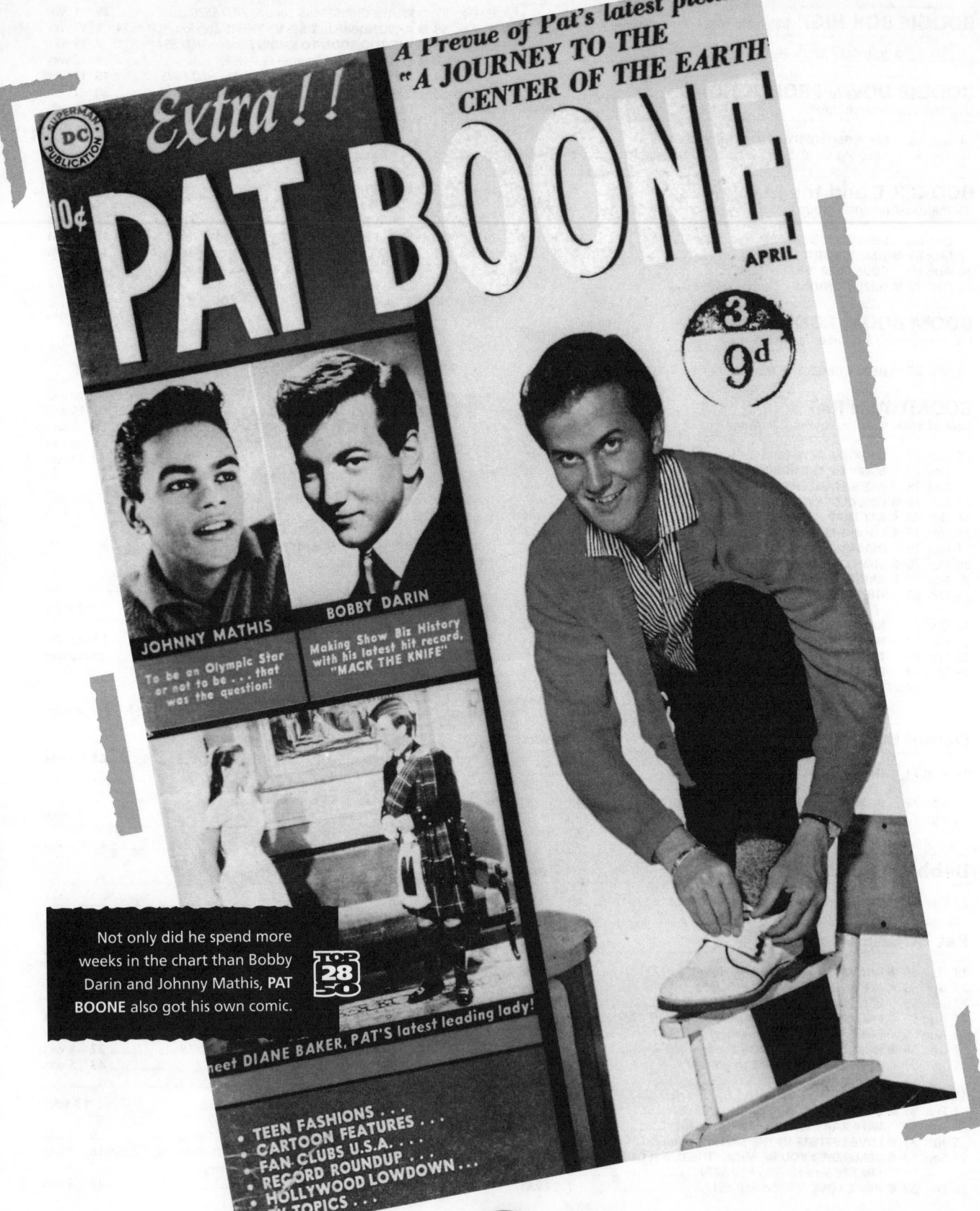

Not only did he spend more weeks in the chart than Bobby Darin and Johnny Mathis, **PAT BOONE** also got his own comic.

La BOUCHE *US, male/female rap/vocal duo*   **1 wk**

24 Sep 94	**SWEET DREAMS** Bell 74321223912 ......**63**	1 wk

Judy BOUCHER *UK, female vocalist*   **23 wks**

4 Apr 87 ●	**CAN'T BE WITH YOU TONIGHT** Orbitone OR 721 ......**2**	14 wks
4 Jul 87	**YOU CAUGHT MY EYE** Orbitone OR 722 ....**18**	9 wks

Peter BOUNCER - *See SHUT UP AND DANCE*

BOUNCING CZECKS
UK, male vocal/instrumental group   **1 wk**

29 Dec 84	**I'M A LITTLE CHRISTMAS CRACKER** RCA 463 ....**72**	1 wk

BOURGEOIS TAGG *US, male vocal/instrumental duo*   **6 wks**

6 Feb 88	**I DON'T MIND AT ALL** Island IS 353 ....**35**	6 wks

BOURGIE BOURGIE
UK, male vocal/instrumental group   **4 wks**

3 Mar 84	**BREAKING POINT** MCA BOU 1 ....**48**	4 wks

BOW WOW WOW
UK, female/male vocal/instrumental group   **54 wks**

26 Jul 80	**C30, C60, C90, GO** EMI 5088 ....**34**	7 wks
6 Dec 80	**YOUR CASSETTE PET** EMI WOW 1 ....**58**	6 wks
28 Mar 81	**W.O.R.K. (N.O. NAH NO NO MY DADDY DON'T)** EMI 5153 ....**62**	3 wks
15 Aug 81	**PRINCE OF DARKNESS** RCA 100 ....**58**	4 wks
7 Nov 81	**CHIHUAHUA** RCA 144 ....**51**	4 wks
30 Jan 82 ●	**GO WILD IN THE COUNTRY** RCA 175 ....**7**	13 wks
1 May 82	**SEE JUNGLE (JUNGLE BOY)/TV SAVAGE** RCA 220 ....**45**	3 wks
5 Jun 82 ●	**I WANT CANDY** RCA 238 ....**9**	8 wks
31 Jul 82	**LOUIS QUATORZE** RCA 263 ....**66**	2 wks
12 Mar 83	**DO YOU WANNA HOLD ME** RCA 314 ....**47**	4 wks

Your Cassette Pet listed as Louis Quatorze on 6 Dec 80 only. Tracks on Your Cassette Pet (available only as a cassette) are: Louis Quatorze/Gold He Said/Umo-Sex-Al Apache/I Want My Baby On Mars/Sexy Eiffel Towers/Giant Sized Baby Thing/Fools Rush In/Radio G.String. RCA 263 is disc version of track on EMI WOW 1 Cassette.

BOWA featuring MALA
US, male/female vocal/instrumental duo   **1 wk**

7 Dec 91	**DIFFERENT STORY** Dead Dead Good GOOD 8 ....**64**	1 wk

David BOWIE *UK, male vocalist*   **418 wks**

6 Sep 69	**SPACE ODDITY** Philips BF 1801 ....**48**	1 wk
20 Sep 69 ●	**SPACE ODDITY (re-entry)** Philips BF 1801 ....**5**	13 wks
24 Jun 72	**STARMAN** RCA 2199 ....**10**	11 wks
16 Sep 72	**JOHN I'M ONLY DANCING** RCA 2263 ....**12**	10 wks
9 Dec 72 ●	**THE JEAN GENIE** RCA 2302 ....**2**	13 wks
14 Apr 73 ●	**DRIVE-IN SATURDAY** RCA 2352 ....**3**	10 wks
30 Jun 73 ●	**LIFE ON MARS** RCA 2316 ....**3**	13 wks
15 Sep 73 ●	**THE LAUGHING GNOME** Deram DM 123 ....**6**	12 wks
20 Oct 73 ●	**SORROW** RCA 2424 ....**3**	15 wks
23 Feb 74 ●	**REBEL REBEL** RCA LPBO 5009 ....**5**	7 wks
20 Apr 74	**ROCK AND ROLL SUICIDE** RCA LPBO 5021 ....**22**	7 wks
22 Jun 74	**DIAMOND DOGS** RCA APBO 0293 ....**21**	6 wks
28 Sep 74	**KNOCK ON WOOD** RCA 2466 ....**10**	6 wks
1 Mar 75	**YOUNG AMERICANS** RCA 2523 ....**18**	7 wks
2 Aug 75	**FAME** RCA 2579 ....**17**	8 wks
11 Oct 75 ★	**SPACE ODDITY (re-issue)** RCA 2593 ....**1**	10 wks
29 Nov 75 ●	**GOLDEN YEARS** RCA 2640 ....**8**	10 wks
22 May 76	**TVC 15** RCA 2682 ....**33**	4 wks
19 Feb 77 ●	**SOUND AND VISION** RCA PB 0905 ....**3**	11 wks

15 Oct 77	**HEROES** RCA PB 1121 ....**24**	8 wks
21 Jan 78	**BEAUTY AND THE BEAST** RCA PB 1190 ....**39**	3 wks
2 Dec 78	**BREAKING GLASS (EP)** RCA BOW 1 ....**54**	7 wks
5 May 79 ●	**BOYS KEEP SWINGING** RCA BOW 2 ....**7**	10 wks
21 Jul 79	**D.J.** RCA BOW 3 ....**29**	5 wks
15 Dec 79	**JOHN I'M ONLY DANCING (AGAIN) (1975)/ JOHN I'M ONLY DANCING (1972)** RCA BOW 4......**12**	8 wks
1 Mar 80	**ALABAMA SONG** RCA BOW 5 ....**23**	5 wks
16 Aug 80 ★	**ASHES TO ASHES** RCA BOW 6 ....**1**	10 wks
1 Nov 80 ●	**FASHION** RCA BOW 7 ....**5**	12 wks
10 Jan 81	**SCARY MONSTERS (AND SUPER CREEPS)** RCA BOW 8 ....**20**	6 wks
28 Mar 81	**UP THE HILL BACKWARDS** RCA BOW 9 ....**32**	6 wks
14 Nov 81 ★	**UNDER PRESSURE** EMI 5250 [1] **1**	11 wks
28 Nov 81	**WILD IS THE WIND** RCA BOW 10 ....**24**	10 wks
6 Mar 82	**BAAL'S HYMN (EP)** RCA BOW 11 ....**29**	5 wks
10 Apr 82	**CAT PEOPLE (PUTTING OUT FIRE)** MCA 770 ....**26**	6 wks
27 Nov 82 ●	**PEACE ON EARTH - LITTLE DRUMMER BOY** RCA BOW 12 [2] **3**	8 wks
26 Mar 83 ★	**LET'S DANCE** EMI America EA 152 ....**1**	14 wks
11 Jun 83 ●	**CHINA GIRL** EMI America EA 157 ....**2**	8 wks
24 Sep 83 ●	**MODERN LOVE** EMI America EA 158 ....**2**	8 wks
5 Nov 83	**WHITE LIGHT, WHITE HEAT** RCA 372 ....**46**	3 wks
22 Sep 84 ●	**BLUE JEAN** EMI America EA 181 ....**6**	8 wks
8 Dec 84	**TONIGHT** EMI America EA 187 ....**53**	4 wks
9 Feb 85	**THIS IS NOT AMERICA** EMI America EA 190 [3] **14**	7 wks
8 Jun 85	**LOVING THE ALIEN** EMI America EA 195 ....**19**	6 wks
27 Jul 85	**LOVING THE ALIEN (re-entry)** EMI America EA 195 **67**	1 wk
7 Sep 85 ★	**DANCING IN THE STREET** EMI America EA 204 [4] **1**	12 wks
15 Mar 86 ●	**ABSOLUTE BEGINNERS** Virgin VS 838 ....**2**	9 wks
21 Jun 86	**UNDERGROUND** EMI America EA 216 ....**21**	6 wks
8 Nov 86	**WHEN THE WIND BLOWS** Virgin VS 906 ....**44**	4 wks
4 Apr 87	**DAY-IN DAY-OUT** EMI America EA 230 ....**17**	6 wks
27 Jun 87	**TIME WILL CRAWL** EMI America EA 237 ....**33**	4 wks
29 Aug 87	**NEVER LET ME DOWN** EMI America EA 239 ....**34**	6 wks
7 Apr 90	**FAME (re-mix)** EMI-USA FAME 90 ....**28**	4 wks
22 Aug 92	**REAL COOL WORLD** Warner Bros. W 0127........................**53**	1 wk
27 Mar 93 ●	**JUMP THEY SAY** Arista 74321139422 ....**9**	6 wks
12 Jun 93	**BLACK TIE WHITE NOISE** Arista 74321148682 [5] **36**	2 wks
23 Oct 93	**MIRACLE GOODNIGHT** Arista 74321162262 ....**40**	2 wks
4 Dec 93	**BUDDHA OF SUBURBIA** Arista 74321177052 ....**35**	3 wks

[1] Queen and David Bowie [2] David Bowie and Bing Crosby [3] David Bowie and the Pat Metheny Group [4] David Bowie and Mick Jagger [5] David Bowie featuring Al B. Sure!

Tracks on Breaking Glass (EP): Breaking Glass/Art Decade/Ziggy Stardust. All three versions of John I'm Only Dancing are different. Tracks on Baal's Hymn (EP): Baal's Hymn/The Drowned Girl/ Remembering Marie/The Dirty Song/Ballad of theAdventurers.

BOX TOPS *US, male vocal/instrumental group*   **33 wks**

13 Sep 67 ●	**THE LETTER** Stateside SS 2044 ....**5**	12 wks
20 Mar 68	**CRY LIKE A BABY** Bell 1001........................**15**	12 wks
23 Aug 69	**SOUL DEEP** Bell 1068........................**22**	9 wks

BOY GEORGE *UK, male vocalist*   **41 wks**

7 Mar 87 ★	**EVERYTHING I OWN** Virgin BOY 100 ....**1**	9 wks
6 Jun 87	**KEEP ME IN MIND** Virgin BOY 101 ....**29**	4 wks
18 Jul 87	**SOLD** Virgin BOY 102 ....**24**	5 wks
21 Nov 87	**TO BE REBORN** Virgin BOY 103 ....**13**	7 wks
5 Mar 88	**LIVE MY LIFE** Virgin BOY 105 ....**62**	2 wks
18 Jun 88	**NO CLAUSE 28** Virgin BOY 106 ....**57**	3 wks
8 Oct 88	**DON'T CRY** Virgin BOY 107 ....**60**	2 wks
4 Mar 89	**DON'T TAKE MY MIND ON A TRIP** Virgin BOY 108 ....**68**	2 wks
19 Sep 92	**THE CRYING GAME** Spaghetti CIAO 6 ....**22**	4 wks
12 Jun 93	**MORE THAN LIKELY** Gee Street GESCD 49 [1] **40**	3 wks

[1] PM Dawn featuring Boy George

BOY MEETS GIRL *US, male/female vocal duo*   **13 wks**

3 Dec 88 ●	**WAITING FOR A STAR TO FALL** RCA PB 49519 ....**9**	13 wks

Jimmy BOYD US, male vocalist　　　22 wks

8 May 53	● TELL ME A STORY *Philips PB 126* [1]	5	15 wks
11 Sep 53	TELL ME A STORY (re-entry) *Philips PB 126* [1]	12	1 wk
27 Nov 53	● I SAW MOMMY KISSING SANTA CLAUS		
	Columbia DB 3365	3	6 wks

[1] Frankie Laine and Jimmy Boyd

Jacqueline BOYER France, female vocalist　　　2 wks

| 28 Apr 60 | TOM PILLIBI *Columbia DB 4452* | 33 | 2 wks |

BOYS US, male vocal group　　　5 wks

| 12 Nov 88 | DIAL MY HEART *Motown ZB 42245* | 61 | 2 wks |
| 29 Sep 90 | CRAZY *Motown ZB 44037* | 57 | 3 wks |

BOYS NEXT DOOR - See June HUTTON and Axel STORDAHL with the
BOYS NEXT DOOR

BOYSTOWN GANG US, male/female vocal group　　　20 wks

22 Aug 81	AIN'T NO MOUNTAIN HIGH ENOUGH -		
	REMEMBER ME (MEDLEY) *WEA DICK 1*	46	6 wks
31 Jul 82	● CAN'T TAKE MY EYES OFF YOU *ERC 101*	4	11 wks
9 Oct 82	SIGNED SEALED DELIVERED (I'M YOURS)		
	ERC 102	50	3 wks

BOYZ - See HEAVY D. and the BOYZ

BOYZ II MEN US, male vocal group　　　48 wks

5 Sep 92	★ END OF THE ROAD *Motown TMG 1411*	1	21 wks
19 Dec 92	MOTOWNPHILLY *Motown TMG 1402*	23	6 wks
27 Feb 93	IN THE STILL OF THE NITE (I'LL REMEMBER)		
	Motown TMGCD 1415	27	4 wks
3 Sep 94	● I'LL MAKE LOVE TO YOU *Motown TMGCD 1431*	5	12 wks
26 Nov 94	ON BENDED KNEE *Motown TMGCD 1433*	20	3 wks
24 Dec 94	I'LL MAKE LOVE TO YOU (re-entry)		
	Motown TMGCD 1433	68†	2 wks

BOYZONE Ireland, male vocal group　　　4 wks

| 10 Dec 94 | ● LOVE ME FOR A REASON *Polydor 8512802* | 3† | 4 wks |

BRAD US, male vocal/instrumental group　　　1 wk

| 26 Jun 93 | 20TH CENTURY *Epic 6592482* | 64 | 1 wk |

Scott BRADLEY UK, male vocalist　　　1 wk

| 15 Oct 94 | ZOOM *Hidden Agenda HIDDCD 1* | 61 | 1 wk |

Billy BRAGG UK, male vocalist　　　49 wks

16 Mar 85	BETWEEN THE WARS (EP) *Go! Discs AGOEP 1*	15	6 wks
28 Dec 85	DAYS LIKE THESE *Go! Discs GOD 8*	43	5 wks
28 Jun 86	LEVI STUBBS TEARS *Go! Discs GOD 12*	29	6 wks
15 Nov 86	GREETINGS TO THE NEW BRUNETTE		
	Go! Discs GOD 15	58	2 wks
14 May 88	★ SHE'S LEAVING HOME *Childline CHILD 1* [1]	1	11 wks
10 Sep 88	WAITING FOR THE GREAT LEAP FORWARDS		
	Go! Discs GOD 23	52	3 wks
8 Jul 89	WON'T TALK ABOUT IT *Go Beat GOD 33* [2]	29	6 wks
6 Jul 91	SEXUALITY *Go! Discs GOD 56*	27	5 wks
7 Sep 91	YOU WOKE UP MY NEIGHBOURHOOD		
	Go! Discs GOD 60	54	2 wks

| 29 Feb 92 | ACCIDENT WAITING TO HAPPEN (EP) | | |
| | *Go! Discs GOD 67* | 33 | 3 wks |

[1] Billy Bragg with Cara Tivey [2] Norman Cook featuring Billy Bragg

Tracks on Between The Wars (EP): *Between The Wars / Which Side Are
You On / World Turned Upside Down / It Says Here. Tracks on* Accident
Waiting To Happen (EP): *Accident Waiting To Happen / Revolution / Sulk /
The Warmest Room.* She's Leaving Home *was listed with the flip side*
With A Little Help From My Friends *by Wet Wet Wet.* Won't Talk About
It *was listed with the flip side* Blame It On The Bassline *by Norman Cook
featuring MC Wildski.*

Wilfrid BRAMBELL and Harry H. CORBETT
UK, male vocal duo　　　12 wks

| 28 Nov 63 | AT THE PALACE (PARTS 1 & 2) *Pye 7N 15588* | 25 | 12 wks |

Bekka BRAMLETT - See Joe COCKER

BRAND NEW HEAVIES
UK/US, male/female vocal/instrumental group　　　40 wks

5 Oct 91	NEVER STOP *ffrr F 165*	43	3 wks
15 Feb 92	DREAM COME TRUE *ffrr F 180*	24	4 wks
18 Apr 92	ULTIMATE TRUNK FUNK EP *ffrr F 185*	19	6 wks
1 Aug 92	DON'T LET IT GO TO YOUR HEAD *ffrr BNH 1*	24	4 wks
19 Dec 92	STAY THIS WAY *ffrr BNH 2*	40	5 wks
26 Mar 94	DREAM ON DREAMER *ffrr BNHCD 3*	15	4 wks
11 Jun 94	BACK TO LOVE *ffrr BNHCD 4*	23	4 wks
13 Aug 94	MIDNIGHT AT THE OASIS *ffrr BNCDP 5*	13	6 wks
5 Nov 94	SPEND SOME TIME *ffrr BNHCD 6*	26	4 wks

*All the above hits are credited 'featuring N'Dea Davenport' on either the
sleeve or the label. Tracks on* Ultimate Trunk Funk EP: *Never Stop / Stay
This Way / Mr Tanaka / Never Stop (re-mix). BNH 2 is a re-mixed version of
the track on the* Ultimate Trunk Funk EP.

Johnny BRANDON UK, male vocalist　　　12 wks

11 Mar 55	● TOMORROW *Polygon P 1131* [1]	8	6 wks
29 Apr 55	TOMORROW (re-entry) *Polygon P 1131* [1]	16	2 wks
1 Jul 55	DON'T WORRY *Polygon P 1163*	18	4 wks

[1] Johnny Brandon and the Phantoms

BRANDY US, female vocalist　　　3 wks

| 10 Dec 94 | I WANNA BE DOWN *Atlantic A7217CD* | 44 | 3 wks |

Laura BRANIGAN US, female vocalist　　　33 wks

18 Dec 82	● GLORIA *Atlantic K 11759*	6	13 wks
7 Jul 84	● SELF CONTROL *Atlantic A 9676*	5	17 wks
6 Oct 84	THE LUCKY ONE *Atlantic A 9636*	56	3 wks

BRASS CONSTRUCTION
US, male vocal/instrumental group　　　35 wks

3 Apr 76	MOVIN' *United Artists UP 36090*	23	6 wks
5 Feb 77	HA CHA CHA (FUNKTION) *United Artists UP 36205*	37	5 wks
26 Jan 80	MUSIC MAKES YOU FEEL LIKE DANCING		
	United Artists UP 615	39	6 wks
28 May 83	WALKIN' THE LINE *Capitol CL 292*	47	3 wks
16 Jul 83	WE CAN WORK IT OUT *Capitol CL 299*	70	2 wks
7 Jul 84	PARTYLINE *Capitol CL 335*	56	4 wks
27 Oct 84	INTERNATIONAL *Capitol CL 341*	70	2 wks
9 Nov 85	GIVE AND TAKE *Capitol CL 377*	62	3 wks
28 May 88	MOVIN' 1988 (re-mix) *Syncopate SY 11*	24	4 wks

British Hit Singles Part One: Alphabetically by Artist
Date of chart entry/Title & catalogue no./Peak position reached/Weeks on chart
★ Number One ● Top Ten † still on chart at 31 Dec 1994
□ = credited to act billed in footnote

BRAT *UK, male vocalist - Roger Kitter*   **8 wks**

| 10 Jul 82 | **CHALK DUST - THE UMPIRE STRIKES BACK** | | |
| | *Hansa SMASH 1* ....**19** | 8 wks |

BRAVADO *UK, male/female vocal/instrumental group*   **3 wks**

| 18 Jun 94 | **HARMONICA MAN** *Peach PEACHCD 5* ....**37** | 3 wks |

Los BRAVOS
Spain/Germany, male vocal/instrumental group   **24 wks**

| 30 Jun 66 | ● **BLACK IS BLACK** *Decca F 22419* ....**2** | 13 wks |
| 8 Sep 66 | **I DON'T CARE** *Decca F 22484* ....**16** | 11 wks |

Dhar BRAXTON *US, female vocalist*   **8 wks**

| 31 May 86 | **JUMP BACK (SET ME FREE)** | |
| | *Fourth & Broadway BRW 47* ....**32** | 8 wks |

Toni BRAXTON *US, female vocalist*   **30 wks**

18 Sep 93	**ANOTHER SAD LOVE SONG** *LaFace 74321163502* ..**51**	2 wks
15 Jan 94	● **BREATHE AGAIN** *LaFace 74321185442* **2**	12 wks
2 Apr 94	**ANOTHER SAD LOVE SONG (re-issue)**	
	LaFace 74321196682 ....**15**	8 wks
9 Jul 94	**YOU MEAN THE WORLD TO ME**	
	LaFace 74321214702 ....**30**	5 wks
3 Dec 94	**LOVE SHOULDA BROUGHT YOU HOME**	
	LaFace 74321249412 ....**33**	3 wks

BREAD *US, male vocal/instrumental group*   **46 wks**

1 Aug 70	● **MAKE IT WITH YOU** *Elektra 2101 010* **5**	14 wks
15 Jan 72	**BABY I'M A WANT YOU** *Elektra K 12033* **14**	10 wks
29 Apr 72	**EVERYTHING I OWN** *Elektra K 12041* **32**	6 wks
30 Sep 72	**GUITAR MAN** *Elektra K 12066* **16**	4 wks
25 Dec 76	**LOST WITHOUT YOUR LOVE** *Elektra K 12241* **27**	7 wks

BREAK MACHINE *US, male vocal/dance group*   **32 wks**

4 Feb 84	● **STREET DANCE** *Record Shack SOHO 13* **3**	14 wks
12 May 84	● **BREAKDANCE PARTY** *Record Shack SOHO 20* **9**	8 wks
14 Jul 84	**BREAKDANCE PARTY (re-entry)**	
	Record Shack SOHO 20 ....**65**	2 wks
11 Aug 84	**ARE YOU READY?** *Record Shack SOHO 24* **27**	8 wks

BREAKFAST CLUB *US, male vocal/instrumental group*   **3 wks**

| 27 Jun 87 | **RIGHT ON TRACK** *MCA MCA 1146* ....**54** | 3 wks |

BREATHE *UK, male vocal/instrumental group*   **27 wks**

30 Jul 88	● **HANDS TO HEAVEN** *Siren SRN 68* **4**	12 wks
22 Oct 88	**JONAH** *Siren SRN 95* **60**	3 wks
3 Dec 88	**HOW CAN I FALL** *Siren SRN 102* **48**	7 wks
11 Mar 89	**DON'T TELL ME LIES** *Siren SRN 109* **45**	5 wks

Freddy BRECK *Germany, male vocalist*   **4 wks**

| 13 Apr 74 | **SO IN LOVE WITH YOU** *Decca F 13481* ....**44** | 4 wks |

BRECKER BROTHERS
US, male vocal/instrumental group   **5 wks**

| 4 Nov 78 | **EAST RIVER** *Arista ARIST 211* ....**34** | 5 wks |

BREEDERS
US/UK, female/male vocal/instrumental group   **6 wks**

18 Apr 92	**SAFARI (EP)** *4AD BAD 2003* **69**	1 wk
21 Aug 93	**CANNONBALL (EP)** *4AD BAD 3011CD* **40**	3 wks
6 Nov 93	**DIVINE HAMMER** *4AD BAD 3017CD* **59**	1 wk
23 Jul 94	**HEAD TO TOE (EP)** *4AD BADD 4012* **68**	1 wk

Tracks on Safari (EP): Do You Love Me Now/Don't Call Home/Safari/So Sad About Us. Tracks on Cannonball (EP): Cannonball/Cro-Aloha/Lord Of The Thighs/900. Tracks on Head To Toe (EP): Head To Toe/Shocker In Gloom Town/Freed Pig/Saints.

BREEKOUT KREW *US, male vocal duo*   **3 wks**

| 24 Nov 84 | **MATT'S MOOD** *London LON 59* ....**51** | 3 wks |

Ann BREEN *Ireland, female vocalist*   **2 wks**

19 Mar 83	**PAL OF MY CRADLE DAYS** *Homespun HS 052* **69**	1 wk
7 Jan 84	**PAL OF MY CRADLE DAYS (re-entry)**	
	Homespun HS 052 ....**74**	1 wk

BRENDON *UK, male vocalist*   **9 wks**

| 19 Mar 77 | **GIMME SOME** *Magnet MAG 80* ....**14** | 9 wks |

Maire BRENNAN *Ireland, female vocalist*   **2 wks**

| 16 May 92 | **AGAINST THE WIND** *RCA PB 45399* ....**64** | 2 wks |

Rose BRENNAN *Ireland, female vocalist*   **9 wks**

| 7 Dec 61 | **TALL DARK STRANGER** *Philips PB 1193* ....**31** | 9 wks |

Walter BRENNAN *US, male vocalist*   **3 wks**

| 28 Jun 62 | **OLD RIVERS** *Liberty LIB 55436* ....**38** | 3 wks |

Tony BRENT *UK, male vocalist*   **52 wks**

19 Dec 52	● **WALKIN' TO MISSOURI** *Columbia DB 3147* **9**	2 wks
2 Jan 53	● **MAKE IT SOON** *Columbia DB 3187* **9**	4 wks
9 Jan 53	● **WALKIN' TO MISSOURI (re-entry)**	
	Columbia DB 3147 ....**7**	5 wks
23 Jan 53	**GOT YOU ON MY MIND** *Columbia DB 3226*............**12**	1 wk
13 Mar 53	● **MAKE IT SOON (re-entry)** *Columbia DB 3187*..........**9**	3 wks
30 Nov 56	**CINDY OH CINDY** *Columbia DB 3844* **16**	6 wks
8 Feb 57	**CINDY OH CINDY (re-entry)** *Columbia DB 3844*......**30**	1 wk
28 Jun 57	**DARK MOON** *Columbia DB 3950* **17**	14 wks
28 Feb 58	**THE CLOUDS WILL SOON ROLL BY**	
	Columbia DB 4066 ....**24**	3 wks
9 May 58	**THE CLOUDS WILL SOON ROLL BY (re-entry)**	
	Columbia DB 4066 ....**20**	2 wks
5 Sep 58	**GIRL OF MY DREAMS** *Columbia DB 4177* **16**	7 wks
24 Jul 59	**WHY SHOULD I BE LONELY** *Columbia DB 4304*........**24**	4 wks

Bernard BRESSLAW *UK, male vocalist*   **11 wks**

| 5 Sep 58 | ● **MAD PASSIONATE LOVE** *HMV POP 522* ....**6** | 11 wks |

See also Michael Medwin, Bernard Bresslaw, Alfie Bass and Leslie Fyson.

Teresa BREWER *US, female vocalist*   **53 wks**

11 Feb 55	● **LET ME GO LOVER** *Vogue/Coral Q 72043* **9**	10 wks
13 Apr 56	● **A TEAR FELL** *Vogue/Coral Q 72146* **2**	15 wks
13 Jul 56	● **SWEET OLD-FASHIONED GIRL**	
	Vogue/Coral Q 72172 ....**3**	15 wks
10 May 57	**NORA MALONE** *Vogue/Coral Q 72224* **26**	2 wks
23 Jun 60	**HOW DO YOU KNOW IT'S LOVE** *Coral Q 72396* **21**	11 wks

BRIAN and MICHAEL UK, male vocal duo **19 wks**

25 Feb 78 ★ **MATCHSTALK MEN AND MATCHSTALK CATS AND DOGS** Pye 7N 46035 ....**1** 19 wks

BRICK US, male vocal / instrumental group **4 wks**

5 Feb 77 **DAZZ** Bang 004 ....**36** 4 wks

Edie BRICKELL and the NEW BOHEMIANS
US, female / male vocal / instrumental group **10 wks**

4 Feb 89 **WHAT I AM** Geffen GEF 49 ....**31** 7 wks
27 May 89 **CIRCLE** Geffen GEF 51 ....**74** 1 wk
1 Oct 94 **GOOD TIMES** Geffen GFSTD 78 [1] ....**40** 2 wks

[1] Edie Brickell

Alicia BRIDGES US, female vocalist **11 wks**

11 Nov 78 **I LOVE THE NIGHT LIFE (DISCO ROUND)**
Polydor 2066 936 ....**32** 10 wks
8 Oct 94 **I LOVE THE NIGHTLIFE (DISCO ROUND) (re-mix)**
Mother MUMCD 57 ....**61** 1 wk

BRIGHOUSE AND RASTRICK BRASS BAND
UK, male brass band **13 wks**

12 Nov 77 ● **THE FLORAL DANCE** Transatlantic BIG 548 ....**2** 13 wks

Bette BRIGHT UK, female vocalist **5 wks**

8 Mar 80 **HELLO I AM YOUR HEART** Korova KOW 3 ....**50** 5 wks

Sarah BRIGHTMAN UK, female vocalist **79 wks**

11 Nov 78 ● **I LOST MY HEART TO A STARSHIP TROOPER**
Ariola/Hansa AHA 527 [1] ....**6** 14 wks
7 Apr 79 **THE ADVENTURES OF THE LOVE CRUSADER**
Ariola/Hansa AHA 538 [2] ....**53** 5 wks
30 Jul 83 **HIM** Polydor POSP 625 [3] ....**55** 4 wks
23 Mar 85 ● **PIE JESU** HMV WEBBER 1 [4] ....**3** 8 wks
11 Jan 86 ● **THE PHANTOM OF THE OPERA** Polydor POSP 800 [5] **7** 10 wks
4 Oct 86 ● **ALL I ASK OF YOU** Polydor POSP 802 [6] ....**3** 16 wks
10 Jan 87 ● **WISHING YOU WERE SOMEHOW HERE AGAIN**
Polydor POSP 803 ....**7** 11 wks
11 Jul 92 **AMIGOS PARA SIEMPRE (FRIENDS FOR LIFE)**
Really Useful RUR 10 [7] ....**11** 11 wks

[1] Sarah Brightman and Hot Gossip [2] Sarah Brightman and the Starship Troopers [3] Sarah Brightman and the Royal Philharmonic Orchestra [4] Sarah Brightman and Paul Miles-Kingston [5] Sarah Brightman and Steve Harley [6] Cliff Richard and Sarah Brightman [7] José Carreras and Sarah Brightman

The listed flip side of Wishing You Were Somehow Here Again was The Music Of The Night by Michael Crawford.

BRIGHTON AND HOVE ALBION F.C.
UK, male football team vocalists **2 wks**

28 May 83 **THE BOYS IN THE OLD BRIGHTON BLUE**
Energy NRG 2 ....**65** 2 wks

BRILLIANT UK, male / female vocal / instrumental group **13 wks**

19 Oct 85 **IT'S A MAN'S MAN'S MAN'S WORLD**
Food FOOD 5 ....**58** 5 wks
22 Mar 86 **LOVE IS WAR** Food FOOD 6 ....**64** 4 wks
2 Aug 86 **SOMEBODY** Food FOOD 7 ....**67** 4 wks

Johnny BRISTOL US, male vocalist **16 wks**

24 Aug 74 ● **HANG ON IN THERE BABY** MGM 2006 443 ....**3** 11 wks

19 Jul 80 **MY GUY - MY GIRL (MEDLEY)**
Atlantic/Hansa K 11550 [1] ....**39** 5 wks

[1] Amii Stewart and Johnny Bristol

BRITS - See VARIOUS ARTISTS (MONTAGES)

BROKEN ENGLISH UK, male vocal / instrumental group **13 wks**

30 May 87 **COMIN' ON STRONG** EMI EM 5 ....**18** 10 wks
3 Oct 87 **LOVE ON THE SIDE** EMI EM 55 ....**69** 3 wks

BRONSKI BEAT UK, male vocal / instrumental group **78 wks**

2 Jun 84 ● **SMALLTOWN BOY** Forbidden Fruit BITE 1 ....**3** 13 wks
22 Sep 84 ● **WHY?** Forbidden Fruit BITE 2 ....**6** 10 wks
1 Dec 84 **IT AIN'T NECESSARILY SO** Forbidden Fruit BITE 3 ..**16** 11 wks
20 Apr 85 ● **I FEEL LOVE (MEDLEY)** Forbidden Fruit BITE 4 [1] .....**3** 12 wks
30 Nov 85 ● **HIT THAT PERFECT BEAT** Forbidden Fruit BITE 6 ....**3** 14 wks
29 Mar 86 **COME ON, COME ON** Forbidden Fruit BITE 7.........**20** 7 wks
1 Jul 89 **CHA CHA HEELS** Arista 112331 [2] ....**32** 7 wks
2 Feb 91 **SMALLTOWN BOY (re-mix)** London LON 287 [3] ....**32** 4 wks

[1] Bronski Beat and Marc Almond [2] Eartha Kitt and Bronski Beat [3] Jimmy Somerville with Bronski Beat

Tracks on medley: I Feel Love / Love To Love You Baby / Johnny Remember Me.

Jet BRONX and the FORBIDDEN
UK, male vocal / instrumental group **1 wk**

17 Dec 77 **AIN'T DOIN' NOTHIN'** Lightning LIG 50 ....**49** 1 wk

BROOK BROTHERS UK, male vocal duo **35 wks**

30 Mar 61 ● **WARPAINT** Pye 7N 15333 ....**5** 14 wks
24 Aug 61 **AIN'T GONNA WASH FOR A WEEK** Pye 7N 15369 ..**13** 10 wks
25 Jan 62 **HE'S OLD ENOUGH TO KNOW BETTER**
Pye 7N 15409 ....**37** 1 wk
16 Aug 62 **WELCOME HOME BABY** Pye 7N 15453.........**33** 6 wks
21 Feb 63 **TROUBLE IS MY MIDDLE NAME** Pye 7N 15498.......**38** 4 wks

Bruno BROOKES - See Liz KERSHAW and Bruno BROOKES

BROOKLYN, BRONX and QUEENS - See BB and Q Band

Elkie BROOKS UK, female vocalist **91 wks**

2 Apr 77 ● **PEARL'S A SINGER** A & M AMS 7275 ....**8** 9 wks
20 Aug 77 ● **SUNSHINE AFTER THE RAIN** A & M AMS 7306 ......**10** 9 wks
25 Feb 78 **LILAC WINE** A & M AMS 7333 ....**16** 7 wks
3 Jun 78 **ONLY LOVE CAN BREAK YOUR HEART**
A & M AMS 7353 ....**43** 5 wks
11 Nov 78 **DON'T CRY OUT LOUD** A & M AMS 7395 ....**12** 11 wks
5 May 79 **THE RUNAWAY** A & M AMS 7428 ....**50** 5 wks
16 Jan 82 **FOOL IF YOU THINK IT'S OVER** A & M AMS 8187....**17** 10 wks
1 May 82 **OUR LOVE** A & M AMS 8214.................**43** 5 wks
17 Jul 82 **NIGHTS IN WHITE SATIN** A & M AMS 8235 ....**33** 5 wks
22 Jan 83 **GASOLINE ALLEY** A & M AMS 8305 ....**52** 5 wks
22 Nov 86 ● **NO MORE THE FOOL** Legend LM 4 ....**5** 16 wks
4 Apr 87 **BREAK THE CHAIN** Legend LM 8.............**55** 3 wks
11 Jul 87 **WE'VE GOT TONIGHT** Legend LM 9 ....**69** 1 wk

Garth BROOKS US, male vocalist **10 wks**

1 Feb 92 **SHAMELESS** Capitol CL 646 ....**71** 1 wk
22 Jan 94 **THE RED STROKES / AIN'T GOING DOWN**
Liberty CDCLS 704 ....**13** 5 wks
16 Apr 94 **STANDING OUTSIDE THE FIRE** Liberty CDCL 712 ....**28** 4 wks

Mel BROOKS US, male vocalist **10 wks**

18 Feb 84 **TO BE OR NOT TO BE (THE HITLER RAP)**
Island IS 158 ....**12** 10 wks

Norman BROOKS *US, male vocalist* — **1 wk**

| 12 Nov 54 | A SKY BLUE SHIRT AND A RAINBOW TIE | | |
| | *London L 1228* ...... **17** | 1 wk |

BROS *UK, male vocal / instrumental group* — **84 wks**

5 Dec 87	WHEN WILL I BE FAMOUS *CBS ATOM 2* **62**	2 wks
9 Jan 88 ●	WHEN WILL I BE FAMOUS (re-entry) *CBS ATOM 2* ..**2**	13 wks
19 Mar 88 ●	DROP THE BOY *CBS ATOM 3* **2**	10 wks
18 Jun 88 ★	I OWE YOU NOTHING *CBS ATOM 4* **1**	11 wks
17 Sep 88 ●	I QUIT *CBS ATOM 5* **4**	8 wks
3 Dec 88 ●	CAT AMONG THE PIGEONS / SILENT NIGHT	
	CBS ATOM 6	**2**	8 wks
29 Jul 89 ●	TOO MUCH *CBS ATOM 7* **2**	7 wks
7 Oct 89 ●	CHOCOLATE BOX *CBS ATOM 8* **9**	6 wks
16 Dec 89 ●	SISTER *CBS ATOM 9* **10**	6 wks
10 Mar 90	MADLY IN LOVE *CBS ATOM 10* **14**	4 wks
13 Jul 91	ARE YOU MINE *Columbia 6569707* **12**	5 wks
21 Sep 91	TRY *Columbia 6574047* **27**	4 wks

Act were duo for last six hits.

BROTHER BEYOND
UK, male vocal / instrumental group — **58 wks**

4 Apr 87	HOW MANY TIMES *EMI EMI 5591* **62**	3 wks
8 Aug 87	CHAIN-GANG SMILE *Parlophone R 6160* **57**	3 wks
23 Jan 88	CAN YOU KEEP A SECRET *Parlophone R 6174* **56**	4 wks
30 Jul 88 ●	THE HARDER I TRY *Parlophone R 6184* **2**	14 wks
5 Nov 88 ●	HE AIN'T NO COMPETITION *Parlophone R 6193* ...**6**	10 wks
21 Jan 89	BE MY TWIN *Parlophone R 6195* **14**	6 wks
1 Apr 89	CAN YOU KEEP A SECRET (re-mix)	
	Parlophone R 6197 ...... **2**	7 wks
28 Oct 89	DRIVE ON *Parlophone R 6233* **39**	4 wks
9 Dec 89	WHEN WILL I SEE YOU AGAIN *Parlophone R 6239*..**43**	5 wks
10 Mar 90	TRUST *Parlophone R 6245* **53**	2 wks
19 Jan 91	THE GIRL I USED TO KNOW *Parlophone R 6265* **48**	2 wks

BROTHER LOVE - *See PRATT and McCLAIN with BROTHER LOVE*

BROTHERHOOD OF MAN
UK, male / female vocal group — **97 wks**

14 Feb 70 ●	UNITED WE STAND *Deram DM 284* **10**	9 wks
4 Jul 70	WHERE ARE YOU GOING TO MY LOVE	
	Deram DM 298 ...... **22**	10 wks
13 Mar 76 ★	SAVE YOUR KISSES FOR ME *Pye 7N 45569* **1**	16 wks
19 Jun 76	MY SWEET ROSALIE *Pye 7N 45602* **30**	7 wks
26 Feb 77 ●	OH BOY (THE MOOD I'M IN) *Pye 7N 45656* **8**	12 wks
9 Jul 77 ★	ANGELO *Pye 7N 45699* **1**	12 wks
14 Jan 78 ★	FIGARO *Pye 7N 46037* **1**	11 wks
27 May 78	BEAUTIFUL LOVER *Pye 7N 46071* **15**	12 wks
30 Sep 78	MIDDLE OF THE NIGHT *Pye 7N 46117* **41**	6 wks
3 Jul 82	LIGHTNING FLASH *EMI 5309* **67**	2 wks

BROTHERS *UK, male vocal group* — **9 wks**

| 29 Jan 77 ● | SING ME *Bus Stop Bus 1054* ...... **8** | 9 wks |

BROTHERS FOUR *US, male vocal group* — **2 wks**

| 23 Jun 60 | GREENFIELDS *Philips PB 1009* ...... **49** | 1 wk |
| 7 Jul 60 | GREENFIELDS (re-entry) *Philips PB 1009* ......**40** | 1 wk |

BROTHERS GRIMM - *See JAZZ and the BROTHERS GRIMM*

BROTHERS IN RHYTHM
UK, male instrumental / production duo — **12 wks**

| 16 Mar 91 | SUCH A GOOD FEELING | |
| | *Fourth & Broadway BRW 228* ...... **64** | 2 wks |

14 Sep 91	SUCH A GOOD FEELING (re-entry)	
	Fourth & Broadway BRW 228 ...... **14**	8 wks
30 Apr 94	FOREVER AND A DAY *Stress CDSTR 36* **51**	2 wks

BROTHERS JOHNSON
US, male vocal / instrumental duo — **34 wks**

9 Jul 77	STRAWBERRY LETTER 23 *A & M AMS 7297* **35**	5 wks
2 Sep 78	AIN'T WE FUNKIN' NOW *A & M AMS 7379* **43**	6 wks
4 Nov 78	RIDE-O-ROCKET *A & M AMS 7400* **50**	4 wks
23 Feb 80 ●	STOMP *A & M AMS 7509* **6**	12 wks
31 May 80	LIGHT UP THE NIGHT *A & M AMS 7526* **47**	4 wks
25 Jul 81	THE REAL THING *A & M AMS 8149* **50**	3 wks

BROTHERS LIKE OUTLAW *UK, male rap duo* — **1 wk**

| 23 Jan 93 | GOOD VIBRATIONS *Gee Street GESCD 44* ......**74** | 1 wk |

Edgar BROUGHTON BAND
UK, male vocal / instrumental group — **10 wks**

18 Apr 70	OUT DEMONS OUT *Harvest HAR 5015* **39**	5 wks
23 Jan 71	APACHE DROPOUT *Harvest HAR 5032* **49**	1 wk
6 Feb 71	APACHE DROPOUT (re-entry) *Harvest HAR 5032* **35**	2 wks
13 Mar 71	APACHE DROPOUT (2nd re-entry)	
	Harvest HAR 5032	**35**	1 wk
27 Mar 71	APACHE DROPOUT (3rd re-entry)	
	Harvest HAR 5032 ...... **33**	1 wk

Alison BROWN - *See BAR-CODES featuring Alison BROWN*

Angie BROWN - *See BIZARRE INC: MOTIV 8*

Crazy World of Arthur BROWN
UK, male vocal / instrumental group — **14 wks**

| 26 Jun 68 ★ | FIRE *Track 604 022* ...... **1** | 14 wks |

Bobby BROWN *US, male vocalist* — **99 wks**

6 Aug 88	DON'T BE CRUEL *MCA MCA 1268* **42**	7 wks
17 Dec 88 ●	MY PREROGATIVE *MCA MCA 1299* **6**	17 wks
25 Mar 89	DON'T BE CRUEL (re-issue) *MCA MCA 1310* **13**	8 wks
20 May 89 ●	EVERY LITTLE STEP *MCA MCA 1338* **6**	9 wks
15 Jul 89 ●	ON OUR OWN (FROM GHOSTBUSTERS II)	
	MCA MCA 1350	**4**	9 wks
23 Sep 89	ROCK WIT'CHA *MCA MCA 1367* **33**	6 wks
25 Nov 89	RONI *MCA MCA 1384* **21**	7 wks
9 Jun 90	THE FREE STYLE MEGA-MIX *MCA MCA 1421* **14**	7 wks
30 Jun 90	SHE AIN'T WORTH IT *London LON 265* [1] **12**	9 wks
22 Aug 92	HUMPIN' AROUND *MCA MCS 1680* **19**	6 wks
17 Oct 92	GOOD ENOUGH *MCA MCS 1704* **41**	4 wks
19 Jun 93	THAT'S THE WAY LOVE IS *MCA MCSTD 1783* **56**	2 wks
22 Jan 94	SOMETHING IN COMMON *MCA MCSTD 1957* [2] **16**	5 wks
25 Jun 94	TWO CAN PLAY THAT GAME *MCA MCSTD 1973*......**38**	3 wks

[1] Glenn Medeiros featuring Bobby Brown [2] Bobby Brown and Whitney Houston

Carl BROWN - *See DOUBLE TROUBLE*

Dennis BROWN *Jamaica, male vocalist* — **18 wks**

3 Mar 79	MONEY IN MY POCKET *Lightning LV 5* **14**	9 wks
3 Jul 82	LOVE HAS FOUND ITS WAY *A & M AMS 8226*......**47**	6 wks
11 Sep 82	HALFWAY UP HALFWAY DOWN *A & M AMS 8250* ..**56**	3 wks

Diana BROWN and Barrie K. SHARPE
UK, female / male vocal duo — **11 wks**

| 2 Jun 90 | THE MASTERPLAN *ffrr F 133* ...... **39** | 6 wks |

1 Sep 90	SUN WORSHIPPERS (POSITIVE THINKING)		
	ffrr F 144	**61**	2 wks
23 Mar 91	LOVE OR NOTHING *ffrr F 152*	**71**	1 wk
27 Jun 92	EATING ME ALIVE *ffrr F 190*	**53**	2 wks

Errol BROWN UK, male vocalist — **10 wks**

4 Jul 87	PERSONAL TOUCH *WEA YZ 130*	**25**	8 wks
28 Nov 87	BODY ROCKIN' *WEA YZ 162*	**51**	2 wks

Gloria D. BROWN US, female vocalist — **3 wks**

8 Jun 85	THE MORE THEY KNOCK, THE MORE I LOVE YOU		
	10 TEN 52	**57**	3 wks

James BROWN US, male vocalist — **101 wks**

23 Sep 65	PAPA'S GOT A BRAND NEW BAG		
	London HL 9990 [1]	**25**	7 wks
24 Feb 66	I GOT YOU *Pye International 7N 25350* [1]	**29**	6 wks
16 Jun 66	IT'S A MAN'S MAN'S MAN'S WORLD		
	Pye International 7N 25371 [1]	**13**	9 wks
10 Oct 70	GET UP I FEEL LIKE BEING A SEX MACHINE		
	Polydor 2001 071	**32**	7 wks
27 Nov 71	HEY AMERICA *Mojo 2093 006*	**47**	3 wks
18 Sep 76	GET UP OFFA THAT THING *Polydor 2066 687*	**22**	6 wks
29 Jan 77	BODY HEAT *Polydor 2066 763*	**36**	4 wks
10 Jan 81	RAPP PAYBACK (WHERE IZ MOSES?) *RCA 28*	**39**	5 wks
2 Jul 83	BRING IT ON ... BRING IT ON *Sonet SON 2258*	**45**	4 wks
1 Sep 84	UNITY (PART 1 - THE THIRD COMING)		
	Tommy Boy AFR 2 [2]	**49**	5 wks
27 Apr 85	FROGGY MIX *Boiling Point FROG 1*	**50**	3 wks
1 Jun 85	GET UP I FEEL LIKE BEING A SEX MACHINE		
	(re-issue) *Boiling Point POSP 751*	**47**	5 wks
25 Jan 86	● LIVING IN AMERICA *Scotti Brothers A 6701*	**5**	10 wks
1 Mar 86	GET UP I FEEL LIKE BEING A SEX MACHINE		
	(re-entry of re-issue) *Boiling Point POSP 751*	**46**	4 wks
18 Oct 86	GRAVITY *Scotti Brothers 650059 7*	**65**	2 wks
30 Jan 88	SHE'S THE ONE *Urban URB 13*	**45**	3 wks
23 Apr 88	THE PAYBACK MIX *Urban URB 17*	**12**	6 wks
4 Jun 88	I'M REAL *Scotti Brothers JSB 1* [3]	**31**	4 wks
23 Jul 88	I GOT YOU (I FEEL GOOD) (re-issue)		
	& M AM 444	**52**	3 wks
16 Nov 91	GET UP (I FEEL LIKE BEING A SEX MACHINE)		
	(2nd re-issue) *Polydor PO 185*	**69**	2 wks
24 Oct 92	I GOT YOU (I FEEL GOOD) (re-mix) *FBI FBI 9* [4]	**72**	1 wk
17 Apr 93	CAN'T GET ANY HARDER *Polydor PZCD 262*	**59**	2 wks

[1] James Brown and The Famous Flames [2] Afrika Bambaataa and James Brown [3] James Brown featuring Full Force [4] James Brown v Dakeyne

Froggy Mix *is a medley of twelve James Brown songs. The listed flip side of* I Got You (I Feel Good) *was* Nowhere To Run *by Martha Reeves and the Vandellas.*

Joanne BROWN - See Tony OSBORNE

Jocelyn BROWN US, female vocalist — **47 wks**

21 Apr 84	SOMEBODY ELSE'S GUY		
	Fourth & Broadway BRW 5	**13**	9 wks
22 Sep 84	I WISH YOU WOULD *Fourth & Broadway BRW 14*	**51**	3 wks
15 Mar 86	LOVE'S GONNA GET YOU *Warner Bros. W 8889*	**70**	1 wk
29 Jun 91	● ALWAYS THERE *Talkin Loud TLK 10* [1]	**6**	9 wks
14 Sep 91	SHE GOT SOUL *A & M AM 819* [2]	**57**	3 wks
7 Dec 91	● DON'T TALK JUST KISS *Tug SNOG 2* [3]	**3**	11 wks
20 Mar 93	TAKE ME UP *A & M AMCD 210* [4]	**61**	1 wk
11 Jun 94	NO MORE TEARS (ENOUGH IS ENOUGH)		
	Ding Dong 74321209032 [5]	**13**	7 wks
8 Oct 94	GIMME ALL YOUR LOVIN'		
	Ding Dong 74321231322 [5]	**22**	3 wks

[1] Incognito featuring Jocelyn Brown [2] Jamestown featuring Jocelyn Brown [3] Right Said Fred. Guest vocals: Jocelyn Brown [4] Sonic Surfers featuring Jocelyn Brown [5] Kym Mazelle and Jocelyn Brown

Joe BROWN and the BRUVVERS
UK, male vocal / instrumental group — **92 wks**

17 Mar 60	DARKTOWN STRUTTERS BALL *Decca F 11207*	**34**	6 wks
26 Jan 61	SHINE *Pye 7N 15322* [1]	**33**	6 wks
11 Jan 62	WHAT A CRAZY WORLD WE'RE LIVING IN		
	Piccadilly 7N 35024	**37**	2 wks
17 May 62	● A PICTURE OF YOU *Piccadilly 7N 35047*	**2**	19 wks
13 Sep 62	YOUR TENDER LOOK *Piccadilly 7N 35058*	**31**	6 wks
15 Nov 62	● IT ONLY TOOK A MINUTE *Piccadilly 7N 35082*	**6**	13 wks
7 Feb 63	● THAT'S WHAT LOVE WILL DO *Piccadilly 7N 35106*	**3**	14 wks
21 Feb 63	IT ONLY TOOK A MINUTE (re-entry)		
	Piccadilly 7N 35082	**50**	1 wk
27 Jun 63	NATURE'S TIME FOR LOVE *Piccadilly 7N 35129*	**26**	6 wks
26 Sep 63	SALLY ANN *Piccadilly 7N 35138*	**28**	9 wks
29 Jun 67	WITH A LITTLE HELP FROM MY FRIENDS		
	Pye 7N 17339 [1]	**32**	4 wks
14 Apr 73	HEY MAMA *Ammo AMO 101* [1]	**33**	6 wks

[1] Joe Brown

Miquel BROWN US, female vocalist — **7 wks**

18 Feb 84	HE'S A SAINT, HE'S A SINNER		
	Record Shack SOHO 15	**68**	4 wks
24 Aug 85	CLOSE TO PERFECTION *Record Shack SOHO 48*	**63**	3 wks

Peter BROWN US, male vocalist — **9 wks**

11 Feb 78	DO YA WANNA GET FUNKY WITH ME		
	TK TKR 6009	**43**	4 wks
17 Jun 78	DANCE WITH ME *TK TKR 6027*	**57**	5 wks

Polly BROWN UK, female vocalist — **5 wks**

14 Sep 74	UP IN A PUFF OF SMOKE *GTO GT 2*	**43**	5 wks

Sam BROWN UK, female vocalist — **34 wks**

11 Jun 88	STOP *A & M AM 440*	**52**	3 wks
4 Feb 89	● STOP (re-entry) *A & M AM 440*	**4**	12 wks
13 May 89	CAN I GET A WITNESS *A & M AM 509*	**15**	7 wks
3 Mar 90	WITH A LITTLE LOVE *A & M AM 539*	**44**	4 wks
5 May 90	KISSING GATE *A & M M AM 549*	**23**	8 wks

Sharon BROWN US, female vocalist — **11 wks**

17 Apr 82	I SPECIALIZE IN LOVE *Virgin VS 494*	**38**	9 wks
26 Feb 94	I SPECIALIZE IN LOVE (re-issue)		
	Deep Distraxion OILYCD 025	**62**	2 wks

BROWN SAUCE UK, male / female vocal group — **12 wks**

12 Dec 81	I WANNA BE A WINNER *BBC RESL 101*	**15**	12 wks

Duncan BROWNE UK, male vocalist — **8 wks**

19 Aug 72	JOURNEY *RAK 135*	**23**	6 wks
22 Dec 84	THEME FROM 'THE TRAVELLING MAN'		
	Towerbell TOW 64	**68**	2 wks

Jackson BROWNE US, male vocalist — **14 wks**

1 Jul 78	STAY *Asylum K 13128*	**12**	11 wks
18 Oct 86	IN THE SHAPE OF A HEART *Elektra EKR 42*	**66**	2 wks
25 Jun 94	EVERYWHERE I GO *Elektra EKR 184CD1*	**67**	1 wk

Ronnie BROWNE - See SCOTTISH RUGBY TEAM with Ronnie BROWNE

Tom BROWNE US, male vocalist — **24 wks**

19 Jul 80	● FUNKIN' FOR JAMAICA (N.Y.) *Arista ARIST 357*	**10**	11 wks

TONI BRAXTON was Best New Artist in the 1993 Grammy Awards. (Ron Wolfson/LFI)

In their home country, **BOYZ II MEN** are the most successful group of the 1990s to date. (Kevin Mazur/LFI)

DAVID BOWIE led the Most Weeks on Chart list in 1973. (LFI)

25 Oct 80	THIGHS HIGH (GRIP YOUR HIPS AND MOVE)		
	Arista ARIST 367 ....**45**	5 wks
30 Jan 82	FUNGI MAMA (BEBOPAFUNKADISCOLYPSO)		
	Arista ARIST 450 ....**58**	4 wks
11 Jan 92	FUNKIN' FOR JAMAICA (re-mix) *Arista 114998* **45**	4 wks

BROWNS *US, male/female vocal group*   **13 wks**

| 18 Sep 59 | ● THE THREE BELLS *RCA 1140* ....**6** | 13 wks |

BROWNSVILLE STATION
US, male vocal/instrumental group   **6 wks**

| 2 Mar 74 | SMOKIN' IN THE BOYS' ROOM *Philips 6073 834* ....**27** | 6 wks |

Dave BRUBECK QUARTET
US, male instrumental group   **30 wks**

26 Oct 61	● TAKE FIVE *Fontana H 339* **6**	15 wks
8 Feb 62	IT'S A RAGGY WALTZ *Fontana H 352* **36**	3 wks
17 May 62	UNSQUARE DANCE *CBS AAG 102* **14**	12 wks

Tommy BRUCE and the BRUISERS
UK, male vocal/instrumental group   **21 wks**

26 May 60	● AIN'T MISBEHAVIN' *Columbia DB 4453* **3**	16 wks
8 Sep 60	BROKEN DOLL *Columbia DB 4498* **36**	4 wks
22 Feb 62	BABETTE *Columbia DB 4776* [1] **50**	1 wk

[1] Tommy Bruce

Claudia BRUCKEN *Germany, female vocalist*   **2 wks**

| 11 Aug 90 | ABSOLUT(E) *Island IS 471* ....**71** | 1 wk |
| 16 Feb 91 | KISS LIKE ETHER *Island IS 479* ....**63** | 1 wk |

BRUISERS *UK, male instrumental group*   **7 wks**

| 8 Aug 63 | BLUE GIRL *Parlophone R 5042* ....**31** | 6 wks |
| 26 Sep 63 | BLUE GIRL (re-entry) *Parlophone R 5042* ....**47** | 1 wk |

See also Tommy Bruce.

BRUNO and LIZ - *See Liz KERSHAW and Bruno BROOKES*

Tyrone BRUNSON *US, male instrumentalist - bass*   **5 wks**

| 25 Dec 82 | THE SMURF *Epic EPC A 3024* ....**52** | 5 wks |

BRUVVERS - *See Joe BROWN and the BRUVVERS*

Dora BRYAN *UK, female vocalist*   **6 wks**

| 5 Dec 63 | ALL I WANT FOR CHRISTMAS IS A BEATLE | | |
| | *Fontana TF 427* ....**20** | 6 wks |

Anita BRYANT *US, female vocalist*   **6 wks**

26 May 60	PAPER ROSES *London HLL 9144* **49**	1 wk
30 Jun 60	PAPER ROSES (re-entry) *London HLL 9144* **45**	1 wk
14 Jul 60	PAPER ROSES (2nd re-entry) *London HLL 9144* **24**	2 wks
6 Oct 60	MY LITTLE CORNER OF THE WORLD		
	London HLL 9171 ....**48**	2 wks

Peabo BRYSON *US, male vocalist*   **35 wks**

20 Aug 83	● TONIGHT I CELEBRATE MY LOVE *Capitol CL 302* [1]..**2**	13 wks
16 May 92	● BEAUTY AND THE BEAST *Epic 6576607* [2] **9**	7 wks
17 Jul 93	BY THE TIME THIS NIGHT IS OVER		
	Arista 74321157142 [3] **56**	3 wks

| 11 Dec 93 | A WHOLE NEW WORLD (ALADDIN'S THEME) | | |
| | *Columbia 6599002* [4] ....**12** | 12 wks |

[1] Peabo Bryson and Roberta Flack [2] Celine Dion and Peabo Bryson
[3] Kenny G with Peabo Bryson [4] Peabo Bryson and Regina Belle

B.T. EXPRESS *US, male instrumental/vocal group*   **11 wks**

29 Mar 75	EXPRESS *Pye International 7N 25674* **34**	6 wks
26 Jul 80	DOES IT FEEL GOOD/GIVE UP THE FUNK		
	(LET'S DANCE) *Calibre CAB 503* **52**	4 wks
23 Apr 94	EXPRESS (re-mix) *PWL International PWCD 285* **67**	1 wk

B-TRIBE *Spain, male/female instrumental/vocal group*   **4 wks**

| 25 Sep 93 | ¡FIESTA FATAL! *East West YZ 770CD* ....**64** | 4 wks |

BUBBLEROCK - *See Jonathan KING*

Catherine BUCHANAN - *See JELLYBEAN*

Roy BUCHANAN *US, male instrumentalist - guitar*   **3 wks**

| 31 Mar 73 | SWEET DREAMS *Polydor 2066 307* ....**40** | 3 wks |

Lindsey BUCKINGHAM *US, male vocalist*   **7 wks**

| 16 Jan 82 | TROUBLE *Mercury MER 85* ....**31** | 7 wks |

BUCKS FIZZ *UK, male/female vocal group*   **150 wks**

28 Mar 81	★ MAKING YOUR MIND UP *RCA 56* **1**	12 wks
6 Jun 81	PIECE OF THE ACTION *RCA 88* **12**	9 wks
15 Aug 81	ONE OF THOSE NIGHTS *RCA 114* **20**	10 wks
28 Nov 81	★ THE LAND OF MAKE BELIEVE *RCA 163* **1**	16 wks
27 Mar 82	★ MY CAMERA NEVER LIES *RCA 202* **1**	8 wks
19 Jun 82	● NOW THOSE DAYS ARE GONE *RCA 241* **8**	9 wks
27 Nov 82	● IF YOU CAN'T STAND THE HEAT *RCA 300* **10**	11 wks
12 Mar 83	RUN FOR YOUR LIFE *RCA FIZ 1* **14**	7 wks
18 Jun 83	● WHEN WE WERE YOUNG *RCA 342* **10**	8 wks
1 Oct 83	LONDON TOWN *RCA 363* **34**	6 wks
17 Dec 83	RULES OF THE GAME *RCA 380* **57**	6 wks
25 Aug 84	TALKING IN YOUR SLEEP *RCA FIZ 2* **15**	9 wks
27 Oct 84	GOLDEN DAYS *RCA FIZ 3* **42**	4 wks
29 Dec 84	I HEAR TALK *RCA FIZ 4* **34**	8 wks
22 Jun 85	YOU AND YOUR HEART SO BLUE *RCA PB 40233* **43**	4 wks
14 Sep 85	MAGICAL *RCA PB 40367* **57**	3 wks
7 Jun 86	● NEW BEGINNING (MAMBA SEYRA)		
	Polydor POSP 794 ....**8**	10 wks
30 Aug 86	LOVE THE ONE YOU'RE WITH *Polydor POSP 813* **47**	3 wks
15 Nov 86	KEEP EACH OTHER WARM *Polydor POSP 835* **45**	4 wks
5 Nov 88	HEART OF STONE *RCA PB 42035* **50**	3 wks

BUDGIE *UK, male vocal/instrumental group*   **2 wks**

| 3 Oct 81 | KEEPING A RENDEZVOUS *RCA BUDGIE 3* ....**71** | 2 wks |

BUG KANN and the PLASTIC JAM
UK, male/female vocal/instrumental group   **2 wks**

31 Aug 91	MADE IN TWO MINUTES		
	Optimum Dance BKPJ 1S [1] **70**	1 wk
26 Feb 94	MADE IN 2 MINUTES (re-mix)		
	PWL International PWCD 286 ....**64**	1 wk

[1] Bug Kann and Plastic Jam featuring Patti Low and Doogie

BUGGLES *UK, male vocal/instrumental duo*   **28 wks**

22 Sep 79	★ VIDEO KILLED THE RADIO STAR *Island WIP 6524* **1**	11 wks
26 Jan 80	THE PLASTIC AGE *Island WIP 6540* **16**	8 wks
5 Apr 80	CLEAN CLEAN *Island WIP 6584* **38**	5 wks
8 Nov 80	ELSTREE *Island WIP 6624* **55**	4 wks

B. BUMBLE and the STINGERS
US, male instrumental group   **26 wks**

19 Apr 62	★ **NUT ROCKER** Top Rank JAR 611	....	**1**	15 wks
3 Jun 72	**NUT ROCKER (re-issue)** Stateside SS 2203	....	**19**	11 wks

BUMP *UK, male instrumental/production duo*   **4 wks**

4 Jul 92	**I'M RUSHING** Good Boy EDGE7 1	....	**40**	4 wks

BUNKER KRU - See HARLEQUIN 4's / BUNKER KRU

BUNNYMEN - See ECHO and the BUNNYMEN

Eric BURDON - See ANIMALS

Geoffrey BURGON *UK, orchestra*   **4 wks**

26 Dec 81	**BRIDESHEAD THEME** Chrysalis CHS 2562	....	**48**	4 wks

Keni BURKE *US, male vocalist*   **4 wks**

27 Jun 81	**LET SOMEBODY LOVE YOU** RCA 93	....	**59**	3 wks
18 Apr 92	**RISIN' TO THE TOP** RCA PB 49103	....	**70**	1 wk

Hank C. BURNETTE
Sweden, male multi-instrumentalist   **8 wks**

30 Oct 76	**SPINNING ROCK BOOGIE** Sonet SON 2094	....	**21**	8 wks

Johnny BURNETTE *US, male vocalist*   **48 wks**

29 Sep 60	● **DREAMIN'** London HLG 9172	....	**5**	16 wks
12 Jan 61	● **YOU'RE SIXTEEN** London HLG 9254	....	**3**	12 wks
13 Apr 61	**LITTLE BOY SAD** London HLG 9315	....	**12**	12 wks
10 Aug 61	**GIRLS** London HLG 9388	....	**37**	5 wks
17 May 62	**CLOWN SHOES** Liberty LIB 55416	....	**35**	3 wks

Rocky BURNETTE *US, male vocalist*   **7 wks**

17 Nov 79	**TIRED OF TOEIN' THE LINE** EMI 2992	....	**58**	7 wks

Jerry BURNS *UK, female vocalist*   **1 wk**

25 Apr 92	**PALE RED** Columbia 6579467	....	**64**	1 wk

Ray BURNS *UK, male vocalist*   **19 wks**

11 Feb 55	● **MOBILE** Columbia DB 3563	....	**4**	13 wks
26 Aug 55	**THAT'S HOW A LOVE SONG WAS BORN** Columbia DB 3640 [1]	....	**14**	6 wks

[1] Ray Burns with the Coronets

Malandra BURROWS *UK, female vocalist*   **8 wks**

1 Dec 90	**JUST THIS SIDE OF LOVE** Yorkshire Television DALE 1	....	**11**	8 wks

Jenny BURTON *US, female vocalist*   **2 wks**

30 Mar 85	**BAD HABITS** Atlantic A 9583	....	**68**	2 wks

BURUNDI STEIPHENSON BLACK
Burundi, drummers and chanters with orchestral additions by Mike Steiphenson of France   **14 wks**

13 Nov 71	**BURUNDI BLACK** Barclay BAR 3	....	**31**	14 wks

Lou BUSCH *US, orchestra and chorus*   **17 wks**

27 Jan 56	● **ZAMBESI** Capitol CL 14504	....	**2**	17 wks

See also Joe 'Fingers' Carr.

Kate BUSH *UK, female vocalist*   **168 wks**

11 Feb 78	★ **WUTHERING HEIGHTS** EMI 2719	....	**1**	12 wks
13 May 78	**WUTHERING HEIGHTS (re-entry)** EMI 2719	....	**75**	1 wk
10 Jun 78	● **MAN WITH THE CHILD IN HIS EYES** EMI 2806	....	**6**	11 wks
11 Nov 78	**HAMMER HORROR** EMI 2887	....	**44**	6 wks
17 Mar 79	**WOW** EMI 2911	....	**14**	10 wks
15 Sep 79	● **KATE BUSH ON STAGE EP** EMI MIEP 2991	....	**10**	9 wks
26 Apr 80	**BREATHING** EMI 5058	....	**16**	7 wks
5 Jul 80	● **BABOOSHKA** EMI 5085	....	**5**	10 wks
4 Oct 80	**ARMY DREAMERS** EMI 5106	....	**16**	9 wks
6 Dec 80	**DECEMBER WILL BE MAGIC AGAIN** EMI 5121	....	**29**	7 wks
11 Jul 81	**SAT IN YOUR LAP** EMI 5201	....	**11**	7 wks
7 Aug 82	**THE DREAMING** EMI 5296	....	**48**	3 wks
17 Aug 85	● **RUNNING UP THAT HILL** EMI KB 1	....	**3**	11 wks
26 Oct 85	**CLOUDBUSTING** EMI KB 2	....	**20**	6 wks
1 Mar 86	**HOUNDS OF LOVE** EMI KB 3	....	**18**	5 wks
10 May 86	**THE BIG SKY** EMI KB 4	....	**37**	3 wks
1 Nov 86	● **DON'T GIVE UP** Virgin PGS 2 [1]	....	**9**	11 wks
8 Nov 86	**EXPERIMENT IV** EMI KB 5	....	**23**	4 wks
30 Sep 89	**THE SENSUAL WORLD** EMI EM 102	....	**12**	5 wks
2 Dec 89	**THIS WOMAN'S WORK** EMI EM 119	....	**25**	5 wks
10 Mar 90	**LOVE AND ANGER** EMI EM 134	....	**38**	3 wks
7 Dec 91	**ROCKET MAN (I THINK IT'S GOING TO BE A LONG LONG TIME)** Mercury TRIBO 2	....	**12**	8 wks
18 Sep 93	**RUBBERBAND GIRL** EMI CDEM 280	....	**12**	5 wks
27 Nov 93	**MOMENTS OF PLEASURE** EMI CDEM 297	....	**26**	3 wks
16 Apr 94	**THE RED SHOES** EMI CDEMS 316	....	**21**	3 wks
30 Jul 94	**THE MAN I LOVE** Mercury MERCD 408 [2]	....	**27**	2 wks
19 Nov 94	**AND SO IS LOVE** EMI CDEMS 355	....	**26**	2 wks

[1] Peter Gabriel and Kate Bush [2] Kate Bush and Larry Adler

Tracks on Kate Bush On Stage EP: Them Heavy People / Don't Push Your Foot on the Heartbrake / James and the Cold Gun / L'Amour Looks Something Like You.

BUSTER *UK, male vocal/instrumental group*   **1 wk**

19 Jun 76	**SUNDAY** RCA 2678	....	**49**	1 wk

Jonathan BUTLER
South Africa, male vocalist/instrumentalist - guitar   **18 wks**

25 Jan 86	**IF YOU'RE READY (COME GO WITH ME)** Jive JIVE 109 [1]	....	**30**	7 wks
8 Aug 87	**LIES** Jive JIVE 141	....	**18**	11 wks

[1] Ruby Turner featuring Jonathan Butler

BUTTERSCOTCH *UK, male vocal group*   **11 wks**

2 May 70	**DON'T YOU KNOW** RCA 1937	....	**17**	11 wks

BUZZCOCKS *UK, male vocal/instrumental group*   **53 wks**

18 Feb 78	**WHAT DO I GET** United Artists UP 36348	....	**37**	3 wks
13 May 78	**I DON'T MIND** United Artists UP 36386	....	**55**	2 wks
15 Jul 78	**LOVE YOU MORE** United Artists UP 36433	....	**34**	6 wks
23 Sep 78	**EVER FALLEN IN LOVE (WITH SOMEONE YOU SHOULDN'T'VE)** United Artists UP 36455	......	**12**	11 wks
25 Nov 78	**PROMISES** United Artists UP 36471	....	**20**	10 wks
10 Mar 79	**EVERYBODY'S HAPPY NOWADAYS** United Artists UP 36499	....	**29**	6 wks
21 Jul 79	**HARMONY IN MY HEAD** United Artists UP 36541	..	**32**	6 wks
25 Aug 79	**SPIRAL SCRATCH EP** New Hormones ORG 1	....	**31**	6 wks
6 Sep 80	**ARE EVERYTHING / WHY SHE'S A GIRL FROM THE CHAINSTORE** United Artists BP 365	....	**61**	3 wks

Tracks on Spiral Scratch EP: Breakdown / Time's Up / Boredom / Friends Of Mine. Sleeve of EP (not the label) credits 'Buzzcocks with Howard Devoto'. Why She's A Girl From The Chainstore listed from 13 Sep 80.

BUZZY BUNCH - *See Celi BEE and the BUZZY BUNCH*

B.V.S.M.P. *US, male vocal group* — **12 wks**

23 Jul 88	● I NEED YOU *Debut DEBT 3044*	...............**3**	12 wks

BY ALL MEANS *US, male vocal group* — **2 wks**

18 Jun 88	I SURRENDER TO YOUR LOVE *Fourth & Broadway BRW 102*	...............**65**	2 wks

Max BYGRAVES *UK, male vocalist* — **131 wks**

14 Nov 52	COWPUNCHER'S CANTATA *HMV B 10250*	...............**11**	1 wk
2 Jan 53	● COWPUNCHER'S CANTATA (re-entry) *HMV B 10250*	...............**8**	1 wk
23 Jan 53	● COWPUNCHER'S CANTATA (2nd re-entry) *HMV B 10250*	...............**6**	5 wks
6 Mar 53	● COWPUNCHER'S CANTATA (3rd re-entry) *HMV B 10250*	...............**10**	1 wk
14 May 54	● HEART OF MY HEART *HMV B 10654*	...............**7**	8 wks
10 Sep 54	● GILLY GILLY OSSENFEFFER KATZENELLEN BOGEN BY THE SEA *HMV B 10734*	...............**7**	7 wks
5 Nov 54	GILLY GILLY OSSENFEFFER KATZENELLEN BOGEN BY THE SEA (re-entry) *HMV B 10734*	...............**20**	1 wk
21 Jan 55	MR. SANDMAN *HMV B 10801*	...............**16**	1 wk
18 Nov 55	● MEET ME ON THE CORNER *HMV POP 116*	...............**2**	11 wks
17 Feb 56	BALLAD OF DAVY CROCKETT *HMV POP 153*	...............**20**	1 wk
25 May 56	OUT OF TOWN *HMV POP 164*	...............**18**	7 wks
5 Apr 57	HEART *Decca F 10862*	...............**14**	8 wks
2 May 58	● YOU NEED HANDS / TULIPS FROM AMSTERDAM *Decca F 11004*	...............**3**	25 wks
22 Aug 58	LITTLE TRAIN / GOTTA HAVE RAIN *Decca F 11046*	...............**28**	2 wks
2 Jan 59	MY UKELELE *Decca F 11077*	...............**19**	4 wks
18 Dec 59	● JINGLE BELL ROCK *Decca F 11176*	...............**7**	4 wks
10 Mar 60	● FINGS AIN'T WOT THEY USED T'BE *Decca F 11214*	...............**5**	15 wks
28 Jul 60	CONSIDER YOURSELF *Decca F 11251*	...............**50**	1 wk
1 Jun 61	BELLS OF AVIGNON *Decca F 11350*	...............**36**	5 wks
19 Feb 69	YOU'RE MY EVERYTHING *Pye 7N 17705*	...............**50**	1 wk
5 Mar 69	YOU'RE MY EVERYTHING (re-entry) *Pye 7N 17705*	...............**34**	3 wks
6 Oct 73	DECK OF CARDS *Pye 7N 45276*	...............**13**	15 wks
9 Dec 89	WHITE CHRISTMAS *Parkfield PMS 5012*	...............**71**	4 wks

See also Various Artists (EPs & LPs) - All Star Hit Parade No. 2.
Cowpuncher's Cantata *is a medley with the following songs: Cry Of The Wild Goose / Riders In The Sky / Mule Train / Jezebel. You Need Hands was listed by itself on 2 May 58. Tulips From Amsterdam was listed beginning 9 May 58.*

BYKER GROOVE! *UK, female vocal group* — **2 wks**

24 Dec 94	LOVE YOUR SEXY...!! *Groove GROVD 01*	...............**48†**	2 wks

Charlie BYRD - *See Stan GETZ*

Debra BYRD - *See Barry MANILOW*

Donald BYRD
US, male vocalist / instrumentalist - trumpet — **6 wks**

26 Sep 81	LOVING YOU / LOVE HAS COME AROUND *Elektra K 12559*	...............**41**	6 wks

Gary BYRD and the GB EXPERIENCE
US, male vocalist and male / female instrumental group — **9 wks**

23 Jul 83	● THE CROWN *Motown TMGT 1312*	...............**6**	9 wks

BYRDS *US, male vocal / instrumental group* — **52 wks**

17 Jun 65	★ MR. TAMBOURINE MAN *CBS 201765*	...............**1**	14 wks
12 Aug 65	● ALL I REALLY WANT TO DO *CBS 201796*	...............**4**	10 wks
11 Nov 65	TURN! TURN! TURN! *CBS 202008*	...............**26**	8 wks
5 May 66	EIGHT MILES HIGH *CBS 202067*	...............**24**	9 wks
5 Jun 68	YOU AIN'T GOIN' NOWHERE *CBS 3411*	...............**45**	3 wks
13 Feb 71	CHESTNUT MARE *CBS 5322*	...............**19**	8 wks

Edward BYRNES - *See Connie STEVENS*

BYSTANDERS *UK, male vocal / instrumental group* — **1 wk**

9 Feb 67	98.6 *Piccadilly 7N 35363*	...............**45**	1 wk

C

Roy C *US, male vocalist* — **24 wks**

21 Apr 66	● SHOTGUN WEDDING *Island WI 273*	...............**6**	11 wks
25 Nov 72	● SHOTGUN WEDDING (re-issue) *UK 19*	...............**8**	13 wks

C & C MUSIC FACTORY / CLIVILLES & COLE
US, male / female vocal / instrumental group — **49 wks**

15 Dec 90	● GONNA MAKE YOU SWEAT (EVERYBODY DANCE NOW) *CBS 6564540* [1]	...............**3**	12 wks
30 Mar 91	HERE WE GO *Columbia 6567557* [1]	...............**20**	7 wks
6 Jul 91	● THINGS THAT MAKE YOU GO HMMM... *Columbia 6566907* [1]	...............**4**	11 wks
23 Nov 91	JUST A TOUCH OF LOVE EVERYDAY *Columbia 6575247* [2]	...............**31**	3 wks
18 Jan 92	PRIDE (IN THE NAME OF LOVE) *Columbia 6577017* [3]	...............**15**	5 wks
14 Mar 92	A DEEPER LOVE *Columbia 6578497* [3]	...............**15**	5 wks
3 Oct 92	KEEP IT COMIN' (DANCE TILL YOU CAN'T DANCE NO MORE) *Columbia 6584307* [4]	...............**34**	3 wks
27 Aug 94	DO YOU WANNA GET FUNKY *Columbia 6607622* [5]	...............**27**	3 wks

[1] C & C Music Factory (featuring Freedom Williams) [2] C & C Music Factory featuring Zelma Davis [3] Clivilles and Cole [4] C & C Music Factory featuring Q Unique and Deborah Cooper [5] C & C Music Factory

ÇA VA ÇA VA *UK, male vocal / instrumental group* — **8 wks**

18 Sep 82	WHERE'S ROMEO *Regard RG 103*	...............**49**	5 wks
19 Feb 83	BROTHER BRIGHT *Regard RG 105*	...............**65**	3 wks

Montserrat CABALLE - *See Freddie MERCURY*

CABARET VOLTAIRE
UK, male vocal / instrumental group — **8 wks**

18 Jul 87	DON'T ARGUE *Parlophone R 6157*	...............**69**	2 wks
4 Nov 89	HYPNOTISED *Parlophone R 6227*	...............**66**	2 wks
12 May 90	KEEP ON *Parlophone R 6250*	...............**55**	2 wks
18 Aug 90	EASY LIFE *Parlophone R 6261*	...............**61**	2 wks

CACIQUE *UK, male / female vocal / instrumental group* — **1 wk**

1 Jun 85	DEVOTED TO YOU *Diamond Duel DISC 1*	...............**69**	1 wk

CACTUS WORLD NEWS
Ireland, male vocal / instrumental group — **7 wks**

8 Feb 86	YEARS LATER *MCA MCA 1024*	...............**59**	3 wks
26 Apr 86	WORLDS APART *MCA MCA 1040*	...............**58**	3 wks
20 Sep 86	THE BRIDGE *MCA MCA 1080*	...............**74**	1 wk

CADETS with Eileen READ
Ireland, male / female vocal group — **1 wk**

3 Jun 65	JEALOUS HEART *Pye 7N 15852*	...............**42**	1 wk

Susan CADOGAN *UK, female vocalist* **19 wks**

5 Apr 75	● HURT SO GOOD *Magnet MAG 23*	4	12 wks
19 Jul 75	LOVE ME BABY *Magnet MAG 36*	...22	7 wks

Al CAIOLA *US, orchestra* **6 wks**

15 Jun 61	THE MAGNIFICENT SEVEN *HMV POP 889*	...34	6 wks

CALIBRE CUTS - *See VARIOUS ARTISTS (MONTAGES)*

CALL *US, male vocal / instrumental group* **6 wks**

30 Sep 89	LET THE DAY BEGIN *MCA MCA 1362*	...42	6 wks

Eddie CALVERT *UK, male instrumentalist - trumpet* **80 wks**

18 Dec 53	★ OH MEIN PAPA *Columbia DB 3337*	...1	21 wks
8 Apr 55	★ CHERRY PINK AND APPLE BLOSSOM WHITE *Columbia DB 3581*	...1	21 wks
13 May 55	STRANGER IN PARADISE *Columbia DB 3594*	...14	4 wks
29 Jul 55	● JOHN AND JULIE *Columbia DB 3624*	...6	11 wks
9 Mar 56	ZAMBESI *Columbia DB 3747*	...18	1 wk
23 Mar 56	ZAMBESI (re-entry) *Columbia DB 3747*	...13	6 wks
7 Feb 58	● MANDY *Columbia DB 3956*	...9	14 wks
20 Jun 58	LITTLE SERENADE *Columbia DB 4105*	...28	2 wks

Donnie CALVIN - *See ROCKER'S REVENGE*

CAMEO *US, male vocal / instrumental group* **66 wks**

31 Mar 84	SHE'S STRANGE *Club JAB 2*	...37	8 wks
13 Jul 85	ATTACK ME WITH YOUR LOVE *Club JAB 16*	...65	2 wks
14 Sep 85	SINGLE LIFE *Club JAB 21*	...15	10 wks
7 Dec 85	SHE'S STRANGE (re-issue) *Club JAB 25*	...22	8 wks
22 Mar 86	A GOODBYE *Club JAB 28*	...65	2 wks
30 Aug 86	● WORD UP *Club JAB 38*	...3	13 wks
29 Nov 86	CANDY *Club JAB 43*	...27	9 wks
25 Apr 87	BACK AND FORTH *Club JAB 49*	...11	9 wks
17 Oct 87	SHE'S MINE *Club JAB 57*	...35	4 wks
29 Oct 88	YOU MAKE ME WORK *Club JAB 70*	...74	1 wk

Andy CAMERON *UK, male vocalist* **8 wks**

4 Mar 78	● ALLY'S TARTAN ARMY *Klub 03*	...6	8 wks

Tony CAMILLO'S BAZUKA
US, male instrumental / vocal group **5 wks**

31 May 75	DYNOMITE (PART 1) *A & M AMS 7168*	...28	5 wks

CAMOUFLAGE featuring MYSTI
UK, male / female vocal / instrumental group **3 wks**

24 Sep 77	BEE STING *State STAT 58*	...48	3 wks

Ali and Robin CAMPBELL - *See Pato BANTON*

Danny CAMPBELL - *See SASHA*

Don CAMPBELL - *See GENERAL SAINT*

Ethna CAMPBELL *UK, female vocalist* **11 wks**

27 Dec 75	THE OLD RUGGED CROSS *Philips 6006 475*	...33	11 wks

Glen CAMPBELL *US, male vocalist* **98 wks**

29 Jan 69	● WICHITA LINEMAN *Ember EMBS 261*	...7	13 wks
7 May 69	GALVESTON *Ember EMBS 263*	...14	10 wks
6 Dec 69	● ALL I HAVE TO DO IS DREAM *Capitol CL 15619* [1]	...3	14 wks
7 Feb 70	TRY A LITTLE KINDNESS *Capitol CL 15622*	...45	2 wks
9 May 70	● HONEY COME BACK *Capitol CL 15638*	...4	19 wks
26 Sep 70	EVERYTHING A MAN COULD EVER NEED *Capitol CL 15653*	...32	5 wks
21 Nov 70	● IT'S ONLY MAKE BELIEVE *Capitol CL 15663*	...4	14 wks
27 Mar 71	DREAM BABY *Capitol CL 15674*	...39	3 wks
4 Oct 75	● RHINESTONE COWBOY *Capitol CL 15824*	...4	12 wks
26 Mar 77	SOUTHERN NIGHTS *Capitol CL 15907*	...28	6 wks

[1] Bobbie Gentry and Glen Campbell

Jo Ann CAMPBELL *US, female vocalist* **3 wks**

8 Jun 61	MOTORCYCLE MICHAEL *HMV POP 873*	...41	3 wks

Junior CAMPBELL *UK, male vocalist* **18 wks**

14 Oct 72	● HALLELUJAH FREEDOM *Deram DM 364*	...10	9 wks
2 Jun 73	SWEET ILLUSION *Deram DM 387*	...15	9 wks

Naomi CAMPBELL *UK, female vocalist* **3 wks**

24 Sep 94	LOVE AND TEARS *Epic 6608352*	...40	3 wks

Pat CAMPBELL *Ireland, male vocalist* **5 wks**

15 Nov 69	THE DEAL *Major Minor MM 648*	...31	5 wks

Stan CAMPBELL *UK, male vocalist* **3 wks**

6 Jun 87	YEARS GO BY *WEA YZ 127*	...65	3 wks

Tevin CAMPBELL *US, male vocalist* **2 wks**

18 Apr 92	TELL ME WHAT YOU WANT ME TO DO *Qwest W 0102*	...63	2 wks

Ian CAMPBELL FOLK GROUP
UK, male vocal / instrumental group **5 wks**

11 Mar 65	THE TIMES THEY ARE A-CHANGIN' *Transatlantic SP 5*	...42	2 wks
1 Apr 65	THE TIMES THEY ARE A-CHANGIN' (re-entry) *Transatlantic SP 5*	...47	1 wk
15 Apr 65	THE TIMES THEY ARE A-CHANGIN' (2nd re-entry) *Transatlantic SP 5*	...46	2 wks

CAN *Germany, male vocal / instrumental group* **10 wks**

28 Aug 76	I WANT MORE *Virgin VS 153*	...26	10 wks

CANDIDO *US, male multi-instrumentalist* **3 wks**

18 Jul 81	JINGO *Excaliber EXC 102*	...55	3 wks

CANDLEWICK GREEN
UK, male vocal / instrumental duo **8 wks**

23 Feb 74	WHO DO YOU THINK YOU ARE *Decca F 13480*	...21	8 wks

CANDY FLIP *UK, male vocal / instrumental duo* **14 wks**

17 Mar 90	● STRAWBERRY FIELDS FOREVER *Debut DEBT 3092*	...3	10 wks
14 Jul 90	THIS CAN BE REAL *Debut DEBT 3099*	...60	4 wks

CANDYLAND *UK, male vocal / instrumental group* **1 wk**

9 Mar 91	FOUNTAIN O' YOUTH *Non Fiction YES 4*	...72	1 wk

CANNED HEAT *US, male vocal / instrumental group* **41 wks**

24 Jul 68	● ON THE ROAD AGAIN *Liberty LBS 15090*	...8	15 wks

1 Jan 69	GOING UP THE COUNTRY *Liberty LBF 15169* **19**	10 wks
17 Jan 70 ●	LET'S WORK TOGETHER *Liberty LBF 15302* **2**	15 wks
11 Jul 70	SUGAR BEE *Liberty LBF 15350* **49**	1 wk

Freddy CANNON US, male vocalist   **51 wks**

14 Aug 59	TALLAHASSEE LASSIE *Top Rank JAR 135*................**17**	8 wks
1 Jan 60 ●	WAY DOWN YONDER IN NEW ORLEANS	
	Top Rank JAR 247 ....**3**	16 wks
10 Mar 60	CALIFORNIA HERE I COME *Top Rank JAR 309*.......**33**	1 wk
17 Mar 60	INDIANA *Top Rank JAR 309* **42**	1 wk
24 Mar 60	CALIFORNIA HERE I COME (re-entry)	
	Top Rank JAR 309 ....**46**	1 wk
19 May 60	THE URGE *Top Rank JAR 369* **18**	10 wks
20 Apr 61	MUSKRAT RAMBLE *Top Rank JAR 548* **32**	5 wks
28 Jun 62	PALISADES PARK *Stateside SS 101* **20**	9 wks

Jim CAPALDI UK, male vocalist   **17 wks**

| 27 Jul 74 | IT'S ALL UP TO YOU *Island WIP 6198* ....**27** | 6 wks |
| 25 Oct 75 ● | LOVE HURTS *Island WIP 6246* ....**4** | 11 wks |

CAPERCAILLIE
UK, male / female vocal / instrumental group   **2 wks**

| 23 May 92 | A PRINCE AMONG ISLANDS EP *Survival ZB 45393*..**39** | 2 wks |

Tracks on A Prince Among Islands EP: Coisich A Ruin (Walk My Beloved) / Fagail Bhearnaraid (Leaving Bernaray) / The Lorn Theme / Gun Teann Mi Ris Na Ruinn Tha Seo (Remembrance).

CAPPELLA Italy, male producer - Gianfranco Bortolotti   **64 wks**

9 Apr 88	PUSH THE BEAT / BAUHAUS *Fast Globe FGL 1* **60**	2 wks
6 May 89	HELYOM HALIB *Music Man MMPS 7004* **11**	9 wks
23 Sep 89	HOUSE ENERGY REVENGE *Music Man MMPS 7009* **73**	1 wk
27 Apr 91	EVERYBODY *ffrr F158* **66**	1 wk
18 Jan 92	TAKE ME AWAY *PWL Continental PWL 210* [1] **25**	5 wks
3 Apr 93 ●	U GOT 2 KNOW *Internal Dance IDC 1* **6**	11 wks
14 Aug 93	U GOT 2 KNOW REVISITED (re-mix)	
	Internal Dance IDCR 2 ....**43**	3 wks
23 Oct 93 ●	U GOT 2 LET THE MUSIC *Internal Dance IDC 3* **2**	12 wks
19 Feb 94 ●	MOVE ON BABY *Internal Dance IDC 4* **7**	7 wks
18 Jun 94 ●	U & ME *Internal Dance IDCC 6* **10**	7 wks
15 Oct 94	MOVE IT UP / BIG BEAT *Internal Dance IDC 7* **16**	6 wks

[1] Cappella featuring Loleatta Holloway

Act was fronted by a UK, male / female vocal duo from U Got 2 Let The Music.

See also 49ers.

Tony CAPSTICK and the CARLTON MAIN/FRICKLEY COLLIERY BAND
UK, male vocalist and male instrumental band   **8 wks**

| 21 Mar 81 ● | THE SHEFFIELD GRINDER / | |
| | CAPSTICK COMES HOME *Dingles SID 27* ....**3** | 8 wks |

CAPTAIN BEAKY - *See Keith MICHELL*

CAPTAIN HOLLYWOOD PROJECT
US / Germany, male / female vocal / instrumental group   **30 wks**

22 Sep 90 ●	I CAN'T STAND IT *BCM BCMR 395* [1] **7**	10 wks
24 Nov 90	ARE YOU DREAMING *BCM BCM 07504* [1] **17**	10 wks
27 Mar 93	ONLY WITH YOU *Pulse 8 CDLOSE 40* **67**	1 wk
6 Nov 93	MORE AND MORE *Pulse 8 CDLOSE 50* **23**	5 wks
5 Feb 94	IMPOSSIBLE *Pulse 8 CDLOSE 54*................................**29**	3 wks
11 Jun 94	ONLY WITH YOU (re-issue) *Pulse 8 CDLOSE 62* **61**	1 wk

[1] Twenty 4 Seven featuring Captain Hollywood

CAPTAIN SENSIBLE UK, male vocalist   **31 wks**

| 26 Jun 82 ★ | HAPPY TALK *A & M CAP 1* ....**1** | 8 wks |

14 Aug 82	WOT *A & M CAP 2* **26**	7 wks
24 Mar 84 ●	GLAD IT'S ALL OVER / DAMNED ON	
	45 *A & M CAP 6* **6**	10 wks
28 Jul 84	THERE ARE MORE SNAKES THAN LADDERS	
	A & M CAP 7 ....**57**	5 wks
10 Dec 94	THE HOKEY COKEY *Have A Nice Day CDHOKEY 1*....**71**	1 wk

CAPTAIN and TENNILLE
US, male instrumentalist - keyboards and female vocalist   **24 wks**

2 Aug 75	LOVE WILL KEEP US TOGETHER	
	A & M AMS 7165 ....**32**	5 wks
24 Jan 76	THE WAY I WANT TO TOUCH YOU	
	A & M AMS 7203 ....**28**	6 wks
4 Nov 78	YOU NEVER DONE IT LIKE THAT	
	A & M AMS 7384 ....**63**	3 wks
16 Feb 80 ●	DO THAT TO ME ONE MORE TIME	
	Casablanca CAN 175 ....**7**	10 wks

Irene CARA US, female vocalist   **33 wks**

3 Jul 82 ★	FAME *RSO 90* **1**	16 wks
4 Sep 82	OUT HERE ON MY OWN *RSO 66* **58**	3 wks
4 Jun 83 ●	FLASHDANCE ... WHAT A FEELING	
	Casablanca CAN 1016...**2**	14 wks

CARAMBA
Sweden, male vocalist / multi-instrumentalist dog impersonator - Michael Tretow   **6 wks**

| 12 Nov 83 | FEDORA (I'LL BE YOUR DAWG) *Billco BILL 101* ......**56** | 6 wks |

CARAVELLES UK, female vocal duo   **13 wks**

| 8 Aug 63 ● | YOU DON'T HAVE TO BE A BABY TO CRY | |
| | *Decca F 11697* ....**6** | 13 wks |

CARE UK, male vocal / instrumental duo   **4 wks**

| 12 Nov 83 | FLAMING SWORD *Arista KBIRD 2* ....**48** | 4 wks |

Mariah CAREY US, female vocalist   **121 wks**

4 Aug 90 ●	VISION OF LOVE *CBS 6559320* **9**	12 wks
10 Nov 90	LOVE TAKES TIME *CBS 6563647* **37**	8 wks
26 Jan 91	SOMEDAY *Columbia 6565837* **38**	5 wks
1 Jun 91	THERE'S GOT TO BE A WAY *Columbia 6569317* **54**	3 wks
5 Oct 91	EMOTIONS *Columbia 6574037* **17**	9 wks
11 Jan 92	CAN'T LET GO *Columbia 6576627* **20**	7 wks
18 Apr 92	MAKE IT HAPPEN *Columbia 6579417* **17**	5 wks
27 Jun 92 ●	I'LL BE THERE *Columbia 6581377* **2**	9 wks
21 Aug 93 ●	DREAMLOVER *Columbia 6594445* **9**	10 wks
6 Nov 93 ●	HERO *Columbia 6598122*...**7**	15 wks
19 Feb 94 ★	WITHOUT YOU *Columbia 6599192*...............................**1**	14 wks
18 Jun 94 ●	ANYTIME YOU NEED A FRIEND *Columbia 6603542*..**8**	10 wks
17 Sep 94 ●	ENDLESS LOVE *Epic 6608062* [1] **3**	10 wks
10 Dec 94 ●	ALL I WANT FOR CHRISTMAS IS YOU	
	Columbia 6610702 ....**2†**	4 wks

[1] Luther Vandross and Mariah Carey

Although he is uncredited, I'll Be There is a duet with Trey Lorenz.

CARL - *See CLUBHOUSE*

Belinda CARLISLE US, female vocalist   **126 wks**

12 Dec 87 ★	HEAVEN IS A PLACE ON EARTH *Virgin VS 1036* **1**	14 wks
27 Feb 88 ●	I GET WEAK *Virgin VS 1046* **10**	9 wks
7 May 88 ●	CIRCLE IN THE SAND *Virgin VS 1074* **4**	11 wks
6 Aug 88	MAD ABOUT YOU *IRS IRM 118* **67**	3 wks
10 Sep 88	WORLD WITHOUT YOU *Virgin VS 1114*.....................**34**	6 wks
10 Dec 88	LOVE NEVER DIES... *Virgin VS 1150* **54**	5 wks
7 Oct 89 ●	LEAVE A LIGHT ON *Virgin VS 1210* **4**	10 wks

9 Dec 89	LA LUNA *Virgin VS 1230*	**38**	6 wks
24 Feb 90	RUNAWAY HORSES *Virgin VS 1244* ...	**40**	5 wks
26 May 90	VISION OF YOU *Virgin VS 1264*	**41**	4 wks
13 Oct 90 ●	(WE WANT) THE SAME THING *Virgin VS 1219* ...	**6**	10 wks
22 Dec 90	SUMMER RAIN *Virgin VS 1323*	**23**	10 wks
20 Apr 91	VISION OF YOU (re-entry) *Virgin VS 1264* ...	**71**	1 wk
28 Sep 91	LIVE YOUR LIFE BE FREE *Virgin VS 1370* ...	**12**	7 wks
16 Nov 91	DO YOU FEEL LIKE I FEEL *Virgin VS 1383* ...	**29**	4 wks
11 Jan 92	HALF THE WORLD *Virgin VS 1388* ...	**35**	4 wks
29 Aug 92	LITTLE BLACK BOOK *Virgin VS 1428* ...	**28**	5 wks
25 Sep 93	BIG SCARY ANIMAL *Virgin VSCDT 1472* ...	**12**	6 wks
27 Nov 93	LAY DOWN YOUR ARMS *Virgin VSCDG 1476* ...	**27**	6 wks

Sara CARLSON - *See MANIC MC's featuring Sara CARLSON*

CARLTON *UK, male vocalist*   **2 wks**

16 Feb 91	LOVE AND PAIN *Smith & Mighty SNM 4* ...	**56**	2 wks

Carl CARLTON *US, male vocalist*   **8 wks**

18 Jul 81	SHE'S A BAD MAMA JAMA (SHE'S BUILT, SHE'S STACKED) *20th Century TC 2488* ...	**34**	8 wks

Larry CARLTON - *See Mike POST*

CARLTON MAIN/FRICKLEY COLLIERY BAND - *See Tony CAPSTICK and the CARLTON MAIN/FRICKLEY COLLIERY BAND*

CARMEL *UK, female / male vocal / instrumental group*   **19 wks**

6 Aug 83	BAD DAY *London LON 29*	**15**	9 wks
11 Feb 84	MORE, MORE, MORE *London LON 44* ...	**23**	7 wks
14 Jun 86	SALLY *London LON 90*	**60**	3 wks

Eric CARMEN *US, male vocalist*   **7 wks**

10 Apr 76	ALL BY MYSELF *Arista 42*	**12**	7 wks

Jean CARN - *See Bobby M featuring Jean CARN*

Kim CARNEGIE *UK, female vocalist*   **1 wk**

19 Jan 91	JAZZ RAP *Best ZB 44085*	**73**	1 wk

Kim CARNES *US, female vocalist*   **15 wks**

9 May 81 ●	BETTE DAVIS EYES *EMI America EA 121* ...	**10**	9 wks
8 Aug 81	DRAW OF THE CARDS *EMI America EA 125* ...	**49**	4 wks
9 Oct 82	VOYEUR *EMI America EA 143*	**68**	2 wks

Renato CAROSONE and his SEXTET
Italy, male vocalist and instrumental backing group   **1 wk**

4 Jul 58	TORERO - CHA CHA CHA *Parlophone R 4433* ...	**25**	1 wk

Mary Chapin CARPENTER *US, female vocalist*   **1 wk**

20 Nov 93	HE THINKS HE'LL KEEP HER *Columbia 6598632* ...	**71**	1 wk

CARPENTERS
US, male / female vocal / instrumental duo   **173 wks**

5 Sep 70 ●	(THEY LONG TO BE) CLOSE TO YOU *A & M AMS 800* ...	**6**	18 wks
9 Jan 71	WE'VE ONLY JUST BEGUN *A & M AMS 813* ...	**28**	7 wks
18 Sep 71	SUPERSTAR / FOR ALL WE KNOW *A & M AMS 864* ...	**18**	13 wks
1 Jan 72	MERRY CHRISTMAS DARLING *A & M AME 601* ...	**45**	1 wk
23 Sep 72 ●	I WON'T LAST A DAY WITHOUT YOU / GOODBYE TO LOVE *A & M AMS 7023* ...	**9**	16 wks

7 Jul 73 ●	YESTERDAY ONCE MORE *A & M AMS 7073* ...	**2**	17 wks
20 Oct 73 ●	TOP OF THE WORLD *A & M AMS 7086* ...	**5**	18 wks
2 Mar 74	JAMBALAYA (ON THE BAYOU) / MR. GUDER *A & M AMS 7098* ...	**12**	11 wks
8 Jun 74	I WON'T LAST A DAY WITHOUT YOU (re-issue) *A & M AMS 7111* ...	**32**	5 wks
18 Jan 75 ●	PLEASE MR. POSTMAN *A & M AMS 7141* ...	**2**	12 wks
19 Apr 75	ONLY YESTERDAY *A & M AMS 7159* ...	**7**	10 wks
30 Aug 75	SOLITAIRE *A & M AMS 7187*	**32**	5 wks
20 Dec 75	SANTA CLAUS IS COMIN' TO TOWN *A & M AMS 7144* ...	**37**	4 wks
27 Mar 76	THERE'S A KIND OF HUSH (ALL OVER THE WORLD) *A & M AMS 7219* ...	**22**	6 wks
3 Jul 76	I NEED TO BE IN LOVE *A & M AMS 7238* ...	**36**	5 wks
8 Oct 77 ●	CALLING OCCUPANTS OF INTERPLANETARY CRAFT (THE RECOGNISED ANTHEM OF WORLD CONTACT DAY) *A & M AMS 7318* ...	**9**	9 wks
11 Feb 78	SWEET SWEET SMILE *A & M AMS 7327* ...	**40**	4 wks
22 Oct 83	MAKE BELIEVE IT'S YOUR FIRST TIME *A & M AM 147* ...	**60**	3 wks
8 Dec 90	MERRY CHRISTMAS DARLING / (THEY LONG TO BE) CLOSE TO YOU (re-issue) *A & M AM 716* ...	**25**	5 wks
13 Feb 93	RAINY DAYS AND MONDAYS *A & M AMCD 0180* ...	**63**	2 wks
24 Dec 94	TRYIN' TO GET THE FEELING AGAIN *A & M 5807612* ...	**44†**	2 wks

I Won't Last A Day Without You AMS 703 listed by itself 23 Sep 72 at position 49. Goodbye To Love, the other side, listed by itself from 30 Sep 72 until the end of the record's chart run. Mr. Guder listed with Jambalaya from 16 Mar 74 until the end of the record's chart run.

Joe 'Fingers' CARR
US, male instrumentalist - piano, Lou Busch under a false name   **5 wks**

29 Jun 56	PORTUGUESE WASHERWOMAN *Capitol CL 14587* ...	**20**	5 wks

See also Lou Busch.

Linda CARR *US, female vocalist*   **12 wks**

12 Jul 75	HIGHWIRE *Chelsea 2005 025* [1] ...	**15**	8 wks
5 Jun 76	SOLD MY ROCK 'N' ROLL (GAVE IT FOR FUNKY SOUL) *Spark SRL 1139* [2] ...	**36**	4 wks

[1] Linda Carr and the Love Squad   [2] Linda and the Funky Boys

Pearl CARR and Teddy JOHNSON
UK, female / male vocal duo   **19 wks**

20 Mar 59	SING LITTLE BIRDIE *Columbia DB 4275* ...	**12**	8 wks
6 Apr 61	HOW WONDERFUL TO KNOW *Columbia DB 4603* ...	**23**	11 wks

Suzi CARR *US, female vocalist*   **1 wk**

8 Oct 94	ALL OVER ME *Cowboy RODEO 947CD* ...	**45**	1 wk

Valerie CARR *US, female vocalist*   **2 wks**

4 Jul 58	WHEN THE BOYS TALK ABOUT THE GIRLS *Columbia DB 4131* ...	**29**	1 wk
18 Jul 58	WHEN THE BOYS TALK ABOUT THE GIRLS (re-entry) *Columbia DB 4131* ...	**30**	1 wk

Vikki CARR *US, female vocalist*   **26 wks**

1 Jun 67 ●	IT MUST BE HIM (SEUL SUR SON ETOILE) *Liberty LIB 55917* ...	**2**	20 wks
30 Aug 67	THERE I GO *Liberty LBF 15022* ...	**50**	1 wk
12 Mar 69	WITH PEN IN HAND *Liberty LBF 15166* ...	**43**	1 wk
26 Mar 69	WITH PEN IN HAND (re-entry) *Liberty LBF 15166* ...	**39**	2 wks
30 Apr 69	WITH PEN IN HAND (2nd re-entry) *Liberty LBF 15166* ...	**40**	2 wks

Raffaella CARRA *Italy, female vocalist*   **12 wks**

15 Apr 78 ● DO IT DO IT AGAIN *Epic EPC 6094* ....**9** 12 wks

Paul CARRACK *UK, male vocalist*   **8 wks**

16 May 87	**WHEN YOU WALK IN THE ROOM** *Chrysalis CHS 3109* **48**	5 wks
18 Mar 89	**DON'T SHED A TEAR** *Chrysalis CHS 3164* **60**	3 wks

José CARRERAS *Spain, male vocalist*   **15 wks**

11 Jul 92	**AMIGOS PARA SIEMPRE (FRIENDS FOR LIFE)** *Really Useful RUR 10* [1] **11**	11 wks
30 Jul 94	**LIBIAMO / LA DONNA E MOBILE** *Teldec YZ 843CD* [2] **21**	4 wks

[1] José Carreras and Sarah Brightman [2] José Carreras, Placido Domingo and Luciano Pavarotti

Tia CARRERE *US, female vocalist*   **6 wks**

30 May 92   **BALLROOM BLITZ** *Reprise W 0105* ....**26** 6 wks

Dina CARROLL *UK, female vocalist*   **74 wks**

2 Feb 91	● **IT'S TOO LATE** *Mercury ITM 3* [1] **8**	14 wks
15 Jun 91	**NAKED LOVE (JUST SAY YOU WANT ME)** *Mercury ITM 4* [2] **39**	3 wks
11 Jul 92	**AIN'T NO MAN** *A & M AM 0001* **16**	8 wks
10 Oct 92	**SPECIAL KIND OF LOVE** *A & M AM 0088* **16**	5 wks
5 Dec 92	**SO CLOSE** *A & M AM 0101* **20**	8 wks
27 Feb 93	**THIS TIME** *A & M AMCD 0184* **23**	6 wks
15 May 93	**EXPRESS** *A & M 5802632* **12**	6 wks
16 Oct 93	● **DON'T BE A STRANGER** *A & M 5803892* **3**	13 wks
11 Dec 93	● **THE PERFECT YEAR** *A & M 5804812* **5**	11 wks

[1] Quartz introducing Dina Carroll [2] Quartz and Dina Carroll

Ronnie CARROLL *UK, male vocalist*   **50 wks**

27 Jul 56	**WALK HAND IN HAND** *Philips PB 605* **13**	8 wks
29 Mar 57	**THE WISDOM OF A FOOL** *Philips PB 667* **20**	2 wks
31 Mar 60	**FOOTSTEPS** *Philips PB 1004* **36**	3 wks
22 Feb 62	**RING A DING GIRL** *Philips PB 1222* **46**	3 wks
2 Aug 62	● **ROSES ARE RED** *Philips 326532 BF* **3**	16 wks
15 Nov 62	**IF ONLY TOMORROW** *Philips 326550 BF* **33**	4 wks
7 Mar 63	● **SAY WONDERFUL THINGS** *Philips 326574 BF*.....**6**	14 wks

Jasper CARROTT *UK, male vocalist*   **15 wks**

16 Aug 75 ● **FUNKY MOPED / MAGIC ROUNDABOUT** *DJM DJS 388* ....**5** 15 wks

CARS *US, male vocal / instrumental group*   **51 wks**

11 Nov 78	● **MY BEST FRIEND'S GIRL** *Elektra K 12301* **3**	10 wks
17 Feb 79	**JUST WHAT I NEEDED** *Elektra K 12312*......**17**	10 wks
28 Jul 79	**LET'S GO** *Elektra K 12371* **51**	4 wks
5 Jun 82	**SINCE YOU'RE GONE** *Elektra K 13177* **37**	4 wks
29 Sep 84	● **DRIVE** *Elektra E 9706* **5**	11 wks
3 Aug 85	● **DRIVE (re-entry)** *Elektra E 9706* **4**	12 wks

CARTER - THE UNSTOPPABLE SEX MACHINE
UK, male vocal / instrumental duo   **41 wks**

26 Jan 91	**BLOODSPORTS FOR ALL** *Rough Trade R 20112687* ..**48**	2 wks
22 Jun 91	**SHERIFF FATMAN** *Big Cat USM 1* **23**	7 wks
26 Oct 91	**AFTER THE WATERSHED** *Big Cat USM 2*..........**11**	5 wks
11 Jan 92	**RUBBISH** *Big Cat USM 3* **14**	5 wks
25 Apr 92	● **THE ONLY LIVING BOY IN NEW CROSS** *Big Cat USM 4* **7**	5 wks
4 Jul 92	**DO RE ME SO FAR SO GOOD** *Chrysalis USM 5*..........**22**	3 wks

28 Nov 92	**THE IMPOSSIBLE DREAM** *Chrysalis USM 6*...........**21**	3 wks
4 Sep 93	**LEAN ON ME I WON'T FALL OVER** *Chrysalis CDUSM 7* **16**	3 wks
16 Oct 93	**LENNY AND TERENCE** *Chrysalis CDUSM 8* **40**	2 wks
12 Mar 94	**GLAM ROCK COPS** *Chrysalis CDUSM 10* **24**	3 wks
19 Nov 94	**LET'S GET TATTOOS** *Chrysalis CDUSMS 30* **30**	3 wks

Clarence CARTER *US, male vocalist*   **13 wks**

10 Oct 70 ● **PATCHES** *Atlantic 2091 030*............................**2** 13 wks

CARVELLS *UK, male vocalist / instrumentalist - Alan Carvell*   **4 wks**

26 Nov 77   **THE L.A. RUN** *Creole CR 143*...........................**31** 4 wks

CASCADES *US, male vocal group*   **16 wks**

28 Feb 63 ● **RHYTHM OF THE RAIN** *Warner Bros. WB 88* ....**5** 16 wks

Natalie CASEY *UK, female vocalist*   **1 wk**

7 Jan 84   **CHICK CHICK CHICKEN** *Polydor CHICK 1* ....**72** 1 wk

Johnny CASH *US, male vocalist*   **59 wks**

3 Jun 65	**IT AIN'T ME BABE** *CBS 201760* **28**	8 wks
6 Sep 69	● **A BOY NAMED SUE** *CBS 4460* **4**	19 wks
23 May 70	**WHAT IS TRUTH** *CBS 4934* **21**	11 wks
15 Apr 72	● **A THING CALLED LOVE** *CBS 7797* [1] **4**	13 wks
22 Jul 72	**A THING CALLED LOVE (re-entry)** *CBS 7797* [1] **48**	1 wk
3 Jul 76	**ONE PIECE AT A TIME** *CBS 4287* [2] **32**	7 wks

[1] Johnny Cash with the Evangel Temple Choir [2] Johnny Cash with the Tennessee Three

Pat CASH - *See John McENROE and Pat CASH with the FULL METAL RACKETS*

CASHFLOW *US, male vocal / instrumental group*   **8 wks**

24 May 86   **MINE ALL MINE / PARTY FREAK** *Club JAB 30* ....**15** 8 wks

CASHMERE *US, male vocal / instrumental group*   **11 wks**

19 Jan 85	**CAN I** *Fourth & Broadway BRW 19*...........................**29**	8 wks
23 Mar 85	**WE NEED LOVE** *Fourth & Broadway BRW 22* **52**	3 wks

CASINOS *US, male vocal group*   **7 wks**

23 Feb 67   **THEN YOU CAN TELL ME GOODBYE** *President PT 123*......................................**28** 7 wks

David CASSIDY *US, male vocalist*   **109 wks**

8 Apr 72	● **COULD IT BE FOREVER / CHERISH** *Bell 1224* **2**	17 wks
16 Sep 72	★ **HOW CAN I BE SURE** *Bell 1258* **1**	11 wks
25 Nov 72	**ROCK ME BABY** *Bell 1268* **11**	9 wks
24 Mar 73	● **I'M A CLOWN / SOME KIND OF A SUMMER** *Bell MABEL 4* **3**	12 wks
13 Oct 73	★ **DAYDREAMER / THE PUPPY SONG** *Bell 1334* **1**	15 wks
11 May 74	● **IF I DIDN'T CARE** *Bell 1350* **9**	8 wks
27 Jul 74	**PLEASE PLEASE ME** *Bell 1371* **16**	6 wks
5 Jul 75	**I WRITE THE SONGS / GET IT UP FOR LOVE** *RCA 2571* **11**	8 wks
25 Oct 75	**DARLIN'** *RCA 2622* **16**	8 wks
23 Feb 85	● **THE LAST KISS** *Arista ARIST 589* **6**	9 wks
11 May 85	**ROMANCE (LET YOUR HEART GO)** *Arista ARIST 620* **54**	6 wks

See also Partridge Family starring Shirley Jones featuring David Cassidy.

Roy CASTLE UK, male vocalist — 3 wks

22 Dec 60	LITTLE WHITE BERRY Philips PB 1087	40	3 wks

CASUALS UK, male vocal / instrumental group — 26 wks

14 Aug 68	● JESAMINE Decca F 22784	2	18 wks
4 Dec 68	TOY Decca F 22852	30	8 wks

CAT UK, male vocalist — 4 wks

23 Oct 93	TONGUE TIED EMI CDEM 286	17	4 wks

CATCH UK, male vocal / instrumental group — 1 wk

17 Nov 90	FREE (C'MON) ffrr F 147	70	1 wk

CATHERINE WHEEL
UK, male vocal / instrumental group — 8 wks

23 Nov 91	BLACK METALLIC (EP) Fontana CW 1	68	1 wk
8 Feb 92	BALLOON Fontana CW 2	59	1 wk
18 Apr 92	I WANT TO TOUCH YOU Fontana CW 3	35	2 wks
9 Jan 93	30 CENTURY MAN Fontana CWCD 4	47	2 wks
10 Jul 93	CRANK Fontana CWCD 5	66	1 wk
16 Oct 93	SHOW ME MARY Fonatana CWCDA 6	62	1 wk

Tracks on Black Metallic (EP): Black Metallic / Crawling Over Me / Let Me Down Again / Saccharine.

Lorraine CATO UK, female vocalist — 2 wks

6 Feb 93	HOW CAN YOU TELL ME IT'S OVER Columbia 6587662	46	2 wks

CATS UK, male instrumental group — 2 wks

9 Apr 69	SWAN LAKE BAF 1	48	1 wk
21 May 69	SWAN LAKE (re-entry) BAF 1	50	1 wk

CATS U.K. UK, female vocal group — 8 wks

6 Oct 79	LUTON AIRPORT WEA K 18075	22	8 wks

Nick CAVE and the BAD SEEDS
Australia / Germany, male vocal / instrumental group — 3 wks

11 Apr 92	STRAIGHT TO YOU / JACK THE RIPPER Mute MUTE 140	68	1 wk
12 Dec 92	WHAT A WONDERFUL WORLD Mute MUTE 151 [1]	72	1 wk
9 Apr 94	DO YOU LOVE ME Mute CDMUTE 160	68	1 wk

[1] Nick Cave and Shane McGowan

CAVEMAN UK, male rap group — 2 wks

9 Mar 91	I'M READY Profile PROF 330	65	2 wks

C.C.S. UK, male vocal / instrumental group — 55 wks

31 Oct 70	WHOLE LOTTA LOVE RAK 104	13	13 wks
27 Feb 71	● WALKIN' RAK 109	7	16 wks
4 Sep 71	● TAP TURNS ON THE WATER RAK 119	5	13 wks
4 Mar 72	BROTHER RAK 126	25	8 wks
4 Aug 73	BAND PLAYED THE BOOGIE RAK 154	36	5 wks

CENTORY US, male rapper — 1 wk

17 Dec 94	POINT OF NO RETURN EMI CDEM 354	67	1 wk

CENTRAL LINE UK, male vocal / instrumental group — 30 wks

31 Jan 81	(YOU KNOW) YOU CAN DO IT Mercury LINE 7	67	3 wks
15 Aug 81	WALKING INTO SUNSHINE Mercury MER 78	42	10 wks
30 Jan 82	DON'T TELL ME Mercury MER 90	55	3 wks
20 Nov 82	YOU'VE SAID ENOUGH Mercury MER 117	58	3 wks
22 Jan 83	NATURE BOY Mercury MER 131	21	8 wks
11 Jun 83	SURPRISE SURPRISE Mercury MER 133	48	3 wks

CERRONE France, male producer / multi-instrumentalist — 20 wks

5 Mar 77	LOVE IN C MINOR Atlantic K 10895	31	4 wks
29 Jul 78	● SUPER NATURE Atlantic K 11089	8	12 wks
13 Jan 79	JE SUIS MUSIC CBS 6918	39	4 wks

A CERTAIN RATIO UK, male vocal / instrumental group — 3 wks

16 Jun 90	WON'T STOP LOVING YOU A & M ACR 540	55	3 wks

Peter CETERA US, male vocalist — 13 wks

2 Aug 86	● GLORY OF LOVE Full Moon W 8662	3	13 wks

Frank CHACKSFIELD UK, orchestra — 41 wks

3 Apr 53	● LITTLE RED MONKEY Parlophone R 3658 [1]	10	3 wks
22 May 53	● TERRY'S THEME FROM 'LIMELIGHT' Decca F 10106	2	24 wks
12 Feb 54	● EBB TIDE Decca F 10122	9	2 wks
24 Feb 56	IN OLD LISBON Decca F 10689	15	4 wks
18 May 56	PORT AU PRINCE Decca F 10727 [2]	18	6 wks
31 Aug 56	DONKEY CART Decca F 10743	26	2 wks

[1] Frank Chacksfield's Tunesmiths, featuring Jack Jordan - clavioline [2] Winifred Atwell and Frank Chacksfield

CHAIRMEN OF THE BOARD US, male vocal group — 77 wks

22 Aug 70	● GIVE ME JUST A LITTLE MORE TIME Invictus INV 501	3	13 wks
14 Nov 70	● YOU'VE GOT ME DANGLING ON A STRING Invictus INV 504	5	13 wks
20 Feb 71	EVERYTHING'S TUESDAY Invictus INV 507	12	9 wks
15 May 71	PAY TO THE PIPER Invictus INV 511	34	7 wks
4 Sep 71	CHAIRMAN OF THE BOARD Invictus INV 516	48	2 wks
15 Jul 72	WORKING ON A BUILDING OF LOVE Invictus INV 519	20	8 wks
7 Oct 72	ELMO JAMES Invictus INV 524	21	7 wks
16 Dec 72	I'M ON MY WAY TO A BETTER PLACE Invictus INV 527	38	1 wk
13 Jan 73	I'M ON MY WAY TO A BETTER PLACE (re-entry) Invictus INV 527	30	5 wks
23 Jun 73	FINDERS KEEPERS Invictus INV 530	21	9 wks
13 Sep 86	LOVERBOY EMI EMI 5585 [1]	56	3 wks

[1] Chairmen Of The Board featuring General Johnson

CHAKACHAS
Belgium, male / female vocal / instrumental group — 8 wks

11 Jan 62	TWIST TWIST RCA 1264	48	1 wk
27 May 72	JUNGLE FEVER Polydor 2121 064	29	7 wks

George CHAKIRIS US, male vocalist — 1 wk

2 Jun 60	HEART OF A TEENAGE GIRL Triumph RGM 1010	49	1 wk

Sue CHALONER UK, female vocalist — 1 wk

22 May 93	MOVE ON UP Pulse 8 CDLOSE 41	64	1 wk

Richard CHAMBERLAIN US, male vocalist — 36 wks

7 Jun 62	THEME FROM 'DR. KILDARE' (THREE STARS WILL SHINE TONIGHT) MGM 1160	12	10 wks
1 Nov 62	LOVE ME TENDER MGM 1173	15	11 wks
21 Feb 63	HI-LILI HI-LO MGM 1189	20	9 wks

18 Jul 63 **TRUE LOVE** *MGM 1205* ....**30** 6 wks

CHAMELEONS - *See LORI and the CHAMELEONS*

CHAMPAIGN
US, male / female vocal / instrumental group   **13 wks**

9 May 81 ● **HOW 'BOUT US** *CBS A 1046* ....**5** 13 wks

CHAMPION LEGEND - *See RAZE*

CHAMPS *US, male instrumental group*   **10 wks**

4 Apr 58 ● **TEQUILA** *London HLU 8580* ....**5** 9 wks
17 Mar 60   **TOO MUCH TEQUILA** *London HLH 9052* ....**49** 1 wk

CHAMPS BOYS *France, male instrumental group*   **6 wks**

19 Jun 76   **TUBULAR BELLS** *Philips 6006 519* ....**41** 6 wks

Gene CHANDLER *US, male vocalist*   **29 wks**

5 Jun 68   **NOTHING CAN STOP ME** *Soul City SC 102* ....**41** 4 wks
3 Feb 79   **GET DOWN** *20th Century BTC 1040* ....**11** 11 wks
1 Sep 79   **WHEN YOU'RE NUMBER 1** *20th Century TC 2411* ....**43** 5 wks
28 Jun 80   **DOES SHE HAVE A FRIEND** *20th Century TC 2451* ..**28** 9 wks

CHANELLE *US, female vocalist*   **9 wks**

11 Mar 89   **ONE MAN** *Cooltempo COOL 183* ....**16** 8 wks
10 Dec 94   **ONE MAN (re-mix)** *Deep Distraxion OILYCD 031* ....**50** 1 wk

CHANGE *US, male / female vocal / instrumental group*   **43 wks**

28 Jun 80   **A LOVER'S HOLIDAY / GLOW OF LOVE**
    WEA K 79141 ....**14** 8 wks
6 Sep 80   **SEARCHING** *WEA K 79156* ....**11** 10 wks
2 Jun 84   **CHANGE OF HEART** *WEA YZ 7* ....**17** 10 wks
11 Aug 84   **YOU ARE MY MELODY** *WEA YZ 14* ....**48** 4 wks
16 Mar 85   **LET'S GO TOGETHER** *Cooltempo COOL 107* ....**37** 7 wks
25 May 85   **OH WHAT A FEELING** *Cooltempo COOL 109* ....**56** 2 wks
13 Jul 85   **MUTUAL ATTRACTION** *Cooltempo COOL 111* ....**60** 2 wks

CHANGING FACES *US, female vocal duo*   **3 wks**

24 Sep 94   **STROKE YOU UP** *Big Beat A 8251CD* ....**43** 3 wks

Bruce CHANNEL *US, male vocalist*   **28 wks**

22 Mar 62 ● **HEY! BABY** *Mercury AMT 1171* ....**2** 12 wks
26 Jun 68   **KEEP ON** *Bell 1010* ....**12** 16 wks

CHANNEL X
Belgium, male / female vocal / instrumental group   **1 wk**

14 Dec 91   **GROOVE TO MOVE** *PWL Continental PWL 209* ....**67** 1 wk

CHANSON *US, male / female vocal group*   **7 wks**

13 Jan 79   **DON'T HOLD BACK** *Ariola ARO 140* ....**33** 7 wks

CHANTAYS *US, male instrumental group*   **14 wks**

18 Apr 63   **PIPELINE** *London HLD 9696* ....**16** 14 wks

CHANTER SISTERS *UK, female vocal group*   **5 wks**

17 Jul 76   **SIDE SHOW** *Polydor 2058 735* ....**43** 5 wks

---

CHAOS *UK, male vocal group*   **2 wks**

3 Oct 92   **FAREWELL MY SUMMER LOVE**
    Arista 74321116397 ....**55** 2 wks

Harry CHAPIN *US, male vocalist*   **5 wks**

11 May 74   **W.O.L.D.** *Elektra K 12133* ....**34** 5 wks

SIMONE CHAPMAN - *See ILLEGAL MOTION featuring SIMONE CHAPMAN*

Tracy CHAPMAN *US, female vocalist*   **15 wks**

11 Jun 88 ● **FAST CAR** *Elektra EKR 73* ....**5** 12 wks
30 Sep 89   **CROSSROADS** *Elektra EKR 95* ....**61** 3 wks

CHAPTERHOUSE *UK, male vocal / instrumental group*   **3 wks**

30 Mar 91   **PEARL** *Dedicated STONE 003* ....**67** 1 wk
12 Oct 91   **MESMERISE** *Dedicated HOUSE 001* ....**60** 2 wks

CHAQUITO *UK, male arranger / conductor - Johnny Gregory*   **1 wk**

27 Oct 60   **NEVER ON SUNDAY** *Fontana H 265* ....**50** 1 wk

CHARLATANS *UK, male vocal / instrumental group*   **35 wks**

2 Jun 90 ● **THE ONLY ONE I KNOW** *Situation Two SIT 70T* ....**9** 9 wks
22 Sep 90   **THEN** *Situation Two SIT 74T* ....**12** 5 wks
9 Mar 91   **OVER RISING** *Situation Two SIT 76* ....**15** 5 wks
17 Aug 91   **INDIAN ROPE** *Dead Dead Good GOOD 1T* ....**57** 1 wk
9 Nov 91   **ME. IN TIME** *Situation Two SIT 84* ....**28** 3 wks
7 Mar 92   **WEIRDO** *Situation Two SIT 88* ....**19** 4 wks
18 Jul 92   **TREMELO SONG (EP)** *Situation Two SIT 97T* ....**44** 2 wks
5 Feb 94   **CAN'T GET OUT OF BED**
    Beggars Banquet BBQ 27CD ....**24** 3 wks
19 Mar 94   **I NEVER WANT AN EASY LIFE IF ME AND HE WERE**
    EVER TO GET THERE *Beggars Banquet BBQ 31CD* ..**38** 1 wk
2 Jul 94   **JESUS HAIRDO** *Beggars Banquet BBQ 32CD1* ....**48** 2 wks

Tracks on Tremelo Song (EP): Tremelo Song / Happen To Die / Normality Swing.

CHARLENE *US, female vocalist*   **12 wks**

15 May 82 ★ **I'VE NEVER BEEN TO ME** *Motown TMG 1260* ....**1** 12 wks

Don CHARLES *UK, male vocalist*   **5 wks**

22 Feb 62   **WALK WITH ME MY ANGEL** *Decca F 11424* ....**39** 5 wks

Ray CHARLES
US, male vocalist / instrumentalist - piano   **130 wks**

1 Dec 60   **GEORGIA ON MY MIND** *HMV POP 792* ....**47** 1 wk
15 Dec 60   **GEORGIA ON MY MIND (re-entry)** *HMV POP 792* ..**24** 7 wks
19 Oct 61 ● **HIT THE ROAD JACK** *HMV POP 935* ....**6** 12 wks
14 Jun 62 ★ **I CAN'T STOP LOVING YOU** *HMV POP 1034* ....**1** 17 wks
13 Sep 62 ● **YOU DON'T KNOW ME** *HMV POP 1064* ....**9** 13 wks
13 Dec 62   **YOUR CHEATING HEART** *HMV POP 1099* ....**13** 8 wks
28 Mar 63   **DON'T SET ME FREE** *HMV POP 1133* ....**37** 3 wks
16 May 63 ● **TAKE THESE CHAINS FROM MY HEART**
    HMV POP 1161 ....**5** 20 wks
12 Sep 63   **NO ONE** *HMV POP 1202* ....**35** 7 wks
31 Oct 63   **BUSTED** *HMV POP 1221* ....**21** 10 wks
24 Sep 64   **NO ONE TO CRY TO** *HMV POP 1333* ....**38** 3 wks
21 Jan 65   **MAKIN' WHOOPEE** *HMV POP 1383* ....**42** 4 wks
10 Feb 66   **CRYIN' TIME** *HMV POP 1502* ....**50** 1 wk
21 Apr 66   **TOGETHER AGAIN** *HMV POP 1519* ....**48** 1 wk
5 Jul 67   **HERE WE GO AGAIN** *HMV POP 1595* ....**38** 1 wk
19 Jul 67   **HERE WE GO AGAIN (re-entry)** *HMV POP 1595* .....**45** 2 wks

20 Dec 67	**YESTERDAY** *Stateside SS 2071*	.....**44**	4 wks
31 Jul 68	**ELEANOR RIGBY** *Stateside SS 2120*	.....**36**	9 wks
13 Jan 90	**I'LL BE GOOD TO YOU** *Qwest W 9992* [1]	.....**21**	7 wks

[1] Quincy Jones featuring Ray Charles and Chaka Khan

See also INXS.

Suzette CHARLES *US, female vocalist*　　　　**2 wks**

| 21 Aug 93 | **FREE TO LOVE AGAIN** *RCA 74321158372* | .....**58** | 2 wks |

Tina CHARLES *UK, female vocalist*　　　　**63 wks**

7 Feb 76	★ **I LOVE TO LOVE (BUT MY BABY LOVES TO DANCE)** *CBS 3937*	.....**1**	12 wks
1 May 76	**LOVE ME LIKE A LOVER** *CBS 4237*	.....**28**	7 wks
21 Aug 76	● **DANCE LITTLE LADY DANCE** *CBS 4480*	.....**6**	13 wks
4 Dec 76	● **DR. LOVE** *CBS 4779*	.....**4**	10 wks
14 May 77	**RENDEZVOUS** *CBS 5174*	.....**27**	6 wks
29 Oct 77	**LOVE BUG–SWEETS FOR MY SWEET (MEDLEY)** *CBS 5680*	.....**26**	4 wks
11 Mar 78	**I'LL GO WHERE YOUR MUSIC TAKES ME** *CBS 6062*	.....**27**	8 wks
30 Aug 86	**I LOVE TO LOVE (re-mix)** *DMC DECK 1*	.....**67**	3 wks

CHARLES and EDDIE *US, male vocal duo*　　　　**26 wks**

31 Oct 92	★ **WOULD I LIE TO YOU** *Capitol CL 673*	.....**1**	17 wks
20 Feb 93	**N.Y.C. (CAN YOU BELIEVE THIS CITY)** *Capitol CDCL 681*	.....**33**	5 wks
22 May 93	**HOUSE IS NOT A HOME** *Capitol CDCLS 688*	.....**29**	4 wks

Dick CHARLESWORTH and his CITY GENTS
UK, male jazz band group, Dick Charlesworth clarinet　　　　**1 wk**

| 4 May 61 | **BILLY BOY** *Top Rank JAR 558* | .....**43** | 1 wk |

CHARLOTTE *UK, female vocalist*　　　　**1 wk**

| 12 Mar 94 | **QUEEN OF HEARTS** *Big Life BLRD 106* | .....**54** | 1 wk |

CHARME *US, male / female vocal group*　　　　**2 wks**

| 17 Nov 84 | **GEORGY PORGY** *RCA 464* | .....**68** | 2 wks |

CHARO and the SALSOUL ORCHESTRA
US, female vocalist and orchestra　　　　**4 wks**

| 29 Apr 78 | **DANCE A LITTLE BIT CLOSER** *Salsoul SSOL 101* | .....**44** | 4 wks |

CHAS and DAVE *UK, male vocal / instrumental duo*　　　　**66 wks**

11 Nov 78	**STRUMMIN'** *EMI 2874* [1]	.....**52**	3 wks
26 May 79	**GERTCHA** *EMI 2947*	.....**20**	8 wks
1 Sep 79	**THE SIDEBOARD SONG (GOT MY BEER IN THE SIDEBOARD HERE)** *EMI 2986*	.....**55**	3 wks
29 Nov 80	● **RABBIT** *Rockney 9*	.....**8**	11 wks
12 Dec 81	**STARS OVER 45** *Rockney KOR 12*	.....**21**	8 wks
13 Mar 82	● **AIN'T NO PLEASING YOU** *Rockney KOR 14*	.....**2**	11 wks
17 Jul 82	**MARGATE** *Rockney KOR 15*	.....**46**	4 wks
19 Mar 83	**LONDON GIRLS** *Rockney KOR 17*	.....**63**	3 wks
3 Dec 83	**MY MELANCHOLY BABY** *Rockney KOR 21*	.....**51**	6 wks
3 May 86	● **SNOOKER LOOPY** *Rockney POT 147* [2]	.....**6**	9 wks

[1] Chas and Dave with Rockney　[2] Matchroom Mob with Chas and Dave

See also Tottenham Hotspur FA Cup Final Squad.

CHEAP TRICK *US, male vocal / instrumental group*　　　　**14 wks**

5 May 79	**I WANT YOU TO WANT ME** *Epic EPC 7258*	.....**29**	9 wks
2 Feb 80	**WAY OF THE WORLD** *Epic EPC 8114*	.....**73**	2 wks
31 Jul 82	**IF YOU WANT MY LOVE** *Epic EPC A 2406*	.....**57**	3 wks

Oliver CHEATHAM *US, male vocalist*　　　　**5 wks**

| 2 Jul 83 | **GET DOWN SATURDAY NIGHT** *MCA 828* | .....**38** | 5 wks |

CHECK 1-2 - *See Craig McLACHLAN*

Chubby CHECKER *US, male vocalist*　　　　**112 wks**

22 Sep 60	**THE TWIST** *Columbia DB 4503*	.....**49**	1 wk
6 Oct 60	**THE TWIST (re-entry)** *Columbia DB 4503*	.....**44**	1 wk
30 Mar 61	**PONY TIME** *Columbia DB 4591*	.....**27**	6 wks
17 Aug 61	**LET'S TWIST AGAIN** *Columbia DB 4691*	.....**37**	3 wks
28 Dec 61	● **LET'S TWIST AGAIN (re-entry)** *Columbia DB 4691*	.....**2**	27 wks
11 Jan 62	**THE TWIST (2nd re-entry)** *Columbia DB 4503*	.....**14**	10 wks
5 Apr 62	**SLOW TWISTIN'** *Columbia DB 4808*	.....**23**	8 wks
19 Apr 62	**TEACH ME TO TWIST** *Columbia DB 4802* [1]	.....**45**	1 wk
9 Aug 62	**DANCIN' PARTY** *Columbia DB 4876*	.....**19**	13 wks
23 Aug 62	**LET'S TWIST AGAIN (2nd re-entry)** *Columbia DB 4691*	.....**46**	1 wk
13 Sep 62	**LET'S TWIST AGAIN (3rd re-entry)** *Columbia DB 4691*	.....**49**	3 wks
1 Nov 62	**LIMBO ROCK** *Cameo-Parkway P 849*	.....**32**	10 wks
20 Dec 62	**JINGLE BELL ROCK** *Cameo-Parkway C 205* [1]	.....**40**	3 wks
31 Oct 63	**WHAT DO YA SAY** *Cameo-Parkway P 806*	.....**37**	4 wks
29 Nov 75	● **LET'S TWIST AGAIN / THE TWIST (re-issue)** *London HL 10512*	.....**5**	10 wks
18 Jun 88	● **THE TWIST (YO, TWIST)** *Urban URB 20* [2]	.....**2**	11 wks

[1] Chubby Checker and Bobby Rydell　[2] Fat Boys and Chubby Checker

CHECKMATES - *See Emile FORD and the CHECKMATES*

CHECKMATES LTD. *US, male vocal / instrumental group*　　　　**8 wks**

| 15 Nov 69 | **PROUD MARY** *A & M AMS 769* | .....**30** | 8 wks |

Judy CHEEKS *US, female vocalist*　　　　**7 wks**

| 13 Nov 93 | **SO IN LOVE (THE REAL DEAL)** *Positiva CDTIV 6* | .....**27** | 3 wks |
| 7 May 94 | **REACH** *Positiva CDTIV 12* | .....**17** | 4 wks |

CHEETAHS *UK, male vocal / instrumental group*　　　　**6 wks**

| 1 Oct 64 | **MECCA** *Philips BF 1362* | .....**36** | 3 wks |
| 21 Jan 65 | **SOLDIER BOY** *Philips BF 1383* | .....**39** | 3 wks |

CHELSEA F.C. *UK, male football team vocalists*　　　　**15 wks**

| 26 Feb 72 | ● **BLUE IS THE COLOUR** *Penny Farthing PEN 782* | .....**5** | 12 wks |
| 14 May 94 | **NO ONE CAN STOP US NOW** *RCA 74321210452* | .....**23** | 3 wks |

CHEQUERS *UK, male vocal / instrumental group*　　　　**10 wks**

| 18 Oct 75 | **ROCK ON BROTHER** *Creole CR 111* | .....**21** | 5 wks |
| 28 Feb 76 | **HEY MISS PAYNE** *Creole CR 116* | .....**32** | 5 wks |

CHER *US, female vocalist*　　　　**142 wks**

19 Aug 65	● **ALL I REALLY WANT TO DO** *Liberty LIB 66114*	.....**9**	10 wks
31 Mar 66	● **BANG BANG (MY BABY SHOT ME DOWN)** *Liberty LIB 66160*	.....**3**	12 wks
4 Aug 66	**I FEEL SOMETHING IN THE AIR** *Liberty LIB 12034*	.....**43**	2 wks
22 Sep 66	**SUNNY** *Liberty LIB 12083*	.....**32**	5 wks
6 Nov 71	● **GYPSYS TRAMPS AND THIEVES** *MCA MU 1142*	.....**4**	13 wks
16 Feb 74	**DARK LADY** *MCA 101*	.....**36**	3 wks
16 Mar 74	**DARK LADY (re-entry)** *MCA 101*	.....**45**	1 wk
19 Dec 87	● **I FOUND SOMEONE** *Geffen GEF 31*	.....**5**	10 wks
2 Apr 88	**WE ALL SLEEP ALONE** *Geffen GEF 35*	.....**47**	5 wks
2 Sep 89	● **IF I COULD TURN BACK TIME** *Geffen GEF 59*	.....**6**	14 wks
13 Jan 90	**JUST LIKE JESSE JAMES** *Geffen GEF 69*	.....**11**	11 wks
7 Apr 90	**HEART OF STONE** *Geffen GEF 75*	.....**43**	5 wks
11 Aug 90	**YOU WOULDN'T KNOW LOVE** *Geffen GEF 77*	.....**55**	3 wks

13 Apr 91	★ THE SHOOP SHOOP SONG (IT'S IN HIS KISS)		
	Epic 6566737	1	15 wks
13 Jul 91	● LOVE AND UNDERSTANDING Geffen GFS 5	10	8 wks
12 Oct 91	SAVE UP ALL YOUR TEARS Geffen GFS 11	37	5 wks
7 Dec 91	LOVE HURTS Geffen GFS 16	43	5 wks
18 Apr 92	COULD'VE BEEN YOU Geffen GFS 19	31	4 wks
14 Nov 92	OH NO NOT MY BABY Geffen GFS 29	33	4 wks
16 Jan 93	MANY RIVERS TO CROSS Geffen GFSTD 31	37	3 wks
6 Mar 93	WHENEVER YOU'RE NEAR Geffen GFSTD 32	72	1 wk
15 Jan 94	I GOT YOU BABE Geffen GFSTD 64 [1]	35	3 wks

[1] Cher with Beavis and Butt-Head

See also Sonny and Cher; Meatloaf.

CHERELLE *US, female vocalist* **25 wks**

28 Dec 85	● SATURDAY LOVE Tabu A 6829 [1]	6	11 wks
1 Mar 86	WILL YOU SATISFY? Tabu A 6927	57	3 wks
6 Feb 88	NEVER KNEW LOVE LIKE THIS Tabu 6513827 [2]	26	7 wks
6 May 89	AFFAIR Tabu 654673 7	67	2 wks
24 Mar 90	SATURDAY LOVE (re-mix) Tabu 6558007 [1]	55	2 wks

[1] Cherelle with Alexander O'Neal [2] Alexander O'Neal featuring Cherelle

CHERI *Canada, female vocal duo* **9 wks**

19 Jun 82	MURPHY'S LAW Polydor POSP 459	13	9 wks

CHEROKEES *UK, male vocal/instrumental group* **5 wks**

3 Sep 64	SEVEN DAFFODILS Columbia DB 7341	33	5 wks

Don CHERRY *US, male vocalist* **11 wks**

10 Feb 56	● BAND OF GOLD Philips PB 549	6	11 wks

Neneh CHERRY *US, female vocalist* **71 wks**

10 Dec 88	● BUFFALO STANCE Circa YR 21	3	13 wks
20 May 89	● MANCHILD Circa YR 30	5	10 wks
12 Aug 89	KISSES ON THE WIND Circa YR 33	20	6 wks
23 Dec 89	INNA CITY MAMMA Circa YR 42	31	7 wks
29 Sep 90	I'VE GOT YOU UNDER MY SKIN Circa YR 53	25	5 wks
3 Oct 92	MONEY LOVE Circa YR 83	23	4 wks
19 Jan 93	BUDDY X Circa YRCD 98	35	3 wks
25 Jun 94	● 7 SECONDS Columbia 6605082 [1]	3	21 wks
24 Dec 94	7 SECONDS (re-entry) Columbia 6605082 [1]	.....60†	2 wks

[1] Youssou N'Dour (featuring Neneh Cherry)

CHIC *US, male/female vocal/instrumental group* **90 wks**

26 Nov 77	● DANCE DANCE DANCE (YOWSAH YOWSAH YOWSAH) Atlantic K 11038	6	12 wks
1 Apr 78	● EVERYBODY DANCE Atlantic K 11097	9	11 wks
18 Nov 78	● LE FREAK Atlantic K 11209	7	16 wks
24 Feb 79	● I WANT YOUR LOVE Atlantic LV 16	4	11 wks
30 Jun 79	● GOOD TIMES Atlantic K 11310	5	11 wks
13 Oct 79	MY FORBIDDEN LOVER Atlantic K 11385	15	8 wks
8 Dec 79	MY FEET KEEP DANCING Atlantic K 11415	21	9 wks
12 Mar 83	HANGIN' Atlantic A 9898	64	1 wk
19 Sep 87	JACK LE FREAK Atlantic A 9198	19	6 wks
14 Jul 90	MEGACHIC - CHIC MEDLEY East West A 7949	58	2 wks
15 Feb 92	CHIC MYSTIQUE Warner Bros. W 0083	48	3 wks

CHICAGO *US, male vocal/instrumental group* **81 wks**

10 Jan 70	● I'M A MAN CBS 4715	8	11 wks
18 Jul 70	● 25 OR 6 TO 4 CBS 5076	7	13 wks
9 Oct 76	★ IF YOU LEAVE ME NOW CBS 4603	1	16 wks
5 Nov 77	BABY WHAT A BIG SURPRISE CBS 5672	41	3 wks
21 Aug 82	● HARD TO SAY I'M SORRY Full Moon K 79301	4	15 wks
27 Oct 84	● HARD HABIT TO BREAK Full Moon W 9214	8	13 wks
26 Jan 85	YOU'RE THE INSPIRATION Warner Bros. W 9126	14	10 wks

CHICKEN SHACK *UK, male/female vocal/instrumental group* **19 wks**

7 May 69	I'D RATHER GO BLIND Blue Horizon 57-3153	14	13 wks
6 Sep 69	TEARS IN THE WIND Blue Horizon 57-3160	29	6 wks

CHICORY TIP *UK, male vocal/instrumental group* **34 wks**

29 Jan 72	★ SON OF MY FATHER CBS 7737	1	13 wks
20 May 72	WHAT'S YOUR NAME CBS 8021	13	8 wks
31 Mar 73	GOOD GRIEF CHRISTINA CBS 1258	17	13 wks

CHIFFONS *US, female vocal group* **40 wks**

11 Apr 63	HE'S SO FINE Stateside SS 172	16	12 wks
18 Jul 63	ONE FINE DAY Stateside SS 202	29	6 wks
26 May 66	SWEET TALKIN' GUY Stateside SS 512	31	8 wks
18 Mar 72	● SWEET TALKIN' GUY (re-issue) London HL 10271	4	14 wks

CHILD *UK, male vocal/instrumental group* **22 wks**

29 Apr 78	WHEN YOU WALK IN THE ROOM		
	Ariola Hansa AHA 511	38	5 wks
22 Jul 78	● IT'S ONLY MAKE BELIEVE Ariola Hansa AHA 522	10	12 wks
28 Apr 79	ONLY YOU (AND YOU ALONE)		
	Ariola Hansa AHA 536	33	5 wks

Jane CHILD *Canada, female vocalist* **8 wks**

12 May 90	DON'T WANNA FALL IN LOVE		
	Warner Bros. W 9817	22	8 wks

CHILDREN FOR RWANDA *UK, male/female choir* **2 wks**

10 Sep 94	LOVE CAN BUILD A BRIDGE East West YZ 849CD	57	2 wks

CHILDREN OF THE NIGHT
UK, male vocalist/producer **2 wks**

26 Nov 88	IT'S A TRIP (TUNE IN, TURN ON, DROP OUT)		
	Jive JIVE 189	52	2 wks

CHILDREN OF THE REVOLUTION - *See KLF*

Toni CHILDS *US, female vocalist* **4 wks**

25 Mar 89	DON'T WALK AWAY A & M AM 462	53	4 wks

CHI-LITES *US, male vocal group* **89 wks**

28 Aug 71	(FOR GOD'S SAKE) GIVE MORE POWER TO THE PEOPLE MCA MU 1138	32	6 wks
15 Jan 72	● HAVE YOU SEEN HER MCA MU 1146	3	12 wks
27 May 72	OH GIRL MCA MU 1156	14	9 wks
23 Mar 74	● HOMELY GIRL Brunswick BR 9	5	13 wks
20 Jul 74	I FOUND SUNSHINE Brunswick BR 12	35	5 wks
2 Nov 74	● TOO GOOD TO BE FORGOTTEN Brunswick BR 13	10	11 wks
21 Jun 75	HAVE YOU SEEN HER/OH GIRL (re-issue)		
	Brunswick BR 20	5	9 wks
13 Sep 75	● IT'S TIME FOR LOVE Brunswick BR 25	5	10 wks
31 Jul 76	● YOU DON'T HAVE TO GO Brunswick BR 34	3	11 wks
13 Aug 83	CHANGING FOR YOU R & B RBS 215	61	3 wks

CHILL FAC-TORR *US, male vocal/instrumental group* **8 wks**

2 Apr 83	TWIST (ROUND `N' ROUND) Phillyworld PWS 109	..37	8 wks

CHIMES *UK, male/female vocal/instrumental group* **28 wks**

19 Aug 89	1-2-3 CBS 655166 7	60	3 wks
2 Dec 89	HEAVEN CBS 655432 7	66	2 wks

6 Jan 90	HEAVEN (re-entry) CBS 655432 7	69	3 wks
19 May 90 ●	STILL HAVEN'T FOUND WHAT I'M LOOKING FOR	6	9 wks
	CBS CHIM 1		
28 Jul 90	TRUE LOVE CBS CHIM 2	48	3 wks
29 Sep 90	HEAVEN (re-issue) CBS CHIM 3	24	6 wks
1 Dec 90	LOVE COMES TO MIND CBS CHIM 4	49	2 wks

CHINA BLACK
UK, male vocal / instrumental duo **26 wks**

16 Jul 94 ●	SEARCHING Wild Card CARDD 7	4	16 wks
29 Oct 94	STARS Wild Card CARDD 9	19	7 wks
17 Dec 94	SEARCHING (re-entry) Wild Card CARDD 7	54†	3 wks

CHINA CRISIS UK, male vocal / instrumental group **66 wks**

7 Aug 82	AFRICAN AND WHITE Inevitable INEV 011	45	5 wks
22 Jan 83	CHRISTIAN Virgin VS 562	12	9 wks
21 May 83	TRAGEDY AND MYSTERY Virgin VS 587	46	6 wks
15 Oct 83	WORKING WITH FIRE AND STEEL Virgin VS 620	48	5 wks
14 Jan 84 ●	WISHFUL THINKING Virgin VS 647	9	8 wks
10 Mar 84	HANNA HANNA Virgin VS 665	44	3 wks
30 Mar 85	BLACK MAN RAY Virgin VS 752	14	9 wks
1 Jun 85	KING IN A CATHOLIC STYLE (WAKE UP)	19	9 wks
	Virgin VS 765		
7 Sep 85	YOU DID CUT ME Virgin VS 799	54	3 wks
8 Nov 86	ARIZONA SKY Virgin VS 898	47	4 wks
24 Jan 87	BEST KEPT SECRET Virgin VS 926	36	5 wks

Jonny CHINGAS US, male vocalist **6 wks**

| 19 Feb 83 | PHONE HOME CBS A 3121 | 43 | 6 wks |

CHIPMUNKS US, male vocalist, David Seville
as himself and a chipmunk vocal trio **11 wks**

| 24 Jul 59 | RAGTIME COWBOY JOE London HLU 8916 | 11 | 8 wks |
| 19 Dec 92 | ACHY BREAKY HEART Epic 6588837 [1] | 53 | 3 wks |

[1] Alvin and the Chipmunks featuring Billy Ray Cyrus. David Seville was by this time deceased.

CHIPPENDALES UK / US, male vocal group **4 wks**

| 31 Oct 92 | GIVE ME YOUR BODY XS Rhythm XSR 3 | 28 | 4 wks |

CHOPS-EMC + EXTENSIVE
UK, male instrumental group and rapper **1 wk**

| 8 Aug 92 | ME' ISRAELITES Faze 2 FAZE 6 | 60 | 1 wk |

CHORDETTES US, female vocal group **25 wks**

17 Dec 54	MR. SANDMAN Columbia DB 3553	11	8 wks
31 Aug 56 ●	BORN TO BE WITH YOU London HLA 8302	8	9 wks
18 Apr 58 ●	LOLLIPOP London HLD 8584	6	8 wks

CHORDS UK, male vocal / instrumental group **17 wks**

6 Oct 79	NOW IT'S GONE Polydor 2059 141	63	2 wks
2 Feb 80	MAYBE TOMORROW Polydor POSP 101	40	5 wks
26 Apr 80	SOMETHING'S MISSING Polydor POSP 146	55	3 wks
12 Jul 80	THE BRITISH WAY OF LIFE Polydor 2059 258	54	3 wks
18 Oct 80	IN MY STREET Polydor POSP 185	50	4 wks

CHRIS and JAMES UK, male production duo **1 wk**

| 17 Sep 94 | CALM DOWN (BASS KEEPS PUMPIN') | 74 | 1 wk |
| | Stress 12STR 38 | | |

Neil CHRISTIAN UK, male vocalist **10 wks**

| 7 Apr 66 | THAT'S NICE Strike JH 301 | 14 | 10 wks |

Roger CHRISTIAN UK, male vocalist **3 wks**

| 30 Sep 89 | TAKE IT FROM ME Island IS 427 | 63 | 3 wks |

CHRISTIANS UK, male vocal / instrumental group **84 wks**

31 Jan 87	FORGOTTEN TOWN Island IS 291	22	11 wks
13 Jun 87	HOOVERVILLE (THEY PROMISED US THE WORLD)	21	10 wks
	Island IS 326		
26 Sep 87	WHEN THE FINGERS POINT Island IS 335	34	7 wks
5 Dec 87	IDEAL WORLD Island IS 347	14	13 wks
23 Apr 88	BORN AGAIN Island IS 365	25	7 wks
15 Oct 88 ●	HARVEST FOR THE WORLD Island IS 395	8	7 wks
20 May 89 ★	FERRY 'CROSS THE MERSEY PWL PWL 41 [1]	1	7 wks
23 Dec 89	WORDS Island IS 450	18	8 wks
7 Apr 90	I FOUND OUT Island IS 453	56	2 wks
15 Sep 90	GREENBANK DRIVE Island IS 466	63	2 wks
5 Sep 92	WHAT'S IN A WORD Island IS 536	33	5 wks
14 Nov 92	FATHER Island IS 543	55	2 wks
6 Mar 93	THE BOTTLE Island CID 549	39	3 wks

[1] Christians, Holly Johnson, Paul McCartney, Gerry Marsden and Stock Aitken Waterman

CHRISTIE UK, male vocal / instrumental group **37 wks**

2 May 70 ★	YELLOW RIVER CBS 4911	1	22 wks
10 Oct 70	SAN BERNADINO CBS 5169	49	1 wk
24 Oct 70 ●	SAN BERNADINO (re-entry) CBS 5169	7	13 wks
25 Mar 72	IRON HORSE CBS 7747	47	1 wk

David CHRISTIE France, male vocalist **12 wks**

| 14 Aug 82 ● | SADDLE UP KR KR 9 | 9 | 12 wks |

John CHRISTIE Australia, male vocalist **6 wks**

| 25 Dec 76 | HERE'S TO LOVE (AULD LANG SYNE) EMI 2554 | 24 | 6 wks |

Lou CHRISTIE US, male vocalist **35 wks**

24 Feb 66	LIGHTNIN' STRIKES MGM 1297	11	8 wks
28 Apr 66	RHAPSODY IN THE RAIN MGM 1308	37	2 wks
13 Sep 69 ●	I'M GONNA MAKE YOU MINE Buddah 201 057	2	17 wks
27 Dec 69	SHE SOLD ME MAGIC Buddah 201 073	25	8 wks

Tony CHRISTIE UK, male vocalist **47 wks**

9 Jan 71	LAS VEGAS MCA MK 5058	21	9 wks
8 May 71 ●	I DID WHAT I DID FOR MARIA MCA MK 5064	2	17 wks
20 Nov 71	IS THIS THE WAY TO AMARILLO MCA MKS 5073	18	13 wks
10 Feb 73	AVENUES AND ALLEYWAYS MCA MKS 5101	37	4 wks
17 Jan 76	DRIVE SAFELY DARLIN' MCA 219	35	4 wks

Shawn CHRISTOPHER US, female vocalist **10 wks**

4 May 91	ANOTHER SLEEPLESS NIGHT Arista 114186	50	4 wks
21 Mar 92	DON'T LOSE THE MAGIC Arista 115097	30	5 wks
2 Jul 94	MAKE MY LOVE BTB BTBCD 502	57	1 wk

CHUBBY CHUNKS UK, male instrumental duo **1 wk**

| 4 Jun 94 | TESTAMENT 4 Cleveland City CLECD 13017 | 52 | 1 wk |

CHUCKS UK, male / female vocal group **7 wks**

| 24 Jan 63 | LOO-BE-LOO Decca F 11569 | 22 | 7 wks |

CHUMBAWAMBA
UK, male / female vocal / instrumental group **3 wks**

| 18 Sep 93 | ENOUGH IS ENOUGH | 56 | 2 wks |
| | One Little Indian 79 TP7CD [1] | | |

4 Dec 93   **TIMEBOMB** One Little Indian 89 TP7CD ....**59**   1 wk

[1] Chumbawamba and Credit To The Nation

CHYNA - See INCOGNITO

CICERO *UK, male vocalist*   **12 wks**

18 Jan 92	**LOVE IS EVERYWHERE** Spaghetti CIAO 3 ....**19**	8 wks
18 Apr 92	**THAT LOVING FEELING** Spaghetti CIAO 4 ....**46**	3 wks
1 Aug 92	**HEAVEN MUST HAVE SENT YOU BACK** Spaghetti CIAO 5 ....**70**	1 wk

CINDERELLA *US, male vocal / instrumental group*   **7 wks**

6 Aug 88	**GYPSY ROAD** Vertigo VER 40 ....**54**	2 wks
4 Mar 89	**DON'T KNOW WHAT YOU GOT** Vertigo VER 43 ....**54**	2 wks
17 Nov 90	**SHELTER ME** Vertigo VER 51 ....**55**	2 wks
27 Apr 91	**HEARTBREAK STATION** Vertigo VER 53 ....**63**	1 wk

CINDY and the SAFFRONS
UK, female vocal group   **3 wks**

15 Jan 83	**PAST, PRESENT AND FUTURE** Stilletto STL 9 ....**56**	3 wks

Gigliola CINQUETTI *Italy, female vocalist*   **27 wks**

23 Apr 64	**NON HO L'ETA PER AMARTI** Decca F 21882............**17**	17 wks
4 May 74	● **GO (BEFORE YOU BREAK MY HEART)** CBS 2294 ......**8**	10 wks

CIRCUIT *UK, male / female vocal / instrumental group*   **2 wks**

20 Jul 91	**SHELTER ME** Cooltempo COOL 237 ....**44**	2 wks

CIRRUS *UK, male vocal group*   **1 wk**

30 Sep 78	**ROLLIN' ON** Jet 123 ....**62**	1 wk

CITY BOY *UK, male vocal / instrumental group*   **20 wks**

8 Jul 78	● **5-7-0-5** Vertigo 6059 207 ....**8**	12 wks
28 Oct 78	**WHAT A NIGHT** Vertigo 6059 211 ....**39**	5 wks
15 Sep 79	**THE DAY THE EARTH CAUGHT FIRE** Vertigo 6059 238 ....**67**	3 wks

CITY GENTS - See Dick CHARLESWORTH and his CITY GENTS

C.J. & CO. *US, male vocal / instrumental group*   **2 wks**

30 Jul 77	**DEVIL'S GUN** Atlantic K 10956............**43**	2 wks

Gary CLAIL ON-U SOUND SYSTEM
UK, male producer   **19 wks**

14 Jul 90	**BEEF** RCA PB 49265 [1] **64**	2 wks
30 Mar 91	● **HUMAN NATURE** Perfecto PB 44401 ....**10**	9 wks
8 Jun 91	**ESCAPE** Perfecto PB 44563 ....**44**	3 wks
14 Nov 92	**WHO PAYS THE PIPER** Perfecto 74321117017 ....**31**	3 wks
22 May 93	**THESE THINGS ARE WORTH FIGHTING FOR** Perfecto 74321147222 ....**45**	2 wks

[1] Gary Clail

See also Various Artists (EPs & LPs) – Gimme Shelter (EP)

CLAIRE and FRIENDS
UK, female vocalist and young male / female friends   **11 wks**

7 Jun 86	● **IT'S 'ORRIBLE BEING IN LOVE (WHEN YOU'RE 8 1/2)** BBC RESL 189 ....**13**	11 wks

CLANNAD *Ireland, male / female vocal group*   **29 wks**

6 Nov 82	● **THEME FROM HARRY'S GAME** RCA 292 ....**5**	10 wks
2 Jul 83	**NEW GRANGE** RCA 340 ....**65**	1 wk
12 May 84	**ROBIN (THE HOODED MAN)** RCA HOOD 1 ....**42**	5 wks
25 Jan 86	**IN A LIFETIME** RCA PB 40535 [1] **20**	5 wks
10 Jun 89	**IN A LIFETIME (re-issue)** RCA PB 42873 [1] **17**	7 wks
10 Aug 91	**BOTH SIDES NOW** MCA MCS 1546 [2] **74**	1 wk

[1] Clannad featuring Bono   [2] Clannad and Paul Young

Jimmy CLANTON *US, male vocalist*   **1 wk**

21 Jul 60	**ANOTHER SLEEPLESS NIGHT** Top Rank JAR 382 ......**50**	1 wk

Eric CLAPTON
UK, male vocalist / instrumentalist - guitar   **131 wks**

20 Dec 69	**COMIN' HOME** Atlantic 584 308 [1] **16**	9 wks
12 Aug 72	● **LAYLA** Polydor 2058 130 [2] **7**	11 wks
27 Jul 74	● **I SHOT THE SHERIFF** RSO 2090 132 ....**9**	9 wks
10 May 75	**SWING LOW SWEET CHARIOT** RSO 2090 158 ....**19**	9 wks
16 Aug 75	**KNOCKIN' ON HEAVEN'S DOOR** RSO 2090 166 ....**38**	4 wks
24 Dec 77	**LAY DOWN SALLY** RSO 2090 264 ....**39**	6 wks
21 Oct 78	**PROMISES** RSO 21 ....**37**	7 wks
6 Mar 82	● **LAYLA (re-issue)** RSO 87 [2] **4**	10 wks
5 Jun 82	**I SHOT THE SHERIFF (re-issue)** RSO 88 ....**64**	2 wks
23 Apr 83	**THE SHAPE YOU'RE IN** Duck W 9701 ....**75**	1 wk
16 Mar 85	**FOREVER MAN** Warner Bros. W 9069 ....**51**	4 wks
4 Jan 86	**EDGE OF DARKNESS** BBC RESL 178 [3] **65**	3 wks
17 Jan 87	**BEHIND THE MASK** Duck W 8461 ....**15**	11 wks
20 Jun 87	**TEARING US APART** Duck W 8299 [4] **56**	3 wks
27 Jan 90	**BAD LOVE** Duck W 2644 ....**25**	7 wks
14 Apr 90	**NO ALIBIS** Duck W 9981 ....**53**	4 wks
16 Nov 91	**WONDERFUL TONIGHT (LIVE)** Duck W 0069 ......**30**	7 wks
8 Feb 92	**TEARS IN HEAVEN** Reprise W 0081 ....**50**	3 wks
7 Mar 92	● **TEARS IN HEAVEN (re-entry)** Reprise W 0081 ....**5**	9 wks
1 Aug 92	**RUNAWAY TRAIN** Rocket EJS 29 [5] **31**	4 wks
29 Aug 92	**IT'S PROBABLY ME** A & M AM 883 [6] **30**	5 wks
3 Oct 92	**LAYLA (ACOUSTIC)** Duck W 0134 ....**45**	3 wks
15 Oct 94	**MOTHERLESS CHILD** Duck W 0271CD **63**	1 wk

[1] Delaney and Bonnie and Friends featuring Eric Clapton [2] Derek and the Dominoes [3] Eric Clapton featuring Michael Kamen [4] Eric Clapton and Tina Turner [5] Elton John and Eric Clapton [6] Sting with Eric Clapton

Layla (Acoustic) is, as its title suggests, a re-recording of Layla.

Dee CLARK *US, male vocalist*   **9 wks**

2 Oct 59	**JUST KEEP IT UP** London HL 8915 ....**26**	1 wk
11 Oct 75	**RIDE A WILD HORSE** Chelsea 2005 037 ....**16**	8 wks

Gary CLARK *UK, male vocalist*   **8 wks**

30 Jan 93	**WE SAIL ON THE STORMY WATERS** Circa YRCDX 93 ....**34**	4 wks
3 Apr 93	**FREEFLOATING** Circa YRCDX 94 ....**50**	3 wks
19 Jun 93	**MAKE A FAMILY** Circa YRCDX 105 ....**70**	1 wk

Loni CLARK *US, female vocalist*   **6 wks**

5 Jun 93	**RUSHING** A & M 5802862 ....**37**	2 wks
22 Jan 94	**U** A & M 5804752 ....**28**	3 wks
17 Dec 94	**LOVE'S GOT ME ON A TRIP SO HIGH** A & M 5808872 ....**59**	1 wk

Petula CLARK *UK, female vocalist*   **247 wks**

11 Jun 54	**THE LITTLE SHOEMAKER** Polygon P 1117 ....**12**	1 wk
25 Jun 54	● **THE LITTLE SHOEMAKER (re-entry)** Polygon P 1117 ....**7**	9 wks
18 Feb 55	**MAJORCA** Polygon P 1146 ....**12**	4 wks
25 Mar 55	**MAJORCA (re-entry)** Polygon P 1146 ....**18**	1 wk
25 Nov 55	● **SUDDENLY THERE'S A VALLEY** Pye Nixa N 15013 ....**7**	10 wks

PETULA CLARK signs an autograph for a delighted Richard Page of Mr. Mister. (LFI)

TOP 42 50

'Twist and Shout' has been a hit song in three different decades but only a number one in the version by **CHAKA DEMUS AND PLIERS**.
(Brian Rasic/REX)

26 Jul 57	● WITH ALL MY HEART *Pye Nixa N 15096*	4	18 wks
15 Nov 57	● ALONE *Pye Nixa N 15112*	8	12 wks
28 Feb 58	BABY LOVER *Pye Nixa N 15126*	12	7 wks
26 Jan 61	★ SAILOR *Pye 7N 15324*	1	15 wks
13 Apr 61	SOMETHING MISSING *Pye 7N 15337*	44	1 wk
13 Jul 61	● ROMEO *Pye 7N 15361*	3	15 wks
16 Nov 61	● MY FRIEND THE SEA *Pye 7N 15389*	7	13 wks
8 Feb 62	I'M COUNTING ON YOU *Pye 7N 15407*	41	2 wks
28 Jun 62	YA YA TWIST *Pye 7N 15448*	14	11 wks
20 Sep 62	YA YA TWIST (re-entry) *Pye 7N 15448*	45	2 wks
2 May 63	CASANOVA/CHARIOT *Pye 7N 15522*	39	7 wks
12 Nov 64	● DOWNTOWN *Pye 7N 15722*	2	15 wks
11 Mar 65	I KNOW A PLACE *Pye 7N 15772*	17	8 wks
12 Aug 65	YOU BETTER COME HOME *Pye 7N 15864*	44	3 wks
14 Oct 65	ROUND EVERY CORNER *Pye 7N 15945*	43	3 wks
4 Nov 65	YOU'RE THE ONE *Pye 7N 15991*	23	9 wks
10 Feb 66	● MY LOVE *Pye 7N 17038*	4	9 wks
21 Apr 66	A SIGN OF THE TIMES *Pye 7N 17071*	49	1 wk
30 Jun 66	● I COULDN'T LIVE WITHOUT YOUR LOVE *Pye 7N 17133*	6	11 wks
2 Feb 67	★ THIS IS MY SONG *Pye 7N 17258*	1	14 wks
25 May 67	DON'T SLEEP IN THE SUBWAY *Pye 7N 17325*	12	11 wks
13 Dec 67	THE OTHER MAN'S GRASS *Pye 7N 17416*	20	9 wks
6 Mar 68	KISS ME GOODBYE *Pye 7N 17466*	50	1 wk
30 Jan 71	THE SONG OF MY LIFE *Pye 7N 45026*	41	1 wk
13 Feb 71	THE SONG OF MY LIFE (re-entry) *Pye 7N 45026*	32	11 wks
15 Jan 72	I DON'T KNOW HOW TO LOVE HIM *Pye 7N 45112*	47	1 wk
29 Jan 72	I DON'T KNOW HOW TO LOVE HIM (re-entry) *Pye 7N 45112*	49	1 wk
19 Nov 88	● DOWNTOWN (re-mix) *PRT PYS 19*	10	11 wks

Dave CLARK FIVE
UK, male vocal / instrumental group **174 wks**

3 Oct 63	DO YOU LOVE ME *Columbia DB 7112*	30	6 wks
21 Nov 63	★ GLAD ALL OVER *Columbia DB 7154*	1	19 wks
20 Feb 64	● BITS AND PIECES *Columbia DB 7210*	2	11 wks
28 May 64	● CAN'T YOU SEE THAT SHE'S MINE *Columbia DB 7291*	10	11 wks
13 Aug 64	THINKING OF YOU BABY *Columbia DB 7335*	26	4 wks
22 Oct 64	ANYWAY YOU WANT IT *Columbia DB 7377*	25	5 wks
14 Jan 65	EVERYBODY KNOWS *Columbia DB 7453*	37	4 wks
11 Mar 65	REELIN' AND ROCKIN' *Columbia DB 7503*	24	8 wks
27 May 65	COME HOME *Columbia DB 7580*	16	8 wks
15 Jul 65	● CATCH US IF YOU CAN *Columbia DB 7625*	5	11 wks
11 Nov 65	OVER AND OVER *Columbia DB 7744*	45	4 wks
19 May 66	LOOK BEFORE YOU LEAP *Columbia DB 7909*	50	1 wk
16 Mar 67	YOU GOT WHAT IT TAKES *Columbia DB 8152*	28	8 wks
1 Nov 67	● EVERYBODY KNOWS *Columbia DB 8286*	2	14 wks
28 Feb 68	NO ONE CAN BREAK A HEART LIKE YOU *Columbia DB 8342*	28	7 wks
18 Sep 68	● RED BALLOON *Columbia DB 8465*	7	11 wks
27 Nov 68	LIVE IN THE SKY *Columbia DB 8505*	39	6 wks
25 Oct 69	PUT A LITTLE LOVE IN YOUR HEART *Columbia DB 8624*	31	4 wks
6 Dec 69	● GOOD OLD ROCK 'N ROLL *Columbia DB 8638*	7	12 wks
7 Mar 70	● EVERYBODY GET TOGETHER *Columbia DB 8660*	8	8 wks
4 Jul 70	HERE COMES SUMMER *Columbia DB 8689*	44	3 wks
7 Nov 70	MORE GOOD OLD ROCK 'N ROLL *Columbia DB 8724*	34	6 wks
1 May 93	GLAD ALL OVER (re-issue) *EMI CDEMCT 8*	37	3 wks

Everybody Knows on *DB 7453* and Everybody Knows on *DB 8286* are two different songs. The two Rock 'N Roll titles are medleys as follows: *Good Old Rock 'N Roll / Sweet Little Sixteen / Long Tall Sally / Whole Lotta Shakin' Goin' On / Blue Suede Shoes / Lucille / Reelin' And Rockin' / Memphis Tennessee*. More Good Old Rock and Roll: *Rock And Roll Music / Blueberry Hill / Good Golly Miss Molly / My Blue Heaven / Keep A Knockin' / Loving You / One Night / Lawdy Miss Clawdy.*

John Cooper CLARKE *UK, male vocalist* **3 wks**

10 Mar 79	GIMMIX! PLAY LOUD *Epic EPC 7009*	39	3 wks

Sharon D. CLARKE - See FPI PROJECT: SERIOUS ROPE

Rick CLARKE *UK, male vocalist* **2 wks**

30 Apr 88	I'LL SEE YOU ALONG THE WAY *WA WA 1*	63	2 wks

Julian CLARY - See JOAN COLLINS FAN CLUB

CLASH *UK, male vocal / instrumental group* **135 wks**

2 Apr 77	WHITE RIOT *CBS 5058*	38	3 wks
8 Oct 77	COMPLETE CONTROL *CBS 5664*	28	2 wks
4 Mar 78	CLASH CITY ROCKERS *CBS 5834*	35	4 wks
24 Jun 78	(WHITE MAN) IN HAMMERSMITH PALAIS *CBS 6383*	32	7 wks
2 Dec 78	TOMMY GUN *CBS 6788*	19	10 wks
3 Mar 79	ENGLISH CIVIL WAR (JOHNNY COMES MARCHING HOME) *CBS 7082*	25	6 wks
19 May 79	THE COST OF LIVING EP *CBS 7324*	22	8 wks
15 Dec 79	LONDON CALLING *CBS 8087*	11	10 wks
9 Aug 80	BANKROBBER *CBS 8323*	12	10 wks
6 Dec 80	THE CALL UP *CBS 9339*	40	6 wks
24 Jan 81	HITSVILLE UK *CBS 9480*	56	4 wks
25 Apr 81	THE MAGNIFICENT SEVEN *CBS 1133*	34	5 wks
28 Nov 81	THIS IS RADIO CLASH *CBS A 1797*	47	6 wks
1 May 82	KNOW YOUR RIGHTS *CBS A 2309*	43	3 wks
26 Jun 82	ROCK THE CASBAH *CBS A 2429*	30	10 wks
25 Sep 82	SHOULD I STAY OR SHOULD I GO / STRAIGHT TO HELL *CBS A 2646*	17	9 wks
12 Oct 85	THIS IS ENGLAND *CBS A 6122*	24	5 wks
12 Mar 88	I FOUGHT THE LAW *CBS CLASH 1*	29	5 wks
7 May 88	LONDON CALLING (re-issue) *CBS CLASH 2*	46	3 wks
21 Jul 90	RETURN TO BRIXTON *CBS 656072 7*	57	2 wks
2 Mar 91	★ SHOULD I STAY OR SHOULD I GO (re-issue) *Columbia 6566677*	1	9 wks
13 Apr 91	ROCK THE CASBAH (re-issue) *Columbia 6568147*	15	6 wks
8 Jun 91	LONDON CALLING (re-issue) *Columbia 6569467*	64	2 wks

Tracks on The Cost Of Living EP: *I Fought The Law / Groovy Times / Gates Of The West / Capital Radio.* CBS CLASH 1 is a re-issue of a track from The Cost of Living EP.

CLASS ACTION featuring Chris WILTSHIRE
US, female vocal group **3 wks**

7 May 83	WEEKEND *Jive JIVE 35*	49	3 wks

CLASSICS IV *US, male vocal / instrumental group* **1 wk**

28 Feb 68	SPOOKY *Liberty LBS 15051*	46	1 wk

CLASSIX NOUVEAUX
UK, male vocal / instrumental group **34 wks**

28 Feb 81	GUILTY *Liberty BP 388*	43	7 wks
16 May 81	TOKYO *Liberty BP 397*	67	3 wks
8 Aug 81	INSIDE OUTSIDE *Liberty BP 403*	45	5 wks
7 Nov 81	NEVER AGAIN (THE DAYS TIME ERASED) *Liberty BP 406*	44	4 wks
13 Mar 82	IS IT A DREAM *Liberty BP 409*	11	9 wks
29 May 82	BECAUSE YOU'RE YOUNG *Liberty BP 411*	43	4 wks
30 Oct 82	THE END ... OR THE BEGINNING *Liberty BP 414*	60	2 wks

CLAWFINGER
Norway / Sweden, male vocal / instrumental group **1 wk**

19 Mar 94	WARFAIR *East West YZ 804CD1*	54	1 wk

Judy CLAY - See William BELL

Merry CLAYTON *US, female vocalist* **1 wk**

21 May 88	YES *RCA PB 49563*	70	1 wk

CLAYTOWN TROUPE
UK, male vocal / instrumental group · **3 wks**

16 Jun 90	WAYS OF LOVE *Island IS 464*	57	2 wks
14 Mar 92	WANTED IT ALL *EMI USA MT 102*	74	1 wk

Johnny CLEGG and SAVUKA
UK / South Africa, male vocal / instrumental group · **1 wk**

16 May 87	SCATTERLINGS OF AFRICA *EMI EMI 5605*	75	1 wk

Jimmy CLIFF *Jamaica, male vocalist* · **33 wks**

25 Oct 69	● WONDERFUL WORLD BEAUTIFUL PEOPLE *Trojan TR 690*	6	13 wks
14 Feb 70	VIETNAM *Trojan TR 7722*	47	1 wk
28 Feb 70	VIETNAM (re-entry) *Trojan TR 7722*	46	2 wks
8 Aug 70	● WILD WORLD *Island WIP 6087*	8	12 wks
19 Mar 94	I CAN SEE CLEARLY NOW *Columbia 6601982*	23	5 wks

Buzz CLIFFORD *US, male vocalist* · **13 wks**

2 Mar 61	BABY SITTIN' BOOGIE *Fontana H 297*	17	13 wks

Linda CLIFFORD *US, female vocalist* · **12 wks**

10 Jun 78	IF MY FRIENDS COULD SEE ME NOW *Curtom K 17163*	50	5 wks
5 May 79	BRIDGE OVER TROUBLED WATER *RSO 30*	28	7 wks

CLIMAX BLUES BAND
UK, male vocal / instrumental group · **9 wks**

9 Oct 76	● COULDN'T GET IT RIGHT *BTM SBT 105*	10	9 wks

Simon CLIMIE *UK, male vocalist* · **2 wks**

19 Sep 92	SOUL INSPIRATION *Epic 6582837*	60	2 wks

CLIMIE FISHER *UK, male vocal / instrumental duo* · **44 wks**

5 Sep 87	LOVE CHANGES (EVERYTHING) *EMI EM 15*	67	2 wks
12 Dec 87	● RISE TO THE OCCASION *EMI EM 33*	10	11 wks
12 Mar 88	● LOVE CHANGES (EVERYTHING) (re-mix) *EMI EM 47*	2	12 wks
21 May 88	THIS IS ME *EMI EM 58*	22	5 wks
20 Aug 88	I WON'T BLEED FOR YOU *EMI EM 66*	35	4 wks
24 Dec 88	LOVE LIKE A RIVER *EMI EM 81*	22	7 wks
23 Sep 89	FACTS OF LOVE *EMI EMI 103*	50	3 wks

Patsy CLINE *US, female vocalist* · **17 wks**

26 Apr 62	SHE'S GOT YOU *Brunswick 05866*	43	1 wk
29 Nov 62	HEARTACHES *Brunswick 05878*	31	5 wks
8 Dec 90	CRAZY *MCA MCA 1465*	14	11 wks

George CLINTON *US, male vocalist* · **10 wks**

4 Dec 82	LOOPZILLA *Capitol CL 271*	57	5 wks
26 Apr 86	DO FRIES GO WITH THAT SHAKE *Capitol CL 402*	57	2 wks
27 Aug 94	BOP GUN (ONE NATION) *Fourth & Broadway BRCD 308* [1]	22	3 wks

[1] Ice Cube featuring George Clinton

CLIVILLES & COLE - See C & C MUSIC FACTORY

CLOCK *UK, male / female vocal / instrumental group* · **6 wks**

30 Oct 93	HOLDING ON *Media MRLCD 007*	66	1 wk
21 May 94	THE RHYTHM *Media MCSTD 1971*	28	2 wks
10 Sep 94	KEEP THE FIRES BURNING *Media MCSTD 1998*	36	3 wks

Rosemary CLOONEY *US, female vocalist* · **81 wks**

14 Nov 52	● HALF AS MUCH *Columbia DB 3129*	3	9 wks
5 Feb 54	● MAN *Philips PB 220*	7	5 wks
8 Oct 54	★ THIS OLE HOUSE *Philips PB 336*	1	18 wks
17 Dec 54	★ MAMBO ITALIANO *Philips PB 382*	1	16 wks
20 May 55	● WHERE WILL THE BABY'S DIMPLE BE *Philips PB 428*	6	13 wks
30 Sep 55	● HEY THERE *Philips PB 494*	4	11 wks
29 Mar 57	MANGOS *Philips PB 671*	25	2 wks
26 Apr 57	MANGOS (re-entry) *Philips PB 671*	17	7 wks

From 19 Feb 54 other side of Man, Woman by José Ferrer, was also credited.

CLOUD *UK, male instrumental group* · **1 wk**

31 Jan 81	ALL NIGHT LONG / TAKE IT TO THE TOP *UK Champagne FUNK 1*	72	1 wk

CLOUT *South Africa, female vocal / instrumental group* · **15 wks**

17 Jun 78	● SUBSTITUTE *Carrere EMI 2788*	2	15 wks

CLUB NOUVEAU
US, male / female vocal / instrumental group · **12 wks**

21 Mar 87	● LEAN ON ME *King Jay W 8430*	3	12 wks

CLUB 69 *Austria / US, male / female vocal / instrumental duo* · **5 wks**

5 Dec 92	LET ME BE YOUR UNDERWEAR *ffrr F 204*	33	5 wks

CLUBHOUSE *Italy, male vocal / instrumental group* · **39 wks**

23 Jul 83	DO IT AGAIN - BILLIE JEAN (MEDLEY) *Island IS 132*	11	6 wks
3 Dec 83	SUPERSTITION - GOOD TIMES (MEDLEY) *Island IS 147*	59	3 wks
1 Jul 89	I'M A MAN - YE KE YE KE (MEDLEY) *Music Man MMPS 7003*	69	3 wks
20 Apr 91	DEEP IN MY HEART *ffrr F 157*	59	2 wks
22 Jun 91	DEEP IN MY HEART (re-entry) *ffrr F 157*	55	2 wks
4 Sep 93	LIGHT MY FIRE *PWL Continental PWCD 272*	59	1 wk
13 Nov 93	LIGHT MY FIRE (re-entry) *PWL Continental PWCD 272*	45	5 wks
25 Dec 93	LIGHT MY FIRE (2nd re-entry) *PWL Continental PWCD 272*	53	6 wks
30 Apr 94	● LIGHT MY FIRE (re-mix) *PWL Continental PWCD 288*	7	8 wks
23 Jul 94	LIVING IN THE SUNSHINE *PWL Continental PWCD 309* [1]	21	3 wks

[1] Clubhouse featuring Carl

CLUBZONE *UK / Germany, male vocal / instrumental group* · **1 wk**

19 Nov 94	HANDS UP *Logic 74321236982*	50	1 wk

Jeremy CLYDE - See Chad STUART and Jeremy CLYDE

CLYDE VALLEY STOMPERS
UK, male instrumental group · **8 wks**

9 Aug 62	PETER AND THE WOLF *Parlophone R 4928*	25	8 wks

COAST TO COAST *UK, male vocal / instrumental group* · **22 wks**

31 Jan 81	● (DO) THE HUCKLEBUCK *Polydor POSP 214*	5	15 wks
23 May 81	LET'S JUMP THE BROOMSTICK *Polydor POSP 249*	28	7 wks

COASTERS US, male vocal group — 32 wks

27 Sep 57	SEARCHIN' London HLE 8450	30	1 wk
15 Aug 58	YAKETY YAK London HLE 8665	12	8 wks
27 Mar 59 ●	CHARLIE BROWN London HLE 8819	6	12 wks
30 Oct 59	POISON IVY London HLE 8938	15	7 wks
9 Apr 94	SORRY BUT I'M GONNA HAVE TO PASS Rhino A 4519CD	41	4 wks

Odia COATES - See Paul ANKA

Luis COBOS - See Placido DOMINGO

Eddie COCHRAN US, male vocalist — 90 wks

7 Nov 58	SUMMERTIME BLUES London HLU 8702	18	6 wks
13 Mar 59 ●	C'MON EVERYBODY London HLU 8792	6	13 wks
16 Oct 59	SOMETHIN' ELSE London HLU 8944	22	3 wks
22 Jan 60	HALLELUJAH I LOVE HER SO London HLW 9022	28	1 wk
5 Feb 60	HALLELUJAH I LOVE HER SO (re-entry) London HLW 9022	22	3 wks
12 May 60 ★	THREE STEPS TO HEAVEN London HLG 9115	1	15 wks
6 Oct 60	SWEETIE PIE London HLG 9196	38	3 wks
3 Nov 60	LONELY London HLG 9196	41	1 wk
15 Jun 61	WEEKEND London HLG 9362	15	16 wks
30 Nov 61	JEANNIE, JEANNIE, JEANNIE London HLG 9460	31	4 wks
25 Apr 63	MY WAY Liberty LIB 10088	23	10 wks
24 Apr 68	SUMMERTIME BLUES (re-issue) Liberty LBF 15071	34	8 wks
13 Feb 88	C'MON EVERYBODY (re-issue) Liberty EDDIE 501	14	7 wks

Tom COCHRANE Canada, male vocalist — 2 wks

27 Jun 92	LIFE IS A HIGHWAY Capitol CL 660	62	2 wks

COCK ROBIN
US, male / female vocal / instrumental group — 12 wks

31 May 86	THE PROMISE YOU MADE CBS A 6764	28	12 wks

Joe COCKER UK, male vocalist — 84 wks

22 May 68	MARJORINE Regal-Zonophone RZ 3006	48	1 wk
2 Oct 68 ★	WITH A LITTLE HELP FROM MY FRIENDS Regal-Zonophone RZ 3013	1	13 wks
27 Sep 69 ●	DELTA LADY Regal-Zonophone RZ 3024	10	11 wks
4 Jul 70	THE LETTER Regal-Zonophone RZ 3027	39	6 wks
26 Sep 81	I'M SO GLAD I'M STANDING HERE TODAY MCA 741 [1]	61	3 wks
15 Jan 83 ●	UP WHERE WE BELONG Island WIP 6830 [2]	7	13 wks
14 Nov 87	UNCHAIN MY HEART Capitol CL 465	46	4 wks
13 Jan 90	WHEN THE NIGHT COMES Capitol CL 535	65	2 wks
7 Mar 92	(ALL I KNOW) FEELS LIKE FOREVER Capitol CL 645	25	5 wks
9 May 92	NOW THAT THE MAGIC HAS GONE Capitol CL 657	28	6 wks
4 Jul 92	UNCHAIN MY HEART (re-issue) Capitol CL 664	17	6 wks
21 Nov 92	WHEN THE NIGHT COMES (re-issue) Capitol CL 674	61	3 wks
13 Aug 94	THE SIMPLE THINGS Capitol CDCLS 722	17	5 wks
22 Oct 94	TAKE ME HOME Capitol CDCLS 729 [3]	45	3 wks
17 Dec 94	LET THE HEALING BEGIN Capitol CDCLS 727	32†	3 wks

[1] Crusaders, featured vocalist Joe Cocker [2] Joe Cocker and Jennifer Warnes [3] Joe Cocker featuring Bekka Bramlett

COCKEREL CHORUS UK, male vocal group — 12 wks

24 Feb 73	NICE ONE CYRIL Youngblood YB 1017	14	12 wks

COCKNEY REBEL - See Steve HARLEY

COCKNEY REJECTS
UK, male vocal / instrumental group — 22 wks

1 Dec 79	I'M NOT A FOOL EMI 5008	65	2 wks
16 Feb 80	BADMAN EMI 5035	65	3 wks
26 Apr 80	THE GREATEST COCKNEY RIPOFF EMI Z 2	21	7 wks
17 May 80	I'M FOREVER BLOWING BUBBLES EMI Z 4	35	5 wks
12 Jul 80	WE CAN DO ANYTHING EMI Z 6	65	2 wks
25 Oct 80	WE ARE THE FIRM EMI Z 10	54	3 wks

CO-CO UK, male / female vocal / instrumental group — 7 wks

22 Apr 78	BAD OLD DAYS Ariola Hansa AHA 513	13	7 wks

El COCO US, male vocal / instrumental group — 4 wks

14 Jan 78	COCOMOTION Pye International 7N 25761	31	4 wks

COCONUTS US, female vocal group — 3 wks

11 Jun 83	DID YOU HAVE TO LOVE ME LIKE YOU DID EMI America EA 156	60	3 wks

See also Kid Creole and the Coconuts.

COCTEAU TWINS
UK, male / female vocal / instrumental group — 20 wks

28 Apr 84	PEARLY-DEWDROPS' DROPS 4AD 405	29	5 wks
30 Mar 85	AIKEA-GUINEA 4AD 501	41	3 wks
23 Nov 85	TINY DYNAMINE EP 4AD BAD 510	52	2 wks
7 Dec 85	ECHOES IN A SHALLOW BAY EP 4AD BAD 511	65	1 wk
25 Oct 86	LOVE'S EASY TEARS 4AD AD 610	53	1 wk
8 Sep 90	ICEBLINK LUCK 4AD AD 0011	38	3 wks
2 Oct 93	EVANGELINE Fontana CTCD 1	34	2 wks
18 Dec 93	WINTER WONDERLAND / FROSTY THE SNOWMAN Fontana COCCD 1	58	1 wk
26 Feb 94	BLUEBEARD Fontana CTCD 2	33	2 wks

Tracks on Tiny Dynamine EP: Pink Orange Red / Ribbed and Veined / Plain Tiger / Sultitan Itan. Tracks on Echoes In A Shallow Bay EP: Great Spangled Fritillary / Melonella / Pale Clouded White / Eggs and Their Shells.

C.O.D. US, male vocal / instrumental group — 2 wks

14 May 83	IN THE BOTTLE Streetwave WAVE 2	54	2 wks

COFFEE US, female vocal group — 13 wks

27 Sep 80	CASANOVA De-Lite MER 38	13	10 wks
6 Dec 80	SLIP AND DIP / I WANNA BE WITH YOU De-Lite DE 1	57	3 wks

Alma COGAN UK, female vocalist — 110 wks

19 Mar 54 ●	BELL BOTTOM BLUES HMV B 10653	4	9 wks
27 Aug 54	LITTLE THINGS MEAN A LOT HMV B 10717	11	2 wks
8 Oct 54	LITTLE THINGS MEAN A LOT (re-entry) HMV B 10717	19	1 wk
22 Oct 54	LITTLE THINGS MEAN A LOT (2nd re-entry) HMV B 10717	18	2 wks
3 Dec 54 ●	I CAN'T TELL A WALTZ FROM A TANGO HMV B 10786	6	11 wks
27 May 55 ★	DREAMBOAT HMV B 10872	1	16 wks
23 Sep 55	BANJO'S BACK IN TOWN HMV B 10917	17	1 wk
14 Oct 55	GO ON BY HMV B 10917	16	4 wks
16 Dec 55	TWENTY TINY FINGERS HMV POP 129	17	1 wk
23 Dec 55 ●	NEVER DO A TANGO WITH AN ESKIMO HMV POP 129	6	5 wks
30 Mar 56	WILLIE CAN HMV POP 187 [1]	13	8 wks
13 Jul 56	THE BIRDS AND THE BEES HMV POP 223	25	4 wks
10 Aug 56	WHY DO FOOLS FALL IN LOVE HMV POP 223	22	3 wks
23 Nov 56	IN THE MIDDLE OF THE HOUSE (re-entry) HMV POP 261	20	3 wks
18 Jan 57	YOU ME AND US HMV POP 284	18	6 wks
29 Mar 57	WHATEVER LOLA WANTS HMV POP 317	26	2 wks
31 Jan 58	THE STORY OF MY LIFE HMV POP 433	25	2 wks

14 Feb 58	**SUGARTIME** *HMV POP 450*..............................**16**	10 wks
2 May 58	**SUGARTIME (re-entry)** *HMV POP 450* **30**	1 wk
23 Jan 59	**LAST NIGHT ON THE BACK PORCH** *HMV POP 573* ..**27**	2 wks
18 Dec 59	**WE GOT LOVE** *HMV POP 670* **26**	4 wks
12 May 60	**DREAM TALK** *HMV POP 728* **48**	1 wk
11 Aug 60	**TRAIN OF LOVE** *HMV POP 760* **27**	5 wks
20 Apr 61	**COWBOY JIMMY JOE** *Columbia DB 4607*............**37**	6 wks

[1] Alma Cogan with Desmond Lane - penny whistle

Shaye COGAN US, female vocalist — 1 wk

24 Mar 60	**MEAN TO ME** *MGM 1063* **40**	1 wk

Izhar COHEN and ALPHABETA
Israel, male/female vocal group — **7 wks**

13 May 78	**A BA NI BI** *Polydor 2001 781* **20**	7 wks

Marc COHN US, male vocalist — 15 wks

25 May 91	**WALKING IN MEMPHIS** *Atlantic A 7747* **66**	4 wks
10 Aug 91	**SILVER THUNDERBIRD** *Atlantic A 7657* **54**	3 wks
12 Oct 91	**WALKING IN MEMPHIS (re-issue)** *Atlantic A 7585* **22**	5 wks
29 May 93	**WALK THROUGH THE WORLD** *Atlantic A 7340CD*....**37**	3 wks

COLA BOY UK, male/female vocal/instrumental duo — 7 wks

6 Jul 91	● **7 WAYS TO LOVE** *Arista 114526* **8**	7 wks

COLD JAM featuring GRACE
US, male/female vocal/instrumental group — **2 wks**

28 Jul 90	**LAST NIGHT A DJ SAVED MY LIFE**	
	Big Wave BWR 39 ....**64**	2 wks

COLDCUT UK, male production duo — 36 wks

20 Feb 88	● **DOCTORIN' THE HOUSE** *Ahead Of Our Time* [1] **6**	9 wks
10 Sep 88	**STOP THIS CRAZY THING** *Ahead Of Our Time* [2] ...**21**	7 wks
25 Mar 89	**PEOPLE HOLD ON** *Ahead Of Our Time* [3] **11**	9 wks
3 Jun 89	**MY TELEPHONE** *Ahead Of Our Time* **52**	2 wks
16 Dec 89	**COLDCUT'S CHRISTMAS BREAK**	
	Ahead Of Our Time **67**	3 wks
26 May 90	**FIND A WAY** *Ahead Of Our Time* [4] **52**	2 wks
4 Sep 93	**DREAMER** *Arista 74321156642* **54**	2 wks
22 Jan 94	**AUTUMN LEAVES** *Arista 74321171052* **50**	2 wks

[1] Coldcut featuring Yazz and the Plastic Population [2] Coldcut featuring Junior Reid and the Ahead Of Our Time Orchestra [3] Coldcut featuring Lisa Stansfield [4] Coldcut featuring Queen Latifah

Cozy COLE US, male instrumentalist - drums — 1 wk

5 Dec 58	**TOPSY (PARTS 1 AND 2)** *London HL 8750* **29**	1 wk

George COLE - *See Dennis WATERMAN*

Lloyd COLE UK, male vocalist — 58 wks

26 May 84	**PERFECT SKIN** *Polydor COLE 1* [1] **71**	1 wk
9 Jun 84	**PERFECT SKIN (re-entry)** *Polydor COLE 1* [1] **26**	8 wks
25 Aug 84	**FOREST FIRE** *Polydor COLE 2* [1] **41**	6 wks
17 Nov 84	**RATTLESNAKES** *Poldor COLE 3* [1] **65**	2 wks
14 Sep 85	**BRAND NEW FRIEND** *Polydor COLE 4* [1] **19**	8 wks
9 Nov 85	**LOST WEEKEND** *Polydor COLE 5* [1] **17**	7 wks
18 Jan 86	**CUT ME DOWN** *Polydor COLE 6* [1] **38**	4 wks
3 Oct 87	**MY BAG** *Polydor COLE 7* [1] **46**	4 wks
9 Jan 88	**JENNIFER SHE SAID** *Polydor COLE 8* [1] **31**	5 wks
23 Apr 88	**FROM THE HIP** EP *Polydor COLE 9* [1] **59**	2 wks
3 Feb 90	**NO BLUE SKIES** *Polydor COLE 11* **42**	4 wks
7 Apr 90	**DON'T LOOK BACK** *Polydor COLE 12* **59**	3 wks
31 Aug 91	**SHE'S A GIRL AND I'M A MAN** *Polydor COLE 14* **55**	2 wks

25 Sep 93	**SO YOU'D LIKE TO SAVE THE WORLD**	
	Fontana VIBED1 14 ....**72**	2 wks

[1] Lloyd Cole and the Commotions

Tracks on From The Hip EP: *From The Hip / Please / Lonely Mile / Love Your Wife.*

Nat 'King' COLE US, male vocalist — 237 wks

14 Nov 52	● **SOMEWHERE ALONG THE WAY** *Capitol CL 13774* ..**3**	7 wks
19 Dec 52	● **BECAUSE YOU'RE MINE** *Capitol CL 13811* **6**	2 wks
2 Jan 53	**FAITH CAN MOVE MOUNTAINS** *Capitol CL 13811* ..**11**	1 wk
16 Jan 53	**FAITH CAN MOVE MOUNTAINS (re-entry)**	
	Capitol CL 13811 ....**12**	2 wks
23 Jan 53	● **BECAUSE YOU'RE MINE (re-entry)**	
	Capitol CL 13811 ....**10**	1 wk
6 Feb 53	● **FAITH CAN MOVE MOUNTAINS (2nd re-entry)**	
	Capitol CL 13811 ....**10**	1 wk
13 Feb 53	**BECAUSE YOU'RE MINE (2nd re-entry)**	
	Capitol CL 13811 ....**11**	1 wk
24 Apr 53	● **PRETEND** *Capitol CL 13878* **2**	18 wks
14 Aug 53	● **CAN'T I?** *Capitol CL 13937* **9**	3 wks
18 Sep 53	● **CAN'T I? (re-entry)** *Capitol CL 13937*................**6**	4 wks
18 Sep 53	● **MOTHER NATURE AND FATHER TIME**	
	Capitol CL 13912 ....**7**	7 wks
30 Oct 53	● **CAN'T I? (2nd re-entry)** *Capitol CL 13937* **10**	1 wk
16 Apr 54	● **TENDERLY** *Capitol CL 14061* **10**	1 wk
10 Sep 54	● **SMILE** *Capitol CL 14149* **2**	14 wks
8 Oct 54	**MAKE HER MINE** *Capitol CL 14149* **11**	2 wks
25 Feb 55	● **A BLOSSOM FELL** *Capitol CL 14235* **3**	10 wks
26 Aug 55	**MY ONE SIN** *Capitol CL 14327* **18**	1 wk
16 Sep 55	**MY ONE SIN (re-entry)** *Capitol CL 14327* **17**	1 wk
27 Jan 56	● **DREAMS CAN TELL A LIE** *Capitol CL 14513*..........**10**	9 wks
11 May 56	● **TOO YOUNG TO GO STEADY** *Capitol CL 14573* **8**	14 wks
14 Sep 56	**LOVE ME AS THOUGH THERE WERE**	
	NO TOMORROW *Capitol CL 14621* **24**	2 wks
5 Oct 56	**LOVE ME AS IF THERE WERE NO TOMORROW**	
	(re-entry) *Capitol CL 14621* **11**	13 wks
19 Apr 57	● **WHEN I FALL IN LOVE** *Capitol CL 14709* **2**	20 wks
5 Jul 57	**WHEN ROCK 'N ROLL CAME TO TRINIDAD**	
	Capitol CL 14733 ....**28**	1 wk
18 Oct 57	**MY PERSONAL POSSESSION** *Capitol CL 14765*......**21**	2 wks
25 Oct 57	**STARDUST** *Capitol CL 14787* **24**	2 wks
29 May 59	**YOU MADE ME LOVE YOU** *Capitol CL 15017* **22**	3 wks
4 Sep 59	**MIDNIGHT FLYER** *Capitol CL 15056*..................**27**	1 wk
18 Sep 59	**MIDNIGHT FLYER (re-entry)** *Capitol CL 15056* **23**	3 wks
12 Feb 60	**TIME AND THE RIVER** *Capitol CL 15111* **29**	1 wk
26 Feb 60	**TIME AND THE RIVER (re-entry)** *Capitol CL 15111* **23**	2 wks
31 Mar 60	**TIME AND THE RIVER (2nd re-entry)**	
	Capitol CL 15111 ....**47**	1 wk
26 May 60	● **THAT'S YOU** *Capitol CL 15129* **10**	8 wks
10 Nov 60	**JUST AS MUCH AS EVER** *Capitol CL 15163* **18**	10 wks
2 Feb 61	**THE WORLD IN MY ARMS** *Capitol CL 15178* **36**	10 wks
16 Nov 61	**LET TRUE LOVE BEGIN** *Capitol CL 15224* **29**	10 wks
22 Mar 62	**BRAZILIAN LOVE SONG** *Capitol CL 15241* **34**	4 wks
31 May 62	**THE RIGHT THING TO SAY** *Capitol CL 15250* **42**	4 wks
19 Jul 62	**LET THERE BE LOVE** *Capitol CL 15257* [1] **11**	14 wks
27 Sep 62	● **RAMBLIN' ROSE** *Capitol CL 15270*....................**5**	14 wks
20 Dec 62	**DEAR LONELY HEARTS** *Capitol CL 15280* **37**	3 wks
12 Dec 87	● **WHEN I FALL IN LOVE (re-issue)** *Capitol CL 15975*....**4**	7 wks
14 Dec 91	**THE CHRISTMAS SONG** *Capitol CL 641* **69**	2 wks
19 Mar 94	**LET'S FACE THE MUSIC AND DANCE** *EMI*	
	CDEM 312 ....**30**	3 wks

[1] Nat 'King' Cole with George Shearing

See also Natalie Cole.

Natalie COLE US, female vocalist — 87 wks

11 Oct 75	**THIS WILL BE** *Capitol CL 15834* **32**	5 wks
8 Aug 87	**JUMP START** *Manhattan MT 22* **44**	8 wks
26 Mar 88	● **PINK CADILLAC** *Manhattan MT 35* **5**	12 wks
25 Jun 88	**EVERLASTING** *Manhattan MT 46* **28**	6 wks
20 Aug 88	**JUMP START (re-issue)** *Manhattan MT 50* **36**	5 wks
26 Nov 88	**I LIVE FOR YOUR LOVE** *Manhattan MT 57*............**23**	14 wks
15 Apr 89	● **MISS YOU LIKE CRAZY** *EMI-USA MT 63* **2**	15 wks

22 Jul 89	**BEST OF THE NIGHT** EMI-USA MT 69	**56**	2 wks
16 Dec 89	**STARTING OVER AGAIN** EMI-USA MT 77	**56**	4 wks
21 Apr 90	**WILD WOMEN DO** EMI-USA MT 81	**16**	7 wks
22 Jun 91	**UNFORGETTABLE** Elektra EKR 128	**19**	8 wks
16 May 92	**THE VERY THOUGHT OF YOU** Elektra EKR 147	**71**	1 wk

Unforgettable *features the uncredited vocals of Nat 'King' Cole.*

COLETTE - See SISTER BLISS with COLETTE

John Ford COLEY - See ENGLAND DAN and John Ford COLEY

COLLAGE
US/Canada/Philippines, male vocal/instrumental group   **5 wks**

| 21 Sep 85 | **ROMEO WHERE'S JULIET?** MCA MCA 1006 | **46** | 5 wks |

Dave and Ansil COLLINS
Jamaica, male vocal/instrumental duo   **27 wks**

| 27 Mar 71 | ★ **DOUBLE BARREL** Technique TE 901 | **1** | 15 wks |
| 26 Jun 71 | ● **MONKEY SPANNER** Technique TE 914 | **7** | 12 wks |

Edwyn COLLINS *UK, male vocalist*   **5 wks**

| 11 Aug 84 | **PALE BLUE EYES** Swamplands SWP 1 [1] | **72** | 2 wks |
| 12 Nov 94 | **A GIRL LIKE YOU** Setanta ZOP 001CD1 | **42** | 3 wks |

[1] Paul Quinn and Edwyn Collins

A Girl Like You *was listed as Expressly EP.*

Felicia COLLINS - See LUKK featuring Felicia COLLINS

Jeff COLLINS *UK, male vocalist*   **8 wks**

| 18 Nov 72 | **ONLY YOU** Polydor 2058 287 | **40** | 8 wks |

Judy COLLINS *US, female vocalist*   **86 wks**

17 Jan 70	**BOTH SIDES NOW** Elektra EKSN 45043	**14**	11 wks
5 Dec 70	● **AMAZING GRACE** Elektra 2101 020	**5**	32 wks
24 Jul 71	**AMAZING GRACE (re-entry)** Elektra 2101 020	**48**	1 wk
4 Sep 71	**AMAZING GRACE (2nd re-entry)** Elektra 2101 020.	**40**	7 wks
20 Nov 71	**AMAZING GRACE (3rd re-entry)** Elektra 2101 020.	**50**	1 wk
18 Dec 71	**AMAZING GRACE (4th re-entry)** Elektra 2101 020.	**48**	2 wks
22 Apr 72	**AMAZING GRACE (5th re-entry)** Elektra 2101 020.	**20**	19 wks
9 Sep 72	**AMAZING GRACE (6th re-entry)** Elektra 2101 020.	**46**	2 wks
23 Dec 72	**AMAZING GRACE (7th re-entry)** Elektra 2101 020.	**49**	3 wks
17 May 75	● **SEND IN THE CLOWNS** Elektra K 12177	**6**	8 wks

Phil COLLINS *UK, male vocalist*   **204 wks**

17 Jan 81	● **IN THE AIR TONIGHT** Virgin VSK 102	**2**	10 wks
7 Mar 81	**I MISSED AGAIN** Virgin VS 402	**14**	8 wks
30 May 81	**IF LEAVING ME IS EASY** Virgin VS 423	**17**	8 wks
23 Oct 82	**THRU' THESE WALLS** Virgin VS 524	**56**	2 wks
4 Dec 82	★ **YOU CAN'T HURRY LOVE** Virgin VS 531	**1**	16 wks
19 Mar 83	**DON'T LET HIM STEAL YOUR HEART AWAY** Virgin VS 572	**45**	5 wks
7 Apr 84	● **AGAINST ALL ODDS (TAKE A LOOK AT ME NOW)** Virgin VS 674	**2**	14 wks
26 Jan 85	● **SUSSUDIO** Virgin VS 736	**12**	9 wks
9 Mar 85	★ **EASY LOVER** CBS A 4915 [1]	**1**	12 wks
13 Apr 85	● **ONE MORE NIGHT** Virgin VS 755	**4**	9 wks
27 Jul 85	**TAKE ME HOME** Virgin VS 777	**19**	9 wks
23 Nov 85	● **SEPARATE LIVES** Virgin VS 818 [2]	**4**	13 wks
18 Jun 88	● **IN THE AIR TONIGHT (re-mix)** Virgin VS 102	**4**	9 wks
3 Sep 88	★ **A GROOVY KIND OF LOVE** Virgin VS 1117	**1**	13 wks
26 Nov 88	● **TWO HEARTS** Virgin VS 1141	**6**	11 wks
4 Nov 89	● **ANOTHER DAY IN PARADISE** Virgin VS 1234	**2**	11 wks
27 Jan 90	● **I WISH IT WOULD RAIN DOWN** Virgin VS 1240	**7**	9 wks
28 Apr 90	**SOMETHING HAPPENED ON THE WAY TO HEAVEN** Virgin VS 1251	**15**	7 wks
28 Jul 90	**THAT'S JUST THE WAY IT IS** Virgin VS 1277	**26**	5 wks
6 Oct 90	**HANG IN LONG ENOUGH** Virgin VS 1300	**34**	3 wks
8 Dec 90	**DO YOU REMEMBER (LIVE)** Virgin VS 1305	**57**	5 wks
15 May 93	**HERO** Atlantic A 7360 [3]	**56**	3 wks
30 Oct 93	● **BOTH SIDES OF THE STORY** Virgin VSCDT 1500	**7**	5 wks
1 Jan 94	**BOTH SIDES OF THE STORY (re-entry)** Virgin VSCDT 1500	**61**	1 wk
15 Jan 94	**EVERYDAY** Virgin VSCDT 1505	**15**	5 wks
7 Mar 94	**WE WAIT AND WE WONDER** Virgin VSCD 1510	**45**	2 wks

[1] Philip Bailey (duet with Phil Collins) [2] Phil Collins and Marilyn Martin [3] David Crosby featuring Phil Collins

Rodger COLLINS *US, male vocalist*   **6 wks**

| 3 Apr 76 | **YOU SEXY SUGAR PLUM (BUT I LIKE IT)** Fantasy FTC 132 | **22** | 6 wks |

Willie COLLINS *US, male vocalist*   **4 wks**

| 28 Jun 86 | **WHERE YOU GONNA BE TONIGHT?** Capitol CL 410 | **46** | 4 wks |

Willie COLON *US, male vocalist*   **7 wks**

| 28 Jun 86 | **SET FIRE TO ME** A & M AM 330 | **41** | 7 wks |

COLOR ME BADD *US, male vocal group*   **31 wks**

18 May 91	★ **I WANNA SEX YOU UP** Giant W 0036	**1**	14 wks
3 Aug 91	● **ALL 4 LOVE** Giant W 0053	**5**	10 wks
12 Oct 91	**I ADORE MI AMOR** Giant W 0067	**44**	2 wks
9 Nov 91	**I ADORE MI AMOR (re-issue)** Giant W 0076	**59**	2 wks
22 Feb 92	**HEARTBREAKER** Giant W 0078	**58**	1 wk
20 Nov 93	**TIME AND CHANCE** Giant 74321168992	**62**	1 wk
16 Apr 94	**CHOOSE** Giant 74321199432	**65**	1 wk

COLORADO *UK, female vocal group*   **3 wks**

| 21 Oct 78 | **CALIFORNIA DREAMIN'** Pinnacle PIN 67 | **45** | 3 wks |

COLOUR FIELD *UK, male vocal/instrumental group*   **18 wks**

21 Jan 84	**THE COLOUR FIELD** Chrysalis COLF 1	**43**	4 wks
28 Jul 84	**TAKE** Chrysalis COLF 2	**70**	1 wk
26 Jan 85	**THINKING OF YOU** Chrysalis COLF 3	**12**	10 wks
13 Apr 85	**CASTLES IN THE AIR** Chrysalis COLF 4	**51**	3 wks

Shawn COLVIN *US, female vocalist*   **3 wks**

27 Nov 93	**I DON'T KNOW WHY** Columbia 6598272	**62**	1 wk
12 Feb 94	**ROUND OF BLUES** Columbia 6594282	**73**	1 wk
3 Sep 94	**EVERY LITTLE THING HE DOES IS MAGIC** Columbia 6607742	**65**	1 wk

COMETS - See Bill HALEY and his COMETS

COMMENTATORS
UK, male impressionist - Rory Bremner   **7 wks**

| 22 Jun 85 | **N-N-NINETEEN NOT OUT** Oval 100 | **13** | 7 wks |

COMMITMENTS
Ireland, male/female vocal/instrumental group   **1 wk**

| 30 Nov 91 | **MUSTANG SALLY** MCA MCS 1598 | **63** | 1 wk |

COMMODORES *US, male vocal/instrumental group*   **121 wks**

24 Aug 74	**MACHINE GUN** Tamla Motown TMG 902	**20**	11 wks
23 Nov 74	**THE ZOO (THE HUMAN ZOO)** Tamla Motown TMG 924	**44**	2 wks
2 Jul 77	● **EASY** Motown TMG 1073	**9**	10 wks
8 Oct 77	**SWEET LOVE / BRICK HOUSE** Motown TMG 1086	**32**	6 wks

PERRY COMO is shown in 1971, the year of his impossible comeback.

Tania Evans and Jay Supreme of **CULTURE BEAT** went to number one in ten European countries with 'Mr. Vain'. (REX)

NAT 'KING' COLE is shown at the piano, the instrument he played when he came to fame in the 1940s with the King Cole Trio. (LFI)

11 Mar 78	**TOO HOT TO TROT / ZOOM** Motown TMG 1096........**38**	4 wks
24 Jun 78	**FLYING HIGH** Motown TMG 1111 ....**37**	7 wks
5 Aug 78	★ **THREE TIMES A LADY** Motown TMG 1113 ....**1**	14 wks
25 Nov 78	**JUST TO BE CLOSE TO YOU** Motown TMG 1127 ....**62**	4 wks
25 Aug 79	● **SAIL ON** Motown TMG 1155 ....**8**	10 wks
3 Nov 79	● **STILL** Motown TMG 1166 ....**4**	11 wks
19 Jan 80	**WONDERLAND** Motown TMG 1172 ....**40**	4 wks
1 Aug 81	**LADY (YOU BRING ME UP)** Motown TMG 1238 .....**56**	5 wks
21 Nov 81	**OH NO** Motown TMG 1245 ....**44**	3 wks
26 Jan 85	● **NIGHTSHIFT** Motown TMG 1371 ....**3**	14 wks
11 May 85	**ANIMAL INSTINCT** Motown ZB 40097 ....**74**	1 wk
25 Oct 86	**GOIN' TO THE BANK** Polydor POSPA 826 ....**43**	4 wks
13 Aug 88	**EASY (re-issue)** Motown ZB 41793 ....**15**	11 wks

Group were US / UK for 1985 and 1986 hits.

COMMOTIONS - See Lloyd COLE

COMMUNARDS *UK, male vocal / instrumental duo* **76 wks**

12 Oct 85	**YOU ARE MY WORLD** London LON 77 ....**30**	8 wks
24 May 86	**DISENCHANTED** London LON 89 ....**29**	5 wks
23 Aug 86	★ **DON'T LEAVE ME THIS WAY** London LON 103 ☐1 ......**1**	14 wks
29 Nov 86	● **SO COLD THE NIGHT** London LON 110 ....**8**	10 wks
21 Feb 87	**YOU ARE MY WORLD ('87) (re-mix)** London LON 123 ....**21**	6 wks
12 Sep 87	**TOMORROW** London LON 143 ....**23**	7 wks
7 Nov 87	● **NEVER CAN SAY GOODBYE** London LON 158...........**4**	11 wks
20 Feb 88	**FOR A FRIEND** London LON 166 ....**28**	7 wks
11 Jun 88	**THERE'S MORE TO LOVE** London LON 173 ....**20**	8 wks

☐1 Communards with Sarah Jane Morris

Perry COMO *US, male vocalist* **294 wks**

16 Jan 53	★ **DON'T LET THE STARS GET IN YOUR EYES** HMV B 10400 ....**1**	15 wks
4 Jun 54	● **WANTED** HMV B 10667 ....**4**	14 wks
25 Jun 54	● **IDLE GOSSIP** HMV B 10710 ....**3**	15 wks
1 Oct 54	**WANTED (re-entry)** HMV B 10667 ....**18**	1 wk
10 Dec 54	**PAPA LOVES MAMBO** HMV B 10776 ....**16**	1 wk
30 Dec 55	**TINA MARIE** HMV POP 103 ....**24**	1 wk
27 Apr 56	**JUKE BOX BABY** HMV POP 191 ....**22**	6 wks
25 May 56	● **HOT DIGGITY** HMV POP 221 ....**4**	13 wks
21 Sep 56	● **MORE** HMV POP 240 ....**10**	11 wks
28 Sep 56	**GLENDORA** HMV POP 240 ....**18**	6 wks
14 Dec 56	**MORE (re-entry)** HMV POP 240 ....**29**	1 wk
7 Feb 58	★ **MAGIC MOMENTS** RCA 1036 ....**1**	17 wks
7 Mar 58	● **CATCH A FALLING STAR** RCA 1036 ....**9**	10 wks
9 May 58	● **KEWPIE DOLL** RCA 1055 ....**9**	7 wks
30 May 58	**I MAY NEVER PASS THIS WAY AGAIN** RCA 1062....**15**	8 wks
5 Sep 58	**MOON TALK** RCA 1071 ....**17**	11 wks
7 Nov 58	● **LOVE MAKES THE WORLD GO ROUND** RCA 1086 ....**6**	14 wks
21 Nov 58	**MANDOLINS IN THE MOONLIGHT** RCA 1086 ....**13**	12 wks
27 Feb 59	● **TOMBOY** RCA 1111 ....**10**	12 wks
10 Jul 59	**I KNOW** RCA 1126 ....**13**	16 wks
26 Feb 60	● **DELAWARE** RCA 1170 ....**3**	13 wks
10 May 62	**CATERINA** RCA 1283 ....**37**	4 wks
14 Jun 62	**CATERINA (re-entry)** RCA 1283 ....**45**	2 wks
30 Jan 71	● **IT'S IMPOSSIBLE** RCA 2043 ....**4**	23 wks
15 May 71	**I THINK OF YOU** RCA 2075 ....**14**	11 wks
21 Apr 73	● **AND I LOVE YOU SO** RCA 2346 ....**3**	31 wks
25 Aug 73	● **FOR THE GOOD TIMES** RCA 2402 ....**7**	27 wks
8 Dec 73	**WALK RIGHT BACK** RCA 2432 ....**33**	10 wks
12 Jan 74	**AND I LOVE YOU SO (re-entry)** RCA 2346 ....**40**	4 wks
25 May 74	**I WANT TO GIVE** RCA LPBO 7518...........................**31**	6 wks

COMPAGNONS DE LA CHANSON
France, male vocal group **3 wks**

9 Oct 59	**THE THREE BELLS (THE JIMMY BROWN SONG)** Columbia DB 4358 ....**27**	1 wk
23 Oct 59	**THE THREE BELLS (THE JIMMY BROWN SONG) (re-entry)** Columbia DB 4358..................................**21**	2 wks

COMSAT ANGELS *UK, male vocal / instrumental group* **2 wks**

21 Jan 84	**INDEPENDENCE DAY** Jive JIVE 54 ....**75**	1 wk
4 Feb 84	**INDEPENDENCE DAY (re-entry)** Jive JIVE 54 ....**71**	1 wk

CON FUNK SHUN *US, male vocal / instrumental group* **2 wks**

19 Jul 86	**BURNIN' LOVE** Club JAB 32 ....**68**	2 wks

CONCEPT *US, male vocalist / instrumentalist - keyboards* **6 wks**

14 Dec 85	**MR. DJ** Fourth & Broadway BRW 40 ....**27**	6 wks

CONFEDERATES - See Elvis COSTELLO

CONGREGATION *UK, male / female choir* **14 wks**

27 Nov 71	● **SOFTLY WHISPERING I LOVE YOU** Columbia DB 8830 ....**4**	14 wks

CONGRESS *UK, male / female vocal / instrumental group* **4 wks**

26 Oct 91	**40 MILES** Inner Rhythm 7HEART 01 ....**26**	4 wks

Arthur CONLEY *US, male vocalist* **15 wks**

27 Apr 67	● **SWEET SOUL MUSIC** Atlantic 584 083........................**7**	14 wks
10 Apr 68	**FUNKY STREET** Atlantic 583 175 ....**46**	1 wk

Harry CONNICK Jr. *US, male vocalist* **11 wks**

25 May 91	**RECIPE FOR LOVE / IT HAD TO BE YOU** Columbia 6568907 ....**32**	6 wks
3 Aug 91	**WE ARE IN LOVE** Columbia 6572847 ....**62**	2 wks
23 Nov 91	**BLUE LIGHT RED LIGHT (SOMEONE'S THERE)** Columbia 6575367 ....**54**	3 wks

Billy CONNOLLY *UK, male vocalist* **31 wks**

1 Nov 75	★ **D.I.V.O.R.C.E.** Polydor 2058 652 ....**1**	10 wks
17 Jul 76	**NO CHANCE (NO CHARGE)** Polydor 2058 748.........**24**	5 wks
25 Aug 79	**IN THE BROWNIES** Polydor 2059 160 ....**38**	7 wks
9 Mar 85	**SUPER GRAN** Stiff BUY 218 ....**32**	9 wks

CONQUERING LION *UK, male vocal group* **1 wk**

8 Oct 94	**CODE RED** Mango CIDM 821 ....**53**	1 wk

Leena CONQUEST *US, female vocalist* **1 wk**

18 Jun 94	**BOUNDARIES** Naturalresponse 74321208522............**67**	1 wk

Jess CONRAD *UK, male vocalist* **13 wks**

30 Jun 60	**CHERRY PIE** Decca F 11236 ....**39**	1 wk
26 Jan 61	**MYSTERY GIRL** Decca F 11315 ....**44**	1 wk
9 Feb 61	**MYSTERY GIRL (re-entry)** Decca F 11315 ....**18**	9 wks
11 Oct 62	**PRETTY JENNY** Decca F 11511 ....**50**	2 wks

CONSORTIUM *UK, male vocal group* **9 wks**

12 Feb 69	**ALL THE LOVE IN THE WORLD** Pye 7N 17635 ....**22**	9 wks

Ann CONSUELO - See SUBTERRANIA featuring Ann CONSUELO

CONTOURS *US, male vocal group* **6 wks**

24 Jan 70	**JUST A LITTLE MISUNDERSTANDING** Tamla Motown TMG 723 ....**31**	6 wks

CONTRABAND
Germany/US, male/female vocal/instrumental group **2 wks**

| 20 Jul 91 | **ALL THE WAY FROM MEMPHIS** *Impact American EM 195*.................**65** | 2 wks |

CONTROL *UK, male/female vocal/instrumental group* **5 wks**

| 2 Nov 91 | **DANCE WITH ME** *All Around The World GLOBE 105* ....**17** | 5 wks |

CONVERT *Belgium, male instrumental/production duo* **6 wks**

| 11 Jan 92 | **NIGHTBIRD** *A & M AM 845*.................**39** | 4 wks |
| 29 May 93 | **ROCKIN' TO THE RHYTHM** *A & M 5802532* ....**42** | 2 wks |

CONWAY BROTHERS *US, male vocal group* **10 wks**

| 22 Jun 85 | **TURN IT UP** *10 TEN 57*.................**11** | 10 wks |

Russ CONWAY *UK, male instrumentalist - piano* **178 wks**

29 Nov 57	**PARTY POPS** *Columbia DB 4031*.................**24**	5 wks
29 Aug 58	**GOT A MATCH** *Columbia DB 4166*.................**30**	1 wk
28 Nov 58	● **MORE PARTY POPS** *Columbia DB 4204* **10**	7 wks
23 Jan 59	**THE WORLD OUTSIDE** *Columbia DB 4234* **24**	1 wk
20 Feb 59	★ **SIDE SADDLE** *Columbia DB 4256*.................**1**	30 wks
6 Mar 59	**THE WORLD OUTSIDE (re-entry)** *Columbia DB 4234*.................**24**	3 wks
15 May 59	★ **ROULETTE** *Columbia DB 4298* **1**	19 wks
21 Aug 59	● **CHINA TEA** *Columbia DB 4337* **5**	13 wks
13 Nov 59	● **SNOW COACH** *Columbia DB 4368* **7**	9 wks
20 Nov 59	● **MORE AND MORE PARTY POPS** *Columbia DB 4373* ..**5**	8 wks
10 Mar 60	**ROYAL EVENT** *Columbia DB 4418* **15**	7 wks
21 Apr 60	**FINGS AIN'T WOT THEY USED T'BE** *Columbia DB 4422* **47**	1 wk
19 May 60	**LUCKY FIVE** *Columbia DB 4457* **14**	9 wks
29 Sep 60	**PASSING BREEZE** *Columbia DB 4508* **16**	10 wks
24 Nov 60	**EVEN MORE PARTY POPS** *Columbia DB 4535* **27**	9 wks
19 Jan 61	**PEPE** *Columbia DB 4564* **19**	9 wks
25 May 61	**PABLO** *Columbia DB 4649* **45**	2 wks
24 Aug 61	**SAY IT WITH FLOWERS** *Columbia DB 4665* [1] **23**	10 wks
30 Nov 61	● **TOY BALLOONS** *Columbia DB 4738* **7**	11 wks
22 Feb 62	**LESSON ONE** *Columbia DB 4784* **21**	7 wks
29 Nov 62	**ALWAYS YOU AND ME** *Columbia DB 4934* **33**	4 wks
3 Jan 63	**ALWAYS YOU AND ME (re-entry)** *Columbia DB 4934* **35**	3 wks

[1] Dorothy Squires and Russ Conway

Always You And Me featured Russ Conway talking as well as playing piano. Several of the discs were medleys as follows: Party Pops: When You're Smiling/I'm Looking Over a Four-Leafed Clover/When You Wore a Tulip/Row Row Row/For Me And My Girl/Shine On Harvest Moon/By The Light Of The Silvery Moon/Side By Side. More Party Pops: Music Music Music/If You Were The Only Girl In The World/Nobody's Sweetheart/Yes Sir That's My Baby/Some Of These Days/Honeysuckle And The Bee/Hello Hello Who's Your Lady Friend/Shanty In Old Shanty Town. More And More Party Pops: Sheik of Araby/Who Were You With Last Night/Any Old Iron/Tiptoe Through The Tulips/If You Were The Only Girl In The World/When I Leave The World Behind. Even More Party Pops: Ain't She Sweet/I Can't Give You Anything But Love/Yes We Have No Bananas/I May Be Wrong/Happy Days And Lonely Nights/Glad Rag Doll. He really did feature If You Were The Only Girl In The World on two different hits.

Martin COOK - See Richard DENTON and Martin COOK

Norman COOK *UK, male producer/multi-instrumentalist* **10 wks**

| 8 Jul 89 | **WON'T TALK ABOUT IT / BLAME IT ON THE BASSLINE** *Go Beat GOD 33* [1] ....**29** | 6 wks |
| 21 Oct 89 | **FOR SPACIOUS LIES** *Go Beat GOD 37* [2] ....**48** | 4 wks |

[1] Norman Cook featuring Billy Bragg/Norman Cook featuring MC Wildski
[2] Norman Cook featuring Lester

Peter COOK *UK, male vocalist* **15 wks**

| 17 Jun 65 | **GOODBYE-EE** *Decca F 12158* [1] ....**18** | 10 wks |
| 15 Jul 65 | **THE BALLAD OF SPOTTY MULDOON** *Decca F 12182*.................**34** | 5 wks |

[1] Peter Cook and Dudley Moore

Brandon COOKE - See Roxanne SHANTE

Sam COOKE *US, male vocalist* **82 wks**

17 Jan 58	**YOU SEND ME** *London HLU 8506* **29**	1 wk
14 Aug 59	**ONLY SIXTEEN** *HMV POP 642* **23**	4 wks
7 Jul 60	**WONDERFUL WORLD** *HMV POP 754* **27**	8 wks
29 Sep 60	● **CHAIN GANG** *RCA 1202* **9**	11 wks
27 Jul 61	● **CUPID** *RCA 1242*.................**7**	14 wks
8 Mar 62	**TWISTIN' THE NIGHT AWAY** *RCA 1277*.................**6**	14 wks
16 May 63	**ANOTHER SATURDAY NIGHT** *RCA 1341*.................**23**	12 wks
5 Sep 63	**FRANKIE AND JOHNNY** *RCA 1361* **30**	6 wks
22 Mar 86	● **WONDERFUL WORLD (re-issue)** *RCA PB 49871* **2**	11 wks
10 May 86	**ANOTHER SATURDAY NIGHT (re-issue)** *RCA PB 49849* **75**	1 wk

COOKIE CREW *UK, female vocal group* **31 wks**

9 Jan 88	● **ROK DA HOUSE** *Rhythm King LEFT 11* [1] **5**	11 wks
7 Jan 89	**BORN THIS WAY (LET'S DANCE)** *ffrr FFR 19* **23**	5 wks
1 Apr 89	**GOT TO KEEP ON** *ffrr FFR 25* **17**	9 wks
15 Jul 89	**COME AND GET SOME** *ffrr F 110* **42**	3 wks
27 Jul 91	**SECRETS OF SUCCESS** *ffrr F159* [2] **53**	3 wks

[1] Beatmasters featuring the Cookie Crew [2] Cookie Crew featuring Danny D

COOKIES *US, female vocal group* **1 wk**

| 10 Jan 63 | **CHAINS** *London HLU 9634* ....**50** | 1 wk |

COOL DOWN ZONE
UK, male/female vocal/instrumental group **4 wks**

| 30 Jun 90 | **HEAVEN KNOWS** *10 TEN 309*.................**52** | 4 wks |

Rita COOLIDGE *US, female vocalist* **24 wks**

25 Jun 77	● **WE'RE ALL ALONE** *A & M AMS 7295* **6**	13 wks
15 Oct 77	**(YOUR LOVE HAS LIFTED ME) HIGHER AND HIGHER** *A & M AMS 7315*.................**49**	1 wk
29 Oct 77	**(YOUR LOVE HAS LIFTED ME) HIGHER AND HIGHER (re-entry)** *A & M AMS 7315*.........**48**	1 wk
4 Feb 78	**WORDS** *A & M AMS 7330* **25**	8 wks
25 Jun 83	**ALL TIME HIGH** *A & M AM 007* **75**	1 wk

COOLIO *US, male rapper* **3 wks**

| 23 Jul 94 | **FANTASTIC VOYAGE** *Tommy Boy TB 0617CD*...........**41** | 2 wks |
| 15 Oct 94 | **I REMEMBER** *Tommy Boy TBXCD 635* ....**73** | 1 wk |

COOLNOTES
UK, male/female vocal/instrumental group **28 wks**

18 Aug 84	**YOU'RE NEVER TOO YOUNG** *Abstract Dance AD 1*	**42**	5 wks
17 Nov 84	**I FORGOT** *Abstract Dance AD 2* **63**	2 wks
23 Mar 85	**SPEND THE NIGHT** *Abstract Dance AD 3* **11**	9 wks
13 Jul 85	**IN YOUR CAR** *Abstract Dance AD 4*.................**13**	9 wks
19 Oct 85	**HAVE A GOOD FOREVER** *Abstract Dance AD 5* **73**	1 wk
17 May 86	**INTO THE MOTION** *Abstract Dance AD 8* **66**	2 wks

Alice COOPER *US, male vocalist* **104 wks**

15 Jul 72	★ **SCHOOL'S OUT** *Warner Bros. K 16188* **1**	12 wks
7 Oct 72	● **ELECTED** *Warner Bros. K 16214* **4**	10 wks
10 Feb 73	● **HELLO HURRAY** *Warner Bros. K 16248* **6**	12 wks

21 Apr 73	● NO MORE MR. NICE GUY *Warner Bros. K 16262*	**10**	10 wks
19 Jan 74	TEENAGE LAMENT '74 *Warner Bros. K 16345*	**12**	7 wks
21 May 77	(NO MORE) LOVE AT YOUR CONVENIENCE		
	Warner Bros. K 16935	**44**	2 wks
23 Dec 78	HOW YOU GONNA SEE ME NOW		
	Warner Bros. K 17270	**61**	6 wks
6 Mar 82	SEVEN AND SEVEN IS (LIVE VERSION)		
	Warner Bros. K 17924	**62**	3 wks
8 May 82	FOR BRITAIN ONLY / UNDER MY WHEELS		
	Warner Bros. K 17940	**66**	2 wks
18 Oct 86	HE'S BACK (THE MAN BEHIND THE MASK)		
	MCA MCA 1090	**61**	2 wks
9 Apr 88	FREEDOM *MCA MCA 1241*	**50**	3 wks
29 Jul 89	● POISON *Epic 655061 7*	**2**	11 wks
7 Oct 89	BED OF NAILS *Epic ALICE 3*	**38**	5 wks
2 Dec 89	HOUSE OF FIRE *Epic ALICE 4*	**65**	2 wks
22 Jun 91	HEY STOOPID *Epic 6569837*	**21**	6 wks
5 Oct 91	LOVE'S A LOADED GUN *Epic 6574387*	**38**	3 wks
6 Jun 92	FEED MY FRANKENSTEIN *Epic 6580927*	**27**	3 wks
28 May 94	LOST IN AMERICA *Epic 6603472*	**22**	3 wks
23 Jul 94	IT'S ME *Epic 6605632*	**34**	2 wks

For the first five hits, 'Alice Cooper' was the name of the entire group, not just of the lead vocalist.

Deborah COOPER - *See C & C MUSIC FACTORY/CLIVILLES & COLE*

Tommy COOPER *UK, male vocalist*   **3 wks**

29 Jun 61	DON'T JUMP OFF THE ROOF DAD *Palette PG 9019* **40**	2 wks
20 Jul 61	DON'T JUMP OFF THE ROOF DAD (re-entry)	
	Palette PG 9019	**50**	1 wk

Julian COPE *UK, male vocalist*   **53 wks**

19 Nov 83	SUNSHINE PLAYROOM *Mercury COPE 1*	**64**	1 wk
31 Mar 84	THE GREATNESS AND PERFECTION OF LOVE		
	Mercury MER 155	**52**	5 wks
27 Sep 86	WORLD SHUT YOUR MOUTH *Island IS 290*	**19**	8 wks
17 Jan 87	TRAMPOLENE *Island IS 305*	**31**	6 wks
11 Apr 87	EVE'S VOLCANO (COVERED IN SIN) *Island IS 318*	**41**	5 wks
24 Sep 88	CHARLOTTE ANNE *Island IS 380*	**35**	6 wks
21 Jan 89	5 O'CLOCK WORLD *Island IS 399*	**42**	4 wks
24 Jun 89	CHINA DOLL *Island IS 406*	**53**	2 wks
9 Feb 91	BEAUTIFUL LOVE *Island IS 483*	**32**	6 wks
20 Apr 91	EAST EASY RIDER *Island IS 492*	**51**	3 wks
3 Aug 91	HEAD *Island IS 497*	**57**	2 wks
8 Aug 92	WORLD SHUT YOUR MOUTH (re-issue)		
	Island IS 534	**44**	3 wks
17 Oct 92	FEAR LOVES THIS PLACE *Island IS 545*	**42**	2 wks

Harry H. CORBETT - *See Wilfrid BRAMBELL and Harry H. CORBETT*

Frank CORDELL *UK, orchestra*   **4 wks**

| 24 Aug 56 | SADIE'S SHAWL *HMV POP 229* | **29** | 2 wks |
| 16 Feb 61 | BLACK BEAR *HMV POP 824* | **44** | 2 wks |

Louise CORDET *France, female vocalist*   **13 wks**

| 5 Jul 62 | I'M JUST A BABY *Decca F 11476* | **13** | 13 wks |

Don CORNELL *US, male vocalist*   **23 wks**

| 3 Sep 54 | ★ HOLD MY HAND *Vogue Q 2013* | **1** | 21 wks |
| 22 Apr 55 | STRANGER IN PARADISE *Vogue Q 72073* | **19** | 2 wks |

Lynn CORNELL *UK, female vocalist*   **9 wks**

| 20 Oct 60 | NEVER ON SUNDAY *Decca F 11277* | **30** | 9 wks |

Charlotte CORNWELL - *See Julie COVINGTON, Rula LENSKA, Charlotte CORNWELL and Sue JONES-DAVIES*

Hugh CORNWELL *UK, male vocalist / instrumentalist - guitar*   **3 wks**

| 24 Jan 87 | FACTS + FIGURES *Virgin VS 922* | **61** | 2 wks |
| 7 May 88 | ANOTHER KIND OF LOVE *Virgin VS 945* | **71** | 1 wk |

CORO featuring TARLISA *Germany, male / female vocal / production group*   **1 wk**

| 12 Dec 92 | BECAUSE THE NIGHT *ZYX ZYX 68227* | **61** | 1 wk |

CORONA *Brazil, female vocalist*   **15 wks**

10 Sep 94	● THE RHYTHM OF THE NIGHT *WEA YZ 837CD1*	**2**	14 wks
31 Dec 94	THE RHYTHM OF THE NIGHT (re-entry)		
	WEA YZ 837CD1	**71†**	1 wk

CORONETS *UK, male / female vocal group*   **7 wks**

26 Aug 55	THAT'S HOW A LOVE SONG WAS BORN		
	Columbia DB 3640 [1]	**14**	6 wks
25 Nov 55	TWENTY TINY FINGERS *Columbia DB 3671*	**20**	1 wk

[1] Ray Burns with the Coronets

Vladimir COSMA *Hungary, orchestra*   **1 wk**

| 14 Jul 79 | DAVID'S SONG (MAIN THEME FROM `KIDNAPPED') | | |
| | *Decca FR 13841* | **64** | 1 wk |

COSMIC BABY *Germany, male producer*   **1 wk**

| 26 Feb 94 | LOOPS OF INFINITY *Logic 74321191432* | **70** | 1 wk |

Don COSTA *US, orchestra*   **10 wks**

| 13 Oct 60 | NEVER ON SUNDAY *London HLT 9195* | **27** | 9 wks |
| 22 Dec 60 | NEVER ON SUNDAY (re-entry) *London HLT 9195* | **41** | 1 wk |

Elvis COSTELLO *UK, male vocalist*   **167 wks**

5 Nov 77	WATCHING THE DETECTIVES *Stiff BUY 20*	**15**	11 wks
11 Mar 78	(I DON'T WANNA GO TO) CHELSEA		
	Radar ADA 3 [1]	**16**	10 wks
13 May 78	PUMP IT UP *Radar ADA 10* [1]	**24**	10 wks
28 Oct 78	RADIO RADIO *Radar ADA 24* [1]	**29**	7 wks
10 Feb 79	● OLIVER'S ARMY *Radar ADA 31* [1]	**2**	12 wks
12 May 79	ACCIDENTS WILL HAPPEN *Radar ADA 35* [1]	**28**	8 wks
16 Feb 80	● I CAN'T STAND UP FOR FALLING DOWN		
	F. Beat XX 1	**4**	8 wks
12 Apr 80	HI FIDELITY *F. Beat XX 3*	**30**	5 wks
7 Jun 80	NEW AMSTERDAM *F. Beat XX 5*	**36**	6 wks
20 Dec 80	CLUBLAND *F. Beat XX 12* [1]	**60**	4 wks
3 Oct 81	● A GOOD YEAR FOR THE ROSES *F. Beat XX 17*	**6**	11 wks
12 Dec 81	SWEET DREAMS *F. Beat XX 19*	**42**	8 wks
10 Apr 82	I'M YOUR TOY *F. Beat XX 21* [2]	**51**	3 wks
19 Jun 82	YOU LITTLE FOOL *F. Beat XX 26*	**52**	3 wks
31 Jul 82	MAN OUT OF TIME *F. Beat XX 28*	**58**	2 wks
25 Sep 82	FROM HEAD TO TOE *F. Beat XX 30*	**43**	4 wks
11 Dec 82	PARTY PARTY *A & M AMS 8267*	**48**	6 wks
11 Jun 83	PILLS AND SOAP *Imp IMP 001* [3]	**16**	4 wks
9 Jul 83	EVERYDAY I WRITE THE BOOK *F. Beat XX 32*	**28**	8 wks
17 Sep 83	LET THEM ALL TALK *F. Beat XX 33*	**59**	2 wks
28 Apr 84	PEACE IN OUR TIME *Imposter TRUCE 1* [3]	**48**	3 wks
16 Jun 84	I WANNA BE LOVED / TURNING THE TOWN RED		
	F. Beat XX 35	**25**	6 wks
25 Aug 84	THE ONLY FLAME IN TOWN *F. Beat XX 37*	**71**	2 wks
4 May 85	GREEN SHIRT *F. Beat ZB 40085*	**71**	1 wk
18 May 85	GREEN SHIRT (re-entry) *F. Beat ZB 40085*	**68**	1 wk

1 Feb 86	DON'T LET ME BE MISUNDERSTOOD		
	F. Beat ZB 40555 [4] **33**	4 wks
30 Aug 86	TOKYO STORM WARNING Imp IMP 007 ....**73**	1 wk
4 Mar 89	VERONICA Warner Bros. W 7558 ....**31**	6 wks
20 May 89	BABY PLAYS AROUND EP Warner Bros. W 2949 ......**65**	1 wk
4 May 91	THE OTHER SIDE OF SUMMER		
	Warner Bros. W 0025 ....**43**	4 wks
5 Mar 94	SULKY GIRL Warner Bros. W 0234CD [1] **22**	3 wks
30 Apr 94	13 STEPS LEAD DOWN Warner Bros. W 0245CD [1] **59**	1 wk
26 Nov 94	LONDON'S BRILLIANT PARADE		
	Warner Bros. W 0270CD1 [1] **48**	2 wks

[1] Elvis Costello and the Attractions [2] Elvis Costello and the Attractions with the Royal Philharmonic Orchestra [3] Imposter [4] Costello Show featuring the Confederates

Tracks on Baby Plays Around (EP): Baby Plays Around / Poisoned Rose / Almost Blue / My Funny Valentine.

COTTAGERS - See Tony REES and the COTTAGERS

Billy COTTON and his BAND
UK, male bandleader, vocalist, with band and chorus **25 wks**

1 May 53	● IN A GOLDEN COACH Decca F 10058 [1] **3**	10 wks
18 Dec 53	I SAW MOMMY KISSING SANTA CLAUS		
	Decca F 10206 [2] **11**	3 wks
30 Apr 54	FRIENDS AND NEIGHBOURS Decca F 10299 [3] **12**	1 wk
14 May 54	● FRIENDS AND NEIGHBOURS (re-entry)		
	Decca F 10299 [3] **3**	11 wks

[1] Billy Cotton and his Band, vocals by Doreen Stephens [2] Billy Cotton and his Band, vocals by the Mill Girls and the Bandits [3] Billy Cotton and his Band, vocals by the Bandits

See also Various Artists (EPs & LPs) - All Stars Hit Parade No. 2.

Mike COTTON'S JAZZMEN
UK, male instrumental band, Mike Cotton trumpet **4 wks**

20 Jun 63	SWING THAT HAMMER Columbia DB 7029 ....**36**	4 wks

John COUGAR - See John Cougar MELLENCAMP

COUGARS *UK, male instrumental group* **8 wks**

28 Feb 63	SATURDAY NITE AT THE DUCK POND		
	Parlophone R 4989 ....**33**	8 wks

COUNCIL COLLECTIVE
UK / US, male / female vocal / instrumental group **6 wks**

22 Dec 84	SOUL DEEP (PART 1) Polydor MINE 1 ....**24**	6 wks

COUNTING CROWS
US, male vocal / instrumental group **6 wks**

30 Apr 94	MR. JONES Geffen GFSTD 69 ....**28**	2 wks
9 Jul 94	ROUND HERE Geffen GFSTD 74 ....**70**	1 wk
15 Oct 94	RAIN KING Geffen GFSTD 82 ....**49**	3 wks

COUNTRYMEN *UK, male vocal group* **2 wks**

3 May 62	I KNOW WHERE I'M GOING Piccadilly 7N 35029 ......**45**	2 wks

Don COVAY *US, male vocalist* **6 wks**

7 Sep 74	IT'S BETTER TO HAVE (AND DON'T NEED)		
	Mercury 6052 634 ....**29**	6 wks

COVENTRY CITY CUP FINAL SQUAD
UK, male football team vocalists **2 wks**

23 May 87	GO FOR IT! Sky Blue SKB 1 ....**61**	2 wks

British Hit Singles Part One: Alphabetically by Artist
Date of chart entry/Title & catalogue no./Peak position reached/Weeks on chart
★ Number One ● Top Ten † still on chart at 31 Dec 1994
□ = credited to act billed in footnote

COVER GIRLS *US, female vocal group* **4 wks**

1 Aug 92	WISHING ON A STAR Epic 6581437 ....**38**	4 wks

COVERDALE PAGE *UK, male vocal / instrumental duo* **3 wks**

3 Jul 93	TAKE ME FOR A LITTLE WHILE EMI CDEM 270 ....**25**	2 wks
23 Oct 93	TAKE A LOOK AT YOURSELF EMI CDEM 279 ....**43**	1 wk

Julie COVINGTON *UK, female vocalist* **29 wks**

25 Dec 76	★ DON'T CRY FOR ME ARGENTINA MCA 260 ....**1**	15 wks
3 Dec 77	ONLY WOMEN BLEED Virgin VS 196 ....**12**	11 wks
15 Jul 78	DON'T CRY FOR ME ARGENTINA (re-entry)		
	MCA 260 ....**63**	3 wks

See also Julie Covington, Rula Lenska, Charlotte Cornwell and Sue Jones-Davies.

Warren COVINGTON - See Tommy DORSEY ORCHESTRA starring Warren COVINGTON

Julie COVINGTON, Rula LENSKA, Charlotte CORNWELL and Sue JONES-DAVIES
UK, female vocal group **6 wks**

21 May 77	● O.K? Polydor 2001 714 ....**10**	6 wks

See also Julie Covington.

Patrick COWLEY - See SYLVESTER

Michael COX *UK, male vocalist* **15 wks**

9 Jun 60	● ANGELA JONES Triumph RGM 1011 ....**7**	13 wks
20 Oct 60	ALONG CAME CAROLINE HMV POP 789 ....**41**	2 wks

CRACKER *US, male vocal / instrumental group* **9 wks**

28 May 94	LOW Virgin America VUSDG 80 ....**43**	4 wks
23 Jul 94	GET OFF THIS Virgin America VUSCD 83 ....**41**	3 wks
3 Dec 94	LOW (re-entry) Virgin America VUSDG 80 ....**54**	2 wks

Floyd CRAMER *US, male instrumentalist - piano* **24 wks**

13 Apr 61	★ ON THE REBOUND RCA 1231 ....**1**	14 wks
20 Jul 61	SAN ANTONIO ROSE RCA 1241 ....**36**	8 wks
23 Aug 62	HOT PEPPER RCA 1301 ....**46**	2 wks

CRAMPS *US, female / male vocal / instrumental group* **4 wks**

9 Nov 85	CAN YOUR PUSSY DO THE DOG?		
	Big Beat NS 110 ....**68**	1 wk
10 Feb 90	BIKINI GIRLS WITH MACHINE GUNS		
	Enigma ENV 17 ....**35**	3 wks

CRANBERRIES
Ireland, male / female vocal / instrumental group **28 wks**

27 Feb 93	LINGER Island CID 556 ....**74**	1 wk
12 Feb 94	LINGER (re-issue) Island CID 559 ....**14**	11 wks
7 May 94	DREAMS Island CIDX 594 ....**27**	5 wks
1 Oct 94	ZOMBIE Island CID 600 ....**14**	6 wks
3 Dec 94	ODE TO MY FAMILY Island CIDX 601 ....**38†**	5 wks

Les CRANE US, male vocalist — 14 wks

| 19 Feb 72 | ● DESIDERATA Warner Bros. K 16119 | **7** | 14 wks |

Whitfield CRANE - See ICE-T: MOTORHEAD

CRANES UK, male/female vocal/instrumental group — 2 wks

| 25 Sep 93 | JEWEL Dedicated CRANE 007CD | **29** | 1 wk |
| 3 Sep 94 | SHINING ROAD Dedicated CRANE 8CD1 | **57** | 1 wk |

CRASH TEST DUMMIES
Canada, male/female vocal/instrumental group — **16 wks**

| 23 Apr 94 | ● MMM MMM MMM MMM RCA 74321201512 | **2** | 11 wks |
| 16 Jul 94 | AFTERNOONS & COFFEESPOONS RCA 74321219622 | **23** | 5 wks |

Beverley CRAVEN UK, female vocalist — 33 wks

20 Apr 91	● PROMISE ME Epic 6559437	**3**	13 wks
20 Jul 91	HOLDING ON Epic 6565507	**32**	7 wks
5 Oct 91	WOMAN TO WOMAN Epic 6574647	**40**	5 wks
7 Dec 91	MEMORIES Epic 6576617	**68**	2 wks
25 Sep 93	LOVE SCENES Epic 6595952	**34**	4 wks
20 Nov 93	MOLLIE'S SONG Epic 6598132	**61**	2 wks

Jimmy CRAWFORD UK, male vocalist — 11 wks

| 8 Jun 61 | LOVE OR MONEY Columbia DB 4633 | **49** | 1 wk |
| 16 Nov 61 | I LOVE HOW YOU LOVE ME Columbia DB 4717 | **18** | 10 wks |

Michael CRAWFORD UK, male vocalist — 14 wks

| 10 Jan 87 | ● THE MUSIC OF THE NIGHT Polydor POSP 803 | **7** | 11 wks |
| 15 Jan 94 | THE MUSIC OF THE NIGHT Columbia 6597382 [1] | **54** | 3 wks |

[1] Barbra Streisand (duet with Michael Crawford)

The flip side of The Music Of The Night/ *in 1987,* Wishing You Were Somehow Here Again *by Sarah Brightman, was also listed.*

Randy CRAWFORD US, female vocalist — 74 wks

21 Jun 80	LAST NIGHT AT DANCELAND Warner Bros. K 17631	**61**	2 wks
30 Aug 80	● ONE DAY I'LL FLY AWAY Warner Bros. K 17680	**2**	11 wks
30 May 81	YOU MIGHT NEED SOMEBODY Warner Bros. K 17803	**11**	13 wks
8 Aug 81	RAINY NIGHT IN GEORGIA Warner Bros. K 17840	**18**	9 wks
31 Oct 81	SECRET COMBINATION Warner Bros. K 17872	**48**	3 wks
30 Jan 82	IMAGINE Warner Bros. K 17906	**60**	1 wk
13 Feb 82	IMAGINE (re-entry) Warner Bros. K 17906	**75**	1 wk
5 Jun 82	ONE HELLO Warner Bros. K 17948	**48**	4 wks
19 Feb 83	HE REMINDS ME Warner Bros. K 17970	**65**	2 wks
8 Oct 83	NIGHT LINE Warner Bros. W 9530	**51**	4 wks
29 Nov 86	● ALMAZ Warner Bros. W 8583	**4**	17 wks
18 Jan 92	DIAMANTE London LON 313 [1]	**44**	7 wks

[1] Zucchero with Randy Crawford

See also Crusaders.

Robert CRAY BAND
US, male vocal/instrumental group — **4 wks**

| 20 Jun 87 | RIGHT NEXT DOOR (BECAUSE OF ME) Mercury CRAY 3 | **50** | 4 wks |

CRAZY ELEPHANT US, male vocal group — 13 wks

| 21 May 69 | GIMME GIMME GOOD LOVIN' Major Minor MM 609 | **12** | 13 wks |

CRAZYHEAD UK, male vocal/instrumental group — 4 wks

| 16 Jul 88 | TIME HAS TAKEN ITS TOLL ON YOU Food FOOD 12 | **65** | 2 wks |
| 25 Feb 89 | HAVE LOVE, WILL TRAVEL EP Food SGE 2025 | **68** | 2 wks |

Tracks on Have Love, Will Travel EP: Have Love Will Travel / Out On A Limb (Live) / Baby Turpentine (Live) / Snake Eyes (Live). *See also Various Artists (EPs & LPs) - The Food Christmas EP.*

CREAM UK, male vocal/instrumental group — 59 wks

20 Oct 66	WRAPPING PAPER Reaction 591 007	**34**	6 wks
15 Dec 66	I FEEL FREE Reaction 591 011	**11**	12 wks
8 Jun 67	STRANGE BREW Reaction 591 015	**17**	9 wks
5 Jun 68	ANYONE FOR TENNIS (THE SAVAGE SEVEN THEME) Polydor 56 258	**40**	3 wks
9 Oct 68	SUNSHINE OF YOUR LOVE Polydor 56 286	**25**	7 wks
15 Jan 69	WHITE ROOM Polydor 56 300	**28**	8 wks
9 Apr 69	BADGE Polydor 56 315	**18**	10 wks
28 Oct 72	BADGE (re-issue) Polydor 2058 285	**42**	4 wks

CREATION UK, male vocal/instrumental group — 3 wks

| 7 Jul 66 | MAKING TIME Planet PLF 116 | **49** | 1 wk |
| 3 Nov 66 | PAINTER MAN Planet PLF 119 | **36** | 2 wks |

CREATURES UK, male/female vocal/instrumental group — 26 wks

3 Oct 81	MAD EYED SCREAMER Polydor POSPD 354	**24**	7 wks
23 Apr 83	MISS THE GIRL Wonderland SHE 1	**21**	7 wks
16 Jul 83	RIGHT NOW Wonderland SHE 2	**14**	10 wks
14 Oct 89	STANDING THERE Wonderland SHE 17	**53**	2 wks

CREDIT TO THE NATION UK, male rap group — 9 wks

22 May 93	CALL IT WHAT YOU WANT One Little Indian 94 TP7CD	**57**	3 wks
18 Sep 93	ENOUGH IS ENOUGH One Little Indian 79 TP7CD [1]	**56**	2 wks
12 Mar 94	TEENAGE SENSATION One Little Indian 124 TP7DC	**24**	3 wks
14 May 94	SOWING THE SEEDS OF HATRED One Little Indian 134 TP7CD	**72**	1 wk

[1] Chumbawamba and Credit To The Nation

CREEDENCE CLEARWATER REVIVAL
US, male vocal/instrumental group — **94 wks**

28 May 69	● PROUD MARY Liberty LBF 15223	**8**	13 wks
16 Aug 69	★ BAD MOON RISING Liberty LBF 15230	**1**	15 wks
15 Nov 69	GREEN RIVER Liberty LBF 15250	**19**	11 wks
14 Feb 70	DOWN ON THE CORNER Liberty LBF 15283	**31**	6 wks
4 Apr 70	● TRAVELLIN' BAND Liberty LBF 15310	**8**	12 wks
20 Jun 70	● UP AROUND THE BEND Liberty LBF 15354	**3**	12 wks
4 Jul 70	TRAVELLIN' BAND (re-entry) Liberty LBF 15310	**46**	1 wk
5 Sep 70	LONG AS I CAN SEE THE LIGHT Liberty LBF 15384	**20**	9 wks
20 Mar 71	HAVE YOU EVER SEEN THE RAIN Liberty LBF 15440	**36**	6 wks
24 Jul 71	SWEET HITCH-HIKER United Artists UP 35261	**36**	8 wks
2 May 92	BAD MOON RISING (re-issue) Epic 6580047	**71**	1 wk

Kid CREOLE and the COCONUTS
US, male vocalist and female vocal group — **58 wks**

13 Jun 81	ME NO POP I Ze WIP 6711 [1]	**32**	7 wks
15 May 82	● I'M A WONDERFUL THING, BABY Ze WIP 6756	**4**	11 wks
24 Jul 82	● STOOL PIGEON Ze WIP 6793	**7**	9 wks
9 Oct 82	● ANNIE I'M NOT YOUR DADDY Ze WIP 6801	**2**	8 wks
11 Dec 82	DEAR ADDY Ze WIP 6840	**29**	7 wks
10 Sep 83	THERE'S SOMETHING WRONG IN PARADISE Island IS 130	**35**	5 wks
19 Nov 83	THE LIFEBOAT PARTY Island IS 142	**49**	4 wks

14 Apr 90	THE SEX OF IT *CBS 655698 7*	**29**	5 wks
10 Apr 93	I'M A WONDERFUL THING BABY (re-mix)		
	Island CID 551	**60**	2 wks

[1] Kid Creole and the Coconuts present Coati Mundi

See also Coconuts.

CREW CUTS *Canada, male vocal group* **29 wks**

1 Oct 54	SH-BOOM *Mercury MB 3140*	**12**	9 wks
15 Apr 55 ●	EARTH ANGEL *Mercury MB 3202*	**4**	20 wks

Bernard CRIBBINS *UK, male vocalist* **29 wks**

15 Feb 62 ●	HOLE IN THE GROUND *Parlophone R 4869*	**9**	13 wks
5 Jul 62 ●	RIGHT SAID FRED *Parlophone R 4923*	**10**	10 wks
13 Dec 62	GOSSIP CALYPSO *Parlophone R 4961*	**25**	6 wks

CRICKETS *US, male vocal/instrumental group* **97 wks**

27 Sep 57 ★	THAT'LL BE THE DAY *Vogue Coral Q 72279*	**1**	14 wks
27 Dec 57 ●	OH BOY *Coral Q 72298*	**3**	15 wks
10 Jan 58	THAT'LL BE THE DAY (re-entry) *Vogue Coral Q 72279*	**29**	1 wk
14 Mar 58 ●	MAYBE BABY *Coral Q 72307*	**4**	10 wks
25 Jul 58	THINK IT OVER *Coral Q 72329*	**11**	7 wks
24 Apr 59	LOVE'S MADE A FOOL OF YOU *Coral Q 72365*	**26**	1 wk
8 May 59	LOVE'S MADE A FOOL OF YOU (re-entry) *Coral Q 72365*	**30**	1 wk
15 Jan 60	WHEN YOU ASK ABOUT LOVE *Coral Q 72382*	**27**	1 wk
12 May 60	MORE THAN I CAN SAY *Coral Q 72395*	**42**	1 wk
26 May 60	BABY MY HEART *Coral Q 72395*	**33**	4 wks
21 Jun 62 ●	DON'T EVER CHANGE *Liberty LIB 55441*	**5**	13 wks
24 Jan 63	MY LITTLE GIRL *Liberty LIB 10067*	**17**	9 wks
6 Jun 63	DON'T TRY TO CHANGE ME *Liberty LIB 10092*	**37**	4 wks
14 May 64	YOU'VE GOT LOVE *Coral Q 72472* [1]	**40**	6 wks
2 Jul 64	(THEY CALL HER) LA BAMBA *Liberty LIB 55696*	**21**	10 wks

[1] Buddy Holly and the Crickets

Although not credited on the records, Buddy Holly was featured on the first four hits.

CRIMINAL ELEMENT ORCHESTRA - *See Wally JUMP Jr. and the CRIMINAL ELEMENT*

CRISPY AND COMPANY
US, male vocal/instrumental group **11 wks**

16 Aug 75	BRAZIL *Creole CR 109*	**26**	5 wks
27 Dec 75	GET IT TOGETHER *Creole CR 114*	**21**	6 wks

CRITTERS *US, male vocal/instrumental group* **5 wks**

30 Jun 66	YOUNGER GIRL *London HL 10047*	**38**	5 wks

Tony CROMBIE and his ROCKETS
UK, male vocal/instrumental group, Tony Crombie – drums **2 wks**

19 Oct 56	TEACH YOU TO ROCK / SHORT'NIN' BREAD *Columbia DB 3822*	**25**	2 wks

Bing CROSBY *US, male vocalist* **93 wks**

14 Nov 52 ●	ISLE OF INNISFREE *Brunswick 04900*	**3**	12 wks
5 Dec 52 ●	ZING A LITTLE ZONG *Brunswick 04981* [1]	**10**	2 wks
19 Dec 52 ●	SILENT NIGHT *Brunswick 03929*	**8**	2 wks
19 Mar 54 ●	CHANGING PARTNERS *Brunswick 05244*	**10**	1 wk
2 Apr 54 ●	CHANGING PARTNERS (re-entry) *Brunswick 05244*	**9**	1 wk
23 Apr 54	CHANGING PARTNERS (2nd re-entry) *Brunswick 05244*	**11**	1 wk
7 Jan 55	COUNT YOUR BLESSINGS *Brunswick 05339*	**18**	1 wk
21 Jan 55	COUNT YOUR BLESSINGS (re-entry) *Brunswick 05339*	**11**	2 wks
29 Apr 55	STRANGER IN PARADISE *Brunswick 05410*	**17**	2 wks
27 Apr 56	IN A LITTLE SPANISH TOWN *Brunswick 05543*	**22**	3 wks
23 Nov 56 ●	TRUE LOVE *Capitol CL 14645* [2]	**4**	27 wks
24 May 57 ●	AROUND THE WORLD *Brunswick 05674*	**5**	15 wks
9 Aug 75	THAT'S WHAT LIFE IS ALL ABOUT *United Artists UP 35852*	**41**	4 wks
3 Dec 77 ●	WHITE CHRISTMAS *MCA 111*	**5**	7 wks
27 Nov 82 ●	PEACE ON EARTH - LITTLE DRUMMER BOY *RCA BOW 12* [3]	**3**	8 wks
17 Dec 83	TRUE LOVE (re-issue) *Capitol CL 315* [2]	**70**	3 wks
21 Dec 85	WHITE CHRISTMAS (re-issue) *MCA BING 1*	**69**	2 wks

[1] Bing Crosby and Jane Wyman [2] Bing Crosby and Grace Kelly [3] David Bowie and Bing Crosby

David CROSBY - *See CROSBY, STILLS, NASH & YOUNG; Phil COLLINS*

CROSBY STILLS NASH and YOUNG
US/UK/Canada, male vocal/instrumental group **12 wks**

16 Aug 69	MARRAKESH EXPRESS *Atlantic 584 283* [1]	**17**	9 wks
21 Jan 89	AMERICAN DREAM *Atlantic A 9003*	**55**	3 wks

[1] Crosby, Stills and Nash

See also Stephen Stills; Neil Young.

CROSS *UK/US, male vocal/instrumental group* **1 wk**

17 Oct 87	COWBOYS AND INDIANS *Virgin VS 1007*	**74**	1 wk

Christopher CROSS *US, male vocalist* **27 wks**

19 Apr 80	RIDE LIKE THE WIND *Warner Bros. K 17582*	**69**	1 wk
14 Feb 81	SAILING *Warner Bros. K 17695*	**48**	6 wks
17 Oct 81	ARTHUR'S THEME (BEST THAT YOU CAN DO) *Warner Bros. K 17847*	**56**	4 wks
9 Jan 82 ●	ARTHUR'S THEME (BEST THAT YOU CAN DO) (re-entry) *Warner Bros. K 17847*	**7**	11 wks
5 Feb 83	ALL RIGHT *Warner Bros. W 9843*	**51**	5 wks

Sheryl CROW *US, female vocalist* **10 wks**

18 Jun 94	LEAVING LAS VEGAS *A & M 5806472*	**66**	1 wk
5 Nov 94 ●	ALL I WANNA DO *A & M 5808452*	**4†**	9 wks

CROWD
Multi-national, male/female vocal/instrumental charity assembly **11 wks**

1 Jun 85 ★	YOU'LL NEVER WALK ALONE *Spartan BRAD 1*	**1**	11 wks

CROWDED HOUSE
Australia/New Zealand/US, male vocal/instrumental group **55 wks**

6 Jun 87	DON'T DREAM IT'S OVER *Capitol CL 438*	**27**	8 wks
22 Jun 91	CHOCOLATE CAKE *Capitol CL 618*	**69**	2 wks
2 Nov 91	FALL AT YOUR FEET *Capitol CL 626*	**17**	7 wks
29 Feb 92 ●	WEATHER WITH YOU *Capitol CL 643*	**7**	9 wks
20 Jun 92	FOUR SEASONS IN ONE DAY *Capitol CL 655*	**26**	5 wks
26 Sep 92	IT'S ONLY NATURAL *Capitol CL 661*	**24**	4 wks
2 Oct 93	DISTANT SUN *Capitol CDCLS 697*	**19**	6 wks
20 Nov 93	NAILS IN MY FEET *Capitol CDCLS 701*	**22**	4 wks
19 Feb 94	LOCKED OUT *Capitol CDCLS 707*	**12**	4 wks
11 Jun 94	FINGERS OF LOVE *Capitol CDCL 715*	**25**	3 wks
24 Sep 94	PINEAPPLE HEAD *Capitol CDCL 723*	**27**	3 wks

Act were Australia/New Zealand only for first six hits.

CROWN HEIGHTS AFFAIR
US, male vocal/instrumental group **34 wks**

19 Aug 78	GALAXY OF LOVE *Mercury 6168 801*	**24**	10 wks
11 Nov 78	I'M GONNA LOVE YOU FOREVER *Mercury 6168 803*	**47**	4 wks
14 Apr 79	DANCE LADY DANCE *Mercury 6168 804*	**44**	4 wks

| 3 May 80 | ● **YOU GAVE ME LOVE** De-Lite MER 9 | **10** | 12 wks |
| 9 Aug 80 | **YOU'VE BEEN GONE** De-Lite MER 28 | **44** | 4 wks |

Julee CRUISE US, female vocalist   **13 wks**

| 10 Nov 90 | ● **FALLING** Warner Bros. W 9544 | **7** | 11 wks |
| 2 Mar 91 | **ROCKIN' BACK INSIDE MY HEART** Warner Bros. W 0004 | **66** | 2 wks |

CRUISERS - See Dave BERRY

CRUSADERS US, male vocal/instrumental group   **16 wks**

18 Aug 79	● **STREET LIFE** MCA 513	**5**	11 wks
26 Sep 81	**I'M SO GLAD I'M STANDING HERE TODAY** MCA 741 [1]	**61**	3 wks
7 Apr 84	**NIGHT LADIES** MCA MCA 853	**55**	2 wks

[1] Crusaders, featured vocalist Joe Cocker

Vocalist on Street Life was Randy Crawford, though uncredited.

Bobby CRUSH UK, male instrumentalist - piano   **4 wks**

| 4 Nov 72 | **BORSALINO** Philips 6006 248 | **37** | 4 wks |

CRY BEFORE DAWN
Ireland, male vocal/instrumental group   **2 wks**

| 17 Jun 89 | **WITNESS FOR THE WORLD** Epic GONE 3 | **67** | 2 wks |

CRY OF LOVE US, male/female vocal/instrumental group   **1 wk**

| 15 Jan 94 | **BAD THING** Columbia 6600462 | **60** | 1 wk |

CRY SISCO! UK, male producer - Barry Blue   **9 wks**

| 2 Sep 89 | **AFRO DIZZI ACT** Escape AWOL 1 | **42** | 8 wks |
| 20 Jan 90 | **AFRO DIZZI ACT** (re-entry) Escape AWOL 1 | **70** | 1 wk |

CRYIN' SHAMES UK, male vocal/instrumental group   **7 wks**

| 31 Mar 66 | **PLEASE STAY** Decca F 12340 | **26** | 7 wks |

CRYPT-KICKERS - See Bobby 'Boris' PICKETT and the CRYPT-KICKERS

CRYSTAL PALACE UK, male football team vocalists   **2 wks**

| 12 May 90 | **GLAD ALL OVER/WHERE EAGLES FLY** Parkfield PMS 5019 | **50** | 2 wks |

CRYSTALS US, female vocal group   **54 wks**

22 Nov 62	**HE'S A REBEL** London HLU 9611	**19**	13 wks
20 Jun 63	● **DA DOO RON RON** London HLU 9732	**5**	16 wks
19 Sep 63	● **THEN HE KISSED ME** London HLU 9773	**2**	14 wks
5 Mar 64	**I WONDER** London HLU 9852	**36**	3 wks
19 Oct 74	**DA DOO RON RON** (re-issue) Warner Spector K 19010	**15**	8 wks

CUBIC 22 Belgium, male instrumental/production duo   **7 wks**

| 22 Jun 91 | **NIGHT IN MOTION** XL XLS 20 | **15** | 7 wks |

CUD UK, male vocal/instrumental group   **16 wks**

19 Oct 91	**OH NO WON'T DO (EP)** A & M AMB 829	**49**	2 wks
28 Mar 92	**THROUGH THE ROOF** A & M AM 857	**44**	2 wks
30 May 92	**RICH AND STRANGE** A & M AM 871	**24**	3 wks
15 Aug 92	**PURPLE LOVE BALLOON** A & M AM 0024	**27**	3 wks
10 Oct 92	**ONCE AGAIN** A & M AM 0081	**45**	1 wk
12 Feb 94	**NEUROTICA** A & M 5805172	**37**	2 wks

| 2 Apr 94 | **STICKS AND STONES** A & M 5805472 | **68** | 1 wk |
| 3 Sep 94 | **ONE GIANT LOVE** A & M 5807292 | **52** | 2 wks |

Tracks on Oh No Won't Do (EP): Oh No Won't Do / Profession / Ariel / Price Of Love.

See also Various Artists (EPs & LPs) – Gimme Shelter (EP).

CUFFLINKS US, male vocal group   **30 wks**

| 29 Nov 69 | ● **TRACY** MCA MU 1101 | **4** | 16 wks |
| 14 Mar 70 | ● **WHEN JULIE COMES AROUND** MCA MU 1112 | **10** | 14 wks |

CULT UK, male vocal/instrumental group   **79 wks**

22 Dec 84	**RESURRECTION JOE** Beggars Banquet BEG 122	**74**	2 wks
25 May 85	**SHE SELLS SANCTUARY** Beggars Banquet BEG 135	**15**	17 wks
28 Sep 85	**SHE SELLS SANCTUARY** (re-entry) Beggars Banquet BEG 135	**61**	2 wks
5 Oct 85	**RAIN** Beggars Banquet BEG 147	**17**	8 wks
30 Nov 85	**REVOLUTION** Beggars Banquet BEG 152	**30**	7 wks
28 Feb 87	**LOVE REMOVAL MACHINE** Beggars Banquet BEG 182	**18**	7 wks
2 May 87	**LIL' DEVIL** Beggars Banquet BEG 188	**11**	7 wks
22 Aug 87	**WILD FLOWER (DOUBLE SINGLE)** Beggars Banquet BEG 195D	**24**	2 wks
29 Aug 87	**WILD FLOWER** Beggars Banquet BEG 195	**30**	4 wks
1 Apr 89	**FIRE WOMAN** Beggars Banquet BEG 228	**15**	4 wks
8 Jul 89	**EDIE (CIAO BABY)** Beggars Banquet BEG 230	**32**	5 wks
18 Nov 89	**SUN KING/EDIE (CIAO BABY)** (re-issue) Beggars Banquet BEG 235	**39**	2 wks
10 Mar 90	**SWEET SOUL SISTER** Beggars Banquet BEG 241	**42**	4 wks
14 Sep 91	**WILD HEARTED SON** Beggars Banquet BEG 255	**40**	2 wks
29 Feb 92	**HEART OF SOUL** Beggars Banquet BEG 260	**51**	1 wk
30 Jan 93	**SHE SELLS SANCTUARY** (re-mix) Beggars Banquet BEG 253CD	**15**	4 wks
8 Oct 94	**COMING DOWN** Beggars Banquet BBQ 40CD	**50**	1 wk

Tracks on double single: Wild Flower / Love Trooper / Outlaw / Horse Nation.

CULT JAM - See LISA LISA and CULT JAM

CULTURE BEAT
UK/US/Germany, male/female vocal/instrumental group   **41 wks**

3 Feb 90	**(CHERRY LIPS) DER ERDBEERMUND** Epic 65563 7	**55**	3 wks
7 Aug 93	★ **MR. VAIN** Epic 6594682	**1**	15 wks
6 Nov 93	● **GOT TO GET IT** Epic 6597212	**4**	11 wks
15 Jan 94	● **ANYTHING** Epic 6600252	**5**	8 wks
2 Apr 94	**WORLD IN YOUR HANDS** Epic 6602292	**20**	4 wks

CULTURE CLUB UK, male vocal/instrumental group   **103 wks**

18 Sep 82	★ **DO YOU REALLY WANT TO HURT ME** Virgin VS 518	**1**	18 wks
27 Nov 82	● **TIME (CLOCK OF THE HEART)** Virgin VS 558	**3**	12 wks
9 Apr 83	● **CHURCH OF THE POISON MIND** Virgin VS 571	**2**	9 wks
17 Sep 83	★ **KARMA CHAMELEON** Virgin VS 612	**1**	20 wks
10 Dec 83	● **VICTIMS** Virgin VS 641	**3**	10 wks
24 Mar 84	● **IT'S A MIRACLE** Virgin VS 662	**4**	9 wks
6 Oct 84	● **THE WAR SONG** Virgin VS 694	**2**	8 wks
1 Dec 84	**THE MEDAL SONG** Virgin VS 730	**32**	4 wks
5 Jan 85	**THE MEDAL SONG** (re-entry) Virgin VS 730	**74**	1 wk
15 Mar 86	● **MOVE AWAY** Virgin VS 845	**7**	7 wks
31 May 86	**GOD THANK YOU WOMAN** Virgin VS 861	**31**	5 wks

Smiley CULTURE UK, male vocalist   **13 wks**

15 Dec 84	**POLICE OFFICER** Fashion FAD 7012	**12**	10 wks
6 Apr 85	**COCKNEY TRANSLATION** Fashion FAD 7028	**71**	1 wk
13 Sep 86	**SCHOOLTIME CHRONICLE** Polydor POSP 815	**59**	2 wks

Larry CUNNINGHAM and the MIGHTY AVONS
Ireland, male vocal/instrumental group   **11 wks**

| 10 Dec 64 | **TRIBUTE TO JIM REEVES** King KG 1016 | **40** | 8 wks |
| 25 Feb 65 | **TRIBUTE TO JIM REEVES** (re-entry) King KG 1016 | **46** | 3 wks |

CUPID'S INSPIRATION
UK, male vocal / instrumental group   **19 wks**

19 Jun 68 ●	YESTERDAY HAS GONE *Nems 56 3500*	4	11 wks
2 Oct 68	MY WORLD *Nems 56 3702*	33	8 wks

CURE *UK, male vocal / instrumental group*   **138 wks**

12 Apr 80	A FOREST *Fiction FICS 10*	31	8 wks
4 Apr 81	PRIMARY *Fiction FICS 12*	43	6 wks
17 Oct 81	CHARLOTTE SOMETIMES *Fiction FICS 14*	44	4 wks
24 Jul 82	HANGING GARDEN *Fiction FICS 15*	34	4 wks
27 Nov 82	LET'S GO TO BED *Fiction FICS 17*	44	4 wks
8 Jan 83	LET'S GO TO BED (re-entry) *Fiction FICS 17*	75	1 wk
9 Jul 83	THE WALK *Fiction FICS 18*	12	8 wks
29 Oct 83 ●	THE LOVE CATS *Fiction FICS 19*	7	11 wks
7 Apr 84	THE CATERPILLAR *Fiction FICS 20*	14	7 wks
27 Jul 85	IN BETWEEN DAYS *Fiction FICS 22*	15	10 wks
21 Sep 85	CLOSE TO ME *Fiction FICS 23*	24	8 wks
3 May 86	BOYS DON'T CRY *Fiction FICS 24*	22	6 wks
18 Apr 87	WHY CAN'T I BE YOU *Fiction FICS 25*	21	5 wks
4 Jul 87	CATCH *Fiction FICS 26*	27	6 wks
17 Oct 87	JUST LIKE HEAVEN *Fiction FICS 27*	29	5 wks
20 Feb 88	HOT HOT HOT!!! *Fiction FICSX 28*	45	3 wks
22 Apr 89 ●	LULLABY *Fiction FICS 29*	5	6 wks
2 Sep 89	LOVESONG *Fiction FICS 30*	18	7 wks
31 Mar 90	PICTURES OF YOU *Fiction FICS 34*	24	6 wks
29 Sep 90	NEVER ENOUGH *Fiction FICS 35*	13	5 wks
3 Nov 90	CLOSE TO ME (re-mix) *Fiction FICS 36*	13	5 wks
28 Mar 92 ●	HIGH *Fiction FICS 39*	8	3 wks
11 Apr 92	HIGH (re-mix) *Fiction FICXS 41*	44	1 wk
23 May 92 ●	FRIDAY I'M IN LOVE *Fiction FICS 42*	6	7 wks
17 Oct 92	A LETTER TO ELISE *Fiction FICS 46*	28	2 wks

CURIOSITY *UK, male vocal / instrumental group*   **58 wks**

13 Dec 86 ●	DOWN TO EARTH *Mercury CAT 2* [1]	3	18 wks
4 Apr 87	ORDINARY DAY *Mercury CAT 3* [1]	11	7 wks
20 Jun 87 ●	MISFIT *Mercury CAT 4* [1]	7	9 wks
19 Sep 87	FREE *Mercury CAT 5* [1]	56	2 wks
16 Sep 89	NAME AND NUMBER *Mercury CAT 6*	14	9 wks
25 Apr 92 ●	HANG ON IN THERE BABY *RCA PB 45377*	3	10 wks
29 Aug 92	I NEED YOUR LOVIN' *RCA 74321111377*	47	2 wks
30 Oct 93	GIMME THE SUNSHINE *RCA 74321168602*	73	1 wk

[1] Curiosity Killed The Cat

CURLS - *See Paul EVANS and the CURLS*

Chantal CURTIS *France, female vocalist*   **3 wks**

14 Jul 79	GET ANOTHER LOVE *Pye 7P 5003*	51	3 wks

T.C. CURTIS *Jamaica, male vocalist / instrumentalist*   **4 wks**

23 Feb 85	YOU SHOULD HAVE KNOWN BETTER *Hot Melt VS 754*	50	4 wks

CURVE *UK, male / female vocal / instrumental duo*   **13 wks**

16 Mar 91	THE BLINDFOLD (EP) *AnXious ANX 27*	68	1 wk
25 May 91	COAST IS CLEAR *AnXious ANX 30*	34	3 wks
9 Nov 91	CLIPPED *AnXious ANX 35*	36	2 wks
7 Mar 92	FAIT ACCOMPLI *AnXious ANXT 36*	22	3 wks
18 Jul 92	HORROR HEAD (EP) *AnXious ANXT 38*	31	2 wks
4 Sep 93	BLACKERTHREETRACKER EP *Anxious ANXCD 42*	39	2 wks

Tracks on The Blindfold (EP): Ten Little Girls / I Speak Your Every Word / Blindfold / No Escape From Heaven. Tracks on Horror Head (EP): Horror Head / Falling Free / Mission From God / Today Is Not The Day. Only track available on all formats of Blackerthreetracker EP: Missing Link.

CURVED AIR *UK, male / female vocal / instrumental group* **12 wks**

7 Aug 71 ●	BACK STREET LUV *Warner Bros. K 16092*	4	12 wks

CUT 'N' MOVE
Denmark, male / female vocal / instrumental group   **2 wks**

2 Oct 93	GIVE IT UP *EMI CDEM 273*	61	2 wks

Adge CUTLER - *See WURZELS*

CUTTING CREW
UK / Canada, male vocal / instrumental group   **37 wks**

16 Aug 86 ●	(I JUST) DIED IN YOUR ARMS *Siren SIREN 21*	4	12 wks
25 Oct 86	I'VE BEEN IN LOVE BEFORE *Siren SIREN 29*	31	9 wks
10 Jan 87	I'VE BEEN IN LOVE BEFORE (re-entry) *Siren SIREN 29*	70	1 wk
7 Mar 87	ONE FOR THE MOCKINGBIRD *Siren SIREN 40*	52	5 wks
21 Nov 87	I'VE BEEN IN LOVE BEFORE (re-mix) *Siren SIREN 29*	24	8 wks
22 Jul 89	(BETWEEN A) ROCK AND A HARD PLACE *Siren SRN 108*	66	2 wks

CYBERSONIK *US, male sampling group*   **1 wk**

10 Nov 90	TECHNARCHY *Champion CHAMP 264*	73	1 wk

Johnny CYMBAL *UK, male vocalist*   **10 wks**

14 Mar 63	MR. BASS MAN *London HLR 9682*	24	10 wks

CYPRESS HILL *US, male rap group*   **22 wks**

31 Jul 93	INSANE IN THE BRAIN *Ruff House 6595332*	32	4 wks
2 Oct 93	WHEN THE SH.. GOES DOWN *Ruff House 6596702*	19	4 wks
11 Dec 93	I AIN'T GOIN' OUT LIKE THAT *Ruff House 6596902*	15	7 wks
26 Feb 94	INSANE IN THE BRAIN (re-issue) *Ruff House 6601762*	21	4 wks
7 May 94	LICK A SHOT *Ruff House 6603192*	20	3 wks

Billy Ray CYRUS *US, male vocalist*   **18 wks**

25 Jul 92 ●	ACHY BREAKY HEART *Mercury MER 373*	3	10 wks
10 Oct 92	COULD'VE BEEN ME *Mercury MER 378*	24	4 wks
28 Nov 92	THESE BOOTS ARE MADE FOR WALKIN' *Mercury MER 384*	63	1 wk
19 Dec 92	ACHY BREAKY HEART *Epic 6588837* [1]	53	3 wks

[1] Alvin and the Chipmunks featuring Billy Ray Cyrus

Chuck D - *See ANTHRAX*

Dimples D *US, female rapper*   **10 wks**

17 Nov 90	SUCKER DJ *FBI FBI 11*	17	10 wks

Longsy D *UK, male vocalist*   **7 wks**

4 Mar 89	THIS IS SKA *Big One BIG 13*	56	7 wks

Nikki D *US, female rapper*   **6 wks**

6 May 89	MY LOVE IS SO RAW *Def Jam 6548987* [1]	34	5 wks
30 Mar 91	DADDY'S LITTLE GIRL *Def Jam 6567347*	75	1 wk

[1] Alyson Williams featuring Nikki D

Vicky D US, female vocalist   **6 wks**

13 Mar 82	**THIS BEAT IS MINE** Virgin VS 486	**42**	6 wks

D.B.M. Germany, male/female vocal/instrumental group   **3 wks**

12 Nov 77	**DISCO BEATLEMANIA** Atlantic K 11027	**45**	3 wks

D, B, M and T UK, male vocal/instrumental group   **8 wks**

1 Aug 70	**MR. PRESIDENT** Fontana 6007 022	**33**	8 wks

See also Dave Dee, Dozy, Beaky, Mick and Tich.

D MOB UK, male producer - Danny D.   **48 wks**

15 Oct 88	● **WE CALL IT ACIEED** ffrr FFR 13 [1]	**3**	12 wks
3 Jun 89	● **IT IS TIME TO GET FUNKY** ffrr F 107 [2]	**9**	10 wks
21 Oct 89	**C'MON AND GET MY LOVE** ffrr F 117 [3]	**15**	10 wks
6 Jan 90	● **PUT YOUR HANDS TOGETHER** ffrr F 124 [4]	**7**	8 wks
7 Apr 90	**THAT'S THE WAY OF THE WORLD** ffrr F 132 [3]	**48**	3 wks
12 Feb 94	**WHY** ffrr FCD 227 [3]	**23**	3 wks
3 Sep 94	**ONE DAY** ffrr FCDP 239	**41**	2 wks

[1] D Mob featuring Gary Haisman [2] D Mob featuring LRS [3] D Mob with Cathy Dennis [4] D Mob featuring Nuff Juice

D TRAIN US, male vocal/instrumental duo   **36 wks**

6 Feb 82	**YOU'RE THE ONE FOR ME** Epic EPC A 2016	**30**	8 wks
8 May 82	**WALK ON BY** Epic EPC A 2298	**44**	6 wks
7 May 83	**MUSIC PART 1** Prelude A 3332	**23**	7 wks
16 Jul 83	**KEEP GIVING ME LOVE** Prelude A 3497	**65**	2 wks
27 Jul 85	**YOU'RE THE ONE FOR ME** (re-mix) Prelude ZB 40302	**15**	11 wks
12 Oct 85	**MUSIC** Prelude ZB 40431	**62**	2 wks

D-INFLUENCE
UK, male/female vocal/instrumental group   **3 wks**

20 Jun 92	**GOOD LOVER** East West A 8573	**46**	2 wks
27 Mar 93	**GOOD LOVER** (re-mix) East West America A 8439CD	**61**	1 wk

J.M.D. - See TYREE

D:REAM UK, male vocal/instrumental duo   **57 wks**

4 Jul 92	**U R THE BEST THING** FXU FXU 3	**72**	1 wk
30 Jan 93	**THINGS CAN ONLY GET BETTER** Magnet MAG 1010CD	**24**	5 wks
24 Apr 93	**U R THE BEST THING** (re-mix) Magnet MAG 1011CD	**19**	8 wks
31 Jul 93	**UNFORGIVEN** Magnet MAG 1016CD	**29**	3 wks
2 Oct 93	**STAR/I LIKE IT** Magnet MAG 1019CD	**26**	4 wks
8 Jan 94	★ **THINGS CAN ONLY GET BETTER** (re-mix) Magnet MAG 1020CD	**1**	16 wks
26 Mar 94	● **U R THE BEST THING** (2nd re-mix) Magnet MAG 1021CD	**4**	10 wks
18 Jun 94	**TAKE ME AWAY** Magnet MAG 1025CD	**18**	5 wks
10 Sep 94	**BLAME IT ON ME** Magnet MAG 1027CD	**25**	5 wks

DA BRAT US, female rapper   **1 wk**

22 Oct 94	**FUNKDAFIED** Columbia 6609212	**65**	1 wk

DA LENCH MOB US, male rap group   **2 wks**

20 Mar 93	**FREEDOM GOT AN A.K.** East West America A 8431CD	**51**	2 wks

Paul DA VINCI UK, male vocalist   **8 wks**

20 Jul 74	**YOUR BABY AIN'T YOUR BABY ANYMORE** Penny Farthing PEN 843	**20**	8 wks

Terry DACTYL and the DINOSAURS
UK, male vocal/instrumental group   **16 wks**

15 Jul 72	● **SEASIDE SHUFFLE** UK 5	**2**	12 wks
13 Jan 73	**ON A SATURDAY NIGHT** UK 21	**45**	4 wks

Terry Dactyl is Jona Lewie.

DADA US, male vocal/instrumental group   **1 wk**

4 Dec 93	**DOG** IRS CDEIRSS 185	**71**	1 wk

DADDY FREDDY - See Simon HARRIS

DAFFY DUCK featuring the GROOVE GANG
Germany, male instrumental/production group   **3 wks**

6 Jul 91	**PARTY ZONE** East West YZ 592	**58**	3 wks

DAINTEES - See Martin STEPHENSON and the DAINTEES

DAISY CHAINSAW
UK, male/female vocal/instrumental group   **6 wks**

18 Jan 92	**LOVE YOUR MONEY** Deva DEVA 001	**26**	5 wks
28 Mar 92	**PINK FLOWER/ROOM ELEVEN** Deva 82 TP7	**65**	1 wk

DAKEYNE - See James BROWN; TINMAN

DAKOTAS UK, male instrumental group   **13 wks**

11 Jul 63	**THE CRUEL SEA** Parlophone R 5044	**18**	13 wks

See also Billy J. Kramer and the Dakotas.

Jim DALE UK, male vocalist   **22 wks**

11 Oct 57	● **BE MY GIRL** Parlophone R 4343	**2**	16 wks
10 Jan 58	**JUST BORN** Parlophone R 4376	**27**	1 wk
17 Jan 58	**CRAZY DREAM** Parlophone R 4376	**24**	2 wks
7 Mar 58	**SUGARTIME** Parlophone R 4402	**25**	3 wks

DALE and GRACE US, male/female vocal duo   **2 wks**

9 Jan 64	**I'M LEAVING IT UP TO YOU** London HL 9807	**42**	2 wks

DALE SISTERS US, female vocal group   **6 wks**

23 Nov 61	**MY SUNDAY BABY** Ember S 140	**36**	6 wks

DALI'S CAR UK, male vocal/instrumental duo   **2 wks**

3 Nov 84	**THE JUDGEMENT IS THE MIRROR** Paradox DOX 1	**66**	2 wks

Roger DALTREY UK, male vocalist   **46 wks**

14 Apr 73	● **GIVING IT ALL AWAY** Track 2094 110	**5**	11 wks
4 Aug 73	**I'M FREE** Ode ODS 66302	**13**	10 wks
14 May 77	**WRITTEN ON THE WIND** Polydor 2121 319	**46**	2 wks
2 Aug 80	**FREE ME** Polydor 2001 980	**39**	6 wks
11 Oct 80	**WITHOUT YOUR LOVE** Polydor POSP 181	**55**	4 wks
3 Mar 84	**WALKING IN MY SLEEP** WEA U 9686	**56**	3 wks
5 Oct 85	**AFTER THE FIRE** 10 TEN 69	**50**	5 wks
8 Mar 86	**UNDER A RAGING MOON** 10 TEN 81	**43**	5 wks

Carolina DAMAS - See SUENO LATINO featuring Carolina DAMAS

DAMIAN UK, male vocalist · 26 wks

26 Dec 87	**THE TIME WARP 2** Jive JIVE 160	**51**	6 wks
27 Aug 88	**THE TIME WARP 2 (re-issue)** Jive JIVE 182	**64**	3 wks
19 Aug 89 ●	**THE TIME WARP (re-mix)** Jive JIVE 209	**7**	13 wks
16 Dec 89	**WIG WAM BAM** Jive JIVE 236	**49**	4 wks

The Time Warp is a re-mix of The Time Warp 2.

DAMNED UK, male vocal/instrumental group · 77 wks

5 May 79	**LOVE SONG** Chiswick CHIS 112	**20**	8 wks
20 Oct 79	**SMASH IT UP** Chiswick CHIS 116	**35**	5 wks
1 Dec 79	**I JUST CAN'T BE HAPPY TODAY** Chiswick CHIS 120	**46**	5 wks
4 Oct 80	**HISTORY OF THE WORLD (PART 1)** Chiswick CHIS 135	**51**	4 wks
28 Nov 81	**FRIDAY 13TH EP** Stale One TRY 1	**50**	4 wks
10 Jul 82	**LOVELY MONEY** Bronze BRO 149	**42**	4 wks
9 Jun 84	**THANKS FOR THE NIGHT** Damned DAMNED 1	**43**	4 wks
30 Mar 85	**GRIMLY FIENDISH** MCA GRIM 1	**21**	7 wks
22 Jun 85	**THE SHADOW OF LOVE** MCA GRIM 2	**25**	8 wks
21 Sep 85	**IS IT A DREAM** MCA GRIM 3	**34**	4 wks
8 Feb 86 ●	**ELOISE** MCA GRIM 4	**3**	9 wks
19 Apr 86	**ELOISE (re-entry)** MCA GRIM 4	**72**	1 wk
22 Nov 86	**ANYTHING** MCA GRIM 5	**32**	4 wks
7 Feb 87	**GIGOLO** MCA GRIM 6	**29**	3 wks
25 Apr 87	**ALONE AGAIN OR** MCA GRIM 7	**27**	6 wks
28 Nov 87	**IN DULCE DECORUM** MCA GRIM 8	**72**	1 wk

Tracks on Friday 13th EP: Disco Man/Limit Club/Billy Bad Breaks/Citadel.

Kenny DAMON US, male vocalist · 1 wk

19 May 66	**WHILE I LIVE** Mercury MF 907	**48**	1 wk

Vic DAMONE US, male vocalist · 22 wks

6 Dec 57	**AN AFFAIR TO REMEMBER** Philips PB 745	**29**	1 wk
31 Jan 58	**AN AFFAIR TO REMEMBER (re-entry)** Philips PB 745	**30**	1 wk
9 May 58 ★	**ON THE STREET WHERE YOU LIVE** Philips PB 819	**1**	17 wks
1 Aug 58	**THE ONLY MAN ON THE ISLAND** Philips PB 837	**24**	3 wks

DANA UK, female vocalist · 75 wks

4 Apr 70 ★	**ALL KINDS OF EVERYTHING** Rex R 11054	**1**	15 wks
25 Jul 70	**ALL KINDS OF EVERYTHING (re-entry)** Rex R 11054	**47**	1 wk
13 Feb 71	**WHO PUT THE LIGHTS OUT** Rex R 11062	**14**	11 wks
25 Jan 75 ●	**PLEASE TELL HIM THAT I SAID HELLO** GTO GT 6	**8**	14 wks
13 Dec 75 ●	**IT'S GONNA BE A COLD COLD CHRISTMAS** GTO GT 45	**4**	6 wks
6 Mar 76	**NEVER GONNA FALL IN LOVE AGAIN** GTO GT 55	**31**	4 wks
16 Oct 76	**FAIRYTALE** GTO GT 66	**13**	16 wks
31 Mar 79	**SOMETHING'S COOKIN' IN THE KITCHEN** GTO GT 243	**44**	5 wks
15 May 82	**I FEEL LOVE COMIN' ON** Creole CR 32	**66**	3 wks

DANCE CONSPIRACY
UK, male instrumental/production duo · 1 wk

3 Oct 92	**DUB WAR** XL XLT 34	**72**	1 wk

DANCE 2 TRANCE
Germany, male instrumental/production duo · 7 wks

24 Apr 93	**P.OWER OF A.MERICAN N.ATIVES** Logic 74321139582	**25**	4 wks
24 Jul 93	**TAKE A FREE FALL** Logic 74321153602	**36**	3 wks

DANGER DANGER US, male vocal/instrumental group · 5 wks

8 Feb 92	**MONKEY BUSINESS** Epic 6577517	**42**	2 wks
28 Mar 92	**I STILL THINK ABOUT YOU** Epic 6578387	**46**	2 wks
13 Jun 92	**COMIN' HOME** Epic 6581337	**75**	1 wk

DAN-I UK, male vocalist · 9 wks

10 Nov 79	**MONKEY CHOP** Island WIP 6520	**30**	9 wks

Charlie DANIELS BAND
US, male vocal/instrumental group · 10 wks

22 Sep 79	**THE DEVIL WENT DOWN TO GEORGIA** Epic EPC 7737	**14**	10 wks

Johnny DANKWORTH
UK, male orchestral/group leader/instrumentalist - alto sax · 33 wks

22 Jun 56 ●	**EXPERIMENTS WITH MICE** Parlophone R 4185	**7**	12 wks
23 Feb 61 ●	**AFRICAN WALTZ** Columbia DB 4590	**9**	21 wks

DANNY and the JUNIORS US, male vocal group · 19 wks

17 Jan 58 ●	**AT THE HOP** HMV POP 436	**3**	14 wks
10 Jul 76	**AT THE HOP (re-issue)** ABC 4123	**39**	5 wks

DANNY WILSON UK, male vocal/instrumental group · 28 wks

22 Aug 87	**MARY'S PRAYER** Virgin VS 934	**42**	7 wks
2 Apr 88 ●	**MARY'S PRAYER (re-entry)** Virgin VS 934	**3**	11 wks
17 Jun 89	**THE SECOND SUMMER OF LOVE** Virgin VS 1186	**23**	9 wks
16 Sep 89	**NEVER GONNA BE THE SAME** Virgin VS 1203	**69**	1 wk

DANSE SOCIETY UK, male vocal/instrumental group · 5 wks

27 Aug 83	**WAKE UP** Society SOC 5	**61**	3 wks
5 Nov 83	**HEAVEN IS WAITING** Society SOC 6	**60**	2 wks

Steven DANTE UK, male vocalist · 16 wks

26 Sep 87	**THE REAL THING** Chrysalis CHS 3167 [1]	**13**	10 wks
9 Jul 88	**I'M TOO SCARED** Cooltempo DANTE 1	**34**	6 wks

[1] Jellybean featuring Steven Dante

Tonja DANTZLER US, female vocalist · 1 wk

17 Dec 94	**IN AND OUT OF MY LIFE** ffrr FCD 246	**66**	1 wk

DANY - See DOUBLE DEE featuring DANY

DANZIG US, male vocal/instrumental group · 1 wk

14 May 94	**MOTHER** American MOMDD 1	**62**	1 wk

Terence Trent D'ARBY US, male vocalist · 70 wks

14 Mar 87 ●	**IF YOU LET ME STAY** CBS TRENT 1	**7**	13 wks
20 Jun 87 ●	**WISHING WELL** CBS TRENT 2	**4**	11 wks
10 Oct 87	**DANCE LITTLE SISTER (PART ONE)** CBS TRENT 3	**20**	7 wks
9 Jan 88 ●	**SIGN YOUR NAME** CBS TRENT 4	**2**	10 wks
20 Jan 90	**TO KNOW SOMEONE DEEPLY IS TO KNOW SOMEONE SOFTLY** CBS TRENT 6	**55**	3 wks
17 Apr 93	**DO YOU LOVE ME LIKE YOU SAY** Columbia 6590732	**14**	6 wks
19 Jun 93	**DELICATE** Columbia 6593312 [1]	**14**	6 wks
28 Aug 93	**SHE KISSED ME** Columbia 6595922	**16**	7 wks
20 Nov 93	**LET HER DOWN EASY** Columbia 6598642	**18**	7 wks

[1] Terence Trent D'Arby featuring Des'ree

Richard DARBYSHIRE US, male vocalist — 7 wks

20 Aug 88	**COMING BACK FOR MORE** Chrysalis JEL 4 [1] 41	3 wks
24 Jul 93	**THIS I SWEAR** Dome CDDOME 1003 50	3 wks
12 Feb 94	**WHEN ONLY LOVE WILL DO** Dome CDDOME 1008...54	1 wk

[1] Jellybean featuring Richard Darbyshire

DARE UK, male vocal/instrumental group — 7 wks

29 Apr 89	**THE RAINDANCE** A & M AM 483 62	2 wks
29 Jul 89	**ABANDON** A & M AM 519 71	2 wks
10 Aug 91	**WE DON'T NEED A REASON** A & M AM 755 52	2 wks
5 Oct 91	**REAL LOVE** A & M AM 824 67	1 wk

Bobby DARIN US, male vocalist — 161 wks

1 Aug 58	**SPLISH SPLASH** London HLE 8666 28	1 wk
15 Aug 58	**SPLISH SPLASH (re-entry)** London HLE 8666 18	6 wks
9 Jan 59	**QUEEN OF THE HOP** London HLE 8737 24	2 wks
29 May 59	★ **DREAM LOVER** London HLE 8867 1	19 wks
25 Sep 59	★ **MACK THE KNIFE** London HLK 8939 1	16 wks
22 Jan 60	**MACK THE KNIFE (re-entry)** London HLK 8939 30	1 wk
29 Jan 60	● **LA MER (BEYOND THE SEA)** London HLK 9034 8	10 wks
10 Mar 60	**MACK THE KNIFE (2nd re-entry)** London HLE 8939 50	1 wk
31 Mar 60	● **CLEMENTINE** London HLK 9086 8	12 wks
21 Apr 60	**LA MER (BEYOND THE SEA) (re-entry)** London HLE 9034 40	2 wks
30 Jun 60	**BILL BAILEY** London HLK 9142 36	1 wk
14 Jul 60	**BILL BAILEY (re-entry)** London HLK 9142 34	1 wk
16 Mar 61	● **LAZY RIVER** London HLK 9303 2	13 wks
6 Jul 61	**NATURE BOY** London HLK 9375 24	7 wks
12 Oct 61	● **YOU MUST HAVE BEEN A BEAUTIFUL BABY** London HLK 9429 10	11 wks
26 Oct 61	**COME SEPTEMBER** London HLK 9407 [1] 50	1 wk
21 Dec 61	● **MULTIPLICATION** London HLK 9474 5	13 wks
19 Jul 62	● **THINGS** London HLK 9575...........................2	17 wks
4 Oct 62	**IF A MAN ANSWERS** Capitol CL 15272 24	6 wks
29 Nov 62	**BABY FACE** London HLK 9624 40	4 wks
25 Jul 63	**EIGHTEEN YELLOW ROSES** Capitol CL 15306 37	4 wks
13 Oct 66	● **IF I WERE A CARPENTER** Atlantic 584 051 9	12 wks
14 Apr 79	**DREAM LOVER/MACK THE KNIFE (re-issues)** Lightning LIG 9017 64	1 wk

[1] Bobby Darin Orchestra

DARKMAN UK, male rapper — 6 wks

14 May 94	**YABBA DABBA DOO** Wild Card CARDD 6 49	2 wks
20 Aug 94	**WHO'S THE DARKMAN** Wild Card CARDD 8 46	2 wks
3 Dec 94	**YABBA DABBA DOO (re-issue)** Wild Card CARDD 11 37	2 wks

DARLING BUDS
UK, male/female vocal/instrumental group — 20 wks

8 Oct 88	**BURST** Epic BLOND 1 50	5 wks
7 Jan 89	**HIT THE GROUND** CBS BLOND 2 27	5 wks
25 Mar 89	**LET'S GO ROUND THERE** CBS BLOND 3 49	4 wks
22 Jul 89	**YOU'VE GOT TO CHOOSE** CBS BLOND 4.........45	3 wks
2 Jun 90	**TINY MACHINE** CBS BLOND 5 60	2 wks
12 Sep 92	**SURE THING** Epic 6582157 71	1 wk

Guy DARRELL UK, male vocalist — 13 wks

18 Aug 73	**I'VE BEEN HURT** Santa Ponsa PNS 4 12	13 wks

James DARREN US, male vocalist — 25 wks

11 Aug 60	**BECAUSE THEY'RE YOUNG** Pye International 7N 25059 29	7 wks
14 Dec 61	**GOODBYE CRUEL WORLD** Pye International 7N 25116 28	9 wks

---

29 Mar 62	**HER ROYAL MAJESTY** Pye International 7N 25125 36	3 wks
21 Jun 62	**CONSCIENCE** Pye International 7N 25138...............30	6 wks

DARTS UK, male/female vocal/instrumental group — 117 wks

5 Nov 77	● **DADDY COOL/THE GIRL CAN'T HELP IT** Magnet MAG 100 6	13 wks
28 Jan 78	● **COME BACK MY LOVE** Magnet MAG 110 2	12 wks
6 May 78	● **BOY FROM NEW YORK CITY** Magnet MAG 116 2	13 wks
5 Aug 78	● **IT'S RAINING** Magnet MAG 126 2	11 wks
11 Nov 78	● **DON'T LET IT FADE AWAY** Magnet MAG 134 ...18	11 wks
10 Feb 79	● **GET IT** Magnet MAG 140 10	9 wks
21 Jul 79	● **DUKE OF EARL** Magnet MAG 147 6	11 wks
20 Oct 79	**CAN'T GET ENOUGH OF YOUR LOVE** Magnet MAG 156 43	6 wks
1 Dec 79	**REET PETITE** Magnet MAG 160 51	7 wks
31 May 80	**LET'S HANG ON** Magnet MAG 174 11	14 wks
6 Sep 80	**PEACHES** Magnet MAG 179 66	3 wks
29 Nov 80	**WHITE CHRISTMAS/SH-BOOM (LIFE COULD BE A DREAM)** Magnet MAG 184 48	7 wks

DAS EFX - *See ICE CUBE*

N'Dea DAVENPORT - *See BRAND NEW HEAVIES; GURU*

Anne-Marie DAVID France, female vocalist — 9 wks

28 Apr 73	**WONDERFUL DREAM** Epic EPC 1446 13	9 wks

F.R. DAVID France, male vocalist — 13 wks

2 Apr 83	● **WORDS** Carrere CAR 248 2	12 wks
18 Jun 83	**MUSIC** Carrere CAR 282 71	1 wk

DAVID and JONATHAN UK, male vocal duo — 22 wks

13 Jan 66	**MICHELLE** Columbia DB 7800..........................11	6 wks
7 Jul 66	● **LOVERS OF THE WORLD UNITE** Columbia DB 7950 ..7	16 wks

Jim DAVIDSON UK, male vocalist — 4 wks

27 Dec 80	**WHITE CHRISTMAS/TOO RISKY** Scratch SCR 001....52	4 wks

Paul DAVIDSON Jamaica, male vocalist — 10 wks

27 Dec 75	● **MIDNIGHT RIDER** Tropical ALO 56 10	10 wks

Dave DAVIES UK, male vocalist — 17 wks

19 Jul 67	● **DEATH OF A CLOWN** Pye 7N 17356.................3	10 wks
6 Dec 67	**SUSANNAH'S STILL ALIVE** Pye 7N 17429...............20	7 wks

Windsor DAVIES and Don ESTELLE
UK, male vocal duo — 16 wks

17 May 75	★ **WHISPERING GRASS** EMI 2290 1	12 wks
25 Oct 75	**PAPER DOLL** EMI 2361 41	4 wks

Billie DAVIS UK, female vocalist — 33 wks

30 Aug 62	**WILL I WHAT** Parlophone R 4932 [1] 18	10 wks
7 Feb 63	● **TELL HIM** Decca F 11572 10	12 wks
30 May 63	**HE'S THE ONE** Decca F 11658 40	3 wks
9 Oct 68	**I WANT YOU TO BE MY BABY** Decca F 12823 33	8 wks

[1] Mike Sarne with Billie Davis

Billy DAVIS Jr. - *See Marilyn McCOO and Billy DAVIS Jr.*

Darlene DAVIS *US, female vocalist*   **5 wks**

| 7 Feb 87 | **I FOUND LOVE** *Serious 7OUS 1* | ...... **55** | 5 wks |

John DAVIS and the MONSTER ORCHESTRA
US, male vocal / instrumental group   **2 wks**

| 10 Feb 79 | **AIN'T THAT ENOUGH FOR YOU** *Miracle M 2* | ...... **70** | 2 wks |

Mac DAVIS *US, male vocalist*   **22 wks**

| 4 Nov 72 | **BABY DON'T GET HOOKED ON ME** *CBS 8250* | ...... **29** | 6 wks |
| 15 Nov 80 | **IT'S HARD TO BE HUMBLE** *Casablanca CAN 210* | ...... **27** | 16 wks |

Ruth DAVIS - *See Bo KIRKLAND and Ruth DAVIS*

Sammy DAVIS Jr. *US, male vocalist*   **35 wks**

29 Jul 55	**SOMETHING'S GOTTA GIVE** *Brunswick 05428*	...... **19**	2 wks
19 Aug 55	**SOMETHING'S GOTTA GIVE (re-entry)** *Brunswick 05428*	...... **11**	5 wks
9 Sep 55	● **LOVE ME OR LEAVE ME** *Brunswick 05428*	...... **8**	6 wks
30 Sep 55	**THAT OLD BLACK MAGIC** *Brunswick 05450*	...... **16**	1 wk
7 Oct 55	**HEY THERE** *Brunswick 05469*	...... **19**	1 wk
4 Nov 55	**LOVE ME OR LEAVE ME (re-entry)** *Brunswick 05428*	...... **18**	2 wks
20 Apr 56	**IN A PERSIAN MARKET** *Brunswick 05518*	...... **28**	1 wk
28 Dec 56	**ALL OF YOU** *Brunswick 05629*	...... **28**	1 wk
16 Jun 60	**HAPPY TO MAKE YOUR ACQUAINTANCE** *Brunswick 05830* [1]	...... **46**	1 wk
22 Mar 62	**WHAT KIND OF FOOL AM I? / GONNA BUILD A MOUNTAIN** *Reprise R 20048*	...... **26**	8 wks
13 Dec 62	**ME AND MY SHADOW** *Reprise R 20128* [2]	...... **20**	7 wks
7 Feb 63	**ME AND MY SHADOW (re-entry)** *Reprise R 20128* [2]	...... **47**	2 wks

[1] Sammy Davis Jr. and Carmen McRae [2] Frank Sinatra and Sammy Davis Jr.

Skeeter DAVIS *US, female vocalist*   **13 wks**

| 14 Mar 63 | **END OF THE WORLD** *RCA 1328* | ...... **18** | 13 wks |

Zelma DAVIS - *See C & C MUSIC FACTORY/CLIVILLES & COLE*

Spencer DAVIS GROUP
UK, male vocal / instrumental group   **71 wks**

5 Nov 64	**I CAN'T STAND IT** *Fontana TF 499*	...... **47**	3 wks
25 Feb 65	**EVERY LITTLE BIT HURTS** *Fontana TF 530*	...... **43**	2 wks
18 Mar 65	**EVERY LITTLE BIT HURTS (re-entry)** *Fontana TF 530*	...... **41**	1 wk
10 Jun 65	**STRONG LOVE** *Fontana TF 571*	...... **50**	1 wk
24 Jun 65	**STRONG LOVE (re-entry)** *Fontana TF 571*	...... **44**	3 wks
2 Dec 65	★ **KEEP ON RUNNING** *Fontana TF 632*	...... **1**	14 wks
24 Mar 66	★ **SOMEBODY HELP ME** *Fontana TF 679*	...... **1**	10 wks
1 Sep 66	**WHEN I COME HOME** *Fontana TF 739*	...... **12**	9 wks
3 Nov 66	● **GIMME SOME LOVING** *Fontana TF 762*	...... **2**	12 wks
26 Jan 67	● **I'M A MAN** *Fontana TF 785*	...... **9**	7 wks
9 Aug 67	**TIME SELLER** *Fontana TF 854*	...... **30**	5 wks
10 Jan 68	**MR. SECOND CLASS** *United Artists UP 1203*	...... **35**	4 wks

DAVIS PINCKNEY PROJECT - *See GO GO LORENZO and the DAVIS PINCKNEY PROJECT*

DAWN *US, male / female vocal group*   **109 wks**

16 Jan 71	● **CANDIDA** *Bell 1118*	...... **9**	11 wks
10 Apr 71	★ **KNOCK THREE TIMES** *Bell 1146*	...... **1**	27 wks
31 Jul 71	● **WHAT ARE YOU DOING SUNDAY** *Bell 1169* [1]	...... **3**	12 wks
10 Mar 73	★ **TIE A YELLOW RIBBON ROUND THE OLD OAK TREE** *Bell 1287* [1]	...... **1**	39 wks
4 Aug 73	**SAY, HAS ANYBODY SEEN MY SWEET GYPSY ROSE** *Bell 1322* [1]	...... **12**	15 wks
5 Jan 74	**TIE A YELLOW RIBBON ROUND THE OLD OAK TREE (re-entry)** *Bell 1287* [1]	...... **41**	1 wk
9 Mar 74	**WHO'S IN THE STRAWBERRY PATCH WITH SALLY** *Bell 1343* [2]	...... **37**	4 wks

[1] Dawn featuring Tony Orlando [2] Tony Orlando and Dawn

Julie DAWN - *See Cyril STAPLETON*

Liz DAWN - *See Joe LONGTHORNE*

Bobby DAY *US, male vocalist*   **2 wks**

| 7 Nov 58 | **ROCKIN' ROBIN** *London HL 8726* | ...... **29** | 2 wks |

Darren DAY *UK, male vocalist*   **2 wks**

| 8 Oct 94 | **YOUNG GIRL** *Bell 74321231082* | ...... **42** | 2 wks |

Doris DAY *US, female vocalist*   **146 wks**

14 Nov 52	● **SUGARBUSH** *Columbia DB 3123* [1]	...... **8**	2 wks
21 Nov 52	● **MY LOVE AND DEVOTION** *Columbia DB 3157*	...... **10**	2 wks
5 Dec 52	● **SUGARBUSH (re-entry)** *Columbia DB 3123* [1]	...... **8**	6 wks
3 Apr 53	● **MA SAYS PA SAYS** *Columbia DB 3242* [2]	...... **12**	1 wk
17 Apr 53	**FULL TIME JOB** *Columbia DB 3242* [2]	...... **11**	1 wk
24 Jul 53	● **LET'S WALK THATA-WAY** *Philips PB 157* [2]	...... **4**	14 wks
2 Apr 54	★ **SECRET LOVE** *Philips PB 230*	...... **1**	29 wks
27 Aug 54	● **BLACK HILLS OF DAKOTA** *Philips PB 287*	...... **7**	8 wks
1 Oct 54	● **IF I GIVE MY HEART TO YOU** *Philips PB 325*	...... **4**	11 wks
8 Apr 55	● **READY WILLING AND ABLE** *Philips PB 402*	...... **7**	9 wks
9 Sep 55	**LOVE ME OR LEAVE ME** *Philips PB 479*	...... **20**	1 wk
21 Oct 55	**I'LL NEVER STOP LOVING YOU** *Philips PB 497*	...... **17**	2 wks
25 Nov 55	**I'LL NEVER STOP LOVING YOU (re-entry)** *Philips PB 497*	...... **19**	1 wk
29 Jun 56	★ **WHATEVER WILL BE WILL BE** *Philips PB 586*	...... **1**	22 wks
13 Jun 58	**A VERY PRECIOUS LOVE** *Philips PB 799*	...... **16**	11 wks
15 Aug 58	**EVERYBODY LOVES A LOVER** *Philips PB 843*	...... **25**	3 wks
26 Sep 58	**EVERYBODY LOVES A LOVER (re-entry)** *Philips PB 843*	...... **27**	1 wk
12 Mar 64	● **MOVE OVER DARLING** *CBS AAG 183*	...... **8**	16 wks
18 Apr 87	**MOVE OVER DARLING (re-issue)** *CBS LEGS 1*	...... **45**	6 wks

[1] Doris Day and Frankie Laine [2] Doris Day and Johnnie Ray

Patti DAY *US, female vocalist*   **1 wk**

| 9 Dec 89 | **RIGHT BEFORE MY EYES** *Debut DEBT 3080* | ...... **69** | 1 wk |

Taylor DAYNE *US, female vocalist*   **49 wks**

23 Jan 88	● **TELL IT TO MY HEART** *Arista 109616*	...... **3**	13 wks
19 Mar 88	● **PROVE YOUR LOVE** *Arista 109830*	...... **8**	10 wks
11 Jun 88	**I'LL ALWAYS LOVE YOU** *Arista 111536*	...... **41**	7 wks
18 Nov 89	**WITH EVERY BEAT OF MY HEART** *Arista 112760*	...... **53**	2 wks
14 Apr 90	**I'LL BE YOUR SHELTER** *Arista 112966*	...... **43**	5 wks
4 Aug 90	**LOVE WILL LEAD YOU BACK** *Arista 113277*	...... **69**	1 wk
3 Jul 93	**CAN'T GET ENOUGH OF YOUR LOVE** *Arista 74321147852*	...... **14**	8 wks
16 Apr 94	**I'LL WAIT** *Arista 74321203472*	...... **29**	3 wks

DAYTON *US, male vocalist*   **1 wk**

| 10 Dec 83 | **THE SOUND OF MUSIC** *Capitol CL 318* | ...... **75** | 1 wk |

DAZZ BAND *US, male vocal / instrumental group*   **12 wks**

| 3 Nov 84 | **LET IT ALL BLOW** *Motown TMG 1361* | ...... **12** | 12 wks |

D'BORA *US, female vocalist*   **1 wk**

| 14 Sep 91 | **DREAM ABOUT YOU** *Polydor PO 161* | ...... **75** | 1 wk |

Nino DE ANGELO *Germany, male vocalist* — **5 wks**

| 21 Jul 84 | GUARDIAN ANGEL *Carrere CAR 335* | **57** | 5 wks |

Chris DE BURGH *Ireland, male vocalist* — **65 wks**

23 Oct 82	DON'T PAY THE FERRYMAN *A & M AMS 8256*	**48**	5 wks
12 May 84	HIGH ON EMOTION *A & M AM 190*	**44**	5 wks
12 Jul 86	★ THE LADY IN RED *A & M AM 331*	**1**	14 wks
20 Sep 86	FATAL HESITATION *A & M AM 348*	**44**	4 wks
13 Dec 86	A SPACEMAN CAME TRAVELLING / THE BALLROOM OF ROMANCE *A & M AM 365*	**40**	5 wks
21 Feb 87	THE LADY IN RED (re-entry) *A & M AM 331*	**74**	1 wk
12 Dec 87	THE SIMPLE TRUTH (A CHILD IS BORN) *A & M AM 427*	**69**	2 wks
2 Jan 88	THE SIMPLE TRUTH (A CHILD IS BORN) (re-entry) *A & M AM 427*	**55**	1 wk
29 Oct 88	● MISSING YOU *A & M AM 474*	**3**	12 wks
7 Jan 89	TENDER HANDS *A & M AM 486*	**43**	6 wks
14 Oct 89	THIS WAITING HEART *A & M AM 528*	**59**	3 wks
25 May 91	THE SIMPLE TRUTH (A CHILD IS BORN) (re-issue) *A & M RELF 1*	**36**	2 wks
11 Apr 92	SEPARATE TABLES *A & M AM 863*	**30**	4 wks
21 May 94	BLONDE HAIR BLUE JEANS *A & M 5805932*	**51**	1 wk

DE CASTRO SISTERS *US, female vocal group* — **1 wk**

| 11 Feb 55 | TEACH ME TONIGHT *London HL 8104* | **20** | 1 wk |

DE LA SOUL *US, male rap / sampling group* — **55 wks**

8 Apr 89	ME MYSELF AND I *Big Life BLR 7*	**22**	8 wks
8 Jul 89	SAY NO GO *Big Life BLR 10*	**18**	7 wks
21 Oct 89	EYE KNOW *Big Life BLR 13*	**14**	7 wks
23 Dec 89	● THE MAGIC NUMBER / BUDDY *Big Life BLR 14*	**7**	8 wks
24 Mar 90	MAMA GAVE BIRTH TO THE SOUL CHILDREN *Gee Street GEE 26* [1]	**14**	7 wks
27 Apr 91	● RING RING RING (HA HA HEY) *Big Life BLR 42*	**10**	7 wks
3 Aug 91	A ROLLER SKATING JAM NAMED 'SATURDAYS' *Big Life BLR 55*	**22**	5 wks
23 Nov 91	KEEPIN' THE FAITH *Big Life BLR 64*	**50**	2 wks
18 Sep 93	BREAKADAWN *Big Life BLRD 103*	**39**	3 wks
2 Apr 94	FALLIN' *Epic 6602622* [2]	**59**	1 wk

[1] Queen Latifah + De La Soul [2] Teenage Fanclub and De La Soul

Buddy only listed for first four weeks peaking at position 13. See also Jungle Brothers.

Donna DE LORY *US, female vocalist* — **1 wk**

| 24 Jul 93 | JUST A DREAM *MCA MCSTD 1750* | **71** | 1 wk |

Lynsey DE PAUL *UK, female vocalist* — **54 wks**

19 Aug 72	● SUGAR ME *MAM 81*	**5**	11 wks
2 Dec 72	GETTING A DRAG *MAM 88*	**18**	8 wks
27 Oct 73	WON'T SOMEBODY DANCE WITH ME *MAM 109*	**14**	7 wks
8 Jun 74	OOH I DO *Warner Bros. K 16401*	**25**	6 wks
2 Nov 74	● NO HONESTLY *Jet 747*	**7**	11 wks
22 Mar 75	MY MAN AND ME *Jet 750*	**40**	4 wks
26 Mar 77	ROCK BOTTOM *Polydor 2058 859* [1]	**19**	7 wks

[1] Lynsey De Paul and Mike Moran

Tullio DE PISCOPO *Italy, male vocalist* — **4 wks**

| 28 Feb 87 | STOP BAJON...PRIMAVERA *Greyhound GREY 9* | **58** | 4 wks |

Rebecca DE RUVO *Sweden, female vocalist* — **1 wk**

| 1 Oct 94 | I CAUGHT YOU OUT *Arista 74321230782* | **72** | 1 wk |

Teri DE SARIO *US, female vocalist* — **5 wks**

| 2 Sep 78 | AIN'T NOTHIN' (GONNA KEEP ME FROM YOU) *Casablanca CAN 128* | **52** | 5 wks |

Stephanie DE SYKES *UK, female vocalist* — **17 wks**

| 20 Jul 74 | ● BORN WITH A SMILE ON MY FACE *Bradley's BRAD 7409* [1] | **2** | 10 wks |
| 19 Apr 75 | WE'LL FIND OUR DAY *Bradley's BRAD 7509* | **17** | 7 wks |

[1] Stephanie De Sykes with Rain

William DE VAUGHN *US, male vocalist* — **10 wks**

| 6 Jul 74 | BE THANKFUL FOR WHAT YOU'VE GOT *Chelsea 2005 002* | **31** | 5 wks |
| 20 Sep 80 | BE THANKFUL FOR WHAT YOU'VE GOT *EMI 5101* | **44** | 5 wks |

EMI version of hit is a new recording.

DEACON BLUE
UK, male / female vocal / instrumental group — **111 wks**

23 Jan 88	DIGNITY *CBS DEAC 4*	**31**	8 wks
9 Apr 88	WHEN WILL YOU MAKE MY TELEPHONE RING *CBS DEAC 5*	**34**	7 wks
16 Jul 88	CHOCOLATE GIRL *CBS DEAC 6*	**43**	7 wks
15 Oct 88	● REAL GONE KID *CBS DEAC 7*	**8**	13 wks
4 Mar 89	WAGES DAY *CBS DEAC 8*	**18**	6 wks
20 May 89	FERGUS SINGS THE BLUES *CBS DEAC 9*	**14**	6 wks
16 Sep 89	LOVE AND REGRET *CBS DEAC 10*	**28**	5 wks
6 Jan 90	QUEEN OF THE NEW YEAR *CBS DEAC 11*	**21**	5 wks
25 Aug 90	● FOUR BACHARACH AND DAVID SONGS EP *CBS DEAC 12*	**2**	9 wks
25 May 91	YOUR SWAYING ARMS *Columbia 6568937*	**23**	4 wks
27 Jul 91	● TWIST AND SHOUT *Columbia 6573027*	**10**	9 wks
12 Oct 91	CLOSING TIME *Columbia 6575027*	**42**	3 wks
14 Dec 91	COVER FROM THE SKY *Columbia 6576737*	**31**	4 wks
28 Nov 92	YOUR TOWN *Columbia 6587867*	**14**	8 wks
13 Feb 93	WILL WE BE LOVERS *Columbia 6589732*	**31**	4 wks
24 Apr 93	ONLY TENDER LOVE *Columbia 6591842*	**22**	4 wks
17 Jul 93	HANG YOUR HEAD *Columbia 6594602*	**21**	4 wks
2 Apr 94	I WAS RIGHT AND YOU WERE WRONG *Columbia 6602222*	**32**	3 wks
28 May 94	DIGNITY *Columbia 6604485*	**20**	3 wks

Tracks on Four Bacharach and David Songs EP: I'll Never Fall In Love Again / The Look Of Love / Message To Michael / Are You There (With Another Girl). Dignity in 94 was the original recording of the song, first issued in 87 but never before a hit.

DEAD DRED *UK, male instrumental / production duo* — **2 wks**

| 5 Nov 94 | DRED BASS *Moving Shadow SHADOW 50CD* | **60** | 2 wks |

DEAD END KIDS *UK, male vocal / instrumental group* — **10 wks**

| 26 Mar 77 | ● HAVE I THE RIGHT *CBS 4972* | **6** | 10 wks |

DEAD KENNEDYS *US, male vocal / instrumental group* — **9 wks**

| 1 Nov 80 | KILL THE POOR *Cherry Red CHERRY 16* | **49** | 3 wks |
| 30 May 81 | TOO DRUNK TO FUCK *Cherry Red CHERRY 24* | **36** | 6 wks |

DEAD OR ALIVE *UK, male vocal / instrumental group* — **70 wks**

24 Mar 84	THAT'S THE WAY (I LIKE IT) *Epic A 4271*	**22**	9 wks
9 Mar 85	★ YOU SPIN ME ROUND (LIKE A RECORD) *Epic A 4861*	**1**	23 wks
20 Apr 85	LOVER COME BACK TO ME *Epic A 6086*	**11**	8 wks
29 Jun 85	IN TOO DEEP *Epic A 6360*	**14**	8 wks
21 Sep 85	MY HEART GOES BANG (GET ME TO THE DOCTOR) *Epic A 6571*	**23**	6 wks

20 Sep 86	**BRAND NEW LOVER** Epic A 650075 7 ....**31**	4 wks
10 Jan 87	**SOMETHING IN MY HOUSE** Epic BURNS 1 ......**12**	7 wks
4 Apr 87	**HOOKED ON LOVE** Epic BURNS 2 ......**69**	2 wks
3 Sep 88	**TURN ROUND AND COUNT 2 TEN** Epic BURNS 4 ...**70**	1 wk
22 Jul 89	**COME HOME WITH ME BABY** Epic BURNS 5 ....**62**	2 wks

DEADLY SINS UK/Italy, male vocal/instrumental duo   **2 wks**

30 Apr 94	**WE ARE GOING ON DOWN** Ffrreedom TABCD 220 ..**45**	2 wks

Hazell DEAN UK, female vocalist   **71 wks**

18 Feb 84	**EVERGREEN / JEALOUS LOVE** Proto ENA 114 ....**63**	3 wks
21 Apr 84	● **SEARCHIN' (I GOTTA FIND A MAN)** Proto ENA 109 ..**6**	15 wks
28 Jul 84	● **WHATEVER I DO (WHEREVER I GO)** Proto ENA 119 ..**4**	11 wks
3 Nov 84	**BACK IN MY ARMS (ONCE AGAIN)** Proto ENA 122 ....**41**	4 wks
2 Mar 85	**NO FOOL (FOR LOVE)** Proto ENA 123 ....**41**	5 wks
12 Oct 85	**THEY SAY IT'S GONNA RAIN** Parlophone R 6107 ....**58**	4 wks
2 Apr 88	● **WHO'S LEAVING WHO** EMI EM 45 ....**4**	11 wks
25 Jun 88	**MAYBE (WE SHOULD CALL IT A DAY)** EMI EM 62 ..**15**	6 wks
24 Sep 88	**TURN IT INTO LOVE** EMI EM 71 ....**21**	7 wks
26 Aug 89	**LOVE PAINS** Lisson DOLE 12 ....**48**	4 wks
23 Mar 91	**BETTER OFF WITHOUT YOU** Lisson DOLE 19 ....**72**	1 wk

Jimmy DEAN US, male vocalist   **17 wks**

26 Oct 61	● **BIG BAD JOHN** Philips PB 1187 ....**2**	13 wks
8 Nov 62	**LITTLE BLACK BOOK** CBS AAG 122 ....**33**	4 wks

Letitia DEAN and Paul MEDFORD
UK, female/male vocal duo   **7 wks**

25 Oct 86	**SOMETHING OUTA NOTHING** BBC RESL 203 ....**12**	7 wks

DeBARGE US, male/female vocal group   **17 wks**

6 Apr 85	● **RHYTHM OF THE NIGHT** Gordy TMG 1376 ....**4**	14 wks
21 Sep 85	**YOU WEAR IT WELL** Gordy ZB 40345 [1] **54**	3 wks

[1] El DeBarge with DeBarge

El DeBARGE US, male vocalist   **3 wks**

28 Jun 86	**WHO'S JOHNNY ('SHORT CIRCUIT' THEME)** Gordy ELD 1 ....**60**	2 wks
31 Mar 90	**SECRET GARDEN** Qwest W 9992 [1] **67**	1 wk

[1] Quincy Jones featuring Al B. Sure, James Ingram, El DeBarge and Barry White

Diana DECKER US, female vocalist   **10 wks**

23 Oct 53	● **POPPA PICCOLINO** Columbia DB 3325 ....**2**	8 wks
8 Jan 54	● **POPPA PICCOLINO (re-entry)** Columbia DB 3325 ......**5**	2 wks

Dave DEE UK, male vocalist   **4 wks**

14 Mar 70	**MY WOMAN'S MAN** Fontana TF 1074 ....**42**	4 wks

See also Dave Dee, Dozy, Beaky, Mick and Tich.

Dave DEE, DOZY, BEAKY, MICK and TICH
UK, male vocal/instrumental group   **141 wks**

23 Dec 65	**YOU MAKE IT MOVE** Fontana TF 630 ....**26**	8 wks
3 Mar 66	● **HOLD TIGHT** Fontana TF 671 ....**4**	17 wks
9 Jun 66	● **HIDEAWAY** Fontana TF 711 ....**10**	11 wks
15 Sep 66	● **BEND IT** Fontana TF 746 ....**2**	12 wks
8 Dec 66	● **SAVE ME** Fontana TF 775 ....**4**	10 wks
9 Mar 67	**TOUCH ME TOUCH ME** Fontana TF 798 ....**13**	9 wks
18 May 67	● **OKAY!** Fontana TF 830 ....**4**	11 wks
11 Oct 67	● **ZABADAK!** Fontana TF 873 ....**3**	14 wks
14 Feb 68	★ **LEGEND OF XANADU** Fontana TF 903 ....**1**	12 wks

3 Jul 68	● **LAST NIGHT IN SOHO** Fontana TF 953 ....**8**	11 wks
2 Oct 68	**WRECK OF THE ANTOINETTE** Fontana TF 971 ....**14**	9 wks
5 Mar 69	**DON JUAN** Fontana TF 1000 ....**23**	9 wks
14 May 69	**SNAKE IN THE GRASS** Fontana TF 1020 ....**23**	8 wks

See also Dave Dee; D, B, M and T.

Jazzy DEE US, male vocalist   **5 wks**

5 Mar 83	**GET ON UP** Laurie LRS 101 ....**53**	5 wks

Joey DEE and the STARLITERS
US, male vocal/instrumental group   **8 wks**

8 Feb 62	**PEPPERMINT TWIST** Columbia DB 4758 ....**33**	8 wks

Kiki DEE UK, female vocalist   **79 wks**

10 Nov 73	**AMOUREUSE** Rocket PIG 4 ....**13**	13 wks
7 Sep 74	**I GOT THE MUSIC IN ME** Rocket PIG 12 [1] **19**	8 wks
12 Apr 75	**(YOU DONT KNOW) HOW GLAD I AM** Rocket PIG 16 [1] **33**	4 wks
3 Jul 76	★ **DON'T GO BREAKING MY HEART** Rocket ROKN 512 [2] **1**	14 wks
11 Sep 76	**LOVING AND FREE / AMOUREUSE (re-issue)** Rocket ROKN 515 ....**13**	8 wks
19 Feb 77	**FIRST THING IN THE MORNING** Rocket ROKN 520 ..**32**	5 wks
11 Jun 77	**CHICAGO** Rocket ROKN 526 ....**28**	4 wks
21 Feb 81	**STAR** Ariola ARO 251 ....**13**	10 wks
23 May 81	**PERFECT TIMING** Ariola ARO 257 ....**66**	3 wks
20 Nov 93	● **TRUE LOVE** Rocket EJSCX 32 [2] **2**	10 wks

[1] Kiki Dee Band [2] Elton John and Kiki Dee

On 18 Sep, 25 Sep and 2 Oct 1976, Loving And Free was listed by itself. Chicago was one side of a double-sided chart entry, the other being Bite Your Lip (Get Up And Dance) by Elton John.

Nancy DEE - See BENELUX and Nancy DEE

DEEE-LITE
US/Russia/Japan, male/female vocal/instrumental group   **30 wks**

18 Aug 90	● **GROOVE IS IN THE HEART / WHAT IS LOVE** Elektra EKR 114 ....**2**	13 wks
24 Nov 90	**POWER OF LOVE / DEEE-LITE THEME** Elektra EKR 117 ....**25**	7 wks
23 Feb 91	**HOW DO YOU SAY...LOVE / GROOVE IS IN THE HEART (re-mix)** Elektra EKR 118 ....**52**	2 wks
27 Apr 91	**GOOD BEAT / RIDING ON THROUGH** Elektra EKR 122 ....**53**	3 wks
13 Jun 92	**RUNAWAY** Elektra EKR 148 ....**45**	3 wks
30 Jul 94	**PICNIC IN THE SUMMERTIME** Elektra EKR 186CD1 ..**43**	2 wks

What Is Love only listed from 25 Aug 90.

Carol DEENE UK, female vocalist   **25 wks**

26 Oct 61	**SAD MOVIES** HMV POP 922 ....**44**	3 wks
25 Jan 62	**NORMAN** HMV POP 973 ....**24**	8 wks
5 Jul 62	**JOHNNY GET ANGRY** HMV POP 1027 ....**32**	4 wks
23 Aug 62	**SOME PEOPLE** HMV POP 1058 ....**25**	10 wks

DEEP BLUE UK, male producer - Sean O'Keefe   **2 wks**

16 Apr 94	**HELICOPTER TUNE** Moving Shadow SHADOW 41CD **68**	2 wks

DEEP C UK, male/female vocal/instrumental group   **3 wks**

19 Jan 91	**AFRICAN REIGN** M & G MAGS 4 ....**75**	1 wk
8 Jun 91	**CHILL TO THE PANIC** M & G MAGS 10 ....**73**	2 wks

DEEP CREED '94
US, male producer - Armand van Helden   **1 wk**

| 7 May 94 | **CAN U FEEL IT** Eastern Bloc BLOCCD 005 ....**59** | 1 wk |

DEEP FEELING UK, male vocal/instrumental group   **5 wks**

| 25 Apr 70 | **DO YOU LOVE ME** Page One POF 165 ....**45** | 1 wk |
| 9 May 70 | **DO YOU LOVE ME (re-entry)** Page One POF 165 ....**34** | 4 wks |

DEEP FOREST France, male instrumental duo   **12 wks**

5 Feb 94	● **SWEET LULLABY** Columbia 6599242...............**10**	6 wks
21 May 94	**DEEP FOREST** Columbia 6604115 ....**20**	4 wks
23 Jul 94	**SAVANNA DANCE** Columbia 6606355 ....**28**	2 wks

DEEP PURPLE UK, male vocal/instrumental group   **84 wks**

15 Aug 70	● **BLACK NIGHT** Harvest HAR 5020 ....**2**	21 wks
27 Feb 71	● **STRANGE KIND OF WOMAN** Harvest HAR 5033 ....**8**	12 wks
13 Nov 71	**FIREBALL** Harvest HAR 5045...............**15**	13 wks
1 Apr 72	**NEVER BEFORE** Purple PUR 102...............**35**	6 wks
16 Apr 77	**SMOKE ON THE WATER** Purple PUR 132 ....**21**	7 wks
15 Oct 77	**NEW LIVE AND RARE EP** Purple PUR 135 ....**31**	4 wks
7 Oct 78	**NEW LIVE AND RARE II EP** Purple PUR 137...............**45**	3 wks
2 Aug 80	**BLACK NIGHT (re-issue)** Harvest HAR 5210...............**43**	6 wks
1 Nov 80	**NEW LIVE AND RARE VOLUME 3 EP** Harvest SHEP 101 ....**48**	3 wks
26 Jan 85	**PERFECT STRANGERS** Polydor POSP 719 ....**48**	3 wks
15 Jun 85	**KNOCKING AT YOUR BACK DOOR/ PERFECT STRANGERS** Polydor POSP 749 ....**68**	1 wk
18 Jun 88	**HUSH** Polydor PO 4 ....**62**	2 wks
20 Oct 90	**KING OF DREAMS** RCA PB 49247 ....**70**	1 wk
2 Mar 91	**LOVE CONQUERS ALL** RCA PB 49225 ....**57**	2 wks

Tracks on New Live And Rare EP: Black Night (Live)/Painted Horse/ When A Blind Man Cries. New Live And Rare II EP: Burn (Edited Version)/ Coronarias Redig/Mistreated (Live)/ Rock Me Baby. New Live And Rare Volume 3 EP: Smoke On The Water/Bird Has Flown/Grabsplatter.

DEEP RIVER BOYS US, male vocal group   **1 wk**

| 7 Dec 56 | **THAT'S RIGHT** HMV POP 263 ....**29** | 1 wk |

Rick DEES and his CAST OF IDIOTS
US, male vocalist with male/female vocal/instrumental group   **9 wks**

| 18 Sep 76 | ● **DISCO DUCK (PART ONE)** RSO 2090 204 ....**6** | 9 wks |

DEF LEPPARD UK, male vocal/instrumental group   **89 wks**

17 Nov 79	**WASTED** Vertigo 6059 247 ....**61**	3 wks
23 Feb 80	**HELLO AMERICA** Vertigo LEPP 1 ....**45**	4 wks
5 Feb 83	**PHOTOGRAPH** Vertigo VER 5 ....**66**	3 wks
27 Aug 83	**ROCK OF AGES** Vertigo VER 6 ....**41**	4 wks
1 Aug 87	● **ANIMAL** Bludgeon Riffola LEP 1 ....**6**	9 wks
19 Sep 87	**POUR SOME SUGAR ON ME** Bludgeon Riffola LEP 2 ....**18**	6 wks
28 Nov 87	**HYSTERIA** Bludgeon Riffola LEP 3 ....**26**	5 wks
9 Jan 88	**HYSTERIA (re-entry)** Bludgeon Riffola LEP 3...............**74**	1 wk
9 Apr 88	**ARMAGEDDON IT** Bludgeon Riffola LEP 4 ....**20**	5 wks
16 Jul 88	**LOVE BITES** Bludgeon Riffola LEP 5...............**11**	8 wks
11 Feb 89	**ROCKET** Bludgeon Riffola LEP 6 ....**15**	7 wks
28 Mar 92	● **LET'S GET ROCKED** Bludgeon Riffola DEF 7 ....**2**	7 wks
27 Jun 92	**MAKE LOVE LIKE A MAN** Bludgeon Riffola LEP 7 ..**12**	5 wks
12 Sep 92	**HAVE YOU EVER NEEDED SOMEONE SO BAD** Bludgeon Riffola LEP 8 ....**16**	5 wks
30 Jan 93	**HEAVEN IS** Bludgeon Riffola LEPCD 9...............**13**	5 wks
1 May 93	**TONIGHT** Bludgeon Riffola LEPCD 10...............**34**	3 wks
18 Sep 93	**TWO STEPS BEHIND** Bludgeon Riffola LEPCD 12...............**32**	4 wks
15 Jan 94	**ACTION** Bludgeon Riffola LEPCD 13...............**14**	5 wks

DEFINITION OF SOUND UK, male rap duo   **20 wks**

9 Mar 91	**WEAR YOUR LOVE LIKE HEAVEN** Circa YR 61 ....**17**	9 wks
1 Jun 91	**NOW IS TOMORROW** Circa YR 66 ....**46**	4 wks
8 Feb 92	**MOIRA JANE'S CAFE** Circa YR 80 ....**34**	4 wks
19 Sep 92	**WHAT ARE YOU UNDER** Circa YR 95...............**68**	1 wk
14 Nov 92	**CAN I GET OVER** Circa YR 97 ....**61**	2 wks

DEGREES OF MOTION featuring BITI
US, female vocal group   **21 wks**

25 Apr 92	**DO YOU WANT IT RIGHT NOW** ffrr F 184...............**31**	5 wks
18 Jul 92	**SHINE ON** ffrr F 192 [1] **43**	3 wks
7 Nov 92	**SOUL FREEDOM - FREE YOUR SOUL** ffrr FX 201......**64**	1 wk
19 Mar 94	● **SHINE ON (re-mix)** ffrr FCD 229 ....**8**	8 wks
25 Jun 94	**DO YOU WANT IT RIGHT NOW (re-mix)** ffrr FCD 246 ....**26**	4 wks

[1] Degrees Of Motion featuring Biti with Kit West

DEJA US, male/female vocal duo   **1 wk**

| 29 Aug 87 | **SERIOUS** 10 TEN 132 ....**75** | 1 wk |

DEJA VU UK, male vocal/instrumental duo   **1 wk**

| 5 Feb 94 | **WHY WHY WHY** Cowboy RODEO 941CD ....**57** | 1 wk |

Desmond DEKKER and the ACES
Jamaica, male vocal/instrumental group   **71 wks**

12 Jul 67	**007** Pyramid PYR 6004...............**14**	11 wks
19 Mar 69	★ **ISRAELITES** Pyramid PYR 6058...............**1**	14 wks
25 Jun 69	● **IT MIEK** Pyramid PYR 6068 ....**7**	11 wks
2 Jul 69	**ISRAELITES (re-entry)** Pyramid PYR 6058 ....**45**	1 wk
10 Jan 70	**PICKNEY GAL** Pyramid PYR 6078...............**42**	3 wks
22 Aug 70	● **YOU CAN GET IT IF YOU REALLY WANT** Trojan TR 7777 [1] **2**	15 wks
10 May 75	● **ISRAELITES (re-issue)** Cactus CT 57 ....**10**	9 wks
30 Aug 75	**SING A LITTLE SONG** Cactus CT 73 ....**16**	7 wks

[1] Desmond Dekker

DEL AMITRI UK, male vocal/instrumental group   **45 wks**

19 Aug 89	**KISS THIS THING GOODBYE** A & M AM 515 ....**59**	2 wks
13 Jan 90	**NOTHING EVER HAPPENS** A & M AM 536 ....**11**	9 wks
24 Mar 90	**KISS THIS THING GOODBYE (re-issue)** A & M AM 551 ....**43**	4 wks
16 Jun 90	**MOVE AWAY JIMMY BLUE** A & M AM 555 ....**36**	6 wks
3 Nov 90	**SPIT IN THE RAIN** A & M AM 589 ....**21**	6 wks
9 May 92	**ALWAYS THE LAST TO KNOW** A & M AM 870...............**13**	7 wks
11 Jul 92	**BE MY DOWNFALL** A & M AM 884 ....**30**	4 wks
12 Sep 92	**JUST LIKE A MAN** A & M AM 0057 ....**25**	4 wks
23 Jan 93	**WHEN YOU WERE YOUNG** A & M AMCD 0132 ....**20**	3 wks

DELAGE UK, female vocal group   **2 wks**

| 15 Dec 90 | **ROCK THE BOAT** PWL/Polydor PO 113...............**63** | 2 wks |

DELANEY and BONNIE and FRIENDS featuring Eric CLAPTON - See *Eric CLAPTON*

DELEGATION UK, male vocal/instrumental group   **7 wks**

| 23 Apr 77 | **WHERE IS THE LOVE (WE USED TO KNOW)** State STAT 40 ....**22** | 6 wks |
| 20 Aug 77 | **YOU'VE BEEN DOING ME WRONG** State STAT 55 ..**49** | 1 wk |

DELFONICS US, male vocal group   **23 wks**

| 10 Apr 71 | **DIDN'T I (BLOW YOUR MIND THIS TIME)** Bell 1099 ....**43** | 1 wk |

24 Apr 71	**DIDN'T I (BLOW YOUR MIND THIS TIME)**		
	(re-entry) Bell 1099 ....**22**	8 wks
10 Jul 71	**LA-LA MEANS I LOVE YOU** Bell 1165 ....**19**	10 wks
16 Oct 71	**READY OR NOT HERE I COME** Bell 1175 ....**41**	4 wks

'DELIVERANCE' SOUNDTRACK
*US, male instrumental duo, Eric Weissberg - banjo and
Steve Mandell - guitar*   **7 wks**

| 31 Mar 73 | **DUELLING BANJOS** Warner Bros. K 16223 ....**17** | 7 wks |

DELLS *US, male vocal group*   **9 wks**

| 16 Jul 69 | **I CAN SING A RAINBOW - LOVE IS BLUE (MEDLEY)** | | |
| | Chess CRS 8099 ....**15** | 9 wks |

DELRONS - *See REPARATA and the DELRONS*

DELUXE *US, female vocalist*   **1 wk**

| 18 Mar 89 | **JUST A LITTLE MORE** Unyque UNQ 5 ....**74** | 1 wk |

Chaka DEMUS and PLIERS
Jamaica, male vocal duo   **52 wks**

12 Jun 93	● **TEASE ME** Mango CIDM 806 ....**3**	15 wks
18 Sep 93	● **SHE DON'T LET NOBODY** Mango CIDM 810 ....**4**	10 wks
18 Dec 93	★ **TWIST AND SHOUT** Mango CIDM 814 [1] **1**	13 wks
12 Mar 94	**MURDER SHE WROTE** Mango CIDM 812 ....**27**	4 wks
18 Jun 94	**I WANNA BE YOUR MAN** Mango CIDM 817 ....**19**	6 wks
27 Aug 94	**GAL WINE** Mango CIDM 818 ....**20**	4 wks

[1] Chaka Demus and Pliers featuring Jack Radics and Taxi Gang

Terry DENE *UK, male vocalist*   **20 wks**

7 Jun 57	**A WHITE SPORT COAT** Decca F 10895 ....**18**	6 wks
19 Jul 57	**START MOVIN'** Decca F 10914 ....**15**	8 wks
26 Jul 57	**A WHITE SPORT COAT (re-entry)** Decca F 10895 ....**30**	1 wk
16 May 58	**STAIRWAY OF LOVE** Decca F 11016 ....**16**	5 wks

Cathy DENNIS *UK, female vocalist*   **60 wks**

21 Oct 89	**C'MON AND GET MY LOVE** ffrr F 117 [1] **15**	10 wks
7 Apr 90	**THAT'S THE WAY OF THE WORLD** ffrr F 132 [1] **48**	3 wks
4 May 91	● **TOUCH ME (ALL NIGHT LONG)** Polydor CATH 3 ....**5**	10 wks
20 Jul 91	**JUST ANOTHER DREAM** Polydor CATH 2 ....**13**	7 wks
5 Oct 91	**TOO MANY WALLS** Polydor CATH 4 ....**17**	7 wks
7 Dec 91	**EVERYBODY MOVE** Polydor CATH 5 ....**25**	8 wks
29 Aug 92	**YOU LIED TO ME** Polydor CATH 6 ....**34**	4 wks
21 Nov 92	**IRRESISTIBLE** Polydor CATH 7 ....**24**	6 wks
6 Feb 93	**FALLING** Polydor CATHD 8 ....**32**	2 wks
12 Feb 94	**WHY** ffrr FCD 227 [1] **23**	3 wks

[1] D Mob with Cathy Dennis

Jackie DENNIS *UK, male vocalist*   **10 wks**

| 14 Mar 58 | ● **LA DEE DAH** Decca F 10992 ....**4** | 9 wks |
| 27 Jun 58 | **PURPLE PEOPLE EATER** Decca F 11033 ....**29** | 1 wk |

Stefan DENNIS *Australia, male vocalist*   **8 wks**

6 May 89	**DON'T IT MAKE YOU FEEL GOOD**		
	Sublime LIME 105 ....**16**	7 wks
7 Oct 89	**THIS LOVE AFFAIR** Sublime LIME 113 ....**67**	1 wk

DENNISONS *UK, male vocal / instrumental group*   **13 wks**

| 15 Aug 63 | **BE MY GIRL** Decca F 11691 ....**46** | 6 wks |
| 7 May 64 | **WALKIN' THE DOG** Decca F 11880 ....**36** | 7 wks |

Richard DENTON and Martin COOK
*UK, male orchestra leaders / instrumental duo,
guitar and keyboards*   **7 wks**

| 15 Apr 78 | **THEME FROM 'THE HONG KONG BEAT'** | | |
| | BBC RESL 52 ....**25** | 7 wks |

John DENVER *US, male vocalist*   **22 wks**

| 17 Aug 74 | ★ **ANNIE'S SONG** RCA APBO 0295 ....**1** | 13 wks |
| 12 Dec 81 | **PERHAPS LOVE** CBS A 1905 [1] ....**46** | 9 wks |

[1] Placido Domingo with John Denver

Karl DENVER *UK, male vocalist*   **127 wks**

22 Jun 61	● **MARCHETA** Decca F 11360 ....**8**	20 wks
19 Oct 61	● **MEXICALI ROSE** Decca F 11395 ....**8**	11 wks
25 Jan 62	● **WIMOWEH** Decca F 11420 ....**4**	17 wks
22 Feb 62	● **NEVER GOODBYE** Decca F 11431 ....**9**	18 wks
7 Jun 62	**A LITTLE LOVE A LITTLE KISS** Decca F 11470 ....**19**	10 wks
20 Sep 62	**BLUE WEEKEND** Decca F 11505 ....**33**	5 wks
21 Mar 63	**CAN YOU FORGIVE ME** Decca F 11608 ....**32**	8 wks
13 Jun 63	**INDIAN LOVE CALL** Decca F 11674 ....**32**	8 wks
22 Aug 63	**STILL** Decca F 11720 ....**13**	15 wks
5 Mar 64	**MY WORLD OF BLUE** Decca F 11828 ....**29**	6 wks
4 Jun 64	**LOVE ME WITH ALL YOUR HEART** Decca F 11905 ....**37**	6 wks
9 Jun 90	**LAZYITIS - ONE ARMED BOXER**		
	Factory FAC 2227 [1] **46**	3 wks

[1] Happy Mondays and Karl Denver

DEODATO *US, male multi-instrumentalist*   **9 wks**

| 5 May 73 | ● **ALSO SPRACH ZARATHUSTRA (2001)** | | |
| | Creed Taylor CTI 4000 ....**7** | 9 wks |

DEPARTMENT S *UK, male vocal / instrumental group*   **13 wks**

| 4 Apr 81 | **IS VIC THERE?** Demon D 1003 ....**22** | 10 wks |
| 11 Jul 81 | **GOING LEFT RIGHT** Stiff BUY 118 ....**55** | 3 wks |

DEPECHE MODE
UK, male vocal / instrumental group   **208 wks**

4 Apr 81	**DREAMING OF ME** Mute MUTE 013 ....**57**	4 wks
13 Jun 81	**NEW LIFE** Mute MUTE 014 ....**11**	15 wks
19 Sep 81	● **JUST CAN'T GET ENOUGH** Mute MUTE 016 ....**8**	10 wks
13 Feb 82	● **SEE YOU** Mute MUTE 018 ....**6**	10 wks
8 May 82	**THE MEANING OF LOVE** Mute MUTE 022 ....**12**	8 wks
28 Aug 82	**LEAVE IN SILENCE** Mute BONG 1 ....**18**	10 wks
12 Feb 83	**GET THE BALANCE RIGHT** Mute 7BONG 2 ....**13**	8 wks
23 Jul 83	● **EVERYTHING COUNTS** Mute 7BONG 3 ....**6**	11 wks
1 Oct 83	**LOVE IN ITSELF.2** Mute 7BONG 4 ....**21**	7 wks
24 Mar 84	● **PEOPLE ARE PEOPLE** Mute 7BONG 5 ....**4**	10 wks
1 Sep 84	● **MASTER AND SERVANT** Mute 7BONG 6 ....**9**	9 wks
10 Nov 84	**SOMEBODY / BLASPHEMOUS RUMOURS**		
	Mute 7BONG 7 ....**16**	6 wks
11 May 85	**SHAKE THE DISEASE** Mute BONG 8 ....**18**	9 wks
28 Sep 85	**IT'S CALLED A HEART** Mute BONG 9 ....**18**	4 wks
22 Feb 86	**STRIPPED** Mute BONG 10 ....**15**	5 wks
26 Apr 86	**A QUESTION OF LUST** Mute BONG 11 ....**28**	5 wks
23 Aug 86	**A QUESTION OF TIME** Mute BONG 12 ....**17**	6 wks
9 May 87	**STRANGELOVE** Mute BONG 13 ....**16**	5 wks
5 Sep 87	**NEVER LET ME DOWN AGAIN** Mute BONG 14 ....**22**	4 wks
9 Jan 88	**BEHIND THE WHEEL** Mute BONG 15 ....**21**	5 wks
28 May 88	**LITTLE 15 (IMPORT)** Mute LITTLE 15 ....**60**	2 wks
25 Feb 89	**EVERYTHING COUNTS** Mute BONG 16 ....**22**	7 wks
9 Sep 89	**PERSONAL JESUS** Mute BONG 17 ....**13**	8 wks
17 Feb 90	● **ENJOY THE SILENCE** Mute BONG 18 ....**6**	9 wks
19 May 90	**POLICY OF TRUTH** Mute BONG 19 ....**16**	6 wks
29 Sep 90	**WORLD IN MY EYES** Mute BONG 20 ....**17**	6 wks
27 Feb 93	● **I FEEL YOU** Mute CDBONG 21 ....**8**	7 wks
8 May 93	**WALKING IN MY SHOES** Mute CDBONG 22 ....**14**	4 wks

25 Sep 93	● **CONDEMNATION** *Mute CDBONG 23* **9**	4 wks
22 Jan 94	● **IN YOUR ROOM** *Mute CDBONG 24* **8**	4 wks

BONG 16 is a live version of BONG 3.

DEREK and the DOMINOES - *See Eric CLAPTON*

DESIRELESS *France, female vocalist*   **19 wks**

31 Oct 87	**VOYAGE VOYAGE** *CBS DESI 1* **53**	6 wks
14 May 88	● **VOYAGE VOYAGE (re-mix)** *CBS DESI 2* **5**	13 wks

DESIYA featuring Melissa YIANNAKOU
UK, male / female vocal / instrumental duo   **1 wk**

1 Feb 92	**COMIN' ON STRONG** *Blackmarket 12MKT 2* **74**	1 wk

DESKEE *UK, male instrumentalist*   **3 wks**

3 Feb 90	**LET THERE BE HOUSE** *Big One VBIG 19* **52**	2 wks
8 Sep 90	**DANCE, DANCE** *Big One VBIG 22* **74**	1 wk

DES'REE *UK, female vocalist*   **35 wks**

31 Aug 91	**FEEL SO HIGH** *Dusted Sound 6573667* **51**	5 wks
11 Jan 92	**FEEL SO HIGH (re-issue)** *Dusted Sound 6576897* **13**	7 wks
21 Mar 92	**MIND ADVENTURES** *Dusted Sound 6578637* **43**	3 wks
27 Jun 92	**WHY SHOULD I LOVE YOU** *Dusted Sound 6580917* **44**	3 wks
19 Jun 93	**DELICATE** *Columbia 6593312* [1] **14**	6 wks
9 Apr 94	**YOU GOTTA BE** *Dusted Sound 6601342* **20**	7 wks
18 Jun 94	**I AIN'T MOVIN'** *Dusted Sound 6604672* **44**	3 wks
3 Sep 94	**LITTLE CHILD** *Dusted Sound 6604515* **69**	1 wk

[1] Terence Trent D'Arby featuring Des'ree

DESTRY - *See ZOO EXPERIENCE featuring DESTRY*

Marcella DETROIT *US, female vocalist*   **16 wks**

12 Mar 94	**I BELIEVE** *London LONCD 347* **11**	8 wks
14 May 94	**AIN'T NOTHING LIKE THE REAL THING** *London LONCD 350* [1] **24**	4 wks
16 Jul 94	**I'M NO ANGEL** *London LOCDP 351* **33**	4 wks

[1] Marcella Detroit and Elton John

DETROIT EMERALDS *US, male vocal group*   **44 wks**

10 Feb 73	● **FEEL THE NEED IN ME** *Janus 6146 020* **4**	15 wks
5 May 73	**YOU WANT IT YOU GOT IT** *Westbound 6146 103* **12**	9 wks
11 Aug 73	**I THINK OF YOU** *Westbound 6146 104* **27**	9 wks
18 Jun 77	**FEEL THE NEED IN ME** *Atlantic K 10945* **12**	11 wks

The second Feel The Need In Me was a re-recording.

DETROIT SPINNERS *US, male vocal group*   **89 wks**

14 Nov 70	**IT'S A SHAME** *Tamla Motown TMG 755* [1] **20**	11 wks
21 Apr 73	**COULD IT BE I'M FALLING IN LOVE** *Atlantic K 10283* **11**	11 wks
29 Sep 73	● **GHETTO CHILD** *Atlantic K 10359* **7**	10 wks
19 Oct 74	**THEN CAME YOU** *Atlantic K 10495* [2] **29**	6 wks
11 Sep 76	**THE RUBBERBAND MAN** *Atlantic K 10807* **16**	11 wks
29 Jan 77	**WAKE UP SUSAN** *Atlantic K 10799* **29**	6 wks
7 May 77	**COULD IT BE I'M FALLING IN LOVE EP** *Atlantic K 10935* **32**	3 wks
23 Feb 80	★ **WORKING MY WAY BACK TO YOU - FORGIVE ME GIRL - (MEDLEY)** *Atlantic K 11432* **1**	14 wks
10 May 80	**BODY LANGUAGE** *Atlantic K 11392* **40**	7 wks
28 Jun 80	● **CUPID - I'VE LOVED YOU FOR A LONG TIME (MEDLEY)** *Atlantic K 11498* **4**	10 wks

[1] Motown Spinners [2] Dionne Warwick and the Detroit Spinners

---

Group was known simply as the Spinners in the US. Tracks on Could It Be I'm Falling In Love EP: Could It Be I'm Falling In Love / You're Throwing A Good Love Away / Games People Play / Lazy Susan.

DETROIT WHEELS - *See Mitch RYDER and the DETROIT WHEELS*

Sidney DEVINE *UK, male vocalist*   **1 wk**

1 Apr 78	**SCOTLAND FOREVER** *Philips SCOT 1* **48**	1 wk

DEVO *US, male vocal / instrumental group*   **23 wks**

22 Apr 78	**(I CAN'T ME GET NO) SATISFACTION** *Stiff BOY 1* ..**41**	8 wks
13 May 78	**JOCKO HOMO** *Stiff DEV 1*.............................**62**	3 wks
12 Aug 78	**BE STIFF** *Stiff BOY 2* **71**	1 wk
2 Sep 78	**COME BACK JONEE** *Virgin VS 223* **60**	4 wks
22 Nov 80	**WHIP IT** *Virgin VS 383* **51**	7 wks

Sheila B. DEVOTION *France, female vocalist*   **33 wks**

11 Mar 78	**SINGIN' IN THE RAIN** PART 1 *Carrere EMI 2751* **11**	13 wks
22 Jul 78	**YOU LIGHT MY FIRE** *Carrere EMI 2828* **44**	6 wks
24 Nov 79	**SPACER** *Carrere CAR 128* [1] **18**	14 wks

[1] Sheila and B. Devotion

DEVOTIONS - *See BELLE and the DEVOTIONS*

Howard DEVOTO - *See BUZZCOCKS*

DEXY'S MIDNIGHT RUNNERS
UK, male vocal / instrumental group   **93 wks**

19 Jan 80	**DANCE STANCE** *Oddball Productions R 6028*...........**40**	6 wks
22 Mar 80	★ **GENO** *Late Night Feelings R 6033*......................**1**	14 wks
12 Jul 80	● **THERE THERE MY DEAR** *Late Night Feelings R 6038*..**7**	9 wks
21 Mar 81	**PLAN B** *Parlophone R 6046*...........................**58**	2 wks
11 Jul 81	**SHOW ME** *Mercury DEXYS 6* **16**	9 wks
20 Mar 82	**THE CELTIC SOUL BROTHERS** *Mercury DEXYS 8* [1] ...**45**	4 wks
3 Jul 82	● **COME ON EILEEN** *Mercury DEXYS 9* [1] **1**	17 wks
2 Oct 82	● **JACKIE WILSON SAID** *Mercury DEXYS 10* [2] **5**	7 wks
4 Dec 82	**LET'S GET THIS STRAIGHT (FROM THE START) / OLD** *Mercury DEXYS 11* [2] **17**	9 wks
2 Apr 83	**THE CELTIC SOUL BROTHERS** *Mercury DEXYS 12* [2] **20**	6 wks
22 Nov 86	**BECAUSE OF YOU** *Mercury BRUSH 1*......................**13**	10 wks

[1] Dexy's Midnight Runners with the Emerald Express [2] Kevin Rowland and Dexy's Midnight Runners

DEXYS 12 is a different version from DEXYS 8.

Tony DI BART *UK, male vocalist*   **16 wks**

9 Apr 94	★ **THE REAL THING** *Cleveland City Blues CCBCD 15001* ..**1**	12 wks
20 Aug 94	**DO IT** *Cleveland City Blues CCBCD 15003* **21**	4 wks

DIAMOND HEAD *UK, male vocal / instrumental group*   **2 wks**

11 Sep 82	**IN THE HEAT OF THE NIGHT** *MCA DHM 102* **67**	2 wks

Jim DIAMOND *UK, male vocalist*   **30 wks**

3 Nov 84	★ **I SHOULD HAVE KNOWN BETTER** *A & M AM 220*......**1**	13 wks
2 Feb 85	**I SLEEP ALONE AT NIGHT** *A & M AM 229* **72**	1 wk
18 May 85	**REMEMBER I LOVE YOU** *A & M AM 247* **42**	5 wks
22 Feb 86	● **HI HO SILVER** *A & M AM 296* **5**	11 wks

Neil DIAMOND *US, male vocalist*   **121 wks**

7 Nov 70	● **CRACKLIN' ROSIE** *Uni UN 529* **3**	17 wks
20 Feb 71	● **SWEET CAROLINE** *Uni UN 531* **8**	11 wks
8 May 71	● **I AM . . . I SAID** *Uni UN 532* **4**	12 wks
13 May 72	**SONG SUNG BLUE** *Uni UN 538* **14**	13 wks

14 Aug 76	IF YOU KNOW WHAT I MEAN CBS 4398	35	4 wks
23 Oct 76	BEAUTIFUL NOISE CBS 4601	13	9 wks
24 Dec 77	DESIREE CBS 5869	39	6 wks
25 Nov 78 ●	YOU DON'T BRING ME FLOWERS CBS 6803 [1]	5	12 wks
3 Mar 79	FOREVER IN BLUE JEANS CBS 7047	16	12 wks
15 Nov 80	LOVE ON THE ROCKS Capitol CL 16173	17	12 wks
14 Feb 81	HELLO AGAIN Capitol CL 16176	51	4 wks
20 Nov 82	HEARTLIGHT CBS A 2814	47	7 wks
21 Nov 92	MORNING HAS BROKEN Columbia 6588267	36	2 wks

[1] Barbra and Neil.

Barbra was Barbra Streisand.

Gregg DIAMOND BIONIC BOOGIE
US, male/female vocal group   **3 wks**

20 Jan 79	CREAM (ALWAYS RISES TO THE TOP) Polydor POSP 18	61	3 wks

DIAMONDS Canada, male vocal group   **17 wks**

31 May 57 ●	LITTLE DARLIN' Mercury MT 148	3	17 wks

DICK and DEEDEE US, male/female vocal duo   **3 wks**

26 Oct 61	THE MOUNTAIN'S HIGH London HLG 9408	37	3 wks

Charles DICKENS UK, male vocalist   **8 wks**

1 Jul 65	THAT'S THE WAY LOVE GOES Pye 7N 15887	37	8 wks

Gwen DICKEY US, female vocalist   **6 wks**

27 Jan 90	CAR WASH Swanyard SYR 7	72	2 wks
2 Jul 94	AIN'T NOBODY (LOVES ME BETTER) X-clusive XCLU 010CD [1]	21	4 wks

[1] KWS and Gwen Dickey

Neville DICKIE UK, male instrumentalist - piano   **10 wks**

25 Oct 69	ROBIN'S RETURN Major Minor MM 644	33	7 wks
20 Dec 69	ROBIN'S RETURN (re-entry) Major Minor MM 644	43	3 wks

DICKIES US, male vocal/instrumental group   **28 wks**

16 Dec 78	SILENT NIGHT A & M AMS 7403	47	4 wks
21 Apr 79 ●	BANANA SPLITS (TRA LA LA SONG) A & M AMS 7431	7	8 wks
21 Jul 79	PARANOID A & M AMS 7368	45	6 wks
15 Sep 79	NIGHTS IN WHITE SATIN A & M AMS 7469	39	5 wks
16 Feb 80	FAN MAIL A & M AMS 7504	57	3 wks
19 Jul 80	GIGANTOR A & M AMS 7544	72	2 wks

Bruce DICKINSON UK, male vocalist   **21 wks**

28 Apr 90	TATTOOED MILLIONAIRE EMI EM 138	18	5 wks
23 Jun 90	ALL THE YOUNG DUDES EMI EM 142	23	5 wks
25 Aug 90	DIVE! DIVE! DIVE! EMI EM 151	45	2 wks
4 Apr 92 ●	(I WANT TO BE) ELECTED London LON 319 [1]	9	5 wks
28 May 94	TEARS OF THE DRAGON EMI CDEM 322	28	2 wks
8 Oct 94	SHOOT ALL THE CLOWNS EMI CDEMS 341	37	2 wks

[1] Mr Bean and Smear Campaign featuring Bruce Dickinson

Barbara DICKSON UK, female vocalist   **49 wks**

17 Jan 76 ●	ANSWER ME RSO 2090 174	9	7 wks
26 Feb 77	ANOTHER SUITCASE IN ANOTHER HALL MCA 266	18	7 wks
19 Jan 80	CARAVAN SONG Epic EPC 8103	41	7 wks
15 Mar 80	JANUARY FEBRUARY Epic EPC 8115	11	10 wks
14 Jun 80	IN THE NIGHT Epic EPC 8593	48	2 wks
5 Jan 85 ★	I KNOW HIM SO WELL RCA CHESS 3 [1]	1	16 wks

[1] Elaine Paige and Barbara Dickson

DICTATORS US, male vocal/instrumental group   **2 wks**

17 Sep 77	SEARCH AND DESTROY Asylum K 13091	49	1 wk
1 Oct 77	SEARCH AND DESTROY (re-entry) Asylum K 13091	50	1 wk

Bo DIDDLEY US, male vocalist/instrumentalist - guitar   **10 wks**

10 Oct 63	PRETTY THING Pye International 7N 25217	34	6 wks
18 Mar 65	HEY GOOD LOOKIN' Chess 8000	39	4 wks

DIDDY US, male producer   **1 wk**

19 Feb 94	GIVE ME LOVE Positiva CDTIV 8	52	1 wk

DIESEL PARK WEST UK, male vocal/instrumental group   **15 wks**

4 Feb 89	ALL THE MYTHS ON SUNDAY Food FOOD 17	66	2 wks
1 Apr 89	LIKE PRINCES DO Food FOOD 19	58	3 wks
5 Aug 89	WHEN THE HOODOO COMES Food FOOD 20	62	2 wks
18 Jan 92	FALL TO LOVE Food FOOD 35	48	3 wks
21 Mar 92	BOY ON TOP OF THE NEWS Food FOOD 36	58	2 wks
5 Sep 92	GOD ONLY KNOWS Food FOOD 39	57	3 wks

See also Various Artists (EPs & LPs) - The Food Christmas EP.

DIFFORD and TILBROOK
UK, male vocal/instrumental duo   **2 wks**

30 Jun 84	LOVE'S CRASHING WAVES A & M AM 193	57	2 wks

DIGABLE PLANETS
US, male/female vocal/instrumental group   **2 wks**

13 Feb 93	REBIRTH OF SLICK (COOL LIKE DAT) Pendulum EKR 159CD	67	2 wks

DIGITAL DREAM BABY UK, male vocalist - Peter Auty   **4 wks**

14 Dec 91	WALKING IN THE AIR Columbia 6576067	49	4 wks

Hit is a dance re-mix of Walking in the Air by Peter Auty.

DIGITAL EXCITATION
Belgium, male producer - Frank De Wulf   **2 wks**

29 Feb 92	PURE PLEASURE R&S RSUK 10	37	2 wks

DIGITAL ORGASM
Belgium, male/female vocal/instrumental group   **14 wks**

7 Dec 91	RUNNING OUT OF TIME Dead Dead Good GOOD 009	16	9 wks
18 Apr 92	STARTOUCHERS DDG International GOOD 13	31	3 wks
25 Jul 92	MOOG ERUPTION DDG International GOOD 17	62	2 wks

DIGITAL UNDERGROUND US, male vocal group   **4 wks**

16 Mar 91	SAME SONG Big Life BLR 40	52	4 wks

Paolo DINI - See FPI PROJECT

Ricky DILLARD - See Farley 'Jackmaster' Funk

Mark DINNING US, male vocalist   **4 wks**

10 Mar 60	TEEN ANGEL MGM 1053	37	3 wks
7 Apr 60	TEEN ANGEL (re-entry) MGM 1053	42	1 wk

DINOSAUR Jr. US, male vocal/instrumental group   **11 wks**

2 Feb 91	THE WAGON blanco y negro NEG 48	49	2 wks

14 Nov 92	**GET ME** blanco y negro NEG 60 ....**44**	1 wk
30 Jan 93	**START CHOPPIN** blanco y negro NEG 61CD **20**	3 wks
12 Jun 93	**OUT THERE** blanco y negro NEG 63CD..................**44**	2 wks
27 Aug 94	**FEEL THE PAIN** blanco y negro NEG 74CD **25**	3 wks

DINOSAURS - See Terry DACTYL and the DINOSAURS

DIO UK / US, male vocal / instrumental group   **22 wks**

20 Aug 83	**HOLY DIVER** Vertigo DIO 1 ....**72**	2 wks
29 Oct 83	**RAINBOW IN THE DARK** Vertigo DIO 2 ....**46**	3 wks
11 Aug 84	**WE ROCK** Vertigo DIO 3 ....**42**	3 wks
29 Sep 84	**MYSTERY** Vertigo DIO 4 ....**34**	4 wks
10 Aug 85	**ROCK `N' ROLL CHILDREN** Vertigo DIO 5 ....**26**	6 wks
2 Nov 85	**HUNGRY FOR HEAVEN** Vertigo DIO 6...................**72**	1 wk
17 May 86	**HUNGRY FOR HEAVEN (re-issue)** Vertigo DIO 7 ...**56**	2 wks
1 Aug 87	**I COULD HAVE BEEN A DREAMER** Vertigo DIO 8....**69**	1 wk

DION US, male vocalist   **35 wks**

26 Jun 59	**A TEENAGER IN LOVE** London HLU 8874 [1] **28**	2 wks
19 Jan 61	**LONELY TEENAGER** Top Rank JAR 521 ....**47**	1 wk
2 Nov 61	**RUNAROUND SUE** Top Rank JAR 586 ....**11**	9 wks
15 Feb 62	● **THE WANDERER** HMV POP 971 ....**10**	12 wks
22 May 76	**THE WANDERER (re-issue)** Philips 6146 700 ....**16**	9 wks
19 Aug 89	**KING OF THE NEW YORK STREET** Arista 112556 ....**74**	2 wks

[1] Dion and the Belmonts

Celine DION Canada, female vocalist   **39 wks**

16 May 92	● **BEAUTY AND THE BEAST** Epic 6576607 [1] **9**	7 wks
4 Jul 92	**IF YOU ASKED ME TO** Epic 6581927 ....**60**	2 wks
14 Nov 92	**LOVE CAN MOVE MOUNTAINS** Epic 6587787 ....**46**	2 wks
26 Dec 92	**IF YOU ASKED ME TO (re-entry)** Epic 6581927 .....**57**	3 wks
3 Apr 93	**WHERE DOES MY HEART BEAT NOW** Epic 6563265 ....**72**	1 wk
29 Jan 94	● **THE POWER OF LOVE** Epic 6597992 ....**4**	10 wks
23 Apr 94	**MISLED** Epic 6602922 ....**40**	3 wks
22 Oct 94	● **THINK TWICE** Epic 6606422 ....**5†**	11 wks

[1] Celine Dion and Peabo Bryson

DIONNE Canada, female vocalist   **2 wks**

23 Sep 89	**COME GET MY LOVIN'** Citybeat CBC 745.................**69**	2 wks

DIRE STRAITS UK, male vocal / instrumental group   **119 wks**

10 Mar 79	● **SULTANS OF SWING** Vertigo 6059 206 ....**8**	11 wks
28 Jul 79	**LADY WRITER** Vertigo 6059 230 ....**51**	6 wks
17 Jan 81	● **ROMEO AND JULIET** Vertigo MOVIE 1 ....**8**	11 wks
4 Apr 81	**SKATEAWAY** Vertigo MOVIE 2 ....**37**	5 wks
10 Oct 81	**TUNNEL OF LOVE** Vertigo MUSIC 3 ....**54**	3 wks
4 Sep 82	● **PRIVATE INVESTIGATIONS** Vertigo DSTR 1 ....**2**	8 wks
22 Jan 83	**TWISTING BY THE POOL** Vertigo DSTR 2 ....**14**	7 wks
18 Feb 84	**LOVE OVER GOLD (LIVE) / SOLID ROCK (LIVE)** Vertigo DSTR 6 ....**50**	3 wks
20 Apr 85	**SO FAR AWAY** Vertigo DSTR 9 ....**20**	6 wks
6 Jul 85	● **MONEY FOR NOTHING** Vertigo DSTR 10 ....**4**	16 wks
26 Oct 85	**BROTHERS IN ARMS** Vertigo DSTR 11 ....**16**	13 wks
11 Jan 86	● **WALK OF LIFE** Vertigo DSTR 12 ....**2**	11 wks
3 May 86	**YOUR LATEST TRICK** Vertigo DSTR 13 ....**26**	6 wks
5 Nov 88	**SULTANS OF SWING (re-issue)** Vertigo DSTR 15......**62**	1 wk
31 Aug 91	**CALLING ELVIS** Vertigo DSTR 16 ....**21**	4 wks
2 Nov 91	**HEAVY FUEL** Vertigo DSTR 17 ....**55**	2 wks
29 Feb 92	**ON EVERY STREET** Vertigo DSTR 18 ....**42**	2 wks
27 Jun 92	**THE BUG** Vertigo DSTR 19...**67**	1 wk
22 May 93	**ENCORES EP** Vertigo DSCD20 ....**31**	3 wks

Tracks on Encores EP: Your Latest Trick / The Bug / Solid Rock / Local Hero–Wild Theme.

DIRECKT UK, male instrumental / production duo   **2 wks**

13 Aug 94	**TWO FATT GUITARS (REVISITED)** UFG UFG 7CD **36**	2 wks

DIRECT DRIVE
UK, male / female vocal / instrumental group   **3 wks**

26 Jan 85	**ANYTHING?** Polydor POSP 728.................................**67**	2 wks
4 May 85	**A.B.C. (FALLING IN LOVE'S NOT EASY)** Boiling Point POSP 742 ....**75**	1 wk

DISCHARGE UK, male vocal / instrumental group   **3 wks**

24 Oct 81	**NEVER AGAIN** Clay CLAY 6 ....**64**	3 wks

DISCO ANTHEM
Holland, male producer - Lex van Coeverden   **2 wks**

18 Jun 94	**SCREAM** Sweat MCSTD 1977 ....**47**	2 wks

DISCO EVANGELISTS
UK, male instrumental / production group   **2 wks**

8 May 93	**DE NIRO** Positiva CDTIV 2 ....**59**	2 wks

DISCO TEX and the SEX-O-LETTES
US, male vocalist / female vocal group   **22 wks**

23 Nov 74	● **GET DANCING** Chelsea 2005 013 ....**8**	12 wks
26 Apr 75	● **I WANNA DANCE WIT CHOO** Chelsea 2005 024 [1]....**6**	10 wks

[1] Disco Tex and the Sex-O-Lettes featuring Sir Monti Rock III

DISPOSABLE HEROES OF HIPHOPRISY
US, male vocal / instrumental duo   **7 wks**

4 Apr 92	**TELEVISION THE DRUG OF THE NATION** Fourth & Broadway BRW 241 ....**57**	2 wks
30 May 92	**LANGUAGE OF VIOLENCE** Fourth & Broadway 12BRW 248 ....**68**	1 wk
19 Dec 92	**TELEVISION THE DRUG OF THE NATION (re-entry)** Fourth & Broadway BRW 241 ....**44**	4 wks

Sacha DISTEL France, male vocalist   **27 wks**

10 Jan 70	**RAINDROPS KEEP FALLING ON MY HEAD** Warner Bros. WB 7345 ....**50**	1 wk
24 Jan 70	● **RAINDROPS KEEP FALLING ON MY HEAD (re-entry)** Warner Bros. WB 7345 ....**10**	20 wks
27 Jun 70	**RAINDROPS KEEP FALLING ON MY HEAD (2nd re-entry)** Warner Bros. WB 7345 ....**43**	4 wks
1 Aug 70	**RAINDROPS KEEP FALLING ON MY HEAD (3rd re-entry)** Warner Bros. WB 7345 ....**47**	1 wk
15 Aug 70	**RAINDROPS KEEP FALLING ON MY HEAD (4th re-entry)** Warner Bros. WB 7345 ....**44**	1 wk

DIVERSIONS UK, male / female vocal / instrumental group   **3 wks**

20 Sep 75	**FATTIE BUM BUM** Gull GULS 18..................................**34**	3 wks

DIVINE US, male vocalist   **24 wks**

15 Oct 83	**LOVE REACTION** Design Communication DES 4........**65**	2 wks
14 Jul 84	**YOU THINK YOU'RE A MAN** Proto ENA 118 ....**16**	10 wks
20 Oct 84	**I'M SO BEAUTIFUL** Proto ENA 121 ....**52**	2 wks
27 Apr 85	**WALK LIKE A MAN** Proto ENA 125 ....**23**	7 wks
20 Jul 85	**TWISTIN' THE NIGHT AWAY** Proto ENA 127 ....**47**	3 wks

DIVINYLS Australia, female / male vocal / instrumental duo   **12 wks**

18 May 91	● **I TOUCH MYSELF** Virgin America VUS 36 ....**10**	12 wks

DIXIE CUPS US, female vocal group — 16 wks

| 18 Jun 64 | **CHAPEL OF LOVE** Pye International 7N 25245 ....**22** | 8 wks |
| 13 May 65 | **IKO IKO** Red Bird RB 10024.................................**23** | 8 wks |

DIZZY HEIGHTS UK, male vocal / instrumental group — 4 wks

| 18 Dec 82 | **CHRISTMAS RAPPING** Polydor WRAP 1 ....**49** | 4 wks |

DJ BOBO Switzerland, male vocalist - René Baumann — 2 wks

| 24 Sep 94 | **EVERYBODY** PWL Continental PWCD 312 ....**47** | 2 wks |

DJ Carl COX UK, male producer — 12 wks

28 Sep 91	**I WANT YOU (FOREVER)** Perfecto PB 44885 ....**23**	7 wks
8 Aug 92	**DOES IT FEEL GOOD TO YOU** Perfecto PB 74321102877 ....**35**	3 wks
6 Nov 93	**THE PLANET OF LOVE** Perfecto 74321161772 [1] **44**	2 wks

[1] Carl Cox

DJ DISCIPLE US, male vocalist — 1 wk

| 12 Nov 94 | **ON THE DANCEFLOOR** Mother MUMCD 55 ......**67** | 1 wk |

DJ DUKE US, male producer — 7 wks

| 8 Jan 94 | **BLOW YOUR WHISTLE** ffrr FCD 228 ....**15** | 5 wks |
| 16 Jul 94 | **TURN IT UP (SAY YEAH)** ffrr FCD 235 ....**31** | 2 wks |

DJ E-Z ROCK - See Rob BASE and DJ E-Z ROCK

DJ 'Fast' EDDIE US, male producer — 15 wks

11 Apr 87	**CAN U DANCE** Champion CHAMP 41 [1] **71**	2 wks
14 Nov 87	**CAN U DANCE (re-entry)** Champion CHAMP 41 [1] ..**67**	2 wks
21 Jan 89	**HIP HOUSE / I CAN DANCE** DJ International DJIN 5 ..**47**	4 wks
11 Mar 89	**YO YO GET FUNKY** DJ International DJIN 7 ....**54**	3 wks
28 Oct 89	**GIT ON UP** DJ International 655366 7 [2] **49**	4 wks

[1] Kenny 'Jammin' Jason and 'Fast' Eddie Smith [2] DJ 'Fast' Eddie featuring Sundance

DJ HYPE UK, male producer — 1 wk

| 20 Mar 93 | **SHOT IN THE DARK** Suburban Base SUBBASE 20CD **63** | 1 wk |

DJ JAZZY JEFF and the FRESH PRINCE - See JAZZY JEFF and FRESH PRINCE

DJ MIKO Italy, male producer — 10 wks

| 13 Aug 94 | ● **WHAT'S UP** Systematic SYSCD 2 ....**6** | 10 wks |

DJ POWER Italy, male producer - Steve Gambaroli — 2 wks

| 7 Mar 92 | **EVERYBODY PUMP** Cooltempo COOL 252 ....**46** | 2 wks |

DJ PROFESSOR Italy, male producer — 5 wks

10 Aug 91	**WE GOTTA DO IT** Fourth & Broadway BRW 225 [1] ..**57**	2 wks
28 Mar 92	**ROCK ME STEADY** PWL Continental PWL 219 ....**49**	2 wks
8 Oct 94	**ROCKIN' ME** Citra CITRA 1CD [2] **56**	1 wk

[1] DJ Professor featuring Francesco Zappala [2] Professor

DJ Doc SCOTT UK, male producer — 2 wks

| 1 Feb 92 | **NHS EP** Absolute 2 ABS 001DJ ....**64** | 2 wks |

Tracks on NHS EP: Surgery / Night Nurse.

DJ SEDUCTION UK, male producer - John Kallum — 8 wks

| 22 Feb 92 | **HARDCORE HEAVEN / YOU AND ME** Ffrreedom TAB 103 ....**26** | 5 wks |
| 11 Jul 92 | **COME ON** Ffrreedom TAB 111 ....**37** | 3 wks |

DJAIMIN Switzerland, male producer — 2 wks

| 19 Sep 92 | **GIVE YOU** Cooltempo COOL 262 ....**45** | 2 wks |

DJH featuring STEFY
Italy, male instrumental / production group — 14 wks

16 Feb 91	**THINK ABOUT...** RCA PB 44385 ....**22**	6 wks
13 Jul 91	**I LIKE IT** RCA PB 44741 ....**16**	7 wks
19 Oct 91	**MOVE YOUR LOVE** RCA PB 44965 ....**73**	1 wk

DJPC Belgium, male producer — 5 wks

| 26 Oct 91 | **INSSOMNIAK** Hype 7PUM 005......................**62** | 4 wks |
| 29 Feb 92 | **INSSOMNIAK (re-issue)** Hype PUMR 005 ....**64** | 1 wk |

DNA UK, male production duo — 29 wks

28 Jul 90	● **TOM'S DINER** A & M AM 592 [1] **2**	10 wks
18 Aug 90	**LA SERENISSIMA** Raw Bass RBASS 006 ....**34**	8 wks
3 Aug 91	**REBEL WOMAN** DNA 7DNA 001 [2] **42**	4 wks
1 Feb 92	**CAN YOU HANDLE IT** EMI EM 219 [3] **17**	5 wks
9 May 92	**BLUE LOVE (CALL MY NAME)** EMI EM 226 [4] **66**	2 wks

[1] DNA featuring Suzanne Vega [2] DNA performed by Jazzi P. [3] DNA featuring Sharon Redd [4] DNA featuring Joe Nye

Carl DOBKINS Jr. US, male vocalist — 1 wk

| 31 Mar 60 | **LUCKY DEVIL** Brunswick 05817 ....**44** | 1 wk |

Anita DOBSON UK, female vocalist — 13 wks

| 9 Aug 86 | ● **ANYONE CAN FALL IN LOVE** BBC RESL 191 [1] ....**4** | 9 wks |
| 18 Jul 87 | **TALKING OF LOVE** Parlophone R 6159 ....**43** | 4 wks |

[1] Anita Dobson featuring the Simon May Orchestra

DOCTOR and the MEDICS
UK, male / female vocal / instrumental group — 25 wks

10 May 86	★ **SPIRIT IN THE SKY** IRS IRM 113 ....**1**	15 wks
9 Aug 86	**BURN** IRS IRM 119 ....**29**	6 wks
22 Nov 86	**WATERLOO** IRS IRM 125 [1] **45**	4 wks

[1] Doctor and the Medics featuring Roy Wood

DR. ALBAN Nigeria, male producer — 27 wks

5 Sep 92	● **IT'S MY LIFE** Logic 7432115330 ....**2**	12 wks
14 Nov 92	**ONE LOVE** Logic 74321108727 ....**45**	2 wks
10 Apr 93	**SING HALLELUJAH!** Logic 74321136202 ....**16**	8 wks
26 Mar 94	**LOOK WHO'S TALKING** Logic 74321195342 ......**55**	3 wks
13 Aug 94	**AWAY FROM HOME** Logic 74321222682 ....**42**	2 wks

DR. DRE US, male rapper — 5 wks

| 22 Jan 94 | **NUTHIN' BUT A 'G' THANG / LET ME RIDE** Death Row A 8328CD ....**31** | 3 wks |
| 3 Sep 94 | **DRE DAY** Death Row A 8292CD ....**59** | 2 wks |

DR. FEELGOOD UK, male vocal / instrumental group — 29 wks

11 Jun 77	**SNEAKIN' SUSPICION** United Artists UP 36255 ....**47**	3 wks
24 Sep 77	**SHE'S A WIND UP** United Artists UP 36304 ....**34**	5 wks
30 Sep 78	**DOWN AT THE DOCTOR'S** United Artists UP 36444 ..**48**	5 wks
20 Jan 79	● **MILK AND ALCOHOL** United Artists UP 36468...........**9**	9 wks

5 May 79	**AS LONG AS THE PRICE IS RIGHT**		
	United Artists YUP 36506 ....**40**	6 wks	
8 Dec 79	**PUT HIM OUT OF YOUR MIND**		
	United Artists BP 306 ....**73**	1 wk	

DR. HOOK US, male vocal / instrumental group   104 wks

24 Jun 72	● **SYLVIA'S MOTHER** CBS 7929 [1] **2**	13 wks
26 Jun 76	● **A LITTLE BIT MORE** Capitol CL 15871 ....**2**	14 wks
30 Oct 76	● **IF NOT YOU** Capitol CL 15885...................**5**	10 wks
25 Mar 78	**MORE LIKE THE MOVIES** Capitol CL 15967 ....**14**	10 wks
22 Sep 79	★ **WHEN YOU'RE IN LOVE WITH**	
	A BEAUTIFUL WOMAN Capitol CL 16039 ....**1**	17 wks
5 Jan 80	● **BETTER LOVE NEXT TIME** Capitol CL 16112 ....**8**	8 wks
29 Mar 80	● **SEXY EYES** Capitol CL 16127 ....**4**	9 wks
23 Aug 80	**YEARS FROM NOW** Capitol CL 16154 ....**47**	6 wks
8 Nov 80	**SHARING THE NIGHT TOGETHER** Capitol CL 16171 **43**	4 wks
22 Nov 80	**GIRLS CAN GET IT** Mercury MER 51 ....**40**	5 wks
1 Feb 92	**WHEN LOVE IN LOVE WITH**	
	A BEAUTIFUL WOMAN (re-issue) Capitol EMCT 4 **44**	4 wks
6 Jun 92	**A LITTLE BIT MORE** (re-issue) EMI EMCT 6 ....**47**	4 wks

[1] Dr. Hook and The Medicine Show

DOCTOR SPIN UK, male instrumental / production duo   8 wks

3 Oct 92	● **TETRIS** Carpet CRPT 4 ....**6**	8 wks

Ken DODD UK, male vocalist   233 wks

7 Jul 60	● **LOVE IS LIKE A VIOLIN** Decca F 11248 ....**8**	18 wks
15 Jun 61	**ONCE IN EVERY LIFETIME** Decca F 11355 ......**28**	7 wks
10 Aug 61	**ONCE IN EVERY LIFETIME** (re-entry)	
	Decca F 11355 ....**47**	1 wk
24 Aug 61	**ONCE IN EVERY LIFETIME** (2nd re-entry)	
	Decca F 11355 ....**31**	10 wks
1 Feb 62	**PIANISSIMO** Decca F 11422 ....**21**	15 wks
29 Aug 63	**STILL** Columbia DB 7094 ....**35**	10 wks
6 Feb 64	**EIGHT BY TEN** Columbia DB 7191 ....**22**	11 wks
23 Jul 64	**HAPPINESS** Columbia DB 7325 ....**31**	13 wks
26 Nov 64	**SO DEEP IS THE NIGHT** Columbia DB 7398 ....**31**	7 wks
2 Sep 65	★ **TEARS** Columbia DB 7659 ....**1**	24 wks
18 Nov 65	● **THE RIVER (LE COLLINE SONO IN FIORO)**	
	Columbia DB 7750 ....**3**	14 wks
12 May 66	● **PROMISES** Columbia DB 7914 ....**6**	14 wks
4 Aug 66	**MORE THAN LOVE** Columbia DB 7976 ....**14**	11 wks
27 Oct 66	**IT'S LOVE** Columbia DB 8031 ....**36**	7 wks
19 Jan 67	**LET ME CRY ON YOUR SHOULDER**	
	Columbia DB 8101 ....**11**	10 wks
30 Jul 69	**TEARS WON'T WASH AWAY MY HEARTACHE**	
	Columbia DB 8600 ....**22**	11 wks
5 Dec 70	**BROKEN HEARTED** Columbia DB 8725 ....**15**	9 wks
13 Feb 71	**BROKEN HEARTED** (re-entry) Columbia DB 8725...**38**	1 wk
10 Jul 71	**WHEN LOVE COMES ROUND AGAIN**	
	(L'ARCA DI NOE) Columbia DB 8796.............**19**	16 wks
18 Nov 72	**JUST OUT OF REACH (OF MY TWO EMPTY ARMS)**	
	Columbia DB 8947 ....**29**	11 wks
29 Nov 75	**(THINK OF ME) WHEREVER YOU ARE** EMI 2342 ....**21**	8 wks
26 Dec 81	**HOLD MY HAND** Images IMGS 0002 ....**44**	5 wks

Rory DODD - See Jim STEINMAN

DODGY UK, male vocal / instrumental group   7 wks

8 May 93	**LOVEBIRDS** A & M AMCD 0177 ....**65**	2 wks
3 Jul 93	**I NEED ANOTHER** (EP) A & M 5803172..........**67**	2 wks
6 Aug 94	**THE MELOD-EP** Bostin 5806772 ....**53**	1 wk
1 Oct 94	**STAYING OUT FOR THE SUMMER** Bostin 5807972 ..**38**	2 wks

Tracks on I Need Another (EP): *I Need Another / Never Again / If I Fall / Hendre DDU. Tracks on* The Melod-EP: *Melodies Haunt You / The Snake / Don't Go / Summer Fayre.*

Tim DOG US, male rapper   1 wk

29 Oct 94	**BITCH WITH A PERM** Dis-stress DISCD 1 ....**49**	1 wk

Nate DOGG - See Warren G

DOGS D'AMOUR UK, male vocal / instrumental group   15 wks

4 Feb 89	**HOW COME IT NEVER RAINS** China CHINA 13 .....**44**	3 wks
5 Aug 89	**SATELLITE KID** China CHINA 17....................**26**	3 wks
14 Oct 89	**TRAIL OF TEARS** China CHINA 20 ....**47**	3 wks
23 Jun 90	**VICTIMS OF SUCCESS** China CHINA 24............**36**	3 wks
15 Sep 90	**EMPTY WORLD** China CHINA 27 ....**61**	2 wks
19 Jun 93	**ALL OR NOTHING** China WOKCD 2033 ....**53**	1 wk

Joe DOLAN Ireland, male vocalist   40 wks

25 Jun 69	● **MAKE ME AN ISLAND** Pye 7N 17738 ....**3**	18 wks
1 Nov 69	**TERESA** Pye 7N 17833 ....**20**	7 wks
8 Nov 69	**MAKE ME AN ISLAND** (re-entry) Pye 7N 17738......**48**	1 wk
28 Feb 70	**YOU'RE SUCH A GOOD LOOKING WOMAN**	
	Pye 7N 17891 ....**17**	13 wks
17 Sep 77	**I NEED YOU** Pye 7N 45702 ....**43**	1 wk

Thomas DOLBY
UK, male vocalist / multi-instrumentalist   51 wks

3 Oct 81	**EUROPA AND THE PIRATE TWINS**	
	Parlophone R 6051 ....**48**	3 wks
14 Aug 82	**WINDPOWER** Venice In Peril VIPS 103 ....**31**	8 wks
6 Nov 82	**SHE BLINDED ME WITH SCIENCE**	
	Venice In Peril VIPS 104 ....**49**	4 wks
16 Jul 83	**SHE BLINDED ME WITH SCIENCE** (re-issue)	
	Venice In Peril VIP 105 ....**56**	4 wks
21 Jan 84	**HYPERACTIVE** Parlophone Odeon R 6065 ....**17**	9 wks
31 Mar 84	**I SCARE MYSELF** Parlophone Odeon R 6067 ....**46**	5 wks
16 Apr 88	**AIRHEAD** Manhattan MT 38........................**53**	3 wks
9 May 92	**CLOSE BUT NO CIGAR** Virgin VS 1410 ....**22**	5 wks
11 Jul 92	**I LOVE YOU GOODBYE** Virgin VS 1417 ....**36**	4 wks
26 Sep 92	**SILK PYJAMAS** Virgin VS 1430 ....**62**	2 wks
22 Jan 94	**HYPERACTIVE!** (re-mix) Parlophone CDEMCTS 10 ..**23**	4 wks

Joe DOLCE MUSIC THEATRE US, male vocalist   10 wks

7 Feb 81	★ **SHADDAP YOU FACE** Epic EPC 9518 ....**1**	10 wks

DOLL UK, male / female vocal / instrumental group   8 wks

13 Jan 79	**DESIRE ME** Beggars Banquet BEG 11 ....**28**	8 wks

DOLLAR UK, male / female vocal duo   128 wks

11 Nov 78	**SHOOTING STAR** Carrere 2871 ....**14**	12 wks
19 May 79	**WHO WERE YOU WITH IN THE MOONLIGHT**	
	Carrere CAR 110 ....**14**	12 wks
18 Aug 79	● **LOVE'S GOTTA HOLD ON ME** Carrere CAR 122 ....**4**	13 wks
24 Nov 79	● **I WANNA HOLD YOUR HAND** Carrere CAR 131 ....**9**	14 wks
25 Oct 80	**TAKIN' A CHANCE ON YOU** WEA K 18353.........**62**	3 wks
15 Aug 81	**HAND HELD IN BLACK AND WHITE** WEA BUCK 1 ..**19**	12 wks
14 Nov 81	● **MIRROR MIRROR (MON AMOUR)** WEA BUCK 2 ......**4**	17 wks
20 Mar 82	**RING RING** Carrere CAR 225 ....**61**	2 wks
27 Mar 82	● **GIVE ME BACK MY HEART** WEA BUCK 3 ....**4**	9 wks
19 Jun 82	**VIDEOTHEQUE** WEA BUCK 4 ....**17**	10 wks
18 Sep 82	**GIVE ME SOME KINDA MAGIC** WEA BUCK 5 ......**34**	6 wks
16 Aug 86	**WE WALKED IN LOVE** Arista DIME 1 ....**61**	4 wks
26 Dec 87	● **O L'AMOUR** London LON 146 ....**7**	11 wks
16 Jul 88	**IT'S NATURE'S WAY (NO PROBLEM)**	
	London LON 179 ....**58**	3 wks

Placido DOMINGO Spain, male vocalist   24 wks

12 Dec 81	**PERHAPS LOVE** CBS A 1905 [1] **46**	9 wks

KEN DODD is surprised to find himself where the likes of Ray Charles, Connie Francis and Cliff Richard have been before – at number one. (LFI)

TOP 49 50

27 May 89	TILL I LOVED YOU CBS 654843 7 [2]	....................**24**	9 wks
16 Jun 90	NESSUN DORMA FROM 'TURANDOT'		
	Epic 656005 7 [3]	....................**59**	2 wks
30 Jul 94	LIBIAMO / LA DONNA E MOBILE		
	Teldec YZ 843CD [4]	....................**21**	4 wks

[1] Placido Domingo with John Denver [2] Placido Domingo and Jennifer Rush [3] Luis Cobos featuring Placido Domingo [4] José Carreras, Placido Domingo and Luciano Pavarotti

DOMINO US, male vocal / instrumental group   **6 wks**

22 Jan 94	GETTO JAM Chaos 6600402	....................**33**	4 wks
14 May 94	SWEET POTATOE PIE Chaos 6603292	....................**42**	2 wks

Fats DOMINO
US, male vocalist / instrumentalist - piano   **109 wks**

27 Jul 56	I'M IN LOVE AGAIN London HLU 8280	........**28**	1 wk
17 Aug 56	I'M IN LOVE AGAIN (re-entry) London HLU 8280 ..**12**		13 wks
30 Nov 56	BLUEBERRY HILL London HLU 8330	........**26**	1 wk
21 Dec 56 ●	BLUEBERRY HILL (re-entry) London HLU 8330 ....**6**		14 wks
25 Jan 57	AIN'T THAT A SHAME London HLU 8173	........**23**	2 wks
1 Feb 57	HONEY CHILE London HLU 8356	........**29**	1 wk
29 Mar 57	BLUE MONDAY London HLP 8377	........**23**	1 wk
19 Apr 57	BLUE MONDAY (re-entry) London HLP 8377	........**30**	1 wk
19 Apr 57	I'M WALKIN' London HLP 8407	........**19**	7 wks
19 Jul 57	VALLEY OF TEARS London HLP 8449	........**25**	1 wk
28 Mar 58	THE BIG BEAT London HLP 8575	........**20**	4 wks
4 Jul 58	SICK AND TIRED London HLP 8628	........**26**	1 wk
22 May 59	MARGIE London HLP 8865	........**18**	5 wks
16 Oct 59	I WANT TO WALK YOU HOME London HLP 8942 ....**14**		5 wks
18 Dec 59	BE MY GUEST London HLP 9005	........**11**	8 wks
19 Feb 60	BE MY GUEST (re-entry) London HLP 9005	........**19**	3 wks
17 Mar 60	COUNTRY BOY London HLP 9073	........**19**	11 wks
21 Jul 60	WALKING TO NEW ORLEANS London HLP 9163 ....**19**		10 wks
10 Nov 60	THREE NIGHTS A WEEK London HLP 9198	........**45**	2 wks
5 Jan 61	MY GIRL JOSEPHINE London HLP 9244	........**32**	4 wks
27 Jul 61	IT KEEPS RAININ' London HLP 9374	........**49**	1 wk
30 Nov 61	WHAT A PARTY London HLP 9456	........**43**	1 wk
29 Mar 62	JAMBALAYA London HLP 9520	........**41**	1 wk
31 Oct 63	RED SAILS IN THE SUNSET HMV POP 1219	........**34**	6 wks
24 Apr 76	BLUEBERRY HILL (re-issue)		
	United Artists UP 35797	........**41**	5 wks

DON PABLO'S ANIMALS
Italy, male instrumental group   **10 wks**

19 May 90 ●	VENUS Rumour RUMA 18	........**4**	10 wks

DON-E UK, male vocalist   **7 wks**

9 May 92	LOVE MAKES THE WORLD GO ROUND		
	Fourth & Broadway BRW 242	........**18**	6 wks
25 Jul 92	PEACE IN THE WORLD Fourth & Broadway BRW 256 **41**		1 wk

Lonnie DONEGAN UK, male vocalist   **321 wks**

6 Jan 56 ●	ROCK ISLAND LINE Decca F 10647	........**8**	13 wks
13 Apr 56	ROCK ISLAND LINE (re-entry) Decca F 10647 ....**16**		3 wks
20 Apr 56	STEWBALL Pye Nixa N 15036	........**27**	1 wk
27 Apr 56 ●	LOST JOHN / STEWBALL Pye Nixa N 15036	........**2**	17 wks
11 May 56	ROCK ISLAND LINE (2nd re-entry) Decca F 10647 ..**19**		6 wks
6 Jul 56	SKIFFLE SESSION EP Pye Nixa NJE 1017	........**20**	2 wks
7 Sep 56 ●	BRING A LITTLE WATER SYLVIE / DEAD OR ALIVE		
	Pye Nixa N 15071	........**7**	12 wks
21 Dec 56	LONNIE DONEGAN SHOWCASE (LP)		
	Pye Nixa NPT 19012	........**26**	3 wks
11 Jan 57	BRING A LITTLE WATER SYLVIE / DEAD OR ALIVE		
	(re-entry) Pye Nixa N 15071	........**30**	1 wk
18 Jan 57 ●	DON'T YOU ROCK ME DADDY-O		
	Pye Nixa N 15080	........**4**	17 wks
5 Apr 57 ★	CUMBERLAND GAP Pye Nixa N 15087	........**1**	12 wks
7 Jun 57 ★	GAMBLIN' MAN / PUTTING ON THE STYLE		
	Pye Nixa N 15093	........**1**	19 wks

11 Oct 57 ●	MY DIXIE DARLING Pye Nixa N 15108	........**10**	15 wks
20 Dec 57	JACK O' DIAMONDS Pye Nixa N 15116	........**10**	15 wks
11 Apr 58 ●	GRAND COOLIE DAM Pye Nixa 7N 15129	........**6**	15 wks
11 Jul 58	SALLY DON'T YOU GRIEVE / BETTY BETTY BETTY		
	Pye Nixa 7N 15148	........**11**	7 wks
26 Sep 58	LONESOME TRAVELLER Pye Nixa 7N 15158	........**28**	1 wk
14 Nov 58	LONNIE'S SKIFFLE PARTY Pye Nixa 7N 15165 ....**23**		5 wks
21 Nov 58 ●	TOM DOOLEY Pye Nixa 7N 15172	........**3**	14 wks
6 Feb 59 ●	DOES YOUR CHEWING GUM LOSE ITS FLAVOUR		
	Pye 7N 15181	........**3**	12 wks
8 May 59	FORT WORTH JAIL Pye 7N 15198	........**14**	5 wks
26 Jun 59 ●	BATTLE OF NEW ORLEANS Pye 7N 15206	........**2**	16 wks
11 Sep 59	SAL'S GOT A SUGAR LIP Pye 7N 15223	........**13**	4 wks
4 Dec 59	SAN MIGUEL Pye 7N 15237	........**19**	4 wks
24 Mar 60 ★	MY OLD MAN'S A DUSTMAN Pye 7N 15256	........**1**	13 wks
26 May 60 ●	I WANNA GO HOME Pye 7N 15267	........**5**	17 wks
25 Aug 60 ●	LORELEI Pye 7N 15275	........**10**	8 wks
24 Nov 60	LIVELY Pye 7N 15312	........**13**	9 wks
8 Dec 60	VIRGIN MARY Pye 7N 15315	........**27**	5 wks
11 May 61 ●	HAVE A DRINK ON ME Pye 7N 15354	........**8**	15 wks
31 Aug 61 ●	MICHAEL ROW THE BOAT / LUMBERED		
	Pye 7N 15371	........**6**	11 wks
18 Jan 62 ●	THE COMANCHEROS Pye 7N 15410	........**14**	10 wks
5 Apr 62 ●	THE PARTY'S OVER Pye 7N 15424	........**9**	12 wks
16 Aug 62 ●	PICK A BALE OF COTTON Pye 7N 15455	........**11**	10 wks

Stewball *had one week on the chart by itself on 20 Apr 56. Lost John, the other side, replaced it on 27 Apr 56 but* Stewball *was given co-billing with* Lost John *for the weeks of 11, 18 and 25 May 56, peaking at position 7.* Dead Or Alive *was not listed with* Bring A Little Water Sylvie *for the week 7 Sep 56.* Putting On The Style *was not listed with* Gamblin' Man *for the weeks of 7 and 14 Jun 56. Tracks on Skiffle Session EP: Railroad Bill / Stockalee / Ballad Of Jesse James / Ol' Riley. Tracks on Lonnie Donegan Showcase (LP): Wabash Cannonball / How Long / How Long Blues / Nobody's Child / I Shall Not Be Moved / I'm Alabammy Bound / I'm A Rambling Man / Wreck Of The Old '97 / Frankie And Johnny.*

Ral DONNER US, male vocalist   **10 wks**

21 Sep 61	YOU DON'T KNOW WHAT YOU'VE GOT		
	Parlophone R 4820	........**25**	10 wks

DONOVAN UK, male vocalist   **100 wks**

25 Mar 65 ●	CATCH THE WIND Pye 7N 15801	........**4**	13 wks
3 Jun 65 ●	COLOURS Pye 7N 15866	........**4**	12 wks
11 Nov 65	TURQUOISE Pye 7N 15984	........**30**	6 wks
8 Dec 66 ●	SUNSHINE SUPERMAN Pye 7N 17241	........**2**	11 wks
9 Feb 67 ●	MELLOW YELLOW Pye 7N 17267	........**8**	8 wks
25 Oct 67 ●	THERE IS A MOUNTAIN Pye 7N 17403	........**8**	11 wks
21 Feb 68 ●	JENNIFER JUNIPER Pye 7N 17457	........**5**	11 wks
29 May 68 ●	HURDY GURDY MAN Pye 7N 17537	........**4**	10 wks
4 Dec 68	ATLANTIS Pye 7N 17660	........**23**	8 wks
9 Jul 69	GOO GOO BARABAJAGAL (LOVE IS HOT)		
	Pye 7N 17778 [1]	........**12**	9 wks
1 Dec 90	JENNIFER JUNIPER Fontana SYP 1 [2]	........**68**	1 wk

[1] Donovan with the Jeff Beck Group [2] Singing Corner meets Donovan

Jason DONOVAN Australia, male vocalist   **137 wks**

10 Sep 88 ●	NOTHING CAN DIVIDE US PWL PWL 17	........**5**	12 wks
10 Dec 88 ★	ESPECIALLY FOR YOU PWL PWL 24 [1]	........**1**	14 wks
4 Mar 89 ★	TOO MANY BROKEN HEARTS PWL PWL 32	........**1**	13 wks
10 Jun 89 ★	SEALED WITH A KISS PWL PWL 39	........**1**	10 wks
9 Sep 89 ●	EVERY DAY (I LOVE YOU MORE) PWL PWL 43	........**2**	9 wks
9 Dec 89 ●	WHEN YOU COME BACK TO ME PWL PWL 46 ....**2**		11 wks
7 Apr 90 ●	HANG ON TO YOUR LOVE PWL PWL 51	........**8**	7 wks
30 Jun 90	ANOTHER NIGHT PWL PWL 58	........**18**	5 wks
1 Sep 90 ●	RHYTHM OF THE RAIN PWL PWL 60	........**9**	6 wks
27 Oct 90	I'M DOING FINE PWL PWL 69	........**22**	6 wks
18 May 91	RSVP PWL PWL 80	........**17**	5 wks
22 Jun 91 ★	ANY DREAM WILL DO Really Useful RUR 7	........**1**	12 wks
24 Aug 91 ●	HAPPY TOGETHER PWL PWL 203	........**10**	6 wks
7 Dec 91	JOSEPH MEGA REMIX Really Useful RUR 9 [2] **13**		8 wks
18 Jul 92	MISSION OF LOVE Polydor PO 222	........**26**	4 wks

| 28 Nov 92 | **AS TIME GOES BY** Polydor PO 245 | **26** | 6 wks |
| 7 Aug 93 | **ALL AROUND THE WORLD** Polydor PZCD 278 | **41** | 3 wks |

[1] Kylie Minogue and Jason Donovan [2] Jason Donovan and Original London Cast featuring Linzi Hately, David Easter and Johnny Amobi

DOOBIE BROTHERS
US, male vocal / instrumental group **45 wks**

9 Mar 74	**LISTEN TO THE MUSIC** Warner Bros. K 16208	**29**	7 wks
7 Jun 75	**TAKE ME IN YOUR ARMS** Warner Bros. K 16559	**29**	5 wks
17 Feb 79	**WHAT A FOOL BELIEVES** Warner Bros. K 17314	**31**	10 wks
5 May 79	**WHAT A FOOL BELIEVES (re-entry)** Warner Bros. K 17314	**72**	1 wk
14 Jul 79	**MINUTE BY MINUTE** Warner Bros. K 17411	**47**	4 wks
24 Jan 87	**WHAT A FOOL BELIEVES (re-issue)** Warner Bros. W 8451 [1]	**57**	3 wks
29 Jul 89	**THE DOCTOR** Capitol CL 536	**73**	2 wks
27 Nov 93	● **LONG TRAIN RUNNIN'** Warner Bros. W 0217CD	**7**	10 wks
14 May 94	**LISTEN TO THE MUSIC (re-mix)** Warner Bros. W 0228CD	**37**	3 wks

[1] Doobie Brothers featuring Michael McDonald

DOOGIE - *See BUG KANN and PLASTIC JAM featuring Patti LOW and DOOGIE*

DOOLEYS
UK, male / female vocal / instrumental group **83 wks**

13 Aug 77	**THINK I'M GONNA FALL IN LOVE WITH YOU** GTO GT 95	**13**	10 wks
12 Nov 77	● **LOVE OF MY LIFE** GTO GT 110	**9**	11 wks
13 May 78	**DON'T TAKE IT LYIN' DOWN** GTO GT 220	**60**	3 wks
2 Sep 78	**A ROSE HAS TO DIE** GTO GT 229	**11**	11 wks
10 Feb 79	**HONEY I'M LOST** GTO GT 242	**24**	9 wks
16 Jun 79	● **WANTED** GTO GT 249	**3**	14 wks
22 Sep 79	● **THE CHOSEN FEW** GTO GT 258	**7**	11 wks
8 Mar 80	**LOVE PATROL** GTO GT 260	**29**	7 wks
6 Sep 80	**BODY LANGUAGE** GTO GT 276	**46**	4 wks
10 Oct 81	**AND I WISH** GTO GT 300	**52**	3 wks

Val DOONICAN
Ireland, male vocalist **143 wks**

15 Oct 64	● **WALK TALL** Decca F 11982	**3**	21 wks
21 Jan 65	● **THE SPECIAL YEARS** Decca F 12049	**7**	12 wks
8 Apr 65	**I'M GONNA GET THERE SOMEHOW** Decca F 12118	**25**	5 wks
22 Apr 65	**THE SPECIAL YEARS (re-entry)** Decca F 12049	**49**	1 wk
17 Mar 66	● **ELUSIVE BUTTERFLY** Decca F 12358	**5**	12 wks
3 Nov 66	● **WHAT WOULD I BE** Decca F 12505	**2**	17 wks
23 Feb 67	**MEMORIES ARE MADE OF THIS** Decca F 12566	**11**	12 wks
25 May 67	**TWO STREETS** Decca F 12608	**39**	4 wks
18 Oct 67	● **IF THE WHOLE WORLD STOPPED LOVING** Pye 7N 17396	**3**	19 wks
21 Feb 68	**YOU'RE THE ONLY ONE** Pye 7N 17465	**37**	4 wks
12 Jun 68	**NOW** Pye 7N 17534	**43**	2 wks
23 Oct 68	**IF I KNEW THEN WHAT I KNOW NOW** Pye 7N 17616	**14**	13 wks
23 Apr 69	**RING OF BRIGHT WATER** Pye 7N 17713	**48**	1 wk
4 Dec 71	**MORNING** Philips 6006 177	**12**	13 wks
10 Mar 73	**HEAVEN IS MY WOMAN'S LOVE** Philips 6028 031	**34**	6 wks
28 Apr 73	**HEAVEN IS MY WOMAN'S LOVE (re-entry)** Philips 6028 031	**47**	1 wk

DOOP
Holland, male instrumental duo **12 wks**

| 12 Mar 94 | ★ **DOOP** Citybeat CBE 774CD | **1** | 12 wks |

DOORS
US, male vocal / instrumental group **42 wks**

16 Aug 67	**LIGHT MY FIRE** Elektra EKSN 45014	**49**	1 wk
28 Aug 68	**HELLO I LOVE YOU** Elektra EKSN 45037	**15**	12 wks
16 Oct 71	**RIDERS ON THE STORM** Elektra K 12021	**50**	1 wk
30 Oct 71	**RIDERS ON THE STORM (re-entry)** Elektra K 12021	**22**	10 wks
20 Mar 76	**RIDERS ON THE STORM (re-issue)** Elektra K 12203	**33**	5 wks
3 Feb 79	**HELLO I LOVE YOU (re-issue)** Elektra K 12215	**71**	2 wks
27 Apr 91	**BREAK ON THROUGH** Elektra EKR 121	**64**	2 wks
1 Jun 91	● **LIGHT MY FIRE (re-issue)** Elektra EKR 125	**7**	8 wks
10 Aug 91	**RIDERS ON THE STORM (re-issue)** Elektra EKR 131	**68**	1 wk

Charlie DORE
UK, female vocalist **2 wks**

| 17 Nov 79 | **PILOT OF THE AIRWAVES** Island WIP 6526 | **66** | 2 wks |

Lee DORSEY
US, male vocalist **36 wks**

3 Feb 66	**GET OUT OF MY LIFE WOMAN** Stateside SS 485	**22**	7 wks
5 May 66	**CONFUSION** Stateside SS 506	**38**	6 wks
11 Aug 66	● **WORKING IN THE COALMINE** Stateside SS 528	**8**	11 wks
27 Oct 66	● **HOLY COW** Stateside SS 552	**6**	12 wks

Tommy DORSEY ORCHESTRA starring Warren COVINGTON
US, orchestra – Warren Covington, male instrumentalist - trombone **19 wks**

| 17 Oct 58 | ● **TEA FOR TWO CHA CHA** Brunswick 05757 | **3** | 19 wks |

DOUBLE
Switzerland, male vocal / instrumental duo **10 wks**

| 25 Jan 86 | ● **THE CAPTAIN OF HER HEART** Polydor POSP 779 | **8** | 9 wks |
| 5 Dec 87 | **DEVIL'S BALL** Polydor POSP 888 | **71** | 1 wk |

DOUBLE DEE featuring DANY
US, male vocal / instrumental group **2 wks**

| 1 Dec 90 | **FOUND LOVE** Epic 6563766 | **63** | 2 wks |

DOUBLE TROUBLE
UK, male instrumental / production duo **35 wks**

27 May 89	**JUST KEEP ROCKIN'** Desire WANT 9 [1]	**11**	12 wks
7 Oct 89	● **STREET TUFF** Desire WANT 18 [1]	**3**	14 wks
12 May 90	**TALK BACK** Desire WANT 27 [2]	**71**	1 wk
30 Jun 90	**LOVE DON'T LIVE HERE ANYMORE** Desire WANT 32 [3]	**21**	6 wks
15 Jun 91	**RUB-A-DUB** Desire WANT 41	**66**	2 wks

[1] Double Trouble and the Rebel MC [2] Double Trouble featuring Janette Sewell [3] Double Trouble featuring Janette Sewell and Carl Brown

DOUBLE YOU?
Italy, male vocalist - Willie Morales **3 wks**

| 2 May 92 | **PLEASE DON'T GO** ZYX ZYX 67487 | **41** | 3 wks |

Carl DOUGLAS
Jamaica, male vocalist **28 wks**

17 Aug 74	★ **KUNG FU FIGHTING** Pye 7N 45377	**1**	13 wks
30 Nov 74	**DANCE THE KUNG FU** Pye 7N 45418	**35**	5 wks
3 Dec 77	**RUN BACK** Pye 7N 46018	**25**	10 wks

Carol DOUGLAS
US, female vocalist **4 wks**

| 22 Jul 78 | **NIGHT FEVER** Gull GULS 61 | **66** | 4 wks |

Craig DOUGLAS
UK, male vocalist **112 wks**

12 Jun 59	**A TEENAGER IN LOVE** Top Rank JAR 133	**13**	11 wks
7 Aug 59	★ **ONLY SIXTEEN** Top Rank JAR 159	**1**	15 wks
22 Jan 60	● **PRETTY BLUE EYES** Top Rank JAR 268	**4**	14 wks
28 Apr 60	● **THE HEART OF A TEENAGE GIRL** Top Rank JAR 340	**10**	9 wks
11 Aug 60	**OH! WHAT A DAY** Top Rank JAR 406	**43**	1 wk
20 Apr 61	● **A HUNDRED POUNDS OF CLAY** Top Rank JAR 555	**9**	9 wks

29 Jun 61	● TIME Top Rank JAR 569	**9**	14 wks
22 Mar 62	● WHEN MY LITTLE GIRL IS SMILING		
	Top Rank JAR 610	**9**	13 wks
28 Jun 62	● OUR FAVOURITE MELODIES Columbia DB 4854 ....**9**		10 wks
18 Oct 62	OH LONESOME ME Decca F 11523	**15**	12 wks
28 Feb 63	TOWN CRIER Decca F 11575	**36**	4 wks

DOWLANDS UK, male vocal duo   **7 wks**

| 9 Jan 64 | ALL MY LOVING Oriole CB 1897 .... | **33** | 7 wks |

Robert DOWNEY Jr. US, male vocalist   **1 wk**

| 30 Jan 93 | SMILE Epic 6589052 .... | **68** | 1 wk |

Don DOWNING US, male vocalist   **10 wks**

| 10 Nov 73 | LONELY DAYS, LONELY NIGHTS People PEO 102 ....**32** | | 10 wks |

Will DOWNING US, male vocalist   **35 wks**

2 Apr 88	A LOVE SUPREME Fourth & Broadway BRW 90 ......**14**		10 wks
25 Jun 88	IN MY DREAMS Fourth & Broadway BRW 104..........**34**		6 wks
1 Oct 88	FREE Fourth & Broadway BRW 112	**58**	5 wks
21 Jan 89	WHERE IS THE LOVE		
	Fourth & Broadway BRW 122 [1]	**19**	7 wks
28 Oct 89	TEST OF TIME Fourth & Broadway BRW 146......**67**		2 wks
24 Feb 90	COME TOGETHER AS ONE		
	Fourth & Broadway BRW 159	**48**	4 wks
18 Sep 93	THERE'S NO LIVING WITHOUT YOU		
	Fourth & Broadway BRCD 278	**67**	1 wk

[1] Mica Paris and Will Downing

Lamont DOZIER - See HOLLAND-DOZIER featuring Lamont DOZIER

Charlie DRAKE UK, male vocalist   **37 wks**

8 Aug 58	● SPLISH SPLASH Parlophone R 4461	**7**	11 wks
24 Oct 58	VOLARE Parlophone R 4478	**28**	2 wks
27 Oct 60	MR. CUSTER Parlophone R 4701	**12**	12 wks
5 Oct 61	MY BOOMERANG WON'T COME BACK		
	Parlophone R 4824	**14**	11 wks
1 Jan 72	PUCKWUDGIE Columbia DB 8829	**47**	1 wk

DRAMATIS UK, male vocal / instrumental group   **8 wks**

5 Dec 81	LOVE NEEDS NO DISGUISE		
	Beggars Banquet BEG 68 [1]	**33**	7 wks
13 Nov 82	I CAN SEE HER NOW Rocket XPRES 83	**57**	1 wk

[1] Gary Numan and Dramatis

Rusty DRAPER US, male vocalist   **4 wks**

| 11 Aug 60 | MULE SKINNER BLUES Mercury AMT 1101 .... | **39** | 4 wks |

DREAD ZEPPELIN US, male vocal / instrumental group   **3 wks**

| 1 Dec 90 | YOUR TIME IS GONNA COME IRS DREAD 1 .... | **59** | 1 wk |
| 13 Jul 91 | STAIRWAY TO HEAVEN IRS DREAD 2 .... | **62** | 2 wks |

DREAM ACADEMY
UK, male / female vocal / instrumental group   **10 wks**

30 Mar 85	LIFE IN A NORTHERN TOWN		
	blanco y negro NEG 10	**15**	8 wks
14 Sep 85	THE LOVE PARADE blanco y negro NEG 16	**68**	2 wks

DREAM FREQUENCY UK, male producer - Ian Bland   **12 wks**

| 12 Jan 91 | LOVE PEACE AND HARMONY Citybeat CBE 756 ....**71** | | 2 wks |

25 Jan 92	FEEL SO REAL Citybeat CBE 763 [1]	**23**	5 wks
25 Apr 92	TAKE ME Citybeat CBE 768	**39**	3 wks
21 May 94	GOOD TIMES / THE DREAM Citybeat CBE 773CD **67**		1 wk
10 Sep 94	YOU MAKE ME FEEL MIGHTY REAL		
	Citybeat CBE 775CD	**65**	1 wk

[1] Dream Frequency featuring Debbie Sharp

DREAM WARRIORS Canada, male rap group   **19 wks**

14 Jul 90	WASH YOUR FACE IN MY SINK		
	Fourth & Broadway BRW 183	**16**	8 wks
24 Nov 90	MY DEFINITION OF A BOOMBASTIC JAZZ STYLE		
	Fourth & Broadway BRW 197	**13**	8 wks
25 Apr 92	LUDI Fourth & Broadway BRW 206	**39**	3 wks

DREAMERS - See FREDDIE and the DREAMERS

DREAMWEAVERS US, male / female vocal group   **18 wks**

| 10 Feb 56 | ★ IT'S ALMOST TOMORROW Brunswick 05515 .... | **1** | 18 wks |

DRELLS - See Archie BELL and the DRELLS

Eddie DRENNON and B.B.S. UNLIMITED
US, male vocal / instrumental group   **6 wks**

| 28 Feb 76 | LET'S DO THE LATIN HUSTLE | | |
| | Pye International 7N 25702 .... | **20** | 6 wks |

Alan DREW UK, male vocalist   **2 wks**

| 26 Sep 63 | ALWAYS THE LONELY ONE Columbia DB 7090 .... | **48** | 2 wks |

DRIFTERS US, male vocal group   **176 wks**

8 Jan 60	DANCE WITH ME London HLE 8988	**17**	4 wks
10 Mar 60	DANCE WITH ME (re-entry) London HLE 8988	**35**	1 wk
3 Nov 60	● SAVE THE LAST DANCE FOR ME London HLK 9201 ..**2**		18 wks
16 Mar 61	I COUNT THE TEARS London HLK 9287	**28**	6 wks
5 Apr 62	WHEN MY LITTLE GIRL IS SMILING		
	London HLK 9522	**31**	3 wks
10 Oct 63	I'LL TAKE YOU HOME London HLK 9785	**37**	5 wks
24 Sep 64	UNDER THE BOARDWALK Atlantic AT 4001	**45**	4 wks
8 Apr 65	AT THE CLUB Atlantic AT 4019	**35**	7 wks
29 Apr 65	COME ON OVER TO MY PLACE Atlantic AT 4023 ....**40**		5 wks
2 Feb 67	BABY WHAT I MEAN Atlantic 584 065	**49**	1 wk
25 Mar 72	AT THE CLUB (re-issue) Atlantic K 10148	**39**	1 wk
8 Apr 72	● AT THE CLUB / SATURDAY NIGHT AT THE MOVIES		
	(re-entry of re-issue) Atlantic K 10148	**3**	19 wks
26 Aug 72	● COME ON OVER TO MY PLACE (re-issue)		
	Atlantic K 10216	**9**	11 wks
4 Aug 73	● LIKE SISTER AND BROTHER Bell 1313	**7**	12 wks
15 Jun 74	● KISSIN' IN THE BACK ROW OF THE MOVIES		
	Bell 1358	**2**	13 wks
12 Oct 74	● DOWN ON THE BEACH TONIGHT Bell 1381	**7**	9 wks
8 Feb 75	LOVE GAMES Bell 1396	**33**	6 wks
6 Sep 75	● THERE GOES MY FIRST LOVE Bell 1433	**3**	12 wks
29 Nov 75	● CAN I TAKE YOU HOME LITTLE GIRL Bell 1462 ......**10**		10 wks
13 Mar 76	HELLO HAPPINESS Bell 1469	**12**	8 wks
11 Sep 76	EVERY NITE'S A SATURDAY NIGHT WITH YOU		
	Bell 1491	**29**	7 wks
18 Dec 76	● YOU'RE MORE THAN A NUMBER IN MY		
	LITTLE RED BOOK Arista 78	**5**	12 wks
14 Apr 79	SAVE THE LAST DANCE FOR ME / WHEN MY LITTLE		
	GIRL IS SMILING (re-issue) Lightning LIG 9014 ....**69**		2 wks

Saturday Night At The Movies only received chart credit with At The
Club after the re-issue's return to the chart on 8 Apr 72.

Julie DRISCOLL, Brian AUGER and the TRINITY
UK, female vocalist / male instrumental group **16 wks**

17 Apr 68 ●	**THIS WHEEL'S ON FIRE** Marmalade 598 006	.........**5**	16 wks

DRIVER 67 *UK, male vocalist - Paul Phillips* **12 wks**

23 Dec 78 ●	**CAR 67** Logo GO 336	..............**7**	12 wks

DRIZA BONE *UK, male instrumental / production duo* **13 wks**

22 Jun 91	**REAL LOVE** Fourth & Broadway BRW 223	...........**16**	7 wks
26 Oct 91	**CATCH THE FIRE** Fourth & Broadway BRW 232	......**54**	2 wks
23 Apr 94	**PRESSURE** Fourth & Broadway BRCD 264	........**33**	2 wks
15 Oct 94	**BRIGHTEST STAR** Fourth & Broadway BRCDX 293	....**45**	2 wks

Frank D'RONE *US, male vocalist* **6 wks**

22 Dec 60	**STRAWBERRY BLONDE** Mercury AMT 1123	..........**24**	6 wks

DRUM CLUB *UK, male instrumental / production duo* **1 wk**

6 Nov 93	**SOUND SYSTEM** Butterfly BFLD 10	..........**62**	1 wk

DRUM THEATRE *UK, male vocal / instrumental group* **8 wks**

15 Feb 86	**LIVING IN THE PAST** Epic A 6798	...........**67**	2 wks
17 Jan 87	**ELDORADO** Epic EMU 1	..............**44**	6 wks

DRUPI *Italy, male vocalist* **12 wks**

1 Dec 73	**VADO VIA** A & M AMS 7083	...........**17**	12 wks

D-SHAKE *Holland, male production duo* **8 wks**

2 Jun 90	**YAAAH / TECHNO TRANCE** Cooltempo COOL 213	....**20**	6 wks
2 Feb 91	**MY HEART THE BEAT** Cooltempo COOL 228	...........**42**	2 wks

DSK *UK, male instrumental / production group* **3 wks**

31 Aug 91	**WHAT WOULD WE DO / READ MY LIPS** Boys' Own BOI 6	...........**46**	3 wks

D-TEK *UK, male instrumental / production group* **1 wk**

6 Nov 93	**DROP THE ROCK (EP)** Positiva 12TIV 5	..........**70**	1 wk

Tracks on Drop The Rock (EP): Drop The Rock / Chunkafunk / Drop The Rock (re-mix) / Don't Breathe.

D.S.M. *US, male rap group* **4 wks**

7 Dec 85	**WARRIOR GROOVE** 10 DAZZ 45-7	...........**68**	4 wks

D.T.I. *US, male vocal / instrumental group* **1 wk**

16 Apr 88	**KEEP THIS FREQUENCY CLEAR / KEEP IT CLEAR** Premiere UK ERE 501	...........**73**	1 wk

DTOX *UK, male / female vocal / instrumental group* **1 wk**

21 Nov 92	**SHATTERED GLASS** Vitality VITal 1	...........**75**	1 wk

John DU CANN *UK, male vocalist* **6 wks**

22 Sep 79	**DON'T BE A DUMMY** Vertigo 6059 241	..........**33**	6 wks

John DU PREZ - See MODERN ROMANCE

DUBLINERS *Ireland, male vocal / instrumental group* **45 wks**

30 Mar 67 ●	**SEVEN DRUNKEN NIGHTS** Major Minor MM 506	......**7**	17 wks
30 Aug 67	**BLACK VELVET BAND** Major Minor MM 530	...........**15**	15 wks
20 Dec 67	**NEVER WED AN OLD MAN** Major Minor MM 551	..**43**	3 wks
28 Mar 87 ●	**THE IRISH ROVER** Stiff BUY 258 [1]	...........**8**	8 wks
16 Jun 90	**JACK'S HEROES / WHISKEY IN THE JAR** Pogue Mahone YZ 500 [1]	...........**63**	2 wks

[1] Pogues and the Dubliners

DUFFO *Australia, male vocalist* **2 wks**

24 Mar 79	**GIVE ME BACK ME BRAIN** Beggars Banquet BEG 15	...........**60**	2 wks

Stephen 'Tin Tin' DUFFY *UK, male vocalist* **24 wks**

9 Jul 83	**HOLD IT** Curve X 9763 [1]	...........**55**	4 wks
2 Mar 85 ●	**KISS ME** 10 TIN 2	...........**4**	11 wks
18 May 85	**ICING ON THE CAKE** 10 TIN 3	...........**14**	9 wks

[1] Tin Tin

George DUKE *US, male vocalist / instrumentalist* **6 wks**

12 Jul 80	**BRAZILIAN LOVE AFFAIR** Epic EPC 8751	.........**36**	6 wks

DUKE BAYSEE *UK, male vocalist* **4 wks**

3 Sep 94	**SUGAR SUGAR** Bell 74321228702	...........**30**	4 wks

DUKES *UK, male vocal duo* **13 wks**

17 Oct 81	**MYSTERY GIRL** WEA K 18867	...........**47**	7 wks
1 May 82	**THANK YOU FOR THE PARTY** WEA K 19136	...........**53**	6 wks

Candy DULFER
Holland, female instrumentalist - saxophone **14 wks**

24 Feb 90 ●	**LILY WAS HERE** RCA ZB 43045 [1]	...........**6**	12 wks
4 Aug 90	**SAXUALITY** RCA PB 43769	...........**60**	2 wks

[1] David A. Stewart featuring Candy Dulfer

Thuli DUMAKUDE *South Africa, male vocalist* **1 wk**

2 Jan 88	**THE FUNERAL (SEPTEMBER 25, 1977)** MCA MCA 1228	...........**75**	1 wk

The listed flip side of The Funeral was Cry Freedom by George Fenton and Jonas Gwangwa.

John DUMMER and Helen APRIL
UK, male / female vocal duo **3 wks**

28 Aug 82	**BLUE SKIES** Speed SPEED 8	...........**54**	3 wks

Johnny DUNCAN and the BLUE GRASS BOYS
US, male vocal / instrumental group **20 wks**

26 Jul 57 ●	**LAST TRAIN TO SAN FERNANDO** Columbia DB 3959	...........**2**	17 wks
25 Oct 57	**BLUE BLUE HEARTACHES** Columbia DB 3996	.........**27**	1 wk
29 Nov 57	**FOOTPRINTS IN THE SNOW** Columbia DB 4029	........**27**	1 wk
3 Jan 58	**FOOTPRINTS IN THE SNOW (re-entry)** Columbia DB 4029	...........**28**	1 wk

David DUNDAS *UK, male vocalist* **14 wks**

24 Jul 76 ●	**JEANS ON** Air CHS 2094	...........**3**	9 wks
9 Apr 77	**ANOTHER FUNNY HONEYMOON** Air CHS 2136	......**29**	5 wks

Peter Cunnah (second from right) was the singer and songwriter of **D:REAM**. (Colin Mason/LFI)

LONNIE DONEGAN captures the informality of a skiffle session with an amused washboard player. (LFI)

The early 1980s line-up of **DURAN DURAN** (left to right: Simon Le Bon, Nick Rhodes, Andy Taylor, John Taylor and Roger Taylor) assemble in the driveway of the Central Park restaurant Tavern on the Green. (LFI)

Erroll DUNKLEY *Jamaica, male vocalist* **14 wks**

| 22 Sep 79 | O.K. FRED *Scope SC 6* ....**11** | 11 wks |
| 2 Feb 80 | SIT DOWN AND CRY *Scope SC 11* ....**52** | 3 wks |

Clive DUNN *UK, male vocalist* **28 wks**

| 28 Nov 70 | ★ GRANDAD *Columbia DB 8726* ....**1** | 27 wks |
| 26 Jun 71 | GRANDAD (re-entry) *Columbia D8 8726*..........**50** | 1 wk |

Simon DUPREE and the BIG SOUND
UK, male vocal / instrumental group **16 wks**

| 22 Nov 67 | ● KITES *Parlophone R 5646* ....**9** | 13 wks |
| 3 Apr 68 | FOR WHOM THE BELL TOLLS *Parlophone R 5670* ....**43** | 3 wks |

DURAN DURAN *UK, male vocal / instrumental group* **207 wks**

21 Feb 81	PLANET EARTH *EMI 5137* **12**	11 wks
9 May 81	CARELESS MEMORIES *EMI 5168* **37**	7 wks
25 Jul 81	● GIRLS ON FILM *EMI 5206* **5**	11 wks
28 Nov 81	MY OWN WAY *EMI 5254* **14**	11 wks
15 May 82	● HUNGRY LIKE THE WOLF *EMI 5295* **5**	12 wks
21 Aug 82	● SAVE A PRAYER *EMI 5327* **2**	9 wks
13 Nov 82	● RIO *EMI 5346* **9**	11 wks
26 Mar 83	★ IS THERE SOMETHING I SHOULD KNOW *EMI 5371* ..**1**	9 wks
29 Oct 83	● UNION OF THE SNAKE *EMI 5429*........**3**	7 wks
24 Dec 83	UNION OF THE SNAKE (re-entry) *EMI 5429* **66**	4 wks
4 Feb 84	● NEW MOON ON MONDAY *EMI DURAN 1* ...**9**	7 wks
28 Apr 84	★ THE REFLEX *EMI DURAN 2* **1**	14 wks
3 Nov 84	● WILD BOYS *Parlophone DURAN 3* **2**	14 wks
18 May 85	● A VIEW TO A KILL *Parlophone DURAN 007* **2**	16 wks
1 Nov 86	● NOTORIOUS *EMI DDN 45* **7**	6 wks
3 Jan 87	NOTORIOUS (re-entry) *EMI DDN 5* **73**	1 wk
21 Feb 87	SKIN TRADE *EMI TRADE 1* **22**	6 wks
25 Apr 87	MEET EL PRESIDENTE *EMI TOUR 1* **24**	5 wks
1 Oct 88	I DON'T WANT YOUR LOVE *EMI YOUR 1* ...**14**	5 wks
7 Jan 89	● ALL SHE WANTS IS *EMI DD 11* **9**	5 wks
22 Apr 89	DO YOU BELIEVE IN SHAME *EMI DD 12* ...**30**	4 wks
16 Dec 89	BURNING THE GROUND *EMI DD 13* **31**	5 wks
4 Aug 90	VIOLENCE OF SUMMER (LOVE'S TAKING OVER) *Parlophone DD 14* **20**	4 wks
17 Nov 90	SERIOUS *Parlophone DD 15* **48**	3 wks
30 Jan 93	● ORDINARY WORLD *Parlophone CDDDS 16* **6**	9 wks
10 Apr 93	COME UNDONE *Parlophone CDDDS 17* **13**	8 wks
4 Sep 93	TOO MUCH INFORMATION *Parlophone CDDDS 18* ..**35**	3 wks

Judith DURHAM *Australia, female vocalist* **5 wks**

| 15 Jun 67 | OLIVE TREE *Columbia DB 8207* ....**33** | 5 wks |

Ian DURY and the BLOCKHEADS
UK, male vocal / instrumental group **55 wks**

29 Apr 78	● WHAT A WASTE *Stiff BUY 27* **9**	12 wks
9 Dec 78	★ HIT ME WITH YOUR RHYTHM STICK *Stiff BUY 38* **1** **1**	15 wks
4 Aug 79	● REASONS TO BE CHEERFUL (PT. 3) *Stiff BUY 50* **3**	8 wks
30 Aug 80	I WANT TO BE STRAIGHT *Stiff BUY 90* **22**	7 wks
15 Nov 80	SUEPERMAN'S BIG SISTER *Stiff BUY 100* **51**	3 wks
25 May 85	HIT ME WITH YOUR RHYTHM STICK (re-mix) *Stiff BUY 214* **55**	4 wks
26 Oct 85	PROFOUNDLY IN LOVE WITH PANDORA *EMI EMI 5534* **2** **45**	5 wks
27 Jul 91	HIT ME WITH YOUR RHYTHM STICK (2nd re-mix) *Flying FLYR 1* **73**	1 wk

1 Ian and the Blockheads **2** Ian Dury

Slim DUSTY *Australia, male vocalist* **15 wks**

| 30 Jan 59 | ● A PUB WITH NO BEER *Columbia DB 4212* ....**3** | 15 wks |

Bob DYLAN *US, male vocalist* **133 wks**

25 Mar 65	● TIMES THEY ARE A-CHANGIN' *CBS 201751* **9**	11 wks
29 Apr 65	● SUBTERRANEAN HOMESICK BLUES *CBS 201753* **9**	9 wks
17 Jun 65	MAGGIE'S FARM *CBS 201781* **22**	8 wks
19 Aug 65	● LIKE A ROLLING STONE *CBS 201811* **4**	12 wks
28 Oct 65	● POSITIVELY FOURTH STREET *CBS 201824* **8**	12 wks
27 Jan 66	CAN YOU PLEASE CRAWL OUT YOUR WINDOW *CBS 201900* **17**	5 wks
14 Apr 66	ONE OF US MUST KNOW (SOONER OR LATER) *CBS 202053* **33**	5 wks
12 May 66	● RAINY DAY WOMEN NOS. 12 & 35 *CBS 202307*.......**7**	8 wks
21 Jul 66	I WANT YOU *CBS 202258* **16**	9 wks
14 May 69	I THREW IT ALL AWAY *CBS 4219*...........**30**	6 wks
13 Sep 69	● LAY LADY LAY *CBS 4434* **5**	12 wks
10 Jul 71	WATCHING THE RIVER FLOW *CBS 7329* **24**	9 wks
6 Oct 73	KNOCKIN' ON HEAVEN'S DOOR *CBS 1762* ...**14**	9 wks
7 Feb 76	HURRICANE *CBS 3878* **43**	4 wks
29 Jul 78	BABY STOP CRYING *CBS 6499* **13**	11 wks
28 Oct 78	IS YOUR LOVE IN VAIN *CBS 6718* **56**	3 wks

DYNAMIX II featuring TOO TOUGH TEE
US, male vocal / instrumental group **4 wks**

| 8 Aug 87 | JUST GIVE THE DJ A BREAK *Cooltempo COOL 151* **50** | 4 wks |

DYNASTY *US, male vocal / instrumental group* **20 wks**

13 Oct 79	I DON'T WANT TO BE A FREAK (BUT I CAN'T HELP MYSELF) *Solar FB 1694*..........**20**	13 wks
9 Aug 80	I'VE JUST BEGUN TO LOVE YOU *Solar SO 10* **51**	4 wks
21 May 83	DOES THAT RING A BELL *Solar E 9911* **53**	3 wks

DYNASTY OF TWO featuring ROWETTA - See *VARIOUS ARTISTS (EPs & LPs)* - The Further Adventures Of North EP.

Ronnie DYSON *US, male vocalist* **6 wks**

| 4 Dec 71 | WHEN YOU GET RIGHT DOWN TO IT *CBS 7449*........**34** | 6 wks |

Katherine E *US, female vocalist* **7 wks**

| 6 Apr 91 | I'M ALRIGHT *Dead Dead Good GOOD 2* ....**41** | 5 wks |
| 18 Jan 92 | THEN I FEEL GOOD *PWL Continental PWL 13* ....**56** | 2 wks |

Lizz E - See FRESH 4 featuring Lizz E

Sheila E *US, female vocalist / instrumentalist - percussion* **9 wks**

| 23 Feb 85 | THE BELLE OF ST MARK *Warner Bros. W 9180* ....**18** | 9 wks |

EAGLES *US, male vocal / instrumental group* **50 wks**

9 Aug 75	ONE OF THESE NIGHTS *Asylum AYM 543*................**23**	7 wks
1 Nov 75	LYIN' EYES *Asylum AYM 548* **23**	7 wks
6 Mar 76	TAKE IT TO THE LIMIT *Asylum K 13029* **12**	7 wks
15 Jan 77	NEW KID IN TOWN *Asylum K 13069* **20**	7 wks
16 Apr 77	● HOTEL CALIFORNIA *Asylum K 13079* **8**	10 wks
16 Dec 78	PLEASE COME HOME FOR CHRISTMAS *Asylum K 13145* **30**	5 wks
13 Oct 79	HEARTACHE TONIGHT *Asylum K 12394* **40**	5 wks
1 Dec 79	THE LONG RUN *Elektra K 12404* **66**	2 wks

Robert EARL *UK, male vocalist* **27 wks**

| 25 Apr 58 | I MAY NEVER PASS THIS WAY AGAIN *Philips PB 805* ....**14** | 13 wks |

24 Oct 58	MORE THAN EVER (COME PRIMA) Philips PB 867	..26	2 wks
21 Nov 58	MORE THAN EVER (COME PRIMA) (re-entry)		
	Philips PB 867	28	2 wks
13 Feb 59	WONDERFUL SECRET OF LOVE Philips PB 891	17	10 wks

Charles EARLAND US, male instrumentalist - keyboards **5 wks**

| 19 Aug 78 | LET THE MUSIC PLAY Mercury 6167 703 | 46 | 5 wks |

Hit features uncredited male vocalist.

Steve EARLE US, male vocalist/instrumentalist - guitar **7 wks**

| 15 Oct 88 | COPPERHEAD ROAD MCA MCA 1280 | 45 | 6 wks |
| 31 Dec 88 | JOHNNY COME LATELY MCA MCA 1301 | 75 | 1 wk |

EARLY MUSIC CONSORT, directed by David MUNROW
UK, male/female instrumental group **1 wk**

| 3 Apr 71 | HENRY VIII SUITE EP BBC RESL 1 | 49 | 1 wk |

Tracks on Henry VIII Suite EP: Fanfare Passomezo Du Roy, Gaillard De Escosse/Pavane, Mille Ducats/Larocque Gaillarde/Allemande/Wedding March, La Morisque/If Love Now Reigned/Ronde, Pourquoi.

EARTH WIND AND FIRE
US, male vocal/instrumental group **125 wks**

12 Feb 77	●	SATURDAY NITE CBS 4835	17	9 wks
11 Feb 78		FANTASY CBS 6056	14	10 wks
13 May 78		JUPITER CBS 6267	41	5 wks
29 Jul 78		MAGIC MIND CBS 6490	75	1 wk
12 Aug 78		MAGIC MIND (re-entry) CBS 6490	54	4 wks
7 Oct 78		GOT TO GET YOU INTO MY LIFE CBS 6553	33	7 wks
9 Dec 78	●	SEPTEMBER CBS 6922	3	13 wks
12 May 79	●	BOOGIE WONDERLAND CBS 7292 □1	4	13 wks
28 Jul 79	●	AFTER THE LOVE HAS GONE CBS 7721	4	10 wks
6 Oct 79		STAR CBS 7092	16	8 wks
15 Dec 79		CAN'T LET GO CBS 8077	46	7 wks
8 Mar 80		IN THE STONE CBS 8252	53	3 wks
11 Oct 80		LET ME TALK CBS 8982	29	5 wks
20 Dec 80		BACK ON THE ROAD CBS 9377	63	4 wks
7 Nov 81	●	LET'S GROOVE CBS A 1679	3	13 wks
6 Feb 82		I'VE HAD ENOUGH CBS A 1959	29	6 wks
5 Feb 83		FALL IN LOVE WITH ME CBS A 2927	47	4 wks
7 Nov 87		SYSTEM OF SURVIVAL CBS EWF 1	54	3 wks

□1 Earth Wind and Fire with the Emotions

EAST OF EDEN UK, male instrumental group **12 wks**

| 17 Apr 71 | ● | JIG A JIG Deram DM 297 | 7 | 12 wks |

EAST 17 UK, male vocal/instrumental group **81 wks**

29 Aug 92	●	HOUSE OF LOVE London LON 325	10	9 wks
14 Nov 92		GOLD London LON 331	28	4 wks
19 Dec 92		GOLD (re-entry) London LON 331	64	4 wks
30 Jan 93	●	DEEP London LOCDP 334	5	10 wks
10 Apr 93		SLOW IT DOWN London LONCD 339	13	7 wks
26 Jun 93		WEST END GIRLS London LONCD 344	11	7 wks
4 Dec 93	●	IT'S ALRIGHT London LONCD 345	3	14 wks
14 May 94	●	AROUND THE WORLD London LONCD 349	3	13 wks
1 Oct 94	●	STEAM London LONCD 353	7	8 wks
3 Dec 94	★	STAY ANOTHER DAY London LONCD 354	1†	5 wks

EAST SIDE BEAT Italy, male vocal/instrumental duo **18 wks**

30 Nov 91	●	RIDE LIKE THE WIND ffrr F 176	3	11 wks
19 Dec 92		ALIVE AND KICKING ffrr F 206	26	6 wks
29 May 93		YOU'RE MY EVERYTHING ffrr FCD 207	65	1 wk

Sheena EASTON UK, female vocalist **103 wks**

5 Apr 80		MODERN GIRL EMI 5042	56	3 wks
19 Jul 80	●	9 TO 5 EMI 5066	3	15 wks
9 Aug 80	●	MODERN GIRL (re-entry) EMI 5042	8	12 wks
25 Oct 80		ONE MAN WOMAN EMI 5114	14	6 wks
14 Feb 81		TAKE MY TIME EMI 5135	44	5 wks
2 May 81		WHEN HE SHINES EMI 5166	12	8 wks
27 Jun 81	●	FOR YOUR EYES ONLY EMI 5195	8	13 wks
12 Sep 81		JUST ANOTHER BROKEN HEART EMI 5232	33	8 wks
5 Dec 81		YOU COULD HAVE BEEN WITH ME EMI 5252	54	5 wks
31 Jul 82		MACHINERY EMI 5326	38	5 wks
12 Feb 83		WE'VE GOT TONIGHT Liberty UP 658 □1	28	7 wks
21 Jan 89		THE LOVER IN ME MCA MCA 1289	15	8 wks
18 Mar 89		DAYS LIKE THIS MCA MCA 1325	43	3 wks
15 Jul 89		101 MCA MCA 1348	54	2 wks
18 Nov 89		THE ARMS OF ORION Warner Bros. W 2757 □2	27	5 wks

□1 Kenny Rogers and Sheena Easton □2 Prince with Sheena Easton

See also Prince.

EASTSIDE CONNECTION US, disco aggregation **3 wks**

| 8 Apr 78 | | YOU'RE SO RIGHT FOR ME Creole CR 149 | 44 | 3 wks |

Clint EASTWOOD US, male vocalist **2 wks**

| 7 Feb 70 | | I TALK TO THE TREES Paramount PARA 3004 | 18 | 2 wks |

This is the flip of Wand'rin Star by Lee Marvin and was listed with Marvin's A-side for two weeks only.

Clint EASTWOOD - See GENERAL SAINT

EASYBEATS Australia, male vocal/instrumental group **24 wks**

| 27 Oct 66 | ● | FRIDAY ON MY MIND United Artists UP 1157 | 6 | 15 wks |
| 10 Apr 68 | | HELLO HOW ARE YOU United Artists UP 2209 | 20 | 9 wks |

EAT UK/US, male/female vocal/instrumental group **1 wk**

| 12 Jun 93 | | BLEED ME WHITE Fiction FICCD 48 | 73 | 1 wk |

Cleveland EATON US, male instrumentalist - keyboards **6 wks**

| 23 Sep 78 | | BAMA BOOGIE WOOGIE Gull GULS 63 | 35 | 6 wks |

EAV Austria, male vocal/instrumental group **4 wks**

| 27 Sep 86 | | BA-BA-BANKROBBERY (ENGLISH VERSION??) | | |
| | | Columbia DB 9139 | 63 | 4 wks |

EAV is short for Erste Allgemeine Verunsicherung.

ECHO and the BUNNYMEN
UK, male vocal/instrumental group **73 wks**

17 May 80		RESCUE Korova KOW 1	62	1 wk
18 Apr 81		CROCODILES Korova ECHO 1	37	4 wks
18 Jul 81		A PROMISE Korova KOW 15	49	4 wks
29 May 82		THE BACK OF LOVE Korova KOW 24	19	7 wks
22 Jan 83	●	THE CUTTER Korova KOW 26	8	8 wks
16 Jul 83		NEVER STOP Korova KOW 28	15	7 wks
28 Jan 84	●	THE KILLING MOON Korova KOW 32	9	6 wks
21 Apr 84		SILVER Korova KOW 34	30	5 wks
14 Jul 84		SEVEN SEAS Korova KOW 35	16	7 wks

EAST 17 are floored by the news that they've achieved the 1994 Christmas number one with 'Stay Another Day'. (LFI)

19 Oct 85	**BRING ON THE DANCING HORSES**		
	Korova KOW 43	**21**	7 wks
13 Jun 87	**THE GAME** *WEA YZ 134*	**28**	4 wks
1 Aug 87	**LIPS LIKE SUGAR** *WEA YZ 144*	**36**	4 wks
20 Feb 88	**PEOPLE ARE STRANGE** *WEA YZ 175*...	**29**	5 wks
2 Mar 91	**PEOPLE ARE STRANGE (re-issue)**		
	East West YZ 567	**34**	4 wks

ECHOBELLY
UK / Sweden, male / female vocal / instrumental group   **4 wks**

2 Apr 94	**INSOMNIAC** *Fauve FAUV 1CD*	**47**	1 wk
2 Jul 94	**I CAN'T IMAGINE THE WORLD WITHOUT ME**		
	Fauve FAUV 2CD	**39**	2 wks
5 Nov 94	**CLOSE...BUT** *Fauve FAUV 4CD*	**59**	1 wk

Billy ECKSTINE *US, male vocalist*   **48 wks**

12 Nov 54	● **NO ONE BUT YOU** *MGM 763*	**3**	17 wks
27 Sep 57	**PASSING STRANGERS** *Mercury MT 164* [1] ...	**22**	2 wks
13 Feb 59	**GIGI** *Mercury AMT 1018*	**8**	14 wks
12 Mar 69	**PASSING STRANGERS (re-issue)**		
	Mercury MF 1082 [1]	**20**	15 wks

[1] Billy Eckstine and Sarah Vaughan

EDDIE and the HOTRODS
UK, male vocal / instrumental group   **26 wks**

11 Sep 76	**LIVE AT THE MARQUEE EP** *Island IEP 2* ...	**43**	5 wks
13 Nov 76	**TEENAGE DEPRESSION** *Island WIP 6354* ...	**35**	4 wks
23 Apr 77	**I MIGHT BE LYING** *Island WIP 6388*........	**44**	3 wks
13 Aug 77	● **DO ANYTHING YOU WANNA DO**		
	Island WIP 6401 [1]	**9**	10 wks
21 Jan 78	**QUIT THIS TOWN** *Island WIP 6411*	**36**	4 wks

[1] Rods

Tracks on Live At The Marquee EP: *96 Tears / Get Out Of Denver / Medley: Gloria / Satisfaction.*

EDDY *UK, female vocalist*   **2 wks**

| 9 Jul 94 | **SOMEDAY** *Positiva CDTIV 14* .... | **49** | 2 wks |

Duane EDDY and the REBELS
US, male instrumentalist - guitar and male instrumental group   **196 wks**

5 Sep 58	**REBEL ROUSER** *London HL 8669*	**19**	10 wks
2 Jan 59	**CANNONBALL** *London HL 8764*	**22**	4 wks
19 Jun 59	● **PETER GUNN THEME** *London HLW 8879*	**6**	10 wks
24 Jul 59	**YEP** *London HLW 8879*	**17**	5 wks
4 Sep 59	**FORTY MILES OF BAD ROAD** *London HLW 8929* ...	**11**	9 wks
11 Sep 59	**PETER GUNN THEME (re-entry)** *London HLW 8879*	**27**	1 wk
18 Dec 59	**SOME KINDA EARTHQUAKE** *London HLW 9007*...	**12**	5 wks
19 Feb 60	**BONNIE CAME BACK** *London HLW 9050*	**12**	10 wks
28 Apr 60	● **SHAZAM!** *London HLW 9104*	**4**	13 wks
21 Jul 60	● **BECAUSE THEY'RE YOUNG** *London HLW 9162*	**2**	18 wks
10 Nov 60	**KOMMOTION** *London HLW 9225*	**13**	10 wks
12 Jan 61	**PEPE** *London HLW 9257*	**2**	14 wks
20 Apr 61	● **THEME FROM DIXIE** *London HLW 9324*	**7**	10 wks
22 Jun 61	**RING OF FIRE** *London HLW 9370*	**17**	10 wks
14 Sep 61	**DRIVIN' HOME** *London HLW 9406*	**30**	4 wks
5 Oct 61	**CARAVAN** *Parlophone R 4826* [1]	**42**	3 wks
24 May 62	**DEEP IN THE HEART OF TEXAS** *RCA 1288* [1]	**19**	8 wks
23 Aug 62	● **BALLAD OF PALADIN** *RCA 1300* [1]	**10**	10 wks
8 Nov 62	● **DANCE WITH THE GUITAR MAN** *RCA 1316* [2]	**4**	16 wks
14 Feb 63	**BOSS GUITAR** *RCA 1329* [2]	**27**	8 wks
30 May 63	**LONELY BOY LONELY GUITAR** *RCA 1344* [2]	**35**	4 wks
29 Aug 63	**YOUR BABY'S GONE SURFIN'** *RCA 1357* [2]	**49**	1 wk
8 Mar 75	● **PLAY ME LIKE YOU PLAY YOUR GUITAR**		
	GTO GT 11 [2]	**9**	9 wks
22 Mar 86	**PETER GUNN** *China WOK 6* [3]	**8**	9 wks

[1] Duane Eddy [2] Duane Eddy and the Rebelettes [3] Art Of Noise featuring Duane Eddy

EDDY and the SOUL BAND
US, male vocal / instrumental group   **7 wks**

| 23 Feb 85 | **THE THEME FROM 'SHAFT'** *Club JAB 11* ...... | **13** | 7 wks |

Randy EDELMAN *US, male vocalist*   **18 wks**

6 Mar 76	**CONCRETE AND CLAY** *20th Century BTC 2261*	**11**	7 wks
18 Sep 76	**UPTOWN UPTEMPO WOMAN**		
	20th Century BTC 2225	**25**	7 wks
15 Jan 77	**YOU** *20th Century BTC 2253*	**49**	2 wks
17 Jul 82	**NOBODY MADE ME** *Rocket XPRES 81*	**60**	2 wks

EDELWEISS
Austria, male / female vocal / instrumental group   **10 wks**

| 29 Apr 89 | ● **BRING ME EDELWEISS** *WEA YZ 353* ...... | **5** | 10 wks |

EDEN
UK / Australia, male / female vocal / instrumental group   **2 wks**

| 6 Mar 93 | **DO U FEEL 4 ME** *Logic 74321135422* ...... | **51** | 2 wks |

EDISON LIGHTHOUSE
UK, male vocal / instrumental group   **13 wks**

24 Jan 70	★ **LOVE GROWS (WHERE MY ROSEMARY GOES)**		
	Bell 1091	**1**	12 wks
30 Jan 71	**IT'S UP TO YOU PETULA** *Bell 1136*	**49**	1 wk

Dave EDMUNDS
UK, male vocalist / multi-instrumentalist   **93 wks**

21 Nov 70	★ **I HEAR YOU KNOCKING** *MAM 1*	**1**	14 wks
20 Jan 73	● **BABY I LOVE YOU** *Rockfield ROC 1*	**8**	13 wks
9 Jun 73	● **BORN TO BE WITH YOU** *Rockfield ROC 2*	**5**	12 wks
2 Jul 77	**I KNEW THE BRIDE** *Swansong SSK 19411*	**26**	8 wks
30 Jun 79	● **GIRLS TALK** *Swansong SSK 19418*	**4**	11 wks
22 Sep 79	**QUEEN OF HEARTS** *Swansong SSK 19419*	**11**	9 wks
24 Nov 79	**CRAWLING FROM THE WRECKAGE**		
	Swansong SSK 19420	**59**	4 wks
9 Feb 80	**SINGING THE BLUES** *Swansong SSK 19422*	**28**	8 wks
28 Mar 81	**ALMOST SATURDAY NIGHT** *Swansong SSK 19424* ...	**58**	3 wks
20 Jun 81	**THE RACE IS ON** *Swansong SSK 19425* [1]	**34**	6 wks
26 Mar 83	**SLIPPING AWAY** *Arista ARIST 522*	**60**	4 wks
7 Apr 90	**KING OF LOVE** *Capitol CL 568*	**68**	1 wk

[1] Dave Edmunds and the Stray Cats

Alton EDWARDS *South Africa, male vocalist*   **9 wks**

| 9 Jan 82 | **I JUST WANNA (SPEND SOME TIME WITH YOU)** | | |
| | *Streetwave STRA 1897* .... | **20** | 9 wks |

Dennis EDWARDS featuring Siedah GARRETT
US, male / female vocal duo   **10 wks**

24 Mar 84	**DON'T LOOK ANY FURTHER** *Gordy TMG 1334*	**45**	5 wks
20 Jun 87	**DON'T LOOK ANY FURTHER (re-entry)**		
	Gordy TMG 1334	**55**	5 wks

See also Michael Jackson.

Rupie EDWARDS *Jamaica, male vocalist*   **16 wks**

| 23 Nov 74 | ● **IRE FEELINGS (SKANGA)** *Cactus CT 38*...... | **9** | 10 wks |
| 8 Feb 75 | **LEGO SKANGA** *Cactus CT 51* ...... | **32** | 6 wks |

Tommy EDWARDS *US, male vocalist*   **18 wks**

| 3 Oct 58 | ★ **IT'S ALL IN THE GAME** *MGM 989* ...... | **1** | 17 wks |
| 7 Aug 59 | **MY MELANCHOLY BABY** *MGM 1020* ...... | **29** | 1 wk |

EFUA
UK, female vocalist **5 wks**

| 3 Jul 93 | **SOMEWHERE** *Virgin VSCDT 1463*.................**42** | 5 wks |

EGYPTIAN EMPIRE *UK, male producer - Tim Taylor* **2 wks**

| 24 Oct 92 | **THE HORN TRACK** *Ffrreedom TAB 115* ....**61** | 2 wks |

808 STATE *UK, male instrumental group* **63 wks**

18 Nov 89	● **PACIFIC STATE** *ZTT ZANG 1* **10**	9 wks
31 Mar 90	**THE EXTENDED PLEASURE OF DANCE EP** *ZTT 2T* ..**56**	1 wk
2 Jun 90	● **THE ONLY RHYME THAT BITES** *ZTT ZANG 3* [1] **10**	10 wks
15 Sep 90	**TUNES SPLITS THE ATOM** *ZTT ZANG 6* [1] **18**	7 wks
10 Nov 90	● **CUBIK / OLYMPIC** *ZTT ZANG 5* **10**	10 wks
16 Feb 91	● **IN YER FACE** *ZTT ZANG 14* **9**	6 wks
27 Apr 91	**OOOPS** *ZTT ZANG 19* [2] **42**	3 wks
17 Aug 91	**LIFT / OPEN YOUR MIND** *ZTT ZANG 20*...............**38**	4 wks
29 Aug 92	**TIME BOMB / NIMBUS** *ZTT ZANG 33* **59**	1 wk
12 Dec 92	**ONE IN TEN** *ZTT ZANG 39* [3] **17**	8 wks
30 Jan 93	**PLAN 9** *ZTT ZANG 38CD* **50**	2 wks
26 Jun 93	**10 X 10** *ZTT ZANG 42CD* **67**	1 wk
13 Aug 94	**BOMBADIN** *ZTT ZANG 54CD* **67**	1 wk

[1] MC Tunes versus 808 State [2] 808 State featuring Bjork [3] 808 State vs UB40

Tracks on The Extended Pleasure Of Dance EP: *Ancodia / Cubik / Cuba Bora.* Cubik *is a re-issue of one of the tracks from* The Extended Pleasure Of Dance EP.

See also Various Artists (EPs & LPs) – Gimme Shelter (EP).

EIGHTH WONDER
UK, male / female vocal / instrumental group **25 wks**

2 Nov 85	**STAY WITH ME** *CBS A 6594* **65**	2 wks
20 Feb 88	● **I'M NOT SCARED** *CBS SCARE 1* **7**	13 wks
25 Jun 88	**CROSS MY HEART** *CBS 651552 7* **13**	8 wks
1 Oct 88	**BABY BABY** *CBS BABE 1* **65**	2 wks

EINSTEIN - *See AMBASSADORS OF FUNK featuring MC MARIO; Simon HARRIS; TECHNOTRONIC*

ELASTICA *UK, female / male vocal / instrumental group* **7 wks**

| 12 Feb 94 | **LINE UP** *Deceptive BLUFF 004CD* ....**20** | 3 wks |
| 22 Oct 94 | **CONNECTION** *Deceptive BLUFF 010CD* ....**17** | 4 wks |

Donnie ELBERT *US, male vocalist* **29 wks**

8 Jan 72	● **WHERE DID OUR LOVE GO?** *London HL 10352* **8**	10 wks
26 Feb 72	**I CAN'T HELP MYSELF** *Avco 6105 009* **11**	10 wks
29 Apr 72	**LITTLE PIECE OF LEATHER** *London HL 10370*...........**27**	9 wks

ELECTRA *UK, male vocal / instrumental group* **7 wks**

| 6 Aug 88 | **JIBARO** *FFRR FFR 9*...............**54** | 3 wks |
| 30 Dec 89 | **IT'S YOUR DESTINY / AUTUMN LOVE** *London F 121* ....**51** | 4 wks |

ELECTRAFIXION *UK, male vocal / instrumental group* **2 wks**

| 19 Nov 94 | **ZEPHYR** *WEA YZ 865CD* ....**47** | 2 wks |

ELECTRIBE 101
UK / Germany, male / female vocal / instrumental group **13 wks**

28 Oct 89	**TELL ME WHEN THE FEVER ENDED** *Mercury MER 310* **32**	5 wks
24 Feb 90	**TALKING WITH MYSELF** *Mercury MER 316* **23**	5 wks
22 Sep 90	**YOU'RE WALKING** *Mercury MER 328* **50**	3 wks

ELECTRIC LIGHT ORCHESTRA
UK, male vocal / instrumental group **255 wks**

29 Jul 72	● **10538 OVERTURE** *Harvest HAR 5053*...............**9**	8 wks
27 Jan 73	● **ROLL OVER BEETHOVEN** *Harvest HAR 5063*...............**6**	10 wks
6 Oct 73	**SHOWDOWN** *Harvest HAR 5077*...............**12**	10 wks
9 Mar 74	**MA-MA-MA-BELLE** *Warner Bros. K 16349* **22**	8 wks
10 Jan 76	● **EVIL WOMAN** *Jet 764* **10**	8 wks
3 Jul 76	**STRANGE MAGIC** *Jet 779* **38**	3 wks
13 Nov 76	● **LIVIN' THING** *Jet UP 36184* **4**	12 wks
19 Feb 77	● **ROCKARIA!** *Jet UP 36209* **9**	9 wks
21 May 77	● **TELEPHONE LINE** *Jet UP 36254* **8**	10 wks
29 Oct 77	**TURN TO STONE** *Jet UP 36313* **18**	12 wks
28 Jan 78	● **MR. BLUE SKY** *Jet UP 36342* **6**	11 wks
10 Jun 78	● **WILD WEST HERO** *Jet JET 109* **6**	14 wks
7 Oct 78	● **SWEET TALKIN' WOMAN** *Jet 121* **6**	9 wks
9 Dec 78	**ELO EP** *Jet ELO 1* **34**	8 wks
19 May 79	● **SHINE A LITTLE LOVE** *Jet 144* **6**	10 wks
21 Jul 79	● **THE DIARY OF HORACE WIMP** *Jet 150* **8**	9 wks
1 Sep 79	● **DON'T BRING ME DOWN** *Jet 153* **3**	9 wks
17 Nov 79	● **CONFUSION / LAST TRAIN TO LONDON** *Jet 166* ...**8**	10 wks
24 May 80	**I'M ALIVE** *Jet 179* **20**	9 wks
21 Jun 80	★ **XANADU** *Jet 185* [1] **1**	11 wks
2 Aug 80	**ALL OVER THE WORLD** *Jet 195* **11**	8 wks
22 Nov 80	**DON'T WALK AWAY** *Jet 7004* **21**	10 wks
1 Aug 81	● **HOLD ON TIGHT** *Jet 7011* **4**	12 wks
24 Oct 81	**TWILIGHT** *Jet 7015* **30**	7 wks
9 Jan 82	**TICKET TO THE MOON / HERE IS THE NEWS** *Jet 7018* **24**	8 wks
18 Jun 83	**ROCK 'N' ROLL IS KING** *Jet A 3500* **13**	9 wks
3 Sep 83	**SECRET MESSAGES** *Jet A 3720* **48**	3 wks
1 Mar 86	**CALLING AMERICA** *Epic A 6844* **28**	7 wks
11 May 91	**HONEST MEN** *Telstar ELO 100* [2] **60**	1 wk

[1] Olivia Newton-John and Electric Light Orchestra [2] Electric Light Orchestra Part 2

Here Is The News *listed from 16 Jan 82. Tracks on ELO EP: Out of My Head / Strange Magic / Ma-Ma-Ma-Belle / Evil Woman.*

ELECTRIC PRUNES *US, male vocal / instrumental group* **5 wks**

| 9 Feb 67 | **I HAD TOO MUCH TO DREAM LAST NIGHT** *Reprise RS 20532* ....**49** | 1 wk |
| 11 May 67 | **GET ME TO THE WORLD ON TIME** *Reprise RS 20564* ....**42** | 4 wks |

ELECTRONIC *UK, male vocal / instrumental group* **25 wks**

16 Dec 89	**GETTING AWAY WITH IT** *Factory FAC 2577* **12**	9 wks
27 Apr 91	● **GET THE MESSAGE** *Factory FAC 2877* **8**	7 wks
21 Sep 91	**FEEL EVERY BEAT** *Factory FAC 3287* **39**	4 wks
4 Jul 92	● **DISAPPOINTED** *Parlophone R 6311* **6**	5 wks

ELECTRONICAS *Holland, male instrumental group* **8 wks**

| 19 Sep 81 | **ORIGINAL BIRD DANCE** *Polydor POSP 360* ....**22** | 8 wks |

ELECTROSET *UK, male instrumental production group* **3 wks**

| 21 Nov 92 | **HOW DOES IT FEEL** *ffrr F 203* ....**27** | 3 wks |

ELEGANTS *US, male vocal group* **2 wks**

| 26 Sep 58 | **LITTLE STAR** *HMV POP 520*...............**25** | 2 wks |

ELEVATION *UK, male instrumental / production duo* **1 wk**

| 23 May 92 | **CAN YOU FEEL IT** *Nova Mute 12NOMU 3*...............**62** | 1 wk |

ELGINS *US, male / female vocal group* **20 wks**

| 1 May 71 | ● **HEAVEN MUST HAVE SENT YOU** *Tamla Motown TMG 771* ....**3** | 13 wks |

Jeff Lynne (right) leads an extremely early line-up of the **ELECTRIC LIGHT ORCHESTRA.** (LFI)

Brian Setzer (left) of the Stray Cats and Bob Geldof are right by the sides of **EURYTHMICS** Annie Lennox and Dave Stewart.

9 Oct 71	**PUT YOURSELF IN MY PLACE** *Tamla Motown TMG 787*	**28**	7 wks

ELIAS and his ZIGZAG JIVE FLUTES
South Africa, male instrumental group **14 wks**

25 Apr 58	● **TOM HARK** *Columbia DB 4109*	**2**	14 wks

Yvonne ELLIMAN *US, female vocalist* **44 wks**

29 Jan 72	**I DON'T KNOW HOW TO LOVE HIM** *MCA MMKS 5077*	**47**	1 wk
6 Nov 76	● **LOVE ME** *RSO 2090 205*	**6**	13 wks
7 May 77	**HELLO STRANGER** *RSO 2090 236*	**26**	5 wks
13 Aug 77	**I CAN'T GET YOU OUT OF MY MIND** *RSO 2090 251*	**17**	13 wks
6 May 78	● **IF I CAN'T HAVE YOU** *RSO 2090 266*	**4**	12 wks

I Don't Know How To Love Him was one of four tracks on a Maxi-Single, two of which were credited during the disc's one week on the chart. The other track credited was Superstar by Murray Head.

Duke ELLINGTON *US, orchestra* **4 wks**

5 Mar 54	● **SKIN DEEP** *Philips PB 243*	**7**	4 wks

Lance ELLINGTON *UK, male vocalist* **1 wk**

21 Aug 93	**LONELY (HAVE WE LOST OUR LOVE)** *RCA 74321158332*	**57**	1 wk

Ray ELLINGTON *UK, orchestra* **4 wks**

15 Nov 62	**THE MADISON** *Ember S 102*	**41**	2 wks
20 Dec 62	**THE MADISON (re-entry)** *Ember S 102*	**36**	2 wks

Bern ELLIOTT and the FENMEN
UK, male vocalist and male vocal / instrumental backing group **22 wks**

21 Nov 63	**MONEY** *Decca F 11770*	**14**	13 wks
19 Mar 64	**NEW ORLEANS** *Decca F 11852*	**24**	9 wks

Joe ELLIOTT - *See Mick RONSON with Joe ELLIOTT*

Greg ELLIS - *See Reva RICE and Greg ELLIS*

Joey B. ELLIS *US, male vocalist* **10 wks**

16 Feb 91	**GO FOR IT (HEART AND FIRE)** *Capitol CL 601* [1] **20**	8 wks
18 May 91	**THOUGHT YOU WERE THE ONE FOR ME** *Capitol CL 614* **58**	2 wks

[1] Rocky V featuring Joey B. Ellis and Tynetta Hare

Shirley ELLIS *US, female vocalist* **17 wks**

6 May 65	● **THE CLAPPING SONG** *London HLR 9961*	**6**	13 wks
8 Jul 78	**THE CLAPPING SONG (EP)** *MCA MCEP 1*	**59**	4 wks

Tracks on The Clapping Song (EP): The Clapping Song / Ever See a Diver Kiss His Wife While The Bubbles Bounce Above The Water / The Name Game / The Nitty Gritty. The Clapping Song itself qualifies as a re-issue.

ELLIS, BEGGS AND HOWARD
UK, male vocal / instrumental group **8 wks**

2 Jul 88	**BIG BUBBLES, NO TROUBLES** *RCA PB 42089* **59**	3 wks
11 Mar 89	**BIG BUBBLES, NO TROUBLES (re-entry)** *RCA PB 42089* **41**	5 wks

E-LUSTRIOUS *UK, male instrumental / production duo* **2 wks**

15 Feb 92	**DANCE NO MORE** *MOS MOS 001T* [1] **58**	1 wk
2 Jul 94	**IN YOUR DANCE** *UFG UFG 6CD* **69**	1 wk

[1] E-Lustrious featuring Deborah French

Keith EMERSON *UK, male instrumentalist - piano* **5 wks**

10 Apr 76	**HONKY TONK TRAIN BLUES** *Manticore K 13513* **21**	5 wks

See also Emerson, Lake and Palmer.

EMERSON, LAKE AND PALMER
UK, male instrumental group **13 wks**

4 Jun 77	● **FANFARE FOR THE COMMON MAN** *Atlantic K 10946*	**2**	13 wks

See also Keith Emerson; Greg Lake.

Dick EMERY *UK, male vocalist* **8 wks**

26 Feb 69	**IF YOU LOVE HER** *Pye 7N 17644*	**32**	4 wks
13 Jan 73	**YOU ARE AWFUL** *Pye 7N 45202*	**43**	4 wks

EMF *UK, male vocal / instrumental group* **38 wks**

3 Nov 90	● **UNBELIEVABLE** *Parlophone R 6273*	**3**	13 wks
2 Feb 91	● **I BELIEVE** *Parlophone R 6279*	**6**	7 wks
27 Apr 91	**CHILDREN** *Parlophone R 6288*	**19**	5 wks
31 Aug 91	**LIES** *Parlophone R 6295*	**28**	3 wks
2 May 92	**UNEXPLAINED EP** *Parlophone SGE 2026*	**18**	4 wks
19 Sep 92	**THEY'RE HERE** *Parlophone R 6321*	**29**	3 wks
21 Nov 92	**IT'S YOU** *Parlophone R 6327*	**23**	3 wks

Tracks on Unexplained EP: Getting Through / Far From Me / The Same / Search And Destroy

EMMA *UK, female vocalist* **6 wks**

28 Apr 90	**GIVE A LITTLE LOVE BACK TO THE WORLD** *Big Wave BWR 33*	**33**	6 wks

An EMOTIONAL FISH
UK, male vocal / instrumental group **5 wks**

23 Jun 90	**CELEBRATE** *East West YZ 489*	**46**	5 wks

EMOTIONS *US, female vocal group* **28 wks**

10 Sep 77	● **BEST OF MY LOVE** *CBS 5555*	**4**	10 wks
24 Dec 77	**I DON'T WANNA LOSE YOUR LOVE** *CBS 5819* **40**	5 wks
12 May 79	● **BOOGIE WONDERLAND** *CBS 7292* [1]	**4**	13 wks

[1] Earth Wind and Fire with the Emotions

EN VOGUE *US, female vocal / instrumental group* **56 wks**

5 May 90	● **HOLD ON** *East West America 7908*	**5**	11 wks
21 Jul 90	**LIES** *East West America 7893*	**44**	4 wks
4 Apr 92	**MY LOVIN'** *East West America A 8578*	**69**	3 wks
9 May 92	● **MY LOVIN' (re-entry)** *East West America A 8578* **4**	9 wks
15 Aug 92	**GIVING HIM SOMETHING HE CAN FEEL** *East West America A 8524*	**44**	3 wks
7 Nov 92	**GIVING HIM SOMETHING HE CAN FEEL (re-issue)** **/ FREE YOUR MIND** *East West America A 8524* **16**	8 wks
16 Jan 93	**GIVE IT UP TURN IT LOOSE** *East West America A 8445CD*	**22**	4 wks
10 Apr 93	**LOVE DON'T LOVE YOU** *East West America A 8424CD*	**64**	1 wk
9 Oct 93	**RUNAWAY LOVE** *East West America A 8359CD* **36**	3 wks
19 Mar 94	● **WHATTA MAN** *ffrr FCD 222* [1]	**7**	10 wks

[1] Salt-N-Pepa with En Vogue

ENERGISE *UK, male vocal / instrumental group* **1 wk**

16 Feb 91	**REPORT TO THE DANCEFLOOR** *Network NWKT 16*	**69**	1 wk

ENERGY ORCHARD
Ireland, male vocal / instrumental group   **6 wks**

| 27 Jan 90 | **BELFAST** *MCA MCA 1392* .... | **52** | 4 wks |
| 7 Apr 90 | **SAILORTOWN** *MCA MCA 1402* .... | **73** | 2 wks |

Harry ENFIELD *UK, male vocalist*   **7 wks**

| 7 May 88 | ● **LOADSAMONEY (DOIN' UP THE HOUSE)** | | |
| | *Mercury DOSH 1* .... | **4** | 7 wks |

ENGLAND DAN and John Ford COLEY
US, male vocal duo   **12 wks**

25 Sep 76	**I'D REALLY LOVE TO SEE YOU TONIGHT**		
	Atlantic K 10810	**26**	7 wks
23 Jun 79	**LOVE IS THE ANSWER** *Big Tree K 11296*	**45**	5 wks

ENGLAND SISTERS *UK, female vocal group*   **1 wk**

| 17 Mar 60 | **HEARTBEAT** *HMV POP 710* .... | **33** | 1 wk |

ENGLAND WORLD CUP SQUAD
UK, male football team vocalists   **46 wks**

18 Apr 70	★ **BACK HOME** *Pye 7N 17920*	**1**	16 wks
15 Aug 70	**BACK HOME (re-entry)** *Pye 7N 17920*	**46**	1 wk
10 Apr 82	● **THIS TIME (WE'LL GET IT RIGHT)** /		
	ENGLAND WE'LL FLY THE FLAG *England ER 1*	**2**	13 wks
19 Apr 86	**WE'VE GOT THE WHOLE WORLD AT OUR FEET** /		
	WHEN WE ARE FAR FROM HOME		
	Columbia DB 9128	**66**	2 wks
21 May 88	**ALL THE WAY** *MCA GOAL 1* [1]	**64**	2 wks
2 Jun 90	★ **WORLD IN MOTION...** *Factory/MCA FAC 2937* [2]	**1**	12 wks

[1] England Football Team and the 'sound' of Stock, Aitken and Waterman
[2] Englandneworder

ENGLAND WORLD CUP SQUAD - *See UNION featuring the ENGLAND WORLD CUP SQUAD*

Kim ENGLISH *US, female vocalist*   **2 wks**

| 23 Jul 94 | **NITE LIFE** *Hi-Life PZCD 323* .... | **35** | 2 wks |

Scott ENGLISH *US, male vocalist*   **10 wks**

| 9 Oct 71 | **BRANDY** *Horse HOSS 7* .... | **12** | 10 wks |

ENIGMA *UK, male vocal / instrumental group*   **15 wks**

| 23 May 81 | **AIN'T NO STOPPING** *Creole CR 9* .... | **11** | 8 wks |
| 8 Aug 81 | **I LOVE MUSIC** *Creole CR 14* .... | **25** | 7 wks |

ENIGMA
Germany / Romania, male / female vocal / instrumental duo   **42 wks**

15 Dec 90	★ **SADNESS PART 1** *Virgin International DINS 101*	**1**	12 wks
30 Mar 91	**MEA CULPA PART II** *Virgin International DINS 104* ..	**55**	3 wks
10 Aug 91	**PRINCIPLES OF LUST**		
	Virgin International DINS 110	**59**	2 wks
11 Jan 92	**THE RIVERS OF BELIEF**		
	Virgin International DINS 112	**68**	2 wks
29 Jan 94	● **RETURN TO INNOCENCE**		
	Virgin International DINSD 123	**3**	14 wks
14 May 94	**THE EYES OF TRUTH**		
	Virgin International DINSD 126	**21**	4 wks
20 Aug 94	**AGE OF LONELINESS**		
	Virgin International DINSD 135	**21**	5 wks

ENYA *Ireland, female vocalist*   **43 wks**

| 15 Oct 88 | ★ **ORINOCO FLOW** *WEA YZ 312* .... | **1** | 13 wks |

24 Dec 88	**EVENING FALLS...** *WEA YZ 356*	**20**	4 wks
10 Jun 89	**STORMS IN AFRICA (PART II)** *WEA YZ 368*	**41**	4 wks
19 Oct 91	**CARIBBEAN BLUE** *WEA YZ 604*	**13**	7 wks
7 Dec 91	**HOW CAN I KEEP FROM SINGING** *WEA YZ 365*	**32**	5 wks
1 Aug 92	● **BOOK OF DAYS** *WEA YZ 640*	**10**	6 wks
14 Nov 92	**THE CELTS** *WEA YZ 705*	**29**	4 wks

EON *UK, male producer - Ian Bela*   **1 wk**

| 17 Aug 91 | **FEAR: THE MINDKILLER** | | |
| | *Vinyl Solution STORM 33* .... | **63** | 1 wk |

EQUALS *UK / Guyana, male vocal / instrumental group*   **69 wks**

21 Feb 68	**I GET SO EXCITED** *President PT 180*	**44**	4 wks
1 May 68	**BABY COME BACK** *President PT 135*	**50**	1 wk
15 May 68	★ **BABY COME BACK (re-entry)** *President PT 135*	**1**	17 wks
21 Aug 68	**LAUREL AND HARDY** *President PT 200*	**35**	5 wks
27 Nov 68	**SOFTLY SOFTLY** *President PT 222*	**48**	3 wks
2 Apr 69	**MICHAEL AND THE SLIPPER TREE**		
	President PT 240	**24**	7 wks
30 Jul 69	● **VIVA BOBBY JOE** *President PT 260*	**6**	14 wks
27 Dec 69	**RUB A DUB DUB** *President PT 275*	**34**	7 wks
19 Dec 70	● **BLACK SKIN BLUE EYED BOYS** *President PT 325*	**9**	11 wks

ERASURE *UK, male vocal / instrumental duo*   **187 wks**

5 Oct 85	**WHO NEEDS LOVE LIKE THAT** *Mute MUTE 40*	**55**	2 wks
25 Oct 86	● **SOMETIMES** *Mute MUTE 51*	**2**	17 wks
28 Feb 87	**IT DOESN'T HAVE TO BE** *Mute MUTE 56*	**12**	9 wks
30 May 87	● **VICTIM OF LOVE** *Mute MUTE 61*	**7**	9 wks
3 Oct 87	● **THE CIRCUS** *Mute MUTE 66*	**6**	10 wks
5 Mar 88	● **SHIP OF FOOLS** *Mute MUTE 74*	**6**	8 wks
11 Jun 88	**CHAINS OF LOVE** *Mute MUTE 83*	**11**	7 wks
1 Oct 88	● **A LITTLE RESPECT** *Mute MUTE 85*	**4**	10 wks
10 Dec 88	● **CRACKERS INTERNATIONAL EP** *Mute MUTE 93*	**2**	13 wks
30 Sep 89	● **DRAMA!** *Mute MUTE 89*	**4**	8 wks
9 Dec 89	**YOU SURROUND ME** *Mute MUTE 99*	**15**	9 wks
10 Mar 90	● **BLUE SAVANNAH** *Mute MUTE 109*	**3**	10 wks
2 Jun 90	**STAR** *Mute MUTE 111*	**11**	7 wks
29 Jun 91	● **CHORUS** *Mute MUTE 125*	**3**	9 wks
21 Sep 91	● **LOVE TO HATE YOU** *Mute MUTE 131*	**4**	9 wks
7 Dec 91	**AM I RIGHT (EP)** *Mute MUTE 134*	**15**	6 wks
11 Jan 92	**AM I RIGHT (EP) (re-mix)** *Mute L12MUTE 134*	**22**	3 wks
28 Mar 92	● **BREATH OF LIFE** *Mute MUTE 142*	**8**	6 wks
13 Jun 92	★ **ABBA-ESQUE EP** *Mute MUTE 144*	**1**	12 wks
7 Nov 92	● **WHO NEEDS LOVE (LIKE THAT) (re-mix)**		
	Mute MUTE 150	**10**	4 wks
23 Apr 94	● **ALWAYS** *Mute CDMUTE 152*	**4**	9 wks
30 Jul 94	● **RUN TO THE SUN** *Mute CDMUTE 153*	**6**	5 wks
3 Dec 94	**I LOVE SATURDAY** *Mute CDMUTE 166*	**20†**	5 wks

Tracks on Crackers International EP: Stop / The Hardest Part / Knocking On Your Door / She Won't Be Home. Tracks on Am I Right (EP): Am I Right / Carry On Clangers / Let It Flow / Waiting For Sex. Tracks on Am I Right (Re-mix EP): Am I Right / Chorus / Love To Hate You / Perfect Stranger. Tracks on Abba-esque EP: Lay All Your Love On Me / SOS / Take A Chance On Me / Voulez-Vous.

ERIC and the GOOD GOOD FEELING
UK, male / female vocal / instrumental group   **1 wk**

| 3 Jun 89 | **GOOD GOOD FEELING** *Equinox EQN 1* .... | **73** | 1 wk |

ERIK *UK, female vocalist*   **5 wks**

10 Apr 93	**LOOKS LIKE I'M IN LOVE AGAIN**		
	PWL Sanctuary PWCD 252 [1]	**46**	2 wks
29 Jan 94	**GOT TO BE REAL** *PWL International PWCD 278*	**42**	2 wks
1 Oct 94	**WE GOT THE LOVE** *PWL International PWCD 305*	**55**	1 wk

[1] Key West featuring Erik

The string of hit singles from the *Always And Forever* album seemed truly **ETERNAL.**

EROTIC DRUM BAND
Canada, male / female vocal / instrumental group **3 wks**

9 Jun 79	**LOVE DISCO STYLE** *Scope SC 1*	....	**47**	3 wks

ERUPTION *US, male / female vocal / instrumental group* **21 wks**

18 Feb 78	● **I CAN'T STAND THE RAIN** *Atlantic K 11068* 1	....	**5**	11 wks
21 Apr 79	● **ONE WAY TICKET** *Atlantic/Hansa K 11266*	....	**9**	10 wks

1 Eruption featuring Precious Wilson

ESCORTS *UK, male vocal / instrumental group* **2 wks**

2 Jul 64	**THE ONE TO CRY** *Fontana TF 474*	....	**49**	2 wks

ESKIMOS & EGYPT
UK, male vocal / instrumental group **4 wks**

13 Feb 93	**FALL FROM GRACE** *One Little Indian EEF 96CD*	....	**51**	2 wks
29 May 93	**UK-USA** *One Little Indian 99 TP7CD*	....	**52**	2 wks

ESPIRITU *UK / France, male / female vocal / instrumental duo* **5 wks**

6 Mar 93	**CONQUISTADOR** *Heavenly HVN 28CD*	....	**47**	2 wks
7 Aug 93	**LOS AMERICANOS** *Heavenly HVN 33CD*	.....	**45**	2 wks
20 Aug 94	**BONITA MANANA** *Columbia 6606925*	.....	**50**	1 wk

ESSEX *US, male / female vocal group* **5 wks**

8 Aug 63	**EASIER SAID THAN DONE** *Columbia DB 7077*	....	**41**	5 wks

David ESSEX *UK, male vocalist* **199 wks**

18 Aug 73	● **ROCK ON** *CBS 1693*	....	**3**	11 wks
10 Nov 73	● **LAMPLIGHT** *CBS 1902*	....	**7**	15 wks
11 May 74	**AMERICA** *CBS 2176*	....	**32**	5 wks
12 Oct 74	★ **GONNA MAKE YOU A STAR** *CBS 2492*	....	**1**	17 wks
14 Dec 74	● **STARDUST** *CBS 2828*	....	**7**	10 wks
5 Jul 75	● **ROLLIN' STONE** *CBS 3425*	....	**5**	7 wks
13 Sep 75	★ **HOLD ME CLOSE** *CBS 3572*	....	**1**	10 wks
6 Dec 75	**IF I COULD** *CBS 3776*	....	**13**	8 wks
20 Mar 76	**CITY LIGHTS** *CBS 4050*	....	**24**	4 wks
16 Oct 76	**COMING HOME** *CBS 4486*	....	**24**	6 wks
17 Sep 77	**COOL OUT TONIGHT** *CBS 5495*	....	**23**	6 wks
11 Mar 78	**STAY WITH ME BABY** *CBS 6063*	....	**45**	5 wks
19 Aug 78	● **OH WHAT A CIRCUS** *Mercury 6007 185*	.....	**3**	11 wks
21 Oct 78	**BRAVE NEW WORLD** *CBS 6705*	....	**55**	3 wks
3 Mar 79	**IMPERIAL WIZARD** *Mercury 6007 202*	......	**32**	8 wks
5 Apr 80	● **SILVER DREAM MACHINE (PART 1)** *Mercury BIKE 1* ..**4**			11 wks
14 Jun 80	**HOT LOVE** *Mercury HOT 11*	....	**57**	4 wks
26 Jun 82	**ME AND MY GIRL (NIGHT-CLUBBING)**			
	Mercury MER 107	....	**13**	10 wks
11 Dec 82	● **A WINTER'S TALE** *Mercury MER 127*	......	**2**	10 wks
4 Jun 83	**THE SMILE** *Mercury ESSEX 1*	....	**52**	4 wks
27 Aug 83	● **TAHITI** *Mercury BOUNT 1*	....	**8**	11 wks
26 Nov 83	**YOU'RE IN MY HEART** *Mercury ESSEX 2*	.....	**67**	2 wks
17 Dec 83	**YOU'RE IN MY HEART (re-entry)** *Mercury ESSEX 2*..**59**			4 wks
23 Feb 85	**FALLING ANGELS RIDING** *Mercury ESSEX 5*	....	**29**	7 wks
18 Apr 87	**MYFANWY** *Arista RIS 11*	....	**41**	7 wks
26 Nov 94	**TRUE LOVE WAYS** *PolyGram TV TLWCD 2* 1	....	**38**	3 wks

1 David Essex and Catherine Zeta Jones

Gloria ESTEFAN *US, female vocalist* **171 wks**

11 Aug 84	● **DR BEAT** *Epic A 4614* 1	....	**6**	14 wks
17 May 86	**BAD BOY** *Epic A 6537* 1	....	**16**	11 wks
16 Jul 88	● **ANYTHING FOR YOU** *Epic 651673 7* 2	.....	**10**	16 wks
22 Oct 88	**1-2-3** *Epic 652958 7* 2	....	**9**	9 wks
17 Dec 88	**RHYTHM IS GONNA GET YOU** *Epic 654514 7* 2 ..**16**			9 wks
31 Dec 88	**1-2-3 (re-entry)** *Epic 652958 7* 2	.....	**72**	1 wk
11 Feb 89	● **CAN'T STAY AWAY FROM YOU** *Epic 651444 7* 2 ..**7**			12 wks
15 Jul 89	● **DON'T WANNA LOSE YOU** *Epic 655054 0*	.....	**6**	10 wks

16 Sep 89	**OYE MI CANTO (HEAR MY VOICE)** *Epic 655287 7* ..**16**			8 wks
25 Nov 89	**GET ON YOUR FEET** *Epic 655450 7*	.....	**23**	7 wks
3 Mar 90	**HERE WE ARE** *Epic 655473 9*	....	**23**	6 wks
26 May 90	**CUTS BOTH WAYS** *Epic 655982 7*	.....	**49**	5 wks
26 Jan 91	**COMING OUT OF THE DARK** *Epic 6565747*	....	**25**	5 wks
6 Apr 91	**SEAL OUR FATE** *Epic 6567737*	....	**24**	7 wks
8 Jun 91	**REMEMBER ME WITH LOVE** *Epic 6569687*	....	**22**	6 wks
21 Sep 91	**LIVE FOR LOVING YOU** *Epic 6573827*	.....	**33**	5 wks
24 Oct 92	● **ALWAYS TOMORROW** *Epic 6583977*	.....	**24**	4 wks
12 Dec 92	● **MIAMI HIT MIX / CHRISTMAS THROUGH YOUR EYES**			
	Epic 6588377	....	**8**	9 wks
13 Feb 93	**I SEE YOUR SMILE** *Epic 6589612*	.....	**48**	2 wks
3 Apr 93	**GO AWAY** *Epic 6590952*	....	**13**	6 wks
3 Jul 93	**MI TIERRA** *Epic 6593512*	....	**36**	3 wks
14 Aug 93	**IF WE WERE LOVERS / CON LOS ANOS**			
	QUE ME QUEDIN *Epic 6595702*	......	**40**	3 wks
18 Dec 93	**MONTUNO** *Epic 6599972*	....	**55**	2 wks
15 Oct 94	**TURN THE BEAT AROUND** *Epic 6606822*	.....	**21**	6 wks
3 Dec 94	**HOLD ME THRILL ME KISS ME** *Epic 6610802* ....**11†**			5 wks

1 Miami Sound Machine 2 Gloria Estefan and Miami Sound Machine

Christmas Through Your Eyes only listed from 19 Dec 92.

Don ESTELLE - *See Windsor DAVIES and Don ESTELLE*

Deon ESTUS *US, male vocalist / instrumentalist - bass* **7 wks**

25 Jan 86	**MY GUY - MY GIRL** *Sedition EDIT 3310* 1	.......**63**	3 wks
29 Apr 89	**HEAVEN HELP ME** *Mika MIKA 2*	......	**41**	4 wks

1 Amii Stewart and Deon Estus

ETERNAL *UK, female vocal group* **44 wks**

2 Oct 93	● **STAY** *EMI CDEM 283*	....	**4**	9 wks
15 Jan 94	● **SAVE OUR LOVE** *EMI CDEM 296*	.....	**8**	7 wks
30 Apr 94	● **JUST A STEP FROM HEAVEN** *EMI CDEM 311* ..**8**			10 wks
20 Aug 94	**SO GOOD** *EMI CDEMS 339*	....	**13**	7 wks
5 Nov 94	● **OH BABY I...** *EMI CDEM 353*	......	**4†**	9 wks
24 Dec 94	**CRAZY** *EMI CDEMX 364*	....	**15†**	2 wks

ETHIOPIANS *Jamaica, male vocal / instrumental group* **6 wks**

13 Sep 67	**TRAIN TO SKAVILLE** *Rio RIO 130*	....	**40**	6 wks

Tony ETORIA *UK, male vocalist* **8 wks**

4 Jun 77	**I CAN PROVE IT** *GTO GT 89*	....	**21**	8 wks

E.U. - *See SALT-N-PEPA*

EUROPE *Sweden, male vocal / instrumental group* **46 wks**

1 Nov 86	★ **THE FINAL COUNTDOWN** *Epic A 7127*	......	**1**	15 wks
31 Jan 87	**ROCK THE NIGHT** *Epic EUR 1*	....	**12**	9 wks
18 Apr 87	**CARRIE** *Epic EUR 2*	....	**22**	8 wks
20 Aug 88	**SUPERSTITIOUS** *Epic EUR 3*	....	**34**	5 wks
1 Feb 92	**I'LL CRY FOR YOU** *Epic 6576977*	.....	**28**	5 wks
21 Mar 92	**HALFWAY TO HEAVEN** *Epic 6578517*	.....	**42**	4 wks

EURYTHMICS
UK, female / male vocal / instrumental duo **198 wks**

4 Jul 81	**NEVER GONNA CRY AGAIN** *RCA 68*	....	**63**	3 wks
20 Nov 82	**LOVE IS A STRANGER** *RCA 54*	....	**54**	5 wks
12 Feb 83	● **SWEET DREAMS (ARE MADE OF THIS)** *RCA DA 2* ..**2**			14 wks
9 Apr 83	● **LOVE IS A STRANGER (re-entry)** *RCA DA 1*	....	**6**	8 wks
9 Jul 83	● **WHO'S THAT GIRL?** *RCA DA 3*	......	**3**	10 wks
5 Nov 83	● **RIGHT BY YOUR SIDE** *RCA DA 4*	.....	**10**	11 wks
21 Jan 84	● **HERE COMES THE RAIN AGAIN** *RCA DA 5*	....	**8**	8 wks
3 Nov 84	● **SEXCRIME (NINETEEN EIGHTY FOUR)**			
	Virgin VS 728	....	**4**	13 wks
19 Jan 85	**JULIA** *Virgin VS 734*	....	**44**	4 wks

20 Apr 85	WOULD I LIE TO YOU? RCA PB 40101 ....**17**	8 wks
6 Jul 85	★ THERE MUST BE AN ANGEL (PLAYING WITH MY HEART) RCA PB 40247 .....**1**	13 wks
2 Nov 85	● SISTERS ARE DOIN' IT FOR THEMSELVES RCA PB 40339 [1] **9**	11 wks
11 Jan 86	IT'S ALRIGHT (BABY'S COMING BACK) RCA PB 40375 ......**12**	8 wks
14 Jun 86	WHEN TOMORROW COMES RCA DA 7 ......**30**	6 wks
6 Sep 86	● THORN IN MY SIDE RCA DA 8 ......**5**	11 wks
29 Nov 86	THE MIRACLE OF LOVE RCA DA 9 ......**23**	9 wks
28 Feb 87	MISSIONARY MAN RCA DA 10 ......**31**	4 wks
24 Oct 87	BEETHOVEN (I LOVE TO LISTEN TO) RCA DA 11 ....**25**	5 wks
26 Dec 87	SHAME RCA DA 14 ......**41**	6 wks
9 Apr 88	I NEED A MAN RCA DA 15 ......**26**	5 wks
11 Jun 88	YOU HAVE PLACED A CHILL IN MY HEART RCA DA 16 ......**16**	8 wks
26 Aug 89	REVIVAL RCA DA 17 ......**26**	6 wks
4 Nov 89	DON'T ASK ME WHY RCA DA 19 ......**25**	6 wks
3 Feb 90	THE KING AND QUEEN OF AMERICA RCA DA 20 ..**29**	5 wks
12 May 90	ANGEL RCA DA 21 ......**23**	6 wks
9 Mar 91	LOVE IS A STRANGER (re-issue) RCA PB 44265 .....**46**	3 wks
16 Nov 91	SWEET DREAMS (ARE MADE OF THIS) (re-mix) RCA PB 45031 ......**48**	2 wks

[1] Eurythmics and Aretha Franklin

EVANGEL TEMPLE CHOIR - *See Johnny CASH*

Maureen EVANS *UK, female vocalist* **37 wks**

22 Jan 60	THE BIG HURT Oriole CB 1533 ......**26**	2 wks
17 Mar 60	LOVE KISSES AND HEARTACHES Oriole CB 1540..**44**	1 wk
2 Jun 60	PAPER ROSES Oriole CB 1550 ......**40**	5 wks
29 Nov 62	● LIKE I DO Oriole CB 1760 ......**3**	18 wks
27 Feb 64	I LOVE HOW YOU LOVE ME Oriole CB 1906 ....**34**	10 wks
14 May 64	I LOVE HOW YOU LOVE ME (re-entry) Oriole CB 1906 ......**50**	1 wk

Paul EVANS *US, male vocalist* **14 wks**

27 Nov 59	SEVEN LITTLE GIRLS SITTING IN THE BACK SEAT London HLL 8968 [1] **25**	1 wk
31 Mar 60	MIDNITE SPECIAL London HLL 9045 ......**41**	1 wk
16 Dec 78	● HELLO THIS IS JOANIE (THE TELEPHONE ANSWERING MACHINE SONG) Spring 2066 932 ....**6**	12 wks

[1] Paul Evans and the Curls

EVASIONS *UK, male / female vocal / instrumental group* **8 wks**

13 Jun 81	WIKKA WRAP Groove GP 107 ......**20**	8 wks

E.V.E. *UK / US, female vocal group* **3 wks**

1 Oct 94	GROOVE OF LOVE Gasoline Alley MCSTD 2007 ......**30**	3 wks

Betty EVERETT *US, female vocalist* **14 wks**

14 Jan 65	GETTING MIGHTY CROWDED Fontana TF 520 ......**29**	7 wks
30 Oct 68	IT'S IN HIS KISS President PT 215 ......**34**	7 wks

Kenny EVERETT *UK, male vocalist* **12 wks**

12 Nov 77	CAPTAIN KREMMEN (RETRIBUTION) DJM DJS 10810 [1] **32**	4 wks
26 Mar 83	● SNOT RAP RCA KEN 1 ......**9**	8 wks

[1] Kenny Everett and Mike Vickers

Phil EVERLY *US, male vocalist* **19 wks**

6 Nov 82	LOUISE Capitol CL 266 ......**47**	6 wks
19 Feb 83	● SHE MEANS NOTHING TO ME Capitol CL 276 [1] **9**	9 wks

10 Dec 94	ALL I HAVE TO DO IS DREAM EMI CDEMS 359 [1]	
	......**14†**	4 wks

[1] Phil Everly and Cliff Richard

All I Have To Do Is Dream was listed with its flip side Miss You Nights *by Cliff Richard.*

See also Everly Brothers.

EVERLY BROTHERS *US, male vocal duo* **337 wks**

12 Jul 57	● BYE BYE LOVE London HLA 8440 ......**6**	16 wks
8 Nov 57	● WAKE UP LITTLE SUSIE London HLA 8498 ......**2**	13 wks
23 May 58	★ ALL I HAVE TO DO IS DREAM / CLAUDETTE London HLA 8618 ......**1**	21 wks
12 Sep 58	● BIRD DOG London HLA 8685 ......**2**	16 wks
23 Jan 59	● PROBLEMS London HLA 8781 ......**6**	12 wks
22 May 59	TAKE A MESSAGE TO MARY London HLA 8863 ......**29**	1 wk
29 May 59	POOR JENNY London HLA 8863 ......**14**	11 wks
19 Jun 59	TAKE A MESSAGE TO MARY (re-entry) London HLA 8863 ......**27**	1 wk
3 Jul 59	TAKE A MESSAGE TO MARY (2nd re-entry) London HLA 8863 ......**20**	8 wks
11 Sep 59	● ('TIL) I KISSED YOU London HLA 8934 ......**2**	15 wks
12 Feb 60	LET IT BE ME London HLA 9039 ......**13**	5 wks
31 Mar 60	LET IT BE ME (re-entry) London HLA 9039 ......**26**	4 wks
14 Apr 60	★ CATHY'S CLOWN Warner Bros. WB 1 ......**1**	18 wks
14 Jul 60	● WHEN WILL I BE LOVED London HLA 9157 ......**4**	16 wks
22 Sep 60	● LUCILLE / SO SAD (TO WATCH GOOD LOVE GO BAD) Warner Bros. WB 19 ......**4**	15 wks
15 Dec 60	LIKE STRANGERS London HLA 9250 ......**11**	10 wks
9 Feb 61	★ WALK RIGHT BACK / EBONY EYES Warner Bros. WB 33 ......**1**	16 wks
15 Jun 61	★ TEMPTATION Warner Bros. WB 42 ......**1**	15 wks
5 Oct 61	MUSKRAT / DON'T BLAME ME Warner Bros. WB 50 ......**20**	6 wks
18 Jan 62	● CRYIN' IN THE RAIN Warner Bros. WB 56 ......**6**	15 wks
17 May 62	HOW CAN I MEET HER Warner Bros. WB 67 ....**12**	10 wks
25 Oct 62	NO ONE CAN MAKE MY SUNSHINE SMILE Warner Bros. WB 79 ......**11**	11 wks
21 Mar 63	SO IT WILL ALWAYS BE Warner Bros. WB 94 ....**23**	11 wks
13 Jun 63	IT'S BEEN NICE Warner Bros. WB 99 ......**26**	5 wks
17 Oct 63	THE GIRL SANG THE BLUES Warner Bros. WB 109 ..**25**	9 wks
16 Jul 64	FERRIS WHEEL Warner Bros. WB 135 ......**22**	10 wks
3 Dec 64	GONE GONE GONE Warner Bros. WB 146 ......**36**	7 wks
6 May 65	THAT'LL BE THE DAY Warner Bros. WB 158 ......**30**	4 wks
20 May 65	● THE PRICE OF LOVE Warner Bros. WB 161 ......**2**	14 wks
26 Aug 65	I'LL NEVER GET OVER YOU Warner Bros. WB 5639 ......**35**	5 wks
21 Oct 65	LOVE IS STRANGE Warner Bros. WB 5649 ......**11**	9 wks
8 May 68	IT'S MY TIME Warner Bros. WB 7192 ......**39**	6 wks
22 Sep 84	ON THE WINGS OF A NIGHTINGALE Mercury MER 170 ......**41**	9 wks

All I Have To Do Is Dream was listed without Claudette for its first week on the chart, but from 30 May 58 both sides were charted for 20 more weeks. See also Phil Everly.

EVERTON 1985 *UK, male football team vocalists* **5 wks**

11 May 85	HERE WE GO Columbia DB 9106 ......**14**	5 wks

EVERYTHING BUT THE GIRL
UK, male / female vocal / instrumental duo **46 wks**

12 May 84	EACH AND EVERYONE blanco y negro NEG 1 ....**28**	7 wks
21 Jul 84	MINE blanco y negro NEG 3 ......**58**	2 wks
6 Oct 84	NATIVE LAND blanco y negro NEG 6 ......**73**	2 wks
2 Aug 86	COME ON HOME blanco y negro NEG 21 ......**44**	7 wks
11 Oct 86	DON'T LEAVE ME BEHIND blanco y negro NEG 23 ..**72**	2 wks
13 Feb 88	THESE EARLY DAYS blanco y negro NEG 30 ....**75**	1 wk
9 Jul 88	● I DON'T WANT TO TALK ABOUT IT blanco y negro NEG 34 ......**3**	9 wks
27 Jan 90	DRIVING blanco y negro NEG 40 ......**54**	2 wks

The **EVERLY BROTHERS**, Don and Phil, had at least one top two hit for five consecutive years. (LFI)

22 Feb 92	**COVERS EP** blanco y negro NEG 54 ....**13**	6 wks
24 Apr 93	**THE ONLY LIVING BOY IN NEW YORK (EP)**	
	blanco y negro NEG 62CD **42**	5 wks
19 Jun 93	**I DIDN'T KNOW I WAS LOOKING FOR LOVE (EP)**	
	blanco y negro NEG 64CD **72**	1 wk
4 Jun 94	**ROLLERCOASTER (EP)** blanco y negro NEG 69CD **65**	1 wk
20 Aug 94	**MISSING** blanco y negro NEG 71CD1 ....**69**	1 wk

Tracks on Covers EP: Love Is Strange / Tougher Than The Rest / Time After Time / Alison. Tracks on The Only Living Boy In New York (EP): The Only Living Boy In New York / Birds / Gabriel / Horses In The Room. Tracks on I Didn't Know I Was Looking For Love (EP): I Didn't Know I Was Looking For Love / My Head Is My Only House Unless It Rains / Political Science / A Piece Of My Mind. Tracks on Rollercoaster (EP): Rollercoaster / Straight Back To You / Lights Of Te Towan / I Didn't Know I Was Looking For Love. The two versions of I Didn't Know I was Looking For Love are different.

EVOLUTION *UK, male / female vocal / instrumental group* **10 wks**

20 Mar 93	**LOVE THING** Deconstruction 74321134272 ....**32**	2 wks
3 Jul 93	**EVERYBODY DANCE** Deconstruction 74321152012 ..**19**	5 wks
8 Jan 94	**EVOLUTIONDANCE PART 1 EP**	
	Deconstruction 74321171912 ....**52**	3 wks

Tracks on Evolutiondance Part 1 EP: Escape 2 Alcatraz / Everybody / Don't Stop The Rain.

EX PISTOLS *UK, male vocal / instrumental group* **2 wks**

| 2 Feb 85 | **LAND OF HOPE AND GLORY** Virginia PISTOL 76......**69** | 2 wks |

EXCITERS *US, male / female vocal group* **7 wks**

| 21 Feb 63 | **TELL HIM** United Artists UP 1011 ....**46** | 1 wk |
| 4 Oct 75 | **REACHING FOR THE BEST** 20th Century BTC 1005 ..**31** | 6 wks |

EXETER BRAMDEAN BOY'S CHOIR
UK, male choir **3 wks**

| 18 Dec 93 | **REMEMBERING CHRISTMAS** | |
| | Golden Sounds DSCC 1 ....**46** | 3 wks |

EXILE *US, male vocal / instrumental group* **18 wks**

19 Aug 78 ●	**KISS YOU ALL OVER** RAK 279 ....**6**	12 wks
12 May 79	**HOW COULD THIS GO WRONG** RAK 293 ....**67**	2 wks
12 Sep 81	**HEART AND SOUL** RAK 333 ....**54**	4 wks

EXOTERIX *UK, male producer - Duncan Millar* **2 wks**

| 24 Apr 93 | **VOID** Positiva CDTIV 1 ....**58** | 1 wk |
| 5 Feb 94 | **SATISFY MY LOVE** Union UCRCD 26 ....**62** | 1 wk |

EXPLOITED *UK, male vocal / instrumental group* **13 wks**

18 Apr 81	**DOGS OF WAR** Secret SHH 110 ....**63**	4 wks
17 Oct 81	**DEAD CITIES** Secret SHH 120 ....**31**	5 wks
5 Dec 81	**DON'T LET 'EM GRIND YOU DOWN**	
	Superville EXP 1003 [1] **70**	1 wk
8 May 82	**ATTACK** Secret SHH 130 ....**50**	3 wks

[1] Exploited and Anti-Pasti

EXPOSÉ *US, female vocal group* **1 wk**

| 28 Aug 93 | **I'LL NEVER GET OVER YOU (GETTING OVER ME)** | |
| | Arista 74321158962 ....**75** | 1 wk |

EXPRESSOS *UK, male / female vocal / instrumental group* **5 wks**

| 21 Jun 80 | **HEY GIRL** WEA K 18246 ....**60** | 3 wks |
| 14 Mar 81 | **TANGO IN MONO** WEA K 18431 ....**70** | 2 wks |

EXTENSIVE - *See CHOPS-EMC + EXTENSIVE*

EXTREME *US, male vocal / instrumental group* **45 wks**

8 Jun 91	**GET THE FUNK OUT** A & M AM 737 ....**19**	7 wks
27 Jul 91 ●	**MORE THAN WORDS** A & M AM 792 ....**2**	11 wks
12 Oct 91	**DECADENCE DANCE** A & M AM 773 ....**36**	3 wks
23 Nov 91	**HOLE HEARTED** A & M AM 839 ....**12**	7 wks
2 May 92	**SONG FOR LOVE** A & M AM 698 ....**12**	6 wks
5 Sep 92	**REST IN PEACE** A & M AM 0055 ....**13**	5 wks
14 Nov 92	**STOP THE WORLD** A & M AM 0096 ....**22**	2 wks
6 Feb 93	**TRAGIC COMIC** A & M AMCD 0156 ....**15**	4 wks

E.Y.C. *US, male vocal group* **30 wks**

11 Dec 93	**FEELIN' ALRIGHT** MCA MCSTD 1952 ....**16**	8 wks
5 Mar 94	**THE WAY YOU WORK IT** MCA MCSTD 1963 ....**14**	7 wks
14 May 94	**NUMBER ONE** MCA MCSTD 1976 ....**27**	5 wks
30 Jul 94	**BLACK BOOK** MCA MCSTD 1987 ....**13**	6 wks
10 Dec 94	**ONE MORE CHANCE** MCA MCSTD 2025 ....**25†**	4 wks

E-ZEE POSSEE
UK, male / female vocal / instrumental group **16 wks**

26 Aug 89	**EVERYTHING STARTS WITH AN 'E'**	
	More Protein PROT 1 ....**69**	1 wk
20 Jan 90	**LOVE ON LOVE** More Protein PROT 3 ....**59**	3 wks
17 Mar 90	**EVERYTHING STARTS WITH AN 'E' (re-entry)**	
	More Protein PROT 1 ....**15**	8 wks
30 Jun 90	**THE SUN MACHINE** More Protein PROT 4 ....**62**	3 wks
21 Sep 91	**BREATHING IS E-ZEE** More Protein PROT 12 [1] **72**	1 wk

[1] E-Zee Possee featuring Tara Newley

FAB *UK, male producers* **11 wks**

7 Jul 90 ●	**THUNDERBIRDS ARE GO**	
	Brothers Organisation FAB 1 [1] **5**	8 wks
20 Oct 90	**THE PRISONER** Brothers Organisation FAB 6 [2] **56**	2 wks
1 Dec 90	**THE STINGRAY MEGAMIX**	
	Brothers Organisation FAB 2 [3] **66**	1 wk

[1] FAB featuring MC Parker [2] FAB featuring MC Number 6 [3] FAB featuring Aqua Marina

Shelley FABARES *US, female vocalist* **4 wks**

| 26 Apr 62 | **JOHNNY ANGEL** Pye International 7N 25132 ....**41** | 4 wks |

FABIAN *US, male vocalist* **1 wk**

| 10 Mar 60 | **HOUND DOG MAN** HMV POP 695 ....**46** | 1 wk |

FACES *UK, male vocal / instrumental group* **46 wks**

18 Dec 71 ●	**STAY WITH ME** Warner Bros. K 16136 ....**6**	14 wks
17 Feb 73 ●	**CINDY INCIDENTALLY** Warner Bros. K 16247 ....**2**	9 wks
8 Dec 73 ●	**POOL HALL RICHARD / I WISH IT WOULD RAIN**	
	Warner Bros. K 16341.................................**8**	11 wks
7 Dec 74	**YOU CAN MAKE ME DANCE SING OR ANYTHING**	
	Warner Bros. K 16494 [1] **12**	9 wks
4 Jun 77	**THE FACES EP** Riva 8 ....**41**	3 wks

[1] Rod Stewart and the Faces

Tracks on The Faces EP: Memphis / You Can Make Me Dance Sing Or Anything / Stay With Me / Cindy Incidentally.

Donald FAGEN *US, male vocalist* — **2 wks**

3 Jul 93	**TOMORROW'S GIRLS** *Reprise W 0180CDX* **46**	2 wks

Joe FAGIN *UK, male vocalist* — **20 wks**

7 Jan 84	● **THAT'S LIVIN' ALRIGHT** *Towerbell TOW 46* **3**	11 wks
5 Apr 86	**BACK WITH THE BOYS AGAIN / GET IT RIGHT** *Towerbell TOW 84* **53**	9 wks

Yvonne FAIR *US, female vocalist* — **11 wks**

24 Jan 76	● **IT SHOULD HAVE BEEN ME** *Tamla Motown TMG 1013* **5**	11 wks

FAIR WEATHER *UK, male vocal / instrumental group* — **12 wks**

18 Jul 70	● **NATURAL SINNER** *RCA 1977* **6**	12 wks

Fair Weather is led by Andy Fairweather-Low.

FAIRGROUND ATTRACTION
UK, female / male vocal / instrumental group — **27 wks**

16 Apr 88	★ **PERFECT** *RCA PB 41845* **1**	13 wks
30 Jul 88	● **FIND MY LOVE** *RCA PB 42079* **7**	10 wks
19 Nov 88	**A SMILE IN A WHISPER** *RCA PB 42249*.................**75**	1 wk
28 Jan 89	**CLARE** *RCA PB 42607*...**49**	3 wks

FAIRPORT CONVENTION
UK, male / female vocal / instrumental group — **9 wks**

23 Jul 69	**SI TU DOIS PARTIR** *Island WIP 6064* **21**	8 wks
27 Sep 69	**SI TU DOIS PARTIR (re-entry)** *Island WIP 6064* **49**	1 wk

Andy FAIRWEATHER-LOW *UK, male vocalist* — **18 wks**

21 Sep 74	● **REGGAE TUNE** *A & M AMS 7129* **10**	8 wks
6 Dec 75	● **WIDE EYED AND LEGLESS** *A & M AMS 7202* **6**	10 wks

Adam FAITH *UK, male vocalist* — **251 wks**

20 Nov 59	★ **WHAT DO YOU WANT** *Parlophone R 4591* **1**	19 wks
22 Jan 60	★ **POOR ME** *Parlophone R 4623* **1**	17 wks
14 Apr 60	● **SOMEONE ELSE'S BABY** *Parlophone R 4643* **2**	13 wks
30 Jun 60	● **WHEN JOHNNY COMES MARCHING HOME / MADE YOU** *Parlophone R 4665* **5**	13 wks
15 Sep 60	● **HOW ABOUT THAT** *Parlophone R 4689* **4**	14 wks
17 Nov 60	● **LONELY PUP (IN A CHRISTMAS SHOP)** *Parlophone R 4708* **4**	11 wks
9 Feb 61	● **WHO AM I / THIS IS IT!** *Parlophone R 4735* **5**	14 wks
27 Apr 61	**EASY GOING ME** *Parlophone R 4766* **12**	10 wks
20 Jul 61	**DON'T YOU KNOW IT** *Parlophone R 4807* **12**	10 wks
26 Oct 61	● **THE TIME HAS COME** *Parlophone R 4837* **4**	14 wks
18 Jan 62	**LONESOME** *Parlophone R 4864* **12**	9 wks
3 May 62	● **AS YOU LIKE IT** *Parlophone R 4896* **5**	15 wks
30 Aug 62	● **DON'T THAT BEAT ALL** *Parlophone R 4930* **8**	11 wks
13 Dec 62	**BABY TAKE A BOW** *Parlophone R 4964* **22**	6 wks
31 Jan 63	**WHAT NOW** *Parlophone R 4990* **31**	5 wks
11 Jul 63	**WALKIN' TALL** *Parlophone R 5039* **23**	6 wks
19 Sep 63	● **THE FIRST TIME** *Parlophone R 5061* [1] **5**	13 wks
12 Dec 63	**WE ARE IN LOVE** *Parlophone R 5091* [1] **11**	12 wks
12 Mar 64	**IF HE TELLS YOU** *Parlophone R 5109* [1] **25**	9 wks
28 May 64	**I LOVE BEING IN LOVE WITH YOU** *Parlophone R 5138* [1] **33**	6 wks
26 Nov 64	**MESSAGE TO MARTHA (KENTUCKY BLUEBIRD)** *Parlophone R 5201* **12**	11 wks
11 Feb 65	**STOP FEELING SORRY FOR YOURSELF** *Parlophone R 5235* **23**	6 wks
17 Jun 65	**SOMEONE'S TAKEN MARIA AWAY** *Parlophone R 5289* **34**	5 wks
20 Oct 66	**CHERYL'S GOIN' HOME** *Parlophone R 5516*............**46**	2 wks

[1] Adam Faith and the Roulettes

Horace FAITH *Jamaica, male vocalist* — **10 wks**

12 Sep 70	**BLACK PEARL** *Trojan TR 7790* **13**	10 wks

Percy FAITH *Canada, orchestra* — **30 wks**

10 Mar 60	● **THEME FROM 'A SUMMER PLACE'** *Philips PB 989* **2**	30 wks

FAITH BROTHERS *UK, male vocal / instrumental group* — **6 wks**

13 Apr 85	**THE COUNTRY OF THE BLIND** *Siren SIREN 2* **63**	3 wks
6 Jul 85	**A STRANGER ON HOME GROUND** *Siren SIREN 4* **69**	3 wks

FAITH, HOPE and CHARITY
US, male / female vocal group — **4 wks**

31 Jan 76	**JUST ONE LOOK** *RCA 2632*..................................**38**	4 wks

FAITH, HOPE and CHARITY
UK, female vocal group — **3 wks**

23 Jun 90	**BATTLE OF THE SEXES** *WEA YZ 480* **53**	3 wks

FAITH NO MORE *US, male vocal / instrumental group* — **46 wks**

6 Feb 88	**WE CARE A LOT** *Slash LASH 17* **53**	3 wks
10 Feb 90	**EPIC** *Slash LASH 21* **37**	4 wks
14 Apr 90	**FROM OUT OF NOWHERE** *Slash LASH 24* **23**	6 wks
14 Jul 90	**FALLING TO PIECES** *Slash LASH 25* **41**	3 wks
8 Sep 90	**EPIC (re-issue)** *Slash LASH 26* **25**	5 wks
6 Jun 92	● **MIDLIFE CRISIS** *Slash LASH 37*.........................**10**	5 wks
15 Aug 92	**A SMALL VICTORY** *Slash LASH 39* **29**	5 wks
12 Sep 92	**A SMALL VICTORY (re-mix)** *Slash LASHX 40*...........**55**	1 wk
21 Nov 92	**EVERYTHING'S RUINED** *Slash LASH 43* **28**	3 wks
16 Jan 93	● **I'M EASY / BE AGGRESSIVE** *Slash LACDP 44* **3**	7 wks
13 Mar 93	**I'M EASY / BE AGGRESSIVE (re-entry)** *Slash LACDP 44* **75**	1 wk
6 Nov 93	**ANOTHER BODY MURDERED** *Epic 6597942* [1] **26**	3 wks

[1] Faith No More & Boo-Yaa T.R.I.B.E.

Marianne FAITHFULL *UK, female vocalist* — **59 wks**

13 Aug 64	● **AS TEARS GO BY** *Decca F 11923* **9**	13 wks
18 Feb 65	● **COME AND STAY WITH ME** *Decca F 12075* **4**	13 wks
6 May 65	● **THIS LITTLE BIRD** *Decca F 12162* **6**	11 wks
22 Jul 65	● **SUMMER NIGHTS** *Decca F 12193* **10**	10 wks
4 Nov 65	**YESTERDAY** *Decca F 12268*..................................**36**	4 wks
9 Mar 67	**IS THIS WHAT I GET FOR LOVING YOU** *Decca F 22524* **43**	2 wks
24 Nov 79	**THE BALLAD OF LUCY JORDAN** *Island WIP 6491* **48**	6 wks

FALCO *Austria, male vocalist* — **26 wks**

22 Mar 86	★ **ROCK ME AMADEUS** *A & M AM 278* **1**	15 wks
31 May 86	● **VIENNA CALLING** *A & M AM 318* **10**	8 wks
2 Aug 86	**JEANNY** *A & M AM 333* **68**	1 wk
27 Sep 86	**THE SOUND OF MUSIK** *WEA U 8591* **61**	2 wks

FALL
UK, male vocalist / multi-instrumentalist – Mark E. Smith — **23 wks**

13 Sep 86	**MR. PHARMACIST** *Beggars Banquet BEG 168* **75**	1 wk
20 Dec 86	**HEY! LUCIANI** *Beggars Banquet BEG 176* **59**	1 wk
9 May 87	**THERE'S A GHOST IN MY HOUSE** *Beggars Banquet BEG 187* **30**	4 wks
31 Oct 87	**HIT THE NORTH** *Beggars Banquet BEG 200* **57**	5 wks
30 Jan 88	**VICTORIA** *Beggars Banquet BEG 206*......................**35**	3 wks
26 Nov 88	**BIG NEW PRINZ / JERUSALEM (DOUBLE SINGLE)** *Beggars Banquet FALL 2/3* **59**	2 wks
27 Jan 90	**TELEPHONE THING** *Cog Sinister SIN 4* **58**	1 wk
8 Sep 90	**WHITE LIGHTNING** *Cog Sinister SIN 6* **56**	2 wks
14 Mar 92	**FREE RANGE** *Cog Sinister SINS 8* **40**	1 wk

17 Apr 93	**WHY ARE PEOPLE GRUDGEFUL**		
	Permanent CDSPERM 9	**43**	1 wk
25 Dec 93	**BEHIND THE COUNTER** *Permanent CDSPERM 13*	**75**	1 wk
30 Apr 94	**15 WAYS** *Permanent CDSPERM 14*	**65**	1 wk

Tracks on Big New Prinz / Jerusalem *double single:* Big New Prinz / Wrong Place Right Time Number Two / Jerusalem / Acid Priest 2088.

Harold FALTERMEYER
Germany, male instrumentalist - keyboards **23 wks**

23 Mar 85	**AXEL F** *MCA MCA 949*	**62**	4 wks
1 Jun 85	● **AXEL F (re-entry)** *MCA MCA 949*	**2**	18 wks
24 Aug 85	**FLETCH THEME** *MCA MCA 991*	**74**	1 wk

Agnetha FALTSKOG *Sweden, female vocalist* **12 wks**

28 May 83	**THE HEAT IS ON** *Epic A 3436*	**35**	6 wks
13 Aug 83	**WRAP YOUR ARMS AROUND ME** *Epic A 3622*	**44**	5 wks
22 Oct 83	**CAN'T SHAKE LOOSE** *Epic A 3812*	**63**	1 wk

Georgie FAME *UK, male vocalist* **115 wks**

17 Dec 64	★ **YEH YEH** *Columbia DB 7428* [1]	**1**	12 wks
4 Mar 65	**IN THE MEANTIME** *Columbia DB 7494* [1]	**22**	8 wks
29 Jul 65	**LIKE WE USED TO BE** *Columbia DB 7633* [1]	**33**	7 wks
28 Oct 65	**SOMETHING** *Columbia DB 7727* [1]	**23**	7 wks
23 Jun 66	★ **GET AWAY** *Columbia DB 7946* [1]	**1**	11 wks
22 Sep 66	**SUNNY** *Columbia DB 8015*	**13**	8 wks
22 Dec 66	**SITTING IN THE PARK** *Columbia DB 8096* [1]	**12**	10 wks
23 Mar 67	**BECAUSE I LOVE YOU** *CBS 202587*	**15**	8 wks
13 Sep 67	**TRY MY WORLD** *CBS 2945*	**37**	5 wks
13 Dec 67	★ **BALLAD OF BONNIE AND CLYDE** *CBS 3124*	**1**	13 wks
9 Jul 69	**PEACEFUL** *CBS 4295*	**16**	9 wks
13 Dec 69	**SEVENTH SON** *CBS 4659*	**25**	7 wks
10 Apr 71	**ROSETTA** *CBS 7108* [2]	**11**	10 wks

[1] Georgie Fame and the Blue Flames [2] Fame and Price Together

FAMILY *UK, male vocal / instrumental group* **44 wks**

1 Nov 69	**NO MULE'S FOOL** *Reprise RS 27001*	**29**	7 wks
22 Aug 70	**STRANGE BAND** *Reprise RS 27009*	**11**	12 wks
17 Jul 71	● **IN MY OWN TIME** *Reprise K 14090*	**4**	13 wks
23 Sep 72	**BURLESQUE** *Reprise K 14196*	**13**	12 wks

FAMILY CAT *UK, male vocal / instrumental group* **4 wks**

28 Aug 93	**AIRPLANE GARDENS / ATMOSPHERIC ROAD**		
	Dedicated FCUK 003CD	**69**	1 wk
21 May 94	**WONDERFUL EXCUSE** *Dedicated 74321208432*	**48**	1 wk
30 Jul 94	**GOLDENBOOK** *Dedicated 74321220072*	**42**	2 wks

FAMILY COOKIN' - *See* LIMMIE *and the* FAMILY COOKIN'

FAMILY DOGG *UK, male / female vocal group* **14 wks**

| 28 May 69 | ● **WAY OF LIFE** *Bell 1055* | **6** | 14 wks |

FAMILY FOUNDATION
UK, male / female vocal / instrumental group **4 wks**

| 13 Jun 92 | **XPRESS YOURSELF** *380 PEW 1* | **42** | 4 wks |

FAMILY STAND
US, male / female vocal / instrumental group **11 wks**

| 31 Mar 90 | ● **GHETTO HEAVEN** *East West A 7997* | **10** | 11 wks |

FAMILY STONE - *See* SLY *and the* FAMILY STONE

FAMOUS FLAMES - *See* James BROWN

FANTASTIC FOUR *US, male vocal group* **4 wks**

| 24 Feb 79 | **B.Y.O.F. (BRING YOUR OWN FUNK)** *Atlantic LV 14* | **62** | 4 wks |

FANTASTICS *US, male vocal group* **12 wks**

| 27 Mar 71 | ● **SOMETHING OLD, SOMETHING NEW** *Bell 1141* | **9** | 12 wks |

FANTASY UFO *UK, male instrumental group* **6 wks**

| 29 Sep 90 | **FANTASY** *XL XLT 15* | **56** | 3 wks |
| 10 Aug 91 | **MIND BODY SOUL** *Strictly Underground YZ 591* [1] | **50** | 3 wks |

[1] Fantasy UFO featuring Jay Groove

FAR CORPORATION
UK / US / Germany / Switzerland, male vocal / instrumental group **11 wks**

| 26 Oct 85 | ● **STAIRWAY TO HEAVEN** *Arista ARIST 639* | **8** | 11 wks |

Don FARDON *UK, male vocalist* **22 wks**

| 18 Apr 70 | **BELFAST BOY** *Young Blood YB 1010* | **32** | 5 wks |
| 10 Oct 70 | ● **INDIAN RESERVATION** *Young Blood YB 1015* | **3** | 17 wks |

FARGETTA and Anne-Marie SMITH
Italy / US, male / female vocal / instrumental duo **2 wks**

| 23 Jan 93 | **MUSIC** *Synthetic CDR 6334* | **34** | 2 wks |

Chris FARLOWE *UK, male vocalist* **36 wks**

27 Jan 66	**THINK** *Immediate IM 023*	**49**	1 wk
10 Feb 66	**THINK (re-entry)** *Immediate IM 023*	**37**	2 wks
23 Jun 66	★ **OUT OF TIME** *Immediate IM 035*	**1**	13 wks
27 Oct 66	**RIDE ON BABY** *Immediate IM 038*	**31**	7 wks
16 Feb 67	**MY WAY OF GIVING IN** *Immediate IM 041*	**48**	1 wk
29 Jun 67	**MOANIN'** *Immediate IM 056*	**46**	2 wks
13 Dec 67	**HANDBAGS AND GLADRAGS** *Immediate IM 065*	**33**	6 wks
27 Sep 75	**OUT OF TIME (re-issue)** *Immediate IMS 101*	**44**	4 wks

FARM *UK, male vocal / instrumental group* **54 wks**

5 May 90	**STEPPING STONE / FAMILY OF MAN**		
	Produce MILK 101	**58**	4 wks
1 Sep 90	● **GROOVY TRAIN** *Produce MILK 102*	**6**	10 wks
8 Dec 90	● **ALL TOGETHER NOW** *Produce MILK 103*	**4**	12 wks
13 Apr 91	**SINFUL!** *Siren SRN 138* [1]	**28**	5 wks
4 May 91	**DON'T LET ME DOWN** *Produce MILK 104*	**36**	3 wks
24 Aug 91	**MIND** *Produce MILK 105*	**31**	4 wks
14 Dec 91	**LOVE SEE NO COLOUR** *Produce MILK 106*	**58**	4 wks
4 Jul 92	**RISING SUN** *End Product 6581737*	**48**	3 wks
17 Oct 92	**DON'T YOU WANT ME** *End Product 6584687*	**18**	5 wks
2 Jan 93	**LOVE SEE NO COLOUR (re-issue)**		
	End Product 6588682	**35**	4 wks

[1] Pete Wylie with the Farm

FARMERS BOYS *UK, male vocal / instrumental group* **17 wks**

9 Apr 83	**MUCK IT OUT** *EMI 5380*	**48**	6 wks
30 Jul 83	**FOR YOU** *EMI 5401*	**66**	3 wks
4 Aug 84	**IN THE COUNTRY** *EMI FAB 2*	**44**	5 wks
3 Nov 84	**PHEW WOW** *EMI FAB 3*	**59**	3 wks

John FARNHAM *Australia, male vocalist* **17 wks**

| 25 Apr 87 | ● **YOU'RE THE VOICE** *Wheatley PB 41093* | **6** | 17 wks |

Joe FARRELL *US, male instrumentalist - saxophone* **4 wks**

| 16 Dec 78 | **NIGHT DANCING** *Warner Bros. LV 2* | **57** | 4 wks |

Gene FARROW and G.F. BAND
UK, male vocal / instrumental group **8 wks**

1 Apr 78	**MOVE YOUR BODY** *Magnet MAG 109* **33**	5 wks
13 May 78	**MOVE YOUR BODY (re-entry)** *Magnet MAG 109*....**67**	1 wk
5 Aug 78	**DON'T STOP NOW** *Magnet MAG 125* **71**	1 wk
19 Aug 78	**DON'T STOP NOW (re-entry)** *Magnet MAG 125*......**74**	1 wk

FASCINATIONS *US, female vocal group* **6 wks**

3 Jul 71	**GIRLS ARE OUT TO GET YOU** *Mojo 2092 004* **32**	6 wks

FASHION *UK, male vocal / instrumental group* **12 wks**

3 Apr 82	**STREETPLAYER (MECHANIK)** *Arista ARIST 456* **46**	5 wks
21 Aug 82	**LOVE SHADOW** *Arista ARIST 483*....................**51**	5 wks
18 Feb 84	**EYE TALK** *De Stijl A 4106* **69**	2 wks

Susan FASSBENDER *UK, female vocalist* **8 wks**

17 Jan 81	**TWILIGHT CAFE** *CBS 9468* **21**	8 wks

FASTWAY *UK, male vocal / instrumental group* **1 wk**

2 Apr 83	**EASY LIVIN'** *CBS A 3196* **74**	1 wk

FAT BOYS *US, male vocal rap group* **29 wks**

4 May 85	**JAIL HOUSE RAP** *Sultra U 9123* **63**	2 wks
22 Aug 87	● **WIPEOUT** *Urban URB 5* [1] **2**	12 wks
18 Jun 88	● **THE TWIST (YO, TWIST)** *Urban URB 20* [2] **2**	11 wks
5 Nov 88	**LOUIE LOUIE** *Urban URB 26* **46**	4 wks

[1] Fat Boys and the Beach Boys [2] Fat Boys and Chubby Checker

FAT LADY SINGS
Ireland, male vocal / instrumental group **2 wks**

17 Jul 93	**DRUNKARD LOGIC** *East West YZ 756CD*....................**56**	2 wks

FAT LARRY'S BAND
US, male vocal / instrumental group **26 wks**

2 Jul 77	**CENTER CITY** *Atlantic K 10951*....................**31**	5 wks
10 Mar 79	**BOOGIE TOWN** *Fantasy FTC 168* [1] **46**	4 wks
18 Aug 79	**LOOKING FOR LOVE TONIGHT** *Fantasy FTC 179* **46**	6 wks
18 Sep 82	● **ZOOM** *Virgin VS 546* **2**	11 wks

[1] F.L.B.

FATBACK BAND *US, male vocal / instrumental group* **67 wks**

6 Sep 75	**YUM YUM (GIMME SOME)** *Polydor 2066 590*..........**40**	6 wks
6 Dec 75	**(ARE YOU READY) DO THE BUS STOP** *Polydor 2066 637* **18**	10 wks
21 Feb 76	● **(DO THE) SPANISH HUSTLE** *Polydor 2066 656*..........**10**	7 wks
29 May 76	**PARTY TIME** *Polydor 2066 682* **41**	4 wks
14 Aug 76	**NIGHT FEVER** *Spring 2066 706* **38**	4 wks
12 Mar 77	**DOUBLE DUTCH** *Spring 2066 777* **31**	4 wks
9 Aug 80	**BACKSTROKIN'** *Spring POSP 149* [1] **41**	9 wks
23 Jun 84	**I FOUND LOVIN'** *Master Mix CHE 8401* **49**	4 wks
4 May 85	**GIRLS ON MY MIND** *Atlantic/Cotillion FBACK 1* [1] ..**69**	12 wks
6 Sep 86	**I FOUND LOVIN' (re-mix)** *Important TAN 10*............**55**	5 wks
5 Sep 87	● **I FOUND LOVIN' (re-entry)** *Master Mix CHE 8401* **7**	12 wks

[1] Fatback

FATHER ABRAHAM and the SMURFS
Holland, male vocalist as himself and Smurfs **36 wks**

3 Jun 78	● **THE SMURF SONG** *Decca F 13759* **2**	17 wks
30 Sep 78	**DIPPETY DAY** *Decca F 13798* **13**	12 wks
2 Dec 78	**CHRISTMAS IN SMURFLAND** *Decca F 13819* **19**	7 wks

---

FATHER ABRAPHART and the SMURPS - *See Jonathan KING*

FATIMA MANSIONS
Ireland, male vocal / instrumental group **11 wks**

23 May 92	**EVIL MAN** *Radioactive SKX 56* **59**	1 wk
1 Aug 92	**1000%** *Radioactive SKX 59* **61**	3 wks
19 Sep 92	● **(EVERYTHING I DO) I DO IT FOR YOU** *Columbia 6583827* **7**	6 wks
6 Aug 94	**THE LOYALISER** *Kitchenware SKCD 67* **58**	1 wk

(Everything I Do) I Do It For You was listed with Theme From M.A.S.H. (Suicide Is Painless) *by Manic Street Preachers.*

FBI - *See REDHEAD KINGPIN and the FBI*

Phil FEARON *UK, vocalist* **63 wks**

23 Apr 83	● **DANCING TIGHT** *Ensign ENY 501* [1] **4**	11 wks
30 Jul 83	**WAIT UNTIL TONIGHT (MY LOVE)** *Ensign ENY 503* [1] **20**	8 wks
22 Oct 83	**FANTASY REAL** *Ensign ENY 507* [2] **41**	6 wks
10 Mar 84	● **WHAT DO I DO** *Ensign ENY 510* [2] **5**	10 wks
14 Jul 84	● **EVERYBODY'S LAUGHING** *Ensign ENY 514* [2] **10**	10 wks
15 Jun 85	**YOU DON'T NEED A REASON** *Ensign ENY 517* [2] **42**	4 wks
27 Jul 85	**THIS KIND OF LOVE** *Ensign ENY 521* [3] **70**	3 wks
2 Aug 86	● **I CAN PROVE IT** *Ensign PF 1* **8**	9 wks
15 Nov 86	**AIN'T NOTHING BUT A HOUSEPARTY** *Ensign PF 2* ..**60**	2 wks

[1] Galaxy featuring Phil Fearon [2] Phil Fearon and Galaxy [3] Phil Fearon and Galaxy featuring Dee Galdes

Wilton FELDER *US, male instrumentalist - tenor sax* **7 wks**

1 Nov 80	**INHERIT THE WIND** *MCA 646*............................**39**	5 wks
16 Feb 85	**(NO MATTER HOW HIGH I GET) I'LL STILL BE LOOKIN' UP TO YOU** *MCA MCA 919*......................**63**	2 wks

Bobby Womack is the uncredited lead vocalist on both hits. Altrina Grayson co-vocalises on MCA 919.

José FELICIANO
US, male vocalist / instrumentalist - guitar **23 wks**

18 Sep 68	● **LIGHT MY FIRE** *RCA 1715*..**6**	16 wks
18 Oct 69	**AND THE SUN WILL SHINE** *RCA 1871*....................**25**	7 wks

FELIX *UK, male producer* **20 wks**

8 Aug 92	● **DON'T YOU WANT ME** *Deconstruction 74321110507* **6**	11 wks
24 Oct 92	**IT WILL MAKE ME CRAZY** *Deconstruction 74321118137* **11**	6 wks
22 May 93	**STARS** *Deconstruction 74321147102* **29**	3 wks

Julie FELIX *US, female vocalist* **19 wks**

18 Apr 70	**IF I COULD (EL CONDOR PASA)** *RAK 101* **19**	11 wks
17 Oct 70	**HEAVEN IS HERE** *RAK 105* **22**	8 wks

FELLY - *See TECHNOTRONIC*

FEMME FATALE
US, male / female vocal / instrumental group **2 wks**

11 Feb 89	**FALLING IN AND OUT OF LOVE** *MCA MCA 1309* **69**	2 wks

FENDERMEN *US, male vocal / instrumental duo - guitars* **9 wks**

18 Aug 60	**MULE SKINNER BLUES** *Top Rank JAR 395* **50**	1 wk
1 Sep 60	**MULE SKINNER BLUES (re-entry)** *Top Rank JAR 395* **37**	2 wks
29 Sep 60	**MULE SKINNER BLUES (2nd re-entry)** *Top Rank JAR 395* **32**	6 wks

ADAM FAITH is pictured with Millicent Martin of the television series *That Was The Week That Was*. (LFI)

For three decades, no disc jockey played the hits in this book more entertainingly than **KENNY EVERETT.** (Capital Radio)

It wasn't fair to **YVONNE FAIR** that Tamla Motown labelmates Gladys Knight And The Pips had the American hit version of 'It Should Have Been Me'.

FENMEN - See Bern ELLIOTT and the FENMEN

George FENTON and Jonas GWANGWA
UK / South Africa, male instrumental production duo   **1 wk**

2 Jan 88	**CRY FREEDOM** MCA MCA 1228	**75**	1 wk

The listed flip side of Cry Freedom was The Funeral by Thuli Dumakude.

Peter FENTON *UK, male vocalist*   **3 wks**

10 Nov 66	**MARBLE BREAKS IRON BENDS** Fontana TF 748	**46**	3 wks

Shane FENTON and the FENTONES
UK, male vocal / instrumental group   **28 wks**

26 Oct 61	**I'M A MOODY GUY** Parlophone R 4827	**22**	8 wks
1 Feb 62	**WALK AWAY** Parlophone R 4866	**38**	5 wks
5 Apr 62	**IT'S ALL OVER NOW** Parlophone R 4883	**29**	7 wks
12 Jul 62	**CINDY'S BIRTHDAY** Parlophone R 4921	**19**	8 wks

Fenton later became Alvin Stardust.

FENTONES *UK, male instrumental group*   **4 wks**

19 Apr 62	**THE MEXICAN** Parlophone R 4899	**41**	3 wks
27 Sep 62	**THE BREEZE AND I** Parlophone R 4937	**48**	1 wk

Sheila FERGUSON *US, female vocalist*   **1 wk**

5 Feb 94	**WHEN WILL I SEE YOU AGAIN** XSrhythm CDSTAS 2711	**60**	1 wk

FERKO STRING BAND
US, male vocal / instrumental group   **2 wks**

12 Aug 55	**ALABAMA JUBILEE** London HL 8140	**20**	2 wks

Luisa FERNANDEZ *Spain, female vocalist*   **8 wks**

11 Nov 78	**LAY LOVE ON YOU** Warner Bros. K 17061	**31**	8 wks

Pamela FERNANDEZ *US, female vocalist*   **2 wks**

17 Sep 94	**KICKIN' IN THE BEAT** Ore AG 5CD	**43**	2 wks

FERRANTE and TEICHER
US, male instrumental duo - pianos   **18 wks**

18 Aug 60	**THEME FROM 'THE APARTMENT'** London HLT 916 4	**44**	1 wk
9 Mar 61	● **THEME FROM 'EXODUS'** London HLT 9298 and HMV POP 881	**6**	17 wks

Theme From 'Exodus' available first on London, then on HMV when the American label, United Artists, changed its UK outlet.

José FERRER *US, male vocalist*   **3 wks**

19 Feb 54	● **WOMAN** Philips PB 220	**7**	3 wks

Woman coupled with Man by Rosemary Clooney.

FERRY AID *International, male / female charity ensemble*   **7 wks**

4 Apr 87	★ **LET IT BE** The Sun AID 1	**1**	7 wks

Bryan FERRY *UK, male vocalist*   **132 wks**

29 Sep 73	● **A HARD RAIN'S GONNA FALL** Island WIP 6170	**10**	9 wks
25 May 74	**THE IN CROWD** Island WIP 6196	**13**	6 wks
31 Aug 74	**SMOKE GETS IN YOUR EYES** Island WIP 6205	**17**	8 wks
5 Jul 75	**YOU GO TO MY HEAD** Island WIP 6234	**33**	3 wks
12 Jun 76	● **LET'S STICK TOGETHER** Island WIP 6307	**4**	10 wks
7 Aug 76	● **EXTENDED PLAY EP** Island IEP 1	**7**	9 wks
5 Feb 77	● **THIS IS TOMORROW** Polydor 2001 704	**9**	9 wks
14 May 77	**TOKYO JOE** Polydor 2001 711	**15**	7 wks
13 May 78	**WHAT GOES ON** Polydor POSP 3	**67**	2 wks
5 Aug 78	**SIGN OF THE TIMES** Polydor 2001 798	**37**	8 wks
11 May 85	● **SLAVE TO LOVE** EG FERRY 1	**10**	9 wks
31 Aug 85	**DON'T STOP THE DANCE** EG FERRY 2	**21**	7 wks
7 Dec 85	**WINDSWEPT** EG FERRY 3	**46**	3 wks
29 Mar 86	**IS YOUR LOVE STRONG ENOUGH?** EG FERRY 4	**22**	7 wks
10 Oct 87	**THE RIGHT STUFF** Virgin VS 940	**37**	6 wks
13 Feb 88	**KISS AND TELL** Virgin VS 1034	**41**	5 wks
29 Oct 88	**LET'S STICK TOGETHER (re-mix)** EG EGO 44	**12**	7 wks
11 Feb 89	**THE PRICE OF LOVE (re-mix)** EG EGO 46	**49**	3 wks
22 Apr 89	**HE'LL HAVE TO GO** EG EGO 48	**63**	1 wk
6 Mar 93	**I PUT A SPELL ON YOU** Virgin VSCDG 1400	**18**	5 wks
29 May 93	**WILL YOU LOVE ME TOMORROW** Virgin VSCDG 1455	**23**	5 wks
4 Sep 93	**GIRL OF MY BEST FRIEND** Virgin VSCDG 1488	**57**	2 wks
29 Oct 94	**YOUR PAINTED SMILE** Virgin VSCDG 1508	**52**	1 wk

Tracks on Extended Play EP: Price Of Love / Shame Shame Shame / Heart On My Sleeve / It's Only Love.

Lena FIAGBE *UK, female vocalist*   **11 wks**

24 Jul 93	**YOU COME FROM EARTH** Mother MUMCD 42 [1]	**69**	1 wk
23 Oct 93	**GOTTA GET IT RIGHT** Mother MUMCD 44	**20**	5 wks
16 Apr 94	**WHAT'S IT LIKE TO BE BEAUTIFUL** Mother MUMCD 49	**52**	3 wks
25 Jun 94	**VISIONS** Mother MUMCD 53	**48**	2 wks

[1] Lena

Karel FIALKA *UK, male vocalist / multi-instrumentalist*   **12 wks**

17 May 80	**THE EYES HAVE IT** Blueprint BLU 2005	**52**	4 wks
5 Sep 87	● **HEY MATTHEW** IRS IRM 140	**9**	8 wks

FIAT LUX *UK, male vocal / instrumental group*   **4 wks**

28 Jan 84	**SECRETS** Polydor FIAT 2	**65**	3 wks
17 Mar 84	**BLUE EMOTION** Polydor FIAT 3	**59**	1 wk

FICTION FACTORY
UK, male vocal / instrumental group   **11 wks**

14 Jan 84	● **(FEELS LIKE) HEAVEN** CBS A 3996	**6**	9 wks
17 Mar 84	**GHOST OF LOVE** CBS A 3819	**64**	2 wks

FIDDLER'S DRAM
UK, male / female vocal / instrumental group   **9 wks**

15 Dec 79	● **DAY TRIP TO BANGOR (DIDN'T WE HAVE A LOVELY TIME)** Dingles SID 211	**3**	9 wks

FIDELFATTI featuring RONNETTE
Italy, male producer and female vocalist   **1 wk**

27 Jan 90	**JUST WANNA TOUCH ME** Urban URB 46	**65**	1 wk

Billy FIELD *Australia, male vocalist*   **3 wks**

12 Jun 82	**YOU WEREN'T IN LOVE WITH ME** CBS A 2344	**67**	3 wks

Ernie FIELDS *US, orchestra*   **8 wks**

25 Dec 59	**IN THE MOOD** London HL 8985	**13**	8 wks

Gracie FIELDS *UK, female vocalist*   **15 wks**

31 May 57	● **AROUND THE WORLD** Columbia DB 3953	**8**	8 wks
2 Aug 57	**AROUND THE WORLD (re-entry)** Columbia DB 3953	**24**	1 wk

6 Nov 59	LITTLE DONKEY *Columbia DB 4360*	**30**	1 wk
20 Nov 59	LITTLE DONKEY (re-entry) *Columbia DB 4360*	**20**	5 wks

Richard 'Dimples' FIELDS *US, male vocalist*   **4 wks**

20 Feb 82	I'VE GOT TO LEARN TO SAY NO *Epic EPC A 1918*	**56**	4 wks

FIELDS OF THE NEPHILIM
UK, male vocal / instrumental group   **9 wks**

24 Oct 87	BLUE WATER *Situation Two SIT 48*	**75**	1 wk
4 Jun 88	MOONCHILD *Situation Two SIT 52*	**28**	3 wks
27 May 89	PSYCHONAUT *Situation Two ST 57*	**35**	3 wks
4 Aug 90	FOR HER LIGHT *Beggars Banquet BEG 244T*	**54**	1 wk
24 Nov 90	SUMERLAND (DREAMED) *Beggars Banquet BEG 250*	**37**	1 wk

FIFTH DIMENSION *US, male / female vocal group*   **21 wks**

16 Apr 69	AQUARIUS / LET THE SUNSHINE IN (MEDLEY) *Liberty LBF 15193*	**11**	12 wks
17 Jan 70	WEDDING BELL BLUES *Liberty LBF 15288*	**16**	9 wks

52ND STREET
UK, male / female vocal / instrumental group   **13 wks**

2 Nov 85	TELL ME (HOW IT FEELS) *10 TEN 74*	**54**	5 wks
11 Jan 86	YOU'RE MY LAST CHANCE *10 TEN 89*	**49**	4 wks
8 Mar 86	I CAN'T LET YOU GO *10 TEN 114*	**57**	4 wks

53RD AND THIRD - *See Jonathan KING*

FINAL CUT - *See TRUE FAITH with FINAL CUT*

FINE YOUNG CANNIBALS
UK, male vocal / instrumental group   **76 wks**

8 Jun 85	● JOHNNY COME HOME *London LON 68*	**8**	13 wks
9 Nov 85	BLUE *London LON 79*	**41**	6 wks
11 Jan 86	● SUSPICIOUS MINDS *London LON 82*	**8**	9 wks
12 Apr 86	FUNNY HOW LOVE IS *London LON 88*	**58**	4 wks
21 Mar 87	● EVER FALLEN IN LOVE *London LON 121*	**9**	10 wks
7 Jan 89	● SHE DRIVES ME CRAZY *London LON 199*	**5**	11 wks
15 Apr 89	● GOOD THING *London LON 218*	**7**	8 wks
19 Aug 89	DON'T LOOK BACK *London LON 220*	**34**	4 wks
18 Nov 89	I'M NOT THE MAN I USED TO BE *London LON 244*	**20**	8 wks
24 Feb 90	I'M NOT SATISFIED *London LON 252*	**46**	3 wks

FINITRIBE *UK, male instrumental / production duo*   **2 wks**

11 Jul 92	FOREVERGREEN *One Little Indian 74 TP12F*	**51**	1 wk
19 Nov 94	BRAND NEW *ffrr FCD 247*	**69**	1 wk

FINK BROTHERS *UK, male vocal / instrumental duo*   **4 wks**

9 Feb 85	MUTANTS IN MEGA CITY ONE *Zarjazz JAZZ 2*	**50**	4 wks

Micky FINN - *See URBAN SHAKEDOWN featuring Micky FINN*

Tim FINN *New Zealand, male vocalist*   **6 wks**

26 Jun 93	PERSUASION *Capitol 6592482*	**43**	3 wks
18 Sep 93	HIT THE GROUND RUNNING *Capitol CDCLS 694*	**50**	3 wks

Elisa FIORILLO *US, female vocalist*   **14 wks**

28 Nov 87	● WHO FOUND WHO *Chrysalis CHS JEL 1* [1]	**10**	10 wks
13 Feb 88	HOW CAN I FORGET YOU *Chrysalis ELISA 1*	**50**	4 wks

[1] Jellybean featuring Elisa Fiorillo

FIRE INC. - *See Jim STEINMAN*

FIRE ISLAND *UK, male instrumental / production group*   **4 wks**

8 Aug 92	IN YOUR BONES / FIRE ISLAND *Boys Own BOIX 11*	**66**	1 wk
12 Mar 94	THERE BUT FOR THE GRACE OF GOD *Junior Boy's Own JBO 18CD* [1]	**32**	3 wks

[1] Fire Island featuring Love Nelson

FIREBALLS *US, male instrumental group*   **17 wks**

27 Jul 61	QUITE A PARTY *Pye International 7N 25092*	**29**	9 wks
14 Nov 63	SUGAR SHACK *London HLD 9789* [1]	**45**	4 wks
19 Dec 63	SUGAR SHACK (re-entry) *London HLD 9789* [1]	**46**	4 wks

[1] Jimmy Gilmer and the Fireballs

FIREHOUSE *US, male vocal / instrumental group*   **2 wks**

13 Jul 91	DON'T TREAT ME BAD *Epic 6567807*	**71**	1 wk
19 Dec 92	WHEN I LOOK INTO YOUR EYES *Epic 6588347*	**65**	1 wk

FIRM *UK, male vocal / instrumental group*   **21 wks**

17 Jul 82	ARTHUR DALEY ('E'S ALRIGHT) *Bark HID 1*	**14**	9 wks
6 Jun 87	★ STAR TREKKIN' *Bark TREK 1*	**1**	12 wks

FIRST CHOICE *US, female vocal group*   **21 wks**

19 May 73	ARMED AND EXTREMELY DANGEROUS *Bell 1297*	**16**	10 wks
4 Aug 73	● SMARTY PANTS *Bell 1324*	**9**	11 wks

FIRST CLASS *UK, male vocal group*   **10 wks**

15 Jun 74	BEACH BABY *UK 66*	**13**	10 wks

FIRST EDITION - *See Kenny ROGERS*

FIRST LIGHT *UK, male vocal / instrumental duo*   **5 wks**

21 May 83	EXPLAIN THE REASONS *London LON 26*	**65**	3 wks
28 Jan 84	WISH YOU WERE HERE *London LON 43*	**71**	2 wks

FISCHER-Z *UK, male vocal / instrumental group*   **7 wks**

26 May 79	THE WORKER *United Artists UP 36509*	**53**	5 wks
3 May 80	SO LONG *United Artists BP 342*	**72**	2 wks

FISH *UK, male vocalist*   **19 wks**

18 Oct 86	SHORT CUT TO SOMEWHERE *Charisma CB 426* [1]	**75**	1 wk
28 Oct 89	STATE OF MIND *EMI EM 109*	**32**	3 wks
6 Jan 90	BIG WEDGE *EMI EM 125*	**25**	4 wks
17 Mar 90	A GENTLEMAN'S EXCUSE ME *EMI EM 135*	**30**	3 wks
28 Sep 91	INTERNAL EXILE *Polydor FISHY 1*	**37**	2 wks
11 Jan 92	CREDO *Polydor FISHY 2*	**38**	2 wks
4 Jul 92	SOMETHING IN THE AIR *Polydor FISHY 3*	**51**	2 wks
16 Apr 94	LADY LET IT LIE *Dick Bros. DDICK 3CD1*	**46**	1 wk
1 Oct 94	FORTUNES OF WAR *Dick Bros. DDICK 008CD1*	**67**	1 wk

[1] Fish and Tony Banks

FISHBONE *US, male vocal / instrumental group*   **3 wks**

1 Aug 92	EVERYDAY SUNSHINE / FIGHT THE YOUTH *Columbia 6581937*	**60**	2 wks
28 Aug 93	SWIM *Columbia 6596252*	**54**	1 wk

Eddie FISHER *US, male vocalist*   **105 wks**

2 Jan 53	★ OUTSIDE OF HEAVEN *HMV B 10362*	**1**	16 wks
23 Jan 53	EVERYTHING I HAVE IS YOURS *HMV B 10398*	**12**	1 wk

6 Feb 53	● **EVERYTHING I HAVE IS YOURS** (re-entry)	
	HMV B 10398 ....**8**	4 wks
1 May 53	● **DOWNHEARTED** HMV B 10450 ....**3**	15 wks
1 May 53	**OUTSIDE OF HEAVEN** (re-entry) HMV B 10362 ...**12**	1 wk
22 May 53	★ **I'M WALKING BEHIND YOU** HMV B 10489 [1] **1**	18 wks
6 Nov 53	● **WISH YOU WERE HERE** HMV B 10564 ....**8**	9 wks
22 Jan 54	**OH MY PAPA** HMV B 10614 ....**9**	1 wk
5 Feb 54	**OH MY PAPA** (re-entry) HMV B 10614 ....**11**	1 wk
26 Feb 54	● **OH MY PAPA** (2nd re-entry) HMV B 10614 ...**10**	1 wk
12 Mar 54	**OH MY PAPA** (3rd re-entry) HMV B 10614 ....**11**	1 wk
29 Oct 54	**I NEED YOU NOW** HMV B 10755 ....**16**	2 wks
19 Nov 54	**I NEED YOU NOW** (re-entry) HMV B 10755 ....**13**	7 wks
21 Jan 55	**I NEED YOU NOW** (2nd re-entry) HMV B 10755 ..**19**	1 wk
18 Mar 55	● **WEDDING BELLS** HMV B 10839 ....**5**	11 wks
23 Nov 56	● **CINDY OH CINDY** HMV POP 273 ....**5**	16 wks

[1] Eddie Fisher with Sally Sweetland (soprano)

Mark FISHER featuring Dotty GREEN
UK, male instrumentalist - keyboards and female vocalist **2 wks**

29 Jun 85	**LOVE SITUATION** Total Control TOCO 3 ....**59**	2 wks

Toni FISHER *US, female vocalist* **1 wk**

12 Feb 60	**THE BIG HURT** Top Rank JAR 261 ....**30**	1 wk

FITS OF GLOOM *UK / Italy, male vocal duo* **4 wks**

4 Jun 94	**HEAVEN** Media MCSTD 1981 ....**47**	2 wks
5 Nov 94	**THE POWER OF LOVE** Media MCSTD 2016 [1] **49**	2 wks

[1] Fits Of Gloom featuring Lizzy Mack

Ella FITZGERALD *US, female vocalist* **29 wks**

23 May 58	**SWINGIN' SHEPHERD BLUES** HMV POP 486 ....**15**	5 wks
16 Oct 59	**BUT NOT FOR ME** HMV POP 657 ....**25**	2 wks
25 Dec 59	**BUT NOT FOR ME** (re-entry) HMV POP 657.......**29**	1 wk
21 Apr 60	**MACK THE KNIFE** HMV POP 736 ....**19**	9 wks
6 Oct 60	**HOW HIGH THE MOON** HMV POP 782 ....**46**	1 wk
22 Nov 62	**DESAFINADO** Verve VS 502 ....**38**	4 wks
27 Dec 62	**DESAFINADO** (re-entry) Verve VS 502 ....**41**	2 wks
30 Apr 64	**CAN'T BUY ME LOVE** Verve VS 519 ....**34**	5 wks

Scott FITZGERALD *UK, male vocalist* **12 wks**

14 Jan 78	● **IF I HAD WORDS** Pepper UP 36333 [1] **3**	10 wks
7 May 88	**GO** PRT PYS 10 ....**52**	2 wks

[1] Scott Fitzgerald and Yvonne Keeley and the St Thomas More School Choir

FIVE SMITH BROTHERS *UK, male vocal group* **1 wk**

22 Jul 55	**I'M IN FAVOUR OF FRIENDSHIP** Decca F 10527 .....**20**	1 wk

FIVE STAR *UK, male / female vocal group* **140 wks**

4 May 85	**ALL FALL DOWN** Tent PB 40039 ....**15**	12 wks
20 Jul 85	**LET ME BE THE ONE** Tent PB 40193 ....**18**	9 wks
14 Sep 85	**LOVE TAKE OVER** Tent PB 40353 ....**25**	9 wks
16 Nov 85	**R.S.V.P.** Tent PB 40445 ....**45**	5 wks
11 Jan 86	● **SYSTEM ADDICT** Tent PB 40515 ....**3**	11 wks
12 Apr 86	● **CAN'T WAIT ANOTHER MINUTE** Tent PB 40697 ....**7**	10 wks
26 Jul 86	● **FIND THE TIME** Tent PB 40799 ....**7**	10 wks
13 Sep 86	● **RAIN OR SHINE** Tent PB 40901 ....**2**	11 wks
22 Nov 86	**IF I SAY YES** Tent PB 40981 ....**15**	9 wks
7 Feb 87	● **STAY OUT OF MY LIFE** Tent PB 41131 ....**9**	8 wks
18 Apr 87	● **THE SLIGHTEST TOUCH** Tent PB 41265 ....**4**	9 wks
22 Aug 87	**WHENEVER YOU'RE READY** Tent PB 41477...........**11**	6 wks
10 Oct 87	**STRONG AS STEEL** Tent PB 41565 ....**16**	7 wks
5 Dec 87	**SOMEWHERE SOMEBODY** Tent PB 41661 ....**23**	6 wks
4 Jun 88	**ANOTHER WEEKEND** Tent PB 42081 ....**18**	4 wks
6 Aug 88	**ROCK MY WORLD** Tent PB 42145 ....**28**	4 wks
17 Sep 88	**THERE'S A BRAND NEW WORLD** Tent PB 42235......**61**	2 wks

British Hit Singles Part One: Alphabetically by Artist
Date of chart entry/Title & catalogue no./Peak position reached/Weeks on chart
★ Number One ● Top Ten † still on chart at 31 Dec 1994
□ = credited to act billed in footnote

19 Nov 88	**LET ME BE YOURS** Tent PB 42343 ....**51**	3 wks
8 Apr 89	**WITH EVERY HEARTBEAT** Tent PB 42693 ....**49**	2 wks
10 Mar 90	**TREAT ME LIKE A LADY** Tent FIVE 1 ....**54**	2 wks
7 Jul 90	**HOT LOVE** Tent FIVE 2 ....**68**	1 wk

FIVE THIRTY *UK, male vocal / instrumental group* **4 wks**

4 Aug 90	**ABSTAIN** East West YZ 530 ....**75**	1 wk
25 May 91	**13TH DISCIPLE** East West YZ 577 ....**67**	1 wk
3 Aug 91	**SUPERNOVA** East West YZ 594 ....**75**	1 wk
2 Nov 91	**YOU** (EP) East West YZ 624 ....**72**	1 wk

Tracks on You (EP): You / Cuddly Drug / Slow Train Into The Ocean.

5000 VOLTS *UK, male / female vocal / insturmental group* **18 wks**

6 Sep 75	● **I'M ON FIRE** Philips 6006 464 ....**4**	9 wks
24 Jul 76	● **DR. KISS KISS** Philips 6006 533 ....**8**	9 wks

FIXX *UK, male vocal / instrumental group* **8 wks**

24 Apr 82	**STAND OR FALL** MCA FIXX 2 ....**54**	4 wks
17 Jul 82	**RED SKIES** MCA FIXX 3 ....**57**	4 wks

F.K.W. *UK, male vocal / instrumental group* **8 wks**

2 Oct 93	**NEVER GONNA** PWL International PWCD 273 ....**48**	2 wks
11 Dec 93	**SEIZE THE DAY** PWL International PWCD 279 ....**45**	2 wks
5 Mar 94	**JINGO** PWL International PWCD 283 ....**30**	3 wks
4 Jun 94	**THIS IS THE WAY** PWL International PWCD 307......**63**	1 wk

Roberta FLACK *US, female vocalist* **79 wks**

27 May 72	**THE FIRST TIME EVER I SAW YOUR FACE**	
	Atlantic K 10161 ....**14**	14 wks
5 Aug 72	**WHERE IS THE LOVE** Atlantic K 10202 [1] **29**	7 wks
17 Feb 73	● **KILLING ME SOFTLY WITH HIS SONG**	
	Atlantic K 10282 ....**6**	14 wks
24 Aug 74	**FEEL LIKE MAKING LOVE** Atlantic K 10467............**34**	7 wks
6 May 78	**THE CLOSER I GET TO YOU** Atlantic K 11099 [1] **42**	4 wks
17 May 80	● **BACK TOGETHER AGAIN** Atlantic K 11481 [1] **3**	11 wks
30 Aug 80	**DON'T MAKE ME WAIT TOO LONG**	
	Atlantic K 11555 ....**44**	7 wks
20 Aug 83	● **TONIGHT I CELEBRATE MY LOVE** Capitol CL 302 [2] ..**2**	13 wks
29 Jul 89	**UH-UH OOH OOH LOOK OUT** (HERE IT COMES)	
	Atlantic A 8941 ....**72**	2 wks

[1] Roberta Flack and Donny Hathaway [2] Peabo Bryson and Roberta Flack

FLAMINGOS *US, male vocal group* **5 wks**

4 Jun 69	**BOOGALOO PARTY** Philips BF 1786..................**26**	5 wks

Michael FLANDERS *UK, male vocalist* **3 wks**

27 Feb 59	**LITTLE DRUMMER BOY** Parlophone R 4528...........**20**	2 wks
17 Apr 59	**LITTLE DRUMMER BOY** (re-entry)	
	Parlophone R 4528 ....**24**	1 wk

FLASH AND THE PAN
Australia, male vocal / instrumental group **15 wks**

23 Sep 78	**AND THE BAND PLAYED ON** (DOWN AMONG	
	THE DEAD MEN) Ensign ENY 15 ....**54**	4 wks
21 May 83	● **WAITING FOR A TRAIN** Easybeat EASY 1 ....**7**	11 wks

Lester FLATT and Earl SCRUGGS
US, male instrumental duo - banjos   **6 wks**

15 Nov 67   **FOGGY MOUNTAIN BREAKDOWN**
     CBS 3038 and Mercury MF 1007 ....**39** 6 wks

The versions on the two labels were not the same cuts; CBS had a 1965 recording, Mercury a 1949. The chart did not differentiate and listed both together.

Fogwell FLAX and the ANKLEBITERS from FREEHOLD JUNIOR SCHOOL
UK, male vocalist and school choir   **2 wks**

26 Dec 81   **ONE NINE FOR SANTA** *EMI 5255*...............**68** 2 wks

F.L.B. - *See FAT LARRY'S BAND*

FLEE-REKKERS UK, male instrumental group   **13 wks**

19 May 60   **GREEN JEANS** *Triumph RGM 1008* ....**23** 13 wks

FLEETWOOD MAC
UK / US, male / female vocal / instrumental group   **223 wks**

Date	Title	Pos	Wks
10 Apr 68	**BLACK MAGIC WOMAN** *Blue Horizon 57 3138*	**37**	7 wks
17 Jul 68	**NEED YOUR LOVE SO BAD** *Blue Horizon 57 3139*	**31**	13 wks
4 Dec 68	★ **ALBATROSS** *Blue Horizon 57 3145*	**1**	20 wks
16 Apr 69	● **MAN OF THE WORLD** *Immediate IM 080*	**2**	14 wks
23 Jul 69	**NEED YOUR LOVE SO BAD (re-issue)** *Blue Horizon 57 3157*	**32**	6 wks
13 Sep 69	**NEED YOUR LOVE SO BAD (re-entry of re-issue)** *Blue Horizon 57 3157*	**42**	3 wks
4 Oct 69	● **OH WELL** *Reprise RS 27000*	**2**	16 wks
23 May 70	● **THE GREEN MANALISHI (WITH THE TWO-PRONG CROWN)** *Reprise RS 27007*	**10**	12 wks
12 May 73	● **ALBATROSS (re-issue)** *CBS 8306*	**2**	15 wks
13 Nov 76	**SAY YOU LOVE ME** *Reprise K 14447*	**40**	4 wks
19 Feb 77	**GO YOUR OWN WAY** *Warner Bros. K 16872*	**38**	4 wks
30 Apr 77	**DON'T STOP** *Warner Bros. K 16930*	**32**	5 wks
9 Jul 77	**DREAMS** *Warner Bros. K 16969*	**24**	9 wks
22 Oct 77	**YOU MAKE LOVING FUN** *Warner Bros. K 17013*	**45**	2 wks
11 Mar 78	**RHIANNON** *Reprise K 14430*	**46**	3 wks
22 Dec 79	**SARA** *Warner Bros. K 17533*	**37**	8 wks
25 Sep 82	**GYPSY** *Warner Bros. K 17997*	**46**	3 wks
18 Dec 82	● **OH DIANE** *Warner Bros. FLEET 1*	**9**	15 wks
4 Apr 87	● **BIG LOVE** *Warner Bros. W 8398*	**9**	12 wks
11 Jul 87	**SEVEN WONDERS** *Warner Bros. W 8317*	**56**	4 wks
26 Sep 87	● **LITTLE LIES** *Warner Bros. W 8291*	**5**	12 wks
26 Dec 87	**FAMILY MAN** *Warner Bros. W 8114*	**54**	5 wks
2 Apr 88	● **EVERYWHERE** *Warner Bros. W 8143*	**4**	10 wks
18 Jun 88	**ISN'T IT MIDNIGHT** *Warner Bros. W 7860*	**60**	2 wks
17 Dec 88	**AS LONG AS YOU FOLLOW** *Warner Bros. W 7644*	**66**	3 wks
5 May 90	**SAVE ME** *Warner Bros. W 9866*	**53**	3 wks
25 Aug 90	**IN THE BACK OF MY MIND** *Warner Bros. W 9739*	**58**	3 wks

Group were UK and male only up to and including the re-issue of Albatross.

FLEETWOODS US, male / female vocal group   **8 wks**

24 Apr 59   ● **COME SOFTLY TO ME** *London HLU 8841* ....**6** 8 wks

Rochelle FLEMING - *See FIRST CHOICE featuring Rochelle FLEMING*

La FLEUR Holland, male / female vocal / instrumental group **4 wks**

30 Jul 83   **BOOGIE NIGHTS** *Proto ENA 111* ....**51** 4 wks

K.C. FLIGHTT US, male rapper   **4 wks**

1 Apr 89   **PLANET E** *RCA PT 49404* ....**48** 4 wks

Dread FLIMSTONE and the NEW TONE AGE FAMILY US, male vocal / instrumental group   **1 wk**

30 Nov 91   **FROM THE GHETTO** *Urban URB 87* ....**66** 1 wk

Berni FLINT UK, male vocalist   **11 wks**

19 Mar 77 ● **I DON'T WANT TO PUT A HOLD ON YOU** *EMI 2599* ..**3** 10 wks
23 Jul 77   **SOUTHERN COMFORT** *EMI 2621* ....**48** 1 wk

FLINTLOCK UK, male vocal / instrumental group   **5 wks**

29 May 76   **DAWN** *Pinnacle P 8419* ....**30** 5 wks

F.L.O. - *See Rahni HARRIS and F.L.O.*

FLOATERS US, male vocal / instrumental group   **11 wks**

23 Jul 77 ★ **FLOAT ON** *ABC 4187* ....**1** 11 wks

A FLOCK OF SEAGULLS
UK, male vocal / instrumental group   **46 wks**

Date	Title	Pos	Wks
27 Mar 82	**I RAN** *Jive JIVE 14*	**43**	6 wks
12 Jun 82	**SPACE AGE LOVE SONG** *Jive JIVE 17*	**34**	6 wks
6 Nov 82	● **WISHING (IF I HAD A PHOTOGRAPH OF YOU)** *Jive JIVE 25*	**10**	12 wks
23 Apr 83	**NIGHTMARES** *Jive JIVE 33*	**53**	3 wks
25 Jun 83	**TRANSFER AFFECTION** *Jive JIVE 41*	**38**	5 wks
14 Jul 84	**THE MORE YOU LIVE, THE MORE YOU LOVE** *Jive JIVE 62*	**26**	11 wks
19 Oct 85	**WHO'S THAT GIRL (SHE'S GOT IT)** *Jive JIVE 106*	**66**	3 wks

FLOWERED UP UK, male vocal / instrumental group   **17 wks**

Date	Title	Pos	Wks
28 Jul 90	**IT'S ON** *Heavenly HVN 3*	**54**	4 wks
24 Nov 90	**PHOBIA** *Heavenly HVN 7*	**75**	1 wk
11 May 91	**TAKE IT** *London FUP 1*	**34**	4 wks
17 Aug 91	**IT'S ON/EGG RUSH** *London FUP 2*	**38**	3 wks
2 May 92	**WEEKENDER** *Heavenly HVN 16*	**20**	5 wks

See also Various Artists (EPs & LPs) - The Fred EP.

FLOWERPOT MEN UK, male vocal group   **12 wks**

23 Aug 67 ● **LET'S GO TO SAN FRANCISCO** *Deram DM 142* ....**4** 12 wks

Eddie FLOYD US, male vocalist   **29 wks**

Date	Title	Pos	Wks
2 Feb 67	**KNOCK ON WOOD** *Atlantic 584 041*	**50**	1 wk
2 Mar 67	**KNOCK ON WOOD (re-entry)** *Atlantic 584 041*	**19**	17 wks
16 Mar 67	**RAISE YOUR HAND** *Stax 601 001*	**42**	3 wks
9 Aug 67	**THINGS GET BETTER** *Stax 601 016*	**31**	8 wks

FLUKE UK, male instrumental / production group   **8 wks**

Date	Title	Pos	Wks
20 Mar 93	**SLID** *Circa YRCD 103*	**59**	1 wk
19 Jun 93	**ELECTRIC GUITAR** *Circa YRCD 104*	**58**	2 wks
11 Sep 93	**GROOVY FEELING** *Circa YRCD 106*	**45**	3 wks
23 Apr 94	**BUBBLE** *Circa YRCD 110*	**37**	2 wks

Tenor FLY - *See REBEL MC*

FLYING LIZARDS
UK, male / female vocal / instrumental group   **16 wks**

Date	Title	Pos	Wks
4 Aug 79	● **MONEY** *Virgin VS 276*	**5**	10 wks
9 Feb 80	**T.V.** *Virgin VS 325*	**43**	6 wks

FLYING PICKETS UK, male vocal group — 20 wks

26 Nov 83	★ ONLY YOU *10 TEN 14*	1	11 wks
21 Apr 84	● WHEN YOU'RE YOUNG AND IN LOVE *10 TEN 20*	7	8 wks
8 Dec 84	WHO'S THAT GIRL *10 GIRL 1*	71	1 wk

FM UK, male vocal / instrumental group — 11 wks

31 Jan 87	FROZEN HEART *Portrait DIDGE 1*	64	2 wks
20 Jun 87	LET LOVE BE THE LEADER *Portrait MERV 1*	71	2 wks
5 Aug 89	BAD LUCK *Epic 655031 7*	54	4 wks
7 Oct 89	SOMEDAY (YOU'LL COME RUNNING) *CBS DINK 1*	64	2 wks
10 Feb 90	EVERYTIME I THINK OF YOU *Epic DINK 2*	73	1 wk

FOCUS Holland, male instrumental group — 21 wks

| 20 Jan 73 | HOCUS POCUS *Polydor 2001 211* | 20 | 10 wks |
| 27 Jan 73 | ● SYLVIA *Polydor 2001 422* | 4 | 11 wks |

FOG US, male / female vocal / instrumental group — 2 wks

| 19 Feb 94 | BEEN A LONG TIME *Columbia 6601212* | 44 | 2 wks |

Dan FOGELBERG US, male vocalist — 4 wks

| 15 Mar 80 | LONGER *Epic EPC 8230* | 59 | 4 wks |

Claudia FONTAINE - See BEATMASTERS

Wayne FONTANA UK, male vocalist — 31 wks

9 Dec 65	IT WAS EASIER TO HURT HER *Fontana TF 642*	36	6 wks
21 Apr 66	COME ON HOME *Fontana TF 684*	16	12 wks
25 Aug 66	GOODBYE BLUEBIRD *Fontana TF 737*	49	1 wk
8 Dec 66	PAMELA PAMELA *Fontana TF 770*	11	12 wks

See also Wayne Fontana and the Mindbenders.

Wayne FONTANA and the MINDBENDERS
UK, male vocalist, male vocal / instrumental backing group — 45 wks

11 Jul 63	HELLO JOSEPHINE *Fontana TF 404*	46	2 wks
28 May 64	STOP LOOK AND LISTEN *Fontana TF 451*	37	4 wks
8 Oct 64	● UM UM UM UM UM UM *Fontana TF 497*	5	15 wks
4 Feb 65	● GAME OF LOVE *Fontana TF 535*	2	11 wks
17 Jun 65	JUST A LITTLE BIT TOO LATE *Fontana TF 579*	20	7 wks
30 Sep 65	SHE NEEDS LOVE *Fontana TF 611*	32	6 wks

See also Wayne Fontana; Mindbenders.

Bill FORBES UK, male vocalist — 1 wk

| 15 Jan 60 | TOO YOUNG *Columbia DB 4386* | 29 | 1 wk |

FORBIDDEN - See Jet BRONX and the FORBIDDEN

FORCE MDs US, male vocal group — 9 wks

| 12 Apr 86 | TENDER LOVE *Tommy Boy IS 269* | 23 | 9 wks |

Baby FORD UK, male instrumentalist - keyboards — 16 wks

10 Sep 88	OOCHY KOOCHY *Rhythm King 7BFORD 1*	58	6 wks
24 Dec 88	CHIKKI CHIKKI AHH AHH *Rhythm King 7BFORD 2*	75	1 wk
7 Jan 89	CHIKKI CHIKKI AHH AHH (re-entry) *Rhythm King 7BFORD 2*	54	3 wks
17 Jun 89	CHILDREN OF THE REVOLUTION *Rhythm King 7BFORD 4*	53	4 wks
17 Feb 90	BEACH BUMP *Rhythm King 7BFORD 6*	68	2 wks

Clinton FORD UK, male vocalist — 25 wks

23 Oct 59	OLD SHEP *Oriole CB 1500*	27	1 wk
17 Aug 61	TOO MANY BEAUTIFUL GIRLS *Oriole CB 1623*	48	1 wk
8 Mar 62	FANLIGHT FANNY *Oriole CB 1706*	22	10 wks
5 Jan 67	RUN TO THE DOOR *Piccadilly 7N 35361*	25	13 wks

Emile FORD and the CHECKMATES
UK, male vocal / instrumental group — 87 wks

30 Oct 59	★ WHAT DO YOU WANT TO MAKE THOSE EYES AT ME FOR *Pye 7N 15225*	1	25 wks
5 Feb 60	● ON A SLOW BOAT TO CHINA *Pye 7N 15245*	3	14 wks
26 May 60	YOU'LL NEVER KNOW WHAT YOU'RE MISSING *Pye 7N 15268*	12	9 wks
1 Sep 60	THEM THERE EYES *Pye 7N 15282* [1]	18	16 wks
8 Dec 60	● COUNTING TEARDROPS *Pye 7N 15314*	4	12 wks
2 Mar 61	WHAT AM I GONNA DO *Pye 7N 15331*	33	6 wks
18 May 61	HALF OF MY HEART *Piccadilly 7N 35003* [1]	50	1 wk
22 Jun 61	HALF OF MY HEART (re-entry) *Piccadilly 7N 35003* [1]	42	3 wks
8 Mar 62	I WONDER WHO'S KISSING HER NOW *Piccadilly 7N 35033*	43	1 wk

[1] Emile Ford

Lita FORD US, female vocalist — 7 wks

17 Dec 88	KISS ME DEADLY *RCA PB 49575*	75	1 wk
20 May 89	CLOSE MY EYES FOREVER *Dreamland PB 49409* [1]	47	3 wks
11 Jan 92	SHOT OF POISON *RCA PB 49145*	63	3 wks

[1] Lita Ford duet with Ozzy Osbourne

Martyn FORD UK, orchestra — 3 wks

| 14 May 77 | LET YOUR BODY GO DOWNTOWN *Mountain TOP 26* | 38 | 3 wks |

Mary FORD - See Les PAUL and Mary FORD

Penny FORD US, female vocalist — 7 wks

| 4 May 85 | DANGEROUS *Total Experience FB 49975* [1] | 43 | 5 wks |
| 29 May 93 | DAYDREAMING *Columbia 6590592* | 43 | 2 wks |

[1] Pennye Ford

Tennessee Ernie FORD US, male vocalist — 42 wks

21 Jan 55	★ GIVE ME YOUR WORD *Capitol CL 14005*	1	24 wks
6 Jan 56	★ SIXTEEN TONS *Capitol CL 14500*	1	11 wks
13 Jan 56	● THE BALLAD OF DAVY CROCKETT *Capitol CL 14506*	3	7 wks

Julia FORDHAM UK, female vocalist — 32 wks

2 Jul 88	HAPPY EVER AFTER *Circa YR 15*	27	9 wks
25 Feb 89	WHERE DOES THE TIME GO *Circa YR 23*	41	5 wks
31 Aug 91	I THOUGHT IT WAS YOU *Circa YR 69*	64	2 wks
18 Jan 92	LOVE MOVES (IN MYSTERIOUS WAYS) *Circa YR 73*	19	9 wks
30 May 92	I THOUGHT IT WAS YOU (re-mix) *Circa YR 90*	45	3 wks
30 Apr 94	DIFFERENT TIME DIFFERENT PLACE *Circa YRCD 111*	41	3 wks
23 Jul 94	I CAN'T HELP MYSELF *Circa YRCD 116*	62	1 wk

FOREIGNER UK / US, male vocal / instrumental group — 78 wks

| 6 May 78 | FEELS LIKE THE FIRST TIME *Atlantic K 11086* | 39 | 6 wks |

15 Jul 78	COLD AS ICE Atlantic K 10986	24	10 wks
28 Oct 78	HOT BLOODED Atlantic K 11167	42	3 wks
24 Feb 79	BLUE MORNING BLUE DAY Atlantic K 11236	45	4 wks
29 Aug 81	URGENT Atlantic K 11665	54	4 wks
10 Oct 81	JUKE BOX HERO Atlantic K 11678	48	4 wks
12 Dec 81	● WAITING FOR A GIRL LIKE YOU Atlantic K 11696	8	13 wks
8 May 82	URGENT (re-issue) Atlantic K 11728	45	5 wks
8 Dec 84	★ I WANT TO KNOW WHAT LOVE IS Atlantic A 9596	1	16 wks
6 Apr 85	THAT WAS YESTERDAY Atlantic A 9571	28	6 wks
22 Jun 85	COLD AS ICE (re-mix) Atlantic A 9539	64	2 wks
19 Dec 87	SAY YOU WILL Atlantic A 9169	71	4 wks
22 Oct 94	WHITE LIE Arista 74321232862	58	1 wk

FORMATIONS US, male vocal group · **11 wks**

| 31 Jul 71 | AT THE TOP OF THE STAIRS Mojo 2027 001 | 50 | 1 wk |
| 14 Aug 71 | AT THE TOP OF THE STAIRS (re-entry) Mojo 2027 001 | 28 | 10 wks |

George FORMBY
UK, male vocalist / instrumentalist - ukelele · **3 wks**

| 21 Jul 60 | HAPPY GO LUCKY ME / BANJO BOY Pye 7N 15269 | 40 | 3 wks |

See also 2 In A Tent.

FORREST US, male vocalist · **20 wks**

26 Feb 83	● ROCK THE BOAT CBS A 3121	4	10 wks
14 May 83	FEEL THE NEED IN ME CBS A 3411	17	8 wks
17 Sep 83	ONE LOVER (DON'T STOP THE SHOW) CBS A 3734	67	2 wks

Lance FORTUNE UK, male vocalist · **17 wks**

| 19 Feb 60 | ● BE MINE Pye 7N 15240 | 4 | 12 wks |
| 5 May 60 | THIS LOVE I HAVE FOR YOU Pye 7N 15260 | 26 | 5 wks |

FORTUNES UK, male vocal / instrumental group · **65 wks**

8 Jul 65	● YOU'VE GOT YOUR TROUBLES Decca F 12173	2	14 wks
7 Oct 65	● HERE IT COMES AGAIN Decca F 12243	4	14 wks
3 Feb 66	THIS GOLDEN RING Decca F 12321	15	9 wks
11 Sep 71	● FREEDOM COME FREEDOM GO Capitol CL 15693	6	17 wks
29 Jan 72	● STORM IN A TEACUP Capitol CL 15707	7	11 wks

45 KING US, male producer - Mark King · **6 wks**

| 28 Oct 89 | THE KING IS HERE / THE 900 NUMBER Dance Trax DRX 9 | 60 | 5 wks |
| 11 Aug 90 | THE KING IS HERE / THE 900 NUMBER (re-entry) Dance Trax DRX 9 | 73 | 1 wk |

49ERS Italy, male producer - Gianfranco Bortolotti · **25 wks**

16 Dec 89	● TOUCH ME Fourth & Broadway BRW 157	3	13 wks
17 Mar 90	DON'T YOU LOVE ME Fourth & Broadway BRW 167	12	6 wks
9 Jun 90	GIRL TO GIRL Fourth & Broadway BRW 174	31	3 wks
6 Jun 92	GOT TO BE FREE Fourth & Broadway BRW 255	46	2 wks
29 Aug 92	THE MESSAGE Fourth & Broadway BRW 257	68	1 wk

See also Cappella.

FOSTER and ALLEN Ireland, male vocal duo · **47 wks**

27 Feb 82	A BUNCH OF THYME Ritz RITZ 5	18	11 wks
30 Oct 82	OLD FLAMES Ritz RITZ 028	51	8 wks
19 Feb 83	MAGGIE Ritz RITZ 025	27	9 wks
29 Oct 83	I WILL LOVE YOU ALL MY LIFE Ritz RITZ 056	49	6 wks
30 Jun 84	JUST FOR OLD TIME'S SAKE Ritz RITZ 066	47	6 wks
29 Mar 86	AFTER ALL THESE YEARS Ritz RITZ 106	43	7 wks

FOUNDATIONS UK, male vocal / instrumental group · **56 wks**

27 Sep 67	★ BABY NOW THAT I'VE FOUND YOU Pye 7N 17366	1	16 wks
24 Jan 68	BACK ON MY FEET AGAIN Pye 7N 17417	18	10 wks
1 May 68	ANY OLD TIME Pye 7N 17503	48	1 wk
15 May 68	ANY OLD TIME (re-entry) Pye 7N 17503	50	1 wk
20 Nov 68	● BUILD ME UP BUTTERCUP Pye 7N 17636	2	15 wks
12 Mar 69	● IN THE BAD BAD OLD DAYS Pye 7N 17702	8	10 wks
13 Sep 69	BORN TO LIVE AND BORN TO DIE Pye 7N 17809	46	3 wks

FOUR ACES US, male vocal group · **40 wks**

30 Jul 54	● THREE COINS IN THE FOUNTAIN Brunswick 05308 [1]	5	5 wks
22 Oct 54	THREE COINS IN THE FOUNTAIN (re-entry) Brunswick 05308 [1]	17	1 wk
7 Jan 55	● MR. SANDMAN Brunswick 05355 [1]	9	5 wks
20 May 55	● STRANGER IN PARADISE Brunswick 05418 [1]	6	6 wks
18 Nov 55	● LOVE IS A MANY SPLENDOURED THING Brunswick 05480 [1]	2	13 wks
19 Oct 56	WOMAN IN LOVE Brunswick 05589 [1]	19	3 wks
4 Jan 57	FRIENDLY PERSUASION Brunswick 05623 [1]	29	1 wk
23 Jan 59	THE WORLD OUTSIDE Brunswick 05773	18	6 wks

[1] Four Aces featuring Al Roberts

FOUR BUCKETEERS UK, male / female vocal group · **6 wks**

| 3 May 80 | BUCKET OF WATER SONG CBS 8393 | 26 | 6 wks |

FOUR ESQUIRES US, male vocal group · **2 wks**

| 31 Jan 58 | LOVE ME FOREVER London HLO 8533 | 23 | 2 wks |

4 HERO UK, male instrumental group · **4 wks**

| 24 Nov 90 | MR. KIRK'S NIGHTMARE Reinforced RIVET 1203 | 73 | 2 wks |
| 9 May 92 | COOKIN' UP YAH BRAIN Reinforced RIVET 1216 | 59 | 2 wks |

400 BLOWS UK, male vocal / instrumental duo · **4 wks**

| 29 Jun 85 | MOVIN' Illuminated ILL 61 | 54 | 4 wks |

FOUR KNIGHTS US, male vocal group · **11 wks**

| 4 Jun 54 | ● I GET SO LONELY Capitol CL 14076 | 5 | 7 wks |
| 30 Jul 54 | ● I GET SO LONELY (re-entry) Capitol CL 14076 | 10 | 4 wks |

FOUR LADS Canada, male vocal group · **23 wks**

19 Dec 52	● FAITH CAN MOVE MOUNTAINS Columbia DB 3154 [1]	7	2 wks
9 Jan 53	● FAITH CAN MOVE MOUNTAINS (re-entry) Columbia DB 3154 [1]	9	1 wk
22 Oct 54	● RAIN RAIN RAIN Philips PB 311 [2]	8	16 wks
28 Apr 60	STANDING ON THE CORNER Philips PB 1000	34	4 wks

[1] Johnnie Ray and the Four Lads [2] Frankie Laine and the Four Lads

4 NON BLONDES
US, female / male vocal / instrumental group · **19 wks**

| 19 Jun 93 | ● WHAT'S UP Interscope A 8412CD | 2 | 17 wks |
| 16 Oct 93 | SPACEMAN Interscope A 8349CD | 53 | 2 wks |

4 OF US Ireland, male vocal / instrumental group · **6 wks**

| 27 Feb 93 | SHE HITS ME Columbia 6589192 | 35 | 4 wks |
| 1 May 93 | I MISS YOU Columbia 6591722 | 62 | 2 wks |

FOUR PENNIES UK, male vocal/instrumental group   **56 wks**

16 Jan 64	**DO YOU WANT ME TO** *Philips BF 1296* **47**	1 wk
6 Feb 64	**DO YOU WANT ME TO (re-entry)** *Philips BF 1296* ...**49**	1 wk
2 Apr 64	★ **JULIET** *Philips BF 1322* **1**	15 wks
16 Jul 64	**I FOUND OUT THE HARD WAY** *Philips BF 1349* ...**14**	11 wks
29 Oct 64	**BLACK GIRL** *Philips BF 1366* **20**	12 wks
7 Oct 65	**UNTIL IT'S TIME FOR YOU TO GO** *Philips BF 1435* ..**19**	11 wks
17 Feb 66	**TROUBLE IS MY MIDDLE NAME** *Philips BF 1469* **32**	5 wks

FOUR PREPS US, male vocal group   **23 wks**

13 Jun 58	● **BIG MAN** *Capitol CL 14873* **2**	13 wks
19 Sep 58	**BIG MAN (re-entry)** *Capitol CL 14873* **22**	1 wk
26 May 60	**GOT A GIRL** *Capitol CL 15128*.............................**28**	6 wks
14 Jul 60	**GOT A GIRL (re-entry)** *Capitol CL 15128* **47**	1 wk
2 Nov 61	**MORE MONEY FOR YOU AND ME (MEDLEY)**	
	Capitol CL 15217 ....**39**	2 wks

Tracks on medley: Mr. Blue / Alley Oop / Smoke Gets In Your Eyes / In This Whole Wide World / A Worried Man / Tom Dooley / A Teenager In Love, all with new lyrics.

FOUR SEASONS US, male vocal group   **151 wks**

4 Oct 62	● **SHERRY** *Stateside SS 122* **8**	16 wks
17 Jan 63	**BIG GIRLS DON'T CRY** *Stateside SS 145* **13**	10 wks
28 Mar 63	**WALK LIKE A MAN** *Stateside SS 169*.................**12**	12 wks
27 Jun 63	**AIN'T THAT A SHAME** *Stateside SS 194* **38**	3 wks
27 Aug 64	● **RAG DOLL** *Philips BF 1347* [1] **2**	13 wks
18 Nov 65	● **LET'S HANG ON** *Philips BF 1439* [1] **4**	16 wks
31 Mar 66	**WORKIN' MY WAY BACK TO YOU**	
	Philips BF 1474 [2] **50**	3 wks
2 Jun 66	**OPUS 17 (DON'T YOU WORRY 'BOUT ME)**	
	Philips BF 1493 [2] **20**	9 wks
29 Sep 66	**I'VE GOT YOU UNDER MY SKIN** *Philips BF 1511* [2] **12**	11 wks
12 Jan 67	**TELL IT TO THE RAIN** *Philips BF 1538* [2] **37**	5 wks
19 Apr 75	● **NIGHT** *Mowest MW 3024* [3] **7**	9 wks
20 Sep 75	● **WHO LOVES YOU** *Warner Bros. K 16602* **6**	9 wks
31 Jan 76	★ **DECEMBER '63 (OH WHAT A NIGHT)**	
	Warner Bros. K 16688 ....**1**	10 wks
24 Apr 76	● **SILVER STAR** *Warner Bros. K 16742* **3**	9 wks
27 Nov 76	**WE CAN WORK IT OUT** *Warner Bros. K 16845* **34**	4 wks
18 Jun 77	**RHAPSODY** *Warner Bros. K 16932* **37**	3 wks
20 Aug 77	**DOWN THE HALL** *Warner Bros. K 16982* **34**	5 wks
29 Oct 88	**DECEMBER '63 (OH WHAT A NIGHT) (re-mix)**	
	BR 45277 [3] **49**	4 wks

[1] Four Seasons with the sound of Frankie Valli [2] Four Seasons with Frankie Valli [3] Frankie Valli and the Four Seasons

FOUR TOPS US, male vocal group   **318 wks**

1 Jul 65	**I CAN'T HELP MYSELF** *Tamla Motown TMG 515*......**23**	9 wks
2 Sep 65	**IT'S THE SAME OLD SONG**	
	Tamla Motown TMG 528 ....**34**	8 wks
21 Jul 66	**LOVING YOU IS SWEETER THAN EVER**	
	Tamla Motown TMG 568 ....**21**	12 wks
13 Oct 66	★ **REACH OUT I'LL BE THERE** *Tamla Motown TMG 579* ..**1**	16 wks
12 Jan 67	● **STANDING IN THE SHADOWS OF LOVE**	
	Tamla Motown TMG 589 ....**6**	8 wks
30 Mar 67	● **BERNADETTE** *Tamla Motown TMG 601*.....................**8**	10 wks
15 Jun 67	**SEVEN ROOMS OF GLOOM**	
	Tamla Motown TMG 612 ....**12**	9 wks
11 Oct 67	**YOU KEEP RUNNING AWAY**	
	Tamla Motown TMG 623 ....**26**	7 wks
13 Dec 67	● **WALK AWAY RENEE** *Tamla Motown TMG 634* **3**	11 wks
13 Mar 68	● **IF I WERE A CARPENTER** *Tamla Motown TMG 647*....**7**	11 wks
21 Aug 68	**YESTERDAY'S DREAMS** *Tamla Motown TMG 665* ..**23**	15 wks
13 Nov 68	**I'M IN A DIFFERENT WORLD**	
	Tamla Motown TMG 675 ....**27**	13 wks
28 May 69	**WHAT IS A MAN** *Tamla Motown TMG 698*...............**16**	11 wks
27 Sep 69	**DO WHAT YOU GOTTA DO** *Tamla Motown TMG 710* **11**	11 wks
21 Mar 70	● **I CAN'T HELP MYSELF (re-issue)**	
	Tamla Motown TMG 732 ....**10**	11 wks
30 May 70	● **IT'S ALL IN THE GAME** *Tamla Motown TMG 736* **5**	14 wks
12 Sep 70	**IT'S ALL IN THE GAME (re-entry)**	
	Tamla Motown TMG 736 ....**48**	2 wks
3 Oct 70	● **STILL WATER (LOVE)** *Tamla Motown TMG 752* **10**	10 wks
19 Dec 70	**STILL WATER (LOVE) (re-entry)**	
	Tamla Motown TMG 752 ....**44**	2 wks
1 May 71	**JUST SEVEN NUMBERS (CAN STRAIGHTEN**	
	OUT MY LIFE) *Tamla Motown TMG 770* **36**	5 wks
26 Jun 71	**RIVER DEEP MOUNTAIN HIGH**	
	Tamla Motown TMG 777 [1] **11**	10 wks
25 Sep 71	● **SIMPLE GAME** *Tamla Motown TMG 785*....................**3**	11 wks
20 Nov 71	**YOU GOTTA HAVE LOVE IN YOUR HEART**	
	Tamla Motown TMG 793 [1] **25**	10 wks
11 Mar 72	**BERNADETTE (re-issue)** *Tamla Motown TMG 803* ..**23**	7 wks
5 Aug 72	**WALK WITH ME TALK WITH ME DARLING**	
	Tamla Motown TMG 823 ....**32**	6 wks
18 Nov 72	**KEEPER OF THE CASTLE** *Probe PRO 575* **18**	9 wks
10 Nov 73	**SWEET UNDERSTANDING LOVE** *Probe PRO 604*.....**29**	10 wks
17 Oct 81	● **WHEN SHE WAS MY GIRL** *Casablanca CAN 1005* ...**3**	10 wks
19 Dec 81	● **DON'T WALK AWAY** *Casablanca CAN 1006* **16**	11 wks
6 Mar 82	**TONIGHT I'M GONNA LOVE YOU ALL OVER**	
	Casablanca CAN 1008 ....**43**	4 wks
26 Jun 82	**BACK TO SCHOOL AGAIN** *RSO 89* **62**	2 wks
23 Jul 88	**REACH OUT I'LL BE THERE (re-mix)**	
	Motown ZB 41943 ....**11**	9 wks
17 Sep 88	**INDESTRUCTIBLE** *Arista 111717* **55**	4 wks
3 Dec 88	● **LOCO IN ACAPULCO** *Arista 111850*.......................**7**	13 wks
25 Feb 89	**INDESTRUCTIBLE** *Arista 112074* [2] **30**	7 wks

[1] Supremes and the Four Tops [2] Four Tops featuring Smokey Robinson

The original US recording of Indestructible was not issued until after the chart run of the UK-only mix.

FOURMOST UK, male vocal/instrumental group   **64 wks**

12 Sep 63	● **HELLO LITTLE GIRL** *Parlophone R 5056*...............**9**	17 wks
26 Dec 63	**I'M IN LOVE** *Parlophone R 5078* **17**	12 wks
23 Apr 64	● **A LITTLE LOVING** *Parlophone R 5128* **6**	13 wks
13 Aug 64	**HOW CAN I TELL HER** *Parlophone R 5157* **33**	4 wks
26 Nov 64	**BABY I NEED YOUR LOVIN'** *Parlophone R 5194* **24**	12 wks
9 Dec 65	**GIRLS GIRLS GIRLS** *Parlophone R 5379* **33**	6 wks

14-18 UK, male vocalist - Peter Waterman   **4 wks**

1 Nov 75	**GOODBYE-EE** *Magnet MAG 48* **33**	4 wks

FOX UK/US, male/female vocal/instrumental group   **29 wks**

15 Feb 75	● **ONLY YOU CAN** *GTO GT 8* **3**	11 wks
10 May 75	**IMAGINE ME IMAGINE YOU** *GTO GT 21* **15**	8 wks
10 Apr 76	**S-S-S-SINGLE BED** *GTO GT 57* **4**	10 wks

Noosha FOX UK, female vocalist   **6 wks**

12 Nov 77	**GEORGINA BAILEY** *GTO GT 106* **31**	6 wks

Samantha FOX UK, female vocalist   **71 wks**

22 Mar 86	● **TOUCH ME (I WANT YOUR BODY)** *Jive FOXY 1* **3**	10 wks
28 Jun 86	● **DO YA DO YA (WANNA PLEASE ME)** *Jive FOXY 2* ..**10**	7 wks
6 Sep 86	**HOLD ON TIGHT** *Jive FOXY 3* **26**	5 wks
13 Dec 86	**I'M ALL YOU NEED** *Jive FOXY 4* **41**	6 wks
30 May 87	● **NOTHING'S GONNA STOP ME NOW** *Jive FOXY 5* **8**	9 wks
25 Jul 87	**I SURRENDER (TO THE SPIRIT OF THE NIGHT)**	
	Jive FOXY 6 ....**25**	7 wks
17 Oct 87	**I PROMISE YOU (GET READY)** *Jive FOXY 7* **58**	3 wks
19 Dec 87	**TRUE DEVOTION** *Jive FOXY 8* **62**	3 wks
21 May 88	**NAUGHTY GIRLS** *Jive FOXY 9* [1] **31**	5 wks
19 Nov 88	**LOVE HOUSE** *Jive FOXY 10* **32**	6 wks
28 Jan 89	**I ONLY WANNA BE WITH YOU** *Jive FOXY 11* **16**	8 wks
17 Jun 89	**I WANNA HAVE SOME FUN** *Jive FOXY 12* **63**	2 wks

[1] Samantha Fox featuring Full Force

See also Various Artists (EPs & LPs) - Gimme Shelter (EP).

The **FOUR TOPS** were promoted in Britain by Beatles manager Brian Epstein. (LFI)

Bruce FOXTON UK, male vocalist — 9 wks

30 Jul 83	FREAK Arista BFOX 1	23	5 wks
29 Oct 83	THIS IS THE WAY Arista BFOX 2	56	3 wks
21 Apr 84	IT MAKES ME WONDER Arista BFOX 3	74	1 wk

Inez FOXX US, female vocalist — 8 wks

23 Jul 64	HURT BY LOVE Sue WI 323	40	3 wks
19 Feb 69	MOCKINGBIRD United Artists UP 2269 [1]	36	2 wks
19 Mar 69	MOCKINGBIRD (re-entry) United Artists UP 2269 [1]	34	3 wks

[1] Inez and Charlie Foxx

John FOXX UK, male vocalist — 31 wks

26 Jan 80	UNDERPASS Virgin VS 318	31	8 wks
29 Mar 80	NO-ONE DRIVING (DOUBLE SINGLE) Virgin VS 338	32	4 wks
19 Jul 80	BURNING CAR Virgin VS 360	35	7 wks
8 Nov 80	MILES AWAY Virgin VS 382	51	3 wks
29 Aug 81	EUROPE (AFTER THE RAIN) Virgin VS 393	40	5 wks
2 Jul 83	ENDLESSLY Virgin VS 543	66	3 wks
17 Sep 83	YOUR DRESS Virgin VS 615	61	1 wk

Tracks on double single: No-One Driving / Glimmer / Mr. No / This City.

FPI PROJECT Italy, male instrumental/production group — 16 wks

9 Dec 89	● GOING BACK TO MY ROOTS / RICH IN PARADISE Rumour RUMAT 9	9	12 wks
9 Mar 91	EVERYBODY (ALL OVER THE WORLD) Rumour RUMA 29	65	3 wks
7 Aug 93	COME ON (AND DO IT) Synthetic SYNTH 006CD	59	1 wk

Going Back To My Roots was a vocal track available in two formats and featured either Paolo Dini or Sharon D. Clarke.

FRAGGLES UK/US, puppets — 8 wks

| 18 Feb 84 | 'FRAGGLE ROCK' THEME RCA 389 | 33 | 8 wks |

Peter FRAMPTON UK, male vocalist — 24 wks

1 May 76	● SHOW ME THE WAY A & M AMS 7218	10	12 wks
11 Sep 76	BABY I LOVE YOUR WAY A & M AMS 7246	43	5 wks
6 Nov 76	DO YOU FEEL LIKE WE DO A & M AMS 7260	39	4 wks
23 Jul 77	I'M IN YOU A & M AMS 7298	41	3 wks

Connie FRANCIS US, female vocalist — 241 wks

4 Apr 58	★ WHO'S SORRY NOW MGM 975	1	25 wks
27 Jun 58	I'M SORRY I MADE YOU CRY MGM 982	11	10 wks
22 Aug 58	★ CAROLINA MOON / STUPID CUPID MGM 985	1	19 wks
31 Oct 58	I'LL GET BY MGM 993	19	6 wks
21 Nov 58	FALLIN' MGM 993	20	5 wks
26 Dec 58	YOU ALWAYS HURT THE ONE YOU LOVE MGM 998	13	7 wks
13 Feb 59	● MY HAPPINESS MGM 1001	4	14 wks
29 May 59	MY HAPPINESS (re-entry) MGM 1001	30	1 wk
3 Jul 59	● LIPSTICK ON YOUR COLLAR MGM 1018	3	16 wks
11 Sep 59	PLENTY GOOD LOVIN' MGM 1036	18	6 wks
4 Dec 59	AMONG MY SOUVENIRS MGM 1046	11	10 wks
17 Mar 60	VALENTINO MGM 1060	27	8 wks
19 May 60	● MAMA / ROBOT MAN MGM 1076	2	19 wks
18 Aug 60	● EVERYBODY'S SOMEBODY'S FOOL MGM 1086	5	13 wks
3 Nov 60	● MY HEART HAS A MIND OF ITS OWN MGM 1100	3	15 wks
12 Jan 61	MANY TEARS AGO MGM 1111	12	9 wks
16 Mar 61	● WHERE THE BOYS ARE / BABY ROO MGM 1121	5	14 wks
15 Jun 61	BREAKIN' IN A BRAND NEW BROKEN HEART MGM 1136	12	11 wks
14 Sep 61	● TOGETHER MGM 1138	6	11 wks
14 Dec 61	BABY'S FIRST CHRISTMAS MGM 1145	30	4 wks
26 Apr 62	DON'T BREAK THE HEART THAT LOVES YOU MGM 1157	39	3 wks
2 Aug 62	● VACATION MGM 1165	10	9 wks
20 Dec 62	I'M GONNA BE WARM THIS WINTER MGM 1185	48	1 wk
10 Jun 65	MY CHILD MGM 1271	26	6 wks
20 Jan 66	JEALOUS HEART MGM 1293	44	2 wks

Baby Roo listed with Where The Boys Are for first eight weeks only.

Jill FRANCIS UK, female vocalist — 1 wk

| 3 Jul 93 | MAKE LOVE TO ME Glady Wax GW 003CD | 70 | 1 wk |

Claude FRANCOIS France, male vocalist — 4 wks

| 10 Jan 76 | TEARS ON THE TELEPHONE Bradley's BRAD 7528 | 35 | 4 wks |

Joe FRANK - See HAMILTON, Joe FRANK and REYNOLDS

FRANK AND WALTERS Ireland, male vocal/instrumental group — 13 wks

21 Mar 92	HAPPY BUSMAN Setanta HOO 2	49	2 wks
12 Sep 92	THIS IS NOT A SONG Setanta HOO 3	46	3 wks
9 Jan 93	AFTER ALL Setanta HOCD 4	11	5 wks
17 Apr 93	FASHION CRISIS HITS NEW YORK Setanta HOOCD 5	42	3 wks

FRANKË UK, male vocalist - Frankë Pharoah — 3 wks

| 7 Nov 92 | UNDERSTAND THIS GROOVE China WOK 2028 | 60 | 2 wks |
| 21 May 94 | LOVE COME HOME Triangle BLUESCD 001 [1] | 73 | 1 wk |

[1] Our Tribe with Frankë Pharoah and Kristine W

FRANKIE GOES TO HOLLYWOOD UK, male vocal/instrumental group — 137 wks

26 Nov 83	★ RELAX ZTT ZTAS 1	1	48 wks
16 Jun 84	★ TWO TRIBES ZTT ZTAS 3	1	20 wks
10 Nov 84	TWO TRIBES (re-entry) ZTT ZTAS 3	73	1 wk
1 Dec 84	★ THE POWER OF LOVE ZTT ZTAS 5	1	11 wks
16 Feb 85	RELAX (re-entry) ZTT ZTAS 1	58	4 wks
23 Feb 85	THE POWER OF LOVE (re-entry) ZTT ZTAS 5	64	1 wk
30 Mar 85	● WELCOME TO THE PLEASURE DOME ZTT ZTAS 7	2	11 wks
6 Sep 86	● RAGE HARD ZTT ZTAS 22	4	7 wks
22 Nov 86	WARRIORS (OF THE WASTELAND) ZTT ZTAS 25	19	8 wks
7 Mar 87	WATCHING THE WILDLIFE ZTT ZTAS 26	28	6 wks
2 Oct 93	● RELAX (re-issue) ZTT FGTH 1CD	5	7 wks
20 Nov 93	WELCOME TO THE PLEASURE DOME (re-mix) ZTT FGTH 2CD	18	3 wks
18 Dec 93	● THE POWER OF LOVE (re-issue) ZTT FGTH 3CD	10	7 wks
26 Feb 94	TWO TRIBES (re-mix) ZTT FGTH 4CD	16	3 wks

Aretha FRANKLIN US, female vocalist — 177 wks

8 Jun 67	● RESPECT Atlantic 584 115	10	14 wks
23 Aug 67	BABY I LOVE YOU Atlantic 584 127	39	4 wks
20 Dec 67	CHAIN OF FOOLS / SATISFACTION Atlantic 584 157	43	2 wks
10 Jan 68	SATISFACTION (re-entry) Atlantic 584 157	37	5 wks
13 Mar 68	SINCE YOU'VE BEEN GONE Atlantic 584 172	47	1 wk
22 May 68	THINK Atlantic 584 186	26	9 wks
7 Aug 68	● I SAY A LITTLE PRAYER Atlantic 584 206	4	14 wks
22 Apr 70	DON'T PLAY THAT SONG Atlantic 2091 027	13	11 wks
2 Oct 71	SPANISH HARLEM Atlantic 2091 138	14	9 wks
8 Sep 73	ANGEL Atlantic K 10346	37	5 wks
16 Feb 74	UNTIL YOU COME BACK TO ME (THAT'S WHAT I'M GONNA DO) Atlantic K 10399	26	8 wks
6 Dec 80	WHAT A FOOL BELIEVES Arista ARIST 377	46	7 wks
19 Sep 81	LOVE ALL THE HURT AWAY Arista ARIST 428 [1]	49	3 wks
4 Sep 82	JUMP TO IT Arista ARIST 479	42	5 wks
23 Jul 83	GET IT RIGHT Arista ARIST 537	74	2 wks
13 Jul 85	FREEWAY OF LOVE Arista ARIST 624	68	3 wks
2 Nov 85	● SISTERS ARE DOIN' IT FOR THEMSELVES RCA PB 40339 [2]	9	11 wks

23 Nov 85	WHO'S ZOOMIN' WHO *Arista ARIST 633* **11**	14 wks
22 Feb 86	ANOTHER NIGHT *Arista ARIST 657* **54**	6 wks
10 May 86	FREEWAY OF LOVE (re-entry) *Arista ARIST 624* **51**	3 wks
25 Oct 86	JUMPIN' JACK FLASH *Arista ARIST 678* **58**	3 wks
31 Jan 87	★ I KNEW YOU WERE WAITING (FOR ME)	
	Epic DUET 1 [3] **1**	9 wks
14 Mar 87	JIMMY LEE *Arista RIS 6* **46**	4 wks
6 May 89	THROUGH THE STORM *Arista 112185* [4] **41**	3 wks
9 Sep 89	IT ISN'T, IT WASN'T, IT AIN'T NEVER GONNA BE	
	Arista 112545 [5] **29**	5 wks
7 Apr 90	THINK *East West A 7951* **31**	2 wks
27 Jul 91	EVERYDAY PEOPLE *Arista 114420* **69**	1 wk
12 Feb 94	● A DEEPER LOVE *Arista 74321187022* **5**	7 wks
25 Jun 94	WILLING TO FORGIVE *Arista 74321213342* **17**	7 wks

[1] Aretha Franklin and George Benson [2] Eurythmics and Aretha Franklin
[3] Aretha Franklin and George Michael [4] Aretha Franklin and Elton John
[5] Aretha Franklin and Whitney Houston

Think *on East West is a re-recording. It was the flip side of Everybody Needs Somebody To Love by Blues Brothers and was listed for the first two weeks of that record's run.*

Erma FRANKLIN *US, female vocalist* **10 wks**

| 10 Oct 92 | ● (TAKE A LITTLE) PIECE OF MY HEART *Epic 6583847*..**9** | 10 wks |

Rodney FRANKLIN *US, male instrumentalist - piano* **9 wks**

| 19 Apr 80 | ● THE GROOVE *CBS 8529* ....**7** | 9 wks |

FRANTIC FIVE - See Don LANG

FRANTIQUE *US, female vocal group* **12 wks**

| 11 Aug 79 | ● STRUT YOUR FUNKY STUFF | |
| | *Philadelphia International PIR 7728* ....**10** | 12 wks |

Elizabeth FRASER - See Ian McCULLOCH

Wendy FRASER - See Patrick SWAYZE featuring Wendy FRASER

FRAZIER CHORUS
UK, male / female vocal / instrumental group **14 wks**

4 Feb 89	DREAM KITCHEN *Virgin VS 1145* **57**	3 wks
15 Apr 89	TYPICAL! *Virgin VS 1174* **53**	2 wks
15 Jul 89	SLOPPY HEART *Virgin VS 1192* **73**	1 wk
9 Jun 90	CLOUD 8 *Virgin VS 1252* **52**	3 wks
25 Aug 90	NOTHING *Virgin VS 1284* **51**	3 wks
16 Feb 91	WALKING ON AIR *Virgin VS 1330* **60**	2 wks

FREAK POWER *UK / US, male vocal / instrumental group* **7 wks**

16 Oct 93	TURN ON TUNE IN DROP OUT	
	Fourth & Broadway BRCD 284 ....**29**	5 wks
26 Feb 94	RUSH *Fourth & Broadway BRCD 291* **62**	2 wks

FREAKY REALISTIC
UK / Japan, male / female vocal / instrumental group **3 wks**

| 3 Apr 93 | KOOCHIE RYDER *Frealism FRECD 2* ....**52** | 2 wks |
| 3 Jul 93 | LEONARD NIMOY *Frealism FRECD 3* ....**71** | 1 wk |

Stan FREBERG *US, male vocalist* **5 wks**

19 Nov 54	SH-BOOM *Capitol CL 14187* [1] **15**	2 wks
27 Jul 56	ROCK ISLAND LINE / HEARTBREAK HOTEL	
	Capitol CL 14608 ....**24**	1 wk
10 Aug 56	ROCK ISLAND LINE / HEARTBREAK HOTEL	
	(re-entry) *Capitol CL 14608* **29**	1 wk
12 May 60	THE OLD PAYOLA ROLL BLUES *Capitol CL 15122* **40**	1 wk

[1] Stan Freberg with the Toads

John FRED and the PLAYBOY BAND
US, male vocal / instrumental group **12 wks**

| 3 Jan 68 | ● JUDY IN DISGUISE (WITH GLASSES) | |
| | *Pye International 7N 25442* ....**3** | 12 wks |

FREDDIE and the DREAMERS
UK, male vocal / instrumental group **85 wks**

9 May 63	● IF YOU GOTTA MAKE A FOOL OF SOMEBODY	
	Columbia DB 7032 ....**3**	14 wks
8 Aug 63	● I'M TELLING YOU NOW *Columbia DB 7086* **2**	11 wks
7 Nov 63	● YOU WERE MADE FOR ME *Columbia DB 7147* **3**	15 wks
20 Feb 64	OVER YOU *Columbia DB 7214* **13**	11 wks
14 May 64	I LOVE YOU BABY *Columbia DB 7286* **16**	8 wks
16 Jul 64	JUST FOR YOU *Columbia DB 7322* **41**	3 wks
5 Nov 64	● I UNDERSTAND *Columbia DB 7381* **5**	15 wks
22 Apr 65	A LITTLE YOU *Columbia DB 7526* **26**	5 wks
4 Nov 65	THOU SHALT NOT STEAL *Columbia DB 7720* **44**	3 wks

FREDERICK - *See NINA and FREDERICK*

Dee FREDRIX *UK, female vocalist* **5 wks**

27 Feb 93	AND SO I WILL WAIT FOR YOU	
	East West YZ 725CD **56**	4 wks
3 Jul 93	DIRTY MONEY *East West YZ 750CD* **74**	1 wk

FREE *UK, male vocal / instrumental group* **75 wks**

6 Jun 70	● ALL RIGHT NOW *Island WIP 6082* **2**	16 wks
1 May 71	● MY BROTHER JAKE *Island WIP 6100* **4**	11 wks
27 May 72	LITTLE BIT OF LOVE *Island WIP 6129* **13**	10 wks
13 Jan 73	● WISHING WELL *Island WIP 6146* **7**	10 wks
21 Jul 73	ALL RIGHT NOW (re-entry) *Island WIP 6082* **15**	9 wks
18 Feb 78	FREE EP *Island IEP 6* **11**	7 wks
23 Oct 82	FREE EP (re-entry) *Island IEP 6* **57**	3 wks
9 Feb 91	● ALL RIGHT NOW (re-mix) *Island IS 486* **8**	9 wks

Tracks on Free EP: All Right Now / My Brother Jake / Wishing Well.

FREEEZ *UK, male vocal / instrumental group* **48 wks**

7 Jun 80	KEEP IN TOUCH *Calibre CAB 103* **49**	3 wks
7 Feb 81	● SOUTHERN FREEEZ *Beggars Banquet BEG 51* **8**	11 wks
18 Apr 81	FLYING HIGH *Beggars Banquet BEG 55* **35**	5 wks
18 Jun 83	● I.O.U. *Beggars Banquet BEG 96* **2**	15 wks
1 Oct 83	POP GOES MY LOVE *Beggars Banquet BEG 98* **26**	6 wks
17 Jan 87	I.O.U. (re-mix) *Citybeat CBE 709* [1] **23**	6 wks
30 May 87	SOUTHERN FREEEZ (re-mix)	
	Total Control TOCO 14 ....**63**	2 wks

[1] Freeez featuring John Rocca

FREEFALL featuring PSYCHOTROPIC
UK / US, male instrumental / production group **1 wk**

| 27 Jul 91 | FEEL SURREAL *ffrr FX 160* ....**63** | 1 wk |

FREEHOLD JUNIOR SCHOOL - *See Fogwell FLAX and the ANKLEBITERS from FREEHOLD JUNIOR SCHOOL*

FREIHEIT *Germany, male vocal / instrumental group* **9 wks**

| 17 Dec 88 | KEEPING THE DREAM ALIVE *CBS 652989 7* ....**14** | 9 wks |

Deborah FRENCH - *See E-LUSTRIOUS featuring Deborah FRENCH*

Nicki FRENCH *UK, female vocalist* **1 wk**

| 15 Oct 94 | TOTAL ECLIPSE OF THE HEART | |
| | *Bags Of Fun BAGSCD 1* ....**54** | 1 wk |

BILLY FURY is shown in February 1964, during the chart run of 'Do You Really Love Me Too'. (LFI)

In 1958 **CONNIE FRANCIS** kicked Marvin Rainwater out of number one, ironic since the previous year they had been duet partners on 'The Majesty Of Love'. (LFI)

Holly Johnston (standing) led **FRANKIE GOES TO HOLLYWOOD** into chart battle. (LFI)

FUNKY POETS US, male vocal group — 1 wk

| 7 May 94 | **BORN IN THE GHETTO** Epic 6603522 | **72** | 1 wk |

FUNKY WORM
UK, male/female vocal/instrumental group — 14 wks

30 Jul 88	**HUSTLE! (TO THE MUSIC...)** Fon FON 15	**13**	8 wks
26 Nov 88	**THE SPELL!** Fon FON 16	**61**	3 wks
20 May 89	**U + ME = LOVE** Fon FON 19	**46**	3 wks

FUREYS Ireland, male vocal group — 14 wks

| 10 Oct 81 | **WHEN YOU WERE SWEET SIXTEEN** Ritz RITZ 003 [1] | **14** | 11 wks |
| 3 Apr 82 | **I WILL LOVE YOU (EV'RY TIME WHEN WE ARE GONE)** Ritz RITZ 012 | **54** | 3 wks |

[1] Fureys with Davey Arthur

FURIOUS FIVE - See GRANDMASTER FLASH, Melle MEL and the FURIOUS FIVE

FURNITURE UK, male/female vocal/instrumental group — 10 wks

| 14 Jun 86 | **BRILLIANT MIND** Stiff BUY 251 | **21** | 10 wks |

Billy FURY UK, male vocalist — 281 wks

27 Feb 59	**MAYBE TOMORROW** Decca F 11102	**22**	3 wks
27 Mar 59	**MAYBE TOMORROW (re-entry)** Decca F 11102	**18**	6 wks
26 Jun 59	**MARGO** Decca F 11128	**28**	1 wk
10 Mar 60	● **COLETTE** Decca F 11200	**9**	10 wks
26 May 60	**THAT'S LOVE** Decca F 11237	**19**	11 wks
22 Sep 60	**WONDROUS PLACE** Decca F 11267	**25**	9 wks
19 Jan 61	**A THOUSAND STARS** Decca F 11311	**14**	10 wks
27 Apr 61	**DON'T WORRY** Decca F 11334	**40**	2 wks
11 May 61	● **HALFWAY TO PARADISE** Decca F 11349	**3**	23 wks
7 Sep 61	● **JEALOUSY** Decca F 11384	**2**	12 wks
14 Dec 61	● **I'D NEVER FIND ANOTHER YOU** Decca F 11409	**5**	15 wks
15 Mar 62	**LETTER FULL OF TEARS** Decca F 11437	**32**	6 wks
3 May 62	● **LAST NIGHT WAS MADE FOR LOVE** Decca F 11458	**4**	16 wks
19 Jul 62	● **ONCE UPON A DREAM** Decca F 11485	**7**	13 wks
25 Oct 62	**BECAUSE OF LOVE** Decca F 11508	**18**	14 wks
14 Feb 63	● **LIKE I'VE NEVER BEEN GONE** Decca F11582	**3**	15 wks
16 May 63	● **WHEN WILL YOU SAY I LOVE YOU** Decca F 11655	**3**	12 wks
25 Jul 63	● **IN SUMMER** Decca F 11701	**5**	11 wks
3 Oct 63	**SOMEBODY ELSE'S GIRL** Decca F 11744	**18**	7 wks
2 Jan 64	**DO YOU REALLY LOVE ME TOO** Decca F 11792	**13**	10 wks
30 Apr 64	**I WILL** Decca F 11888	**14**	12 wks
23 Jul 64	● **IT'S ONLY MAKE BELIEVE** Decca F 11939	**10**	10 wks
14 Jan 65	**I'M LOST WITHOUT YOU** Decca F 12048	**16**	10 wks
22 Jul 65	● **IN THOUGHTS OF YOU** Decca F 12178	**9**	11 wks
16 Sep 65	**RUN TO MY LOVIN' ARMS** Decca F 12230	**25**	7 wks
10 Feb 66	**I'LL NEVER QUITE GET OVER YOU** Decca F 12325	**35**	5 wks
4 Aug 66	**GIVE ME YOUR WORD** Decca F 12459	**27**	7 wks
4 Sep 82	**LOVE OR MONEY** Polydor POSP 488	**57**	5 wks
13 Nov 82	**DEVIL OR ANGEL** Polydor POSP 528	**58**	4 wks
4 Jun 83	**FORGET HIM** Polydor POSP 558	**59**	4 wks

FUTURE SOUND OF LONDON
UK, male instrumental/production duo — 13 wks

23 May 92	**PAPUA NEW GUINEA** Jumpin' & Pumpin' TOT 17	**22**	6 wks
6 Nov 93	**CASCADE** Virgin VSCDT 1478	**27**	3 wks
30 Jul 94	**EXPANDER** Jumpin' & Pumpin' CDSTOT 37	**72**	1 wk
13 Aug 94	**LIFEFORMS** Virgin VSCD 1484	**14**	3 wks

FUZZBOX - See WE'VE GOT A FUZZBOX AND WE'RE GONNA USE IT

Leslie FYSON - See Michael MEDWIN, Bernard BRESSLAW, Alfie BASS and Leslie FYSON

Bobby G UK, male vocalist — 12 wks

1 Dec 84	**BIG DEAL** BBC RESL 151	**75**	1 wk
15 Dec 84	**BIG DEAL (re-entry)** BBC RESL 151	**65**	5 wks
19 Oct 85	**BIG DEAL (2nd re-entry)** BBC RESL 151	**46**	6 wks

Kenny G US, male instrumentalist - saxophone — 22 wks

21 Apr 84	**HI! HOW YA DOIN'?** Arista ARIST 561	**70**	3 wks
30 Aug 86	**WHAT DOES IT TAKE (TO WIN YOUR LOVE)** Arista ARIST 672	**64**	2 wks
4 Jul 87	**SONGBIRD** Arista RIS 18	**22**	7 wks
9 May 92	**MISSING YOU NOW** Columbia 6579917 [1]	**28**	4 wks
24 Apr 93	**FOREVER IN LOVE** Arista 74321145552	**47**	3 wks
17 Jul 93	**BY THE TIME THIS NIGHT IS OVER** Arista 74321157142 [2]	**56**	3 wks

[1] Michael Bolton featuring Kenny G [2] Kenny G with Peabo Bryson

Warren G US, male rapper — 20 wks

23 Jul 94	● **REGULATE** Death Row A 8290CD [1]	**5**	14 wks
12 Nov 94	**THIS DJ** RAL RALCD 1	**12**	5 wks
31 Dec 94	**THIS DJ (re-entry)** RAL RALCD 1	**72†**	1 wk

[1] Warren G and Nate Dogg

Eric GABLE US, male vocalist — 1 wk

| 19 Mar 94 | **PROCESS OF ELIMINATION** Epic 6602282 | **63** | 1 wk |

Peter GABRIEL UK, male vocalist — 112 wks

9 Apr 77	**SOLSBURY HILL** Charisma CB 301	**13**	9 wks
9 Feb 80	● **GAMES WITHOUT FRONTIERS** Charisma CB 354	**4**	11 wks
10 May 80	**NO SELF CONTROL** Charisma CB 360	**33**	6 wks
23 Aug 80	**BIKO** Charisma CB 370	**38**	3 wks
25 Sep 82	**SHOCK THE MONKEY** Charisma SHOCK 1	**58**	5 wks
9 Jul 83	**I DON'T REMEMBER** Charisma GAB 1	**62**	3 wks
2 Jun 84	**WALK THROUGH THE FIRE** Virgin VS 689	**69**	3 wks
26 Apr 86	● **SLEDGEHAMMER** Virgin PGS 1	**4**	16 wks
1 Nov 86	**DON'T GIVE UP** Virgin PGS 2 [1]	**9**	11 wks
28 Mar 87	**BIG TIME** Charisma PGS 3	**13**	7 wks
11 Jul 87	**RED RAIN** Charisma PGS 4	**46**	3 wks
21 Nov 87	**BIKO (LIVE)** Charisma PGS 6	**49**	6 wks
3 Jun 89	**SHAKING THE TREE** Virgin VS 1167 [2]	**61**	3 wks
22 Dec 90	**SOLSBURY HILL / SHAKING THE TREE (re-issue)** Virgin VS 1322 [3]	**57**	4 wks
19 Sep 92	**DIGGING IN THE DIRT** Realworld PGS 7	**24**	4 wks
16 Jan 93	● **STEAM** Realworld PGSDG 8	**10**	7 wks
3 Apr 93	**BLOOD OF EDEN** Realworld PGSDG 9	**43**	4 wks
25 Sep 93	**KISS THAT FROG** Realworld PGSDG 10	**46**	3 wks
25 Jun 94	**LOVETOWN** Epic 6604802	**49**	2 wks
3 Sep 94	**SW LIVE EP** Realworld PGSCD 11	**39**	2 wks

[1] Peter Gabriel and Kate Bush [2] Youssou N'Dour and Peter Gabriel [3] Peter Gabriel/Youssou N'Dour and Peter Gabriel

Tracks available on all formats of SW Live EP: Red Rain/San Jacinto. Red Rain is a live version of his '87 hit.

GABRIELLE UK, female vocalist — 32 wks

19 Jun 93	★ **DREAMS** Go.Beat GODCD 99	**1**	15 wks
2 Oct 93	● **GOING NOWHERE** Go.Beat GODCD 106	**9**	7 wks
11 Dec 93	**I WISH** Go.Beat GODCD 108	**26**	5 wks
26 Feb 94	**BECAUSE OF YOU** Go.Beat GOLCD 109	**24**	5 wks

Yvonne GAGE US, female vocalist — 4 wks

| 16 Jun 84 | **DOIN' IT IN A HAUNTED HOUSE** Epic A 4519 | **45** | 4 wks |

GABRIELLE performs at Gay and Lesbian Pride in June 1993.
(Steve Gillett)

Danni'elle GAHA *Australia, female vocalist* — **7 wks**

1 Aug 92	**STUCK IN THE MIDDLE** *Epic 6581247*	**68**	2 wks
27 Feb 93	**DO IT FOR LOVE** *Epic 6584612*	**52**	2 wks
12 Jun 93	**SECRET LOVE** *Epic 6592212*	**41**	3 wks

Serge GAINSBOURG - *See Jane BIRKIN and Serge GAINSBOURG*

GALAXY - *See Phil FEARON*

Dee GALDES - *See Phil FEARON*

Eve GALLAGHER *UK, female vocalist* — **4 wks**

1 Dec 90	**LOVE COME DOWN** *More Protein PROT 6*	**61**	3 wks
29 Dec 90	**LOVE COME DOWN (re-entry)** *More Protein PROT 6*	**68**	1 wk

GALLAGHER and LYLE
UK, male vocal / instrumental duo — **27 wks**

28 Feb 76	● **I WANNA STAY WITH YOU** *A & M AMS 7211*	**6**	9 wks
22 May 76	● **HEART ON MY SLEEVE** *A & M AMS 7227*	**6**	10 wks
11 Sep 76	**BREAKAWAY** *A & M AMS 7245*	**35**	4 wks
29 Jan 77	**EVERY LITTLE TEARDROP** *A & M AMS 7274*	**32**	4 wks

Patsy GALLANT *Canada, female vocalist* — **9 wks**

10 Sep 77	● **FROM NEW YORK TO L.A.** *EMI 2620*	**6**	9 wks

GALLIANO *UK, male / female vocal / instrumental group* — **12 wks**

30 May 92	**SKUNK FUNK** *Talkin Loud TLK 23*	**41**	2 wks
1 Aug 92	**PRINCE OF PEACE** *Talkin Loud TLK 24*	**47**	3 wks
10 Oct 92	**JUS' REACH (RECYCLED)** *Talkin Loud TLK 29*	**66**	2 wks
28 May 94	**LONG TIME GONE** *Talkin Loud TLKCD 48*	**15**	3 wks
30 Jul 94	**TWYFORD DOWN** *Talkin Loud TLKDD 49*	**37**	2 wks

James GALWAY *UK, male instrumentalist - flute* — **13 wks**

27 May 78	● **ANNIE'S SONG** *RCA Red Seal RB 5085*	**3**	13 wks

GANG OF FOUR *UK, male vocal / instrumental group* — **5 wks**

16 Jun 79	**AT HOME HE'S A TOURIST** *EMI 2956*	**58**	3 wks
22 May 82	**I LOVE A MAN IN UNIFORM** *EMI 5299*	**65**	2 wks

GANG STARR *US, male rap group* — **8 wks**

13 Oct 90	**JAZZ THING** *CBS 356377 7*	**66**	2 wks
23 Feb 91	**TAKE A REST** *Cooltempo COOL 230*	**63**	1 wk
25 May 91	**LOVESICK** *Cooltempo COOL 234*	**50**	3 wks
13 Jun 92	**2 DEEP** *Cooltempo COOL 256*	**67**	2 wks

GAP BAND *US, male vocal / instrumental group* — **82 wks**

12 Jul 80	● **OOPS UP SIDE YOUR HEAD** *Mercury MER 22*	**6**	14 wks
27 Sep 80	**PARTY LIGHTS** *Mercury MER 37*	**30**	8 wks
27 Dec 80	**BURN RUBBER ON ME (WHY YOU WANNA HURT ME)** *Mercury MER 52*	**22**	11 wks
11 Apr 81	**HUMPIN'** *Mercury MER 63*	**36**	6 wks
27 Jun 81	**YEARNING FOR YOUR LOVE** *Mercury MER 73*	**47**	4 wks
5 Jun 82	**EARLY IN THE MORNING** *Mercury MER 97*	**55**	3 wks
19 Feb 83	**OUTSTANDING** *Total Experience TE 001*	**68**	2 wks
31 Mar 84	**SOMEDAY** *Total Experience TE 5*	**17**	8 wks
23 Jun 84	**JAMMIN' IN AMERICA** *Total Experience TE 6*	**64**	2 wks
13 Dec 86	● **BIG FUN** *Total Experience FB 49779*	**4**	12 wks
14 Mar 87	**HOW MUSIC CAME ABOUT (BOP B DA B DA DA)** *Total Experience FB 49755*	**61**	2 wks
11 Jul 87	**OOPS UPSIDE YOUR HEAD (re-mix)** *Club JAB 54*	**20**	8 wks
18 Feb 89	**I'M GONNA GIT YOU SUCKA** *Arista 112016*	**63**	2 wks

Boris GARDINER
Jamaica, male vocalist / instrumentalist — **38 wks**

17 Jan 70	**ELIZABETHAN REGGAE** *Duke DU 39*	**48**	1 wk
31 Jan 70	**ELIZABETHAN REGGAE (re-entry)** *Duke DU 39*	**14**	13 wks
26 Jul 86	★ **I WANT TO WAKE UP WITH YOU** *Revue REV 733*	**1**	15 wks
4 Oct 86	**YOU'RE EVERYTHING TO ME** *Revue REV 735*	**11**	8 wks
27 Dec 86	**THE MEANING OF CHRISTMAS** *Revue REV 740*	**69**	1 wk

The first copies of Elizabethan Reggae, an instrumental, were printed with the label incorrectly crediting Byron Lee as the performer. The charts for the first entry, and the first four weeks of the re-entry, all reprinted this error. All charts and discs printed after 28 Feb 1970 gave Boris Gardiner the credit he deserved.

Paul GARDINER *UK, male instrumentalist - bass* — **4 wks**

25 Jul 81	**STORMTROOPER IN DRAG** *Beggars Banquet BEG 61*	**49**	4 wks

Uncredited vocalist is Gary Numan.

Art GARFUNKEL *US, male vocalist* — **37 wks**

13 Sep 75	★ **I ONLY HAVE EYES FOR YOU** *CBS 3575*	**1**	11 wks
3 Mar 79	★ **BRIGHT EYES** *CBS 6947*	**1**	19 wks
7 Jul 79	**SINCE I DON'T HAVE YOU** *CBS 7371*	**38**	7 wks

Judy GARLAND *US, female vocalist* — **2 wks**

10 Jun 55	**THE MAN THAT GOT AWAY** *Philips PB 366*	**18**	2 wks

Lee GARRETT *US, male vocalist* — **7 wks**

29 May 76	**YOU'RE MY EVERYTHING** *Chrysalis CHS 2087*	**15**	7 wks

Leif GARRETT *US, male vocalist* — **14 wks**

20 Jan 79	● **I WAS MADE FOR DANCIN'** *Scotti Brothers K 11202*	**4**	10 wks
21 Apr 79	**FEEL THE NEED** *Scotti Brothers K 11274*	**38**	4 wks

Lesley GARRETT and Amanda THOMPSON
UK, female vocal / instrumental duo — **10 wks**

6 Nov 93	**AVE MARIA** *Internal Affairs KGBD 012*	**16**	10 wks

Siedah GARRETT - *See Dennis EDWARDS; Michael JACKSON*

David GARRICK *UK, male vocalist* — **16 wks**

9 Jun 66	**LADY JANE** *Piccadilly 7N 35317*	**28**	7 wks
22 Sep 66	**DEAR MRS. APPLEBEE** *Piccadilly 7N 35335*	**22**	9 wks

GARY'S GANG *US, male vocal / instrumental group* — **18 wks**

24 Feb 79	● **KEEP ON DANCIN'** *CBS 7109*	**8**	10 wks
2 Jun 79	**LET'S LOVE DANCE TONIGHT** *CBS 7328*	**49**	4 wks
6 Nov 82	**KNOCK ME OUT** *Arista ARIST 499*	**45**	4 wks

Barbara GASKIN - *See Dave STEWART*

GAT DECOR *UK, male instrumental group* — **4 wks**

16 May 92	**PASSION** *Effective EFFS 1*	**29**	4 wks

David GATES *US, male vocalist* — **2 wks**

22 Jul 78	**TOOK THE LAST TRAIN** *Elektra K 12307*	**50**	2 wks

GAY GORDON and the MINCE PIES
UK, male/female vocal/instrumental group   **5 wks**

| 6 Dec 86 | THE ESSENTIAL WALLY PARTY MEDLEY | | |
| | *Lifestyle XY 2* | **60** | 5 wks |

GAYE BYKERS ON ACID
UK, male vocal/instrumental group   **2 wks**

| 31 Oct 87 | GIT DOWN (SHAKE YOUR THANG) | | |
| | *Purple Fluid VS 1008* | **54** | 2 wks |

Marvin GAYE *US, male vocalist*   **200 wks**

30 Jul 64	ONCE UPON A TIME *Stateside SS 316* [1]	**50**	1 wk
10 Dec 64	HOW SWEET IT IS *Stateside SS 360*	**49**	1 wk
29 Sep 66	LITTLE DARLIN' *Tamla Motown TMG 574*	**50**	1 wk
26 Jan 67	IT TAKES TWO *Tamla Motown TMG 590* [2]	**16**	11 wks
17 Jan 68	IF I COULD BUILD MY WHOLE WORLD		
	AROUND YOU *Tamla Motown TMG 635* [3]	**41**	7 wks
12 Jun 68	AIN'T NOTHIN' LIKE THE REAL THING		
	Tamla Motown TMG 655 [3]	**34**	7 wks
2 Oct 68	YOU'RE ALL I NEED TO GET BY		
	Tamla Motown TMG 668 [3]	**19**	19 wks
22 Jan 69	YOU AIN'T LIVIN' 'TILL YOU'RE LOVIN'		
	Tamla Motown TMG 681 [3]	**21**	8 wks
12 Feb 69	★ I HEARD IT THROUGH THE GRAPEVINE		
	Tamla Motown TMG 686	**1**	15 wks
4 Jun 69	GOOD LOVIN' AIN'T EASY TO COME BY		
	Tamla Motown TMG 697 [3]	**26**	7 wks
23 Jul 69	● TOO BUSY THINKING 'BOUT MY BABY		
	Tamla Motown TMG 705	**5**	16 wks
30 Jul 69	GOOD LOVIN' AIN'T EASY TO COME BY (re-entry)		
	Tamla Motown TMG 697 [3]	**48**	1 wk
15 Nov 69	● ONION SONG *Tamla Motown TMG 715* [3]	**9**	12 wks
9 May 70	● ABRAHAM MARTIN AND JOHN		
	Tamla Motown TMG 734	**9**	14 wks
11 Dec 71	SAVE THE CHILDREN *Tamla Motown TMG 796*	**41**	6 wks
22 Sep 73	LET'S GET IT ON *Tamla Motown TMG 868*	**31**	7 wks
23 Mar 74	● YOU ARE EVERYTHING *Tamla Motown TMG 890* [4]	**5**	12 wks
20 Jul 74	STOP LOOK LISTEN (TO YOUR HEART)		
	Tamla Motown TMG 906 [4]	**25**	8 wks
7 May 77	● GOT TO GIVE IT UP *Motown TMG 1069*	**7**	10 wks
24 Feb 79	POPS WE LOVE YOU *Motown TMG 1136* [5]	**66**	5 wks
30 Oct 82	● (SEXUAL) HEALING *CBS A 2855*	**4**	14 wks
8 Jan 83	MY LOVE IS WAITING *CBS A 3048*	**34**	5 wks
18 May 85	SANCTIFIED LADY *CBS A 4894*	**51**	4 wks
26 Apr 86	● I HEARD IT THRU THE GRAPEVINE (re-issue)		
	Tamla Motown ZB 40701	**8**	8 wks
14 May 94	LUCKY LUCKY ME *Motown TMGCD 1426*	**67**	1 wk

[1] Marvin Gaye and Mary Wells [2] Marvin Gaye and Kim Weston [3] Marvin Gaye and Tammi Terrell [4] Diana Ross and Marvin Gaye [5] Diana Ross, Marvin Gaye, Smokey Robinson and Stevie Wonder

GAYLE & GILLIAN *Australia, female vocal duo*   **2 wks**

| 3 Jul 93 | MAD IF YA DON'T *Mushroom CDMUSH 1* | **75** | 1 wk |
| 19 Mar 94 | WANNA BE YOUR LOVER *Mushroom D 11598* | **62** | 1 wk |

Crystal GAYLE *US, female vocalist*   **28 wks**

12 Nov 77	● DON'T IT MAKE MY BROWN EYES BLUE		
	United Artists UP 36307	**5**	14 wks
26 Aug 78	TALKING IN YOUR SLEEP *United Artists UP 36422*	**11**	14 wks

Michelle GAYLE *UK, female vocalist*   **24 wks**

7 Aug 93	LOOKING UP *RCA 74321154532*	**11**	6 wks
24 Sep 94	● SWEETNESS *RCA 74321230192*	**4†**	15 wks
17 Dec 94	I'LL FIND YOU *RCA 74321247762*	**26†**	3 wks

Roy GAYLE - *See MIRAGE*

Gloria GAYNOR *US, female vocalist*   **72 wks**

7 Dec 74	● NEVER CAN SAY GOODBYE *MGM 2006 463*	**2**	13 wks
8 Mar 75	REACH OUT I'LL BE THERE *MGM 2006 499*	**14**	8 wks
9 Aug 75	ALL I NEED IS YOUR SWEET LOVIN'		
	MGM 2006 531	**44**	3 wks
17 Jan 76	HOW HIGH THE MOON *MGM 2006 558*	**33**	4 wks
3 Feb 79	★ I WILL SURVIVE *Polydor 2095 017*	**1**	15 wks
6 Oct 79	LET ME KNOW (I HAVE A RIGHT) *Polydor STEP 5*	**32**	7 wks
24 Dec 83	I AM WHAT I AM *Chrysalis CHS 2765*	**13**	12 wks
26 Jun 93	● I WILL SURVIVE (re-mix) *Polydor PZCD 270*	**5**	10 wks

GAZ *US, male vocal/instrumental group*   **4 wks**

| 24 Feb 79 | SING SING *Salsoul SSOL 116* | **60** | 4 wks |

GAZZA *UK, male vocalist - Paul Gascoigne*   **14 wks**

| 10 Nov 90 | ● FOG ON THE TYNE (REVISITED) *Best ZB 44083* [1] | **2** | 9 wks |
| 22 Dec 90 | GEORDIE BOYS (GAZZA RAP) *Best ZB 44229* | **31** | 5 wks |

[1] Gazza and Lindisfarne

GBH *UK, male vocal/instrumental group*   **5 wks**

| 6 Feb 82 | NO SURVIVORS *Clay CLAY 8* | **63** | 2 wks |
| 20 Nov 82 | GIVE ME FIRE *Clay CLAY 16* | **69** | 3 wks |

G-CLEFS *US, male vocal group*   **12 wks**

| 30 Nov 61 | I UNDERSTAND *London HLU 9433* | **17** | 12 wks |

J. GEILS BAND *US, male vocal/instrumental group*   **20 wks**

9 Jun 79	ONE LAST KISS *EMI America AM 507*	**74**	1 wk
13 Feb 82	● CENTERFOLD *EMI America EA 135*	**3**	9 wks
10 Apr 82	FREEZE-FRAME *EMI America EA 134*	**27**	7 wks
26 Jun 82	ANGEL IN BLUE *EMI America EA 138*	**55**	3 wks

Bob GELDOF *Ireland, male vocalist*   **15 wks**

1 Nov 86	THIS IS THE WORLD CALLING *Mercury BOB 101*	**25**	5 wks
21 Feb 87	LOVE LIKE A ROCKET *Mercury BOB 102*	**61**	3 wks
23 Jun 90	THE GREAT SONG OF INDIFFERENCE		
	Mercury BOB 104	**15**	6 wks
7 May 94	CRAZY *Vertigo VERCX 85*	**65**	1 wk

GEM - *See ONE TRIBE featuring GEM*

GENE *UK, male vocal/instrumental group*   **3 wks**

13 Aug 94	BE MY LIGHT BE MY GUIDE		
	Costermonger COST 002CD	**54**	1 wk
12 Nov 94	SLEEP WELL TONIGHT		
	Costermonger COST 003CD	**36**	2 wks

GENE AND JIM ARE INTO SHAKES
UK, male vocal/instrumental duo   **2 wks**

| 19 Mar 88 | SHAKE! (HOW ABOUT A SAMPLING GENE) | | |
| | *Rough Trade RT 216* | **68** | 2 wks |

GENE LOVES JEZEBEL
UK, male vocal/instrumental group   **7 wks**

29 Mar 86	SWEETEST THING *Beggars Banquet BEG 156*	**75**	1 wk
14 Jun 86	HEARTACHE *Beggars Banquet BEG 161*	**71**	2 wks
5 Sep 87	THE MOTION OF LOVE *Beggars Banquet BEG 192*	**56**	3 wks
5 Dec 87	GORGEOUS *Beggars Banquet BEG 202*	**68**	1 wk

GENERAL LEVY UK, male vocalist — **13 wks**

4 Sep 93	**MONKEY MAN** ffrr FCD 214	............**75**	1 wk
18 Jun 94	**INCREDIBLE** Renk RENKT 42CD [1]	............**39**	3 wks
10 Sep 94	● **INCREDIBLE (re-mix)** Renk CDRENK 44 [1]	............**8**	9 wks

[1] M-Beat featuring General Levy

GENERAL PUBLIC UK, male vocal/instrumental group — **4 wks**

| 10 Mar 84 | **GENERAL PUBLIC** Virgin VS 659 | ....**60** | 3 wks |
| 2 Jul 94 | **I'LL TAKE YOU THERE** Epic 6605532 | ....**73** | 1 wk |

GENERAL SAINT UK, male vocalist — **9 wks**

29 Sep 84	**LAST PLANE (ONE WAY TICKET)** MCA MCA 910 [1]	............**51**	3 wks
2 Apr 94	**OH CAROL!** Copasetic COPCD 0009 [2]	............**54**	5 wks
6 Aug 94	**SAVE THE LAST DANCE FOR ME** Copasetic COPCD 12 [2]	............**75**	1 wk

[1] Clint Eastwood and General Saint [2] General Saint featuring Don Campbell

GENERATION X UK, male vocal/instrumental group — **31 wks**

17 Sep 77	**YOUR GENERATION** Chrysalis CHS 2165	............**36**	4 wks
11 Mar 78	**READY STEADY GO** Chrysalis CHS 2207	............**47**	3 wks
20 Jan 79	**KING ROCKER** Chrysalis CHS 2261	............**11**	9 wks
7 Apr 79	**VALLEY OF THE DOLLS** Chrysalis CHS 2310	............**23**	7 wks
30 Jun 79	**FRIDAY'S ANGELS** Chrysalis CHS 2330	............**62**	2 wks
18 Oct 80	**DANCING WITH MYSELF** Chrysalis CHS 2444 [1]	............**62**	2 wks
24 Jan 81	**DANCING WITH MYSELF (EP)** Chrysalis CHS 2488 [1]	............**60**	4 wks

[1] Gen X

Tracks on Dancing With Myself (EP): Dancing With Myself / Untouchables / Rock On / King Rocker.

GENESIS UK, male vocal/instrumental group — **183 wks**

6 Apr 74	**I KNOW WHAT I LIKE (IN YOUR WARDROBE)** Charisma CB 224	............**21**	7 wks
26 Feb 77	**YOUR OWN SPECIAL WAY** Charisma CB 300	............**43**	3 wks
28 May 77	**SPOT THE PIGEON EP** Charisma GEN 001	............**14**	7 wks
11 Mar 78	● **FOLLOW YOU FOLLOW ME** Charisma CB 309	............**7**	13 wks
8 Jul 78	**MANY TOO MANY** Charisma CB 315	............**43**	5 wks
15 Mar 80	● **TURN IT ON AGAIN** Charisma CB 356	............**8**	10 wks
17 May 80	**DUCHESS** Charisma CB 363	............**46**	5 wks
13 Sep 80	**MISUNDERSTANDING** Charisma CB 369	............**42**	5 wks
22 Aug 81	● **ABACAB** Charisma CB 388	............**9**	8 wks
31 Oct 81	**KEEP IT DARK** Charisma CB 391	............**33**	4 wks
13 Mar 82	**MAN ON THE CORNER** Charisma CB 393	............**41**	5 wks
22 May 82	**3 X 3 EP** Charisma GEN 1	............**10**	8 wks
3 Sep 83	● **MAMA** Virgin/Charisma MAMA 1	............**4**	10 wks
12 Nov 83	**THAT'S ALL** Charisma/Virgin TATA 1	............**16**	11 wks
11 Feb 84	**ILLEGAL ALIEN** Charisma/Virgin AL1	............**46**	3 wks
10 Mar 84	**ILLEGAL ALIEN (re-entry)** Charisma/Virgin AL1	............**70**	1 wk
31 May 86	**INVISIBLE TOUCH** Virgin GENS 1	............**15**	8 wks
30 Aug 86	**IN TOO DEEP** Virgin GENS 2	............**19**	9 wks
22 Nov 86	**LAND OF CONFUSION** Virgin GENS 3	............**14**	12 wks
14 Mar 87	**TONIGHT TONIGHT TONIGHT** Virgin GENS 4	............**18**	6 wks
20 Jun 87	**THROWING IT ALL AWAY** Virgin GENS 5	............**22**	8 wks
2 Nov 91	● **NO SON OF MINE** Virgin GENS 6	............**6**	6 wks
4 Jan 92	**NO SON OF MINE (re-entry)** Virgin GENS 6	............**70**	1 wk
11 Jan 92	● **I CAN'T DANCE** Virgin GENS 7	............**7**	9 wks
18 Apr 92	**HOLD ON MY HEART** Virgin GENS 8	............**16**	5 wks
25 Jul 92	**JESUS HE KNOWS ME** Virgin GENS 9	............**20**	7 wks
21 Nov 92	● **INVISIBLE TOUCH (LIVE)** Virgin GENS 10	............**7**	4 wks

---

| 20 Feb 93 | **TELL ME WHY** Virgin GENDG 11 | ....**40** | 3 wks |

Tracks on Spot The Pigeon EP: Match Of The Day / Pigeons / Inside and Out. Tracks on 3 X 3 EP: Paperlate / You Might Recall / Me And Virgil.

GENEVIEVE France, female vocalist — **1 wk**

| 5 May 66 | **ONCE** CBS 202061 | ....**43** | 1 wk |

Bobbie GENTRY US, female vocalist — **48 wks**

13 Sep 67	**ODE TO BILLY JOE** Capitol CL 15511	............**13**	11 wks
30 Aug 69	★ **I'LL NEVER FALL IN LOVE AGAIN** Capitol CL 15606	..**1**	19 wks
6 Dec 69	● **ALL I HAVE TO DO IS DREAM** Capitol CL 15619 [1]	....**3**	14 wks
21 Feb 70	**RAINDROPS KEEP FALLIN' ON MY HEAD** Capitol CL 15626	............**40**	4 wks

[1] Bobbie Gentry and Glen Campbell

GEORDIE UK, vocal/instrumental group — **35 wks**

2 Dec 72	**DON'T DO THAT** Regal Zonophone RZ 3067	............**32**	7 wks
17 Mar 73	● **ALL BECAUSE OF YOU** EMI 2008	............**6**	13 wks
16 Jun 73	**CAN YOU DO IT** EMI 2031	............**13**	9 wks
25 Aug 73	**ELECTRIC LADY** EMI 2048	............**32**	6 wks

Robin GEORGE
UK, male vocalist/instrumentalist - guitar — **2 wks**

| 27 Apr 85 | **HEARTLINE** Bronze BRO 191 | ....**68** | 2 wks |

Sophia GEORGE Jamaica, female vocalist — **11 wks**

| 7 Dec 85 | ● **GIRLIE GIRLIE** Winner WIN 01 | ....**7** | 11 wks |

GEORGIA SATELLITES
US, male vocal/instrumental group — **8 wks**

7 Feb 87	**KEEP YOUR HANDS TO YOURSELF** Elektra EKR 50	............**69**	1 wk
16 May 87	**BATTLESHIP CHAINS** Elektra EKR 58	............**44**	4 wks
21 Jan 89	**HIPPY HIPPY SHAKE** Elektra EKR 86	............**63**	3 wks

GEORGIO US, male vocalist — **3 wks**

| 20 Feb 88 | **LOVER'S LANE** Motown ZB 41611 | ....**54** | 3 wks |

Danyel GERARD France, male vocalist — **12 wks**

| 18 Sep 71 | **BUTTERFLY** CBS 7454 | ....**11** | 12 wks |

GERIDEAU - See PROJECT featuring GERIDEAU

GERRY and the PACEMAKERS
UK, male vocal/instrumental group — **114 wks**

14 Mar 63	★ **HOW DO YOU DO IT?** Columbia DB 4987	............**1**	18 wks
30 May 63	★ **I LIKE IT** Columbia DB 7041	............**1**	15 wks
10 Oct 63	★ **YOU'LL NEVER WALK ALONE** Columbia DB 7126	......**1**	19 wks
16 Jan 64	● **I'M THE ONE** Columbia DB 7189	............**2**	15 wks
16 Apr 64	● **DON'T LET THE SUN CATCH YOU CRYING** Columbia DB 7268	............**6**	11 wks
3 Sep 64	**IT'S GONNA BE ALL RIGHT** Columbia DB 7353	............**24**	7 wks
17 Dec 64	● **FERRY ACROSS THE MERSEY** Columbia DB 7437	............**8**	13 wks
25 Mar 65	**I'LL BE THERE** Columbia DB 7504	............**15**	9 wks
18 Nov 65	**WALK HAND IN HAND** Columbia DB 7738	............**29**	7 wks

GET FRESH CREW - See Doug E. FRESH and the GET FRESH CREW

Stan GETZ *US, male instrumentalist - tenor sax* · **29 wks**

8 Nov 62	**DESAFINADO** *HMV POP 1061* [1]	**11**	13 wks
23 Jul 64	**THE GIRL FROM IPANEMA (GAROTA DE IPANEMA)** *Verve VS 520* [2]	**29**	10 wks
25 Aug 84	**THE GIRL FROM IPANEMA (re-issue)** *Verve IPA 1* [3]	**55**	6 wks

[1] Stan Getz and Charlie Byrd [2] Stan Getz and Joao Gilberto [3] Astrud Gilberto

The re-issue of The Girl From Ipanema was credited only to Astrud Gilberto, the vocalist, even though it was exactly the same recording as the original hit.

GHOST DANCE *UK, male vocal / instrumental group* · **2 wks**

| 17 Jun 89 | **DOWN TO THE WIRE** *Chrysalis CHS 3376* | **66** | 2 wks |

Andy GIBB *UK, male vocalist* · **30 wks**

25 Jun 77	**I JUST WANNA BE YOUR EVERYTHING** *RSO 2090 237*	**26**	7 wks
13 May 78	**SHADOW DANCING** *RSO 001*	**42**	6 wks
12 Aug 78	● **AN EVERLASTING LOVE** *RSO 015*	**10**	10 wks
27 Jan 79	**(OUR LOVE) DON'T THROW IT ALL AWAY** *RSO 26*	**32**	7 wks

Barry GIBB - *See Barbra STREISAND*

Robin GIBB *UK, male vocalist* · **21 wks**

9 Jul 69	● **SAVED BY THE BELL** *Polydor 56-337*	**2**	16 wks
15 Nov 69	**SAVED BY THE BELL (re-entry)** *Polydor 56-337*	**49**	1 wk
7 Feb 70	**AUGUST OCTOBER** *Polydor 56-371*	**45**	3 wks
11 Feb 84	**ANOTHER LONELY NIGHT IN NEW YORK** *Polydor POSP 668*	**71**	1 wk

Steve GIBBONS BAND
UK, male vocal / instrumental group · **14 wks**

| 6 Aug 77 | **TULANE** *Polydor 2058 889* | **12** | 10 wks |
| 13 May 78 | **EDDY VORTEX** *Polydor 2059 017* | **56** | 4 wks |

Georgia GIBBS *US, female vocalist* · **2 wks**

| 22 Apr 55 | **TWEEDLE DEE** *Mercury MB 3196* | **20** | 1 wk |
| 13 Jul 56 | **KISS ME ANOTHER** *Mercury MT 110* | **24** | 1 wk |

Debbie GIBSON *US, female vocalist* · **70 wks**

26 Sep 87	**ONLY IN MY DREAMS** *Atlantic A 9322*	**54**	5 wks
23 Jan 88	● **SHAKE YOUR LOVE** *Atlantic A 9187*	**7**	8 wks
19 Mar 88	**ONLY IN MY DREAMS (re-entry)** *Atlantic A 9322*	**11**	7 wks
7 May 88	**OUT OF THE BLUE** *Atlantic A 9091*	**19**	7 wks
9 Jul 88	● **FOOLISH BEAT** *Atlantic A 9059*	**9**	9 wks
15 Oct 88	**STAYING TOGETHER** *Atlantic A 9020*	**53**	2 wks
28 Jan 89	**LOST IN YOUR EYES** *Atlantic A 8970*	**34**	7 wks
29 Apr 89	**ELECTRIC YOUTH** *Atlantic A 8919*	**14**	8 wks
19 Aug 89	**WE COULD BE TOGETHER** *Atlantic A 8896*	**22**	8 wks
9 Mar 91	**ANYTHING IS POSSIBLE** *Atlantic A 7735*	**51**	2 wks
3 Apr 93	**SHOCK YOUR MAMA** *Atlantic A 7386CD*	**74**	1 wk
24 Jul 93	**YOU'RE THE ONE THAT I WANT** *Epic 6595222* [1]	**13**	6 wks

[1] Craig McLachlan and Debbie Gibson

Don GIBSON *US, male vocalist* · **16 wks**

| 31 Aug 61 | **SEA OF HEARTBREAK** *RCA 1243* | **14** | 13 wks |
| 1 Feb 62 | **LONESOME NUMBER ONE** *RCA 1272* | **47** | 3 wks |

Wayne GIBSON *UK, male vocalist* · **13 wks**

| 3 Sep 64 | **KELLY** *Pye 7N 15680* | **48** | 2 wks |
| 23 Nov 74 | **UNDER MY THUMB** *Pye Disco Demand DDS 2001* | **17** | 11 wks |

GIBSON BROTHERS
Martinique, male vocal / instrumental group · **54 wks**

10 Mar 79	**CUBA** *Island WIP 6483*	**41**	9 wks
21 Jul 79	● **OOH! WHAT A LIFE** *Island WIP 6503*	**10**	12 wks
17 Nov 79	● **QUE SERA MI VIDA (IF YOU SHOULD GO)** *Island WIP 6525*	**5**	11 wks
23 Feb 80	**CUBA / BETTER DO IT SALSA (re-issue)** *Island WIP 6561*	**12**	9 wks
12 Jul 80	**MARIANA** *Island WIP 6617*	**11**	10 wks
9 Jul 83	**MY HEART'S BEATING WILD (TIC TAC TIC TAC)** *Stiff BUY 184*	**56**	3 wks

GIDEA PARK
UK, male vocal / instrumentalist - Adrian Baker · **19 wks**

| 4 Jul 81 | **BEACHBOY GOLD** *Stone SON 2162* | **11** | 13 wks |
| 12 Sep 81 | **SEASONS OF GOLD** *Polo POLO 14* | **28** | 6 wks |

GIGOLO AUNTS *US, male vocal / instrumental group* · **1 wk**

| 23 Apr 94 | **MRS. WASHINGTON** *Fire BLAZE 68CD* | **74** | 1 wk |

Astrud GILBERTO - *See Stan GETZ*

Joao GILBERTO - *See Stan GETZ*

Donna GILES *US, male vocalist* · **2 wks**

| 13 Aug 94 | **AND I'M TELLING YOU I'M NOT GOING** *Ore AG 4CD* | **43** | 2 wks |

Johnny GILL *US, male vocalist* · **12 wks**

23 Feb 91	**WRAP MY BODY TIGHT** *Motown ZB 44271*	**57**	2 wks
28 Nov 92	**SLOW AND SEXY** *Epic 6587727* [1]	**17**	7 wks
17 Jul 93	**THE FLOOR** *Motown TMGCD 1416*	**53**	1 wk
29 Jan 94	**A CUTE SWEET LOVE ADDICTION** *Motown TMGCD 1420*	**46**	2 wks

[1] Shabba Ranks featuring Johnny Gill

GILLAN *UK, male vocal / instrumental group* · **46 wks**

14 Jun 80	**SLEEPIN' ON THE JOB** *Virgin VS 355*	**55**	3 wks
4 Oct 80	**TROUBLE** *Virgin VS 377*	**14**	6 wks
14 Feb 81	**MUTUALLY ASSURED DESTRUCTION** *Virgin VS 103*	**32**	5 wks
21 Mar 81	**NEW ORLEANS** *Virgin VS 406*	**17**	10 wks
20 Jun 81	**NO LAUGHING IN HEAVEN** *Virgin VS 425*	**31**	6 wks
10 Oct 81	**NIGHTMARE** *Virgin VS 441*	**36**	6 wks
23 Jan 82	**RESTLESS** *Virgin VS 465*	**25**	7 wks
4 Sep 82	**LIVING FOR THE CITY** *Virgin VS 519*	**50**	3 wks

GILLETTE - *See 20 FINGERS featuring GILLETTE*

Stuart GILLIES *UK, male vocalist* · **10 wks**

| 31 Mar 73 | **AMANDA** *Philips 6006 293* | **13** | 10 wks |

Jimmy GILMER - *See FIREBALLS*

James GILREATH US, male vocalist   **10 wks**

2 May 63	**LITTLE BAND OF GOLD** Pye International 7N 25150 ..**29**	10 wks

Jim GILSTRAP US, male vocalist   **11 wks**

15 Mar 75	● **SWING YOUR DADDY** Chelsea 2005 021 ....**4**	11 wks

Gordon GILTRAP UK, male instrumentalist - guitar   **10 wks**

14 Jan 78	**HEARTSONG** Electric WOT 19.........................**21**	7 wks
28 Apr 79	**FEAR OF THE DARK** Electric WOT 29 [1] **58**	3 wks

[1] Gordon Giltrap Band

GIN BLOSSOMS US, male vocal / instrumental group   **8 wks**

5 Feb 94	**HEY JEALOUSY** Fontana GINCD 3 ....**24**	5 wks
16 Apr 94	**FOUND OUT ABOUT YOU** Fontana GINCD 4 ....**40**	3 wks

GINGERBREADS - See GOLDIE and the GINGERBREADS

GIPSY KINGS France, male vocal / instrumental group   **2 wks**

3 Sep 94	**HITS MEDLEY** Columbia 6606022 ....**53**	2 wks

Martine GIRAULT US, female vocalist   **5 wks**

29 Aug 92	**REVIVAL** ffrr FX 195 ....**53**	2 wks
30 Jan 93	**REVIVAL (re-issue)** ffrr FCD 205 ....**37**	3 wks

GIRL UK, male vocal / instrumental group   **3 wks**

12 Apr 80	**HOLLYWOOD TEASE** Jet 176 ....**50**	3 wks

GIRLFRIEND Australia, female vocal group   **6 wks**

30 Jan 93	**TAKE IT FROM ME** Arista 74321114252 ....**47**	4 wks
15 May 93	**GIRL'S LIFE** Arista 74321138452......................**68**	2 wks

GIRLSCHOOL UK, female vocal / instrumental group   **25 wks**

2 Aug 80	**RACE WITH THE DEVIL** Bronze BRO 100 ....**49**	6 wks
21 Feb 81	● **ST. VALENTINE'S DAY MASSACRE EP** Bronze BRO 116 [1] **5**	8 wks
11 Apr 81	**HIT AND RUN** Bronze BRO 118 ....**32**	6 wks
11 Jul 81	**C'MON LET'S GO** Bronze BRO 126 ....**42**	4 wks
3 Apr 82	**WILDLIFE (EP)** Bronze BRO 144 ....**58**	2 wks

[1] Motorhead and Girlschool (also known as Headgirl)

Tracks on St. Valentine's Day Massacre EP: Please Don't Touch / Emergency / Bomber. Tracks on Wildlife (EP): Don't Call It Love / Wildlife / Don't Stop.

Junior GISCOMBE - See JUNIOR

GLADIATORS - See NERO and the GLADIATORS

GLAM Italy, male instrumental / production group   **2 wks**

1 May 93	**HELL'S PARTY** Six6 SIXCD 001 ....**42**	2 wks

GLASS TIGER Canada, male vocal / instrumental group   **18 wks**

18 Oct 86	**DON'T FORGET ME (WHEN I'M GONE)** Manhattan MT 13 ....**29**	9 wks
31 Jan 87	**SOMEDAY** Manhattan MT 17..........................**66**	2 wks
26 Oct 91	**MY TOWN** EMI EM 212 ....**33**	7 wks

My Town features the uncredited vocals of Rod Stewart.

Mayson GLEN ORCHESTRA - See Paul HENRY and the Mayson GLEN ORCHESTRA

GLENN and CHRIS UK, male vocal duo   **8 wks**

18 Apr 87	**DIAMOND LIGHTS** Record Shack KICK 1.................**12**	8 wks

Gary GLITTER UK, male vocalist   **168 wks**

10 Jun 72	● **ROCK AND ROLL (PARTS 1 & 2)** Bell 1216 ....**2**	15 wks
23 Sep 72	● **I DIDN'T KNOW I LOVED YOU (TILL I SAW YOU ROCK `N' ROLL)** Bell 1259 ....**4**	11 wks
20 Jan 73	● **DO YOU WANNA TOUCH ME? (OH YEAH)** Bell 1280 ....**2**	11 wks
7 Apr 73	● **HELLO HELLO I'M BACK AGAIN** Bell 1299 ....**2**	14 wks
21 Jul 73	★ **I'M THE LEADER OF THE GANG (I AM)** Bell 1321 ....**1**	12 wks
17 Nov 73	★ **I LOVE YOU LOVE ME LOVE** Bell 1337 ....**1**	14 wks
30 Mar 74	● **REMEMBER ME THIS WAY** Bell 1349 ....**3**	8 wks
15 Jun 74	★ **ALWAYS YOURS** Bell 1359 ....**1**	9 wks
23 Nov 74	● **OH YES! YOU'RE BEAUTIFUL** Bell 1391 ....**2**	10 wks
3 May 75	● **LOVE LIKE YOU AND ME** Bell 1423 ....**10**	6 wks
21 Jun 75	● **DOING ALRIGHT WITH THE BOYS** Bell 1429 ....**6**	7 wks
8 Nov 75	**PAPA OOM MOW MOW** Bell 1451 ....**38**	5 wks
13 Mar 76	**YOU BELONG TO ME** Bell 1473 ....**40**	5 wks
22 Jan 77	**IT TAKES ALL NIGHT LONG** Arista 85 ....**25**	6 wks
16 Jul 77	**A LITTLE BOOGIE WOOGIE IN THE BACK OF MY MIND** Arista 112 ....**31**	5 wks
20 Sep 80	**GARY GLITTER EP** GTO GT 282 ....**57**	3 wks
10 Oct 81	**AND THEN SHE KISSED ME** Bell BELL 1497 ....**39**	5 wks
5 Dec 81	**ALL THAT GLITTERS** Bell BELL 1498....................**48**	5 wks
23 Jun 84	**DANCE ME UP** Arista ARIST 570 ....**25**	5 wks
1 Dec 84	● **ANOTHER ROCK AND ROLL CHRISTMAS** Arista ARIST 592 ....**7**	7 wks
10 Oct 92	**AND THE LEADER ROCKS ON** EMI EM 252 ....**58**	2 wks
21 Nov 92	**THROUGH THE YEARS** EMI EM 256.....................**49**	3 wks

Rock And Roll Part 1 not listed with Part 2 for weeks of 10 and 17 Jun 72. Tracks on Gary Glitter EP: I'm The Leader Of The Gang (I Am) / Rock And Roll (Part 2) / Hello Hello I'm Back Again / Do You Wanna Touch Me?(Oh Yeah). All were re-issues.

GLITTER BAND UK, male vocal / instrumental group   **60 wks**

23 Mar 74	● **ANGEL FACE** Bell 1348 ....**4**	10 wks
3 Aug 74	● **JUST FOR YOU** Bell 1368 ....**10**	8 wks
19 Oct 74	● **LET'S GET TOGETHER AGAIN** Bell 1383 ....**8**	8 wks
18 Jan 75	● **GOODBYE MY LOVE** Bell 1395 ....**2**	9 wks
12 Apr 75	● **THE TEARS I CRIED** Bell 1416 ....**8**	8 wks
9 Aug 75	**LOVE IN THE SUN** Bell 1437 ....**15**	8 wks
28 Feb 76	● **PEOPLE LIKE YOU AND PEOPLE LIKE ME** Bell 1471 ....**5**	9 wks

GLOVE UK, male vocal / instrumental group   **3 wks**

20 Aug 83	**LIKE AN ANIMAL** Wonderland SHE 3 ....**52**	3 wks

GLOWORM UK / US, male vocal / instrumental group   **17 wks**

6 Feb 93	**I LIFT MY CUP** Pulse 8 CDLOSE 37 ....**20**	4 wks
14 May 94	● **CARRY ME HOME** Go.Beat GODCD 112 ....**9**	11 wks
6 Aug 94	**I LIFT MY CUP (re-issue)** Pulse 8 CDLOSE 67 ....**46**	2 wks

GO GO LORENZO and the DAVIS PINCKNEY PROJECT
US, male vocal / instrumental group   **8 wks**

6 Dec 86	**YOU CAN DANCE (IF YOU WANT TO)** Boiling Point POSP 836 ....**46**	8 wks

GO-GOS US, female vocal / instrumental group   **7 wks**

15 May 82	**OUR LIPS ARE SEALED** IRS GDN 102 ....**47**	6 wks
26 Jan 91	**COOL JERK** IRS AM 712.................................**60**	1 wk

GO WEST UK, male vocal / instrumental duo · 85 wks

23 Feb 85	● WE CLOSE OUR EYES Chrysalis CHS 2850 ...... **5**	14 wks
11 May 85	CALL ME Chrysalis GOW 1 ...... **12**	10 wks
3 Aug 85	GOODBYE GIRL Chrysalis GOW 2 ...... **25**	7 wks
23 Nov 85	DON'T LOOK DOWN - THE SEQUEL Chrysalis GOW 3 ...... **13**	10 wks
29 Nov 86	TRUE COLOURS Chrysalis GOW 4 ...... **48**	7 wks
9 May 87	I WANT TO HEAR IT FROM YOU Chrysalis GOW 5 .. **43**	3 wks
12 Sep 87	THE KING IS DEAD Chrysalis GOW 6 ...... **67**	2 wks
28 Jul 90	THE KING OF WISHFUL THINKING Chrysalis GOW 8 ...... **18**	10 wks
17 Oct 92	FAITHFUL Chrysalis GOW 9 ...... **13**	6 wks
16 Jan 93	WHAT YOU WON'T DO FOR LOVE Chrysalis CDGOWS 10 ...... **15**	5 wks
27 Mar 93	STILL IN LOVE Chrysalis CDGOWS 11 ...... **43**	3 wks
2 Oct 93	TRACKS OF MY TEARS Chrysalis CDGOWS 12 ...... **16**	5 wks
4 Dec 93	WE CLOSE OUR EYES (re-mix) Chrysalis CDGOWS 13 ...... **40**	3 wks

GOATS US, male rap group · 2 wks

| 29 May 93 | AAAH D YAAA / TYPICAL AMERICAN Ruff House 6593032 ...... **53** | 2 wks |

Typical American *only listed from 5 Jun, peaking at position 65.*

GOD MACHINE US, male vocal / instrumental group · 2 wks

| 30 Jan 93 | HOME Fiction FICCD 47 ...... **65** | 2 wks |

GODIEGO Japan / US, male vocal / instrumental group · 11 wks

| 15 Oct 77 | THE WATER MARGIN BBC RESL 50 ...... **37** | 4 wks |
| 16 Feb 80 | GANDHARA BBC RESL 66 ...... **56** | 7 wks |

The Water Margin *is the English version of the song, which shared chart credit with the Japanese language version by Pete Mac Jr.*

GODLEY and CREME UK, male vocal / instrumental duo · 36 wks

12 Sep 81	● UNDER YOUR THUMB Polydor POSP 322 ...... **3**	11 wks
21 Nov 81	● WEDDING BELLS Polydor POSP 369 ...... **7**	11 wks
30 Mar 85	CRY Polydor POSP 732 ...... **19**	11 wks
16 Aug 86	CRY (re-entry) Polydor POSP 732 ...... **66**	3 wks

Andrew GOLD US, male vocalist / instrumentalist - piano · 36 wks

2 Apr 77	LONELY BOY Asylum K 13076 ...... **11**	9 wks
25 Mar 78	● NEVER LET HER SLIP AWAY Asylum K 13112 ...... **5**	13 wks
24 Jun 78	HOW CAN THIS BE LOVE Asylum K 13126 ...... **19**	10 wks
14 Oct 78	THANK YOU FOR BEING A FRIEND Asylum K 13135 ...... **42**	4 wks

Brian and Tony GOLD - *See RED DRAGON with Brian and Tony GOLD*

GOLDEN EARRING Holland, male vocal / instrumental group · 16 wks

| 8 Dec 73 | ● RADAR LOVE Track 2094 116 ...... **7** | 13 wks |
| 8 Oct 77 | RADAR LOVE Polydor 2121 335 ...... **44** | 3 wks |

These are two different recordings of the same song.

GOLDIE UK, male vocal / instrumental group · 11 wks

| 27 May 78 | ● MAKING UP AGAIN Bronze BRO 50 ...... **7** | 11 wks |

GOLDIE and the GINGERBREADS US, female vocal / instrumental group · 5 wks

| 25 Feb 65 | CAN'T YOU HEAR MY HEART BEAT? Decca F 12070 ...... **25** | 5 wks |

GOLDIE presents METALHEADS UK, male / female vocal / instrumental duo · 2 wks

| 3 Dec 94 | INNER CITY LIFE ffrr FCD 251 ...... **49** | 2 wks |

Bobby GOLDSBORO US, male vocalist · 47 wks

17 Apr 68	● HONEY United Artists UP2215 ...... **2**	15 wks
4 Aug 73	● SUMMER (THE FIRST TIME) United Artists UP35558 .. **9**	10 wks
3 Aug 74	HELLO SUMMERTIME United Artists UP35705 ...... **14**	10 wks
29 Mar 75	● HONEY (re-issue) United Artists UP35633 ...... **2**	12 wks

Glen GOLDSMITH US, male vocalist · 24 wks

7 Nov 87	I WON'T CRY Reproduction PB 41493 ...... **34**	7 wks
12 Mar 88	DREAMING Reproduction PB 41711 ...... **12**	11 wks
11 Jun 88	WHAT YOU SEE IS WHAT YOU GET Reproduction PB 42075 ...... **33**	5 wks
3 Sep 88	SAVE A LITTLE BIT Reproduction PB 42147 ...... **73**	1 wk

Leroy GOMEZ - *See SANTA ESMERALDA and Leroy GOMEZ*

GONZALEZ UK / US, male vocal / instrumental group · 11 wks

| 31 Mar 79 | HAVEN'T STOPPED DANCING YET Sidewalk SID 102 ...... **15** | 11 wks |

GOOD GIRLS US, female vocal group · 1 wk

| 24 Jul 93 | JUST CALL ME Motown TMGCD 1417 ...... **75** | 1 wk |

GOODBYE MR. MACKENZIE UK, male / female vocal / instrumental group · 13 wks

20 Aug 88	GOODBYE MR MACKENZIE Capitol CL 501 ...... **62**	2 wks
11 Mar 89	THE RATTLER Capitol CL 522 ...... **37**	6 wks
29 Jul 89	GOODWILL CITY / I'M SICK OF YOU Capitol CL 538 ...... **49**	2 wks
21 Apr 90	LOVE CHILD Parlophone R 6247 ...... **52**	2 wks
23 Jun 90	BLACKER THAN BLACK Parlophone R 6257 ...... **61**	1 wk

GOODIES UK, male vocal group · 38 wks

7 Dec 74	● THE IN BETWEENIES / FATHER CHRISTMAS DO NOT TOUCH ME Bradley's BRAD 7421 ...... **7**	9 wks
15 Mar 75	● FUNKY GIBBON / SICK MAN BLUES Bradley's BRAD 7504 ...... **4**	10 wks
21 Jun 75	BLACK PUDDING BERTHA Bradley's BRAD 7517 ...... **19**	7 wks
27 Sep 75	NAPPY LOVE / WILD THING Bradley's BRAD 7524 .... **21**	6 wks
13 Dec 75	MAKE A DAFT NOISE FOR CHRISTMAS Bradley's BRAD 7533 ...... **20**	6 wks

Cuba GOODING US, male vocalist · 2 wks

| 19 Nov 83 | HAPPINESS IS JUST AROUND THE BEND London LON 41 ...... **72** | 2 wks |

GOODMEN Holland, male instrumental / production duo · 19 wks

| 7 Aug 93 | GIVE IT UP Fresh Fruit TABCD 118 ...... **23** | 5 wks |
| 9 Oct 93 | ● GIVE IT UP (re-entry) Fresh Fruit TABCD 118 ...... **5** | 14 wks |

Ron GOODWIN UK, orchestra · 24 wks

| 15 May 53 | ● TERRY'S THEME FROM `LIMELIGHT' Parlophone R 3686 ...... **3** | 23 wks |
| 28 Oct 55 | BLUE STAR (THE MEDIC THEME) Parlophone R 4074 ...... **20** | 1 wk |

See also Eamonn Andrews.

GOODY GOODY US, female vocal duo · 5 wks

| 2 Dec 78 | NUMBER ONE DEE JAY Atlantic LV 3 ...... **55** | 5 wks |

GOOMBAY DANCE BAND
Germany / Montserrat, male / female vocal / instrumental group **16 wks**

| 27 Feb 82 | ★ SEVEN TEARS *Epic EPC A 1242* | 1 | 12 wks |
| 15 May 82 | SUN OF JAMAICA *Epic EPC A 2345* | 50 | 4 wks |

GOONS *UK, male vocal group* **30 wks**

29 Jun 56	● I'M WALKING BACKWARDS FOR CHRISTMAS / BLUEBOTTLE BLUES *Decca F 10756*	4	10 wks
14 Sep 56	● BLOODNOK'S ROCK 'N' ROLL CALL / YING TONG SONG *Decca E 10780*	3	10 wks
21 Jul 73	● YING TONG SONG (re-issue) *Decca F 13414*	9	10 wks

Bluebottle Blues only listed from 13 Jul 56. It peaked at position 5.

Lonnie GORDON *US, female vocalist* **21 wks**

24 Jun 89	(I'VE GOT YOUR) PLEASURE CONTROL *ffrr F 106* [1]	60	3 wks
27 Jan 90	● HAPPENIN' ALL OVER AGAIN *Supreme SUPE 159*	4	10 wks
11 Aug 90	BEYOND YOUR WILDEST DREAMS *Supreme SUPE 167*	48	2 wks
17 Nov 90	IF I HAVE TO STAND ALONE *Supreme SUPE 181*	68	1 wk
4 May 91	GONNA CATCH YOU *Supreme SUPE 185*	32	5 wks

[1] Simon Harris featuring Lonnie Gordon

Lesley GORE *US, female vocalist* **20 wks**

| 20 Jun 63 | ● IT'S MY PARTY *Mercury AMT 1205* | 9 | 12 wks |
| 24 Sep 64 | MAYBE I KNOW *Mercury MF 829* | 20 | 8 wks |

Eydie GORMÉ *US, female vocalist* **33 wks**

24 Jan 58	LOVE ME FOREVER *HMV POP 432*	21	5 wks
21 Jun 62	● YES MY DARLING DAUGHTER *CBS AAG 105*	10	9 wks
31 Jan 63	BLAME IT ON THE BOSSA NOVA *CBS AAG 131*	32	6 wks
22 Aug 63	● I WANT TO STAY HERE *CBS AAG 163* [1]	3	13 wks

[1] Steve and Eydie

Luke GOSS and the BAND OF THIEVES
UK, male vocal / instrumental group **3 wks**

| 12 Jun 93 | SWEETER THAN THE MIDNIGHT RAIN
Sabre CDSAB 1 | 52 | 2 wks |
| 21 Aug 93 | GIVE ME ONE MORE CHANCE *Sabre CDSAB 2* | 68 | 1 wk |

Nigel GOULDING - See Abigail MEAD and Nigel GOULDING

G.O.S.H. *UK, male / female charity ensemble* **11 wks**

| 28 Nov 87 | THE WISHING WELL *MBS GOSH 1* | 22 | 11 wks |

Graham GOULDMAN *UK, male vocalist* **4 wks**

| 23 Jun 79 | SUNBURN *Mercury SUNNY 1* | 52 | 4 wks |

G.Q. *US, male vocal / instrumental group* **6 wks**

| 10 Mar 79 | DISCO NIGHTS (ROCK FREAK) *Arista ARIST 245* | 42 | 6 wks |

Charlie GRACIE *US, male vocalist* **39 wks**

19 Apr 57	BUTTERFLY *Parlophone R 4290*	12	8 wks
14 Jun 57	● FABULOUS *Parlophone R 4313*	8	16 wks
23 Aug 57	I LOVE YOU SO MUCH IT HURTS / WANDERIN' EYES *London HLU 8467*	14	2 wks
6 Sep 57	● WANDERIN' EYES *London HLU 8467*	6	12 wks
6 Sep 57	I LOVE YOU SO MUCH IT HURTS *London HLU 8467*	20	2 wks

---

| 10 Jan 58 | COOL BABY *London HLU 8521* | 26 | 1 wk |

I Love You So Much It Hurts and Wanderin' Eyes were listed together for two weeks, then listed separately for a further two and 12 weeks respectively.

Eve GRAHAM - See NEW SEEKERS

Jaki GRAHAM *UK, female vocalist* **73 wks**

23 Mar 85	● COULD IT BE I'M FALLING IN LOVE *Chrysalis GRAN 6* [1]	5	11 wks
29 Jun 85	● ROUND AND ROUND *EMI JAKI 4*	9	11 wks
31 Aug 85	HEAVEN KNOWS *EMI JAKI 5*	59	3 wks
16 Nov 85	MATED *EMI JAKI 6* [1]	20	10 wks
3 May 86	● SET ME FREE *EMI JAKI 7*	7	12 wks
9 Aug 86	BREAKING AWAY *EMI JAKI 8*	16	8 wks
15 Nov 86	STEP RIGHT UP *EMI JAKI 9*	15	12 wks
9 Jul 88	NO MORE TEARS *EMI JAKI 12*	60	2 wks
24 Jun 89	FROM NOW ON *EMI JAKI 15*	73	2 wks
16 Jul 94	AIN'T NOBODY *Pulse 8 CDLOSE 64*	44	2 wks

[1] David Grant and Jaki Graham

Larry GRAHAM *US, male vocalist* **4 wks**

| 3 Jul 82 | SOONER OR LATER *Warner Bros. K 17925* | 54 | 4 wks |

Ron GRAINER ORCHESTRA *UK, orchestra* **7 wks**

| 9 Dec 78 | A TOUCH OF VELVET A STING OF BRASS
Casino Classics CC 5 | 60 | 7 wks |

GRAND FUNK RAILROAD
US, male vocal / instrumental group **1 wk**

| 6 Feb 71 | INSIDE LOOKING OUT *Capitol CL 15668* | 40 | 1 wk |

GRAND PLAZ *UK, production group* **4 wks**

| 8 Sep 90 | WOW WOW - NA NA *Urban URB 6 0* | 41 | 4 wks |

GRAND PRIX *UK, male vocal / instrumental group* **1 wk**

| 27 Feb 82 | KEEP ON BELIEVING *RCA 162* | 75 | 1 wk |

GRANDMASTER FLASH, Melle MEL and the FURIOUS FIVE
US, male vocal duo and male vocal group **87 wks**

28 Aug 82	● THE MESSAGE *Sugarhill SHL 117* [1]	8	9 wks
22 Jan 83	MESSAGE II (SURVIVAL) *Sugarhill SH 119* [2]	74	2 wks
19 Nov 83	WHITE LINES (DON'T DON'T DO IT) *Sugarhill SH 130* [3]	60	3 wks
11 Feb 84	● WHITE LINES (DON'T DON'T DO IT) (re-entry) *Sugarhill SH 130* [3]	7	38 wks
30 Jun 84	BEAT STREET BREAKDOWN *Atlantic A9659* [4]	42	7 wks
22 Sep 84	WE DON'T WORK FOR FREE *Sugarhill SH 136* [4]	45	4 wks
24 Nov 84	WHITE LINES (DON'T DON'T DO IT) (2nd re-entry) *Sugarhill SH 130* [3]	75	1 wk
15 Dec 84	● STEP OFF (PART 1) *Sugarhill SH 139* [4]	8	12 wks
5 Jan 85	WHITE LINES (DON'T DON'T DO IT) (3rd re-entry) *Sugarhill SH 130* [3]	73	1 wk
16 Feb 85	SIGN OF THE TIMES *Elektra E 9677* [5]	72	1 wk
16 Mar 85	PUMP ME UP *Sugarhill SH 142* [4]	45	6 wks
8 Jan 94	WHITE LINES (DON'T DO IT) (re-mix) *WGAF WGAFCD 103* [3]	59	3 wks

[1] Grandmaster Flash and the Furious Five [2] Melle Mel and Duke Bootee [3] Grandmaster Flash and Melle Mel [4] Grandmaster Melle Mel and the Furious Five [5] Grandmaster Flash

GRANDMIXER US, male 'scratch' DJ — 3 wks

24 Dec 83	**CRAZY CUTS** Island IS 146	**73**	2 wks
14 Jan 84	**CRAZY CUTS (re-entry)** Island IS 146	**71**	1 wk

GRANGE HILL CAST
UK, male/female vocal charity assembly — 6 wks

19 Apr 86	● **JUST SAY NO** BBC RESL 183	**5**	6 wks

Gerri GRANGER US, female vocalist — 3 wks

30 Sep 78	**I GO TO PIECES (EVERYTIME)** Casino Classics CC3 ..	**50**	3 wks

Amy GRANT US, female vocalist — 27 wks

11 May 91	● **BABY BABY** A & M AM 727	**2**	13 wks
3 Aug 91	**EVERY HEARTBEAT** A & M AM 783	**25**	7 wks
2 Nov 91	**THAT'S WHAT LOVE IS FOR** A & M AM 666	**60**	3 wks
15 Feb 92	**GOOD FOR ME** A & M AM 810	**60**	1 wk
13 Aug 94	**LUCKY ONE** A & M 5807322	**60**	1 wk
22 Oct 94	**SAY YOU'LL BE MINE** A & M 5808292	**41**	2 wks

Boysie GRANT - *See Ezz RECO and the LAUNCHERS with Boysie GRANT*

David GRANT UK, male vocalist — 59 wks

30 Apr 83	**STOP AND GO** Chrysalis GRAN 1	**19**	9 wks
16 Jul 83	● **WATCHING YOU WATCHING ME** Chrysalis GRAN 2..	**10**	13 wks
8 Oct 83	**LOVE WILL FIND A WAY** Chrysalis GRAN 3	**24**	6 wks
26 Nov 83	**ROCK THE MIDNIGHT** Chrysalis GRAN 4	**46**	4 wks
23 Mar 85	● **COULD IT BE I'M FALLING IN LOVE** Chrysalis GRAN 6 [1]	**5**	11 wks
16 Nov 85	**MATED** EMI JAKI 6 [1]	**20**	10 wks
1 Aug 87	**CHANGE** Polydor POSP 871	**55**	4 wks
12 May 90	**KEEP IT TOGETHER** Fourth & Broadway BRW 169	**56**	2 wks

[1] David Grant and Jaki Graham

Eddy GRANT
Guyana, male vocalist/multi-instrumentalist — 94 wks

2 Jun 79	**LIVING ON THE FRONT LINE** Ensign ENY 26	**11**	11 wks
15 Nov 80	● **DO YOU FEEL MY LOVE** Ensign ENY 45	**8**	11 wks
4 Apr 81	**CAN'T GET ENOUGH OF YOU** Ensign ENY 207	**13**	10 wks
25 Jul 81	**I LOVE YOU, YES I LOVE YOU** Ensign ENY 216	**37**	6 wks
16 Oct 82	★ **I DON'T WANNA DANCE** Ice ICE 56	**1**	15 wks
15 Jan 83	● **ELECTRIC AVENUE** Ice ICE 57	**2**	9 wks
19 Mar 83	**LIVING ON THE FRONT LINE/DO YOU FEEL MY LOVE (re-issue)** Mercury MER 135	**47**	4 wks
23 Apr 83	**WAR PARTY** Ice ICE 58	**42**	4 wks
29 Oct 83	**TILL I CAN'T TAKE LOVE NO MORE** Ice ICE 60	**42**	7 wks
19 May 84	**ROMANCING THE STONE** Ice ICE 61	**52**	3 wks
23 Jan 88	● **GIMME HOPE JO'ANNA** Ice ICE 78701	**7**	12 wks
27 May 89	**WALKING ON SUNSHINE** Blue Wave R 6217	**63**	2 wks

Gogi GRANT US, female vocalist — 11 wks

29 Jun 56	● **WAYWARD WIND** London HLB 8282	**9**	11 wks

Julie GRANT UK, female vocalist — 17 wks

3 Jan 63	**UP ON THE ROOF** Pye 7N 15483	**33**	3 wks
28 Mar 63	**COUNT ON ME** Pye 7N 15508	**24**	9 wks
24 Sep 64	**COME TO ME** Pye 7N 15684	**31**	5 wks

Rudy GRANT Guyana, male vocalist — 3 wks

14 Feb 81	**LATELY** Ensign ENY 202	**58**	3 wks

GRAPEFRUIT UK, male vocal/instrumental group — 19 wks

14 Feb 68	**DEAR DELILAH** RCA 1656	**21**	9 wks
14 Aug 68	**C'MON MARIANNE** RCA 1716	**31**	10 wks

Dobie GRAY US, male vocalist — 11 wks

25 Feb 65	**THE IN CROWD** London HL 9953	**25**	7 wks
27 Sep 75	**OUT ON THE FLOOR** Black Magic BM 107	**42**	4 wks

Dorian GRAY UK, male vocalist — 7 wks

27 Mar 68	**I'VE GOT YOU ON MY MIND** Parlophone R 5667	**36**	7 wks

Les GRAY UK, male vocalist — 5 wks

26 Feb 77	**A GROOVY KIND OF LOVE** Warner Bros. K 16883 ..	**32**	5 wks

Barry GRAY ORCHESTRA UK, orchestra — 8 wks

11 Jul 81	**THUNDERBIRDS** PRT 7P 216	**61**	2 wks
14 Jun 86	**JOE 90/CAPTAIN SCARLET THEME** PRT 7PX 345 [1]	**53**	6 wks

[1] Barry Gray Orchestra with Peter Beckett - keyboards

Altrina GRAYSON - *See Wilton FELDER*

GREAT WHITE US, male vocal/instrumental group — 5 wks

24 Feb 90	**HOUSE OF BROKEN LOVE** Capitol CL 562	**44**	2 wks
16 Feb 91	**CONGO SQUARE** Capitol CL 605	**62**	1 wk
7 Sep 91	**CALL IT ROCK 'N' ROLL** Capitol CL 625	**67**	2 wks

Buddy GRECO US, male vocalist — 8 wks

7 Jul 60	**LADY IS A TRAMP** Fontana H 225	**26**	8 wks

GREEDIES Ireland/UK/US, male vocal/instrumental group — 5 wks

15 Dec 79	**A MERRY JINGLE** Vertigo GREED 1	**28**	5 wks

Al GREEN US, male vocalist — 68 wks

9 Oct 71	● **TIRED OF BEING ALONE** London HL 10337	**4**	13 wks
8 Jan 72	● **LET'S STAY TOGETHER** London HL 10348	**7**	12 wks
20 May 72	**LOOK WHAT YOU DONE FOR ME** London HL 10369	**44**	4 wks
19 Aug 72	**I'M STILL IN LOVE WITH YOU** London HL 10382	**35**	5 wks
16 Nov 74	**SHA-LA-LA (MAKE ME HAPPY)** London HL 10470 ..	**20**	11 wks
15 Mar 75	**L. O. V. E.** London HL 10482	**24**	8 wks
3 Dec 88	**PUT A LITTLE LOVE IN YOUR HEART** A & M AM 484 [1]	**28**	8 wks
21 Oct 89	**THE MESSAGE IS LOVE** Breakout USA 668 [2]	**38**	5 wks
2 Oct 93	**LOVE IS A BEAUTIFUL THING** Arista 74321162692 ..	**56**	2 wks

[1] Annie Lennox and Al Green [2] Arthur Baker and the Backbeat Disciples featuring Al Green

Dotty GREEN - *See Mark FISHER featuring Dotty GREEN*

Jesse GREEN US, male vocalist — 26 wks

7 Aug 76	**NICE AND SLOW** EMI 2492	**17**	12 wks
18 Dec 76	**FLIP** EMI 2564	**26**	8 wks
11 Jun 77	**COME WITH ME** EMI 2615	**29**	6 wks

GREEN DAY US, male vocal/instrumental group — 5 wks

20 Aug 94	**BASKET CASE** Reprise W 0257CD	**55**	2 wks
29 Oct 94	**WELCOME TO PARADISE** Reprise W 0269CDX	**20**	3 wks

GREEN JELLY US, male vocal / instrumental group — **15 wks**

5 Jun 93 ●	THREE LITTLE PIGS Zoo 74321151422	**5**	8 wks
14 Aug 93	ANARCHY IN THE UK Zoo 74321159052	**27**	3 wks
25 Dec 93	I'M THE LEADER OF THE GANG Arista 74321174892 [1]	**25**	4 wks

[1] Hulk Hogan with Green Jelly

Norman GREENBAUM US, male vocalist — **20 wks**

21 Mar 70 ★	SPIRIT IN THE SKY Reprise RS 20885	**1**	20 wks

Lorne GREENE Canada, male vocalist — **8 wks**

17 Dec 64	RINGO RCA 1428	**22**	8 wks

Lee GREENWOOD US, male vocalist — **6 wks**

19 May 84	THE WIND BENEATH MY WINGS MCA 877	**49**	6 wks

Iain GREGORY UK, male vocalist — **2 wks**

4 Jan 62	CAN'T YOU HEAR THE BEAT OF A BROKEN HEART Pye 7N 15397	**39**	2 wks

Johnny GREGORY - See CHAQUITO

Band of the GRENADIER GUARDS - See ST. JOHN'S COLLEGE SCHOOL CHOIR and the Band of the GRENADIER GUARDS

GREYHOUND Jamaica, male vocal / instrumental group — **33 wks**

26 Jun 71 ●	BLACK AND WHITE Trojan TR 7820	**6**	13 wks
8 Jan 72	MOON RIVER Trojan TR 7848	**12**	11 wks
25 Mar 72	I AM WHAT I AM Trojan TR 7853	**20**	9 wks

GRID UK, male instrumental / production duo — **44 wks**

7 Jul 90	FLOATATION East West YZ 475	**60**	2 wks
29 Sep 90	A BEAT CALLED LOVE East West YZ 498	**64**	4 wks
25 Jul 92	FIGURE OF 8 Virgin VSTG 1421	**50**	3 wks
3 Oct 92	HEARTBEAT Virgin VST 1427	**72**	2 wks
13 Mar 93	CRYSTAL CLEAR Virgin VSCDT 1442	**27**	4 wks
30 Oct 93	TEXAS COWBOYS Deconstruction 74321167762	**21**	3 wks
4 Jun 94 ●	SWAMP THING Deconstruction 74321205842	**3**	17 wks
17 Sep 94	ROLLERCOASTER Deconstruction 74321230772	**19**	4 wks
3 Dec 94	TEXAS COWBOYS (re-issue) Deconstruction 74321244032	**17†**	5 wks

Zaine GRIFF New Zealand, male vocalist — **6 wks**

16 Feb 80	TONIGHT Automatic K 17547	**54**	3 wks
31 May 80	ASHES AND DIAMONDS Automatic K 17610	**68**	3 wks

Billy GRIFFIN US, male vocalist — **12 wks**

8 Jan 83	HOLD ME TIGHTER IN THE RAIN CBS A 2935	**17**	9 wks
14 Jan 84	SERIOUS CBS A 4053	**64**	3 wks

Clive GRIFFIN UK, male vocalist — **5 wks**

24 Jun 89	HEAD ABOVE WATER Mercury STEP 4	**60**	2 wks
11 May 91	I'LL BE WAITING Mercury STEP 6	**56**	3 wks

Ronnie GRIFFITH US, female vocalist — **4 wks**

30 Jun 84	(THE BEST PART OF) BREAKING UP Making Waves SURF 101	**63**	4 wks

GRIMETHORPE COLLIERY BAND - See Peter SKELLERN

GROOVE CORPORATION
UK / Italy, male / female vocal / instrumental group — **1 wk**

16 Apr 94	RAIN Six6 SIXCD 109	**71**	1 wk

GROOVE GANG - See DAFFY DUCK featuring the GROOVE GANG

Jay GROOVE - See FANTASY U.F.O.

Henry GROSS US, male vocalist — **4 wks**

28 Aug 76	SHANNON Life Song ELS 45002	**32**	4 wks

GROUND LEVEL
Australia, male instrumental / production group — **2 wks**

30 Jan 93	DREAMS OF HEAVEN Faze 2 CDFAZE 14	**54**	2 wks

Boring Bob GROVER - See PIRANHAS

GSP UK, male instrumental / production duo — **3 wks**

3 Oct 92	THE BANANA SONG Yoyo YOYO 1	**37**	3 wks

G.T.O. Holland, male instrumental group — **7 wks**

4 Aug 90	PURE Cooltempo COOL 218	**57**	3 wks
7 Sep 91	LISTEN TO THE RHYTHM FLOW / BULLFROG React REACT 7001	**72**	2 wks
2 May 92	ELEVATION React REACT 4	**59**	2 wks

GUESS WHO Canada, male vocal / instrumental group — **14 wks**

16 Feb 67	HIS GIRL King KG 1044	**45**	1 wk
9 May 70	AMERICAN WOMAN RCA 1943	**45**	2 wks
30 May 70	AMERICAN WOMAN (re-entry) RCA 1943	**19**	11 wks

GUN UK, male vocal / instrumental group — **11 wks**

20 Nov 68 ●	RACE WITH THE DEVIL CBS 3734	**8**	11 wks

GUN UK, male vocal / instrumental group — **38 wks**

1 Jul 89	BETTER DAYS A & M AM 505	**33**	9 wks
16 Sep 89	MONEY (EVERYBODY LOVES HER) A & M AM 520	**73**	2 wks
11 Nov 89	INSIDE OUT A & M AM 531	**57**	2 wks
10 Feb 90	TAKING ON THE WORLD A & M AM 541	**50**	3 wks
14 Jul 90	SHAME ON YOU A & M AM 573	**33**	4 wks
14 Mar 92	STEAL YOUR FIRE A & M AM 851	**24**	4 wks
2 May 92	HIGHER GROUND A & M AM 869	**48**	2 wks
4 Jul 92	WELCOME TO THE REAL WORLD A & M AM 885	**43**	2 wks
9 Jul 94 ●	WORD UP A & M 5806672	**8**	7 wks
24 Sep 94	DON'T SAY IT'S OVER A & M 5807572	**19**	3 wks

GUNS N' ROSES US, male vocal / instrumental group — **101 wks**

3 Oct 87	WELCOME TO THE JUNGLE Geffen GEF 30	**67**	2 wks
20 Aug 88	SWEET CHILD O' MINE Geffen GEF 43	**24**	8 wks
29 Oct 88	WELCOME TO THE JUNGLE (re-issue) / NIGHTTRAIN Geffen GEF 47	**24**	5 wks
18 Mar 89 ●	PARADISE CITY Geffen GEF 50	**6**	9 wks
3 Jun 89 ●	SWEET CHILD O' MINE (re-mix) Geffen GEF 55	**6**	9 wks
1 Jul 89 ●	PATIENCE Geffen GEF 56	**10**	7 wks
2 Sep 89	NIGHTTRAIN (re-issue) Geffen GEF 60	**17**	5 wks
13 Jul 91 ●	YOU COULD BE MINE Geffen GFS 6	**3**	10 wks
21 Sep 91 ●	DON'T CRY Geffen GFS 9	**8**	4 wks
21 Dec 91 ●	LIVE AND LET DIE Geffen GFS 17	**5**	7 wks
7 Mar 92 ●	NOVEMBER RAIN Geffen GFS 18	**4**	5 wks
23 May 92 ●	KNOCKIN' ON HEAVEN'S DOOR Geffen GFS 21	**2**	9 wks
21 Nov 92 ●	YESTERDAYS / NOVEMBER RAIN (re-issue) Geffen GFS 27	**8**	9 wks

29 May 93	THE CIVIL WAR EP Geffen GEFSTD 43 ....**11**	3 wks
20 Nov 93 ●	AIN'T IT FUN Geffen GFSTD 62 ....**9**	3 wks
4 Jun 94 ●	SINCE I DON'T HAVE YOU Geffen GFSTD 70 ....**10**	6 wks

The re-issue of November Rain only listed from 28 Nov 92. Tracks on The Civil War EP: Civil War / Garden Of Eden / Dead Horse / Interview.

GURU US, male instrumentalist   **5 wks**

11 Sep 93	TRUST ME Cooltempo CDCOOL 278 [1] **34**	2 wks
13 Nov 93	NO TIME TO PLAY Cooltempo CDCOOL 282 [2] **25**	3 wks

[1] Guru featuring N'Dea Davenport [2] Guru featuring D.C. Lee

GURU JOSH UK, male vocal / instrumental group   **14 wks**

24 Feb 90 ●	INFINITY Deconstruction PB 43475 ....**5**	10 wks
16 Jun 90	WHOSE LAW (IS IT ANYWAY)	
	Deconstruction PB 43647 ....**26**	4 wks

Adrian GURVITZ UK, male vocalist   **16 wks**

30 Jan 82 ●	CLASSIC RAK 339 ....**8**	13 wks
12 Jun 82	YOUR DREAM RAK 343 ....**61**	3 wks

Gwen GUTHRIE US, female vocalist   **25 wks**

19 Jul 86 ●	AIN'T NOTHING GOIN' ON BUT THE RENT	
	Boiling Point POSP 807 ....**5**	12 wks
11 Oct 86	(THEY LONG TO BE) CLOSE TO YOU	
	Boiling Point POSP 822 ....**25**	7 wks
14 Feb 87	GOOD TO GO LOVER / OUTSIDE IN THE RAIN	
	Boiling Point POSP 841 ....**37**	4 wks
4 Sep 93	AIN'T NOTHIN' GOIN' ON BUT THE RENT (re-mix)	
	Polydor PZCD 276 ....**42**	2 wks

GUY US, male vocal group   **4 wks**

4 May 91	HER MCA MCS 1575 ....**58**	4 wks

A GUY CALLED GERALD
UK, male producer - Gerald Simpson   **23 wks**

8 Apr 89	VOODOO RAY Rham! RS 804 ....**55**	8 wks
24 Jun 89	VOODOO RAY (re-entry) Rham! RS 804 ....**12**	10 wks
16 Dec 89	FX / EYES OF SORROW Subscape AGCG 1 ....**52**	5 wks

GUYS and DOLLS UK, male / female vocal group   **33 wks**

1 Mar 75 ●	THERE'S A WHOLE LOT OF LOVING	
	Magnet MAG 20 ....**2**	11 wks
17 May 75	HERE I GO AGAIN Magnet MAG 30 ....**33**	5 wks
21 Feb 76 ●	YOU DON'T HAVE TO SAY YOU LOVE ME	
	Magnet MAG 50 ....**5**	8 wks
6 Nov 76	STONEY GROUND Magnet MAG 76 ....**38**	4 wks
13 May 78	ONLY LOVIN' DOES IT Magnet MAG 115 ....**42**	5 wks

Jonas GWANGWA - *See George FENTON and Jonas GWANGA*

HABIT UK, male vocal / instrumental group   **2 wks**

30 Apr 88	LUCY Virgin VS 1063 ....**56**	2 wks

Steve HACKETT
UK, male vocalist / instrumentalist - guitar   **2 wks**

2 Apr 83	CELL 151 Charisma CELL 1 ....**66**	2 wks

HADDAWAY Trinidad & Tobago, male vocalist   **47 wks**

5 Jun 93 ●	WHAT IS LOVE Logic 74321148502 ....**2**	15 wks
25 Sep 93 ●	LIFE Logic 74321164212 ....**6**	9 wks
18 Dec 93 ●	I MISS YOU Logic 74321181522 ....**9**	14 wks
2 Apr 94 ●	ROCK MY HEART Logic 74321194122 ....**9**	9 wks

Tony HADLEY UK, male vocalist   **7 wks**

7 Mar 92	LOST IN YOUR LOVE EMI EM 222 ....**42**	4 wks
29 Aug 92	FOR YOUR BLUE EYES ONLY EMI EM 234 ....**67**	2 wks
16 Jan 93	GAME OF LOVE EMI CDEM 254 ....**72**	1 wk

Sammy HAGAR
US, male vocalist / instrumentalist - guitar   **15 wks**

15 Dec 79	THIS PLANET'S ON FIRE / SPACE STATION NO. 5	
	Capitol CL 16114 ....**52**	5 wks
16 Feb 80	I'VE DONE EVERYTHING FOR YOU	
	Capitol CL 16120 ....**36**	5 wks
24 May 80	HEARTBEAT / LOVE OR MONEY Capitol RED 1 ....**67**	2 wks
16 Jan 82	PIECE OF MY HEART Geffen GEFA 1884 ....**67**	1 wk
30 Jan 82	PIECE OF MY HEART (re-entry) Geffen GEFA 1884 ..**67**	2 wks

Paul HAIG UK, male vocalist   **3 wks**

28 May 83	HEAVEN SENT Island IS 111 ....**74**	3 wks

HAIRCUT 100 UK, male vocal / instrumental group   **47 wks**

24 Oct 81 ●	FAVOURITE SHIRTS (BOY MEETS GIRL)	
	Arista CLIP 1 ....**4**	14 wks
30 Jan 82 ●	LOVE PLUS ONE Arista CLIP 2 ....**3**	12 wks
10 Apr 82 ●	FANTASTIC DAY Arista CLIP 3 ....**9**	9 wks
21 Aug 82 ●	NOBODY'S FOOL Arista CLIP 4 ....**9**	7 wks
6 Aug 83	PRIME TIME Polydor HC 1 ....**46**	5 wks

Curtis HAIRSTON US, male vocalist   **16 wks**

15 Oct 83	I WANT YOU (ALL TONIGHT) RCA 368 ....**44**	5 wks
27 Apr 85	I WANT YOUR LOVIN' (JUST A LITTLE BIT)	
	London LON 66 ....**13**	7 wks
6 Dec 86	CHILLIN' OUT Atlantic A 9335 ....**57**	4 wks

Gary HAISMAN - *See D MOB*

HALE and PACE and the STONKERS
UK, male comedy duo and backing group   **7 wks**

9 Mar 91 ★	THE STONK London LON 296 ....**1**	7 wks

Bill HALEY and his COMETS
US, male vocal / instrumental group   **199 wks**

17 Dec 54 ●	SHAKE RATTLE AND ROLL Brunswick 05338 ....**4**	14 wks
7 Jan 55	ROCK AROUND THE CLOCK Brunswick 05317.........**17**	2 wks
15 Apr 55	MAMBO ROCK Brunswick 05405 ....**14**	2 wks
14 Oct 55 ★	ROCK AROUND THE CLOCK (re-entry)	
	Brunswick 05317 ....**1**	17 wks
30 Dec 55 ●	ROCK-A-BEATIN' BOOGIE Brunswick 05509 ....**4**	9 wks
9 Mar 56 ●	SEE YOU LATER ALLIGATOR Brunswick 05530 ....**7**	13 wks
25 May 56 ●	THE SAINTS ROCK 'N ROLL Brunswick 05565 ....**5**	24 wks
17 Aug 56 ●	ROCKIN' THROUGH THE RYE Brunswick 05582 ....**3**	18 wks
14 Sep 56	RAZZLE DAZZLE Brunswick 05453 ....**13**	8 wks
21 Sep 56 ●	ROCK AROUND THE CLOCK (2nd re-entry)	
	Brunswick 05317 ....**5**	11 wks
21 Sep 56	SEE YOU LATER ALLIGATOR (re-entry)	
	Brunswick 05530 ....**12**	8 wks
9 Nov 56 ●	RIP IT UP Brunswick 05615 ....**4**	18 wks
9 Nov 56	ROCK 'N ROLL STAGE SHOW (LP)	
	Brunswick LAT 8139 ....**30**	1 wk
23 Nov 56	RUDY'S ROCK Brunswick 05616 ....**30**	1 wk

14 Dec 56	**ROCK AROUND THE CLOCK (3rd re-entry)**		
	Brunswick 05317	.....**24**	2 wks
14 Dec 56	**RUDY'S ROCK (re-entry)** *Brunswick 05616*	.....**26**	4 wks
4 Jan 57	**ROCK AROUND THE CLOCK (4th re-entry)**		
	Brunswick 05317	.....**25**	2 wks
4 Jan 57	**ROCKIN' THROUGH THE RYE (re-entry)**		
	Brunswick 05582	.....**19**	5 wks
25 Jan 57	**ROCK AROUND THE CLOCK (5th re-entry)**		
	Brunswick 05317	.....**22**	2 wks
1 Feb 57	**ROCK THE JOINT** *London HLF 8371*	.....**20**	4 wks
8 Feb 57	● **DON'T KNOCK THE ROCK** *Brunswick 05640*	.....**7**	8 wks
3 Apr 68	**ROCK AROUND THE CLOCK (re-issue)**		
	MCA MU 1013	.....**20**	11 wks
16 Mar 74	**ROCK AROUND THE CLOCK (2nd re-issue)**		
	MCA 128	.....**12**	10 wks
25 Apr 81	**HALEY'S GOLDEN MEDLEY** *MCA 694*	.....**50**	5 wks

Tracks on Rock 'N Roll Stage Show (LP): *Calling All Comets / Rockin' Through The Rye / A Rockin' Little Tune / Hide And Seek / Hey There Now / Goofin' Around / Hook Line and Sinker / Rudy's Rock / Choo Choo Ch'Boogie / Blue Comets Rock / Hot Dog Buddy Buddy / Tonight's The Night.* Occasionally, some of the Rock Around The Clock labels billed the song as (We're Gonna) Rock Around The Clock.

Aaron HALL *US, male vocalist*   3 wks

13 Jun 92	**DON'T BE AFRAID** *MCA MCS 1632*	.....**56**	2 wks
23 Oct 93	**GET A LITTLE FREAKY WITH ME**		
	MCA MCSTD 1936	.....**66**	1 wk

Audrey HALL *Jamaica, female vocalist*   20 wks

| 25 Jan 86 | **ONE DANCE WON'T DO** *Germain DG7-1985* | .....**20** | 11 wks |
| 5 Jul 86 | **SMILE** *Germain DG 15* | .....**14** | 9 wks |

Daryl HALL *US, male vocalist*   23 wks

2 Aug 86	**DREAMTIME** *RCA HALL 1*	.....**28**	8 wks
25 Sep 93	**I'M IN A PHILLY MOOD** *Epic 6595555*	.....**59**	2 wks
8 Jan 94	**STOP LOVING ME STOP LOVING YOU**		
	Epic 6599982	.....**30**	6 wks
26 Mar 94	**I'M IN A PHILLY MOOD (re-entry)** *Epic 6595555*	.....**52**	2 wks
14 May 94	**HELP ME FIND A WAY TO YOUR HEART**		
	Epic 6604102	.....**70**	1 wk
2 Jul 94	**GLORYLAND** *Mercury MERCD 404* [1]	.....**36**	4 wks

[1] Daryl Hall and the Sounds Of Blackness

See also Daryl Hall and John Oates.

Daryl HALL and John OATES
US, male vocal / instrumental duo   84 wks

16 Oct 76	**SHE'S GONE** *Atlantic K 10828*	.....**42**	4 wks
14 Jun 80	**RUNNING FROM PARADISE** *RCA RUN 1*	.....**41**	6 wks
20 Sep 80	**YOU'VE LOST THAT LOVIN' FEELIN'** *RCA 1*	.....**55**	3 wks
15 Nov 80	**KISS ON MY LIST** *RCA 15*	.....**33**	8 wks
23 Jan 82	● **I CAN'T GO FOR THAT (NO CAN DO)** *RCA 172*	.....**8**	10 wks
10 Apr 82	**PRIVATE EYES** *RCA 134*	.....**32**	7 wks
30 Oct 82	● **MANEATER** *RCA 290*	.....**6**	11 wks
22 Jan 83	**ONE ON ONE** *RCA 305*	.....**63**	3 wks
30 Apr 83	**FAMILY MAN** *RCA 323*	.....**15**	7 wks
12 Nov 83	**SAY IT ISN'T SO** *RCA 375*	.....**69**	3 wks
10 Mar 84	**ADULT EDUCATION** *RCA 396*	.....**63**	2 wks
20 Oct 84	**OUT OF TOUCH** *RCA 449*	.....**48**	5 wks
9 Feb 85	**METHOD OF MODERN LOVE** *RCA RCA 472*	.....**21**	8 wks
22 Jun 85	**OUT OF TOUCH (re-mix)** *RCA PB 4 9967*	.....**62**	3 wks
21 Sep 85	**A NIGHT AT THE APOLLO LIVE!** *RCA PB 49935* [1]	..**58**	2 wks
29 Sep 90	**SO CLOSE** *Arista 113600* [2]	.....**69**	1 wk
26 Jan 91	**EVERYWHERE I LOOK** *Arista 113980*	.....**74**	1 wk

[1] Daryl Hall and John Oates featuring David Ruffin and Eddie Kendrick [2] Hall and Oates

A Night At The Apollo Live! is a medley of The Way You Do The Things You Do / My Girl. See also Daryl Hall.

Pam HALL *Jamaica, female vocalist*   4 wks

| 16 Aug 86 | **DEAR BOOPSIE** *Bluemountain BM 027* | .....**54** | 4 wks |

Terry HALL *UK, male vocalist*   4 wks

11 Nov 89	**MISSING** *Chrysalis CHS 3381*	.....**75**	1 wk
27 Aug 94	**FOREVER J** *Anxious ANX 1024CDX*	.....**67**	1 wk
12 Nov 94	**SENSE** *Anxious ANX 1027CD*	.....**54**	2 wks

The sleeve, not the label, of Missing credits Terry, Blair and Anouchka.

HALO JAMES *UK, male vocal / instrumental group*   24 wks

7 Oct 89	**WANTED** *Epic HALO 1*	.....**45**	5 wks
23 Dec 89	● **COULD HAVE TOLD YOU SO** *Epic HALO 2*	.....**6**	12 wks
17 Mar 90	**BABY** *Epic HALO 3*	.....**43**	4 wks
19 May 90	**MAGIC HOUR** *Epic HALO 4*	.....**59**	3 wks

George HAMILTON IV *US, male vocalist*   13 wks

7 Mar 58	**WHY DON'T THEY UNDERSTAND** *HMV POP 429*	....**22**	9 wks
18 Jul 58	**I KNOW WHERE I'M GOING** *HMV POP 505*	.....**29**	1 wk
8 Aug 58	**I KNOW WHERE I'M GOING (re-entry)**		
	HMV POP 505	.....**23**	3 wks

Lynne HAMILTON *Australia, female vocalist*   11 wks

| 29 Apr 89 | ● **ON THE INSIDE (THEME FROM 'PRISONER CELL** | | |
| | **BLOCK H')** *A.1. A1 311* | .....**3** | 11 wks |

Russ HAMILTON *UK, male vocalist*   26 wks

| 24 May 57 | ● **WE WILL MAKE LOVE** *Oriole CB 1359* | .....**2** | 20 wks |
| 27 Sep 57 | **WEDDING RING** *Oriole CB 1388* | .....**20** | 6 wks |

HAMILTON, Joe FRANK and REYNOLDS
US, male vocal group   6 wks

| 13 Sep 75 | **FALLIN' IN LOVE** *Pye International 7N 25690* | .....**33** | 6 wks |

Marvin HAMLISCH *US, male instrumentalist - piano*   13 wks

| 30 Mar 74 | **THE ENTERTAINER** *MCA 121* | .....**25** | 13 wks |

HAMMER *US, male rapper*   67 wks

9 Jun 90	● **U CAN'T TOUCH THIS** *Capitol CL 578* [1]	.....**3**	16 wks
6 Oct 90	● **HAVE YOU SEEN HER** *Capitol CL 590* [1]	.....**8**	7 wks
8 Dec 90	● **PRAY** *Capitol CL 599* [1]	.....**8**	10 wks
23 Feb 91	**HERE COMES THE HAMMER** *Capitol CL 610* [1]	....**15**	5 wks
1 Jun 91	**YO!! SWEETNESS** *Capitol CL 616* [1]	.....**16**	5 wks
20 Jul 91	**(HAMMER HAMMER) THEY PUT ME IN THE MIX**		
	Capitol CL 607 [1]	.....**20**	4 wks
26 Oct 91	**2 LEGIT 2 QUIT** *Capitol CL 636*	.....**60**	2 wks
21 Dec 91	● **ADDAMS GROOVE** *Capitol CL 642*	.....**4**	9 wks
21 Mar 92	**DO NOT PASS ME BY** *Capitol CL 650*	.....**14**	6 wks
12 Mar 94	**IT'S ALL GOOD** *RCA 74321188612*	.....**52**	2 wks
13 Aug 94	**DON'T STOP** *RCA 74321220012*	.....**72**	1 wk

[1] MC Hammer

Jan HAMMER
Czechoslovakia, male instrumentalist - keyboards   26 wks

12 Oct 85	● **MIAMI VICE THEME** *MCA MCA 1000*	.....**5**	8 wks
19 Sep 87	● **CROCKETT'S THEME** *MCA MCA 1193*	.....**2**	12 wks
1 Jun 91	**CROCKETT'S THEME (re-issue)** *MCA MCS 1541*	....**47**	6 wks

Albert HAMMOND *UK, male vocalist*   11 wks

| 30 Jun 73 | **FREE ELECTRIC BAND** *Mums 1494* | .....**19** | 11 wks |

Beres HAMMOND - *See Maxi PRIEST*

Herbie HANCOCK
US, male vocalist / instrumentalist - keyboards　　　　**41 wks**

26 Aug 78	**I THOUGHT IT WAS YOU** *CBS 6530*	**15**	9 wks
3 Feb 79	**YOU BET YOUR LOVE** *CBS 7010*	**18**	10 wks
30 Jul 83	● **ROCKIT** *CBS A 3577*	**8**	12 wks
8 Oct 83	**AUTO DRIVE** *CBS A 3802*	**33**	4 wks
21 Jan 84	**FUTURE SHOCK** *CBS A 4075*	**54**	3 wks
4 Aug 84	**HARDROCK** *CBS A 4616*	**65**	3 wks

HANDLEY FAMILY *UK, male / female vocal group*　　**7 wks**

7 Apr 73	**WAM BAM** *GL 100*	**30**	7 wks

HANNAH and her SISTERS - *See Hannah JONES*

HANOI ROCKS
Finland / UK, male vocal / instrumental group　　**2 wks**

7 Jul 84	**UP AROUND THE BEND** *CBS A 4513*	**61**	2 wks

HAPPENINGS *US, male vocal group*　　**14 wks**

18 May 67	**I GOT RHYTHM** *Stateside SS 2013*	**28**	9 wks
16 Aug 67	**MY MAMMY**		
	Pye Int 7N 25501 and B.T. Puppy BTS 45530	**34**	5 wks

Pye gave the American B.T. Puppy label its own identification halfway through the success of My Mammy.

HAPPY MONDAYS
UK, male vocal / instrumental group　　**51 wks**

30 Sep 89	**WFL** *Factory FAC 2327*	**68**	2 wks
25 Nov 89	**MADCHESTER RAVE ON EP** *Factory FAC 2427*	**19**	14 wks
7 Apr 90	● **STEP ON** *Factory FAC 2727*	**5**	11 wks
9 Jun 90	**LAZYITIS - ONE ARMED BOXER**		
	Factory FAC 2227 [1]	**46**	3 wks
20 Oct 90	● **KINKY AFRO** *Factory FAC 3027*	**5**	7 wks
9 Mar 91	**LOOSE FIT** *Factory FAC 3127*	**17**	7 wks
30 Nov 91	**JUDGE FUDGE** *Factory FAC 3327*	**24**	3 wks
19 Sep 92	**STINKIN THINKIN** *Factory FAC 3627*	**31**	3 wks
21 Nov 92	**SUNSHINE AND LOVE** *Factory FAC 3727*	**62**	1 wk

[1] Happy Mondays and Karl Denver

Tracks on Madchester Rave On EP: *Hallelujah / Holy Ghost / Clap Your Hands / Rave On.*

Paul HARDCASTLE *UK, male producer*　　**66 wks**

7 Apr 84	**YOU'RE THE ONE FOR ME - DAYBREAK - A.M.**		
	Total Control TOCO 1	**41**	4 wks
28 Jul 84	**GUILTY** *Total Control TOCO 2*	**55**	3 wks
22 Sep 84	**RAIN FOREST** *Bluebird BR 8*	**41**	5 wks
17 Nov 84	**EAT YOUR HEART OUT** *Cool Tempo COOL 102*	**59**	4 wks
4 May 85	★ **NINETEEN** *Chrysalis CHS 2860*	**1**	16 wks
15 Jun 85	**RAIN FOREST** (re-issue) *Bluebird 10 BR 15*	**53**	4 wks
9 Nov 85	**JUST FOR MONEY** *Chrysalis CASH 1*	**19**	5 wks
1 Feb 86	● **DON'T WASTE MY TIME** *Chrysalis PAUL 1* [1]	**8**	11 wks
21 Jun 86	**FOOLIN' YOURSELF** *Chrysalis PAUL 2*	**51**	3 wks
11 Oct 86	**THE WIZARD** *Chrysalis PAUL 3*	**15**	6 wks
9 Apr 88	**WALK IN THE NIGHT** *Chrysalis PAUL 4*	**54**	3 wks
4 Jun 88	**40 YEARS** *Chrysalis PAUL 5*	**53**	2 wks

[1] Paul Hardcastle featuring Carol Kenyon

Just for Money features the voices of Laurence Olivier, Bob Hoskins, Ed O'Ross and Alan Talbot, who are credited on the sleeve only. See also Silent Underdog.

HARDCORE RHYTHM TEAM
UK, male vocal / production group　　**1 wk**

14 Mar 92	**HARDCORE - THE FINAL CONFLICT**		
	Furious FRUT 001	**69**	1 wk

HARDFLOOR
Germany, male instrumental / production group　　**5 wks**

26 Dec 92	**HARDTRANCE ACPERIENCE**		
	Harthouse UK HARTUK 1	**56**	4 wks
10 Apr 93	**TRANCESCRIPT** *Harthouse UK HARTUK 5CD*	**72**	1 wk

Tim HARDIN *US, male vocalist*　　**1 wk**

5 Jan 67	**HANG ON TO A DREAM** *Verve VS 1504*	**50**	1 wk

Mike HARDING *UK, male vocalist*　　**8 wks**

2 Aug 75	**ROCHDALE COWBOY** *Rubber ADUB 3*	**22**	8 wks

Francoise HARDY *France, female vocalist*　　**26 wks**

25 Jun 64	**TOUS LES GARCONS ET LES FILLES** *Pye 7N 15653*	**36**	7 wks
7 Jan 65	**ET MEME** *Pye 7N 15740*	**31**	4 wks
25 Mar 65	**ALL OVER THE WORLD** *Pye 7N 15802*	**16**	15 wks

Tynetta HARE - *See Joey B. ELLIS*

HARLEM COMMUNITY CHOIR - *See John LENNON*

HARLEQUIN 4's / BUNKER KRU
US, male vocal / instrumental group with UK, male production duo　　**4 wks**

19 Mar 88	**SET IT OFF** *Champion CHAMP 64*	**55**	4 wks

HARLEY QUINNE *UK, male vocal group*　　**8 wks**

14 Oct 72	**NEW ORLEANS** *Bell 1255*	**19**	8 wks

Steve HARLEY and COCKNEY REBEL
UK, male vocalist and male vocal / instrumental backing group　　**66 wks**

11 May 74	● **JUDY TEEN** *EMI 2128* [1]	**5**	11 wks
10 Aug 74	● **MR. SOFT** *EMI 2191* [1]	**8**	9 wks
8 Feb 75	★ **MAKE ME SMILE (COME UP AND SEE ME)**		
	EMI 2263	**1**	9 wks
7 Jun 75	**MR. RAFFLES (MAN IT WAS MEAN)** *EMI 2299*	**13**	6 wks
31 Jul 76	● **HERE COMES THE SUN** *EMI 2505* [2]	**10**	7 wks
6 Nov 76	**LOVE'S A PRIMA DONNA** *EMI 2539* [2]	**41**	4 wks
20 Oct 79	**FREEDOM'S PRISONER** *EMI 2994* [2]	**58**	3 wks
13 Aug 83	**BALLERINA (PRIMA DONNA)** *Stilletto STL 14* [2]	**51**	5 wks
11 Jan 86	● **THE PHANTOM OF THE OPERA**		
	Polydor POSP 800 [3]	**7**	10 wks
25 Apr 92	**MAKE ME SMILE (COME UP AND SEE ME)**		
	(re-issue) *EMI EMCT 5* [2]	**46**	2 wks

[1] Cockney Rebel [2] Steve Harley [3] Sarah Brightman and Steve Harley

HARMONY GRASS
UK, male vocal / instrumental group　　**7 wks**

29 Jan 69	**MOVE IN A LITTLE CLOSER** *RCA 1772*	**24**	7 wks

Charlie HARPER *UK, male vocalist*　　**1 wk**

19 Jul 80	**BARMY LONDON ARMY** *Gem GEMS 35*	**68**	1 wk

HARPERS BIZARRE *US, male vocal group*　　**13 wks**

30 Mar 67	**59TH STREET BRIDGE SONG (FEELING GROOVY)**		
	Warner Bros. WB 5890	**34**	7 wks
4 Oct 67	**ANYTHING GOES** *Warner Bros. WB 7063*	**33**	6 wks

HARPO *Sweden, male vocalist*   **6 wks**

| 17 Apr 76 | **MOVIE STAR** DJM DJS 400 ....**24** | 6 wks |

T. HARRINGTON - See Rahni HARRIS and F.L.O.

Anita HARRIS *UK, female vocalist*   **50 wks**

29 Jun 67 ●	**JUST LOVING YOU** CBS 2724 ....**6**	30 wks
11 Oct 67	**PLAYGROUND** CBS 2991 ....**46**	3 wks
24 Jan 68	**ANNIVERSARY WALTZ** CBS 3211 ....**21**	9 wks
14 Aug 68	**DREAM A LITTLE DREAM OF ME** CBS 3637 ......**33**	8 wks

Emmylou HARRIS *US, female vocalist*   **6 wks**

| 6 Mar 76 | **HERE THERE AND EVERYWHERE** Reprise K 14415 ..**30** | 6 wks |

Jet HARRIS *UK, male instrumentalist - bass guitar*   **18 wks**

| 24 May 62 | **BESAME MUCHO** Decca F 11466 ....**22** | 7 wks |
| 16 Aug 62 | **MAIN TITLE THEME FROM 'MAN WITH THE GOLDEN ARM'** Decca F 11488 ....**12** | 11 wks |

See also Jet Harris and Tony Meehan.

Jet HARRIS and Tony MEEHAN
UK, male instrumental duo - bass guitar and drums   **39 wks**

10 Jan 63 ★	**DIAMONDS** Decca F 11563 ....**1**	13 wks
25 Apr 63 ●	**SCARLETT O'HARA** Decca F 11644 ....**2**	13 wks
5 Sep 63 ●	**APPLEJACK** Decca F 11710 ....**4**	13 wks

See also Jet Harris; Tony Meehan.

Keith HARRIS and ORVILLE
UK, male ventriloquist vocalist with feathered dummy   **20 wks**

18 Dec 82 ●	**ORVILLE'S SONG** BBC RESL 124 ....**4**	11 wks
24 Dec 83	**COME TO MY PARTY** BBC RESL 138 [1] **44**	4 wks
14 Dec 85	**WHITE CHRISTMAS** Columbia DB 9121 ....**40**	5 wks

[1] Keith Harris and Orville with Dippy

Major HARRIS *US, male vocalist*   **9 wks**

| 9 Aug 75 | **LOVE WON'T LET ME WAIT** Atlantic K 10585 ....**37** | 7 wks |
| 5 Nov 83 | **ALL MY LIFE** London LON 37 ....**61** | 2 wks |

Max HARRIS *UK, orchestra*   **10 wks**

| 1 Dec 60 | **GURNEY SLADE** Fontana H 282 ....**11** | 10 wks |

Rahni HARRIS and F.L.O.
US, male instrumental group   **7 wks**

| 16 Dec 78 | **SIX MILLION STEPS (WEST RUNS SOUTH)** Mercury 6007 198 ....**43** | 7 wks |

Hit has credit 'vocals by T. Harrington and O. Rasbury'.

Richard HARRIS *Ireland, male vocalist*   **18 wks**

| 26 Jun 68 ● | **MACARTHUR PARK** RCA 1699 ....**4** | 12 wks |
| 8 Jul 72 | **MACARTHUR PARK (re-issue)** Probe GFF 101 ....**38** | 6 wks |

Rolf HARRIS *Australia, male vocalist*   **70 wks**

21 Jul 60 ●	**TIE ME KANGAROO DOWN SPORT** Columbia DB 4483 ....**9**	13 wks
25 Oct 62 ●	**SUN ARISE** Columbia DB 4888 ....**3**	16 wks
28 Feb 63	**JOHNNY DAY** Columbia DB 4979 ....**44**	2 wks
16 Apr 69	**BLUER THAN BLUE** Columbia DB 8553 ....**30**	8 wks

22 Nov 69 ★	**TWO LITTLE BOYS** Columbia DB 8630 ....**1**	24 wks
20 Jun 70	**TWO LITTLE BOYS (re-entry)** Columbia DB 8630 ....**50**	1 wk
13 Feb 93 ●	**STAIRWAY TO HEAVEN** Vertigo VERCD 73 ....**7**	6 wks

Ronnie HARRIS *UK, male vocalist*   **3 wks**

| 24 Sep 54 | **STORY OF TINA** Columbia DB 3499 ....**12** | 3 wks |

Sam HARRIS *UK, male vocalist*   **2 wks**

| 9 Feb 85 | **HEARTS ON FIRE / OVER THE RAINBOW** Motown TMG 1370 ....**67** | 2 wks |

Simon HARRIS *UK, male producer*   **17 wks**

19 Mar 88	**BASS (HOW LOW CAN YOU GO)** ffrr FFR 4 ....**12**	6 wks
29 Oct 88	**HERE COMES THAT SOUND** ffrr FFR 12 ....**38**	4 wks
24 Jun 89	**(I'VE GOT YOUR) PLEASURE CONTROL** ffrr F 106 [1] **60**	3 wks
18 Nov 89	**ANOTHER MONSTERJAM** ffrr F 116 [2] **65**	1 wk
10 Mar 90	**RAGGA HOUSE (ALL NIGHT LONG)** Living Beat 7SMASH 9 [3] **56**	3 wks

[1] Simon Harris featuring Lonnie Gordon [2] Simon Harris featuring Einstein
[3] Simon Harris featuring Daddy Freddy

George HARRISON *UK, male vocalist*   **82 wks**

23 Jan 71 ★	**MY SWEET LORD** Apple R 5884 ....**1**	17 wks
14 Aug 71 ●	**BANGLA DESH** Apple R 5912 ....**10**	9 wks
2 Jun 73 ●	**GIVE ME LOVE (GIVE ME PEACE ON EARTH)** Apple R 5988 ....**8**	10 wks
21 Dec 74	**DING DONG** Apple R 6002 ....**38**	5 wks
11 Oct 75	**YOU** Apple R 6007 ....**38**	5 wks
10 Mar 79	**BLOW AWAY** Dark Horse K 17327 ....**51**	5 wks
23 May 81	**ALL THOSE YEARS AGO** Dark Horse K 17807 ....**13**	7 wks
24 Oct 87 ●	**GOT MY MIND SET ON YOU** Dark Horse W 8178 ......**2**	14 wks
6 Feb 88	**WHEN WE WAS FAB** Dark Horse W 8131 ....**25**	7 wks
25 Jun 88	**THIS IS LOVE** Dark Horse W 7913 ....**55**	3 wks

Noel HARRISON *UK, male vocalist*   **14 wks**

| 26 Feb 69 ● | **WINDMILLS OF YOUR MIND** Reprise RS 20758 ....**8** | 14 wks |

Deborah HARRY *US, female vocalist*   **52 wks**

1 Aug 81	**BACKFIRED** Chrysalis CHS 2526 [1] **32**	6 wks
15 Nov 86 ●	**FRENCH KISSIN' IN THE USA** Chrysalis CHS 3066 [1] ..**8**	10 wks
28 Feb 87	**FREE TO FALL** Chrysalis CHS 3093 [1] **46**	4 wks
9 May 87	**IN LOVE WITH LOVE** Chrysalis CHS 3128 [1] **45**	5 wks
7 Oct 89	**I WANT THAT MAN** Chrysalis CHS 3369 ....**13**	10 wks
2 Dec 89	**BRITE SIDE** Chrysalis CHS 3452 ....**59**	4 wks
31 Mar 90	**SWEET AND LOW** Chrysalis CHS 3491 ....**57**	3 wks
5 Jan 91	**WELL DID YOU EVAH!** Chrysalis CHS 3646 [2] **42**	4 wks
3 Jul 93	**I CAN SEE CLEARLY NOW** Chrysalis CDCHSS 4900 ....**23**	4 wks
18 Sep 93	**STRIKE ME PINK** Chrysalis CDCHSS 5000 ....**46**	2 wks

[1] Debbie Harry [2] Deborah Harry and Iggy Pop

HARRY J. ALL STARS
Jamaica, male instrumental group   **25 wks**

| 25 Oct 69 ● | **LIQUIDATOR** Trojan TR 675 ....**9** | 20 wks |
| 29 Mar 80 | **LIQUIDATOR (re-issue)** Trojan TRO 9063 ....**42** | 5 wks |

Re-issue of Liquidator coupled with re-issue of Long Shot Kick De Bucket by the Pioneers.

Richard HARTLEY/Michael REED ORCHESTRA
UK, male instrumentalist - synthesizer, orchestra   **10 wks**

| 25 Feb 84 ● | **THE MUSIC OF TORVILL AND DEAN EP** Safari SKATE 1 ....**9** | 10 wks |

Tracks on EP: Bolero / Capriccio Espagnole Opus. 34 (Nos.4 and 5) by Richard Hartley; Barnum On Ice / Discoskate by the Michael Reed Orchestra.

Dan HARTMAN US, male vocalist — **33 wks**

Date	Title	Pos	Wks
21 Oct 78	● **INSTANT REPLAY** Sky 6706	8	15 wks
13 Jan 79	**THIS IS IT** Blue Sky SKY 6999	17	8 wks
18 May 85	**SECOND NATURE** MCA MCA 957	66	2 wks
24 Aug 85	**I CAN DREAM ABOUT YOU** MCA MCA 988	12	8 wks

Steve HARVEY UK, male vocalist — **6 wks**

Date	Title	Pos	Wks
28 May 83	**SOMETHING SPECIAL** London LON 25	46	4 wks
29 Oct 83	**TONIGHT** London LON 36	63	2 wks

Sensational Alex HARVEY BAND
UK, male vocal / instrumental group — **25 wks**

Date	Title	Pos	Wks
26 Jul 75	● **DELILAH** Vertigo ALEX 001	7	7 wks
22 Nov 75	**GAMBLIN' BAR ROOM BLUES** Vertigo ALEX 002	38	8 wks
19 Jun 76	**THE BOSTON TEA PARTY** Mountain TOP 12	13	10 wks

P.J. HARVEY - See PJ HARVEY

David HASSELHOFF US, male vocalist — **2 wks**

Date	Title	Pos	Wks
13 Nov 93	**IF I COULD ONLY SAY GOODBYE** Arista 74321172262	35	2 wks

Tony HATCH UK, orchestra — **1 wk**

Date	Title	Pos	Wks
4 Oct 62	**OUT OF THIS WORLD** Pye 7N 15460	50	1 wk

Juliana HATFIELD THREE
US, female / male vocal / instrumental group — **1 wk**

Date	Title	Pos	Wks
11 Sep 93	**MY SISTER** Mammoth YZ 767CD	71	1 wk

Donny HATHAWAY - See Roberta FLACK

Lalah HATHAWAY US, female vocalist — **10 wks**

Date	Title	Pos	Wks
1 Sep 90	**HEAVEN KNOWS** Virgin America VUS 28	66	2 wks
2 Feb 91	**BABY DON'T CRY** Virgin America VUS 35	54	3 wks
27 Jul 91	**FAMILY AFFAIR** Ten TEN 369 [1]	37	5 wks

[1] B.E.F. featuring Lalah Hathaway

HAVANA UK, male instrumental / production group — **1 wk**

Date	Title	Pos	Wks
6 Mar 93	**ETHNIC PRAYER** Limbo LIMBO 007CD	71	1 wk

Nic HAVERSON UK, male vocalist — **3 wks**

Date	Title	Pos	Wks
30 Jan 93	**HEAD OVER HEELS** Telstar CDHOH 1	48	3 wks

Chesney HAWKES UK, male vocalist — **25 wks**

Date	Title	Pos	Wks
23 Feb 91	★ **THE ONE AND ONLY** Chrysalis CHS 3627	1	16 wks
22 Jun 91	**I'M A MAN NOT A BOY** Chrysalis CHS 3708	27	5 wks
28 Sep 91	**SECRETS OF THE HEART** Chrysalis CHS 3681	57	3 wks
29 May 93	**WHAT'S WRONG WITH THIS PICTURE** Chrysalis CDCHS 3969	63	1 wk

Edwin HAWKINS SINGERS featuring Dorothy Combs MORRISON
US, male / female vocal group — **13 wks**

Date	Title	Pos	Wks
21 May 69	● **OH HAPPY DAY** Buddah 201 048	2	12 wks
23 Aug 69	**OH HAPPY DAY** (re-entry) Buddah 201 048	43	1 wk

Screamin' Jay HAWKINS US, male vocalist — **3 wks**

Date	Title	Pos	Wks
3 Apr 93	**HEART ATTACK AND VINE** Columbia 6591092	42	3 wks

Sophie B. HAWKINS US, female vocalist — **31 wks**

Date	Title	Pos	Wks
4 Jul 92	**DAMN I WISH I WAS YOUR LOVER** Columbia 6581077	14	9 wks
12 Sep 92	**CALIFORNIA HERE I COME** Columbia 6583177	53	3 wks
6 Feb 93	**I WANT YOU** Columbia 6587772	49	2 wks
13 Aug 94	**RIGHT BESIDE YOU** Columbia 6606915	13	12 wks
26 Nov 94	**DON'T DON'T TELL ME NO** Columbia 6610152	36	5 wks

HAWKWIND
UK, male vocal / instrumental group with female dancer — **28 wks**

Date	Title	Pos	Wks
1 Jul 72	● **SILVER MACHINE** United Artists UP 35381	3	15 wks
11 Aug 73	**URBAN GUERRILLA** United Artists UP 35566	39	3 wks
21 Oct 78	**SILVER MACHINE** (re-entry) United Artists UP 35381	34	5 wks
19 Jul 80	**SHOT DOWN IN THE NIGHT** Bronze BRO 98	59	3 wks
15 Jan 83	**SILVER MACHINE** (2nd re-entry) United Artists UP 35381	67	2 wks

See also Various Artists (EPs & LPs) - Gimme Shelter (EP).

Bill HAYES US, male vocalist — **9 wks**

Date	Title	Pos	Wks
6 Jan 56	● **BALLAD OF DAVY CROCKETT** London HLA 8220	2	9 wks

Isaac HAYES US, male vocalist / multi-instrumentalist — **21 wks**

Date	Title	Pos	Wks
4 Dec 71	● **THEME FROM 'SHAFT'** Stax 2025 069	4	12 wks
3 Apr 76	● **DISCO CONNECTION** ABC 4100 [1]	10	9 wks

[1] Isaac Hayes Movement

HAYSI FANTAYZEE UK, male / female vocal duo — **25 wks**

Date	Title	Pos	Wks
24 Jul 82	**JOHN WAYNE IS BIG LEGGY** Regard RG 100	11	10 wks
13 Nov 82	**HOLY JOE** Regard RG 104	51	3 wks
22 Jan 83	**SHINY SHINY** Regard RG 106	16	10 wks
25 Jun 83	**SISTER FRICTION** Regard RG 108	62	2 wks

Justin HAYWARD UK, male vocalist — **20 wks**

Date	Title	Pos	Wks
25 Oct 75	● **BLUE GUITAR** Threshold TH 21 [1]	8	7 wks
8 Jul 78	● **FOREVER AUTUMN** CBS 6368	5	13 wks

[1] Justin Hayward and John Lodge

Leon HAYWOOD US, male vocalist — **11 wks**

Date	Title	Pos	Wks
15 Mar 80	**DON'T PUSH IT, DON'T FORCE IT** 20th Century Fox TC 2443	12	11 wks

HAYWOODE UK, female vocalist — **31 wks**

Date	Title	Pos	Wks
17 Sep 83	**A TIME LIKE THIS** CBS A 3651	48	7 wks
29 Sep 84	**I CAN'T LET YOU GO** CBS A 4664	63	4 wks
13 Apr 85	**ROSES** CBS A 6069	65	3 wks
5 Oct 85	**GETTING CLOSER** CBS A 6582	67	2 wks
21 Jun 86	**ROSES** (re-issue) CBS A 7224	11	11 wks
13 Sep 86	**I CAN'T LET YOU GO** (re-issue) CBS 650076 7	50	4 wks

Ofra HAZA Israel, female vocalist — **8 wks**

Date	Title	Pos	Wks
30 Apr 88	**IM NIN'ALU** WEA YZ 190	15	8 wks

Lee HAZLEWOOD - See Nancy SINATRA

Murray HEAD UK, male vocalist — **15 wks**

Date	Title	Pos	Wks
29 Jan 72	**SUPERSTAR** MCA MMKS 5077	47	1 wk
10 Nov 84	**ONE NIGHT IN BANGKOK** RCA CHESS 1	12	13 wks

16 Feb 85   **ONE NIGHT IN BANGKOK (re-entry)** *RCA CHESS 1* ..**74**   1 wk

Superstar was one of four tracks on a maxi single, two of which were credited during the disc's one week on the chart. The other track credited was I Don't Know How To Love Him by Yvonne Elliman.

Roy HEAD *US, male vocalist*   **5 wks**

4 Nov 65   **TREAT HER RIGHT** *Vocalion V-P 9248* ....**30**   5 wks

HEADBANGERS *UK, male vocal / instrumental group*   **3 wks**

10 Oct 81   **STATUS ROCK** *Magnet MAG 206* ....**60**   3 wks

HEADBOYS *UK, male vocal / instrumental group*   **8 wks**

22 Sep 79   **THE SHAPE OF THINGS TO COME** *RSO 40* ....**45**   8 wks

HEADGIRL - *See MOTORHEAD; GIRLSCHOOL*

Max HEADROOM - *See ART OF NOISE*

HEADS *UK, male instrumental group*   **4 wks**

21 Jun 86   **AZTEC LIGHTNING (THEME FROM BBC WORLD CUP GRANDSTAND)** *BBC RESL 184* ....**45**   4 wks

HEAR 'N AID
International, male / female vocal / instrumental charity assembly   **6 wks**

19 Apr 86   **STARS** *Vertigo HEAR 1* ....**26**   6 wks

HEART *US, female / male vocal / instrumental group*   **76 wks**

29 Mar 86	**THESE DREAMS** *Capitol CL 394* **62**	4 wks
13 Jun 87	● **ALONE** *Capitol CL 448* **3**	16 wks
19 Sep 87	**WHO WILL YOU RUN TO** *Capitol CL 457* **30**	7 wks
12 Dec 87	**THERE'S THE GIRL** *Capitol CL 473* **34**	7 wks
5 Mar 88	● **NEVER / THESE DREAMS (re-issue)** *Capitol CL 482* ..**8**	9 wks
14 May 88	**WHAT ABOUT LOVE** *Capitol CL 487* **14**	6 wks
22 Oct 88	**NOTHIN' AT ALL** *Capitol CL 507* **38**	3 wks
24 Mar 90	● **ALL I WANNA DO IS MAKE LOVE TO YOU** *Capitol CL 569* **8**	13 wks
28 Jul 90	**I DIDN'T WANT TO NEED YOU** *Capitol CL 580* **47**	3 wks
17 Nov 90	**STRANDED** *Capitol CL 595* **60**	2 wks
14 Sep 91	**YOU'RE THE VOICE** *Capitol CLS 624* **56**	2 wks
20 Nov 93	**WILL YOU BE THERE (IN THE MORNING)** *Capitol CDCLS 700* **19**	4 wks

HEARTBEAT *UK, male / female vocal / instrumental group*   **5 wks**

24 Oct 87   **TEARS FROM HEAVEN** *Priority P 17* ....**32**   4 wks
23 Apr 88   **THE WINNER** *Priority P 19* ....**70**   1 wk

HEARTBEAT COUNTRY
UK, male vocalist - Bill Maynard   **1 wk**

31 Dec 94   **HEARTBEAT** *MMM MMM 01CD* ....**75**   1 wk

HEARTBREAKERS - *See Tom PETTY and the HEARTBREAKERS; Stevie NICKS*

Ted HEATH *UK, orchestra*   **56 wks**

16 Jan 53	**VANESSA** *Decca F 9983* **11**	1 wk
3 Jul 53	● **HOT TODDY** *Decca F 10093* **6**	11 wks
23 Oct 53	**DRAGNET** *Decca F 10176* **12**	1 wk
27 Nov 53	● **DRAGNET (re-entry)** *Decca F 10176* **9**	1 wk
11 Dec 53	**DRAGNET (2nd re-entry)** *Decca F 10176* **11**	1 wk
15 Jan 54	**DRAGNET (3rd re-entry)** *Decca F 10176* **11**	1 wk
5 Feb 54	**DRAGNET (4th re-entry)** *Decca F 10176* **12**	1 wk
12 Feb 54	● **SKIN DEEP** *Decca F 10246* **9**	3 wks
6 Jul 56	**THE FAITHFUL HUSSAR** *Decca F 10746* **18**	9 wks
14 Mar 58	● **SWINGIN' SHEPHERD BLUES** *Decca F 11000* **3**	14 wks
11 Apr 58	**TEQUILA** *Decca F 11003* **21**	6 wks
4 Jul 58	**TOM HARK** *Decca F 11025* **24**	2 wks
5 Oct 61	**SUCU SUCU** *Decca F 11392* **36**	4 wks
9 Nov 61	**SUCU SUCU (re-entry)** *Decca F 11392* **47**	1 wk

HEATWAVE *UK / US, male vocal / instrumental group*   **80 wks**

22 Jan 77	● **BOOGIE NIGHTS** *GTO GT 77* **2**	14 wks
7 May 77	**TOO HOT TO HANDLE / SLIP YOUR DISC TO THIS** *GTO GT 91* **15**	11 wks
14 Jan 78	**THE GROOVE LINE** *GTO GT 115* **12**	8 wks
3 Jun 78	**MIND BLOWING DECISIONS** *GTO GT 226* **12**	11 wks
4 Nov 78	● **ALWAYS AND FOREVER / MIND BLOWING DECISIONS (re-mix)** *GTO GT 236* **9**	14 wks
26 May 79	**RAZZLE DAZZLE** *GTO GT 248* **43**	5 wks
17 Jan 81	**GANGSTERS OF THE GROOVE** *GTO GT 285* **19**	8 wks
21 Mar 81	**JITTERBUGGIN'** *GTO GT 290* **34**	7 wks
1 Sep 90	**MIND BLOWING DECISIONS (re-issue)** *Brothers Organisation HW 1* **65**	2 wks

Mind Blowing Decisions on GT 236 is an extended remixed version of GT 226.

HEAVEN 17 *UK, male vocal / instrumental group*   **87 wks**

21 Mar 81	**(WE DON'T NEED THIS) FASCIST GROOVE THANG** *Virgin VS 400* **45**	5 wks
5 Sep 81	**PLAY TO WIN** *Virgin VS 433* **46**	7 wks
14 Nov 81	**PENTHOUSE AND PAVEMENT** *Virgin VS 455* **57**	3 wks
30 Oct 82	**LET ME GO** *Virgin VS 532* **41**	6 wks
16 Apr 83	● **TEMPTATION** *Virgin VS 570* **2**	13 wks
25 Jun 83	● **COME LIVE WITH ME** *Virgin VS 607* **5**	11 wks
10 Sep 83	**CRUSHED BY THE WHEELS OF INDUSTRY** *Virgin VS 628* **17**	7 wks
1 Sep 84	**SUNSET NOW** *Virgin VS 708* **24**	6 wks
27 Oct 84	**THIS IS MINE** *Virgin VS 722* **23**	7 wks
19 Jan 85	**...(AND THAT'S NO LIE)** *Virgin VS 740* **52**	5 wks
17 Jan 87	**TROUBLE** *Virgin VS 920* **51**	3 wks
21 Nov 92	● **TEMPTATION (re-mix)** *Virgin VS 1446* **4**	11 wks
27 Feb 93	**(WE DON'T NEED THIS) FASCIST GROOVE THANG** *Virgin VSCDT 1451* **40**	2 wks
10 Apr 93	**PENTHOUSE AND PAVEMENT (re-mix)** *Virgin VSCDT 1457* **54**	1 wk

Carol Kenyon is the uncredited vocalist on Temptation. Fascist Groove Thang in '93 is a re-recording. See also Various Artists (EPs & LPs) - Gimme Shelter (EP).

HEAVY D. and the BOYZ
Jamaica / US, male vocal / instrumental group   **28 wks**

6 Dec 86	**MR. BIG STUFF** *MCA MCA 1106* **61**	8 wks
15 Jul 89	**WE GOT OUR OWN THANG** *MCA MCA 23942* **69**	2 wks
6 Jul 91	● **NOW THAT WE FOUND LOVE** *MCA MCS 1550* **2**	12 wks
28 Sep 91	**IS IT GOOD TO YOU** *MCA MCS 1564* **46**	3 wks
8 Oct 94	**THIS IS YOUR NIGHT** *MCA MCSTD 2010* **30**	3 wks

HEAVY PETTIN' *UK, male vocal / instrumental group*   **2 wks**

17 Mar 84   **LOVE TIMES LOVE** *Polydor HEP 3* ....**69**   2 wks

Bobby HEBB *US, male vocalist*   **15 wks**

8 Sep 66   **SUNNY** *Philips BF 1503* ....**12**   9 wks
19 Aug 72   **LOVE LOVE LOVE** *Philips 6051 023* ....**32**   6 wks

HED BOYS *UK, male instrumental / production duo*   **4 wks**

6 Aug 94   **GIRLS + BOYS** *Deconstruction 74321223322* ....**21**   4 wks

HEDGEHOPPERS ANONYMOUS
UK, male vocal / instrumental group   **12 wks**

30 Sep 65	● IT'S GOOD NEWS WEEK *Decca F 12241*	**5**	12 wks

Neal HEFTI *US, male orchestra*   **4 wks**

9 Apr 88	BATMAN THEME *RCA PB 49571*	**55**	4 wks

Den HEGARTY *UK, male vocalist*   **2 wks**

31 Mar 79	VOODOO VOODOO *Magnet MAG 143*	**73**	2 wks

Anita HEGERLAND - *See Mike OLDFIELD*

HEINZ *UK, male vocalist*   **35 wks**

8 Aug 63	● JUST LIKE EDDIE *Decca F 11693*	**5**	15 wks
28 Nov 63	COUNTRY BOY *Decca F 11768*	**26**	9 wks
27 Feb 64	YOU WERE THERE *Decca F 11831*	**26**	8 wks
15 Oct 64	QUESTIONS I CAN'T ANSWER *Columbia DB 7374*	**39**	2 wks
18 Mar 65	DIGGIN' MY POTATOES *Columbia DB 7482*	**49**	1 wk

HELICOPTER *UK, male instrumental / production duo*   **2 wks**

27 Aug 94	ON YA WAY '94 *Helicopter TIG 007CD*	**32**	2 wks

HELLO *UK, male vocal / instrumental group*   **21 wks**

9 Nov 74	● TELL HIM *Bell 1377*	**6**	12 wks
18 Oct 75	● NEW YORK GROOVE *Bell 1438*	**9**	9 wks

HELLOWEEN *US, male vocal / instrumental group*   **7 wks**

27 Aug 88	DR STEIN *Noise International 7HELLO 1*	**57**	3 wks
12 Nov 88	I WANT OUT *Noise International 7HELLO 2*	**69**	2 wks
2 Mar 91	KIDS OF THE CENTURY *EMI EM 178*	**56**	2 wks

Bobby HELMS *US, male vocalist*   **7 wks**

29 Nov 57	MY SPECIAL ANGEL *Brunswick 05721*	**22**	3 wks
21 Feb 58	NO OTHER BABY *Brunswick 05730*	**30**	1 wk
1 Aug 58	JACQUELINE *Brunswick 05748*	**20**	3 wks

Jimmy HELMS *UK, male vocalist*   **10 wks**

24 Feb 73	● GONNA MAKE YOU AN OFFER YOU CAN'T REFUSE *Cube BUG 27*	**8**	10 wks

Eddie HENDERSON
US, male vocalist / instrumentalist - trumpet   **6 wks**

28 Oct 78	PRANCE ON *Capitol CL 16015*	**44**	6 wks

Joe 'Mr. Piano' HENDERSON
UK, male instrumentalist - piano   **23 wks**

3 Jun 55	SING IT WITH JOE *Polygon P 1167*	**14**	4 wks
2 Sep 55	SING IT AGAIN WITH JOE *Polygon P 1184*	**18**	3 wks
25 Jul 58	TRUDIE *Pye Nixa N 15147*	**14**	12 wks
24 Oct 58	TRUDIE (re-entry) *Pye Nixa N 15147*	**23**	1 wk
23 Oct 59	TREBLE CHANCE *Pye 7N 15224*	**28**	1 wk
24 Mar 60	OOH LA LA *Pye 7N 15257*	**46**	1 wk

First two hits are medleys as follows: Sing It With Joe: Margie / I'm Nobody's Sweetheart / Somebody Stole My Gal / Moonlight Bay / By The Light Of The Silvery Moon / Cuddle Up A Little Closer. Sing It Again With Joe: Put Your Arms Around Me Honey / Ain't She Sweet / When You're Smiling / Shine On Harvest Moon / My Blue Heaven / Show Me The Way To Go Home.

Wayne HENDERSON - *See Roy AYERS*

Jimi HENDRIX EXPERIENCE
US / UK, male vocal / instrumental group, Jimi Hendrix, vocalist / instrumentalist - guitar   **87 wks**

5 Jan 67	● HEY JOE *Polydor 56 139* [1]	**6**	10 wks
23 Mar 67	● PURPLE HAZE *Track 604 001*	**3**	14 wks
11 May 67	● THE WIND CRIES MARY *Track 604 004*	**6**	11 wks
30 Aug 67	BURNING OF THE MIDNIGHT LAMP *Track 604 007*	**18**	9 wks
23 Oct 68	● ALL ALONG THE WATCHTOWER *Track 604 025*	**5**	11 wks
16 Apr 69	CROSSTOWN TRAFFIC *Track 604 029*	**37**	3 wks
7 Nov 70	★ VOODOO CHILE *Track 2095 001*	**1**	13 wks
30 Oct 71	GYPSY EYES / REMEMBER *Track 2094 010*	**35**	5 wks
12 Feb 72	JOHNNY B. GOODE *Polydor 2001 277* [1]	**35**	5 wks
21 Apr 90	CROSSTOWN TRAFFIC (re-issue) *Polydor PO 71* [1]	**61**	3 wks
20 Oct 90	ALL ALONG THE WATCHTOWER (EP) *Polydor PO 100* [1]	**52**	3 wks

[1] Jimi Hendrix

Tracks on All Along The Watchtower (EP): All Along The Watchtower / Voodoo Chile / Hey Joe.

Nona HENDRYX *US, female vocalist*   **2 wks**

16 May 87	WHY SHOULD I CRY *EMI America EA 234*	**60**	2 wks

Don HENLEY *US, male vocalist*   **24 wks**

12 Feb 83	DIRTY LAUNDRY *Asylum E 9894*	**59**	3 wks
9 Feb 85	THE BOYS OF SUMMER *Geffen A 4945*	**12**	10 wks
29 Jul 89	THE END OF THE INNOCENCE *Geffen GEF 57*	**48**	5 wks
3 Oct 92	SOMETIMES LOVE JUST AIN'T ENOUGH *MCA MCS 1692* [1]	**22**	6 wks

[1] Patty Smyth with Don Henley

Clarence 'Frogman' HENRY *US, male vocalist*   **35 wks**

4 May 61	● BUT I DO *Pye International 7N 25078*	**3**	19 wks
13 Jul 61	● YOU ALWAYS HURT THE ONE YOU LOVE *Pye International 7N 25089*	**6**	12 wks
21 Sep 61	LONELY STREET / WHY CAN'T YOU *Pye International 7N 25108*	**42**	2 wks
17 Jul 93	(I DON'T KNOW WHY) BUT I DO (re-issue) *MCA MCSTD 1797*	**65**	2 wks

Kevin HENRY - *See L.A. MIX*

Paul HENRY and the Mayson GLEN ORCHESTRA *UK, male vocalist / orchestra*   **2 wks**

14 Jan 78	BENNY'S THEME *Pye 7N 46027*	**39**	2 wks

Pauline HENRY *UK, female vocalist*   **13 wks**

18 Sep 93	TOO MANY PEOPLE *Sony S2 6595942*	**38**	2 wks
6 Nov 93	FEEL LIKE MAKING LOVE *Sony S2 6597972*	**12**	7 wks
29 Jan 94	CAN'T TAKE YOUR LOVE *Sony S2 6599902*	**30**	3 wks
21 May 94	WATCH THE MIRACLE START *Sony S2 6602772*	**54**	1 wk

HERD *UK, male vocal / instrumental group*   **35 wks**

13 Sep 67	● FROM THE UNDERWORLD *Fontana TF 856*	**6**	13 wks
20 Dec 67	PARADISE LOST *Fontana TF 887*	**15**	9 wks
10 Apr 68	● I DON'T WANT OUR LOVING TO DIE *Fontana TF 925*	**5**	13 wks

HERMAN'S HERMITS
UK, male vocal / instrumental group   **211 wks**

20 Aug 64	★ I'M INTO SOMETHING GOOD *Columbia DB 7338*	**1**	15 wks
19 Nov 64	SHOW ME GIRL *Columbia DB 7408*	**19**	9 wks
18 Feb 65	● SILHOUETTES *Columbia DB 7475*	**3**	12 wks

29 Apr 65	● WONDERFUL WORLD Columbia DB 7546 ....**7**	9 wks
2 Sep 65	JUST A LITTLE BIT BETTER Columbia DB 7670 ....**15**	9 wks
23 Dec 65	● A MUST TO AVOID Columbia DB 7791 ....**6**	11 wks
24 Mar 66	YOU WON'T BE LEAVING Columbia DB 7861 ....**20**	7 wks
23 Jun 66	THIS DOOR SWINGS BOTH WAYS	
	Columbia DB 7947 ....**18**	7 wks
6 Oct 66	● NO MILK TODAY Columbia DB 8012 ....**7**	11 wks
1 Dec 66	EAST WEST Columbia DB 8076 ....**37**	7 wks
9 Feb 67	● THERE'S A KIND OF HUSH Columbia DB 8123 ....**7**	11 wks
17 Jan 68	I CAN TAKE OR LEAVE YOUR LOVING	
	Columbia DB 8327 ....**11**	9 wks
1 May 68	SLEEPY JOE Columbia DB 8404 ....**12**	10 wks
17 Jul 68	● SUNSHINE GIRL Columbia DB 8446 ....**8**	14 wks
18 Dec 68	● SOMETHING'S HAPPENING Columbia DB 8504.........**6**	15 wks
23 Apr 69	● MY SENTIMENTAL FRIEND Columbia DB 8563 ....**2**	12 wks
8 Nov 69	HERE COMES THE STAR Columbia DB 8626...........**33**	9 wks
7 Feb 70	● YEARS MAY COME, YEARS MAY GO	
	Columbia DB 8656 ....**7**	11 wks
2 May 70	YEARS MAY COME, YEARS MAY GO (re-entry)	
	Columbia DB 8656 ....**45**	1 wk
23 May 70	BET YER LIFE I DO RAK 102 ....**22**	10 wks
14 Nov 70	LADY BARBARA RAK 106 [1] **13**	12 wks

[1] Peter Noone and Herman's Hermits

See also Peter Noone.

HERNANDEZ UK, male vocalist — 3 wks

15 Apr 89	ALL MY LOVE Epic HER 1 ....**58**	3 wks

Patrick HERNANDEZ Guadeloupe, male vocalist — 14 wks

16 Jun 79	● BORN TO BE ALIVE Gem GEM 4 ....**10**	14 wks

HERREYS Sweden, male vocal group — 3 wks

26 May 84	DIGGI LOO-DIGGI LEY Panther PAN 5 ....**46**	3 wks

Kristin HERSH US, female vocalist — 3 wks

22 Jan 94	YOUR GHOST 4AD BAD 4001CD **45**	2 wks
16 Apr 94	STRINGS 4AD BAD 4006CD............................**60**	1 wk

Nick HEYWARD UK, male vocalist — 61 wks

19 Mar 83	WHISTLE DOWN THE WIND Arista HEY 1 ....**13**	8 wks
4 Jun 83	TAKE THAT SITUATION Arista HEY 2...............**11**	10 wks
24 Sep 83	BLUE HAT FOR A BLUE DAY Arista HEY 3 ....**14**	8 wks
3 Dec 83	ON A SUNDAY Arista HEY 4..........................**52**	5 wks
2 Jun 84	LOVE ALL DAY Arista HEY 5 ....**31**	6 wks
3 Nov 84	WARNING SIGN Arista HEY 6 ....**25**	8 wks
5 Jan 85	WARNING SIGN (re-entry) Arista HEY 6 ....**72**	1 wk
8 Jun 85	LAURA Arista HEY 8 ....**45**	4 wks
10 May 86	OVER THE WEEKEND Arista HEY 9 ....**43**	5 wks
10 Sep 88	YOU'RE MY WORLD Warner Bros. W 7758 ....**67**	2 wks
21 Aug 93	KITE Epic 6594882 ....**44**	2 wks
16 Oct 93	HE DOESN'T LOVE YOU LIKE I DO Epic 6597282 ....**58**	2 wks

HI-FIVE US, male vocal group — 8 wks

1 Jun 91	I LIKE THE WAY (THE KISSING GAME)	
	Jive JIVE 271 ....**43**	6 wks
24 Oct 92	SHE'S PLAYING HARD TO GET Jive JIVE 316 ....**55**	2 wks

HI GLOSS US, disco aggregation — 13 wks

8 Aug 81	YOU'LL NEVER KNOW Epic EPC A 1387 ....**12**	13 wks

HI POWER Germany, male rap group — 1 wk

1 Sep 90	CULT OF SNAP / SIMBA GROOVE	
	Rumour RUMAT 24.................................**73**	1 wk

HI TENSION UK, male vocal / instrumental group — 23 wks

6 May 78	HI TENSION Island WIP 6422 ....**13**	12 wks
12 Aug 78	● BRITISH HUSTLE / PEACE ON EARTH	
	Island WIP 6446 ....**8**	11 wks

Peace On Earth credited with British Hustle from 2 Sep 78 to end of record's chart run.

Al HIBBLER US, male vocalist — 17 wks

13 May 55	● UNCHAINED MELODY Brunswick 05420 ....**2**	17 wks

Bertie HIGGINS US, male vocalist — 4 wks

5 Jun 82	KEY LARGO Epic EPC A 2168 ....**60**	4 wks

HIGH UK, male vocal group — 10 wks

25 Aug 90	UP AND DOWN London LON 272 ....**53**	4 wks
27 Oct 90	TAKE YOUR TIME London LON 280 ....**56**	2 wks
12 Jan 91	BOX SET GO London LONG 286 ....**28**	3 wks
8 Apr 91	MORE... London LON 297 ....**67**	1 wk

HIGH NUMBERS UK, male vocal / instrumental group — 4 wks

5 Apr 80	I'M THE FACE Back Door DOOR 4 ....**49**	4 wks

The High Numbers were an early version of the Who. See also the Who.

HIGH SOCIETY UK, male vocal / instrumental group — 4 wks

15 Nov 80	I NEVER GO OUT IN THE RAIN Eagle ERS 002 ....**53**	4 wks

HIGHLY LIKELY UK, male vocal / instrumental group — 4 wks

21 Apr 73	WHATEVER HAPPENED TO YOU	
	('LIKELY LADS' THEME) BBC RESL 10 ....**35**	4 wks

HIGHWAYMEN US, male vocal group — 18 wks

7 Sep 61	★ MICHAEL HMV POP 910 ....**1**	14 wks
7 Dec 61	GYPSY ROVER HMV POP 948 ....**41**	3 wks
11 Jan 62	GYPSY ROVER (re-entry) HMV POP 948 ....**43**	1 wk

HIJACK UK, male producer — 3 wks

6 Jan 90	THE BADMAN IS ROBBIN'	
	Rhyme Syndicate 655517 7 ....**56**	3 wks

Benny HILL UK, male vocalist — 43 wks

16 Feb 61	GATHER IN THE MUSHROOMS Pye 7N 15327 ....**12**	8 wks
1 Jun 61	TRANSISTOR RADIO Pye 7N 15359 ....**24**	6 wks
16 May 63	HARVEST OF LOVE Pye 7N 15520 ....**20**	8 wks
13 Nov 71	★ ERNIE (THE FASTEST MILKMAN IN THE WEST)	
	Columbia DB 8833 ....**1**	17 wks
30 May 92	ERNIE (THE FASTEST MILKMAN IN THE WEST)	
	(re-issue) EMI ERN 1 ....**29**	4 wks

Chris HILL UK, male vocalist / producer — 14 wks

6 Dec 75	● RENTA SANTA Philips 6006 491 ....**10**	7 wks
4 Dec 76	● BIONIC SANTA Philips 6006 551 ....**10**	7 wks

Dan HILL Canada, male vocalist — 13 wks

18 Feb 78	SOMETIMES WHEN WE TOUCH	
	20th Century BTC 2355 ....**46**	1 wk
4 Mar 78	SOMETIMES WHEN WE TOUCH (re-entry)	
	20th Century BTC 2355 ....**13**	12 wks

Lonnie HILL — US, male vocalist — 4 wks

22 Mar 86	**GALVESTON BAY** *10 TEN 111*............**51**	4 wks

Roni HILL — US, female vocalist — 4 wks

7 May 77	**YOU KEEP ME HANGIN' ON - STOP IN THE NAME OF LOVE** (MEDLEY) *Creole CR 138* **36**	4 wks

Vince HILL — UK, male vocalist — 91 wks

7 Jun 62	**THE RIVER'S RUN DRY** *Piccadilly 7N 35043* **49**	1 wk
28 Jun 62	**THE RIVER'S RUN DRY (re-entry)** *Piccadilly 7N 35043* **41**	1 wk
6 Jan 66	**TAKE ME TO YOUR HEART AGAIN** *Columbia DB 7781* **13**	11 wks
17 Mar 66	**HEARTACHES** *Columbia DB 7852* **28**	5 wks
2 Jun 66	**MERCI CHERI** *Columbia DB 7924* **36**	6 wks
9 Feb 67	● **EDELWEISS** *Columbia DB 8127* **2**	17 wks
11 May 67	**ROSES OF PICARDY** *Columbia DB 8185* **13**	11 wks
27 Sep 67	**LOVE LETTERS IN THE SAND** *Columbia DB 8268* ...**23**	9 wks
26 Jun 68	**IMPORTANCE OF YOUR LOVE** *Columbia DB 8414*....**32**	12 wks
12 Feb 69	**DOESN'T ANYBODY KNOW MY NAME?** *Columbia DB 8515* **50**	1 wk
25 Oct 69	**LITTLE BLUE BIRD** *Columbia DB 8616* **42**	1 wk
25 Sep 71	**LOOK AROUND** *Columbia DB 8804* **12**	16 wks

HILLTOPPERS — US, male vocal group — 30 wks

27 Jan 56	● **ONLY YOU** *London HLD 8221* **3**	22 wks
10 Aug 56	**ONLY YOU (re-entry)** *London HLD 8221* **24**	1 wk
14 Sep 56	**TRYIN'** *London HLD 8298* **30**	1 wk
5 Apr 57	**MARIANNE** *London HLD 8381* **20**	2 wks
26 Apr 57	**MARIANNE (re-entry)** *London HLD 8381* **23**	4 wks

Ronnie HILTON — UK, male vocalist — 128 wks

26 Nov 54	● **I STILL BELIEVE** *HMV B 10785* **3**	14 wks
10 Dec 54	**VENI VIDI VICI** *HMV B 10785* **12**	8 wks
11 Mar 55	● **A BLOSSOM FELL** *HMV B 10808* **10**	5 wks
26 Aug 55	**STARS SHINE IN YOUR EYES** *HMV B 10901*...........**13**	7 wks
11 Nov 55	**YELLOW ROSE OF TEXAS** *HMV B 10924* **15**	2 wks
10 Feb 56	**YOUNG AND FOOLISH** *HMV POP 154*...........**17**	1 wk
24 Feb 56	**YOUNG AND FOOLISH (re-entry)** *HMV POP 154* **20**	1 wk
9 Mar 56	**YOUNG AND FOOLISH (2nd re-entry)** *HMV POP 154* **19**	1 wk
20 Apr 56	★ **NO OTHER LOVE** *HMV POP 198* **1**	14 wks
29 Jun 56	● **WHO ARE WE** *HMV POP 221* **6**	12 wks
21 Sep 56	**WOMAN IN LOVE** *HMV POP 248* **30**	1 wk
9 Nov 56	**TWO DIFFERENT WORLDS** *HMV POP 274* **13**	13 wks
24 May 57	● **AROUND THE WORLD** *HMV POP 338* **4**	18 wks
2 Aug 57	**WONDERFUL WONDERFUL** *HMV POP 364*...........**27**	2 wks
21 Feb 58	**MAGIC MOMENTS** *HMV POP 446*...........**22**	2 wks
18 Apr 58	**I MAY NEVER PASS THIS WAY AGAIN** *HMV POP 468* [1] **30**	1 wk
2 May 58	**I MAY NEVER PASS THIS WAY AGAIN (re-entry)** *HMV POP 468* [1] **30**	1 wk
6 Jun 58	**I MAY NEVER PASS THIS WAY AGAIN (2nd re-entry)** *HMV POP 468* [1] **27**	1 wk
9 Jan 59	**THE WORLD OUTSIDE** *HMV POP 559* [1] **18**	6 wks
21 Aug 59	**THE WONDER OF YOU** *HMV POP 638*...........**22**	3 wks
21 May 64	**DON'T LET THE RAIN COME DOWN** *HMV POP 1291* **21**	10 wks
11 Feb 65	**A WINDMILL IN OLD AMSTERDAM** *HMV POP 1378* **23**	13 wks

[1] Ronnie Hilton with the Michael Sammes Singers

HINDSIGHT — UK, male vocal / instrumental group — 3 wks

5 Sep 87	**LOWDOWN** *Circa YR 5* **62**	3 wks

Gregory HINES - *See Luther VANDROSS*

HIPSWAY — UK, male vocal / instrumental group — 21 wks

13 Jul 85	**THE BROKEN YEARS** *Mercury MER 193* **72**	3 wks
14 Sep 85	**ASK THE LORD** *Mercury MER 195* **72**	1 wk
22 Feb 86	**THE HONEYTHIEF** *Mercury MER 212* **17**	9 wks
10 May 86	**ASK THE LORD** *Mercury LORD 1* **50**	5 wks
20 Sep 86	**LONG WHITE CAR** *Mercury MER 230* **55**	2 wks
1 Apr 89	**YOUR LOVE** *Mercury MER 279* **66**	1 wk

LORD 1 was a re-recording of MER 195.

HISTORY featuring Q-TEE — US, male / female rap group — 5 wks

21 Apr 90	**AFRIKA** *SBK SBK 7008* **42**	5 wks

Carol HITCHCOCK — Australia, female vocalist — 5 wks

30 May 87	**GET READY** *A & M AM 391* **56**	5 wks

HI-TEK 3 featuring YA KID K — Belgium, male / female vocal / instrumental group — 10 wks

3 Feb 90	**SPIN THAT WHEEL** *Brothers Organisation BORG 1* ..**69**	3 wks
29 Sep 90	**SPIN THAT WHEEL (TURTLES GET REAL) (re-issue)** *Brothers Organisation BORG 16* **15**	7 wks

See also Technotronic.

HITHOUSE — Holland, male producer - Peter Slaghuis — 13 wks

5 Nov 88	**JACK TO THE SOUND OF THE UNDERGROUND** *Supreme SUPE 137* **14**	12 wks
19 Aug 89	**MOVE YOUR FEET TO THE RHYTHM OF THE BEAT** *Supreme SUPE 149* **69**	1 wk

HITMAN HOWIE TEE - *See REAL ROXANNE*

Edmund HOCKRIDGE — Canada, male vocalist — 18 wks

17 Feb 56	● **YOUNG AND FOOLISH** *Nixa N 15039* **10**	7 wks
13 Apr 56	**YOUNG AND FOOLISH (re-entry)** *Nixa N 15039*......**28**	1 wk
4 May 56	**YOUNG AND FOOLISH (2nd re-entry)** *Nixa N 15039* **26**	1 wk
11 May 56	**NO OTHER LOVE** *Nixa N 15048* **24**	2 wks
1 Jun 56	**NO OTHER LOVE (re-entry)** *Nixa N 15048* **29**	1 wk
15 Jun 56	**NO OTHER LOVE (2nd re-entry)** *Nixa N 15048* **30**	1 wk
31 Aug 56	**BY THE FOUNTAINS OF ROME** *Pye Nixa N 15063* **17**	5 wks

Eddie HODGES — US, male vocalist — 10 wks

28 Sep 61	**I'M GONNA KNOCK ON YOUR DOOR** *London HLA 9369*...........**37**	6 wks
9 Aug 62	**MADE TO LOVE (GIRLS GIRLS GIRLS)** *London HLA 9576*...........**37**	4 wks

Roger HODGSON - *See SUPERTRAMP*

Susanna HOFFS — US, female vocalist — 6 wks

2 Mar 91	**MY SIDE OF THE BED** *Columbia 6565547*...........**44**	4 wks
11 May 91	**UNCONDITIONAL LOVE** *Columbia 6567827*...........**65**	2 wks

Hulk HOGAN - *See GREEN JELLY*

HOLE — US, female / male vocal / instrumental group — 2 wks

17 Apr 93	**BEAUTIFUL SON** *City Slang EFA 0491603* **54**	1 wk
9 Apr 94	**MS. WORLD** *City Slang EFA 049362* **64**	1 wk

The **HOLLIES** are pictured in April 1968, eight months before Graham Nash (back right) left to join David Crosby and Stephen Stills. (LFI)

David Ball (seated) was in Soft Cell before going on to find 1990s success with the **GRID**. (Dave Hogan/REX)

RICHARD HARRIS (right) talks to songwriter Jim Webb in 1968, the year of their international success with 'MacArthur Park'.

HOLLAND-DOZIER featuring Lamont DOZIER
US, male vocal duo **5 wks**

28 Oct 72	**WHY CAN'T WE BE LOVERS** *Invictus INV 525*	..........**29**	5 wks

Jennifer HOLLIDAY *US, female vocalist* **6 wks**

4 Sep 82	**AND I'M TELLING YOU I'M NOT GOING** *Geffen GEF A 2644*	..........**32**	6 wks

Michael HOLLIDAY *UK, male vocalist* **63 wks**

30 Mar 56	**NOTHIN' TO DO** *Columbia DB 3746*	..........**20**	1 wk
27 Apr 56	**NOTHIN' TO DO (re-entry)** *Columbia DB 3746*	..........**23**	2 wks
15 Jun 56	**GAL WITH THE YALLER SHOES** *Columbia DB 3783*	..........**13**	3 wks
22 Jun 56	**HOT DIGGITY** *Columbia DB 3783*	..........**14**	5 wks
3 Aug 56	**HOT DIGGITY / GAL WITH THE YALLER SHOES (re-entry)** *Columbia DB 3783*	..........**17**	3 wks
5 Oct 56	**TEN THOUSAND MILES** *Columbia DB 3813*	..........**24**	3 wks
17 Jan 58	★ **THE STORY OF MY LIFE** *Columbia DB 4058*	..........**1**	15 wks
14 Mar 58	**IN LOVE** *Columbia DB 4087*	..........**26**	3 wks
16 May 58	● **STAIRWAY OF LOVE** *Columbia DB 4121*	..........**3**	13 wks
11 Jul 58	**I'LL ALWAYS BE IN LOVE WITH YOU** *Columbia DB 4155*	..........**27**	1 wk
1 Jan 60	★ **STARRY EYED** *Columbia DB 4378*	..........**1**	12 wks
14 Apr 60	**SKYLARK** *Columbia DB 4437*	..........**39**	3 wks
1 Sep 60	**LITTLE BOY LOST** *Columbia DB 4475*	..........**50**	1 wk

When Hot Diggity / Gal With The Yaller Shoes *re-entered the chart on 3 Aug 56* Hot Diggity *was listed by itself on 3 Aug and 10 Aug. Both sides were listed on 17 Aug,* Gal With The Yaller Shoes *peaking at position 25.*

HOLLIES *UK, male vocal / instrumental group* **318 wks**

30 May 63	**JUST LIKE ME** *Parlophone R 5030*	..........**25**	10 wks
29 Aug 63	**SEARCHIN'** *Parlophone R 5052*	..........**12**	14 wks
21 Nov 63	● **STAY** *Parlophone R 5077*	..........**8**	16 wks
27 Feb 64	● **JUST ONE LOOK** *Parlophone R 5104*	..........**2**	13 wks
21 May 64	● **HERE I GO AGAIN** *Parlophone R 5137*	..........**4**	12 wks
17 Sep 64	● **WE'RE THROUGH** *Parlophone R 5178*	..........**7**	11 wks
28 Jan 65	● **YES I WILL** *Parlophone R 5232*	..........**9**	13 wks
27 May 65	★ **I'M ALIVE** *Parlophone R 5287*	..........**1**	14 wks
2 Sep 65	● **LOOK THROUGH ANY WINDOW** *Parlophone R 5322*	..........**4**	11 wks
9 Dec 65	**IF I NEEDED SOMEONE** *Parlophone R 5392*	..........**20**	9 wks
24 Feb 66	● **I CAN'T LET GO** *Parlophone R 5409*	..........**2**	10 wks
23 Jun 66	● **BUS STOP** *Parlophone R 5469*	..........**5**	9 wks
13 Oct 66	● **STOP STOP STOP** *Parlophone R 5508*	..........**2**	12 wks
16 Feb 67	● **ON A CAROUSEL** *Parlophone R 5562*	..........**4**	11 wks
1 Jun 67	● **CARRIE-ANNE** *Parlophone R 5602*	..........**3**	11 wks
27 Sep 67	**KING MIDAS IN REVERSE** *Parlophone R 5637*	..........**18**	8 wks
27 Mar 68	● **JENNIFER ECCLES** *Parlophone R 5680*	..........**7**	11 wks
2 Oct 68	**LISTEN TO ME** *Parlophone R 5733*	..........**11**	11 wks
5 Mar 69	● **SORRY SUZANNE** *Parlophone R 5765*	..........**3**	12 wks
4 Oct 69	● **HE AIN'T HEAVY, HE'S MY BROTHER** *Parlophone R 5806*	..........**3**	15 wks
18 Apr 70	● **I CAN'T TELL THE BOTTOM FROM THE TOP** *Parlophone R 5837*	..........**7**	10 wks
3 Oct 70	**GASOLINE ALLEY BRED** *Parlophone R 5862*	..........**14**	7 wks
22 May 71	**HEY WILLY** *Parlophone R 5905*	..........**22**	7 wks
26 Feb 72	**THE BABY** *Polydor 2058 199*	..........**26**	6 wks
2 Sep 72	**LONG COOL WOMAN IN A BLACK DRESS** *Parlophone R 5939*	..........**32**	8 wks
13 Oct 73	**THE DAY THAT CURLY BILLY SHOT DOWN CRAZY SAM MCGHEE** *Polydor 2058 403*	..........**24**	6 wks
9 Feb 74	● **THE AIR THAT I BREATHE** *Polydor 2058 435*	..........**2**	13 wks
14 Jun 80	**SOLDIER'S SONG** *Polydor 2059 246*	..........**58**	3 wks
29 Aug 81	**HOLLIEDAZE (MEDLEY)** *EMI 5229*	..........**28**	7 wks
3 Sep 88	★ **HE AIN'T HEAVY, HE'S MY BROTHER (re-issue)** *EMI EM 74*	..........**1**	11 wks
3 Dec 88	**THE AIR THAT I BREATHE (re-issue)** *EMI EM 80*	..........**60**	5 wks
20 Mar 93	**THE WOMAN I LOVE** *EMI CDEM 264*	..........**42**	2 wks

Loleatta HOLLOWAY *US, female vocalist* **13 wks**

31 Aug 91	**GOOD VIBRATIONS** *Interscope A 8764* [1]	..........**14**	7 wks
18 Jan 92	**TAKE ME AWAY** *PWL Continental PWL 210* [2]	..........**25**	5 wks
26 Mar 94	**STAND UP** *Six6 SIXCD 111*	..........**68**	1 wk

[1] Marky Mark and the Funky Bunch featuring Loleatta Holloway [2] Cappella featuring Loleatta Holloway

Buddy HOLLY *US, male vocalist* **190 wks**

6 Dec 57	● **PEGGY SUE** *Coral Q 72293*	..........**6**	17 wks
14 Mar 58	**LISTEN TO ME** *Coral Q 72288*	..........**16**	2 wks
20 Jun 58	● **RAVE ON** *Coral Q 72325*	..........**5**	14 wks
29 Aug 58	**EARLY IN THE MORNING** *Coral Q 72333*	..........**17**	4 wks
16 Jan 59	**HEARTBEAT** *Coral Q 72346*	..........**30**	1 wk
27 Feb 59	★ **IT DOESN'T MATTER ANYMORE** *Coral Q 72360*	..........**1**	21 wks
31 Jul 59	**MIDNIGHT SHIFT** *Brunswick 05800*	..........**26**	3 wks
11 Sep 59	**PEGGY SUE GOT MARRIED** *Coral Q 72376*	..........**13**	10 wks
28 Apr 60	**HEARTBEAT (re-issue)** *Coral Q 72392*	..........**30**	3 wks
26 May 60	**TRUE LOVE WAYS** *Coral Q 72397*	..........**25**	7 wks
20 Oct 60	**LEARNIN' THE GAME** *Coral Q 72411*	..........**36**	3 wks
26 Jan 61	**WHAT TO DO** *Coral Q 72419*	..........**34**	6 wks
6 Jul 61	**BABY I DON'T CARE / VALLEY OF TEARS** *Coral Q 72432*	..........**12**	14 wks
15 Mar 62	**LISTEN TO ME (re-issue)** *Coral Q 72449*	..........**48**	1 wk
13 Sep 62	**REMINISCING** *Coral Q 72455*	..........**17**	11 wks
14 Mar 63	● **BROWN-EYED HANDSOME MAN** *Coral Q 72459*	..........**3**	17 wks
6 Jun 63	● **BO DIDDLEY** *Coral Q 72463*	..........**4**	12 wks
5 Sep 63	● **WISHING** *Coral Q 72466*	..........**10**	11 wks
19 Dec 63	**WHAT TO DO** *Coral Q 72469*	..........**27**	8 wks
14 May 64	**YOU'VE GOT LOVE** *Coral Q 72472* [1]	..........**40**	6 wks
10 Sep 64	**LOVE'S MADE A FOOL OF YOU** *Coral Q 72475*	..........**39**	6 wks
3 Apr 68	**PEGGY SUE / RAVE ON (re-issue)** *MCA MU 1012*	..........**32**	9 wks
10 Dec 88	**TRUE LOVE WAYS (re-issue)** *MCA MCA 1302*	..........**65**	4 wks

[1] Buddy Holly and the Crickets

Buddy Holly's version of Love's Made A Fool Of You *is not the same version as the Crickets' hit of 1959, on which Holly did not appear.* Valley Of Tears *was not listed together with* Baby I Don't Care *until 13 Jul 61.* What To Do *on Q 72469 was a re-recording.*

HOLLY and the IVYS
UK, male / female vocal / instrumental group **4 wks**

19 Dec 81	**CHRISTMAS ON 45** *Decca SANTA 1*	..........**40**	4 wks

HOLLYWOOD ARGYLES *US, male vocal group* **10 wks**

21 Jul 60	**ALLEY OOP** *London HLU 9146*	..........**24**	10 wks

HOLLYWOOD BEYOND *UK, male vocalist* **14 wks**

12 Jul 86	● **WHAT'S THE COLOUR OF MONEY?** *WEA YZ 76*	..........**7**	10 wks
20 Sep 86	**NO MORE TEARS** *WEA YZ 81*	..........**47**	4 wks

Eddie HOLMAN *US, male vocalist* **13 wks**

19 Oct 74	● **(HEY THERE) LONELY GIRL** *ABC 4012*	..........**4**	13 wks

Rupert HOLMES *US, male vocalist* **14 wks**

12 Jan 80	**ESCAPE (THE PINA COLADA SONG)** *Infinity INF 120*	..........**23**	7 wks
22 Mar 80	**HIM** *MCA 565*	..........**31**	7 wks

John HOLT *Jamaica, male vocalist* **14 wks**

14 Dec 74	● **HELP ME MAKE IT THROUGH THE NIGHT** *Trojan TR 7909*	..........**6**	14 wks

A HOMEBOY, A HIPPIE and A FUNKI DREDD
UK, male vocal / instrumental group **9 wks**

13 Oct 90	**TOTAL CONFUSION** *Tam Tam 7TTT 031*	..........**56**	3 wks

| 29 Dec 90 | FREEDOM *Tam Tam 7TTT 039*........................**68** | 4 wks |
| 8 Jan 94 | HERE WE GO AGAIN *Polydor PZCD 302* ....**57** | 2 wks |

HONEYBUS *UK, male vocal / instrumental group*   **12 wks**

| 20 Mar 68 | ● I CAN'T LET MAGGIE GO *Deram DM 182*..................**8** | 12 wks |

HONEYCOMBS
UK, male / female vocal / instrumental group   **39 wks**

23 Jul 64	★ HAVE I THE RIGHT *Pye 7N 15664* **1**	15 wks
22 Oct 64	IS IT BECAUSE *Pye 7N 15705* **38**	6 wks
29 Apr 65	SOMETHING BETTER BEGINNING *Pye 7N 15827*...**39**	4 wks
5 Aug 65	THAT'S THE WAY *Pye 7N 15890* **12**	14 wks

HONEYDRIPPERS
UK / US, male vocal / instrumental group   **3 wks**

| 2 Feb 85 | SEA OF LOVE *Es Paranza YZ 33* ....**56** | 3 wks |

HONKY *UK, male vocal / instrumental group*   **5 wks**

| 28 May 77 | JOIN THE PARTY *Creole CR 137* ....**28** | 5 wks |

HONKY *UK, male vocal / instrumental group*   **3 wks**

| 30 Oct 93 | THE HONKY DOODLE DAY (EP) *ZTT ZANG 45CD* ....**61** | 1 wk |
| 19 Feb 94 | THE WHISTLER *ZTT ZANG 48CD* ....**41** | 2 wks |

Tracks on The Honky Doodle Day (EP): KKK (Boom Boom Tra La La La) / Honky Doodle Day / Chains.

Frank HOOKER and POSITIVE PEOPLE
US, male vocal / instrumental group   **4 wks**

| 5 Jul 80 | THIS FEELIN' *DJM DJS 10947* ....**48** | 4 wks |

John Lee HOOKER *US, male vocalist*   **20 wks**

11 Jun 64	DIMPLES *Stateside SS 297*........................**23**	10 wks
24 Oct 92	BOOM BOOM *Pointblank POB 3* **16**	5 wks
16 Jan 93	BOOGIE AT RUSSIAN HILL *Pointblank POBDX 4* **53**	2 wks
15 May 93	GLORIA *Exile VANCD 11* ☐1 ....**31**	3 wks

☐1 Van Morrison and John Lee Hooker

HOOTERS *US, male vocal / instrumental group*   **9 wks**

| 21 Nov 87 | SATELLITE *CBS 651168 7* ....**22** | 9 wks |

HOPE A.D. *UK, male producer - David Hope*   **1 wk**

| 4 Jun 94 | TREE FROG *Sun-Up SUN 003CD* ....**73** | 1 wk |

See also Mind Of Kane.

Mary HOPKIN *UK, female vocalist*   **74 wks**

4 Sep 68	★ THOSE WERE THE DAYS *Apple 2* **1**	21 wks
2 Apr 69	● GOODBYE *Apple 10* **2**	14 wks
31 Jan 70	● TEMMA HARBOUR *Apple 22* **6**	11 wks
28 Mar 70	● KNOCK KNOCK WHO'S THERE *Apple 26* **2**	14 wks
31 Oct 70	THINK ABOUT YOUR CHILDREN *Apple 30*...**19**	7 wks
2 Jan 71	THINK ABOUT YOUR CHILDREN (re-entry) *Apple 30* **46**	2 wks
31 Jul 71	LET MY NAME BE SORROW *Apple 34* **46**	1 wk
20 Mar 76	IF YOU LOVE ME *Good Earth GD 2* **32**	4 wks

See also Various Artists (EPs & LPs) - The Apple EP.

Anthony HOPKINS *UK, male vocalist*   **1 wk**

| 27 Dec 86 | DISTANT STAR *Juice AA 5* ....**75** | 1 wk |

Bruce HORNSBY and the RANGE
US, male vocal / instrumental group   **15 wks**

2 Aug 86	THE WAY IT IS *RCA PB 49805* **15**	10 wks
25 Apr 87	MANDOLIN RAIN *RCA PB 49769* **70**	1 wk
28 May 88	THE VALLEY ROAD *RCA PB 49561* **44**	4 wks

HORSE *UK, female / male vocal / instrumental group*   **8 wks**

24 Nov 90	CAREFUL *Capitol CL 587* **52**	3 wks
21 Aug 93	SHAKE THIS MOUNTAIN *Oxygen GASPD 7* **52**	2 wks
23 Oct 93	GOD'S HOME MOVIE *Oxygen GASXD 10* **56**	1 wk
15 Jan 94	CELEBRATE *Oxygen GASPD 11* **49**	2 wks

Johnny HORTON *US, male vocalist*   **15 wks**

| 26 Jun 59 | BATTLE OF NEW ORLEANS *Philips PB 932* ....**16** | 4 wks |
| 19 Jan 61 | NORTH TO ALASKA *Philips PB 1062* ....**23** | 11 wks |

HOT BLOOD *France, male instrumental group*   **5 wks**

| 9 Oct 76 | SOUL DRACULA *Creole CR 132* ....**32** | 5 wks |

HOT BUTTER *US, male instrumental group*   **19 wks**

| 22 Jul 72 | ● POPCORN *Pye International 7N 25583*.........................**5** | 16 wks |
| 23 Dec 72 | POPCORN (re-entry) *Pye International 7N 25583* ....**50** | 3 wks |

HOT CHOCOLATE
UK, male vocal / instrumental group   **272 wks**

15 Aug 70	● LOVE IS LIFE *RAK 103* **6**	12 wks
6 Mar 71	YOU COULD HAVE BEEN A LADY *RAK 110*...**22**	9 wks
28 Aug 71	● I BELIEVE (IN LOVE) *RAK 118* **8**	11 wks
28 Oct 72	YOU'LL ALWAYS BE A FRIEND *RAK 139* **23**	8 wks
14 Apr 73	● BROTHER LOUIE *RAK 149* **7**	10 wks
18 Aug 73	RUMOURS *RAK 157* **44**	3 wks
16 Mar 74	● EMMA *RAK 168* **3**	10 wks
30 Nov 74	CHERI BABE *RAK 188* **31**	9 wks
24 May 75	DISCO QUEEN *RAK 202* **11**	9 wks
9 Aug 75	● A CHILD'S PRAYER *RAK 212* **7**	10 wks
8 Nov 75	● YOU SEXY THING *RAK 221* **2**	12 wks
20 Mar 76	DON'T STOP IT NOW *RAK 230*.........................**11**	8 wks
26 Jun 76	MAN TO MAN *RAK 238* **14**	8 wks
21 Aug 76	HEAVEN IS IN THE BACK SEAT OF MY CADILLAC *RAK 240* **25**	8 wks
18 Jun 77	★ SO YOU WIN AGAIN *RAK 259* **1**	11 wks
26 Nov 77	● PUT YOUR LOVE IN ME *RAK 266* **10**	9 wks
4 Mar 78	EVERY 1'S A WINNER *RAK 270* **12**	11 wks
2 Dec 78	I'LL PUT YOU TOGETHER AGAIN *RAK 286* **13**	11 wks
19 May 79	MINDLESS BOOGIE *RAK 292* **46**	5 wks
28 Jul 79	GOING THROUGH THE MOTIONS *RAK 296* **53**	4 wks
3 May 80	● NO DOUBT ABOUT IT *RAK 310* **2**	11 wks
19 Jul 80	ARE YOU GETTING ENOUGH OF WHAT MAKES YOU HAPPY *RAK 318* **17**	7 wks
13 Dec 80	LOVE ME TO SLEEP *RAK 324* **50**	5 wks
30 May 81	YOU'LL NEVER BE SO WRONG *RAK 331* **52**	4 wks
17 Apr 82	● GIRL CRAZY *RAK 341* **7**	11 wks
10 Jul 82	● IT STARTED WITH A KISS *RAK 344* **5**	12 wks
25 Sep 82	CHANCES *RAK 350* **32**	5 wks
7 May 83	● WHAT KINDA BOY YOU LOOKING FOR (GIRL) *RAK 357* **10**	9 wks
17 Sep 83	TEARS ON THE TELEPHONE *RAK 363* **37**	5 wks
4 Feb 84	I GAVE YOU MY HEART (DIDN'T I) *RAK 369* **13**	10 wks
17 Jan 87	● YOU SEXY THING (re-mix) *EMI 5592* **10**	10 wks
4 Apr 87	EVERY 1'S A WINNER (re-mix) *EMI 5607* **69**	2 wks
6 Mar 93	IT STARTED WITH A KISS (re-issue) *EMI CDEMCTS 7* **31**	5 wks

HOT GOSSIP - *See Sarah BRIGHTMAN*

HOT HOUSE UK, male/female vocal/instrumental group — 3 wks

| 14 Feb 87 | DON'T COME TO STAY Deconstruction CHEZ 1 | 74 | 1 wk |
| 24 Sep 88 | DON'T COME TO STAY (re-issue) Deconstruction PB 42233 | 70 | 2 wks |

HOT STREAK US, male vocal/instrumental group — 8 wks

| 10 Sep 83 | BODY WORK Polydor POSP 642 | 19 | 8 wks |

HOTHOUSE FLOWERS
Ireland, male vocal/instrumental group — 35 wks

14 May 88	DON'T GO London LON 174	11	8 wks
23 Jul 88	I'M SORRY London LON 187	53	3 wks
12 May 90	GIVE IT UP London LON 258	30	5 wks
28 Jul 90	I CAN SEE CLEARLY NOW London LON 269	23	7 wks
20 Oct 90	MOVIES London LON 276	68	2 wks
13 Feb 93	EMOTIONAL TIME London LONCD 335	38	4 wks
8 May 93	ONE TONGUE London LOCDP 340	45	3 wks
19 Jun 93	ISN'T IT AMAZING London LOCDP 343	46	2 wks
27 Nov 93	THIS IS IT (YOUR SOUL) London LONCD 346	67	1 wk

HOTLEGS UK, male vocal/instrumental group — 14 wks

| 4 Jul 70 | ● NEANDERTHAL MAN Fontana 6007 019 | 2 | 14 wks |

HOTRODS - See EDDIE and the HOTRODS

HOTSHOTS UK, male vocal group — 15 wks

| 2 Jun 73 | ● SNOOPY VS. THE RED BARON Mooncrest MOON 5 | 4 | 15 wks |

A HOUSE Ireland, male vocal/instrumental group — 8 wks

13 Jun 92	ENDLESS ART Setanta AHOU 1	46	3 wks
8 Aug 92	TAKE IT EASY ON ME Setanta AHOU 2	55	2 wks
25 Jun 94	WHY ME Setanta CDAHOU 4	52	1 wk
1 Oct 94	HERE COME THE GOOD TIMES Setanta CDAHOUS 5	37	2 wks

HOUSE ENGINEERS UK, male vocal/instrumental duo — 2 wks

| 5 Dec 87 | GHOST HOUSE Syncopate SY 8 | 69 | 2 wks |

HOUSE OF LOVE UK, male vocal/instrumental group — 21 wks

22 Apr 89	NEVER Fontana HOL 1	41	2 wks
18 Nov 89	I DON'T KNOW WHY I LOVE YOU Fontana HOL 2	41	3 wks
3 Feb 90	SHINE ON Fontana HOL 3	20	4 wks
7 Apr 90	BEATLES AND THE STONES Fontana HOL 4	36	4 wks
26 Oct 91	THE GIRL WITH THE LONELIEST EYES Fontana HOL 5	58	1 wk
2 May 92	FEEL Fontana HOL 6	45	3 wks
27 Jun 92	YOU DON'T UNDERSTAND Fontana HOL 7	46	3 wks
5 Dec 92	CRUSH ME Fontana HOL 810	67	1 wk

HOUSE OF PAIN US, male rap group — 20 wks

10 Oct 92	JUMP AROUND Ruffness XLS 32	32	4 wks
22 May 93	● JUMP AROUND (re-issue)/TOP O' THE MORNING TO YA Ruffness XLS 43CD	8	7 wks
23 Oct 93	SHAMROCKS AND SHENANIGANS/ WHO'S THE MAN Ruffness XLS 46CD	23	4 wks
16 Jul 94	ON POINT Ruffness XLS 52CD	19	3 wks
12 Nov 94	IT AIN'T A CRIME Ruffness XLS 55CD1	37	2 wks

HOUSE OF VIRGINISM
Sweden, male vocal/instrumental group — 5 wks

| 20 Nov 93 | I'LL BE THERE FOR YOU (DOYA DODODO DOYA) ffrr FCD 221 | 29 | 3 wks |
| 30 Jul 94 | REACHIN ffrr FCD 238 | 35 | 2 wks |

HOUSE OF ZEKKARIYAS - See WOMACK and WOMACK

HOUSEMARTINS UK, male vocal/instrumental group — 59 wks

8 Mar 86	SHEEP Go! Discs GOD 9	54	3 wks
5 Apr 86	SHEEP (re-entry) Go! Discs GOD 9	71	1 wk
7 Jun 86	● HAPPY HOUR Go! Discs GOD 11	3	13 wks
4 Oct 86	THINK FOR A MINUTE Go! Discs GOD 13	18	8 wks
6 Dec 86	★ CARAVAN OF LOVE Go! Discs GOD 16	1	11 wks
23 May 87	FIVE GET OVER EXCITED Go! Discs GOD 18	11	6 wks
5 Sep 87	ME AND THE FARMER Go! Discs GOD 19	15	5 wks
21 Nov 87	BUILD Go! Discs GOD 21	15	8 wks
23 Apr 88	THERE IS ALWAYS SOMETHING THERE TO REMIND ME Go! Discs GOD 22	35	4 wks

HOUSEMASTER BOYZ and the RUDE BOY OF HOUSE
US, male vocal/instrumental group — 14 wks

| 9 May 87 | HOUSE NATION Magnetic Dance MAGD 1 | 48 | 6 wks |
| 12 Sep 87 | ● HOUSE NATION (re-entry) Magnetic Dance MAGD 1 | 8 | 8 wks |

Thelma HOUSTON US, female vocalist — 20 wks

5 Feb 77	DON'T LEAVE ME THIS WAY Motown TMG 1060	13	8 wks
27 Jun 81	IF YOU FEEL IT RCA 77	48	4 wks
1 Dec 84	YOU USED TO HOLD ME SO TIGHT MCA MCA 932	49	8 wks

Whitney HOUSTON US, female vocalist — 204 wks

16 Nov 85	★ SAVING ALL MY LOVE FOR YOU Arista ARIST 640	1	16 wks
25 Jan 86	● HOW WILL I KNOW Arista ARIST 656	5	12 wks
25 Jan 86	HOLD ME Asylum EKR 32 [1]	44	5 wks
12 Apr 86	● GREATEST LOVE OF ALL Arista ARIST 658	8	11 wks
23 May 87	★ I WANNA DANCE WITH SOMEBODY (WHO LOVES ME) Arista RIS 1	1	16 wks
22 Aug 87	DIDN'T WE ALMOST HAVE IT ALL Arista RIS 31	14	8 wks
14 Nov 87	● SO EMOTIONAL Arista RIS 43	5	11 wks
12 Mar 88	WHERE DO BROKEN HEARTS GO Arista 109793	14	8 wks
28 May 88	● LOVE WILL SAVE THE DAY Arista 111516	10	7 wks
24 Sep 88	★ ONE MOMENT IN TIME Arista 111613	1	12 wks
9 Sep 89	IT ISN'T, IT WASN'T, IT AIN'T NEVER GONNA BE Arista 112545 [2]	29	5 wks
20 Oct 90	● I'M YOUR BABY TONIGHT Arista 113594	5	9 wks
22 Dec 90	ALL THE MAN THAT I NEED Arista 114000	13	10 wks
29 Dec 90	I'M YOUR BABY TONIGHT (re-entry) Arista 113594	69	1 wk
6 Jul 91	MY NAME IS NOT SUSAN Arista 114510	29	5 wks
28 Sep 91	I BELONG TO YOU Arista 114727	54	2 wks
14 Nov 92	★ I WILL ALWAYS LOVE YOU Arista 74321120657	1	23 wks
20 Feb 93	● I'M EVERY WOMAN Arista 74321131502	4	11 wks
24 Apr 93	● I HAVE NOTHING Arista 74321146142	3	10 wks
31 Jul 93	RUN TO YOU Arista 74321153332	15	6 wks
6 Nov 93	QUEEN OF THE NIGHT Arista 74321169302	14	5 wks
18 Dec 93	I WILL ALWAYS LOVE YOU (re-entry) Arista 74321120652	25	6 wks
22 Jan 94	SOMETHING IN COMMON MCA MCSTD 1957 [3]	16	5 wks

[1] Teddy Pendergrass with Whitney Houston [2] Aretha Franklin and Whitney Houston [3] Bobby Brown and Whitney Houston

Billy HOWARD *UK, male vocalist* — **12 wks**

13 Dec 75	● KING OF THE COPS *Penny Farthing PEN 892*	6	12 wks

Miki HOWARD *US, female vocalist* — **2 wks**

26 May 90	UNTIL YOU COME BACK (THAT'S WHAT I'M GONNA DO) *East West 7935*	67	2 wks

Robert HOWARD - *See Kym MAZELLE*

HOWLIN' WOLF *US, male vocalist* — **5 wks**

4 Jun 64	SMOKESTACK LIGHTNIN' *Pye International 7N 25244*	42	5 wks

H₂O *UK, male vocal / instrumental group* — **16 wks**

H$_2$O

21 May 83	DREAM TO SLEEP *RCA 330*	17	10 wks
13 Aug 83	JUST OUTSIDE OF HEAVEN *RCA 349*	38	6 wks

Al HUDSON *US, male vocalist* — **22 wks**

9 Sep 78	DANCE, GET DOWN / HOW DO YOU DO *ABC 4229*	57	4 wks
15 Sep 79	YOU CAN DO IT *MCA 511* [1]	15	10 wks
8 Dec 79	MUSIC *MCA 542* [2]	56	6 wks
29 Jun 85	LET'S TALK *MCA 972* [2]	64	2 wks

[1] Al Hudson and the Partners [2] One Way featuring Al Hudson

Lavine HUDSON *UK, female vocalist* — **3 wks**

21 May 88	INTERVENTION *Virgin VS 1067*	57	3 wks

HUDSON-FORD *UK, male vocal / instrumental duo* — **20 wks**

18 Aug 73	● PICK UP THE PIECES *A & M AMS 7078*	8	9 wks
16 Feb 74	BURN BABY BURN *A & M AMS 7096*	15	9 wks
29 Jun 74	FLOATING IN THE WIND *A & M AMS 7116*	35	2 wks

See also Monks.

HUE AND CRY *UK, male vocal / instrumental duo* — **59 wks**

13 Jun 87	● LABOUR OF LOVE *Circa YR 4*	6	16 wks
19 Sep 87	STRENGTH TO STRENGTH *Circa YR 6*	46	5 wks
30 Jan 88	I REFUSE *Circa YR 8*	47	3 wks
22 Oct 88	ORDINARY ANGEL *Circa YR 18*	42	6 wks
28 Jan 89	LOOKING FOR LINDA *Circa YR 24*	15	9 wks
6 May 89	VIOLENTLY (EP) *Circa YR 29*	21	6 wks
30 Sep 89	SWEET INVISIBILITY *Circa YR 37*	55	3 wks
25 May 91	MY SALT HEART *Circa YR 64*	47	3 wks
3 Aug 91	LONG TERM LOVERS OF PAIN (EP) *Circa YR 71*	48	3 wks
11 Jul 92	PROFOUNDLY YOURS *Fidelity FIDEL 1*	74	1 wk
13 Mar 93	LABOUR OF LOVE (re-mix) *Circa HUESCD 1*	25	4 wks

Tracks on Violently (EP): Violently / The Man With The Child In His Eyes / Calamity John. Tracks on Long Term Lovers Of Pain (EP): Long Term Lovers Of Pain / Heart Of Saturday Night / Remember And Gold / Stars Crash Down.

HUES CORPORATION *US, male / female vocal group* — **16 wks**

27 Jul 74	● ROCK THE BOAT *RCA APBO 0232*	6	10 wks
19 Oct 74	ROCKIN' SOUL *RCA PB 10066*	24	6 wks

David HUGHES *UK, male vocalist* — **1 wk**

21 Sep 56	BY THE FOUNTAINS OF ROME *Philips PB 606*	27	1 wk

HUGO and LUIGI *US, male vocal duo* — **2 wks**

24 Jul 59	LA PLUME DE MA TANTE *RCA 1127*	29	2 wks

HUMAN LEAGUE
UK, male / female vocal / instrumental group — **131 wks**

3 May 80	HOLIDAY 80 (DOUBLE SINGLE) *Virgin SV 105*	56	5 wks
21 Jun 80	EMPIRE STATE HUMAN *Virgin VS 351*	62	2 wks
28 Feb 81	BOYS AND GIRLS *Virgin VS 395*	48	4 wks
2 May 81	THE SOUND OF THE CROWD *Virgin VS 416*	12	10 wks
8 Aug 81	● LOVE ACTION (I BELIEVE IN LOVE) *Virgin VS 435*	3	13 wks
10 Oct 81	● OPEN YOUR HEART *Virgin VS 453*	6	9 wks
5 Dec 81	★ DON'T YOU WANT ME *Virgin VS 466*	1	13 wks
9 Jan 82	● BEING BOILED *EMI FAST 4*	6	9 wks
6 Feb 82	HOLIDAY 80 (DOUBLE SINGLE) (re-entry) *Virgin SV 105*	46	5 wks
20 Nov 82	● MIRROR MAN *Virgin VS 522*	2	10 wks
23 Apr 83	● (KEEP FEELING) FASCINATION *Virgin VS 569*	2	9 wks
5 May 84	THE LEBANON *Virgin VS 672*	11	6 wks
23 Jun 84	THE LEBANON (re-entry) *Virgin VS 672*	75	1 wk
30 Jun 84	LIFE ON YOUR OWN *Virgin VS 688*	16	6 wks
17 Nov 84	LOUISE *Virgin VS 723*	13	10 wks
23 Aug 86	● HUMAN *Virgin VS 880*	8	8 wks
22 Nov 86	I NEED YOUR LOVING *Virgin VS 900*	72	1 wk
15 Oct 88	LOVE IS ALL THAT MATTERS *Virgin VS 1025*	41	5 wks
18 Aug 90	HEART LIKE A WHEEL *Virgin VS 1262*	29	5 wks

Tracks on double single: Being Boiled / Marianne / Rock And Roll - Nightclubbing / Dancevision.

HUMAN RESOURCE
Holland, male instrumental / production group — **14 wks**

14 Sep 91	DOMINATOR *R&S RSUK 4*	36	7 wks
21 Dec 91	THE COMPLETE DOMINATOR (re-mix) *R&S RSUK 4X*	18	7 wks

HUMANOID *UK, male producer* — **13 wks**

26 Nov 88	STAKKER HUMANOID *Westside WSR 12*	17	8 wks
22 Apr 89	SLAM *Westside WSR 14*	54	2 wks
8 Aug 92	STAKKER HUMANOID (re-issue) *Jumpin' + Pumpin' TOT 27*	40	3 wks

HUMBLE PIE *UK, male vocal / instrumental group* — **10 wks**

23 Aug 69	● NATURAL BORN BUGIE *Immediate IM 082*	4	10 wks

Engelbert HUMPERDINCK *UK, male vocalist* — **235 wks**

26 Jan 67	★ RELEASE ME *Decca F 12541*	1	56 wks
25 May 67	● THERE GOES MY EVERYTHING *Decca F 12610*	2	29 wks
23 Aug 67	★ THE LAST WALTZ *Decca F 12655*	1	27 wks
10 Jan 68	● AM I THAT EASY TO FORGET *Decca F 12722*	3	13 wks
24 Apr 68	● A MAN WITHOUT LOVE *Decca F 12770*	2	15 wks
25 Sep 68	● LES BICYCLETTES DE BELSIZE *Decca F 12834*	5	15 wks
5 Feb 69	● THE WAY IT USED TO BE *Decca F 12879*	3	14 wks
9 Aug 69	I'M A BETTER MAN *Decca F 12957*	15	13 wks
15 Nov 69	● WINTER WORLD OF LOVE *Decca F 12980*	7	13 wks
30 May 70	MY MARIE *Decca F 13032*	31	7 wks
12 Sep 70	SWEETHEART *Decca F 13068*	22	6 wks
31 Oct 70	SWEETHEART (re-entry) *Decca F 13068*	50	1 wk
11 Sep 71	ANOTHER TIME ANOTHER PLACE *Decca F 13212*	13	12 wks
4 Mar 72	TOO BEAUTIFUL TO LAST *Decca F 13281*	14	10 wks
20 Oct 73	LOVE IS ALL *Decca F 13443*	44	3 wks
17 Nov 73	LOVE IS ALL (re-entry) *Decca F 13443*	45	1 wk

Peter HUNNIGALE - *See ARSENAL F.C. TEAM SQUAD*

Geraldine HUNT *Canada, female vocalist* — **5 wks**

25 Oct 80	CAN'T FAKE THE FEELING *Champagne FIZZ 501*	44	5 wks

Lisa HUNT - *See LOVESTATION*

It is 23 October 1989, and **ENGELBERT HUMPERDINCK** gets his star on the Hollywood Walk of Fame. (LFI)

WHITNEY HOUSTON is shown with her mother Cissy at a songwriting awards dinner in the New York Hilton Hotel on 30 May 1990. (LFI)

HOT CHOCOLATE recorded on Apple before beginning their string of hits on RAK. (LFI)

Marsha HUNT US, female vocalist   **3 wks**

21 May 69	**WALK ON GILDED SPLINTERS** Track 604 030	46	2 wks
2 May 70	**KEEP THE CUSTOMER SATISFIED** Track 604 037	41	1 wk

Tommy HUNT US, male vocalist   **17 wks**

11 Oct 75	**CRACKIN' UP** Spark SRL 1132	39	5 wks
21 Aug 76	**LOVING ON THE LOSING SIDE** Spark SRL 1146	28	9 wks
4 Dec 76	**ONE FINE MORNING** Spark SRL 1148	44	3 wks

Ian HUNTER UK, male vocalist   **10 wks**

3 May 75	**ONCE BITTEN TWICE SHY** CBS 3194	14	10 wks

Tab HUNTER US, male vocalist   **30 wks**

8 Feb 57	★ **YOUNG LOVE** London HLD 8380	1	18 wks
12 Apr 57	● **99 WAYS** London HLD 8410	5	11 wks
5 Jul 57	**99 WAYS (re-entry)** London HLD 8410	29	1 wk

Steve 'Silk' HURLEY US, male vocalist   **9 wks**

10 Jan 87	★ **JACK YOUR BODY** DJ International LON 117	1	9 wks

HURRICANES - See JOHNNY and the HURRICANES

Phil HURTT US, male vocalist   **5 wks**

11 Nov 78	**GIVING IT BACK** Fantasy FTC 161	36	5 wks

Willie HUTCH US, male vocalist   **8 wks**

4 Dec 82	**IN AND OUT** Motown TMG 1285	51	7 wks
6 Jul 85	**KEEP ON JAMMIN'** Motown ZB 40173	73	1 wk

June HUTTON and Axel STORDAHL with the BOYS NEXT DOOR
US, female vocalist and male orchestra with male vocal group   **7 wks**

7 Aug 53	● **SAY YOU'RE MINE AGAIN** Capitol CL 13918	10	3 wks
4 Sep 53	● **SAY YOU'RE MINE AGAIN (re-entry)** Capitol CL 13918	6	4 wks

HWA featuring SONIC THE HEDGEHOG
UK, male producer - Jeremy Healey   **6 wks**

5 Dec 92	**SUPERSONIC** Internal Affairs	33	6 wks

Brian HYLAND US, male vocalist   **72 wks**

7 Jul 60	● **ITSY BITSY TEENY WEENY YELLOW POLKA DOT BIKINI** London HLR 9161	8	13 wks
20 Oct 60	**FOUR LITTLE HEELS** London HLR 9203	29	6 wks
10 May 62	● **GINNY COME LATELY** HMV POP 1013	5	15 wks
2 Aug 62	● **SEALED WITH A KISS** HMV POP 1051	3	15 wks
8 Nov 62	**WARMED OVER KISSES** HMV POP 1079	28	6 wks
27 Mar 71	**GYPSY WOMAN** Uni UN 530	45	1 wk
10 Apr 71	**GYPSY WOMAN (re-entry)** Uni UN 530	42	5 wks
28 Jun 75	● **SEALED WITH A KISS (re-issue)** ABC 4059	7	11 wks

Sheila HYLTON Jamaica, female vocalist   **12 wks**

15 Sep 79	**BREAKFAST IN BED** United Artists BP 304	57	5 wks
17 Jan 81	**THE BED'S TOO BIG WITHOUT YOU** Island WIP 6671	35	7 wks

Phyllis HYMAN US, female vocalist   **9 wks**

16 Feb 80	**YOU KNOW HOW TO LOVE ME** Arista ARIST 323	47	6 wks
12 Sep 81	**YOU SURE LOOK GOOD TO ME** Arista ARIST 424	56	3 wks

Dick HYMAN TRIO
US, male instrument, Dick Hyman, keyboards   **10 wks**

16 Mar 56	● **THEME FROM 'THE THREEPENNY OPERA'** MGM 890	9	10 wks

Chrissie HYNDE - See MOODSWINGS featuring Chrissie HYNDE; UB40

HYPER GO GO UK, male instrumental / production duo   **11 wks**

22 Aug 92	**HIGH** Deconstruction 74321110497	30	5 wks
31 Jul 93	**NEVER LET GO** Positiva CDTIV 3	45	3 wks
5 Feb 94	**RAISE** Positiva CDTIV 9	36	2 wks
26 Nov 94	**IT'S ALRIGHT** Positiva CDTIV 20	49	1 wk

HYPERSTATE UK, male / female vocal / instrumental duo   **1 wk**

6 Feb 93	**TIME AFTER TIME** M & G MAGCD 34	71	1 wk

HYPNOTIST UK, male producer - Caspar Pound   **5 wks**

28 Sep 91	**THE HOUSE IS MINE** Rising High RSN 4	65	2 wks
21 Dec 91	**THE HARDCORE EP** Rising High RSN 13	68	3 wks

Tracks on The Hardcore EP: Hardcore U Know The Score / The Ride / Night Of The Livin' E Heads / God Of The Universe.

HYSTERICS UK, male vocal / instrumental group   **5 wks**

12 Dec 81	**JINGLE BELLS LAUGHING ALL THE WAY** Record Delivery KA 5	44	5 wks

HYSTERIX UK, male / female vocal / instrumental group   **3 wks**

7 May 94	**MUST BE THE MUSIC** Deconstruction 74321207362	40	3 wks

Janis IAN US, female vocalist   **10 wks**

17 Nov 79	**FLY TOO HIGH** CBS 7936	44	7 wks
28 Jun 80	**THE OTHER SIDE OF THE SUN** CBS 8611	44	3 wks

ICE CUBE US, male rapper   **18 wks**

27 Mar 93	**IT WAS A GOOD DAY** Fourth & Broadway BRCD 270	27	4 wks
7 Aug 93	**CHECK YO SELF** Fourth & Broadway BRCD 283 [1]	36	4 wks
11 Sep 93	**WICKED** Fourth & Broadway BRCD 282	62	1 wk
18 Dec 93	**REALLY DOE** Fourth & Broadway BRCD 302	66	1 wk
26 Mar 94	**YOU KNOW HOW WE DO IT** Fourth & Broadway BRCD 303	41	3 wks
27 Aug 94	**BOP GUN (ONE NATION)** Fourth & Broadway BRCD 308 [2]	22	3 wks
24 Dec 94	**YOU KNOW HOW WE DO IT (re-entry)** Fourth & Broadway BRCD 303	46†	2 wks

[1] Ice Cube featuring Das EFX   [2] Ice Cube featuring George Clinton

ICEHOUSE New Zealand, male vocal / instrumental group   **28 wks**

5 Feb 83	**HEY LITTLE GIRL** Chrysalis CHS 2670	17	10 wks
23 Apr 83	**STREET CAFE** Chrysalis COOL 1	62	4 wks

3 May 86	NO PROMISES Chrysalis CHS 2978	72	1 wk
29 Aug 87	CRAZY Chrysalis CHS 3156	74	1 wk
13 Feb 88	CRAZY (re-entry) Chrysalis CHS 3156	38	8 wks
14 May 88	ELECTRIC BLUE Chrysalis CHS 3239	53	4 wks

ICE MC Italy, male rapper — 2 wks

6 Aug 94	THINK ABOUT THE WAY (BOM DIGI DIGI BOM...) WEA YZ 829CD	42	2 wks

ICE-T US, male rapper — 21 wks

18 Mar 89	HIGH ROLLERS Sire W 7574	63	2 wks
17 Feb 90	YOU PLAYED YOURSELF Sire W 9994	64	2 wks
29 Sep 90	SUPERFLY 1990 Capitol CL 586 [1]	48	3 wks
8 May 93	I AIN'T NEW TA THIS Rhyme Syndicate SYNDD 1	62	2 wks
18 Dec 93	THAT'S HOW I'M LIVIN' Rhyme Syndicate SYNDD 2	21	6 wks
9 Apr 94	GOTTA LOTTA LOVE Rhyme Syndicate SYNDD 3	24	2 wks
10 Dec 94	BORN TO RAISE HELL Fox 74321230152 [2]	47	2 wks

[1] Curtis Mayfield and Ice-T [2] Motorhead/Ice-T/Whitfield Crane

ICICLE WORKS UK, male vocal / instrumental group — 28 wks

24 Dec 83	LOVE IS A WONDERFUL COLOUR Beggars Banquet BEG 99	15	8 wks
10 Mar 84	BIRDS FLY (WHISPER TO A SCREAM) / IN THE CAULDRON OF LOVE Beggars Banquet BEG 108	53	4 wks
26 Jul 86	UNDERSTANDING JANE Beggars Banquet BEG 160	52	3 wks
4 Oct 86	WHO DO YOU WANT FOR YOUR LOVE Beggars Banquet BEG 172	54	4 wks
14 Feb 87	EVANGELINE Beggars Banquet BEG 181	53	4 wks
30 Apr 88	LITTLE GIRL LOST Beggars Banquet BEG 215	59	4 wks
17 Mar 90	MOTORCYCLE RIDER Epic WORKS 100	73	1 wk

IDEAL LIFE UK, male producer - Jon Da Silva — 2 wks

6 Aug 94	HOT Cleveland City CLECD 13019	49	2 wks

IDES OF MARCH US, male vocal / instrumental group — 9 wks

6 Jun 70	VEHICLE Warner Bros. WB 7378	31	9 wks

Eric IDLE featuring Richard WILSON
UK, male vocal duo — 3 wks

17 Dec 94	ONE FOOT IN THE GRAVE Victa CDVICTA 1	50†	3 wks

Billy IDOL UK, male vocalist — 106 wks

11 Sep 82	HOT IN THE CITY Chrysalis CHS 2625	58	4 wks
24 Mar 84	REBEL YELL Chrysalis IDOL 2	62	2 wks
30 Jun 84	EYES WITHOUT A FACE Chrysalis IDOL 3	18	11 wks
29 Sep 84	FLESH FOR FANTASY Chrysalis IDOL 4	54	3 wks
13 Jul 85	● WHITE WEDDING Chrysalis IDOL 5	6	15 wks
14 Sep 85	● REBEL YELL (re-issue) Chrysalis IDOL 6	6	12 wks
4 Oct 86	TO BE A LOVER Chrysalis IDOL 8	22	8 wks
7 Mar 87	DON'T NEED A GUN Chrysalis IDOL 9	26	5 wks
13 Jun 87	SWEET SIXTEEN Chrysalis IDOL 10	17	9 wks
3 Oct 87	● MONY MONY Chrysalis IDOL 11	7	10 wks
16 Jan 88	HOT IN THE CITY (re-mix) Chrysalis IDOL 12	13	9 wks
13 Aug 88	CATCH MY FALL Chrysalis IDOL 13	63	3 wks
28 Apr 90	CRADLE OF LOVE Chrysalis IDOL 14	34	4 wks
11 Aug 90	L.A. WOMAN Chrysalis IDOL 15	70	2 wks
22 Dec 90	PRODIGAL BLUES Chrysalis IDOL 16	47	4 wks
26 Jun 93	SHOCK TO THE SYSTEM Chrysalis CDCHS 3994	30	3 wks
10 Sep 94	SPEED Fox 74321223472	47	2 wks

Frank IFIELD UK, male vocalist — 162 wks

19 Feb 60	LUCKY DEVIL Columbia DB 4399	22	5 wks
7 Apr 60	LUCKY DEVIL (re-entry) Columbia DB 4399	33	2 wks
29 Sep 60	GOTTA GET A DATE Columbia DB 4496	49	1 wk
5 Jul 62	★ I REMEMBER YOU Columbia DB 4856	1	28 wks
25 Oct 62	★ LOVESICK BLUES Columbia DB 4913	1	17 wks
24 Jan 63	★ WAYWARD WIND Columbia DB 4960	1	13 wks
11 Apr 63	● NOBODY'S DARLIN' BUT MINE Columbia DB 7007	4	16 wks
27 Jun 63	★ CONFESSIN' Columbia DB 7062	1	16 wks
17 Oct 63	MULE TRAIN Columbia DB 7131	22	6 wks
9 Jan 64	● DON'T BLAME ME Columbia DB 7184	8	13 wks
23 Apr 64	ANGRY AT THE BIG OAK TREE Columbia DB 7263	25	8 wks
23 Jul 64	I SHOULD CARE Columbia DB 7319	33	3 wks
1 Oct 64	SUMMER IS OVER Columbia DB 7355	25	6 wks
19 Aug 65	PARADISE Columbia DB 7655	26	9 wks
23 Jun 66	NO ONE WILL EVER KNOW Columbia DB 7940	25	4 wks
8 Dec 66	CALL HER YOUR SWEETHEART Columbia DB 8078	24	11 wks
7 Dec 91	THE YODELLING SONG EMI 7YODEL 1 [1]	40	4 wks

[1] Frank Ifield featuring the Backroom Boys

Julio IGLESIAS Spain, male vocalist — 74 wks

24 Oct 81	★ BEGIN THE BEGUINE (VOLVER A EMPEZAR) CBS A 1612	1	14 wks
6 Mar 82	● QUIEREME MUCHO (YOURS) CBS A 1939	3	9 wks
9 Oct 82	AMOR CBS A 2801	32	7 wks
9 Apr 83	HEY! CBS JULIO 1	31	7 wks
7 Apr 84	TO ALL THE GIRLS I'VE LOVED BEFORE CBS A 4252 [1]	17	10 wks
7 Jul 84	ALL OF YOU CBS A 4522 [2]	43	8 wks
6 Aug 88	● MY LOVE CBS JULIO 2 [3]	5	11 wks
4 Jun 94	CRAZY Columbia 6603695	43	3 wks
27 Aug 94	CRAZY (re-entry) Columbia 6603695	50	2 wks
26 Nov 94	FRAGILE Columbia 6610192	53	2 wks
31 Dec 94	FRAGILE (re-entry) Columbia 6610192	66†	1 wk

[1] Julio Iglesias and Willie Nelson [2] Julio Iglesias and Diana Ross [3] Julio Iglesias featuring Stevie Wonder

IGNORANTS UK, male vocal duo — 3 wks

25 Dec 93	PHAT GIRLS Spaghetti CIOCD 8	59	3 wks

I-LEVEL UK, male vocal / instrumental group — 9 wks

16 Apr 83	MINEFIELD Virgin VS 563	52	6 wks
18 Jun 83	TEACHER Virgin VS 595	56	3 wks

ILLEGAL MOTION featuring Simone CHAPMAN UK, male / female vocal / instrumental duo — 1 wk

9 Oct 93	SATURDAY LOVE Arista 74321163032	67	1 wk

IMAGINATION UK, male vocal / instrumental group — 105 wks

16 May 81	● BODY TALK R & B RBS 201	4	18 wks
5 Sep 81	IN AND OUT OF LOVE R & B RBS 202	16	9 wks
14 Nov 81	FLASHBACK R & B RBS 206	16	13 wks
6 Mar 82	● JUST AN ILLUSION R & B RBS 208	2	11 wks
26 Jun 82	● MUSIC AND LIGHTS R & B RBS 210	5	9 wks
25 Sep 82	IN THE HEAT OF THE NIGHT R & B RBS 211	22	8 wks
11 Dec 82	CHANGES R & B RBS 213	31	8 wks
4 Jun 83	LOOKING AT MIDNIGHT R & B RBS 214	29	7 wks
5 Nov 83	NEW DIMENSIONS R & B RBS 216	56	3 wks
26 May 84	STATE OF LOVE R & B RBS 218	67	2 wks
24 Nov 84	THANK YOU MY LOVE R & B RBS 219	22	15 wks
16 Jan 88	INSTINCTUAL RCA PB 41697	62	2 wks

IMMACULATE FOOLS
UK, male vocal / instrumental group — 4 wks

26 Jan 85	IMMACULATE FOOLS A & M AM 227	51	4 wks

IMPALAS US, male vocal group — 1 wk

21 Aug 59	SORRY (I RAN ALL THE WAY HOME) MGM 1015	28	1 wk

IMPEDANCE UK, male producer - Daniel Haydon   **4 wks**

11 Nov 89	**TAINTED LOVE** Jumpin' & Pumpin' TOT 4 ....**54**	4 wks

IMPERIALS - See LITTLE ANTHONY and the IMPERIALS

IMPOSTER - See Elvis COSTELLO

IMPRESSIONS US, male vocal group   **10 wks**

22 Nov 75	**FIRST IMPRESSIONS** Curtom K 16638...............**16**	10 wks

IN CROWD UK, male vocal / instrumental group   **1 wk**

20 May 65	**THAT'S HOW STRONG MY LOVE IS** Parlophone R 5276 ....**48**	1 wk

IN TUA NUA
Ireland, male / female vocal / instrumental group   **2 wks**

14 May 88	**ALL I WANTED** Virgin VS 1072 ....**69**	2 wks

INCANTATION UK, male instrumental group   **12 wks**

4 Dec 82	**CACHARPAYA (ANDES PUMPSA DAESI)** Beggars Banquet BEG 84 ....**12**	12 wks

INCOGNITO
France / UK, male / female instrumental group   **27 wks**

15 Nov 80	**PARISIENNE GIRL** Ensign ENY 44 ....**73**	2 wks
29 Jun 91	● **ALWAYS THERE** Talkin Loud TLK 10 [1] **6**	9 wks
14 Sep 91	**CRAZY FOR YOU** Talkin Loud TLK 14 [2] **59**	2 wks
6 Jun 92	**DON'T YOU WORRY 'BOUT A THING** Talkin Loud TLK 21 ....**19**	6 wks
15 Aug 92	**CHANGE** Talkin Loud TLK 26 ....**52**	2 wks
21 Aug 93	**STILL A FRIEND OF MINE** Talkin Loud TLKCD 42......**47**	2 wks
20 Nov 93	**GIVIN' IT UP** Talkin Loud TLKCD 44 ....**43**	2 wks
12 Mar 94	**PIECES OF A DREAM** Talkin Loud TLKCD 46 ....**35**	2 wks

[1] Incognito featuring Jocelyn Brown [2] Incognito featuring Chyna

INDEEP US, male / female vocal duo   **11 wks**

22 Jan 83	**LAST NIGHT A DJ SAVED MY LIFE** Sound Of New York SNY 1...............**13**	9 wks
14 May 83	**WHEN BOYS TALK** Sound Of New York SNY 3...............**67**	2 wks

INDIAN VIBES UK, male vocal / instrumental group   **1 wk**

24 Sep 94	**MATHAR** Virgin International DINSD 136 ....**68**	1 wk

Los INDIOS TABAJARAS
Brazil, male instrumental duo - guitars   **17 wks**

31 Oct 63	● **MARIA ELENA** RCA 1365 ....**5**	17 wks

INGRAM US, male vocal / instrumental group   **2 wks**

11 Jun 83	**SMOOTHIN' GROOVIN'** Streetwave WAVE 3 ....**56**	2 wks

James INGRAM US, male vocalist   **42 wks**

12 Feb 83	**BABY COME TO ME** Qwest K 15005 [1] **11**	10 wks
18 Feb 84	**YAH MO B THERE** Qwest W 9394 [2] **44**	5 wks
7 Apr 84	**YAH MO B THERE (re-entry)** Qwest W 9394 [2] **69**	3 wks
12 Jan 85	**YAH MO B THERE (re-mix)** Qwest W 9394 [2] **12**	8 wks
11 Jul 87	● **SOMEWHERE OUT THERE** MCA MCA 1132 [3] **8**	13 wks
31 Mar 90	**SECRET GARDEN** Qwest W 9992 [4] **67**	1 wk
16 Apr 94	**THE DAY I FALL IN LOVE** Columbia 6600282 [5] **64**	2 wks

[1] Patti Austin and James Ingram [2] James Ingram with Michael McDonald
[3] Linda Ronstadt and James Ingram [4] Quincy Jones featuring Al B. Sure!, James Ingram, El DeBarge and Barry White [5] Dolly Parton and James Ingram

INK SPOTS US, male vocal group   **4 wks**

29 Apr 55	● **MELODY OF LOVE** Parlophone R 3977 ....**10**	4 wks

John INMAN UK, male vocalist   **6 wks**

25 Oct 75	**ARE YOU BEING SERVED SIR** DJM DJS 602 ....**39**	6 wks

INMATES UK, male vocal / instrumental group   **9 wks**

8 Dec 79	**THE WALK** Radar ADA 47 ....**36**	9 wks

INNER CIRCLE Jamaica, male vocal / instrumental group   **35 wks**

24 Feb 79	**EVERYTHING IS GREAT** Island WIP 6472 ....**37**	8 wks
12 May 79	**STOP BREAKING MY HEART** Island WIP 6488 ....**50**	3 wks
31 Oct 92	**SWEAT (A LA LA LA LA LONG)** Magnet 9031776802 ....**43**	5 wks
1 May 93	● **SWEAT (A LA LA LA LA LONG) (re-entry)** Magnet 9031776802 ....**3**	14 wks
31 Jul 93	**BAD BOYS** Magnet MAG 1017CD **52**	3 wks
10 Sep 94	**GAMES PEOPLE PLAY** Magnet MAG 1026CD **67**	2 wks

INNER CITY US, male / female vocal / instrumental duo   **71 wks**

3 Sep 88	● **BIG FUN** 10 TEN 240 [1] **8**	14 wks
10 Dec 88	● **GOOD LIFE** 10 TEN 249 ....**4**	12 wks
22 Apr 89	● **AIN'T NOBODY BETTER** 10 TEN 252 ....**10**	7 wks
29 Jul 89	**DO YOU LOVE WHAT YOU FEEL** 10 TEN 237 ....**16**	7 wks
18 Nov 89	**WATCHA GONNA DO WITH MY LOVIN'** 10 TEN 290 ....**12**	9 wks
13 Oct 90	**THAT MAN (HE'S ALL MINE)** 10 TEN 334...............**42**	4 wks
23 Feb 91	**TILL WE MEET AGAIN** Ten TEN 337 ....**47**	2 wks
7 Dec 91	**LET IT REIGN** Ten TEN 392 ....**51**	2 wks
4 Apr 92	**HALLELUJAH '92** Ten TEN 398 ....**22**	4 wks
13 Jun 92	**PENNIES FROM HEAVEN** Ten TEN 405 ....**24**	4 wks
12 Sep 92	**PRAISE** Ten TENX 408 ....**59**	2 wks
27 Feb 93	**TILL WE MEET AGAIN (re-mix)** Ten TENCD 414 ....**55**	1 wk
5 Feb 94	**DO YA** Six6 SIXCD 107 ....**44**	2 wks
9 Jul 94	**SHARE MY LIFE** Six6 SIXCD 114 ....**62**	1 wk

[1] Inner City featuring Kevin Saunderson

INNOCENCE UK, male / female vocal / instrumental group   **33 wks**

3 Mar 90	**NATURAL THING** Cooltempo COOL 201 ....**16**	7 wks
21 Jul 90	**SILENT VOICE** Cooltempo COOL 212 ....**37**	5 wks
13 Oct 90	**LET'S PUSH IT** Cooltempo COOL 220...............**25**	6 wks
8 Dec 90	**A MATTER OF FACT** Cooltempo COOL 223...............**37**	7 wks
30 Mar 91	**REMEMBER THE DAY** Cooltempo COOL 226 ....**56**	2 wks
20 Jun 92	**I'LL BE THERE** Cooltempo COOL 255...............**26**	3 wks
3 Oct 92	**ONE LOVE IN MY LIFETIME** Cooltempo COOL 263..**40**	2 wks
21 Nov 92	**BUILD** Cooltempo COOL 267 ....**72**	1 wk

INSPIRAL CARPETS
UK, male vocal / instrumental group   **48 wks**

18 Nov 89	**MOVE** Cow DUNG 6...............**49**	2 wks
17 Mar 90	**THIS IS HOW IT FEELS** Cow DUNG 7 ....**14**	8 wks
30 Jun 90	**SHE COMES IN THE FALL** Cow DUNG 10 ....**27**	6 wks
17 Nov 90	**ISLAND HEAD EP** Cow DUNG 11 ....**21**	4 wks
30 Mar 91	**CARAVAN** Cow DUNG 13 ....**30**	5 wks
22 Jun 91	**PLEASE BE CRUEL** Cow DUNG 15 ....**50**	2 wks
29 Feb 92	**DRAGGING ME DOWN** Cow DUNG 16 ....**12**	5 wks
30 May 92	**TWO WORLDS COLLIDE** Cow DUNG 17 ....**32**	2 wks
19 Sep 92	**GENERATIONS** Cow DUNG 18T **28**	3 wks
14 Nov 92	**BITCHES BREW** Cow DUNG 20T **36**	2 wks
5 Jun 93	**HOW IT SHOULD BE** Cow DUNG 22CD **49**	1 wk
22 Jan 94	**SATURN 5** Cow DUNG 23CD **20**	4 wks
5 Mar 94	**I WANT YOU** Cow DUNG 24CD [1] **18**	3 wks
7 May 94	**UNIFORM** Cow DUNG 26CD **51**	1 wk

[1] Inspiral Carpets featuring Mark E. Smith

Tracks on Island Head EP: Biggest Mountain / Gold Top / Weakness / I'll Keep It In Mind.

INSPIRATIONAL CHOIR US, male / female choir   **11 wks**

22 Dec 84	**ABIDE WITH ME** Epic A 4997	**44**	5 wks
14 Dec 85	**ABIDE WITH ME (re-issue)** Portrait A 4997	**36**	6 wks

Label credits the Royal Choral Society.

INSTANT FUNK US, male vocal / instrumental group   **5 wks**

20 Jan 79	**GOT MY MIND MADE UP** Salsoul SSOL 114	**46**	5 wks

INTASTELLA UK, male / female vocal / instrumental group   **5 wks**

25 May 91	**DREAM SOME PARADISE** MCA MCS 1520	**69**	1 wk
24 Aug 91	**PEOPLE** MCA MCS 1559	**74**	2 wks
16 Nov 91	**CENTURY** MCA MCS 1585	**70**	2 wks

INTELLIGENT HOODLUM US, male rap group   **3 wks**

6 Oct 90	**BACK TO REALITY** A & M AM 598	**55**	3 wks

INTRUDERS US, male vocal group   **21 wks**

13 Apr 74	**I'LL ALWAYS LOVE MY MAMA** Philadelphia International PIR 2149	**32**	7 wks
6 Jul 74	**(WIN PLACE OR SHOW) SHE'S A WINNER** Philadelphia International PIR 2212	**14**	9 wks
22 Dec 84	**WHO DO YOU LOVE?** Streetwave KHAN 34	**65**	5 wks

INVADERS OF THE HEART - *See Jah WOBBLE'S INVADERS OF THE HEART*

INVISIBLE GIRLS - *See Pauline MURRAY and the INVISIBLE GIRLS*

INXS Australia, male vocal / instrumental group   **116 wks**

19 Apr 86	**WHAT YOU NEED** Mercury INXS 5	**51**	6 wks
28 Jun 86	**LISTEN LIKE THIEVES** Mercury INXS 6	**46**	7 wks
30 Aug 86	**KISS THE DIRT (FALLING DOWN THE MOUNTAIN)** Mercury INXS 7	**54**	3 wks
24 Oct 87	**NEED YOU TONIGHT** Mercury INXS 8	**58**	3 wks
9 Jan 88	**NEW SENSATION** Mercury INXS 9	**25**	6 wks
12 Mar 88	**DEVIL INSIDE** Mercury INXS 10	**47**	5 wks
25 Jun 88	**NEVER TEAR US APART** Mecury INXS 11	**24**	7 wks
12 Nov 88 ●	**NEED YOU TONIGHT (re-issue)** Mercury INXS 12	**2**	11 wks
8 Apr 89	**MYSTIFY** Mercury INXS 13	**14**	7 wks
15 Sep 90	**SUICIDE BLONDE** Mercury INXS 14	**11**	6 wks
8 Dec 90	**DISAPPEAR** Mercury INXS 15	**21**	8 wks
26 Jan 91	**GOOD TIMES** Atlantic A 7751 [1]	**18**	8 wks
30 Mar 91	**BY MY SIDE** Mercury INXS 16	**42**	4 wks
13 Jul 91	**BITTER TEARS** Mercury INXS 17	**30**	3 wks
2 Nov 91	**SHINING STAR (EP)** Mercury INXS 18	**27**	3 wks
18 Jul 92	**HEAVEN SENT** Mercury INXS 19	**31**	3 wks
5 Sep 92	**BABY DON'T CRY** Mercury INXS 20	**20**	5 wks
14 Nov 92	**TASTE IT** Mercury INXS 23	**21**	4 wks
13 Feb 93	**BEAUTIFUL GIRL** Mercury INXCD 24	**23**	5 wks
23 Oct 93	**THE GIFT** Mercury INXCD 25	**11**	4 wks
11 Dec 93	**PLEASE (YOU GOT THAT...)** Mercury INXCD 26	**50**	3 wks
22 Oct 94	**THE STRANGEST PARTY (THESE ARE THE TIMES)** Mercury INXCD 27	**15**	5 wks

[1] Jimmy Barnes and INXS

Tracks on Shining Star (EP): *Shining Star / Send A Message (Live) / Faith In Each Other (Live) / Bitter Tears (Live). Although uncredited* Please (You Got That...) *is a duet with Ray Charles.*

Sweetie IRIE - *See ASWAD; SCRITTI POLITTI*

Tippa IRIE UK, male vocalist   **13 wks**

22 Mar 86	**HELLO DARLING** Greensleeves/UK Bubb TIPPA 4	**22**	7 wks
19 Jul 86	**HEARTBEAT** Greensleeves/UK Bubb TIPPA 5	**59**	3 wks
15 May 93	**SHOUTING FOR THE GUNNERS** London LONCD 342 [1]	**34**	3 wks

[1] Arsenal FA Cup Squad featuring Tippa Irie and Peter Hunnigale

IRON MAIDEN UK, male vocal / instrumental group   **138 wks**

23 Feb 80	**RUNNING FREE** EMI 5032	**34**	5 wks
7 Jun 80	**SANCTUARY** EMI 5065	**29**	5 wks
8 Nov 80	**WOMEN IN UNIFORM** EMI 5105	**35**	4 wks
14 Mar 81	**TWILIGHT ZONE / WRATH CHILD** EMI 5145	**31**	5 wks
27 Jun 81	**PURGATORY** EMI 5184	**52**	3 wks
26 Sep 81	**MAIDEN JAPAN** EMI 5219	**43**	4 wks
20 Feb 82 ●	**RUN TO THE HILLS** EMI 5263	**7**	10 wks
15 May 82	**THE NUMBER OF THE BEAST** EMI 5287	**18**	8 wks
23 Apr 83	**FLIGHT OF ICARUS** EMI 5378	**11**	6 wks
2 Jul 83	**THE TROOPER** EMI 5397	**12**	7 wks
18 Aug 84	**2 MINUTES TO MIDNIGHT** EMI 5849	**11**	6 wks
3 Nov 84	**ACES HIGH** EMI 5502	**20**	4 wks
5 Oct 85	**RUNNING FREE (LIVE)** EMI EMI 5532	**19**	5 wks
14 Dec 85	**RUN TO THE HILLS (LIVE)** EMI 5542	**26**	6 wks
6 Sep 86	**WASTED YEARS** EMI 5583	**18**	4 wks
22 Nov 86	**STRANGER IN A STRANGE LAND** EMI EMI 5589	**22**	4 wks
27 Dec 86	**STRANGER IN A STRANGE LAND (re-entry)** EMI EMI 5589	**71**	2 wks
26 Mar 88 ●	**CAN I PLAY WITH MADNESS** EMI EM 49	**3**	6 wks
13 Aug 88 ●	**THE EVIL THAT MEN DO** EMI EM 64	**5**	6 wks
19 Nov 88 ●	**THE CLAIRVOYANT** EMI EM 79	**6**	8 wks
18 Nov 89 ●	**INFINITE DREAMS** EMI EM 117	**6**	5 wks
30 Dec 89	**INFINITE DREAMS (re-entry)** EMI EM 117	**74**	1 wk
22 Sep 90 ●	**HOLY SMOKE** EMI EM 153	**3**	4 wks
5 Jan 91 ★	**BRING YOUR DAUGHTER...TO THE SLAUGHTER** EMI EMPD 171	**1**	5 wks
25 Apr 92 ●	**BE QUICK OR BE DEAD** EMI EM 229	**2**	4 wks
11 Jul 92	**FROM HERE TO ETERNITY** EMI EMS 240	**21**	4 wks
13 Mar 93 ●	**FEAR OF THE DARK (LIVE)** EMI CDEMS 263	**8**	3 wks
16 Oct 93 ●	**HALLOWED BE THY NAME (LIVE)** EMI CDEM 288	**9**	3 wks

IRONHORSE Canada, male vocal / instrumental group   **3 wks**

5 May 79	**SWEET LUI-LOUISE** Scotti Brothers K 11271	**60**	3 wks

Big Dee IRWIN US, male vocalist   **17 wks**

21 Nov 63 ●	**SWINGING ON A STAR** Colpix PX 11010	**7**	17 wks

This hit was in fact a vocal duet by Big Dee Irwin and Little Eva, though she was not credited.

Chris ISAAK US, male vocalist   **21 wks**

24 Nov 90 ●	**WICKED GAME** London LON 279	**10**	10 wks
2 Feb 91	**BLUE HOTEL** Reprise W 0005	**17**	7 wks
3 Apr 93	**CAN'T DO A THING (TO STOP ME)** Reprise W 0161CD	**36**	3 wks
10 Jul 93	**SAN FRANCISCO DAYS** Reprise W 0182CD	**62**	1 wk

Ronald ISLEY - *See Rod STEWART*

ISLEY BROTHERS US, male vocal / instrumental group   **108 wks**

25 Jul 63	**TWIST AND SHOUT** Stateside SS 112	**42**	1 wk
28 Apr 66	**THIS OLD HEART OF MINE** Tamla Motown TMG 555	**47**	1 wk
1 Sep 66	**I GUESS I'LL ALWAYS LOVE YOU** Tamla Motown TMG 572	**45**	2 wks
23 Oct 68 ●	**THIS OLD HEART OF MINE (re-entry)** Tamla Motown TMG 555	**3**	16 wks
15 Jan 69	**I GUESS I'LL ALWAYS LOVE YOU (re-issue)** Tamla Motown TMG 683	**11**	9 wks
16 Apr 69 ●	**BEHIND A PAINTED SMILE** Tamla Motown TMG 693	**5**	12 wks
25 Jun 69	**IT'S YOUR THING** Major Minor MM 621	**30**	5 wks
30 Aug 69	**PUT YOURSELF IN MY PLACE** Tamla Motown TMG 708	**13**	11 wks

22 Sep 73	**THAT LADY** Epic EPC 1704	**14**	9 wks
19 Jan 74	**HIGHWAY OF MY LIFE** Epic EPC 1980	**25**	8 wks
25 May 74	**SUMMER BREEZE** Epic EPC 2244	**16**	8 wks
10 Jul 76	● **HARVEST FOR THE WORLD** Epic EPC 4369	**10**	8 wks
13 May 78	**TAKE ME TO THE NEXT PHASE** Epic EPC 6292	**50**	4 wks
3 Nov 79	**IT'S A DISCO NIGHT (ROCK DON'T STOP)** Epic EPC 7911	**14**	11 wks
16 Jul 83	**BETWEEN THE SHEETS** Epic A 3513	**52**	3 wks

ISLEY JASPER ISLEY
US, male vocal / instrumental group **5 wks**

23 Nov 85	**CARAVAN OF LOVE** Epic A 6612	**52**	5 wks

ISOTONIK
UK, male producer - Chris Paul **9 wks**

11 Jan 92	**DIFFERENT STROKES** Ffrreedom TAB 101	**12**	5 wks
2 May 92	**EVERYWHERE I GO / LET'S GET DOWN** Ffrreedom TAB 108	**25**	4 wks

Let's Get Down only listed from 9 May 92.

IT BITES
UK, male vocal / instrumental group **21 wks**

12 Jul 86	● **CALLING ALL THE HEROES** Virgin VS 872	**6**	12 wks
18 Oct 86	**WHOLE NEW WORLD** Virgin VS 896	**54**	3 wks
23 May 87	**THE OLD MAN AND THE ANGEL** Virgin VS 941	**72**	1 wk
13 May 89	**STILL TOO YOUNG TO REMEMBER** Virgin VS 1184	**66**	3 wks
24 Feb 90	**STILL TOO YOUNG TO REMEMBER (re-issue)** Virgin VS 1238	**60**	2 wks

IT'S IMMATERIAL
UK, male vocal / instrumental group **10 wks**

12 Apr 86	**DRIVING AWAY FROM HOME (JIM'S TUNE)** Siren SIREN 15	**18**	7 wks
2 Aug 86	**ED'S FUNKY DINER (FRIDAY NIGHT, SATURDAY MORNING)** Siren SIREN 24	**65**	3 wks

Burl IVES
US, male vocalist **25 wks**

25 Jan 62	● **A LITTLE BITTY TEAR** Brunswick 05863	**9**	15 wks
17 May 62	**FUNNY WAY OF LAUGHIN'** Brunswick 05868	**29**	10 wks

IVY LEAGUE
UK, male vocal group **31 wks**

4 Feb 65	● **FUNNY HOW LOVE CAN BE** Piccadilly 7N 35222	**8**	9 wks
6 May 65	**THAT'S WHY I'M CRYING** Piccadilly 7N 35228	**22**	8 wks
24 Jun 65	● **TOSSING AND TURNING** Piccadilly 7N 35251	**3**	13 wks
14 Jul 66	**WILLOW TREE** Piccadilly 7N 35326	**50**	1 wk

IZIT
UK, male / female vocal / instrumental group **3 wks**

2 Dec 89	**STORIES** ffrr F 122	**52**	3 wks

J

Lady J - See *RAZE*

JACK 'N' CHILL
UK, male instrumental group **21 wks**

6 Jun 87	**THE JACK THAT HOUSE BUILT** Oval TEN 174	**48**	5 wks
9 Jan 88	● **THE JACK THAT HOUSE BUILT (re-entry)** Oval TEN 174	**6**	11 wks
9 Jul 88	**BEATIN' THE HEAT** 10 TEN 234	**42**	5 wks

Terry JACKS
Canada, male vocalist **21 wks**

23 Mar 74	★ **SEASONS IN THE SUN** Bell 1344	**1**	12 wks
29 Jun 74	● **IF YOU GO AWAY** Bell 1362	**8**	9 wks

Chad JACKSON
UK, male producer **10 wks**

2 Jun 90	● **HEAR THE DRUMMER (GET WICKED)** Big Wave BWR 36	**3**	10 wks

Dee D. JACKSON
UK, female vocalist **14 wks**

22 Apr 78	● **AUTOMATIC LOVER** Mercury 6007 171	**4**	9 wks
2 Sep 78	**METEOR MAN** Mercury 6007 182	**48**	5 wks

Freddie JACKSON
US, male vocalist **31 wks**

23 Nov 85	**YOU ARE MY LADY** Capitol CL 379	**49**	4 wks
22 Feb 86	**ROCK ME TONIGHT (FOR OLD TIME'S SAKE)** Capitol CL 358	**18**	9 wks
11 Oct 86	**TASTY LOVE** Capitol CL 428	**73**	1 wk
7 Feb 87	**HAVE YOU EVER LOVED SOMEBODY** Capitol CL 437	**33**	6 wks
9 Jul 88	**NICE 'N' SLOW** Capitol CL 502	**56**	2 wks
15 Oct 88	**CRAZY (FOR ME)** Capitol CL 510	**41**	3 wks
5 Sep 92	**ME AND MRS JONES** Capitol CL 668	**32**	5 wks
15 Jan 94	**MAKE LOVE EASY** RCA 74321179162	**70**	1 wk

Janet JACKSON
US, female vocalist **149 wks**

22 Mar 86	● **WHAT HAVE YOU DONE FOR ME LATELY** A & M AM 308	**3**	14 wks
31 May 86	**NASTY** A & M AM 316	**19**	9 wks
9 Aug 86	● **WHEN I THINK OF YOU** A & M AM 337	**10**	10 wks
1 Nov 86	**CONTROL** A & M AM 359	**42**	5 wks
21 Mar 87	● **LET'S WAIT AWHILE** Breakout USA 601	**3**	10 wks
13 Jun 87	**PLEASURE PRINCIPLE** Breakout USA 604	**24**	5 wks
14 Nov 87	**FUNNY HOW TIME FLIES (WHEN YOU'RE HAVING FUN)** Breakout USA 613	**59**	2 wks
2 Sep 89	**MISS YOU MUCH** Breakout USA 663	**22**	7 wks
4 Nov 89	**RHYTHM NATION** Breakout USA 673	**23**	5 wks
27 Jan 90	**COME BACK TO ME** Breakout USA 681	**20**	7 wks
31 Mar 90	**ESCAPADE** Breakout USA 684	**17**	7 wks
7 Jul 90	**ALRIGHT** A & M USA 693	**20**	5 wks
8 Sep 90	**BLACK CAT** A & M EM 587	**15**	6 wks
27 Oct 90	**LOVE WILL NEVER DO (WITHOUT YOU)** A & M EM 700	**34**	4 wks
15 Aug 92	● **THE BEST THINGS IN LIFE ARE FREE** Perspective PERSS 7400 [1]	**2**	13 wks
8 May 93	● **THAT'S THE WAY LOVE GOES** Virgin VSCDG 1460	**2**	10 wks
31 Jul 93	**IF** Virgin VSCDT 1474	**14**	7 wks
20 Nov 93	**AGAIN** Virgin VSCDG 1481	**6**	11 wks
12 Mar 94	**BECAUSE OF LOVE** Virgin VSCDG 1488	**19**	4 wks
18 Jun 94	**ANY TIME ANY PLACE** Virgin VSCDT 1501	**13**	5 wks
26 Nov 94	**YOU WANT THIS** Virgin VSCDT 1519	**14**	3 wks

[1] Luther Vandross and Janet Jackson with special guests BBD and Ralph Tresvant

See also Herb Alpert.

Jermaine JACKSON
US, male vocalist **43 wks**

10 May 80	● **LET'S GET SERIOUS** Motown TMG 1183	**8**	11 wks
26 Jul 80	**BURNIN' HOT** Motown TMG 1194	**32**	6 wks
30 May 81	**YOU LIKE ME DON'T YOU** Motown TMG 1222	**41**	5 wks
12 May 84	**SWEETEST SWEETEST** Arista JJK 1	**52**	4 wks
27 Oct 84	**WHEN THE RAIN BEGINS TO FALL** Arista ARIST 584 [1]	**68**	2 wks
16 Feb 85	● **DO WHAT YOU DO** Arista ARIST 609	**6**	13 wks
21 Oct 89	**DON'T TAKE IT PERSONAL** Arista 112634	**69**	2 wks

[1] Jermaine Jackson and Pia Zadora

Joe JACKSON
UK, male vocalist **49 wks**

4 Aug 79	**IS SHE REALLY GOING OUT WITH HIM?** A & M AMS 7459	**13**	9 wks
12 Jan 80	● **IT'S DIFFERENT FOR GIRLS** A & M AMS 7493	**5**	9 wks
4 Jul 81	**JUMPIN' JIVE** A & M AMS 8145 [1]	**43**	5 wks

8 Jan 83	● STEPPIN' OUT *A & M AMS 8262*	6	8 wks
12 Mar 83	BREAKING US IN TWO *A & M AM 101*	59	4 wks
28 Apr 84	HAPPY ENDING *A & M AM 186*	58	3 wks
7 Jul 84	BE MY NUMBER TWO *A & M AM 200*	70	2 wks
7 Jun 86	LEFT OF CENTER *A & M AM 320* [2]	32	9 wks

[1] Joe Jackson's Jumpin' Jive [2] Suzanne Vega featuring Joe Jackson

Michael JACKSON *US, male vocalist* — 382 wks

12 Feb 72	● GOT TO BE THERE *Tamla Motown TMG 797*	5	11 wks
20 May 72	● ROCKIN' ROBIN *Tamla Motown TMG 816*	3	14 wks
19 Aug 72	● AIN'T NO SUNSHINE *Tamla Motown TMG 826*	8	11 wks
25 Nov 72	● BEN *Tamla Motown TMG 834*	7	14 wks
18 Nov 78	EASE ON DOWN THE ROAD *MCA 396* [1]	45	4 wks
15 Sep 79	● DON'T STOP TILL YOU GET ENOUGH *Epic EPC 7763*	3	12 wks
24 Nov 79	● OFF THE WALL *Epic EPC 8045*	7	10 wks
9 Feb 80	● ROCK WITH YOU *Epic EPC 8206*	7	9 wks
3 May 80	● SHE'S OUT OF MY LIFE *Epic EPC 8384*	3	9 wks
26 Jul 80	GIRLFRIEND *Epic EPC 8782*	41	5 wks
23 May 81	★ ONE DAY IN YOUR LIFE *Motown TMG 976*	1	14 wks
1 Aug 81	WE'RE ALMOST THERE *Motown TMG 977*	46	4 wks
6 Nov 82	● THE GIRL IS MINE *Epic EPC A 2729* [2]	8	9 wks
15 Jan 83	THE GIRL IS MINE (re-entry) *Epic EPC A 2729* [2]	75	1 wk
29 Jan 83	★ BILLIE JEAN *Epic EPC A 3084*	1	15 wks
9 Apr 83	● BEAT IT *Epic EPC A 3258*	3	12 wks
11 Jun 83	● WANNA BE STARTIN' SOMETHING *Epic A 3427*	8	9 wks
23 Jul 83	HAPPY (LOVE THEME FROM 'LADY SINGS THE BLUES') *Tamla Motown TMG 986*	52	3 wks
15 Oct 83	● SAY SAY SAY *Parlophone R 6062* [3]	2	15 wks
19 Nov 83	● THRILLER *Epic A 3643*	10	18 wks
31 Mar 84	P.Y.T. (PRETTY YOUNG THING) *Epic A 4136*	11	8 wks
2 Jun 84	● FAREWELL MY SUMMER LOVE *Motown TMG 1342*	7	12 wks
11 Aug 84	GIRL YOU'RE SO TOGETHER *Motown TMG 1355*	33	8 wks
8 Aug 87	★ I JUST CAN'T STOP LOVING YOU *Epic 650202 7*	1	10 wks
26 Sep 87	● BAD *Epic 651155 7*	3	11 wks
5 Dec 87	● THE WAY YOU MAKE ME FEEL *Epic 651275 7*	3	10 wks
20 Feb 88	MAN IN THE MIRROR *Epic 651388 7*	21	5 wks
28 May 88	GET IT *Motown ZB 41883* [4]	37	4 wks
16 Jul 88	● DIRTY DIANA *Epic 651546 7*	4	8 wks
10 Sep 88	ANOTHER PART OF ME *Epic 652844 7*	15	6 wks
26 Nov 88	● SMOOTH CRIMINAL *Epic 653026 7*	8	10 wks
25 Feb 89	● LEAVE ME ALONE *Epic 654672 7*	2	9 wks
15 Jul 89	LIBERIAN GIRL *Epic 654947 0*	13	6 wks
23 Nov 91	★ BLACK OR WHITE *Epic 6575987*	1	10 wks
18 Jan 92	BLACK OR WHITE (re-mix) *Epic 6577316*	14	4 wks
15 Feb 92	● REMEMBER THE TIME / COME TOGETHER *Epic 6577747*	3	8 wks
2 May 92	● IN THE CLOSET *Epic 6580187*	8	6 wks
25 Jul 92	● WHO IS IT *Epic 6581797*	10	7 wks
12 Sep 92	JAM *Epic 6583607*	13	5 wks
5 Dec 92	● HEAL THE WORLD *Epic 6584887*	2	15 wks
27 Feb 93	● GIVE IN TO ME *Epic 6590692*	2	9 wks
10 Jul 93	● WILL YOU BE THERE *Epic 6592222*	9	8 wks
18 Dec 93	GONE TOO SOON *Epic 6599762*	33	5 wks

[1] Diana Ross and Michael Jackson [2] Michael Jackson and Paul McCartney [3] Paul McCartney and Michael Jackson [4] Stevie Wonder and Michael Jackson

The sleeve of I Just Can't Stop Loving You credits Siedah Garrett, but the label does not. Come Together only listed from 7 Mar 92. It peaked at position 10.

Mick JACKSON *UK, male vocalist* — 16 wks

30 Sep 78	BLAME IT ON THE BOOGIE *Atlantic K 11102*	15	8 wks
3 Feb 79	WEEKEND *Atlantic K 11224*	38	8 wks

Millie JACKSON *US, female vocalist* — 8 wks

18 Nov 72	MY MAN A SWEET MAN *Mojo 2093 022*	50	1 wk
10 Mar 84	I FEEL LIKE WALKIN' IN THE RAIN *Sire W 9348*	55	2 wks
15 Jun 85	ACT OF WAR *Rocket EJS 8* [1]	32	5 wks

[1] Elton John and Millie Jackson

Stonewall JACKSON *US, male vocalist* — 2 wks

17 Jul 59	WATERLOO *Philips PB 941*	24	2 wks

Tony JACKSON - *See Q*

Tony JACKSON and the VIBRATIONS

UK, male vocal / instrumental group — 3 wks

8 Oct 64	BYE BYE BABY *Pye 7N 15685*	38	3 wks

Wanda JACKSON *US, female vocalist* — 11 wks

1 Sep 60	LET'S HAVE A PARTY *Capitol CL 15147*	32	8 wks
26 Jan 61	MEAN MEAN MAN *Capitol CL 15176*	46	1 wk
9 Feb 61	MEAN MEAN MAN (re-entry) *Capitol CL 15176*	40	2 wks

JACKSON SISTERS *US, female vocal group* — 2 wks

20 Jun 87	I BELIEVE IN MIRACLES *Urban URB 4*	72	2 wks

JACKSONS *US, male vocal group* — 235 wks

31 Jan 70	● I WANT YOU BACK *Tamla Motown TMG 724* [1]	2	13 wks
16 May 70	● ABC *Tamla Motown TMG 738* [1]	8	11 wks
1 Aug 70	● THE LOVE YOU SAVE *Tamla Motown TMG 746* [1]	7	9 wks
21 Nov 70	● I'LL BE THERE *Tamla Motown TMG 758* [1]	4	16 wks
10 Apr 71	MAMA'S PEARL *Tamla Motown TMG 769* [1]	25	7 wks
17 Jul 71	NEVER CAN SAY GOODBYE *Tamla Motown TMG 778* [1]	33	7 wks
11 Nov 72	● LOOKIN' THROUGH THE WINDOWS *Tamla Motown TMG 833* [1]	9	11 wks
23 Dec 72	SANTA CLAUS IS COMING TO TOWN *Tamla Motown TMG 837* [1]	43	3 wks
17 Feb 73	● DOCTOR MY EYES *Tamla Motown TMG 842* [1]	9	10 wks
9 Jun 73	HALLELUJAH DAY *Tamla Motown TMG 856* [1]	20	9 wks
8 Sep 73	SKYWRITER *Tamla Motown TMG 865* [1]	25	8 wks
9 Apr 77	ENJOY YOURSELF *Epic EPC 5063*	42	4 wks
4 Jun 77	★ SHOW YOU THE WAY TO GO *Epic EPC 5266*	1	10 wks
13 Aug 77	DREAMER *Epic EPC 5458*	22	9 wks
5 Nov 77	GOIN' PLACES *Epic EPC 5732*	26	7 wks
11 Feb 78	EVEN THOUGH YOU'VE GONE *Epic EPC 5919*	31	4 wks
23 Sep 78	● BLAME IT ON THE BOOGIE *Epic EPC 6683*	8	12 wks
3 Feb 79	DESTINY *Epic EPC 6983*	39	6 wks
24 Mar 79	● SHAKE YOUR BODY (DOWN TO THE GROUND) *Epic EPC 7181*	4	12 wks
25 Oct 80	LOVELY ONE *Epic EPC 9302*	29	6 wks
13 Dec 80	HEARTBREAK HOTEL *Epic EPC 9391*	44	6 wks
28 Feb 81	● CAN YOU FEEL IT *Epic EPC 9554*	6	15 wks
4 Jul 81	● WALK RIGHT NOW *Epic EPC A 1294*	7	11 wks
7 Jul 84	STATE OF SHOCK *Epic A 4431* [2]	14	8 wks
8 Sep 84	TORTURE *Epic A 4675*	26	6 wks
16 Apr 88	● I WANT YOU BACK (re-mix) *Motown ZB 41913* [3]	8	9 wks
13 May 89	NOTHIN' (THAT COMPARES 2 U) *Epic 654808 7*	33	6 wks

[1] Jackson Five [2] Jacksons, lead vocals Mick Jagger and Michael Jackson [3] Michael Jackson with the Jackson Five

JACKY - *See Jackie LEE*

JADE *US, female vocal group* — 23 wks

20 Mar 93	● DON'T WALK AWAY *Giant W 0160CD*	7	8 wks
3 Jul 93	I WANNA LOVE YOU *Giant 74321151662*	13	7 wks
18 Sep 93	ONE WOMAN *Giant 74321165122*	22	5 wks
5 Feb 94	ALL THRU THE NITE *Giant 74321187552* [1]	32	3 wks

[1] P.O.V. featuring Jade

JADE 4 U - *See Praga KHAN*

JAGGED EDGE *UK, male vocal / instrumental group* — 2 wks

15 Sep 90	YOU DON'T LOVE ME *Polydor PO 97*	66	2 wks

Mick JAGGER *UK, male vocalist* — 42 wks

14 Nov 70	MEMO FROM TURNER *Decca F 13067*	32	5 wks

The **JACKSON FIVE** and brother Randy (second from right) arrive at Heathrow on 29 October, 1972, for the Royal Variety Performance the following evening.

JANET JACKSON attends the premiere of her video for 'When I Think Of You'. (Scott Downie/LFI)

7 Jul 84	**STATE OF SHOCK** *Epic A 4431* [1]	....	**14**	8 wks
16 Feb 85	**JUST ANOTHER NIGHT** *CBS A 4722*	....	**32**	6 wks
7 Sep 85	★ **DANCING IN THE STREET** *EMI America EA 204* [2]	....**1**	12 wks
12 Sep 87	**LET'S WORK** *CBS 651028 7*	....	**31**	7 wks
6 Feb 93	**SWEET THING** *Atlantic A 7410CD*	....	**24**	4 wks

[1] Jacksons, lead vocals Mick Jagger and Michael Jackson [2] David Bowie and Mick Jagger

JAGS UK, *male vocal/instrumental group* — **11 wks**

8 Sep 79	**BACK OF MY HAND** *Island WIP 6501*	....	**17**	10 wks
2 Feb 80	**WOMAN'S WORLD** *Island WIP 6531*	....	**75**	1 wk

J.A.L.N. BAND
UK/Jamaica, male vocal/instrumental group — **17 wks**

11 Sep 76	**DISCO MUSIC/I LIKE IT** *Magnet MAG 73*	......	**21**	9 wks
27 Aug 77	**I GOT TO SING** *Magnet MAG 97*	......	**40**	4 wks
1 Jul 78	**GET UP** *Magnet MAG 118*	....	**53**	4 wks

JAM UK, *male vocal/instrumental group* — **203 wks**

7 May 77	**IN THE CITY** *Polydor 2058 866*	......	**40**	6 wks
23 Jul 77	**ALL AROUND THE WORLD** *Polydor 2058 903*	......	**13**	8 wks
5 Nov 77	**THE MODERN WORLD** *Polydor 2058 945*	......	**36**	4 wks
11 Mar 78	**NEWS OF THE WORLD** *Polydor 2058 995*	......	**27**	5 wks
26 Aug 78	**DAVID WATTS/'A' BOMB IN WARDOUR STREET** *Polydor 2059 054*	......	**25**	8 wks
21 Oct 78	**DOWN IN THE TUBE STATION AT MIDNIGHT** *Polydor POSP 8*	......	**15**	7 wks
17 Mar 79	**STRANGE TOWN** *Polydor POSP 34*	......	**15**	9 wks
25 Aug 79	**WHEN YOU'RE YOUNG** *Polydor POSP 69*	......	**17**	7 wks
3 Nov 79	● **THE ETON RIFLES** *Polydor POSP 83*	......	**3**	12 wks
22 Mar 80	★ **GOING UNDERGROUND/DREAMS OF CHILDREN** *Polydor POSP 113*	......	**1**	9 wks
26 Apr 80	**ALL AROUND THE WORLD (re-entry)** *Polydor 2058 903*	......	**43**	3 wks
26 Apr 80	**DAVID WATTS/'A' BOMB IN WARDOUR STREET (re-entry)** *Polydor 2059 054*	......	**54**	3 wks
26 Apr 80	**IN THE CITY (re-entry)** *Polydor 2058 866*	......	**40**	4 wks
26 Apr 80	**NEWS OF THE WORLD (re-entry)** *Polydor 2058 995*	......	**53**	3 wks
26 Apr 80	**STRANGE TOWN (re-entry)** *Polydor POSP 34*	......	**44**	4 wks
26 Apr 80	**THE MODERN WORLD (re-entry)** *Polydor 2058 945*	......	**52**	3 wks
23 Aug 80	★ **START** *Polydor 2059 266*	......	**1**	8 wks
7 Feb 81	**THAT'S ENTERTAINMENT (IMPORT)** *Metronome 0030 364*	......	**21**	7 wks
6 Jun 81	● **FUNERAL PYRE** *Polydor POSP 257*	......	**4**	6 wks
24 Oct 81	● **ABSOLUTE BEGINNERS** *Polydor POSP 350*	......	**4**	6 wks
13 Feb 82	★ **TOWN CALLED MALICE/PRECIOUS** *Polydor POSP 400*	......	**1**	8 wks
3 Jul 82	● **JUST WHO IS THE FIVE O'CLOCK HERO** *Polydor 2059 504*	......	**8**	5 wks
18 Sep 82	● **THE BITTEREST PILL (I EVER HAD TO SWALLOW)** *Polydor POSP 505*	......	**2**	7 wks
4 Dec 82	★ **BEAT SURRENDER** *Polydor POSP 540*	......	**1**	9 wks
22 Jan 83	**ALL AROUND THE WORLD (2nd re-entry)** *Polydor 2058 903*	......	**38**	4 wks
22 Jan 83	**DAVID WATTS/'A'BOMB IN WARDOUR STREET (2nd re-entry)** *Polydor 2059 054*	......	**50**	4 wks
22 Jan 83	**DOWN IN THE TUBE STATION AT MIDNIGHT (re-entry)** *Polydor POSP 8*	......	**30**	6 wks
22 Jan 83	**GOING UNDERGROUND/DREAMS OF CHILDREN (re-entry)** *Polydor POSP 113*	......	**21**	6 wks
22 Jan 83	**IN THE CITY (2nd re-entry)** *Polydor 2058 866*	......	**47**	4 wks
22 Jan 83	**NEWS OF THE WORLD (2nd re-entry)** *Polydor 2058 995*	......	**39**	4 wks
22 Jan 83	**STRANGE TOWN (2nd re-entry)** *Polydor POSP 34*	..**42**	5 wks
22 Jan 83	**THE MODERN WORLD (2nd re-entry)** *Polydor 2058 945*	......	**51**	4 wks
22 Jan 83	**WHEN YOU'RE YOUNG (re-entry)** *Polydor POSP 69*..**53**		4 wks
29 Jan 83	**THAT'S ENTERTAINMENT (re-issue)** *Polydor POSP 482*	......	**60**	3 wks
5 Feb 83	**START (re-entry)** *Polydor 2059 266*	......	**62**	2 wks

5 Feb 83	**THE ETON RIFLES (re-entry)** *Polydor POSP 83*	......**54**	3 wks
5 Feb 83	**TOWN CALLED MALICE/PRECIOUS (re-entry)** *Polydor POSP 400*	......	**73**	1 wk
29 Jun 91	**THAT'S ENTERTAINMENT (2nd re-issue)** *Polydor PO 155*	......	**57**	2 wks

JAM AND SPOON
Germany, male instrumental/production duo — **10 wks**

2 May 92	**TALES FROM A DANCEOGRAPHIC OCEAN EP** *R & S RSUK 14*	......	**49**	1 wk
6 Jun 92	**THE COMPLETE STELLA (re-mix)** *R & S RSUK 14X* ..**66**		2 wks
26 Feb 94	**RIGHT IN THE NIGHT (FALL IN LOVE WITH MUSIC)** *Epic 6600822* [1]	......	**31**	4 wks
24 Sep 94	**FIND ME (ODYSSEY TO ANYOONA)** *Epic 6608082* [1]	......	**37**	3 wks

[1] Jam and Spoon featuring Plavka

Tracks on Tales From A Danceographic Ocean EP: *Stella/Keep On Movin'/My First Fantastic FF. The Complete Stella is a re-mix of a track from the EP.*

JAM MACHINE *Italy/US, male vocal/instrumental group* — **1 wk**

23 Dec 89	**EVERYDAY** *Deconstruction PB 43299*	......	**68**	1 wk

JAM ON THE MUTHA
UK, male vocal/instrumental group — **2 wks**

11 Aug 90	**HOTEL CALIFORNIA** *M & G MAGS 3*	......	**62**	2 wks

JAM TRONIK
Germany, male/female vocal/instrumental group — **7 wks**

24 Mar 90	**ANOTHER DAY IN PARADISE** *Debut DEBT 3093* **19**		7 wks

JAMES UK, *male vocal/instrumental group* — **51 wks**

12 May 90	**HOW WAS IT FOR YOU** *Fontana JIM 5* **32**		3 wks
7 Jul 90	**COME HOME** *Fontana JIM 6*	......	**32**	4 wks
8 Dec 90	**LOSE CONTROL** *Fontana JIM 7*	......	**38**	5 wks
30 Mar 91	● **SIT DOWN** *Fontana JIM 8*	......	**2**	10 wks
30 Nov 91	● **SOUND** *Fontana JIM 9*	......	**9**	7 wks
1 Feb 92	**BORN OF FRUSTRATION** *Fontana JIM 10*	......	**13**	6 wks
4 Apr 92	**RING THE BELLS** *Fontana JIM 11*	......	**37**	2 wks
18 Jul 92	**SEVEN (EP)** *Fontana JIM 12*	......	**46**	2 wks
11 Sep 93	**SOMETIMES** *Fontana JIMCD 13*	......	**18**	4 wks
13 Nov 93	**LAID** *Fontana JIMCD 14*	......	**25**	4 wks
2 Apr 94	**JAM J/SAY SOMETHING** *Fontana JIMCD 152* **24**		4 wks

Tracks on Seven (EP): *Seven/Goalie's Ball/William Burroughs/Still Alive. Say Something only listed with Jam J for first two weeks of record's run.*

Dick JAMES UK, *male vocalist* — **13 wks**

20 Jan 56	**ROBIN HOOD** *Parlophone R 4117*	......	**14**	8 wks
18 May 56	**ROBIN HOOD/BALLAD OF DAVY CROCKETT (re-entry)** *Parlophone R 4117*	......	**29**	1 wk
11 Jan 57	**GARDEN OF EDEN** *Parlophone R 4255*	......	**18**	4 wks

Robin Hood is with Stephen James and his Chums.

Freddie JAMES *Canada, male vocalist* — **3 wks**

24 Nov 79	**GET UP AND BOOGIE** *Warner Bros. K 17478* **54**		3 wks

Jimmy JAMES and the VAGABONDS
UK, male vocal/instrumental group — **25 wks**

11 Sep 68	**RED RED WINE** *Pye 7N 17579*	......	**36**	8 wks

24 Apr 76	I'LL GO WHERE YOUR MUSIC TAKES ME		
	Pye 7N 45585	**23**	8 wks
17 Jul 76	● NOW IS THE TIME *Pye 7N 45606*	**5**	9 wks

Joni JAMES US, female vocalist   **2 wks**

| 6 Mar 53 | WHY DON'T YOU BELIEVE ME *MGM 582* | **11** | 1 wk |
| 30 Jan 59 | THERE MUST BE A WAY *MGM 1002* | **24** | 1 wk |

Rick JAMES US, male vocalist   **30 wks**

8 Jul 78	YOU AND I *Motown TMG 1110*	**46**	7 wks
7 Jul 79	I'M A SUCKER FOR YOUR LOVE		
	Motown TMG 1146 1	**43**	8 wks
6 Sep 80	BIG TIME *Motown TMG 1198*	**41**	6 wks
4 Jul 81	GIVE IT TO ME BABY *Motown TMG 1229*	**47**	3 wks
12 Jun 82	STANDING ON THE TOP (PART 1)		
	Motown TMG 1263 2	**53**	3 wks
3 Jul 82	DANCE WIT' ME *Motown TMG 1266*	**53**	3 wks

1 Teena Marie, co-lead vocals Rick James 2 Temptations featuring Rick James

Sonny JAMES US, male vocalist   **8 wks**

| 30 Nov 56 | THE CAT CAME BACK *Capitol CL 14635* | **30** | 1 wk |
| 8 Feb 57 | YOUNG LOVE *Capitol CL 14683* | **11** | 7 wks |

Tommy JAMES and the SHONDELLS
US, male vocal / instrumental group   **25 wks**

| 21 Jul 66 | HANKY PANKY *Roulette RK 7000* | **38** | 7 wks |
| 5 Jun 68 | ★ MONY MONY *Major Minor MM 567* | **1** | 18 wks |

Wendy JAMES UK, female vocalist   **4 wks**

| 20 Feb 93 | THE NAMELESS ONE *MCA MCSTD 1732* | **34** | 3 wks |
| 17 Apr 93 | LONDON'S BRILLIANT *MCA MCSTD 1763* | **62** | 1 wk |

JAMES BOYS UK, male vocal duo   **6 wks**

| 19 May 73 | OVER AND OVER *Penny Farthing PEN 806* | **39** | 6 wks |

JAMESTOWN - *See Jocelyn BROWN*

JAMIROQUAI UK, male vocal / instrumental group   **34 wks**

31 Oct 92	WHEN YOU GONNA LEARN *Acid Jazz JAZID 46T*	**52**	2 wks
20 Feb 93	WHEN YOU GONNA LEARN (re-entry)		
	Acid Jazz JAZID 46	**69**	1 wk
13 Mar 93	● TOO YOUNG TO DIE *Sony S2 6590112*	**12**	6 wks
5 Jun 93	BLOW YOUR MIND *Sony S2 6592972*	**10**	7 wks
14 Aug 93	EMERGENCY ON PLANET EARTH		
	Sony S2 6595782	**32**	3 wks
25 Sep 93	WHEN YOU GONNA LEARN (re-issue)		
	Sony S2 6596952	**28**	3 wks
8 Oct 94	SPACE COWBOY *Sony S2 6608512*	**17**	5 wks
19 Nov 94	HALF THE MAN *Sony S2 6610032*	**15†**	7 wks

JAMMERS US, male vocal / instrumental group   **2 wks**

| 29 Jan 83 | BE MINE TONIGHT *Salsoul SAL 101* | **65** | 2 wks |

JAN and DEAN US, male vocal duo   **18 wks**

| 24 Aug 61 | HEART AND SOUL *London HLH 9395* | **24** | 8 wks |
| 15 Aug 63 | SURF CITY *Liberty LIB 55580* | **26** | 10 wks |

JAN and KJELD Denmark, male vocal duo   **4 wks**

| 21 Jul 60 | BANJO BOY *Ember S 101* | **36** | 4 wks |

JANE'S ADDICTION
US, male vocal / instrumental group   **4 wks**

| 23 Mar 91 | BEEN CAUGHT STEALING *Warner Bros. W 0011* | **34** | 3 wks |
| 1 Jun 91 | CLASSIC GIRL *Warner Bros. W 0031* | **60** | 1 wk |

Horst JANKOWSKI
Germany, male instrumentalist - piano   **18 wks**

| 29 Jul 65 | ● A WALK IN THE BLACK FOREST *Mercury MF 861* | **3** | 18 wks |

Samantha JANUS UK, female vocalist   **3 wks**

| 11 May 91 | A MESSAGE TO YOUR HEART | | |
| | *Hollywood HWD 104* | **30** | 3 wks |

Philip JAP UK, male vocalist   **8 wks**

| 31 Jul 82 | SAVE US *A & M AMS 8217* | **53** | 4 wks |
| 25 Sep 82 | TOTAL ERASURE *A & M JAP 1* | **41** | 4 wks |

JAPAN UK, male vocal / instrumental group   **81 wks**

18 Oct 80	GENTLEMEN TAKE POLAROIDS *Virgin VS 379*	**60**	2 wks
9 May 81	THE ART OF PARTIES *Virgin VS 409*	**48**	5 wks
19 Sep 81	QUIET LIFE *Hansa HANSA 6*	**19**	9 wks
7 Nov 81	VISIONS OF CHINA *Virgin VS 436*	**32**	12 wks
23 Jan 82	EUROPEAN SON *Hansa HANSA 10*	**31**	6 wks
20 Mar 82	● GHOSTS *Virgin VS 472*	**5**	8 wks
22 May 82	CANTONESE BOY *Virgin VS 502*	**24**	6 wks
3 Jul 82	● I SECOND THAT EMOTION *Hansa HANSA 12*	**9**	11 wks
9 Oct 82	LIFE IN TOKYO *Hansa HANSA 17*	**28**	6 wks
20 Nov 82	NIGHT PORTER *Virgin VS 554*	**29**	9 wks
12 Mar 83	ALL TOMORROW'S PARTIES *Hansa HANSA 18*	**38**	4 wks
21 May 83	CANTON (LIVE) *Virgin VS 581*	**42**	3 wks

See also Rain Tree Crow

Jean-Michel JARRE
France, male instrumentalist / producer   **28 wks**

27 Aug 77	● OXYGENE PART IV *Polydor 2001 721*	**4**	9 wks
20 Jan 79	EQUINOXE PART 5 *Polydor POSP 20*	**45**	5 wks
23 Aug 86	FOURTH RENDEZ-VOUS *Polydor POSP 788*	**65**	4 wks
5 Nov 88	REVOLUTIONS *Polydor PO 25*	**52**	6 wks
7 Jan 89	LONDON KID *Polydor PO 32* 1	**52**	3 wks
7 Oct 89	OXYGENE PART IV (re-mix) *Polydor PO 55*	**65**	2 wks
26 Jun 93	CHRONOLOGIE PART 4 *Polydor POCS 274*	**55**	2 wks
30 Oct 93	CHRONOLOGIE PART 4 (re-mix)		
	Polydor POCS 274	**56**	1 wk

1 Jean-Michel Jarre featuring Hank Marvin

Al JARREAU US, male vocalist   **30 wks**

26 Sep 81	WE'RE IN THIS LOVE TOGETHER		
	Warner Bros. K 17849	**55**	4 wks
14 May 83	MORNIN' *WEA U9929*	**28**	6 wks
16 Jul 83	TROUBLE IN PARADISE *WEA International U 9871*	**36**	5 wks
24 Sep 83	BOOGIE DOWN *WEA U 9814*	**63**	3 wks
16 Nov 85	DAY BY DAY *Polydor POSP 770* 1	**53**	3 wks
5 Apr 86	THE MUSIC OF GOODBYE (LOVE THEME		
	FROM 'OUT OF AFRICA') *MCA MCA 1038* 2	**75**	1 wk
7 Mar 87	● 'MOONLIGHTING' THEME *WEA U 8407*	**8**	8 wks

1 Shakatak with Al Jarreau 2 Melissa Manchester and Al Jarreau

Kenny 'Jammin' JASON - *See DJ 'FAST' EDDIE*

JAVELLS featuring Nosmo KING
UK, male / female vocal group   **8 wks**

| 9 Nov 74 | GOODBYE NOTHING TO SAY | | |
| | *Pye Disco Demand DDS 2003* | **26** | 8 wks |

Peter JAY and the JAYWALKERS
UK, male instrumental group, Peter Jay - drums **11 wks**

8 Nov 62	**CAN CAN 62** Decca F 11531	31	11 wks

JAZZ and the BROTHERS GRIMM
UK, male vocal / instrumental group **2 wks**

9 Jul 88	**(LET'S ALL GO BACK) DISCO NIGHTS** Ensign ENY 616	57	2 wks

JAZZY JEFF and the FRESH PRINCE
US, male vocal / instrumental rap duo **45 wks**

4 Oct 86	**GIRLS AIN'T NOTHING BUT TROUBLE** Champion CHAMP 18 [1]	21	8 wks
3 Aug 91 ●	**SUMMERTIME** Jive JIVE 279 [1]	8	8 wks
9 Nov 91	**RING MY BELL** Jive JIVE 288 [1]	53	2 wks
11 Sep 93 ★	**BOOM! SHAKE THE ROOM** Jive JIVECD 335	1	13 wks
20 Nov 93	**I'M LOOKING FOR THE ONE (TO BE WITH ME)** Jive JIVECD 345	24	4 wks
19 Feb 94	**CAN'T WAIT TO BE WITH YOU** Jive JIVECD 348	29	4 wks
4 Jun 94	**TWINKLE TWINKLE (I'M NOT A STAR)** Jive JIVECD 354	62	2 wks
6 Aug 94	**SUMMERTIME (re-entry)** Jive JIVECD 279	29	4 wks

[1] DJ Jazzy Jeff and the Fresh Prince

JB's ALL STARS
UK, male / female vocal / instrumental group **4 wks**

11 Feb 84	**BACKFIELD IN MOTION** RCA Victor RCA 384	48	4 wks

J.C. 001 *UK, male rapper* **4 wks**

24 Apr 93	**NEVER AGAIN** Anxious ANX 1012CD	67	2 wks
26 Jun 93	**CUPID** Anxious ANX 1014CD	56	2 wks

JEFFERSON *UK, male vocalist* **8 wks**

9 Apr 69	**COLOUR OF MY LOVE** Pye 7N 17706	22	8 wks

JEFFERSON STARSHIP - See STARSHIP

Garland JEFFREYS *US, male vocalist* **1 wk**

8 Feb 92	**HAIL HAIL ROCK 'N' ROLL** RCA PB 49171	72	1 wk

Garland JELLYBEAN *US, male producer* **47 wks**

1 Feb 86	**SIDEWALK TALK** EMI America EA 210 [1]	47	4 wks
26 Sep 87	**THE REAL THING** Chrysalis CHS 3167 [2]	13	10 wks
28 Nov 87 ●	**WHO FOUND WHO** Chrysalis CHS JEL 1 [3]	10	10 wks
12 Dec 87	**JINGO** Chrysalis JEL 2	12	10 wks
12 Mar 88	**JUST A MIRAGE** Chrysalis JEL 3 [4]	13	10 wks
20 Aug 88	**COMING BACK FOR MORE** Chrysalis JEL 4 [5]	41	3 wks

[1] Jellybean featuring Catherine Buchanan [2] Jellybean featuring Steven Dante [3] Jellybean featuring Elisa Fiorillo [4] Jellybean featuring Adele Bertei [5] Jellybean featuring Richard Darbyshire

JELLYFISH *US, male vocal / instrumental group* **20 wks**

26 Jan 91	**THE KING IS HALF UNDRESSED** Charisma CUSS 1	39	6 wks
27 Apr 91	**BABY'S COMING BACK** Charisma CUSS 2	51	4 wks
3 Aug 91	**THE SCARY-GO-ROUND EP** Charisma CUSS 3	49	3 wks
26 Oct 91	**I WANNA STAY HOME** Charisma CUSS 4	59	2 wks
1 May 93	**THE GHOST AT NUMBER ONE** Charisma CUSDG 10	43	3 wks
17 Jul 93	**NEW MISTAKE** Charisma CUSDG 11	55	2 wks

Tracks on The Scary-Go-Round EP: Now She Knows She's Wrong / Bedspring Kiss / She Still Loves Him (Live) / Baby's Coming Back (Live).

JESUS AND MARY CHAIN
UK, male vocal / instrumental group **55 wks**

2 Mar 85	**NEVER UNDERSTAND** blanco y negro NEG 8	47	4 wks
8 Jun 85	**YOU TRIP ME UP** blanco y negro NEG 13	55	3 wks
12 Oct 85	**JUST LIKE HONEY** blanco y negro NEG 17	45	3 wks
26 Jul 86	**SOME CANDY TALKING** blanco y negro NEG 19	13	5 wks
2 May 87 ●	**APRIL SKIES** blanco y negro NEG 24	8	6 wks
15 Aug 87	**HAPPY WHEN IT RAINS** blanco y negro NEG 25	25	5 wks
7 Nov 87	**DARKLANDS** blanco y negro NEG 29	33	4 wks
9 Apr 88	**SIDEWALKING** blanco y negro NEG 32	30	3 wks
23 Sep 89	**BLUES FROM A GUN** blanco y negro NEG 41	32	2 wks
18 Nov 89	**HEAD ON** blanco y negro NEG 42	57	2 wks
8 Sep 90	**ROLLERCOASTER (EP)** blanco y negro NEG 45	46	2 wks
15 Feb 92 ●	**REVERENCE** blanco y negro NEG 55	10	4 wks
14 Mar 92	**FAR GONE AND OUT** blanco y negro NEG 56	23	3 wks
4 Jul 92	**ALMOST GOLD** blanco y negro NEG 57	41	2 wks
10 Jul 93	**SOUND OF SPEED (EP)** blanco y negro NEG 66CD	30	2 wks
30 Jul 94	**SOMETIMES ALWAYS** blanco y negro NEG 70CD	22	3 wks
22 Oct 94	**COME ON** blanco y negro NEG 73CD1	52	2 wks

Tracks on Rollercoaster (EP): Rollercoaster / Silverblade / Lowlife / Tower Of Song. Tracks on Sound Of Speed EP: Snakedriver / Something I Can't Have / Write Record Release Blues / Little Red Rooster.

JESUS JONES *UK, male vocal / instrumental group* **50 wks**

25 Feb 89	**INFO-FREAKO** Food FOOD 18	42	3 wks
8 Jul 89	**NEVER ENOUGH** Food FOOD 21	42	3 wks
23 Sep 89	**BRING IT ON DOWN** Food FOOD 22	46	3 wks
7 Apr 90	**REAL REAL REAL** Food FOOD 24	19	8 wks
6 Oct 90	**RIGHT HERE RIGHT NOW** Food FOOD 25	31	4 wks
12 Jan 91 ●	**INTERNATIONAL BRIGHT YOUNG THING** Food FOOD 27	7	7 wks
2 Mar 91	**WHO WHERE WHY** Food FOOD 28	21	7 wks
20 Jul 91	**RIGHT HERE RIGHT NOW (re-issue)** Food FOOD 30	31	4 wks
9 Jan 93 ●	**THE DEVIL YOU KNOW** Food CDPERV 1	10	5 wks
10 Apr 93	**THE RIGHT DECISION** Food CDPERV 2	36	3 wks
10 Jul 93	**ZEROES & ONES** Food CDFOODS 44	30	3 wks

See also Various Artists (EPs & LPs) - The Food Christmas EP.

JESUS LIZARD *US, male vocal / instrumental group* **2 wks**

6 Mar 93	**PUSS** Touch And Go TG 83CD	12	2 wks

The listed flip side of Puss was Oh, The Guilt by Nirvana.

JESUS LOVES YOU *UK, male vocalist - Boy George* **18 wks**

11 Nov 89	**AFTER THE LOVE** More Protein PROT 2	68	1 wk
23 Feb 91	**BOW DOWN MISTER** More Protein PROT 8	27	8 wks
8 Jun 91	**GENERATIONS OF LOVE** More Protein PROT 10	35	8 wks
12 Dec 92	**SWEET TOXIC LOVE** Virgin VS 1449	65	1 wk

JETHRO TULL *UK, male vocal / instrumental group* **68 wks**

1 Jan 69	**LOVE STORY** Island WIP 6048	29	8 wks
14 May 69 ●	**LIVING IN THE PAST** Island WIP 6056	3	14 wks
1 Nov 69 ●	**SWEET DREAM** Chrysalis WIP 6070	7	11 wks
24 Jan 70 ●	**TEACHER / THE WITCH'S PROMISE** Chrysalis WIP 6077	4	9 wks
18 Sep 71	**LIFE IS A LONG SONG / UP THE POOL** Chrysalis WIP 6106	11	8 wks
11 Dec 76	**RING OUT SOLSTICE BELLS (EP)** Chrysalis CXP 2	28	6 wks
15 Sep 84	**LAP OF LUXURY** Chrysalis TULL 1	70	2 wks
16 Jan 88	**SAID SHE WAS A DANCER** Chrysalis TULL 4	55	4 wks
21 Mar 92	**ROCKS ON THE ROAD** Chrysalis TULLX 7	47	3 wks
22 May 93	**LIVING IN THE (SLIGHTLY MORE RECENT) PAST** Chrysalis CDCHSS 3970	32	3 wks

Tracks on Ring Out Solstice Bells (EP): Ring Out Solstice Bells / March the Mad Scientist / The Christmas Song / Pan Dance. Living In The (Slightly More Recent) Past is a live version of the original.

JETS UK, male vocal / instrumental group — **38 wks**

22 Aug 81	SUGAR DOLL EMI 5211	55	3 wks
31 Oct 81	YES TONIGHT JOSEPHINE EMI 5247	25	11 wks
6 Feb 82	LOVE MAKES THE WORLD GO ROUND EMI 5262	21	9 wks
24 Apr 82	THE HONEYDRIPPER EMI 5289	58	3 wks
9 Oct 82	SOMEBODY TO LOVE EMI 5342	56	3 wks
6 Aug 83	BLUE SKIES EMI 5405	53	3 wks
17 Dec 83	ROCKIN' AROUND THE CHRISTMAS TREE PRT 7P 297	62	4 wks
13 Oct 84	PARTY DOLL PRT JETS 2	72	2 wks

JETS US, male / female vocal / instrumental group — **19 wks**

31 Jan 87	● CRUSH ON YOU MCA MCA 1048	5	13 wks
25 Apr 87	CURIOSITY MCA MCA 1119	41	4 wks
28 May 88	ROCKET 2 U MCA MCA 1226	69	2 wks

Joan JETT and the BLACKHEARTS
US, female vocalist with male vocal / instrumental group — **21 wks**

24 Apr 82	● I LOVE ROCK 'N' ROLL Epic EPC A 2087	4	10 wks
10 Jul 82	CRIMSON AND CLOVER Epic EPC A 2485	60	3 wks
20 Aug 88	I HATE MYSELF FOR LOVING YOU London LON 195	46	6 wks
31 Mar 90	DIRTY DEEDS Chrysalis CHS 3518 [1]	69	1 wk
19 Feb 94	I LOVE ROCK & ROLL (RE-ISSUE) Reprise W 0232CD	75	1 wk

[1] Joan Jett

JIGSAW UK, male vocal / instrumental group — **16 wks**

1 Nov 75	● SKY HIGH Splash CP1 1	9	11 wks
6 Aug 77	IF I HAVE TO GO AWAY Splash CP 11	36	5 wks

JILTED JOHN UK, male vocalist — **12 wks**

12 Aug 78	● JILTED JOHN EMI International INT 567	4	12 wks

JIMMY THE HOOVER
UK, male / female vocal / instrumental group — **8 wks**

25 Jun 83	TANTALISE (WO WO EE YEH YEH) Innervision A 3406	18	8 wks

JINGLE BELLES US / UK, female vocal group — **4 wks**

17 Dec 83	CHRISTMAS SPECTRE Passion PASH 14	37	4 wks

JINNY Italy, female vocalist — **4 wks**

29 Jun 91	KEEP WARM Virgin VS 1356	68	3 wks
22 May 93	FEEL THE RHYTHM Logic 401633001022	74	1 wk

JIVE BUNNY and the MASTERMIXERS
UK, male production / mixing group — **68 wks**

15 Jul 89	★ SWING THE MOOD Music Factory Dance MFD 001	1	19 wks
14 Oct 89	★ THAT'S WHAT I LIKE Music Factory Dance MFD 002	1	12 wks
16 Dec 89	★ LET'S PARTY Music Factory Dance MFD 003	1	6 wks
17 Mar 90	● THAT SOUNDS GOOD TO ME Music Factory Dance MFD 004	4	6 wks
25 Aug 90	● CAN CAN YOU PARTY Music Factory Dance MFD 007	8	6 wks
17 Nov 90	LET'S SWING AGAIN Music Factory Dance MFD 009	19	5 wks
22 Dec 90	THE CRAZY PARTY MIXES Music Factory Dance MFD 010	13	5 wks
23 Mar 91	OVER TO YOU JOHN (HERE WE GO AGAIN) Music Factory Dance MFD 012	28	5 wks
20 Jul 91	HOT SUMMER SALSA Music Factory Dance MFD 013	43	2 wks
23 Nov 91	ROCK 'N' ROLL DANCE PARTY Music Factory Dance MFD 015	48	2 wks

See also Liz Kershaw and Bruno Brookes.

JJ UK, male / female vocal / instumental duo — **3 wks**

9 Feb 91	IF THIS IS LOVE Columbia 6566097	55	3 wks

JKD BAND UK, male vocal / instrumental group — **4 wks**

1 Jul 78	DRAGON POWER Satril SAT 132	58	4 wks

J.M.D - See Tyree

J.M. SILK US, male vocal / instrumental duo — **6 wks**

25 Oct 86	I CAN'T TURN AROUND RCA PB 49793	62	3 wks
7 Mar 87	LET THE MUSIC TAKE CONTROL RCA PB 49767	47	3 wks

JO BOXERS UK, male vocal / instrumental group — **33 wks**

19 Feb 83	● BOXER BEAT RCA BOXX 1	3	15 wks
21 May 83	● JUST GOT LUCKY RCA BOXX 2	7	9 wks
13 Aug 83	JOHNNY FRIENDLY RCA BOXX 3	31	8 wks
12 Nov 83	JEALOUS LOVE RCA BOXX 4	72	1 wk

JO JO GUNNE US, male vocal / instrumental group — **12 wks**

25 Mar 72	● RUN RUN RUN Asylum AYM 501	6	12 wks

JOAN COLLINS FAN CLUB
UK, male vocalist - Julian Clary — **3 wks**

18 Jun 88	LEADER OF THE PACK 10 TEN 227	60	3 wks

John Paul JOANS UK, male vocalist — **7 wks**

19 Dec 70	MAN FROM NAZARETH RAK 107	41	3 wks
16 Jan 71	MAN FROM NAZARETH (re-entry) RAK 107	25	4 wks

JOCKMASTER B.A. - See MAD JOCKS featuring JOCKMASTER B.A.

JOCKO US, male vocalist — **3 wks**

23 Feb 80	RHYTHM TALK Philadelphia International PIR 8222	56	3 wks

JODECI US, male vocal group — **6 wks**

16 Jan 93	CHERISH MCA MCSTD 1726	56	2 wks
11 Dec 93	CRY FOR YOU MCA MCSTD 1951	56	1 wk
16 Jul 94	FEENIN' MCA MCSTD 1984	18	3 wks

JOE US, male vocalist — **7 wks**

22 Jan 94	I'M IN LUV Mercury JOECD 1	22	4 wks
25 Jun 94	THE ONE FOR ME Mercury JOECD 2	34	2 wks
22 Oct 94	ALL OR NOTHING Mercury JOECD 3	56	1 wk

JOE PUBLIC US, male rap group — **5 wks**

11 Jul 92	LIVE AND LEARN Columbia 6575267	43	4 wks
28 Nov 92	I'VE BEEN WATCHIN' Columbia 6587657	75	1 wk

Billy JOEL US, male vocalist / instrumentalist - piano — **146 wks**

11 Feb 78	JUST THE WAY YOU ARE CBS 5872	19	9 wks
24 Jun 78	MOVIN' OUT (ANTHONY'S SONG) CBS 6412	35	6 wks
2 Dec 78	MY LIFE CBS 6821	12	15 wks
28 Apr 79	UNTIL THE NIGHT CBS 7242	50	3 wks

Little did the young **ELTON JOHN** know that in addition to his historic solo career he would have more duet partners than any other chart artist. (LFI)

12 Apr 80	ALL FOR LEYNA *CBS 8325* **40**	4 wks
9 Aug 80	IT'S STILL ROCK AND ROLL TO ME *CBS 8753* **14**	11 wks
15 Oct 83	★ UPTOWN GIRL *CBS A 3775* **1**	17 wks
10 Dec 83	● TELL HER ABOUT IT *CBS A 3655* **4**	10 wks
18 Feb 84	● AN INNOCENT MAN *CBS A 4142* **8**	10 wks
28 Apr 84	THE LONGEST TIME *CBS A 4280* **25**	8 wks
23 Jun 84	LEAVE A TENDER MOMENT ALONE / GOODNIGHT SAIGON *CBS A 4521* **29**	7 wks
22 Feb 86	SHE'S ALWAYS A WOMAN / JUST THE WAY YOU ARE (re-issue) *CBS A 6862* **53**	1 wk
20 Sep 86	A MATTER OF TRUST *CBS 650057 7* **52**	4 wks
30 Sep 89	● WE DIDN'T START THE FIRE *CBS JOEL 1* **7**	10 wks
16 Dec 89	LENINGRAD *CBS JOEL 3* **53**	4 wks
10 Mar 90	I GO TO EXTREMES *CBS JOEL 2* **70**	2 wks
29 Aug 92	ALL SHOOK UP *Columbia 6583437* **27**	4 wks
31 Jul 93	● THE RIVER OF DREAMS *Columbia 6595432* **3**	14 wks
23 Oct 93	ALL ABOUT SOUL *Columbia 6597362* **32**	4 wks
26 Feb 94	NO MAN'S LAND *Columbia 6599202* **50**	3 wks

Goodnight Saigon only listed from 30 Jun 84.

Elton JOHN *UK, male vocalist / instrumentalist - piano* **508 wks**

23 Jan 71	● YOUR SONG *DJM DJS 233* **7**	12 wks
22 Apr 72	● ROCKET MAN *DJM DJX 501* **2**	13 wks
9 Sep 72	HONKY CAT *DJM DJS* **31**	6 wks
4 Nov 72	● CROCODILE ROCK *DJM DJS 271* **5**	14 wks
20 Jan 73	● DANIEL *DJM DJS 275* **4**	10 wks
7 Jul 73	● SATURDAY NIGHT'S ALRIGHT FOR FIGHTING *DJM DJX 502* **7**	9 wks
29 Sep 73	● GOODBYE YELLOW BRICK ROAD *DJM DJS 285* ..**6**	16 wks
8 Dec 73	STEP INTO CHRISTMAS *DJM DJS 290* **24**	7 wks
2 Mar 74	CANDLE IN THE WIND *DJM DJS 297* **11**	9 wks
1 Jun 74	DON'T LET THE SUN GO DOWN ON ME *DJM DJS 302* **16**	8 wks
14 Sep 74	THE BITCH IS BACK *DJM DJS 322* **15**	7 wks
23 Nov 74	● LUCY IN THE SKY WITH DIAMONDS *DJM DJS 340*..**10**	10 wks
8 Mar 75	PHILADELPHIA FREEDOM *DJM DJS 354* [1] **12**	9 wks
28 Jun 75	SOMEONE SAVED MY LIFE TONIGHT *DJM DJS 385* **22**	5 wks
4 Oct 75	ISLAND GIRL *DJM DJS 610* **14**	8 wks
20 Mar 76	● PINBALL WIZARD *DJM DJS 652* **7**	7 wks
3 Jul 76	★ DON'T GO BREAKING MY HEART *Rocket ROKN 512* [2] **1**	14 wks
25 Sep 76	BENNIE AND THE JETS *DJM DJS 10705* **37**	5 wks
13 Nov 76	SORRY SEEMS TO BE THE HARDEST WORD *Rocket ROKN 517* **11**	10 wks
26 Feb 77	CRAZY WATER *Rocket ROKN 521* **27**	6 wks
11 Jun 77	BITE YOUR LIP (GET UP AND DANCE) *Rocket ROKN 526* **28**	4 wks
15 Apr 78	EGO *Rocket ROKN 538* **34**	6 wks
21 Oct 78	PART TIME LOVE *Rocket XPRES 1* **15**	13 wks
16 Dec 78	SONG FOR GUY *Rocket XPRES 5* **4**	10 wks
12 May 79	ARE YOU READY FOR LOVE *Rocket XPRES 13* ..**42**	6 wks
24 May 80	LITTLE JEANNIE *Rocket XPRES 32* **33**	7 wks
23 Aug 80	SARTORIAL ELOQUENCE *Rocket XPRES 41* **44**	5 wks
21 Mar 81	I SAW HER STANDING THERE [3] *DJM DJS 10965* ..**40**	4 wks
23 May 81	NOBODY WINS *Rocket XPRES 54* **42**	5 wks
27 Mar 82	● BLUE EYES *Rocket XPRES 71* **8**	10 wks
12 Jun 82	EMPTY GARDEN *Rocket XPRES 77* **51**	4 wks
30 Apr 83	● I GUESS THAT'S WHY THEY CALL IT THE BLUES *Rocket XPRES 91* **5**	15 wks
30 Jul 83	● I'M STILL STANDING *Rocket EJS 1* **4**	11 wks
15 Oct 83	KISS THE BRIDE *Rocket EJS 2* **20**	7 wks
10 Dec 83	COLD AS CHRISTMAS *Rocket EJS 3* **33**	6 wks
26 May 84	SAD SONGS (SAY SO MUCH) *Rocket PH 7* **7**	12 wks
11 Aug 84	● PASSENGERS *Rocket EJS 5* **5**	11 wks
20 Oct 84	WHO WEARS THESE SHOES *Rocket EJS 6* **50**	3 wks
2 Mar 85	BREAKING HEARTS (AIN'T WHAT IT USED TO BE) *Rocket EJS 7* **59**	3 wks
15 Jun 85	ACT OF WAR *Rocket EJS 8* [4] **32**	5 wks
12 Oct 85	● NIKITA *Rocket EJS 9* **3**	13 wks
9 Nov 85	THAT'S WHAT FRIENDS ARE FOR *Arista ARIST 638* [5] **16**	9 wks
7 Dec 85	WRAP HER UP *Rocket EJS 10* **12**	10 wks
1 Mar 86	CRY TO HEAVEN *Rocket EJS 11* **47**	4 wks
4 Oct 86	HEARTACHE ALL OVER THE WORLD *Rocket EJS 12* **45**	4 wks
29 Nov 86	SLOW RIVERS *Rocket EJS 13* [6] **44**	8 wks
20 Jun 87	FLAMES OF PARADISE *CBS 6508657* [7] **59**	3 wks
16 Jan 88	CANDLE IN THE WIND *Rocket EJS 15* **5**	11 wks
4 Jun 88	I DON'T WANNA GO ON WITH YOU LIKE THAT *Rocket EJS 16* **30**	8 wks
3 Sep 88	TOWN OF PLENTY *Rocket EJS 17* **74**	1 wk
6 May 89	THROUGH THE STORM *Arista 112185* [8] **41**	3 wks
26 Aug 89	HEALING HANDS *Rocket EJS 19* **45**	5 wks
4 Nov 89	SACRIFICE *Rocket EJS 20* **55**	3 wks
9 Jun 90	★ SACRIFICE / HEALING HANDS (re-issues) *Rocket EJS 22* **1**	15 wks
18 Aug 90	CLUB AT THE END OF THE STREET / WHISPERS *Rocket EJS 23* **47**	3 wks
20 Oct 90	YOU GOTTA LOVE SOMEONE *Rocket EJS 24* ...**33**	4 wks
15 Dec 90	EASIER TO WALK AWAY *Rocket EJS 25* **67**	1 wk
29 Dec 90	EASIER TO WALK AWAY (re-entry) *Rocket EJS 25*..**63**	1 wk
7 Dec 91	★ DON'T LET THE SUN GO DOWN ON ME *Epic 6576467* [9] **1**	10 wks
6 Jun 92	● THE ONE *Rocket EJS 28* **10**	8 wks
1 Aug 92	RUNAWAY TRAIN *Rocket EJS 29* [10] **31**	4 wks
7 Nov 92	THE LAST SONG *Rocket EJS 30* **21**	4 wks
22 May 93	SIMPLE LIFE *Rocket EJSCD 31* **44**	2 wks
20 Nov 93	● TRUE LOVE *Rocket EJSCX 32* [2] **2**	10 wks
26 Feb 94	● DON'T GO BREAKING MY HEART *Rocket EJCD 33* [11] **7**	7 wks
14 May 94	AIN'T NOTHING LIKE THE REAL THING *London LONCD 350* [12] **24**	4 wks
9 Jul 94	CAN YOU FEEL THE LOVE TONIGHT *Mercury EJCD 34* **14**	9 wks
8 Oct 94	CIRCLE OF LIFE *Rocket EJSCD 35* **11**	12 wks

[1] Elton John Band [2] Elton John and Kiki Dee [3] Elton John Band featuring John Lennon and the Muscle Shoals Horns [4] Elton John and Millie Jackson [5] Dionne Warwick and Friends featuring Elton John, Stevie Wonder and Gladys Knight [6] Elton John and Cliff Richard [7] Jennifer Rush and Elton John [8] Aretha Franklin and Elton John [9] George Michael and Elton John [10] Elton John and Eric Clapton [11] Elton John with RuPaul [12] Marcella Detroit and Elton John

Bite Your Lip (Get Up And Dance) was one side of a double-sided chart entry, the other being Chicago by Kiki Dee. Wrap Her Up features George Michael as uncredited co-vocalist. The 1988 version of Candle In The Wind was a live recording.

Robert JOHN *US, male vocalist* **13 wks**

17 Jul 68	IF YOU DON'T WANT MY LOVE *CBS 3436* **42**	5 wks
20 Oct 79	SAD EYES *EMI American EA 101* **31**	8 wks

JOHNNY and CHARLEY *Spain, male vocal duo* **1 wk**

14 Oct 65	LA YENKA *Pye International 7N 25326* **49**	1 wk

JOHNNY HATES JAZZ
UK, male vocal / instrumental group **45 wks**

11 Apr 87	● SHATTERED DREAMS *Virgin VS 948* **5**	14 wks
29 Aug 87	I DON'T WANT TO BE A HERO *Virgin VS 1000* ...**11**	10 wks
21 Nov 87	TURN BACK THE CLOCK *Virgin VS 1017* **12**	11 wks
27 Feb 88	HEART OF GOLD *Virgin VS 1045* **19**	7 wks
9 Jul 88	DON'T SAY IT'S LOVE *Virgin VS 1081* **48**	3 wks

JOHNNY and the HURRICANES
US, male instrumental group **88 wks**

9 Oct 59	● RED RIVER ROCK *London HL 8948* **3**	16 wks
25 Dec 59	REVEILLE ROCK *London HL 9017* **14**	5 wks
17 Mar 60	● BEATNIK FLY *London HLI 9072* **8**	19 wks
16 Jun 60	● DOWN YONDER *London HLX 9134* **8**	11 wks
29 Sep 60	● ROCKING GOOSE *London HLX 9190* **3**	20 wks
2 Mar 61	JA-DA *London HLX 9289* **14**	9 wks
6 Jul 61	OLD SMOKEY / HIGH VOLTAGE *London HLX 9378* ..**24**	8 wks

Bryan JOHNSON *UK, male vocalist* **11 wks**

10 Mar 60	LOOKING HIGH HIGH HIGH *Decca F 11213* **20**	11 wks

Carey JOHNSON *Australia, male vocalist* **8 wks**

25 Apr 87	**REAL FASHION REGGAE STYLE** *Oval TEN 170* **19**	8 wks

Denise JOHNSON *UK, female vocalist* **4 wks**

24 Aug 91	**DON'T FIGHT IT FEEL IT** *Creation CRE 110* [1] **41**	2 wks
14 May 94	**RAYS OF THE RISING SUN** *Magnet MAG 1022CD* **45**	2 wks

[1] Primal Scream featuring Denise Johnson

Don JOHNSON *US, male vocalist* **12 wks**

18 Oct 86	**HEARTBEAT** *Epic 650064 7* **46**	5 wks
5 Nov 88	**TILL I LOVED YOU (LOVE THEME FROM 'GOYA')** *CBS BARB 2* [1] **16**	7 wks

[1] Barbra Streisand and Don Johnson

General JOHNSON - *See CHAIRMEN OF THE BOARD*

Holly JOHNSON *UK, male vocalist* **36 wks**

14 Jan 89	● **LOVE TRAIN** *MCA MCA 1306* **4**	11 wks
1 Apr 89	● **AMERICANOS** *MCA MCA 1323* **4**	11 wks
20 May 89	★ **FERRY 'CROSS THE MERSEY** *PWL PWL 41* [1] **1**	7 wks
24 Jun 89	**ATOMIC CITY** *MCA MCA 1342* **18**	4 wks
30 Sep 89	**HEAVEN'S HERE** *MCA MCA 1365* **62**	2 wks
1 Dec 90	**WHERE HAS LOVE GONE** *MCA MCA 1460* **73**	1 wk

[1] Christians, Holly Johnson, Paul McCartney, Gerry Marsden and Stock Aitken Waterman

Howard JOHNSON *US, male vocalist* **6 wks**

4 Sep 82	**KEEPIN' LOVE NEW / SO FINE** *A & M USA 1221* **45**	6 wks

Keepin' Love New listed 4 Sep 82 only, peaking at position 64.

Johnny JOHNSON and the BANDWAGON
US, male vocal group **50 wks**

16 Oct 68	● **BREAKIN' DOWN THE WALLS OF HEARTACHE** *Direction 58-3670* [1] **4**	15 wks
5 Feb 69	**YOU** *Direction 58-3923* [1] **34**	4 wks
28 May 69	**LET'S HANG ON** *Direction 58-4180* [1] **36**	6 wks
25 Jul 70	● **SWEET INSPIRATION** *Bell 1111* **10**	12 wks
24 Oct 70	**SWEET INSPIRATION (re-entry)** *Bell 1111* **46**	1 wk
28 Nov 70	● **BLAME IT ON THE PONY EXPRESS** *Bell 1128* **7**	12 wks

[1] Bandwagon

Kevin JOHNSON *Australia, male vocalist* **6 wks**

11 Jan 75	**ROCK 'N ROLL (I GAVE YOU THE BEST YEARS OF MY LIFE)** *UK UKR 84* **23**	6 wks

Laurie JOHNSON *UK, orchestra* **12 wks**

28 Sep 61	● **SUCU SUCU** *Pye 7N 15383* **9**	12 wks

L. J. JOHNSON *US, male vocalist* **6 wks**

7 Feb 76	**YOUR MAGIC PUT A SPELL ON ME** *Philips 6006 492* **27**	6 wks

Lou JOHNSON *US, male vocalist* **2 wks**

26 Nov 64	**MESSAGE TO MARTHA** *London HL 9929* **36**	2 wks

Marv JOHNSON *US, male vocalist* **39 wks**

12 Feb 60	● **YOU GOT WHAT IT TAKES** *London HLT 9013* **7**	16 wks
5 May 60	**I LOVE THE WAY YOU LOVE** *London HLT 9109* **35**	3 wks
11 Aug 60	**AIN'T GONNA BE THAT WAY** *London HLT 9165* **50**	1 wk
22 Jan 69	● **I'LL PICK A ROSE FOR MY ROSE** *Tamla Motown TMG 680* **10**	11 wks
25 Oct 69	**I MISS YOU BABY** *Tamla Motown TMG 713* **25**	8 wks

Orlando JOHNSON - *See SECCHI featuring Orlando JOHNSON*

Paul JOHNSON *UK, male vocalist* **7 wks**

21 Feb 87	**WHEN LOVE COMES CALLING** *CBS PJOHN 1* **52**	5 wks
25 Feb 89	**NO MORE TOMORROWS** *CBS PJOHN 7* **67**	2 wks

Teddy JOHNSON - *See Pearl CARR and Teddy JOHNSON*

Bruce JOHNSTON *US, male instrumentalist - keyboards* **4 wks**

27 Aug 77	**PIPELINE** *CBS 5514* **33**	4 wks

Sabrina JOHNSTON *US, female vocalist* **19 wks**

7 Sep 91	● **PEACE** *East West YZ 616* **8**	10 wks
7 Dec 91	**FRIENDSHIP** *East West YZ 637* **58**	4 wks
11 Jul 92	**I WANNA SING** *East West YZ 661* **46**	2 wks
3 Oct 92	**PEACE (re-mix)** *Epic 6584377* **35**	2 wks
13 Aug 94	**SATISFY MY LOVE** *Champion CHAMPCD 311* **62**	1 wk

The listed flipside of Peace (re-mix) was Gypsy Woman (re-mix) by Crystal Waters.

JOHNSTON BROTHERS *UK, male vocal group* **33 wks**

3 Apr 53	● **OH HAPPY DAY** *Decca F 10071* **4**	8 wks
5 Nov 54	**WAIT FOR ME DARLING** *Decca F 10362* [1] **18**	1 wk
21 Jan 55	**HAPPY DAYS AND LONELY NIGHTS** *Decca F 10389* [2] **14**	2 wks
7 Oct 55	★ **HERNANDO'S HIDEAWAY** *Decca F 10608* **1**	13 wks
30 Dec 55	● **JOIN IN AND SING AGAIN** *Decca F 10636* **9**	1 wk
13 Apr 56	**NO OTHER LOVE** *Decca F 10721* **22**	1 wk
30 Nov 56	**IN THE MIDDLE OF THE HOUSE** *Decca F 10781* **27**	1 wk
7 Dec 56	**JOIN IN AND SING (NO. 3)** *Decca F 10814* **30**	1 wk
28 Dec 56	**JOIN IN AND SING (NO. 3) (re-entry)** *Decca F 10814* **24**	1 wk
8 Feb 57	**GIVE HER MY LOVE** *Decca F 10828* **27**	1 wk
19 Apr 57	**HEART** *Decca F 10860* **23**	3 wks

[1] Joan Regan and the Johnston Brothers [2] Suzi Miller and the Johnston Brothers

The following two hits were medleys: Join In And Sing Again: Sheik Of Araby / Yes Sir That's My Baby / California Here I Come / Some Of These Days / Charleston / Margie. Join In And Sing (No.3): Coal Black Morning / When You're Smiling / Alexander's Ragtime Band / Sweet Sue Just You / When You Wore A Tulip / If You Were The Only Girl In The World. See also Various Artists (EPs & LPs) - All Star Hit Parade No. 2.

JOLLY BROTHERS
Jamaica, male vocal / instrumental group **7 wks**

28 Jul 79	**CONSCIOUS MAN** *United Artists UP 36415* **46**	7 wks

JOLLY ROGER *UK, male vocalist* **12 wks**

10 Sep 88	**ACID MAN** *10 TEN 236* **23**	12 wks

JOMANDA *US, female vocal group* **10 wks**

22 Apr 89	**MAKE MY BODY ROCK** *RCA PB 42749* **44**	3 wks
29 Jun 91	**GOT A LOVE FOR YOU** *Giant W 0040* **43**	4 wks
11 Sep 93	**I LIKE IT** *Big Beat A 8377CD* **67**	1 wk
13 Nov 93	**NEVER** *Big Beat A 8347CD* **40**	2 wks

JON and VANGELIS
UK, male vocalist / Greece, male multi-instrumentalist **28 wks**

5 Jan 80	● **I HEAR YOU NOW** *Polydor POSP 96* **8**	11 wks

12 Dec 81	● I'LL FIND MY WAY HOME Polydor JV 1	6	13 wks
30 Jul 83	HE IS SAILING Polydor JV 4	61	2 wks
18 Aug 84	STATE OF INDEPENDENCE Polydor JV 5	67	2 wks

See also Vangelis.

Aled JONES UK, male vocalist — 24 wks

20 Jul 85	MEMORY BBC RESL 175	42	4 wks
30 Nov 85	● WALKING IN THE AIR HMV ALED 1	5	11 wks
14 Dec 85	PICTURES IN THE DARK Virgin VS 836 [1]	50	6 wks
20 Dec 86	A WINTER STORY HMV ALED 2	51	3 wks

[1] Mike Oldfield featuring Aled Jones, Anita Hegerland and Barry Palmer

Barbara JONES Jamaica, female vocalist — 7 wks

| 31 Jan 81 | JUST WHEN I NEEDED YOU MOST Sonet SON 2221 | 31 | 7 wks |

Catherine Zeta JONES UK, female vocalist — 8 wks

| 19 Sep 92 | FOR ALL TIME Columbia 6583547 | 36 | 5 wks |
| 26 Nov 94 | TRUE LOVE WAYS PolyGram TV TLWCD 2 [1] | 38 | 3 wks |

[1] David Essex and Catherine Zeta Jones

Grace JONES US, female vocalist — 45 wks

26 Jul 80	PRIVATE LIFE Island WIP 6629	17	8 wks
20 Jun 81	PULL UP TO THE BUMPER Island WIP 6696	53	4 wks
30 Oct 82	THE APPLE STRETCHING / NIPPLE TO THE BOTTLE Island WIP 6779	50	4 wks
9 Apr 83	MY JAMAICAN GUY Island IS 103	56	3 wks
12 Oct 85	SLAVE TO THE RHYTHM ZTT IS 206	12	8 wks
18 Jan 86	PULL UP TO THE BUMPER (re-issue) / LA VIE ENROSE Island IS 240	12	9 wks
1 Mar 86	LOVE IS THE DRUG Island IS 266	35	4 wks
15 Nov 86	I'M NOT PERFECT (BUT I'M PERFECT FOR YOU) Manhattan MT 15	56	3 wks
7 May 94	SLAVE TO THE RHYTHM (re-mix) Zance ZANG 50CD1	28	2 wks

La Vie En Rose was only listed from 1 Feb 86.

Hannah JONES US, female vocalist — 9 wks

| 14 Sep 91 | BRIDGE OVER TROUBLED WATER Dance Pool 6565467 [1] | 21 | 8 wks |
| 30 Jan 93 | KEEP IT ON TMRC CDTMRC 7 | 67 | 1 wk |

[1] PJB featuring Hannah and her Sisters

Howard JONES UK, male vocalist — 103 wks

17 Sep 83	● NEW SONG WEA HOW 1	3	12 wks
26 Nov 83	● WHAT IS LOVE WEA HOW 2	2	15 wks
14 Jan 84	NEW SONG (re-entry) WEA HOW 1	60	3 wks
18 Feb 84	HIDE AND SEEK WEA HOW 3	12	9 wks
26 May 84	PEARL IN THE SHELL WEA HOW 4	7	10 wks
11 Aug 84	LIKE TO GET TO KNOW YOU WELL WEA HOW 5	4	12 wks
9 Feb 85	● THINGS CAN ONLY GET BETTER WEA HOW 6	6	8 wks
20 Apr 85	● LOOK MAMA WEA HOW 7	10	6 wks
29 Jun 85	LIFE IN ONE DAY WEA HOW 8	14	7 wks
15 Mar 86	NO ONE IS TO BLAME WEA HOW 9	16	7 wks
4 Oct 86	ALL I WANT WEA HOW 10	35	4 wks
29 Nov 86	YOU KNOW I LOVE YOU...DON'T YOU? WEA HOW 11	43	3 wks
21 Mar 87	A LITTLE BIT OF SNOW WEA HOW 12	70	1 wk
4 Mar 89	EVERLASTING LOVE WEA HOW 13	62	3 wks
11 Apr 92	LIFT ME UP East West HOW 15	52	3 wks

Janie JONES UK, female vocalist — 3 wks

| 27 Jan 66 | WITCHES' BREW HMV POP 1495 | 46 | 3 wks |

Jimmy JONES US, male vocalist — 47 wks

17 Mar 60	● HANDY MAN MGM 1051	3	21 wks
16 Jun 60	★ GOOD TIMIN' MGM 1078	1	15 wks
18 Aug 60	HANDY MAN (re-entry) MGM 1051	32	3 wks
8 Sep 60	I JUST GO FOR YOU MGM 1091	35	4 wks
17 Nov 60	READY FOR LOVE MGM 1103	46	1 wk
30 Mar 61	I TOLD YOU SO MGM 1123	33	3 wks

Juggy JONES US, male multi-instrumentalist — 4 wks

| 7 Feb 76 | INSIDE AMERICA Contempo CS 2080 | 39 | 4 wks |

Mick JONES - See AZTEC CAMERA

Oran 'Juice' JONES US, male vocalist — 14 wks

| 15 Nov 86 | ● THE RAIN Def Jam A 7303 | 4 | 14 wks |

Paul JONES UK, male vocalist — 34 wks

6 Oct 66	● HIGH TIME HMV POP 1554	4	15 wks
19 Jan 67	● I'VE BEEN A BAD BAD BOY HMV POP 1576	5	9 wks
23 Aug 67	THINKIN' AIN'T FOR ME HMV POP 1602	47	1 wk
13 Sep 67	THINKIN' AIN'T FOR ME (re-entry) HMV POP 1602	32	7 wks
5 Feb 69	AQUARIUS Columbia DB 8514	45	2 wks

Quincy JONES
US, male producer / instrumentalist - keyboards — 39 wks

29 Jul 78	STUFF LIKE THAT A & M AMS 7367	34	9 wks
11 Apr 81	AI NO CORRIDA (I-NO-KO-REE-DA) A & M AMS 8109	14	10 wks
20 Jun 81	RAZZAMATAZZ A & M AMS 8140 [1]	11	9 wks
5 Sep 81	BETCHA' WOULDN'T HURT ME A & M AMS 8157	52	3 wks
13 Jan 90	I'LL BE GOOD TO YOU Qwest W 2697 [2]	21	7 wks
31 Mar 90	SECRET GARDEN Qwest W 9992 [3]	67	1 wk

[1] Quincy Jones featuring Patti Austin [2] Quincy Jones featuring Ray Charles and Chaka Khan [3] Quincy Jones featuring Al B. Sure!, James Ingram, El DeBarge and Barry White

Uncredited vocals on Stuff Like That were by Ashford and Simpson and Chaka Khan, and on Ai No Corrida by Dune.

Rickie Lee JONES US, female vocalist — 9 wks

| 23 Jun 79 | CHUCK E.'S IN LOVE Warner Bros. K 17390 | 18 | 9 wks |

Shirley JONES - See PARTRIDGE FAMILY starring Shirley JONES featuring David CASSIDY; VARIOUS ARTISTS (EPs & LPs) - Carousel Soundtrack

Tammy JONES UK, female vocalist — 10 wks

| 26 Apr 75 | ● LET ME TRY AGAIN Epic EPC 3211 | 5 | 10 wks |

Tom JONES UK, male vocalist — 356 wks

11 Feb 65	★ IT'S NOT UNUSUAL Decca F 12062	1	14 wks
6 May 65	ONCE UPON A TIME Decca F 12121	32	4 wks
8 Jul 65	WITH THESE HANDS Decca F 12191	13	11 wks
12 Aug 65	WHAT'S NEW PUSSYCAT Decca F 12203	11	10 wks
13 Jan 66	THUNDERBALL Decca F 12292	35	4 wks
19 May 66	ONCE THERE WAS A TIME / NOT RESPONSIBLE Decca F 12390	18	9 wks
18 Aug 66	THIS AND THAT Decca F 12461	44	3 wks
10 Nov 66	★ GREEN GREEN GRASS OF HOME Decca F 22511	1	22 wks
16 Feb 67	● DETROIT CITY Decca F 22555	8	10 wks
13 Apr 67	● FUNNY FAMILIAR FORGOTTEN FEELINGS Decca F 12599	7	15 wks
26 Jul 67	● I'LL NEVER FALL IN LOVE AGAIN Decca F 12639	2	25 wks
22 Nov 67	● I'M COMING HOME Decca F 12693	2	16 wks

TOM JONES seems furious his microphone is not plugged in. (LFI)

28 Feb 68	● DELILAH Decca F 12747	2	17 wks
17 Jul 68	● HELP YOURSELF Decca F 12812	5	26 wks
27 Nov 68	A MINUTE OF YOUR TIME Decca F 12854	..14	15 wks
14 May 69	● LOVE ME TONIGHT Decca F 12924	9	12 wks
13 Dec 69	● WITHOUT LOVE Decca F 12990	..10	11 wks
14 Mar 70	WITHOUT LOVE (re-entry) Decca F 12990	..49	1 wk
18 Apr 70	● DAUGHTER OF DARKNESS Decca F 13013	5	15 wks
15 Aug 70	I (WHO HAVE NOTHING) Decca F 13061	..16	8 wks
17 Oct 70	I (WHO HAVE NOTHING) (re-entry) Decca F 13061	.47	3 wks
16 Jan 71	SHE'S A LADY Decca F 13113	..13	9 wks
27 Mar 71	SHE'S A LADY (re-entry) Decca F 13113	..47	1 wk
5 Jun 71	PUPPET MAN Decca F 13183	..49	1 wk
19 Jun 71	PUPPET MAN (re-entry) Decca F 13183	..50	1 wk
23 Oct 71	● TILL Decca F 13236	2	15 wks
1 Apr 72	● THE YOUNG NEW MEXICAN PUPPETEER Decca F 13298	6	12 wks
14 Apr 73	LETTER TO LUCILLE Decca F 13393	..31	8 wks
7 Sep 74	SOMETHING 'BOUT YOU BABY I LIKE Decca F 13550	..36	5 wks
16 Apr 77	SAY YOU'LL STAY UNTIL TOMORROW EMI 2583	..40	3 wks
18 Apr 87	● A BOY FROM NOWHERE Epic OLE 1	2	12 wks
30 May 87	IT'S NOT UNUSUAL (re-issue) Decca F 103	..17	8 wks
2 Jan 88	I WAS BORN TO BE ME Epic OLE 4	..61	1 wk
29 Oct 88	● KISS China CHINA 11 [1]	5	7 wks
29 Apr 89	MOVE CLOSER Jive JIVE 203	..49	3 wks
26 Jan 91	COULDN'T SAY GOODBYE Dover ROJ 10	..51	2 wks
16 Mar 91	CARRYING A TORCH Dover ROJ 12	..57	2 wks
4 Jul 92	DELILAH (re-issue) The Hit Label TOM 10	..68	2 wks
6 Feb 93	ALL YOU NEED IS LOVE Childline CHILDCD 93	..19	4 wks
5 Nov 94	IF I ONLY KNEW ZTT ZANG 59CD	..11†	9 wks

[1] Art Of Noise featuring Tom Jones

See also Various Artists (EPs & LPs) - Gimme Shelter (EP).

Sue JONES-DAVIES - *See Julie COVINGTON, Rula LENSKA, Charlotte CORNWELL and Sue JONES-DAVIES*

Alison JORDAN *UK, female vocalist*   **4 wks**

| 9 May 92 | BOY FROM NEW YORK CITY Arista 74321100427 | ..23 | 4 wks |

Dick JORDAN *UK, male vocalist*   **4 wks**

| 17 Mar 60 | HALLELUJAH I LOVE HER SO Oriole CB 1534 | ..47 | 1 wk |
| 9 Jun 60 | LITTLE CHRISTINE Oriole CB 1548 | ..39 | 3 wks |

Jack JORDAN - *See Frank CHACKSFIELD*

Ronny JORDAN *UK, male instrumentalist - guitar*   **7 wks**

1 Feb 92	SO WHAT! Antilles ANN 14	..32	4 wks
25 Sep 93	UNDER YOUR SPELL Island CID 565	..72	1 wk
15 Jan 94	TINSEL TOWN Island CID 566	..64	1 wk
28 May 94	COME WITH ME Island CID 584	..63	1 wk

David JOSEPH *UK, male vocalist*   **21 wks**

26 Feb 83	YOU CAN'T HIDE (YOUR LOVE FROM ME) Island IS 101	..13	9 wks
28 May 83	LET'S LIVE IT UP (NITE PEOPLE) Island IS 116	..26	5 wks
18 Feb 84	JOYS OF LIFE Island IS 153	..61	2 wks
31 May 86	EXPANSIONS '86 (EXPAND YOUR MIND) Fourth & Broadway BRW 48 [1]	..58	5 wks

[1] Chris Paul featuring David Joseph

Martyn JOSEPH *UK, male vocalist*   **8 wks**

20 Jun 92	DOLPHINS MAKE ME CRY Epic 6581347	..34	4 wks
12 Sep 92	WORKING MOTHER Epic 6582937	..65	1 wk
9 Jan 93	PLEASE SIR Epic 6588552	..45	3 wks

JOURNEY *US, male vocal / instrumental group*   **9 wks**

| 27 Feb 82 | DON'T STOP BELIEVIN' CBS A 1728 | ..62 | 4 wks |
| 11 Sep 82 | WHO'S CRYING NOW CBS A 2725 | ..46 | 5 wks |

Ruth JOY *UK, female vocalist*   **3 wks**

| 26 Aug 89 | DON'T PUSH IT MCA RJOY 1 | ..66 | 2 wks |
| 22 Feb 92 | FEEL MCA MCS 1574 | ..67 | 1 wk |

JOY DIVISION *UK, male vocal / instrumental group*   **21 wks**

28 Jun 80	LOVE WILL TEAR US APART Factory FAC 23	..13	9 wks
29 Oct 83	LOVE WILL TEAR US APART (re-entry) Factory FAC 23	..19	7 wks
18 Jun 88	ATMOSPHERE Factory FAC 2137	..34	5 wks

JOY STRINGS
UK, male / female vocal / instrumental group   **11 wks**

| 27 Feb 64 | IT'S AN OPEN SECRET Regal Zonophone RZ 501 | ..32 | 7 wks |
| 17 Dec 64 | A STARRY NIGHT Regal Zonophone RZ 504 | ..35 | 4 wks |

JT and the BIG FAMILY
Italy, male / female vocal / instrumental group   **8 wks**

| 3 Mar 90 | ● MOMENTS IN SOUL Champion CHAMP 237 | ....7 | 8 wks |

J.T.Q. with Noel McKOY
UK, male instrumental group with male vocalist   **5 wks**

| 3 Apr 93 | LOVE THE LIFE Big Life BLRD 93 | ..34 | 3 wks |
| 3 Jul 93 | SEE A BRIGHTER DAY Big Life BLRDA 97 | ..49 | 2 wks |

JUDAS PRIEST *UK, male vocal / instrumental group*   **51 wks**

20 Jan 79	TAKE ON THE WORLD CBS 6915	..14	10 wks
12 May 79	EVENING STAR CBS 7312	..53	4 wks
29 Mar 80	LIVING AFTER MIDNIGHT CBS 8379	..12	7 wks
7 Jun 80	BREAKING THE LAW CBS 8644	..12	6 wks
23 Aug 80	UNITED CBS 8897	..26	8 wks
21 Feb 81	DON'T GO CBS 9520	..51	3 wks
25 Apr 81	HOT ROCKIN' CBS 1153	..60	3 wks
21 Aug 82	YOU'VE GOT ANOTHER THING COMIN' CBS A 2611	..66	2 wks
21 Jan 84	FREEWHEEL BURNIN' CBS A 4054	..42	3 wks
23 Apr 88	JOHNNY B. GOODE Atlantic A 9114	..64	2 wks
15 Sep 90	PAINKILLER CBS 656273 7	..74	1 wk
23 Mar 91	A TOUCH OF EVIL Columbia 6565897	..58	1 wk
24 Apr 93	NIGHT CRAWLER Columbia 6590972	..63	1 wk

JUDGE DREAD *UK, male vocalist*   **95 wks**

26 Aug 72	BIG SIX Big Shot BI 608	..11	27 wks
9 Dec 72	● BIG SEVEN Big Shot BI 613	8	18 wks
21 Apr 73	BIG EIGHT Big Shot BI 619	..14	10 wks
5 Jul 75	● JE T'AIME (MOI NON PLUS) Cactus CT 65	9	9 wks
27 Sep 75	BIG TEN Cactus CT 77	..14	7 wks
6 Dec 75	CHRISTMAS IN DREADLAND / COME OUTSIDE Cactus CT 80	..14	7 wks
8 May 76	THE WINKLE MAN Cactus CT 90	..35	4 wks
28 Aug 76	Y VIVA SUSPENDERS Cactus CT 99	..27	4 wks
2 Apr 77	5TH ANNIVERSARY EP Cactus CT 98	..31	4 wks
14 Jan 78	UP WITH THE COCK / BIG PUNK Cactus CT 110	..49	1 wk
16 Dec 78	HOKEY COKEY / JINGLE BELLS EMI 2881	..59	4 wks

Tracks on 5th Anniversary EP: Jamaica Jerk (Off) / Bring Back The Skins / End Of The World / Big Everything.

JUICY *US, male / female vocal duo*   **5 wks**

| 22 Feb 86 | SUGAR FREE Epic A 6917 | ..45 | 5 wks |

JUICY LUCY UK, male vocal/instrumental group — 17 wks

7 Mar 70	**WHO DO YOU LOVE** Vertigo V 1	**14**	12 wks
10 Oct 70	**PRETTY WOMAN** Vertigo 6059 015	**45**	2 wks
31 Oct 70	**PRETTY WOMAN (re-entry)** Vertigo 6059 015	**44**	3 wks

JULIA and COMPANY US, male/female vocal group — 10 wks

3 Mar 84	**BREAKIN' DOWN (SUGAR SAMBA)** London LON 46	**15**	8 wks
23 Feb 85	**I'M SO HAPPY** Next Plateau LON 61	**56**	2 wks

JULUKA
UK/South Africa, male/female vocal/instrumental group — 4 wks

12 Feb 83	**SCATTERLINGS OF AFRICA** Safari ZULU 1	**44**	4 wks

Wally JUMP Jr. and the CRIMINAL ELEMENT
US, male producer - Arthur Baker — 19 wks

28 Feb 87	**TURN ME LOOSE** London LON 126	**60**	2 wks
5 Sep 87	**PUT THE NEEDLE TO THE RECORD** Cooltempo COOL 150 [1]	**63**	3 wks
12 Dec 87	**TIGHTEN UP - I JUST CAN'T STOP DANCING** Breakout USA 621	**24**	7 wks
19 Mar 88	**PRIVATE PARTY** Breakout USA 624	**57**	3 wks
6 Oct 90	**EVERYBODY (RAP)** Deconstruction PB 44701 [2]	**30**	4 wks

[1] Criminal Element Orchestra [2] Criminal Element Orchestra and Wendell Williams

JUMPING JACKS - See Danny PEPPERMINT and the JUMPING JACKS

Rosemary JUNE US, female vocalist — 9 wks

23 Jan 59	**I'LL BE WITH YOU IN APPLE BLOSSOM TIME** Pye International 7N 25005	**14**	9 wks

JUNGLE BOOK US, male/female vocal group — 8 wks

8 May 93	**THE JUNGLE BOOK GROOVE** Hollywood HWCD 128	**14**	8 wks

JUNGLE BROTHERS US, male rap group — 17 wks

22 Oct 88	**I'LL HOUSE YOU** Gee Street GEE 003 [1]	**22**	5 wks
18 Mar 89	**BLACK IS BLACK/STRAIGHT OUT OF THE JUNGLE** Gee Street GEE 15	**72**	1 wk
31 Mar 90	**WHAT 'U' WAITIN' '4'** Eternal W 9865	**35**	5 wks
21 Jul 90	**DOIN' OUR OWN DANG** Eternal W 9754	**33**	6 wks

[1] Richie Rich meets the Jungle Brothers

Doin' Our Own Dang features the uncredited De La Soul and Monie Love.

JUNGLE HIGH - See BLUE PEARL

JUNIOR UK, male vocalist — 57 wks

24 Apr 82	● **MAMA USED TO SAY** Mercury MER 98	**7**	13 wks
10 Jul 82	**TOO LATE** Mercury MER 112	**20**	9 wks
25 Sep 82	**LET ME KNOW/I CAN'T HELP IT** Mercury MER 116	**53**	3 wks
23 Apr 83	**COMMUNICATION BREAKDOWN** Mercury MER 134	**57**	3 wks
8 Sep 84	**SOMEBODY** London LON 50	**64**	2 wks
9 Feb 85	**DO YOU REALLY (WANT MY LOVE)** London LON 60	**47**	4 wks
30 Nov 85	**OH LOUISE** London LON 75	**74**	3 wks
4 Apr 87	● **ANOTHER STEP CLOSER TO YOU** MCA KIM 5 [1]	**6**	11 wks
25 Aug 90	**STEP OFF** MCA MCA 1432 [2]	**63**	3 wks
15 Aug 92	**THEN CAME YOU** MCA MCS 1676 [2]	**32**	5 wks

31 Oct 92	**ALL OVER THE WORLD** MCA MCS 1691 [2]	**74**	1 wk

[1] Kim Wilde and Junior [2] Junior Giscombe

JUNIORS - See DANNY and the JUNIORS

Jimmy JUSTICE UK, male vocalist — 35 wks

29 Mar 62	● **WHEN MY LITTLE GIRL IS SMILING** Pye 7N 15421	**9**	13 wks
14 Jun 62	● **AIN'T THAT FUNNY** Pye 7N 15443	**8**	11 wks
23 Aug 62	**SPANISH HARLEM** Pye 7N 15457	**20**	11 wks

JUSTIFIED ANCIENTS OF MU MU
UK, male production duo - The KLF under an assumed name — 6 wks

9 Nov 91	● **IT'S GRIM UP NORTH** KLF Communications JAMS 028	**10**	5 wks
4 Jan 92	**IT'S GRIM UP NORTH (re-entry)** KLF Communications JAMS 028	**67**	1 wk

Bill JUSTIS US, male instrumentalist - alto sax — 8 wks

10 Jan 58	**RAUNCHY** London HLS 8517	**24**	2 wks
31 Jan 58	**RAUNCHY (re-entry)** London HLS 8517	**11**	6 wks

Patrick JUVET France, male vocalist — 19 wks

2 Sep 78	**GOT A FEELING** Casablanca CAN 127	**34**	7 wks
4 Nov 78	**I LOVE AMERICA** Casablanca CAN 132	**12**	12 wks

J.X. UK, male producer - Jake Williams — 6 wks

2 Apr 94	**SON OF A GUN** Internal Dance IDC 5	**13**	6 wks

K

Frank K featuring Wiston OFFICE
Italy/US, male vocal/instrumental duo — 1 wk

26 Jan 91	**EVERYBODY LET'S SOMEBODY LOVE** Urban URB 66	**61**	1 wk

Leila K Sweden, female vocalist — 22 wks

25 Nov 89	● **GOT TO GET** Arista 112696 [1]	**8**	14 wks
17 Mar 90	**ROK THE NATION** Arista 112971 [1]	**41**	3 wks
23 Jan 93	**OPEN SESAME** Polydor PQCD 1	**23**	4 wks
3 Jul 93	**CA PLANE POUR MOI** Polydor PQCD 3	**69**	1 wk

[1] Rob 'N' Raz featuring Leila K

Joshua KADISON US, male vocalist — 6 wks

26 Feb 94	**JESSIE** SBK CDSBK 43	**69**	2 wks
1 Oct 94	**JESSIE (re-entry)** SBK CDSBK 43	**48**	3 wks
12 Nov 94	**BEAUTIFUL IN MY EYES** SBK CDSBK 50	**65**	1 wk

Bert KAEMPFERT Germany, orchestra — 10 wks

23 Dec 65	**BYE BYE BLUES** Polydor BM 56 504	**24**	10 wks

KAJAGOOGOO UK, male vocal/instrumental group — 50 wks

22 Jan 83	★ **TOO SHY** EMI 5359	**1**	13 wks
2 Apr 83	● **OOH TO BE AH** EMI 5383	**7**	8 wks
4 Jun 83	**HANG ON NOW** EMI 5394	**13**	7 wks
17 Sep 83	● **BIG APPLE** EMI 5423	**8**	8 wks
3 Mar 84	**THE LION'S MOUTH** EMI 5449	**25**	7 wks

5 May 84	**TURN YOUR BACK ON ME** EMI 5646 ....**47**	4 wks
21 Sep 85	**SHOULDN'T DO THAT** Parlophone R 6106 [1] **63**	3 wks

[1] Kaja

KALIN TWINS US, male vocal duo — **18 wks**

18 Jul 58	★ **WHEN** Brunswick 05751 ....**1**	18 wks

Kitty KALLEN US, female vocalist — **23 wks**

2 Jul 54	★ **LITTLE THINGS MEAN A LOT** Brunswick 05287 ....**1**	23 wks

Gunter KALLMAN CHOIR
Germany, male/female vocal group — **3 wks**

24 Dec 64	**ELISABETH SERENADE** Polydor NH 24678 ....**45**	3 wks

Nick KAMEN UK, male vocalist — **33 wks**

8 Nov 86	● **EACH TIME YOU BREAK MY HEART** WEA YZ 90 ......**5**	12 wks
28 Feb 87	**LOVING YOU IS SWEETER THAN EVER**	
	WEA YZ 106 ....**16**	9 wks
16 May 87	**NOBODY ELSE** WEA YZ 122 ....**47**	3 wks
28 May 88	**TELL ME** WEA YZ 184 ....**40**	5 wks
28 Apr 90	**I PROMISED MYSELF** WEA YZ 454 ....**50**	4 wks

KANDIDATE UK, male vocal/instrumental group — **28 wks**

19 Aug 78	**DON'T WANNA SAY GOODNIGHT** RAK 280 ....**47**	6 wks
17 Mar 79	**I DON'T WANNA LOSE YOU** RAK 289 ....**11**	12 wks
4 Aug 79	**GIRLS GIRLS GIRLS** RAK 295 ....**34**	7 wks
22 Mar 80	**LET ME ROCK YOU** RAK 306 ....**58**	3 wks

Eden KANE UK, male vocalist — **73 wks**

1 Jun 61	★ **WELL I ASK YOU** Decca F 11353 ....**1**	21 wks
14 Sep 61	● **GET LOST** Decca F 11381 ....**10**	11 wks
18 Jan 62	● **FORGET ME NOT** Decca F 11418 ....**3**	14 wks
10 May 62	● **I DON'T KNOW WHY** Decca F 11460 ....**7**	13 wks
30 Jan 64	● **BOYS CRY** Fontana TF 438 ....**8**	14 wks

KANE GANG UK, male vocal/instrumental group — **37 wks**

19 May 84	**SMALL TOWN CREED** Kitchenware SK 11 ....**60**	2 wks
7 Jul 84	**CLOSEST THING TO HEAVEN** Kitchenware SK 15 ....**12**	11 wks
10 Nov 84	**RESPECT YOURSELF** Kitchenware SK 16..............**21**	10 wks
26 Jan 85	**RESPECT YOURSELF (re-entry)** Kitchenware SK 16..**75**	1 wk
9 Mar 85	**GUN LAW** Kitchenware SK 20....................**53**	4 wks
27 Jun 87	**MOTORTOWN** Kitchenware SK 30 ....**45**	5 wks
16 Apr 88	**DON'T LOOK ANY FURTHER** Kitchenware SK 33.....**52**	4 wks

KANSAS US, male vocal/instrumental group — **7 wks**

1 Jul 78	**CARRY ON WAYWARD SON** Kirshner KIR 4932........**51**	7 wks

Mory KANTÉ Guinea, male vocalist — **9 wks**

23 Jul 88	**YE KE YE KE** London LON 171 ....**29**	9 wks

KAOMA France, male/female vocal/instrumental group — **20 wks**

21 Oct 89	● **LAMBADA** CBS 655011 7 ....**4**	18 wks
27 Jan 90	**DANCANDO LAMBADA** CBS 655235 7 ....**62**	2 wks

KAOTIC CHEMISTRY
UK, male instrumental/production group — **1 wk**

31 Oct 92	**LSD (EP)** Moving Shadow SHADOW 20 ....**68**	1 wk

Tracks on LSD (EP): Space Cakes/LSD/Illegal Substances/Drumtrip II.

KARIN - See UNIQUE 3

KARIYA US, female vocalist — **9 wks**

8 Jul 89	**LET ME LOVE YOU FOR TONIGHT**	
	Sleeping Bag SBUK 4 ....**44**	6 wks
21 Oct 89	**LET ME LOVE YOU FOR TONIGHT (re-entry)**	
	Sleeping Bag SBUK 4 ....**57**	3 wks

Mick KARN UK, male instrumentalist - saxophone — **6 wks**

9 Jul 83	**AFTER A FASHION** Musicfest FEST 1 [1] **39**	4 wks
17 Jan 87	**BUOY** Virgin VS 910 [2] **63**	2 wks

[1] Midge Ure and Mick Karn [2] Mick Karn featuring David Sylvian

KARTOON KREW US, male vocal/instrumental group — **6 wks**

7 Dec 85	**INSPECTOR GADGET** Champion CHAMP 6..............**58**	6 wks

KASENETZ-KATZ SINGING ORCHESTRAL CIRCUS US, male vocal/instrumental group — **15 wks**

20 Nov 68	**QUICK JOEY SMALL (RUN JOEY RUN)**	
	Buddah 201 022 ....**19**	15 wks

KATRINA and the WAVES
UK/US, female/male vocal/instrumental group — **21 wks**

4 May 85	● **WALKING ON SUNSHINE** Capitol CL 354 ....**8**	12 wks
5 Jul 86	**SUN STREET** Capitol CL 407 ....**22**	9 wks

Niamh KAVANAGH Ireland, female vocalist — **5 wks**

12 Jun 93	**IN YOUR EYES** Arista 74321154152 ....**24**	5 wks

Janet KAY UK, female vocalist — **24 wks**

9 Jun 79	● **SILLY GAMES** Scope SC 2 ....**2**	14 wks
11 Aug 90	**SILLY GAMES** Arista 113452 [1] **22**	7 wks
11 Aug 90	**SILLY GAMES (re-mix)**	
	Music Factory Dance MFD 006....................**62**	3 wks

[1] Lindy Layton featuring Janet Kay

Danny KAYE US, male vocalist — **10 wks**

27 Feb 53	● **WONDERFUL COPENHAGEN** Brunswick 05023 ....**5**	10 wks

KAYE SISTERS UK, female vocal group — **45 wks**

25 May 56	**IVORY TOWER** HMV POP 209 [1] **20**	5 wks
1 Nov 57	● **GOTTA HAVE SOMETHING IN THE BANK FRANK**	
	Philips PB 751 [2] **8**	11 wks
3 Jan 58	**SHAKE ME I RATTLE / ALONE** Philips PB 752 ....**27**	1 wk
1 May 59	● **COME SOFTLY TO ME** Philips PB 913 [2] **9**	9 wks
7 Jul 60	● **PAPER ROSES** Philips PB 1024 ....**7**	19 wks

[1] Three Kayes [2] Frankie Vaughan and The Kaye Sisters

KC and the SUNSHINE BAND
US, male vocal/instrumental group — **104 wks**

17 Aug 74	● **QUEEN OF CLUBS** Jayboy BOY 88 ....**7**	12 wks
23 Nov 74	**SOUND YOUR FUNKY HORN** Jayboy BOY 83..........**17**	9 wks
29 Mar 75	**GET DOWN TONIGHT** Jayboy BOY 93 ....**21**	9 wks
2 Aug 75	● **THAT'S THE WAY (I LIKE IT)** Jayboy BOY 99 ....**4**	10 wks
22 Nov 75	**I'M SO CRAZY** Jayboy BOY 101 ....**34**	3 wks
17 Jul 76	**(SHAKE SHAKE SHAKE) SHAKE YOUR BOOTY**	
	Jayboy BOY 110 ....**22**	8 wks
11 Dec 76	**KEEP IT COMIN' LOVE** Jayboy BOY 112 ....**31**	8 wks
30 Apr 77	**I'M YOUR BOOGIE MAN** TK XB 2167 ....**41**	4 wks

6 May 78	**BOOGIE SHOES** TK TKR 6025	**34**	5 wks
22 Jul 78	**IT'S THE SAME OLD SONG** TK TKR 6037	**49**	5 wks
8 Dec 79	● **PLEASE DON'T GO** TK TKR 7558	**3**	12 wks
16 Jul 83	★ **GIVE IT UP** Epic EPC A 3017	**1**	14 wks
24 Sep 83	**(YOU SAID) YOU'D GIMME SOME MORE** Epic A 2760	**41**	3 wks
11 May 91	**THAT'S THE WAY I LIKE IT (re-mix)** Music Factory Dance M7FAC 2	**59**	2 wks

K-CREATIVE UK, male vocal / instrumental group **2 wks**

7 Mar 92	**THREE TIMES A MAYBE** Talkin Loud TLK 17	**58**	2 wks

The listed flipside of Three Times A Maybe was Feed The Feeling by Perception.

Ernie K-DOE US, male vocalist **7 wks**

11 May 61	**MOTHER-IN-LAW** London HLU 9330	**29**	7 wks

Johnny KEATING UK, orchestra **14 wks**

1 Mar 62	● **THEME FROM 'Z CARS'** Piccadilly 7N 35032	**8**	14 wks

Kevin KEEGAN UK, male vocalist **6 wks**

9 Jun 79	**HEAD OVER HEELS IN LOVE** EMI 2965	**31**	6 wks

Yvonne KEELEY - See Scott FITZGERALD

Nelson KEENE UK, male vocalist **5 wks**

25 Aug 60	**IMAGE OF A GIRL** HMV POP 771	**37**	4 wks
29 Sep 60	**IMAGE OF A GIRL (re-entry)** HMV POP 771	**45**	1 wk

KEITH US, male vocalist **8 wks**

26 Jan 67	**98.6** Mercury MF 955	**24**	7 wks
16 Mar 67	**TELL ME TO MY FACE** Mercury MF 968	**50**	1 wk

Jerry KELLER US, male vocalist **14 wks**

28 Aug 59	★ **HERE COMES SUMMER** London HLR 8890	**1**	14 wks

Frank KELLY Ireland, male vocalist **5 wks**

24 Dec 83	**CHRISTMAS COUNTDOWN** Ritz RITZ 062	**26**	4 wks
29 Dec 84	**CHRISTMAS COUNTDOWN (re-entry)** Ritz RITZ 062	**54**	1 wk

Frankie KELLY US, male vocalist / instrumentalist **2 wks**

2 Nov 85	**AIN'T THAT THE TRUTH** 10 TEN 87	**65**	2 wks

Grace KELLY - See Bing CROSBY

Keith KELLY UK, male vocalist **5 wks**

5 May 60	**TEASE ME** Parlophone R 4640	**46**	1 wk
19 May 60	**TEASE ME (re-entry)** Parlophone R 4640	**27**	3 wks
18 Aug 60	**LISTEN LITTLE GIRL** Parlophone R 4676	**47**	1 wk

R KELLY US, male vocalist **21 wks**

9 May 92	**SHE'S GOT THAT VIBE** Jive JIVET 292 [1]	**57**	2 wks
20 Nov 93	**SEX ME** Jive JIVECD 346 [1]	**75**	1 wk
14 May 94	**YOUR BODY'S CALLIN'** Jive JIVECD 353	**19**	4 wks
3 Sep 94	**SUMMER BUNNIES** Jive JIVECD 358	**23**	3 wks
22 Oct 94	● **SHE'S GOT THAT VIBE (re-issue)** Jive JIVECD 364	**3†**	11 wks

[1] R Kelly and Public Announcement

Roberta KELLY US, female vocalist **3 wks**

21 Jan 78	**ZODIACS** Oasis/Hansa 3	**48**	1 wk
4 Feb 78	**ZODIACS (re-entry)** Oasis/Hansa 3	**44**	2 wks

Johnny KEMP Barbados, male vocalist **1 wk**

27 Aug 88	**JUST GOT PAID** CBS 651470 7	**68**	1 wk

Tara KEMP US, female vocalist **2 wks**

20 Apr 91	**HOLD YOU TIGHT** Giant W 0020	**69**	2 wks

Graham KENDRICK UK, male vocalist **4 wks**

9 Sep 89	**LET THE FLAME BURN BRIGHTER** Power P 30	**55**	4 wks

Eddie KENDRICKS US, male vocalist **20 wks**

3 Nov 73	**KEEP ON TRUCKIN'** Tamla Motown TMG 873	**18**	14 wks
16 Mar 74	**BOOGIE DOWN** Tamla Motown TMG 888	**39**	4 wks
21 Sep 85	**A NIGHT AT THE APOLLO LIVE!** RCA PB 49935 [1] ..	**58**	2 wks

[1] Daryl Hall and John Oates featuring David Ruffin and Eddie Kendrick

A Night At The Apollo Live! is a medley of The Way You Do The Things You Do / My Girl. Kendricks dropped the 's' from his name for last hit.

Jane KENNAWAY and STRANGE BEHAVIOUR
UK, female vocalist, male instrumental group **3 wks**

24 Jan 81	**I.O.U.** Deram DM 436	**65**	3 wks

KENNY Ireland, male vocalist **16 wks**

3 Mar 73	**HEART OF STONE** RAK 144	**11**	13 wks
30 Jun 73	**GIVE IT TO ME NOW** RAK 153	**38**	3 wks

KENNY UK, male vocal / instrumental group **39 wks**

7 Dec 74	● **THE BUMP** RAK 186	**3**	15 wks
8 Mar 75	● **FANCY PANTS** RAK 196	**4**	9 wks
7 Jun 75	**BABY I LOVE YOU OK** RAK 207	**12**	7 wks
16 Aug 75	● **JULIE ANN** RAK 214	**10**	8 wks

Gerard KENNY US, male vocalist **21 wks**

9 Dec 78	**NEW YORK, NEW YORK** RCA PB 5117	**43**	8 wks
21 Jun 80	**FANTASY** RCA PB 5256	**65**	1 wk
5 Jul 80	**FANTASY (re-entry)** RCA PB 5256	**34**	5 wks
18 Feb 84	**THE OTHER WOMAN, THE OTHER MAN** Impression IMS 3	**69**	4 wks
4 May 85	**NO MAN'S LAND** WEA YZ 38	**56**	3 wks

Klark KENT US, male vocalist / multi-instrumentalist **4 wks**

26 Aug 78	**DON'T CARE** A & M AMS 7376	**48**	4 wks

Carol KENYON - See Paul HARDCASTLE; HEAVEN 17; RAPINATION

KERBDOG Ireland, male vocal / instrumental group **3 wks**

12 Mar 94	**DRY RISER** Vertigo VERCC 83	**60**	1 wk
6 Aug 94	**DUMMY CRUSHER** Vertigo VERCD 86	**37**	2 wks

KERRI and MICK Australia, female / male vocal duo **3 wks**

28 Apr 84	**'SONS AND DAUGHTERS' THEME** A1 A1 286	**68**	3 wks

Liz KERSHAW and Bruno BROOKES
UK, male / female vocal duo　　　　　　　　　**3 wks**

2 Dec 89	**IT TAKES TWO BABY** *Spartan CIN 101* [1] **53**	2 wks
1 Dec 90	**LET'S DANCE** *Jive BRUNO 1* [2] **54**	1 wk

[1] Liz Kershaw, Bruno Brookes, Jive Bunny and Londonbeat [2] Bruno and Liz and the Radio 1 DJ Posse

See also Jive Bunny and the Mastermixers; Londonbeat.

Nik KERSHAW *UK, male vocalist*　　　　**87 wks**

19 Nov 83	**I WON'T LET THE SUN GO DOWN ON ME** *MCA MCA 816* **47**	5 wks
28 Jan 84 ●	**WOULDN'T IT BE GOOD** *MCA NIK 2* **4**	14 wks
14 Apr 84	**DANCING GIRLS** *MCA NIK 3* **13**	9 wks
16 Jun 84 ●	**I WON'T LET THE SUN GO DOWN ON ME (re-issue)** *MCA NIK 4* **2**	13 wks
15 Sep 84	**HUMAN RACING** *MCA NIK 5* **19**	7 wks
17 Nov 84 ●	**THE RIDDLE** *MCA NIK 6* **3**	11 wks
16 Mar 85 ●	**WIDE BOY** *MCA NIK 7* **9**	8 wks
3 Aug 85 ●	**DON QUIXOTE** *MCA NIK 8* **10**	7 wks
30 Nov 85	**WHEN A HEART BEATS** *MCA NIK 9*..........**27**	7 wks
11 Oct 86	**NOBODY KNOWS** *MCA NIK 10* **44**	3 wks
13 Dec 86	**RADIO MUSICOLA** *MCA NIK 11* **43**	2 wks
4 Feb 89	**ONE STEP AHEAD** *MCA NIK 12* **55**	1 wk

KEVIN THE GERBIL *UK, male gerbil vocalist*　　**6 wks**

4 Aug 84	**SUMMER HOLIDAY** *Magnet RAT 3* **50**	6 wks

KEY WEST - *See ERIK*

KEYNOTES - *See Dave KING*

Chaka KHAN *US, female vocalist*　　　　**90 wks**

2 Dec 78	**I'M EVERY WOMAN** *Warner Bros. K 17269* **11**	13 wks
31 Mar 84 ●	**AIN'T NOBODY** *Warner Bros. RCK 1* [1] **8**	12 wks
20 Oct 84 ★	**I FEEL FOR YOU** *Warner Bros. W 9209* **1**	16 wks
19 Jan 85	**THIS IS MY NIGHT** *Warner Bros. W 9097* **14**	6 wks
20 Apr 85	**EYE TO EYE** *Warner Bros. W 9009* **16**	7 wks
12 Jul 86	**LOVE OF A LIFETIME** *Warner Bros. W 8671* **52**	4 wks
21 Jan 89	**IT'S MY PARTY** *Warner Bros. W 7678* **71**	2 wks
6 May 89 ●	**I'M EVERY WOMAN (re-mix)** *Warner Bros. W 2963*..**8**	8 wks
8 Jul 89 ●	**AIN'T NOBODY (re-mix)** *Warner Bros. W 2880* [1] **6**	9 wks
7 Oct 89	**I FEEL FOR YOU (re-mix)** *Warner Bros. W 2764* **45**	2 wks
13 Jan 90	**I'LL BE GOOD TO YOU** *Qwest W 2697* [2] **21**	7 wks
28 Mar 92	**LOVE YOU ALL MY LIFETIME** *Warner Bros. W 0087* **49**	3 wks
17 Jul 93	**DON'T LOOK AT ME THAT WAY** *Warner Bros. W 0192CD* **73**	1 wk

[1] Rufus and Chaka Khan [2] Quincy Jones featuring Ray Charles and Chaka Khan

See also Quincy Jones.

Praga KHAN *Belgium, male producer*　　　**8 wks**

4 Apr 92	**FREE YOUR BODY / INJECTED WITH A POISON** *Profile PROFT 347* [1] **16**	6 wks
11 Jul 92	**RAVE ALERT** *Profile PROF 369* **39**	2 wks

[1] Praga Khan featuring Jade 4 U

KICK SQUAD
UK / Germany, male vocal / instrumental group　　**2 wks**

10 Nov 90	**SOUND CLASH (CHAMPION SOUND)** *Kickin KICK 2*.**59**	2 wks

KICKING BACK with TAXMAN
UK, male / female vocal / instrumental duo with male rapper　　**8 wks**

17 Mar 90	**DEVOTION** *10 TEN 297* **47**	4 wks
7 Jul 90	**EVERYTHING** *10 TEN 307* **54**	4 wks

---

British Hit Singles Part One: Alphabetically by Artist
Date of chart entry/Title & catalogue no./Peak position reached/Weeks on chart
★ Number One　● Top Ten　† still on chart at 31 Dec 1994
□ = credited to act billed in footnote

KICKS LIKE A MULE
UK, male instrumental / production duo　　　**6 wks**

1 Feb 92 ●	**THE BOUNCER** *Tribal Bass TRIBE 3S* **7**	6 wks

K.I.D. *Antilles, male / female vocal / instrumental group*　　**4 wks**

28 Feb 81	**DON'T STOP** *EMI 5143* **49**	4 wks

KID 'N' PLAY *US, male vocal / instrumental duo*　　**7 wks**

18 Jul 87	**LAST NIGHT** *Cooltempo COOL 148* **71**	1 wk
26 Mar 88	**DO THIS MY WAY** *Cooltempo COOL 164* **48**	3 wks
17 Sep 88	**GITTIN' FUNKY** *Cooltempo COOL 168* **55**	3 wks

KID UNKNOWN *UK, male producer - Paul Fitzpatrick*　　**1 wk**

2 May 92	**NIGHTMARE** *Warp WAP 20CD* **64**	1 wk

Carol KIDD featuring Terry WAITE
UK, female / male vocal duo　　　　**3 wks**

17 Oct 92	**WHEN I DREAM** *The Hit Label HLS 1* **58**	3 wks

Johnny KIDD and the PIRATES
UK, male vocal / instrumental group　　　**62 wks**

12 Jun 59	**PLEASE DON'T TOUCH** *HMV POP 615* [1] **26**	3 wks
17 Jul 59	**PLEASE DON'T TOUCH (re-entry)** *HMV POP 615* [1] **25**	2 wks
12 Feb 60	**YOU GOT WHAT IT TAKES** *HMV POP 698*...........**25**	3 wks
16 Jun 60 ★	**SHAKIN' ALL OVER** *HMV POP 753* **1**	19 wks
6 Oct 60	**RESTLESS** *HMV POP 790* **22**	7 wks
13 Apr 61	**LINDA LU** *HMV POP 853* **47**	1 wk
10 Jan 63	**SHOT OF RHYTHM AND BLUES** *HMV POP 1088* **48**	1 wk
25 Jul 63 ●	**I'LL NEVER GET OVER YOU** *HMV POP 1173*.......**4**	15 wks
28 Nov 63	**HUNGRY FOR LOVE** *HMV POP 1228* **20**	10 wks
30 Apr 64	**ALWAYS AND EVER** *HMV POP 1269*...........**46**	1 wk

[1] Johnny Kidd

KIDS FROM 'FAME' *US, male / female vocal group*　　**36 wks**

14 Aug 82 ●	**HI-FIDELITY** *RCA 254* [1] **5**	10 wks
2 Oct 82 ●	**STARMAKER** *RCA 280* **3**	10 wks
11 Dec 82	**MANNEQUIN** *RCA 299* [2] **50**	6 wks
9 Apr 83	**FRIDAY NIGHT (LIVE VERSION)** *RCA 320* **13**	10 wks

[1] Kids From Fame featuring Valerie Landsberg [2] Kids From Fame featuring Gene Anthony Ray

Greg KIHN BAND *US, male vocal / instrumental group*　　**2 wks**

23 Apr 83	**JEOPARDY** *Beserkley E 9847*...................**63**	2 wks

KILLING JOKE *UK, male vocal / instrumental group*　　**46 wks**

23 May 81	**FOLLOW THE LEADERS** *Malicious Damage EGMDS 101* **55**	5 wks
20 Mar 82	**EMPIRE SONG** *Malicious Damage EGO 4* **43**	4 wks
30 Oct 82	**BIRDS OF A FEATHER** *EG EGO 10* **64**	2 wks
25 Jun 83	**LET'S ALL (GO TO THE FIRE DANCES)** *EG EGO 11* ..**51**	3 wks
15 Oct 83	**ME OR YOU?** *EG EGO 14* **57**	1 wk
7 Apr 84	**EIGHTIES** *EG EGO 16* **60**	5 wks
21 Jul 84	**A NEW DAY** *EG EGO 17* **56**	2 wks
2 Feb 85	**LOVE LIKE BLOOD** *EG EGO 20* **16**	9 wks
30 Mar 85	**KINGS AND QUEENS** *EG EGO 21*...........**58**	3 wks

16 Aug 86	ADORATIONS EG EGO 27	42	6 wks
18 Oct 86	SANITY EG EGO 30	70	1 wk
7 May 94	MILLENIUM Butterfly BFLD 12	34	2 wks
16 Jul 94	THE PANDEMONIUM SINGLE Butterfly BFLDA 17	28	3 wks

Andy KIM Canada, male vocalist   12 wks

24 Aug 74	● ROCK ME GENTLY Capitol CL 15787	2	12 wks

KING UK / Ireland, male vocal / instrumental group   44 wks

12 Jan 85	● LOVE AND PRIDE CBS A 4988	2	14 wks
23 Mar 85	WON'T YOU HOLD MY HAND NOW CBS A 6094	24	8 wks
17 Aug 85	● ALONE WITHOUT YOU CBS A 6308	8	9 wks
19 Oct 85	THE TASTE OF YOUR TEARS CBS A 6618	11	9 wks
11 Jan 86	TORTURE CBS A 6761	23	4 wks

Albert KING - *See Gary MOORE*

B.B. KING US, male vocalist / instrumentalist - guitar   10 wks

15 Apr 89	● WHEN LOVE COMES TO TOWN Island IS 411 [1]	6	7 wks
18 Jul 92	SINCE I MET YOU BABY Virgin VS 1423 [2]	59	3 wks

[1] U2 with B.B. King [2] Gary Moore and B.B. King

Ben E. KING US, male vocalist   35 wks

2 Feb 61	FIRST TASTE OF LOVE London HLK 9258	27	11 wks
22 Jun 61	STAND BY ME London HLK 9358	50	1 wk
6 Jul 61	STAND BY ME (re-entry) London HLK 9358	27	6 wks
5 Oct 61	AMOR AMOR London HLK 9416	38	4 wks
14 Feb 87	★ STAND BY ME (re-issue) Atlantic A 9361	1	11 wks
4 Jul 87	SAVE THE LAST DANCE FOR ME Manhattan MT 25	69	2 wks

Carole KING US, female vocalist   29 wks

20 Sep 62	● IT MIGHT AS WELL RAIN UNTIL SEPTEMBER London HLU 9591	3	13 wks
7 Aug 71	● IT'S TOO LATE A & M AMS 849	6	12 wks
28 Oct 72	IT MIGHT AS WELL RAIN UNTIL SEPTEMBER (re-issue) London HL 10391	43	4 wks

Dave KING Canada, male vocalist   29 wks

17 Feb 56	● MEMORIES ARE MADE OF THIS Decca F 10684 [1]	5	15 wks
13 Apr 56	YOU CAN'T BE TRUE TO TWO Decca F 10720 [1]	11	9 wks
21 Dec 56	CHRISTMAS AND YOU Decca F 10791	23	2 wks
24 Jan 58	THE STORY OF MY LIFE Decca F 10973	20	3 wks

[1] Dave King featuring The Keynotes

See also Various Artists (EPs & LPs) - All Star Hit Parade.

Denis KING - *See STUTZ BEARCATS and the Denis KING ORCHESTRA*

Evelyn 'Champagne' KING US, female vocalist   76 wks

13 May 78	SHAME RCA PC 1122	39	23 wks
3 Feb 79	I DON'T KNOW IF IT'S RIGHT RCA PB 1386	67	2 wks
27 Jun 81	I'M IN LOVE RCA 95 [1]	27	11 wks
26 Sep 81	IF YOU WANT MY LOVIN' RCA 131 [1]	43	6 wks
28 Aug 82	● LOVE COME DOWN RCA 249 [1]	7	13 wks
20 Nov 82	BACK TO LOVE RCA 287 [1]	40	4 wks
19 Feb 83	GET LOOSE RCA 315 [1]	45	5 wks
9 Nov 85	YOUR PERSONAL TOUCH RCA PB 49915	37	5 wks
29 Mar 86	HIGH HORSE RCA PB 49891	55	3 wks
23 Jul 88	HOLD ON TO WHAT YOU'VE GOT Manhattan MT 49	47	3 wks
10 Oct 92	SHAME (re-mix) Network NWKTEN 56 [2]	74	1 wk

[1] Evelyn King [2] Altern 8 vs Evelyn King

Jonathan KING UK, male vocalist   128 wks

29 Jul 65	● EVERYONE'S GONE TO THE MOON Decca F 12187	4	11 wks
10 Jan 70	LET IT ALL HANG OUT Decca F 12988	26	7 wks
16 Jan 71	IT'S THE SAME OLD SONG B & C CB 139 [1]	19	9 wks
3 Apr 71	SUGAR SUGAR RCA 2064 [2]	12	14 wks
29 May 71	LAZY BONES Decca F 13177	23	8 wks
20 Nov 71	HOOKED ON A FEELING Decca F 13241	23	10 wks
5 Feb 72	FLIRT Decca F 13276	22	9 wks
14 Oct 72	● LOOP DI LOVE UK 7 [3]	4	13 wks
26 Jan 74	(I CAN'T GET NO) SATISFACTION UK 53 [4]	29	5 wks
6 Sep 75	● UNA PALOMA BLANCA UK 105	5	11 wks
20 Sep 75	CHICK-A-BOOM (DON'T YA JES LOVE IT) UK 2012 002 [5]	36	4 wks
7 Feb 76	IN THE MOOD UK 121 [6]	46	3 wks
26 Jun 76	● IT ONLY TAKES A MINUTE UK 135 [7]	9	9 wks
7 Oct 78	ONE FOR YOU ONE FOR ME GTO GT 237	29	6 wks
16 Dec 78	LICK A SMURP FOR CHRISTMAS (ALL FALL DOWN) Petrol GAS 1	58	4 wks
16 Jun 79	YOU'RE THE GREATEST LOVER UK International INT 586	67	2 wks
3 Nov 79	GLORIA Ariola ARO 198	65	3 wks

[1] Weathermen [2] Sakkarin [3] Shag [4] Bubblerock [5] 53rd and 3rd featuring the Sound Of Shag [6] Sound 9418 [7] One Hundred Ton And A Feather [8] Father Abraphart and the Smurps

Petrol GAS 1 transferred to Magnet MAG 139 after the first week on chart.

Nosmo KING - *See JAVELLS featuring Nosmo KING*

Paul KING UK, male vocalist   3 wks

2 May 87	I KNOW CBS PKING 1	59	3 wks

Solomon KING US, male vocalist   28 wks

3 Jan 68	● SHE WEARS MY RING Columbia DB 8325	3	18 wks
1 May 68	WHEN WE WERE YOUNG Columbia DB 8402	21	10 wks

Tony KING - *See Kylie MINOGUE*

KING BEE UK, male rapper   6 wks

26 Jan 91	MUST BEE THE MUSIC Columbia 6565827	44	4 wks
23 Mar 91	BACK BY DOPE DEMAND First Bass 7RUFF 6X	61	2 wks

KING BROTHERS UK, male vocal / instrumental group   74 wks

31 May 57	● A WHITE SPORT COAT Parlophone R 4310	6	14 wks
9 Aug 57	IN THE MIDDLE OF AN ISLAND Parlophone R 4338	19	13 wks
6 Dec 57	WAKE UP LITTLE SUSIE Parlophone R 4367	22	3 wks
31 Jan 58	PUT A LIGHT IN THE WINDOW Parlophone R 4389	29	1 wk
14 Feb 58	PUT A LIGHT IN THE WINDOW (re-entry) Parlophone R 4389	28	1 wk
28 Feb 58	PUT A LIGHT IN THE WINDOW (2nd re-entry) Parlophone R 4389	25	2 wks
14 Apr 60	● STANDING ON THE CORNER Parlophone R 4639	4	11 wks
28 Jul 60	MAIS OUI Parlophone R 4672	16	10 wks
12 Jan 61	DOLL HOUSE Parlophone R 4715	21	8 wks
2 Mar 61	76 TROMBONES Parlophone R 4737	19	11 wks

KING KURT UK, male vocal / instrumental group   16 wks

15 Oct 83	DESTINATION ZULULAND Stiff BUY 189	36	6 wks
28 Apr 84	MACK THE KNIFE Stiff BUY 199	55	4 wks
4 Aug 84	BANANA BANANA Stiff BUY 206	54	4 wks
15 Nov 86	AMERICA Polydor KURT 1	73	1 wk
2 May 87	THE LAND OF RING DANG DO Polydor KURT 2	67	1 wk

KING SUN-D'MOET US, male rap/scratch duo · **3 wks**

| 11 Jul 87 | HEY LOVE Flame MELT 5 .... | 66 | 3 wks |

KING TRIGGER
UK, male/female vocal/instrumental group · **4 wks**

| 14 Aug 82 | THE RIVER Chrysalis CHS 2623 .... | 57 | 4 wks |

KINGDOM COME US, male vocal/instrumental group · **2 wks**

| 16 Apr 88 | GET IT ON Polydor KCS 1 .... | 75 | 1 wk |
| 6 May 89 | DO YOU LIKE IT Polydor KCS 3 .... | 73 | 1 wk |

KINGMAKER UK, male vocal/instrumental group · **17 wks**

18 Jan 92	IDIOTS AT THE WHEEL EP Scorch SCORCH 3	30	3 wks
23 May 92	EAT YOURSELF WHOLE Scorch SCORCHG 5	15	3 wks
31 Oct 92	ARMCHAIR ANARCHIST Scorch SCORCHG 6	47	2 wks
8 May 93	10 YEARS ASLEEP Scorch CDSCORCHS 8	15	4 wks
19 Jun 93	QUEEN JANE Scorch CDSCORS 9	29	4 wks
30 Oct 93	SATURDAY'S NOT WHAT IT USED TO BE		
	Scorch CDSCORCH 10	63	1 wk

Tracks on Idiots At The Wheel EP: Really Scrape The Sky / Revelation /
Every Teenage Suicide / Strip Away.
See also Various Artists (EPs & LPs) - Gimme Shelter (EP).

KINGS OF SWING ORCHESTRA
Australia, orchestra · **5 wks**

| 1 May 82 | SWITCHED ON SWING Philips Swing 1 .... | 48 | 5 wks |

KINGSMEN US, male vocal/instrumental group · **7 wks**

| 30 Jan 64 | LOUIE LOUIE Pye International 7N 25231 ...... | 26 | 7 wks |

KINGSTON TRIO US, male vocal/instrumental group · **15 wks**

| 21 Nov 58 | ● TOM DOOLEY Capitol CL 14951 .... | 5 | 14 wks |
| 4 Dec 59 | SAN MIGUEL Capitol CL 15073 .... | 29 | 1 wk |

KINKS UK, male vocal/instrumental group · **213 wks**

13 Aug 64	★ YOU REALLY GOT ME Pye 7N 15673	1	12 wks
29 Oct 64	● ALL DAY AND ALL OF THE NIGHT Pye 7N 15714	2	14 wks
21 Jan 65	★ TIRED OF WAITING FOR YOU Pye 7N 15759	1	10 wks
25 Mar 65	EVERYBODY'S GONNA BE HAPPY Pye 7N 15813	17	8 wks
27 May 65	● SET ME FREE Pye 7N 15854	9	11 wks
5 Aug 65	● SEE MY FRIEND Pye 7N 15919	10	9 wks
2 Dec 65	● TILL THE END OF THE DAY Pye 7N 15981	8	12 wks
3 Mar 66	● DEDICATED FOLLOWER OF FASHION		
	Pye 7N 17064	4	11 wks
9 Jun 66	★ SUNNY AFTERNOON Pye 7N 17125	1	13 wks
24 Nov 66	● DEAD END STREET Pye 7N 17222	5	11 wks
11 May 67	● WATERLOO SUNSET Pye 7N 17321	2	11 wks
18 Oct 67	● AUTUMN ALMANAC Pye 7N 17400	3	11 wks
17 Apr 68	WONDERBOY Pye 7N 17468	36	5 wks
17 Jul 68	DAYS Pye 7N 17573	12	10 wks
16 Apr 69	PLASTIC MAN Pye 7N 17724	31	4 wks
10 Jan 70	VICTORIA Pye 7N 17865	33	4 wks
4 Jul 70	● LOLA Pye 7N 17961	2	14 wks
12 Dec 70	APEMAN Pye 7N 45010	5	14 wks
27 May 72	SUPERSONIC ROCKET SHIP RCA 2211	16	8 wks
27 Jun 81	BETTER THINGS Arista ARIST 415	46	5 wks
6 Aug 83	COME DANCING Arista ARIST 502	12	9 wks
15 Oct 83	DON'T FORGET TO DANCE Arista ARIST 524	58	3 wks
15 Oct 83	YOU REALLY GOT ME (re-issue) PRT KD1	47	4 wks

KINKY MACHINE UK, male vocal/instrumental group · **4 wks**

| 6 Mar 93 | SUPERNATURAL GIVER Lemon LEMON 006CD | 70 | 1 wk |
| 29 May 93 | SHOCKAHOLIC Oxygen GASPD 5 .... | 70 | 1 wk |

| 14 Aug 93 | GOING OUT WITH GOD Oxygen GASPD 9 .... | 74 | 1 wk |
| 2 Jul 94 | 10 SECOND BIONIC MAN Oxygen GASPD 14 ..... | 66 | 1 wk |

Fern KINNEY US, female vocalist · **11 wks**

| 16 Feb 80 | ★ TOGETHER WE ARE BEAUTIFUL WEA K 79111 | 1 | 11 wks |

KINSHASA BAND - See Johnny WAKELIN

Kathy KIRBY UK, female vocalist · **54 wks**

15 Aug 63	DANCE ON Decca F 11682	11	13 wks
7 Nov 63	● SECRET LOVE Decca F 11759	4	18 wks
20 Feb 64	● LET ME GO LOVER Decca F 11832	10	11 wks
7 May 64	YOU'RE THE ONE Decca F 11892	17	9 wks
4 Mar 65	I BELONG Decca F 12087	36	3 wks

Bo KIRKLAND and Ruth DAVIS
US, male/female vocal duo · **9 wks**

| 4 Jun 77 | YOU'RE GONNA GET NEXT TO ME | | |
| | EMI International INT 532 .... | 12 | 9 wks |

KISS US, male vocal/instrumental group · **57 wks**

30 Jun 79	I WAS MADE FOR LOVIN' YOU		
	Casablanca CAN 152	50	7 wks
20 Feb 82	A WORLD WITHOUT HEROES Casablanca KISS 002	55	3 wks
30 Apr 83	CREATURES OF THE NIGHT Casablanca KISS 4	34	4 wks
29 Oct 83	LICK IT UP Vertigo KISS 5	31	5 wks
8 Sep 84	HEAVEN'S ON FIRE Vertigo VER 12	43	3 wks
9 Nov 85	TEARS ARE FALLING Vertigo KISS 6	57	3 wks
3 Oct 87	● CRAZY CRAZY NIGHTS Vertigo KISS 7	4	9 wks
5 Dec 87	REASON TO LIVE Vertigo KISS 8	33	7 wks
10 Sep 88	TURN ON THE NIGHT Vertigo KISS 9	41	3 wks
18 Nov 89	HIDE YOUR HEART Vertigo KISS 10	59	2 wks
31 Mar 90	FOREVER Vertigo KISS 11	65	2 wks
11 Jan 92	● GOD GAVE ROCK AND ROLL TO YOU II		
	Interscope A 8696	4	8 wks
9 May 92	UNHOLY Mercury KISS 12	26	2 wks

KISS AMC UK, female vocal duo · **5 wks**

1 Jul 89	A BIT OF... Syncopate SY 29	58	2 wks
19 Aug 89	A BIT OF U2 (re-entry) Syncopate SY 29	58	2 wks
3 Feb 90	MY DOCS Syncopate XAMC 1	66	1 wk

Before the re-entry of A Bit Of U2, copyright problems meant that the
disc was unable to be given its full title.

KISSING THE PINK
UK, male/female vocal/instrumental group · **14 wks**

| 5 Mar 83 | LAST FILM Magnet KTP 3 .... | 19 | 14 wks |

Mac and Katie KISSOON
UK, male/female vocal duo · **33 wks**

19 Jun 71	CHIRPY CHIRPY CHEEP CHEEP		
	Young Blood YB 1026	41	1 wk
18 Jan 75	● SUGAR CANDY KISSES Polydor 2058 531	3	10 wks
3 May 75	● DON'T DO IT BABY State STAT 4	9	8 wks
30 Aug 75	LIKE A BUTTERFLY State STAT 9	18	9 wks
15 May 76	THE TWO OF US State STAT 21	46	5 wks

Kevin KITCHEN UK, male vocalist · **3 wks**

| 20 Apr 85 | PUT MY ARMS AROUND YOU China WOK 1 | 64 | 3 wks |

Eartha KITT US, female vocalist · **34 wks**

| 1 Apr 55 | ● UNDER THE BRIDGES OF PARIS HMV B 10647 | 7 | 9 wks |

10 Jun 55	UNDER THE BRIDGES OF PARIS (re-entry)		
	HMV B 10647	20	1 wk
3 Dec 83	WHERE IS MY MAN Record Shack SOHO 11	36	11 wks
7 Jul 84	I LOVE MEN Record Shack SOHO 21	50	3 wks
12 Apr 86	THIS IS MY LIFE Record Shack SOHO 61	73	1 wk
1 Jul 89	CHA CHA HEELS Arista 112331 [1]	32	7 wks
5 Mar 94	IF I LOVE YA THEN I NEED YA IF I NEED YA THEN I WANT YOU AROUND RCA 74321190342	43	2 wks

[1] Eartha Kitt and Bronski Beat

K-KLASS UK, male/female vocal/instrumental group — 30 wks

4 May 91	RHYTHM IS A MYSTERY		
	Deconstruction CREED 11	61	2 wks
9 Nov 91	● RHYTHM IS A MYSTERY (re-issue)		
	Deconstruction R 6302	3	10 wks
25 Apr 92	SO RIGHT Deconstruction R 6309	20	5 wks
7 Nov 92	DON'T STOP Deconstruction R 6325	32	3 wks
27 Nov 93	LET ME SHOW YOU Deconstruction CDR 6367	13	7 wks
28 May 94	WHAT YOU'RE MISSING		
	Deconstruction CDRS 6380	24	3 wks

KLAXONS Belgium, male vocal/instrumental group — 6 wks

10 Dec 83	THE CLAP CLAP SOUND PRT 7P 290	45	6 wks

KLEEER US, male/female vocal/instrumental group — 10 wks

17 Mar 79	KEEEP YOUR BODY WORKING Atlantic LV 21	51	6 wks
14 Mar 81	GET TOUGH Atlantic 11560	49	4 wks

KLF UK, male vocal/instrumental duo — 51 wks

11 Aug 90	● WHAT TIME IS LOVE (LIVE AT TRANCENTRAL)		
	KLF Communications KLF 004 [1]	5	12 wks
19 Jan 91	★ 3 AM ETERNAL KLF Communications KLF 005 [1]	1	11 wks
4 May 91	● LAST TRAIN TO TRANCENTRAL		
	KLF Communications KLF 008 [1]	2	9 wks
7 Dec 91	● JUSTIFIED AND ANCIENT		
	KLF Communications KLF 099 [2]	2	12 wks
7 Mar 92	● AMERICA: WHAT TIME IS LOVE		
	KLF Communications KLFUSA 004	4	7 wks

[1] KLF featuring the Children Of The Revolution [2] KLF, guest vocals: Tammy Wynette

See also Justified Ancients Of Mu Mu.

KNACK US, male vocal/instrumental group — 12 wks

30 Jun 79	● MY SHARONA Capitol CL 16087	6	10 wks
13 Oct 79	GOOD GIRLS DON'T Capitol CL 16097	66	2 wks

Frederick KNIGHT US, male vocalist — 10 wks

10 Jun 72	I'VE BEEN LONELY SO LONG Stax 2025 098	22	10 wks

Gladys KNIGHT and the PIPS
US, female vocalist and male vocal backing group — 187 wks

8 Jun 67	TAKE ME IN YOUR ARMS AND LOVE ME		
	Tamla Motown TMG 604	13	15 wks
27 Dec 67	I HEARD IT THROUGH THE GRAPEVINE		
	Tamla Motown TMG 629	47	1 wk
17 Jun 72	JUST WALK IN MY SHOES		
	Tamla Motown TMG 813	35	8 wks
25 Nov 72	HELP ME MAKE IT THROUGH THE NIGHT		
	Tamla Motown TMG 830	11	17 wks
3 Mar 73	LOOK OF LOVE Tamla Motown TMG 844	21	9 wks
26 May 73	NEITHER ONE OF US Tamla Motown TMG 855	31	7 wks
5 Apr 75	● THE WAY WE WERE - TRY TO REMEMBER		
	Buddah BDS 428	4	15 wks
2 Aug 75	● BEST THING THAT EVER HAPPENED TO ME		
	Buddah BDS 432	7	10 wks

15 Nov 75	PART TIME LOVE Buddah BDS 438	30	5 wks
8 May 76	● MIDNIGHT TRAIN TO GEORGIA Buddah BDS 444	10	9 wks
21 Aug 76	MAKE YOURS A HAPPY HOME Buddah BDS 447	35	4 wks
6 Nov 76	SO SAD THE SONG Buddah BDS 448	20	9 wks
15 Jan 77	NOBODY BUT YOU Buddah BDS 451	34	2 wks
28 May 77	● BABY DON'T CHANGE YOUR MIND		
	Buddah BDS 458	4	12 wks
24 Sep 77	HOME IS WHERE THE HEART IS Buddah BDS 460	35	4 wks
8 Apr 78	THE ONE AND ONLY Buddah BDS 470	32	4 wks
13 May 78	THE ONE AND ONLY (re-entry) Buddah BDS 470	66	1 wk
24 Jun 78	COME BACK AND FINISH WHAT YOU STARTED		
	Buddah BDS 473	15	13 wks
30 Sep 78	IT'S A BETTER THAN GOOD TIME		
	Buddah BDS 478	59	4 wks
30 Aug 80	TASTE OF BITTER LOVE CBS 8890	35	6 wks
8 Nov 80	BOURGIE BOURGIE CBS 9081	32	6 wks
26 Dec 81	WHEN A CHILD IS BORN CBS S 1758 [1]	74	2 wks
9 Nov 85	THAT'S WHAT FRIENDS ARE FOR		
	Arista ARIST 638 [2]	16	9 wks
16 Jan 88	LOVE OVERBOARD MCA MCA 1223	42	4 wks
10 Jun 89	● LICENCE TO KILL MCA MCA 1339 [3]	6	11 wks

[1] Johnny Mathis and Gladys Knight [2] Dionne Warwick and Friends featuring Elton John, Stevie Wonder and Gladys Knight [3] Gladys Knight

Robert KNIGHT US, male vocalist — 26 wks

17 Jan 68	EVERLASTING LOVE Monument MON 1008	40	2 wks
24 Nov 73	● LOVE ON A MOUNTAIN TOP		
	Monument MNT 1875	10	16 wks
9 Mar 74	EVERLASTING LOVE (re-issue)		
	Monument MNT 2106	19	8 wks

Mark KNOPFLER
UK, male vocalist/instrumentalist - guitar — 3 wks

12 Mar 83	GOING HOME (THEME OF 'LOCAL HERO')		
	Vertigo DSTR 4	56	3 wks

Buddy KNOX US, male vocalist — 5 wks

10 May 57	PARTY DOLL Columbia DB 3914	29	3 wks
16 Aug 62	SHE'S GONE Liberty LIB 55473	45	2 wks

Frankie KNUCKLES US, male producer — 15 wks

17 Jun 89	TEARS ffrr F 108 [1]	50	3 wks
21 Oct 89	YOUR LOVE Trax TRAXT 3	59	4 wks
27 Jul 91	THE WHISTLE SONG Virgin America VUS 47	17	5 wks
23 Nov 91	IT'S HARD SOMETIMES Virgin America VUS 52	67	1 wk
6 Jun 92	RAIN FALLS Virgin America VUST 60 [2]	48	2 wks

[1] Frankie Knuckles presents Satoshi Tomiie [2] Frankie Knuckles featuring Lisa Michaelis

Moe KOFFMAN QUARTETTE
Canada, male instrumental group, Moe Koffman - flute — 2 wks

28 Mar 58	SWINGIN' SHEPHERD BLUES London HLJ 8549	23	2 wks

KOKOMO US, male instrumentalist - piano — 7 wks

13 Apr 61	ASIA MINOR London HLU 9305	35	7 wks

KOKOMO UK, male/female vocal/instrumental group — 3 wks

29 May 82	A LITTLE BIT FURTHER AWAY CBS A 2064	45	3 wks

KON KAN Canada, male vocal/instrumental duo — 13 wks

4 Mar 89	● I BEG YOUR PARDON Atlantic A 8969	5	13 wks

John KONGOS
South Africa, male vocalist / multi-instrumentalist   **25 wks**

22 May 71	● HE'S GONNA STEP ON YOU AGAIN *Fly BUG 8* **4**	14 wks
20 Nov 71	● TOKOLOSHE MAN *Fly BUG 14* **4**	11 wks

KOOL and the GANG
US, male vocal / instrumental group   **207 wks**

27 Oct 79	● LADIES NIGHT *Mercury KOOL 7* **9**	12 wks
19 Jan 80	TOO HOT *Mercury KOOL 8* **23**	8 wks
12 Jul 80	HANGIN' OUT *De-Lite KOOL 9* **52**	4 wks
1 Nov 80	● CELEBRATION *De-Lite KOOL 10* **7**	13 wks
21 Feb 81	JONES VS JONES / SUMMER MADNESS *De-Lite KOOL 11* **17**	11 wks
30 May 81	TAKE IT TO THE TOP *De-Lite DE 2* **15**	9 wks
31 Oct 81	STEPPIN' OUT *De-Lite DE 4* **12**	13 wks
19 Dec 81	● GET DOWN ON IT *De-Lite DE 5* **3**	12 wks
6 Mar 82	TAKE MY HEART (YOU CAN HAVE IT IF YOU WANT IT) *De-Lite DE 6* **29**	7 wks
7 Aug 82	BIG FUN *De-Lite DE 7* **14**	8 wks
16 Oct 82	● OOH LA LA LA (LET'S GO DANCIN') *De-Lite DE 9* **6**	9 wks
4 Dec 82	HI DE HI, HI DE HO *De-Lite DE 14* **29**	8 wks
10 Dec 83	STRAIGHT AHEAD *De-Lite DE 15*.............**15**	10 wks
11 Feb 84	● JOANNA / TONIGHT *De-Lite DE 16* **2**	11 wks
14 Apr 84	(WHEN YOU SAY YOU LOVE SOMEBODY) IN THE HEART *De-Lite DE 17* **7**	8 wks
24 Nov 84	FRESH *De-Lite DE 18* **11**	12 wks
9 Feb 85	MISLED *De-Lite DE 19* **28**	5 wks
11 May 85	● CHERISH *De-Lite DE 20* **4**	22 wks
2 Nov 85	EMERGENCY *De-Lite DE 21* **50**	3 wks
22 Nov 86	VICTORY *Club JAB 44* **67**	2 wks
20 Dec 86	VICTORY (re-entry) *Club JAB 44* **30**	10 wks
21 Mar 87	STONE LOVE *Club JAB 47* **45**	4 wks
31 Dec 88	CELEBRATION (re-mix) *Club JAB 78*.........**56**	5 wks
6 Jul 91	GET DOWN ON IT (re-mix) *Mercury MER 346* **69**	1 wk

Funky Stuff and Hollywood Swinging only appeared on 12-inch and EP versions of Kool 11, although the chart listed all four songs.

KOOLROCK STEADY - See TYREE

KORGIS
UK, male vocal / instrumental duo   **27 wks**

23 Jun 79	IF I HAD YOU *Rialto TREB 103* **13**	12 wks
24 May 80	● EVERYBODY'S GOT TO LEARN SOMETIME *Rialto TREB 115* **5**	12 wks
30 Aug 80	IF IT'S ALRIGHT WITH YOU BABY *Rialto TREB 118*..**56**	3 wks

KRAFTWERK
Germany, male instrumental / vocal group   **69 wks**

10 May 75	AUTOBAHN *Vertigo 6147 012* **11**	9 wks
28 Oct 78	NEON LIGHTS *Capitol CL 15998* **53**	3 wks
9 May 81	POCKET CALCULATOR *EMI 5175* **39**	6 wks
11 Jul 81	COMPUTER LOVE / THE MODEL *EMI 5207* .**36**	8 wks
26 Dec 81	★ COMPUTER LOVE / THE MODEL (re-entry) *EMI 5207* **1**	13 wks
20 Feb 82	SHOWROOM DUMMIES *EMI 5272* **25**	5 wks
6 Aug 83	TOUR DE FRANCE *EMI 5413* **22**	8 wks
25 Aug 84	TOUR DE FRANCE (re-entry) *EMI 5413* **24**	11 wks
1 Jun 91	THE ROBOTS *EMI EM 192* **20**	4 wks
2 Nov 91	RADIOACTIVITY *EMI EM 201* **43**	2 wks

Billy J. KRAMER and the DAKOTAS
UK, male vocalist and male instrumental backing group   **71 wks**

2 May 63	● DO YOU WANT TO KNOW A SECRET? *Parlophone R 5023* **2**	15 wks
1 Aug 63	★ BAD TO ME *Parlophone R 5049* **1**	14 wks
7 Nov 63	● I'LL KEEP YOU SATISFIED *Parlophone R 5073* **4**	13 wks
27 Feb 64	★ LITTLE CHILDREN *Parlophone R 5105* **1**	13 wks
23 Jul 64	● FROM A WINDOW *Parlophone R 5156* **10**	8 wks
20 May 65	TRAINS AND BOATS AND PLANES *Parlophone R 5285* **12**	8 wks

KRANKIES
UK, male / female vocal duo   **6 wks**

7 Feb 81	FAN'DABI'DOZI *Monarch MON 21* **71**	1 wk
7 Mar 81	FAN'DABI'DOZI (re-entry) *Monarch MON 21* **46**	5 wks

Lenny KRAVITZ
US, male vocalist   **45 wks**

2 Jun 90	MR. CABDRIVER *Virgin America VUS 20* **58**	2 wks
4 Aug 90	LET LOVE RULE *Virgin America VUS 26* **39**	4 wks
30 Mar 91	ALWAYS ON THE RUN *Virgin America VUS 34*.........**41**	3 wks
15 Jun 91	IT AIN'T OVER TIL IT'S OVER *Virgin America VUS 43* **11**	8 wks
14 Sep 91	STAND BY MY WOMAN *Virgin America VUS 45* **55**	3 wks
20 Feb 93	● ARE YOU GONNA GO MY WAY *Virgin America VUSDG 65* **4**	11 wks
22 May 93	BELIEVE *Virgin America VUSCD 72* **30**	5 wks
28 Aug 93	HEAVEN HELP *Virgin America VUSDG 73* **20**	7 wks
4 Dec 93	IS THERE ANY LOVE IN YOUR HEART *Virgin America VUSDG 76* **52**	2 wks

KRAZE
US, male / female vocal / instrumental group   **6 wks**

22 Oct 88	THE PARTY *MCA MCA 1288* **29**	5 wks
17 Jun 89	LET'S PLAY HOUSE *MCA MCA 1337* **71**	1 wk

KREW-KATS
UK, male instrumental group   **10 wks**

9 Mar 61	TRAMBONE *HMV POP 840* **33**	9 wks
18 May 61	TRAMBONE (re-entry) *HMV POP 840*..........**49**	1 wk

KRIS KROSS
US, male vocal duo   **22 wks**

30 May 92	● JUMP *Ruff House 6578547* **2**	8 wks
25 Jul 92	WARM IT UP *Ruff House 6582187* **16**	6 wks
17 Oct 92	I MISSED THE BUS *Ruff House 6583927* **57**	1 wk
19 Dec 92	IT'S A SHAME *Ruff House 6588587* **31**	5 wks
11 Sep 93	ALRIGHT *Ruff House 6595652* **47**	2 wks

Marty KRISTIAN - See NEW SEEKERS

KROKUS
Switzerland / Argenti, male vocal / instrumental group   **2 wks**

16 May 81	INDUSTRIAL STRENGTH EP *Ariola ARO 258* **62**	2 wks

Tracks on Industrial Strength EP: Bedside Radio / Easy Rocker / Celebration / Bye Bye Baby.

KRUSH
UK, male / female vocal / instrumental group   **16 wks**

5 Dec 87	● HOUSE ARREST *Club JAB 63* **3**	15 wks
14 Nov 92	WALKING ON SUNSHINE *Network NWK 55* **71**	1 wk

KRUSH PERSPECTIVE
US, female vocal group   **2 wks**

16 Jan 93	LET'S GET TOGETHER (SO GROOVY NOW) *Perspective PERD 7416* **61**	2 wks

K7
US, male vocalist   **22 wks**

11 Dec 93	● COME BABY COME *Big Life BLRD 105* **3**	16 wks
2 Apr 94	HI DE HO *Big Life BLRD 108* [1] **17**	5 wks
25 Jun 94	ZUNGA ZENG *Big Life BLRD 111* [1] **63**	1 wk

[1] K7 and the Swing Kids

K3M
Italy, male / female vocal / instrumental duo   **1 wk**

21 Mar 92	LISTEN TO THE RHYTHM *PWL Continental PWL 214*..............................**71**	1 wk

Charlie KUNZ US, male instrumentalist - piano   4 wks

| 17 Dec 54 | **PIANO MEDLEY NO. 114** Decca F 10419 | **20** | 3 wks |
| 14 Jan 55 | **PIANO MEDLEY NO. 114 (re-entry)** Decca F 10419 | **16** | 1 wk |

Medley titles: There Must Be A Reason / Hold My Hand / If I Give My Heart To You / Little Things Mean A Lot / Make Her Mine / My Son My Son.

KURSAAL FLYERS UK, male vocal / instrumental group   10 wks

| 20 Nov 76 | **LITTLE DOES SHE KNOW** CBS 4689 | **14** | 10 wks |

Li KWAN UK, male producer - Joey Negro   2 wks

| 17 Dec 94 | **I NEED A MAN** Deconstruction 74321252192 | **51** | 2 wks |

See also Joey Negro.

KWS UK, male vocal / instrumental group   36 wks

25 Apr 92	★ **PLEASE DON'T GO / GAME BOY** Network NWK 46	**1**	16 wks
22 Aug 92	● **ROCK YOUR BABY** Network NWK 54	**8**	7 wks
12 Dec 92	**HOLD BACK THE NIGHT** Network NWK 65 [1]	**30**	5 wks
5 Jun 93	**CAN'T GET ENOUGH OF YOUR LOVE** Network NWKCD 72	**71**	1 wk
9 Apr 94	**IT SEEMS TO HANG ON** X-clusive XCLU 006CD	**58**	1 wk
2 Jul 94	**AIN'T NOBODY (LOVES ME BETTER)** X-clusive XCLU 010CD [2]	**21**	4 wks
19 Nov 94	**THE MORE I GET THE MORE I WANT** X-clusive XCLU 011CD [3]	**35**	2 wks

[1] KWS features guest vocal from the Trammps [2] KWS and Gwen Dickey [3] KWS featuring Teddy Pendergrass

Game Boy *was only listed from 9 May 92.*

L

Jonny L UK, male vocalist   1 wk

| 28 Aug 93 | **OOH I LIKE IT** XL XLS 44CD | **73** | 1 wk |

L.A. GUNS US, male / female vocal / instrumental group   4 wks

| 30 Nov 91 | **SOME LIE 4 LOVE** Mercury MER 358 | **61** | 1 wk |
| 21 Dec 91 | **THE BALLAD OF JAYNE** Mercury MER 361 | **53** | 3 wks |

L.A. MIX UK, male / female vocal / instrumental duo   25 wks

10 Oct 87	**DON'T STOP (JAMMIN')** Breakout USA 615	**47**	4 wks
21 May 88	● **CHECK THIS OUT** Breakout USA 629	**6**	7 wks
8 Jul 89	**GET LOOSE** Breakout USA 659 [1]	**25**	6 wks
16 Sep 89	**LOVE TOGETHER** Breakout USA 662 [2]	**66**	2 wks
15 Sep 90	**COMING BACK FOR MORE** A & M AM 579	**50**	3 wks
19 Jan 91	**MYSTERIES OF LOVE** A & M AM 707	**46**	2 wks
23 Mar 91	**WE SHOULDN'T HOLD HANDS IN THE DARK** A & M AM 755	**69**	1 wk

[1] L.A. Mix performed by Jazzi P [2] L.A. Mix featuring Kevin Henry

LA NA NEE NEE NOO NOO - *See BANANARAMA*

Danny LA RUE UK, male vocalist   9 wks

| 18 Dec 68 | **ON MOTHER KELLY'S DOORSTEP** Page One POF 108 | **33** | 9 wks |

Denise LA SALLE US, female vocalist   13 wks

| 15 Jun 85 | ● **MY TOOT TOOT** Epic A 6334 | **6** | 13 wks |

LABELLE US, female vocal group   9 wks

| 22 Mar 75 | **LADY MARMALADE (VOULEZ-VOUS COUCHER AVEC MOI CE SOIR?)** Epic EPC 2852 | **17** | 9 wks |

See also Patti Labelle.

Patti LABELLE US, female vocalist   21 wks

3 May 86	● **ON MY OWN** MCA MCA 1045 [1]	**2**	13 wks
2 Aug 86	**OH, PEOPLE** MCA MCA 1075	**26**	6 wks
3 Sep 94	**THE RIGHT KINDA LOVER** MCA MCSTD 1995	**50**	2 wks

[1] Patti Labelle and Michael McDonald

See also Labelle.

LADIES CHOICE UK, male vocalist   4 wks

| 25 Jan 86 | **FUNKY SENSATION** Sure Delight SD 01 | **41** | 4 wks |

LADY OF RAGE US, female rapper   1 wk

| 8 Oct 94 | **AFRO PUFFS** Interscope A 8288CD | **72** | 1 wk |

LAID BACK Norway, male vocal / instrumental duo   4 wks

| 5 May 90 | **BAKERMAN** Arista 112356 | **44** | 4 wks |

Cleo LAINE UK, female vocalist   14 wks

| 29 Dec 60 | **LET'S SLIP AWAY** Fontana H 269 | **42** | 1 wk |
| 14 Sep 61 | ● **YOU'LL ANSWER TO ME** Fontana H 326 | **5** | 13 wks |

Frankie LAINE US, male vocalist   281 wks

14 Nov 52	● **HIGH NOON** Columbia DB 3113	**7**	7 wks
14 Nov 52	● **SUGARBUSH** Columbia DB 3123 [1]	**8**	2 wks
5 Dec 52	● **SUGARBUSH (re-entry)** Columbia DB 3123 [1]	**8**	6 wks
20 Mar 53	**GIRL IN THE WOOD** Columbia DB 2907	**11**	1 wk
3 Apr 53	★ **I BELIEVE** Philips PB 117	**1**	36 wks
8 May 53	● **TELL ME A STORY** Philips PB 126 [2]	**5**	15 wks
4 Sep 53	● **WHERE THE WINDS BLOW** Philips PB 167	**2**	12 wks
11 Sep 53	**TELL ME A STORY (re-entry)** Philips PB 126 [2]	**12**	1 wk
16 Oct 53	★ **HEY JOE** Philips PB 172	**1**	8 wks
30 Oct 53	★ **ANSWER ME** Philips PB 196	**1**	17 wks
8 Jan 54	● **BLOWING WILD** Philips PB 207	**2**	12 wks
26 Mar 54	● **GRANADA** Philips PB 242	**10**	1 wk
9 Apr 54	● **GRANADA (re-entry)** Philips PB 242	**9**	1 wk
16 Apr 54	● **THE KID'S LAST FIGHT** Philips PB 258	**3**	10 wks
13 Aug 54	● **MY FRIEND** Philips PB 316	**3**	15 wks
8 Oct 54	● **THERE MUST BE A REASON** Philips PB 306	**9**	9 wks
22 Oct 54	● **RAIN RAIN RAIN** Philips PB 311 [3]	**8**	16 wks
11 Mar 55	**IN THE BEGINNING** Philips PB 404	**20**	1 wk
24 Jun 55	● **COOL WATER** Philips PB 465	**2**	22 wks
15 Jul 55	● **STRANGE LADY IN TOWN** Philips PB 478	**6**	13 wks
11 Nov 55	**HUMMING BIRD** Philips PB 498	**16**	1 wk
25 Nov 55	● **HAWKEYE** Philips PB 519	**7**	8 wks
20 Jan 56	● **SIXTEEN TONS** Philips PB 539	**10**	3 wks
4 May 56	**HELL HATH NO FURY** Philips PB 585	**28**	1 wk
7 Sep 56	★ **A WOMAN IN LOVE** Philips PB 617	**1**	21 wks
28 Dec 56	**MOONLIGHT GAMBLER** Philips PB 638	**13**	12 wks
29 Mar 57	**MOONLIGHT GAMBLER (re-entry)** Philips PB 638	**28**	1 wk
26 Apr 57	**LOVE IS A GOLDEN RING** Philips PB 676	**19**	5 wks
4 Oct 57	**GOOD EVENING FRIENDS / UP ABOVE MY HEAD** Philips PB 708 [4]	**25**	4 wks
13 Nov 59	● **RAWHIDE** Philips PB 965	**6**	17 wks
31 Mar 60	**RAWHIDE (re-entry)** Philips PB 965	**41**	2 wks
11 May 61	**GUNSLINGER** Philips PB 1135	**50**	1 wk

[1] Doris Day and Frankie Laine [2] Frankie Laine and Jimmy Boyd [3] Frankie Laine and the Four Lads [4] Frankie Laine and Johnnie Ray

15 year-old **BRENDA LEE** receives a gold disc for 'I'm Sorry' from Milton Rachmil, President of Decca Records in the United States.

FRANKIE LAINE is shown in 1953, the year he was number one more weeks than all other artists put together. (LFI)

The **KINGSMEN** were kept out of number one in the American Hot 100 by the Singing Nun.

STEVE LAWRENCE AND EYDIE GORME had a top three single, 'I Want To Stay Here', and a Broadway musical, *Golden Rainbow*, among their many collaborations.

MAJOR LANCE died in 1994, 30 years after 'Um'ing his way into the chart with a Curtis Mayfield song.

Greg LAKE UK, male vocalist — **12 wks**

6 Dec 75	● I BELIEVE IN FATHER CHRISTMAS		
	Manticore K 13511	**2**	7 wks
25 Dec 82	I BELIEVE IN FATHER CHRISTMAS (re-entry)		
	Manticore K 13511	**72**	3 wks
24 Dec 83	I BELIEVE IN FATHER CHRISTMAS (2nd re-entry)		
	Manticore K 13511	**65**	2 wks

See also Emerson, Lake and Palmer.

Annabel LAMB UK, female vocalist — **7 wks**

27 Aug 83	RIDERS ON THE STORM A & M AM 131	**27**	7 wks

LAMBRETTAS UK, male vocal / instrumental group — **24 wks**

1 Mar 80	● POISON IVY Rocket XPRESS 25	**7**	12 wks
24 May 80	D-A-A-ANCE Rocket XPRESS 33	**12**	8 wks
23 Aug 80	ANOTHER DAY (ANOTHER GIRL)		
	Rocket XPRESS 36	**49**	4 wks

LANCASTRIANS UK, male vocal / instrumental group — **2 wks**

24 Dec 64	WE'LL SING IN THE SUNSHINE Pye 7N 15732	**47**	2 wks

Major LANCE US, male vocalist — **2 wks**

13 Feb 64	UM UM UM UM UM UM Columbia DB 7205	**40**	2 wks

Valerie LANDSBERG - See KIDS FROM FAME

LANDSCAPE UK, male vocal / instrumental group — **20 wks**

28 Feb 81	● EINSTEIN A GO-GO RCA 22	**5**	13 wks
23 May 81	NORMAN BATES RCA 60	**40**	7 wks

Desmond LANE - See Alma COGAN; Cyril STAPLETON

Ronnie LANE and SLIM CHANCE
UK, male vocalist and male instrumental group — **12 wks**

12 Jan 74	HOW COME GM GMS 011	**11**	8 wks
15 Jun 74	THE POACHER GM GMS 024	**36**	4 wks

Don LANG UK, male vocalist — **18 wks**

4 Nov 55	CLOUDBURST HMV POP 115	**16**	2 wks
2 Dec 55	CLOUDBURST (re-entry) HMV POP 115	**18**	1 wk
13 Jan 56	CLOUDBURST (2nd re-entry) HMV POP 115	**20**	1 wk
5 Jul 57	SCHOOL DAY HMV POP 350 [1]	**26**	2 wks
23 May 58	● WITCH DOCTOR HMV POP 488 [1]	**5**	11 wks
10 Mar 60	SINK THE BISMARCK HMV POP 714	**43**	1 wk

[1] Don Lang and his Frantic Five

k.d. lang Canada, female vocalist — **22 wks**

16 May 92	CONSTANT CRAVING Sire W 0100	**52**	4 wks
22 Aug 92	CRYING Virgin America VUS 63 [1]	**13**	6 wks
27 Feb 93	CONSTANT CRAVING (re-issue) Sire W 0157CD	**15**	8 wks
1 May 93	THE MIND OF LOVE Sire W 0170CD1	**72**	1 wk
26 Jun 93	MISS CHATELAINE Sire W 0181CDX	**68**	2 wks
11 Dec 93	JUST KEEP ME MOVING Sire W 0227CD	**59**	1 wk

[1] Roy Orbison (duet with k.d. lang)

Thomas LANG UK, male vocalist — **3 wks**

30 Jan 88	THE HAPPY MAN Epic VOW 4	**67**	3 wks

Mario LANZA US, male vocalist — **32 wks**

14 Nov 52	● BECAUSE YOU'RE MINE HMV DA 2017	**3**	24 wks
4 Feb 55	DRINKING SONG HMV DA 2065	**13**	1 wk
18 Feb 55	I'LL WALK WITH GOD HMV DA 2062	**18**	1 wk
22 Apr 55	SERENADE HMV DA 2065	**19**	1 wk
6 May 55	I'LL WALK WITH GOD (re-entry) HMV DA 2062	**20**	1 wk
6 May 55	SERENADE (re-entry) HMV DA 2065	**15**	2 wks
14 Sep 56	SERENADE HMV DA 2085	**25**	1 wk
12 Oct 56	SERENADE (re-entry) HMV DA 2085	**29**	1 wk

DA 2065 and DA 2085 are two different songs.

Julius LAROSA US, male vocalist — **9 wks**

4 Jul 58	TORERO RCA 1063	**15**	9 wks

LA'S UK, male vocal / instrumental group — **18 wks**

14 Jan 89	THERE SHE GOES Go! Discs GOLAS 2	**59**	4 wks
15 Sep 90	TIMELESS MELODY Go! Discs GOLAS 4	**57**	2 wks
3 Nov 90	THERE SHE GOES (re-issue) Go! Discs GOLAS 5	**13**	9 wks
16 Feb 91	FEELIN' Go! Discs GOLAS 6	**43**	3 wks

James LAST BAND Germany, male orchestra — **4 wks**

3 May 80	THE SEDUCTION (LOVE THEME) Polydor PD 2071	**48**	4 wks

LATE SHOW UK, male vocal / instrumental group — **6 wks**

3 Mar 79	BRISTOL STOMP Decca F 13822	**40**	6 wks

LATIN QUARTER
UK, male / female vocal / instrumental group — **10 wks**

18 Jan 86	RADIO AFRICA Rockin' Horse RH 102	**19**	9 wks
18 Apr 87	NOMZAMO (ONE PEOPLE ONE CAUSE)		
	Rockin' Horse RH 113	**73**	1 wk

Gino LATINO Italy, male producer — **7 wks**

20 Jan 90	WELCOME ffrr F 126	**17**	7 wks

LATINO RAVE - See VARIOUS ARTISTS (MONTAGES)

LATOUR US, male vocalist / producer — **7 wks**

8 Jun 91	PEOPLE ARE STILL HAVING SEX Polydor PO 147	**15**	7 wks

Stacy LATTISAW US, female vocalist — **14 wks**

14 Jun 80	● JUMP TO THE BEAT Atlantic/Cotillion K 11496	**3**	11 wks
30 Aug 80	DYNAMITE Atlantic K 11554	**51**	3 wks

LAUNCHERS - See Ezz RECO and the LAUNCHERS with Boysie GRANT

Cyndi LAUPER US, female vocalist — **97 wks**

14 Jan 84	● GIRLS JUST WANT TO HAVE FUN Portrait A 3943	**2**	12 wks
24 Mar 84	TIME AFTER TIME Portrait A 4290	**54**	4 wks
16 Jun 84	TIME AFTER TIME (re-entry) Portrait A 4290	**3**	13 wks
1 Sep 84	SHE BOP Portrait A 4620	**46**	5 wks
17 Nov 84	ALL THROUGH THE NIGHT Portrait A 4849	**64**	2 wks
20 Sep 86	TRUE COLOURS Portrait 650026 7	**12**	11 wks
27 Dec 86	CHANGE OF HEART Portrait CYNDI 1	**74**	1 wk
10 Jan 87	CHANGE OF HEART Portrait CYNDI 1	**67**	1 wk
28 Mar 87	WHAT'S GOING ON Portrait CYN 1	**57**	3 wks
20 May 89	● I DROVE ALL NIGHT Epic CYN 4	**7**	12 wks
5 Aug 89	MY FIRST NIGHT WITHOUT YOU Epic CYN 5	**53**	4 wks
30 Dec 89	HEADING WEST Epic CYN 6	**68**	1 wk
6 Jun 92	THE WORLD IS STONE Epic 6579707	**15**	7 wks

13 Nov 93	**THAT'S WHAT I THINK** Epic 6598782	**31**	4 wks
8 Jan 94	**WHO LET IN THE RAIN** Epic 6590392	**32**	4 wks
17 Sep 94	● **HEY NOW (GIRLS JUST WANT TO HAVE FUN)** Epic 6608072	**4**	13 wks

Hey Now (Girls Just Want To Have Fun) is a re-recording of her first hit.

LAUREL and HARDY
UK, male vocal / instrumental duo   **2 wks**

2 Apr 83	**CLUNK CLINK** CBS A 3213	**65**	2 wks

LAUREL and HARDY with the AVALON BOYS featuring Chill WILLS
UK / US, male vocal duo with US, male vocal group   **10 wks**

22 Nov 75	● **THE TRAIL OF THE LONESOME PINE** United Artists UP 36026	**2**	10 wks

Joanna LAW *UK, female vocalist*   **3 wks**

7 Jul 90	**FIRST TIME EVER** Citybeat CBE 752	**67**	3 wks

Joey LAWRENCE *US, male vocalist*   **14 wks**

26 Jun 93	**NOTHIN' MY LOVE CAN'T FIX** EMI CDEM 271	**13**	7 wks
28 Aug 93	**I CAN'T HELP MYSELF** EMI CDEM 277	**27**	4 wks
30 Oct 93	**STAY FOREVER** EMI CDEM 289	**41**	3 wks

Lee LAWRENCE *UK, male vocalist*   **10 wks**

20 Nov 53	**CRYING IN THE CHAPEL** Decca F 10177	**11**	1 wk
11 Dec 53	● **CRYING IN THE CHAPEL (re-entry)** Decca F 10177	**7**	5 wks
2 Dec 55	**SUDDENLY THERE'S A VALLEY** Columbia DB 3681	**19**	1 wk
16 Dec 55	**SUDDENLY THERE'S A VALLEY (re-entry)** Columbia DB 3681	**14**	3 wks

Sophie LAWRENCE *UK, female vocalist*   **7 wks**

3 Aug 91	**LOVE'S UNKIND** IQ ZB 44821	**21**	7 wks

Steve LAWRENCE *US, male vocalist*   **27 wks**

21 Apr 60	● **FOOTSTEPS** HMV POP 726	**4**	13 wks
18 Aug 60	**GIRLS GIRLS GIRLS** London HLT 9166	**49**	1 wk
22 Aug 63	● **I WANT TO STAY HERE** CBS AAG 163 [1]	**3**	13 wks

[1] Steve and Eydie

Lindy LAYTON *UK, female vocalist*   **15 wks**

11 Aug 90	**SILLY GAMES** Arista 113452 [1]	**22**	7 wks
26 Jan 91	**ECHO MY HEART** Arista 113845	**42**	2 wks
31 Aug 91	**WITHOUT YOU (ONE AND ONE)** Arista 114636	**71**	2 wks
24 Apr 93	**WE GOT THE LOVE** PWL International PWCD 250	**38**	3 wks
30 Oct 93	**SHOW ME** PWL International PWCD 275	**47**	1 wk

[1] Lindy Layton featuring Janet Kay

See also Beats International.

Doug LAZY *US, male vocalist*   **9 wks**

15 Jul 89	**LET IT ROLL** Atlantic A 8866 [1]	**27**	5 wks
4 Nov 89	**LET THE RHYTHM PUMP** Atlantic A 8784	**45**	3 wks
26 May 90	**LET THE RHYTHM PUMP (re-mix)** East West A 7919	**63**	1 wk

[1] Raze presents Doug Lazy

Keith LE BLANC - *See Malcolm X*

Vicky LEANDROS *Greece, female vocalist*   **29 wks**

8 Apr 72	● **COME WHAT MAY** Philips 6000 049	**2**	16 wks
23 Dec 72	**THE LOVE IN YOUR EYES** Philips 6000 081	**48**	3 wks
20 Jan 73	**THE LOVE IN YOUR EYES (re-entry)** Philips 6000 081	**40**	4 wks
7 Apr 73	**THE LOVE IN YOUR EYES (2nd re-entry)** Philips 6000 081	**46**	1 wk
7 Jul 73	**WHEN BOUZOUKIS PLAYED** Philips 6000 111	**44**	2 wks
28 Jul 73	**WHEN BOUZOUKIS PLAYED (re-entry)** Philips 6000 111	**45**	3 wks

Brenda LEE *US, female vocalist*   **210 wks**

17 Mar 60	**SWEET NOTHIN'S** Brunswick 05819	**45**	1 wk
7 Apr 60	● **SWEET NOTHIN'S (re-entry)** Brunswick 05819	**4**	18 wks
30 Jun 60	**I'M SORRY** Brunswick 05833	**12**	16 wks
20 Oct 60	**I WANT TO BE WANTED** Brunswick 05839	**31**	6 wks
19 Jan 61	**LET'S JUMP THE BROOMSTICK** Brunswick 05823	**12**	15 wks
6 Apr 61	**EMOTIONS** Brunswick 05847	**45**	1 wk
20 Jul 61	**DUM DUM** Brunswick 05854	**22**	8 wks
16 Nov 61	**FOOL NUMBER ONE** Brunswick 05860	**38**	3 wks
8 Feb 62	**BREAK IT TO ME GENTLY** Brunswick 05864	**46**	2 wks
5 Apr 62	● **SPEAK TO ME PRETTY** Brunswick 05867	**3**	12 wks
21 Jun 62	● **HERE COMES THAT FEELING** Brunswick 05871	**5**	12 wks
13 Sep 62	**IT STARTED ALL OVER AGAIN** Brunswick 05876	**15**	11 wks
29 Nov 62	● **ROCKIN' AROUND THE CHRISTMAS TREE** Brunswick 05880	**6**	7 wks
17 Jan 63	● **ALL ALONE AM I** Brunswick 05882	**7**	17 wks
28 Mar 63	● **LOSING YOU** Brunswick 05886	**10**	16 wks
18 Jul 63	**I WONDER** Brunswick 05891	**14**	9 wks
31 Oct 63	**SWEET IMPOSSIBLE YOU** Brunswick 05896	**28**	6 wks
9 Jan 64	● **AS USUAL** Brunswick 05899	**5**	15 wks
9 Apr 64	**THINK** Brunswick 05903	**26**	8 wks
10 Sep 64	**IS IT TRUE** Brunswick 05915	**17**	8 wks
10 Dec 64	**CHRISTMAS WILL BE JUST ANOTHER LONELY DAY** Brunswick 05921	**29**	5 wks
4 Feb 65	**THANKS A LOT** Brunswick 05927	**41**	2 wks
29 Jul 65	**TOO MANY RIVERS** Brunswick 05936	**22**	12 wks

Byron LEE - *See Boris GARDINER*

Curtis LEE *US, male vocalist*   **2 wks**

31 Aug 61	**PRETTY LITTLE ANGEL EYES** London HLX 9397	**47**	1 wk
14 Sep 61	**PRETTY LITTLE ANGEL EYES (re-entry)** London HLX 9397	**48**	1 wk

Dee C. LEE *UK, female vocalist*   **20 wks**

9 Nov 85	● **SEE THE DAY** CBS A 6570	**3**	12 wks
8 Mar 86	**COME HELL OR WATERS HIGH** CBS A 6869	**46**	5 wks
13 Nov 93	**NO TIME TO PLAY** Cooltempo CDCOOL 282 [1]	**25**	3 wks

[1] Guru featuring D.C. Lee

Garry LEE and SHOWDOWN
Canada, male vocal / instrumental group   **3 wks**

31 Jul 93	**THE RODEO SONG** Party Dish VCD 101	**44**	3 wks

Jackie LEE *UK, female vocalist*   **31 wks**

10 Apr 68	● **WHITE HORSES** Philips BF 1674 [1]	**10**	14 wks
2 Jan 71	**RUPERT** Pye 7N 45003	**14**	17 wks

[1] Jacky

Leapy LEE *UK, male vocalist*   **28 wks**

21 Aug 68	● **LITTLE ARROWS** MCA MU 1028	**2**	21 wks
20 Dec 69	**GOOD MORNING** MCA MK 5021	**47**	1 wk
10 Jan 70	**GOOD MORNING (re-entry)** MCA MK 5021	**29**	6 wks

Peggy LEE US, female vocalist — 29 wks

24 May 57	● MR. WONDERFUL *Brunswick 05671*	5	13 wks
15 Aug 58	● FEVER *Capitol CL 14902*	5	11 wks
23 Mar 61	TILL THERE WAS YOU *Capitol CL 15184*	40	1 wk
6 Apr 61	TILL THERE WAS YOU (re-entry) *Capitol CL 15184*	30	3 wks
22 Aug 92	FEVER (re-issue) *Capitol PEG 1*	75	1 wk

Toney LEE US, male vocalist — 4 wks

29 Jan 83	REACH UP *TMT TMT 2*	64	4 wks

LEEDS UNITED FC UK, male football team vocalists — 13 wks

29 Apr 72	● LEEDS UNITED *Chapter One SCH 168*	10	10 wks
25 Apr 92	LEEDS LEEDS LEEDS *Q Music LUFC 2*	61	1 wk
9 May 92	LEEDS LEEDS LEEDS (re-entry) *Q Music LUFC 2*	54	2 wks

Raymond LEFEVRE France, orchestra — 2 wks

15 May 68	SOUL COAXING *Major Minor MM 559*	46	2 wks

LEFTFIELD UK, male instrumental / production duo — 6 wks

12 Dec 92	SONG OF LIFE *Hard Hands HAND 002T*	59	1 wk
13 Nov 93	OPEN UP *Hard Hands HAND 009CD* [1]	13	5 wks

[1] Leftfield Lydon

Paul LEKAKIS US, male vocalist — 4 wks

30 May 87	BOOM BOOM (LET'S GO BACK TO MY ROOM) *Champion CHAMP 43*	60	4 wks

LEMON PIPERS US, male vocal / instrumental group — 16 wks

7 Feb 68	● GREEN TAMBOURINE *Pye International 7N 25444*	7	11 wks
1 May 68	RICE IS NICE *Pye International 7N 25454*	41	5 wks

LEMON TREES UK, male vocal / instrumental group — 9 wks

26 Sep 92	LOVE IS IN YOUR EYES *Oxygen GASP 1*	75	1 wk
7 Nov 92	THE WAY I FEEL *Oxygen GASP 2*	62	2 wks
13 Feb 93	LET IT LOOSE *Oxygen GASPD 3*	55	2 wks
17 Apr 93	CHILD OF LOVE *Oxygen GASPD 4*	55	3 wks
3 Jul 93	I CAN'T FACE THE WORLD *Oxygen GASPD 6*	52	1 wk

LEMONHEADS
US / Australia, male vocal / instrumental group — 23 wks

17 Oct 92	IT'S A SHAME ABOUT RAY *Atlantic A 7423*	70	1 wk
5 Dec 92	MRS ROBINSON / BEIN' AROUND *Atlantic A 7401*	19	9 wks
6 Feb 93	CONFETTI / MY DRUG BUDDY *Atlantic A 7430CD*	44	2 wks
10 Apr 93	IT'S A SHAME ABOUT RAY (re-issue) *Atlantic A 5764CD*	31	3 wks
16 Oct 93	INTO YOUR ARMS *Atlantic A 7302CD*	14	4 wks
27 Nov 93	IT'S ABOUT TIME *Atlantic A 7296CD*	57	2 wks
14 May 94	BIG GAY HEART *Atlantic A 7259CD*	55	2 wks

LENA - See Lena FIAGBE

John LENNON UK, male vocalist — 184 wks

9 Jul 69	● GIVE PEACE A CHANCE *Apple 13* [1]	2	13 wks
1 Nov 69	COLD TURKEY *Apple APPLES 1001* [1]	14	8 wks
21 Feb 70	● INSTANT KARMA *Apple APPLES 1003* [2]	5	9 wks
20 Mar 71	● POWER TO THE PEOPLE *Apple R 5892* [3]	7	9 wks
9 Dec 72	● HAPPY XMAS (WAR IS OVER) *Apple R 5970* [4]	4	8 wks
24 Nov 73	MIND GAMES *Apple R 5994*	26	9 wks
19 Oct 74	WHATEVER GETS YOU THROUGH THE NIGHT *Apple R 5998* [5]	36	4 wks
4 Jan 75	HAPPY XMAS (WAR IS OVER) (re-entry) *Apple R 5970* [4]	48	1 wk
8 Feb 75	NUMBER 9 DREAM *Apple R 6003*	23	8 wks
3 May 75	STAND BY ME *Apple R 6005*	30	7 wks
1 Nov 75	● IMAGINE *Apple R 6009*	6	11 wks
8 Nov 80	★ (JUST LIKE) STARTING OVER *Geffen K 79186*	1	15 wks
20 Dec 80	● HAPPY XMAS (WAR IS OVER) (2nd re-entry) *Apple R 5970* [4]	2	9 wks
27 Dec 80	★ IMAGINE (re-entry) *Apple R 6009*	1	13 wks
24 Jan 81	★ WOMAN *Geffen K 79195*	1	11 wks
24 Jan 81	GIVE PEACE A CHANCE (re-entry) *Apple 13*	33	5 wks
21 Mar 81	I SAW HER STANDING THERE *DJM DJS 10965* [6]	40	4 wks
4 Apr 81	WATCHING THE WHEELS *Geffen K 79207*	30	6 wks
19 Dec 81	HAPPY XMAS (WAR IS OVER) (3rd re-entry) *Apple R 5970* [4]	28	5 wks
20 Nov 82	LOVE *Parlophone R 6059*	41	7 wks
25 Dec 82	HAPPY XMAS (WAR IS OVER) (4th re-entry) *Apple R 5970* [4]	56	3 wks
21 Jan 84	● NOBODY TOLD ME *Ono Music/Polydor POSP 700*	6	6 wks
17 Mar 84	BORROWED TIME *Polydor POSP 701*	32	6 wks
30 Nov 85	JEALOUS GUY *Parlophone R 6117*	65	2 wks
10 Dec 88	IMAGINE / JEALOUS GUY / HAPPY XMAS (WAR IS OVER) (re-issue) *Parlophone R 6199*	45	5 wks

[1] Plastic Ono Band [2] Lennon, Ono and the Plastic Ono Band [3] John Lennon and the Plastic Ono Band [4] John and Yoko and the Plastic Ono Band with the Harlem Community Choir [5] John Lennon with the Plastic Ono Nuclear Band [6] The Elton John Band featuring John Lennon and the Muscle Shoals Horns

Julian LENNON UK, male vocalist — 46 wks

6 Oct 84	● TOO LATE FOR GOODBYES *Charisma JL 1*	6	11 wks
15 Dec 84	VALOTTE *Charisma JL 2*	55	6 wks
9 Mar 85	SAY YOU'RE WRONG *Charisma JL 3*	75	1 wk
7 Dec 85	BECAUSE *EMI 5538*	40	7 wks
11 Mar 89	NOW YOU'RE IN HEAVEN *Virgin VS 1154*	59	3 wks
24 Aug 91	● SALTWATER *Virgin VS 1361*	6	13 wks
30 Nov 91	HELP YOURSELF *Virgin VS 1379*	53	2 wks
25 Apr 92	GET A LIFE *Virgin VS 1398*	56	3 wks

Annie LENNOX UK, female vocalist — 45 wks

3 Dec 88	PUT A LITTLE LOVE IN YOUR HEART *A & M AM 484* [1]	28	8 wks
28 Mar 92	● WHY *RCA PB 45317*	5	8 wks
6 Jun 92	PRECIOUS *RCA 74321100257*	23	5 wks
22 Aug 92	● WALKING ON BROKEN GLASS *RCA 74321107227*	8	8 wks
31 Oct 92	COLD *RCA 74321116902*	26	4 wks
13 Feb 93	● LITTLE BIRD / LOVE SONG FOR A VAMPIRE *RCA 743211233832*	3	12 wks

[1] Annie Lennox and Al Green

Rula LENSKA - See Julie COVINGTON, Rula LENSKA, Charlotte CORN-WELL and Sue JONES-DAVIES

Phillip LEO UK, male vocalist — 2 wks

23 Jul 94	SECOND CHANCE *EMI CDEM 327*	57	2 wks

LESTER - See Norman COOK

Ketty LESTER US, female vocalist — 16 wks

19 Apr 62	● LOVE LETTERS *London HLN 9527*	4	12 wks
19 Jul 62	BUT NOT FOR ME *London HLN 9574*	45	4 wks

LET LOOSE UK, male vocal / instrumental group — 33 wks

24 Apr 93	CRAZY FOR YOU *Vertigo VERCD 74*	44	3 wks
9 Apr 94	SEVENTEEN *Mercury MERCD 400*	44	2 wks
25 Jun 94	● CRAZY FOR YOU (re-issue) *Mercury MERCD 402*	2	20 wks
22 Oct 94	SEVENTEEN (re-issue) *Mercury MERCD 406*	11	6 wks

| 24 Dec 94 | CRAZY FOR YOU (re-entry of re-issue) | | |
| | Mercury MERCD 402 | 52† | 2 wks |

Gerald LETHAN - See WALL OF SOUND featuring Gerald LETHAN

LETTERMEN US, male vocal group — **3 wks**

| 23 Nov 61 | THE WAY YOU LOOK TONIGHT Capitol CL 15222 | 36 | 3 wks |

LEVEL 42 UK, male vocal / instrumental group — **177 wks**

30 Aug 80	LOVE MEETING LOVE Polydor POSP 170	61	4 wks
18 Apr 81	LOVE GAMES Polydor POSP 234	38	6 wks
8 Aug 81	TURN IT ON Polydor POSP 286	57	6 wks
14 Nov 81	STARCHILD Polydor POSP 343	47	4 wks
8 May 82	ARE YOU HEARING (WHAT I HEAR)?		
	Polydor POSP 396	49	5 wks
2 Oct 82	WEAVE YOUR SPELL Polydor POSP 500	43	4 wks
15 Jan 83	THE CHINESE WAY Polydor POSP 538	24	8 wks
16 Apr 83	OUT OF SIGHT, OUT OF MIND Polydor POSP 570	41	4 wks
30 Jul 83	● THE SUN GOES DOWN (LIVING IT UP)		
	Polydor POSP 622	10	12 wks
22 Oct 83	MICRO KID Polydor POSP 643	37	5 wks
1 Sep 84	HOT WATER Polydor POSP 697	18	9 wks
3 Nov 84	THE CHANT HAS BEGUN Polydor POSP 710	41	5 wks
21 Sep 85	● SOMETHING ABOUT YOU Polydor POSP 759	6	17 wks
7 Dec 85	LEAVING ME NOW Polydor POSP 776	15	11 wks
26 Apr 86	● LESSONS IN LOVE Polydor POSP 790	3	13 wks
14 Feb 87	● RUNNING IN THE FAMILY Polydor POSP 842	6	10 wks
25 Apr 87	● TO BE WITH YOU AGAIN Polydor POSP 855	10	7 wks
12 Sep 87	● IT'S OVER Polydor POSP 900	10	8 wks
12 Dec 87	CHILDREN SAY Polydor POSP 911	22	6 wks
3 Sep 88	HEAVEN IN MY HANDS Polydor PO 14	12	5 wks
29 Oct 88	TAKE A LOOK Polydor PO 24	32	4 wks
21 Jan 89	TRACIE Polydor PO 34	25	5 wks
28 Oct 89	TAKE CARE OF YOURSELF Polydor PO 58	39	3 wks
17 Aug 91	GUARANTEED RCA PB 44745	17	4 wks
19 Oct 91	OVERTIME RCA PB 44997	62	2 wks
18 Apr 92	MY FATHER'S SHOES RCA PB 45271	55	1 wk
26 Feb 94	FOREVER NOW RCA 74321190272	19	4 wks
30 Apr 94	ALL OVER YOU RCA 74321205662	26	2 wks
6 Aug 94	LOVE IN A PEACEFUL WORLD RCA 74321220332	31	3 wks

LEVELLERS UK, male vocal / instrumental group — **20 wks**

21 Sep 91	ONE WAY China WOK 2008	51	2 wks
7 Dec 91	FAR FROM HOME China WOK 2010	71	1 wk
23 May 92	15 YEARS (EP) China WOKX 2020	11	5 wks
10 Jul 93	BELARUSE China WOKCD 2034	12	5 wks
30 Oct 93	THIS GARDEN China WOKCD 2039	12	4 wks
14 May 94	JULIE (EP) China WOKCD 2042	17	3 wks

Tracks on 15 Years (EP): 15 Years / Dance Before The Storm / The River Flow (Live) / Plastic Jeezus. Tracks on Julie (EP): Julie / English Civil War / Lowlands Of Holland / 100 years.

LEVERT UK, male vocal group — **10 wks**

| 22 Aug 87 | ● CASANOVA Atlantic A 9217 | 9 | 10 wks |

Hank LEVINE US, orchestra — **4 wks**

| 21 Dec 61 | IMAGE HMV POP 947 | 45 | 4 wks |

Barrington LEVY Jamaica, male vocalist — **11 wks**

2 Feb 85	HERE I COME London LON 62	41	4 wks
15 Jun 91	TRIBAL BASE Desire WANT 44 [1]	20	6 wks
24 Sep 94	WORK MCA MCSTD 2003	65	1 wk

[1] Rebel MC featuring Tenor Fly and Barrington Levy

Jona LEWIE UK, male vocalist — **20 wks**

| 10 May 80 | YOU'LL ALWAYS FIND ME IN THE KITCHEN | | |
| | AT PARTIES Stiff BUY 73 | 16 | 9 wks |

| 29 Nov 80 | ● STOP THE CAVALRY Stiff BUY 104 | 3 | 11 wks |

On some copies first title was simply Kitchen At Parties. See also Terry Dactyl and the Dinosaurs.

C.J. LEWIS UK, male vocalist — **29 wks**

23 Apr 94	● SWEETS FOR MY SWEET Black Market BMITD 017	3	13 wks
23 Jul 94	● EVERYTHING IS ALRIGHT (UPTIGHT)		
	Black Market BMITD 019	10	7 wks
8 Oct 94	BEST OF MY LOVE Black Market BMITD 021	13	6 wks
17 Dec 94	DOLLARS Black Market BMITD 023	34†	3 wks

DARLENE LEWIS US, female vocalist — **4 wks**

| 16 Apr 94 | ● LET THE MUSIC (LIFT YOU UP) | | |
| | KMS / Eastern Bloc KMSCD 10 [1] | 16 | 4 wks |

[1] Loveland featuring Rachel McFarlane vs Darlene Lewis

All formats of Let the Music (Lift You Up) featured versions by Loveland featuring Rachel McFarlane and also by Darlene Lewis.

Dee LEWIS UK, female vocalist — **5 wks**

| 18 Jun 88 | BEST OF MY LOVE Mercury DEE 3 | 47 | 5 wks |

Gary LEWIS and the PLAYBOYS
US, male vocal / instrumental group — **7 wks**

| 8 Feb 75 | MY HEART'S SYMPHONY United Artists UP 35780 | 36 | 7 wks |

Huey LEWIS and the NEWS
US, male vocal / instrumental group — **66 wks**

27 Oct 84	IF THIS IS IT Chrysalis CHS 2829	39	6 wks
31 Aug 85	THE POWER OF LOVE Chrysalis HUEY 1	11	10 wks
23 Nov 85	HEART AND SOUL (EP) Chrysalis HUEY 2	61	4 wks
8 Feb 86	● THE POWER OF LOVE (re-issue) DO YOU BELIEVE		
	IN LOVE Chrysalis HUEY 3	9	12 wks
10 May 86	THE HEART OF ROCK AND ROLL Chrysalis HUEY 4	49	3 wks
23 Aug 86	STUCK WITH YOU Chrysalis HUEY 5	12	12 wks
6 Dec 86	HIP TO BE SQUARE Chrysalis HUEY 6	41	5 wks
21 Mar 87	SIMPLE AS THAT Chrysalis HUEY 7	47	5 wks
16 Jul 88	PERFECT WORLD Chrysalis HUEY 10	48	6 wks

Tracks on Heart and Soul (EP): Heart and Soul / Hope You Love Me Like You Say You Do / Heart of Rock And Roll / Buzz Buzz Buzz. Do You Believe In Love only listed from 15 Feb 86.

Jerry LEWIS US, male vocalist — **8 wks**

8 Feb 57	ROCK-A-BYE YOUR BABY (WITH A DIXIE		
	MELODY) Brunswick 05636	12	7 wks
5 Apr 57	ROCK-A-BYE YOUR BABY (WITH A DIXIE		
	MELODY) (re-entry) Brunswick 05636	22	1 wk

Jerry Lee LEWIS
US, male vocalist / instrumentalist - piano — **68 wks**

27 Sep 57	● WHOLE LOTTA SHAKIN' GOIN' ON		
	London HLS 8457	8	10 wks
20 Dec 57	★ GREAT BALLS OF FIRE London HLS 8529	1	12 wks
27 Dec 57	WHOLE LOTTA SHAKIN' GOIN' ON (re-entry)		
	London HLS 8457	26	1 wk
11 Apr 58	● BREATHLESS London HLS 8592	8	7 wks
23 Jan 59	HIGH SCHOOL CONFIDENTIAL London HLS 8780	12	6 wks
1 May 59	LOVIN' UP A STORM London HLS 8840	28	1 wk
9 Jun 60	BABY BABY BYE BYE London HLS 9131	47	1 wk
4 May 61	● WHAT'D I SAY London HLS 9335	10	12 wks
3 Aug 61	WHAT'D I SAY (re-entry) London HLS 9335	49	1 wk
6 Sep 62	SWEET LITTLE SIXTEEN London HLS 9584	38	5 wks
14 Mar 63	GOOD GOLLY MISS MOLLY London HLS 9688	31	6 wks
6 May 72	CHANTILLY LACE Mercury 6052 141	33	5 wks

Linda LEWIS — UK, female vocalist — 30 wks

Date	Title	Pos	Wks
2 Jun 73	ROCK-A-DOODLE-DOO Raft RA 18502	15	11 wks
12 Jul 75	● IT'S IN HIS KISS Arista 17	6	8 wks
17 Apr 76	BABY I'M YOURS Arista 43	33	6 wks
2 Jun 79	I'D BE SURPRISINGLY GOOD FOR YOU Ariola ARO 166	40	5 wks

Ramsey LEWIS — US, male instrumentalist - piano — 8 wks

Date	Title	Pos	Wks
15 Apr 72	WADE IN THE WATER Chess 6145 004	31	8 wks

Shirley LEWIS - See Arthur BAKER

John LEYTON — UK, male vocalist — 70 wks

Date	Title	Pos	Wks
3 Aug 61	★ JOHNNY REMEMBER ME Top Rank JAR 577	1	15 wks
5 Oct 61	● WILD WIND Top Rank JAR 585	2	10 wks
28 Dec 61	SON THIS IS SHE HMV POP 956	15	10 wks
15 Mar 62	LONE RIDER HMV POP 992	40	5 wks
3 May 62	LONELY CITY HMV POP 1014	14	11 wks
23 Aug 62	DOWN THE RIVER NILE HMV POP 1054	42	3 wks
21 Feb 63	CUPBOARD LOVE HMV POP 1122	22	12 wks
18 Jul 63	I'LL CUT YOUR TAIL OFF HMV POP 1175	50	1 wk
8 Aug 63	I'LL CUT YOUR TAIL OFF (re-entry) HMV POP 1175	36	2 wks
20 Feb 64	MAKE LOVE TO ME HMV POP 1264	49	1 wk

LEYTON BUZZARDS — UK, male vocal / instrumental group — 5 wks

Date	Title	Pos	Wks
3 Mar 79	SATURDAY NIGHT (BENEATH THE PLASTIC PALM TREES) Chrysalis CHS 2288	53	5 wks

LFO — UK, male instrumental group — 15 wks

Date	Title	Pos	Wks
14 Jul 90	LFO Warp WAP 5	12	10 wks
6 Jul 91	WE ARE BACK / NURTURE Warp 7WAP 14	47	3 wks
1 Feb 92	WHAT IS HOUSE (EP) Warp WAP 17	62	2 wks

Tracks on What Is House (EP): Tan Ta Ra / Mashed Potato / What Is House / Syndrome.

LIBERACE — US, male instrumentalist - piano — 2 wks

Date	Title	Pos	Wks
17 Jun 55	UNCHAINED MELODY Philips PB 430	20	1 wk
19 Oct 56	I DON'T CARE Columbia DB 3834	28	1 wk

I Don't Care featured Liberace as vocalist too.

LIBERATION — UK, male instrumental / production duo — 3 wks

Date	Title	Pos	Wks
24 Oct 92	LIBERATION ZYX ZYX 68657	28	3 wks

LICK THE TINS — UK, male / female vocal / instrumental group — 8 wks

Date	Title	Pos	Wks
29 Mar 86	CAN'T HELP FALLING IN LOVE Sedition EDIT 3308	42	8 wks

Ben LIEBRAND — Holland, male producer / multi-instrumentalist — 2 wks

Date	Title	Pos	Wks
9 Jun 90	PULS(T)AR Epic LIEB 1	68	2 wks

LIEUTENANT PIGEON — UK, male / female instrumental group — 29 wks

Date	Title	Pos	Wks
16 Sep 72	★ MOULDY OLD DOUGH Decca F 13278	1	19 wks
16 Dec 72	DESPERATE DAN Decca F 13365	17	10 wks

LIGHT OF THE WORLD — UK, male vocal / instrumental group — 25 wks

Date	Title	Pos	Wks
14 Apr 79	SWINGIN' Ensign ENY 22	45	5 wks
14 Jul 79	MIDNIGHT GROOVIN' Ensign ENY 29	72	1 wk

Date	Title	Pos	Wks
18 Oct 80	LONDON TOWN Ensign ENY 43	41	5 wks
17 Jan 81	I SHOT THE SHERIFF Ensign ENY 46	40	5 wks
28 Mar 81	I'M SO HAPPY Ensign MER 64	35	6 wks
21 Nov 81	RIDE THE LOVE TRAIN EMI 5242	49	3 wks

LIGHTER SHADE OF BROWN — US, male vocal duo — 3 wks

Date	Title	Pos	Wks
9 Jul 94	HEY DJ Mercury MERCD 401	33	3 wks

Gordon LIGHTFOOT — Canada, male vocalist — 26 wks

Date	Title	Pos	Wks
19 Jun 71	IF YOU COULD READ MY MIND Reprise RS 20974	30	9 wks
3 Aug 74	SUNDOWN Reprise K 14327	33	7 wks
15 Jan 77	THE WRECK OF THE EDMUND FITZGERALD Reprise K 14451	40	4 wks
16 Sep 78	DAYLIGHT KATY Warner Bros. K 17214	41	6 wks

Terry LIGHTFOOT and his NEW ORLEANS JAZZMEN — UK, male jazz band, Terry Lightfoot vocalist / instrumentalist - clarinet — 17 wks

Date	Title	Pos	Wks
7 Sep 61	TRUE LOVE Columbia DB 4696	33	4 wks
23 Nov 61	KING KONG Columbia SCD 2165	29	12 wks
3 May 62	TAVERN IN THE TOWN Columbia DB 4822	49	1 wk

LIGHTNING SEEDS — UK, male vocalist - Ian Broudie — 21 wks

Date	Title	Pos	Wks
22 Jul 89	PURE Ghetto GTG 4	16	8 wks
14 Mar 92	THE LIFE OF RILEY Virgin VS 1402	28	6 wks
30 May 92	SENSE Virgin VS 1414	31	5 wks
20 Aug 94	LUCKY YOU Epic 6606282	43	2 wks

LIL' LOUIS — US, male producer — 18 wks

Date	Title	Pos	Wks
29 Jul 89	● FRENCH KISS ffrr FX 115	2	11 wks
13 Jan 90	I CALLED U ffrr F 123	16	6 wks
26 Sep 92	SAVED MY LIFE ffrr FX 197 [1]	74	1 wk

[1] Lil' Louis and the World

LIMAHL — UK, male vocalist — 25 wks

Date	Title	Pos	Wks
5 Nov 83	ONLY FOR LOVE EMI LML 1	16	7 wks
7 Jan 84	ONLY FOR LOVE (re-entry) EMI LML 1	75	1 wk
2 Jun 84	TOO MUCH TROUBLE EMI LML 2	64	3 wks
13 Oct 84	● NEVER ENDING STORY EMI LML 3	4	14 wks

Alison LIMERICK — UK, female vocalist — 29 wks

Date	Title	Pos	Wks
30 Mar 91	WHERE LOVE LIVES Arista 144208	27	8 wks
12 Oct 91	COME BACK (FOR REAL LOVE) Arista 114530	53	2 wks
21 Dec 91	MAGIC'S BACK (THEME FROM THE GHOSTS OF OXFORD STREET) RCA PB 45223 [1]	42	4 wks
29 Feb 92	MAKE IT ON MY OWN Arista 114996	16	6 wks
18 Jul 92	GETTIN' IT RIGHT Arista 74321102867	57	2 wks
28 Nov 92	HEAR MY CALL Arista 115337	73	1 wk
8 Jan 94	TIME OF OUR LIVES Arista 74321180332	36	4 wks
19 Mar 94	LOVE COME DOWN Arista 74321191952	36	2 wks

[1] Malcolm McLaren featuring Alison Limerick

LIMIT — Holland, male vocal / instrumental duo — 8 wks

Date	Title	Pos	Wks
5 Jan 85	SAY YEAH Portrait A 4808	17	8 wks

LIMMIE and the FAMILY COOKIN' — US, male / female vocal group — 28 wks

Date	Title	Pos	Wks
21 Jul 73	● YOU CAN DO MAGIC Avco 6105 019	3	13 wks
20 Oct 73	DREAMBOAT Avco 6105 025	31	5 wks
6 Apr 74	● A WALKIN' MIRACLE Avco 6105 027	6	10 wks

Bob LIND US, male vocalist — 10 wks

10 Mar 66	● ELUSIVE BUTTERFLY Fontana TF 670	5	9 wks
26 May 66	REMEMBER THE RAIN Fontana TF 702	46	1 wk

LINDISFARNE UK, male vocal/instrumental group — 55 wks

26 Feb 72	● MEET ME ON THE CORNER Charisma CB 173	5	11 wks
13 May 72	● LADY ELEANOR Charisma CB 153	3	11 wks
23 Sep 72	ALL FALL DOWN Charisma CB 191	34	5 wks
3 Jun 78	● RUN FOR HOME Mercury 6007 177	10	15 wks
7 Oct 78	JUKE BOX GYPSY Mercury 6007 187	56	4 wks
10 Nov 90	● FOG ON THE TYNE (REVISITED) Best ZB 44083 [1]	2	9 wks

[1] Gazza and Lindisfarne

LINER UK, male vocal/instrumental group — 6 wks

10 Mar 79	KEEP REACHING OUT FOR LOVE Atlantic K 11235	49	3 wks
26 May 79	YOU AND ME Atlantic K 11285	44	3 wks

Laurie LINGO and the DIPSTICKS
UK, male vocal duo, disc jockeys Dave Lee Travis and Paul Burnett — 7 wks

17 Apr 76	● CONVOY G. B. State STAT 23	4	7 wks

LINX UK, male vocal/instrumental duo — 45 wks

20 Sep 80	YOU'RE LYING Chrysalis CHS 2461	15	10 wks
7 Mar 81	● INTUITION Chrysalis CHS 2500	7	11 wks
13 Jun 81	THROW AWAY THE KEY Chrysalis CHS 2519	21	9 wks
5 Sep 81	SO THIS IS ROMANCE Chrysalis CHS 2546	15	4 wks
21 Nov 81	CAN'T HELP MYSELF Chrysalis CHS 2565	55	3 wks
10 Jul 82	PLAYTHING Chrysalis CHS 2621	48	3 wks

LIONROCK UK, male producer - Justin Robertson — 7 wks

5 Dec 92	LIONROCK Deconstruction 74321124381	63	1 wk
8 May 93	PACKET OF PEACE Deconstruction 74321144372	32	3 wks
23 Oct 93	CARNIVAL Deconstruction 74321164862	34	2 wks
27 Aug 94	TRIPWIRE Deconstruction 74321204702	44	1 wk

LIPPS INC. US, male/female vocal/instrumental group — 13 wks

17 May 80	● FUNKYTOWN Casablanca CAN 194	2	13 wks

LIQUID UK, male instrumental/production duo — 10 wks

21 Mar 92	SWEET HARMONY XL XLS 28	15	6 wks
5 Sep 92	THE FUTURE MUSIC EP XL XLT 33	59	2 wks
20 Mar 93	TIME TO GET UP XL XLS 40CD	46	2 wks

Tracks on The Future Music EP: Liquid Is Liquid/Music/House (Is A Feeling)/The Year 3000.

LIQUID GOLD
UK, male/female vocal/instrumental group — 46 wks

2 Dec 78	ANYWAY YOU DO IT Creole CR 159	41	7 wks
23 Feb 80	● DANCE YOURSELF DIZZY Polo POLO 1	2	14 wks
31 May 80	● SUBSTITUTE Polo POLO 4	8	9 wks
1 Nov 80	THE NIGHT THE WINE AND THE ROSES Polo POLO 6	32	7 wks
28 Mar 81	DON'T PANIC Polo POLO 8	42	5 wks
21 Aug 82	WHERE DID WE GO WRONG Polo POLO 23	56	4 wks

LIQUID OXYGEN US, male producer — 2 wks

28 Apr 90	THE PLANET DANCE Champion CHAMP 242	56	2 wks

LISA LISA US, female vocalist — 32 wks

4 May 85	I WONDER IF I TAKE YOU HOME CBS A 6057 [1]	53	6 wks
3 Aug 85	I WONDER IF I TAKE YOU HOME (re-entry) CBS A 6057 [1]	12	11 wks
31 Oct 87	LOST IN EMOTION CBS 651036 7 [2]	58	4 wks
13 Jul 91	LET THE BEAT HIT 'EM Columbia 6572867 [2]	17	6 wks
24 Aug 91	LET THE BEAT HIT 'EM PART 2 Columbia 6573747 [2]	49	2 wks
26 Mar 94	SKIP TO MY LU Chrysalis CDCHS 5006	34	3 wks

[1] Lisa Lisa and Cult Jam with Full Force [2] Lisa Lisa and Cult Jam

LISA MARIE - See Malcolm McLAREN

De Etta LITTLE and Nelson PIGFORD
US, female/male vocal duo — 5 wks

13 Aug 77	YOU TAKE MY HEART AWAY United Artists UP 36257	35	5 wks

LITTLE ANGELS UK, male vocal/instrumental group — 41 wks

4 Mar 89	BIG BAD EP Polydor LTLEP 2	74	1 wk
24 Feb 90	KICKING UP DUST Polydor LTL 5	46	4 wks
12 May 90	RADICAL YOUR LOVER Polydor LTL 7 [1]	34	4 wks
4 Aug 90	SHE'S A LITTLE ANGEL Polydor LTL 7	21	3 wks
2 Feb 91	BONEYARD Polydor LTL 8	33	4 wks
30 Mar 91	PRODUCT OF THE WORKING CLASS Polydor LTL 9	40	2 wks
1 Jun 91	YOUNG GODS Polydor LTL 10	34	2 wks
20 Jul 91	I AIN'T GONNA CRY Polydor LTL 11	26	3 wks
7 Nov 92	TOO MUCH TOO YOUNG Polydor LTL 12	22	3 wks
9 Jan 93	WOMANKIND Polydor LTLCD 13	12	5 wks
24 Apr 93	SOAPBOX Polydor LTLCD 14	33	4 wks
25 Sep 93	SAIL AWAY Polydor LTLCD 15	45	3 wks
9 Apr 94	TEN MILES HIGH Polydor LTLCD 16	18	3 wks

[1] Little Angels featuring the Big Bad Horns

Tracks on Big Bad EP: She's A Little Angel/Don't Waste My Time/Better Than The Rest/Sex In Cars.

See also Various Artists (EPs & LPs) - Gimme Shelter (EP).

LITTLE ANTHONY and the IMPERIALS
US, male vocal group — 17 wks

31 Jul 76	BETTER USE YOUR HEAD United Artists UP 36141	42	4 wks
24 Dec 77	WHO'S GONNA LOVE ME Power Exchange PX 266 [1]	17	9 wks

[1] Imperials

LITTLE BENNY and the MASTERS US, male rapper/
instrumentalist - trumpet, and male instrumental group — 7 wks

2 Feb 85	WHO COMES TO BOOGIE Bluebird 10 BR 13	33	7 wks

LITTLE CAESAR UK, male vocalist — 3 wks

9 Jun 90	THE WHOLE OF THE MOON A1 EAU 1	68	3 wks

LITTLE EVA US, female vocalist — 45 wks

6 Sep 62	● THE LOCO-MOTION London HL 9581	2	17 wks
3 Jan 63	KEEP YOUR HANDS OFF MY BABY London HLU 9633	30	5 wks
7 Mar 63	LET'S TURKEY TROT London HLU 9687	13	12 wks
29 Jul 72	THE LOCO-MOTION (re-entry) London HL 9581	11	11 wks

See also Big Dee Irwin.

LITTLE RICHARD
US, male vocalist/instrumentalist - piano — 108 wks

14 Dec 56	RIP IT UP London HLO 8336	30	1 wk
8 Feb 57	● LONG TALL SALLY London HLO 8366	3	16 wks
22 Feb 57	TUTTI FRUTTI London HLO 8366	29	1 wk
8 Mar 57	SHE'S GOT IT London HLO 8382	15	7 wks

15 Mar 57	● THE GIRL CAN'T HELP IT *London HLO 8382*	**9**	11 wks
24 May 57	SHE'S GOT IT (re-entry) *London HLO 8382*	**28**	2 wks
28 Jun 57	LUCILLE *London HLO 8446*	**10**	9 wks
13 Sep 57	JENNY JENNY *London HLO 8470*	**11**	5 wks
29 Nov 57	KEEP A KNOCKIN' *London HLO 8509*	**21**	7 wks
28 Feb 58	● GOOD GOLLY MISS MOLLY *London HLU 8560*	**8**	9 wks
11 Jul 58	OOH MY SOUL *London HLO 8647*	**30**	1 wk
25 Jul 58	OOH MY SOUL (re-entry) *London HLO 8647*	**22**	3 wks
2 Jan 59	● BABY FACE *London HLU 8770*	**2**	15 wks
3 Apr 59	BY THE LIGHT OF THE SILVERY MOON *London HLU 8831*	**17**	5 wks
5 Jun 59	KANSAS CITY *London HLU 8868*	**26**	5 wks
11 Oct 62	HE GOT WHAT HE WANTED *Mercury AMT 1189*	**38**	4 wks
4 Jun 64	BAMA LAMA BAMA LOO *London HL 9896*	**20**	7 wks
2 Jul 77	GOOD GOLLY MISS MOLLY / RIP IT UP *Creole CR 140*	**37**	4 wks
14 Jun 86	GREAT GOSH A'MIGHTY (IT'S A MATTER OF TIME) *MCA MCA 1049*	**62**	2 wks
25 Oct 86	OPERATOR *WEA YZ 89*	**67**	2 wks

The versions of Good Golly Miss Molly and Rip It Up on Creole are re-recordings.

LITTLE STEVEN *US, male vocalist / instrumentalist - guitar* **3 wks**

23 May 87	BITTER FRUIT *Manhattan MT 21*	**66**	3 wks

LITTLE T - *See REBEL MC*

LITTLE TONY *Italy, male vocalist* **3 wks**

15 Jan 60	TOO GOOD *Decca F 11190*	**19**	3 wks

LIVE REPORT *UK, male vocal / instrumental group* **1 wk**

20 May 89	WHY DO I ALWAYS GET IT WRONG *Brouhaha CUE 7*	**73**	1 wk

LIVERPOOL EXPRESS
UK, male vocal / instrumental group **26 wks**

26 Jun 76	YOU ARE MY LOVE *Warner Bros. K 16743*	**11**	9 wks
16 Oct 76	HOLD TIGHT *Warner Bros. K 16799*	**46**	2 wks
18 Dec 76	EVERY MAN MUST HAVE A DREAM *Warner Bros. K 16854*	**17**	11 wks
4 Jun 77	DREAMIN' *Warner Bros. K 16933*	**40**	4 wks

LIVERPOOL FC *UK, male football team vocalists* **16 wks**

28 May 77	WE CAN DO IT (EP) *State STAT 50*	**15**	4 wks
23 Apr 83	LIVERPOOL (WE'RE NEVER GONNA...) / LIVERPOOL (ANTHEM) *Mean MEAN 102*	**54**	4 wks
17 May 86	SITTING ON THE TOP OF THE WORLD *Columbia DB 9116*	**50**	2 wks
14 May 88	● ANFIELD RAP (RED MACHINE IN FULL EFFECT) *Virgin LFC 1*	**3**	6 wks

Tracks on We Can Do It (EP): *We Can Do It / Liverpool Lou / We Shall Not Be Moved / You'll Never Walk Alone.*

LIVIN' JOY
US / Italy, male / female vocal / instrumental group **6 wks**

3 Sep 94	DREAMER *Undiscovered MCSTD 1993*	**18**	6 wks

LIVING COLOUR *US, male vocal / instrumental group* **22 wks**

27 Oct 90	TYPE *Epic LCL 7*	**75**	1 wk
2 Feb 91	LOVE REARS ITS UGLY HEAD *Epic 6565937*	**12**	11 wks
1 Jun 91	SOLACE OF YOU *Epic 6569087*	**33**	5 wks
26 Oct 91	CULT OF PERSONALITY *Epic 6575357*	**67**	2 wks
20 Feb 93	LEAVE IT ALONE *Epic 6589762*	**34**	2 wks
17 Apr 93	AUSLANDER *Epic 6591732*	**53**	1 wk

LIVING IN A BOX *UK, male vocal / instrumental group* **62 wks**

4 Apr 87	● LIVING IN A BOX *Chrysalis LIB 1*	**5**	13 wks
13 Jun 87	SCALES OF JUSTICE *Chrysalis LIB 2*	**30**	6 wks
26 Sep 87	SO THE STORY GOES *Chrysalis LIB 3* [1]	**34**	8 wks
30 Jan 88	LOVE IS THE ART *Chrysalis LIB 4*	**45**	4 wks
18 Feb 89	● BLOW THE HOUSE DOWN *Chrysalis LIB 5*	**10**	9 wks
10 Jun 89	GATECRASHING *Chrysalis LIB 6*	**36**	6 wks
23 Sep 89	● ROOM IN YOUR HEART *Chrysalis LIB 7*	**5**	13 wks
30 Dec 89	DIFFERENT AIR *Chrysalis LIB 8*	**64**	1 wk
13 Jan 90	DIFFERENT AIR (re-entry) *Chrysalis LIB 8*	**57**	2 wks

[1] Living In A Box featuring Bobby Womack

Dandy LIVINGSTONE *Jamaica, male vocalist* **19 wks**

2 Sep 72	SUZANNE BEWARE OF THE DEVIL *Horse HOSS 16*	**14**	11 wks
13 Jan 73	BIG CITY / THINK ABOUT THAT *Horse HOSS 25*	**26**	8 wks

LL COOL J *US, male rapper* **32 wks**

4 Jul 87	I'M BAD *Def Jam 650856 7*	**71**	1 wk
12 Sep 87	● I NEED LOVE *Def Jam 651101 7*	**8**	10 wks
21 Nov 87	GO CUT CREATOR GO *Def Jam LLCJ 1*	**66**	2 wks
13 Feb 88	GOING BACK TO CALI / JACK THE RIPPER *Def Jam LLCJ 2*	**37**	4 wks
10 Jun 89	I'M THAT TYPE OF GUY *Def Jam LLCJ 3*	**43**	5 wks
1 Dec 90	AROUND THE WAY GIRL / MAMA SAID KNOCK YOU OUT *Def Jam 6564470*	**41**	4 wks
9 Mar 91	AROUND THE WAY GIRL (re-issue) *Columbia 6564470*	**36**	4 wks
10 Apr 93	HOW I'M COMIN' *Def Jam 6591692*	**37**	2 wks

Jack The Ripper *only listed from 20 Feb 88.*

Kelly LLORENNA - *See N-TRANCE*

L.N.R. *US, male vocal / instrumental duo* **2 wks**

3 Jun 89	WORK IT TO THE BONE *Kool Kat KOOL 501*	**64**	2 wks

LOBO *US, male vocalist* **25 wks**

19 Jun 71	● ME AND YOU AND A DOG NAMED BOO *Philips 6073 801*	**4**	14 wks
8 Jun 74	● I'D LOVE YOU TO WANT ME *UK 68*	**5**	11 wks

LOBO *Holland, male vocalist* **11 wks**

25 Jul 81	● THE CARIBBEAN DISCO SHOW *Polydor POSP 302*	**8**	11 wks

Los LOBOS *US, male vocal / instrumental group* **24 wks**

6 Apr 85	DON'T WORRY BABY / WILL THE WOLF SURVIVE *London LASH 4*	**57**	4 wks
18 Jul 87	★ LA BAMBA *Slash LASH 13*	**1**	11 wks
26 Sep 87	COME ON LET'S GO *Slash LASH 14*	**18**	9 wks

Tone LOC *US, male rapper* **19 wks**

11 Feb 89	WILD THING / LOC'ED AFTER DARK *Fourth & Broadway BRW 121*	**21**	8 wks
20 May 89	FUNKY COLD MEDINA / ON FIRE *Fourth & Broadway BRW 129*	**13**	9 wks
5 Aug 89	I GOT IT GOIN' ON *Fourth & Broadway BRW 140*	**55**	2 wks

Hank LOCKLIN *US, male vocalist* **41 wks**

11 Aug 60	● PLEASE HELP ME I'M FALLING *RCA 1188*	**9**	19 wks
15 Feb 62	FROM HERE TO THERE TO YOU *RCA 1273*	**44**	3 wks
15 Nov 62	WE'RE GONNA GO FISHIN' *RCA 1305*	**18**	11 wks
5 May 66	I FEEL A CRY COMING ON *RCA 1510*	**29**	8 wks

LOCKSMITH US, male vocal / instrumental group — 6 wks

23 Aug 80	**UNLOCK THE FUNK** Arista ARIST 364	42	6 wks

LOCOMOTIVE UK, male vocal / instrumental group — 8 wks

16 Oct 68	**RUDI'S IN LOVE** Parlophone R 5718	25	8 wks

John LODGE - See Justin HAYWARD

Lisa LOEB and NINE STORIES
US, female / male vocal / instrumental group — 15 wks

3 Sep 94 ●	**STAY (I MISSED YOU)** RCA 74321212522	6	15 wks

Nils LOFGREN US, male vocalist / instrumentalist - guitar — 3 wks

8 Jun 85	**SECRETS IN THE STREET** Towerbell TOW 68	53	3 wks

Johnny LOGAN Ireland, male vocalist — 24 wks

3 May 80 ★	**WHAT'S ANOTHER YEAR** Epic EPC 8572	1	8 wks
23 May 87 ●	**HOLD ME NOW** Epic LOG 1	2	11 wks
22 Aug 87	**I'M NOT IN LOVE** Epic LOG 2	51	5 wks

Kenny LOGGINS US, male vocalist — 21 wks

28 Apr 84 ●	**FOOTLOOSE** CBS A 4101	6	10 wks
1 Nov 86	**DANGER ZONE** CBS A 7188	45	11 wks

LOLA US, female vocalist — 1 wk

28 Mar 87	**WAX THE VAN** Syncopate SY 1	65	1 wk

Jackie LOMAX - See VARIOUS ARTISTS (EPs & LPs) - The Apple EP.

Alain LOMBARD - See Mady MESPLÉ and Danielle MILLET

Julie LONDON US, female vocalist — 3 wks

5 Apr 57	**CRY ME A RIVER** London HLU 8240	22	3 wks

Laurie LONDON UK, male vocalist — 12 wks

8 Nov 57	**HE'S GOT THE WHOLE WORLD IN HIS HANDS** Parlophone R 4359	12	12 wks

LONDON BOYS UK, male vocal duo — 46 wks

10 Dec 88	**REQUIEM** WEA YZ 345	59	6 wks
1 Apr 89 ●	**REQUIEM (re-entry)** WEA YZ 345	4	15 wks
1 Jul 89 ●	**LONDON NIGHTS** WEA YZ 393	2	9 wks
16 Sep 89	**HARLEM DESIRE** WEA YZ 415	17	7 wks
2 Dec 89	**MY LOVE** WEA YZ 433	46	6 wks
16 Jun 90	**CHAPEL OF LOVE** East West YZ 458	75	1 wk
19 Jan 91	**FREEDOM** East West YZ 554	54	2 wks

LONDON COMMUNITY GOSPEL CHOIR - See Sal SOLO

LONDON PHILHARMONIC ORCHESTRA - See Cliff RICHARD

LONDON STRING CHORALE UK, orchestra / choir — 13 wks

15 Dec 73	**GALLOPING HOME** Polydor 2058 280	49	3 wks
19 Jan 74	**GALLOPING HOME (re-entry)** Polydor 2058 280	31	10 wks

LONDON SYMPHONY ORCHESTRA
UK, orchestra conducted by John Williams. — 5 wks

6 Jan 79	**THEME FROM 'SUPERMAN' (MAIN TITLE)** Warner Bros. K 17292	32	5 wks

LONDONBEAT UK / US, male vocal group — 43 wks

26 Nov 88	**9 A.M. (THE COMFORT ZONE)** Anxious ANX 008	19	10 wks
18 Feb 89	**FAILING IN LOVE AGAIN** Anxious ANX 007	60	2 wks
1 Sep 90 ●	**I'VE BEEN THINKING ABOUT YOU** Anxious ANX 14	2	13 wks
24 Nov 90	**A BETTER LOVE** Anxious ANX 21	52	5 wks
2 Mar 91	**NO WOMAN NO CRY** Anxious ANX 25	64	2 wks
20 Jul 91	**A BETTER LOVE (re-issue)** Anxious ANX 32	23	6 wks
27 Jun 92	**YOU BRING ON THE SUN** Anxious ANX 37	32	4 wks
24 Oct 92	**THAT'S HOW I FEEL ABOUT YOU** Anxious ANX 40	69	1 wk

LONE JUSTICE
US, female / male vocal / instrumental group — 4 wks

7 Mar 87	**I FOUND LOVE** Geffen GEF 18	45	4 wks

Shorty LONG US, male vocalist — 7 wks

17 Jul 68	**HERE COMES THE JUDGE** Tamla Motown TMG 663	30	7 wks

LONG AND THE SHORT
UK, male vocal / instrumental group — 8 wks

10 Sep 64	**THE LETTER** Decca F 11964	35	5 wks
24 Dec 64	**CHOC ICE** Decca F 12043	49	3 wks

LONG RYDERS US, male vocal / instrumental group — 4 wks

5 Oct 85	**LOOKING FOR LEWIS AND CLARK** Island IS 237	59	4 wks

Joe LONGTHORNE UK, male vocalist — 6 wks

30 Apr 94	**YOUNG GIRL** EMI CDEM 310	61	2 wks
10 Dec 94	**PASSING STRANGERS** EMI CDEM 362 [1]	34†	4 wks

[1] Joe Longthorne and Liz Dawn

LOOK UK, male vocal / instrumental group — 15 wks

20 Dec 80 ●	**I AM THE BEAT** MCA 647	6	12 wks
29 Aug 81	**FEEDING TIME** MCA 736	50	3 wks

LOOSE ENDS
UK, male / female vocal / instrumental group — 76 wks

25 Feb 84	**TELL ME WHAT YOU WANT** Virgin VS 658	74	1 wk
28 Apr 84	**EMERGENCY (DIAL 999)** Virgin VS 677	41	6 wks
21 Jul 84	**CHOOSE ME (RESCUE ME)** Virgin VS 697	59	3 wks
23 Feb 85	**HANGIN' ON A STRING (CONTEMPLATING)** Virgin VS 748	13	13 wks
11 May 85	**MAGIC TOUCH** Virgin VS 761	16	7 wks
27 Jul 85	**GOLDEN YEARS** Virgin VS 795	59	4 wks
14 Jun 86	**STAY A LITTLE WHILE, CHILD** Virgin VS 819	52	5 wks
20 Sep 86	**SLOW DOWN** Virgin VS 884	27	5 wks
29 Nov 86	**NIGHTS OF PLEASURE** Virgin VS 919	42	7 wks
4 Jun 88	**MR BACHELOR** Virgin VS 1080	50	4 wks
25 Aug 90	**DON'T BE A FOOL** 10 TEN 312	13	9 wks
17 Nov 90	**LOVE'S GOT ME** 10 TEN 330	40	4 wks
20 Jun 92	**HANGIN' ON A STRING (re-mix)** Ten TEN 406	25	5 wks
5 Sep 92	**MAGIC TOUCH (re-mix)** Ten TEN 409	75	1 wk

Trini LOPEZ US, male vocalist — 37 wks

12 Sep 63 ●	**IF I HAD A HAMMER** Reprise R 20198	4	17 wks
12 Dec 63	**KANSAS CITY** Reprise R 20236	35	5 wks
12 May 66	**I'M COMING HOME CINDY** Reprise R 20455	28	5 wks
6 Apr 67	**GONNA GET ALONG WITHOUT YA NOW** Reprise R 20547	41	5 wks
19 Dec 81	**TRINI TRACKS** RCA 154	59	5 wks

LO-PRO - See X-PRESS 2

LORD ROCKINGHAM'S XI
UK, male instrumental group **21 wks**

24 Oct 58	★ HOOTS MON Decca F 11059	**1**	17 wks
6 Feb 59	WEE TOM Decca F 11104	**16**	3 wks
25 Sep 93	HOOTS MON (re-issue) Decca 8820982	**60**	1 wk

Both of the group's hits contain a little spoken Scottish.

LORD TANAMO *Trinidad & Tobago, male vocalist* **2 wks**

1 Dec 90	I'M IN THE MOOD FOR LOVE Mooncrest MOON 1009	**58**	2 wks

Jerry LORDAN *UK, male vocalist* **15 wks**

8 Jan 60	I'LL STAY SINGLE Parlophone R 4588	**26**	2 wks
26 Feb 60	WHO COULD BE BLUER Parlophone R 4627	**17**	9 wks
10 Mar 60	I'LL STAY SINGLE (re-entry) Parlophone R 4588	**41**	1 wk
19 May 60	WHO COULD BE BLUER (re-entry) Parlophone R 4627	**45**	1 wk
2 Jun 60	SING LIKE AN ANGEL Parlophone R 4653	**36**	2 wks

Sophia LOREN - *See Peter SELLERS*

Trey LORENZ *US, male vocalist* **5 wks**

21 Nov 92	SOMEONE TO HOLD Epic 6587857	**65**	2 wks
30 Jan 93	PHOTOGRAPH OF MARY Epic 6589542	**38**	3 wks

See also Mariah Carey.

LORI and the CHAMELEONS
UK, female / male vocal / instrumental group **1 wk**

8 Dec 79	TOUCH Sire SIR 4025	**70**	1 wk

LORRAINE - *See BOMB THE BASS*

Joe LOSS *UK, orchestra* **53 wks**

29 Jun 61	WHEELS CHA CHA HMV POP 880	**21**	21 wks
19 Oct 61	SUCU SUCU HMV POP 937	**48**	1 wk
29 Mar 62	THE MAIGRET THEME HMV POP 995	**20**	10 wks
1 Nov 62	MUST BE MADISON HMV POP 1075	**20**	13 wks
5 Nov 64	MARCH OF THE MODS HMV POP 1351	**35**	4 wks
24 Dec 64	MARCH OF THE MODS (re-entry) HMV POP 1351	**31**	4 wks

LOST *UK, male / instrumental / production duo* **1 wk**

22 Jun 91	TECHNO FUNK Perfecto PT 44560	**75**	1 wk

LOTUS EATERS *UK, male vocal / instrumental duo* **16 wks**

2 Jul 83	FIRST PICTURE OF YOU Sylvan SYL 1	**15**	12 wks
8 Oct 83	YOU DON'T NEED SOMEONE NEW Sylvan SYL 2	**53**	4 wks

Bonnie LOU *US, female vocalist* **10 wks**

5 Feb 54	● TENNESSEE WIG WALK Parlophone R 3730	**4**	10 wks

Louchie LOU and Michie ONE
UK, female vocal duo **10 wks**

29 May 93	● SHOUT ffrr FCD 211	**7**	8 wks
14 Aug 93	SOMEBODY ELSE'S GUY ffrr FCD 216	**54**	2 wks

LOUD *UK, male vocal / instrumental group* **2 wks**

28 Mar 92	EASY China WOK 2016	**67**	2 wks

John D. LOUDERMILK *US, male vocalist* **10 wks**

4 Jan 62	THE LANGUAGE OF LOVE RCA 1269	**13**	10 wks

Louie LOUIE *US, male vocalist* **5 wks**

19 Dec 92	THE THOUGHT OF IT Hardback YZ 724	**34**	5 wks

Darlene LOVE *US, female vocalist* **5 wks**

19 Dec 92	ALL ALONE ON CHRISTMAS Arista 7432112476	**31**	4 wks
1 Jan 94	ALL ALONE ON CHRISTMAS (re-entry) Arista 7432112476	**72**	1 wk

Geoff LOVE - *See MANUEL and his MUSIC OF THE MOUNTAINS*

Monie LOVE *UK, female rapper* **49 wks**

4 Feb 89	I CAN DO THIS Cooltempo COOL 177	**37**	4 wks
24 Jun 89	GRANDPA'S PARTY Cooltempo COOL 184	**16**	9 wks
14 Jul 90	MONIE IN THE MIDDLE Cooltempo COOL 210	**46**	3 wks
22 Sep 90	IT'S A SHAME (MY SISTER) Cooltempo COOL 219 [1]	**12**	8 wks
1 Dec 90	DOWN TO EARTH Cooltempo COOL 222	**31**	6 wks
6 Apr 91	RING MY BELL Cooltempo COOL 224 [2]	**20**	5 wks
25 Jul 92	FULL TERM LOVE Cooltempo COOL 258	**34**	4 wks
13 Mar 93	BORN 2 B.R.E.E.D. Cooltempo CDCOOL 269	**18**	5 wks
12 Jun 93	IN A WORD OR 2 / THE POWER Cooltempo CDCOOL 273	**33**	3 wks
21 Aug 93	NEVER GIVE UP Cooltempo CDCOOL 276	**41**	2 wks

[1] Monie Love featuring True Image [2] Monie Love vs Adeva

See also Jungle Brothers.

Vikki LOVE - *See NUANCE featuring Vikki LOVE*

LOVE AFFAIR *UK, male vocal / instrumental group* **56 wks**

3 Jan 68	★ EVERLASTING LOVE CBS 3125	**1**	12 wks
17 Apr 68	● RAINBOW VALLEY CBS 3366	**5**	13 wks
11 Sep 68	● A DAY WITHOUT LOVE CBS 3674	**6**	12 wks
19 Feb 69	ONE ROAD CBS 3994	**16**	9 wks
16 Jul 69	● BRINGING ON BACK THE GOOD TIMES CBS 4300	**9**	10 wks

LOVE AND MONEY
UK, male vocal / instrumental group **23 wks**

24 May 86	CANDYBAR EXPRESS Mercury MONEY 1	**56**	4 wks
25 Apr 87	LOVE AND MONEY Mercury MONEY 4	**68**	4 wks
17 Sep 88	HALLELUJAH MAN Fontana MONEY 5	**63**	4 wks
14 Jan 89	STRANGE KIND OF LOVE Fontana MONEY 6	**45**	5 wks
25 Mar 89	JOCELYN SQUARE Fontana MONEY 7	**51**	4 wks
16 Nov 91	WINTER Fontana MONEY 9	**52**	2 wks

LOVE DECADE
UK, male / female vocal / instrumental group **13 wks**

6 Jul 91	DREAM ON (IS THIS A DREAM) All Around The World GLOBE 100	**52**	2 wks
23 Nov 91	SO REAL All Around The World GLOBE 106	**14**	7 wks
11 Apr 92	I FEEL YOU All Around The World GLOBE 107	**34**	3 wks
6 Feb 93	WHEN THE MORNING COMES All Around The World CDGLOBE 114	**69**	1 wk

LOVE DECREE *UK, male vocal / instrumental group* **4 wks**

16 Sep 89	SOMETHING SO REAL (CHINHEADS THEME) Ariola 112642	**61**	4 wks

LOVE/HATE *US, male vocal / instrumental group* **4 wks**

30 Nov 91	EVIL TWIN Columbia 6575967	**59**	1 wk
4 Apr 92	WASTED IN AMERICA Columbia 6578897	**38**	3 wks

LOVE INC UK, male vocal / production duo **3 wks**

9 Feb 91 **LOVE IS THE MESSAGE** Love EVOL 1 ....**59** 3 wks

LOVE NELSON - See FIRE ISLAND

LOVE REACTION - See Zodiac MINDWARP and the LOVE REACTION

LOVE SCULPTURE UK, instrumental group **14 wks**

27 Nov 68 ● **SABRE DANCE** Parlophone R 5744 ....**5** 14 wks

LOVE SQUAD - See Linda CARR

LOVE UNLIMITED US, female vocal group **25 wks**

17 Jun 72 **WALKIN' IN THE RAIN WITH THE ONE I LOVE**
Uni UN 539 ....**14** 10 wks
25 Jan 75 **IT MAY BE WINTER OUTSIDE (BUT IN MY HEART**
IT'S SPRING) 20th Century BTC 2149 ....**11** 9 wks

LOVE UNLIMITED ORCHESTRA US, orchestra **10 wks**

2 Feb 74 ● **LOVE'S THEME** Pye International 7N 25635 ....**10** 10 wks

LOVEBUG STARSKI US, male vocalist **9 wks**

31 May 86 **AMITYVILLE (THE HOUSE ON THE HILL)**
Epic A 7182 ....**12** 9 wks

Bill LOVELADY UK, male vocalist **10 wks**

18 Aug 79 **REGGAE FOR IT NOW** Charisma CB 337 ....**12** 10 wks

LOVELAND featuring Rachel McFARLANE
UK, male / female vocal / instrumental group **6 wks**

16 Apr 94 **LET THE MUSIC (LIFT YOU UP)**
KMS/Eastern Bloc KMSCD 10 [1] ....**16** 4 wks
5 Nov 94 **(KEEP ON) SHINING / HOPE (NEVER GIVE UP)**
Eastern Bloc BLOCCD 016 ....**37** 2 wks

[1] Loveland featuring Rachel McFarlane vs Darlene Lewis

All formats of Let The Music (Lift You Up) featured versions by Loveland
featuring Rachel McFarlane and also by Darlene Love.

LOVER SPEAKS UK, male vocal / instrumental duo **5 wks**

16 Aug 86 **NO MORE 'I LOVE YOU'S** A & M AM 326.................**58** 5 wks

Michael LOVESMITH US, male vocalist **1 wk**

5 Oct 85 **AIN'T NOTHIN' LIKE IT** Motown ZB 40369 ....**75** 1 wk

LOVESTATION UK, male production group **2 wks**

13 Mar 93 **SHINE ON ME** RCA 743211337912 [1] ....**71** 1 wk
13 Nov 93 **BEST OF MY LOVE** Fresh FRSHD 1 ....**73** 1 wk

[1] Lovestation featuring Lisa Hunt

Lene LOVICH US, female vocalist **38 wks**

17 Feb 79 ● **LUCKY NUMBER** Stiff BUY 42 ....**3** 11 wks
12 May 79 **SAY WHEN** Stiff BUY 46 ....**19** 10 wks
20 Oct 79 **BIRD SONG** Stiff BUY 53 ....**39** 7 wks
29 Mar 80 **WHAT WILL I DO WITHOUT YOU** Stiff BUY 69.......**58** 3 wks
14 Mar 81 **NEW TOY** Stiff BUY 97 ....**53** 5 wks
27 Nov 82 **IT'S YOU ONLY YOU (MEIN SCHMERZ)**
Stiff BUY 164 ....**68** 2 wks

LOVIN' SPOONFUL
US / Canada, male vocal / instrumental group **33 wks**

14 Apr 66 ● **DAYDREAM** Pye International 7N 25361 ....**2** 13 wks
14 Jul 66 ● **SUMMER IN THE CITY** Kama Sutra KAS 200.........**8** 11 wks
5 Jan 67 **NASHVILLE CATS** Kama Sutra KAS 204..............**26** 7 wks
9 Mar 67 **DARLING BE HOME SOON** Kama Sutra KAS 207......**44** 2 wks

LOVINDEER UK, male vocalist **3 wks**

27 Sep 86 **MAN SHORTAGE** TSOJ TS 1 ....**69** 3 wks

Gary LOW Italy, male vocalist **3 wks**

8 Oct 83 **I WANT YOU** Savoir Faire FAIS 004...........................**52** 3 wks

Patti LOW - See BUG KANN and the PLASTIC JAM

Jim LOWE US, male vocalist **9 wks**

26 Oct 56 ● **THE GREEN DOOR** London HLD 8317 ....**8** 9 wks

Nick LOWE UK, male vocalist **27 wks**

11 Mar 78 ● **I LOVE THE SOUND OF BREAKING GLASS**
Radar ADA ....**7** 8 wks
9 Jun 79 **CRACKIN' UP** Radar ADA 34 ....**34** 5 wks
25 Aug 79 **CRUEL TO BE KIND** Radar ADA 43 ....**12** 11 wks
26 May 84 **HALF A BOY HALF A MAN** F. Beat XX 34.................**53** 3 wks

LOWRELL US, male vocalist **9 wks**

24 Nov 79 **MELLOW MELLOW RIGHT ON** AVI AVIS 108 ....**37** 9 wks

LRS - See D MOB

L7 US, female vocal / instrumental group **18 wks**

4 Apr 92 **PRETEND WE'RE DEAD** Slash LASH 34 ....**21** 7 wks
30 May 92 **EVERGLADE** Slash LASH 36 ....**27** 3 wks
12 Sep 92 **MONSTER** Slash LASH 38 ....**33** 3 wks
28 Nov 92 **PRETEND WE'RE DEAD (re-issue)** Slash LASH 42 ....**50** 3 wks
9 Jul 94 **ANDRES** Slash LASCD 48..............................**34** 2 wks

L.T.D. US, male vocal / instrumental group **3 wks**

9 Sep 78 **HOLDING ON (WHEN LOVE IS GONE)**
A & M AMS 7378 ....**70** 3 wks

LUCAS US, male vocalist **4 wks**

6 Aug 94 **LUCAS WITH THE LID OFF** WEA YZ 832CD...............**37** 4 wks

Carrie LUCAS US, female vocalist **6 wks**

16 Jun 79 **DANCE WITH YOU** Solar FB 1482............................**40** 6 wks

Tammy LUCAS - See Teddy RILEY

LUCIANA UK, female vocalist **5 wks**

23 Apr 94 **GET IT UP FOR LOVE** Chrysalis CDCHS 5008 ....**55** 2 wks
6 Aug 94 **IF YOU WANT** Chrysalis CDCHS 5009 ....**47** 2 wks
5 Nov 94 **WHAT GOES AROUND / ONE MORE RIVER**
Chrysalis CDCHS 5015......................................**67** 1 wk

Robin LUKE US, male vocalist **6 wks**

17 Oct 58 **SUSIE DARLIN'** London HLD 8676 ....**24** 3 wks

| 21 Nov 58 | SUSIE DARLIN' (re-entry) *London HLD 8676* | **23** | 1 wk |
| 5 Dec 58 | SUSIE DARLIN' (2nd re-entry) *London HLD 8676* | **23** | 2 wks |

LUKK featuring Felicia COLLINS
US, male / female vocal / instrumental group **1 wk**

| 28 Sep 85 | ON THE ONE *Important TAN 6* | **72** | 1 wk |

LULU *UK, female vocalist* **165 wks**

14 May 64	● SHOUT *Decca F 11884* [1]	**7**	13 wks
12 Nov 64	HERE COMES THE NIGHT *Decca F 12017*	**50**	1 wk
17 Jun 65	● LEAVE A LITTLE LOVE *Decca F 12169*	**8**	11 wks
2 Sep 65	TRY TO UNDERSTAND *Decca F 12214*	**25**	8 wks
13 Apr 67	● THE BOAT THAT I ROW *Columbia DB 8169*	**6**	11 wks
29 Jun 67	LET'S PRETEND *Columbia DB 8221*	**11**	11 wks
8 Nov 67	LOVE LOVES TO LOVE LOVE *Columbia DB 8295*	**32**	6 wks
28 Feb 68	● ME THE PEACEFUL HEART *Columbia DB 8358*	**9**	9 wks
5 Jun 68	BOY *Columbia DB 8425*	**15**	7 wks
6 Nov 68	● I'M A TIGER *Columbia DB 8500*	**9**	13 wks
12 Mar 69	● BOOM BANG-A-BANG *Columbia DB 8550*	**2**	13 wks
22 Nov 69	OH ME OH MY (I'M A FOOL FOR YOU BABY) *Atco 226008*	**47**	2 wks
26 Jan 74	● THE MAN WHO SOLD THE WORLD *Polydor 2001 490*	**3**	9 wks
19 Apr 75	TAKE YOUR MAMA FOR A RIDE *Chelsea 2005 022*	**37**	4 wks
12 Dec 81	I COULD NEVER MISS YOU (MORE THAN I DO) *Alfa ALFA 1700*	**62**	4 wks
16 Jan 82	I COULD NEVER MISS YOU (MORE THAN I DO) (re-entry) *Alfa ALFA 1700*	**63**	1 wk
19 Jul 86	● SHOUT *Jive LULU1 / Decca SHOUT 1*	**8**	10 wks
30 Jan 93	INDEPENDENCE *Dome CDDOME 1001*	**11**	5 wks
3 Apr 93	I'M BACK FOR MORE *Dome CDDOME 1002* [2]	**27**	5 wks
4 Sep 93	LET ME WAKE UP IN YOUR ARMS *Dome CDDOME 1005*	**51**	2 wks
9 Oct 93	★ RELIGHT MY FIRE *RCA 74321167722* [3]	**1**	12 wks
27 Nov 93	HOW 'BOUT US *Dome CDDOME 1007*	**46**	3 wks
27 Aug 94	GOODBYE BABY AND AMEN *Dome CDDOME 1011*	**40**	2 wks
26 Nov 94	EVERY WOMAN KNOWS *Dome CDDOME 1013*	**44**	2 wks

[1] Lulu and the Luvvers [2] Lulu and Bobby Womack [3] Take That featuring Lulu

The newly recorded Shout entered the chart on 19 Jul 86, and the next week the original Decca version by Lulu and the Luvvers also charted. For all subsequent weeks Gallup amalgamated both versions under one entry.

Bob LUMAN *US, male vocalist* **21 wks**

8 Sep 60	● LET'S THINK ABOUT LIVING *Warner Bros. WB 18*	**6**	18 wks
15 Dec 60	WHY WHY BYE BYE *Warner Bros. WB 28*	**46**	1 wk
4 May 61	THE GREAT SNOWMAN *Warner Bros. WB 37*	**49**	2 wks

LURKERS *UK, male vocal / instrumental group* **11 wks**

3 Jun 78	AIN'T GOT A CLUE *Beggars Banquet BEG 6*	**45**	3 wks
5 Aug 78	I DON'T NEED TO TELL HER *Beggars Banquet BEG 9*	**49**	4 wks
3 Feb 79	JUST THIRTEEN *Beggars Banquet BEG 14*	**66**	2 wks
9 Jun 79	OUT IN THE DARK / CYANIDE *Beggars Banquet BEG 19*	**72**	1 wk
17 Nov 79	NEW GUITAR IN TOWN *Beggars Banquet BEG 28*	**72**	1 wk

LUSH *UK, male / female vocal / instrumental group* **10 wks**

10 Mar 90	MAD LOVE EP *4AD BAD 003*	**55**	1 wk
27 Oct 90	SWEETNESS AND LIGHT *4AD BAD 0013*	**47**	2 wks
19 Oct 91	NOTHING NATURAL *4AD AD 1016*	**43**	2 wks
11 Jan 92	FOR LOVE (EP) *4AD BAD 2001*	**35**	2 wks
11 Jun 94	HYPOCRITE *4AD BAD 4008CD*	**52**	2 wks
11 Jun 94	DESIRE LINES *4AD BAD 4010CD*	**60**	1 wk

Tracks on Mad Love EP: De-Luxe / Leaves Me Cold / Downer / Thoughtforms. Tracks on For Love (EP): For Love / Starlust / Outdoor Miner / Astronaut.

LUVVERS - *See LULU*

L.W.S. *Italy, male instrumental group* **1 wk**

| 29 Oct 94 | GOSP *Transworld TRANNY 4CD* | **65** | 1 wk |

Frankie LYMON and the TEENAGERS
US, male vocal group **33 wks**

29 Jun 56	★ WHY DO FOOLS FALL IN LOVE *Columbia DB 3772* [1]	**1**	16 wks
29 Mar 57	I'M NOT A JUVENILE DELINQUENT *Columbia DB 3878*	**12**	7 wks
12 Apr 57	● BABY BABY *Columbia DB 3878*	**4**	12 wks
20 Sep 57	GOODY GOODY *Columbia DB 3983*	**24**	3 wks

[1] Teenagers featuring Frankie Lymon

Kenny LYNCH *UK, male vocalist* **59 wks**

30 Jun 60	MOUNTAIN OF LOVE *HMV POP 751*	**33**	3 wks
13 Sep 62	PUFF *HMV POP 1057*	**33**	5 wks
25 Oct 62	PUFF (re-entry) *HMV POP 1057*	**46**	1 wk
6 Dec 62	● UP ON THE ROOF *HMV POP 1090*	**10**	12 wks
20 Jun 63	● YOU CAN NEVER STOP ME LOVING YOU *HMV POP 1165*	**10**	14 wks
16 Apr 64	STAND BY ME *HMV POP 1280*	**39**	7 wks
27 Aug 64	WHAT AM I TO YOU *HMV POP 1321*	**37**	4 wks
1 Oct 64	WHAT AM I TO YOU (re-entry) *HMV POP 1321*	**44**	2 wks
17 Jun 65	I'LL STAY BY YOU *HMV POP 1430*	**29**	7 wks
20 Aug 83	HALF THE DAY'S GONE AND WE HAVEN'T EARNT A PENNY *Satril SAT 510*	**50**	4 wks

Cheryl LYNN *US, female vocalist* **2 wks**

| 8 Sep 84 | ENCORE *Streetwave KHAN 23* | **68** | 2 wks |

Patti LYNN *UK, female vocalist* **5 wks**

| 10 May 62 | JOHNNY ANGEL *Fontana H 391* | **37** | 5 wks |

Tami LYNN *US, female vocalist* **20 wks**

| 22 May 71 | ● I'M GONNA RUN AWAY FROM YOU *Mojo 2092 001* | **4** | 14 wks |
| 3 May 75 | I'M GONNA RUN AWAY FROM YOU (re-issue) *Contempo Raries CS 9026* | **36** | 6 wks |

Vera LYNN *UK, female vocalist* **46 wks**

14 Nov 52	● AUF WIEDERSEHEN *Decca F 9927*	**10**	1 wk
14 Nov 52	● FORGET ME NOT *Decca F 9985*	**7**	1 wk
14 Nov 52	● HOMING WALTZ *Decca F 9959*	**9**	3 wks
28 Nov 52	● FORGET ME NOT (re-entry) *Decca F 9985*	**5**	5 wks
5 Jun 53	WINDSOR WALTZ *Decca F 10092*	**11**	1 wk
15 Oct 54	★ MY SON MY SON *Decca F 10372* [1]	**1**	14 wks
8 Jun 56	WHO ARE WE *Decca F 10715*	**30**	1 wk
26 Oct 56	A HOUSE WITH LOVE IN IT *Decca F 10799*	**17**	13 wks
15 Mar 57	THE FAITHFUL HUSSAR (DON'T CRY MY LOVE) *Decca F 10846*	**29**	2 wks
21 Jun 57	TRAVELLIN' HOME *Decca F 10903*	**20**	5 wks

[1] Vera Lynn with Frank Weir, his saxophone, his Orchestra and Chorus

Jeff LYNNE *UK, male vocalist* **4 wks**

| 30 Jun 90 | EVERY LITTLE THING *Reprise W 9799* | **59** | 4 wks |

Philip LYNOTT *Ireland, male vocalist* **36 wks**

5 Apr 80	DEAR MISS LONELY HEARTS *Vertigo SOLO 1*	**32**	6 wks
21 Jun 80	KING'S CALL *Vertigo SOLO 2*	**35**	6 wks
21 Mar 81	YELLOW PEARL *Vertigo SOLO 3*	**56**	3 wks

Heather Small of **M PEOPLE** sings at the 1994 Glastonbury Festival.
(Steve Gillett)

'Stay (I Missed You)' by **LISA LOEB AND NINE STORIES** came from the soundtrack of the film *Reality Bites*.
(Brian Rasic/REX)

PATTI LYNN scored her only chart hit with 'Johnny Angel' in May 1962.
(Patti Lynn collection)

26 Dec 81	**YELLOW PEARL** (re-entry) *Vertigo SOLO 3*	.....**14**	9 wks
18 May 85	● **OUT IN THE FIELDS** *10 TEN 49* [1]	.....**5**	10 wks
24 Jan 87	**KING'S CALL** (re-mix) *Vertigo LYN 1*	.....**68**	2 wks

[1] Gary Moore and Phil Lynott

See also Gary Moore.

LYNYRD SKYNYRD *US, male vocal / instrumental group* **21 wks**

11 Sep 76	**FREE BIRD EP** *MCA 251*	.....**31**	4 wks
22 Dec 79	**FREE BIRD EP** (re-entry) *MCA 251*	.....**43**	8 wks
19 Jun 82	**FREE BIRD EP** (2nd re-entry) *MCA 251*	.....**21**	9 wks

Tracks on Free Bird EP: Free Bird / Sweet Home Alabama / Double Trouble.

Barbara LYON *US, female vocalist* **12 wks**

| 24 Jun 55 | **STOWAWAY** *Columbia DB 3619* | .....**12** | 8 wks |
| 21 Dec 56 | **LETTER TO A SOLDIER** *Columbia DB 3865* | .....**27** | 4 wks |

Humphrey LYTTELTON BAND
UK, male jazz band, Humphrey Lyttelton - trumpet **6 wks**

| 13 Jul 56 | **BAD PENNY BLUES** *Parlophone R 4184* | .....**19** | 6 wks |

M *UK, male vocalist / multi-instrumentalist - Robin Scott* **39 wks**

7 Apr 79	● **POP MUZIK** *MCA 413*	.....**2**	14 wks
8 Dec 79	**MOONLIGHT AND MUZAK** *MCA 541*	.....**33**	9 wks
15 Mar 80	**THAT'S THE WAY THE MONEY GOES** *MCA 570*	.....**45**	5 wks
22 Nov 80	**OFFICIAL SECRETS** *MCA 650*	.....**64**	2 wks
10 Jun 89	**POP MUZIK** (re-mix) *Freestyle FRS 1*	.....**15**	9 wks

Bobby M featuring Jean CARN
US, male / female vocal / instrumental duo **3 wks**

| 29 Jan 83 | **LET'S STAY TOGETHER** *Gordy TMG 1288* | .....**53** | 3 wks |

M-BEAT *UK, male producer* **15 wks**

18 Jun 94	**INCREDIBLE** *Renk RENK 42CD* [1]	.....**39**	3 wks
10 Sep 94	● **INCREDIBLE** (re-mix) *Renk CDRENK 44* [1]	.....**8**	9 wks
17 Dec 94	**SWEET LOVE** *Renk CDRENK 49* [2]	.....**18†**	3 wks

[1] M-Beat featuring General Levy [2] M-Beat featuring Nazlyn

M-D-EMM *UK, male producer - Mark Ryder* **3 wks**

| 22 Feb 92 | **GET DOWN** *Strictly Underground 7STUR 13* | .....**55** | 2 wks |
| 30 May 92 | **MOVE YOUR FEET** *Strictly Underground STUR 15* | .....**67** | 1 wk |

M + M *Canada, male / female vocal duo* **4 wks**

| 28 Jul 84 | **BLACK STATIONS WHITE STATIONS** *RCA 426* | .....**46** | 4 wks |

See also Martha and the Muffins.

M and O BAND *UK, male vocal / instrumental group* **6 wks**

| 28 Feb 76 | **LET'S DO THE LATIN HUSTLE** *Creole CR 120* | .....**16** | 6 wks |

M PEOPLE *UK, male / female vocal / instrumental group* **77 wks**

26 Oct 91	**HOW CAN I LOVE YOU MORE** *Deconstruction PB 44855*	.....**29**	9 wks
7 Mar 92	**COLOUR MY LIFE** *Deconstruction PB 45241*	.....**35**	4 wks
18 Apr 92	**SOMEDAY** *Deconstruction PB 45369* [1]	.....**38**	3 wks
10 Oct 92	**EXCITED** *Deconstruction 74321116337*	.....**29**	5 wks
5 Feb 93	● **HOW CAN I LOVE YOU MORE** (re-mix) *Deconstruction 74321130232*	.....**8**	8 wks
26 Jun 93	● **ONE NIGHT IN HEAVEN** *Deconstruction 74321151852*	.....**6**	11 wks
25 Sep 93	● **MOVING ON UP** *Deconstruction 74321166162*	.....**2**	11 wks
4 Dec 93	● **DON'T LOOK ANY FURTHER** *Deconstruction 74321177112*	.....**9**	10 wks
12 Mar 94	● **RENAISSANCE** *Deconstruction 74321194132*	.....**5**	7 wks
17 Sep 94	**ELEGANTLY AMERICAN: ONE NIGHT IN HEAVEN / MOVING ON UP** (re-mixes) *Deconstruction 74321231882*	.....**31**	2 wks
19 Nov 94	● **SIGHT FOR SORE EYES** *Deconstruction 74321245472*	.....**6†**	7 wks

[1] M People with Heather Small

Pete MAC Jr. *US, male vocalist* **4 wks**

| 15 Oct 77 | **THE WATER MARGIN** *BBC RESL 50* | .....**37** | 4 wks |

This is the Japanese version of the song which shared chart credit with the English language version by Godiego. See also Godiego.

MAC BAND featuring the McCAMPBELL BROTHERS *US, male vocal group* **17 wks**

| 18 Jun 88 | ● **ROSES ARE RED** *MCA MCA 1264* | .....**8** | 13 wks |
| 10 Sep 88 | **STALEMATE** *MCA MCA 1271* | .....**40** | 4 wks |

Stalemate credits the McCampbell Brothers on the sleeve only, not on the label.

Keith MAC PROJECT
UK, male / female vocal / instrumental group **1 wk**

| 25 Jun 94 | **DE DAH DAH (SPICE OF LIFE)** *Public Demand PPDCD 3* | .....**66** | 1 wk |

Neil MacARTHUR *UK, male vocalist* **5 wks**

| 5 Feb 69 | **SHE'S NOT THERE** *Deram DM 225* | .....**34** | 5 wks |

Neil MacArthur is Colin Blunstone under a false name.

David MacBETH *UK, male vocalist* **4 wks**

| 30 Oct 59 | **MR. BLUE** *Pye 7N 15231* | .....**18** | 4 wks |

Nicko McBRAIN
UK, male vocalist / instrumentalist - drums **1 wk**

| 13 Jul 91 | **RHYTHM OF THE BEAST** *EMI NICK 01* | .....**72** | 1 wk |

Frankie McBRIDE *Ireland, male vocalist* **15 wks**

| 9 Aug 67 | **FIVE LITTLE FINGERS** *Emerald MD 1081* | .....**19** | 15 wks |

Dan McCAFFERTY *UK, male vocalist* **3 wks**

| 13 Sep 75 | **OUT OF TIME** *Mountain TOP 1* | .....**41** | 3 wks |

C.W. McCALL *US, male vocalist* **10 wks**

| 14 Feb 76 | ● **CONVOY** *MGM 2006 560* | .....**2** | 10 wks |

David McCALLUM *UK, male vocalist* **4 wks**

| 14 Apr 66 | **COMMUNICATION** *Capitol CL 15439* | .....**32** | 4 wks |

McCAMPBELL BROTHERS - *See MAC BAND featuring the McCAMPBELL BROTHERS*

Paul McCARTNEY UK, male vocalist — **397 wks**

27 Feb 71	● ANOTHER DAY *Apple R 5889*		**2**	12 wks
28 Aug 71	BACK SEAT OF MY CAR *Apple R 5914* [1]		**39**	5 wks
26 Feb 72	GIVE IRELAND BACK TO THE IRISH *Apple R 5936* [2]		**16**	8 wks
27 May 72	● MARY HAD A LITTLE LAMB *Apple R 5949* [2]		**9**	11 wks
9 Dec 72	HI HI HI / C MOON *Apple R 5973* [2]		**5**	13 wks
7 Apr 73	● MY LOVE *Apple R 5985* [3]		**9**	11 wks
9 Jun 73	● LIVE AND LET DIE *Apple R 5987* [2]		**9**	13 wks
15 Sep 73	LIVE AND LET DIE (re-entry) *Apple R 5987* [2]		**49**	1 wk
3 Nov 73	HELEN WHEELS *Apple R 5993* [3]		**12**	12 wks
2 Mar 74	● JET *Apple R 5996* [3]		**7**	9 wks
6 Jul 74	● BAND ON THE RUN *Apple R 5997* [3]		**3**	11 wks
9 Nov 74	JUNIOR'S FARM *Apple R 5999* [3]		**16**	10 wks
31 May 75	● LISTEN TO WHAT THE MAN SAID *Capitol R 6006* [2]		**6**	8 wks
18 Oct 75	LETTING GO *Capitol R 6008* [2]		**41**	3 wks
15 May 76	● SILLY LOVE SONGS *Parlophone R 6014* [2]		**2**	11 wks
7 Aug 76	● LET 'EM IN *Parlophone R 6015* [2]		**2**	10 wks
19 Feb 77	MAYBE I'M AMAZED *Parlophone R 6017* [2]		**28**	5 wks
19 Nov 77	★ MULL OF KINTYRE / GIRLS' SCHOOL *Capitol R 6018* [2]		**1**	17 wks
1 Apr 78	● WITH A LITTLE LUCK *Parlophone R 6019* [2]		**5**	9 wks
1 Jul 78	I'VE HAD ENOUGH *Parlophone R 6020* [2]		**42**	7 wks
9 Sep 78	LONDON TOWN *Parlophone R 6021* [2]		**60**	4 wks
7 Apr 79	● GOODNIGHT TONIGHT *Parlophone R 6023* [2]		**5**	10 wks
16 Jun 79	OLD SIAM SIR *MPL R 6026* [2]		**35**	6 wks
1 Sep 79	GETTING CLOSER / BABY'S REQUEST *R 6027* [2]		**60**	3 wks
1 Dec 79	● WONDERFUL CHRISTMAS TIME *Parlophone R 6029*		**6**	8 wks
19 Apr 80	● COMING UP *Parlophone R 6035*		**2**	9 wks
21 Jun 80	● WATERFALLS *Parlophone R 6037*		**9**	8 wks
10 Apr 82	★ EBONY AND IVORY *Parlophone R 6054* [4]		**1**	10 wks
3 Jul 82	TAKE IT AWAY *Parlophone R 6056*		**15**	10 wks
9 Oct 82	TUG OF WAR *Parlophone R 6057*		**53**	3 wks
6 Nov 82	● THE GIRL IS MINE *Epic EPC A 2729* [5]		**8**	9 wks
15 Jan 83	THE GIRL IS MINE (re-entry) *Epic EPC A 2729* [5]		**75**	1 wk
15 Oct 83	● SAY SAY SAY *Parlophone R 6062* [6]		**2**	15 wks
17 Dec 83	★ PIPES OF PEACE *Parlophone R 6064*		**1**	12 wks
6 Oct 84	● NO MORE LONELY NIGHTS (BALLAD) *Parlophone R 6080*		**2**	15 wks
24 Nov 84	● WE ALL STAND TOGETHER *Parlophone R 6086* [7]		**3**	13 wks
30 Nov 85	SPIES LIKE US *Parlophone R 6118*		**13**	10 wks
21 Dec 85	WE ALL STAND TOGETHER (re-entry) *Parlophone R 6086*		**32**	5 wks
26 Jul 86	PRESS *Parlophone R 6133*		**25**	8 wks
13 Dec 86	ONLY LOVE REMAINS *Parlophone R 6148*		**34**	5 wks
28 Nov 87	● ONCE UPON A LONG AGO *Parlophone R 6170*		**10**	7 wks
20 May 89	★ FERRY 'CROSS THE MERSEY *PWL PWL 41* [8]		**1**	7 wks
20 May 89	MY BRAVE FACE *Parlophone R 6213*		**18**	5 wks
29 Jul 89	THIS ONE *Parlophone R 6223*		**18**	6 wks
25 Nov 89	FIGURE OF EIGHT *Parlophone R 6235*		**42**	4 wks
17 Feb 90	PUT IT THERE *Parlophone R 6246*		**32**	2 wks
20 Oct 90	BIRTHDAY *Parlophone R 6271*		**29**	3 wks
8 Dec 90	ALL MY TRIALS *Parlophone R 6278*		**35**	5 wks
5 Feb 93	HOPE OF DELIVERANCE *Parlophone CDR 6330*		**18**	6 wks
6 Mar 93	C'MON PEOPLE *Parlophone CDRS 6338*		**41**	3 wks

[1] Paul and Linda McCartney [2] Wings [3] Paul McCartney and Wings [4] Paul McCartney with Stevie Wonder [5] Michael Jackson and Paul McCartney [6] Paul McCartney and Michael Jackson [7] Paul McCartney and the Frog Chorus [8] Christians, Holly Johnson, Paul McCartney, Gerry Marsden and Stock Aitken Waterman

R 6027 credits no label at all, although the number is a Parlophone one.

Kirsty MacCOLL UK, female vocalist — **57 wks**

13 Jun 81	THERE'S A GUY WORKS DOWN THE CHIPSHOP SWEARS HE'S ELVIS *Polydor POSP 250*		**14**	9 wks
19 Jan 85	● A NEW ENGLAND *Stiff BUY 216*		**7**	10 wks
5 Dec 87	● FAIRYTALE OF NEW YORK *Pogue Mahone NY 7* [1]		**2**	9 wks
8 Apr 89	FREE WORLD *Virgin KMA 1*		**43**	6 wks
1 Jul 89	DAYS *Virgin KMA 2*		**12**	9 wks
25 May 91	WALKING DOWN MADISON *Virgin VS 1348*		**23**	7 wks
24 Aug 91	MY AFFAIR *Virgin VS 1354*		**68**	2 wks
14 Dec 91	FAIRYTALE OF NEW YORK (re-issue) *PM YZ 628* [1]		**36**	5 wks

[1] Pogues featuring Kirsty MacColl

Marilyn McCOO and Billy DAVIS Jr. US, female / male vocal duo — **9 wks**

19 Mar 77	● YOU DON'T HAVE TO BE A STAR (TO BE IN MY SHOW) *ABC 4147*		**7**	9 wks

Van McCOY US, orchestra — **36 wks**

31 May 75	● THE HUSTLE *Avco 6105 038* [1]		**3**	12 wks
1 Nov 75	CHANGE WITH THE TIMES *Avco 6105 042*		**36**	4 wks
12 Feb 77	SOUL CHA CHA *H & L 6105 065*		**34**	6 wks
9 Apr 77	● THE SHUFFLE *H & L 6105 076*		**4**	14 wks

[1] Van McCoy with the Soul City Symphony

McCOYS US, male vocal / instrumental group — **18 wks**

2 Sep 65	● HANG ON SLOOPY *Immediate IM 001*		**5**	14 wks
16 Dec 65	FEVER *Immediate IM 021*		**44**	4 wks

George McCRAE US, male vocalist — **62 wks**

29 Jun 74	★ ROCK YOUR BABY *Jayboy BOY 85*		**1**	14 wks
5 Oct 74	● I CAN'T LEAVE YOU ALONE *Jayboy BOY 90*		**9**	9 wks
14 Dec 74	YOU CAN HAVE IT ALL *Jayboy BOY 92*		**23**	9 wks
22 Mar 75	SING A HAPPY SONG *Jayboy BOY 95*		**38**	4 wks
19 Jul 75	● IT'S BEEN SO LONG *Jayboy BOY 100*		**4**	11 wks
18 Oct 75	I AIN'T LYIN' *Jayboy BOY 105*		**12**	7 wks
24 Jan 76	HONEY I *Jayboy BOY 107*		**33**	4 wks
25 Feb 84	ONE STEP CLOSER (TO LOVE) *President PT 522*		**57**	4 wks

Gwen McCRAE US, female vocalist — **5 wks**

30 Apr 88	ALL THIS LOVE THAT I'M GIVING *Flame MELT 7*		**63**	2 wks
13 Feb 93	ALL THIS LOVE I'M GIVING *KTDA CDKTDA 2* [1]		**36**	3 wks

[1] Music And Mystery featuring Gwen McCrae

All This Love I'm Giving is a re-recording of her first hit.

MacCRARYS US, male vocal / instrumental group — **4 wks**

31 Jul 82	LOVE ON A SUMMER NIGHT *Capitol CL 251*		**52**	4 wks

Ian McCULLOCH UK, male vocalist — **14 wks**

15 Dec 84	SEPTEMBER SONG *Korova KOW 40*		**51**	5 wks
2 Sep 89	PROUD TO FALL *WEA YZ 417*		**51**	4 wks
12 May 90	CANDLELAND (THE SECOND COMING) *East West YZ 452* [1]		**75**	1 wk
22 Feb 92	LOVER LOVER LOVER *East West YZ 643*		**47**	4 wks

[1] Ian McCulloch featuring Elizabeth Fraser

Gene McDANIELS US, male vocalist — **2 wks**

16 Nov 61	TOWER OF STRENGTH *London HLG 9448*		**49**	1 wk
30 Nov 61	TOWER OF STRENGTH (re-entry) *London HLG 9448*		**49**	1 wk

Charles McDEVITT SKIFFLE GROUP featuring Nancy WHISKEY UK, male / female vocal / instrumental group — **20 wks**

12 Apr 57	● FREIGHT TRAIN *Oriole CB 1352*		**5**	17 wks

MADNESS policed the chart beat for ten consecutive years.
(Paul Cox/LFI)

TOP 38

PAUL McCARTNEY remains the only artist to have number ones as a soloist and as a member of a duo (with Stevie Wonder), trio (Wings), quartet (Beatles), quintet (Beatles with Billy Preston) and charity aggregation (with the Christians, Holly Johnson, Gerry Marsden and Stock Aitken Waterman). His totals of 21 number ones as a featured artist and 86 weeks at number one are the all-time highs.

TOP 11

14 Jun 57	**GREENBACK DOLLAR** Oriole CB 1371 ....**28**	1 wk
5 Jul 57	**GREENBACK DOLLAR (re-entry)** Oriole CB 1371 ....**30**	1 wk
20 Sep 57	**FREIGHT TRAIN (re-entry)** Oriole CB 1352 ....**27**	1 wk

Michael McDONALD US, male vocalist — 45 wks

18 Feb 84	**YAH MO B THERE** Qwest W 9394 [1] **44**	5 wks
7 Apr 84	**YAH MO B THERE (re-entry)** Qwest W 9394 [1] **69**	3 wks
12 Jan 85	**YAH MO B THERE (2nd re-entry)** Qwest W 9394 [1] **12**	8 wks
3 May 86	● **ON MY OWN** MCA MCA 1045 [2] **2**	13 wks
26 Jul 86	**I KEEP FORGETTIN'** Warner Bros. K 17992 ....**43**	6 wks
6 Sep 86	**SWEET FREEDOM** MCA MCA 1073 ....**12**	10 wks

[1] James Ingram with Michael McDonald [2] Patti Labelle and Michael McDonald

The '85 entry of Yah Mo B There is a re-mix of the original hit with the same catalogue number. See also Doobie Brothers.

Carrie McDOWELL US, female vocalist — 3 wks

26 Sep 87	**UH UH NO NO CASUAL SEX** Motown ZV 41501 ......**68**	3 wks

John McENROE and Pat CASH with the FULL METAL RACKETS US/Australia, male vocal/instrumental duo with UK backing group — 1 wk

13 Jul 91	**ROCK 'N' ROLL** Music For Nations KUT 141 ....**66**	1 wk

MACEO and the MACS US, male vocal/instrumental group — 5 wks

16 May 87	**CROSS THE TRACK (WE BETTER GO BACK)** Urban URBX 1.......................**54**	5 wks

McFADDEN and WHITEHEAD US, male vocal duo — 10 wks

19 May 79	● **AIN'T NO STOPPIN' US NOW** Philadelphia International PIR 7365 ....**5**	10 wks

Rachel McFARLANE - See LOVELAND featuring Rachel McFARLANE

Bobby McFERRIN US, male vocalist — 15 wks

24 Sep 88	● **DON'T WORRY BE HAPPY** Manhattan MT 56 ....**2**	11 wks
17 Dec 88	**THINKIN' ABOUT YOUR BODY** Manhattan BLUE 6..**46**	4 wks

Mike McGEAR UK, male vocalist — 4 wks

5 Oct 74	**LEAVE IT** Warner Bros. K 16446 ....**36**	4 wks

Maureen McGOVERN US, female vocalist — 8 wks

5 Jun 76	**THE CONTINENTAL** 20th Century BTC 2222 ....**16**	8 wks

Shane McGOWAN and the POPES UK, male vocal/instrumental group — 5 wks

12 Dec 92	**WHAT A WONDERFUL WORLD** Mute MUTE 151 [1] **72**	1 wk
3 Sep 94	**THE CHURCH OF THE HOLY SPOOK** ZTT ZANG 57CD **74**	1 wk
15 Oct 94	**THAT WOMAN'S GOT ME DRINKING** ZTT ZANG 57CD **34**	3 wks

[1] Nick Cave and Shane McGowan

Freddie McGREGOR Jamaica, male vocalist — 16 wks

27 Jun 87	● **JUST DON'T WANT TO BE LONELY** Germain DG 24 ..**9**	11 wks
19 Sep 87	**THAT GIRL (GROOVY SITUATION)** Polydor POSP 884 ....**47**	5 wks

Mary MacGREGOR US, female vocalist — 10 wks

19 Feb 77	● **TORN BETWEEN TWO LOVERS** Ariola America AA 111 ....**4**	10 wks

McGUINNESS FLINT UK, male vocal/instrumental group — 26 wks

21 Nov 70	● **WHEN I'M DEAD AND GONE** Capitol CL 15662........**2**	14 wks
1 May 71	● **MALT AND BARLEY BLUES** Capitol CL 15682 ....**5**	12 wks

Barry McGUIRE US, male vocalist — 13 wks

9 Sep 65	● **EVE OF DESTRUCTION** RCA 1469 ....**3**	13 wks

McGUIRE SISTERS US, female vocal group — 24 wks

1 Apr 55	**NO MORE** Vogue Coral Q 72050 ....**20**	1 wk
15 Jul 55	**SINCERELY** Vogue Coral Q 72050 ....**14**	4 wks
1 Jun 56	**DELILAH JONES** Vogue Coral Q 72161 ....**24**	2 wks
14 Feb 58	**SUGARTIME** Coral Q 72305 ....**14**	6 wks
1 May 59	**MAY YOU ALWAYS** Coral Q 72356 ....**15**	10 wks
17 Jul 59	**MAY YOU ALWAYS (re-entry)** Coral Q 72356........**28**	1 wk

Craig MACK US, male rapper — 2 wks

12 Nov 94	**FLAVA IN YA EAR** Bad Boy 74321242582 ....**57**	2 wks

Lizzy MACK - See FITS OF GLOOM

Lonnie MACK US, male instrumentalist - guitar — 3 wks

14 Apr 79	**MEMPHIS** Lightning LIG 9011 ....**47**	3 wks

Memphis was coupled with Let's Dance by Chris Montez as a double A-side.

Maria McKEE US, female vocalist — 23 wks

15 Sep 90	★ **SHOW ME HEAVEN** Epic 656303 7.......................**1**	14 wks
26 Jan 91	**BREATHE** Geffen GFS 1 ....**59**	1 wk
1 Aug 92	**SWEETEST CHILD** Geffen GFS 23 ....**45**	4 wks
22 May 93	**I'M GONNA SOOTHE YOU** Geffen GFSTD 39 ....**35**	3 wks
18 Sep 93	**I CAN'T MAKE IT ALONE** Geffen GFSTD 53 ....**74**	1 wk

Kenneth McKELLAR UK, male vocalist — 4 wks

10 Mar 66	**A MAN WITHOUT LOVE** Decca F 12341 ....**30**	4 wks

Terence McKENNA - See SHAMEN

Gisele McKENZIE Canada, female vocalist — 6 wks

17 Jul 53	**SEVEN LONELY DAYS** Capitol CL 13920 ....**12**	1 wk
31 Jul 53	**SEVEN LONELY DAYS (re-entry)** Capitol CL 13920 ..**11**	1 wk
21 Aug 53	● **SEVEN LONELY DAYS (2nd re-entry)** Capitol CL 13920.......................**6**	4 wks

Scott McKENZIE US, male vocalist — 18 wks

12 Jul 67	★ **SAN FRANCISCO (BE SURE TO WEAR SOME FLOWERS IN YOUR HAIR)** CBS 2816.......................**1**	17 wks
1 Nov 67	**LIKE AN OLD TIME MOVIE** CBS 3009 [1] **50**	1 wk

[1] The Voice Of Scott McKenzie

Ken MACKINTOSH *UK, orchestra* — 9 wks

15 Jan 54	**THE CREEP** *HMV BD 1295*	**12**	1 wk
29 Jan 54	● **THE CREEP (re-entry)** *HMV BD 1295*	**10**	1 wk
7 Feb 58	**RAUNCHY** *HMV POP 426*	**19**	6 wks
10 Mar 60	**NO HIDING PLACE** *HMV POP 713*	**45**	1 wk

Vivienne McKONE *UK, female vocalist* — 5 wks

| 25 Jul 92 | **SING (OOH-EE-OOH)** *ffrr F 183* .... | **47** | 4 wks |
| 31 Oct 92 | **BEWARE** *ffrr F 202* .... | **69** | 1 wk |

McKOY *UK, male / female vocal group* — 2 wks

| 6 Mar 93 | **FIGHT** *Rightrack CDTUM 1* .... | **54** | 2 wks |

Noel McKOY - *See J.T.Q. with Noel McKOY; McKOY*

Craig McLACHLAN *Australia, male vocalist* — 38 wks

16 Jun 90	● **MONA** *Epic 655784 7* [1]	**2**	11 wks
4 Aug 90	**AMANDA** *Epic 656170 7* [1]	**19**	6 wks
10 Nov 90	**I ALMOST FELT LIKE CRYING** *Epic 656310 7* [1]	**50**	3 wks
23 May 92	**ONE REASON WHY** *Epic 6580677*	**29**	6 wks
14 Nov 92	**ON MY OWN** *Epic 6584677*	**59**	2 wks
24 Jul 93	**YOU'RE THE ONE THAT I WANT** *Epic 6595222* [2] ..**13**		6 wks
25 Dec 93	**GREASE** *Epic 6600242*	**44**	4 wks

[1] Craig McLachlan and Check 1-2 [2] Craig McLachlan and Debbie Gibson

Tommy McLAIN *US, male vocalist* — 1 wk

| 8 Sep 66 | **SWEET DREAMS** *London HL 10065* .... | **49** | 1 wk |

Malcolm McLAREN *UK, male vocalist* — 64 wks

4 Dec 82	● **BUFFALO GALS** *Charisma MALC 1* [1]	**9**	12 wks
26 Feb 83	**SOWETO** *Charisma MALC 2* [2]	**32**	5 wks
2 Jul 83	● **DOUBLE DUTCH** *Charisma MALC 3*	**3**	13 wks
17 Dec 83	**DUCK FOR THE OYSTER** *Charisma MALC 4*	**54**	5 wks
1 Sep 84	**MADAM BUTTERFLY (UN BEL DI VEDREMO)** *Charisma MALC 5*	**13**	9 wks
27 May 89	**WALTZ DARLING** *Epic WALTZ 2* [3]	**31**	8 wks
19 Aug 89	**SOMETHING'S JUMPIN' IN YOUR SHIRT** *Epic WALTZ 3* [4]	**29**	7 wks
25 Nov 89	**HOUSE OF THE BLUE DANUBE** *Epic WALTZ 4* [3] **73**		1 wk
21 Dec 91	**MAGIC'S BACK (THEME FROM THE GHOSTS OF OXFORD STREET)** *RCA PB 45223* [5]	**42**	4 wks

[1] Malcolm McLaren and the World's Famous Supreme Team [2] Malcolm McLaren and the McLarenettes [3] Malcolm McLaren and the Bootzilla Orchestra [4] Malcolm McLaren and the Bootzilla Orchestra featuring Lisa Marie [5] Malcolm McLaren featuring Alison Limerick

Bitty McLEAN *UK, male vocalist* — 37 wks

31 Jul 93	● **IT KEEP RAININ' (TEARS FROM MY EYES)** *Brilliant CDBRIL 1*	**2**	15 wks
30 Oct 93	**PASS IT ON** *Brilliant CDBRIL 2*	**35**	3 wks
15 Jan 94	● **HERE I STAND** *Brilliant CDBRIL 3*	**10**	6 wks
9 Apr 94	● **DEDICATED TO THE ONE I LOVE** *Brilliant CDBRIL 4* ..**6**		10 wks
6 Aug 94	**WHAT GOES AROUND** *Brilliant CDBRIL 5*	**36**	3 wks

Don McLEAN *US, male vocalist* — 68 wks

22 Jan 72	● **AMERICAN PIE** *United Artists UP 35325*	**2**	16 wks
13 May 72	★ **VINCENT** *United Artists UP 35359*	**1**	15 wks
14 Apr 73	**EVERYDAY** *United Artists UP 35519*	**38**	5 wks
10 May 80	★ **CRYING** *EMI 5051*	**1**	14 wks
17 Apr 82	**CASTLES IN THE AIR** *EMI 5258*	**47**	8 wks
5 Oct 91	**AMERICAN PIE (re-issue)** *Liberty EMCT 3*	**12**	10 wks

Jackie McLEAN *US, male instrumentalist - alto sax* — 4 wks

| 7 Jul 79 | **DR. JACKYLL AND MISTER FUNK** *RCA PB 1575* ......**53** | | 4 wks |

Phil McLEAN *US, male vocalist* — 4 wks

| 18 Jan 62 | **SMALL SAD SAM** *Top Rank JAR 597* .... | **34** | 4 wks |

Ian McNABB *UK, male vocalist* — 4 wks

23 Jan 93	**IF LOVE WAS LIKE GUITARS** *This Way Up WAY 233*	**67**	1 wk
2 Jul 94	**YOU MUST BE PREPARED TO DREAM** *This Way Up WAY 3199* [1]	**54**	1 wk
17 Sep 94	**GO INTO THE LIGHT** *This Way Up WAY 3699* **66**		2 wks

[1] Ian McNabb featuring Ralph Molina and Billy Talbot

Patrick MACNEE and Honor BLACKMAN
UK, male / female vocal duo — 7 wks

| 1 Dec 90 | ● **KINKY BOOTS** *Deram KINKY 1* .... | **5** | 7 wks |

Rita MacNEIL *Canada, female vocalist* — 10 wks

| 6 Oct 90 | **WORKING MAN** *Polydor PO 98* .... | **11** | 10 wks |

Clyde McPHATTER *US, male vocalist* — 1 wk

| 24 Aug 56 | **TREASURE OF LOVE** *London HLE 8293* .... | **27** | 1 wk |

Carmen McRAE - *See Sammy DAVIS Jr.*

Gordon MacRAE - *See VARIOUS ARTISTS (EPs & LPs) - Carousel Soundtrack.*

Ralph McTELL *UK, male vocalist* — 18 wks

| 7 Dec 74 | ● **STREETS OF LONDON** *Reprise K 14380* .... | **2** | 12 wks |
| 20 Dec 75 | **DREAMS OF YOU** *Warner Bros. K 16648* .... | **36** | 6 wks |

MAD COBRA featuring Ritchie STEPHENS
Jamaica / UK, male vocal duo — 2 wks

| 15 May 93 | **LEGACY** *Columbia 6592852* .... | **64** | 2 wks |

MAD JOCKS featuring JOCKMASTER B.A.
UK, male vocal / instrumental group — 9 wks

| 19 Dec 87 | **JOCK MIX 1** *Debut DEBT 3037* .... | **46** | 5 wks |
| 18 Dec 93 | **PARTY FOUR EP** *SMP CDSSKM 24* .... | **57** | 4 wks |

Tracks on Party Four EP: No Lager / Here We Go Again / Jock Party Mix / Jock Jak Mix.

MAD STUNTMAN - *See REEL 2 REAL featuring the MAD STUNTMAN*

Danny MADDEN *US, male vocalist* — 2 wks

| 14 Jul 90 | **THE FACTS OF LIFE** *Eternal YZ 473* .... | **72** | 2 wks |

MADDER ROSE
US, male / female vocal / instrumental group — 2 wks

| 26 Mar 94 | **PANIC ON** *Atlantic A 8301CD* .... | **65** | 1 wk |
| 16 Jul 94 | **CAR SONG** *Seed A 7256CD* .... | **68** | 1 wk |

MADNESS *UK, male vocal / instrumental group* — 258 wks

| 1 Sep 79 | **THE PRINCE** *2 Tone TT 3* .... | **16** | 11 wks |
| 10 Nov 79 | ● **ONE STEP BEYOND** *Stiff BUY 56* .... | **7** | 14 wks |

5 Jan 80	● MY GIRL Stiff BUY 62	3	10 wks
5 Apr 80	● WORK REST AND PLAY EP Stiff BUY 71	6	8 wks
13 Sep 80	● BAGGY TROUSERS Stiff BUY 84	3	20 wks
22 Nov 80	● EMBARRASSMENT Stiff BUY 102	4	12 wks
24 Jan 81	● THE RETURN OF THE LOS PALMAS SEVEN Stiff BUY 108	7	11 wks
25 Apr 81	● GREY DAY Stiff BUY 112	4	10 wks
26 Sep 81	● SHUT UP Stiff BUY 126	7	9 wks
5 Dec 81	● IT MUST BE LOVE Stiff BUY 134	4	12 wks
20 Feb 82	CARDIAC ARREST Stiff BUY 140	14	10 wks
22 May 82	★ HOUSE OF FUN Stiff BUY 146	1	9 wks
24 Jul 82	● DRIVING IN MY CAR Stiff BUY 153	4	8 wks
27 Nov 82	● OUR HOUSE Stiff BUY 163	5	13 wks
19 Feb 83	● TOMORROW'S (JUST ANOTHER DAY) / MADNESS (IS ALL IN THE MIND) Stiff BUY 169	8	9 wks
20 Aug 83	● WINGS OF A DOVE Stiff BUY 181	2	10 wks
5 Nov 83	● THE SUN AND THE RAIN Stiff BUY 192	5	10 wks
11 Feb 84	MICHAEL CAINE Stiff BUY 196	11	8 wks
2 Jun 84	ONE BETTER DAY Stiff BUY 201	17	7 wks
31 Aug 85	YESTERDAY'S MEN Zarjazz JAZZ 5	18	7 wks
26 Oct 85	UNCLE SAM Zarjazz JAZZ 7	21	11 wks
1 Feb 86	SWEETEST GIRL Zarjazz JAZZ 8	35	6 wks
8 Nov 86	(WAITING FOR) THE GHOST TRAIN Zarjazz JAZZ 9	18	7 wks
3 Jan 87	(WAITING FOR) THE GHOST TRAIN (re-entry) Zarjazz JAZZ 9	74	1 wk
19 Mar 88	I PRONOUNCE YOU Virgin VS 1054 [1]	44	4 wks
15 Feb 92	● IT MUST BE LOVE (re-issue) Virgin VS 1405	6	9 wks
25 Apr 92	HOUSE OF FUN (re-issue) Virgin VS 1413	40	3 wks
8 Aug 92	MY GIRL (re-issue) Virgin VS 1425	27	4 wks
28 Nov 92	THE HARDER THEY COME Go! Discs GOD 93	44	3 wks
27 Feb 93	NIGHT BOAT TO CAIRO Virgin VSCDT 1447	56	2 wks

[1] The Madness

Tracks on Work Rest and Play EP: Night Boat to Cairo / Deceives The Eye / The Young And The Old / Don't Quote Me On That. Night Boat To Cairo in '93 is a re-issue of a track from the Work Rest And Play EP.

See also Various Artists (EPs & LPs) - The Two Tone EP.

MADONNA US, female vocalist 382 wks

14 Jan 84	● HOLIDAY Sire W 9405	6	11 wks
17 Mar 84	LUCKY STAR Sire W 9522	14	9 wks
2 Jun 84	BORDERLINE Sire W 9260	56	4 wks
17 Nov 84	● LIKE A VIRGIN Sire W 9210	3	15 wks
2 Mar 85	● MATERIAL GIRL Sire W 9083	3	10 wks
8 Jun 85	● CRAZY FOR YOU Geffen A 6323	2	15 wks
27 Jul 85	★ INTO THE GROOVE Sire W 8934	1	14 wks
3 Aug 85	● HOLIDAY (re-entry) Sire W 9405	2	10 wks
21 Sep 85	● ANGEL Sire W 8881	5	9 wks
12 Oct 85	● GAMBLER Geffen A 6585	4	11 wks
7 Dec 85	● DRESS YOU UP Sire W 8848	5	11 wks
4 Jan 86	GAMBLER (re-entry) Geffen A 6585	61	1 wk
25 Jan 86	● BORDERLINE (re-entry) Sire W 9260	2	9 wks
26 Apr 86	● LIVE TO TELL Sire W 8717	2	12 wks
28 Jun 86	★ PAPA DON'T PREACH Sire W 8636	1	14 wks
4 Oct 86	● TRUE BLUE Sire W 8550	1	15 wks
13 Dec 86	● OPEN YOUR HEART Sire W 8480	4	9 wks
4 Apr 87	★ LA ISLA BONITA Sire W 8378	1	11 wks
18 Jul 87	★ WHO'S THAT GIRL Sire W 8341	1	10 wks
19 Sep 87	● CAUSING A COMMOTION Sire W 8224	4	9 wks
12 Dec 87	● THE LOOK OF LOVE Sire W 8115	9	7 wks
18 Mar 89	★ LIKE A PRAYER Sire W 7539	1	12 wks
3 Jun 89	● EXPRESS YOURSELF Sire W 2948	5	10 wks
16 Sep 89	● CHERISH Sire W 2883	3	8 wks
16 Dec 89	● DEAR JESSIE Sire W 2668	5	9 wks
7 Apr 90	★ VOGUE Sire W 9851	1	14 wks
21 Jul 90	● HANKY PANKY Sire W 9789	2	9 wks
8 Dec 90	● JUSTIFY MY LOVE Sire W 9000	2	10 wks
2 Mar 91	● CRAZY FOR YOU (re-mix) Sire W 0008	2	8 wks
13 Apr 91	● RESCUE ME Sire W 0024	3	8 wks
8 Jun 91	● HOLIDAY (re-issue) Sire W 0037	5	7 wks
25 Jul 92	● THIS USED TO BE MY PLAYGROUND Sire W 0122	3	9 wks
17 Oct 92	● EROTICA Maverick W 0138	3	8 wks
12 Dec 92	● DEEPER AND DEEPER Maverick W 0146	6	9 wks
9 Jan 93	EROTICA (re-entry) Maverick W 0138	65	1 wk
6 Mar 93	● BAD GIRL Maverick W 0145CD	10	7 wks

3 Apr 93	● FEVER Maverick W 0168CD	6	6 wks
31 Jul 93	● RAIN Maverick W 0190CD	7	8 wks
2 Apr 94	● I'LL REMEMBER Maverick W 0240CD	7	8 wks
8 Oct 94	● SECRET Maverick W 0268CD	5	9 wks
17 Dec 94	TAKE A BOW Maverick W 0278CD	16†	3 wks

MAGAZINE UK, male vocal / instrumental group 7 wks

| 11 Feb 78 | SHOT BY BOTH SIDES Virgin VS 200 | 41 | 4 wks |
| 26 Jul 80 | SWEET HEART CONTRACT Virgin VS 368 | 54 | 3 wks |

MAGIC AFFAIR
US / Germany, male / female vocal / instrumental group 8 wks

4 Jun 94	OMEN III EMI CDEM 317	17	4 wks
27 Aug 94	GIVE ME ALL YOUR LOVE EMI CDEM 340	30	2 wks
5 Nov 94	IN THE MIDDLE OF THE NIGHT EMI CDEM 349	38	2 wks

MAGIC LADY US, female vocal duo 3 wks

| 14 May 88 | BETCHA CAN'T LOSE (WITH MY LOVE) Motown ZB 42003 | 58 | 3 wks |

MAGIC LANTERNS
UK, male vocal / instrumental group 3 wks

7 Jul 66	EXCUSE ME BABY CBS 202094	46	1 wk
28 Jul 66	EXCUSE ME BABY (re-entry) CBS 202094	44	1 wk
11 Aug 66	EXCUSE ME BABY (2nd re-entry) CBS 202094	46	1 wk

MAGNUM UK, male vocal / instrumental group 26 wks

22 Mar 80	MAGNUM (DOUBLE SINGLE) Jet 175	47	6 wks
12 Jul 86	LONELY NIGHT Polydor POSP 798	70	2 wks
19 Mar 88	DAYS OF NO TRUST Polydor POSP 910	32	4 wks
7 May 88	START TALKING LOVE Polydor POSP 920	22	4 wks
2 Jul 88	IT MUST HAVE BEEN LOVE Polydor POSP 930	33	4 wks
23 Jun 90	ROCKIN' CHAIR Polydor PO 88	27	4 wks
25 Aug 90	HEARTBROKE AND BUSTED Polydor PO 94	49	2 wks

Tracks on double single: Invasion / Kingdom of Madness / All of My Life / Great Adventure.

Sean MAGUIRE UK, male vocalist 12 wks

20 Aug 94	SOMEONE TO LOVE Parlophone CDRS 6390	14	7 wks
5 Nov 94	TAKE THIS TIME Parlophone CDR 6395	27	4 wks
31 Dec 94	TAKE THIS TIME (re-entry) Parlophone CDR 6395	74†	1 wk

Siobhan MAHER - See OCEANIC

MAHLATHINI and the MAHOTELLA QUEENS - See ART OF NOISE

MAI TAI Holland, female vocal group 30 wks

25 May 85	● HISTORY Virgin VS 773	8	13 wks
3 Aug 85	● BODY AND SOUL Virgin VS 801	9	13 wks
15 Feb 86	FEMALE INTUITION Virgin VS 844	54	4 wks

MAIN INGREDIENT US, male vocal group 7 wks

| 29 Jun 74 | JUST DON'T WANT TO BE LONELY RCA APBO 0205 | 27 | 7 wks |

MAISONETTES UK, male / female vocal group 12 wks

| 11 Dec 82 | ● HEARTACHE AVENUE Ready Steady Go! RSG 1 | 7 | 12 wks |

Raven MAIZE US, male vocalist 1 wk

| 5 Aug 89 | FOREVER TOGETHER Republic LIC 014 | 67 | 1 wk |

It may appear that **MADONNA** is expressing an aversion to the Kid Creole and the Coconuts Present Coati Mundi hit 'Me No Pop I', but she is actually threatening Coati in a still from the film *Who's That Girl*. (Warner Bros Inc)

MANCHESTER UNITED FOOTBALL SQUAD were the first club side to both lead the table and score two top ten goals.

MEAT LOAF won the Best Selling Single award at the February 1994 Brits ceremony. (JM International)

The MANCHESTER UNITED Football Squad

CD SINGLE

COME ON YOU REDS

MAKADOPOULOS and his GREEK SERENADERS
Greece, male vocal / instrumental group **14 wks**

20 Oct 60	**NEVER ON SUNDAY** *Palette PG 9005* **36**	14 wks

Jack E. MAKOSSA
Kenya, male producer **5 wks**

12 Sep 87	**THE OPERA HOUSE** *Champion CHAMP 50* **48**	5 wks

MALA - *See BOWA featuring MALA*

MALAIKA
US, female vocalist **1 wk**

31 Jul 93	**GOTTA KNOW (YOUR NAME)** *A & M 5802732* **68**	1 wk

Carl MALCOLM
Jamaica, male vocalist **8 wks**

13 Sep 75	● **FATTIE BUM BUM** *UK 108*.............**8**	8 wks

Timmy MALLETT - *See BOMBALURINA*

MAMA CASS
US, female vocalist **27 wks**

14 Aug 68	**DREAM A LITTLE DREAM OF ME** *RCA 1726* **11**	12 wks
16 Aug 69	● **IT'S GETTING BETTER** *Stateside SS 8021* **8**	15 wks

See also Mamas and the Papas.

MAMAS and the PAPAS
US, female / male vocal group **64 wks**

28 Apr 66	**CALIFORNIA DREAMIN'** *RCA 1503* **23**	9 wks
12 May 66	● **MONDAY MONDAY** *RCA 1516*.............**3**	13 wks
28 Jul 66	**I SAW HER AGAIN** *RCA 1533* **11**	11 wks
9 Feb 67	**WORDS OF LOVE** *RCA 1564*.............**47**	9 wks
6 Apr 67	● **DEDICATED TO THE ONE I LOVE** *RCA 1576* ...**2**	17 wks
26 Jul 67	● **CREEQUE ALLEY** *RCA 1613* **9**	11 wks

See also Mama Cass.

MAMBAS - *See Marc ALMOND*

A MAN CALLED ADAM
UK, male / female vocal / instrumental group **4 wks**

29 Sep 90	**BAREFOOT IN THE HEAD** *Big Life BLR 28*.............**70**	2 wks
20 Oct 90	**BAREFOOT IN THE HEAD (re-entry)**	
	Big Life BLR 28 ....**60**	2 wks

MAN TO MAN
US, male vocal / instrumental duo **19 wks**

13 Sep 86	**MALE STRIPPER** *Bolts BOLTS 4* [1] **64**	3 wks
3 Jan 87	**MALE STRIPPER (re-entry)** *Bolts BOLTS 4* [1] **63**	1 wk
7 Feb 87	● **MALE STRIPPER (2nd re-entry)** *Bolts BOLTS 4* [1] **4**	12 wks
4 Jul 87	**I NEED A MAN / ENERGY IS EUROBEAT**	
	Bolts BOLTS 5 ....**43**	3 wks

[1] Man 2 Man meet Man Parrish

Melissa MANCHESTER - *See Al JARREAU*

MANCHESTER UNITED FOOTBALL CLUB
UK, male football team vocalists **28 wks**

8 May 76	**MANCHESTER UNITED** *Decca F 13633* **50**	1 wk
21 May 83	**GLORY GLORY MAN. UNITED** *EMI 5390* **13**	5 wks
18 May 85	● **WE ALL FOLLOW MAN. UNITED**	
	Columbia DB 9107 ....**10**	5 wks
19 Jun 93	**UNITED (WE LOVE YOU)**	
	Living Beat LBECD 026 [1] **37**	2 wks
30 Apr 94	★ **COME ON YOU REDS** *PolyGram TV MANU 2* **1**	15 wks

[1] Manchester United and the Champions

Henry MANCINI
US, orchestra / chorus **23 wks**

7 Dec 61	**MOON RIVER** *RCA 1256* **46**	2 wks
28 Dec 61	**MOON RIVER (re-entry)** *RCA 1256* **44**	1 wk
24 Sep 64	**HOW SOON** *RCA 1414* **10**	12 wks
25 Mar 72	**THEME FROM 'CADE'S COUNTY'** *RCA 2182* **42**	1 wk
11 Feb 84	**MAIN THEME FROM 'THE THORNBIRDS'**	
	Warner Bros. 9677 ....**23**	7 wks

Steve MANDELL - *See 'DELIVERANCE' SOUNDTRACK*

MANFRED MANN
South Africa / UK, male vocal / instrumental group **217 wks**

23 Jan 64	● **5-4-3-2-1** *HMV POP 1252* **5**	13 wks
16 Apr 64	**HUBBLE BUBBLE TOIL AND TROUBLE**	
	HMV POP 1282 ....**11**	8 wks
16 Jul 64	★ **DO WAH DIDDY DIDDY** *HMV POP 1320* **1**	14 wks
15 Oct 64	● **SHA LA LA** *HMV POP 1346* **3**	12 wks
14 Jan 65	● **COME TOMORROW** *HMV POP 1381* **4**	9 wks
15 Apr 65	**OH NO NOT MY BABY** *HMV POP 1413* **11**	10 wks
16 Sep 65	● **IF YOU GOTTA GO GO NOW** *HMV POP 1466* **2**	12 wks
21 Apr 66	★ **PRETTY FLAMINGO** *HMV POP 1523* **1**	12 wks
7 Jul 66	**YOU GAVE ME SOMEBODY TO LOVE**	
	HMV POP 1541 ....**36**	4 wks
4 Aug 66	● **JUST LIKE A WOMAN** *Fontana TF 730* **10**	10 wks
27 Oct 66	● **SEMI-DETACHED SUBURBAN MR. JAMES**	
	Fontana TF 757 ....**2**	12 wks
30 Mar 67	● **HA HA SAID THE CLOWN** *Fontana TF 812* **4**	11 wks
25 May 67	**SWEET PEA** *Fontana TF 828* **36**	4 wks
24 Jan 68	★ **MIGHTY QUINN** *Fontana TF 897* **1**	11 wks
12 Jun 68	● **MY NAME IS JACK** *Fontana TF 943* **8**	11 wks
18 Dec 68	● **FOX ON THE RUN** *Fontana TF 985* **5**	12 wks
30 Apr 69	● **RAGAMUFFIN MAN** *Fontana TF 1013* **8**	11 wks
8 Sep 73	● **JOYBRINGER** *Vertigo 6059 083* [1] **9**	10 wks
28 Aug 76	● **BLINDED BY THE LIGHT** *Bronze BRO 29* [1] **6**	10 wks
20 May 78	● **DAVY'S ON THE ROAD AGAIN** *Bronze BRO 52* [1] ...**6**	12 wks
17 Mar 79	**YOU ANGEL YOU** *Bronze BRO 68* [1] **54**	5 wks
7 Jul 79	**DON'T KILL IT CAROL** *Bronze BRO 77* [1] **45**	4 wks

[1] Manfred Mann's Earth Band

MANHATTAN TRANSFER
US, male / female vocal group **72 wks**

7 Feb 76	**TUXEDO JUNCTION** *Atlantic K 10670* **24**	6 wks
5 Feb 77	★ **CHANSON D'AMOUR** *Atlantic K 10886* **1**	13 wks
28 May 77	**DON'T LET GO** *Atlantic K 10930* **32**	6 wks
18 Feb 78	**WALK IN LOVE** *Atlantic K 11075* **48**	1 wk
4 Mar 78	**WALK IN LOVE (re-entry)** *Atlantic K 11075* **12**	11 wks
20 May 78	**ON A LITTLE STREET IN SINGAPORE**	
	Atlantic K 11136...........**20**	9 wks
16 Sep 78	**WHERE DID OUR LOVE GO / JE VOULAIS TE DIRE**	
	(QUE JE T'ATTENDS) *Atlantic K 11182* **40**	4 wks
23 Dec 78	**WHO WHAT WHEN WHERE WHY** *Atlantic K 11233*..**49**	6 wks
17 May 80	**TWILIGHT ZONE - TWILIGHT TONE** (MEDLEY)	
	Atlantic K 11476 ....**25**	8 wks
21 Jan 84	**SPICE OF LIFE** *Atlantic A 9728* **19**	8 wks

MANHATTANS
US, male vocal group **31 wks**

19 Jun 76	● **KISS AND SAY GOODBYE** *CBS 4317* **4**	11 wks
2 Oct 76	● **HURT** *CBS 4562* **4**	11 wks
23 Apr 77	**IT'S YOU** *CBS 5093* **43**	3 wks
26 Jul 80	**SHINING STAR** *CBS 8624*...........**45**	4 wks
6 Aug 83	**CRAZY** *CBS A 3578*...........**63**	2 wks

M.A.N.I.C.
UK, male vocal / production duo **1 wk**

18 Apr 92	**I'M COMIN' HARDCORE** *Union City UCRT 2* **60**	1 wk

MANIC MC's featuring Sara CARLSON
UK, male production duo and female vocalist **5 wks**

12 Aug 89	**MENTAL** *RCA PB 43037* **30**	5 wks

MANIC STREET PREACHERS
UK, male vocal / instrumental group **54 wks**

25 May 91	**YOU LOVE US** *Heavenly HVN 10*	**62**	2 wks
10 Aug 91	**STAY BEAUTIFUL** *Columbia 6573377*	**40**	3 wks
9 Nov 91	**LOVE'S SWEET EXILE / REPEAT** *Columbia 6575827..*	**26**	3 wks
1 Feb 92	**YOU LOVE US (re-issue)** *Columbia 6577247*	**16**	4 wks
28 Mar 92	**SLASH 'N' BURN** *Columbia 6578737*	**20**	4 wks
13 Jun 92	**MOTORCYCLE EMPTINESS** *Columbia 6580837*	**17**	6 wks
19 Sep 92	● **THEME FROM M.A.S.H. (SUICIDE IS PAINLESS)** *Columbia 6583827*	**7**	6 wks
21 Nov 92	**LITTLE BABY NOTHING** *Columbia 6587967*	**29**	3 wks
12 Jun 93	**FROM DESPAIR TO WHERE** *Columbia 6593372*	**25**	4 wks
31 Jul 93	**LA TRISTESSE DURERA (SCREAM TO A SIGH)** *Columbia 6594772*	**22**	5 wks
2 Oct 93	**ROSES IN THE HOSPITAL** *Columbia 6597272*	**15**	3 wks
12 Feb 94	**LIFE BECOMING A LANDSLIDE** *Columbia 6600702..*	**36**	2 wks
11 Jun 94	**FASTER / PCP** *Epic 6604472*	**16**	3 wks
13 Aug 94	**REVOL** *Epic 6606862*	**22**	3 wks
15 Oct 94	**SHE IS SUFFERING** *Epic 6608952*	**25**	3 wks

The listed flipside of Theme From M.A.S.H. (Suicide Is Painless) was with (Everything I Do) I Do It For You by Fatima Mansions.

Barry MANILOW *US, male vocalist* **136 wks**

22 Feb 75	**MANDY** *Arista 1*	**11**	9 wks
6 May 78	**CAN'T SMILE WITHOUT YOU** *Arista 176*	**43**	7 wks
29 Jul 78	**SOMEWHERE IN THE NIGHT / COPACABANA (AT THE COPA)** *Arista 196*	**42**	10 wks
23 Dec 78	**COULD IT BE MAGIC** *Arista ARIST 229*	**25**	10 wks
8 Nov 80	**LONELY TOGETHER** *Arista ARIST 373*	**21**	13 wks
7 Feb 81	**I MADE IT THROUGH THE RAIN** *Arista ARIST 384*	**37**	6 wks
11 Apr 81	**BERMUDA TRIANGLE** *Arista ARIST 406*	**15**	9 wks
26 Sep 81	**LET'S HANG ON** *Arista ARIST 429*	**12**	11 wks
12 Dec 81	**THE OLD SONGS** *Arista ARIST 443*	**48**	8 wks
20 Feb 82	**IF I SHOULD LOVE AGAIN** *Arista ARIST 453*	**66**	2 wks
17 Apr 82	**STAY** *Arista ARIST 464*	**23**	8 wks
16 Oct 82	● **I WANNA DO IT WITH YOU** *Arista ARIST 495*	**8**	8 wks
4 Dec 82	**I'M GONNA SIT RIGHT DOWN AND WRITE MYSELF A LETTER** *Arista ARIST 503*	**36**	7 wks
25 Jun 83	**SOME KIND OF FRIEND** *Arista ARIST 516*	**48**	2 wks
27 Aug 83	**YOU'RE LOOKING HOT TONIGHT** *Arista ARIST 542..*	**47**	6 wks
10 Dec 83	**READ 'EM AND WEEP** *Arista ARIST 551*	**17**	7 wks
8 Apr 89	**PLEASE DON'T BE SCARED** *Arista 112186*	**35**	5 wks
10 Apr 93	**COPACABANA (AT THE COPA) (re-mix)** *Arista 74321136912*	**22**	4 wks
20 Nov 93	**COULD IT BE MAGIC (re-mix)** *Arista 74321174882..*	**36**	3 wks
6 Aug 94	**LET ME BE YOUR WINGS** *EMI CDEM 336* [1]	**73**	1 wk

[1] Barry Manilow and Debra Byrd

ARIST 464 was available as both a live and studio recording. Could It Be Magic in '93 is a re-recording.

MANIX *UK, male / female vocal / instrumental group* **6 wks**

23 Nov 91	**MANIC MINDS** *Reinforced RIVET 1209*	**63**	2 wks
7 Mar 92	**OBLIVION (HEAD IN THE CLOUDS)(EP)** *Reinforced RIVET 1212*	**43**	3 wks
8 Aug 92	**RAINBOW PEOPLE** *Reinforced RIVET 1221*	**57**	1 wk

Tracks on Oblivion (Head In The Clouds) (EP): Oblivion (Head In The Clouds) / Never Been To Belgium (Gotta Rush) / I Can't Stand It / You Held My Hand.

MANKIND *UK, male instrumental group* **12 wks**

25 Nov 78	**DR. WHO** *Pinnacle PIN 71*	**25**	12 wks

Aimee MANN *US, female vocalist* **9 wks**

31 Oct 87	**TIME STAND STILL** *Imago RUSH 13* [1]	**42**	3 wks
28 Aug 93	**I SHOULD'VE KNOWN** *Imago 72787250432*	**55**	2 wks
20 Nov 93	**STUPID THING** *Imago 72787250522*	**47**	2 wks
5 Mar 94	**I SHOULD'VE KNOWN (re-issue)** *Imago 72787250602*	**45**	2 wks

[1] Rush with Aimee Mann

Johnny MANN SINGERS
US, male / female vocal group **13 wks**

12 Jul 67	● **UP, UP AND AWAY** *Liberty LIB 55972*	**6**	13 wks

MANTOVANI *UK, orchestra* **52 wks**

19 Dec 52	● **WHITE CHRISTMAS** *Decca F 10017*	**6**	3 wks
29 May 53	★ **MOULIN ROUGE** *Decca F 10094*	**1**	21 wks
23 Oct 53	● **SWEDISH RHAPSODY** *Decca F 10168*	**2**	17 wks
13 Nov 53	**MOULIN ROUGE (re-entry)** *Decca F 10094*	**10**	1 wk
4 Dec 53	**MOULIN ROUGE (2nd re-entry)** *Decca F 10094*	**12**	1 wk
26 Feb 54	**SWEDISH RHAPSODY (re-entry)** *Decca F 10168*	**12**	1 wk
11 Feb 55	**LONELY BALLERINA** *Decca F 10395*	**16**	3 wks
18 Mar 55	**LONELY BALLERINA (re-entry)** *Decca F 10395*	**18**	1 wk
31 May 57	**AROUND THE WORLD** *Decca F 10888*	**20**	4 wks

See also David Whitfield.

MANTRONIX *US / Jamaica, male vocal / instrumental duo* **48 wks**

22 Feb 86	**LADIES** *10 TEN 116*	**55**	4 wks
17 May 86	**BASSLINE** *10 TEN 118*	**34**	6 wks
7 Feb 87	**WHO IS IT** *10 TEN 137*	**40**	6 wks
4 Jul 87	**SCREAM (PRIMAL SCREAM)** *10 TEN 169*	**46**	4 wks
30 Jan 88	**SING A SONG (BREAK IT DOWN)** *10 TEN 206*	**61**	2 wks
12 Mar 88	**SIMPLE SIMON (YOU GOTTA REGARD)** *10 TEN 217*	**72**	2 wks
6 Jan 90	● **GOT TO HAVE YOUR LOVE** *Capitol CL 559* [1]	**4**	11 wks
12 May 90	● **TAKE YOUR TIME** *Capitol CL 573* [1]	**10**	7 wks
2 Mar 91	**DON'T GO MESSIN' WITH MY HEART** *Capitol CL 608*	**22**	5 wks
22 Jun 91	**STEP TO ME (DO ME)** *Capitol CL 613*	**59**	1 wk

[1] Mantronix featuring Wondress

MANUEL and his MUSIC OF THE MOUNTAINS
UK, orchestra, leader Geoff Love **31 wks**

28 Aug 59	**THEME FROM HONEYMOON** *Columbia DB 4323*	**29**	2 wks
25 Sep 59	**THEME FROM HONEYMOON (re-entry)** *Columbia DB 4323*	**22**	5 wks
6 Nov 59	**THEME FROM HONEYMOON (2nd re-entry)** *Columbia DB 4323*	**27**	2 wks
13 Oct 60	**NEVER ON SUNDAY** *Columbia DB 4515*	**29**	10 wks
13 Oct 66	**SOMEWHERE MY LOVE** *Columbia DB 7969*	**42**	2 wks
31 Jan 76	● **RODRIGO'S GUITAR CONCERTO DE ARANJUEZ (THEME FROM 2ND MOVEMENT)** *EMI 2383*	**3**	10 wks

MARATHON
Germany / UK, male vocal / instrumental group **3 wks**

25 Jan 92	**MOVIN'** *Ten TEN 395*	**36**	3 wks

MARAUDERS *UK, male vocal / instrumental group* **4 wks**

8 Aug 63	**THAT'S WHAT I WANT** *Decca F 11695*	**48**	1 wk
22 Aug 63	**THAT'S WHAT I WANT (re-entry)** *Decca F 11695*	**43**	3 wks

MARBLES *UK, male vocal duo* **18 wks**

25 Sep 68	● **ONLY ONE WOMAN** *Polydor 56 272*	**5**	12 wks
26 Mar 69	**THE WALLS FELL DOWN** *Polydor 56 310*	**28**	6 wks

MARC and the MAMBAS - See Marc ALMOND

MARCELS *US, male vocal group* **17 wks**

13 Apr 61	★ **BLUE MOON** *Pye International 7N 25073*	**1**	13 wks
8 Jun 61	**SUMMERTIME** *Pye International 7N 25083*	**46**	4 wks

Little Peggy MARCH US, female vocalist — **7 wks**

12 Sep 63	HELLO HEARTACHE GOODBYE LOVE RCA 1362	29	7 wks

MARDI GRAS UK, male vocal / instrumental group — **9 wks**

5 Aug 72	TOO BUSY THINKING 'BOUT MY BABY Bell 1226	19	9 wks

Kelly MARIE UK, female vocalist — **36 wks**

2 Aug 80	★ FEELS LIKE I'M IN LOVE Calibre PLUS 1	1	16 wks
18 Oct 80	LOVING JUST FOR FUN Calibre PLUS 4	21	7 wks
7 Feb 81	HOT LOVE Calibre PLUS 5	22	10 wks
30 May 81	LOVE TRIAL Calibre PLUS 7	51	3 wks

Teena MARIE US, female vocalist — **28 wks**

7 Jul 79	I'M A SUCKER FOR YOUR LOVE Motown TMG 1146 [1]	43	8 wks
31 May 80	● BEHIND THE GROOVE Motown TMG 1185	6	10 wks
11 Oct 80	I NEED YOUR LOVIN' Motown TMG 1203	28	6 wks
26 Mar 88	OO LA LA LA Epic 651423 7	74	2 wks
10 Nov 90	SINCE DAY ONE Epic 656429 7	69	2 wks

[1] Teena Marie, co-lead vocals Rick James

MARILLION UK, male vocal / instrumental group — **101 wks**

20 Nov 82	MARKET SQUARE HEROES EMI 5351	60	2 wks
12 Feb 83	HE KNOWS YOU KNOW EMI 5362	35	4 wks
16 Apr 83	MARKET SQUARE HEROES (re-entry) EMI 5351	53	6 wks
18 Jun 83	GARDEN PARTY EMI 5393	16	5 wks
11 Feb 84	PUNCH AND JUDY EMI MARIL 1	29	4 wks
12 May 84	ASSASSING EMI MARIL 2	22	5 wks
18 May 85	● KAYLEIGH EMI MARIL 3	2	14 wks
7 Sep 85	● LAVENDER EMI MARIL 4	5	9 wks
30 Nov 85	HEART OF LOTHIAN EMI MARIL 5	29	6 wks
23 May 87	● INCOMMUNICADO EMI MARIL 6	6	5 wks
25 Jul 87	SUGAR MICE EMI MARIL 7	22	5 wks
7 Nov 87	WARM WET CIRCLES EMI MARIL 8	22	4 wks
26 Nov 88	FREAKS (LIVE) EMI MARIL 9	24	3 wks
9 Sep 89	HOOKS IN YOU Capitol MARIL 10	30	3 wks
9 Dec 89	UNINVITED GUEST EMI MARIL 11	53	2 wks
14 Apr 90	EASTER EMI MARIL 12	34	2 wks
8 Jun 91	COVER MY EYES (PAIN AND HEAVEN) EMI MARIL 13	34	4 wks
3 Aug 91	NO ONE CAN EMI MARIL 14	33	4 wks
5 Oct 91	DRY LAND EMI MARIL 15	34	2 wks
23 May 92	SYMPATHY EMI MARIL 16	17	3 wks
1 Aug 92	NO ONE CAN (re-issue) EMI MARIL 17	26	4 wks
26 Mar 94	THE HOLLOW MAN EMI CDEMS 307	30	2 wks
7 May 94	ALONE AGAIN IN THE LAP OF LUXURY EMI CDEMS 318	53	3 wks

MARILYN UK, male vocalist — **26 wks**

5 Nov 83	● CALLING YOUR NAME Mercury MAZ 1	4	12 wks
11 Feb 84	CRY AND BE FREE Mercury MAZ 2	31	6 wks
21 Apr 84	YOU DON'T LOVE ME Mercury MAZ 3	40	7 wks
13 Apr 85	BABY U LEFT ME (IN THE COLD) Mercury MAZ 4	70	1 wk

Marino MARINI and his QUARTET
Italy, male vocalist and instrumental group — **17 wks**

3 Oct 58	VOLARE Durium DC 16632	13	7 wks
10 Oct 58	● COME PRIMA Durium DC 16632	2	14 wks
20 Mar 59	CIAO CIAO BAMBINA Durium DC 16636	25	1 wk
3 Apr 59	CIAO CIAO BAMBINA (re-entry) Durium DC 16636	24	1 wk

Pigmeat MARKHAM US, male vocalist — **8 wks**

17 Jul 68	HERE COMES THE JUDGE Chess CRS 8077	19	8 wks

Biz MARKIE US, male rapper — **2 wks**

26 May 90	JUST A FRIEND Cold Chillin' W 9823	55	2 wks

Yannis MARKOPOULOS Greece, orchestra — **8 wks**

17 Dec 77	WHO PAYS THE FERRYMAN BBC RESL 51	11	8 wks

Guy MARKS Australia, male vocalist — **8 wks**

13 May 78	LOVING YOU HAS MADE ME BANANAS ABC 4211	25	8 wks

MARKY MARK and the FUNKY BUNCH
US, male / female vocal / instrumental group — **14 wks**

31 Aug 91	GOOD VIBRATIONS Interscope A 8764 [1]	14	7 wks
2 Nov 91	WILDSIDE Interscope A 8674	42	3 wks
12 Dec 92	YOU GOTTA BELIEVE Interscope A 8480	54	4 wks

[1] Marky Mark and the Funky Bunch featuring Loleatta Holloway

Bob MARLEY and the WAILERS
Jamaica, male vocal / instrumental group — **137 wks**

27 Sep 75	NO WOMAN NO CRY Island WIP 6244	22	7 wks
25 Jun 77	EXODUS Island WIP 6390	14	9 wks
10 Sep 77	WAITING IN VAIN Island WIP 6402	27	6 wks
10 Dec 77	● JAMMING / PUNKY REGGAE PARTY Island WIP 6410	9	12 wks
25 Feb 78	● IS THIS LOVE Island WIP 6420	9	9 wks
10 Jun 78	SATISFY MY SOUL Island WIP 6440	21	10 wks
20 Oct 79	SO MUCH TROUBLE IN THE WORLD Island WIP 6510	56	4 wks
21 Jun 80	● COULD YOU BE LOVED Island WIP 6610	5	12 wks
13 Sep 80	THREE LITTLE BIRDS Island WIP 6641	17	9 wks
13 Jun 81	● NO WOMAN NO CRY (re-entry) Island WIP 6244	8	11 wks
7 May 83	● BUFFALO SOLDIER Island/Tuff Gong IS 108	4	12 wks
21 Apr 84	● ONE LOVE - PEOPLE GET READY Island IS 169	5	11 wks
23 Jun 84	WAITING IN VAIN (re-issue) Island IS 180	31	7 wks
8 Dec 84	COULD YOU BE LOVED (re-issue) Island IS 210	71	2 wks
18 May 91	ONE LOVE - PEOPLE GET READY (re-issue) Tuff Gong TGX 1	42	3 wks
19 Sep 92	● IRON LION ZION Tuff Gong TGX 2	5	9 wks
28 Nov 92	WHY SHOULD I / EXODUS Tuff Gong TGX 3	42	3 wks
2 Jan 93	WHY SHOULD I / EXODUS (re-entry) Tuff Gong TGX 3	75	1 wk

Exodus on Tuff Gong TGX 3 only listed with Why Should I from 5 Dec 92 and is a different version from the Island hit. It peaked at position 53.

Ziggy MARLEY and the MELODY MAKERS
Jamaica, male / female vocal / instrumental group — **11 wks**

11 Jun 88	TOMORROW PEOPLE Virgin VS 1049	22	10 wks
23 Sep 89	LOOK WHO'S DANCING Virgin America VUS 5	65	1 wk

MARMALADE UK, male vocal / instrumental group — **130 wks**

22 May 68	● LOVIN' THINGS CBS 3412	6	13 wks
23 Oct 68	WAIT FOR ME MARIANNE CBS 3708	30	5 wks
4 Dec 68	★ OB-LA-DI OB-LA-DA CBS 3892	1	20 wks
11 Jun 69	● BABY MAKE IT SOON CBS 4287	9	13 wks
20 Dec 69	● REFLECTIONS OF MY LIFE Decca F 12982	3	12 wks
18 Jul 70	● RAINBOW Decca F 13035	3	14 wks
27 Mar 71	MY LITTLE ONE Decca F 13135	15	11 wks
4 Sep 71	● COUSIN NORMAN Decca F 13214	6	11 wks
27 Nov 71	BACK ON THE ROAD Decca F 13251	35	7 wks
22 Jan 72	BACK ON THE ROAD (re-entry) Decca F 13251	50	1 wk
1 Apr 72	● RADANCER Decca F 13297	6	12 wks
21 Feb 76	● FALLING APART AT THE SEAMS Target TGT 105	9	11 wks

MARRADONA
UK, male / female vocal / instrumental group   **3 wks**

| 26 Feb 94 | OUT OF MY HEAD Peach PWCD 282 | 38 | 3 wks |

M/A/R/R/S UK, male instrumental / scratch group   **14 wks**

| 5 Sep 87 ★ | PUMP UP THE VOLUME / ANITINA (THE FIRST TIME I SEE SHE DANCE) 4AD AD 70 | 1 | 14 wks |

The b-side of this record was listed on the chart at the record company's request without evidence of consumer interest.

Gerry MARSDEN - See CHRISTIANS; Holly JOHNSON; Paul McCARTNEY; STOCK AITKEN WATERMAN; GERRY and the PACEMAKERS

Stevie MARSH UK, female vocalist   **4 wks**

| 4 Dec 59 | THE ONLY BOY IN THE WORLD Decca F 11181 | 29 | 2 wks |
| 25 Dec 59 | THE ONLY BOY IN THE WORLD (re-entry) Decca F 11181 | 24 | 2 wks |

Joy MARSHALL UK, female vocalist   **2 wks**

| 23 Jun 66 | THE MORE I SEE YOU Decca F 12422 | 34 | 2 wks |

Keith MARSHALL UK, male vocalist   **10 wks**

| 4 Apr 81 | ONLY CRYING Arrival PIK 2 | 12 | 10 wks |

Wayne MARSHALL UK, male vocalist   **3 wks**

| 1 Oct 94 | OOH AAH (G-SPOT) Soultown SOULCDS 322 | 29 | 3 wks |

MARSHALL HAIN
UK, male / female vocal / instrumental duo   **19 wks**

| 3 Jun 78 ● | DANCING IN THE CITY Harvest HAR 5157 | 3 | 15 wks |
| 14 Oct 78 | COMING HOME Harvest HAR 5168 | 39 | 4 wks |

Lena MARTELL UK, female vocalist   **18 wks**

| 29 Sep 79 ★ | ONE DAY AT A TIME Pye 7N 46021 | 1 | 18 wks |

MARTHA and the MUFFINS
Canada, female / male vocal / instrumental group   **10 wks**

| 1 Mar 80 ● | ECHO BEACH Dindisc DIN 9 | 10 | 10 wks |

See also M + M, who are Martha and a Muffin.

MARTHA and the VANDELLAS - See Martha REEVES and the VANDELLAS

MARTIKA US, female vocalist   **57 wks**

29 Jul 89 ●	TOY SOLDIERS CBS 655049 7	5	11 wks
14 Oct 89 ●	I FEEL THE EARTH MOVE CBS 655294 7	7	14 wks
13 Jan 90	MORE THAN YOU KNOW CBS 655526 7	15	7 wks
17 Mar 90	WATER CBS 655731 7	59	3 wks
17 Aug 91 ●	LOVE...THY WILL BE DONE Columbia 6573137	9	9 wks
30 Nov 91	MARTIKA'S KITCHEN Columbia 6575687	17	10 wks
22 Feb 92	COLOURED KISSES Columbia 6577097	41	3 wks

Billie Ray MARTIN Germany, female vocalist   **3 wks**

| 19 Nov 94 | YOUR LOVING ARMS Magnet MAG 1028CD | 38 | 3 wks |

Dean MARTIN US, male vocalist   **154 wks**

18 Sep 53 ●	KISS Capitol CL 13893	9	1 wk
2 Oct 53 ●	KISS (re-entry) Capitol CL 13893	5	7 wks
22 Jan 54 ●	THAT'S AMORE Capitol CL 14008	2	11 wks
1 Oct 54 ●	SWAY Capitol CL 14138	6	7 wks
22 Oct 54	HOW DO YOU SPEAK TO AN ANGEL Capitol CL 14150	15	2 wks
19 Nov 54	HOW DO YOU SPEAK TO AN ANGEL (re-entry) Capitol CL 14150	17	4 wks
28 Jan 55 ●	NAUGHTY LADY OF SHADY LANE Capitol CL 14226	5	10 wks
4 Feb 55	MAMBO ITALIANO Capitol CL 14227	14	2 wks
25 Feb 55 ●	LET ME GO LOVER Capitol CL 14226	3	9 wks
1 Apr 55 ●	UNDER THE BRIDGES OF PARIS Capitol CL 14255	6	8 wks
10 Feb 56 ★	MEMORIES ARE MADE OF THIS Capitol CL 14523	1	16 wks
2 Mar 56	YOUNG AND FOOLISH Capitol CL 14519	20	1 wk
27 Apr 56	INNAMORATA Capitol CL 14507	21	3 wks
22 Mar 57	THE MAN WHO PLAYS THE MANDOLINO Capitol CL 14690	21	2 wks
13 Jun 58 ●	RETURN TO ME Capitol CL 14844	2	22 wks
29 Aug 58 ●	VOLARE Capitol CL 14910	2	14 wks
27 Aug 64	EVERYBODY LOVES SOMEBODY Reprise R 20281	11	13 wks
12 Nov 64	THE DOOR IS STILL OPEN TO MY HEART Reprise R 20307	42	4 wks
5 Feb 69 ●	GENTLE ON MY MIND Reprise RS 23343	2	23 wks
30 Aug 69	GENTLE ON MY MIND (re-entry) Reprise RS 23343	49	1 wk

Juan MARTIN Spain, male instrumentalist - guitar   **7 wks**

| 28 Jan 84 ● | LOVE THEME FROM 'THE THORN BIRDS' WEA X 9518 | 10 | 7 wks |

Linda MARTIN Ireland, female vocalist   **2 wks**

| 30 May 92 | WHY ME Columbia 6581317 | 59 | 2 wks |

Marilyn MARTIN - See Phil COLLINS

Ray MARTIN UK, orchestra   **11 wks**

14 Nov 52 ●	BLUE TANGO Columbia DB 3051	8	1 wk
28 Nov 52 ●	BLUE TANGO (re-entry) Columbia DB 3051	10	3 wks
4 Dec 53 ●	SWEDISH RHAPSODY Columbia DB 3346	10	1 wk
18 Dec 53 ●	SWEDISH RHAPSODY (re-entry) Columbia DB 3346	4	3 wks
15 Jun 56	CAROUSEL WALTZ Columbia DB 3771	28	1 wk
3 Aug 56	CAROUSEL WALTZ (re-entry) Columbia DB 3771	24	2 wks

Tony MARTIN US, male vocalist   **28 wks**

| 22 Apr 55 ● | STRANGER IN PARADISE HMV B 10849 | 6 | 13 wks |
| 13 Jul 56 ● | WALK HAND IN HAND HMV POP 222 | 2 | 15 wks |

Vince MARTIN - See TARRIERS

Wink MARTINDALE US, male vocalist   **41 wks**

4 Dec 59	DECK OF CARDS London HLD 8962	18	5 wks
15 Jan 60	DECK OF CARDS (re-entry) London HLD 8962	28	2 wks
31 Mar 60	DECK OF CARDS (2nd re-entry) London HLD 8962	45	1 wk
18 Apr 63 ●	DECK OF CARDS (3rd re-entry) London HLD 8962	5	21 wks
20 Oct 73	DECK OF CARDS (re-issue) Dot DOT 109	22	12 wks

Al MARTINO US, male vocalist   **87 wks**

14 Nov 52 ★	HERE IN MY HEART Capitol CL 13779	1	18 wks
21 Nov 52 ●	TAKE MY HEART Capitol CL 13769	9	1 wk
30 Jan 53 ●	NOW Capitol CL 13835	3	12 wks
10 Jul 53 ●	RACHEL Capitol CL 13879	10	4 wks
11 Sep 53	RACHEL (re-entry) Capitol CL 13879	12	1 wk
4 Jun 54	WANTED Capitol CL 14128	12	1 wk
18 Jun 54 ●	WANTED (re-entry) Capitol CL 14128	4	14 wks
1 Oct 54 ●	THE STORY OF TINA Capitol CL 14163	10	8 wks
1 Oct 54	WANTED (2nd re-entry) Capitol CL 14128	17	1 wk
23 Sep 55	THE MAN FROM LARAMIE Capitol CL 14343	19	2 wks

28 Oct 55	THE MAN FROM LARAMIE (re-entry)		
	Capitol CL 14343	**20**	1 wk
31 Mar 60	SUMMERTIME *Top Rank JAR 312*	**49**	1 wk
29 Aug 63	I LOVE YOU BECAUSE *Capitol CL 15300*	**48**	1 wk
22 Aug 70	SPANISH EYES *Capitol CL 15430*	**49**	1 wk
14 Jul 73 ●	SPANISH EYES (re-entry) *Capitol CL 15430*	**5**	21 wks

MARVELETTES *US, female vocal group*   **10 wks**

15 Jun 67	WHEN YOU'RE YOUNG AND IN LOVE		
	Tamla Motown TMG 609	**13**	10 wks

Hank MARVIN
UK, male vocalist/instrumentalist - guitar   **36 wks**

13 Sep 69 ●	THROW DOWN A LINE *Columbia DB 8615* [1]	**7**	9 wks
21 Feb 70	JOY OF LIVING *Columbia DB 8657* [1]	**25**	8 wks
6 Mar 82	DON'T TALK *Polydor POSP 420*	**49**	4 wks
22 Mar 86 ★	LIVING DOLL *WEA YZ 65* [2]	**1**	11 wks
7 Jan 89	LONDON KID *Polydor PO 32* [3]	**52**	3 wks
17 Oct 92	WE ARE THE CHAMPIONS		
	PolyGram TV TV PO 229 [4]	**66**	1 wk

[1] Cliff and Hank [2] Cliff Richard and the Young Ones featuring Hank B. Marvin [3] Jean-Michel Jarre featuring Hank Marvin [4] Hank Marvin featuring Brian May

Lee MARVIN *US, male vocalist*   **23 wks**

7 Feb 70 ★	WAND'RIN' STAR *Paramount PARA 3004*	**1**	18 wks
20 Jun 70	WAND'RIN' STAR (re-entry)		
	Paramount PARA 3004	**42**	3 wks
15 Aug 70	WAND'RIN' STAR (2nd re-entry)		
	Paramount PARA 3004	**47**	2 wks

I Talk To The Trees *by Clint Eastwood, the flip side of* Wand'rin' Star *was listed with* Wand'rin' Star *for 7 Feb 70 and 14 Feb 70 only.*

MARVIN THE PARANOID ANDROID *UK, robot* **4 wks**

16 May 81	MARVIN *Polydor POSP 261*	**53**	4 wks

Richard MARX *US, male vocalist*   **75 wks**

27 Feb 88	SHOULD'VE KNOWN BETTER *Manhattan MT 32*	**50**	5 wks
14 May 88	ENDLESS SUMMER NIGHTS *Manhattan MT 39*	**50**	3 wks
17 Jun 89	SATISFIED *EMI-USA MT 64*	**52**	4 wks
2 Sep 89 ●	RIGHT HERE WAITING *EMI-USA MT 72*	**2**	10 wks
11 Nov 89	ANGELIA *EMI-USA MT 74*	**45**	4 wks
24 Mar 90	TOO LATE TO SAY GOODBYE *EMI-USA MT 80*	**38**	3 wks
7 Jul 90	CHILDREN OF THE NIGHT *EMI-USA MT 84*	**54**	2 wks
1 Sep 90	ENDLESS SUMMER NIGHTS (re-issue)		
	EMI-USA MT 89	**60**	2 wks
19 Oct 91	KEEP COMING BACK *Capitol CL 634*	**55**	2 wks
9 May 92 ●	HAZARD *Capitol CL 654*	**3**	15 wks
29 Aug 92	TAKE THIS HEART *Capitol CL 667*	**13**	6 wks
28 Nov 92	CHAINS AROUND MY HEART *Capitol CL 676*	**29**	6 wks
29 Jan 94	NOW AND FOREVER *Capitol CDCLS 703*	**13**	6 wks
30 Apr 94	SILENT SCREAM *Capitol CDCLS 714*	**32**	4 wks
13 Aug 94	THE WAY SHE LOVES ME *Capitol CDCL 721*	**38**	3 wks

MARXMAN *UK/Ireland, rap/instrumental group*   **5 wks**

6 Mar 93	ALL ABOUT EVE *Talkin Loud TLKCD 35*	**28**	4 wks
1 May 93	SHIP AHOY *Talkin Loud TLKCD 39*	**64**	1 wk

Sinead O'Connor provides uncredited vocals on Ship Ahoy.

MARY JANE GIRLS *US, female vocal group*   **14 wks**

21 May 83	CANDY MAN *Motown TMG 1301*	**60**	4 wks
25 Jun 83	ALL NIGHT LONG *Gordy TMG 1309*	**13**	9 wks
8 Oct 83	BOYS *Gordy TMG 1315*	**74**	1 wk

Carolyne MAS *US, female vocalist*   **2 wks**

2 Feb 80	QUOTE GOODBYE QUOTE *Mercury 6167 873*	**71**	2 wks

MASH *US, male vocal/instrumental group*   **12 wks**

10 May 80 ★	THEME FROM M*A*S*H* (SUICIDE IS PAINLESS) *CBS 8536*	**1**	12 wks

MASH! *UK/US, male/female vocal group*   **2 wks**

21 May 94	U DON'T HAVE TO SAY U LOVE ME		
	React CDREACT 37	**37**	2 wks

Barbara MASON *US, female vocalist*   **5 wks**

21 Jan 84	ANOTHER MAN *Streetwave KHAN 3*	**45**	5 wks

Glen MASON *UK, male vocalist*   **7 wks**

28 Sep 56	GLENDORA *Parlophone R 4203*	**28**	2 wks
16 Nov 56	GREEN DOOR *Parlophone R 4244*	**24**	5 wks

Mary MASON *UK, female vocalist*   **6 wks**

8 Oct 77	ANGEL OF THE MORNING - ANY WAY THAT YOU WANT ME (MEDLEY) *Epic EPC 5552*	**27**	6 wks

MASQUERADE *UK, male/female vocal group*   **10 wks**

11 Jan 86	ONE NATION *Streetwave KHAN 59*	**54**	6 wks
5 Jul 86	(SOLUTION TO) THE PROBLEM		
	Streetwave KHAN 67	**65**	2 wks
26 Jul 86	(SOLUTION TO) THE PROBLEM (re-entry)		
	Streetwave KHAN 67	**64**	2 wks

MASS ORDER *US, male vocal/instrumental duo*   **5 wks**

14 Mar 92	LIFT EVERY VOICE (TAKE ME AWAY)		
	Columbia 6577487	**35**	3 wks
23 May 92	LET'S GET HAPPY *Columbia 6580737*	**45**	2 wks

MASS PRODUCTION
US, male vocal/instrumental group   **7 wks**

12 Mar 77	WELCOME TO OUR WORLD (OF MERRY MUSIC)		
	Atlantic K 10898	**44**	3 wks
17 May 80	SHANTE *Atlantic K 11475*	**59**	4 wks

Zeitia MASSIAH *UK, female vocalist*   **2 wks**

12 Mar 94	I SPECIALIZE IN LOVE *Union City UCRCD 27* [1]	**74**	1 wk
24 Sep 94	THIS IS THE PLACE *Virgin VSCDT 1511*	**62**	1 wk

[1] Arizona featuring Zeitia

MASSIEL *Spain, female vocalist*   **4 wks**

24 Apr 68	LA LA LA *Philips BF 1667*	**35**	4 wks

MASSIVE ATTACK
UK, male/female vocal/instrumental group   **23 wks**

23 Feb 91	UNFINISHED SYMPATHY *Wild Bunch WBRS 2* [1]	**13**	9 wks
8 Jun 91	SAFE FROM HARM *Wild Bunch WBRS 3*	**25**	6 wks
22 Feb 92	MASSIVE ATTACK EP *Wild Bunch WBRS 4*	**27**	4 wks
29 Oct 94	SLY *Wild Bunch WBRDX 5*	**24**	4 wks

[1] Massive

Tracks on Massive Attack EP: *Hymn Of The Big Wheel / Home Of The Whale / Be Thankful / Any Love.*

MASSIVO featuring TRACY
UK, male / female vocal / instrumental group **11 wks**

26 May 90	LOVING YOU *Debut DEBT 3097* **25**	11 wks

MASTER SINGERS *UK, male vocal group* **7 wks**

| 14 Apr 66 | HIGHWAY CODE *Parlophone R 5428* ....**25** | 6 wks |
| 17 Nov 66 | WEATHER FORECAST *Parlophone R 5523* ....**50** | 1 wk |

MASTERMIXERS - See JIVE BUNNY and the MASTERMIXERS

Sammy MASTERS *US, male vocalist* **5 wks**

| 9 Jun 60 | ROCKIN' RED WING *Warner Bros. WB 10* ....**36** | 5 wks |

MATCH *UK, male vocal / instrumental group* **3 wks**

| 16 Jun 79 | BOOGIE MAN *Flamingo FM 2* ....**48** | 3 wks |

MATCHBOX *UK, male vocal / instrumental group* **66 wks**

3 Nov 79	ROCKABILLY REBEL *Magnet MAG 155* **18**	12 wks
19 Jan 80	BUZZ BUZZ A DIDDLE IT *Magnet MAG 157* **22**	8 wks
10 May 80	MIDNITE DYNAMOS *Magnet MAG 169* **14**	12 wks
27 Sep 80	● WHEN YOU ASK ABOUT LOVE *Magnet MAG 191* **4**	12 wks
29 Nov 80	OVER THE RAINBOW - YOU BELONG TO ME (MEDLEY) *Magnet MAG 192* **15**	11 wks
4 Apr 81	BABES IN THE WOOD *Magnet MAG 193* **46**	6 wks
1 Aug 81	LOVE'S MADE A FOOL OF YOU *Magnet MAG 194*..**63**	3 wks
29 May 82	ONE MORE SATURDAY NIGHT *Magnet MAG 223*....**63**	2 wks

MATCHROOM MOB - See CHAS and DAVE

Mireille MATHIEU *France, female vocalist* **7 wks**

| 13 Dec 67 | LA DERNIERE VALSE *Columbia DB 8323* ....**26** | 7 wks |

Johnny MATHIS *US, male vocalist* **137 wks**

23 May 58	TEACHER TEACHER *Fontana H 130* **27**	5 wks
26 Sep 58	● A CERTAIN SMILE *Fontana H 142* **4**	16 wks
19 Dec 58	WINTER WONDERLAND *Fontana H 165* **17**	3 wks
7 Aug 59	● SOMEONE *Fontana H 199* **6**	15 wks
27 Nov 59	THE BEST OF EVERYTHING *Fontana H 218* **30**	1 wk
29 Jan 60	MISTY *Fontana H 219* **12**	9 wks
24 Mar 60	YOU ARE BEAUTIFUL *Fontana H 234* **38**	8 wks
14 Apr 60	MISTY (re-entry) *Fontana H 219* **46**	2 wks
26 May 60	YOU ARE BEAUTIFUL (re-entry) *Fontana H 234*..**46**	1 wk
28 Jul 60	STARBRIGHT *Fontana H 254* **47**	2 wks
6 Oct 60	● MY LOVE FOR YOU *Fontana H 267* **9**	18 wks
4 Apr 63	WHAT WILL MARY SAY *CBS AAG 135* **49**	1 wk
25 Jan 75	● I'M STONE IN LOVE WITH YOU *CBS 2653* **10**	12 wks
13 Nov 76	★ WHEN A CHILD IS BORN (SOLEADO) *CBS 4599* **1**	12 wks
25 Mar 78	● TOO MUCH TOO LITTLE TOO LATE *CBS 6164* [1] **3**	14 wks
29 Jul 78	YOU'RE ALL I NEED TO GET BY *CBS 6483* [1] **45**	6 wks
11 Aug 79	GONE GONE GONE *CBS 7730* **15**	10 wks
26 Dec 81	WHEN A CHILD IS BORN *CBS S 1758* [2] **74**	2 wks

[1] Johnny Mathis and Deniece Williams [2] Johnny Mathis and Gladys Knight

MATT BIANCO
UK / Poland male / female vocal / instrumental group **65 wks**

11 Feb 84	GET OUT OF YOUR LAZY BED *WEA BIANCO 1* **15**	8 wks
14 Apr 84	SNEAKING OUT THE BACK DOOR / MATT'S MOOD *WEA YZ 3* **44**	7 wks
10 Nov 84	HALF A MINUTE *WEA YZ 26* **23**	10 wks
2 Mar 85	MORE THAN I CAN BEAR *WEA YZ 34* **50**	7 wks
5 Oct 85	YEH YEH *WEA YZ 46* **13**	10 wks
1 Mar 86	JUST CAN'T STAND IT *WEA YZ 62* **66**	2 wks
14 Jun 86	DANCING IN THE STREET *WEA YZ 72* **64**	3 wks

4 Jun 88	DON'T BLAME IT ON THAT GIRL / WAP-BAM-BOOGIE *WEA YZ 188*..................**11**	13 wks
27 Aug 88	GOOD TIMES *WEA YZ 302* **55**	3 wks
4 Feb 89	NERVOUS / WAP BAM BOOGIE (re-mix) *WEA YZ 328* **59**	2 wks

Matt's Mood only credited from 5 May 84. Act was just UK, male vocalist after the first five hits.

Al MATTHEWS *US, male vocalist* **8 wks**

| 23 Aug 75 | FOOL *CBS 3429* ....**16** | 8 wks |

John MATTHEWS - See UNDERCOVER

MATTHEWS' SOUTHERN COMFORT
UK, male vocal / instrumental group **18 wks**

| 26 Sep 70 | ★ WOODSTOCK *Uni UNS 526* ....**1** | 18 wks |

MATUMBI *UK, male vocal / instrumental group* **7 wks**

| 29 Sep 79 | POINT OF VIEW *Matumbi RIC 101* ....**35** | 7 wks |

Susan MAUGHAN *UK, female vocalist* **25 wks**

11 Oct 62	● BOBBY'S GIRL *Philips 326544 BF* **3**	19 wks
14 Feb 63	HAND A HANDKERCHIEF TO HELEN *Philips 326562 BF* **41**	3 wks
9 May 63	SHE'S NEW TO YOU *Philips 326586 BF* **45**	3 wks

MAUREEN *UK, female vocalist* **22 wks**

26 Nov 88	● SAY A LITTLE PRAYER *Rhythm King DOOD 3* [1] **10**	10 wks
16 Jun 90	THINKING OF YOU *Urban URB 55* **11**	9 wks
12 Jan 91	WHERE HAS ALL THE LOVE GONE *Urban URB 65* ..**51**	3 wks

[1] Bomb The Bass featuring Maureen

Some copies of Thinking Of You are credited to the fuller name of Maureen Walsh.

Paul MAURIAT *France, orchestra* **14 wks**

| 21 Feb 68 | LOVE IS BLUE (L'AMOUR EST BLEU) *Philips BF 1637* ....**12** | 14 wks |

MAX Q *Australia, male vocal / instrumental duo* **3 wks**

| 17 Feb 90 | SOMETIMES *Mercury MXQ 2* ....**53** | 3 wks |

MAX WEBSTER *Canada, male vocal / instrumental group* **3 wks**

| 19 May 79 | PARADISE SKIES *Capitol CL 16079* ....**43** | 3 wks |

MAXIMA featuring LILY
UK / Spain, male / female vocal / instrumental duo **2 wks**

| 14 Aug 93 | IBIZA *Yo! Yo! CDLILY 1* ....**55** | 2 wks |

MAXX *UK / Sweden / Germany, male / female vocal / instrumental group* **23 wks**

21 May 94	● GET-A-WAY *Pulse 8 CDLOSE 59*..................**4**	12 wks
6 Aug 94	● NO MORE (I CAN'T STAND IT) *Pulse 8 CDLOSE 66* **8**	8 wks
29 Oct 94	YOU CAN GET IT *Pulse 8 CDLOSE 75* **21**	3 wks

Billy MAY *US, orchestra* **10 wks**

| 27 Apr 56 | ● MAIN TITLE THEME FROM 'MAN WITH THE GOLDEN ARM' *Capitol CL 14551* ....**9** | 10 wks |

Brian MAY UK, male vocalist/instrumentalist - guitar — 31 wks

5 Nov 83	**STAR FLEET** EMI 5436 [1]	.........**65**	3 wks
7 Dec 91	● **DRIVEN BY YOU** Parlophone R 6304	.........**6**	9 wks
5 Sep 92	● **TOO MUCH LOVE WILL KILL YOU** Parlophone R 6320	.........**5**	9 wks
17 Oct 92	**WE ARE THE CHAMPIONS** PolyGram TV TV PO 229 [2]	.........**66**	1 wk
21 Nov 92	**BACK TO THE LIGHT** Parlophone R 6329	.........**19**	4 wks
19 Jun 93	**RESURRECTION** Parlophone CDRS 6351 [3]	.........**23**	3 wks
18 Dec 93	**LAST HORIZON** Parlophone CDR 6371	.........**51**	2 wks

[1] Brian May and Friends [2] Hank Marvin featuring Brian May [3] Brian May with Cozy Powell

Mary MAY UK, female vocalist — 1 wk

27 Feb 64	**ANYONE WHO HAD A HEART** Fontana TF 440	.......**49**	1 wk

Simon MAY UK, male vocalist — 21 wks

9 Oct 76	● **SUMMER OF MY LIFE** Pye 7N 45627	.........**7**	8 wks
21 May 77	**WE'LL GATHER LILACS - ALL MY LOVING (MEDLEY)** Pye 7N 45688	.........**49**	1 wk
4 Jun 77	**WE'LL GATHER LILACS - ALL MY LOVING (MEDLEY) (re-entry)** Pye 7N 45688	.........**50**	1 wk
26 Oct 85	**HOWARD'S WAY** BBC RESL 174 [1]	.........**21**	11 wks

[1] Simon May Orchestra

See also Anita Dobson; Marti Webb.

Curtis MAYFIELD US, male vocalist — 18 wks

31 Jul 71	**MOVE ON UP** Buddah 2011 080	.........**12**	10 wks
2 Dec 78	**NO GOODBYES** Atlantic LV 1	.........**65**	3 wks
30 May 87	**(CELEBRATE) THE DAY AFTER YOU** RCA MONK 6 [1]	.........**52**	2 wks
29 Sep 90	**SUPERFLY 1990** Capitol CL 586 [2]	.........**48**	3 wks

[1] Blow Monkeys with Curtis Mayfield [2] Curtis Mayfield and Ice-T

MAYTALS Jamaica, male vocal/instrumental group — 4 wks

25 Apr 70	**MONKEY MAN** Trojan TR 7711	.........**50**	1 wk
9 May 70	**MONKEY MAN (re-entry)** Trojan TR 7711	.........**47**	3 wks

MAZE featuring Frankie BEVERLY
US, male vocal/instrumental group — 14 wks

20 Jul 85	**TOO MANY GAMES** Capitol CL 363	.........**36**	7 wks
23 Aug 86	**I WANNA BE WITH YOU** Capitol CL 421	.........**55**	3 wks
27 May 89	**JOY AND PAIN** Capitol CL 531 [1]	.........**57**	4 wks

[1] Maze

Kym MAZELLE US, female vocalist — 57 wks

12 Nov 88	**USELESS (I DON'T NEED YOU NOW)** Syncopate SY 18	.........**53**	3 wks
14 Jan 89	● **WAIT** RCA PB 42595 [1]	.........**7**	10 wks
25 Mar 89	**GOT TO GET YOU BACK** Syncopate SY 25	.........**29**	4 wks
7 Oct 89	**LOVE STRAIN** Syncopate SY 30	.........**52**	3 wks
20 Jan 90	**WAS THAT ALL IT WAS** Syncopate SY 32	.........**33**	6 wks
26 May 90	**USELESS (I DON'T NEED YOU NOW) (re-mix)** Syncopate SY 36	.........**48**	2 wks
24 Nov 90	**MISSING YOU** Ten TEN 345 [2]	.........**22**	7 wks
25 May 91	**NO ONE CAN LOVE YOU MORE THAN ME** Parlophone R 6287	.........**62**	2 wks
26 Dec 92	**LOVE ME THE RIGHT WAY** Logic 74321128097 [3]	.........**22**	10 wks
11 Jun 94	**NO MORE TEARS (ENOUGH IS ENOUGH)** Ding Dong 74321209032 [4]	.........**13**	7 wks
8 Oct 94	**GIMME ALL YOUR LOVIN'** Ding Dong 74321231322 [4]	.........**22**	3 wks

[1] Robert Howard and Kym Mazelle [2] Soul II Soul featuring Kym Mazelle [3] Rapination and Kym Mazelle [4] Kym Mazelle and Jocelyn Brown

MAZZY STAR US, male/female vocal/instrumental duo — 1 wk

27 Aug 94	**FADE INTO YOU** Capitol CDCL 720	.........**48**	1 wk

MC DUKE UK, male rapper — 1 wk

11 Mar 89	**I'M RIFFIN (ENGLISH RASTA)** Music Of Life 7NOTE 25	.........**75**	1 wk

MC ERIC - See TECHNOTRONIC

MC FIX IT - See ANTICAPPELLA

MC Mikee FREEDOM - See NOMAD

MC HAMMER - See HAMMER

MC LETHAL UK, male producer — 1 wk

14 Nov 92	**THE RAVE DIGGER** Network NWKT 60	.........**66**	1 wk

MC LYTE US, female rapper — 1 wk

15 Jan 94	**RUFFNECK** Atlantic A 8336CD	.........**67**	1 wk

MC MARIO - See AMBASSADORS OF FUNK featuring MC MARIO

MC MIKER 'G' and Deejay SVEN
Holland, male vocal/instrumental rap duo — 7 wks

6 Sep 86	● **HOLIDAY RAP** Debut DEBT 3008	.........**6**	7 wks

MC SAR - See REAL McCOY

MC SKAT KAT and the STRAY MOB
US, male vocal/instrumental group — 2 wks

9 Nov 91	**SKAT STRUT** Virgin America VUS 51	.........**64**	2 wks

MC SOLAAR - See URBAN SPECIES

MC TUNES UK, male rapper — 18 wks

2 Jun 90	● **THE ONLY RHYME THAT BITES** ZTT ZANG 3 [1]	.........**10**	10 wks
15 Sep 90	**TUNES SPLITS THE ATOM** ZTT ZANG 6 [1]	.........**18**	7 wks
1 Dec 90	**PRIMARY RHYMING** ZTT ZANG 10	.........**67**	1 wk

[1] MC Tunes versus 808 State

MC WILDSKI UK, male rapper — 10 wks

8 Jul 89	**BLAME IT ON THE BASSLINE** Go.Beat GOD 33 [1]	..**29**	6 wks
3 Mar 90	**WARRIOR** Arista 112956	.........**49**	4 wks

[1] Norman Cook featuring MC Wildski

Blame It On The Bassline was listed with Won't Talk About It *by Norman Cook featuring Billy Bragg.*

ME AND YOU featuring WE THE PEOPLE BAND Jamaica/UK, male/female vocal/instrumental group — 9 wks

28 Jul 79	**YOU NEVER KNOW WHAT YOU'VE GOT** Laser LAS 8	.........**31**	9 wks

Abigail MEAD and Nigel GOULDING
UK/US, female/male producers — 10 wks

26 Sep 87	● **FULL METAL JACKET (I WANNA BE YOUR DRILL INSTRUCTOR)** Warner Bros. W 8187	.........**2**	10 wks

MEAT BEAT MANIFESTO
UK, male instrumental / production duo   **1 wk**

20 Feb 93	**MINDSTREAM** *Play It Again Sam BIAS 232CD*	**55**	1 wk

MEAT LOAF *US, male vocalist*   **122 wks**

20 May 78	**YOU TOOK THE WORDS RIGHT OUT OF MY MOUTH**		
	Epic EPC 5980	**33**	8 wks
19 Aug 78	**TWO OUT OF THREE AIN'T BAD** *Epic EPC 6281*	**32**	8 wks
10 Feb 79	**BAT OUT OF HELL** *Epic EPC 7018*	**15**	7 wks
26 Sep 81	**I'M GONNA LOVE HER FOR BOTH OF US**		
	Epic EPCA 1580	**62**	3 wks
28 Nov 81	● **DEAD RINGER FOR LOVE** *Epic EPCA 1697*	**5**	17 wks
28 May 83	**IF YOU REALLY WANT TO** *Epic A 3357*	**59**	2 wks
24 Sep 83	**MIDNIGHT AT THE LOST AND FOUND**		
	Epic A 3748	**17**	8 wks
14 Jan 84	**RAZOR'S EDGE** *Epic A 4080*	**41**	3 wks
6 Oct 84	**MODERN GIRL** *Arista ARIST 585*	**17**	9 wks
22 Dec 84	**NOWHERE FAST** *Arista ARIST 600*	**67**	4 wks
23 Mar 85	**PIECE OF THE ACTION** *Arista ARIST 603*	**47**	5 wks
30 Aug 86	**ROCK 'N' ROLL MERCENARIES**		
	Arista ARIST 666 [1]	**31**	6 wks
22 Jun 91	**DEAD RINGER FOR LOVE (re-issue)** *Epic 6569827*	**53**	2 wks
27 Jun 92	**TWO OUT OF THREE AIN'T BAD (re-issue)**		
	Epic 6574917	**69**	1 wk
9 Oct 93	★ **I'D DO ANYTHING FOR LOVE**		
	(BUT I WON'T DO THAT) *Virgin VSCDT 1443*	**1**	19 wks
18 Dec 93	● **BAT OUT OF HELL (re-issue)** *Epic 6600062*	**8**	9 wks
19 Feb 94	**ROCK AND ROLL DREAMS COME THROUGH**		
	Virgin VSCDT 1479	**11**	7 wks
7 May 94	**OBJECTS IN THE REAR VIEW MIRROR MAY**		
	APPEAR CLOSER THAN THEY ARE		
	Virgin VSCDT 1492	**26**	4 wks

[1] Meat Loaf featuring John Parr

Dead Ringer For Love *features Cher as uncredited co-vocalist.*

MECHANICS - *See MIKE + the MECHANICS*

MECO *US, orchestra*   **9 wks**

1 Oct 77	● **STAR WARS THEME-CANTINA BAND** *RCA XB 1028*	**7**	9 wks

Glenn MEDEIROS *US, male vocalist*   **26 wks**

18 Jun 88	★ **NOTHING'S GONNA CHANGE MY LOVE FOR YOU**		
	London LON 184	**1**	13 wks
3 Sep 88	**LONG AND LASTING LOVE (ONCE IN A LIFETIME)**		
	London LON 202	**42**	4 wks
30 Jun 90	**SHE AIN'T WORTH IT** *London LON 265* [1]	**12**	9 wks

[1] Glenn Medeiros featuring Bobby Brown

Paul MEDFORD - *See Letitia DEAN and Paul MEDFORD*

MEDICINE HEAD *UK, male vocal / instrumental duo*   **37 wks**

26 Jun 71	**(AND THE) PICTURES IN THE SKY**		
	Dandelion DAN 7003	**22**	8 wks
5 May 73	● **ONE AND ONE IS ONE** *Polydor 2001 432*	**3**	13 wks
4 Aug 73	**RISING SUN** *Polydor 2058 389*	**11**	9 wks
9 Feb 74	**SLIP AND SLIDE** *Polydor 2058 436*	**22**	7 wks

MEDICINE SHOW - *See DR. HOOK*

Bill MEDLEY *US, male vocalist*   **29 wks**

31 Oct 87	● **(I'VE HAD) THE TIME OF MY LIFE**		
	RCA PB 49625 [1]	**6**	12 wks
27 Aug 88	**HE AIN'T HEAVY, HE'S MY BROTHER**		
	Scotti Brothers PO 10	**25**	6 wks
15 Dec 90	● **(I'VE HAD) THE TIME THE TIME OF MY LIFE**		
	(re-entry) *RCA PB 49625* [1]	**8**	11 wks

[1] Bill Medley and Jennifer Warnes

Michael MEDWIN, Bernard BRESSLAW, Alfie BASS and Leslie FYSON *UK, male vocal group*   **9 wks**

30 May 58	● **THE SIGNATURE TUNE OF 'THE ARMY GAME'**		
	HMV POP 490	**5**	9 wks

See also Bernard Bresslaw.

Tony MEEHAN COMBO
UK, male instrumental group, Tony Meehan - drums   **4 wks**

16 Jan 64	**SONG OF MEXICO** *Decca F 11801*	**39**	4 wks

See also Jet Harris and Tony Meehan.

MEGA CITY FOUR *UK, male vocal / instrumental group*   **7 wks**

19 Oct 91	**WORDS THAT SAY** *Big Life MEGA 2*	**66**	1 wk
8 Feb 92	**STOP (EP)** *Big Life MEGA 3*	**36**	2 wks
16 May 92	**SHIVERING SAND** *Big Life MEGA 4*	**35**	2 wks
1 May 93	**IRON SKY** *Big Life MEGAD 5*	**48**	1 wk
17 Jul 93	**WALLFLOWER** *Big Life MEGAD 6*	**69**	1 wk

Tracks on Stop (EP): *Stop / Desert Song / Back To Zero / Overlap.*

MEGABASS - *See VARIOUS ARTISTS (MONTAGES)*

MEGADETH *US, male vocal / instrumental group*   **29 wks**

19 Dec 87	**WAKE UP DEAD** *Capitol CL 476*	**65**	2 wks
27 Feb 88	**ANARCHY IN THE UK** *Capitol CL 480*	**45**	3 wks
21 May 88	**MARY JANE** *Capitol CL 489*	**46**	2 wks
13 Jan 90	**NO MORE MR. NICE GUY** *SBK SBK 4*	**13**	6 wks
29 Sep 90	**HOLY WARS...THE PUNISHMENT DUE**		
	Capitol CLP 588	**24**	3 wks
16 Mar 91	**HANGAR 18** *Capitol CLS 604*	**26**	4 wks
27 Jun 92	**SYMPHONY OF DESTRUCTION** *Capitol CLS 662*	**15**	3 wks
24 Oct 92	**SKIN O' MY TEETH** *Capitol CLP 669*	**13**	3 wks
29 May 93	**SWEATING BULLETS** *Capitol CDCL 682*	**26**	3 wks

Melle MEL - *See GRANDMASTER FLASH, Melle MEL and the FURIOUS FIVE*

MEL and KIM - *See Mel SMITH; Kim WILDE*

MEL and KIM *UK, female vocal duo*   **51 wks**

20 Sep 86	● **SHOWING OUT (GET FRESH AT THE WEEKEND)**		
	Supreme SUPE 107	**3**	19 wks
7 Mar 87	★ **RESPECTABLE** *Supreme SUPE 111*	**1**	15 wks
11 Jul 87	● **F.L.M.** *Supreme SUPE 113*	**7**	10 wks
27 Feb 88	● **THAT'S THE WAY IT IS** *Supreme SUPE 117*	**10**	7 wks

Melle MEL - *See GRANDMASTER FLASH, Melle MEL and the FURIOUS FIVE*

George MELACHRINO ORCHESTRA
UK, orchestra   **9 wks**

12 Oct 56	**AUTUMN CONCERTO** *HMV B 10958*	**18**	9 wks

MELANIE *US, female vocalist*   **35 wks**

26 Sep 70	● **RUBY TUESDAY** *Buddah 2011 038*	**9**	14 wks
9 Jan 71	**RUBY TUESDAY (re-entry)** *Buddah 2011 038*	**43**	1 wk
16 Jan 71	**WHAT HAVE THEY DONE TO MY SONG MA**		
	Buddah 2011 038	**39**	1 wk
1 Jan 72	● **BRAND NEW KEY** *Buddah 2011 105*	**4**	12 wks

16 Feb 74	**WILL YOU LOVE ME TOMORROW**		
	Neighbourhood NBH 9 ....**37**	5 wks
24 Sep 83	**EVERY BREATH OF THE WAY**		
	Neighbourhood HOOD NB1 ....**70**	2 wks

John Cougar MELLENCAMP US, male vocalist   18 wks

23 Oct 82	**JACK AND DIANE** *Riva RIVA 37* [1] **25**	8 wks
1 Feb 86	**SMALL TOWN** *Riva JCM 5*.....................**53**	4 wks
10 May 86	**R.O.C.K. IN THE U.S.A.** *Riva JCM 6*............**67**	3 wks
3 Sep 94	**WILD NIGHT** *Mercury MERCD 409* [2] **34**	3 wks

[1] John Cougar [2] John Mellencamp featuring Me'Shell NdegeoCello

MELODIANS *Jamaica, male vocal / instrumental group*   1 wk

10 Jan 70	**SWEET SENSATION** *Trojan TR 695*.........**41**	1 wk

MELODY MAKERS - *See Ziggy MARLEY and the MELODY MAKERS*

Harold MELVIN and the BLUENOTES
US, male vocal group   **52 wks**

13 Jan 73	● **IF YOU DON'T KNOW ME BY NOW** *CBS 8496* **9**	9 wks
12 Jan 74	**THE LOVE I LOST**	
	Philadelphia International PIR 1879 ....**21**	8 wks
13 Apr 74	**SATISFACTION GUARANTEED (OR TAKE YOUR LOVE BACK)** *Philadelphia International PIR 2187* ..**32**	6 wks
31 May 75	**GET OUT** *Route RT 06* **35**	5 wks
28 Feb 76	**WAKE UP EVERYBODY**	
	Philadelphia International PIR 3866 ....**23**	7 wks
22 Jan 77	● **DON'T LEAVE ME THIS WAY**	
	Philadelphia International PIR 4909 ....**5**	10 wks
2 Apr 77	**REACHING FOR THE WORLD** *ABC 4161* **48**	1 wk
28 Apr 84	**DON'T GIVE ME UP** *London LON 47* **59**	4 wks
4 Aug 84	**TODAY'S YOUR LUCKY DAY** *London LON 52* ...**66**	2 wks

MEMBERS *UK, male vocal / instrumental group*   14 wks

3 Feb 79	**THE SOUND OF THE SUBURBS** *Virgin VS 242* ...**12**	9 wks
7 Apr 79	**OFFSHORE BANKING BUSINESS** *Virgin VS 248*........**31**	5 wks

MEN AT WORK
Australia, male vocal / instrumental group   **39 wks**

30 Oct 82	**WHO CAN IT BE NOW?** *Epic EPC A 2392*...............**45**	5 wks
8 Jan 83	★ **DOWN UNDER** *Epic EPC A 1980* **1**	12 wks
9 Apr 83	**OVERKILL** *Epic EPC A 3220* **21**	10 wks
2 Jul 83	**IT'S A MISTAKE** *Epic EPC A 3475* **33**	6 wks
10 Sep 83	**DR. HECKYLL AND MR. JIVE** *Epic EPC A 3668*..........**31**	6 wks

MEN THEY COULDN'T HANG
UK, male vocal / instrumental group   **4 wks**

2 Apr 88	**THE COLOURS** *Magnet SELL 6* **61**	4 wks

MEN WITHOUT HATS
Canada, male vocal / instrumental group   **11 wks**

8 Oct 83	● **THE SAFETY DANCE** *Statik TAK 1* **6**	11 wks

Sergio MENDES *Brazil, male conductor*   5 wks

9 Jul 83	**NEVER GONNA LET YOU GO** *A & M AM 118*............**45**	5 wks

Uncredited vocals by Joe Pizzulo and Leza Miller.

MENTAL AS ANYTHING
Australia, male vocal / instrumental group   **13 wks**

7 Feb 87	● **LIVE IT UP** *Epic ANY 1* **3**	13 wks

Freddie MERCURY *UK, male vocalist*   79 wks

22 Sep 84	● **LOVE KILLS** *CBS A 4735* **10**	8 wks
20 Apr 85	**I WAS BORN TO LOVE YOU** *CBS A 6019*...................**11**	10 wks
13 Jul 85	**MADE IN HEAVEN** *CBS A 6413* **57**	4 wks
21 Sep 85	**LIVING ON MY OWN** *CBS A 6555* **50**	3 wks
24 May 86	**TIME** *EMI EMI 5559* **32**	5 wks
7 Mar 87	● **THE GREAT PRETENDER** *Parlophone R 6151* **4**	9 wks
7 Nov 87	● **BARCELONA** *Polydor POSP 887* [1] **8**	9 wks
8 Aug 92	● **BARCELONA (re-issue)** *Polydor PO 221* [1] **2**	8 wks
12 Dec 92	● **IN MY DEFENCE** *Parlophone R 6331* **8**	7 wks
6 Feb 93	**THE GREAT PRETENDER (re-issue)**	
	Parlophone CDR 6336 ....**29**	3 wks
31 Jul 93	★ **LIVING ON MY OWN (re-mix)**	
	Parlophone CDR 6355 ....**1**	13 wks

[1] Freddie Mercury and Montserrat Caballe

MERCY MERCY *UK, male vocal / instrumental group*   2 wks

21 Sep 85	**WHAT ARE WE GONNA DO ABOUT IT?**	
	Ensign ENY 522 ....**59**	2 wks

Tony MERRICK *UK, male vocalist*   1 wks

2 Jun 66	**LADY JANE** *Columbia DB 7913* **49**	1 wk

MERSEYBEATS *UK, male vocal / instrumental group*   64 wks

12 Sep 63	**IT'S LOVE THAT REALLY COUNTS** *Fontana TF 412* ..**24**	12 wks
16 Jan 64	● **I THINK OF YOU** *Fontana TF 431* **5**	17 wks
16 Apr 64	**DON'T TURN AROUND** *Fontana TF 459* **13**	11 wks
9 Jul 64	**WISHIN' AND HOPIN'** *Fontana TF 482* **13**	10 wks
5 Nov 64	**LAST NIGHT** *Fontana TF 504* **40**	3 wks
14 Oct 65	**I LOVE YOU, YES I DO** *Fontana TF 607* **22**	8 wks
20 Jan 66	**I STAND ACCUSED** *Fontana TF 645* **38**	3 wks

MERSEYS *UK, male vocal duo*   13 wks

28 Apr 66	● **SORROW** *Fontana TF 694* **4**	13 wks

MERTON PARKAS *UK, male vocal / instrumental group*   6 wks

4 Aug 79	**YOU NEED WHEELS** *Beggars Banquet BEG 22* **40**	6 wks

Mady MESPLÉ and Danielle MILLET with the PARIS OPERA-COMIQUE ORCHESTRA conducted by Alain LOMBARD
France, female vocal duo and orchestra   **4 wks**

6 Apr 85	**FLOWER DUET (FROM LAKME)** *EMI 5481* **47**	4 wks

MESSIAH *UK, male instrumental / production group*   13 wks

20 Jun 92	**TEMPLE OF DREAMS** *Kickin KICK 12S* **20**	5 wks
26 Sep 92	**I FEEL LOVE** *Kickin KICK 22S* [1] **19**	5 wks
27 Nov 93	**THUNDERDOME** *WEA YZ 790CD1* **29**	3 wks

[1] Messiah featuring Precious Wilson

METAL GURUS *UK, male vocal / instrumental group*   2 wks

8 Dec 90	**MERRY XMAS EVERYBODY** *Mercury GURU 1*..........**55**	2 wks

METALHEADS - *See GOLDIE presents METALHEADS*

METALLICA
US / Denmark, male vocal / instrumental group   **35 wks**

22 Aug 87	**THE $5.98 EP - GARAGE DAYS REVISITED**	
	Vertigo METAL 112 ....**27**	4 wks
3 Sep 88	**HARVESTER OF SORROW** *Vertigo METAL 212*..........**20**	3 wks
22 Apr 89	**ONE** *Vertigo METAL 5* **13**	7 wks
10 Aug 91	● **ENTER SANDMAN** *Vertigo METAL 7* **5**	4 wks
9 Nov 91	**THE UNFORGIVEN** *Vertigo METAL 8* **15**	4 wks
2 May 92	● **NOTHING ELSE MATTERS** *Vertigo METAL 10*..........**6**	6 wks

GEORGE MICHAEL is shown with Linda Evangelista as she appeared in the 'Too Funky' video.
(Kevin Mazur/LFI)

| 31 Oct 92 | **WHEREVER I MAY ROAM** Vertigo METAL 9 | **25** | 4 wks |
| 20 Feb 93 | **SAD BUT TRUE** Vertigo METCD 11 | **20** | 3 wks |

Tracks on The $5.98 EP: Garage Days Revisited / Helpless / Crash Course in Brain Surgery / The Small Hours / Last Caress / Green Hell.

METEORS UK, male vocal / instrumental group — 2 wks

| 26 Feb 83 | **JOHNNY REMEMBER ME** ID EYE 1 | **66** | 2 wks |

Pat METHENY GROUP - See David BOWIE

MEZZOFORTE Iceland, male instrumental group — 10 wks

| 5 Mar 83 | **GARDEN PARTY** Steinar STE 705 | **17** | 9 wks |
| 11 Jun 83 | **ROCKALL** Steinar STE 710 | **75** | 1 wk |

MFSB US, orchestra — 18 wks

27 Apr 74	**TSOP (THE SOUND OF PHILADELPHIA)** Philadelphia International PIR 2289 [1]	**22**	9 wks
26 Jul 75	**SEXY** Philadelphia International PIR 3381	**37**	5 wks
31 Jan 81	**MYSTERIES OF THE WORLD** Sound Of Philadelphia PIR 9501	**41**	4 wks

[1] MFSB featuring the Three Degrees

M.G.'s - See BOOKER T. and the M.G.'s

MIAMI SOUND MACHINE - See Gloria ESTEFAN

George MICHAEL UK, male vocalist — 139 wks

4 Aug 84	★ **CARELESS WHISPER** Epic A 4603	**1**	17 wks
5 Apr 86	★ **A DIFFERENT CORNER** Epic A 7033	**1**	10 wks
31 Jan 87	★ **I KNEW YOU WERE WAITING (FOR ME)** Epic DUET 2 [1]	**1**	9 wks
13 Jun 87	● **I WANT YOUR SEX** Epic LUST 1	**3**	10 wks
24 Oct 87	● **FAITH** Epic EMU 3	**2**	12 wks
9 Jan 88	**FATHER FIGURE** Epic EMU 4	**11**	6 wks
23 Apr 88	● **ONE MORE TRY** Epic EMU 5	**8**	7 wks
16 Jul 88	**MONKEY** Epic EMU 6	**13**	6 wks
3 Dec 88	**KISSING A FOOL** Epic EMU 7	**18**	6 wks
25 Aug 90	● **PRAYING FOR TIME** Epic GEO 1	**6**	7 wks
27 Oct 90	**WAITING FOR THAT DAY** Epic GEO 2	**23**	5 wks
15 Dec 90	**FREEDOM 90** Epic GEO 3	**28**	6 wks
16 Feb 91	**HEAL THE PAIN** Epic 6566477	**31**	4 wks
30 Mar 91	**COWBOYS AND ANGELS** Epic 6567747	**45**	3 wks
7 Dec 91	★ **DON'T LET THE SUN GO DOWN ON ME** Epic 6576467 [2]	**1**	10 wks
13 Jun 92	● **TOOFUNKY** Epic 6580587	**4**	9 wks
1 May 93	★ **FIVE LIVE EP** Parlophone CDRS 6340 [3]	**1**	11 wks
24 Jul 93	**FIVE LIVE EP** (re-entry) Parlophone CDRS 6340 [3]	**74**	1 wk

[1] Aretha Franklin and George Michael [2] George Michael and Elton John [3] George Michael and Queen with Lisa Stansfield

Tracks on Five Live EP: Somebody To Love / These Are The Days Of Our Lives / Calling You / Papa Was A Rolling Stone-Killer (medley). The first track on the EP features Queen, the second Queen and Lisa Stansfield. See also Elton John.

MICHAELA UK, female vocalist — 6 wks

| 2 Sep 89 | **H-A-P-P-Y RADIO** London H 1 | **62** | 4 wks |
| 28 Apr 90 | **TAKE GOOD CARE OF MY HEART** London WAC 90 | **66** | 2 wks |

Lisa MICHAELIS - See Frankie KNUCKLES

Keith MICHELL Australia, male vocalist — 25 wks

27 Mar 71	**I'LL GIVE YOU THE EARTH (TOUS LES BATEAUX, TOUS LES OISEAUX)** Spark SRL 1046	**43**	1 wk
17 Apr 71	**I'LL GIVE YOU THE EARTH (TOUS LES BATEAUX, TOUS LES OISEAUX)** (re-entry) Spark SRL 1046	**30**	10 wks
26 Jan 80	● **CAPTAIN BEAKY / WILFRED THE WEASEL** Polydor POSP 106	**5**	10 wks
29 Mar 80	**THE TRIAL OF HISSING SID** Polydor HISS 1 [1]	**53**	4 wks

[1] Keith Michell, Captain Beaky and his Band

Lloyd MICHELS - See MISTURA featuring Lloyd MICHELS

MICK and PAT - See PAT and MICK

MICROBE UK, male vocalist — 7 wks

| 14 May 69 | **GROOVY BABY** CBS 4158 | **29** | 7 wks |

MICRODISNEY Ireland, male vocal / instrumental group — 3 wks

| 21 Feb 87 | **TOWN TO TOWN** Virgin VS 927 | **55** | 3 wks |

MIDDLE OF THE ROAD UK, male / female vocal / instrumental group — 76 wks

5 Jun 71	★ **CHIRPY CHIRPY CHEEP CHEEP** RCA 2047	**1**	34 wks
4 Sep 71	● **TWEEDLE DEE TWEEDLE DUM** RCA 2110	**2**	17 wks
11 Dec 71	● **SOLEY SOLEY** RCA 2151	**5**	12 wks
25 Mar 72	**SACRAMENTO** RCA 2184	**49**	1 wk
8 Apr 72	**SACRAMENTO** (re-entry) RCA 2184	**23**	6 wks
29 Jul 72	**SAMSON AND DELILAH** RCA 2237	**26**	6 wks

Bette MIDLER US, female vocalist — 26 wks

17 Jun 89	● **WIND BENEATH MY WINGS** Atlantic A 8972	**5**	12 wks
13 Oct 90	**FROM A DISTANCE** Atlantic A 7820	**45**	5 wks
15 Jun 91	● **FROM A DISTANCE** (re-entry) Atlantic A 7820	**6**	9 wks

MIDNIGHT BAND - See Tony RALLO and the MIDNIGHT BAND

MIDNIGHT COWBOY SOUNDTRACK US, orchestra — 4 wks

| 8 Nov 80 | **MIDNIGHT COWBOY** United Artists UP 634 | **47** | 4 wks |

MIDNIGHT OIL Australia, male vocal / instrumental group — 32 wks

23 Apr 88	**BEDS ARE BURNING** Sprint OIL 1	**48**	5 wks
2 Jul 88	**THE DEAD HEART** Spring OIL 2	**68**	2 wks
25 Mar 89	● **BEDS ARE BURNING** (re-issue) Sprint OIL 3	**6**	13 wks
1 Jul 89	**THE DEAD HEART** (re-issue) Sprint OIL 4	**62**	4 wks
10 Feb 90	**BLUE SKY MINE** CBS OIL 5	**66**	2 wks
17 Apr 93	**TRUGANINI** Columbia 6590492	**29**	4 wks
3 Jul 93	**MY COUNTRY** Columbia 6593702	**66**	1 wk
6 Nov 93	**IN THE VALLEY** Columbia 6598492	**60**	1 wk

MIDNIGHT STAR US, male / female vocal / instrumental group — 26 wks

23 Feb 85	**OPERATOR** Solar MCA 942	**66**	2 wks
28 Jun 86	**HEADLINES** Solar MCA 1065	**16**	8 wks
4 Oct 86	● **MIDAS TOUCH** Solar MCA 1096	**8**	10 wks
7 Feb 87	**ENGINE NO.9** Solar MCA 1117	**64**	3 wks
2 May 87	**WET MY WHISTLE** Solar MCA 1127	**60**	3 wks

MIGHTY AVENGERS UK, male vocal / instrumental group — 2 wks

| 26 Nov 64 | **SO MUCH IN LOVE** Decca F 11962 | **46** | 2 wks |

MIGHTY AVONS - See Larry CUNNINGHAM and the MIGHTY AVONS

MIGHTY DIAMONDS - See VARIOUS ARTISTS - Gimme Shelter (EP).

MIGHTY LEMON DROPS
UK, male vocal / instrumental group **7 wks**

13 Sep 86	**THE OTHER SIDE OF YOU** *Blue Guitar AZUR 1* **51**	2 wks
18 Apr 87	**OUT OF HAND** *Blue Guitar AZUR 4* **66**	3 wks
23 Jan 88	**INSIDE OUT** *Blue Guitar AZUR 6* **74**	2 wks

MIGHTY MORPH'N POWER RANGERS
US, male / female vocal group **3 wks**

| 17 Dec 94 | ● **POWER RANGERS** *RCA 74321253022* ....**3†** | 3 wks |

MIGHTY WAH - *See WAH!*

MIGIL FIVE *UK, male vocal / instrumental group* **20 wks**

| 19 Mar 64 | ● **MOCKINGBIRD HILL** *Pye 7N 15597* ....**10** | 13 wks |
| 4 Jun 64 | **NEAR YOU** *Pye 7N 15645* ....**31** | 7 wks |

MIG29 *Italy, male instrumental / production group* **2 wks**

| 22 Feb 92 | **MIG29** *Champion CHAMP 292* ....**62** | 2 wks |

MIKE *UK, male producer - Mark Jolley* **2 wks**

| 19 Nov 94 | **TWANGLING THREE FINGERS IN A BOX** *Pukka CDMIKE 100* ....**40** | 2 wks |

MIKE + the MECHANICS
UK, male vocal / instrumental group **41 wks**

15 Feb 86	**SILENT RUNNING (ON DANGEROUS GROUND)** *WEA U 8908* **21**	9 wks
31 May 86	**ALL I NEED IS A MIRACLE** *WEA U 8765* **53**	4 wks
14 Jan 89	● **THE LIVING YEARS** *WEA U 7717* **2**	11 wks
16 Mar 91	**WORD OF MOUTH** *Virgin VS 1345* **13**	10 wks
15 Jun 91	**A TIME AND PLACE** *Virgin VS 1351* **58**	3 wks
8 Feb 92	**EVERYBODY GETS A SECOND CHANCE** *Virgin VS 1396* **56**	4 wks

MIKI and GRIFF *UK, female / male vocal duo* **25 wks**

2 Oct 59	**HOLD BACK TOMORROW** *Pye 7N 15213* **26**	2 wks
13 Oct 60	**ROCKIN' ALONE** *Pye 7N 15296* **44**	3 wks
1 Feb 62	**LITTLE BITTY TEAR** *Pye 7N 15412* **16**	13 wks
22 Aug 63	**I WANNA STAY HERE** *Pye 7N 15555* **23**	7 wks

John MILES *UK, male vocalist / multi-instrumentalist* **30 wks**

18 Oct 75	**HIGH FLY** *Decca F 13595* **17**	6 wks
20 Mar 76	● **MUSIC** *Decca F 13627* **3**	9 wks
16 Oct 76	**REMEMBER YESTERDAY** *Decca F 13667* **32**	5 wks
18 Jun 77	● **SLOW DOWN** *Decca F 13709* **10**	10 wks

June MILES-KINGSTON - *See Jimmy SOMERVILLE*

Paul MILES-KINGSTON - *See Sarah BRIGHTMAN*

MILK AND HONEY featuring Gali ATARI
Israel, male / female vocal / instrumental group **8 wks**

| 14 Apr 79 | ● **HALLELUJAH** *Polydor 2001 870* ....**5** | 8 wks |

MILL GIRLS - *See Billy COTTON*

MILLA *US, female vocalist* **1 wk**

| 18 Jun 94 | **GENTLEMAN WHO FELL** *SBK CDSBK 49* ....**65** | 1 wk |

Frankie MILLER *UK, male vocalist* **32 wks**

4 Jun 77	**BE GOOD TO YOURSELF** *Chrysalis CHS 2147* **27**	6 wks
14 Oct 78	● **DARLIN'** *Chrysalis CHS 2255* **6**	15 wks
20 Jan 79	**WHEN I'M AWAY FROM YOU** *Chrysalis CHS 2276* **42**	5 wks
21 Mar 92	**CALEDONIA** *MCS MCS 2001* **45**	6 wks

Gary MILLER *UK, male vocalist* **35 wks**

21 Oct 55	**YELLOW ROSE OF TEXAS** *Nixa N 15004* **13**	5 wks
13 Jan 56	● **ROBIN HOOD** *Nixa N 15020* **10**	6 wks
11 Jan 57	**GARDEN OF EDEN** *Pye Nixa N 15070* **14**	6 wks
1 Mar 57	**GARDEN OF EDEN (re-entry)** *Pye Nixa N 15070* **27**	1 wk
19 Jul 57	**WONDERFUL WONDERFUL** *Pye Nixa N 15094* **29**	1 wk
17 Jan 58	**STORY OF MY LIFE** *Pye Nixa N 15120* **14**	6 wks
21 Dec 61	**THERE GOES THAT SONG AGAIN / THE NIGHT IS YOUNG** *Pye 7N 15404* **29**	9 wks
1 Mar 62	**THERE GOES THAT SONG AGAIN (re-entry)** *Pye 7N 15404* **48**	1 wk

The Night Is Young *only listed with* There Goes That Song Again *for weeks 21 and 28 Dec 61 and 4 Jan 62. It peaked at position 32.*

Glenn MILLER *US, orchestra, Glenn Miller, trombone* **9 wks**

| 12 Mar 54 | **MOONLIGHT SERENADE** *HMV BD 5942* ....**12** | 1 wk |
| 24 Jan 76 | **MOONLIGHT SERENADE / LITTLE BROWN JUG / IN THE MOOD (re-issue)** *RCA 2644* ....**13** | 8 wks |

Jody MILLER *US, female vocalist* **1 wk**

| 21 Oct 65 | **HOME OF THE BRAVE** *Capitol CL 15415* ....**49** | 1 wk |

Leza MILLER - *See Sergio MENDES*

Mitch MILLER *US, orchestra and chorus* **13 wks**

| 7 Oct 55 | ● **YELLOW ROSE OF TEXAS** *Philips PB 505* ....**2** | 13 wks |

Ned MILLER *US, male vocalist* **22 wks**

| 14 Feb 63 | ● **FROM A JACK TO A KING** *London HL 9658* ....**2** | 21 wks |
| 18 Feb 65 | **DO WHAT YOU DO DO WELL** *London HL 9937* ....**48** | 1 wk |

Roger MILLER *US, male vocalist* **42 wks**

18 Mar 65	★ **KING OF THE ROAD** *Philips BF 1397* **1**	15 wks
3 Jun 65	**ENGINE ENGINE NO. 9** *Philips BF 1416* **33**	5 wks
21 Oct 65	**KANSAS CITY STAR** *Philips BF 1437* **48**	1 wk
16 Dec 65	**ENGLAND SWINGS** *Philips BF 1456* **45**	1 wk
6 Jan 66	**ENGLAND SWINGS (re-entry)** *Philips BF 1456* **13**	7 wks
27 Mar 68	**LITTLE GREEN APPLES** *Mercury MF 1021* **19**	10 wks
2 Apr 69	**LITTLE GREEN APPLES (re-entry)** *Mercury MF 1021* **48**	1 wk
7 May 69	**LITTLE GREEN APPLES (2nd re-entry)** *Mercury MF 1021* **39**	2 wks

Suzi MILLER - *See JOHNSTON BROTHERS*

Steve MILLER BAND
US, male vocal / instrumental group **36 wks**

23 Oct 76	**ROCK 'N ME** *Mercury 6078 804* **11**	9 wks
19 Jun 82	● **ABRACADABRA** *Mercury STEVE 3* **2**	11 wks
4 Sep 82	**KEEPS ME WONDERING WHY** *Mercury STEVE 4* **52**	3 wks
11 Aug 90	★ **THE JOKER** *Capitol CL 583* **1**	13 wks

Lisa MILLETT - *See SHEER BRONZE*

213

MILLI VANILLI France / Germany, male duo — **50 wks**

1 Oct 88 ●	GIRL YOU KNOW IT'S TRUE Cooltempo COOL 170 ...**3**	13 wks
17 Dec 88	BABY DON'T FORGET MY NUMBER Cooltempo COOL 178 ....**16**	11 wks
22 Jul 89	BLAME IT ON THE RAIN Cooltempo COOL 180 ....**53**	5 wks
30 Sep 89 ●	GIRL I'M GONNA MISS YOU Cooltempo COOL 191 ..**2**	15 wks
2 Dec 89	BLAME IT ON THE RAIN (re-entry) Cooltempo COOL 180 ....**52**	5 wks
10 Mar 90	ALL OR NOTHING Cooltempo COOL 199 ....**74**	1 wk

MILLICAN and NESBITT UK, male vocal duo — **14 wks**

1 Dec 73	VAYA CON DIOS Pye 7N 45310 ....**20**	11 wks
18 May 74	FOR OLD TIME'S SAKE Pye 7N 45357 ....**38**	3 wks

MILLIE Jamaica, female vocalist — **33 wks**

12 Mar 64 ●	MY BOY LOLLIPOP Fontana TF 449 ....**2**	18 wks
25 Jun 64	SWEET WILLIAM Fontana TF 479 ....**30**	9 wks
11 Nov 65	BLOODSHOT EYES Fontana TF 617 ....**48**	1 wk
25 Jul 87	MY BOY LOLLIPOP (re-issue) Island WIP 6574 ..**46**	5 wks

MILLIONAIRE HIPPIES
UK, male producer - Danny Rampling — **4 wks**

18 Dec 93	I AM THE MUSIC HEAR ME! Deconstruction 74321175432 ....**52**	3 wks
10 Sep 94	C'MON Deconstruction 74321229372 ....**59**	1 wk

Garry MILLS UK, male vocalist — **31 wks**

7 Jul 60 ●	LOOK FOR A STAR Top Rank JAR 336 ....**7**	14 wks
20 Oct 60	TOP TEEN BABY Top Rank JAR 500 ....**24**	12 wks
22 Jun 61	I'LL STEP DOWN Decca F 11358 ....**39**	5 wks

Hayley MILLS UK, female vocalist — **11 wks**

19 Oct 61	LET'S GET TOGETHER Decca F 21396 ....**17**	11 wks

Mrs. MILLS UK, female instrumentalist - piano — **5 wks**

14 Dec 61	MRS MILLS' MEDLEY Parlophone R 4856 ....**18**	5 wks

Mrs Mills' Medley consisted of the following tunes: I Want To Be Happy/ Sheik Of Araby/Baby Face/Somebody Stole My Gal/Ma (He's Making Eyes At Me)/Swanee/Ain't She Sweet/California Here I Come.

Stephanie MILLS US, female vocalist — **33 wks**

18 Oct 80 ●	NEVER KNEW LOVE LIKE THIS BEFORE 20th Century TC 2460 ....**4**	14 wks
23 May 81	TWO HEARTS 20th Century TC 2492 ⬚1 ....**49**	5 wks
15 Sep 84	THE MEDICINE SONG Club JAB 8 ....**29**	9 wks
5 Sep 87	(YOU'RE PUTTIN') A RUSH ON ME MCA MCA 1187..**62**	2 wks
1 May 93	NEVER DO YOU WRONG MCA MCSTD 1767 ......**57**	2 wks
10 Jul 93	ALL DAY ALL NIGHT MCA MCSTD 1778 ....**68**	1 wk

1 Stephanie Mills featuring Teddy Pendergrass

Warren MILLS Zambia, male vocalist — **1 wk**

28 Sep 85	SUNSHINE Jive JIVE 99 ....**74**	1 wk

MILLS BROTHERS US, male vocal group — **1 wk**

30 Jan 53 ●	GLOW WORM Brunswick 05007 ....**10**	1 wk

MILLTOWN BROTHERS
UK, male vocal / instrumental group — **16 wks**

2 Feb 91	WHICH WAY SHOULD I JUMP A & M AM 711 ....**38**	5 wks

13 Apr 91	HERE I STAND A & M AM 758 ....**41**	4 wks
6 Jul 91	APPLE GREEN A & M AM 787 ....**43**	4 wks
22 May 93	TURN OFF A & M 5802692 ....**55**	1 wk
17 Jul 93	IT'S ALL OVER NOW BABY BLUE A & M 5803332 ..**48**	2 wks

C.B. MILTON Holland, male vocalist — **2 wks**

21 May 94	IT'S A LOVING THING Logic 74321208062 ....**49**	2 wks

Garnet MIMMS and TRUCKIN' CO.
US, male vocalist and male instrumental group — **1 wk**

25 Jun 77	WHAT IT IS Arista 109 ....**44**	1 wk

MIND OF KANE UK, male producer - David Hope — **1 wk**

27 Jul 91	STABBED IN THE BACK Deja Vu DJV 007 ....**64**	1 wk

See also Hope AD.

MINDBENDERS UK, male vocal / instrumental group — **34 wks**

13 Jan 66 ●	A GROOVY KIND OF LOVE Fontana TF 644 ....**2**	14 wks
5 May 66	CAN'T LIVE WITH YOU (CAN'T LIVE WITHOUT YOU) Fontana TF 697 ....**28**	7 wks
25 Aug 66	ASHES TO ASHES Fontana TF 731 ....**14**	9 wks
20 Sep 67	THE LETTER Fontana TF 869 ....**42**	4 wks

See also Wayne Fontana and the Mindbenders.

Zodiac MINDWARP and the LOVE REACTION
UK, male / female vocal / instrumental group — **11 wks**

9 May 87	PRIME MOVER Mercury ZOD 1 ....**18**	6 wks
14 Nov 87	BACKSEAT EDUCATION Mercury ZOD 2 ....**49**	3 wks
2 Apr 88	PLANET GIRL Mercury ZOD 3......................**63**	2 wks

Sal MINEO US, male vocalist — **11 wks**

12 Jul 57	START MOVIN' Philips PB 707 ....**16**	11 wks

Marcello MINERBI Italy, orchestra — **16 wks**

22 Jul 65 ●	ZORBA'S DANCE Durium DRS 54001 ....**6**	16 wks

MINI POPS UK, male / female vocal group — **2 wks**

26 Dec 87	SONGS FOR CHRISTMAS '87 EP Bright BULB 9........**39**	2 wks

Tracks on Songs For Christmas '87 EP: Thanks For Giving Us Christmas/ The Man In Red/Christmas Time Around The World/Shine On.

MINISTRY US, male vocal / instrumental group — **1 wk**

8 Aug 92	NWO Sire W 0125TE.............................**49**	1 wk

MINK DE VILLE US, male vocal / instrumental group — **9 wks**

6 Aug 77	SPANISH STROLL Capitol CLX 103 ....**20**	9 wks

Liza MINNELLI US, female vocalist — **15 wks**

12 Aug 89 ●	LOSING MY MIND Epic ZEE 1 ....**6**	7 wks
7 Oct 89	DON'T DROP BOMBS Epic ZEE 2 ....**46**	3 wks
25 Nov 89	SO SORRY I SAID Epic ZEE 3 ....**62**	2 wks
3 Mar 90	LOVE PAINS Epic ZEE 4 ....**41**	3 wks

Dannii MINOGUE Australia, female vocalist — **52 wks**

30 Mar 91 ●	LOVE AND KISSES MCA MCS 1529 ....**8**	8 wks
18 May 91	SUCCESS MCA MCS 1538 ....**11**	7 wks
27 Jul 91 ●	JUMP TO THE BEAT MCA MCS 1556 ....**8**	6 wks

19 Oct 91	**BABY LOVE** *MCA MCS 1580*	**14**	6 wks
14 Dec 91	**I DON'T WANNA TAKE THIS PAIN** *MCA MCS 1600*..**40**		5 wks
1 Aug 92	**SHOW YOU THE WAY TO GO** *MCA MCS 1671*	**30**	3 wks
12 Dec 92	**LOVE'S ON EVERY CORNER** *MCA MCSR 1723* **44**		4 wks
17 Jul 93	● **THIS IS IT** *MCA MCSTD 1790*	**10**	8 wks
2 Oct 93	**THIS IS THE WAY** *MCA MCSTD 1935*	**27**	3 wks
11 Jun 94	**GET INTO YOU** *Mushroom D 11751*	**36**	2 wks

Kylie MINOGUE *Australia, female vocalist*   **191 wks**

23 Jan 88	★ **I SHOULD BE SO LUCKY** *PWL PWL 8*......**1**		16 wks
14 May 88	● **GOT TO BE CERTAIN** *PWL PWL 12* **2**		12 wks
6 Aug 88	● **THE LOCO-MOTION** *PWL PWL 14*......**2**		11 wks
22 Oct 88	● **JE NE SAIS PAS POURQUOI** *PWL PWL 21* **2**		13 wks
10 Dec 88	★ **ESPECIALLY FOR YOU** *PWL PWL 24* [1] **1**		14 wks
6 May 89	★ **HAND ON YOUR HEART** *PWL PWL 35* **1**		11 wks
5 Aug 89	● **WOULDN'T CHANGE A THING** *PWL PWL 42* **2**		9 wks
4 Nov 89	● **NEVER TOO LATE** *PWL PWL 45* **4**		10 wks
20 Jan 90	★ **TEARS ON MY PILLOW** *PWL PWL 47*......**1**		8 wks
12 May 90	● **BETTER THE DEVIL YOU KNOW** *PWL PWL 56* **2**		10 wks
3 Nov 90	● **STEP BACK IN TIME** *PWL PWL 64* **4**		8 wks
2 Feb 91	● **WHAT DO I HAVE TO DO** *PWL PWL 72* **6**		8 wks
1 Jun 91	● **SHOCKED** *PWL PWL 81* **6**		7 wks
7 Sep 91	**WORD IS OUT** *PWL PWL 204* **16**		5 wks
2 Nov 91	● **IF YOU WERE WITH ME NOW** *PWL PWL 208* [2] **4**		7 wks
30 Nov 91	**KEEP ON PUMPIN' IT** *PWL PWL 207* [3] **49**		1 wk
25 Jan 92	● **GIVE ME JUST A LITTLE MORE TIME** *PWL PWL 212* ..**2**		8 wks
25 Apr 92	**FINER FEELINGS** *PWL International PWL 227*......**11**		6 wks
22 Aug 92	**WHAT KIND OF FOOL (HEARD IT ALL BEFORE)** *PWL International PWL 241* **14**		5 wks
28 Nov 92	**CELEBRATION** *PWL International PWL 257* **20**		7 wks
10 Sep 94	● **CONFIDE IN ME** *Deconstruction 74321227482* **2**		9 wks
26 Nov 94	**PUT YOURSELF IN MY PLACE** *Deconstruction 74321246572* ......**11†**		6 wks

[1] Kylie Minogue and Jason Donovan [2] Kylie Minogue and Keith Washington [3] Visionmasters with Tony King featuring Kylie Minogue

Morris MINOR and the MAJORS
UK, male vocal group   **11 wks**

19 Dec 87	● **STUTTER RAP (NO SLEEP 'TIL BEDTIME)** *10 TEN 203* **4**		11 wks

Sugar MINOTT *UK, male vocalist*   **16 wks**

28 Mar 81	● **GOOD THING GOING (WE'VE GOT A GOOD THING GOING)** *RCA 58* **4**		12 wks
17 Oct 81	**NEVER MY LOVE** *RCA 138* **52**		4 wks

MINT JULEPS *UK, female vocal group*   **7 wks**

22 Mar 86	**ONLY LOVE CAN BREAK YOUR HEART** *Stiff BUY 241* **62**		2 wks
30 May 87	**EVERY KINDA PEOPLE** *Stiff BUY 257* **58**		5 wks

MIRACLES *US, male vocal group*   **10 wks**

10 Jan 76	● **LOVE MACHINE** *Tamla Motown TMG 1015* **3**		10 wks

See also Smokey Robinson and the Miracles.

MIRAGE *UK, male vocal / instrumental group*   **35 wks**

14 Jan 84	**GIVE ME THE NIGHT** *Passion PASH 15* [1] **49**		4 wks
9 May 87	● **JACK MIX II/III** *Debut DEBT 3022*......**4**		11 wks
25 Jul 87	**SERIOUS MIX** *Debut DEBT 3028* **42**		4 wks
7 Nov 87	● **JACK MIX IV** *Debut DEBT 3035* **8**		10 wks
27 Feb 88	**JACK MIX VII** *Debut DEBT 3042* **50**		3 wks
2 Jul 88	**PUSH THE BEAT** *Debut DEBT 3050*......**67**		2 wks
11 Nov 89	**LATINO HOUSE** *Debut DEBT 3085* **70**		1 wk

[1] Mirage featuring Roy Gayle

Jack Mix III *only listed with Jack Mix II from 6 Jun 87.*

Danny MIRROR *Holland, male vocalist*   **9 wks**

17 Sep 77	● **I REMEMBER ELVIS PRESLEY (THE KING IS DEAD)** *Sonet SON 2121* **4**		9 wks

MISSION *UK, male vocal / instrumental group*   **57 wks**

14 Jun 86	**SERPENTS KISS** *Chapter 22 CHAP 6* **70**		3 wks
26 Jul 86	**GARDEN OF DELIGHT / LIKE A HURRICANE** *Chapter 22 CHAP 7* **49**		4 wks
18 Oct 86	**STAY WITH ME** *Mercury MYTH 1* **30**		4 wks
17 Jan 87	**WASTELAND** *Mercury MYTH 2* **11**		6 wks
14 Mar 87	**SEVERINA** *Mercury MYTH 3*......**25**		5 wks
13 Feb 88	**TOWER OF STRENGTH** *Mercury MYTH 4* **12**		7 wks
23 Apr 88	**BEYOND THE PALE** *Mercury MYTH 6* **32**		4 wks
13 Jan 90	**BUTTERFLY ON A WHEEL** *Mercury MYTH 8* **12**		4 wks
10 Mar 90	**DELIVERANCE** *Mercury MYTH 9* **27**		4 wks
2 Jun 90	**INTO THE BLUE** *Mercury MYTH 10* **32**		3 wks
17 Nov 90	**HANDS ACROSS THE OCEAN** *Mercury MYTH 11* **28**		2 wks
25 Apr 92	**NEVER AGAIN** *Mercury MYTH 12* **34**		3 wks
20 Jun 92	**LIKE A CHILD AGAIN** *Mercury MYTH 13* **30**		2 wks
17 Oct 92	**SHADES OF GREEN** *Vertigo MYTH 14* **49**		2 wks
8 Jan 94	**TOWER OF STRENGTH (re-mix)** *Vertigo MYTCD 15*..**33**		3 wks
26 Mar 94	**AFTERGLOW** *Vertigo MYTCD 16* **53**		1 wk

MISTA E *UK, male producer - Damon Rochort*   **5 wks**

10 Dec 88	**DON'T BELIEVE THE HYPE** *Urban URB 28* **41**		5 wks

MR. BEAN and SMEAR CAMPAIGN featuring Bruce DICKINSON
UK, male comedian - Rowan Atkinson and vocal / instrumental group   **5 wks**

4 Apr 92	● **(I WANT TO BE) ELECTED** *London LON 319* **9**		5 wks

MR. BIG *UK, male vocal / instrumental group*   **14 wks**

12 Feb 77	● **ROMEO** *EMI 2567*......**4**		10 wks
21 May 77	**FEEL LIKE CALLING HOME** *EMI 2610* **35**		4 wks

MR. BIG *US, male vocal / instrumental group*   **17 wks**

7 Mar 92	● **TO BE WITH YOU** *Atlantic A 7514* **3**		11 wks
23 May 92	**JUST TAKE MY HEART** *Atlantic A 7490*......**26**		4 wks
8 Aug 92	**GREEN TINTED SIXTIES MIND** *Atlantic A 7468*......**72**		1 wk
20 Nov 93	**WILD WORLD** *Atlantic A 7310CD*......**59**		1 wk

MR. BLOBBY *UK, male vocalist*   **12 wks**

4 Dec 93	★ **MR. BLOBBY** *Destiny Music CDDMUS 104*......**1**		12 wks

MR. BLOE *UK, male instrumentalist - harmonica*   **18 wks**

9 May 70	● **GROOVIN' WITH MR. BLOE** *DJM DJS 216*......**2**		18 wks

MR. FINGERS *US, male producer - Larry Heard*   **5 wks**

17 Mar 90	**WHAT ABOUT THIS LOVE** *ffrr F 131* **74**		1 wk
7 Mar 92	**CLOSER** *MCA MCS 1601* **50**		3 wks
23 May 92	**ON MY WAY** *MCA MCS 1630* **71**		1 wk

MR. FOOD *UK, male vocalist*   **3 wks**

9 Jun 90	**...AND THAT'S BEFORE ME TEA!** *Tangible TGB 005* **62**		3 wks

MR. LEE *US, male producer - Leroy Haggard*   **6 wks**

6 Aug 88	**PUMP UP LONDON** *Breakout USA 639* **64**		2 wks

One of the earliest hit songs from soap operas was taken to the top 20 by **SUE NICHOLLS**, perhaps better known as Audrey Roberts of *Coronation Street*.

MR. BLOBBY fell from the number one spot but soon bounced back. (Colin Mason/LFI)

11 Nov 89	GET BUSY *Jive JIVE 231*	**71**	1 wk
24 Feb 90	GET BUSY (re-entry) *Jive JIVE 231*	**41**	3 wks

MR. MISTER US, male vocal/instrumental group　　22 wks

21 Dec 85	● BROKEN WINGS *RCA PB 49945*	**4**	13 wks
1 Mar 86	● KYRIE *RCA PB 49927*	**11**	9 wks

MR. ROY UK, male instrumental/production group　　1 wk

7 May 94	SOMETHING ABOUT YOU *Fresh FRSHD 11*	**74**	1 wk

MR. V UK, male producer - Rob Villiers　　2 wks

6 Aug 94	GIVE ME LIFE *Cheeky CHEKCD 005*	**40**	2 wks

MISTURA featuring Lloyd MICHELS
US, male instrumental group, Lloyd Michels - trumpet　　10 wks

15 May 76	THE FLASHER *Route RT 30*	**23**	10 wks

Cameron MITCHELL - *See VARIOUS ARTISTS (EPs & LPs) - Carousel Soundtrack.*

Guy MITCHELL US, male vocalist　　163 wks

14 Nov 52	● FEET UP *Columbia DB 3151*	**2**	10 wks
13 Feb 53	★ SHE WEARS RED FEATHERS *Columbia DB 3238*	**1**	15 wks
24 Apr 53	● PRETTY LITTLE BLACK EYED SUSIE *Columbia DB 3255*	**2**	11 wks
12 Jun 53	SHE WEARS RED FEATHERS (re-entry) *Columbia DB 3238*	**12**	1 wk
28 Aug 53	★ LOOK AT THAT GIRL *Philips PB 162*	**1**	14 wks
6 Nov 53	● CHICKA BOOM *Philips PB 178*	**5**	9 wks
18 Dec 53	● CLOUD LUCKY SEVEN *Philips PB 210*	**1**	16 wks
15 Jan 54	● CHICKA BOOM (re-entry) *Philips PB 178*	**4**	6 wks
19 Feb 54	● CUFF OF MY SHIRT *Philips PB 225*	**9**	1 wk
26 Feb 54	SIPPIN' SODA *Philips PB 210*	**11**	1 wk
19 Mar 54	CUFF OF MY SHIRT (re-entry) *Philips PB 225*	**12**	1 wk
2 Apr 54	CUFF OF MY SHIRT (2nd re-entry) *Philips PB 225*	**11**	1 wk
30 Apr 54	● DIME AND A DOLLAR *Philips PB 248*	**8**	1 wk
14 May 54	● DIME AND A DOLLAR (re-entry) *Philips PB 248*	**8**	4 wks
7 Dec 56	★ SINGING THE BLUES *Philips PB 650*	**1**	22 wks
15 Feb 57	● KNEE DEEP IN THE BLUES *Philips PB 669*	**3**	12 wks
26 Apr 57	★ ROCK-A-BILLY *Philips PB 685*	**1**	14 wks
26 Jul 57	IN THE MIDDLE OF A DARK DARK NIGHT / SWEET STUFF *Philips PB 712*	**27**	2 wks
23 Aug 57	IN THE MIDDLE OF A DARK DARK NIGHT / SWEET STUFF (re-entry) *Philips PB 712*	**25**	2 wks
11 Oct 57	CALL ROSIE ON THE PHONE *Philips PB 743*	**17**	6 wks
27 Nov 59	● HEARTACHES BY THE NUMBER *Philips PB 964*	**26**	2 wks
18 Dec 59	● HEARTACHES BY THE NUMBER (re-entry) *Philips PB 964*	**5**	13 wks

Joni MITCHELL Canada, female vocalist　　15 wks

13 Jun 70	BIG YELLOW TAXI *Reprise RS 20906*	**11**	15 wks

Willie MITCHELL US, male instrumentalist - guitar　　3 wks

24 Apr 68	SOUL SERENADE *London HLU 10186*	**43**	1 wk
11 Dec 76	THE CHAMPION *London HL 10545*	**47**	2 wks

MIX FACTORY
UK, male/female vocal/instrumental group　　2 wks

30 Jan 93	TAKE ME AWAY (PARADISE) *All Around The World CDGLOBE 120*	**51**	2 wks

MIXMASTER Italy, male producer - Daniele Daroli　　10 wks

4 Nov 89	● GRAND PIANO *BCM BCM 344*	**9**	10 wks

MIXTURES Australia, male vocal/instrumental group　　21 wks

16 Jan 71	● THE PUSHBIKE SONG *Polydor 2058 083*	**2**	21 wks

Hank MIZELL US, male vocalist　　13 wks

20 Mar 76	● JUNGLE ROCK *Charly CS 1005*	**3**	13 wks

M.N.O. Belgium, male instrumental/production group　　2 wks

28 Sep 91	GOD OF ABRAHAM *A & M AM 820*	**66**	2 wks

MOBILES UK, male/female vocal/instrumental group　　14 wks

9 Jan 82	● DROWNING IN BERLIN *Rialto RIA 3*	**9**	10 wks
27 Mar 82	AMOUR AMOUR *Rialto RIA 5*	**45**	4 wks

MOBY US, male producer - Richard Hall　　22 wks

27 Jul 91	GO *Outer Rhythm FOOT 15*	**46**	3 wks
19 Oct 91	● GO (re-entry) *Outer Rhythm FOOT 15*	**10**	7 wks
3 Jul 93	I FEEL IT *Equinox AXISCD 001*	**38**	3 wks
11 Sep 93	MOVE *Mute CDMUTE 158*	**21**	5 wks
28 May 94	HYMN *Mute CDMUTE 161*	**31**	2 wks
29 Oct 94	FEELING SO REAL *Mute CDMUTE 173*	**30**	2 wks

MOCK TURTLES UK, male vocal/instrumental group　　15 wks

9 Mar 91	CAN YOU DIG IT *Siren SRN 136*	**18**	11 wks
29 Jun 91	AND THEN SHE SMILES *Siren SRN 139*	**44**	4 wks

MODERN LOVERS - *See Jonathan RICHMAN and the MODERN LOVERS*

MODERN ROMANCE
UK, male vocal/instrumental group　　77 wks

15 Aug 81	EVERYBODY SALSA *WEA K 18815*	**12**	10 wks
7 Nov 81	● AY AY AY AY MOOSEY *WEA K 18883*	**10**	12 wks
30 Jan 82	QUEEN OF THE RAPPING SCENE (NOTHING EVER GOES THE WAY YOU PLAN) *WEA K 18928*	**37**	8 wks
14 Aug 82	CHERRY PINK AND APPLE BLOSSOM WHITE *WEA K 19245* 1	**15**	8 wks
13 Nov 82	● BEST YEARS OF OUR LIVES *WEA ROM 1*	**4**	13 wks
26 Feb 83	● HIGH LIFE *WEA ROM 2*	**8**	8 wks
7 May 83	DON'T STOP THAT CRAZY RHYTHM *WEA ROM 3*	**14**	6 wks
6 Aug 83	● WALKING IN THE RAIN *WEA X 9733*	**7**	12 wks

1 Modern Romance featuring John du Prez

MODERN TALKING
Germany, male vocal/instrumental duo　　22 wks

15 Jun 85	YOU'RE MY HEART, YOU'RE MY SOUL *Magnet MAG 277*	**69**	2 wks
17 Aug 85	YOU'RE MY HEART, YOU'RE MY SOUL (re-entry) *Magnet MAG 277*	**56**	5 wks
12 Oct 85	YOU CAN WIN IF YOU WANT *Magnet MAG 282*	**70**	2 wks
16 Aug 86	● BROTHER LOUIE *RCA PB 40875*	**4**	10 wks
4 Oct 86	ATLANTIS IS CALLING (S.O.S. FOR LOVE) *RCA PB 40969*	**55**	3 wks

MODETTES UK, female vocal/instrumental group　　6 wks

12 Jul 80	PAINT IT BLACK *Deram DET-R 1*	**42**	5 wks
18 Jul 81	TONIGHT *Deram DET 3*	**68**	1 wk

Domenico MODUGNO Italy, male vocalist　　13 wks

5 Sep 58	● VOLARE *Oriole ICB 5000*	**10**	12 wks
27 Mar 59	CIAO CIAO BAMBINA *Oriole CB 1489*	**29**	1 wk

MOHAWKS Jamaica, male vocal / instrumental group — 2 wks

| 24 Jan 87 | THE CHAMP Pama PM 1 | 58 | 2 wks |

MOIST Canada, male vocal / instrumental group — 3 wks

| 12 Nov 94 | PUSH Chrysalis CDCHS 5016 | 35 | 3 wks |

MOJO UK, male instrumental group — 3 wks

| 22 Aug 81 | DANCE ON Creole CR 17 | 70 | 3 wks |

MOJOS UK, male vocal / instrumental group — 26 wks

26 Mar 64	● EVERYTHING'S ALRIGHT Decca F 11853	9	11 wks
11 Jun 64	WHY NOT TONIGHT Decca F 11918	25	10 wks
10 Sep 64	SEVEN DAFFODILS Decca F 11959	30	5 wks

Ralph MOLINA - See Ian McNABB

Sam MOLLISON - See SASHA

MOMENTS US, male vocal group — 32 wks

8 Mar 75	● GIRLS All Platinum 6146 302 [1]	3	10 wks
19 Jul 75	● DOLLY MY LOVE All Platinum 6146 306	10	9 wks
25 Oct 75	LOOK AT ME (I'M IN LOVE) All Platinum 6146 309	42	4 wks
22 Jan 77	● JACK IN THE BOX All Platinum 6146 318	7	9 wks

[1] Moments and Whatnauts

Jay MONDI and the LIVING BASS
US, male / female vocal / instrumental group — 3 wks

| 24 Mar 90 | ALL NIGHT LONG 10 TEN 304 | 63 | 3 wks |

MONDO KANE UK, male vocal / instrumental group — 2 wks

| 16 Aug 86 | NEW YORK AFTERNOON Lisson DOLE 2 | 70 | 2 wks |

Zoot MONEY and the BIG ROLL BAND
UK, male vocal / instrumental — 8 wks

| 18 Aug 66 | BIG TIME OPERATOR Columbia DB 7975 | 25 | 8 wks |

T.S. MONK US, male / female vocal / instrumental group — 6 wks

| 7 Mar 81 | BON BON VIE Mirage K 11653 | 63 | 2 wks |
| 25 Apr 81 | CANDIDATE FOR LOVE Mirage K 11648 | 58 | 4 wks |

MONKEES US / UK, male vocal / instrumental group — 101 wks

5 Jan 67	★ I'M A BELIEVER RCA 1560	1	17 wks
26 Jan 67	LAST TRAIN TO CLARKSVILLE RCA 1547	23	7 wks
6 Apr 67	● A LITTLE BIT ME A LITTLE BIT YOU RCA 1580	3	12 wks
22 Jun 67	● ALTERNATE TITLE RCA 1604	2	12 wks
16 Aug 67	PLEASANT VALLEY SUNDAY RC 1620	11	8 wks
15 Nov 67	● DAYDREAM BELIEVER RCA 1645	5	17 wks
27 Mar 68	VALLERI RCA 1673	12	8 wks
26 Jun 68	D.W. WASHBURN RCA 1706	17	6 wks
26 Mar 69	TEARDROP CITY RCA 1802	46	1 wk
25 Jun 69	SOMEDAY MAN RCA 1824	47	1 wk
15 Mar 80	THE MONKEES EP Arista ARIST 326	33	9 wks
18 Oct 86	THAT WAS THEN, THIS IS NOW Arista ARIST 673	68	1 wk
1 Apr 89	THE MONKEES EP Arista 112157	62	2 wks

Tracks on Arista 326 EP: I'm a Believer / Daydream Believer / Last Train to Clarksville / A Little Bit Me A Little Bit You. Tracks on Arista 112157 EP: Daydream Believer / Monkees Theme / Last Train To Clarksville.

MONKS UK, male vocal / instrumental duo — 9 wks

| 21 Apr 79 | NICE LEGS SHAME ABOUT HER FACE Carrere CAR 104 | 19 | 9 wks |

The Monks were Hudson-Ford under a different name.

Matt MONRO UK, male vocalist — 127 wks

15 Dec 60	● PORTRAIT OF MY LOVE Parlophone R 4714	3	16 wks
9 Mar 61	● MY KIND OF GIRL Parlophone R 4755	5	12 wks
18 May 61	WHY NOT NOW / CAN THIS BE LOVE Parlophone R 4775	24	9 wks
28 Sep 61	GONNA BUILD A MOUNTAIN Parlophone R 4819	44	3 wks
8 Feb 62	● SOFTLY AS I LEAVE YOU Parlophone R 4868	10	18 wks
14 Jun 62	WHEN LOVE COMES ALONG Parlophone R 4911	46	3 wks
8 Nov 62	MY LOVE AND DEVOTION Parlophone R 4954	29	5 wks
14 Nov 63	FROM RUSSIA WITH LOVE Parlophone R 5068	20	13 wks
17 Sep 64	● WALK AWAY Parlophone R 5171	4	20 wks
24 Dec 64	FOR MAMA Parlophone R 5215	36	4 wks
25 Mar 65	WITHOUT YOU Parlophone R 5251	37	4 wks
21 Oct 65	● YESTERDAY Parlophone R 5348	8	12 wks
24 Nov 73	AND YOU SMILED EMI 2091	28	8 wks

Gerry MONROE UK, male vocalist — 57 wks

23 May 70	● SALLY Chapter One CH 122	4	20 wks
19 Sep 70	CRY Chapter One CH 128	38	5 wks
14 Nov 70	● MY PRAYER Chapter One CH 132	9	12 wks
17 Apr 71	IT'S A SIN TO TELL A LIE Chapter One CH 144	13	12 wks
21 Aug 71	LITTLE DROPS OF SILVER Chapter One CH 152	37	6 wks
12 Feb 72	GIRL OF MY DREAMS Chapter One CH 159	43	2 wks

MONSOON UK, male / female vocal / instrumental group — 12 wks

| 3 Apr 82 | EVER SO LONELY Mobile Suit Corp CORP 2 | 12 | 9 wks |
| 5 Jun 82 | SHAKTI (THE MEANING OF WITHIN) Mobile Suit Corp CORP 4 | 41 | 3 wks |

MONSTER MAGNET
US, male vocal / instrumental group — 1 wk

| 29 May 93 | TWIN EARTH A & M 5802812 | 67 | 1 wk |

MONTANA SEXTET
US, male / female vocal / instrumental group — 1 wk

| 15 Jan 83 | HEAVY VIBES Virgin VS 560 | 59 | 1 wk |

Hugo MONTENEGRO US, orchestra — 26 wks

11 Sep 68	★ THE GOOD THE BAD AND THE UGLY RCA 1727	1	24 wks
8 Jan 69	HANG 'EM HIGH RCA 1771	50	1 wk
19 Mar 69	THE GOOD THE BAD AND THE UGLY (re-entry) RCA 1727	48	1 wk

Chris MONTEZ US, male vocalist — 61 wks

4 Oct 62	● LET'S DANCE London HLU 9596	2	18 wks
17 Jan 63	● SOME KINDA FUN London HLU 9650	10	9 wks
30 Jun 66	● THE MORE I SEE YOU Pye International 7N 25369	3	13 wks
22 Sep 66	THERE WILL NEVER BE ANOTHER YOU Pye International 7N 25381	37	4 wks
14 Oct 72	● LET'S DANCE (re-issue) London HL 10205	9	14 wks
14 Apr 79	LET'S DANCE (2nd re-issue) Lightning LIG 9011	47	3 wks

The second re-issue of Let's Dance on Lightning was coupled with Memphis by Lonnie Mack as a double A-side.

MONTROSE US, male vocal / instrumental group — 2 wks

| 28 Jun 80 | SPACE STATION NO. 5 / GOOD ROCKIN' TONIGHT WB HM 9 | 71 | 2 wks |

MONTY PYTHON UK, male comedy group — 9 wks

| 5 Oct 91 | ● ALWAYS LOOK ON THE BRIGHT SIDE OF LIFE Virgin PYTH 1 | 3 | 9 wks |

MONYAKA US / Jamaica, male vocal / instrumental group — 8 wks

| 10 Sep 83 | GO DEH YAKA (GO TO THE TOP) Polydor POSP 641 | 14 | 8 wks |

MOOD *UK, male vocal / instrumental group*   **10 wks**

6 Feb 82	**DON'T STOP** *RCA 171*	**59**	4 wks
22 May 82	**PARIS IS ONE DAY AWAY** *RCA 211*	**42**	5 wks
30 Oct 82	**PASSION IN DARK ROOMS** *RCA 276*	**74**	1 wk

MOODSWINGS featuring Chrissie HYNDE
UK / US, male / female vocal / instrumental group   **4 wks**

12 Oct 91	**SPIRITUAL HIGH (STATE OF INDEPENDENCE)** *Arista 114528*	**66**	2 wks
23 Jan 93	**SPIRITUAL HIGH (re-issue)** *Arista 74321127712*	**47**	2 wks

MOODY BLUES *UK, male vocal / instrumental group*   **114 wks**

10 Dec 64	★ **GO NOW** *Decca F 12022*	**1**	14 wks
4 Mar 65	**I DON'T WANT TO GO ON WITHOUT YOU** *Decca F 12095*	**33**	9 wks
10 Jun 65	**FROM THE BOTTOM OF MY HEART** *Decca F 12166* ..	**22**	9 wks
18 Nov 65	**EVERYDAY** *Decca F 12266*	**44**	2 wks
27 Dec 67	**NIGHTS IN WHITE SATIN** *Deram DM 161*	**19**	11 wks
7 Aug 68	**VOICES IN THE SKY** *Deram DM 196*	**27**	10 wks
4 Dec 68	**RIDE MY SEE-SAW** *Deram DM 213*	**42**	1 wk
2 May 70	● **QUESTION** *Threshold TH 4*	**2**	12 wks
6 May 72	**ISN'T LIFE STRANGE** *Threshold TH 9*	**13**	10 wks
2 Dec 72	● **NIGHTS IN WHITE SATIN (re-entry)** *Deram DM 161* ..	**9**	11 wks
10 Feb 73	**I'M JUST A SINGER (IN A ROCK 'N' ROLL BAND)** *Threshold TH 13*	**36**	4 wks
10 Nov 79	**NIGHTS IN WHITE SATIN (2nd re-entry)** *Deram DM 161*	**14**	12 wks
20 Aug 83	**BLUE WORLD** *Threshold TH 30*	**35**	5 wks
25 Jun 88	**I KNOW YOU'RE OUT THERE SOMEWHERE** *Polydor POSP 921*	**52**	4 wks

MOONTREKKERS *UK, male instrumental group*   **1 wk**

2 Nov 61	**NIGHT OF THE VAMPIRE** *Parlophone R 4814*	**50**	1 wk

Chante MOORE *US, female vocalist*   **3 wks**

20 Mar 93	**LOVE'S TAKEN OVER** *MCA MCSTD 1744*	**54**	3 wks

Dorothy MOORE *US, female vocalist*   **24 wks**

19 Jun 76	● **MISTY BLUE** *Contempo CS 2087*	**5**	12 wks
16 Oct 76	**FUNNY HOW TIME SLIPS AWAY** *Contempo CS 2092*	**38**	3 wks
15 Oct 77	**I BELIEVE YOU** *Epic EPC 5573*	**20**	9 wks

Dudley MOORE - *See Peter COOK*

Gary MOORE
UK, male vocalist / instrumentalist - guitar   **101 wks**

21 Apr 79	● **PARISIENNE WALKWAYS** *MCA 419*	**8**	11 wks
21 Jan 84	**HOLD ON TO LOVE** *10 TEN 13*	**65**	3 wks
11 Aug 84	**EMPTY ROOMS** *10 TEN 25*	**51**	5 wks
18 May 85	● **OUT IN THE FIELDS** *10 TEN 49* [1]	**5**	10 wks
27 Jul 85	**EMPTY ROOMS (re-issue)** *10 TEN 58*	**23**	8 wks
20 Dec 86	**OVER THE HILLS AND FAR AWAY** *10 TEN 134*	**20**	8 wks
28 Feb 87	**WILD FRONTIER** *10 TEN 159*	**35**	5 wks
9 May 87	**FRIDAY ON MY MIND** *10 TEN 164*	**26**	6 wks
29 Aug 87	**THE LONER** *10 TEN 178*	**53**	5 wks
5 Dec 87	**TAKE A LITTLE TIME (DOUBLE SINGLE)** *10 TEN 190* ..	**75**	1 wk
14 Jan 89	**AFTER THE WAR** *Virgin GMS 1*	**37**	4 wks
18 Mar 89	**READY FOR LOVE** *Virgin GMS 2*	**56**	2 wks
24 Mar 90	**OH PRETTY WOMAN** *Virgin VS 1233* [2]	**48**	3 wks
12 May 90	**STILL GOT THE BLUES (FOR YOU)** *Virgin VS 1267*	**31**	7 wks
18 Aug 90	**WALKING BY MYSELF** *Virgin VS 1281*	**48**	5 wks
15 Dec 90	**TOO TIRED** *Virgin VS 1306*	**71**	1 wk
22 Feb 92	**COLD DAY IN HELL** *Virgin VS 1393*	**24**	5 wks
9 May 92	**STORY OF THE BLUES** *Virgin VS 1412*	**40**	4 wks
18 Jul 92	**SINCE I MET YOU BABY** *Virgin VS 1423* [3]	**59**	3 wks
24 Oct 92	**SEPARATE WAYS** *Virgin VS 1437*	**59**	1 wk
8 May 93	**PARISIENNE WALKWAYS (re-mix)** *Virgin VSCDX 1456*	**32**	4 wks

[1] Gary Moore and Phil Lynott [2] Gary Moore featuring Albert King [3] Gary Moore and B.B. King

Parisienne Walkways features uncredited vocals by Phil Lynott. Tracks on double single: Take A Little Time / Out In The Fields / All Messed Up / Thunder Rising.

Jackie MOORE *US, female vocalist*   **5 wks**

15 Sep 79	**THIS TIME BABY** *CBS 7722*	**49**	5 wks

Melba MOORE *US, female vocalist*   **29 wks**

15 May 76	● **THIS IS IT** *Buddah BDS 443*	**9**	8 wks
26 May 79	**PICK ME UP I'LL DANCE** *Epic EPC 7234*	**48**	5 wks
9 Oct 82	**LOVE'S COMIN' AT YA** *EMI America EA 146*	**15**	8 wks
15 Jan 83	**MIND UP TONIGHT** *Capitol CL 272*	**22**	6 wks
5 Mar 83	**UNDERLOVE** *Capitol CL 281*	**60**	2 wks

Ray MOORE *UK, male vocalist*   **9 wks**

29 Nov 86	**O' MY FATHER HAD A RABBIT** *Play PLAY 213*	**24**	7 wks
5 Dec 87	**BOG EYED JOG** *Play PLAY 224*	**61**	2 wks

Sam MOORE - *See SAM and DAVE; Lou REED*

David MORALES and the BAD YARD CLUB
US, male producer   **4 wks**

10 Jul 93	**GIMME LUV (EENIE MEENIE MINY MO)** *Mercury MERCD 390*	**37**	3 wks
20 Nov 93	**THE PROGRAM** *Mercury MERCD 396*	**66**	1 wk

See also Boss.

Mike MORAN - *See Lynsey DE PAUL*

MORE *UK, male vocal / instrumental group*   **2 wks**

14 Mar 81	**WE ARE THE BAND** *Atlantic K 11561*	**59**	2 wks

Derrick MORGAN *Jamaica, male vocalist*   **1 wk**

17 Jan 70	**MOON HOP** *Crab 32*	**49**	1 wk

Jamie J. MORGAN *US, male vocalist*   **6 wks**

10 Feb 90	**WALK ON THE WILD SIDE** *Tabu 655596 7*	**27**	6 wks

Jane MORGAN *US, female vocalist*   **22 wks**

5 Dec 58	★ **THE DAY THE RAINS CAME** *London HLR 8751*	**1**	16 wks
22 May 59	**IF ONLY I COULD LIVE MY LIFE AGAIN** *London HLR 8810*	**27**	1 wk
21 Jul 60	**ROMANTICA** *London HLR 9120*	**39**	5 wks

Meli'sa MORGAN *US, female vocalist*   **7 wks**

9 Aug 86	**FOOL'S PARADISE** *Capitol CL 415*	**41**	5 wks
25 Jun 88	**GOOD LOVE** *Capitol CL 483*	**59**	2 wks

Ray MORGAN *UK, male vocalist*   **6 wks**

25 Jul 70	**THE LONG AND WINDING ROAD** *B & C CB 128*	**32**	6 wks

Giorgio MORODER
Italy, male instrumentalist - synthesizer   **34 wks**

24 Sep 77	**FROM HERE TO ETERNITY** *Oasis 1* [1]	**16**	10 wks

17 Mar 79	**CHASE** Casablanca CAN 144	**48** 6 wks
22 Sep 84	● **TOGETHER IN ELECTRIC DREAMS**	
	Virgin VS 713 [2]	**3** 13 wks
29 Jun 85	**GOODBYE BAD TIMES** Virgin VS 772 [2]	**44** 5 wks

[1] Giorgio [2] Giorgio Moroder and Phil Oakey

Ennio MORRICONE *Italy, orchestra*　　　**12 wks**

11 Apr 81	● **CHI MAI (THEME FROM THE TV SERIES 'THE LIFE AND TIMES OF DAVID LLOYD GEORGE')**	
	BBC RESL 92	**2** 12 wks

Sarah Jane MORRIS - *See COMMUNARDS*

Diana MORRISON - *See Michael BALL*

Dorothy Combs MORRISON - *See Edwin HAWKINS SINGERS featuring Dorothy Combs MORRISON*

Van MORRISON *UK, male vocalist*　　　**13 wks**

20 Oct 79	**BRIGHT SIDE OF THE ROAD** Mercury 6001 121	**63** 3 wks
1 Jul 89	**HAVE I TOLD YOU LATELY** Polydor VANS 1	**74** 1 wk
9 Dec 89	**WHENEVER GOD SHINES HIS LIGHT**	
	Polydor VANS 2 [1]	**20** 6 wks
15 May 93	**GLORIA** Exile VANCD 11 [2]	**31** 3 wks

[1] Van Morrison with Cliff Richard [2] Van Morrison and John Lee Hooker

MORRISSEY *UK, male vocalist*　　　**59 wks**

27 Feb 88	● **SUEDEHEAD** HMV POP 1618	**5** 6 wks
11 Jun 88	● **EVERYDAY IS LIKE SUNDAY** HMV POP 1619	**9** 6 wks
11 Feb 89	● **LAST OF THE FAMOUS INTERNATIONAL PLAYBOYS**	
	HMV POP 1620	**6** 5 wks
29 Apr 89	● **INTERESTING DRUG** HMV POP 1621	**9** 4 wks
25 Nov 89	**OUIJA BOARD OUIJA BOARD** HMV POP 1622	**18** 4 wks
5 May 90	**NOVEMBER SPAWNED A MONSTER**	
	HMV POP 1623	**12** 4 wks
20 Oct 90	**PICCADILLY PALARE** HMV POP 1624	**18** 2 wks
23 Feb 91	**OUR FRANK** HMV POP 1625	**26** 3 wks
13 Apr 91	**SING YOUR LIFE** HMV POP 1626	**33** 2 wks
27 Jul 91	**PREGNANT FOR THE LAST TIME** HMV POP 1627	**25** 4 wks
12 Oct 91	**MY LOVE LIFE** HMV POP 1628	**29** 2 wks
9 May 92	**WE HATE IT WHEN OUR FRIENDS BECOME SUCCESSFUL** HMV POP 1629	**17** 3 wks
18 Jul 92	**YOU'RE THE ONE FOR ME, FATTY** HMV POP 1630	**19** 3 wks
19 Dec 92	**CERTAIN PEOPLE I KNOW** HMV POP 1631	**35** 4 wks
12 Mar 94	● **THE MORE YOU IGNORE ME THE CLOSER I GET**	
	Parlophone CDR 6372	**8** 3 wks
11 Jun 94	**HOLD ON TO YOUR FRIENDS**	
	Parlophone CDR 6383	**47** 2 wks
20 Aug 94	**INTERLUDE** Parlophone CDR 6365 [1]	**25** 2 wks

[1] Morrissey and Siouxsie

MORRISTON ORPHEUS MALE VOICE CHOIR - *See ALARM*

Buddy MORROW *US, orchestra*　　　**1 wk**

20 Mar 53	**NIGHT TRAIN** HMV B 10347	**12** 1 wk

Mickie MOST *UK, male vocalist*　　　**1 wk**

25 Jul 63	**MISTER PORTER** Decca F 11664	**45** 1 wk

MOTELS *US/UK, male/female vocal/instrumental group*　　　**7 wks**

11 Oct 80	**WHOSE PROBLEM?** Capitol CL 16162	**42** 4 wks
10 Jan 81	**DAYS ARE O.K.** Capitol CL 16149	**41** 3 wks

Wendy MOTEN *US, female vocalist*　　　**13 wks**

5 Feb 94	● **COME IN OUT OF THE RAIN** EMI-USA CDMT 105	**8** 9 wks
14 May 94	**SO CLOSE TO LOVE** EMI-USA CDMTS 106	**35** 4 wks

MOTHER *UK, male instrumental/production duo*　　　**3 wks**

12 Jun 93	**ALL FUNKED UP** Bosting BYSNCD 101	**34** 2 wks
1 Oct 94	**GET BACK** Six6 SIXT 119	**73** 1 wk

MOTIV 8 *UK, male producer - Steve Rodway*　　　**5 wks**

17 Jul 93	**ROCKIN' FOR MYSELF**	
	Nuff Respect NUFF 002CD [1]	**67** 1 wk
7 May 94	**ROCKIN' FOR MYSELF (re-mix)** WEA YZ 814CD	**18** 4 wks

[1] Motiv 8 featuring Angie Brown

MOTLEY CRUE *US, male vocal/instrumental group*　　　**27 wks**

24 Aug 85	**SMOKIN' IN THE BOYS ROOM** Elektra EKR 16	**71** 2 wks
8 Feb 86	**HOME SWEET HOME/SMOKIN' IN THE BOYS ROOM (re-issue)** Elektra EKR 33	**51** 3 wks
1 Aug 87	**GIRLS GIRLS GIRLS** Elektra EKR 59	**26** 6 wks
16 Jan 88	**YOU'RE ALL I NEED/WILD SIDE** Elektra EKR 65	**23** 4 wks
4 Nov 89	**DR. FEELGOOD** Elektra EKR 97	**50** 3 wks
12 May 90	**WITHOUT YOU** Elektra EKR 109	**39** 3 wks
7 Sep 91	**PRIMAL SCREAM** Elektra EKR 133	**32** 2 wks
11 Jan 92	**HOME SWEET HOME (re-mix)** Elektra EKR 136	**37** 2 wks
5 Mar 94	**HOOLIGAN'S HOLIDAY** Elektra EKR 180CDX	**36** 2 wks

Wild Side only listed with You're All I Need from 30 Jan 88. It peaked at position 26.

MOTORHEAD *UK, male vocal/instrumental group*　　　**81 wks**

16 Sep 78	**LOUIE LOUIE** Bronze BRO 60	**75** 1 wk
30 Sep 78	**LOUIE LOUIE (re-entry)** Bronze BRO 60	**68** 1 wk
10 Mar 79	**OVERKILL** Bronze BRO 67	**39** 4 wks
14 Apr 79	**OVERKILL (re-entry)** Bronze BRO 67	**57** 3 wks
30 Jun 79	**NO CLASS** Bronze BRO 78	**61** 4 wks
1 Dec 79	**BOMBER** Bronze BRO 85	**34** 7 wks
3 May 80	● **THE GOLDEN YEARS EP** Bronze BRO 92	**8** 7 wks
1 Nov 80	**ACE OF SPADES** Bronze BRO 106	**15** 12 wks
22 Nov 80	**BEER DRINKERS AND HELL RAISERS**	
	Big Beat SWT 61	**43** 4 wks
21 Feb 81	● **ST. VALENTINE'S DAY MASSACRE EP**	
	Bronze BRO 116 [1]	**5** 8 wks
11 Jul 81	● **MOTORHEAD LIVE** Bronze BRO 124	**6** 7 wks
3 Apr 82	**IRON FIST** Bronze BRO 146	**29** 5 wks
21 May 83	**I GOT MINE** Bronze BRO 165	**46** 2 wks
30 Jul 83	**SHINE** Bronze BRO 167	**59** 2 wks
1 Sep 84	**KILLED BY DEATH** Bronze BRO 185	**51** 2 wks
5 Jul 86	**DEAF FOREVER** GWR GWR 2	**67** 1 wk
5 Jan 91	**THE ONE TO SING THE BLUES** Epic 6565787	**45** 3 wks
14 Nov 92	**'92 TOUR EP** Epic 6588096	**63** 1 wk
11 Sep 93	**ACE OF SPADES (re-mix)** WGAF CDWGAF 101	**23** 5 wks
10 Dec 94	**BORN TO RAISE HELL** Fox 74321230152 [2]	**47** 2 wks

[1] Motorhead and Girlschool (also known as Headgirl) [2] Motorhead/Ice-T/Whitfield Crane

Tracks on The Golden Years EP: Dead Men Tell No Tales/Too Late Too Late/Leaving Here/Stone Dead Forever. Tracks on St. Valentine's Day Massacre EP: Please Don't Touch/Emergency/Bomber. Tracks on '92 Tour EP: Hellraiser/You Better Run/Going To Brazil/Ramones.

MOTORS *UK, male vocal/instrumental group*　　　**29 wks**

24 Sep 77	**DANCING THE NIGHT AWAY** Virgin VS 186	**42** 4 wks
10 Jun 78	● **AIRPORT** Virgin VS 219	**4** 13 wks
19 Aug 78	**FORGET ABOUT YOU** Virgin VS 222	**13** 9 wks
12 Apr 80	**LOVE AND LONELINESS** Virgin VS 263	**58** 3 wks

MOTOWN SPINNERS - *See DETROIT SPINNERS*

MOTT THE HOOPLE
UK, male vocal/instrumental group　　　**55 wks**

12 Aug 72	● **ALL THE YOUNG DUDES** CBS 8271	**3** 11 wks

British Hit Singles Part One: Alphabetically by Artist
Date of chart entry/Title & catalogue no./Peak position reached/Weeks on chart
★ Number One ● Top Ten † still on chart at 31 Dec 1994
□ = credited to act billed in footnote

16 Jun 73	**HONALOOCHIE BOOGIE** CBS 1530	**12**	9 wks
8 Sep 73 ●	**ALL THE WAY FROM MEMPHIS** CBS 1764	**10**	8 wks
24 Nov 73 ●	**ROLL AWAY THE STONE** CBS 1895	**8**	12 wks
30 Mar 74	**GOLDEN AGE OF ROCK AND ROLL** CBS 2177	**16**	7 wks
22 Jun 74	**FOXY FOXY** CBS 2439	**33**	5 wks
2 Nov 74	**SATURDAY GIGS** CBS 2754	**41**	3 wks

Nana MOUSKOURI Greece, female vocalist   11 wks

11 Jan 86 ●	**ONLY LOVE** Philips PH 38	**2**	11 wks

MOUTH and MACNEAL
Holland, male/female vocal duo   10 wks

4 May 74 ●	**I SEE A STAR** Decca F 13504	**8**	10 wks

MOVE UK, male vocal/instrumental group   110 wks

5 Jan 67 ●	**NIGHT OF FEAR** Deram DM 109	**2**	10 wks
6 Apr 67 ●	**I CAN HEAR THE GRASS GROW** Deram DM 117	**5**	10 wks
6 Sep 67 ●	**FLOWERS IN THE RAIN** Regal Zonophone RZ3001	**2**	13 wks
7 Feb 68 ●	**FIRE BRIGADE** Regal Zonophone RZ3005	**3**	11 wks
25 Dec 68 ★	**BLACKBERRY WAY** Regal Zonophone RZ3015	**1**	12 wks
23 Jul 69	**CURLY** Regal Zonophone RZ3021	**12**	12 wks
25 Apr 70 ●	**BRONTOSAURUS** Regal Zonophone RZ3026	**7**	10 wks
3 Jul 71	**TONIGHT** Harvest HAR 5038	**11**	10 wks
23 Oct 71	**CHINATOWN** Harvest HAR 5043	**23**	8 wks
13 May 72 ●	**CALIFORNIA MAN** Harvest HAR 5050	**7**	14 wks

MOVEMENT US, male vocal/instrumental group   2 wks

24 Oct 92	**JUMP!** Arista 74321116677	**57**	2 wks

MOVEMENT 98 featuring Carroll THOMPSON
UK, male/female vocal/instrumental group   8 wks

19 May 90	**JOY AND HEARTBREAK** Circa YR 45	**27**	5 wks
15 Sep 90	**SUNRISE** Circa YR 51	**58**	3 wks

See also Courtney Pine.

MOVIN MELODIES PRODUCTION
UK, male instrumental/production duo   1 wk

22 Oct 94	**LA LUNA** Effective EFFS 017CD	**64**	1 wk

Alison MOYET UK, female vocalist   105 wks

23 Jun 84 ●	**LOVE RESURRECTION** CBS A 4497	**10**	11 wks
13 Oct 84 ●	**ALL CRIED OUT** CBS A 4757	**8**	11 wks
1 Dec 84	**INVISIBLE** CBS A 4930	**21**	10 wks
16 Mar 85 ●	**THAT OLE DEVIL CALLED LOVE** CBS A 6044	**2**	10 wks
29 Nov 86 ●	**IS THIS LOVE?** CBS MOYET 1	**3**	16 wks
7 Mar 87 ●	**WEAK IN THE PRESENCE OF BEAUTY** CBS MOYET 2	**6**	10 wks
30 May 87	**ORDINARY GIRL** CBS MOYET 3	**43**	4 wks
28 Nov 87 ●	**LOVE LETTERS** CBS MOYET 5	**4**	10 wks
6 Apr 91	**IT WON'T BE LONG** Columbia 6567577	**50**	4 wks
1 Jun 91	**WISHING YOU WERE HERE** Columbia 6569397	**72**	1 wk
12 Oct 91	**THIS HOUSE** Columbia 6575157	**40**	5 wks
12 Mar 93	**WHISPERING YOUR NAME** Columbia 6601622	**18**	7 wks
16 Oct 93	**FALLING** Columbia 6595962	**42**	3 wks
28 May 94	**GETTING INTO SOMETHING** Columbia 6603565	**51**	2 wks
22 Oct 94	**ODE TO BOY** Columbia 6607952	**59**	1 wk

MTUME US, male/female vocal/instrumental group   12 wks

14 May 83	**JUICY FRUIT** Epic A 3424	**34**	9 wks
22 Sep 84	**PRIME TIME** Epic A 4720	**57**	3 wks

MUD UK, male vocal/instrumental group   139 wks

10 Mar 73	**CRAZY** RAK 146	**12**	12 wks
23 Jun 73	**HYPNOSIS** RAK 152	**16**	13 wks
27 Oct 73 ●	**DYNA-MITE** RAK 159	**4**	12 wks
19 Jan 74 ★	**TIGER FEET** RAK 166	**1**	11 wks
13 Apr 74 ●	**THE CAT CREPT IN** RAK 170	**2**	9 wks
27 Jul 74 ●	**ROCKET** RAK 178	**6**	9 wks
30 Nov 74 ●	**LONELY THIS CHRISTMAS** RAK 187	**1**	10 wks
15 Feb 75 ●	**THE SECRETS THAT YOU KEEP** RAK 194	**3**	9 wks
26 Apr 75 ★	**OH BOY** RAK 201	**1**	9 wks
21 Jun 75 ●	**MOONSHINE SALLY** RAK 208	**10**	7 wks
2 Aug 75	**ONE NIGHT** RAK 213	**32**	4 wks
4 Oct 75 ●	**L-L-LUCY** Private Stock PVT 41	**10**	6 wks
29 Nov 75 ●	**SHOW ME YOU'RE A WOMAN** Private Stock PVT 45	**8**	8 wks
15 May 76 ●	**SHAKE IT DOWN** Private Stock PVT 65	**12**	8 wks
27 Nov 76 ●	**LEAN ON ME** Private Stock PVT 85	**7**	9 wks
21 Dec 85	**LONELY THIS CHRISTMAS** (re-entry) RAK 187	**61**	3 wks

MUDHONEY US, male vocal/instrumental group   2 wks

17 Aug 91	**LET IT SLIDE** Subpop SP 15154	**60**	1 wk
24 Oct 92	**SUCK YOU DRY** Reprise W 0137	**65**	1 wk

MUDLARKS UK, male/female vocal group   19 wks

2 May 58 ●	**LOLLIPOP** Columbia DB 4099	**2**	9 wks
6 Jun 58 ●	**BOOK OF LOVE** Columbia DB 4133	**8**	9 wks
27 Feb 59	**THE LOVE GAME** Columbia DB 4250	**30**	1 wk

MUFFINS - See MARTHA and the MUFFINS

Idris MUHAMMAD US, male vocalist   3 wks

17 Sep 77	**COULD HEAVEN EVER BE LIKE THIS** Kudu 935	**42**	3 wks

MUKKAA UK, male instrumental/production duo   1 wk

27 Feb 93	**BURUCHACCA** Limbo LIMBO 008	**74**	1 wk

Maria MULDAUR US, female vocalist   8 wks

29 Jun 74	**MIDNIGHT AT THE OASIS** Reprise K 14331	**21**	8 wks

Arthur MULLARD - See Hylda BAKER and Arthur MULLARD

Coati MUNDI - See Kid CREOLE and the COCONUTS

MUNGO JERRY UK, male vocal/instrumental group   87 wks

6 Jun 70 ★	**IN THE SUMMERTIME** Dawn DNX 2502	**1**	20 wks
6 Feb 71	**BABY JUMP** Dawn DNX 2505	**32**	1 wk
20 Feb 71 ★	**BABY JUMP** (re-entry) Dawn DNX 2505	**1**	12 wks
29 May 71 ●	**LADY ROSE** Dawn DNX 2510	**5**	12 wks
18 Sep 71	**YOU DON'T HAVE TO BE IN THE ARMY TO FIGHT IN THE WAR** Dawn DNX 2513	**13**	8 wks
22 Apr 72	**OPEN UP** Dawn DNX 2514	**21**	8 wks
7 Jul 73 ●	**ALRIGHT ALRIGHT ALRIGHT** Dawn DNS 1037	**3**	12 wks
10 Nov 73	**WILD LOVE** Dawn DNS 1051	**32**	5 wks
6 Apr 74	**LONGLEGGED WOMAN DRESSED IN BLACK** Dawn DNS 1061	**13**	9 wks

MUNICH MACHINE
Germany, male instrumental group   8 wks

10 Dec 77	**GET ON THE FUNK TRAIN** Oasis OASIS 2	**41**	4 wks

4 Nov 78 **A WHITER SHADE OF PALE** *Oasis* OASIS 5 [1] ....**42** 4 wks

[1] Munich Machine introducing Chris Bennett

David MUNROW - *See EARLY MUSIC CONSORT*

MUPPETS *US, puppets*   **15 wks**

28 May 77 ● **HALFWAY DOWN THE STAIRS** *Pye 7N 45698*.............**7** 8 wks
17 Dec 77   **THE MUPPET SHOW MUSIC HALL EP**
        Pye 7NX 8004 ....**19** 7 wks

Halfway Down the Stairs is sung by Jerry Nelson as Kermit the Frog's nephew, Robin. Tracks on The Muppet Show Music Hall EP: Don't Dilly Dally On The Way / Waiting At The Church / The Boy In The Gallery / Wotcher (Knocked 'Em In The Old Kent Road).

Lydia MURDOCK *US, female vocalist*   **9 wks**

24 Sep 83   **SUPERSTAR** *Korova KOW 30* ....**14** 9 wks

Shirley MURDOCK *US, female vocalist*   **2 wks**

12 Apr 86   **TRUTH OR DARE** *Elektra EKR 36* ....**60** 2 wks

Eddie MURPHY *US, male vocalist*   **1 wk**

6 Mar 93   **I WAS A KING** *Motown TMGCD 1414* ....**64** 1 wk

Noel MURPHY *Ireland, male vocalist*   **4 wks**

27 Jun 87   **MURPHY AND THE BRICKS** *Murphy's STACK 1* ....**57** 4 wks

Walter MURPHY and the BIG APPLE BAND
US, orchestra   **9 wks**

10 Jul 76   **A FIFTH OF BEETHOVEN** *Private Stock PVT 59* ....**28** 9 wks

Anne MURRAY *Canada, female vocalist*   **40 wks**

24 Oct 70   **SNOWBIRD** *Capitol CL 15654* ....**23** 17 wks
21 Oct 72   **DESTINY** *Capitol CL 15734* ....**41** 4 wks
9 Dec 78   **YOU NEEDED ME** *Capitol CL 16011*.......**22** 14 wks
21 Apr 79   **I JUST FALL IN LOVE AGAIN** *Capitol CL 16069* ....**58** 2 wks
19 Apr 80   **DAYDREAM BELIEVER** *Capitol CL 16123* ....**61** 3 wks

Pauline MURRAY and the INVISIBLE GIRLS
UK, female vocalist with male (really) vocal / instrumental group   **2 wks**

2 Aug 80   **DREAM SEQUENCE (ONE)** *Illusive IVE 1* ....**67** 2 wks

Ruby MURRAY *UK, female vocalist*   **110 wks**

3 Dec 54 ● **HEARTBEAT** *Columbia DB 3542* ....**3** 16 wks
28 Jan 55 ★ **SOFTLY SOFTLY** *Columbia DB 3558* ....**1** 22 wks
4 Feb 55 ● **HAPPY DAYS AND LONELY NIGHTS**
        Columbia DB 3577 ....**6** 8 wks
4 Mar 55 ● **LET ME GO LOVER** *Columbia DB 3577* ....**5** 7 wks
18 Mar 55 ● **IF ANYONE FINDS THIS I LOVE YOU**
        Columbia DB 3580 [1] ....**4** 11 wks
1 Jul 55 ● **EVERMORE** *Columbia DB 3617* ....**3** 17 wks
8 Jul 55   **SOFTLY SOFTLY (re-entry)** *Columbia DB 3558* ....**20** 1 wk
14 Oct 55 ● **I'LL COME WHEN YOU CALL** *Columbia DB 3643* ....**6** 7 wks
31 Aug 56   **YOU ARE MY FIRST LOVE** *Columbia DB 3770* ....**16** 4 wks
5 Oct 56   **YOU ARE MY FIRST LOVE (re-entry)**
        Columbia DB 3770 ....**21** 1 wk
12 Dec 58   **REAL LOVE** *Columbia DB 4192*.......**18** 6 wks
5 Jun 59 ● **GOODBYE JIMMY GOODBYE** *Columbia DB 4305* ....**10** 13 wks
9 Oct 59   **GOODBYE JIMMY GOODBYE (re-entry)**
        Columbia DB 4305 ....**26** 1 wk

[1] Ruby Murray with Anne Warren

Junior MURVIN *Jamaica, male vocalist*   **9 wks**

3 May 80   **POLICE AND THIEVES** *Island WIP 6539*.......**23** 9 wks

MUSIC AND MYSTERY - *See Gwen McCRAE*

MUSIC RELIEF '94
UK, male / female vocal / instrumental group   **1 wk**

5 Nov 94   **WHAT'S GOING ON** *Jive RWANDACD 1* ....**70** 1 wk

MUSICAL YOUTH *UK, male vocal / instrumental group*   **55 wks**

25 Sep 82 ★ **PASS THE DUTCHIE** *MCA YOU 1* ....**1** 12 wks
20 Nov 82   **YOUTH OF TODAY** *MCA YOU 2* ....**13** 9 wks
8 Jan 83   **PASS THE DUTCHIE (re-entry)** *MCA YOU 1*.......**65** 1 wk
12 Feb 83 ● **NEVER GONNA GIVE YOU UP** *MCA YOU 3* ....**6** 10 wks
16 Apr 83   **HEARTBREAKER** *MCA YOU 4*.......**44** 3 wks
9 Jul 83   **TELL ME WHY** *MCA YOU 5*.......**33** 6 wks
22 Oct 83   **007** *MCA YOU 6* ....**26** 6 wks
14 Jan 84   **SIXTEEN** *MCA YOU 7* ....**23** 8 wks

See also Donna Summer.

MUSIQUE *US, female vocal group*   **12 wks**

18 Nov 78   **IN THE BUSH** *CBS 6791* ....**16** 12 wks

MUSTAFAS - *See STAIFFI and his MUSTAFAS*

MXM *Italy, male / female vocal / instrumental group*   **1 wk**

2 Jun 90   **NOTHING COMPARES 2 U** *London LON 267* ....**68** 1 wk

MY BLOODY VALENTINE
UK, male / female vocal / instrumental group   **5 wks**

5 May 90   **SOON** *Creation CRE 073* ....**41** 3 wks
16 Feb 91   **TO HERE KNOWS WHEN** *Creation CRE 085* ....**29** 2 wks

Tim MYCROFT - *See SOUNDS NICE*

Alicia MYERS *US, female vocalist*   **3 wks**

1 Sep 84   **YOU GET THE BEST FROM ME (SAY SAY SAY)**
        MCA MCA 914 ....**58** 3 wks

Richard MYHILL *UK, male vocalist*   **9 wks**

1 Apr 78   **IT TAKES TWO TO TANGO** *Mercury 6007 167* ....**17** 9 wks

Alannah MYLES *Canada, female vocalist*   **17 wks**

17 Mar 90 ● **BLACK VELVET** *East West A 8742* ....**2** 15 wks
16 Jun 90   **LOVE IS** *East West A 8918* ....**61** 2 wks

Marie MYRIAM *France, female vocalist*   **4 wks**

28 May 77   **L'OISEAU ET L'ENFANT** *Polydor 2056 634*.......**42** 4 wks

MYSTERIANS - *See ?(QUESTION MARK) and the MYSTERIANS*

MYSTI - *See CAMOUFLAGE featuring MYSTI*

MYSTIC MERLIN
US, male vocal / instrumental and magic group   **9 wks**

26 Apr 80   **JUST CAN'T GIVE YOU UP** *Capitol CL 16133* ....**20** 9 wks

Jimmy NAIL UK, male vocalist — 31 wks

27 Apr 85	● LOVE DON'T LIVE HERE ANYMORE Virgin VS 764	...3	11 wks
11 Jul 92	★ AIN'T NO DOUBT East West YZ 686	...1	12 wks
3 Oct 92	LAURA East West YZ 702	...58	2 wks
26 Nov 94	● CROCODILE SHOES East West YZ 867CD	...4†	6 wks

NAKED EYES UK, male vocal / instrumental duo — 3 wks

23 Jul 83	ALWAYS SOMETHING THERE TO REMIND ME RCA 348	...59	3 wks

NANCY AND LEE - See Nancy Sinatra

NAPOLEON XIV US, male vocalist — 10 wks

4 Aug 66	● THEY'RE COMING TO TAKE ME AWAY HA-HAAAA! Warner Bros. WB 5831	...4	10 wks

NARADA - See Narada Michael WALDEN

NAS US, male rapper — 1 wk

28 May 94	IT AIN'T HARD TO TELL Columbia 6604702	...64	1 wk

Johnny NASH US, male vocalist — 106 wks

7 Aug 68	● HOLD ME TIGHT Regal Zonophone RZ 3010	...5	16 wks
8 Jan 69	● YOU GOT SOUL Major Minor MM 586	...6	12 wks
2 Apr 69	● CUPID Major Minor MM 603	...6	11 wks
25 Jun 69	CUPID (re-entry) Major Minor MM 603	...50	1 wk
1 Apr 72	STIR IT UP CBS 7800	...13	12 wks
24 Jun 72	● I CAN SEE CLEARLY NOW CBS 8113	...5	15 wks
7 Oct 72	● THERE ARE MORE QUESTIONS THAN ANSWERS CBS 8351	...9	9 wks
14 Jun 75	★ TEARS ON MY PILLOW CBS 3220	...1	11 wks
11 Oct 75	LET'S BE FRIENDS CBS 3597	...42	3 wks
12 Jun 76	(WHAT A) WONDERFUL WORLD Epic EPC 4294	...25	7 wks
9 Nov 85	ROCK ME BABY 2000 A.D. FED 19	...47	4 wks
15 Apr 89	I CAN SEE CLEARLY NOW (re-mix) Epic JN 1	...54	5 wks

NASHVILLE TEENS
UK, male vocal / instrumental group — 37 wks

9 Jul 64	● TOBACCO ROAD Decca F 11930	...6	13 wks
22 Oct 64	● GOOGLE EYE Decca F 12000	...10	11 wks
4 Mar 65	FIND MY WAY BACK HOME Decca F 12089	...34	6 wks
20 May 65	THIS LITTLE BIRD Decca F 12143	...38	4 wks
3 Feb 66	THE HARD WAY Decca F 12316	...45	2 wks
24 Feb 66	THE HARD WAY (re-entry) Decca F 12316	...48	1 wk

NATASHA UK, female vocalist — 16 wks

5 Jun 82	● IKO IKO Towerbell TOW 22	...10	11 wks
4 Sep 82	THE BOOM BOOM ROOM Towerbell TOW 25	...44	5 wks

Ultra NATÉ US, female vocalist — 5 wks

9 Dec 89	IT'S OVER NOW Eternal YZ 440	...62	3 wks
23 Feb 91	IS IT LOVE Eternal YZ 509	...71	1 wk
29 Jan 94	SHOW ME Warner Bros. W 0219CD	...62	1 wk

NATURAL LIFE
UK, male / female vocal / instrumental group — 3 wks

7 Mar 92	NATURAL LIFE Tribe NLIFE 3	...47	3 wks

NATURAL SELECTION
US, male vocal / instrumental duo — 2 wks

9 Nov 91	DO ANYTHING East West A 8724	...69	2 wks

NATURALS UK, male vocal / instrumental group — 9 wks

20 Aug 64	I SHOULD HAVE KNOWN BETTER Parlophone R 5165	...24	9 wks

David NAUGHTON US, male vocalist — 6 wks

25 Aug 79	MAKIN' IT RSO 32	...44	6 wks

NAUGHTY BY NATURE US, male rap group — 13 wks

9 Nov 91	O.P.P. Big Life BLR 62	...73	1 wk
20 Jun 92	O.P.P. (re-issue) Big Life BLR 74	...35	3 wks
30 Jan 93	HIP HOP HOORAY Big Life BLRD 89	...22	3 wks
19 Jun 93	IT'S ON Big Life BLRD 99	...48	2 wks
27 Nov 93	HIP HOP HOORAY (re-mix) Big Life BLRDA 104	...20	4 wks

NAZARETH UK, male vocal / instrumental group — 75 wks

5 May 73	● BROKEN DOWN ANGEL Mooncrest MOON 1	...9	11 wks
21 Jul 73	● BAD BAD BOY Mooncrest MOON 9	...10	9 wks
13 Oct 73	THIS FLIGHT TONIGHT Mooncrest MOON 14	...11	13 wks
23 Mar 74	SHANGHAI'D IN SHANGHAI Mooncrest MOON 22	...41	4 wks
14 Jun 75	MY WHITE BICYCLE Mooncrest MOON 47	...14	8 wks
15 Nov 75	HOLY ROLLER Mountain TOP 3	...36	4 wks
24 Sep 77	HOT TRACKS EP Mountain NAZ 1	...15	11 wks
18 Feb 78	GONE DEAD TRAIN Mountain NAZ 002	...49	2 wks
13 May 78	PLACE IN YOUR HEART Mountain TOP 37	...70	1 wk
27 May 78	PLACE IN YOUR HEART (re-entry) Mountain TOP 37	...74	1 wk
27 Jan 79	MAY THE SUN SHINE Mountain NAZ 003	...22	8 wks
28 Jul 79	STAR Mountain TOP 45	...54	3 wks

Tracks on Hot Tracks EP: Love Hurts / This Flight Tonight / Broken Down Angel / Hair of the Dog.

NAZLYN - See M-BEAT

Me'Shell NDEGEOCELLO
US, female vocalist / instrumentalist - bass — 4 wks

12 Feb 94	IF THAT'S YOUR BOYFRIEND (HE WASN'T LAST NIGHT) Maverick W 0223CD1	...74	1 wk
3 Sep 94	WILD NIGHT Mercury MERCD 409 [1]	...34	3 wks

[1] John Mellencamp featuring Me'Shell NdegeoCello

Youssou N'DOUR Senegal, male vocalist — 30 wks

3 Jun 89	SHAKING THE TREE Virgin VS 1167 [1]	...61	3 wks
22 Dec 90	SHAKING THE TREE (re-issue) Virgin VS 1322 [1]	..57	4 wks
25 Jun 94	● 7 SECONDS Columbia 6605082 [2]	...3	21 wks
24 Dec 94	7 SECONDS (re-entry) Columbia 6605082 [2]	...60†	2 wks

[1] Youssou N'Dour and Peter Gabriel [2] Youssou N'Dour (featuring Neneh Cherry)

The re-issue of Shaking The Tree was listed with its flip side, Solsbury Hill by Peter Gabriel.

Terry NEASON UK, female vocalist — 1 wk

25 Jun 94	LIFEBOAT WEA YZ 830	...72	1 wk

NEBULA II UK, male instrumental / production group — 3 wks

1 Feb 92	SEANCE / ATHEAMA Reinforced RIVET 1211	...55	2 wks
16 May 92	FLATLINERS J4M 12NEBULA 2	...54	1 wk

NED'S ATOMIC DUSTBIN
UK, male vocal/instrumental group **21 wks**

14 Jul 90	**KILL YOUR TELEVISION** Chapter 22 CHAP 48 ....**53**	2 wks
27 Oct 90	**UNTIL YOU FIND OUT** Chapter 22 CHAP 52 ....**51**	2 wks
9 Mar 91	**HAPPY** Columbia 6566807 ....**16**	4 wks
21 Sep 91	**TRUST** Furtive 6574627 ....**21**	4 wks
10 Oct 92	**NOT SLEEPING AROUND** Furtive 6583866 ......**19**	3 wks
5 Dec 92	**INTACT** Furtive 6588166 ....**36**	6 wks

Joey NEGRO *UK, male producer - Dave Lee* **10 wks**

18 Mar 89	**REACHIN'** Republic LIC 006 [1] **70**	1 wk
16 Nov 91	**DO WHAT YOU FEEL** Ten TEN 391 ....**36**	3 wks
21 Dec 91	**REACHIN' (re-mix)** Republic LIC 160 [2] **70**	1 wk
18 Jul 92	**ENTER YOUR FANTASY EP** Ten TEN 397..........**35**	3 wks
25 Sep 93	**WHAT HAPPENED TO THE MUSIC** Virgin VSCD 1466 ....**51**	2 wks

[1] Phase II [2] Joey Negro presents Phase II

Tracks on Enter Your Fantasy EP: Love Fantasy/Get Up/Enter Your Mind/ Everybody.

See also Li Kwan.

neil *UK, male vocalist* **10 wks**

14 Jul 84	● **HOLE IN MY SHOE** WEA YZ 10 ....**2**	10 wks

Vince NEIL *US, male vocalist* **1 wk**

3 Oct 92	**YOU'RE INVITED (BUT YOUR FRIEND CAN'T COME)** Hollywood HWD 123 ....**63**	1 wk

NELSON *US, male vocal duo* **3 wks**

27 Oct 90	**(CAN'T LIVE WITHOUT YOUR) LOVE AND AFFECTION** DGC GEF 82 ....**54**	3 wks

Bill NELSON
UK, male vocalist/instrumentalist - guitar and synthesizer **12 wks**

24 Feb 79	**FURNITURE MUSIC** Harvest HAR 5176 [1] **59**	3 wks
5 May 79	**REVOLT INTO STYLE** Harvest HAR 5183 [1] **69**	2 wks
5 Jul 80	**DO YOU DREAM IN COLOUR?** Cocteau COQ 1 ...**52**	4 wks
13 Jun 81	**YOUTH OF NATION ON FIRE** Mercury WILL 2 ....**73**	3 wks

[1] Bill Nelson's Red Noise

Phyllis NELSON *US, female vocalist* **24 wks**

23 Feb 85	★ **MOVE CLOSER** Carrerre CAR 337..................**1**	21 wks
21 May 94	**MOVE CLOSER (re-issue)** EMI CDEMCT 9 ......**34**	3 wks

Ricky NELSON *US, male vocalist* **137 wks**

21 Feb 58	**STOOD UP** London HLP 8542 ....**27**	1 wk
7 Mar 58	**STOOD UP (re-entry)** London HLP 8542 ....**29**	1 wk
22 Aug 58	● **POOR LITTLE FOOL** London HLP 8670 ....**4**	13 wks
7 Nov 58	● **SOMEDAY** London HLP 8732 ....**9**	13 wks
21 Nov 58	**I GOT A FEELING** London HLP 8732 ....**27**	1 wk
28 Nov 58	**POOR LITTLE FOOL (re-entry)** London HLP 8670 ....**28**	1 wk
17 Apr 59	● **IT'S LATE** London HLP 8817 ....**3**	20 wks
15 May 59	**NEVER BE ANYONE ELSE BUT YOU** London HLP 8817 ....**19**	1 wk
5 Jun 59	**NEVER BE ANYONE ELSE BUT YOU (re-entry)** London HLP 8817 ....**14**	9 wks
4 Sep 59	**SWEETER THAN YOU** London HLP 8927 ....**19**	3 wks
11 Sep 59	**JUST A LITTLE TOO MUCH** London HLP 8927.........**11**	8 wks
15 Jan 60	**I WANNA BE LOVED** London HLP 9021 ....**30**	1 wk
7 Jul 60	**YOUNG EMOTIONS** London HLP 9121 ....**48**	1 wk
1 Jun 61	● **HELLO MARY LOU/TRAVELLIN' MAN** London HLP 9347 ....**2**	18 wks
16 Nov 61	**EVERLOVIN'** London HLP 9440 [1] **23**	5 wks

29 Mar 62	**YOUNG WORLD** London HLP 9524 ....**19**	13 wks
30 Aug 62	**TEENAGE IDOL** London HLP 9583 [1] **39**	4 wks
17 Jan 63	**IT'S UP TO YOU** London HLP 9648 [1] **22**	9 wks
17 Oct 63	**FOOLS RUSH IN** Brunswick 05895 [1] **12**	9 wks
30 Jan 64	**FOR YOU** Brunswick 05900 [1] **14**	10 wks
21 Oct 72	**GARDEN PARTY** MCA MU 1165 [1] **41**	4 wks
24 Aug 91	**HELLO MARY LOU (GOODBYE HEART) (re-issue)** Liberty EMCT 2 ....**45**	5 wks

[1] Rick Nelson

Sandy NELSON *US, male instrumentalist - drums* **42 wks**

6 Nov 59	● **TEEN BEAT** Top Rank JAR 197.....................**9**	11 wks
5 Feb 60	**TEEN BEAT (re-entry)** Top Rank JAR 197 ....**25**	1 wk
14 Dec 61	● **LET THERE BE DRUMS** London HLP 9466 ....**3**	16 wks
22 Mar 62	**DRUMS ARE MY BEAT** London HLP 9521 ....**30**	6 wks
7 Jun 62	**DRUMMIN' UP A STORM** London HLP 9558 ....**39**	8 wks

Shara NELSON *UK, female vocalist* **20 wks**

24 Jul 93	**DOWN THAT ROAD** Cooltempo CDCOOL 275 ....**19**	6 wks
18 Sep 93	**ONE GOODBYE IN TEN** Cooltempo CDCOOL 279 ...**21**	5 wks
12 Feb 94	**UPTIGHT** Cooltempo CDCOOL 286 ....**19**	5 wks
4 Jun 94	**NOBODY** Cooltempo CDCOOL 290 ....**49**	1 wk
10 Sep 94	**INSIDE OUT/DOWN THAT ROAD (re-mix)** Cooltempo CDCOOLX 295 ....**34**	3 wks

Willie NELSON *US, male vocalist* **13 wks**

31 Jul 82	**ALWAYS ON MY MIND** CBS A 2511 ....**49**	3 wks
7 Apr 84	**TO ALL THE GIRLS I'VE LOVED BEFORE** CBS A 4252 [1] **17**	10 wks

[1] Julio Iglesias and Willie Nelson

NENA *Germany, female/male vocal/instrumental group* **14 wks**

4 Feb 84	★ **99 RED BALLOONS** Epic A 4074...................**1**	12 wks
5 May 84	**JUST A DREAM** Epic H 3249 ....**70**	2 wks

Frances NERO *US, female vocalist* **9 wks**

13 Apr 91	**FOOTSTEPS FOLLOWING ME** Debut DEBT 3109 ......**17**	9 wks

NERO and the GLADIATORS
UK, male instrumental group **6 wks**

23 Mar 61	**ENTRY OF THE GLADIATORS** Decca F 11329 ....**50**	1 wk
6 Apr 61	**ENTRY OF THE GLADIATORS (re-entry)** Decca F 11329 ....**37**	4 wks
27 Jul 61	**IN THE HALL OF THE MOUNTAIN KING** Decca F 11367 ....**48**	1 wk

Michael NESMITH *US, male vocalist* **6 wks**

26 Mar 77	**RIO** Island WIP 6373................................**28**	6 wks

NETWORK *UK, male vocal/instrumental group* **4 wks**

12 Dec 92	**BROKEN WINGS** Chrysalis CHS 3923 ....**46**	4 wks

NEVADA *UK, male/female vocal/instrumental group* **1 wk**

8 Jan 83	**IN THE BLEAK MID WINTER** Polydor POSP 203 ....**71**	1 wk

Robbie NEVIL *US, male vocalist* **24 wks**

20 Dec 86	● **C'EST LA VIE** Manhattan MT 14...................**3**	11 wks
2 May 87	**DOMINOES** Manhattan MT 19......................**26**	6 wks
11 Jul 87	**WOT'S IT TO YA** Manhattan MT 24 ....**43**	7 wks

Aaron NEVILLE - *See Linda RONSTADT: NEVILLE BROTHERS*

NEVILLE BROTHERS
US, male vocal / instrumental group **7 wks**

25 Nov 89	WITH GOD ON OUR SIDE *A & M AM 545*	**47**	6 wks
7 Jul 90	BIRD ON A WIRE *A & M AM 568*	**72**	1 wk

NEW ATLANTIC
UK, male instrumental / production duo **15 wks**

29 Feb 92	I KNOW *3 Beat 3BT 1*	**12**	7 wks
3 Oct 92	INTO THE FUTURE *3 Beat 3BT 2*	**70**	1 wk
13 Feb 93	TAKE OFF SOME TIME *3 Beat 3BTCD 14*	**64**	1 wk
26 Nov 94	THE SUNSHINE AFTER THE RAIN *3 Beat TABCD 223* [1]	**26†**	6 wks

[1] New Atlantic/U4EA featuring Berri

NEW BOHEMIANS - *See Edie BRICKELL and the NEW BOHEMIANS*

NEW EDITION *US, male vocal group* **28 wks**

16 Apr 83	★ CANDY GIRL *London LON 21*	**1**	13 wks
13 Aug 83	POPCORN LOVE *London LON 31*	**43**	5 wks
23 Feb 85	MR. TELEPHONE MAN *MCA MCA 938*	**19**	9 wks
15 Apr 89	CRUCIAL *MCA MCA 23934*	**70**	1 wk

NEW GENERATION
UK, male vocal / instrumental group **5 wks**

26 Jun 68	SMOKEY BLUES AWAY *Spark SRL 1007*	**38**	5 wks

NEW KIDS ON THE BLOCK *US, male vocal group* **90 wks**

16 Sep 89	HANGIN' TOUGH *CBS BLOCK 1*	**52**	4 wks
11 Nov 89	★ YOU GOT IT (THE RIGHT STUFF) *CBS BLOCK 2*	**1**	13 wks
6 Jan 90	★ HANGIN' TOUGH (re-issue) *CBS BLOCK 3*	**1**	9 wks
17 Mar 90	● I'LL BE LOVING YOU (FOREVER) *CBS BLOCK 4*	**5**	8 wks
12 May 90	● COVER GIRL *CBS BLOCK 5*	**4**	8 wks
16 Jun 90	● STEP BY STEP *CBS BLOCK 6*	**2**	7 wks
4 Aug 90	● TONIGHT *CBS BLOCK 7*	**3**	10 wks
13 Oct 90	● LET'S TRY AGAIN / DIDN'T I BLOW YOUR MIND *CBS BLOCK 8*	**8**	5 wks
8 Dec 90	● THIS ONE'S FOR THE CHILDREN *CBS BLOCK 9*	**9**	7 wks
9 Feb 91	GAMES *CBS 6566267*	**14**	4 wks
18 May 91	CALL IT WHAT YOU WANT *Columbia 6567857*	**12**	5 wks
14 Dec 91	IF YOU GO AWAY *Columbia 6576667*	**9**	5 wks
19 Feb 94	DIRTY DAWG *Columbia 6600362* [1]	**27**	3 wks
26 Mar 94	NEVER LET YOU GO *Columbia 6602072* [1]	**42**	2 wks

[1] NKOTB

NEW MODEL ARMY
UK, male vocal / instrumental group **33 wks**

27 Apr 85	NO REST *EMI NMA 1*	**28**	5 wks
3 Aug 85	BETTER THAN THEM / NO SENSE *EMI NMA 2*	**49**	2 wks
30 Nov 85	BRAVE NEW WORLD *EMI NMA 3*	**57**	1 wk
8 Nov 86	FIFTY-FIRST STATE *EMI NMA 4*	**71**	2 wks
28 Feb 87	POISON STREET *EMI NMA 5*	**64**	1 wk
26 Sep 87	WHITE COATS EP *EMI NMA 6*	**50**	3 wks
21 Jan 89	STUPID QUESTION *EMI NMA 7*	**31**	3 wks
11 Mar 89	VAGABONDS *EMI NMA 8*	**37**	3 wks
10 Jun 89	GREEN AND GREY *EMI NMA 9*	**37**	3 wks
8 Sep 90	GET ME OUT *EMI NMA 10*	**34**	3 wks
3 Nov 90	PURITY *EMI NMA 11*	**61**	2 wks
8 Jun 91	SPACE *EMI NMA 12*	**39**	2 wks
20 Feb 93	HERE COMES THE WAR *Epic 6589352*	**25**	2 wks
24 Jul 93	LIVING IN THE ROSE (THE BALLADS EP) *Epic 6592492*	**51**	1 wk

Tracks on White Coats EP: *The Charge / Chinese Whispers / My Country.*
Tracks on Living In The Rose (The Ballads EP): *Living In The Rose, Drummy B, Marry The Sea, Sleepwalking.*

See also Various Artists (EPs & LPs) - Gimme Shelter (EP).

NEW MUSIK *UK, male vocal / instrumental group* **27 wks**

6 Oct 79	STRAIGHT LINES *GTO GT 255*	**53**	5 wks
19 Jan 80	LIVING BY NUMBERS *GTO GT 261*	**13**	8 wks
26 Apr 80	THIS WORLD OF WATER *GTO GT 268*	**31**	7 wks
12 Jul 80	SANCTUARY *GTO GT 275*	**31**	7 wks

NEW ORDER
UK, male / female vocal / instrumental group **170 wks**

14 Mar 81	CEREMONY *Factory FAC 33*	**34**	5 wks
3 Oct 81	PROCESSION / EVERYTHING'S GONE GREEN *Factory FAC 53*	**38**	5 wks
22 May 82	TEMPTATION *Factory FAC 63*	**29**	7 wks
19 Mar 83	BLUE MONDAY *Factory FAC 73*	**12**	17 wks
13 Aug 83	● BLUE MONDAY (re-entry) *Factory FAC 73*	**9**	17 wks
3 Sep 83	CONFUSION *Factory FAC 93*	**12**	7 wks
7 Jan 84	BLUE MONDAY (2nd re-entry) *Factory FAC 73*	**52**	4 wks
28 Apr 84	THIEVES LIKE US *Factory FAC 103*	**18**	5 wks
25 May 85	THE PERFECT KISS *Factory FAC 123*	**46**	4 wks
9 Nov 85	SUB-CULTURE *Factory FAC 133*	**63**	4 wks
29 Mar 86	SHELLSHOCK *Factory FAC 143*	**28**	5 wks
27 Sep 86	STATE OF THE NATION *Factory FAC 153*	**30**	3 wks
27 Sep 86	THE PEEL SESSIONS (1ST JUNE 1982) *Strange Fruit SFPS 001*	**54**	1 wk
15 Nov 86	BIZARRE LOVE TRIANGLE *Factory FAC 163*	**56**	2 wks
1 Aug 87	● TRUE FAITH *Factory FAC 183/7*	**4**	10 wks
19 Dec 87	TOUCHED BY THE HAND OF GOD *Factory FAC 1937*	**20**	7 wks
7 May 88	● BLUE MONDAY (re-mix) *Factory FAC 737*	**3**	11 wks
10 Dec 88	FINE TIME *Factory FAC 2237*	**11**	8 wks
11 Mar 89	ROUND AND ROUND *Factory FAC 2637*	**21**	7 wks
9 Sep 89	RUN 2 *Factory FAC 273*	**49**	2 wks
2 Jun 90	★ WORLD IN MOTION... *Factory/MCA FAC 2937* [1]	**1**	12 wks
17 Apr 93	● REGRET *Centredate Co. NUOCD 1*	**4**	7 wks
3 Jul 93	RUINED IN A DAY *Centredate Co. NUOCD 2*	**22**	4 wks
4 Sep 93	WORLD (THE PRICE OF LOVE) *Centredate Co. NUOCD 3*	**13**	5 wks
18 Dec 93	SPOOKY *Centredate Co. NUOCD 4*	**22**	4 wks
19 Nov 94	● TRUE FAITH (re-mix) *Centredate Co. NUOCD 5*	**9†**	7 wks

[1] Englandneworder

Group male only on first hit. Blue Monday 1988 is a re-mixed version of the original 1983 hit which was made available on 7-inch for the first time, hence the slight difference in catalogue number. Sales for the re-mix and the original were combined from 7 May 1988 onwards when calculating its chart position.

NEW ORLEANS JAZZMEN - *See Terry LIGHTFOOT and his NEW ORLEANS JAZZMEN*

NEW POWER GENERATION - *See PRINCE*

NEW SEEKERS
UK, male / female vocal / instrumental group **143 wks**

17 Oct 70	WHAT HAVE THEY DONE TO MY SONG MA *Philips 6006 027*	**48**	1 wk
31 Oct 70	WHAT HAVE THEY DONE TO MY SONG MA (re-entry) *Philips 6006 027*	**44**	1 wk
10 Jul 71	● NEVER ENDING SONG OF LOVE *Philips 6006 125*	**2**	19 wks
18 Dec 71	★ I'D LIKE TO TEACH THE WORLD TO SING (IN PERFECT HARMONY) *Polydor 2058 184*	**1**	21 wks
4 Mar 72	● BEG STEAL OR BORROW *Polydor 2058 201*	**2**	13 wks
10 Jun 72	● CIRCLES *Polydor 2058 242*	**4**	16 wks
2 Dec 72	COME SOFTLY TO ME *Polydor 2058 315* [1]	**20**	11 wks
24 Feb 73	PINBALL WIZARD - SEE ME FEEL ME (MEDLEY) *Polydor 2058 338*	**16**	8 wks
7 Apr 73	NEVERTHELESS *Polydor 2068 340* [2]	**34**	5 wks
16 Jun 73	GOODBYE IS JUST ANOTHER WORD *Polydor 2058 368*	**36**	5 wks
24 Nov 73	★ YOU WON'T FIND ANOTHER FOOL LIKE ME *Polydor 2058 421*	**1**	16 wks
9 Mar 74	● I GET A LITTLE SENTIMENTAL OVER YOU *Polydor 2058 439*	**5**	9 wks

14 Aug 76	IT'S SO NICE (TO HAVE YOU HOME) CBS 4391	**44**	4 wks
29 Jan 77	I WANNA GO BACK CBS 4786	**25**	4 wks
15 Jul 78	ANTHEM (ONE DAY IN EVERY WEEK) CBS 6413	**21**	10 wks

[1] New Seekers featuring Marty Kristian [2] Eve Graham and the New Seekers

NEW TONE AGE FAMILY - *See Dread FLIMSTONE and the NEW TONE AGE FAMILY*

NEW VAUDEVILLE BAND
UK, male vocal / instrumental group   **43 wks**

8 Sep 66	● WINCHESTER CATHEDRAL Fontana TF 741	**4**	19 wks
26 Jan 67	● PEEK-A-BOO Fontana TF 784 [1]	**7**	11 wks
11 May 67	FINCHLEY CENTRAL Fontana TF 824	**11**	9 wks
2 Aug 67	GREEN STREET GREEN Fontana TF 853	**37**	4 wks

[1] New Vaudeville Band featuring Tristram

NEW WORLD *Australia, male vocal / instrumental group*   **53 wks**

27 Feb 71	ROSE GARDEN RAK 111	**15**	11 wks
3 Jul 71	● TOM TOM TURNAROUND RAK 117	**6**	15 wks
4 Dec 71	KARA KARA RAK 123	**17**	13 wks
13 May 72	● SISTER JANE RAK 130	**9**	13 wks
12 May 73	ROOF TOP SINGING RAK 148	**50**	1 wk

NEW YORK CITY *US, male vocal group*   **11 wks**

| 21 Jul 73 | I'M DOING FINE NOW RCA 2351 | **20** | 11 wks |

NEW YORK SKYY
US, male / female vocal / instrumental group   **2 wks**

| 16 Jan 82 | LET'S CELEBRATE Epic EPC A 1898 | **71** | 1 wk |
| 30 Jan 82 | LET'S CELEBRATE (re-entry) Epic EPC A 1898 | **67** | 1 wk |

NEWBEATS *US, male vocal group*   **22 wks**

| 10 Sep 64 | BREAD AND BUTTER Hickory 1269 | **15** | 9 wks |
| 23 Oct 71 | ● RUN BABY RUN London HL 10341 | **10** | 13 wks |

Booker NEWBURY III *US, male vocalist*   **11 wks**

| 28 May 83 | ● LOVE TOWN Polydor POSP 613 | **6** | 8 wks |
| 8 Oct 83 | TEDDY BEAR Polydor POSP 637 | **44** | 3 wks |

Mickey NEWBURY *US, male vocalist*   **5 wks**

| 1 Jul 72 | AMERICAN TRILOGY Elektra K 12047 | **42** | 5 wks |

NEWCLEUS *US, male vocal / instrumental group*   **6 wks**

| 3 Sep 83 | JAM ON REVENGE (THE WIKKI WIKKI SONG) Beckett BKS 8 | **44** | 6 wks |

Anthony NEWLEY *UK, male vocalist*   **129 wks**

1 May 59	● I'VE WAITED SO LONG Decca F 11127	**3**	15 wks
8 May 59	IDLE ON PARADE EP Decca DFE 6566	**13**	4 wks
12 Jun 59	● PERSONALITY Decca F 11142	**6**	12 wks
15 Jan 60	★ WHY Decca F 11194	**1**	17 wks
24 Mar 60	★ DO YOU MIND Decca F 11220	**1**	15 wks
14 Jul 60	● IF SHE SHOULD COME TO YOU Decca F 11254	**4**	15 wks
24 Nov 60	● STRAWBERRY FAIR Decca F 11295	**3**	11 wks
16 Mar 61	● AND THE HEAVENS CRIED Decca F 11331	**6**	12 wks
15 Jun 61	POP GOES THE WEASEL / BEE BOM Decca F 11362	**12**	9 wks
3 Aug 61	WHAT KIND OF FOOL AM I? Decca F 11376	**36**	8 wks
25 Jan 62	D-DARLING Decca F 11419	**25**	6 wks
26 Jul 62	THAT NOISE Decca F 11486	**34**	5 wks

Bee Bom *only listed together with* Pop Goes The Weasel *for weeks of 15 and 22 June 61. It peaked at position 15. Tracks on* Idle On Parade EP: I've Waited So Long / Idle Rock-A-Boogie / Idle On Parade / Saturday Night Rock-A-Boogie.

Tara NEWLEY - *See E-ZEE POSSEE*

Alfred NEWMAN - *See VARIOUS ARTISTS (EPs & LPs) - Carousel Soundtrack*

Brad NEWMAN *UK, male vocalist*   **1 wk**

| 22 Feb 62 | SOMEBODY TO LOVE Fontana H 357 | **47** | 1 wk |

Dave NEWMAN *UK, male vocalist*   **6 wks**

| 15 Apr 72 | THE LION SLEEPS TONIGHT Pye 7N 45134 | **48** | 1 wk |
| 29 Apr 72 | THE LION SLEEPS TONIGHT (re-entry) Pye 7N 45134 | **34** | 5 wks |

NEWS - *See Huey LEWIS and the NEWS*

NEWS *UK, male vocal / instrumental group*   **3 wks**

| 29 Aug 81 | AUDIO VIDEO George GEORGE 1 | **52** | 3 wks |

Juice NEWTON *US, female vocalist*   **6 wks**

| 2 May 81 | ANGEL OF THE MORNING Capitol CL 16189 | **43** | 6 wks |

Olivia NEWTON-JOHN *UK, female vocalist*   **221 wks**

20 Mar 71	● IF NOT FOR YOU Pye International 7N 25543	**7**	11 wks
23 Oct 71	● BANKS OF THE OHIO Pye International 7N 25568	**6**	17 wks
11 Mar 72	WHAT IS LIFE Pye International 7N 25575	**16**	8 wks
13 Jan 73	TAKE ME HOME COUNTRY ROADS Pye International 7N 25599	**15**	13 wks
16 Mar 74	LONG LIVE LOVE Pye International 7N 25638	**11**	8 wks
12 Oct 74	I HONESTLY LOVE YOU EMI 2216	**22**	6 wks
11 Jun 77	● SAM EMI 2616	**6**	11 wks
20 May 78	★ YOU'RE THE ONE THAT I WANT RSO 006 [1]	**1**	26 wks
16 Sep 78	★ SUMMER NIGHTS RSO 18 [1]	**1**	19 wks
4 Nov 78	● HOPELESSLY DEVOTED TO YOU RSO 17	**2**	11 wks
16 Dec 78	● A LITTLE MORE LOVE EMI 2879	**4**	12 wks
30 Jun 79	DEEPER THAN THE NIGHT EMI 2954	**64**	3 wks
21 Jun 80	★ XANADU Jet 185 [2]	**1**	11 wks
23 Aug 80	MAGIC Jet 196	**32**	7 wks
25 Oct 80	SUDDENLY Jet 7002 [3]	**15**	7 wks
10 Oct 81	● PHYSICAL EMI 5234	**7**	16 wks
16 Jan 82	LANDSLIDE EMI 5257	**18**	9 wks
17 Apr 82	MAKE A MOVE ON ME EMI 5291	**43**	3 wks
23 Oct 82	HEART ATTACK EMI 5347	**46**	4 wks
15 Jan 83	I HONESTLY LOVE YOU (re-issue) EMI 5360	**52**	4 wks
12 Nov 83	TWIST OF FATE EMI 5438	**57**	2 wks
22 Dec 90	● THE GREASE MEGAMIX Polydor PO 114 [1]	**3**	10 wks
23 Mar 91	GREASE - THE DREAM MIX PWL/Polydor PO 136 [4]	**47**	2 wks
4 Jul 92	I NEED LOVE Mercury MER 370	**75**	1 wk

[1] John Travolta and Olivia Newton-John [2] Olivia Newton-John and Electric Light Orchestra [3] Olivia Newton-John and Cliff Richard [4] Frankie Valli, John Travolta and Olivia Newton-John

NICE *UK, male instrumental group*   **15 wks**

| 10 Jul 68 | AMERICA Immediate IM 068 | **21** | 15 wks |

Paul NICHOLAS *UK, male vocalist*   **31 wks**

17 Apr 76	REGGAE LIKE IT USED TO BE RSO 2090 185	**17**	8 wks
9 Oct 76	● DANCING WITH THE CAPTAIN RSO 2090 206	**8**	9 wks
4 Dec 76	● GRANDMA'S PARTY RSO 2090 216	**9**	11 wks
9 Jul 77	HEAVEN ON THE 7TH FLOOR RSO 2090 249	**40**	3 wks

Sue NICHOLLS *UK, female vocalist*   **8 wks**

| 3 Jul 68 | WHERE WILL YOU BE Pye 7N 17565 | **17** | 8 wks |

Stevie NICKS *US, female vocalist* — **30 wks**

Date	Title	Pos	Wks
15 Aug 81	**STOP DRAGGIN' MY HEART AROUND** *WEA K 79231* [1]	50	4 wks
25 Jan 86	**I CAN'T WAIT** *Parlophone R 6110*	54	4 wks
29 Mar 86	**TALK TO ME** *Parlophone R 6124*	68	2 wks
6 May 89	**ROOMS ON FIRE** *EMI EM 90*	16	7 wks
12 Aug 89	**LONG WAY TO GO** *EMI EM 97*	60	2 wks
11 Nov 89	**WHOLE LOTTA TROUBLE** *EMI EM 114*	62	4 wks
24 Aug 91	**SOMETIMES IT'S A BITCH** *EMI EM 203*	40	4 wks
9 Nov 91	**I CAN'T WAIT (re-issue)** *EMI EM 214*	47	2 wks
2 Jul 94	**MAYBE LOVE** *EMI CDEMS 328*	42	3 wks

[1] Stevie Nicks with Tom Petty and the Heartbreakers

NICOLE *Germany, female vocalist* — **10 wks**

Date	Title	Pos	Wks
8 May 82	★ **A LITTLE PEACE** *CBS A 2365*	1	9 wks
21 Aug 82	**GIVE ME MORE TIME** *CBS A 2467*	75	1 wk

NICOLE - See SOURCE; Timmy THOMAS

NIGHTCRAWLERS
UK, male instrumental / production duo — **5 wks**

Date	Title	Pos	Wks
15 Oct 94	**PUSH THE FEELING ON** *ffrr FCD 245*	22	5 wks

Maxine NIGHTINGALE *UK, female vocalist* — **16 wks**

Date	Title	Pos	Wks
1 Nov 75	● **RIGHT BACK WHERE WE STARTED FROM** *United Artists UP 36015*	8	8 wks
12 Mar 77	**LOVE HIT ME** *United Artists UP 36215*	11	8 wks

NIGHTMARES ON WAX
UK, male instrumental group — **5 wks**

Date	Title	Pos	Wks
27 Oct 90	**AFTERMATH / I'M FOR REAL** *Warp WAP 6*	38	5 wks

NIGHTWRITERS *US, male vocal / instrumental duo* — **2 wks**

Date	Title	Pos	Wks
23 May 92	**LET THE MUSIC USE YOU** *Ffrreedom TABX 112*	51	2 wks

NIKKE? NICOLE! *US, female rapper* — **1 wk**

Date	Title	Pos	Wks
1 Jun 91	**NIKKE DOES IT BETTER** *Love EVOL 5*	73	1 wk

NILSSON *US, male vocalist* — **55 wks**

Date	Title	Pos	Wks
27 Sep 69	**EVERYBODY'S TALKIN'** *RCA 1876*	50	1 wk
11 Oct 69	**EVERYBODY'S TALKIN' (re-entry)** *RCA 1876*	23	9 wks
14 Mar 70	**EVERYBODY'S TALKIN' (2nd re-entry)** *RCA 1876*	39	5 wks
5 Feb 72	★ **WITHOUT YOU** *RCA 2165*	1	20 wks
3 Jun 72	**COCONUT** *RCA 2214*	42	5 wks
16 Oct 76	**WITHOUT YOU (re-issue)** *RCA 2733*	22	8 wks
20 Aug 77	**ALL I THINK ABOUT IS YOU** *RCA PB 9104*	43	3 wks
19 Feb 94	**WITHOUT YOU (re-issue)** *RCA 74321193092*	47	4 wks

NINA and FREDERICK
Denmark, female / male vocal duo — **29 wks**

Date	Title	Pos	Wks
18 Dec 59	**MARY'S BOY CHILD** *Columbia DB 4375*	26	1 wk
10 Mar 60	**LISTEN TO THE OCEAN** *Columbia DB 4332*	47	1 wk
7 Apr 60	**LISTEN TO THE OCEAN (re-entry)** *Columbia DB 4332*	46	1 wk
17 Nov 60	● **LITTLE DONKEY** *Columbia DB 4536*	3	10 wks
28 Sep 61	**LONGTIME BOY** *Columbia DB 4703*	43	3 wks
5 Oct 61	**SUCU SUCU** *Columbia DB 4632*	23	13 wks

NINE INCH NAILS
US, male vocalist - Trent Reznor and backing musicians — **12 wks**

Date	Title	Pos	Wks
14 Sep 91	**HEAD LIKE A HOLE** *TVT IS 484*	45	4 wks
16 Nov 91	**SIN** *TVT IS 508*	35	2 wks
9 Apr 94	**MARCH OF THE PIGS** *TVT CID 592*	45	3 wks
18 Jun 94	**CLOSER** *TVT CID 596*	25	3 wks

999 *UK, male vocal / instrumental group* — **13 wks**

Date	Title	Pos	Wks
25 Nov 78	**HOMICIDE** *United Artists UP 36467*	40	3 wks
27 Oct 79	**FOUND OUT TOO LATE** *Radar ADA 46*	69	2 wks
16 May 81	**OBSESSED** *Albion ION 1011*	71	1 wk
18 Jul 81	**LIL RED RIDING HOOD** *Albion ION 1017*	59	3 wks
14 Nov 81	**INDIAN RESERVATION** *Albion ION 1023*	51	4 wks

9.9 *US, female / male vocal group* — **3 wks**

Date	Title	Pos	Wks
6 Jul 85	**ALL OF ME FOR ALL OF YOU** *RCA PB 49951*	53	3 wks

1910 FRUITGUM CO.
US, male vocal / instrumental group — **16 wks**

Date	Title	Pos	Wks
20 Mar 68	● **SIMON SAYS** *Pye International 7N 25447*	2	16 wks

1927 *Australia, male vocal / instrumental group* — **6 wks**

Date	Title	Pos	Wks
22 Apr 89	**THAT'S WHEN I THINK OF YOU** *WEA YZ 351*	46	6 wks

NIRVANA *UK / Ireland, male vocal / instrumental duo* — **6 wks**

Date	Title	Pos	Wks
15 May 68	**RAINBOW CHASER** *Island WIP 6029*	34	6 wks

NIRVANA *US, male vocal / instrumental group* — **36 wks**

Date	Title	Pos	Wks
30 Nov 91	● **SMELLS LIKE TEEN SPIRIT** *DGC DGCS 5*	7	6 wks
14 Mar 92	● **COME AS YOU ARE** *DGC DGCS 7*	9	5 wks
25 Jul 92	**LITHIUM** *DGC DGCS 9*	11	6 wks
12 Dec 92	**IN BLOOM** *Geffen GFS 34*	28	7 wks
6 Mar 93	**OH THE GUILT** *Touch And Go TG 83CD*	12	1 wk
11 Sep 93	● **HEART-SHAPED BOX** *Geffen GFSTD 54*	5	5 wks
18 Dec 93	**ALL APOLOGIES / RAPE ME** *Geffen GFSTD 66*	32	5 wks

The listed flip side of Oh The Guilt was Puss by Jesus Lizard.

NITRO DELUXE
US, male multi-instrumentalist - Lee Junior — **16 wks**

Date	Title	Pos	Wks
14 Feb 87	**THIS BRUTAL HOUSE** *Cooltempo COOL 142*	47	7 wks
13 Jun 87	**THIS BRUTAL HOUSE (re-entry)** *Cooltempo COOL 142*	62	4 wks
6 Feb 88	**LET'S GET BRUTAL** *Cooltempo COOL 142*	24	5 wks

Let's Get Brutal is a re-mixed version of This Brutal House.

NITZER EBB *UK, male vocal / instrumental group* — **2 wks**

Date	Title	Pos	Wks
11 Jan 92	**GODHEAD** *Mute 1MUTE 135T*	56	1 wk
11 Apr 92	**ASCEND** *Mute 110MUTE 145*	52	1 wk

N-JOI *UK, male instrumental / production group* — **27 wks**

Date	Title	Pos	Wks
27 Oct 90	**ANTHEM** *Deconstruction PB 44041*	45	5 wks
2 Mar 91	**ADRENALIN (EP)** *Deconstruction PT 44344*	23	5 wks
6 Apr 91	● **ANTHEM (re-issue)** *Deconstruction PB 44445*	8	8 wks
22 Feb 92	**LIVE IN MANCHESTER (PARTS 1 + 2)** *Deconstruction PT 45252*	12	5 wks
24 Jul 93	**THE DRUMSTRUCK (EP)** *Deconstruction 74321154832*	33	3 wks
17 Dec 94	**PAPILLON** *Deconstruction 74321252132*	70	1 wk

Tracks on Adrenalin (EP): *Adrenalin / The Kraken / Rhythm Zone / Phoenix. Tracks on* The Drumstruck (EP): *The Void / Boom Bass / Drumstruck.*

N.K.O.T.B. - *See NEW KIDS ON THE BLOCK*

NO DICE *UK, male vocal / instrumental group*   **2 wks**

5 May 79	**COME DANCING** *EMI 2927*	**65**	2 wks

NO SWEAT *Ireland, male vocal / instrumental group*   **5 wks**

13 Oct 90	**HEART AND SOUL** *London LON 274*	**64**	4 wks
2 Feb 91	**TEAR DOWN THE WALLS** *London LON 288*	**61**	1 wk

NO WAY JOSÉ *US, male instrumental group*   **6 wks**

3 Aug 85	**TEQUILA** *Fourth & Broadway BRW 28*	**47**	6 wks

NOLANS *Ireland, female vocal group*   **89 wks**

6 Oct 79	● **SPIRIT BODY AND SOUL** *Epic EPC 7796* [1]	**34**	6 wks
22 Dec 79	● **I'M IN THE MOOD FOR DANCING** *Epic EPC 8068*	**3**	15 wks
12 Apr 80	**DON'T MAKE WAVES** *Epic EPC 8349*	**12**	11 wks
13 Sep 80	● **GOTTA PULL MYSELF TOGETHER** *Epic EPC 8878*	**9**	13 wks
6 Dec 80	**WHO'S GONNA ROCK YOU** *Epic EPC 9325*	**12**	11 wks
14 Mar 81	● **ATTENTION TO ME** *Epic EPC 9571*	**9**	13 wks
15 Aug 81	**CHEMISTRY** *Epic EPC A1485*	**15**	8 wks
20 Feb 82	**DON'T LOVE ME TOO HARD** *Epic EPC A 1927*	**14**	12 wks

[1] Nolan Sisters

NOMAD *UK, male / female vocal / instrumental duo*   **20 wks**

2 Feb 91	● **(I WANNA GIVE YOU) DEVOTION** *Rumour RUMA 25* [1]	**2**	10 wks
4 May 91	**JUST A GROOVE** *Rumour RUMA 33*	**16**	6 wks
28 Sep 91	**SOMETHING SPECIAL** *Rumour RUMA 35*	**73**	1 wk
25 Apr 92	**YOUR LOVE IS LIFTING ME** *Rumour RUMA 48*	**60**	2 wks
7 Nov 92	**24 HOURS A DAY** *Rumour RUMA 60*	**61**	1 wk

[1] Nomad featuring MC Mikee Freedom

Peter NOONE *UK, male vocalist*   **9 wks**

22 May 71	**OH YOU PRETTY THING** *RAK 114*	**12**	9 wks

See also Herman's Hermits.

Ken NORDENE - *See Billy VAUGHN*

Chris NORMAN - *See Suzi QUATRO*

NORTHSIDE *UK, male vocal / instrumental group*   **12 wks**

9 Jun 90	**SHALL WE TAKE A TRIP / MOODY PLACES** *Factory FAC 268*	**50**	5 wks
3 Nov 90	**MY RISING STAR** *Factory FAC 2987*	**32**	3 wks
1 Jun 91	**TAKE 5** *Factory FAC 3087*	**40**	4 wks

Freddie NOTES and the RUDIES
Jamaica, male vocal / instrumental group   **2 wks**

10 Oct 70	**MONTEGO BAY** *Trojan TR 7791*	**45**	2 wks

NOTORIOUS B.I.G. *US, male rapper*   **1 wk**

29 Oct 94	**JUICY** *Bad Boy 74321240102*	**72**	1 wk

NOTTINGHAM FOREST F.C. - *See PAPER LACE*

Nancy NOVA *UK, female vocalist*   **2 wks**

4 Sep 82	**NO NO NO** *EMI 5328*	**63**	2 wks

N.T. GANG *Germany, male vocal / instrumental group*   **1 wk**

2 Apr 88	**WAM BAM** *Cooltempo COOL 163*	**71**	1 wk

N-TRANCE *UK, male / female vocal / instrumental group*   **7 wks**

7 May 94	**SET YOU FREE** *All Around The World CDGLOBE 124* [1]	**39**	4 wks
22 Oct 94	**TURN UP THE POWER** *All Around The World CDGLOBE 125*	**23**	3 wks

[1] N-Trance featuring Kelly Llorenna

NU COLOURS *UK, male / female vocal / instrumental group*   **7 wks**

6 Jun 92	**TEARS** *Wild Card CARD 1*	**55**	2 wks
10 Oct 92	**POWER** *Wild Card CARD 3*	**64**	1 wk
5 Jun 93	**WHAT IN THE WORLD** *Wild Card CARDD 4*	**57**	2 wks
27 Nov 93	**POWER (re-issue)** *Wild Card CARDD 5*	**40**	2 wks

NU MATIC *UK, male instrumental / production duo*   **1 wk**

8 Aug 92	**SPRING IN MY STEP** *XL XLS 31*	**58**	1 wk

NU SHOOZ *US, male / female vocal duo*   **17 wks**

24 May 86	● **I CAN'T WAIT** *Atlantic A 9446*	**2**	14 wks
26 Jul 86	**POINT OF NO RETURN** *Atlantic A 9392*	**48**	3 wks

NUANCE featuring Vikki LOVE
US, male / female vocal / instrumental group   **3 wks**

19 Jan 85	**LOVERIDE** *Fourth & Broadway BRW 20*	**59**	3 wks

NUBIAN PRINZ - *See POWERCUT featuring NUBIAN PRINZ*

NUFF JUICE - *See D MOB*

Gary NUMAN *UK, male vocalist*   **160 wks**

19 May 79	★ **ARE 'FRIENDS' ELECTRIC?** *Beggars Banquet BEG 18* [1]	**1**	16 wks
1 Sep 79	★ **CARS** *Beggars Banquet BEG 23*	**1**	11 wks
24 Nov 79	● **COMPLEX** *Beggars Banquet BEG 29*	**6**	9 wks
24 May 80	● **WE ARE GLASS** *Beggars Banquet BEG 35*	**5**	7 wks
30 Aug 80	● **I DIE: YOU DIE** *Beggars Banquet BEG 46*	**6**	7 wks
20 Dec 80	**THIS WRECKAGE** *Beggars Banquet BEG 50*	**20**	7 wks
29 Aug 81	● **SHE'S GOT CLAWS** *Beggars Banquet BEG 62*	**6**	6 wks
5 Dec 81	**LOVE NEEDS NO DISGUISE** *Beggars Banquet BEG 68* [2]	**33**	7 wks
6 Mar 82	**MUSIC FOR CHAMELEONS** *Beggars Banquet BEG 70*	**19**	7 wks
19 Jun 82	● **WE TAKE MYSTERY (TO BED)** *Beggars Banquet BEG 77*	**9**	4 wks
28 Aug 82	**WHITE BOYS AND HEROES** *Beggars Banquet BEG 81*	**20**	4 wks
3 Sep 83	**WARRIORS** *Beggars Banquet BEG 95*	**20**	5 wks
22 Oct 83	**SISTER SURPRISE** *Beggars Banquet BEG 101*	**32**	3 wks
3 Nov 84	**BERSERKER** *Numa NU 4*	**32**	5 wks
22 Dec 84	**MY DYING MACHINE** *Numa NU 6*	**66**	1 wk
9 Feb 85	**CHANGE YOUR MIND** *Polydor POSP 722* [3]	**17**	8 wks
25 May 85	**THE LIVE EP** *Numa NUM 7*	**27**	4 wks
10 Aug 85	**YOUR FASCINATION** *Numa NU 9*	**46**	5 wks
21 Sep 85	**CALL OUT THE DOGS** *Numa NU 11*	**49**	2 wks
16 Nov 85	**MIRACLES** *Numa NU 13*	**49**	3 wks
19 Apr 86	**THIS IS LOVE** *Numa NU 16*	**28**	3 wks
28 Jun 86	**I CAN'T STOP** *Numa NU 17*	**27**	4 wks
4 Oct 86	**NEW THING FROM LONDON TOWN** *Numa NU 19* [3]	**52**	3 wks
6 Dec 86	**I STILL REMEMBER** *Numa NU 21*	**74**	1 wk
28 Mar 87	**RADIO HEART** *GFM GFM 109* [4]	**35**	6 wks
13 Jun 87	**LONDON TIMES** *GFM GFM 112* [4]	**48**	2 wks
19 Sep 87	**CARS (E REG MODEL) / ARE 'FRIENDS' ELECTRIC?** (re-mix) *Beggars Banquet BEG 199*	**16**	7 wks
30 Jan 88	**NO MORE LIES** *Polydor POSP 894* [3]	**34**	3 wks
1 Oct 88	**NEW ANGER** *Illegal ILS 1003*	**46**	2 wks
3 Dec 88	**AMERICA** *Illegal ILS 1004*	**49**	1 wk

3 Jun 89	**I'M ON AUTOMATIC** *Polydor PO 43* [3] **44**	2 wks
16 Mar 91	**HEART** *IRS NUMAN 1* **43**	2 wks
21 Mar 92	**THE SKIN GAME** *Numa NU 23* **68**	1 wk
1 Aug 92	**MACHINE + SOUL** *Numa NUM 124* **72**	1 wk
4 Sep 93	**CARS (2nd re-mix)** *Beggars Banquet BEG 264CD* **53**	1 wk

[1] Tubeway Army [2] Gary Numan and Dramatis [3] Sharpe and Numan [4] Radio Heart featuring Gary Numan

Tracks on The Live EP: *Are 'Friends' Electric / Berserker / Cars / We Are Glass. See also Paul Gardiner.*

Bobby NUNN *US, male vocalist / multi-instrumentalist* **3 wks**

4 Feb 84	**DON'T KNOCK IT (UNTIL YOU TRY IT)** *Motown TMG 1323* **65**	3 wks

NUSH *UK, male instrumental / production duo* **1 wk**

23 Jul 94	**U GIRLS** *Blunted Vinyl BLNCDX 006* **58**	1 wk

N.W.A. *US, male rap group* **15 wks**

9 Sep 89	**EXPRESS YOURSELF** *Fourth & Broadway BRW 144* ..**50**	4 wks
26 May 90	**EXPRESS YOURSELF (re-entry)** *Fourth & Broadway BRW 144* **26**	5 wks
1 Sep 90	**GANGSTA, GANGSTA** *Fourth & Broadway BRW 191* **70**	1 wk
10 Nov 90	**100 MILES AND RUNNIN'** *Fourth & Broadway BRW 200* **38**	3 wks
23 Nov 91	**ALWAYZ INTO SOMETHIN'** *Fourth & Broadway BRW 238* **60**	2 wks

Joe NYE - *See DNA*

Michael NYMAN *UK, male instrumentalist - piano* **2 wks**

19 Mar 94	**THE HEART ASKS PLEASURE FIRST - THE PROMISE** *Virgin VEND 3* **60**	2 wks

O

Phil OAKEY - *See Giorgio MORODER*

OASIS *UK, male vocal / instrumental group* **21 wks**

23 Apr 94	**SUPERSONIC** *Creation CRESCD 176* **31**	3 wks
2 Jul 94	**SHAKERMAKER** *Creation CRESCD 182* **11**	5 wks
20 Aug 94	● **LIVE FOREVER** *Creation CRESCD 185* **10**	5 wks
22 Oct 94	● **CIGARETTES AND ALCOHOL** *Creation CRESCD 190* ..**7**	6 wks
31 Dec 94	● **WHATEVER** *Creation CRESCD 195* ....**3†**	1 wk
31 Dec 94	**CIGARETTES AND ALCOHOL (re-entry)** *Creation CRESCD 190* ....**69†**	1 wk

John OATES - *See Daryl HALL and John OATES*

OBERNKIRCHEN CHILDREN'S CHOIR
Germany, children's choir **26 wks**

22 Jan 54	● **HAPPY WANDERER** *Parlophone R 3799* **2**	23 wks
9 Jul 54	● **HAPPY WANDERER (re-entry)** *Parlophone R 3799* **8**	3 wks

Dermot O'BRIEN *Ireland, male vocalist* **2 wks**

20 Oct 66	**THE MERRY PLOUGHBOY** *Envoy ENV 016* **46**	1 wk
3 Nov 66	**THE MERRY PLOUGHBOY (re-entry)** *Envoy ENV 016* **50**	1 wk

Billy OCEAN *UK, male vocalist* **153 wks**

21 Feb 76	● **LOVE REALLY HURTS WITHOUT YOU** *GTO GT 52* **2**	10 wks
10 Jul 76	**L.O.D. (LOVE ON DELIVERY)** *GTO GT 62* **19**	8 wks
13 Nov 76	**STOP ME (IF YOU'VE HEARD IT ALL BEFORE)** *GTO GT 72* **12**	11 wks
19 Mar 77	● **RED LIGHT SPELLS DANGER** *GTO GT 85* **2**	10 wks
1 Sep 79	**AMERICAN HEARTS** *GTO GT 244* **54**	5 wks
19 Jan 80	**ARE YOU READY** *GTO GT 259* **42**	7 wks
13 Oct 84	● **CARIBBEAN QUEEN (NO MORE LOVE ON THE RUN)** *Jive Jive 77* **6**	14 wks
19 Jan 85	● **LOVERBOY** *Jive JIVE 80* **15**	10 wks
11 May 85	● **SUDDENLY** *Jive JIVE 90* **4**	14 wks
17 Aug 85	**MYSTERY LADY** *Jive JIVE 98* **49**	4 wks
25 Jan 86	★ **WHEN THE GOING GETS TOUGH, THE TOUGH GET GOING** *Jive JIVE 114* **1**	13 wks
12 Apr 86	**THERE'LL BE SAD SONGS (TO MAKE YOU CRY)** *Jive JIVE 117* **12**	13 wks
9 Aug 86	**LOVE ZONE** *Jive JIVE 124* **49**	3 wks
11 Oct 86	**BITTERSWEET** *Jive JIVE 133* **44**	4 wks
10 Jan 87	**LOVE IS FOREVER** *Jive JIVE 134* **34**	7 wks
6 Feb 88	● **GET OUTTA MY DREAMS GET INTO MY CAR** *Jive BOS 1* **3**	11 wks
7 May 88	**CALYPSO CRAZY** *Jive BOS 2* **35**	4 wks
6 Aug 88	**THE COLOUR OF LOVE** *Jive BOS 3* **65**	3 wks
6 Feb 93	**PRESSURE** *Jive BOSCD 6* **55**	2 wks

OCEAN COLOUR SCENE
UK, male vocal / instrumental group **1 wk**

23 Mar 91	**YESTERDAY TODAY** *!Phfft FIT 2* **49**	1 wk

OCEANIC *UK, male / female vocal / instrumental group* **26 wks**

24 Aug 91	● **INSANITY** *Dead Dead Good GOOD 4* **3**	15 wks
30 Nov 91	**WICKED LOVE** *Dead Dead Good GOOD 5* **25**	3 wks
28 Dec 91	**WICKED LOVE (re-entry)** *Dead Dead Good GOOD 5* **65**	2 wks
13 Jun 92	**CONTROLLING ME** *Dead Dead Good GOOD 14* **14**	5 wks
14 Nov 92	**IGNORANCE** *Dead Dead Good GOOD 22* [1] **72**	1 wk

[1] Oceanic featuring Siobhan Maher

Des O'CONNOR *UK, male vocalist* **117 wks**

1 Nov 67	● **CARELESS HANDS** *Columbia DB 8275* **6**	17 wks
8 May 68	★ **I PRETEND** *Columbia DB 8397* **1**	36 wks
20 Nov 68	● **1-2-3 O'LEARY** *Columbia DB 8492* **4**	11 wks
7 May 69	**DICK-A-DUM-DUM (KING'S ROAD)** *Columbia DB 8566* **14**	10 wks
29 Nov 69	**LONELINESS** *Columbia DB 8632* **18**	11 wks
14 Mar 70	**I'LL GO ON HOPING** *Columbia DB 8661* **30**	7 wks
26 Sep 70	**THE TIPS OF MY FINGERS** *Columbia DB 8713* **15**	15 wks
8 Nov 86	● **THE SKYE BOAT SONG** *Tembo TML 119* [1] **10**	10 wks

[1] Roger Whittaker and Des O'Connor

Hazel O'CONNOR *UK, female vocalist* **46 wks**

16 Aug 80	● **EIGHTH DAY** *A & M AMS 7553* **5**	11 wks
25 Oct 80	**GIVE ME AN INCH** *A & M AMS 7569* **41**	4 wks
21 Mar 81	● **D-DAYS** *Albion ION 1009* **10**	9 wks
23 May 81	● **WILL YOU** *A & M AMS 8131* **8**	10 wks
1 Aug 81	**(COVER PLUS) WE'RE ALL GROWN UP** *Albion ION 1018* **41**	6 wks
3 Oct 81	**HANGING AROUND** *Albion ION 1022* **45**	3 wks
23 Jan 82	**CALLS THE TUNE** *A & M AMS 8203* **60**	3 wks

Sinead O'CONNOR *Ireland, female vocalist* **56 wks**

16 Jan 88	**MANDINKA** *Ensign ENY 611* **17**	9 wks
20 Jan 90	★ **NOTHING COMPARES 2 U** *Ensign ENY 630* **1**	14 wks
21 Jul 90	**THE EMPEROR'S NEW CLOTHES** *Ensign ENY 633* **31**	5 wks
20 Oct 90	**THREE BABIES** *Ensign ENY 635* **42**	4 wks
8 Jun 91	**MY SPECIAL CHILD** *Ensign ENY 646* **42**	3 wks

Midnight. It must be OASIS.
The biggest-selling indie band
of 1994, Oasis were fronted by
brothers Noel and Liam
Gallagher.

14 Dec 91	**SILENT NIGHT** Ensign ENY 652............**60**	4 wks
12 Sep 92	**SUCCESS HAS MADE A FAILURE OF OUR HOME**	
	Ensign ENY 656 ....**18**	4 wks
12 Dec 92	**DON'T CRY FOR ME ARGENTINA** Ensign ENY 657 ..**53**	4 wks
19 Feb 94	**YOU MADE ME THE THIEF OF YOUR HEART**	
	Island CID 588 ....**42**	3 wks
26 Nov 94	**THANK YOU FOR HEARING ME**	
	Ensign CDENYS 662 ....**13†**	6 wks

See also Jah Wobble's Invaders Of The Heart: Marxman.

Alan O'DAY US, male vocalist　　　　　　**3 wks**

2 Jul 77	**UNDERCOVER ANGEL** Atlantic K 10926 ....**43**	3 wks

ODETTA - See Harry BELAFONTE

Daniel O'DONNELL Ireland, male vocalist　　**22 wks**

12 Sep 92	**I JUST WANT TO DANCE WITH YOU** Ritz RITZ 250P..**20**	7 wks
2 Jan 93	**THE THREE BELLS** Ritz RITZCD 239 ....**71**	1 wk
8 May 93	**THE LOVE IN YOUR EYES** Ritz RITZCD 257............**47**	3 wks
7 Aug 93	**WHAT EVER HAPPENED TO OLD FASHIONED LOVE**	
	Ritz RITZCD 262 ....**21**	5 wks
16 Apr 94	**SINGING THE BLUES** Ritz RITZCD 270 ....**23**	3 wks
26 Nov 94	**THE GIFT** Ritz RITZCD 275 ....**46**	3 wks

ODYSSEY US, male/female vocal group　　　　**82 wks**

24 Dec 77	● **NATIVE NEW YORKER** RCA PC 1129 ....**5**	11 wks
21 Jun 80	★ **USE IT UP AND WEAR IT OUT** RCA PB 1962 ....**1**	12 wks
13 Sep 80	● **IF YOU'RE LOOKIN' FOR A WAY OUT** RCA 5............**6**	15 wks
17 Jan 81	**HANG TOGETHER** RCA 23 ....**36**	7 wks
30 May 81	● **GOING BACK TO MY ROOTS** RCA 85 ....**4**	12 wks
19 Sep 81	**IT WILL BE ALRIGHT** RCA 128 ....**43**	5 wks
12 Jun 82	● **INSIDE OUT** RCA 226 ....**3**	11 wks
11 Sep 82	**MAGIC TOUCH** RCA 275 ....**41**	5 wks
17 Aug 85	**(JOY) I KNOW IT** Mirror BUTCH 12 ....**51**	4 wks

Esther and Abi OFARIM
Israel, female/male vocal duo　　　　　　　**22 wks**

14 Feb 68	★ **CINDERELLA ROCKEFELLA** Philips BF 1640 ....**1**	13 wks
19 Jun 68	**ONE MORE DANCE** Philips BF 1678............**13**	9 wks

OFF-SHORE Germany, male instrumental/production duo **12 wks**

22 Dec 90	● **I CAN'T TAKE THE POWER** CBS 6565707 ....**7**	11 wks
17 Aug 91	**I GOT A LITTLE SONG** Dance Pool 6568257 ....**64**	1 wk

Wiston OFFICE - See Frank K featuring Wiston OFFICE

OH WELL Germany, male producer - Ackim Faulker　**7 wks**

14 Oct 89	**OH WELL** Parlophone R 6236 ....**28**	6 wks
3 Mar 90	**RADAR LOVE** Parlophone R 6244 ....**65**	1 wk

OHIO EXPRESS US, male vocal/instrumental group　**15 wks**

5 Jun 68	● **YUMMY YUMMY YUMMY**	
	Pye International 7N 25459 ....**5**	15 wks

OHIO PLAYERS US, male vocal/instrumental group　**4 wks**

10 Jul 76	**WHO'D SHE COO** Mercury PLAY 001 ....**43**	4 wks

O'JAYS US, male vocal group　　　　　　　**72 wks**

23 Sep 72	**BACK STABBERS** CBS 8270............**14**	9 wks
3 Mar 73	● **LOVE TRAIN** CBS 1181 ....**9**	13 wks
31 Jan 76	**I LOVE MUSIC** Philadelphia International PIR 3879 ..**13**	9 wks
12 Feb 77	**DARLIN' DARLIN' BABY (SWEET, TENDER, LOVE)**	
	Philadelphia International PIR 4834 ....**24**	6 wks

8 Apr 78	**I LOVE MUSIC (re-issue)**	
	Philadelphia International PIR 6093 ....**36**	3 wks
17 Jun 78	**USED TA BE MY GIRL**	
	Philadelphia International PIR 6332 ....**12**	12 wks
30 Sep 78	**BRANDY** Philadelphia International PIR 6658............**21**	9 wks
29 Sep 79	**SING A HAPPY SONG**	
	Philadelphia International PIR 7825 ....**39**	6 wks
30 Jul 83	**PUT OUR HEADS TOGETHER**	
	Philadelphia International A 3642 ....**45**	5 wks

John O'KANE UK, male vocalist　　　　　　**4 wks**

9 May 92	**STAY WITH ME** Circa YR 88 ....**41**	4 wks

Mike OLDFIELD
UK, male multi-instrumentalist/vocalist　　　**110 wks**

13 Jul 74	**MIKE OLDFIELD'S SINGLE (THEME FROM**	
	TUBULAR BELLS) Virgin VS 101 ....**31**	6 wks
20 Dec 75	● **IN DULCE JUBILO/ON HORSEBACK** Virgin VS 131....**4**	10 wks
27 Nov 76	● **PORTSMOUTH** Virgin VS 163 ....**3**	12 wks
23 Dec 78	**TAKE 4 EP** Virgin VS 238 ....**72**	3 wks
21 Apr 79	**GUILTY** Virgin VS 245 ....**22**	8 wks
8 Dec 79	**BLUE PETER** Virgin VS 317 ....**19**	9 wks
20 Mar 82	**FIVE MILES OUT** Virgin VS 464 [1] **43**	5 wks
12 Jun 82	**FAMILY MAN** Virgin VS 489 [1] **45**	6 wks
28 May 83	● **MOONLIGHT SHADOW** Virgin VS 586 [1] **4**	17 wks
14 Jan 84	**CRIME OF PASSION** Virgin VS 648 [1] **61**	3 wks
30 Jun 84	**TO FRANCE** Virgin VS 686 [1] **48**	7 wks
14 Dec 85	**PICTURES IN THE DARK** Virgin VS 836 [2] **50**	6 wks
3 Oct 92	● **SENTINEL** WEA YZ 698 ....**10**	6 wks
19 Dec 92	**TATTOO** WEA YZ 708 ....**33**	5 wks
17 Apr 93	**THE BELL** WEA YZ 737CD **50**	2 wks
9 Oct 93	**MOONLIGHT SHADOW (re-issue)**	
	Virgin VSCDT 1477 ....**52**	2 wks
17 Dec 94	**HIBERNACULUM** WEA YZ 871CD ....**47†**	3 wks

[1] Mike Oldfield featuring Maggie Reilly [2] Mike Oldfield featuring Aled Jones, Anita Hegerland and Barry Palmer

Tracks on Take 4 EP: Portsmouth/In Dulce Jubilo/Wrekorder Wrondo/Sailors Hornpipe. The Bell credits Viv Stanshall.

Sally OLDFIELD UK, female vocalist　　　　**13 wks**

9 Dec 78	**MIRRORS** Bronze BRO 66 ....**19**	13 wks

Misty OLDLAND UK, female vocalist　　　　**7 wks**

16 Oct 93	**GOT ME A FELLING** Columbia 6597872 ....**59**	2 wks
12 Mar 94	**A FAIR AFFAIR (JE T'AIME)** Columbia 6601612........**49**	4 wks
9 Jul 94	**I WROTE YOU A SONG** Columbia 6603732............**73**	1 wk

OLGA Italy, female vocalist　　　　　　　**1 wk**

1 Oct 94	**I'M A BITCH** UMM UMM 144UKCD **68**	1 wk

OLIVER US, male vocalist　　　　　　　　**18 wks**

9 Aug 69	● **GOOD MORNING STARSHINE** CBS 4435............**6**	16 wks
27 Dec 69	**GOOD MORNING STARSHINE (re-entry)** CBS 4435.**39**	2 wks

OLLIE and JERRY US, male vocal duo　　　**14 wks**

23 Jun 84	● **BREAKIN'...THERE'S NO STOPPING US**	
	Polydor POSP 690 ....**5**	11 wks
9 Mar 85	**ELECTRIC BOOGALOO** Polydor POSP 730 ....**57**	3 wks

OLYMPIC ORCHESTRA UK, orchestra　　　**15 wks**

1 Oct 83	**REILLY** Red Bus RBUS 82 ....**26**	15 wks

OLYMPIC RUNNERS
UK, male vocal/instrumental group　　　　　**21 wks**

13 May 78	**WHATEVER IT TAKES** RCA PC 5078 ....**61**	2 wks

14 Oct 78	**GET IT WHILE YOU CAN** Polydor RUN 7 ....**35**	6 wks
20 Jan 79	**SIR DANCEALOT** Polydor POSP 17 ....**35**	6 wks
28 Jul 79	**THE BITCH** Polydor POSP 63 ....**37**	7 wks

OLYMPICS *US, male vocal group*   **9 wks**

| 3 Oct 58 | **WESTERN MOVIES** HMV POP 528 ....**12** | 8 wks |
| 19 Jan 61 | **I WISH I COULD SHIMMY LIKE MY SISTER KATE** Vogue V 9174 ....**40** | 1 wk |

OMAR *UK, male vocalist*   **14 wks**

22 Jun 91	**THERE'S NOTHING LIKE THIS** Talkin Loud TLK 9......**14**	7 wks
23 May 92	**YOUR LOSS MY GAIN** Talkin Loud TLK 22 ....**47**	2 wks
26 Sep 92	**MUSIC** Talkin Loud TLK 28 ....**53**	2 wks
23 Jul 94	**OUTSIDE / SATURDAY** RCA 74321213982 ....**43**	2 wks
15 Oct 94	**KEEP STEPPIN'** RCA 74321233682 ....**57**	1 wk

OMD - *See* ORCHESTRAL MANOEUVRES IN THE DARK

Michie ONE - *See* Louchie LOU and Michie ONE

ONE DOVE *UK, male/female vocal/instrumental group*   **9 wks**

7 Aug 93	**WHITE LOVE** Boy's Own BOICD 14 ....**43**	3 wks
16 Oct 93	**BREAKDOWN** Boy's Own BOICD 15 ....**24**	3 wks
15 Jan 94	**WHY DON'T YOU TAKE ME** Boy's Own BOICD 16 ...**30**	3 wks

ONE HUNDRED TON AND A FEATHER - *See* Jonathan KING

ONE THE JUGGLER *UK, male vocal/instrumental group* **1 wk**

| 19 Feb 83 | **PASSION KILLER** Regard RG 107 ....**71** | 1 wk |

ONE TRIBE featuring GEM
UK, male/female vocal/instrumental duo   **2 wks**

| 20 Jun 92 | **WHAT HAVE YOU DONE (IS THIS ALL)** Inner Rhythm HEART 03 ....**52** | 2 wks |

ONE 2 MANY
Norway, male/female vocal/instrumental group   **11 wks**

| 12 Nov 88 | **DOWNTOWN** A & M AM 476 ....**65** | 4 wks |
| 3 Jun 89 | **DOWNTOWN (re-issue)** A & M AM 456 ....**43** | 7 wks |

ONE WAY featuring Al HUDSON - *See* Al HUDSON

Alexander O'NEAL *US, male vocalist*   **106 wks**

28 Dec 85	● **SATURDAY LOVE** Tabu A 6829 [1] **6**	11 wks
15 Feb 86	**IF YOU WERE HERE TONIGHT** Tabu A 6391 ....**13**	10 wks
5 Apr 86	**A BROKEN HEART CAN MEND** Tabu A 6244 ....**53**	4 wks
6 Jun 87	**FAKE** Tabu 650891 7 ....**33**	6 wks
31 Oct 87	● **CRITICIZE** Tabu 651211 7 ....**4**	14 wks
6 Feb 88	**NEVER KNEW LOVE LIKE THIS** Tabu 651382 7 [2] ...**26**	7 wks
28 May 88	**THE LOVERS** Tabu 651595 7 ....**28**	4 wks
23 Jul 88	**(WHAT CAN I SAY) TO MAKE YOU LOVE ME** Tabu 652852 7 ....**27**	5 wks
24 Sep 88	**FAKE '88 (re-mix)** Tabu 652949 7 ....**16**	7 wks
10 Dec 88	**CHRISTMAS SONG / THANK YOU FOR A GOOD YEAR** Tabu 653182 7 ....**30**	5 wks
25 Feb 89	**HEARSAY '89** Tabu 654466 7 ....**56**	2 wks
2 Sep 89	**SUNSHINE** Tabu 655191 7 ....**72**	1 wk
9 Dec 89	**HITMIX (OFFICIAL BOOTLEG MEGA-MIX)** Tabu 655504 7 ....**19**	7 wks
24 Mar 90	**SATURDAY LOVE (re-mix)** Tabu 655680 7 [1] **55**	2 wks
12 Jan 91	**ALL TRUE MAN** Tabu 6565717 ....**18**	6 wks
23 Mar 91	**WHAT IS THIS THING CALLED LOVE** Tabu 6567317..**53**	2 wks
11 May 91	**SHAME ON ME** Tabu 6568737 ....**71**	1 wk
9 May 92	**SENTIMENTAL** Tabu 6580147 ....**53**	2 wks
30 Jan 93	**LOVE MAKES NO SENSE** Tabu AMCD 7708 ....**28**	6 wks

---

| 3 Jul 93 | **IN THE MIDDLE** Tabu 5877152 ....**32** | 3 wks |
| 25 Sep 93 | **ALL THAT MATTERS TO ME** Tabu 5877232 ....**67** | 1 wk |

[1] Cherelle with Alexander O'Neal   [2] Alexander O'Neal featuring Cherelle

Shaquille O'NEAL *US, male rapper*   **1 wk**

| 26 Mar 94 | **I'M OUTSTANDING** Jive JIVECD 349 ....**70** | 1 wk |

ONLY ONES *UK, male vocal/instrumental group*   **2 wks**

| 1 Feb 92 | **ANOTHER GIRL - ANOTHER PLANET** Columbia 6577507 ....**57** | 2 wks |

Yoko ONO *Japan, female vocalist*   **5 wks**

| 28 Feb 81 | **WALKING ON THIN ICE** Geffen K 79202 ....**35** | 5 wks |

See also John Lennon.

ONSLAUGHT *UK, male vocal/instrumental group*   **3 wks**

| 6 May 89 | **LET THERE BE ROCK** London LON 224 ....**50** | 3 wks |

ONYX *US, male rap group*   **7 wks**

| 28 Aug 93 | **SLAM** Columbia 6596302 ....**31** | 4 wks |
| 27 Nov 93 | **THROW YA GUNZ** Columbia 6598312 ....**34** | 3 wks |

OO LA LA *UK, male vocal/instrumental group*   **2 wks**

| 5 Sep 92 | **OO...AH...CANTONA** North Speed OOAH 1 ....**64** | 2 wks |

OPTIMYSTIC *UK, male/female vocal group*   **5 wks**

| 17 Sep 94 | **CAUGHT UP IN MY HEART** WEA YZ 841CD ....**49** | 3 wks |
| 10 Dec 94 | **NOTHING BUT LOVE** WEA YZ 864CD1 ....**37** | 2 wks |

OPUS *Austria, male vocal/instrumental group*   **15 wks**

| 15 Jun 85 | ● **LIVE IS LIFE** Polydor POSP 743 ....**6** | 15 wks |

OPUS III *UK, male/female vocal/instrumental group*   **10 wks**

22 Feb 92	● **IT'S A FINE DAY** PWL International PWL 215 ....**5**	8 wks
27 Jun 92	**I TALK TO THE WIND** PWL Continental PWL 235 ...**52**	1 wk
11 Jun 94	**WHEN YOU MADE THE MOUNTAIN** PWL International PWCD 302 ....**71**	1 wk

ORANGE *UK, male vocal/instrumental group*   **1 wk**

| 8 Oct 94 | **JUDY OVER THE RAINBOW** Chrysalis CDCHS 5012 ..**73** | 1 wk |

ORANGE JUICE *UK, male vocal/instrumental group*   **34 wks**

7 Nov 81	**L.O.V.E...LOVE** Polydor POSP 357 ....**65**	2 wks
30 Jan 82	**FELICITY** Polydor POSP 386 ....**63**	3 wks
21 Aug 82	**TWO HEARTS TOGETHER / HOKOYO** Polydor POSP 470 ....**60**	2 wks
23 Oct 82	**I CAN'T HELP MYSELF** Polydor POSP 522 ....**42**	3 wks
19 Feb 83	● **RIP IT UP** Polydor POSP 547 ....**8**	11 wks
4 Jun 83	**FLESH OF MY FLESH** Polydor OJ 4 ....**41**	2 wks
25 Feb 84	**BRIDGE** Polydor OJ 5 ....**67**	2 wks
12 May 84	**WHAT PRESENCE?** Polydor OJ 6 ....**47**	4 wks
27 Oct 84	**LEAN PERIOD** Polydor OJ 7 ....**74**	1 wk

ORB *UK, male instrumental/production duo*   **22 wks**

15 Jun 91	**PERPETUAL DAWN** Big Life BLR 46 ....**61**	1 wk
20 Jun 92	● **BLUE ROOM** Big Life BLRT 75 ....**8**	6 wks
17 Oct 92	**ASSASSIN** Big Life BLRT 81 ....**12**	5 wks
13 Nov 93	● **LITTLE FLUFFY CLOUDS** Big Life BLRD 98 ....**10**	5 wks
5 Feb 94	**PERPETUAL DAWN (re-entry)** Big Life BLRD 46 ......**18**	5 wks

Roy ORBISON US, male vocalist — **345 wks**

Date	Title	Pos	Wks
28 Jul 60	**ONLY THE LONELY** London HLU 9149	**36**	1 wk
11 Aug 60 ★	**ONLY THE LONELY (re-entry)** London HLU 9149	**1**	23 wks
27 Oct 60	**BLUE ANGEL** London HLU 9207	**11**	16 wks
25 May 61 ●	**RUNNING SCARED** London HLU 9342	**9**	13 wks
21 Sep 61	**CRYIN'** London HLU 9405	**25**	9 wks
8 Mar 62 ●	**DREAM BABY** London HLU 9511	**2**	14 wks
28 Jun 62	**THE CROWD** London HLU 9561	**40**	4 wks
8 Nov 62	**WORKIN' FOR THE MAN** London HLU 9607	**50**	1 wk
28 Feb 63	**IN DREAMS** London HLU 9676	**6**	23 wks
30 May 63 ●	**FALLING** London HLU 9727	**9**	11 wks
19 Sep 63 ●	**BLUE BAYOU / MEAN WOMAN BLUES** London HLU 9777	**3**	19 wks
20 Feb 64	**BORNE ON THE WIND** London HLU 9845	**15**	10 wks
30 Apr 64 ★	**IT'S OVER** London HLU 9882	**1**	18 wks
10 Sep 64 ★	**OH PRETTY WOMAN** London HLU 9919	**1**	18 wks
19 Nov 64 ●	**PRETTY PAPER** London HLU 9930	**6**	11 wks
11 Feb 65	**GOODNIGHT** London HLU 9951	**14**	9 wks
22 Jul 65	**(SAY) YOU'RE MY GIRL** London HLU 9978	**23**	8 wks
9 Sep 65	**RIDE AWAY** London HLU 9986	**34**	6 wks
4 Nov 65	**CRAWLIN' BACK** London HLU 10000	**19**	9 wks
27 Jan 66	**BREAKIN' UP IS BREAKIN' MY HEART** London HL 10015	**22**	6 wks
7 Apr 66	**TWINKLE TOES** London HLU 10034	**29**	5 wks
16 Jun 66	**LANA** London HL 10051	**15**	9 wks
18 Aug 66 ●	**TOO SOON TO KNOW** London HLU 10067	**3**	17 wks
1 Dec 66	**THERE WON'T BE MANY COMING HOME** London HL 10096	**18**	9 wks
23 Feb 67	**SO GOOD** London HL 10113	**32**	6 wks
24 Jul 68	**WALK ON** London HLU 10206	**39**	10 wks
25 Sep 68	**HEARTACHE** London HLU 10222	**44**	4 wks
30 Apr 69	**MY FRIEND** London HL 10261	**35**	4 wks
13 Sep 69	**PENNY ARCADE** London HL 10285	**40**	3 wks
11 Oct 69	**PENNY ARCADE (re-entry)** London HL 10285	**27**	11 wks
14 Jan 89 ●	**YOU GOT IT** Virgin VS 1166	**3**	10 wks
1 Apr 89	**SHE'S A MYSTERY TO ME** Virgin VS 1173	**27**	5 wks
4 Jul 92 ●	**I DROVE ALL NIGHT** MCA MCS 1652	**7**	10 wks
22 Aug 92	**CRYING** Virgin America VUS 63 [1]	**13**	6 wks
7 Nov 92	**HEARTBREAK RADIO** Virgin America VUS 68	**36**	3 wks
13 Nov 93	**I DROVE ALL NIGHT (re-issue)** Virgin America VUSCD 79	**47**	2 wks

[1] Roy Orbison (duet with k.d. lang)

William ORBIT UK, male producer — **1 wk**

Date	Title	Pos	Wks
26 Jun 93	**WATER FROM A VINE LEAF** Guerilla VSCDT 1465	**59**	1 wk

ORBITAL UK, male instrumental duo — **23 wks**

Date	Title	Pos	Wks
24 Mar 90	**CHIME** ffrr F B5	**17**	7 wks
22 Sep 90	**OMEN** ffrr F 145	**46**	3 wks
19 Jan 91	**SATAN** ffrr FX 149	**31**	4 wks
15 Feb 92	**MUTATIONS EP** ffrr FX 181	**24**	3 wks
26 Sep 92	**RADICCIO EP** Internal LIARX 1	**37**	2 wks
21 Aug 93	**LUSH** Internal LIECD 7	**43**	2 wks
24 Sep 94	**ARE WE HERE** Internal LIECD 15	**33**	2 wks

Tracks on Mutations EP: Chime Chime / Oolaa / Farenheit 3D 3 / Speed Freak. Tracks on Radiccio EP: Halcyon / The Naked And The Dead / Sunday.

ORCHESTRA ON THE HALF SHELL
US, male vocal / instrumental group — **6 wks**

Date	Title	Pos	Wks
15 Dec 90	**TURTLE RHAPSODY** SBK SBK 17	**36**	6 wks

ORCHESTRAL MANOEUVRES IN THE DARK
UK, male vocal / instrumental group — **193 wks**

Date	Title	Pos	Wks
9 Feb 80	**RED FRAME WHITE LIGHT** Dindisc DIN 6	**67**	2 wks
10 May 80	**MESSAGES** Dindisc DIN 15	**13**	11 wks
4 Oct 80 ●	**ENOLA GAY** Dindisc DIN 22	**8**	15 wks
29 Aug 81 ●	**SOUVENIR** Dindisc DIN 24	**3**	12 wks
24 Oct 81 ●	**JOAN OF ARC** Dindisc DIN 36	**5**	14 wks
23 Jan 82 ●	**MAID OF ORLEANS (THE WALTZ JOAN OF ARC)** Dindisc DIN 40	**4**	10 wks
19 Feb 83	**GENETIC ENGINEERING** Virgin VS 527	**20**	8 wks
9 Apr 83	**TELEGRAPH** Virgin VS 580	**42**	4 wks
14 Apr 84 ●	**LOCOMOTION** Virgin VS 660	**5**	11 wks
16 Jun 84	**TALKING LOUD AND CLEAR** Virgin VS 685	**11**	10 wks
8 Sep 84	**TESLA GIRLS** Virgin VS 705	**21**	8 wks
10 Nov 84	**NEVER TURN AWAY** Virgin VS 727	**70**	2 wks
25 May 85	**SO IN LOVE** Virgin VS 766	**27**	7 wks
20 Jul 85	**SECRET** Virgin VS 796	**34**	7 wks
26 Oct 85	**LA FEMME ACCIDENT** Virgin VS 811	**42**	4 wks
3 May 86	**IF YOU LEAVE** Virgin VS 843	**48**	4 wks
6 Sep 86	**(FOREVER) LIVE AND DIE** Virgin VS 888	**11**	10 wks
15 Nov 86	**WE LOVE YOU** Virgin VS 911	**54**	5 wks
2 May 87	**SHAME** Virgin VS 938	**52**	3 wks
6 Feb 88	**DREAMING** Virgin VS 987	**50**	3 wks
2 Jul 88	**DREAMING (re-entry)** Virgin VS 987	**60**	3 wks
30 Mar 91 ●	**SAILING ON THE SEVEN SEAS** Virgin VS 1310	**3**	13 wks
6 Jul 91 ●	**PANDORA'S BOX** Virgin VS 1331	**7**	10 wks
14 Sep 91	**THEN YOU TURN AWAY** Virgin VS 1368	**50**	4 wks
7 Dec 91	**CALL MY NAME** Virgin VS 1380	**50**	2 wks
15 May 93	**STAND ABOVE ME** Virgin VSCDG 1444	**21**	4 wks
17 Jul 93	**DREAM OF ME (BASED ON LOVE'S THEME)** Virgin VSCDT 1461	**24**	5 wks
18 Sep 93	**EVERYDAY** Virgin VSCDT 1471	**59**	2 wks

Group often known as OMD.

Raul ORELLANA Italy, male producer — **8 wks**

Date	Title	Pos	Wks
30 Sep 89	**THE REAL WILD HOUSE** RCA BCM 322	**29**	8 wks

Tony ORLANDO US, male vocalist — **11 wks**

Date	Title	Pos	Wks
5 Oct 61 ●	**BLESS YOU** Fontana H 330	**5**	11 wks

See also Dawn.

ORLONS US, female / male vocal group — **3 wks**

Date	Title	Pos	Wks
27 Dec 62	**DON'T HANG UP** Cameo Parkway C 231	**50**	1 wk
10 Jan 63	**DON'T HANG UP (re-entry)** Cameo Parkway C 231	**39**	2 wks

ORVILLE - See Keith HARRIS

Jeffrey OSBORNE US, male vocalist — **38 wks**

Date	Title	Pos	Wks
17 Sep 83	**DON'T YOU GET SO MAD** A & M AM 140	**54**	2 wks
14 Apr 84	**STAY WITH ME TONIGHT** A & M AM 188	**18**	11 wks
23 Jun 84	**ON THE WINGS OF LOVE** A & M AM 198	**11**	14 wks
20 Oct 84	**DON'T STOP** A & M AM 222	**61**	2 wks
26 Jul 86	**SOWETO** A & M AM 334	**44**	5 wks
6 Sep 86	**SOWETO (re-entry)** A & M AM 334	**75**	1 wk
15 Aug 87	**LOVE POWER** Arista RIS 27 [1]	**63**	3 wks

[1] Dionne Warwick and Jeffrey Osborne

Tony OSBORNE SOUND UK, orchestra — **3 wks**

Date	Title	Pos	Wks
23 Feb 61	**MAN FROM MADRID** HMV POP 827 [1]	**50**	1 wk
3 Feb 73	**THE SHEPHERD'S SONG** Philips 6006 266	**46**	2 wks

[1] Tony Osborne Sound featuring Joanne Brown

Ozzy OSBOURNE UK, male vocalist — **39 wks**

Date	Title	Pos	Wks
13 Sep 80	**CRAZY TRAIN** Jet 197 [1]	**49**	4 wks
15 Nov 80	**MR. CROWLEY** Jet 7003 [1]	**46**	3 wks
26 Nov 83	**BARK AT THE MOON** Epic A 3915	**21**	8 wks
2 Jun 84	**SO TIRED** Epic A 4452	**20**	9 wks
1 Feb 86	**SHOT IN THE DARK** Epic A 6859	**20**	6 wks
9 Aug 86	**THE ULTIMATE SIN / LIGHTNING STRIKES** Epic A 7311	**72**	1 wk
20 May 89	**CLOSE MY EYES FOREVER** Dreamland PB 49409 [2]	**47**	3 wks

28 Sep 91	**NO MORE TEARS** Epic 6574407 ....**32**	3 wks
30 Nov 91	**MAMA I'M COMING HOME** Epic 6576177 ....**46**	2 wks

[1] Ozzy Osbourne's Blizzard of Ozz [2] Lita Ford duet with Ozzy Osbourne

OSIBISA Ghana / Nigeria, male vocal / instrumental group　　12 wks

17 Jan 76	**SUNSHINE DAY** Bronze BRO 20 ....**17**	6 wks
5 Jun 76	**DANCE THE BODY MUSIC** Bronze BRO 26 ....**31**	6 wks

OSMOND BOYS US, male vocal group　　6 wks

9 Nov 91	**BOYS WILL BE BOYS** Curb 6573847 ....**65**	2 wks
11 Jan 92	**SHOW ME THE WAY** Curb 6577227...................**60**	4 wks

Donny OSMOND US, male vocalist　　118 wks

17 Jun 72	★ **PUPPY LOVE** MGM 2006 104 ....**1**	17 wks
16 Sep 72	● **TOO YOUNG** MGM 2006 113 ....**5**	12 wks
21 Oct 72	**PUPPY LOVE (re-entry)** MGM 2006 104 ....**45**	2 wks
11 Nov 72	● **WHY** MGM 2006 119 ....**3**	20 wks
23 Dec 72	**PUPPY LOVE (2nd re-entry)** MGM 2006 104..........**46**	3 wks
23 Dec 72	**TOO YOUNG (re-entry)** MGM 2006 113 ....**47**	3 wks
27 Jan 73	**PUPPY LOVE (3rd re-entry)** MGM 2006 104 ....**48**	1 wk
10 Mar 73	★ **THE TWELFTH OF NEVER** MGM 2006 199.............**1**	14 wks
18 Aug 73	★ **YOUNG LOVE** MGM 2006 300 ....**1**	10 wks
10 Nov 73	● **WHEN I FALL IN LOVE** MGM 2006 365 ....**4**	13 wks
9 Nov 74	**WHERE DID ALL THE GOOD TIMES GO** MGM 2006 468 ....**18**	10 wks
26 Sep 87	**I'M IN IT FOR LOVE** Virgin VS 994 ....**70**	1 wk
6 Aug 88	**SOLDIER OF LOVE** Virgin VS 1094 ....**29**	8 wks
12 Nov 88	**IF IT'S LOVE THAT YOU WANT** Virgin VS 1140 .....**70**	2 wks
9 Feb 91	**MY LOVE IS A FIRE** Capitol CL 600 ....**64**	2 wks

See also Donny and Marie Osmond; Osmonds.

Donny and Marie OSMOND
US, male / female vocal duo　　37 wks

3 Aug 74	● **I'M LEAVING IT (ALL) UP TO YOU** MGM 2006 446 ....**2**	12 wks
14 Dec 74	● **MORNING SIDE OF THE MOUNTAIN** MGM 2006 274 ....**5**	12 wks
21 Jun 75	**MAKE THE WORLD GO AWAY** MGM 2006 523 ....**18**	6 wks
17 Jan 76	**DEEP PURPLE** MGM 2006 561 ....**25**	7 wks

See also Donny Osmond; Marie Osmond.

Little Jimmy OSMOND US, male vocalist　　50 wks

25 Nov 72	★ **LONG HAIRED LOVER FROM LIVERPOOL** MGM 2006 109 ....**1**	24 wks
31 Mar 73	● **TWEEDLE DEE** MGM 2006 175 ....**4**	13 wks
19 May 73	**LONG HAIRED LOVER FROM LIVERPOOL (re-entry)** MGM 2006 109 ....**41**	3 wks
23 Mar 74	**I'M GONNA KNOCK ON YOUR DOOR** MGM 2006 389 ....**11**	10 wks

Marie OSMOND US, female vocalist　　15 wks

17 Nov 73	● **PAPER ROSES** MGM 2006 315 ....**2**	15 wks

See also Donny and Marie Osmond.

OSMONDS US, male vocal / instrumental group　　91 wks

25 Mar 72	**DOWN BY THE LAZY RIVER** MGM 2006 096 ....**40**	5 wks
11 Nov 72	● **CRAZY HORSES** MGM 2006 142 ....**2**	18 wks
14 Jul 73	● **GOING HOME** MGM 2006 288 ....**4**	10 wks
27 Oct 73	● **LET ME IN** MGM 2006 321 ....**2**	14 wks
20 Apr 74	**I CAN'T STOP** MCA 129 ....**12**	10 wks
24 Aug 74	★ **LOVE ME FOR A REASON** MGM 2006 458 ....**1**	9 wks
1 Mar 75	**HAVING A PARTY** MGM 2006 492 ....**28**	8 wks
24 May 75	● **THE PROUD ONE** MGM 2006 520...................**5**	8 wks
15 Nov 75	**I'M STILL GONNA NEED YOU** MGM 2006 551 ....**32**	4 wks
30 Oct 76	**I CAN'T LIVE A DREAM** Polydor 2066 726 ....**37**	5 wks

Gilbert O'SULLIVAN Ireland, male vocalist　　145 wks

28 Nov 70	● **NOTHING RHYMED** MAM 3 ....**8**	11 wks
3 Apr 71	**UNDERNEATH THE BLANKET GO** MAM 13 ....**40**	1 wk
17 Apr 71	**UNDERNEATH THE BLANKET GO (re-entry)** MAM 13 ....**42**	3 wks
24 Jul 71	**WE WILL** MAM 30 ....**16**	11 wks
27 Nov 71	● **NO MATTER HOW I TRY** MAM 53 ....**5**	15 wks
4 Mar 72	● **ALONE AGAIN (NATURALLY)** MAM 66 ....**3**	12 wks
17 Jun 72	● **OOH-WAKKA-DOO-WAKKA-DAY** MAM 78 ....**8**	11 wks
21 Oct 72	★ **CLAIR** MAM 84 ....**1**	14 wks
17 Mar 73	★ **GET DOWN** MAM 96 ....**1**	13 wks
15 Sep 73	**OOH BABY** MAM 107 ....**18**	7 wks
10 Nov 73	● **WHY OH WHY OH WHY** MAM 111 ....**6**	14 wks
9 Feb 74	**HAPPINESS IS ME AND YOU** MAM 114 ....**19**	7 wks
24 Aug 74	**A WOMAN'S PLACE** MAM 122 ....**42**	3 wks
14 Dec 74	**CHRISTMAS SONG** MAM 124 ....**12**	6 wks
14 Jun 75	**I DON'T LOVE YOU BUT I THINK I LIKE YOU** MAM 130 ....**14**	6 wks
27 Sep 80	**WHAT'S IN A KISS?** CBS 8929 ....**19**	9 wks
24 Feb 90	**SO WHAT** Dover ROJ 3 ....**70**	2 wks

O.T. QUARTET - *See OUR TRIBE*

OTHER TWO UK, male / female vocal / instrumental duo　　5 wks

9 Nov 91	**TASTY FISH** Factory FAC 3297 ....**41**	3 wks
6 Nov 93	**SELFISH** London TWOCD 1 ....**46**	2 wks

Johnny OTIS SHOW US, orchestra and chorus　　22 wks

22 Nov 57	● **MA HE'S MAKING EYES AT ME** Capitol CL 14794 [1] **2**	15 wks
10 Jan 58	**BYE BYE BABY** Capitol CL 14817 [2] **20**	7 wks

[1] Johnny Otis and his orchestra with Marie Adams and the Three Tons of Joy
[2] Johnny Otis Show, vocals by Marie Adams and Johnny Otis

OTTAWAN France, male / female vocal duo　　45 wks

13 Sep 80	● **D.I.S.C.O.** Carrere CAR 161 ....**2**	18 wks
13 Dec 80	**YOU'RE O.K.** Carrere CAR 168 ....**56**	6 wks
29 Aug 81	● **HANDS UP (GIVE ME YOUR HEART)** Carrere CAR 183 ....**3**	15 wks
5 Dec 81	**HELP, GET ME SOME HELP!** Carrere CAR 215 ....**49**	6 wks

John OTWAY and Wild Willy BARRETT
UK, male vocal / instrumental duo　　12 wks

3 Dec 77	**REALLY FREE** Polydor 2058 951 ....**27**	8 wks
5 Jul 80	**DK 50-80** Polydor 2059 250 [1] **45**	4 wks

[1] Otway and Barrett

OUI 3
UK / US / Switzerland, male / female vocal / instrumental group　　19 wks

20 Feb 93	**FOR WHAT IT'S WORTH** MCA MCSTD 1736 ....**28**	6 wks
24 Apr 93	**ARMS OF SOLITUDE** MCA MCSTD 1759 ....**54**	2 wks
17 Jul 93	**BREAK FROM THE OLD ROUTINE** MCA MCSTD 1793 ....**17**	6 wks
23 Oct 93	**FOR WHAT IT'S WORTH (re-mix)** MCA MCSTD 1941 ....**26**	3 wks
29 Jan 94	**FACT OF LIFE** MCA MCSTD 1939 ....**38**	2 wks

OUR DAUGHTER'S WEDDING
US, male vocal / instrumental group　　6 wks

1 Aug 81	**LAWNCHAIRS** EMI America EA 124 ....**49**	6 wks

OUR KID UK, male vocal group　　11 wks

29 May 76	● **YOU JUST MIGHT SEE ME CRY** Polydor 2058 729 ......**2**	11 wks

OUR TRIBE
UK/US, male/female vocal/instrumental group **6 wks**

27 Mar 93	**I BELIEVE IN YOU** Ffrreedom TABCD 117 42	2 wks
30 Apr 94	**HOLD THAT SUCKER DOWN** Cheeky CHEKCD 004 [1] 24	3 wks
21 May 94	**LOVE COME HOME** Triangle BLUESCD 001 [2] 73	1 wk

[1] O.T. Quartet [2] Our Tribe with Frankë Pharoah and Kristine W

OUTLANDER
Belgium, male producer - Marcos Salon **2 wks**

31 Aug 91	**VAMP** R & S RSUK 1 51	2 wks

OUTLAWS
UK, male instrumental group **4 wks**

13 Apr 61	**SWINGIN' LOW** HMV POP 844 46	2 wks
8 Jun 61	**AMBUSH** HMV POP 877 43	2 wks

See also Mike Berry.

OVERLANDERS
UK, male vocal/instrumental group **10 wks**

13 Jan 66	★ **MICHELLE** Pye 7N 17034 1	10 wks

OVERWEIGHT POOCH - See Ce Ce PENISTON

Reg OWEN
UK, orchestra **10 wks**

27 Feb 59	**MANHATTAN SPIRITUAL** Pye International 7N 25009 20	8 wks
27 Oct 60	**OBSESSION** Palette PG 9004 43	2 wks

Robert OWENS
US, male vocalist **2 wks**

7 Dec 91	**I'LL BE YOUR FRIEND** Perfecto PB 45161 75	2 wks

See also Various Artists (EPs & LPs) - Gimme Shelter (EP).

P

Jazzi P
US, female vocalist **12 wks**

8 Jul 89	**GET LOOSE** Breakout USA 659 [1] 25	6 wks
9 Jun 90	**FEEL THE RHYTHM** A & M AMUSA 691 51	2 wks
3 Aug 91	**REBEL WOMAN** DNA 7DNA 001 [2] 42	4 wks

[1] L.A. Mix performed by Jazzi P [2] DNA performed by Jazzi P

Thom PACE
US, male vocalist **15 wks**

19 May 79	**MAYBE** RSO 34.........................14	15 wks

PACEMAKERS - See GERRY and the PACEMAKERS

PACK featuring Nigel BENN
UK, male vocal/instrumental group **2 wks**

8 Dec 90	**STAND AND FIGHT** IQ ZB 44237 61	2 wks

PACKABEATS
UK, male instrumental group **1 wk**

23 Feb 61	**GYPSY BEAT** Parlophone R 4729 49	1 wk

Hal PAGE and the WHALERS
US, male vocal/instrumental group **1 wk**

25 Aug 60	**GOING BACK TO MY HOME TOWN** Melodisc MEL 1553 50	1 wk

Jimmy PAGE - *See Robert PLANT*

Patti PAGE
US, female vocalist **5 wks**

27 Mar 53	● **(HOW MUCH IS) THAT DOGGIE IN THE WINDOW** Oriole CB 1156 9	5 wks

Tommy PAGE
US, male vocalist **3 wks**

26 May 90	**I'LL BE YOUR EVERYTHING** Sire W 9959 53	3 wks

PAGLIARO
Canada, male vocalist **6 wks**

19 Feb 72	**LOVING YOU AIN'T EASY** Pye 7N 45111 31	6 wks

Elaine PAIGE
UK, female vocalist **38 wks**

21 Oct 78	**DON'T WALK AWAY TILL I TOUCH YOU** EMI 2862 ..46	5 wks
6 Jun 81	● **MEMORY** Polydor POSP 279 6	12 wks
30 Jan 82	**MEMORY (re-entry)** Polydor POSP 279 67	3 wks
14 Apr 84	**SOMETIMES (THEME FROM 'CHAMPIONS')** Island IS 174 72	1 wk
5 Jan 85	★ **I KNOW HIM SO WELL** RCA CHESS 3 [1] 1	16 wks
21 Nov 87	**THE SECOND TIME (THEME FROM 'BILITIS')** WEA YZ 163 69	1 wk

[1] Elaine Paige and Barbara Dickson

Orchestre De Chambre Jean-Francois PAILLARD
France, male conductor and orchestra **3 wks**

20 Aug 88	**THEME FROM 'VIETNAM'(CANON IN D)** Debut DEBT 3053 61	3 wks

PALE
Ireland, male vocal/instrumental group **2 wks**

13 Jun 92	**DOGS WITH NO TAILS** A & M AM 866 51	2 wks

PALE FOUNTAINS
UK, male vocal/instrumental group **6 wks**

27 Nov 82	**THANK YOU** Virgin VS 557 48	6 wks

PALE SAINTS
Australia, male/female vocal/instrumental group **1 wk**

6 Jul 91	**KINKY LOVE** 4AD AD 1009........................72	1 wk

Barry PALMER - *See Mike OLDFIELD*

Robert PALMER
UK, male vocalist **124 wks**

20 May 78	**EVERY KINDA PEOPLE** Island WIP 6425 53	4 wks
7 Jul 79	**BAD CASE OF LOVIN' YOU (DOCTOR DOCTOR)** Island WIP 6481 61	2 wks
6 Sep 80	**JOHNNY AND MARY** Island WIP 6638 44	8 wks
22 Nov 80	**LOOKING FOR CLUES** Island WIP 6651 33	9 wks
13 Feb 82	**SOME GUYS HAVE ALL THE LUCK** Island WIP 6754 16	8 wks
2 Apr 83	**YOU ARE IN MY SYSTEM** Island IS 104 53	4 wks
18 Jun 83	**YOU CAN HAVE IT (TAKE MY HEART)** Island IS 121 66	2 wks
10 May 86	● **ADDICTED TO LOVE** Island IS 270 5	15 wks
19 Jul 86	● **I DIDN'T MEAN TO TURN YOU ON** Island IS 283 9	9 wks
1 Nov 86	**DISCIPLINE OF LOVE** Island IS 242 68	1 wk
26 Mar 88	**SWEET LIES** Island IS 352 58	3 wks
11 Jun 88	**SIMPLY IRRESISTIBLE** EMI EM 61 44	4 wks
15 Oct 88	● **SHE MAKES MY DAY** EMI EM 65 6	12 wks
13 May 89	**CHANGE HIS WAYS** EMI EM 85 28	7 wks
26 Aug 89	**IT COULD HAPPEN TO YOU** EMI EM 99 71	1 wk
3 Nov 90	● **I'LL BE YOUR BABY TONIGHT** EMI EM 167 [1] 6	10 wks
5 Jan 91	● **MERCY MERCY ME - I WANT YOU** EMI EM 173 9	9 wks

15 Jun 91	**DREAMS TO REMEMBER** EMI EM 193 ....**68**	1 wk
7 Mar 92	**EVERY KINDA PEOPLE (re-issue)** Island IS 498........**43**	3 wks
17 Oct 92	**WITCHCRAFT** EMI EM 251 ....**50**	3 wks
9 Jul 94	**GIRL U WANT** EMI CDEMS 331 ....**57**	2 wks
3 Sep 94	**KNOW BY NOW** EMI CDEMS 343 ....**25**	5 wks
24 Dec 94	**YOU BLOW ME AWAY** EMI CDEMS 350 ....**38†**	2 wks

[1] Robert Palmer and UB40

PAN POSITION
Italy / Venezuela, male instrumental / production group **1 wk**

18 Jun 94	**ELEPHANT PAW (GET DOWN TO THE FUNK)** Positiva CDTIV 13 ....**55**	1 wk

PANDORA'S BOX
US, male / female vocal / instrumental group **3 wks**

21 Oct 89	**IT'S ALL COMING BACK TO ME NOW** Virgin VS 1216 ....**51**	3 wks

Johnny PANIC and the BIBLE OF DREAMS
UK, male / female vocal / instrumental group **2 wks**

2 Feb 91	**JOHNNY PANIC AND THE BIBLE OF DREAMS** Fontana PANIC 1 ....**70**	2 wks

PANTERA *US, male vocal / instrumental group* **8 wks**

10 Oct 92	**MOUTH FOR WAR** Atco A 5845T **73**	1 wk
27 Feb 93	**WALK** Atco B 6076CD **35**	2 wks
19 Mar 94	**I'M BROKEN** Atco B 5932CD1 ....**19**	2 wks
22 Oct 94	**PLANET CARAVAN** East West A 5836CD1................**26**	3 wks

PAPER DOLLS *UK, female vocal group* **13 wks**

13 Mar 68	**SOMETHING HERE IN MY HEART** **(KEEPS A-TELLIN' ME NO)** Pye 7N 17456...............**11**	13 wks

PAPER LACE *UK, male vocal / instrumental group* **41 wks**

23 Feb 74	★ **BILLY DON'T BE A HERO** Bus Stop BUS 1014 ....**1**	14 wks
4 May 74	● **THE NIGHT CHICAGO DIED** Bus Stop BUS 1016 ....**3**	11 wks
24 Aug 74	**THE BLACK EYED BOYS** Bus Stop BUS 1019 ....**11**	10 wks
4 Mar 78	**WE'VE GOT THE WHOLE WORLD IN OUR HANDS** Warner Bros. K17110 [1] **24**	6 wks

[1] Nottingham Forest F.C. and Paper Lace

Vanessa PARADIS *France, female vocalist* **30 wks**

13 Feb 88	● **JOE LE TAXI** FA Productions POSP 902 ....**3**	10 wks
10 Oct 92	● **BE MY BABY** Remark PO 235 ....**6**	15 wks
27 Feb 93	**SUNDAY MONDAYS** Remark PZCD 251 ....**49**	4 wks
24 Jul 93	**JUST AS LONG AS YOU ARE THERE** Remark PZCD 272 ....**57**	1 wk

PARADISE *UK, male vocal / instrumental group* **4 wks**

10 Sep 83	**ONE MIND, TWO HEARTS** Priority P 1 ....**42**	4 wks

PARADISE ORGANISATION
UK, male instrumental / production group **1 wk**

23 Jan 93	**PRAYER TOWER** Cowboy RODEO 13 ....**70**	1 wk

PARADOX *UK, male instrumental duo* **2 wks**

24 Feb 90	**JAILBREAK** Ronin 7R2...**66**	2 wks

Norrie PARAMOR *UK, orchestra* **8 wks**

17 Mar 60	**THEME FROM 'A SUMMER PLACE'** Columbia DB 4419 ....**36**	2 wks

22 Mar 62	**THEME FROM 'Z CARS'** Columbia DB 4789 ....**33**	6 wks

PARAMOUNT JAZZ BAND - *See Mr. Acker BILK and his PARAMOUNT JAZZ BAND*

PARAMOUNTS *UK, male vocal / instrumental group* **7 wks**

16 Jan 64	**POISON IVY** Parlophone R 5093 ....**35**	7 wks

PARCHMENT *UK, male / female vocal / instrumental group* **5 wks**

16 Sep 72	**LIGHT UP THE FIRE** Pye 7N 45178 ....**31**	5 wks

PARIS *UK, male / female vocal group* **4 wks**

19 Jun 82	**NO GETTING OVER YOU** RCA 222 ....**49**	4 wks

Mica PARIS *UK, female vocalist* **56 wks**

7 May 88	● **MY ONE TEMPTATION** Fourth & Broadway BRW 85 ..**7**	11 wks
30 Jul 88	**LIKE DREAMERS DO** Fourth & Broadway BRW 108 [1] **26**	5 wks
22 Oct 88	**BREATHE LIFE INTO ME** Fourth & Broadway BRW 115 ....**26**	10 wks
21 Jan 89	**WHERE IS THE LOVE** Fourth & Broadway BRW 122 [2] **19**	7 wks
6 Oct 90	**CONTRIBUTION** Fourth & Broadway BRW 188 ....**33**	4 wks
1 Dec 90	**SOUTH OF THE RIVER** Fourth & Broadway BRW 199 ....**50**	2 wks
23 Feb 91	**IF I LOVE U 2 NITE** Fourth & Broadway BRW 207 ....**43**	3 wks
31 Aug 91	**YOUNG SOUL REBELS** Big Life BLR 57 ....**61**	3 wks
3 Apr 93	**I NEVER FELT LIKE THIS BEFORE** Fourth & Broadway BRCD 263 ....**15**	5 wks
5 Jun 93	**I WANNA HOLD ON TO YOU** Fourth & Broadway BRCD 275....................................**27**	3 wks
7 Aug 93	**TWO IN A MILLION** Fourth & Broadway BRCD 285 ..**51**	2 wks
4 Dec 93	**WHISPER A PRAYER** Fourth & Broadway BRCD 287 ....**65**	1 wk

[1] Mica Paris featuring Courtney Pine [2] Mica Paris and Will Downing

Ryan PARIS *France, male vocalist* **10 wks**

3 Sep 83	● **DOLCE VITA** Carrere CAR 289...**5**	10 wks

PARIS ANGELS *Ireland, male vocal / instrumental group* **5 wks**

3 Nov 90	**SCOPE** Sheer Joy SHEER 0047 ....**75**	1 wk
20 Jul 91	**PERFUME** Virgin VS 1360 ....**55**	3 wks
21 Sep 91	**FADE** Virgin VS 1365 ....**70**	1 wk

PARIS RED
US / Germany, male / female vocal / instrumental duo **2 wks**

29 Feb 92	**GOOD FRIEND** Columbia 6569417.........................**61**	1 wk
15 May 93	**PROMISES** Columbia 6592342 ....**59**	1 wk

Simon PARK *UK, orchestra* **23 wks**

25 Nov 72	**EYE LEVEL** Columbia DB 8946 ....**41**	2 wks
15 Sep 73	★ **EYE LEVEL (re-entry)** Columbia DB 8946 ....**1**	21 wks

Graham PARKER and the RUMOUR
UK, male vocal / instrumental group **16 wks**

19 Mar 77	**THE PINK PARKER EP** Vertigo PARK 001...................**24**	5 wks
22 Apr 78	**HEY LORD DON'T ASK ME QUESTIONS** Vertigo PARK 002 ....**32**	7 wks
20 Mar 82	**TEMPORARY BEAUTY** RCA PARK 100 [1] **50**	4 wks

[1] Graham Parker

Tracks on The Pink Parker EP: Hold Back The Night / (Let Me Get) Sweet On You / White Honey / Soul Shoes.

Ray PARKER Jr. *US, male vocalist* — **47 wks**

25 Aug 84	● **GHOSTBUSTERS** Arista ARIST 580	**2** 31 wks
18 Jan 86	**GIRLS ARE MORE FUN** Arista ARIST 641	**46** 4 wks
3 Oct 87	**I DON'T THINK THAT MAN SHOULD SLEEP ALONE** Geffen GEF 27	**13** 10 wks
30 Jan 88	**OVER YOU** Geffen GEF 33	**65** 2 wks

Robert PARKER *US, male vocalist* — **8 wks**

4 Aug 66	**BAREFOOTIN'** Island WI 286	**24** 8 wks

Jimmy PARKINSON *Australia, male vocalist* — **19 wks**

2 Mar 56	● **THE GREAT PRETENDER** Columbia DB 3729	**9** 13 wks
17 Aug 56	**WALK HAND IN HAND** Columbia DB 3775	**30** 1 wk
5 Oct 56	**WALK HAND IN HAND (re-entry)** Columbia DB 3775	**26** 1 wk
9 Nov 56	**IN THE MIDDLE OF THE HOUSE** Columbia DB 3833	**26** 2 wks
30 Nov 56	**IN THE MIDDLE OF THE HOUSE (re-entry)** Columbia DB 3833	**20** 2 wks

John PARR *UK, male vocalist* — **22 wks**

14 Sep 85	● **ST ELMO'S FIRE (MAN IN MOTION)** London LON 73	**6** 13 wks
18 Jan 86	**NAUGHTY NAUGHTY** London LON 80	**58** 3 wks
30 Aug 86	**ROCK 'N' ROLL MERCENARIES** Arista ARIST 666 [1]	**31** 6 wks

[1] Meat Loaf featuring John Parr

Dean PARRISH *US, male vocalist* — **5 wks**

8 Feb 75	**I'M ON MY WAY** UK USA 2	**38** 5 wks

Man PARRISH *US, mixer* — **26 wks**

26 Mar 83	**HOP HOP, BE BOP (DON'T STOP)** Polydor POSP 575	**41** 6 wks
23 Mar 85	**BOOGIE DOWN (BRONX)** Boiling Point POSP 731	**56** 4 wks
13 Sep 86	**MALE STRIPPER** Bolts BOLTS 4 [1]	**64** 3 wks
3 Jan 87	**MALE STRIPPER (re-entry)** Bolts BOLTS 4 [1]	**63** 1 wk
7 Feb 87	● **MALE STRIPPER (2nd re-entry)** Bolts BOLTS 4 [1]	**4** 12 wks

[1] Man 2 Man meet Man Parrish

Bill PARSONS *US, male vocalist* — **2 wks**

10 Apr 59	**ALL AMERICAN BOY** London HL 8798	**22** 2 wks

Record erroneously credited to Bill Parsons, actual vocalist is Bobby Bare.

Alan PARSONS PROJECT
UK, male vocal / instrumental group — **4 wks**

15 Jan 83	**OLD AND WISE** Arista ARIST 494	**74** 1 wk
10 Mar 84	**DON'T ANSWER ME** Arista ARIST 553	**58** 3 wks

PARTNERS - *See Al HUDSON*

PARTNERS IN KRYME
US, male vocal / instrumental duo — **10 wks**

21 Jul 90	★ **TURTLE POWER** SBK TURTLE 1	**1** 10 wks

David PARTON *UK, male vocalist* — **9 wks**

15 Jan 77	● **ISN'T SHE LOVELY** Pye 7N 45663	**4** 9 wks

Dolly PARTON *US, female vocalist* — **33 wks**

15 May 76	● **JOLENE** RCA 2675	**7** 10 wks
21 Feb 81	**9 TO 5** RCA 25	**47** 5 wks
12 Nov 83	● **ISLANDS IN THE STREAM** RCA 378 [1]	**7** 15 wks
7 Apr 84	**HERE YOU COME AGAIN** RCA 395	**75** 1 wk
16 Apr 94	**THE DAY I FALL IN LOVE** Columbia 6600282 [2]	**64** 2 wks

[1] Kenny Rogers and Dolly Parton [2] Dolly Parton and James Ingram

Stella PARTON *US, female vocalist* — **4 wks**

22 Oct 77	**THE DANGER OF A STRANGER** Elektra K 12272	**35** 4 wks

Don PARTRIDGE *UK, male vocalist* — **32 wks**

7 Feb 68	● **ROSIE** Columbia DB 8330	**4** 12 wks
29 May 68	● **BLUE EYES** Columbia DB 8416	**3** 13 wks
19 Feb 69	**BREAKFAST ON PLUTO** Columbia DB 8538	**26** 7 wks

PARTRIDGE FAMILY *US, male / female vocal group* — **53 wks**

13 Feb 71	**I THINK I LOVE YOU** Bell 1130 [1]	**18** 9 wks
26 Feb 72	**IT'S ONE OF THOSE NIGHTS (YES LOVE)** Bell 1203 [1]	**11** 11 wks
8 Jul 72	● **BREAKING UP IS HARD TO DO** Bell MABEL 1 [1]	**3** 13 wks
3 Feb 73	● **LOOKING THROUGH THE EYES OF LOVE** Bell 1278 [2]	**9** 9 wks
19 May 73	● **WALKING IN THE RAIN** Bell 1293 [2]	**10** 11 wks

[1] Partridge Family starring Shirley Jones featuring David Cassidy [2] Partridge Family starring David Cassidy

PASADENAS *UK, male vocal group* — **57 wks**

28 May 88	● **TRIBUTE (RIGHT ON)** CBS PASA 1	**5** 14 wks
17 Sep 88	**RIDING ON A TRAIN** CBS PASA 2	**13** 9 wks
26 Nov 88	**ENCHANTED LADY** CBS PASA 3	**31** 6 wks
12 May 90	**LOVE THING** CBS PASA 4	**22** 5 wks
14 Jul 90	**REELING** CBS PASA 5	**75** 1 wk
1 Feb 92	● **I'M DOING FINE NOW** Columbia 6577187	**4** 10 wks
4 Apr 92	**MAKE IT WITH YOU** Columbia 6579257	**20** 4 wks
6 Jun 92	**I BELIEVE IN MIRACLES** Columbia 6580567	**34** 3 wks
29 Aug 92	**MOVING IN THE RIGHT DIRECTION** Columbia 6583417	**49** 2 wks
21 Nov 92	**LET'S STAY TOGETHER** Columbia 6587747	**22** 3 wks

PASSIONS *UK, male / female vocal / instrumental group* — **8 wks**

31 Jan 81	**I'M IN LOVE WITH A GERMAN FILM STAR** Polydor POSP 222	**25** 8 wks

PAT and MICK *UK, male vocal duo* — **27 wks**

9 Apr 88	**LET'S ALL CHANT / ON THE NIGHT** PWL PWL 10 [1]	**11** 9 wks
25 Mar 89	**I HAVEN'T STOPPED DANCING YET** PWL PWL 33	**9** 8 wks
14 Apr 90	**USE IT UP AND WEAR IT OUT** PWL PWL 55	**22** 6 wks
23 Mar 91	**GIMME SOME** PWL PWL 75	**53** 2 wks
15 May 93	**HOT HOT HOT** PWL International PARKCD 1	**47** 2 wks

[1] Mick and Pat

On The Night only listed from 4 Jun 88. It peaked at position 70.

PATIENCE and PRUDENCE *US, female vocal duo* — **8 wks**

2 Nov 56	**TONIGHT YOU BELONG TO ME** London HLU 8321	**28** 3 wks
1 Mar 57	**GONNA GET ALONG WITHOUT YA NOW** London HLU 8369	**22** 4 wks
12 Apr 57	**GONNA GET ALONG WITHOUT YA NOW (re-entry)** London HLU 8369	**24** 1 wk

PATRA - *See Shabba RANKS*

PATRIC *UK, male vocalist* — **2 wks**

9 Jul 94	**LOVE ME** Bell 7432125352	**54** 2 wks

Kellee PATTERSON *US, female vocalist* — **7 wks**

Date	Title	Pos	Wks
18 Feb 78	**IF IT DON'T FIT DON'T FORCE IT** EMI International INT 544	**44**	7 wks

Billy PAUL *US, male vocalist* — **44 wks**

Date	Title	Pos	Wks
13 Jan 73	**ME AND MRS JONES** Epic EPC 1055	**12**	9 wks
12 Jan 74	**THANKS FOR SAVING MY LIFE** Philadelphia International PIR 1928	**33**	6 wks
22 May 76	**LET'S MAKE A BABY** Philadelphia International PIR 4144	**30**	5 wks
30 Apr 77	**LET 'EM IN** Philadelphia International PIR 5143	**26**	5 wks
16 Jul 77	**YOUR SONG** Philadelphia International PIR 5391	**37**	7 wks
19 Nov 77	**ONLY THE STRONG SURVIVE** Philadelphia International PIR 5699	**33**	7 wks
14 Jul 79	**BRING THE FAMILY BACK** Philadelphia International PIR 7456	**51**	5 wks

Chris PAUL *UK, male instrumentalist - guitar* — **8 wks**

Date	Title	Pos	Wks
31 May 86	**EXPANSIONS '86 (EXPAND YOUR MIND)** Fourth & Broadway BRW 48 [1]	**58**	5 wks
21 Nov 87	**BACK IN MY ARMS** Syncopate SY 5	**74**	2 wks
13 Aug 88	**TURN THE MUSIC UP** Syncopate SY 13	**73**	1 wk

[1] Chris Paul featuring David Joseph

Les PAUL and Mary FORD
US, male instrumentalist - guitar, and female vocalist — **4 wks**

Date	Title	Pos	Wks
20 Nov 53	● **VAYA CON DIOS** Capitol CL 13943	**7**	4 wks

Lyn PAUL *UK, female vocalist* — **6 wks**

Date	Title	Pos	Wks
28 Jun 75	**IT OUGHTA SELL A MILLION** Polydor 2058 602	**37**	6 wks

Owen PAUL *UK, male vocalist* — **14 wks**

Date	Title	Pos	Wks
31 May 86	● **MY FAVOURITE WASTE OF TIME** Epic A 7125	**3**	14 wks

PAUL and PAULA *US, male / female vocal duo* — **31 wks**

Date	Title	Pos	Wks
14 Feb 63	● **HEY PAULA** Philips 304012 BF	**8**	12 wks
18 Apr 63	● **YOUNG LOVERS** Philips 304016 BF	**9**	14 wks
16 May 63	**HEY PAULA (re-entry)** Philips 304012 BF	**37**	5 wks

Luciano PAVAROTTI *Italy, male vocalist* — **20 wks**

Date	Title	Pos	Wks
16 Jun 90	● **NESSUN DORMA** Decca PAV 03	**2**	11 wks
24 Oct 92	**MISERERE** London LON 329 [1]	**15**	5 wks
30 Jul 94	**LIBIAMO / LA DONNA E MOBILE** Teldec YZ 843CD [2]	**21**	4 wks

[1] Zucchero with Luciano Pavarotti [2] José Carreras, Placido Domingo and Luciano Pavarotti

PAVEMENT *UK, male vocal / instrumental group* — **2 wks**

Date	Title	Pos	Wks
28 Nov 92	**WATERY DOMESTIC EP** Big Cat ABB 38T	**58**	1 wk
12 Feb 94	**CUT YOUR HAIR** Big Cat ABB 55SCD	**52**	1 wk

Tracks on Watery Domestic EP: Brick Wall / Sick Profile / Annual Report / Fear The Panzers.

Rita PAVONE *Italy, female vocalist* — **19 wks**

Date	Title	Pos	Wks
1 Dec 66	**HEART** RCA 1553	**27**	12 wks
19 Jan 67	**YOU ONLY YOU** RCA 1561	**21**	7 wks

Freda PAYNE *US, female vocalist* — **30 wks**

Date	Title	Pos	Wks
5 Sep 70	★ **BAND OF GOLD** Invictus INV 502	**1**	19 wks
21 Nov 70	**DEEPER AND DEEPER** Invictus INV 505	**33**	9 wks
27 Mar 71	**CHERISH WHAT IS DEAR TO YOU** Invictus INV 509	**46**	2 wks

Tammy PAYNE *UK, female vocalist* — **2 wks**

Date	Title	Pos	Wks
20 Jul 91	**TAKE ME NOW** Talkin Loud TLK 12	**55**	2 wks

PEACHES and HERB *US, female / male vocal duo* — **23 wks**

Date	Title	Pos	Wks
20 Jan 79	**SHAKE YOUR GROOVE THING** Polydor 2066 992	**26**	10 wks
21 Apr 79	● **REUNITED** Polydor POSP 43	**4**	13 wks

PEARL JAM *US, male vocal / instrumental group* — **25 wks**

Date	Title	Pos	Wks
15 Feb 92	**ALIVE** Epic 6575727	**16**	6 wks
18 Apr 92	**EVEN FLOW** Epic 6578577	**27**	3 wks
26 Sep 92	**JEREMY** Epic 6582587	**15**	4 wks
1 Jan 94	**DAUGHTER** Epic 6600202	**18**	5 wks
28 May 94	**DISSIDENT** Epic 6604415	**14**	4 wks
26 Nov 94	● **SPIN THE BLACK CIRCLE** Epic 6610362	**10**	3 wks

PEARLS *UK, female vocal duo* — **24 wks**

Date	Title	Pos	Wks
27 May 72	**THIRD FINGER, LEFT HAND** Bell 1217	**31**	6 wks
23 Sep 72	**YOU CAME YOU SAW YOU CONQUERED** Bell 1254	**32**	5 wks
24 Mar 73	**YOU ARE EVERYTHING** Bell 1284	**41**	3 wks
1 Jun 74	● **GUILTY** Bell 1352	**10**	10 wks

Johnny PEARSON
UK, orchestra, Johnny Pearson featured pianist — **15 wks**

Date	Title	Pos	Wks
18 Dec 71	● **SLEEPY SHORES** Penny Farthing PEN 778	**8**	15 wks

PEBBLES *US, female vocalist* — **17 wks**

Date	Title	Pos	Wks
19 Mar 88	● **GIRLFRIEND** MCA MCA 1233	**8**	11 wks
28 May 88	**MERCEDES BOY** MCA MCA 1248	**42**	4 wks
27 Oct 90	**GIVING YOU THE BENEFIT** MCA MCA 1448	**73**	2 wks

PEDDLERS *UK, male vocal / instrumental group* — **14 wks**

Date	Title	Pos	Wks
7 Jan 65	**LET THE SUNSHINE IN** Philips BF 1375	**50**	1 wk
23 Aug 69	**BIRTH** CBS 4449	**17**	9 wks
31 Jan 70	**GIRLIE** CBS 4720	**34**	4 wks

PEE BEE SQUAD *UK, male vocalist - Paul Burnett* — **3 wks**

Date	Title	Pos	Wks
5 Oct 85	**RUGGED AND MEAN, BUTCH AND ON SCREEN** Project PRO 3	**52**	3 wks

Ann PEEBLES *US, female vocalist* — **3 wks**

Date	Title	Pos	Wks
20 Apr 74	**I CAN'T STAND THE RAIN** London HL 10428	**50**	1 wk
4 May 74	**I CAN'T STAND THE RAIN (re-entry)** London HL 10428	**41**	2 wks

PEECH BOYS *UK, male vocal / instrumental group* — **3 wks**

Date	Title	Pos	Wks
30 Oct 82	**DON'T MAKE ME WAIT** TMT QTMT 7001	**49**	3 wks

Donald PEERS *UK, male vocalist* — **27 wks**

Date	Title	Pos	Wks
18 Dec 68	● **PLEASE DON'T GO** Columbia DB 8502	**3**	18 wks
30 Apr 69	**PLEASE DON'T GO (re-entry)** Columbia DB 8502	**38**	3 wks
24 Jun 72	**GIVE ME ONE MORE CHANCE** Decca F 13302	**36**	6 wks

PELE *UK, male / female vocal / instrumental group* — **3 wks**

Date	Title	Pos	Wks
15 Feb 92	**MEGALOMANIA** M & G MAGS 20	**73**	1 wk
13 Jun 92	**FAIR BLOWS THE WIND FOR FRANCE** M & G MAGS 24	**62**	1 wk
31 Jul 93	**FAT BLACK HEART** M & G MAGCD 43	**75**	1 wk

Teddy PENDERGRASS US, male vocalist　24 wks

21 May 77	THE WHOLE TOWN'S LAUGHING AT ME		
	Philadelphia International PIR 5116 ......**44**	3 wks
28 Oct 78	ONLY YOU / CLOSE THE DOOR		
	Philadelphia International PIR 6713 ......**41**	6 wks
23 May 81	TWO HEARTS 20th Century TC 2492 [1] **49**	5 wks
25 Jan 86	HOLD ME Asylum EKR 32 [2] **44**	5 wks
28 May 88	JOY Elektra EKR 75 ......**58**	3 wks
19 Nov 94	THE MORE I GET THE MORE I WANT		
	X-clusive XCLU 011CD [3] **35**	2 wks

[1] Stephanie Mills featuring Teddy Pendergrass [2] Teddy Pendergrass with Whitney Houston [3] KWS featuring Teddy Pendergrass

Ce Ce PENISTON US, female vocalist　44 wks

12 Oct 91	FINALLY A & M AM 822 ......**29**	7 wks
11 Jan 92	● WE GOT A LOVE THANG A & M AM 846 ......**6**	8 wks
18 Jan 92	I LIKE IT A & M AM 847 [1] **58**	2 wks
21 Mar 92	● FINALLY (re-issue) A & M AM 858 ......**2**	8 wks
23 May 92	● KEEP ON WALKIN' A & M AM 878 ......**10**	6 wks
5 Sep 92	CRAZY LOVE A & M AM 0060 ......**44**	3 wks
12 Dec 92	INSIDE THAT I CRIED A & M AM 0121 ......**42**	2 wks
15 Jan 94	I'M IN THE MOOD A & M 5804552 ......**16**	4 wks
2 Apr 94	KEEP GIVIN' ME YOUR LOVE A & M 5805492 ......**36**	2 wks
6 Aug 94	HIT BY LOVE A & M 5806932 ......**33**	2 wks

[1] Overweight Pooch featuring Ce Ce Peniston

Dawn PENN Jamaica, female vocalist　12 wks

| 11 Jun 94 | ● YOU DON'T LOVE ME (NO, NO, NO) | | |
| | Big Beat A 8295CD ......**3** | 12 wks |

Barbara PENNINGTON US, female vocalist　8 wks

| 27 Apr 85 | FAN THE FLAME Record Shack SOHO 37 ......**62** | 3 wks |
| 27 Jul 85 | ON A CROWDED STREET Record Shack SOHO 49 ....**57** | 5 wks |

PENTANGLE UK, male / female vocal / instrumental group　4 wks

28 May 69	ONCE I HAD A SWEETHEART Big T BIG 124 ......**46**	1 wk
14 Feb 70	LIGHT FLIGHT Big T BIG 128 ......**43**	1 wk
28 Feb 70	LIGHT FLIGHT (re-entry) Big T BIG 128 ......**45**	2 wks

PENTHOUSE 4 UK, male vocal / instrumental duo　3 wks

| 23 Apr 88 | BUST THIS HOUSE DOWN Syncopate SY 10 ......**56** | 3 wks |

PEOPLES CHOICE US, male vocal / instrumental group　9 wks

20 Sep 75	DO IT ANYWAY YOU WANNA		
	Philadelphia International PIR 3500 ......**36**	5 wks
21 Jan 78	JAM JAM JAM Philadelphia International PIR 5891 **40**	4 wks

Danny PEPPERMINT and the JUMPING JACKS US, male vocal / instrumental group　8 wks

| 18 Jan 62 | PEPPERMINT TWIST London HLL 9478 ......**26** | 8 wks |

PEPPERS France, male instrumental group　12 wks

| 26 Oct 74 | ● PEPPER BOX Spark SRL 1100 ......**6** | 12 wks |

PEPSI and SHIRLIE UK, female vocal duo　24 wks

17 Jan 87	● HEARTACHE Polydor POSP 837 ......**2**	12 wks
30 May 87	● GOODBYE STRANGER Polydor POSP 865 ......**9**	7 wks
26 Sep 87	CAN'T GIVE ME LOVE Polydor POSP 885 ......**58**	3 wks
12 Dec 87	ALL RIGHT NOW Polydor POSP 896 ......**50**	2 wks

PERCEPTION UK, male vocal group　2 wks

| 7 Mar 92 | FEED THE FEELING Talkin Loud TLK 17 ......**58** | 2 wks |

The listed flip side of Feed The Feeling was Three Times A Maybe by K-Creative.

Lance PERCIVAL UK, male vocalist　3 wks

| 28 Oct 65 | SHAME AND SCANDAL IN THE FAMILY | | |
| | Parlophone R 5335 ......**37** | 3 wks |

PERFECT DAY UK, male vocal / instrumental group　4 wks

| 21 Jan 89 | LIBERTY TOWN London LON 214 ......**58** | 3 wks |
| 1 Apr 89 | JANE London LON 188 ......**68** | 1 wk |

PERFECTLY ORDINARY PEOPLE
UK, male vocal / instrumental group　3 wks

| 22 Oct 88 | THEME FROM P.O.P. Urban URB 25 ......**61** | 3 wks |

Emilio PERICOLI Italy, male vocalist　14 wks

| 28 Jun 62 | AL DI LA Warner Bros. WB 69 ......**30** | 14 wks |

Carl PERKINS US, male vocalist　8 wks

| 18 May 56 | ● BLUE SUEDE SHOES London HLU 8271 ......**10** | 8 wks |

Steve PERRY UK, male vocalist　1 wk

| 4 Aug 60 | STEP BY STEP HMV POP 745 ......**41** | 1 wk |

Jon PERTWEE UK, male vocalist　7 wks

| 1 Mar 80 | WORZEL'S SONG Decca F 13885 ......**33** | 7 wks |

PET SHOP BOYS UK, male vocal / instrumental duo　188 wks

23 Nov 85	★ WEST END GIRLS Parlophone R 6115 ......**1**	15 wks
8 Mar 86	LOVE COMES QUICKLY Parlophone R 6116 ......**19**	9 wks
31 May 86	OPPORTUNITIES (LET'S MAKE LOTS OF MONEY)		
	Parlophone R 6129 ......**11**	8 wks
4 Oct 86	● SUBURBIA Parlophone R 6140 ......**8**	9 wks
27 Jun 87	★ IT'S A SIN Parlophone R 6158 ......**1**	11 wks
22 Aug 87	● WHAT HAVE I DONE TO DESERVE THIS		
	Parlophone R 6163 [1] **2**	9 wks
24 Oct 87	● RENT Parlophone R 6168 ......**8**	7 wks
12 Dec 87	★ ALWAYS ON MY MIND Parlophone R 6171 ......**1**	11 wks
2 Apr 88	★ HEART Parlophone R 6177 ......**1**	10 wks
24 Sep 88	● DOMINO DANCING Parlophone R 6190 ......**7**	8 wks
26 Nov 88	● LEFT TO MY OWN DEVICES Parlophone R 6198 ......**4**	8 wks
8 Jul 89	● IT'S ALRIGHT Parlophone R 6220 ......**5**	8 wks
6 Oct 90	● SO HARD Parlophone R 6269 ......**4**	6 wks
24 Nov 90	BEING BORING Parlophone R 6275 ......**20**	8 wks
23 Mar 91	● WHERE THE STREETS HAVE NO NAME - CAN'T TAKE MY EYES OFF YOU / HOW CAN YOU EXPECT TO BE TAKEN SERIOUSLY		
	Parlophone R 6285 ......**4**	8 wks
8 Jun 91	JEALOUSY Parlophone R 6283 ......**12**	5 wks
26 Oct 91	DJ CULTURE Parlophone R 6301 ......**13**	3 wks
23 Nov 91	DJ CULTURE (re-mix) Parlophone 12RX 6301 ......**40**	2 wks
21 Dec 91	WAS IT WORTH IT Parlophone R 6306 ......**24**	4 wks
12 Jun 93	● CAN YOU FORGIVE HER Parlophone CDR 6348 ......**7**	7 wks
18 Sep 93	● GO WEST Parlophone CDR 6356 ......**2**	9 wks
11 Dec 93	I WOULDN'T NORMALLY DO THIS KIND OF THING		
	Parlophone CDR 6370 ......**13**	7 wks
16 Apr 94	LIBERATION Parlophone CDRS 6377 ......**14**	5 wks
11 Jun 94	● ABSOLUTELY FABULOUS Spaghetti CDR 6382 [2] **6**	7 wks
10 Sep 94	YESTERDAY WHEN I WAS MAD		
	Parlophone CDRS 6386 ......**13**	4 wks

[1] Pet Shop Boys and Dusty Springfield [2] Absolutely Fabulous

PETER and GORDON UK, male vocal duo
77 wks

12 Mar 64	★ A WORLD WITHOUT LOVE Columbia DB 7225	1	14 wks
4 Jun 64	● NOBODY I KNOW Columbia DB 7292	10	11 wks
8 Apr 65	● TRUE LOVE WAYS Columbia DB 7524	2	15 wks
24 Jun 65	● TO KNOW YOU IS TO LOVE YOU		
	Columbia DB 7617	5	10 wks
21 Oct 65	BABY I'M YOURS Columbia DB 7729	19	9 wks
24 Feb 66	WOMAN Columbia DB 7834	28	7 wks
22 Sep 66	LADY GODIVA Columbia DB 8003	16	11 wks

PETER, PAUL and MARY
US, male/female vocal/instrumental group
38 wks

10 Oct 63	BLOWING IN THE WIND Warner Bros. WB 104	13	16 wks
16 Apr 64	TELL IT ON THE MOUNTAIN Warner Bros. WB 127	33	4 wks
15 Oct 64	THE TIMES THEY ARE A-CHANGIN'		
	Warner Bros. WB 142	44	2 wks
17 Jan 70	● LEAVIN' ON A JET PLANE Warner Bros. WB 7340	2	16 wks

PETERS and LEE UK, male/female vocal duo
57 wks

26 May 73	★ WELCOME HOME Philips 6006 307	1	24 wks
3 Nov 73	BY YOUR SIDE Philips 6006 339	39	4 wks
20 Apr 74	● DON'T STAY AWAY TOO LONG Philips 6006 388	3	15 wks
17 Aug 74	RAINBOW Philips 6006 406	17	7 wks
6 Mar 76	HEY MR. MUSIC MAN Philips 6006 502	16	7 wks

Ray PETERSON US, male vocalist
9 wks

4 Sep 59	THE WONDER OF YOU RCA 1131	23	1 wk
24 Mar 60	ANSWER ME RCA 1175	47	1 wk
19 Jan 61	CORRINE, CORRINA London HLX 9246	48	1 wk
2 Feb 61	CORRINE, CORRINA (re-entry) London HLX 9246	41	6 wks

Tom PETTY and the HEARTBREAKERS
US, male vocal/instrumental group
43 wks

25 Jun 77	ANYTHING THAT'S ROCK 'N' ROLL		
	Shelter WIP 6396	36	3 wks
13 Aug 77	AMERICAN GIRL Shelter WIP 6403	40	5 wks
15 Aug 81	STOP DRAGGIN' MY HEART AROUND		
	WEA K 79231 [1]	50	4 wks
13 Apr 85	DON'T COME AROUND HERE NO MORE		
	MCA MCA 926	50	4 wks
13 May 89	I WON'T BACK DOWN MCA MCA 1334 [2]	28	10 wks
12 Aug 89	RUNNIN' DOWN A DREAM MCA MCA 1359 [2]	55	4 wks
25 Nov 89	FREE FALLIN' MCA MCA 1381 [2]	64	3 wks
29 Jun 91	LEARNING TO FLY MCA MCS 1555	46	4 wks
4 Apr 92	TOO GOOD TO BE TRUE MCA MCS 1616	34	3 wks
30 Oct 93	SOMETHING IN THE AIR MCA MCSTD 1945 [2]	53	2 wks
12 Mar 94	MARY JANE'S LAST DANCE MCA MCSTD 1966	52	2 wks

[1] Stevie Nicks with Tom Petty and the Heartbreakers [2] Tom Petty

PHANTOMS - See Johnny BRANDON

PHARAOHS - See SAM THE SHAM and the PHARAOHS

PHARCYDE US, male rap group
3 wks

31 Jul 93	PASSIN' ME BY Atlantic A 8360CD	55	3 wks

Frankë PHAROAH - See FRANKË

PhD UK, male vocal/instrumental duo
14 wks

3 Apr 82	● I WON'T LET YOU DOWN WEA K 79209	3	14 wks

Barrington PHELOUNG Australia, male composer
2 wks

13 Mar 93	INSPECTOR MORSE THEME Virgin VSCDT 1458	61	2 wks

PHILADELPHIA INTERNATIONAL ALL-STARS
US, amalgamation of various acts
8 wks

13 Aug 77	LET'S CLEAN UP THE GHETTO		
	Philadelphia International PIR 5451	34	8 wks

PHILHARMONIA ORCHESTRA, conductor Lorin MAAZEL UK, orchestra, US, male conductor
7 wks

30 Jul 69	THUS SPAKE ZARATHUSTRA Columbia DB 8607	33	7 wks

Esther PHILLIPS US, female vocalist
8 wks

4 Oct 75	● WHAT A DIFFERENCE A DAY MADE Kudu 925	6	8 wks

Paul PHOENIX UK, male vocalist
4 wks

3 Nov 79	NUNC DIMITTIS Different HAVE 20	56	4 wks

Full artist credit on hit as follows: Paul Phoenix (treble) with Instrumental Ensemble - James Watson (trumpet), John Scott (organ), conducted by Barry Rose.

PHOTOS UK, male/female vocal/instrumental group
4 wks

17 May 80	IRENE Epic EPC 8517	56	4 wks

PHUTURE ASSASSINS
UK, male instrumental/production group
1 wk

6 Jun 92	FUTURE SOUND (EP) Suburban Base SUBBASE 010	64	1 wk

Tracks on Future Sound (EP): Future Sound / African Sanctus / Rydim Come Foward / Freedom Sound.

PIA - See Pia ZADORA

Edith PIAF France, female vocalist
15 wks

12 May 60	MILORD Columbia DC 754	41	4 wks
3 Nov 60	MILORD (re-entry) Columbia DC 754	24	11 wks

Bobby 'Boris' PICKETT and the CRYPT-KICKERS
US, male vocalist, male vocal/instrumental backing group
13 wks

1 Sep 73	● MONSTER MASH London HL 10320	3	13 wks

Wilson PICKETT US, male vocalist
61 wks

23 Sep 65	IN THE MIDNIGHT HOUR Atlantic AT 4036	12	11 wks
25 Nov 65	DON'T FIGHT IT Atlantic AT 4052	29	8 wks
10 Mar 66	634-5789 Atlantic AT 4072	36	5 wks
1 Sep 66	LAND OF 1000 DANCES Atlantic 584-039	22	9 wks
15 Dec 66	MUSTANG SALLY Atlantic 584-066	28	7 wks
27 Sep 67	FUNKY BROADWAY Atlantic 584-130	43	3 wks
11 Sep 68	I'M A MIDNIGHT MOVER Atlantic 584-203	38	6 wks
8 Jan 69	HEY JUDE Atlantic 584-236	16	9 wks
21 Nov 87	IN THE MIDNIGHT HOUR Motown ZB 41583	62	3 wks

In The Midnight Hour on Motown is a re-recording.

PICKETTYWITCH
UK, male/female vocal/instrumental group
34 wks

28 Feb 70	● THAT SAME OLD FEELING Pye 7N 17887	5	14 wks
4 Jul 70	(IT'S LIKE A) SAD OLD KINDA MOVIE		
	Pye 7N 17951	16	10 wks
7 Nov 70	BABY I WON'T LET YOU DOWN Pye 7N 45002	27	10 wks

PIGBAG *UK, male instrumental group* **20 wks**

7 Nov 81	**SUNNY DAY** *Y Records Y 12*	**53**	3 wks
27 Feb 82	**GETTING UP** *Y Records Y 16*	**61**	3 wks
3 Apr 82	● **PAPA'S GOT A BRAND NEW PIGBAG** *Y Records Y 10*	**3**	11 wks
10 Jul 82	**THE BIG BEAN** *Y Records Y 24*	**40**	3 wks

Nelson PIGFORD - *See De Etta LITTLE and Nelson PIGFORD*

PIGLETS *UK, female vocal group* **12 wks**

6 Nov 71	● **JOHNNY REGGAE** *Bell 1180*	**3**	12 wks

Dick PIKE - *See Ruby WRIGHT*

P.I.L. - *See PUBLIC IMAGE LTD.*

PILOT *UK, male vocal / instrumental group* **29 wks**

2 Nov 74	**MAGIC** *EMI 2217*	**11**	11 wks
18 Jan 75	★ **JANUARY** *EMI 2255*	**1**	10 wks
19 Apr 75	**CALL ME ROUND** *EMI 2287*	**34**	4 wks
27 Sep 75	**JUST A SMILE** *EMI 2338*	**31**	4 wks

PILTDOWN MEN *US, male instrumental group* **36 wks**

8 Sep 60	**MACDONALD'S CAVE** *Capitol CL 15149*	**14**	18 wks
12 Jan 61	**PILTDOWN RIDES AGAIN** *Capitol CL 15175*	**14**	10 wks
9 Mar 61	**GOODNIGHT MRS. FLINTSTONE** *Capitol CL 15186* ..	**18**	8 wks

Courtney PINE *UK, male instrumentalist - saxophone* **6 wks**

30 Jul 88	**LIKE DREAMERS DO** *Fourth & Broadway BRW 108* 1	**26**	5 wks
7 Jul 90	**I'M STILL WAITING** *Mango MNG 749* 2	**66**	1 wk

1 Mica Paris featuring Courtney Pine 2 Courtney Pine featuring Carroll Thompson

See also Movement 98 featuring Carroll Thompson.

PING PING and Al VERLAINE
Belgium, male vocal duo **4 wks**

28 Sep 61	**SUCU SUCU** *Oriole CB 1589*	**41**	4 wks

PINK FLOYD *UK, male vocal / instrumental group* **55 wks**

30 Mar 67	**ARNOLD LAYNE** *Columbia DB 8156*	**20**	8 wks
22 Jun 67	● **SEE EMILY PLAY** *Columbia DB 8214*	**6**	12 wks
1 Dec 79	★ **ANOTHER BRICK IN THE WALL (PART 2)** *Harvest HAR 5194*	**1**	12 wks
7 Aug 82	**WHEN THE TIGERS BROKE FREE** *Harvest HAR 5222*	**39**	5 wks
7 May 83	**NOT NOW JOHN** *Harvest HAR 5224*	**30**	4 wks
19 Dec 87	**ON THE TURNING AWAY** *EMI EM 34*	**55**	4 wks
25 Jun 88	**ONE SLIP** *EMI EM 52*	**50**	3 wks
4 Jun 94	**TAKE IT BACK** *EMI CDEMS 309*	**23**	4 wks
29 Oct 94	**HIGH HOPES / KEEP TALKING** *EMI CDEMS 342*	**26**	3 wks

PINKEES *UK, male vocal / instrumental group* **9 wks**

18 Sep 82	● **DANGER GAMES** *Creole CR 39*	**8**	9 wks

PINKERTON'S ASSORTED COLOURS
UK, male vocal / instrumental group **12 wks**

13 Jan 66	● **MIRROR MIRROR** *Decca F 12307*	**9**	11 wks
21 Apr 66	**DON'T STOP LOVIN' ME BABY** *Decca F 12377*	**50**	1 wk

PINKY and PERKY *UK, puppet duo* **3 wks**

29 May 93	**REET PETITE** *Telstar CDPIGGY 1*	**47**	3 wks

PIONEERS *Jamaica, male vocal / instrumental group* **34 wks**

18 Oct 69	**LONG SHOT KICK DE BUCKET** *Trojan TR 672*	**21**	10 wks
10 Jan 70	**LONG SHOT KICK DE BUCKET (re-entry)** *Trojan TR 672*	**40**	1 wk
31 Jul 71	● **LET YOUR YEAH BE YEAH** *Trojan TR 7825*	**5**	12 wks
15 Jan 72	**GIVE AND TAKE** *Trojan TR 7846*	**35**	6 wks
29 Mar 80	**LONG SHOT KICK DE BUCKET (re-issue)** *Trojan TRO 9063*	**42**	5 wks

Re-issue of Long Shot Kick De Bucket *coupled with re-issue of* Liquidator *by Harry J. All Stars.*

PIPKINS *UK, male vocal duo* **10 wks**

28 Mar 70	● **GIMME DAT DING** *Columbia DB 8662*	**6**	10 wks

PIPS - *See Gladys KNIGHT and the PIPS*

PIRANHAS *UK, male vocal / instrumental group* **21 wks**

2 Aug 80	● **TOM HARK** *Sire SIR 4044*	**6**	12 wks
16 Oct 82	**ZAMBESI** *Dakota DAK 6* 1	**17**	9 wks

1 Piranhas featuring Boring Bob Grover

PIRATES - *See Johnny KIDD and the PIRATES*

Gene PITNEY *US, male vocalist* **212 wks**

23 Mar 61	**I WANNA LOVE MY LIFE AWAY** *London HL 9270* ..	**26**	11 wks
8 Mar 62	**TOWN WITHOUT PITY** *HMV POP 952*	**32**	6 wks
5 Dec 63	● **TWENTY FOUR HOURS FROM TULSA** *United Artists UP 1035*	**5**	19 wks
5 Mar 64	● **THAT GIRL BELONGS TO YESTERDAY** *United Artists UP 1045*	**7**	12 wks
15 Oct 64	**IT HURTS TO BE IN LOVE** *United Artists UP 1063*	**36**	4 wks
12 Nov 64	● **I'M GONNA BE STRONG** *Stateside SS 358*	**2**	14 wks
18 Feb 65	● **I MUST BE SEEING THINGS** *Stateside SS 390*	**6**	10 wks
10 Jun 65	● **LOOKING THROUGH THE EYES OF LOVE** *Stateside SS 420*	**3**	12 wks
4 Nov 65	● **PRINCESS IN RAGS** *Stateside SS 471*	**9**	12 wks
17 Feb 66	● **BACKSTAGE** *Stateside SS 490*	**4**	10 wks
9 Jun 66	● **NOBODY NEEDS YOUR LOVE** *Stateside SS 518*	**2**	13 wks
10 Nov 66	● **JUST ONE SMILE** *Stateside SS 558*	**8**	12 wks
23 Feb 67	**COLD LIGHT OF DAY** *Stateside SS 597*	**38**	6 wks
15 Nov 67	● **SOMETHING'S GOTTEN HOLD OF MY HEART** *Stateside SS 2060*	**5**	13 wks
3 Apr 68	**SOMEWHERE IN THE COUNTRY** *Stateside SS 2103*	**19**	9 wks
27 Nov 68	**YOURS UNTIL TOMORROW** *Stateside SS 2131*	**34**	7 wks
5 Mar 69	**MARIA ELENA** *Stateside SS 2142*	**25**	6 wks
14 Mar 70	**A STREET CALLED HOPE** *Stateside SS 2164*	**37**	5 wks
3 Oct 70	**SHADY LADY** *Stateside SS 2177*	**29**	8 wks
28 Apr 73	**24 SYCAMORE** *Pye International 7N 25606*	**34**	7 wks
2 Nov 74	**BLUE ANGEL** *Bronze BRO 11*	**49**	1 wk
16 Nov 74	**BLUE ANGEL (re-entry)** *Bronze BRO 11*	**39**	3 wks
14 Jan 89	★ **SOMETHING'S GOTTEN HOLD OF MY HEART** *Parlophone R 6201* 1	**1**	12 wks

1 Marc Almond featuring special guest star Gene Pitney

PIXIES *US, male / female vocal / instrumental group* **11 wks**

1 Apr 89	**MONKEY GONE TO HEAVEN** *4AD AD 904*	**60**	3 wks
1 Jul 89	**HERE COMES YOUR MAN** *4AD AD 909*	**54**	1 wk
28 Jul 90	**VELOURIA** *4AD AD 0009*	**28**	3 wks
10 Nov 90	**DIG FOR FIRE** *4AD AD 0014*	**62**	1 wk
8 Jun 91	**PLANET OF SOUND** *4AD AD 1008*	**27**	3 wks

PIZZAMAN *UK, male instrumental / production group* **2 wks**

27 Aug 94	**TRIPPIN ON SUNSHINE** *Loaded CDLOAD 16* **33**	2 wks

Joe PIZZULO - *See Sergio MENDES*

P.J. and DUNCAN *UK, male vocal duo* **30 wks**

18 Dec 93	**TONIGHT I'M FREE** *Telstar CDSTAS 2706*.................**62**	3 wks
23 Apr 94	**WHY ME** *Telstar CDSTAS 2719* **27**	4 wks
23 Jul 94	● **LET'S GET READY TO RHUMBLE**	
	XSrhythm CDDEC 1 ....**9**	11 wks
8 Oct 94	**IF I GIVE YOU MY NUMBER** *XSrhythm CDDEC 2*......**15**	7 wks
3 Dec 94	**ETERNAL LOVE** *XSrhythm CDDEC 3* ....**12†**	5 wks

PJB featuring HANNAH and her SISTERS - *See Hannah JONES*

PJ HARVEY *UK, female / male vocal / instrumental group* **5 wks**

29 Feb 92	**SHEELA-NA-GIG** *Too Pure PURE 008* **69**	1 wk
1 May 93	**50 FT QUEENIE** *Island CID 538* **27**	2 wks
17 Jul 93	**MAN-SIZE** *Island CID 569* **42**	2 wks

PKA *UK, male producer - Phil Kelsey* **2 wks**

20 Apr 91	**TEMPERATURE RISING** *Stress SS 4* **68**	1 wk
7 Mar 92	**POWERGEN (ONLY YOUR LOVE)** *Stress PKA 1* **70**	1 wk

PLANET PATROL *US, male vocal / instrumental group* **3 wks**

17 Sep 83	**CHEAP THRILLS** *Polydor POSP 639* **64**	3 wks

PLANETS *UK, male vocal / instrumental group* **8 wks**

18 Aug 79	**LINES** *Rialto TREB 104* **36**	6 wks
25 Oct 80	**DON'T LOOK DOWN** *Rialto TREB 116* **66**	2 wks

Robert PLANT *UK, male vocalist* **31 wks**

9 Oct 82	**BURNING DOWN ONE SIDE** *Swansong SSK 19429* ..**73**	1 wk
16 Jul 83	**BIG LOG** *WEA B 9848* **11**	10 wks
30 Jan 88	**HEAVEN KNOWS** *Es Paranza A 9373*................**33**	5 wks
28 Apr 90	**HURTING KIND (I'VE GOT MY EYES ON YOU)**	
	Es Paranza A 8985 ....**45**	3 wks
8 May 93	**29 PALMS** *Fontana FATEX 1* **21**	5 wks
3 Jul 93	**I BELIEVE** *Fontana FATEX 2* **64**	2 wks
25 Dec 93	**IF I WERE A CARPENTER** *Fontana FATEX 4* **63**	2 wks
17 Dec 94	**GALLOWS POLE** *Fontana PPCD 2* [1] ....**35†**	3 wks

[1] Jimmy Page and Robert Plant

PLASMATICS *US, female / male vocal / instrumental group* **4 wks**

26 Jul 80	**BUTCHER BABY** *Stiff BUY 76* **55**	4 wks

PLASTIC BERTRAND *Belgium, male vocalist* **17 wks**

13 May 78	● **CA PLANE POUR MOI** *Sire 6078 616* **8**	12 wks
5 Aug 78	**SHA LA LA LA LEE** *Vertigo 6059 209* **39**	5 wks

PLASTIC JAM - *See BUG KANN and PLASTIC JAM*

PLASTIC ONO BAND - *See John LENNON*

PLASTIC PENNY *UK, male vocal / instrumental group* **10 wks**

3 Jan 68	● **EVERYTHING I AM** *Page One POF 051* **6**	10 wks

PLASTIC POPULATION - *See YAZZ*

PLATINUM HOOK *US, male vocal / instrumental group* **1 wk**

2 Sep 78	**STANDING ON THE VERGE (OF GETTING IT ON)**	
	Motown TMG 1115 ....**72**	1 wk

PLATTERS *US, male / female vocal group* **91 wks**

7 Sep 56	● **THE GREAT PRETENDER / ONLY YOU**		
	Mercury MT 117 ....**5**	12 wks
2 Nov 56	● **MY PRAYER** *Mercury MT 120* **4**	10 wks
7 Dec 56	**THE GREAT PRETENDER / ONLY YOU (re-entry)**		
	Mercury MT 117 ....**21**	1 wk
18 Jan 57	**MY PRAYER (re-entry)** *Mercury MT 120* ...**28**	2 wks
25 Jan 57	**YOU'LL NEVER NEVER KNOW / IT ISN'T RIGHT**		
	Mercury MT 130 ....**23**	1 wk
8 Feb 57	**YOU'LL NEVER NEVER KNOW / IT ISN'T RIGHT**		
	(re-entry) *Mercury MT 130* **29**	1 wk
29 Mar 57	**MY PRAYER (2nd re-entry)** *Mercury MT 120* **22**	1 wk
29 Mar 57	**ONLY YOU (2nd re-entry)** *Mercury MT 117*........**18**	3 wks
12 Apr 57	**YOU'LL NEVER NEVER KNOW / IT ISN'T RIGHT**		
	(2nd re-entry) *Mercury MT 130* **29**	1 wk
17 May 57	**I'M SORRY** *Mercury MT 145* **18**	6 wks
5 Jul 57	**I'M SORRY (re-entry)** *Mercury MT 145* **23**	1 wk
19 Jul 57	**I'M SORRY (2nd re-entry)** *Mercury MT 145* **22**	1 wk
16 May 58	● **TWILIGHT TIME** *Mercury MT 214* **3**	18 wks
16 Jan 59	★ **SMOKE GETS IN YOUR EYES** *Mercury AMT 1016* ..**1**	20 wks
28 Aug 59	**REMEMBER WHEN** *Mercury AMT 1053* **25**	2 wks
29 Jan 60	**HARBOUR LIGHTS** *Mercury AMT 1081* **11**	11 wks

PLAVKA - *See JAM and SPOON*

PLAYBOY BAND - *See John FRED and the PLAYBOY BAND*

PLAYBOYS - *See Gary LEWIS and the PLAYBOYS*

PLAYER *US / UK, male vocal / instrumental group* **7 wks**

25 Feb 78	**BABY COME BACK** *RSO 2090 254* **32**	7 wks

PLAYERS ASSOCIATION
US, male / female vocal / instrumental group **17 wks**

10 Mar 79	● **TURN THE MUSIC UP** *Vanguard VS 5011* **8**	9 wks
5 May 79	**RIDE THE GROOVE** *Vanguard VS 5012* **42**	5 wks
9 Feb 80	**WE GOT THE GROOVE** *Vanguard VS 5016* **61**	3 wks

PLUS ONE featuring SIRRON
UK, male / female vocal / instrumental group **4 wks**

19 May 90	**IT'S HAPPENIN'** *MCA MCA 1405* **40**	4 wks

PLUTO - *See Pluto SHERVINGTON*

PM DAWN *US, male vocal / instrumental duo* **35 wks**

8 Jun 91	**A WATCHER'S POINT OF VIEW** *Gee Street GEE 32* ..**36**	5 wks
17 Aug 91	● **SET ADRIFT ON MEMORY BLISS** *Gee Street GEE 33*..**3**	8 wks
19 Oct 91	**PAPER DOLL** *Gee Street GEE 35* **49**	3 wks
22 Feb 92	**REALITY USED TO BE A FRIEND OF MINE**	
	Gee Street GEE 37 ....**29**	4 wks
7 Nov 92	**I'D DIE WITHOUT YOU** *Gee Street GEE 39* **30**	5 wks
13 Mar 93	**LOOKING THROUGH PATIENT EYES**	
	Gee Street GESCD 47 ....**11**	7 wks
12 Jun 93	**MORE THAN LIKELY** *Gee Street GESCD 49* [1] **40**	3 wks

[1] PM Dawn featuring Boy George

POETS *UK, male vocal / instrumental group* **5 wks**

29 Oct 64	**NOW WE'RE THRU** *Decca F 11995* **31**	5 wks

POGUES
Ireland / UK, male / female vocal / instrumental group **70 wks**

6 Apr 85	**A PAIR OF BROWN EYES** *Stiff BUY 220* **72**	2 wks
22 Jun 85	**SALLY MACLENNANE** *Stiff BUY 224*................**51**	4 wks
14 Sep 85	**DIRTY OLD TOWN** *Stiff BUY 229* **62**	3 wks
8 Mar 86	**POGUETRY IN MOTION EP** *Stiff BUY 243* **29**	6 wks
30 Aug 86	**HAUNTED** *MCA MCA 1084* **42**	4 wks

28 Mar 87	● THE IRISH ROVER *Stiff BUY 258* [1]	...8	8 wks
5 Dec 87	● FAIRYTALE OF NEW YORK *Pogue Mahone NY 7* [2]	.2	9 wks
5 Mar 88	IF I SHOULD FALL FROM GRACE WITH GOD *Pogue Mahone PG 1*	.58	3 wks
16 Jul 88	FIESTA *Pogue Mahone PG 2*	.24	5 wks
17 Dec 88	YEAH YEAH YEAH YEAH *Pogue Mahone YZ 355*	.43	4 wks
8 Jul 89	MISTY MORNING, ALBERT BRIDGE *PM YZ 407*	.41	3 wks
16 Jun 90	JACK'S HEROES / WHISKEY IN THE JAR *PM YZ 500* [1]	.63	2 wks
15 Sep 90	SUMMER IN SIAM *PM YZ 519*	.64	2 wks
21 Sep 91	A RAINY NIGHT IN SOHO *PM YZ 603*	.67	1 wk
14 Dec 91	FAIRYTALE OF NEW YORK (re-issue) *PM YZ 628* [2]	.36	5 wks
30 May 92	HONKY TONK WOMEN *PM YZ 673*	.56	2 wks
21 Aug 93	TUESDAY MORNING *PM YZ 758CD*	.18	5 wks
22 Jan 94	ONCE UPON A TIME *PM YZ 771CD*	.66	2 wks

[1] Pogues and the Dubliners [2] Pogues featuring Kirsty MacColl

Tracks on Poguetry In Motion EP: London Girl / The Body of an American / A Rainy Night in Soho / Planxty Noel Hill.

POINTER SISTERS *US, female vocal group* **87 wks**

3 Feb 79	EVERYBODY IS A STAR *Planet K 12324*	.61	3 wks
17 Mar 79	FIRE *Planet K 12339*	.34	8 wks
22 Aug 81	● SLOWHAND *Planet K 12530*	.10	11 wks
5 Dec 81	SHOULD I DO IT? *Planet K 12578*	.50	5 wks
14 Apr 84	● AUTOMATIC *Planet RPS 105*	.2	15 wks
23 Jun 84	● JUMP (FOR MY LOVE) *Planet RPS 106*	.6	10 wks
11 Aug 84	I NEED YOU *Planet RPS 107*	.25	9 wks
27 Oct 84	I'M SO EXCITED *Planet RPS 108*	.11	11 wks
12 Jan 85	NEUTRON DANCE *Planet RPS 109*	.31	7 wks
20 Jul 85	DARE ME *RCA PB 49957*	.17	8 wks

POISON *US, male vocal / instrumental group* **43 wks**

23 May 87	TALK DIRTY TO ME *Music For Nations KUT 125*	.67	1 wk
7 May 88	NOTHIN' BUT A GOOD TIME *Capitol CL 486*	.35	3 wks
5 Nov 88	FALLEN ANGEL *Capitol CL 500*	.59	1 wk
11 Feb 89	EVERY ROSE HAS ITS THORN *Capitol CL 520*	.13	9 wks
29 Apr 89	YOUR MAMA DON'T DANCE *Capitol CL 523*	.13	7 wks
23 Sep 89	NOTHIN' BUT A GOOD TIME (re-issue) *Capitol CL 539*	.48	3 wks
30 Jun 90	UNSKINNY BOP *Capitol CL 582*	.15	7 wks
27 Oct 90	SOMETHING TO BELIEVE IN *Enigma CL 594*	.35	4 wks
23 Nov 91	SO TELL ME WHY *Capitol CL 640*	.25	2 wks
13 Feb 93	STAND *Capitol CDCL 679*	.25	3 wks
24 Apr 93	UNTIL YOU SUFFER SOME (FIRE AND ICE) *Capitol CDCL 685*	.32	3 wks

POLECATS *UK, male vocal / instrumental group* **18 wks**

7 Mar 81	JOHN I'M ONLY DANCING / BIG GREEN CAR *Mercury POLE 1*	.35	8 wks
16 May 81	ROCKABILLY GUY *Mercury POLE 2*	.35	6 wks
22 Aug 81	JEEPSTER / MARIE CELESTE *Mercury POLE 3*	.53	4 wks

POLICE *UK / US, male vocal / instrumental group* **142 wks**

7 Oct 78	CAN'T STAND LOSING YOU *A & M AMS 7381*	.42	5 wks
28 Apr 79	ROXANNE *A & M AMS 7348*	.12	9 wks
7 Jul 79	● CAN'T STAND LOSING YOU (re-entry) *A & M AMS 7381*	.2	11 wks
22 Sep 79	★ MESSAGE IN A BOTTLE *A & M AMS 7474*	.1	11 wks
17 Nov 79	FALL OUT *Illegal IL 001*	.47	4 wks
1 Dec 79	★ WALKING ON THE MOON *A & M AMS 7494*	.1	10 wks
16 Feb 80	● SO LONELY *A & M AMS 7402*	.6	10 wks
14 Jun 80	SIX PACK *A & M AMPP 6001*	.17	4 wks
27 Sep 80	★ DON'T STAND SO CLOSE TO ME *A & M AMS 7564*	.1	10 wks
13 Dec 80	● DE DO DO DO, DE DA DA DA *A & M AMS 7578*	.5	8 wks
26 Sep 81	● INVISIBLE SUN *A & M AMS 8164*	.2	8 wks
24 Oct 81	★ EVERY LITTLE THING SHE DOES IS MAGIC *A & M AMS 8174*	.1	13 wks
12 Dec 81	SPIRITS IN THE MATERIAL WORLD *A & M AMS 8194*	.12	8 wks

28 May 83	★ EVERY BREATH YOU TAKE *A & M AM 117*	.1	11 wks
23 Jul 83	● WRAPPED AROUND YOUR FINGER *A & M AM 127*	.7	7 wks
5 Nov 83	SYNCHRONICITY II *A & M AM 153*	.17	4 wks
14 Jan 84	KING OF PAIN *A & M AM 176*	.17	5 wks
11 Oct 86	DON'T STAND SO CLOSE TO ME '86 (re-mix) *A & M AM 354*	.24	4 wks

Six Pack consists of six separate Police singles as follows: The Bed's Too Big Without You / Roxanne / Message In A Bottle / Walking On The Moon / So Lonely / Can't Stand Losing You. The last five titles were re-issues.

Su POLLARD *UK, female vocalist* **11 wks**

5 Oct 85	COME TO ME (I AM WOMAN) *Rainbow RBR 1*	.71	1 wk
1 Feb 86	● STARTING TOGETHER *Rainbow RBR 4*	.2	10 wks

Jimi POLO *US, male producer* **4 wks**

9 Nov 91	NEVER GOIN' DOWN *MCA MCS 1578* [1]	.51	2 wks
1 Aug 92	EXPRESS YOURSELF *Perfecto 74321101827*	.59	2 wks

[1] Adamski featuring Jimi Polo

The listed flip side of Never Goin' Down was Born To Be Alive by Adamski featuring Soho.

Peter POLYCARPOU *UK, male vocalist* **4 wks**

20 Feb 93	LOVE HURTS *Soundtrack Music CDEM 259*	.26	4 wks

POLYGON WINDOW *UK, male producer - Richard James* **1 wk**

3 Apr 93	QUOTH *Warp WAP 33CD*	.49	1 wk

See also Aphex Twin.

PONI-TAILS *US, female vocal group* **14 wks**

19 Sep 58	● BORN TOO LATE *HMV POP 516*	.5	11 wks
10 Apr 59	EARLY TO BED *HMV POP 596*	.26	3 wks

Brian POOLE and the TREMELOES
UK, male vocalist, male vocal / instrumental backing group **90 wks**

4 Jul 63	● TWIST AND SHOUT *Decca F 11694*	.4	14 wks
12 Sep 63	★ DO YOU LOVE ME *Decca F 11739*	.1	14 wks
28 Nov 63	I CAN DANCE *Decca F 11771*	.31	8 wks
30 Jan 64	● CANDY MAN *Decca F 11823*	.6	13 wks
7 May 64	● SOMEONE SOMEONE *Decca F 11893*	.2	17 wks
20 Aug 64	TWELVE STEPS TO LOVE *Decca F 11951*	.32	7 wks
7 Jan 65	THREE BELLS *Decca F 12037*	.17	9 wks
22 Jul 65	I WANT CANDY *Decca F 12197*	.25	8 wks

See also Tremeloes.

Glyn POOLE *UK, male vocalist* **8 wks**

20 Oct 73	MILLY MOLLY MANDY *York SYK 565*	.35	8 wks

Iggy POP *US, male vocalist* **23 wks**

13 Dec 86	● REAL WILD CHILD (WILD ONE) *A & M AM 368*	.10	11 wks
10 Feb 90	LIVIN' ON THE EDGE OF THE NIGHT *Virgin America VUS 18*	.51	4 wks
13 Oct 90	CANDY *Virgin America VUS 29*	.67	1 wk
5 Jan 91	WELL DID YOU EVAH! *Chrysalis CHS 3646* [1]	.42	4 wks
4 Sep 93	THE WILD AMERICA (EP) *Virgin America VUSCD 74*	.63	1 wk
21 May 94	BESIDE YOU *Virgin America VUSCD 77*	.47	2 wks

[1] Deborah Harry and Iggy Pop

Tracks on The Wild America (EP): Wild America / Credit Card / Come Back Tomorrow / My Angel.

POP TOPS *Spain, male vocal group* **6 wks**

9 Oct 71	MAMY BLUE *A & M AMS 859*	.35	6 wks

POP WILL EAT ITSELF
UK, male vocal / instrumental group   **43 wks**

30 Jan 88	**THERE IS NO LOVE BETWEEN US ANYMORE**		
	Chapter 22 CHAP 20......................**66**	1 wk
23 Jul 88	**DEF. CON ONE** Chapter 22 PWE 001 ....**63**	4 wks
11 Feb 89	**CAN U DIG IT** RCA PB 42621 ....**38**	4 wks
22 Apr 89	**WISE UP! SUCKER** RCA PB 42761 ....**41**	3 wks
2 Sep 89	**VERY METAL NOISE POLLUTION EP** RCA PB 42883.**45**	3 wks
9 Jun 90	**TOUCHED BY THE HAND OF CICCIOLINA**		
	RCA PB 43735 ....**28**	4 wks
13 Oct 90	**DANCE OF THE MAD** RCA PB 44023 ....**32**	2 wks
12 Jan 91	**X Y & ZEE** RCA PB 44243 ....**15**	4 wks
1 Jun 91	**92 DEGREES** RCA PB 44555 ....**23**	3 wks
6 Jun 92	**KARMADROME / EAT ME DRINK ME LOVE ME**		
	RCA PB 45467 ....**17**	2 wks
29 Aug 92	**BULLETPROOF!** RCA 74321110137.............**24**	3 wks
16 Jan 93 ●	**GET THE GIRL! KILL THE BADDIES!**		
	RCA 74321128802................................**9**	4 wks
16 Oct 93	**RSVP / FAMILIUS HORRIBILUS**		
	Infectious INFECT 1CD.......................**27**	2 wks
12 Mar 94	**ICH BIN EIN AUSLANDER** Infectious INFECT 4CD **28**	2 wks
10 Sep 94	**EVERYTHING'S COOL** Infectious INFECT 9CD ...**23**	2 wks

Tracks on Very Metal Noise Pollution EP: *Def Con. 1989 AD including the Twilight Zone / Preaching To The Perverted / P.W.E.I.-zation / 92°F.*

See also Various Artists (EPs & LPs) - Gimme Shelter (EP).

POPES - *See Shane MacGOWAN and the POPES*

POPPY FAMILY
Canada, male / female vocal / instrumental group   **14 wks**

| 15 Aug 70 ● | **WHICH WAY YOU GOIN' BILLY** Decca F 22976 ....**7** | 14 wks |

PORNO FOR PYROS
US, male vocal / instrumental group   **2 wks**

| 5 Jun 93 | **PETS** Warner Bros. 0777CDX ....**53** | 2 wks |

PORTISHEAD   UK, male / female vocal / instrumental duo   **1 wk**

| 13 Aug 94 | **SOUR TIMES** Go.Beat GODCD 116 ....**57** | 1 wk |

Gary PORTNOY   US, male vocalist   **3 wks**

| 25 Feb 84 | **THEME FROM 'CHEERS'** Starblend CHEER 1 ....**58** | 3 wks |

PORTRAIT   US, male vocal group   **3 wks**

| 27 Mar 93 | **HERE WE GO AGAIN** Capitol CDCL 683 ....**37** | 3 wks |

PORTSMOUTH SINFONIA   UK, orchestra   **4 wks**

| 12 Sep 81 | **CLASSICAL MUDDLEY** Island WIP 6736 ....**38** | 4 wks |

Sandy POSEY   US, female vocalist   **32 wks**

15 Sep 66	**BORN A WOMAN** MGM 1321 ....**24**	11 wks
5 Jan 67	**SINGLE GIRL** MGM 1330 ....**15**	13 wks
13 Apr 67	**WHAT A WOMAN IN LOVE WON'T DO** MGM 1335..**48**	3 wks
6 Sep 75	**SINGLE GIRL (re-issue)** MGM 2006 533 ....**35**	5 wks

POSIES   US, male vocal / instrumental group   **1 wk**

| 19 Mar 94 | **DEFINITE DOOR** Geffen GFSTD 68.........**67** | 1 wk |

POSITIVE FORCE   US, female vocal duo   **9 wks**

| 22 Dec 79 | **WE GOT THE FUNK** Sugarhill SHL 102 ....**18** | 9 wks |

POSITIVE GANG
UK, male / female instrumental / vocal group   **5 wks**

| 17 Apr 93 | **SWEET FREEDOM** PWL Continental PWCD 261 ....**34** | 4 wks |

| 31 Jul 93 | **SWEET FREEDOM PART 2** | | |
| | PWL Continental PWCD 264 ....**67** | 1 wk |

POSITIVE K   US, male rapper   **2 wks**

| 15 May 93 | **I GOT A MAN** Fourth & Broadway BRCD 280 ....**43** | 2 wks |

Mike POST   US, orchestra   **18 wks**

9 Aug 75	**AFTERNOON OF THE RHINO**		
	Warner Bros. K 16588 [1] **48**	1 wk
23 Aug 75	**AFTERNOON OF THE RHINO (re-entry)**		
	Warner Bros. K 16588 [1] **47**	1 wk
16 Jan 82	**THEME FROM 'HILL STREET BLUES'**		
	Elektron K 12576 [2] **25**	11 wks
29 Sep 84	**THE A TEAM** RCA 443 ....**45**	5 wks

[1] Mike Post Coalition [2] Mike Post featuring Larry Carlton

POTTERS   UK, male vocal group   **2 wks**

| 1 Apr 72 | **WE'LL BE WITH YOU** Pye JT 100 ....**34** | 2 wks |

P.O.V. - *See JADE*

Bryan POWELL   UK, male vocalist   **3 wks**

13 Mar 93	**IT'S ALRIGHT** Talkin Loud TLKCD 34 ....**73**	1 wk
15 May 93	**I THINK OF YOU** Talkin Loud TLKCD 38.........**61**	1 wk
7 Aug 93	**NATURAL** Talkin Loud TLKCD 41 ....**73**	1 wk

Cozy POWELL   UK, male instrumentalist - drums   **38 wks**

8 Dec 73 ●	**DANCE WITH THE DEVIL** RAK 164 ....**3**	15 wks
25 May 74	**THE MAN IN BLACK** RAK 173 ....**18**	8 wks
10 Aug 74 ●	**NA NA NA** RAK 180 ....**10**	10 wks
10 Nov 79	**THEME ONE** Ariola ARO 189 ....**62**	2 wks
19 Jun 93	**RESURRECTION** Parlophone CDRS 6351 [1] **23**	3 wks

[1] Brian May with Cozy Powell

Kobie POWELL - *See US3*

POWER OF DREAMS
Ireland, male vocal / instrumental group   **2 wks**

| 19 Jan 91 | **AMERICAN DREAM** Polydor PO 117.........**74** | 1 wk |
| 11 Apr 92 | **THERE I GO AGAIN** Polydor PO 200 ....**65** | 1 wk |

POWER STATION
UK / US, male vocal / instrumental group   **16 wks**

16 Mar 85	**SOME LIKE IT HOT** Parlophone R 6091 ...**14**	8 wks
11 May 85	**GET IT ON** Parlophone R 6096 ....**22**	7 wks
9 Nov 85	**COMMUNICATION** Parlophone R 6114 ....**75**	1 wk

POWERCUT featuring NUBIAN PRINZ
US, male vocal / instrumental group   **4 wks**

| 22 Jun 91 | **GIRLS** Eternal YZ 570.....................**50** | 4 wks |

POWERPILL   UK, male instrumental / production group   **3 wks**

| 6 Jun 92 | **PAC-MAN** Ffrreedom TABX 110 ....**43** | 3 wks |

Will POWERS   US, female vocalist - Lyn Goldsmith   **9 wks**

| 1 Oct 83 | **KISSING WITH CONFIDENCE** Island IS 134.........**17** | 9 wks |

Hit features uncredited vocals by Carly Simon.

Perez PRADO   Cuba, orchestra   **37 wks**

| 25 Mar 55 ★ | **CHERRY PINK AND APPLE BLOSSOM WHITE** | | |
| | HMV B 10833 [1] ....**1** | 17 wks |

| 25 Jul | 58 | ● **PATRICIA** RCA 1067 | .....**8** | 16 wks |
| 10 Dec | 94 | **GUAGLIONE** RCA 74321250192 [2] | .....**41†** | 4 wks |

[1] Perez 'Prez' Prado and his Orchestra, the King of the Mambo [2] Perez 'Prez' Prado and his Orchestra

PRAISE *UK, male / female vocal / instrumental group* **7 wks**

| 2 Feb | 91 | ● **ONLY YOU** Epic 6566117 | .....**4** | 7 wks |

PRATT and McCLAIN with BROTHERLOVE
US, male vocal duo with male instrumental group **6 wks**

| 1 Oct | 77 | **HAPPY DAYS** Reprise K 14435 | .....**31** | 6 wks |

PRAYING MANTIS *UK, male vocal / instrumental group* **2 wks**

| 31 Jan | 81 | **CHEATED** Arista ARIST 378 | .....**69** | 2 wks |

PREFAB SPROUT
UK, male / female vocal / instrumental group **57 wks**

28 Jan	84	**DON'T SING** Kitchenware SK 9	.....**62**	2 wks
20 Jul	85	**FARON YOUNG** Kitchenware SK 22	.....**74**	1 wk
9 Nov	85	**WHEN LOVE BREAKS DOWN** Kitchenware SK 21	.....**25**	10 wks
8 Feb	86	**JOHNNY JOHNNY** Kitchenware SK 24	.....**64**	2 wks
13 Feb	88	**CARS AND GIRLS** Kitchenware SK 35	.....**44**	5 wks
30 Apr	88	**THE KING OF ROCK 'N' ROLL** Kitchenware SK 37	.....**7**	10 wks
23 Jul	88	**HEY MANHATTAN!** Kitchenware SK 38	.....**72**	1 wk
18 Aug	90	**LOOKING FOR ATLANTIS** Kitchenware SK 47	.....**51**	3 wks
20 Oct	90	**WE LET THE STARS GO** Kitchenware SK 48	.....**50**	3 wks
5 Jan	91	**JORDAN: THE EP** Kitchenware SK 49	.....**35**	4 wks
13 Jun	92	**THE SOUND OF CRYING** Kitchenware SK 58	.....**23**	5 wks
8 Aug	92	**IF YOU DON'T LOVE ME** Kitchenware SK 60	.....**33**	4 wks
3 Oct	92	**ALL THE WORLD LOVES LOVERS** Kitchenware SK 62	.....**61**	2 wks
9 Jan	93	**LIFE OF SURPRISES** Kitchenware SKCD 63	.....**24**	4 wks

Tracks on Jordan: The EP: Carnival 2000 / The Ice Maiden / One Of The Broken / Jordan: The Comeback.

PRELUDE *UK, male / female vocal group* **26 wks**

26 Jan	74	**AFTER THE GOLDRUSH** Dawn DNS 1052	.....**21**	9 wks
26 Apr	80	**PLATINUM BLONDE** EMI 5046	.....**45**	7 wks
22 May	82	**AFTER THE GOLDRUSH (re-issue)** After Hours AFT 02	.....**28**	7 wks
31 Jul	82	**ONLY THE LONELY** After Hours AFT 06	.....**55**	3 wks

AFT 02 was a re-recording of DNS 1052. Both songs are a capella.

Elvis PRESLEY *US, male vocalist* **1145 wks**

11 May	56	● **HEARTBREAK HOTEL** HMV POP 182	.....**2**	21 wks
25 May	56	● **BLUE SUEDE SHOES** HMV POP 213	.....**9**	8 wks
13 Jul	56	**I WANT YOU I NEED YOU I LOVE YOU** HMV POP 235	.....**25**	2 wks
3 Aug	56	**I WANT YOU I NEED YOU I LOVE YOU (re-entry)** HMV POP 235	.....**14**	9 wks
17 Aug	56	**BLUE SUEDE SHOES (re-entry)** HMV POP 213	.....**26**	2 wks
21 Sep	56	● **HOUND DOG** HMV POP 249	.....**2**	23 wks
26 Oct	56	**HEARTBREAK HOTEL (re-entry)** HMV POP 182	.....**23**	1 wk
16 Nov	56	● **BLUE MOON** HMV POP 272	.....**9**	11 wks
23 Nov	56	**I DON'T CARE IF THE SUN DON'T SHINE** HMV POP 272	.....**29**	1 wk
7 Dec	56	**LOVE ME TENDER** HMV POP 253	.....**11**	9 wks
21 Dec	56	**I DON'T CARE IF THE SUN DON'T SHINE (re-entry)** HMV POP 272	.....**23**	3 wks
15 Feb	57	**MYSTERY TRAIN** HMV POP 295	.....**25**	5 wks
8 Mar	57	**RIP IT UP** HMV POP 305	.....**27**	1 wk
10 May	57	● **TOO MUCH** HMV POP 330	.....**6**	8 wks
14 Jun	57	**ALL SHOOK UP** HMV POP 359	.....**24**	1 wk
28 Jun	57	★ **ALL SHOOK UP (re-entry)** HMV POP 359	.....**1**	20 wks
12 Jul	57	● **TEDDY BEAR** RCA 1013	.....**3**	19 wks
12 Jul	57	**TOO MUCH (re-entry)** HMV POP 330	.....**26**	1 wk

30 Aug	57	● **PARALYSED** HMV POP 378	.....**8**	10 wks
4 Oct	57	● **PARTY** RCA 1020	.....**2**	15 wks
18 Oct	57	**GOT A LOT O' LIVIN' TO DO** RCA 1020	.....**17**	4 wks
1 Nov	57	**LOVING YOU** RCA 1013	.....**24**	2 wks
1 Nov	57	**TRYING TO GET TO YOU** RCA 1013	.....**16**	4 wks
8 Nov	57	**LAWDY MISS CLAWDY** HMV POP 408	.....**15**	5 wks
15 Nov	57	● **SANTA BRING MY BABY BACK TO ME** RCA 1025	.....**7**	8 wks
17 Jan	58	**I'M LEFT YOU'RE RIGHT SHE'S GONE** HMV POP 428	.....**21**	2 wks
24 Jan	58	★ **JAILHOUSE ROCK** RCA 1028	.....**1**	14 wks
31 Jan	58	**JAILHOUSE ROCK EP** RCA RCX 106	.....**18**	5 wks
7 Feb	58	**I'M LEFT YOU'RE RIGHT SHE'S GONE (re-entry)** HMV POP 428	.....**29**	1 wk
28 Feb	58	● **DON'T** RCA 1043	.....**2**	11 wks
2 May	58	● **WEAR MY RING AROUND YOUR NECK** RCA 1058	.....**3**	10 wks
25 Jul	58	● **HARD HEADED WOMAN** RCA 1070	.....**2**	11 wks
3 Oct	58	● **KING CREOLE** RCA 1081	.....**2**	15 wks
23 Jan	59	★ **ONE NIGHT / I GOT STUNG** RCA 1100	.....**1**	12 wks
24 Apr	59	● **A FOOL SUCH AS I / I NEED YOUR LOVE TONIGHT** RCA 1113	.....**1**	15 wks
24 Jul	59	● **A BIG HUNK O' LOVE** RCA 1136	.....**4**	9 wks
12 Feb	60	**STRICTLY ELVIS EP** RCA RCX 175	.....**26**	1 wk
7 Apr	60	● **STUCK ON YOU** RCA 1187	.....**3**	14 wks
28 Jul	60	● **A MESS OF BLUES** RCA 1194	.....**2**	18 wks
3 Nov	60	★ **IT'S NOW OR NEVER** RCA 1207	.....**1**	19 wks
19 Jan	61	★ **ARE YOU LONESOME TONIGHT** RCA 1216	.....**1**	15 wks
9 Mar	61	★ **WOODEN HEART** RCA 1226	.....**1**	27 wks
25 May	61	★ **SURRENDER** RCA 1227	.....**1**	15 wks
7 Sep	61	● **WILD IN THE COUNTRY / I FEEL SO BAD** RCA 1244	.....**4**	12 wks
2 Nov	61	★ **HIS LATEST FLAME / LITTLE SISTER** RCA 1258	.....**1**	13 wks
1 Feb	62	★ **ROCK A HULA BABY / CAN'T HELP FALLING IN LOVE** RCA 1270	.....**1**	20 wks
10 May	62	★ **GOOD LUCK CHARM** RCA 1280	.....**1**	17 wks
21 Jun	62	**FOLLOW THAT DREAM EP** RCA RCX 211	.....**34**	2 wks
30 Aug	62	★ **SHE'S NOT YOU** RCA 1303	.....**1**	14 wks
29 Nov	62	★ **RETURN TO SENDER** RCA 1320	.....**1**	14 wks
28 Feb	63	**ONE BROKEN HEART FOR SALE** RCA 1337	.....**12**	9 wks
4 Jul	63	★ **DEVIL IN DISGUISE** RCA 1355	.....**1**	12 wks
24 Oct	63	**BOSSA NOVA BABY** RCA 1374	.....**13**	8 wks
19 Dec	63	**KISS ME QUICK** RCA 1375	.....**14**	10 wks
12 Mar	64	**VIVA LAS VEGAS** RCA 1390	.....**17**	12 wks
25 Jun	64	● **KISSIN' COUSINS** RCA 1404	.....**10**	11 wks
20 Aug	64	**SUCH A NIGHT** RCA 1411	.....**13**	10 wks
29 Oct	64	**AIN'T THAT LOVIN' YOU BABY** RCA 1422	.....**15**	8 wks
3 Dec	64	**BLUE CHRISTMAS** RCA 1430	.....**11**	7 wks
11 Mar	65	**DO THE CLAM** RCA 1443	.....**19**	8 wks
27 May	65	★ **CRYING IN THE CHAPEL** RCA 1455	.....**1**	15 wks
11 Nov	65	**TELL ME WHY** RCA 1489	.....**15**	10 wks
24 Feb	66	**BLUE RIVER** RCA 1504	.....**22**	7 wks
7 Apr	66	**FRANKIE AND JOHNNY** RCA 1509	.....**21**	9 wks
7 Jul	66	● **LOVE LETTERS** RCA 1526	.....**6**	10 wks
13 Oct	66	**ALL THAT I AM** RCA 1545	.....**18**	8 wks
1 Dec	66	**IF EVERY DAY WAS LIKE CHRISTMAS** RCA 1557	.....**13**	7 wks
9 Feb	67	**INDESCRIBABLY BLUE** RCA 1565	.....**21**	5 wks
11 May	67	**YOU GOTTA STOP / LOVE MACHINE** RCA 1593	.....**38**	5 wks
16 Aug	67	**LONG LEGGED GIRL** RCA 1616	.....**49**	2 wks
21 Feb	68	**GUITAR MAN** RCA 1663	.....**19**	8 wks
15 May	68	**U. S. MALE** RCA 1688	.....**15**	8 wks
17 Jul	68	**YOUR TIME HASN'T COME YET BABY** RCA 1714	.....**22**	11 wks
16 Oct	68	**YOU'LL NEVER WALK ALONE** RCA 1747	.....**44**	3 wks
26 Feb	69	**IF I CAN DREAM** RCA 1795	.....**11**	10 wks
11 Jun	69	● **IN THE GHETTO** RCA 1831	.....**2**	16 wks
6 Sep	69	**CLEAN UP YOUR OWN BACK YARD** RCA 1869	.....**21**	7 wks
18 Oct	69	**IN THE GHETTO (re-entry)** RCA 1831	.....**50**	1 wk
29 Nov	69	**SUSPICIOUS MINDS** RCA 1900	.....**2**	14 wks
28 Feb	70	● **DON'T CRY DADDY** RCA 1916	.....**8**	11 wks
16 May	70	**KENTUCKY RAIN** RCA 1949	.....**21**	11 wks
11 Jul	70	★ **THE WONDER OF YOU** RCA 1974	.....**1**	20 wks
8 Aug	70	**KENTUCKY RAIN (re-entry)** RCA 1949	.....**46**	1 wk
14 Nov	70	**I'VE LOST YOU** RCA 1999	.....**9**	12 wks
9 Jan	71	● **YOU DON'T HAVE TO SAY YOU LOVE ME** RCA 2046	.....**9**	7 wks
23 Jan	71	**THE WONDER OF YOU (re-entry)** RCA 1974	.....**47**	1 wk
6 Mar	71	**YOU DON'T HAVE TO SAY YOU LOVE ME (re-entry)** RCA 2046	.....**35**	3 wks
20 Mar	71	● **THERE GOES MY EVERYTHING** RCA 2060	.....**6**	11 wks
15 May	71	● **RAGS TO RICHES** RCA 2084	.....**9**	11 wks

ELVIS PRESLEY reminds us he was a guitarist as well as the most successful vocalist of the rock era. (LFI)

ROY ORBISON is shown on the roof of ATV House in London in October 1964, after breaking a British television record by signing a £10,000 contract for two ITV appearances. (LFI)

Pictured in the mid 1970s, **FREDA PAYNE** performed in 1994 in the Boston version of the Broadway hit *Jelly's Last Jam*. (REX)

17 Jul 71	● **HEARTBREAK HOTEL / HOUND DOG** (re-issue) *RCA Maximillion 2104* **10**	12 wks
2 Oct 71	**I'M LEAVIN'** *RCA 2125* **23**	9 wks
4 Dec 71	● **I JUST CAN'T HELP BELIEVING** *RCA 2158* **6**	16 wks
11 Dec 71	**JAILHOUSE ROCK** (re-issue) *RCA Maximillion 2153.* .**42**	5 wks
1 Apr 72	● **UNTIL IT'S TIME FOR YOU TO GO** *RCA 2188* **5**	9 wks
17 Jun 72	● **AMERICAN TRILOGY** *RCA 2229* **8**	11 wks
30 Sep 72	● **BURNING LOVE** *RCA 2267* **7**	9 wks
16 Dec 72	● **ALWAYS ON MY MIND** *RCA 2304* **9**	13 wks
26 May 73	**POLK SALAD ANNIE** *RCA 2359* **23**	7 wks
11 Aug 73	**FOOL** *RCA 2393* **15**	10 wks
24 Nov 73	**RAISED ON ROCK** *RCA 2435* **36**	7 wks
16 Mar 74	**I'VE GOT A THING ABOUT YOU BABY** *RCA APBO 0196* **33**	5 wks
13 Jul 74	**IF YOU TALK IN YOUR SLEEP** *RCA APBO 0280* **40**	3 wks
16 Nov 74	● **MY BOY** *RCA 2458* **5**	13 wks
18 Jan 75	● **PROMISED LAND** *RCA PB 10074* **9**	8 wks
24 May 75	**T. R. O. U. B. L. E.** *RCA 2562* **31**	4 wks
29 Nov 75	**GREEN GREEN GRASS OF HOME** *RCA 2635* **29**	7 wks
1 May 76	**HURT** *RCA 2674* **37**	5 wks
4 Sep 76	● **GIRL OF MY BEST FRIEND** *RCA 2729* **9**	12 wks
25 Dec 76	● **SUSPICION** *RCA 2768* **9**	12 wks
5 Mar 77	● **MOODY BLUE** *RCA PB 0857* **6**	9 wks
13 Aug 77	★ **WAY DOWN** *RCA PB 0998* **1**	13 wks
3 Sep 77	**ALL SHOOK UP** (re-issue) *RCA PB 2694* **41**	2 wks
3 Sep 77	**ARE YOU LONESOME TONIGHT** (re-issue) *RCA PB 2699* **46**	1 wk
3 Sep 77	**CRYING IN THE CHAPEL** (re-issue) *RCA PB 2708* .**43**	2 wks
3 Sep 77	**IT'S NOW OR NEVER** (re-issue) *RCA PB 2698* **39**	2 wks
3 Sep 77	**JAILHOUSE ROCK** (2nd re-issue) *RCA PB 2695* **44**	2 wks
3 Sep 77	**RETURN TO SENDER** (re-issue) *RCA PB 2706* **42**	3 wks
3 Sep 77	**THE WONDER OF YOU** (re-issue) *RCA PB 2709* ..**48**	1 wk
3 Sep 77	**WOODEN HEART** (re-issue) *RCA PB 2700* **49**	1 wk
10 Dec 77	● **MY WAY** *RCA PB 1165* **9**	8 wks
24 Jun 78	**DON'T BE CRUEL** *RCA PB 9265* **24**	12 wks
15 Dec 79	**IT WON'T SEEM LIKE CHRISTMAS** (WITHOUT YOU) *RCA PB 9464* **13**	6 wks
30 Aug 80	● **IT'S ONLY LOVE / BEYOND THE REEF** *RCA 4* **3**	10 wks
6 Dec 80	**SANTA CLAUS IS BACK IN TOWN** *RCA 16* **41**	6 wks
14 Feb 81	**GUITAR MAN** *RCA 43* **43**	4 wks
18 Apr 81	**LOVING ARMS** *RCA 48* **47**	6 wks
13 Mar 82	**ARE YOU LONESOME TONIGHT** *RCA 196* **25**	7 wks
26 Jun 82	**THE SOUND OF YOUR CRY** *RCA 232* **59**	2 wks
5 Feb 83	**JAILHOUSE ROCK** (re-entry) *RCA 1028* **27**	6 wks
7 May 83	**BABY I DON'T CARE** *RCA 332* **61**	3 wks
3 Dec 83	**I CAN HELP** *RCA 369* **30**	9 wks
10 Nov 84	**THE LAST FAREWELL** *RCA 459* **48**	6 wks
19 Jan 85	**THE ELVIS MEDLEY** *RCA 476* **51**	3 wks
10 Aug 85	**ALWAYS ON MY MIND** *RCA PB 49944* **59**	4 wks
11 Apr 87	**AIN'T THAT LOVIN' YOU BABY / BOSSA NOVA BABY** *RCA ARON 1* **47**	5 wks
22 Aug 87	**LOVE ME TENDER / IF I CAN DREAM** (re-issue) *RCA ARON 2* **56**	3 wks
16 Jan 88	**STUCK ON YOU** *RCA PB 49595* **58**	2 wks
17 Aug 91	**ARE YOU LONESOME TONIGHT** (LIVE) (re-issue) *RCA PB 49177* **68**	2 wks
29 Aug 92	**DON'T BE CRUEL** (re-issue) *RCA 74321110777* **42**	2 wks

Tracks on Jailhouse Rock *(EP):* Jailhouse Rock / Young And Beautiful / I Want To Be Free / Don't Leave Me Now / Baby I Don't Care. *On* Strictly Elvis *(EP):* Old Shep / Any Place Is Paradise / Paralysed / Is It So Strange. *On* Follow That Dream *(EP):* Follow That Dream / Angel / What A Wonderful Life / I'm Not The Marrying Kind. *On 5 July 62 a note on the Top 50 for that week stated 'Due to difficulties in assessing returns of* Follow That Dream EP, *it has been decided not to include it in Britain's Top 50. It is of course No.1 in the EP charts'. Therefore this EP only had a two week run on the chart when its sales would certainly have justified a much longer one.* Beyond The Reef *listed only 30 Aug to 13 Sep 80. It peaked at position 7.* Are You Lonesome Tonight *on RCA 196 is a live version. RCA PB 49177 is a re-issue of RCA 196.* Can't Help Falling In Love *credited from 1 Mar 62.*

Tracks on The Elvis Medley: Jailhouse Rock / Teddy Bear / Hound Dog / Don't Be Cruel / Burning Love / Suspicious Minds. *Both sides of RCA ARON 1 are alternate versions to the original hits. RCA PB 49944 is also an alternate version.*

Billy PRESTON
US, male vocalist / instrumentalist - keyboards   **51 wks**

23 Apr 69	★ **GET BACK** *Apple R 5777* [1] **1**	17 wks
2 Jul 69	**THAT'S THE WAY GOD PLANNED IT** *Apple 12* **11**	10 wks
16 Sep 72	**OUTA SPACE** *A & M AMS 7007* **44**	3 wks
3 Apr 76	**GET BACK** (re-entry) *Apple R 5777* [1] **28**	5 wks
15 Dec 79	● **WITH YOU I'M BORN AGAIN** *Motown TMG 1159* [2] **2**	11 wks
8 Mar 80	**IT WILL COME IN TIME** *Motown TMG 1175* [2] **47**	4 wks
22 Apr 89	**GET BACK** (2nd re-entry) *Apple R 5777* [1] **74**	1 wk

[1] Beatles with Billy Preston [2] Billy Preston and Syreeta

See also Various Artists (EPs & LPs) - The Apple EP.

Johnny PRESTON
US, male vocalist   **45 wks**

12 Feb 60	★ **RUNNING BEAR** *Mercury AMT 1079* **1**	14 wks
21 Apr 60	● **CRADLE OF LOVE** *Mercury AMT 1092* **2**	16 wks
2 Jun 60	**RUNNING BEAR** (re-entry) *Mercury AMT 1079* **41**	1 wk
28 Jul 60	**I'M STARTING TO GO STEADY** *Mercury AMT 1104*	49 1 wk
11 Aug 60	**FEEL SO FINE** *Mercury AMT 1104* **18**	10 wks
8 Dec 60	**CHARMING BILLY** *Mercury AMT 1114* **34**	1 wk
22 Dec 60	**CHARMING BILLY** (re-entry) *Mercury AMT 1114* .**42**	2 wks

Mike PRESTON
UK, male vocalist   **33 wks**

30 Oct 59	**MR. BLUE** *Decca F 11167* **12**	8 wks
25 Aug 60	**I'D DO ANYTHING** *Decca F 11255* **23**	13 wks
22 Dec 60	**TOGETHERNESS** *Decca F 11287* **41**	5 wks
9 Mar 61	**MARRY ME** *Decca F 11335* **14**	10 wks

PRETENDERS
US / UK, female / male vocal / instrumental group   **127 wks**

10 Feb 79	**STOP YOUR SOBBING** *Real ARE 6* **34**	9 wks
14 Jul 79	**KID** *Real ARE 9* **33**	7 wks
17 Nov 79	★ **BRASS IN POCKET** *Real ARE 11* **1**	17 wks
5 Apr 80	● **TALK OF THE TOWN** *Real ARE 12* **8**	8 wks
14 Feb 81	**MESSAGE OF LOVE** *Real ARE 15* **11**	7 wks
12 Sep 81	**DAY AFTER DAY** *Real ARE 17* **45**	4 wks
14 Nov 81	● **I GO TO SLEEP** *Real ARE 18* **7**	10 wks
2 Oct 82	**BACK ON THE CHAIN GANG** *Real ARE 19* **17**	9 wks
26 Nov 83	**2000 MILES** *Real ARE 20* **15**	9 wks
9 Jun 84	**THIN LINE BETWEEN LOVE AND HATE** *Real ARE 22* **49**	3 wks
11 Oct 86	● **DON'T GET ME WRONG** *Real YZ 85* **10**	9 wks
13 Dec 86	● **HYMN TO HER** *Real YZ 93* **8**	12 wks
15 Aug 87	**IF THERE WAS A MAN** *Real YZ 149* [1] **49**	6 wks
23 Apr 94	● **I'LL STAND BY YOU** *WEA YZ 815CD* **10**	10 wks
2 Jul 94	**NIGHT IN MY VEINS** *WEA YZ 825CD* **25**	5 wks
15 Oct 94	**977** *WEA YZ 848CD1* **66**	2 wks

[1] Pretenders For 007

PRETTY BOY FLOYD
US, male vocal / instrumental group   **1 wk**

10 Mar 90	**ROCK AND ROLL (IS GONNA SET THE NIGHT ON FIRE)** *MCA MCA 1393* **75**	1 wk

PRETTY THINGS
UK, male vocal / instrumental group   **41 wks**

18 Jun 64	**ROSALYN** *Fontana TF 469* **41**	5 wks
22 Oct 64	● **DON'T BRING ME DOWN** *Fontana TF 503* **10**	11 wks
25 Feb 65	**HONEY I NEED** *Fontana TF 537* **13**	10 wks
15 Jul 65	**CRY TO ME** *Fontana TF 585* **28**	7 wks
20 Jan 66	**MIDNIGHT TO SIX MAN** *Fontana TF 647* **46**	1 wk
5 May 66	**COME SEE ME** *Fontana TF 688* **43**	5 wks
21 Jul 66	**A HOUSE IN THE COUNTRY** *Fontana TF 722* **50**	1 wk
4 Aug 66	**A HOUSE IN THE COUNTRY** (re-entry) *Fontana TF 722* **50**	1 wk

Alan PRICE
UK, male vocalist / instrumentalist - keyboards   **88 wks**

31 Mar 66	● **I PUT A SPELL ON YOU** *Decca F 12367* [1] **9**	10 wks
14 Jul 66	**HI LILI HI LO** *Decca F 12442* [1] **11**	12 wks
2 Mar 67	● **SIMON SMITH AND HIS AMAZING DANCING BEAR** *Decca F 12570* [1] **4**	12 wks

2 Aug 67	● THE HOUSE THAT JACK BUILT Decca F 12641 [1] 4	10 wks
15 Nov 67	SHAME Decca F 12691 [1] 45	2 wks
31 Jan 68	DON'T STOP THE CARNIVAL Decca F 12731 [1] 13	8 wks
10 Apr 71	ROSETTA CBS 7108 [2] 11	10 wks
25 May 74	● JARROW SONG Warner Bros. K 16372 6	9 wks
29 Apr 78	JUST FOR YOU Jet UP 36358 43	8 wks
17 Feb 79	BABY OF MINE / JUST FOR YOU (re-issue) Jet 135..32	3 wks
30 Apr 88	CHANGES Ariola 109911....................54	4 wks

[1] Alan Price Set [2] Fame and Price Together

Lloyd PRICE US, male vocalist — **36 wks**

13 Feb 59	● STAGGER LEE HMV POP 580 7	14 wks
15 May 59	WHERE WERE YOU HMV POP 598...............15	6 wks
12 Jun 59	● PERSONALITY HMV POP 626 9	8 wks
14 Aug 59	PERSONALITY (re-entry) HMV POP 626 25	2 wks
11 Sep 59	I'M GONNA GET MARRIED HMV POP 650.........23	5 wks
21 Apr 60	LADY LUCK HMV POP 712....................45	1 wk

Dickie PRIDE UK, male vocalist — **1 wk**

| 30 Oct 59 | PRIMROSE LANE Columbia DB 4340...........28 | 1 wk |

Maxi PRIEST UK, male vocalist — **97 wks**

29 Mar 86	STROLLIN' ON 10 TEN 84 32	9 wks
12 Jul 86	IN THE SPRINGTIME 10 TEN 127 54	3 wks
8 Nov 86	CRAZY LOVE 10 TEN 135 67	5 wks
4 Apr 87	LET ME KNOW 10 TEN 156 49	4 wks
24 Oct 87	SOME GUYS HAVE ALL THE LUCK 10 TEN 198 12	12 wks
20 Feb 88	HOW CAN WE EASE THE PAIN 10 TEN 207 [1] 41	6 wks
4 Jun 88	● WILD WORLD 10 TEN 221 5	9 wks
27 Aug 88	GOODBYE TO LOVE AGAIN 10 TEN 238 57	3 wks
9 Jun 90	● CLOSE TO YOU 10 TEN 294 7	10 wks
1 Sep 90	PEACE THROUGHOUT THE WORLD	
	10 TEN 317 [2] 41	4 wks
1 Dec 90	HUMAN WORK OF ART 10 TEN 328 75	1 wk
15 Dec 90	HUMAN WORK OF ART (re-entry) 10 TEN 328 71	3 wks
24 Aug 91	HOUSECALL Epic 6573477 [3] 31	7 wks
5 Oct 91	THE MAXI PRIEST EP Ten TEN 343 62	3 wks
26 Sep 92	GROOVIN' IN THE MIDNIGHT Ten TEN 412 50	2 wks
28 Nov 92	JUST WANNA KNOW / FE' REAL Ten TEN 416 [4] ..33	3 wks
20 Mar 93	ONE MORE CHANCE Ten TENCD 420 40	3 wks
8 May 93	● HOUSECALL (re-mix) Epic 6592842 [3] 8	8 wks
31 Jul 93	WAITING IN VAIN GRP MCSC 1921 [5] 65	2 wks

[1] Maxi Priest featuring Beres Hammond [2] Maxi Priest featuring Jazzie B [3] Shabba Ranks featuring Maxi Priest [4] Maxi Priest / Maxi Priest featuring Apache Indian [5] Lee Ritenour and Maxi Priest

Tracks on The Maxi Priest EP: *Just A Little Bit Longer / Best Of Me / Searching / Fever.*

Louis PRIMA US, male vocalist — **1 wk**

| 21 Feb 58 | BUONA SERA Capitol CL 14841 ....25 | 1 wk |

PRIMA DONNA UK, male / female vocal group — **4 wks**

| 26 Apr 80 | LOVE ENOUGH FOR TWO Ariola ARO 221 ....48 | 4 wks |

PRIMAL SCREAM UK, male vocal / instrumental group — **34 wks**

3 Mar 90	LOADED Creation CRE 070 16	9 wks
18 Aug 90	COME TOGETHER Creation CRE 0778 26	6 wks
22 Jun 91	HIGHER THAN THE SUN Creation CRE 096.......40	2 wks
24 Aug 91	DON'T FIGHT IT FEEL IT Creation CRE 110 [1] ...41	2 wks
8 Feb 92	DIXIE-NARCO EP Creation CRE 117............11	6 wks
12 Mar 94	● ROCKS / FUNKY JAM Creation CRESCD 129 7	5 wks
18 Jun 94	JAILBIRD Creation CRESCD 145 29	2 wks
10 Dec 94	(I'M GONNA) CRY MYSELF BLIND	
	Creation CRESCD 183 49	2 wks

[1] Primal Scream featuring Denise Johnson

Tracks on Dixie-Narco EP: *Movin' On Up / Stone My Soul / Carry Me Home / Screamadelica.*

PRIME MOVERS US, male vocal / instrumental group — **1 wk**

| 8 Feb 86 | ON THE TRAIL Island IS 263 ....74 | 1 wk |

PRIMITIVES UK, male / female vocal / instrumental group — **27 wks**

27 Feb 88	● CRASH Lazy PB 41761 5	10 wks
30 Apr 88	OUT OF REACH Lazy PB 42011 25	4 wks
3 Sep 88	WAY BEHIND ME Lazy PB 42209 36	4 wks
29 Jul 89	SICK OF IT Lazy PB 42947 24	4 wks
30 Sep 89	SECRETS Lazy PB 43173 49	3 wks
3 Aug 91	YOU ARE THE WAY RCA PB 44481 58	2 wks

♀ PRINCE US, male vocalist — **269 wks**

19 Jan 80	I WANNA BE YOUR LOVER Warner Bros. K 17537 ..41	3 wks
29 Jan 83	1999 Warner Bros. W 9896 25	7 wks
30 Apr 83	LITTLE RED CORVETTE Warner Bros. W 9688..........54	6 wks
26 Nov 83	LITTLE RED CORVETTE (re-issue)	
	Warner Bros. W 9436 66	2 wks
30 Jun 84	● WHEN DOVES CRY Warner Bros. W 9286 4	15 wks
22 Sep 84	● PURPLE RAIN Warner Bros. W 9174 [1] 8	9 wks
8 Dec 84	I WOULD DIE 4 U Warner Bros. W 9121 [1] 58	6 wks
19 Jan 85	● 1999 / LITTLE RED CORVETTE (re-issue)	
	Warner Bros. W 1999 2	10 wks
23 Feb 85	● LET'S GO CRAZY / TAKE ME WITH YOU	
	Warner Bros. W 2000 [1] 7	9 wks
25 May 85	PAISLEY PARK WEA W 9052 [1] 18	10 wks
27 Jul 85	RASPBERRY BERET WEA W 8929 [1] 25	8 wks
26 Oct 85	POP LIFE Paisley Park W 8858 [1] 60	2 wks
8 Mar 86	● KISS Paisley Park W 8751 [1] 6	9 wks
14 Jun 86	MOUNTAINS Paisley Park W 8711 [1] 45	4 wks
16 Aug 86	GIRLS AND BOYS Paisley Park W 8586 [1] 11	8 wks
1 Nov 86	ANOTHERLOVERHOLENYOHEAD	
	Paisley Park W 8521 [1] 36	3 wks
14 Mar 87	● SIGN 'O' THE TIMES Paisley Park W 8399......10	9 wks
20 Jun 87	IF I WAS YOUR GIRLFRIEND Paisley Park W 8334....20	6 wks
15 Aug 87	U GOT THE LOOK Paisley Park W 8289 11	9 wks
28 Nov 87	I COULD NEVER TAKE THE PLACE OF YOUR MAN	
	Paisley Park W 8288 29	6 wks
7 May 88	● ALPHABET STREET Paisley Park W 7900 9	6 wks
23 Jul 88	GLAM SLAM Paisley Park W 7806 29	4 wks
5 Nov 88	I WISH U HEAVEN Paisley Park W 7745.........24	5 wks
24 Jun 89	● BATDANCE Warner Bros. W 2924 2	12 wks
9 Sep 89	PARTYMAN Warner Bros. W 2814 14	6 wks
18 Nov 89	THE ARMS OF ORION Warner Bros. W 2757 [2] ..27	5 wks
4 Aug 90	● THIEVES IN THE TEMPLE Paisley Park W 9751 ...7	6 wks
10 Nov 90	NEW POWER GENERATION Paisley Park W 9525.....26	4 wks
31 Aug 91	● GETT OFF Paisley Park W 0056 [3] 4	8 wks
21 Sep 91	CREAM Paisley Park W 0061 [3] 15	7 wks
7 Dec 91	DIAMONDS AND PEARLS Paisley Park W 0075 [3] ..25	6 wks
28 Mar 92	MONEY DON'T MATTER 2 NIGHT	
	Paisley Park W 0091 [3] 19	5 wks
27 Jun 92	THUNDER Paisley Park W 01132P [3] 28	3 wks
18 Jul 92	● SEXY MF / STROLLIN' Paisley Park W 0123 [3] ...4	7 wks
10 Oct 92	● MY NAME IS PRINCE Paisley Park W 0132 [3] ...7	5 wks
14 Nov 92	MY NAME IS PRINCE (re-mix)	
	Paisley Park W 0142T [3] 51	1 wk
5 Dec 92	7 Paisley Park W 0147 [3] 27	6 wks
13 Mar 93	THE MORNING PAPERS Paisley Park W 0162CD [3] 52	3 wks
16 Oct 93	PEACH Paisley Park W 0210CD 14	5 wks
11 Dec 93	● CONTROVERSY Paisley Park W 0215CD1.......5	5 wks
9 Apr 94	★ THE MOST BEAUTIFUL GIRL IN THE WORLD	
	NPG NPG 60155 [4] 1	12 wks
4 Jun 94	THE BEAUTIFUL EXPERIENCE (re-mix)	
	NPG NPG 60212 [4] 18	3 wks
10 Sep 94	LETITGO Warner Bros. W 0260CD 30	4 wks

[1] Prince and the Revolution [2] Prince with Sheena Easton [3] Prince and the New Power Generation [4] ♀

Although uncredited, Sheena Easton also vocalises on U Got The Look. The Beautiful Experience *was a seven track CD featuring* The Most Beautiful Girl In The World *and six further mixes of the track.*

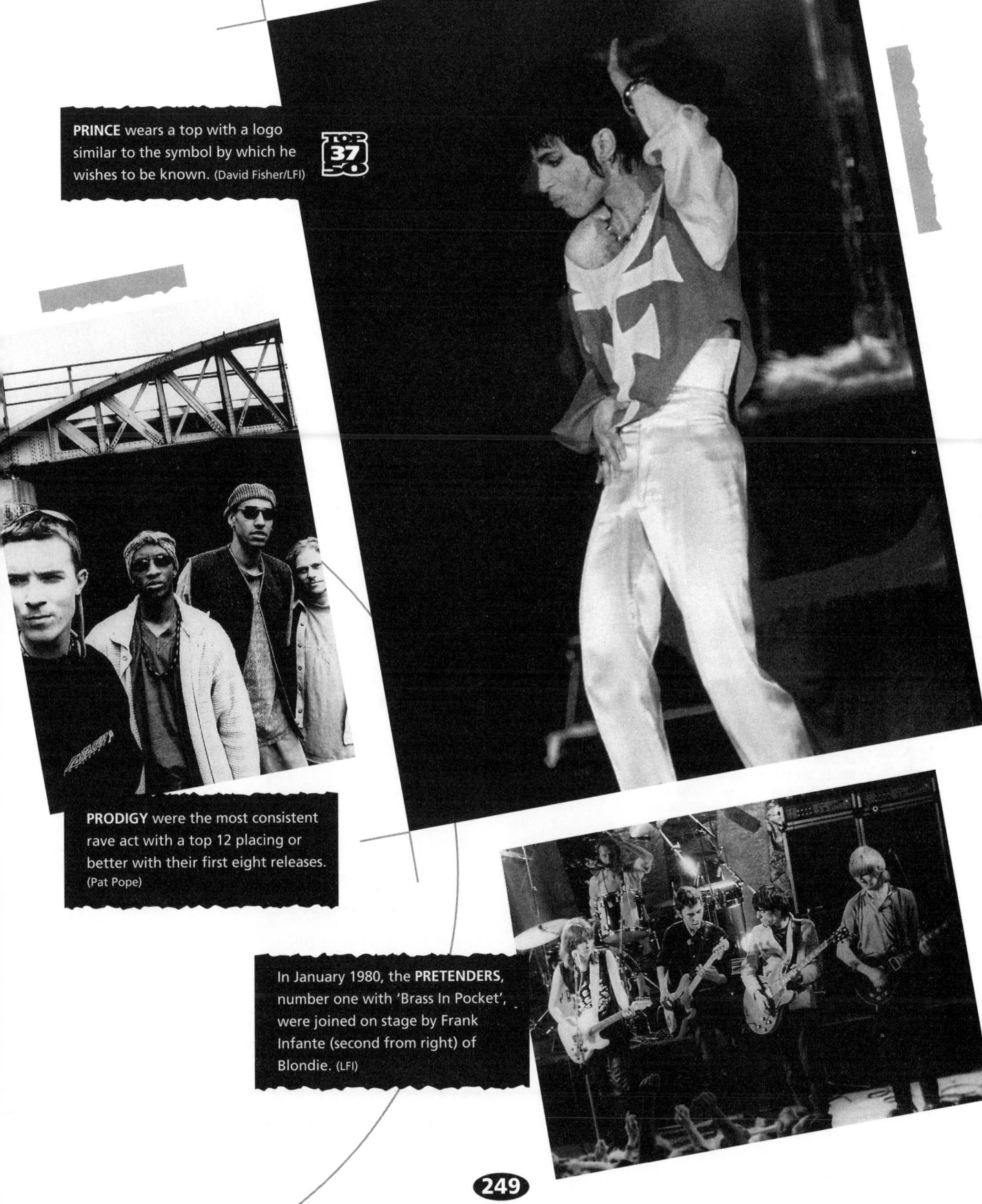

PRINCE wears a top with a logo similar to the symbol by which he wishes to be known. (David Fisher/LFI)

TOP 37 50

PRODIGY were the most consistent rave act with a top 12 placing or better with their first eight releases. (Pat Pope)

In January 1980, the **PRETENDERS**, number one with 'Brass In Pocket', were joined on stage by Frank Infante (second from right) of Blondie. (LFI)

PRINCE BUSTER *Jamaica, male vocalist*   **13 wks**

23 Feb 67   **AL CAPONE** *Blue Beat BB 324* ....**18** 13 wks

PRINCE CHARLES and the CITY BEAT BAND
US, male vocalist with male vocal/instrumental group   **2 wks**

22 Feb 86   **WE CAN MAKE IT HAPPEN** *PRT 7P 348* ....**56** 2 wks

PRINCESS *UK, female vocalist*   **44 wks**

3 Aug 85 ● **SAY I'M YOU'RE NO. 1** *Supreme SUPE 101* ....**7** 12 wks
9 Nov 85   **AFTER THE LOVE HAS GONE** *Supreme SUPE 103* ...**28** 13 wks
19 Apr 86   **I'LL KEEP ON LOVING YOU** *Supreme SUPE 105*........**16** 8 wks
5 Jul 86   **TELL ME TOMORROW** *Supreme SUPE 106* ....**34** 5 wks
25 Oct 86   **IN THE HEAT OF A PASSIONATE MOMENT**
              Supreme SUPE 109 ....**74** 1 wk
13 Jun 87   **RED HOT** *Polydor POSP 868* ....**58** 5 wks

PRINCESS IVORI *US, female rapper*   **2 wks**

17 Mar 90   **WANTED** *Supreme SUPE 163* ....**69** 2 wks

PRIVATE LIVES *UK, male vocal/instrumental duo*   **4 wks**

11 Feb 84   **LIVING IN A WORLD (TURNED UPSIDE DOWN)**
              EMI PRIV 2 ....**53** 4 wks

P.J. PROBY *US, male vocalist*   **89 wks**

28 May 64 ● **HOLD ME** *Decca F 11904* ....**3** 15 wks
3 Sep 64 ● **TOGETHER** *Decca F 11967* ....**8** 11 wks
10 Dec 64 ● **SOMEWHERE** *Liberty LIB 10182* ....**6** 12 wks
25 Feb 65   **I APOLOGISE** *Liberty LIB 10188* ....**11** 8 wks
8 Jul 65   **LET THE WATER RUN DOWN** *Liberty LIB 10206*........**19** 8 wks
30 Sep 65   **THAT MEANS A LOT** *Liberty LIB 10215* ....**30** 6 wks
25 Nov 65 ● **MARIA** *Liberty LIB 10218* ....**8** 9 wks
10 Feb 66   **YOU'VE COME BACK** *Liberty LIB 10223* ......**25** 7 wks
16 Jun 66   **TO MAKE A BIG MAN CRY** *Liberty LIB 10236* ......**34** 3 wks
27 Oct 66   **I CAN'T MAKE IT ALONE** *Liberty LIB 10250* ......**37** 5 wks
6 Mar 68   **IT'S YOUR DAY TODAY** *Liberty LBF 15046* ......**32** 5 wks

PROCLAIMERS *UK, male vocal/instrumental duo*   **50 wks**

14 Nov 87 ● **LETTER FROM AMERICA** *Chrysalis CHS 3178* ....**3** 10 wks
5 Mar 88   **MAKE MY HEART FLY** *Chrysalis CLAIM 1* ....**63** 3 wks
27 Aug 88   **I'M GONNA BE** *Chrysalis CLAIM 2* ....**11** 11 wks
12 Nov 88   **SUNSHINE ON LEITH** *Chrysalis CLAIM 3* ....**41** 5 wks
11 Feb 89   **I'M ON MY WAY** *Chrysalis CLAIM 4* ....**43** 4 wks
24 Nov 90 ● **KING OF THE ROAD (EP)** *Chrysalis CLAIM 5*...............**9** 8 wks
19 Feb 94   **LET'S GET MARRIED** *Chrysalis CDCLAIMS 6* ......**21** 4 wks
16 Apr 94   **WHAT MAKES YOU CRY** *Chrysalis CDCLAIMS 7*........**38** 3 wks
22 Oct 94   **THESE ARMS OF MINE** *Chrysalis CDCLAIM 8* ....**51** 2 wks

*Tracks on King Of The Road (EP): King Of The Road/Long Black Veil/
Lulu Selling Tea/Not Ever.*

PROCOL HARUM *UK, male vocal/instrumental group*   **56 wks**

25 May 67 ★ **A WHITER SHADE OF PALE** *Deram DM 126* ....**1** 15 wks
4 Oct 67 ● **HOMBURG** *Regal Zonophone RZ 3003*........................**6** 10 wks
24 Apr 68   **QUITE RIGHTLY SO** *Regal Zonophone RZ 3007* ....**50** 1 wk
18 Jun 69   **SALTY DOG** *Regal Zonophone RZ 3019*......................**44** 1 wk
2 Jul 69   **SALTY DOG (re-entry)** *Regal Zonophone RZ 3019* ..**44** 1 wk
16 Jul 69   **SALTY DOG (2nd re-entry)**
              Regal Zonophone RZ 3019 ....**44** 1 wk
22 Apr 72   **A WHITER SHADE OF PALE (re-issue)**
              Magnifly ECHO 10 ....**13** 13 wks
5 Aug 72   **CONQUISTADOR** *Chrysalis CHS 2003* ......**22** 7 wks
23 Aug 75   **PANDORA'S BOX** *Chrysalis CHS 2073* ......**16** 7 wks

PRODIGY *UK, male producer - Liam Howlett and dancers*   **65 wks**

24 Aug 91 ● **CHARLY** *XL XLS 21* ....**3** 10 wks
4 Jan 92 ● **EVERYBODY IN THE PLACE (EP)** *XL XLS 26* ....**2** 9 wks
26 Sep 92   **FIRE/JERICHO** *XL XLS 30* ....**11** 4 wks
21 Nov 92 ● **OUT OF SPACE/RUFF IN THE JUNGLE BIZNESS**
              XL XLS 35 ....**5** 12 wks
17 Apr 93   **WIND IT UP (REWOUND)** *XL XLS 39CD*...............**11** 7 wks
16 Oct 93 ● **ONE LOVE** *XL XLS 47CD* ....**8** 6 wks
28 May 94 ● **NO GOOD (START THE DANCE)** *XL XLS 51CD* ....**4** 12 wks
24 Sep 94   **VOODOO PEOPLE** *XL XLS 54CD* ....**13** 5 wks

*Tracks on Everybody In The Place (EP): Everybody In The Place/Crazy
Man/G-Force/Rip Up The Sound System. Ruff In The Jungle Bizness only
listed 27 Nov and 5 Dec 92.*

PROFESSIONALS *UK, male vocal/instrumental group*   **4 wks**

11 Oct 80   **1-2-3** *Virgin VS 376* ....**43** 4 wks

PROFESSOR - *See DJ PROFESSOR*

PROGRAM 2 BELTRAM - *See BELTRAM*

PROJECT 1 *UK, male producer - Mark Williams*   **3 wks**

16 May 92   **ROUGHNECK EP** *Rising High RSN 22* ....**49** 2 wks
29 Aug 92   **DON CARGON COMIN'** *Rising High RSN 35* ....**64** 1 wk

*Tracks on Roughneck EP: Come My Selector/Can't Take The Heartbreak/
Live Vibe 4 (Summer Vibes).*

PROJECT featuring GERIDEAU
US, male vocal/instrumental duo   **1 wk**

27 Aug 94   **BRING IT BACK 2 LUV** *Fruittree FTREE 10CD* ....**65** 1 wk

PRONG *US, male vocal/instrumental group*   **1 wk**

25 Apr 92   **WHOSE FIST IS THIS ANYWAY EP** *Epic 6580026*......**58** 1 wk

*Tracks on Whose Fist Is This Anyway EP: Prove You Wrong/Hell If I Could/
(Get A) Grip (On Yourself)/Prove You Wrong (re-mix).*

PROPAGANDA
Germany, male/female vocal/instrumental group   **35 wks**

17 Mar 84   **DR MABUSE** *ZTT ZTAS 2* ....**27** 9 wks
4 May 85   **DUEL** *ZTT ZTAS 8* ....**21** 12 wks
10 Aug 85   **P MACHINERY** *ZTT ZTAS 12* ....**50** 5 wks
28 Apr 90   **HEAVEN GIVE ME WORDS** *Virgin VS 1245* ....**36** 5 wks
8 Sep 90   **ONLY ONE WORD** *Virgin VS 1271* ....**71** 4 wks

Brian PROTHEROE *UK, male vocalist*   **6 wks**

7 Sep 74   **PINBALL** *Chrysalis CHS 2043* ....**22** 6 wks

Dorothy PROVINE *US, female vocalist*   **15 wks**

7 Dec 61   **DON'T BRING LULU** *Warner Bros. WB 53* ....**17** 12 wks
28 Jun 62   **CRAZY WORDS CRAZY TUNE** *Warner Bros. WB 70*..**45** 3 wks

PSEUDO ECHO
Australia, male vocal/instrumental group   **12 wks**

18 Jul 87 ● **FUNKY TOWN** *RCA PB 49705* ....**8** 12 wks

PSYCHEDELIC FURS
UK, male vocal/instrumental group   **31 wks**

2 May 81   **DUMB WAITERS** *CBS 1166* ....**59** 2 wks
27 Jun 81   **PRETTY IN PINK** *CBS A 1327* ....**43** 5 wks
31 Jul 82   **LOVE MY WAY** *CBS A 2549* ....**42** 6 wks

31 Mar 84	**HEAVEN** CBS A 4300	**29**	6 wks
16 Jun 84	**GHOST IN YOU** CBS A 4470	**68**	2 wks
23 Aug 86	**PRETTY IN PINK** CBS A 7242	**18**	9 wks
9 Jul 88	**ALL THAT MONEY WANTS** CBS FURS 4	**75**	1 wk

A 7242 was a re-recording of A 1327.

PSYCHIC TV *UK, male / female vocal / instrumental group* **4 wks**

| 26 Apr 86 | **GODSTAR** Temple TOPY 009 [1] | **67** | 2 wks |
| 20 Sep 86 | **GOOD VIBRATIONS / ROMAN P.** Temple TOPY 23 | **65** | 2 wks |

[1] Psychic TV and the Angels of Light

PSYCHOTROPIC - See FREEFALL featuring PSYCHOTROPIC; SALT-N-PEPA

PUBLIC ANNOUNCEMENT - See R KELLY and PUBLIC ANNOUNCEMENT

PUBLIC ENEMY *US, male rap duo* **47 wks**

21 Nov 87	**REBEL WITHOUT A PAUSE** Def Jam 651245 7	**37**	5 wks
2 Jan 88	**REBEL WITHOUT A PAUSE (re-entry)** Def Jam 651245 7	**71**	2 wks
9 Jan 88	**BRING THE NOISE** Def Jam 651335 7	**32**	5 wks
2 Jul 88	**DON'T BELIEVE THE HYPE** Def Jam 652833 7	**18**	5 wks
15 Oct 88	**NIGHT OF THE LIVING BASEHEADS** Def Jam 6530460	**63**	2 wks
24 Jun 89	**FIGHT THE POWER** Motown ZB 42877	**29**	5 wks
20 Jan 90	**WELCOME TO THE TERRORDOME** Def Jam 655476 0	**18**	4 wks
7 Apr 90	**911 IS A JOKE** Def Jam 655830 7	**41**	3 wks
23 Jun 90	**BROTHERS GONNA WORK IT OUT** Def Jam 656018 1	**46**	2 wks
3 Nov 90	**CAN'T DO NUTTIN' FOR YA MAN** Def Jam 656385 7	**53**	2 wks
12 Oct 91	**CAN'T TRUSS IT** Def Jam 6575307	**22**	4 wks
25 Jan 92	**SHUT 'EM DOWN** Def Jam 6577617	**21**	3 wks
11 Apr 92	**NIGHTTRAIN** Def Jam 6578647	**55**	2 wks
13 Aug 94	**GIVE IT UP** Def Jam DEFCD1	**18**	3 wks

PUBLIC IMAGE LTD.
UK, male vocal / instrumental group **61 wks**

21 Oct 78	● **PUBLIC IMAGE** Virgin VS 228	**9**	8 wks
7 Jul 79	**DEATH DISCO (PARTS 1 & 2)** Virgin VS 274	**20**	7 wks
20 Oct 79	**MEMORIES** Virgin VS 299	**60**	7 wks
4 Apr 81	**FLOWERS OF ROMANCE** Virgin VS 397	**24**	7 wks
17 Sep 83	● **THIS IS NOT A LOVE SONG** Virgin VS 529	**5**	10 wks
19 May 84	**BAD LIFE** Virgin VS 675	**71**	2 wks
1 Feb 86	**RISE** Virgin VS 841	**11**	8 wks
3 May 86	**HOME** Virgin VS 855	**75**	1 wk
22 Aug 87	**SEATTLE** Virgin VS 988	**47**	4 wks
6 May 89	**DISAPPOINTED** Virgin VS 1181	**38**	5 wks
20 Oct 90	**DON'T ASK ME** Virgin VS 1231	**22**	5 wks
22 Feb 92	**CRUEL** Virgin VS 1390	**49**	2 wks

Group often known as P.I.L.

Gary PUCKETT - See UNION GAP featuring Gary PUCKETT

PULP *UK, male / female vocal / instrumental group* **10 wks**

27 Nov 93	**LIP GLOSS** Island CID 567	**50**	2 wks
2 Apr 94	**DO YOU REMEMBER THE FIRST TIME** Island CID 574	**33**	4 wks
4 Jun 94	**THE SISTERS EP** Island CID 595	**19**	4 wks

Tracks on The Sisters EP: Babies / Your Sister's Clothes / Seconds / His 'N' Hers.

James and Bobby PURIFY *US, male vocal duo* **16 wks**

| 24 Apr 76 | **I'M YOUR PUPPET** Mercury 6167 324 | **12** | 10 wks |
| 7 Aug 76 | **MORNING GLORY** Mercury 6167 380 | **27** | 6 wks |

British Hit Singles Part One: Alphabetically by Artist
Date of chart entry / Title & catalogue no. / Peak position reached / Weeks on chart
★ Number One ● Top Ten † still on chart at 31 Dec 1994
□ = credited to act billed in footnote

PURPLE HEARTS *UK, male vocal / instrumental group* **5 wks**

| 22 Sep 79 | **MILLIONS LIKE US** Fiction FICS 003 | **57** | 3 wks |
| 8 Mar 80 | **JIMMY** Fiction FICS 9 | **60** | 2 wks |

PURPLE KINGS *UK, male vocal / instrumental duo* **3 wks**

| 15 Oct 94 | **THAT'S THE WAY YOU DO IT** Positiva CDTIV 21 | **26** | 3 wks |

PUSSYCAT
Holland, male / female vocal / instrumental group **30 wks**

| 28 Aug 76 | ★ **MISSISSIPPI** Sonet SON 2077 | **1** | 22 wks |
| 25 Dec 76 | **SMILE** Sonet SON 2096 | **24** | 8 wks |

PYRAMIDS *Jamaica, male vocal / instrumental group* **4 wks**

| 22 Nov 67 | **TRAIN TOUR TO RAINBOW CITY** President PT 161 | **35** | 4 wks |

PYTHON LEE JACKSON
Australia, male vocal / instrumental group **12 wks**

| 30 Sep 72 | ● **IN A BROKEN DREAM** Youngblood YB 1002 | **3** | 12 wks |

Uncredited lead vocals by Rod Stewart.

Q *UK, male instrumental / production duo* **9 wks**

| 5 Jun 93 | **GET HERE** Arista 74321145972 [1] | **37** | 4 wks |
| 12 Mar 94 | **(EVERYTHING I DO) I DO IT FOR YOU** Bell 74321193062 [2] | **47** | 2 wks |

[1] Q featuring Tracy Ackerman [2] Q featuring Tony Jackson

Q UNIQUE - See C&C MUSIC FACTORY / CLIVILLES & COLE

Q-BASS *UK, male production / instrumental group* **1 wk**

| 8 Feb 92 | **HARDCORE WILL NEVER DIE** Suburban Base SUBBASE 007 | **64** | 1 wk |

See also Various Artists (EPs & LPs) - Subplates Volume 1 EP.

Q-TEE - See HISTORY featuring Q-TEE

Q-TEX *UK, male / female vocal / instrumental group* **3 wks**

| 9 Apr 94 | **THE POWER OF LOVE** Stoatin' STOAT 002CD | **65** | 1 wk |
| 26 Nov 94 | **BELIEVE** 23rd Precinct THIRD 2CD | **41** | 2 wks |

QUADROPHONIA
Belgium, male instrumental / production group **15 wks**

13 Apr 91	**QUADROPHONIA** ARS 6567687	**14**	9 wks
6 Jul 91	**THE WAVE OF THE FUTURE** ARS 6569937	**40**	3 wks
21 Dec 91	**FIND THE TIME (PART ONE)** ARS 6576260	**41**	3 wks

QUADS *UK, male vocal / instrumental group* **2 wks**

| 22 Sep 79 | **THERE MUST BE THOUSANDS** Big Bear BB 23 | **66** | 2 wks |

QUANTUM JUMP *UK, male vocal/instrumental group* **10 wks**

2 Jun 79	● THE LONE RANGER *Electric WOT 33*	**5**	10 wks

QUARTERFLASH
US, male/female vocal/instrumental group **5 wks**

27 Feb 82	HARDEN MY HEART *Geffen GEF A 1838*	**49**	5 wks

QUARTZ *UK, male instrumental group* **19 wks**

17 Mar 90	WE'RE COMIN' AT YA *Mercury ITMR 2* 1	**65**	2 wks
2 Feb 91	● IT'S TOO LATE *Mercury ITM 3* 2	**8**	14 wks
15 Jun 91	NAKED LOVE (JUST SAY YOU WANT ME) *Mercury ITM 4* 3	**39**	3 wks

1 Quartz featuring Stepz 2 Quartz introducing Dina Carroll 3 Quartz and Dina Carroll

Jakie QUARTZ *France, female vocalist* **3 wks**

11 Mar 89	A LA VIE, A L'AMOUR *PWL PWL 30*	**55**	3 wks

Suzi QUATRO
US, female vocalist/instrumentalist - bass guitar **122 wks**

19 May 73	★ CAN THE CAN *RAK 150*	**1**	14 wks
28 Jul 73	● 48 CRASH *RAK 158*	**3**	9 wks
27 Oct 73	DAYTONA DEMON *RAK 161*	**14**	13 wks
9 Feb 74	★ DEVIL GATE DRIVE *RAK 167*	**1**	11 wks
29 Jun 74	TOO BIG *RAK 175*	**14**	6 wks
9 Nov 74	● THE WILD ONE *RAK 185*	**7**	10 wks
8 Feb 75	YOUR MAMA WON'T LIKE ME *RAK 191*	**31**	4 wks
5 Mar 77	TEAR ME APART *RAK 248*	**27**	6 wks
18 Mar 78	● IF YOU CAN'T GIVE ME LOVE *RAK 271*	**4**	13 wks
22 Jul 78	THE RACE IS ON *RAK 278*	**43**	5 wks
11 Nov 78	STUMBLIN' IN *RAK 285* 1	**41**	8 wks
20 Oct 79	SHE'S IN LOVE WITH YOU *RAK 299*	**11**	9 wks
19 Jan 80	MAMA'S BOY *RAK 303*	**34**	5 wks
5 Apr 80	I'VE NEVER BEEN IN LOVE *RAK 307*	**56**	3 wks
25 Oct 80	ROCK HARD *Dreamland DLSP 6*	**68**	2 wks
13 Nov 82	HEART OF STONE *Polydor POSP 477*	**60**	3 wks

1 Suzi Quatro and Chris Norman

QUEEN *UK, male vocal/instrumental group* **357 wks**

9 Mar 74	● SEVEN SEAS OF RHYE *EMI 2121*	**10**	10 wks
26 Oct 74	● KILLER QUEEN *EMI 2229*	**2**	12 wks
25 Jan 75	NOW I'M HERE *EMI 2256*	**11**	7 wks
8 Nov 75	★ BOHEMIAN RHAPSODY *EMI 2375*	**1**	17 wks
3 Jul 76	● YOU'RE MY BEST FRIEND *EMI 2494*	**7**	8 wks
27 Nov 76	● SOMEBODY TO LOVE *EMI 2565*	**2**	9 wks
19 Mar 77	TIE YOUR MOTHER DOWN *EMI 2593*	**31**	4 wks
4 Jun 77	QUEEN'S FIRST EP *EMI 2623*	**17**	10 wks
22 Oct 77	● WE ARE THE CHAMPIONS *EMI 2708*	**2**	11 wks
25 Feb 78	SPREAD YOUR WINGS *EMI 2757*	**34**	4 wks
28 Oct 78	BICYCLE RACE/FAT BOTTOMED GIRLS *EMI 2870*	**11**	12 wks
10 Feb 79	● DON'T STOP ME NOW *EMI 2910*	**9**	12 wks
14 Jul 79	LOVE OF MY LIFE *EMI 2959*	**63**	2 wks
20 Oct 79	● CRAZY LITTLE THING CALLED LOVE *EMI 5001*	**2**	14 wks
2 Feb 80	SAVE ME *EMI 5022*	**11**	6 wks
14 Jun 80	PLAY THE GAME *EMI 5076*	**14**	8 wks
6 Sep 80	● ANOTHER ONE BITES THE DUST *EMI 5102*	**7**	9 wks
6 Dec 80	● FLASH *EMI 5126*	**10**	13 wks
14 Nov 81	★ UNDER PRESSURE *EMI 5250* 1	**1**	11 wks
1 May 82	BODY LANGUAGE *EMI 5293*	**25**	6 wks
12 Jun 82	LAS PALABRAS DE AMOR *EMI 5316*	**17**	8 wks
21 Aug 82	BACKCHAT *EMI 5325*	**40**	4 wks
4 Feb 84	● RADIO GA GA *EMI QUEEN 1*	**2**	9 wks
14 Apr 84	● I WANT TO BREAK FREE *EMI QUEEN 2*	**3**	15 wks
28 Jul 84	● IT'S A HARD LIFE *EMI QUEEN 3*	**6**	9 wks
22 Sep 84	HAMMER TO FALL *EMI QUEEN 4*	**13**	7 wks
8 Dec 84	THANK GOD IT'S CHRISTMAS *EMI QUEEN 5*	**21**	6 wks
16 Nov 85	● ONE VISION *EMI QUEEN 6*	**7**	10 wks
29 Mar 86	● A KIND OF MAGIC *EMI QUEEN 7*	**3**	11 wks
21 Jun 86	FRIENDS WILL BE FRIENDS *EMI QUEEN 8*	**14**	8 wks
27 Sep 86	WHO WANTS TO LIVE FOREVER *EMI QUEEN 9*	**24**	5 wks
13 May 89	● I WANT IT ALL *Parlophone QUEEN 10*	**3**	7 wks
1 Jul 89	● BREAKTHRU' *Parlophone QUEEN 11*	**7**	7 wks
19 Aug 89	THE INVISIBLE MAN *Parlophone QUEEN 12*	**12**	6 wks
21 Oct 89	SCANDAL *Parlophone QUEEN 14*	**25**	4 wks
9 Dec 89	THE MIRACLE *Parlophone QUEEN 15*	**21**	5 wks
26 Jan 91	★ INNUENDO *Parlophone QUEEN 16*	**1**	6 wks
16 Mar 91	I'M GOING SLIGHTLY MAD *Parlophone QUEEN 17*	**22**	4 wks
25 May 91	HEADLONG *Parlophone QUEEN 18*	**14**	4 wks
26 Oct 91	THE SHOW MUST GO ON *Parlophone QUEEN 19*	**16**	5 wks
7 Dec 91	THE SHOW MUST GO ON (re-entry) *Parlophone QUEEN 19*	**27**	5 wks
21 Dec 91	★ BOHEMIAN RHAPSODY (re-issue) *Parlophone QUEEN 20*	**1**	14 wks
1 May 93	★ FIVE LIVE EP *Parlophone CDRS 6340* 2	**1**	11 wks
24 Jul 93	FIVE LIVE EP (re-entry) *Parlophone CDRS 6340*	**74**	1 wk

1 Queen and David Bowie 2 George Michael and Queen with Lisa Stansfield

Tracks on Queen's First EP: Good Old Fashioned Lover Boy / Death On Two Legs (Dedicated To...) / Tenement Funster / White Queen (As It Began). Tracks on Five Live EP: Somebody To Love / These Are The Days Of Our Lives / Calling You / Papa Was A Rolling Stone - Killer (medley). Queen only appear on the first two tracks. The first credits George Michael and Queen and the second George Michael and Queen with Lisa Stansfield.

QUEEN LATIFAH *US, female rapper* **15 wks**

24 Mar 90	MAMA GAVE BIRTH TO THE SOUL CHILDREN *Gee Street GEE 26* 1	**14**	7 wks
26 May 90	FIND A WAY *Ahead Of Our Time CCUT 8* 2	**52**	2 wks
31 Aug 91	FLY GIRL *Gee Street GEE 34*	**67**	1 wk
26 Jun 93	WHAT'CHA GONNA DO *Epic 6593072* 3	**21**	4 wks
26 Mar 94	U.N.I.T.Y. *Motown TMGCD 1422*	**74**	1 wk

1 Queen Latifah + De La Soul 2 Coldcut featuring Queen Latifah 3 Shabba Ranks featuring Queen Latifah

QUEENSRYCHE *US, male vocal/instrumental group* **16 wks**

13 May 89	EYES OF A STRANGER *EMI USA MT 65*	**59**	1 wk
10 Nov 90	EMPIRE *EMI USA MT 90*	**61**	1 wk
20 Apr 91	SILENT LUCIDITY *EMI USA MT 94*	**34**	5 wks
6 Jul 91	BEST I CAN *EMI USA MT 97*	**36**	3 wks
7 Sep 91	JET CITY WOMAN *EMI USA MT 98*	**39**	2 wks
8 Aug 92	SILENT LUCIDITY (re-issue) *EMI USA MT 104*	**18**	4 wks

? (QUESTION MARK) and the MYSTERIANS
US, male vocal/instrumental group **4 wks**

17 Nov 66	96 TEARS *Cameo Parkway C428*	**37**	4 wks

QUESTIONS *UK, male vocal/instrumental group* **8 wks**

23 Apr 83	PRICE YOU PAY *Respond KOB 702*	**56**	3 wks
17 Sep 83	TEAR SOUP *Respond KOB 705*	**66**	1 wk
10 Mar 84	TUESDAY SUNSHINE *Respond KOB 707*	**46**	4 wks

QUICK *UK, male vocal/instrumental group* **7 wks**

15 May 82	RHYTHM OF THE JUNGLE *Epic EPC A 2013*	**41**	7 wks

Tommy QUICKLY *UK, male vocalist* **8 wks**

22 Oct 64	WILD SIDE OF LIFE *Pye 7N 15708*	**33**	8 wks

QUIET FIVE *UK, male vocal/instrumental group* **3 wks**

13 May 65	WHEN THE MORNING SUN DRIES THE DEW *Parlophone R 5273*	**45**	1 wk
21 Apr 66	HOMEWARD BOUND *Parlophone R 5421*	**44**	2 wks

QUIET RIOT US, male vocal / instrumental group — 5 wks

Date	Title	Pos	Wks
3 Dec 83	**METAL HEALTH / CUM ON FEEL THE NOIZE** Epic A 3968	45	5 wks

Cum on Feel the Noize *only credited from 10 Dec 83.*

Paul QUINN - *See Edwyn COLLINS*

QUIREBOYS UK, male vocal / instrumental group — 27 wks

Date	Title	Pos	Wks
4 Nov 89	**7 O'CLOCK** Parlophone R 6230	36	4 wks
6 Jan 90	**HEY YOU** Parlophone R 6241	14	7 wks
7 Apr 90	**I DON'T LOVE YOU ANYMORE** Parlophone R 6248	24	6 wks
8 Sep 90	**THERE SHE GOES AGAIN / MISLED** Parlophone R 6267	37	4 wks
10 Oct 92	**TRAMPS AND THIEVES** Parlophone RS 6323	41	3 wks
20 Feb 93	**BROTHER LOUIE** Parlophone CDR 6335	31	3 wks

QUIVER - *See SUTHERLAND BROTHERS and QUIVER*

QUIVVER UK, male instrumental / production duo — 2 wks

Date	Title	Pos	Wks
5 Mar 94	**SAXY LADY** A & M 5805152	56	2 wks

R

Eddie RABBITT US, male vocalist — 14 wks

Date	Title	Pos	Wks
27 Jan 79	**EVERY WHICH WAY BUT LOOSE** Elektra K 12331	41	9 wks
28 Feb 81	**I LOVE A RAINY NIGHT** Elektra K 12498	53	5 wks

Steve RACE UK, male instrumentalist - piano — 9 wks

Date	Title	Pos	Wks
28 Feb 63	**PIED PIPER (THE BEEJE)** Parlophone R 4981	29	9 wks

RACEY UK, male vocal / instrumental group — 44 wks

Date	Title	Pos	Wks
25 Nov 78	● **LAY YOUR LOVE ON ME** RAK 284	3	14 wks
31 Mar 79	● **SOME GIRLS** RAK 291	2	11 wks
18 Aug 79	**BOY OH BOY** RAK 297	22	9 wks
20 Dec 80	**RUNAROUND SUE** RAK 325	13	10 wks

RACING CARS UK, male vocal / instrumental group — 7 wks

Date	Title	Pos	Wks
12 Feb 77	**THEY SHOOT HORSES DON'T THEY** Chrysalis CHS 2129	14	7 wks

RACKETEERS - *See Elbow BONES and the RACKETEERS*

Jimmy RADCLIFFE US, male vocalist — 2 wks

Date	Title	Pos	Wks
4 Feb 65	**LONG AFTER TONIGHT IS ALL OVER** Stateside SS 374	40	2 wks

RADHA KRISHNA TEMPLE
Oxford Street, male / female vocal / instrumental group — 17 wks

Date	Title	Pos	Wks
13 Sep 69	**HARE KRISHNA MANTRA** Apple 15	12	9 wks
28 Mar 70	**GOVINDA** Apple 25	23	8 wks

RADICAL ROB UK, male producer - Rob McLuan — 1 wk

Date	Title	Pos	Wks
11 Jan 92	**MONKEY WAH** R & S RSUK 8	67	1 wk

RADIO HEART - *See Gary NUMAN*

RADIO 1 DJ POSSE - *See Liz KERSHAW and Bruno BROOKES*

RADIO REVELLERS - *See Anthony STEEL and the RADIO REVELLERS*

RADIO STARS UK, male vocal / instrumental group — 3 wks

Date	Title	Pos	Wks
4 Feb 78	**NERVOUS WRECK** Chiswick NS 23	39	3 wks

RADIOHEAD UK, male vocal / instrumental group — 12 wks

Date	Title	Pos	Wks
13 Feb 93	**ANYONE CAN PLAY GUITAR** Parlophone CDR 6333	32	2 wks
22 May 93	**POP IS DEAD** Parlophone CDR 6345	42	2 wks
18 Sep 93	● **CREEP** Parlophone CDR 6359	7	6 wks
8 Oct 94	**MY IRON LUNG** Parlophone CDR 6394	24	2 wks

Fonda RAE US, female vocalist — 4 wks

Date	Title	Pos	Wks
6 Oct 84	**TUCH ME** Streetwave KHAN 28	49	4 wks

Jesse RAE UK, male vocalist — 2 wks

Date	Title	Pos	Wks
11 May 85	**OVER THE SEA** Scotland-Video YZ 36	65	2 wks

RAF Italy, male / female vocal / instrumental group — 4 wks

Date	Title	Pos	Wks
14 Mar 92	**WE'VE GOT TO LIVE TOGETHER** PWL Continental PWL 218	34	3 wks
5 Mar 94	**TAKE ME HIGHER** Media MRLCD 0012	71	1 wk

Gerry RAFFERTY UK, male vocalist — 47 wks

Date	Title	Pos	Wks
18 Feb 78	● **BAKER STREET** United Artists UP 36346	3	15 wks
26 May 79	**NIGHT OWL** United Artists UP 36512	5	13 wks
18 Aug 79	**GET IT RIGHT NEXT TIME** United Artists BP 301	30	9 wks
22 Mar 80	**BRING IT ALL HOME** United Artists BP 340	54	4 wks
21 Jun 80	**ROYAL MILE** United Artists BP 354	67	2 wks
10 Mar 90	**BAKER STREET (re-mix)** EMI EM 132	53	4 wks

RAGE UK, male vocal / instrumental group — 15 wks

Date	Title	Pos	Wks
31 Oct 92	● **RUN TO YOU** Pulse 8 LOSE 33	3	11 wks
27 Feb 93	**WHY DON'T YOU** Pulse 8 CDLOSE 39	44	2 wks
15 May 93	**HOUSE OF THE RISING SUN** Pulse 8 CDLOSE 43	41	2 wks

RAGE AGAINST THE MACHINE
US, male vocal / instrumental group — 10 wks

Date	Title	Pos	Wks
27 Feb 93	**KILLING IN THE NAME** Epic 6584922	25	4 wks
8 May 93	**BULLET IN THE HEAD** Epic 6592582	16	4 wks
4 Sep 93	**BOMBTRACK** Epic 6594712	37	2 wks

RAGGA TWINS UK, male vocal group — 10 wks

Date	Title	Pos	Wks
10 Nov 90	**ILLEGAL GUNSHOT / SPLIFFHEAD** Shut Up And Dance SUAD 7	51	2 wks
6 Apr 91	**WIPE THE NEEDLE / JUGGLING** Shut Up And Dance SUAD 12S	71	2 wks
6 Jul 91	**HOOLIGAN 69** Shut Up And Dance SUAD 16S	56	2 wks
7 Mar 92	**MIXED TRUTH / BRING UP THE MIC SOME MORE** Shut Up And Dance SUAD 27S	65	2 wks
11 Jul 92	**SHINE EYE** Shut Up And Dance SUAD 32S 1	63	2 wks

1 Ragga Twins featuring Junior Reid

RAGTIMERS UK, male instrumental group — 8 wks

Date	Title	Pos	Wks
16 Mar 74	**THE STING** Pye 7N 45323	46	1 wk
30 Mar 74	**THE STING (re-entry)** Pye 7N 45323	31	7 wks

RAH BAND UK, male/female vocal/instrumental group   50 wks

9 Jul 77	● THE CRUNCH Good Earth GD 7	6	12 wks
1 Nov 80	FALCON DJM DJS 10954	35	7 wks
7 Feb 81	SLIDE DJM DJS 10964	50	7 wks
1 May 82	PERFUMED GARDEN KR KR 5	45	7 wks
9 Jul 83	MESSAGES FROM THE STARS TMT TMT 5	42	5 wks
19 Jan 85	ARE YOU SATISFIED? (FUNKA NOVA) RCA RCA 470	70	2 wks
30 Mar 85	● CLOUDS ACROSS THE MOON RCA PB 40025	6	10 wks

RAHSAAN - See US3

RAILWAY CHILDREN
UK, male vocal/instrumental group   13 wks

24 Mar 90	EVERY BEAT OF THE HEART Virgin VS 1237	68	2 wks
2 Jun 90	MUSIC STOP Virgin VS 1255	66	2 wks
20 Oct 90	SO RIGHT Virgin VS 1289	68	1 wk
2 Feb 91	EVERY BEAT OF THE HEART (re-entry) Virgin VS 1237	24	6 wks
20 Apr 91	SOMETHING SO GOOD Virgin VS 1318	57	2 wks

RAIN - See Stephanie DE SYKES

RAIN TREE CROW UK, male vocal/instrumental group - Japan under an assumed name   1 wk

30 Mar 91	BLACKWATER Virgin VS 1340	62	1 wk

RAINBOW UK, male vocal/instrumental group   62 wks

17 Sep 77	KILL THE KING Polydor 2066 845	44	3 wks
8 Apr 78	LONG LIVE ROCK 'N' ROLL Polydor 2066 913	33	3 wks
30 Sep 78	L. A. CONNECTION Polydor 2066 968	40	4 wks
15 Sep 79	● SINCE YOU'VE BEEN GONE Polydor POSP 70	6	10 wks
16 Feb 80	● ALL NIGHT LONG Polydor POSP 104	5	11 wks
31 Jan 81	● I SURRENDER Polydor POSP 221	3	10 wks
20 Jun 81	CAN'T HAPPEN HERE Polydor POSP 251	20	8 wks
11 Jul 81	KILL THE KING (re-issue) Polydor POSP 274	41	4 wks
3 Apr 82	STONE COLD Polydor POSP 421	34	4 wks
27 Aug 83	STREET OF DREAMS Polydor POSP 631	52	3 wks
5 Nov 83	CAN'T LET YOU GO Polydor POSP 654	43	2 wks

RAINBOW COTTAGE
UK, male vocal/instrumental group   4 wks

6 Mar 76	SEAGULL Penny Farthing PEN 906	33	4 wks

RAINMAKERS US, male vocal/instrumental group   11 wks

7 Mar 87	LET MY PEOPLE GO-GO Mercury MER 238	18	11 wks

Marvin RAINWATER US, male vocalist   22 wks

7 Mar 58	★ WHOLE LOTTA WOMAN MGM 974	1	15 wks
6 Jun 58	I DIG YOU BABY MGM 980	19	7 wks

Bonnie RAITT US, female vocalist   7 wks

14 Dec 91	I CAN'T MAKE YOU LOVE ME Capitol CL 639	50	4 wks
9 Apr 94	LOVE SNEAKIN' UP ON YOU Capitol CDCL 713	69	1 wk
18 Jun 94	YOU Capitol CDCLS 718	31	2 wks

Tony RALLO and the MIDNIGHT BAND
France/US, male vocal/instrumental group   8 wks

23 Feb 80	HOLDIN' ON Calibre CAB 150	34	8 wks

Sheryl Lee RALPH US, female vocalist   2 wks

26 Jan 85	IN THE EVENING Arista ARIST 595	64	2 wks

RAM JAM US, male vocal/instrumental group   20 wks

10 Sep 77	● BLACK BETTY Epic EPC 5492	7	12 wks
17 Feb 90	BLACK BETTY (re-mix) Epic 655430 7	13	8 wks

RAM JAM BAND - See Geno WASHINGTON and the RAM JAM BAND

RAMBLERS (from the Abbey Hey Junior School) UK, children's choir   15 wks

13 Oct 79	THE SPARROW Decca F 13860	11	15 wks

RAMONES US, male vocal/instrumental group   32 wks

21 May 77	SHEENA IS A PUNK ROCKER Sire RAM 001	22	7 wks
6 Aug 77	SWALLOW MY PRIDE Sire 6078 607	36	3 wks
30 Sep 78	DON'T COME CLOSE Sire SRE 1031	39	5 wks
8 Sep 79	ROCK 'N' ROLL HIGH SCHOOL Sire SIR 4021	67	2 wks
26 Jan 80	● BABY I LOVE YOU Sire SIR 4031	8	9 wks
19 Apr 80	DO YOU REMEMBER ROCK 'N' ROLL RADIO Sire SIR 4037	54	3 wks
10 May 86	SOMEBODY PUT SOMETHING IN MY DRINK / SOMETHING TO BELIEVE IN Beggars Banquet BEG 157	69	1 wk
19 Dec 92	POISON HEART Chrysalis CHS 3917	69	2 wks

RAMRODS US, male/female instrumental group   12 wks

23 Feb 61	● RIDERS IN THE SKY London HLU 9282	8	12 wks

RANGE - See Bruce HORNSBY and the RANGE

RANKING ANN - See SCRITTI POLITTI

RANKING ROGER - See Various Artists (EPs & LPs) - Gimme Shelter (EP).

Shabba RANKS Jamaica, male vocalist   61 wks

16 Mar 91	SHE'S A WOMAN Virgin VS 1333 [1]	20	7 wks
18 May 91	TRAILER LOAD A GIRLS Epic 6568747	63	2 wks
24 Aug 91	HOUSECALL Epic 6573477 [2]	31	7 wks
8 Aug 92	MR LOVERMAN Epic 6582517	23	7 wks
28 Nov 92	SLOW AND SEXY Epic 6587727 [3]	17	7 wks
13 Mar 93	● MR. LOVERMAN (re-issue) Epic 6590782	3	11 wks
8 May 93	● HOUSECALL (re-mix) Epic 6592842 [2]	8	8 wks
26 Jun 93	WHAT'CHA GONNA DO Epic 6593072 [4]	21	4 wks
25 Dec 93	FAMILY AFFAIR Polydor PZCD 304 [5]	18	8 wks

[1] Scritti Politti featuring Shabba Ranks [2] Shabba Ranks featuring Maxi Priest [3] Shabba Ranks featuring Johnny Gill [4] Shabba Ranks featuring Queen Latifah [5] Shabba Ranks featuring Patra and Terry & Monica

RAPINATION Italy, male instrumental/production duo   11 wks

26 Dec 92	LOVE ME THE RIGHT WAY Logic 74321128097 [1]	22	10 wks
10 Jul 93	HERE'S MY A Logic 74321153092 [2]	69	1 wk

[1] Rapination featuring Kym Mazelle [2] Rapination featuring Carol Kenyon

RARE BIRD UK, male vocal/instrumental group   8 wks

14 Feb 70	SYMPATHY Charisma CB 120	27	8 wks

O. RASBURY - See Rahni HARRIS and F.L.O.

Roland RAT SUPERSTAR UK, male rat vocalist   20 wks

19 Nov 83	RAT RAPPING Rodent RAT 1	14	12 wks
28 Apr 84	LOVE ME TENDER Rodent RAT 2	32	7 wks
2 Mar 85	NO. 1 RAT FAN Rodent RAT 4	72	1 wk

RATPACK UK, male instrumental / production duo — 3 wks

6 Jun 92	SEARCHIN' FOR MY RIZLA Big Giant BIGT 02	58	3 wks

RATTLES Germany, male vocal / instrumental group — 15 wks

3 Oct 70	● THE WITCH Decca F 23058	8	15 wks

RAVESIGNAL III
Belgium, male producer - Raymond Bolland — 2 wks

14 Dec 91	HORSEPOWER R & S RSUK 6	61	2 wks

RAW SILK US, female vocal group — 12 wks

16 Oct 82	DO IT TO THE MUSIC KR KR 14	18	9 wks
10 Sep 83	JUST IN TIME West End WEND 2	49	3 wks

Lou RAWLS US, male vocalist — 10 wks

31 Jul 76	● YOU'LL NEVER FIND ANOTHER LOVE LIKE MINE		
	Philadelphia International PIR 4372	10	10 wks

Gene Anthony RAY - See KIDS FROM FAME

Johnnie RAY US, male vocalist — 152 wks

14 Nov 52	WALKING MY BABY BACK HOME		
	Columbia DB 3060	12	1 wk
19 Dec 52	● FAITH CAN MOVE MOUNTAINS		
	Columbia DB 3154 [1]	7	2 wks
9 Jan 53	● FAITH CAN MOVE MOUNTAINS (re-entry)		
	Columbia DB 3154 [1]	9	1 wk
3 Apr 53	MA SAYS PA SAYS Columbia DB 3242 [2]	12	1 wk
10 Apr 53	● SOMEBODY STOLE MY GAL Philips PB 123	6	1 wk
17 Apr 53	FULL TIME JOB Columbia DB 3242 [2]	11	1 wk
24 Apr 53	● SOMEBODY STOLE MY GAL (re-entry)		
	Philips PB 123	6	4 wks
29 May 53	SOMEBODY STOLE MY GAL (2nd re-entry)		
	Philips PB 123	12	1 wk
24 Jul 53	● LET'S WALK THAT-A-WAY Philips PB 157 [2]	4	14 wks
7 Aug 53	SOMEBODY STOLE MY GAL (3rd re-entry)		
	Philips PB 123	11	1 wk
9 Apr 54	★ SUCH A NIGHT Philips PB 244	1	18 wks
8 Apr 55	● IF YOU BELIEVE Philips PB 379	15	1 wk
13 May 55	● IF YOU BELIEVE (re-entry) Philips PB 379	7	10 wks
20 May 55	PATHS OF PARADISE Philips PB 441	20	1 wk
7 Oct 55	HERNANDO'S HIDEAWAY Philips PB 495	11	5 wks
14 Oct 55	● HEY THERE Philips PB 495	5	9 wks
28 Oct 55	● SONG OF THE DREAMER Philips PB 516	10	5 wks
17 Feb 56	WHO'S SORRY NOW Philips PB 546	17	2 wks
20 Apr 56	AIN'T MISBEHAVIN' Philips PB 580	17	6 wks
8 Jun 56	AIN'T MISBEHAVIN' (re-entry) Philips PB 580	24	1 wk
12 Oct 56	★ JUST WALKIN' IN THE RAIN Philips PB 624	1	19 wks
18 Jan 57	YOU DON'T OWE ME A THING Philips PB 655	12	15 wks
8 Feb 57	● LOOK HOMEWARD ANGEL Philips PB 655	7	16 wks
10 May 57	★ YES TONIGHT JOSEPHINE Philips PB 686	1	16 wks
6 Sep 57	BUILD YOUR LOVE Philips PB 721	17	7 wks
4 Oct 57	GOOD EVENING FRIENDS / UP ABOVE MY HEAD		
	Philips PB 708 [3]	25	4 wks
4 Dec 59	I'LL NEVER FALL IN LOVE AGAIN Philips PB 952	26	4 wks
8 Jan 60	I'LL NEVER FALL IN LOVE AGAIN (re-entry)		
	Philips PB 952	26	1 wk
5 Feb 60	I'LL NEVER FALL IN LOVE AGAIN (2nd re-entry)		
	Philips PB 952	28	1 wk

[1] Johnnie Ray and the Four Lads [2] Doris Day and Johnnie Ray [3] Frankie Laine and Johnnie Ray

The chart history of You Don't Owe Me A Thing / Look Homeward Angel is complicated, as follows: You Don't Owe Me A Thing entered the chart by itself on 18 Jan 57. On 8 and 15 Feb 57 Look Homeward Angel was coupled with You Don't Owe Me A Thing but from 22 Feb 57 the two sides went their individual ways on the chart and were listed separately, You Don't Owe Me A Thing for a further ten weeks and Look Homeward Angel for a further 14 weeks.

RAYDIO US, male / female vocal / instrumental group — 21 wks

8 Apr 78	JACK AND JILL Arista 161	11	12 wks
8 Jul 78	IS THIS A LOVE THING Arista 193	27	9 wks

RAZE US, male / female vocal / instrumental group — 47 wks

1 Nov 86	JACK THE GROOVE Champion CHAMP 23	57	7 wks
3 Jan 87	JACK THE GROOVE (re-entry)		
	Champion CHAMP 23	20	8 wks
28 Feb 87	LET THE MUSIC MOVE U Champion CHAMP 27	57	3 wks
31 Dec 88	BREAK 4 LOVE Champion CHAMP 67	28	11 wks
15 Jul 89	LET IT ROLL Atlantic A 8866 [1]	27	5 wks
2 Sep 89	BREAK 4 LOVE (re-entry) Champion CHAMP 67	59	5 wks
27 Jan 90	ALL 4 LOVE (BREAK 4 LOVE 1990)		
	Champion CHAMP 228 [2]	30	5 wks
10 Feb 90	CAN YOU FEEL IT / CAN YOU FEEL IT		
	Champion CHAMP 227 [3]	62	1 wk
24 Sep 94	BREAK 4 LOVE (2nd re-mix)		
	Champion CHAMPCD 314	44	2 wks

[1] Raze presents Doug Lazy [2] Raze featuring Lady J and Secretary of Entertainment [3] Raze / Champion Legend

Can You Feel It by Champion Legend, is a montage of six Raze tracks.

Chris REA UK, male vocalist — 118 wks

7 Oct 78	FOOL (IF YOU THINK IT'S OVER)		
	Magnet MAG 111	30	7 wks
21 Apr 79	DIAMONDS Magnet MAG 144	44	3 wks
27 Mar 82	LOVING YOU Magnet MAG 215	65	3 wks
1 Oct 83	I CAN HEAR YOUR HEARTBEAT Magnet MAG 244	60	2 wks
17 Mar 84	I DON'T KNOW WHAT IT IS BUT I LOVE IT		
	Magnet MAG 255	65	2 wks
30 Mar 85	STAINSBY GIRLS Magnet MAG 276	25	10 wks
29 Jun 85	JOSEPHINE Magnet MAG 280	67	2 wks
29 Mar 86	IT'S ALL GONE Magnet MAG 283	69	1 wk
31 May 86	ON THE BEACH Magnet MAG 294	57	3 wks
28 Jun 86	ON THE BEACH (re-entry) Magnet MAG 294	75	1 wk
12 Jul 86	ON THE BEACH (2nd re-entry) Magnet MAG 294	66	4 wks
6 Jun 87	LET'S DANCE Magnet MAG 299	12	10 wks
29 Aug 87	LOVING YOU AGAIN Magnet MAG 300	47	4 wks
5 Dec 87	JOYS OF CHRISTMAS Magnet MAG 314	67	1 wk
13 Feb 88	QUE SERA Magnet MAG 318	73	2 wks
13 Aug 88	ON THE BEACH SUMMER '88 WEA YZ 195	12	6 wks
22 Oct 88	I CAN HEAR YOUR HEARTBEAT WEA YZ 320	74	2 wks
17 Dec 88	DRIVING HOME FOR CHRISTMAS EP WEA YZ 325	53	3 wks
18 Feb 89	WORKING ON IT WEA YZ 50	53	3 wks
14 Oct 89	● THE ROAD TO HELL (PART 2) WEA YZ 431	10	9 wks
10 Feb 90	TELL ME THERE'S A HEAVEN East West YZ 455	24	6 wks
5 May 90	TEXAS East West YZ 468	69	1 wk
16 Feb 91	AUBERGE East West YZ 555	16	6 wks
6 Apr 91	HEAVEN East West YZ 566	57	2 wks
29 Jun 91	LOOKING FOR THE SUMMER East West YZ 584	49	3 wks
9 Nov 91	WINTER SONG East West YZ 629	27	4 wks
24 Oct 92	NOTHING TO FEAR East West YZ 699	16	4 wks
28 Nov 92	GOD'S GREAT BANANA SKIN East West YZ 706	31	3 wks
30 Jan 93	SOFT TOP HARD SHOULDER East West YZ 710CD	53	2 wks
23 Oct 93	JULIA East West YZ 772CD	18	5 wks
12 Nov 94	YOU CAN GO YOUR OWN WAY		
	East West YZ 835CD	28	3 wks
24 Dec 94	TELL ME THERE'S A HEAVEN (re-issue)		
	East West YZ 885CD	70	1 wk

Both On The Beach Summer '88 and I Can Hear Your Heartbeat in 1988 are re-recordings. Tracks on Driving Home For Christmas EP: Driving Home For Christmas / Footsteps In The Snow / Joys Of Christmas / Smile.

Eileen READ - See CADETS

Eddi READER UK, female vocalist — 10 wks

4 Jun 94	PATIENCE OF ANGELS blanco y negro NEG 68CD	33	5 wks
13 Aug 94	JOKE (I'M LAUGHING) blanco y negro NEG 72CD	42	3 wks
5 Nov 94	DEAR JOHN blanco y negro NEG 75CD1	48	2 wks

READY FOR THE WORLD
US, male vocal / instrumental group　　　**8 wks**

26 Oct 85	**OH SHEILA** MCA MCA 1005	**50**	5 wks
14 Mar 87	**LOVE YOU DOWN** MCA MCA 1110	**60**	3 wks

REAL McCOY
Germany, male / female vocal / instrumental duo　　**10 wks**

6 Nov 93	**ANOTHER NIGHT** Logic 74321173732	**61**	1 wk
5 Nov 94	**ANOTHER NIGHT** (re-issue) Logic 74321236992 [1]	**2†**	9 wks

[1] (MC Sar &) the Real McCoy

REAL PEOPLE *UK, male vocal / instrumental group*　**8 wks**

16 Feb 91	**OPEN UP YOUR MIND (LET ME IN)** CBS 6566127	**70**	1 wk
20 Apr 91	**THE TRUTH** Columbia 6567877	**73**	1 wk
6 Jul 91	**WINDOW PANE (EP)** Columbia 6569327	**60**	1 wk
11 Jan 92	**THE TRUTH** (re-issue) Columbia 6576987	**41**	3 wks
23 May 92	**BELIEVER** Columbia 6580067	**38**	2 wks

Tracks on Window Pane (EP): *Window Pane / See Through You / Everything Must Change.*

REAL ROXANNE *US, female vocalist*　　**10 wks**

28 Jun 86	**BANG ZOOM (LET'S GO GO)** Cooltempo COOL 124 [1]	**11**	9 wks
12 Nov 88	**RESPECT** Cooltempo COOL 176	**71**	1 wk

[1] Real Roxanne with Hitman Howie Tee

REAL THING *UK, male vocal / instrumental group*　**114 wks**

5 Jun 76	★ **YOU TO ME ARE EVERYTHING** Pye International 7N 25709	**1**	11 wks
4 Sep 76	● **CAN'T GET BY WITHOUT YOU** Pye 7N 45618	**2**	10 wks
12 Feb 77	**YOU'LL NEVER KNOW WHAT YOU'RE MISSING** Pye 7N 45662	**16**	9 wks
30 Jul 77	**LOVE'S SUCH A WONDERFUL THING** Pye 7N 45701	**33**	5 wks
4 Mar 78	**WHENEVER YOU WANT MY LOVE** Pye 7N 46045	**18**	9 wks
3 Jun 78	**LET'S GO DISCO** Pye 7N 46078	**39**	7 wks
12 Aug 78	**RAININ' THROUGH MY SUNSHINE** Pye 7N 46113	**40**	8 wks
17 Feb 79	● **CAN YOU FEEL THE FORCE** Pye 7N 46147	**5**	11 wks
21 Jul 79	**BOOGIE DOWN (GET FUNKY NOW)** Pye 7P 109	**33**	6 wks
22 Nov 80	**SHE'S A GROOVY FREAK** Calibre CAB 105	**52**	4 wks
8 Mar 86	● **YOU TO ME ARE EVERYTHING (THE DECADE REMIX 76-86)** PRT 7P 349	**5**	12 wks
24 May 86	● **CAN'T GET BY WITHOUT YOU (THE SECOND DECADE REMIX)** PRT 7P 352	**6**	13 wks
7 Jun 86	**YOU TO ME ARE EVERYTHING (THE DECADE REMIX 76-86) (re-entry)** PRT 7P 349	**72**	1 wk
2 Aug 86	**CAN YOU FEEL THE FORCE ('86 REMIX)** PRT 7P 358	**24**	6 wks
25 Oct 86	**STRAIGHT TO THE HEART** Jive JIVE 129	**71**	2 wks

REAL TO REEL *US, male vocal / instrumental group*　**2 wks**

21 Apr 84	**LOVE ME LIKE THIS** Arista ARIST 565	**68**	2 wks

REBEL MC *UK, male vocalist*　　**52 wks**

27 May 89	**JUST KEEP ROCKIN'** Desire WANT 9 [1]	**11**	12 wks
7 Oct 89	● **STREET TUFF** Desire WANT 18 [2]	**3**	14 wks
31 Mar 90	**BETTER WORLD** Desire WANT 25	**20**	6 wks
2 Jun 90	**REBEL MUSIC** Desire WANT 31	**53**	2 wks
6 Apr 91	**WICKEDEST SOUND** Desire WANT 40 [3]	**43**	6 wks
15 Jun 91	**TRIBAL BASE** Desire WANT 44 [4]	**20**	6 wks
31 Aug 91	**BLACK MEANING GOOD** Desire WANT 47	**73**	1 wk
21 Mar 92	**RICH AH GETTING RICHER** Big Life BLR 70 [5]	**48**	4 wks
8 Aug 92	**HUMANITY** Big Life BLR 78 [6]	**62**	1 wk

[1] Double Trouble and the Rebel MC [2] Rebel MC and Double Trouble [3] Rebel MC featuring Tenor Fly [4] Rebel MC featuring Tenor Fly and Barrington Levy [5] Rebel MC introducing Little T [6] Rebel MC featuring Lincoln Thompson

---

Ezz RECO and the LAUNCHERS with Boysie GRANT *Jamaica, male vocal / instrumental group*　**4 wks**

5 Mar 64	**KING OF KINGS** Columbia DB 7217	**44**	4 wks

RECOIL *UK, male vocal / instrumental group*　**1 wk**

21 Mar 92	**FAITH HEALER** Mute MUTE 110	**60**	1 wk

RED BOX *UK, male vocal / instrumental duo*　**28 wks**

24 Aug 85	● **LEAN ON ME (AH-LI-AYO)** Sire W 8926	**3**	14 wks
25 Oct 86	● **FOR AMERICA** Sire YZ 84	**10**	12 wks
31 Jan 87	**HEART OF THE SUN** Sire YZ 100	**71**	2 wks

RED CAR AND THE BLUE CAR
UK, male vocal / instrumental group　**4 wks**

14 Dec 91	**HOME FOR CHRISTMAS DAY** Virgin VS 1394	**44**	4 wks

RED DRAGON with Brian and Tony GOLD
Jamaica, male vocal group　**14 wks**

30 Jul 94	● **COMPLIMENTS ON YOUR KISS** Mango CIDM 820	**2**	13 wks
31 Dec 94	**COMPLIMENTS ON YOUR KISS (re-entry)** Mango CIDM 820	**49†**	1 wk

RED EYE *UK, male instrumental / production duo*　**1 wk**

3 Dec 94	**KUT IT** Champion CHAMPCD 315	**62**	1 wk

RED HOT CHILI PEPPERS
US, male vocal / instrumental group　**26 wks**

10 Feb 90	**HIGHER GROUND** EMI-USA MT 75	**55**	3 wks
23 Jun 90	**TASTE THE PAIN** EMI-USA MT 85	**29**	3 wks
8 Sep 90	**HIGHER GROUND (re-issue)** EMI-USA MT 88	**54**	3 wks
14 Mar 92	**UNDER THE BRIDGE** Warner Bros. W 0084	**26**	3 wks
15 Aug 92	**BREAKING THE GIRL** Warner Bros. W 0126	**41**	3 wks
5 Feb 94	● **GIVE IT AWAY** Warner Bros. W0225CD1	**9**	4 wks
30 Apr 94	**UNDER THE BRIDGE (re-issue)** Warner Bros. W 0237CDX	**13**	6 wks

REDBONE *US, male vocal / instrumental group*　**12 wks**

25 Sep 71	● **WITCH QUEEN OF NEW ORLEANS** Epic EPC 7351	**2**	12 wks

Sharon REDD *US, female vocalist*　**32 wks**

28 Feb 81	**CAN YOU HANDLE IT** Epic EPC 9572	**31**	8 wks
2 Oct 82	**NEVER GIVE YOU UP** Prelude PRL A2755	**20**	9 wks
15 Jan 83	**IN THE NAME OF LOVE** Prelude PRL A2905	**31**	5 wks
22 Oct 83	**LOVE HOW YOU FEEL** Prelude A3868	**39**	5 wks
1 Feb 92	**CAN YOU HANDLE IT** EMI EM 219 [1]	**17**	5 wks

[1] DNA featuring Sharon Redd

REDD KROSS *US, male vocal / instrumental group*　**3 wks**

5 Feb 94	**VISIONARY** This Way Up WAY 2733	**75**	1 wk
10 Sep 94	**YESTERDAY ONCE MORE** A & M 5807932	**45**	2 wks

The listed flip side of Yesterday Once More *was* Superstar *by Sonic Youth.*

Otis REDDING US, male vocalist — 124 wks

Date	Title	Pos	Wks
25 Nov 65	**MY GIRL** Atlantic AT 4050	**11**	16 wks
7 Apr 66	**SATISFACTION** Atlantic AT 4080	**33**	4 wks
14 Jul 66	**MY LOVER'S PRAYER** Atlantic 584 019	**37**	6 wks
25 Aug 66	**I CAN'T TURN YOU LOOSE** Atlantic 584 030	**29**	8 wks
24 Nov 66	**FA FA FA FA FA (SAD SONG)** Atlantic 584 049	**23**	9 wks
26 Jan 67	**TRY A LITTLE TENDERNESS** Atlantic 584 070	**46**	4 wks
23 Mar 67	**DAY TRIPPER** Stax 601 005	**43**	6 wks
4 May 67	**LET ME COME ON HOME** Stax 601 007	**48**	1 wk
15 Jun 67	**SHAKE** Stax 601 011	**28**	10 wks
19 Jul 67	**TRAMP** Stax 601 012 [1]	**18**	11 wks
11 Oct 67	**KNOCK ON WOOD** Stax 601 021 [1]	**35**	5 wks
14 Feb 68	**MY GIRL (re-issue)** Atlantic 584 092	**36**	9 wks
21 Feb 68	● **(SITTIN' ON) THE DOCK OF THE BAY** Stax 601 031	**3**	15 wks
29 May 68	**HAPPY SONG** Stax 601 040	**24**	5 wks
31 Jul 68	**HARD TO HANDLE** Atlantic 584 199	**15**	12 wks
9 Jul 69	**LOVE MAN** Atco 226 001	**43**	3 wks

[1] Otis Redding and Carla Thomas

Helen REDDY Australia, female vocalist — 18 wks

Date	Title	Pos	Wks
18 Jan 75	● **ANGIE BABY** Capitol CL 15799	**5**	10 wks
28 Nov 81	**I CAN'T SAY GOODBYE TO YOU** MCA 744	**43**	8 wks

REDHEAD KINGPIN and the FBI
US, male vocalist — 11 wks

Date	Title	Pos	Wks
22 Jul 89	**DO THE RIGHT THING** 10 TEN 271	**13**	10 wks
2 Dec 89	**SUPERBAD SUPERSLICK** 10 TEN 286	**68**	1 wk

REDNEX Sweden, male/female vocal/instrumental group — 3 wks

Date	Title	Pos	Wks
17 Dec 94	● **COTTON EYE JOE** Internal Affairs KGBCD 016	**5†**	3 wks

REDSKINS UK, male vocal/instrumental duo — 12 wks

Date	Title	Pos	Wks
10 Nov 84	**KEEP ON KEEPIN' ON** Decca F 1	**43**	5 wks
22 Jun 85	**BRING IT DOWN (THIS INSANE THING)** Decca F 2	**33**	5 wks
22 Feb 86	**THE POWER IS YOURS** Decca F 3	**59**	2 wks

Jimmy REED US, male vocalist — 2 wks

Date	Title	Pos	Wks
10 Sep 64	**SHAME SHAME SHAME** Stateside SS 330	**45**	2 wks

Lou REED US, male vocalist — 19 wks

Date	Title	Pos	Wks
12 May 73	● **WALK ON THE WILD SIDE** RCA 2303	**10**	9 wks
17 Jan 87	**SOUL MAN** A & M AM 364 [1]	**30**	10 wks

[1] Sam Moore and Lou Reed

Dan REED NETWORK
US, male vocal/instrumental group — 16 wks

Date	Title	Pos	Wks
20 Jan 90	**COME BACK BABY** Mercury DRN 2	**51**	3 wks
17 Mar 90	**RAINBOW CHILD** Mercury DRN 3	**60**	3 wks
21 Jul 90	**STARDATE 1990 / RAINBOW CHILD (re-issue)** Mercury DRN 4	**39**	4 wks
8 Sep 90	**LOVER / MONEY** Mercury DRN 5	**45**	3 wks
13 Jul 91	**MIX IT UP** Mercury MER 345	**49**	2 wks
21 Sep 91	**BABY NOW I** Mercury MER 352	**65**	1 wk

Michael REED ORCHESTRA - See Richard HARTLEY / Michael REED ORCHESTRA

REEL 2 REAL featuring the MAD STUNTMAN
US, male vocal/instrumental duo — 39 wks

Date	Title	Pos	Wks
12 Feb 94	● **I LIKE TO MOVE IT** Positiva CDTIV 10	**5**	20 wks
2 Jul 94	● **GO ON MOVE** Positiva CDTIV 15	**7**	9 wks
1 Oct 94	**CAN YOU FEEL IT** Positiva CDTIV 22	**13**	5 wks
3 Dec 94	**RAISE YOUR HANDS** Positiva CDTIV 27	**14†**	5 wks

Tony REES and the COTTAGERS
UK, male vocal group — 1 wk

Date	Title	Pos	Wks
10 May 75	**VIVA EL FULHAM** Sonet SON 2059	**46**	1 wk

REESE PROJECT US, male producer - Kevin Saunderson — 6 wks

Date	Title	Pos	Wks
8 Aug 92	**THE COLOUR OF LOVE** Network NWK 51	**52**	2 wks
12 Dec 92	**I BELIEVE** Network NWKT 63	**74**	1 wk
13 Mar 93	**SO DEEP** Network NWKCD 68	**54**	2 wks
24 Sep 94	**THE COLOUR OF LOVE (re-mix)** Network NWKCD 81	**55**	1 wk

Jim REEVES US, male vocalist — 322 wks

Date	Title	Pos	Wks
24 Mar 60	**HE'LL HAVE TO GO** RCA 1168	**36**	1 wk
7 Apr 60	**HE'LL HAVE TO GO (re-entry)** RCA 1168	**12**	30 wks
16 Mar 61	**WHISPERING HOPE** RCA 1223	**50**	1 wk
23 Nov 61	**YOU'RE THE ONLY GOOD THING** RCA 1261	**17**	19 wks
28 Jun 62	**ADIOS AMIGO** RCA 1293	**23**	21 wks
22 Nov 62	**I'M GONNA CHANGE EVERYTHING** RCA 1317	**42**	2 wks
13 Jun 63	● **WELCOME TO MY WORLD** RCA 1342	**6**	15 wks
17 Oct 63	**GUILTY** RCA 1364	**29**	7 wks
20 Feb 64	● **I LOVE YOU BECAUSE** RCA 1385	**5**	39 wks
18 Jun 64	● **I WON'T FORGET YOU** RCA 1400	**3**	25 wks
5 Nov 64	● **THERE'S A HEARTACHE FOLLOWING ME** RCA 1423	**6**	13 wks
7 Jan 65	**I WON'T FORGET YOU (re-entry)** RCA 1400	**47**	1 wk
4 Feb 65	● **IT HURTS SO MUCH** RCA 1437	**8**	10 wks
15 Apr 65	**NOT UNTIL THE NEXT TIME** RCA 1446	**13**	12 wks
6 May 65	**HOW LONG HAS IT BEEN** RCA 1445	**45**	5 wks
15 Jul 65	**THIS WORLD IS NOT MY HOME** RCA 1412	**22**	9 wks
11 Nov 65	**IS IT REALLY OVER** RCA 1488	**17**	9 wks
18 Aug 66	★ **DISTANT DRUMS** RCA 1537	**1**	25 wks
2 Feb 67	**I WON'T COME IN WHILE HE'S THERE** RCA 1563	**12**	11 wks
26 Jul 67	**TRYING TO FORGET** RCA 1611	**33**	5 wks
22 Nov 67	**I HEARD A HEART BREAK LAST NIGHT** RCA 1643	**38**	6 wks
27 Mar 68	**PRETTY BROWN EYES** RCA 1672	**33**	5 wks
25 Jun 69	**WHEN TWO WORLDS COLLIDE** RCA 1830	**17**	17 wks
6 Dec 69	**BUT YOU LOVE ME DADDY** RCA 1899	**15**	16 wks
21 Mar 70	**NOBODY'S FOOL** RCA 1915	**32**	5 wks
12 Sep 70	**ANGELS DON'T LIE** RCA 1997	**44**	1 wk
26 Sep 70	**ANGELS DON'T LIE (re-entry)** RCA 1997	**32**	2 wks
26 Jun 71	**I LOVE YOU BECAUSE / HE'LL HAVE TO GO / MOONLIGHT & ROSES (re-issue)** RCA Maximillion 2092	**34**	8 wks
19 Feb 72	**YOU'RE FREE TO GO** RCA 2174	**48**	2 wks

Martha REEVES and the VANDELLAS
US, female vocal group — 85 wks

Date	Title	Pos	Wks
29 Oct 64	**DANCING IN THE STREET** Stateside SS 345 [1]	**28**	8 wks
1 Apr 65	**NOWHERE TO RUN** Tamla Motown TMG 502 [1]	**26**	8 wks
1 Dec 66	**I'M READY FOR LOVE** Tamla Motown TMG 582 [1]	**29**	8 wks
30 Mar 67	**JIMMY MACK** Tamla Motown TMG 599 [1]	**21**	9 wks
17 Jan 68	**HONEY CHILE** Tamla Motown TMG 636	**30**	9 wks
15 Jan 69	● **DANCING IN THE STREET (re-issue)** Tamla Motown TMG 684	**4**	12 wks
16 Apr 69	**NOWHERE TO RUN (re-issue)** Tamla Motown TMG 694	**42**	3 wks
29 Aug 70	**JIMMY MACK (re-entry)** Tamla Motown TMG 599	**21**	12 wks
13 Feb 71	**FORGET ME NOT** Tamla Motown TMG 762	**11**	8 wks
8 Jan 72	**BLESS YOU** Tamla Motown TMG 794	**33**	5 wks
23 Jan 88	**NOWHERE TO RUN (2nd re-issue)** A & M AM 444	**52**	3 wks

[1] Martha and the Vandellas

The listed flip side of Nowhere To Run in 1988 was I Got You (I Feel Good) by James Brown.

Vic REEVES UK, male vocalist — 21 wks

Date	Title	Pos	Wks
27 Apr 91	● **BORN FREE** Sense SIGH 710 [1]	**6**	6 wks
26 Oct 91	★ **DIZZY** Sense SIGH 712 [2]	**1**	12 wks
14 Dec 91	**ABIDE WITH ME** Sense SIGH 713	**47**	3 wks

[1] Vic Reeves and the Roman Numerals [2] Vic Reeves and the Wonder Stuff

JIM REEVES appears at a reception to promote his recordings. Tragically, his own death in a plane crash on 31 July 1964 will prove to be his greatest promotion. (LFI)

The first British hit by **R.E.M.** was also the Georgia group's first American top ten success. (LFI)

QUEEN perform with the Frank Kelly Freas robot from the *News Of The World* album sleeve on Roger Taylor's bass drum. (LFI)

RE-FLEX UK, male vocal/instrumental group   **9 wks**

28 Jan 84   **THE POLITICS OF DANCING** EMI FLEX 2 ....**28** 9 wks

Joan REGAN UK, female vocalist   **62 wks**

11 Dec 53 ● **RICOCHET** Decca F 10193 [1] ....**8** 1 wk
 8 Jan 54 ● **RICOCHET (re-entry)** Decca F 10193 [1] ....**9** 4 wks
14 May 54 ● **SOMEONE ELSE'S ROSES** Decca F 10257 ....**5** 8 wks
 1 Oct 54   **IF I GIVE MY HEART TO YOU** Decca F 10373 ...**20** 1 wk
29 Oct 54 ● **IF I GIVE MY HEART TO YOU (re-entry)**
              Decca F 10373 ....**3** 10 wks
 5 Nov 54   **WAIT FOR ME DARLING** Decca F 10362 [2] ....**18** 1 wk
25 Mar 55 ● **PRIZE OF GOLD** Decca F 10432 ....**6** 8 wks
 6 May 55   **OPEN UP YOUR HEART** Decca F 10474 ....**19** 1 wk
 1 May 59 ● **MAY YOU ALWAYS** HMV POP 593 ....**9** 16 wks
 5 Feb 60   **HAPPY ANNIVERSARY** Pye 7N 15238 ....**29** 1 wk
19 Feb 60   **HAPPY ANNIVERSARY (re-entry)** Pye 7N 15238 ....**29** 1 wk
28 Jul 60   **PAPA LOVES MAMA** Pye 7N 15278...................**29** 8 wks
24 Nov 60   **ONE OF THE LUCKY ONES** Pye 7N 15310 ....**47** 1 wk
 5 Jan 61   **IT MUST BE SANTA** Pye 7N 15303 ....**42** 1 wk

[1] Joan Regan with the Squadronaires [2] Joan Regan and the Johnston Brothers

See also Various Artists (EPs & LPs) - All Star Hit Parade.

REGENTS UK, male/female vocal/instrumental group   **14 wks**

22 Dec 79   **7 TEEN** Rialto TREB 111 ....**11** 12 wks
 7 Jun 80   **SEE YOU LATER** Arista ARIST 350 ....**55** 2 wks

REGGAE PHILHARMONIC ORCHESTRA
UK, male/female vocal/instrumental group   **11 wks**

19 Nov 88   **MINNIE THE MOOCHER** Mango IS 378 ....**35** 9 wks
28 Jul 90   **LOVELY THING** Mango MNG 742....................**71** 2 wks

REGINA US, female vocalist   **3 wks**

 1 Feb 86   **BABY LOVE** Funkin' Marvellous MARV 01 ....**50** 3 wks

REID UK, male vocal group   **12 wks**

 8 Oct 88   **ONE WAY OUT** Syncopate SY 16 ....**66** 2 wks
11 Feb 89   **REAL EMOTION** Syncopate SY 24 ....**65** 2 wks
15 Apr 89   **GOOD TIMES** Syncopate SY 27....................**55** 6 wks
21 Oct 89   **LOVIN' ON THE SIDE** Syncopate REID 1 ....**71** 2 wks

Junior REID - *See COLDCUT; RAGGA TWINS; SOUPDRAGONS*

Mike REID UK, male vocalist   **8 wks**

22 Mar 75 ● **THE UGLY DUCKLING** Pye 7N 45434 ....**10** 8 wks

Neil REID UK, male vocalist   **26 wks**

 1 Jan 72 ● **MOTHER OF MINE** Decca F 13264 ....**2** 20 wks
 8 Apr 72   **THAT'S WHAT I WANT TO BE** Decca F 13300 ....**49** 1 wk
22 Apr 72   **THAT'S WHAT I WANT TO BE (re-entry)**
              Decca F 13300 ....**45** 5 wks

Maggie REILLY - *See Mike OLDFIELD*

Keith RELF UK, male vocalist   **1 wk**

26 May 66   **MR. ZERO** Columbia DB 7920 ....**50** 1 wk

R.E.M. US, male vocal/instrumental group   **105 wks**

28 Nov 87   **THE ONE I LOVE** IRS IRM 46 ....**51** 8 wks
30 Apr 88   **FINEST WORKSONG** IRS IRM 161 ....**50** 2 wks

 4 Feb 89   **STAND** Warner Bros. W 7577 ....**51** 3 wks
 3 Jun 89   **ORANGE CRUSH** Warner Bros. W 2960 ....**28** 5 wks
12 Aug 89   **STAND (re-issue)** Warner Bros. W 2833 ....**48** 2 wks
 9 Mar 91   **LOSING MY RELIGION** Warner Bros. W 0015........**19** 9 wks
18 May 91 ● **SHINY HAPPY PEOPLE** Warner Bros. W 0027.....**6** 11 wks
17 Aug 91   **NEAR WILD HEAVEN** Warner Bros. W 0055........**27** 4 wks
21 Sep 91   **THE ONE I LOVE (re-issue)** IRS IRM 178 ....**16** 6 wks
16 Nov 91   **RADIO SONG** Warner Bros. W 0072.....................**28** 3 wks
14 Dec 91   **IT'S THE END OF THE WORLD AS WE KNOW**
              IT IRS IRM 180..**39** 4 wks
 3 Oct 92   **DRIVE** Warner Bros. W 0136 ....**11** 5 wks
28 Nov 92   **MAN ON THE MOON** Warner Bros. W 0143 ....**18** 8 wks
20 Feb 93   **THE SIDEWINDER SLEEPS TONITE**
              Warner Bros. W 0152CD1 ....**17** 6 wks
17 Apr 93 ● **EVERYBODY HURTS** Warner Bros. W 0169CD1 ....**7** 12 wks
24 Jul 93   **NIGHTSWIMMING** Warner Bros. W 0184CD.........**27** 5 wks
11 Dec 93   **FIND THE RIVER** Warner Bros. W 0211CD............**54** 1 wk
17 Sep 94 ● **WHAT'S THE FREQUENCY, KENNETH**
              Warner Bros. W 0265CD...............................**9** 7 wks
12 Nov 94   **BANG AND BLAME** Warner Bros. W 0275CD...........**15** 4 wks

RENAISSANCE
UK, male/female vocal/instrumental group   **11 wks**

15 Jul 78 ● **NORTHERN LIGHTS** Warner Bros. K 17177 ....**10** 11 wks

RENÉ and ANGELA US, male/female vocal duo   **15 wks**

15 Jun 85   **SAVE YOUR LOVE (FOR NUMBER 1)**
              Club JAB 14 [1] ....**66** 2 wks
 7 Sep 85   **I'LL BE GOOD** Club JAB 18 ....**22** 10 wks
 2 Nov 85   **SECRET RENDEZVOUS** Champion CHAMP 5 ....**54** 3 wks

[1] René and Angela featuring Kuris Blow

RENÉ and YVETTE UK, male/female vocal duo   **4 wks**

22 Nov 86   **JE T'AIME (ALLO ALLO) / RENE D.M.C.**
              (DEVASTATING MACHO CHARISMA)
              Sedition EDIT 3319 ....**57** 4 wks

RENÉE and RENATO
UK/Italy, female/male vocal duo   **22 wks**

30 Oct 82 ★ **SAVE YOUR LOVE** Hollywood HWD 003 ....**1** 16 wks
12 Feb 83   **JUST ONE MORE KISS** Hollywood HWD 006 ....**48** 6 wks

RENEGADE SOUNDWAVE
UK, male vocal/instrumental group   **7 wks**

 3 Feb 90   **PROBABLY A ROBBERY** Mute MUTE 102 ....**38** 6 wks
 5 Feb 94   **RENEGADE SOUNDWAVE** Mute CDMUTE 146 ....**64** 1 wk

REO SPEEDWAGON
US, male vocal/instrumental group   **38 wks**

11 Apr 81 ● **KEEP ON LOVING YOU** Epic EPC 9544 ....**7** 14 wks
27 Jun 81   **TAKE IT ON THE RUN** Epic EPC A 1207 ....**19** 14 wks
16 Mar 85   **CAN'T FIGHT THIS FEELING** Epic A 4880 ....**16** 10 wks

REPARATA and the DELRONS
US, female vocal group   **12 wks**

20 Mar 68   **CAPTAIN OF YOUR SHIP** Bell 1002 ....**13** 10 wks
18 Oct 75   **SHOES** Dart 2066 562 [1] ....**43** 2 wks

[1] Reparata

REUNION US, male vocal group   **4 wks**

21 Sep 74   **LIFE IS A ROCK (BUT THE RADIO ROLLED ME)**
              RCA PB 10056 ....**33** 4 wks

REVILLOS - *See REZILLOS*

REVOLTING COCKS US, male vocal/instrumental group   **1 wk**

18 Sep 93   **DA YA THINK I'M SEXY** Devotion CDDVN 111 ....**61**   1 wk

REVOLUTION - See PRINCE

Debbie REYNOLDS US, female vocalist   **17 wks**

30 Aug 57 ● **TAMMY** Vogue Coral Q 72274 ....**2** 17 wks

Jody REYNOLDS US, male vocalist   **1 wk**

14 Apr 79   **ENDLESS SLEEP** Lightning LIG 9015 ....**66** 1 wk

Endless Sleep was coupled with To Know Him Is To Love Him by the Teddy Bears as a double A-side.

L.J. REYNOLDS US, male vocalist   **3 wks**

30 Jun 84   **DON'T LET NOBODY HOLD YOU DOWN**
Club JAB 5...............................**53** 3 wks

REYNOLDS GIRLS UK, female vocal duo   **12 wks**

25 Feb 89 ● **I'D RATHER JACK** PWL PWL 25 ....**8** 12 wks

REZILLOS UK, male/female vocal/instrumental group   **21 wks**

12 Aug 78   **TOP OF THE POPS** Sire SIR 4001 ....**17** 9 wks
25 Nov 78   **DESTINATION VENUS** Sire SIR 4008 ....**43** 4 wks
18 Aug 79   **I WANNA BE YOUR MAN / I CAN'T STAND MY BABY**
Sensible SAB 1 ....**71** 1 wk
1 Sep 79   **I WANNA BE YOUR MAN / I CAN'T STAND MY BABY**
(re-entry) Sensible SAB 1 ....**75** 1 wk
26 Jan 80   **MOTORBIKE BEAT** Dindisc DIN 5 [1] ....**45** 6 wks

[1] Revillos

RHC Belgium, male/female vocal/instrumental duo   **1 wk**

11 Jan 92   **FEVER CALLED LOVE** R & S RSUK 9............**65** 1 wk

RHODA - See SPECIALS

RHYTHM ETERNITY
UK, male/female vocal/instrumental group   **1 wk**

23 May 92   **PINK CHAMPAGNE** Dead Dead Good GOOD 15T ....**72** 1 wk

RHYTHM IS RHYTHM US, male instrumental duo   **1 wk**

11 Nov 89   **STRINGS OF LIFE '89** Kool Kat KOOL 509 ....**74** 1 wk

RHYTHM-N-BASS UK, male rap group   **4 wks**

19 Sep 92   **ROSES** Epic 6582907 ....**56** 2 wks
3 Jul 93   **CAN'T STOP THIS FEELING** Epic 6592002..........**59** 2 wks

RHYTHM QUEST UK, male producer - Mark Hadfield   **2 wks**

20 Jun 92   **CLOSER TO ALL YOUR DREAMS**
Network NWK 40 ....**45** 2 wks

RHYTHM SECTION UK, male vocal/instrumental group   **1 wk**

18 Jul 92   **MIDSUMMER MADNESS EP**
Rhythm Section RSEC 006 ....**66** 1 wk

Tracks on Midsummer Madness EP: Dreamworld / Burnin' Up / Perfect Love 2am / Perfect Love 8am.

RHYTHMATIC UK, male instrumental group   **3 wks**

12 May 90   **TAKE ME BACK** Network NWK 8.........................**74** 1 wk
26 May 90   **TAKE ME BACK** (re-entry) Network NWK 8 ....**71** 1 wk
3 Nov 90   **FREQUENCY** Network NWK 13 ....**62** 1 wk

Reva RICE and Greg ELLIS
UK, male/female vocal duo   **2 wks**

27 Mar 93   **NEXT TIME YOU FALL IN LOVE**
Really Useful RURCD 12 ....**59** 2 wks

Charlie RICH US, male vocalist   **29 wks**

16 Feb 74 ● **THE MOST BEAUTIFUL GIRL** CBS 1897 ....**2** 14 wks
13 Apr 74   **BEHIND CLOSED DOORS** Epic EPC 1539...........**16** 10 wks
1 Feb 75   **WE LOVE EACH OTHER** Epic EPC 2868 ....**37** 5 wks

Richie RICH UK, male vocalist   **15 wks**

16 Jul 88   **TURN IT UP** Club JAB 68 ....**48** 3 wks
22 Oct 88   **I'LL HOUSE YOU** Gee Street GEE 003 [1] ....**22** 5 wks
10 Dec 88   **MY DJ (PUMP IT UP SOME)** Gee Street GEE 7 ....**74** 1 wk
2 Sep 89   **SALSA HOUSE** ffrr F 113 ....**50** 3 wks
9 Mar 91   **YOU USED TO SALSA** ffrr F 156 [2] ....**52** 3 wks

[1] Richie Rich meets the Jungle Brothers [2] Richie Rich's Salsa House featuring Ralphi Rosario

RICH KIDS UK, male vocal/instrumental group   **5 wks**

28 Jan 78   **RICH KIDS** EMI 2738 ....**24** 5 wks

Cliff RICHARD UK, male vocalist   **1100 wks**

12 Sep 58 ● **MOVE IT** Columbia DB 4178 ....**2** 17 wks
21 Nov 58 ● **HIGH CLASS BABY** Columbia DB 4203 ....**7** 10 wks
30 Jan 59   **LIVIN' LOVIN' DOLL** Columbia DB 4249 ....**20** 6 wks
8 May 59 ● **MEAN STREAK** Columbia DB 4290 ....**10** 9 wks
15 May 59   **NEVER MIND** Columbia DB 4290 ....**21** 2 wks
10 Jul 59 ★ **LIVING DOLL** Columbia DB 4306 ....**1** 21 wks
9 Oct 59 ★ **TRAVELLIN' LIGHT** Columbia DB 4351 ....**1** 17 wks
9 Oct 59   **DYNAMITE** Columbia DB 4351 ....**16** 2 wks
30 Oct 59   **DYNAMITE** (re-entry) Columbia DB 4351 ....**21** 2 wks
11 Dec 59   **LIVING DOLL** (re-entry) Columbia DB 4306 ....**26** 1 wk
1 Jan 60   **LIVING DOLL** (2nd re-entry) Columbia DB 4306..**28** 1 wk
15 Jan 60   **EXPRESSO BONGO EP** Columbia SEG 7971 ......**14** 7 wks
22 Jan 60 ● **VOICE IN THE WILDERNESS** Columbia DB 4398 ..**2** 13 wks
24 Mar 60 ● **FALL IN LOVE WITH YOU** Columbia DB 4431 ......**2** 15 wks
5 May 60   **VOICE IN THE WILDERNESS** (re-entry)
Columbia DB 4398 ....**36** 2 wks
30 Jun 60 ★ **PLEASE DON'T TEASE** Columbia DB 4479 ......**1** 18 wks
22 Sep 60 ● **NINE TIMES OUT OF TEN** Columbia DB 4506 ...**3** 12 wks
1 Dec 60 ★ **I LOVE YOU** Columbia DB 4547 ....**1** 16 wks
2 Mar 61 ● **THEME FOR A DREAM** Columbia DB 4593 ....**3** 14 wks
30 Mar 61 ● **GEE WHIZ IT'S YOU** Columbia DC 756 ....**4** 14 wks
22 Jun 61 ● **A GIRL LIKE YOU** Columbia DB 4667 ....**3** 14 wks
19 Oct 61 ● **WHEN THE GIRL IN YOUR ARMS IS THE GIRL
IN YOUR HEART** Columbia DB 4716 ....**3** 15 wks
11 Jan 62 ★ **THE YOUNG ONES** Columbia DB 4761 ....**1** 21 wks
10 May 62 ● **I'M LOOKING OUT THE WINDOW/DO YOU
WANNA DANCE** Columbia DB 4828 ....**2** 17 wks
6 Sep 62 ● **IT'LL BE ME** Columbia DB 4886 ....**2** 12 wks
6 Dec 62 ★ **THE NEXT TIME / BACHELOR BOY**
Columbia DB 4950 ....**1** 18 wks
21 Feb 63 ★ **SUMMER HOLIDAY** Columbia DB 4977..........**1** 18 wks
9 May 63 ● **LUCKY LIPS** Columbia DB 7034 ....**4** 15 wks
22 Aug 63 ● **IT'S ALL IN THE GAME** Columbia DB 7089 ....**2** 13 wks
7 Nov 63 ● **DON'T TALK TO HIM** Columbia DB 7150.........**2** 13 wks
6 Feb 64 ● **I'M THE LONELY ONE** Columbia DB 7203 ....**8** 10 wks
13 Feb 64   **DON'T TALK TO HIM** (re-entry) Columbia DB 7150..**50** 1 wk
30 Apr 64 ● **CONSTANTLY** Columbia DB 7272 ....**4** 13 wks
2 Jul 64 ● **ON THE BEACH** Columbia DB 7305 ....**7** 13 wks
8 Oct 64 ● **THE TWELFTH OF NEVER** Columbia DB 7372 ...**8** 11 wks

Date	Title	Pos	Wks
10 Dec 64	● I COULD EASILY FALL *Columbia DB 7420*	9	11 wks
11 Mar 65	★ THE MINUTE YOU'RE GONE *Columbia DB 7496*	1	14 wks
10 Jun 65	ON MY WORD *Columbia DB 7596*	12	10 wks
19 Aug 65	THE TIME IN BETWEEN *Columbia DB 7660*	22	8 wks
4 Nov 65	● WIND ME UP (LET ME GO) *Columbia DB 7745*	2	16 wks
24 Mar 66	BLUE TURNS TO GREY *Columbia DB 7866*	15	9 wks
21 Jul 66	VISIONS *Columbia DB 7968*	7	12 wks
13 Oct 66	● TIME DRAGS BY *Columbia DB 8017*	10	12 wks
15 Dec 66	● IN THE COUNTRY *Columbia DB 8094*	6	10 wks
16 Mar 67	● IT'S ALL OVER *Columbia DB 8150*	9	10 wks
8 Jun 67	I'LL COME RUNNING *Columbia DB 8210*	26	8 wks
16 Aug 67	THE DAY I MET MARIE *Columbia DB 8245*	10	14 wks
15 Nov 67	● ALL MY LOVE *Columbia DB 8293*	6	12 wks
20 Mar 68	★ CONGRATULATIONS *Columbia DB 8376*	1	13 wks
26 Jun 68	I'LL LOVE YOU FOREVER TODAY *Columbia DB 8437*	27	6 wks
25 Sep 68	MARIANNE *Columbia DB 8476*	22	8 wks
27 Nov 68	DON'T FORGET TO CATCH ME *Columbia DB 8503*	21	10 wks
26 Feb 69	GOOD TIMES (BETTER TIMES) *Columbia DB 8548*	12	11 wks
28 May 69	BIG SHIP *Columbia DB 8581*	8	10 wks
13 Sep 69	● THROW DOWN A LINE *Columbia DB 8615* [1]	7	9 wks
6 Dec 69	WITH THE EYES OF A CHILD *Columbia DB 8641*	20	11 wks
21 Feb 70	JOY OF LIVING *Columbia DB 8657* [1]	25	8 wks
6 Jun 70	● GOODBYE SAM HELLO SAMANTHA *Columbia DB 8685*	6	15 wks
5 Sep 70	I AIN'T GOT TIME ANYMORE *Columbia DB 8708*	21	7 wks
23 Jan 71	SUNNY HONEY GIRL *Columbia DB 8747*	19	8 wks
10 Apr 71	SILVERY RAIN *Columbia DB 8774*	27	6 wks
17 Jul 71	FLYING MACHINE *Columbia DB 8797*	37	7 wks
13 Nov 71	SING A SONG OF FREEDOM *Columbia DB 8836*	13	12 wks
11 Mar 72	JESUS *Columbia DB 8864*	35	3 wks
26 Aug 72	LIVING IN HARMONY *Columbia DB 8917*	12	10 wks
17 Mar 73	● POWER TO ALL OUR FRIENDS *EMI 2012*	4	12 wks
12 May 73	HELP IT ALONG / TOMORROW RISING *EMI 2022*	29	6 wks
1 Dec 73	TAKE ME HIGH *EMI 2088*	27	12 wks
18 May 74	(YOU KEEP ME) HANGIN' ON *EMI 2150*	13	8 wks
7 Feb 76	MISS YOU NIGHTS *EMI 2376*	15	10 wks
8 May 76	● DEVIL WOMAN *EMI 2458*	9	8 wks
21 Aug 76	I CAN'T ASK FOR ANYMORE THAN YOU *EMI 2499*	17	8 wks
4 Dec 76	HEY MR. DREAM MAKER *EMI 2559*	31	5 wks
5 Mar 77	MY KINDA LIFE *EMI 2584*	15	8 wks
16 Jul 77	WHEN TWO WORLDS DRIFT APART *EMI 2633*	46	3 wks
31 Mar 79	GREEN LIGHT *EMI 2920*	57	3 wks
21 Jul 79	★ WE DON'T TALK ANYMORE *EMI 2975*	1	14 wks
3 Nov 79	HOT SHOT *EMI 5003*	46	5 wks
2 Feb 80	● CARRIE *EMI 5006*	4	10 wks
16 Aug 80	● DREAMIN' *EMI 5095*	8	10 wks
25 Oct 80	SUDDENLY *Jet 7002* [2]	15	7 wks
24 Jan 81	A LITTLE IN LOVE *EMI 5123*	15	8 wks
29 Aug 81	● WIRED FOR SOUND *EMI 5221*	4	9 wks
21 Nov 81	● DADDY'S HOME *EMI 5251*	2	12 wks
17 Jul 82	● THE ONLY WAY OUT *EMI 5318*	10	9 wks
25 Sep 82	WHERE DO WE GO FROM HERE *EMI 5341*	60	3 wks
4 Dec 82	LITTLE TOWN *EMI 5348*	11	7 wks
19 Feb 83	● SHE MEANS NOTHING TO ME *Capitol CL 276* [3]	9	9 wks
16 Apr 83	● TRUE LOVE WAYS *EMI 5385* [4]	8	8 wks
4 Jun 83	DRIFTING *DJM SHEIL 1* [5]	64	2 wks
3 Sep 83	NEVER SAY DIE (GIVE A LITTLE BIT MORE) *EMI 5415*	15	7 wks
26 Nov 83	● PLEASE DON'T FALL IN LOVE *EMI 5437*	7	9 wks
31 Mar 84	BABY YOU'RE DYNAMITE / OCEAN DEEP *EMI 5457*	27	6 wks
19 May 84	OCEAN DEEP / BABY YOU'RE DYNAMITE (re-entry) *EMI 5457*	72	1 wk
3 Nov 84	SHOOTING FROM THE HEART *EMI RICH 1*	51	4 wks
9 Feb 85	HEART USER *EMI RICH 2*	46	3 wks
14 Sep 85	SHE'S SO BEAUTIFUL *EMI 5531*	17	9 wks
7 Dec 85	IT'S IN EVERY ONE OF US *EMI 5537*	45	6 wks
22 Mar 86	★ LIVING DOLL *WEA YZ 65* [6]	1	11 wks
4 Oct 86	● ALL I ASK OF YOU *Polydor POSP 802* [7]	3	16 wks
29 Nov 86	SLOW RIVERS *Rocket EJS 13* [8]	44	8 wks
20 Jun 87	● MY PRETTY ONE *EMI EM 4*	6	10 wks
29 Aug 87	● SOME PEOPLE *EMI EM 18*	3	10 wks
31 Oct 87	REMEMBER ME *EMI EM 31*	35	4 wks
13 Feb 88	TWO HEARTS *EMI EM 42*	34	3 wks

Date	Title	Pos	Wks
3 Dec 88	★ MISTLETOE AND WINE *EMI EM 78*	1	8 wks
10 Jun 89	● THE BEST OF ME *EMI EM 78*	2	7 wks
26 Aug 89	● I JUST DON'T HAVE THE HEART *EMI EM 101*	3	8 wks
14 Oct 89	LEAN ON YOU *EMI EM 105*	17	6 wks
9 Dec 89	WHENEVER GOD SHINES HIS LIGHT *Polydor VANS 2* [9]	20	6 wks
24 Feb 90	STRONGER THAN THAT *EMI EM 129*	14	5 wks
25 Aug 90	● SILHOUETTES *EMI EM 152*	10	7 wks
13 Oct 90	FROM A DISTANCE *EMI EM 155*	11	6 wks
8 Dec 90	● SAVIOUR'S DAY *EMI XMAS 90*	1	7 wks
14 Sep 91	MORE TO LIFE *EMI EM 205*	23	4 wks
7 Dec 91	● WE SHOULD BE TOGETHER *EMI XMAS 91*	10	6 wks
11 Jan 92	THIS NEW YEAR *EMI EMS 216*	30	2 wks
5 Dec 92	● I STILL BELIEVE IN YOU *EMI EM 255*	7	5 wks
27 Mar 93	● PEACE IN OUR TIME *EMI CDEMS 265*	8	5 wks
12 Jun 93	HUMAN WORK OF ART *EMI CDEMS 267*	24	4 wks
2 Oct 93	NEVER LET GO *EMI CDEM 281*	32	3 wks
18 Dec 93	HEALING LOVE *EMI CDEM 294*	19	5 wks
10 Dec 94	ALL I HAVE TO DO IS DREAM / MISS YOU NIGHTS (re-issue) *EMI CDEMS 359* [10]	14†	4 wks

[1] Cliff and Hank [2] Olivia Newton-John and Cliff Richard [3] Phil Everly and Cliff Richard [4] Cliff Richard with the London Philharmonic Orchestra [5] Sheila Walsh and Cliff Richard [6] Cliff Richard and the Young Ones fea turing Hank B. Marvin [7] Cliff Richard and Sarah Brightman [8] Elton John and Cliff Richard [9] Van Morrison with Cliff Richard [10] Cliff Richard with Phil Everly/Cliff Richard

The Shadows appear on all Cliff's hits from Move It *to* A Girl Like You. *After that they are on the following hits:* The Young Ones, Do You Wanna Dance, It'll Be Me, The Next Time, Bachelor Boy, Summer Holiday, Lucky Lips, Don't Talk To Him, I'm The Lonely One, On The Beach, I Could Easily Fall, The Time In Between, Blue Turns To Grey, Time Drags By, In The Country *and* Don't Forget To Catch Me. *Tracks on the* Expresso Bongo EP: Love / A Voice in The Wilderness / The Shrine On The Second Floor / Bongo Blues. Bongo Blues *features only the Shadows. The Shadows were the Drifters on Cliff's hits before* Living Doll. Bachelor Boy *was only listed with* The Next Time *from 10 Jan 63.* Ocean Deep *listed from 28 Apr 84 onwards. It peaked at position 41.*

Wendy RICHARD - *See Mike SARNE*

Lionel RICHIE US, male vocalist   159 wks

Date	Title	Pos	Wks
12 Sep 81	● ENDLESS LOVE *Motown TMG 1240* [1]	7	12 wks
20 Nov 82	● TRULY *Motown TMG 1284*	6	11 wks
29 Jan 83	YOU ARE *Motown TMG 1290*	43	7 wks
7 May 83	MY LOVE *Motown TMG 1300*	70	3 wks
1 Oct 83	● ALL NIGHT LONG (ALL NIGHT) *Motown TMG 1319*	2	16 wks
3 Dec 83	● RUNNING WITH THE NIGHT *Motown TMG 1324*	9	12 wks
10 Mar 84	★ HELLO *Motown TMG 1330*	1	15 wks
23 Jun 84	STUCK ON YOU *Motown TMG 1341*	12	12 wks
20 Oct 84	PENNY LOVER *Motown TMG 1356*	18	7 wks
16 Nov 85	● SAY YOU, SAY ME *Motown ZB 40421*	8	11 wks
26 Jul 86	● DANCING ON THE CEILING *Motown L10 1*	7	11 wks
11 Oct 86	LOVE WILL CONQUER ALL *Motown L10 2*	45	5 wks
20 Dec 86	BALLERINA GIRL / DEEP RIVER WOMAN *Motown L10 3*	17	8 wks
28 Mar 87	SELA *Motown L10 4*	43	6 wks
9 May 92	DO IT TO ME *Motown TMG 1407*	33	6 wks
22 Aug 92	● MY DESTINY *Motown TMG 1408*	7	13 wks
28 Nov 92	LOVE OH LOVE *Motown TMG 1413*	52	3 wks
26 Dec 92	LOVE OH LOVE (re-entry) *Motown TMG 1413*	73†	1 wk

[1] Diana Ross and Lionel Richie

Deep River Woman *only listed from 17 Jan 87. It has the credit: background vocal 'Alabama'.*

Jonathan RICHMAN and the MODERN LOVERS US, male vocal / instrumental group   27 wks

Date	Title	Pos	Wks
16 Jul 77	ROADRUNNER *Beserkley BZZ 1*	11	9 wks
29 Oct 77	● EGYPTIAN REGGAE *Beserkley BZZ 2*	5	14 wks
21 Jan 78	MORNING OF OUR LIVES *Beserkley BZZ 7* [1]	29	4 wks

[1] Modern Lovers

RIDE *UK, male vocal/instrumental group*   **21 wks**

27 Jan 90	**RIDE EP** *Creation CRE 07T2*...................**71**	2 wks
14 Apr 90	**PLAY EP** *Creation CRE 075T* **32**	3 wks
29 Sep 90	**FALL EP** *Creation CRE 087T*...................**34**	3 wks
16 Mar 91	**TODAY FOREVER** *Creation CRE 100T* **14**	4 wks
15 Feb 92	● **LEAVE THEM ALL BEHIND** *Creation CRE 123T*...........**9**	3 wks
25 Apr 92	**TWISTERELLA** *Creation CRE 150T* **36**	2 wks
30 Apr 94	**BIRDMAN** *Creation CRESCD 155* **38**	2 wks
25 Jun 94	**HOW DOES IT FEEL TO FEEL** *Creation CRESCD 184*..**58**	1 wk
8 Oct 94	**I DON'T KNOW WHERE IT COMES FROM** *Creation CRESCD 189R*...................**46**	1 wk

Tracks on Ride EP: *Chelsea Girl / Drive Blind / All I See / Close My Eyes.*
Tracks on Play EP: *Like A Daydream / Silver / Furthest Sense / Perfect Time.* Tracks on Fall EP: *Dreams Burn Down / Taste / Hear And Now / Nowhere.*

Andrew RIDGELEY *UK, male vocalist*   **3 wks**

31 Mar 90	**SHAKE** *Epic AJR 1* **58**	3 wks

Stan RIDGWAY *US, male vocalist*   **12 wks**

5 Jul 86	● **CAMOUFLAGE** *IRS IRM 114* **4**	12 wks

RIGHEIRA *Spain, male vocal duo*   **3 wks**

24 Sep 83	**VAMOS A LA PLAYA** *A & M AM 137*...................**53**	3 wks

RIGHT SAID FRED
UK, male vocal/instrumental group   **61 wks**

27 Jul 91	● **I'M TOO SEXY** *Tug SNOG 1* **2**	16 wks
7 Dec 91	● **DON'T TALK JUST KISS** *Tug SNOG 2* [1] **3**	11 wks
21 Mar 92	★ **DEEPLY DIPPY** *Tug SNOG 3* **1**	14 wks
1 Aug 92	**THOSE SIMPLE THINGS / DAYDREAM** *Tug SNOG 4*...................**29**	5 wks
27 Feb 93	● **STICK IT OUT** *Tug CDCOMIC 1* [2] **4**	7 wks
23 Oct 93	**BUMPED** *Tug CDSNOG 7*...................**32**	4 wks
18 Dec 93	**HANDS UP (4 LOVERS)** *Tug CDSNOG 8* **60**	3 wks
19 Mar 94	**WONDERMAN** *Tug CDSNOG 9*...................**55**	1 wk

[1] Right Said Fred, guest vocals: Jocelyn Brown [2] Right Said Fred and Friends

RIGHTEOUS BROTHERS *US, male vocal duo*   **86 wks**

14 Jan 65	★ **YOU'VE LOST THAT LOVIN' FEELIN'** *London HLU 9943*...................**1**	10 wks
12 Aug 65	**UNCHAINED MELODY** *London HL 9975* **14**	12 wks
13 Jan 66	**EBB TIDE** *London HL 10011* **48**	2 wks
14 Apr 66	**(YOU'RE MY) SOUL AND INSPIRATION** *Verve VS 535*...................**15**	10 wks
10 Nov 66	**WHITE CLIFFS OF DOVER** *London HL 10086* **21**	9 wks
22 Dec 66	**ISLAND IN THE SUN** *Verve VS 547*...................**36**	5 wks
12 Feb 69	● **YOU'VE LOST THAT LOVIN' FEELIN' (re-issue)** *London HL 10241*...................**10**	11 wks
19 Nov 77	**YOU'VE LOST THAT LOVIN' FEELIN' (2nd re-issue)** *Phil Spector International 2010 022*...................**42**	4 wks
27 Oct 90	★ **UNCHAINED MELODY (re-issue)** *Verve/Polydor PO 101*...................**1**	14 wks
15 Dec 90	● **YOU'VE LOST THAT LOVIN' FEELIN' (3rd re-issue)** *Verve/Polydor PO 116*...................**3**	9 wks

Cheryl Pepsii RILEY *US, female vocalist*   **1 wk**

28 Jan 89	**THANKS FOR MY CHILD** *CBS 653153 7*...................**75**	1 wk

Jeannie C. RILEY *US, female vocalist*   **15 wks**

16 Oct 68	**HARPER VALLEY P. T. A.** *Polydor 56748* **12**	15 wks

Teddy RILEY *US, male producer*   **5 wks**

21 Mar 92	**IS IT GOOD TO YOU** *MCA MCS 1611* [1] **53**	2 wks
19 Jun 93	**BABY BE MINE** *MCA MCSTD 1772* [2] **37**	3 wks

[1] Teddy Riley featuring Tammy Lucas [2] Blackstreet featuring Teddy Riley

RIMSHOTS *US, male instrumental/vocal group*   **5 wks**

19 Jul 75	**7-6-5-4-3-2-1 (BLOW YOUR WHISTLE)** *All Platinum 6146 304* **26**	5 wks

Miguel RIOS *Spain, male vocalist*   **12 wks**

11 Jul 70	**SONG OF JOY** *A & M AMS 790*...................**16**	12 wks

Waldo de los RIOS *Argentina, orchestra*   **16 wks**

10 Apr 71	● **MOZART SYMPHONY NO. 40 IN G MINOR K550 1ST MOVEMENT (ALLEGRO MOLTO)** *A & M AMS 836*...................**5**	16 wks

Minnie RIPERTON *US, female vocalist*   **10 wks**

12 Apr 75	● **LOVING YOU** *Epic EPC 3121* **2**	10 wks

RITCHIE FAMILY *US, female vocal group*   **19 wks**

23 Aug 75	**BRAZIL** *Polydor 2058 625* **41**	4 wks
18 Sep 76	● **THE BEST DISCO IN TOWN** *Polydor 2058 777* **10**	9 wks
17 Feb 79	**AMERICAN GENERATION** *Mercury 6007 199*...........**49**	6 wks

Lee RITENOUR - *See Maxi PRIEST*

Tex RITTER *US, male vocalist*   **14 wks**

22 Jun 56	● **WAYWARD WIND** *Capitol CL 14581* **8**	14 wks

RIVER CITY PEOPLE
UK, male/female vocal/instrumental group   **27 wks**

12 Aug 89	**(WHAT'S WRONG WITH) DREAMING** *EMI EM 95* **70**	3 wks
3 Mar 90	**WALKING ON ICE** *EMI EM 130* **62**	2 wks
30 Jun 90	**CARRY THE BLAME / CALIFORNIA DREAMIN'** *EMI EM 145*...................**13**	10 wks
22 Sep 90	**(WHAT'S WRONG WITH) DREAMING (re-issue)** *EMI EM 156*...................**40**	3 wks
2 Mar 91	**WHEN I WAS YOUNG** *EMI EM 176* **62**	2 wks
28 Sep 91	**SPECIAL WAY** *EMI EM 207* **44**	3 wks
22 Feb 92	**STANDING IN THE NEED OF LOVE** *EMI EM 216* **36**	4 wks

RIVER DETECTIVES *UK, male vocal/instrumental duo*   **4 wks**

29 Jul 89	**CHAINS** *WEA YZ 383* **51**	4 wks

RIVER OCEAN featuring INDIA
US, male/female vocal/instrumental duo   **2 wks**

26 Feb 94	**LOVE AND HAPPINESS (YEMAYA Y OCHUN)** *Cooltempo CDCOOL 287* **50**	2 wks

Danny RIVERS *UK, male vocalist*   **3 wks**

12 Jan 61	**CAN'T YOU HEAR MY HEART** *Decca F 11294* **36**	3 wks

ROACH MOTEL
UK, male instrumental/production group   **2 wks**

21 Aug 93	**AFRO SLEEZE / TRANSATLANTIC** *Junior Boy's Own JBO 1412* **73**	1 wk
10 Dec 94	**HAPPY BIZZNESS / WILD LUV** *Junior Boy's Own JBO 24* **75**	1 wk

ROACHFORD
UK, male / female vocal / instrumental group   **50 wks**

18 Jun 88	**CUDDLY TOY** CBS ROA 2	**61**	4 wks
14 Jan 89	● **CUDDLY TOY (re-issue)** CBS ROA 4	**4**	9 wks
18 Mar 89	**FAMILY MAN** CBS ROA 5	**25**	6 wks
1 Jul 89	**KATHLEEN** CBS ROA 6	**43**	5 wks
13 Apr 91	**GET READY!** Columbia 6567057	**22**	8 wks
19 Mar 94	**ONLY TO BE WITH YOU** Columbia 6601562	**21**	7 wks
18 Jun 94	**LAY YOUR LOVE ON ME** Columbia 6603722	**36**	5 wks
20 Aug 94	**THIS GENERATION** Columbia 6607452	**38**	4 wks
3 Dec 94	**CRY FOR ME** Columbia 6610742	**46**	2 wks

ROB 'N' RAZ - See Leila K

Kate ROBBINS and BEYOND
UK, female / male vocal / instrumental group   **10 wks**

30 May 81	● **MORE THAN IN LOVE** RCA 69	**2**	10 wks

Marty ROBBINS US, male vocalist   **32 wks**

29 Jan 60	**EL PASO** Fontana H 233	**19**	7 wks
7 Apr 60	**EL PASO (re-entry)** Fontana H 233	**44**	1 wk
26 May 60	**BIG IRON** Fontana H 229	**48**	1 wk
27 Sep 62	● **DEVIL WOMAN** CBS AAG 114	**5**	17 wks
17 Jan 63	**RUBY ANN** CBS AAG 128	**24**	6 wks

Al ROBERTS - See FOUR ACES

Austin ROBERTS US, male vocalist   **7 wks**

25 Oct 75	**ROCKY** Private Stock PVT 33	**22**	7 wks

Joe ROBERTS UK, male vocalist   **12 wks**

28 Aug 93	**BACK IN MY LIFE** ffrr FCD 215	**59**	1 wk
29 Jan 94	**LOVER** ffrr FCD 220	**22**	5 wks
14 May 94	**BACK IN MY LIFE (re-issue)** ffrr FCD 230	**39**	3 wks
6 Aug 94	**ADORE** ffrr FCD 240	**45**	3 wks

Juliet ROBERTS UK, female vocalist   **20 wks**

31 Jul 93	**CAUGHT IN THE MIDDLE** Cooltempo CDCOOL 272	**24**	6 wks
6 Nov 93	**FREE LOVE** Cooltempo CDCOOL 281	**25**	3 wks
19 Mar 94	**AGAIN / I WANT YOU** Cooltempo CDCOOL 285	**33**	3 wks
2 Jul 94	**CAUGHT IN THE MIDDLE (re-mix)** Cooltempo CDCOOL 291	**14**	5 wks
15 Oct 94	**I WANT YOU (re-issue)** Cooltempo CDCOOL 297	**28**	3 wks

Malcolm ROBERTS UK, male vocalist   **29 wks**

11 May 67	**TIME ALONE WILL TELL** RCA 1578	**45**	2 wks
30 Oct 68	● **MAY I HAVE THE NEXT DREAM WITH YOU** Major Minor MM 581	**8**	14 wks
12 Feb 69	**MAY I HAVE THE NEXT DREAM WITH YOU (re-entry)** Major Minor MM 581	**45**	1 wk
22 Nov 69	**LOVE IS ALL** Major Minor MM 637	**12**	12 wks

B.A. ROBERTSON UK, male vocalist   **60 wks**

28 Jul 79	● **BANG BANG** Asylum K 13152	**2**	12 wks
27 Oct 79	● **KNOCKED IT OFF** Asylum K 12396	**8**	12 wks
1 Mar 80	**KOOL IN THE KAFTAN** Asylum K 12427	**17**	12 wks
31 May 80	● **TO BE OR NOT TO BE** Asylum K 12449	**9**	11 wks
17 Oct 81	**HOLD ME** Swansong BAM 1 [1]	**11**	8 wks
17 Dec 83	**TIME** Epic A 3983 [2]	**45**	5 wks

[1] B.A. Robertson and Maggie Bell [2] Frida and B.A. Robertson

Don ROBERTSON
US, male instrumentalist - piano and whistler   **9 wks**

11 May 56	● **THE HAPPY WHISTLER** Capitol CL 14575	**8**	9 wks

Robbie ROBERTSON Canada, male vocalist   **10 wks**

23 Jul 88	**SOMEWHERE DOWN THE CRAZY RIVER** Geffen GEF 40	**15**	10 wks

Ivo ROBIC Yugoslavia, male vocalist   **1 wk**

6 Nov 59	**MORGEN** Polydor 23923	**23**	1 wk

Floyd ROBINSON US, male vocalist   **9 wks**

16 Oct 59	● **MAKIN' LOVE** RCA 1146	**9**	9 wks

Smokey ROBINSON US, male vocalist   **41 wks**

23 Feb 74	**JUST MY SOUL RESPONDING** Tamla Motown TMG 883	**35**	6 wks
24 Feb 79	**POPS WE LOVE YOU** Motown TMG 1136 [1]	**66**	5 wks
9 May 81	★ **BEING WITH YOU** Motown TMG 1223	**1**	13 wks
13 Mar 82	**TELL ME TOMORROW** Motown TMG 1255	**51**	4 wks
28 Mar 87	**JUST TO SEE HER** Motown ZB 41147	**52**	6 wks
25 Feb 89	**INDESTRUCTIBLE** Arista 112074 [2]	**30**	7 wks

[1] Diana Ross, Marvin Gaye, Smokey Robinson and Stevie Wonder [2] Four Tops featuring Smokey Robinson

See also Smokey Robinson and the Miracles.

Smokey ROBINSON and the MIRACLES
US, male vocal group   **71 wks**

24 Feb 66	**GOING TO A GO-GO** Tamla Motown TMG 547	**44**	5 wks
22 Dec 66	**(COME 'ROUND HERE) I'M THE ONE YOU NEED** Tamla Motown TMG 584	**45**	2 wks
27 Dec 67	**I SECOND THAT EMOTION** Tamla Motown TMG 631	**27**	11 wks
3 Apr 68	**IF YOU CAN WANT** Tamla Motown TMG 648	**50**	1 wk
7 May 69	● **TRACKS OF MY TEARS** Tamla Motown TMG 696	**9**	13 wks
1 Aug 70	★ **TEARS OF A CLOWN** Tamla Motown TMG 745	**1**	14 wks
30 Jan 71	**(COME 'ROUND HERE) I'M THE ONE YOU NEED (re-issue)** Tamla Motown TMG 761	**13**	9 wks
5 Jun 71	**I DON'T BLAME YOU AT ALL** Tamla Motown TMG 774	**11**	10 wks
2 Oct 76	**TEARS OF A CLOWN (re-issue)** Tamla Motown TMG 1048	**34**	6 wks

See also Miracles; Smokey Robinson.

Tom ROBINSON UK, male vocalist   **41 wks**

22 Oct 77	● **2-4-6-8 MOTORWAY** EMI 2715 [1]	**5**	9 wks
18 Feb 78	**DON'T TAKE NO FOR AN ANSWER** EMI 2749 [1]	**18**	6 wks
13 May 78	**UP AGAINST THE WALL** EMI 2787 [1]	**33**	6 wks
17 Mar 79	**BULLY FOR YOU** EMI 2916 [1]	**68**	2 wks
25 Jun 83	● **WAR BABY** Panic NIC 2	**6**	9 wks
12 Nov 83	**LISTEN TO THE RADIO: ATMOSPHERICS** Panic NIC 3	**39**	6 wks
15 Sep 84	**RIKKI DON'T LOSE THAT NUMBER** Castaway TR 2	**58**	3 wks

[1] Tom Robinson Band

John ROCCA - See FREEEZ

ROCHELLE US, female vocalist   **6 wks**

1 Feb 86	**MY MAGIC MAN** Warner Bros. W 8838	**27**	6 wks

ROCK AID ARMENIA
UK, male vocal / instrumental charity ensemble   **5 wks**

16 Dec 89	**SMOKE ON THE WATER** Life Aid Armenia ARMEN 001	**39**	5 wks

ROCK CANDY UK, male vocal / instrumental group   **6 wks**

11 Sep 71	**REMEMBER** MCA MK 5069	**32**	6 wks

Chubb ROCK US, male rapper — **1 wk**

19 Jan 91	**TREAT 'EM RIGHT** Champion CHAMP 272 ....**67**	1 wk

ROCK GODDESS UK, female vocal / instrumental group — **5 wks**

5 Mar 83	**MY ANGEL** A & M AMS 8311 ....**64**	2 wks
24 Mar 84	**I DIDN'T KNOW I LOVED YOU (TILL I SAW YOU ROCK 'N' ROLL)** A & M AMS 185...........................**57**	3 wks

Sir Monti ROCK III - See DISCO TEX and the SEX-O-LETTES

ROCKER'S REVENGE
US, male / female vocal / instrumental group — **20 wks**

14 Aug 82	● **WALKING ON SUNSHINE** London LON 11 [1] **4**	13 wks
29 Jan 83	**THE HARDER THEY COME** London LON 18 ....**30**	7 wks

[1] Rocker's Revenge featuring Donnie Calvin

ROCKETS - See Tony CROMBIE and his ROCKETS

ROCKIN' BERRIES UK, male vocal / instrumental group — **41 wks**

1 Oct 64	**I DIDN'T MEAN TO HURT YOU** Piccadilly 7N 35197..**43**	1 wk
15 Oct 64	● **HE'S IN TOWN** Piccadilly 7N 35203 ....**3**	13 wks
21 Jan 65	**WHAT IN THE WORLD'S COME OVER YOU** Piccadilly 7N 35217...........................**23**	7 wks
13 May 65	● **POOR MAN'S SON** Piccadilly 7N 35236 ....**5**	11 wks
26 Aug 65	**YOU'RE MY GIRL** Piccadilly 7N 35254 ....**40**	7 wks
6 Jan 66	**THE WATER IS OVER MY HEAD** Piccadilly 7N 35270...........................**43**	1 wk
20 Jan 66	**THE WATER IS OVER MY HEAD (re-entry)** Piccadilly 7N 35270...........................**50**	1 wk

LORD ROCKINGHAM'S XI - See LORD Rockingham's XI

ROCKNEY - See CHAS and DAVE

ROCKSTEADY CREW US, male / female vocal group — **16 wks**

1 Oct 83	● **(HEY YOU) THE ROCKSTEADY CREW** Charisma/Virgin RSC 1...........................**6**	12 wks
5 May 84	**UPROCK** Charisma/Virgin RSC 2 ....**64**	4 wks

ROCKWELL US, male vocalist — **11 wks**

4 Feb 84	● **SOMEBODY'S WATCHING ME** Motown TMG 1331....**6**	11 wks

ROCKY V - See Joey B. ELLIS

ROCOCO UK / Italy, male / female vocal / instrumental group — **5 wks**

16 Dec 89	**ITALO HOUSE MIX** Mercury MER 314 ....**54**	5 wks

RODEO JONES
UK / Grenada, male / female vocal / instrumental group — **2 wks**

30 Jan 93	**NATURAL WORLD** A & M AMCD 0165 ....**75**	1 wk
3 Apr 93	**SHADES OF SUMMER** A & M AMCD 212 ....**59**	1 wk

Clodagh RODGERS Ireland, female vocalist — **59 wks**

26 Mar 69	● **COME BACK AND SHAKE ME** RCA 1792 ....**3**	14 wks
9 Jul 69	● **GOODNIGHT MIDNIGHT** RCA 1852 ....**4**	11 wks
4 Oct 69	**GOODNIGHT MIDNIGHT (re-entry)** RCA 1852 ....**48**	1 wk
8 Nov 69	**BILJO** RCA 1891 ....**22**	9 wks
4 Apr 70	**EVERYBODY GO HOME THE PARTY'S OVER** RCA 1930 ....**47**	2 wks
20 Mar 71	● **JACK IN THE BOX** RCA 2066 ....**4**	10 wks
9 Oct 71	**LADY LOVE BUG** RCA 2117 ....**28**	12 wks

Jimmie RODGERS US, male vocalist — **37 wks**

1 Nov 57	**HONEYCOMB** Columbia DB 3986...........................**30**	1 wk
20 Dec 57	● **KISSES SWEETER THAN WINE** Columbia DB 4052 ..**7**	11 wks
28 Mar 58	**OH OH, I'M FALLING IN LOVE AGAIN** Columbia DB 4078...........................**18**	6 wks
19 Dec 58	**WOMAN FROM LIBERIA** Columbia DB 4206 ....**18**	6 wks
14 Jun 62	● **ENGLISH COUNTRY GARDEN** Columbia DB 4847 ......**5**	13 wks

Paul RODGERS UK, male vocalist — **2 wks**

12 Feb 94	**MUDDY WATER BLUES** Creation CRESCD 178 ....**45**	2 wks

RODS - See EDDIE and the HOT RODS

Tommy ROE US, male vocalist — **74 wks**

6 Sep 62	● **SHEILA** HMV POP 1060 ....**3**	14 wks
6 Dec 62	**SUSIE DARLIN'** HMV POP 1092 ....**37**	5 wks
21 Mar 63	● **THE FOLK SINGER** HMV POP 1138...........................**4**	13 wks
26 Sep 63	● **EVERYBODY** HMV POP 1207 ....**9**	11 wks
19 Dec 63	**EVERYBODY (re-entry)** HMV POP 1207 ....**49**	3 wks
16 Apr 69	★ **DIZZY** Stateside SS 2143 ....**1**	19 wks
23 Jul 69	**HEATHER HONEY** Stateside SS 2152 ....**24**	9 wks

ROFO UK, male instrumental / production duo — **3 wks**

1 Aug 92	**ROFO'S THEME** PWL Continental PWLT 236 ....**44**	3 wks

ROGER US, male vocalist — **7 wks**

17 Oct 87	**I WANT TO BE YOUR MAN** Reprise W 8229.............**61**	4 wks
12 Nov 88	**BOOM! THERE SHE WAS** Virgin VS 1143 [1] **55**	3 wks

[1] Scritti Politti featuring Roger

Julie ROGERS UK, female vocalist — **38 wks**

13 Aug 64	● **THE WEDDING** Mercury MF 820...........................**3**	23 wks
10 Dec 64	**LIKE A CHILD** Mercury MF 838...........................**21**	9 wks
25 Mar 65	**HAWAIIAN WEDDING SONG** Mercury MF 849 ....**31**	6 wks

Kenny ROGERS US, male vocalist — **109 wks**

18 Oct 69	● **RUBY DON'T TAKE YOUR LOVE TO TOWN** Reprise RS 20829 [1] **2**	23 wks
7 Feb 70	● **SOMETHING'S BURNING** Reprise RS 20888 [1] **8**	14 wks
30 Apr 77	★ **LUCILLE** United Artists UP 36242 ....**1**	14 wks
17 Sep 77	**DAYTIME FRIENDS** United Artists UP 36289 ....**39**	4 wks
2 Jun 79	**SHE BELIEVES IN ME** United Artists UP 36533 ....**42**	7 wks
26 Jan 80	★ **COWARD OF THE COUNTY** United Artists UP 614 ......**1**	12 wks
15 Nov 80	**LADY** United Artists UP 635 ....**12**	12 wks
12 Feb 83	**WE'VE GOT TONIGHT** Liberty UP 658 [2] **28**	7 wks
22 Oct 83	**EYES THAT SEE IN THE DARK** RCA 358 ....**61**	1 wk
12 Nov 83	● **ISLANDS IN THE STREAM** RCA 378 [3] **7**	15 wks

[1] Kenny Rogers and the First Edition [2] Kenny Rogers and Sheena Easton [3] Kenny Rogers and Dolly Parton

ROKOTTO UK, male vocal / instrumental group — **10 wks**

22 Oct 77	**BOOGIE ON UP** State STAT 62 ....**40**	4 wks
10 Jun 78	**FUNK THEORY** State STAT 80 ....**49**	6 wks

ROLLING STONES
UK, male vocal / instrumental group — **352 wks**

25 Jul 63	**COME ON** Decca F 11675 ....**21**	14 wks
14 Nov 63	**I WANNA BE YOUR MAN** Decca F 11764 ....**12**	16 wks
27 Feb 64	● **NOT FADE AWAY** Decca F 11845 ....**3**	15 wks
2 Jul 64	★ **IT'S ALL OVER NOW** Decca F 11934 ....**1**	15 wks
19 Nov 64	★ **LITTLE RED ROOSTER** Decca F 12014 ....**1**	12 wks

Date	Title	Pos	Wks
4 Mar 65	★ THE LAST TIME Decca F 12104	1	13 wks
26 Aug 65	★ (I CAN'T GET NO) SATISFACTION Decca F 12220	1	12 wks
28 Oct 65	★ GET OFF OF MY CLOUD Decca F 12263	1	12 wks
10 Feb 66	● NINETEENTH NERVOUS BREAKDOWN Decca F 12331	2	8 wks
19 May 66	★ PAINT IT, BLACK Decca F 12395	1	10 wks
29 Sep 66	● HAVE YOU SEEN YOUR MOTHER BABY STANDING IN THE SHADOW Decca F 12497	5	8 wks
19 Jan 67	● LET'S SPEND THE NIGHT TOGETHER / RUBY TUESDAY Decca F 12546	3	10 wks
23 Aug 67	● WE LOVE YOU / DANDELION Decca F 12654	8	8 wks
29 May 68	★ JUMPING JACK FLASH Decca F 12782	1	11 wks
9 Jul 69	★ HONKY TONK WOMEN Decca F 12952	1	17 wks
24 Apr 71	● BROWN SUGAR / BITCH / LET IT ROCK Rolling Stones RS 19100	2	13 wks
3 Jul 71	STREET FIGHTING MAN Decca F 13195	21	8 wks
29 Apr 72	● TUMBLING DICE Rolling Stones RS 19103	5	8 wks
1 Sep 73	● ANGIE Rolling Stones RS 19105	5	10 wks
3 Aug 74	● IT'S ONLY ROCK AND ROLL Rolling Stones RS 19114	10	7 wks
20 Sep 75	OUT OF TIME Decca F 13597	45	2 wks
1 May 76	● FOOL TO CRY Rolling Stones RS 19121	6	10 wks
3 Jun 78	● MISS YOU / FAR AWAY EYES Rolling Stones EMI 2802	3	13 wks
30 Sep 78	RESPECTABLE Rolling Stones EMI 2861	23	9 wks
5 Jul 80	● EMOTIONAL RESCUE Rolling Stones RSR 105	9	8 wks
4 Oct 80	SHE'S SO COLD Rolling Stones RSR 106	33	6 wks
29 Aug 81	★ START ME UP Rolling Stones RSR 108	7	9 wks
12 Dec 81	WAITING ON A FRIEND Rolling Stones RSR 109	50	6 wks
12 Jun 82	GOING TO A GO GO Rolling Stones RSR 110	26	6 wks
2 Oct 82	TIME IS ON MY SIDE Rolling Stones RSR 111	62	2 wks
12 Nov 83	UNDERCOVER OF THE NIGHT Rolling Stones RSR 113	11	9 wks
11 Feb 84	SHE WAS HOT Rolling Stones RSR 114	42	4 wks
21 Jul 84	BROWN SUGAR (re-issue) Rolling Stones SUGAR 1	58	2 wks
15 Mar 86	HARLEM SHUFFLE Rolling Stones A 6864	13	7 wks
2 Sep 89	MIXED EMOTIONS Rolling Stones 655193 7	36	5 wks
2 Dec 89	ROCK AND A HARD PLACE Rolling Stones 655422 7	63	1 wk
23 Jun 90	PAINT IT, BLACK (re-issue) London LON 264	61	3 wks
30 Jun 90	ALMOST HEAR YOU SIGH Rolling Stones 656065 7	31	5 wks
30 Mar 91	HIGHWIRE Rolling Stones 6567567	29	4 wks
1 Jun 91	RUBY TUESDAY (LIVE) Rolling Stones 6568927	59	2 wks
16 Jul 94	LOVE IS STRONG Virgin VSCDT 1503	14	5 wks
8 Oct 94	YOU GOT ME ROCKING Virgin VSCDG 1518	23	3 wks
10 Dec 94	OUT OF TEARS Virgin VSCDT 1524	36†	4 wks

Far Away Eyes was listed from 15 Jul 78 with a peak position of 10.

ROLLINS BAND US, male vocal / instrumental group   4 wks

12 Sep 92	TEARING Imago 72787250187	54	2 wks
10 Sep 94	LIAR / DISCONNECTED Imago 74321213052	27	2 wks

ROLLO GOES CAMPING
UK, male producer - Rollo Armstrong   4 wks

29 Jan 94	GET OFF YOUR HIGH HORSE Cheeky CHEKCD 003	43	2 wks
1 Oct 94	GET OFF YOUR HIGH HORSE (re-entry) Cheeky CHEKCD 003	47	2 wks

ROMAN HOLIDAY
UK, male vocal / instrumental group   19 wks

2 Apr 83	STAND BY Jive JIVE 31	61	3 wks
2 Jul 83	DON'T TRY TO STOP IT Jive JIVE 39	14	9 wks
24 Sep 83	MOTORMANIA Jive JIVE 49	40	7 wks

ROMAN NUMERALS - See Vic REEVES

ROMANTICS - See RUBY and the ROMANTICS

Max ROMEO Jamaica, male vocalist   25 wks

28 May 69	● WET DREAM Unity UN 503	10	24 wks
29 Nov 69	WET DREAM (re-entry) Unity UN 503	50	1 wk

RONDO VENEZIANA Italy, orchestra   3 wks

22 Oct 83	LA SERENISSIMA (THEME FROM 'VENICE IN PERIL') Ferroway 7 RON 1	58	3 wks

RONETTES US, female vocal group   34 wks

17 Oct 63	● BE MY BABY London HLU 9793	4	13 wks
9 Jan 64	BABY I LOVE YOU London HLU 9826	11	14 wks
27 Aug 64	BEST PART OF BREAKING UP London HLU 9905	43	3 wks
8 Oct 64	DO I LOVE YOU London HLU 9922	35	4 wks

RONNETTE - See FIDELFATTI featuring RONNETTE

Mick RONSON with Joe ELLIOTT
UK, male instrumental / vocal duo   1 wk

7 May 94	DON'T LOOK DOWN Epic 6603582	55	1 wk

Linda RONSTADT US, female vocalist   34 wks

8 May 76	TRACKS OF MY TEARS Asylum K 13034	42	3 wks
28 Jan 78	BLUE BAYOU Asylum K 13106	35	4 wks
26 May 79	ALISON Asylum K 13149	66	2 wks
11 Jul 87	● SOMEWHERE OUT THERE MCA MCA 1132 [1]	8	13 wks
11 Nov 89	● DON'T KNOW MUCH Elektra EKR 100 [1]	2	12 wks

[1] Linda Ronstadt and James Ingram

Don't Know Much features the uncredited vocals of Aaron Neville.

ROOFTOP SINGERS US, male / female vocal group   12 wks

31 Jan 63	● WALK RIGHT IN Fontana TF 271700	10	12 wks

Ralphi ROSARIO - See Richie RICH

ROSE MARIE UK, female vocalist   5 wks

19 Nov 83	WHEN I LEAVE THE WORLD BEHIND A1 284	75	1 wk
3 Dec 83	WHEN I LEAVE THE WORLD BEHIND (re-entry) A1 284	63	2 wks
24 Dec 83	WHEN I LEAVE THE WORLD BEHIND (2nd re-entry) A1 284	66	2 wks

ROSE OF ROMANCE ORCHESTRA UK, orchestra   1 wk

9 Jan 82	TARA'S THEME FROM 'GONE WITH THE WIND' BBC RESL 108	71	1 wk

ROSE ROYCE
US, male / female vocal / instrumental group   110 wks

25 Dec 76	● CAR WASH MCA 267	9	12 wks
22 Jan 77	PUT YOUR MONEY WHERE YOUR MOUTH IS MCA 259	44	5 wks
2 Apr 77	I WANNA GET NEXT TO YOU MCA 278	14	8 wks
24 Sep 77	DO YOUR DANCE Whitfield K 17006	30	6 wks
14 Jan 78	● WISHING ON A STAR Warner Bros. K 17060	3	14 wks
6 May 78	IT MAKES YOU FEEL LIKE DANCIN' Warner Bros. K 17148	16	10 wks
16 Sep 78	● LOVE DON'T LIVE HERE ANYMORE Whitfield K 17236	2	10 wks
3 Feb 79	I'M IN LOVE (AND I LOVE THE FEELING) Whitfield K 17291	51	4 wks
17 Nov 79	IS IT LOVE YOU'RE AFTER Whitfield K 17456	13	13 wks
8 Mar 80	OOH BOY Whitfield K 17575	46	7 wks
21 Nov 81	ROSE ROYCE EXPRESS Warner Bros. K 17875	52	3 wks
1 Sep 84	MAGIC TOUCH Streetwave KHAN 21	43	8 wks
6 Apr 85	LOVE ME RIGHT NOW Streetwave KHAN 39	60	3 wks
11 Jun 88	CAR WASH / IS IT LOVE YOU'RE AFTER (re-issue) MCA MCA 1253	20	7 wks

CLIFF RICHARD and the **SHADOWS** are both among the all-time top 20 acts, and would remain so even if their collaborations were not included in Cliff's hit list. (LFI)

The **ROLLING STONES** are all dressed for a beggars' banquet, but only Mick Jagger (third from left) has brought a fork. (LFI)

ROSE TATTOO *Australia, male vocal / instrumental group*　**4 wks**

| 11 Jul 81 | ROCK 'N' ROLL OUTLAW *Carrere CAR 200*............**60** | 4 wks |

Jimmy ROSELLI *US, male vocalist*　**8 wks**

| 5 Mar 83 | WHEN YOUR OLD WEDDING RING WAS NEW *A1 282*..**51** | 5 wks |
| 20 Jun 87 | WHEN YOUR OLD WEDDING RING WAS NEW (re-issue) *First Night SCORE 9* ....**52** | 3 wks |

Diana ROSS *US, female vocalist*　**415 wks**

18 Jul 70	REACH OUT AND TOUCH *Tamla Motown TMG 743* **33**	5 wks
12 Sep 70	● AIN'T NO MOUNTAIN HIGH ENOUGH *Tamla Motown TMG 751* **6**	12 wks
3 Apr 71	● REMEMBER ME *Tamla Motown TMG 768*...............**7**	12 wks
31 Jul 71	★ I'M STILL WAITING *Tamla Motown TMG 781* **1**	14 wks
30 Oct 71	● SURRENDER *Tamla Motown TMG 792* **10**	11 wks
13 May 72	DOOBEDOOD'NDOOBE DOOBEDOOD'NDOOBE *Tamla Motown TMG 812* **12**	9 wks
14 Jul 73	● TOUCH ME IN THE MORNING *Tamla Motown TMG 861* **9**	12 wks
13 Oct 73	TOUCH ME IN THE MORNING (re-entry) *Tamla Motown TMG 861* **50**	1 wk
5 Jan 74	● ALL OF MY LIFE *Tamla Motown TMG 880* **9**	13 wks
23 Mar 74	● YOU ARE EVERYTHING *Tamla Motown TMG 890* [1] **5**	12 wks
4 May 74	LAST TIME I SAW HIM *Tamla Motown TMG 893*.....**35**	4 wks
20 Jul 74	STOP LOOK LISTEN (TO YOUR HEART) *Tamla Motown TMG 906* [1] **25**	8 wks
28 Sep 74	LOVE ME *Tamla Motown TMG 917* **38**	5 wks
29 Mar 75	SORRY DOESN'T ALWAYS MAKE IT RIGHT *Tamla Motown TMG 941* **23**	9 wks
3 Apr 76	● THEME FROM MAHOGANY (DO YOU KNOW WHERE YOU'RE GOING TO) *Tamla Motown TMG 1010* **5**	8 wks
24 Apr 76	● LOVE HANGOVER *Tamla Motown TMG 1024*.........**10**	10 wks
10 Jul 76	I THOUGHT IT TOOK A LITTLE TIME *Tamla Motown TMG 1032* **32**	5 wks
16 Oct 76	I'M STILL WAITING (re-issue) *Tamla Motown TMG 1041* **41**	4 wks
19 Nov 77	GETTIN' READY FOR LOVE *Motown TMG 1090* **23**	7 wks
22 Jul 78	LOVIN' LIVIN' AND GIVIN' *Motown TMG 1112* **54**	6 wks
18 Nov 78	EASE ON DOWN THE ROAD *MCA 396* [2] **45**	4 wks
24 Feb 79	POPS WE LOVE YOU *Tamla Motown TMG 1136* [3] ..**66**	5 wks
21 Jul 79	THE BOSS *Motown TMG 1150* **40**	7 wks
6 Oct 79	NO ONE GETS THE PRIZE *Motown TMG 1160* **59**	3 wks
24 Nov 79	IT'S MY HOUSE *Motown TMG 1169* **32**	10 wks
19 Jul 80	● UPSIDE DOWN *Motown TMG 1195* **2**	12 wks
20 Sep 80	● MY OLD PIANO *Motown TMG 1202* **5**	9 wks
15 Nov 80	I'M COMING OUT *Motown TMG 1210* **13**	10 wks
17 Jan 81	IT'S MY TURN *Motown TMG 1217* **16**	8 wks
28 Mar 81	ONE MORE CHANCE *Motown TMG 1227* **49**	5 wks
13 Jun 81	CRYIN' MY HEART OUT FOR YOU *Motown TMG 1233* **58**	3 wks
12 Sep 81	● ENDLESS LOVE *Motown TMG 1240* [4] **7**	12 wks
7 Nov 81	● WHY DO FOOLS FALL IN LOVE *Capitol CL 226* **4**	12 wks
23 Jan 82	TENDERNESS *Motown TMG 1248*...................**73**	1 wk
30 Jan 82	MIRROR MIRROR *Capitol CL 234*...................**36**	5 wks
6 Feb 82	TENDERNESS (re-entry) *Motown TMG 1248*........**75**	1 wk
29 May 82	● WORK THAT BODY *Capitol CL 241* **7**	11 wks
7 Aug 82	IT'S NEVER TOO LATE *Capitol CL 256* **41**	4 wks
23 Oct 82	MUSCLES *Capitol CL 268* **15**	9 wks
15 Jan 83	SO CLOSE *Capitol CL 277* **43**	4 wks
23 Jul 83	PIECES OF ICE *Capitol CL 298* **46**	3 wks
7 Jul 84	ALL OF YOU *CBS A 4522* [5] **43**	8 wks
15 Sep 84	TOUCH BY TOUCH *Capitol CL 337* **47**	6 wks
28 Sep 85	EATEN ALIVE *Capitol CL 372* **71**	1 wk
25 Jan 86	★ CHAIN REACTION *Capitol CL 386* **1**	17 wks
3 May 86	EXPERIENCE *Capitol CL 400* **47**	3 wks
13 Jun 87	DIRTY LOOKS *EMI EM 2* **49**	3 wks
8 Oct 88	MR. LEE *EMI EM 73* **58**	2 wks
26 Nov 88	LOVE HANGOVER (re-mix) *Motown ZB 42307* **75**	1 wk
6 May 89	WORKIN' OVERTIME *EMI EM 91* **32**	5 wks
29 Jul 89	PARADISE *EMI EM 94* **61**	2 wks
7 Jul 90	I'M STILL WAITING (re-mix) *Motown ZB 43781* **21**	6 wks
30 Nov 91	● WHEN YOU TELL ME THAT YOU LOVE ME *EMI EM 217* **2**	11 wks
15 Feb 92	THE FORCE BEHIND THE POWER *EMI EM 221*........**27**	3 wks
20 Jun 92	ONE SHINING MOMENT *EMI EM 239* **10**	8 wks
28 Nov 92	IF WE HOLD ON TOGETHER *EMI EM 257* **11**	10 wks
13 Mar 93	HEART (DON'T CHANGE MY MIND) *EMI CDEM 261* **31**	3 wks
9 Oct 93	CHAIN REACTION (re-issue) *EMI CDEM 290* **20**	5 wks
11 Dec 93	YOUR LOVE *EMI CDEM 299* **14**	8 wks
2 Apr 94	THE BEST YEARS OF MY LIFE *EMI CDEM 305*........**28**	4 wks
9 Jul 94	WHY DO FOOLS FALL IN LOVE (re-issue)/ I'M COMING OUT (re-mix) *EMI CDEM 332*...........**36**	4 wks

[1] Diana Ross and Marvin Gaye [2] Diana Ross and Michael Jackson [3] Diana Ross, Marvin Gaye, Smokey Robinson and Stevie Wonder [4] Diana Ross and Lionel Richie [5] Julio Iglesias and Diana Ross

See also Supremes.

Francis ROSSI and Bernard FROST
UK, male vocal / instrumental duo　**4 wks**

| 11 May 85 | MODERN ROMANCE (I WANT TO FALL IN LOVE AGAIN) *Vertigo FROS 1* ....**54** | 4 wks |

Laurent ROSSI - *See BIMBO JET*

Nini ROSSO *Italy, male instrumentalist - trumpet*　**14 wks**

| 26 Aug 65 | ● IL SILENZIO *Durium DRS 54000* ....**8** | 14 wks |

David Lee ROTH *US, male vocalist*　**15 wks**

23 Feb 85	CALIFORNIA GIRLS *Warner Bros. W 9102* **68**	2 wks
5 Mar 88	JUST LIKE PARADISE *Warner Bros. W 8119* **27**	7 wks
3 Sep 88	DAMN GOOD / STAND UP *Warner Bros. W 7753* **72**	1 wk
12 Jan 91	A LIL' AIN'T ENOUGH *Warner Bros. W 0002* **32**	3 wks
19 Feb 94	SHE'S MY MACHINE *Reprise W 0229CD*.............**64**	1 wk
28 May 94	NIGHT LIFE *Reprise W 0249CD* **72**	1 wk

ROTTERDAM TERMINATION SOURCE
Holland, male instrumental / production duo　**6 wks**

| 7 Nov 92 | POING *SEP EDGE 74*................................**27** | 4 wks |
| 25 Dec 93 | MERRY X-MESS *React CDREACT 33* ....**73** | 2 wks |

ROULETTES - *See Adam FAITH*

Robert ROUNSEVILLE - *See VARIOUS ARTISTS (EPs & LPs)* - Carousel Soundtrack

Demis ROUSSOS *Greece, male vocalist*　**44 wks**

22 Nov 75	● HAPPY TO BE ON AN ISLAND IN THE SUN *Philips 6042 033* **5**	10 wks
28 Feb 76	CAN'T SAY HOW MUCH I LOVE YOU *Philips 6042 114* **35**	5 wks
26 Jun 76	★ THE ROUSSOS PHENOMENON EP *Philips DEMIS 001* **1**	12 wks
2 Oct 76	● WHEN FOREVER HAS GONE *Philips 6042 186* **2**	10 wks
19 Mar 77	BECAUSE *Philips 6042 245* **39**	4 wks
18 Jun 77	KYRILA (EP) *Philips Demis 002* **33**	3 wks

Tracks on The Roussos Phenomenon EP: Forever And Ever / Sing An Ode To Love / So Dreamy / My Friend The Wind. Tracks on Kyrila (EP): Kyrila / I'm Gonna Fall In Love / I Dig You / Sister Emilyne.

ROUTERS *US, male instrumental group*　**7 wks**

| 27 Dec 62 | LET'S GO *Warner Bros. WB 77* ....**32** | 7 wks |

Kevin ROWLAND - *See DEXY'S MIDNIGHT RUNNERS*

John ROWLES *New Zealand, male vocalist* — **28 wks**

13 Mar 68 ●	IF I ONLY HAD TIME *MCA MU 1000* **3**	18 wks
19 Jun 68	HUSH NOT A WORD TO MARY *MCA MU 1023* **12**	10 wks

ROXETTE *Sweden, male / female vocal / instrumental duo* — **126 wks**

22 Apr 89 ●	THE LOOK *EMI EM 87* **7**	10 wks
15 Jul 89	DRESSED FOR SUCCESS *EMI EM 96* **48**	5 wks
28 Oct 89	LISTEN TO YOUR HEART *EMI EM 108* **62**	3 wks
2 Jun 90 ●	IT MUST HAVE BEEN LOVE *EMI EM 141* **3**	14 wks
11 Aug 90 ●	LISTEN TO YOUR HEART (re-issue) *EMI EM 149* ...**6**	9 wks
27 Oct 90	DRESSED FOR SUCCESS (re-issue) *EMI EM 162* **18**	7 wks
9 Mar 91 ●	JOYRIDE *EMI EM 177* **4**	10 wks
11 May 91	FADING LIKE A FLOWER *EMI EM 190* **12**	6 wks
7 Sep 91	THE BIG L *EMI EM 204* **21**	6 wks
23 Nov 91	SPENDING MY TIME *EMI EM 215* **22**	4 wks
28 Mar 92	CHURCH OF YOUR HEART *EMI EM 227* **21**	4 wks
1 Aug 92	HOW DO YOU DO! *EMI EM 241* **13**	7 wks
7 Nov 92	QUEEN OF RAIN *EMI EM 253* **28**	4 wks
24 Jul 93 ●	ALMOST UNREAL *EMI CDEM 268* **7**	9 wks
18 Sep 93	IT MUST HAVE BEEN LOVE (re-issue)	
	EMI CDEM 285 ....**10**	8 wks
26 Mar 94	SLEEPING IN MY CAR *EMI CDEM 314* **14**	6 wks
4 Jun 94	CRASH! BOOM! BANG! *EMI CDEMS 324* **26**	5 wks
17 Sep 94	FIREWORKS *EMI CDEMS 345* **30**	4 wks
3 Dec 94	RUN TO YOU *EMI CDEMS 360* ....**27†**	5 wks

ROXY MUSIC *UK, male vocal / instrumental group* — **153 wks**

19 Aug 72 ●	VIRGINIA PLAIN *Island WIP 6144* **4**	12 wks
10 Mar 73 ●	PYJAMARAMA *Island WIP 6159* **10**	12 wks
17 Nov 73 ●	STREET LIFE *Island WIP 6173* **9**	12 wks
12 Oct 74	ALL I WANT IS YOU *Island WIP 6208* **12**	8 wks
11 Oct 75 ●	LOVE IS THE DRUG *Island WIP 6248* **2**	10 wks
27 Dec 75	BOTH ENDS BURNING *Island WIP 6262* **25**	7 wks
22 Oct 77	VIRGINIA PLAIN (re-issue) *Polydor 2001 739* **11**	6 wks
3 Mar 79	TRASH *Polydor POSP 32* **40**	6 wks
28 Apr 79 ●	DANCE AWAY *Polydor POSP 44* **2**	14 wks
11 Aug 79 ●	ANGEL EYES *Polydor POSP 67* **4**	11 wks
17 May 80 ●	OVER YOU *Polydor POSP 93* **5**	9 wks
2 Aug 80 ●	OH YEAH (ON THE RADIO) *Polydor 2001 972* **5**	8 wks
8 Nov 80	THE SAME OLD SCENE *Polydor ROXY 1*...............**12**	7 wks
21 Feb 81 ★	JEALOUS GUY *EG ROXY 2* **1**	11 wks
3 Apr 82 ●	MORE THAN THIS *EG ROXY 3* **6**	8 wks
19 Jun 82	AVALON *EG ROXY 4* **13**	6 wks
25 Sep 82	TAKE A CHANCE WITH ME *EG ROXY 5* **26**	6 wks

Billy Joe ROYAL *US, male vocalist* — **18 wks**

7 Oct 65	DOWN IN THE BOONDOCKS *CBS 201802*..................**38**	4 wks

The Central Band of the ROYAL AIR FORCE, Conductor W/Cdr. A.E. SIMS O.B.E.
UK, military band — **1 wk**

21 Oct 55	THE DAMBUSTERS MARCH *HMV B 10877*...............**18**	1 wk

ROYAL GUARDSMEN
US, male vocal / instrumental group — **17 wks**

19 Jan 67 ●	SNOOPY VS. THE RED BARON *Stateside SS 574* **8**	13 wks
6 Apr 67	RETURN OF THE RED BARON *Stateside SS 2010* **37**	4 wks

ROYAL HOUSE
US, male / female vocal / instrumental group — **18 wks**

10 Sep 88	CAN YOU PARTY *Champion CHAMP 79* **14**	14 wks
7 Jan 89	YEAH! BUDDY *Champion CHAMP 91* **35**	4 wks

ROYAL PHILHARMONIC ORCHESTRA arranged and conducted by Louis CLARK
UK, orchestra and conductor — **19 wks**

25 Jul 81 ●	HOOKED ON CLASSICS *RCA 109*............................**2**	11 wks
24 Oct 81	HOOKED ON CAN-CAN *RCA 151* **47**	3 wks
10 Jul 82	BBC WORLD CUP GRANDSTAND *BBC RESL 116* **61**	3 wks
7 Aug 82	IF YOU KNEW SOUSA (AND FRIENDS) *RCA 256* **71**	2 wks

See also Elvis Costello. Louis Clark did not conduct the third hit.

The Pipes and Drums and Military Band of the ROYAL SCOTS DRAGOON GUARDS
UK, military band — **43 wks**

1 Apr 72 ★	AMAZING GRACE *RCA 2191* **1**	24 wks
19 Aug 72	HEYKENS SERENADE / THE DAY IS ENDED	
	RCA 2251 ....**30**	7 wks
2 Dec 72	LITTLE DRUMMER BOY *RCA 2301*......................**13**	9 wks
23 Dec 72	AMAZING GRACE (re-entry) *RCA 2191* **42**	3 wks

ROYALLE DELITE *US, female vocal group* — **6 wks**

14 Sep 85	(I'LL BE A) FREAK FOR YOU *Streetwave KHAN 51* ..**45**	6 wks

Lita ROZA *UK, female vocalist* — **18 wks**

13 Mar 53 ★	(HOW MUCH IS) THAT DOGGIE IN THE WINDOW	
	Decca F 10070 ....**1**	11 wks
7 Oct 55	HEY THERE *Decca F 10611* **17**	2 wks
23 Mar 56	JIMMY UNKNOWN *Decca F 10679* **15**	5 wks

See also Various Artists (EPs & LPs) - All Star Hit Parade.

ROZALLA *Zimbabwe, female vocalist* — **43 wks**

27 Apr 91	FAITH (IN THE POWER OF LOVE) *Pulse 8 LOSE 7* **65**	2 wks
7 Sep 91 ●	EVERYBODY'S FREE (TO FEEL GOOD)	
	Pulse 8 LOSE 13 ....**6**	11 wks
16 Nov 91	FAITH (IN THE POWER OF LOVE) (re-issue)	
	Pulse 8 LOSE 15 ....**11**	6 wks
22 Feb 92	ARE YOU READY TO FLY *Pulse 8 LOSE 21* **14**	6 wks
9 May 92	LOVE BREAKDOWN *Pulse 8 LOSE 25* **65**	2 wks
15 Aug 92	IN 4 CHOONS LATER *Pulse 8 LOSE 29* **50**	2 wks
30 Oct 93	DON'T PLAY WITH ME *Pulse 8 CDLOSE 52* **50**	1 wk
5 Feb 94	I LOVE MUSIC *Epic 6598932* **18**	5 wks
6 Aug 94	THIS TIME I FOUND LOVE *Epic 6603742*..............**33**	3 wks
29 Oct 94	YOU NEVER LOVE THE SAME WAY TWICE	
	Epic 6609052 ....**16**	5 wks

RTE CONCERT ORCHESTRA - *See Bill WHELAN featuring ANUNA and the RTE CONCERT ORCHESTRA*

RUBETTES *UK, male vocal / instrumental group* — **68 wks**

4 May 74 ★	SUGAR BABY LOVE *Polydor 2058 442* **1**	10 wks
13 Jul 74	TONIGHT *Polydor 2058 499*..............................**12**	9 wks
16 Nov 74 ●	JUKE BOX JIVE *Polydor 2058 529* **3**	12 wks
8 Mar 75 ●	I CAN DO IT *State STAT 1* **7**	9 wks
21 Jun 75	FOE-DEE-O-DEE *State STAT 7* **15**	6 wks
22 Nov 75	LITTLE DARLING *State STAT 13* **30**	5 wks
1 May 76	YOU'RE THE REASON WHY *State STAT 20* **28**	4 wks
25 Sep 76	UNDER ONE ROOF *State STAT 27* **40**	3 wks
12 Feb 77 ●	BABY I KNOW *State STAT 37* **10**	10 wks

RUBY and the ROMANTICS
US, female / male vocal group — **6 wks**

28 Mar 63	OUR DAY WILL COME *London HLR 9679* **38**	6 wks

RUDE BOY OF HOUSE - *See HOUSEMASTER BOYZ and the RUDE BOY OF HOUSE*

RUDIES - *See Freddie NOTES and the RUDIES*

Frances RUFFELLE *UK, female vocalist* **6 wks**

16 Apr 94	**LONELY SYMPHONY** *Virgin VSCDT 1499*	**25**	6 wks

Bruce RUFFIN *Jamaica, male vocalist* **23 wks**

1 May 71	**RAIN** *Trojan TR 7814*	**19**	11 wks
24 Jun 72	● **MAD ABOUT YOU** *Rhino RNO 101*	**9**	12 wks

David RUFFIN *US, male vocalist* **10 wks**

17 Jan 76	● **WALK AWAY FROM LOVE** *Tamla Motown TMG 1017*	**10**	8 wks
21 Sep 85	**A NIGHT AT THE APOLLO LIVE!** *RCA PB 49935* [1]	**58**	2 wks

[1] Hall and Oates featuring David Ruffin and Eddie Kendrick

Jimmy RUFFIN *US, male vocalist* **106 wks**

27 Oct 66	● **WHAT BECOMES OF THE BROKENHEARTED** *Tamla Motown TMG 577*	**10**	15 wks
9 Feb 67	**I'VE PASSED THIS WAY BEFORE** *Tamla Motown TMG 593*	**29**	7 wks
20 Apr 67	**GONNA GIVE HER ALL THE LOVE I'VE GOT** *Tamla Motown TMG 603*	**26**	6 wks
9 Aug 69	**I'VE PASSED THIS WAY BEFORE (re-issue)** *Tamla Motown TMG 703*	**33**	6 wks
28 Feb 70	● **FAREWELL IS A LONELY SOUND** *Tamla Motown TMG 726*	**8**	16 wks
4 Jul 70	● **I'LL SAY FOREVER MY LOVE** *Tamla Motown TMG 740*	**7**	12 wks
17 Oct 70	● **IT'S WONDERFUL** *Tamla Motown TMG 753*	**6**	14 wks
27 Jul 74	● **WHAT BECOMES OF THE BROKENHEARTED (re-issue)** *Tamla Motown TMG 911*	**4**	12 wks
2 Nov 74	**FAREWELL IS A LONELY SOUND (re-issue)** *Tamla Motown TMG 922*	**30**	5 wks
16 Nov 74	**TELL ME WHAT YOU WANT** *Polydor 2058 433*	**39**	4 wks
3 May 80	● **HOLD ON TO MY LOVE** *RSO 57*	**7**	8 wks
26 Jan 85	**THERE WILL NEVER BE ANOTHER YOU** *EMI 5541*	**68**	1 wk

RUFUS - *See Chaka KHAN*

Barbara RUICK - *See VARIOUS ARTISTS (EPs & LPs)* - Carousel Soundtrack

RUMOUR - *See Graham PARKER and the RUMOUR*

RUMPLE-STILTS-SKIN
US, male / female vocal / instrumental group **4 wks**

24 Sep 83	**I THINK I WANT TO DANCE WITH YOU** *Polydor POSP 649*	**51**	4 wks

RUN D.M.C. *US, male rap group* **38 wks**

19 Jul 86	**MY ADIDAS / PETER PIPER** *London LON 101*	**62**	2 wks
6 Sep 86	● **WALK THIS WAY** *London LON 104*	**8**	10 wks
7 Feb 87	**YOU BE ILLIN'** *Profile LON 118*	**42**	4 wks
30 May 87	**IT'S TRICKY** *Profile LON 130*	**16**	7 wks
12 Dec 87	**CHRISTMAS IN HOLLIS** *Profile LON 163*	**56**	4 wks
21 May 88	**RUN'S HOUSE** *London LON 177*	**37**	4 wks
2 Sep 89	**GHOSTBUSTERS** *MCA Profile MCA 1360*	**65**	2 wks
1 Dec 90	**WHAT'S IT ALL ABOUT** *Profile PROF 315*	**48**	3 wks
27 Mar 93	**DOWN WITH THE KING** *Profile PROFCD 39*	**69**	2 wks

RUN TINGS *UK, male instrumental / production duo* **1 wk**

16 May 92	**FIRES BURNING** *Suburban Base SUBBASE 009*	**58**	1 wk

See also Various Artists (EPs & LPs) - Subplates Volume 1 EP.

Todd RUNDGREN *US, male vocalist* **8 wks**

30 Jun 73	**I SAW THE LIGHT** *Bearsville K 15506*	**36**	6 wks
14 Dec 85	**LOVING YOU'S A DIRTY JOB BUT SOMEBODY'S GOTTA DO IT** *CBS A 6662* [1]	**73**	2 wks

[1] Bonnie Tyler, guest vocals Todd Rundgren

RUNRIG *UK, male vocal / instrumental group* **14 wks**

29 Sep 90	**CAPTURE THE HEART EP** *Chrysalis CHS 3594*	**49**	2 wks
7 Sep 91	**HEARTHAMMER (EP)** *Chrysalis CHS 3754*	**25**	4 wks
9 Nov 91	**FLOWER OF THE WEST** *Chrysalis CHS 3805*	**43**	2 wks
6 Mar 93	**WONDERFUL** *Chrysalis CDCHS 3952*	**29**	3 wks
15 May 93	**THE GREATEST FLAME** *Chrysalis CDCHS 3975*	**36**	3 wks

Tracks on Capture The Heart EP: *Stepping Down The Glory Road / Satellite Flood / Harvest Moon / The Apple Came Down. Tracks on* Hearthammer (EP): *Hearthammer / Pride Of The Summer (Live) / Loch Lomond (Live) / Solus Na Madainn.*

RuPAUL *US, male vocalist* **16 wks**

26 Jun 93	**SUPERMODEL (YOU BETTER WORK)** *Union City UCRD 21*	**39**	4 wks
18 Sep 93	**HOUSE OF LOVE / BACK TO MY ROOTS** *Union City UCRD 23*	**40**	2 wks
22 Jan 94	**SUPERMODEL (re-mix) / LITTLE DRUMMER BOY** *Union City UCRD 25*	**61**	2 wks
26 Feb 94	● **DON'T GO BREAKING MY HEART** *Rocket EJCD 33* [1]	**7**	7 wks
21 May 94	**HOUSE OF LOVE (re-mix)** *Union City UCRDG 29*	**68**	1 wk

[1] Elton John with RuPaul

RUSH *Canada, male vocal / instrumental group* **43 wks**

11 Feb 78	**CLOSER TO THE HEART** *Mercury RUSH 7*	**36**	3 wks
15 Mar 80	**SPIRIT OF RADIO** *Mercury RADIO 7*	**13**	7 wks
28 Mar 81	**VITAL SIGNS / A PASSAGE TO BANGKOK** *Mercury VITAL7*	**41**	4 wks
31 Oct 81	**TOM SAWYER** *Exit EXIT 7*	**25**	6 wks
4 Sep 82	**NEW WORLD MAN** *Mercury RUSH 8*	**42**	3 wks
30 Oct 82	**SUBDIVISIONS** *Mercury RUSH 9*	**53**	2 wks
7 May 83	**COUNTDOWN / NEW WORLD MAN** *Mercury RUSH 10*	**36**	5 wks
26 May 84	**THE BODY ELECTRIC** *Vertigo RUSH 11*	**56**	3 wks
12 Oct 85	**THE BIG MONEY** *Vertigo RUSH 12*	**46**	3 wks
31 Oct 87	**TIME STAND STILL** *Vertigo RUSH 13* [1]	**42**	3 wks
23 Apr 88	**PRIME MOVER** *Vertigo RUSH 14*	**43**	3 wks
7 Mar 92	**ROLL THE BONES** *Atlantic A 7524*	**49**	1 wk

[1] Rush with Aimee Mann

New World Man on RUSH 10 *is a live version of* RUSH 8.

Donell RUSH *US, male vocalist* **1 wk**

5 Dec 92	**SYMPHONY** *ID 6587977*	**66**	1 wk

Jennifer RUSH *US, female vocalist* **58 wks**

29 Jun 85	★ **THE POWER OF LOVE** *CBS A 5003*	**1**	32 wks
14 Dec 85	**RING OF ICE** *CBS A 4745*	**14**	10 wks
20 Dec 86	**THE POWER OF LOVE (re-entry)** *CBS A 5003*	**55**	4 wks
20 Jun 87	**FLAMES OF PARADISE** *CBS 650865 7* [1]	**59**	3 wks
27 May 89	**TILL I LOVED YOU** *CBS 654843 7* [2]	**24**	9 wks

[1] Jennifer Rush and Elton John [2] Placido Domingo and Jennifer Rush

Patrice RUSHEN *US, female vocalist* **25 wks**

1 Mar 80	**HAVEN'T YOU HEARD** *Elektra K 12414*	**62**	3 wks
24 Jan 81	**NEVER GONNA GIVE YOU UP (WON'T LET YOU BE)** *Elektra K 12494*	**66**	3 wks
24 Apr 82	● **FORGET ME NOTS** *Elektra K 13173*	**8**	11 wks

10 Jul 82	**I WAS TIRED OF BEING ALONE** Elektra K 13184......**39**	5 wks
9 Jun 84	**FEELS SO REAL (WON'T LET GO)** Elektra E 9742 ....**51**	3 wks

Brenda RUSSELL US, female vocalist — 17 wks

19 Apr 80	**SO GOOD SO RIGHT / IN THE THICK OF IT** A & M AM 7515 ....**51**	5 wks
12 Mar 88	**PIANO IN THE DARK** Breakout USA 623......**23**	12 wks

Paul RUTHERFORD UK, male vocalist — 6 wks

8 Oct 88	**GET REAL** Fourth & Broadway BRW 113 ......**47**	3 wks
19 Aug 89	**OH WORLD** Fourth & Broadway BRW 136......**61**	3 wks

RUTHLESS RAP ASSASSINS UK, male rappers — 2 wks

9 Jun 90	**JUST MELLOW** Syncopate SY 35 ......**75**	1 wk
1 Sep 90	**AND IT WASN'T A DREAM** Syncopate SY 38......**75**	1 wk

RUTLES UK, male vocal group — 4 wks

15 Apr 78	**I MUST BE IN LOVE** Warner Bros. K 17125 ......**39**	3 wks
13 May 78	**I MUST BE IN LOVE (re-entry)** Warner Bros. K 17125 ......**64**	1 wk

RUTS UK, male vocal / instrumental group — 28 wks

16 Jun 79	● **BABYLON'S BURNING** Virgin VS 271 ......**7**	11 wks
8 Sep 79	**SOMETHING THAT I SAID** Virgin VS 285 ......**29**	5 wks
19 Apr 80	**STARING AT THE RUDE BOYS** Virgin VS 327 ......**22**	8 wks
30 Aug 80	**WEST ONE (SHINE ON ME)** Virgin VS 370 ......**43**	4 wks

Barry RYAN UK, male vocalist — 33 wks

23 Oct 68	● **ELOISE** MGM 1442......**2**	12 wks
19 Feb 69	**LOVE IS LOVE** MGM 1464 ......**25**	4 wks
4 Oct 69	**HUNT** Polydor 56 348......**34**	5 wks
21 Feb 70	**MAGICAL SPIEL** Polydor 56 370 ......**49**	1 wk
16 May 70	**KITSCH** Polydor 2001 035 ......**37**	6 wks
15 Jan 72	**CAN'T LET YOU GO** Polydor 2001 256 ......**32**	5 wks

See also Paul and Barry Ryan.

Marion RYAN UK, female vocalist — 11 wks

24 Jan 58	● **LOVE ME FOREVER** Pye Nixa N 15121......**5**	11 wks

Paul and Barry RYAN UK, male vocal duo — 43 wks

11 Nov 65	**DON'T BRING ME YOUR HEARTACHES** Decca F 12260......**13**	9 wks
3 Feb 66	**HAVE PITY ON THE BOY** Decca F 12319 ......**18**	6 wks
12 May 66	**I LOVE HER** Decca F 12391 ......**17**	8 wks
14 Jul 66	**I LOVE HOW YOU LOVE ME** Decca F 12445 ......**21**	7 wks
29 Sep 66	**HAVE YOU EVER LOVED SOMEBODY** Decca F 12494 ......**49**	1 wk
8 Dec 66	**MISSY MISSY** Decca F 12520 ......**43**	4 wks
2 Mar 67	**KEEP IT OUT OF SIGHT** Decca F 12567 ......**30**	6 wks
29 Jun 67	**CLAIRE** Decca F 12633 ......**47**	2 wks

See also Barry Ryan.

Bobby RYDELL US, male vocalist — 60 wks

10 Mar 60	● **WILD ONE** Columbia DB 4429 ......**7**	14 wks
23 Jun 60	**WILD ONE (re-entry)** Columbia DB 4429 ......**47**	1 wk
30 Jun 60	**SWINGING SCHOOL** Columbia DB 4471 ......**44**	1 wk
1 Sep 60	**VOLARE** Columbia DB 4495 ......**46**	1 wk
15 Sep 60	**VOLARE (re-entry)** Columbia DB 4495 ......**22**	5 wks
15 Dec 60	**SWAY** Columbia DB 4545 ......**12**	13 wks
23 Mar 61	**GOOD TIME BABY** Columbia DB 4600 ......**42**	7 wks
19 Apr 62	**TEACH ME TO TWIST** Columbia DB 4802 [1] **45**	1 wk
20 Dec 62	**JINGLE BELL ROCK** Cameo Parkway C 205 [1] **40**	3 wks

---

23 May 63	**FORGET HIM** Cameo Parkway C 108 ......**13**	14 wks

[1] Chubby Checker and Bobby Rydell

Mitch RYDER and the DETROIT WHEELS
US, male vocalist, male vocal / instrumental backing group — 5 wks

10 Feb 66	**JENNY TAKE A RIDE** Stateside SS 481 ......**44**	1 wk
24 Feb 66	**JENNY TAKE A RIDE (re-entry)** Stateside SS 481 ....**33**	4 wks

RYTHM SYNDICATE US, male vocal / instrumental group — 5 wks

27 Jul 91	**P.A.S.S.I.O.N.** Impact American EM 197 ......**58**	5 wks

S

Robin S US, female vocalist — 29 wks

16 Jan 93	**SHOW ME LOVE** Champion CHAMPCD 300 ......**59**	4 wks
13 Mar 93	● **SHOW ME LOVE (re-entry)** Champion CHAMPCD 300 ......**6**	13 wks
31 Jul 93	**LUV 4 LUV** Champion CHAMPCD 301 ......**11**	7 wks
4 Dec 93	**WHAT I DO BEST** Champion CHAMPCD 307 ......**43**	2 wks
19 Mar 94	**I WANT TO THANK YOU** Champion CHAMPCD 310 **48**	1 wk
5 Nov 94	**BACK IT UP** Champion CHAMPCD 312 ......**43**	2 wks

S EXPRESS UK, male / female vocal / instrumental group — 46 wks

16 Apr 88	★ **THEME FROM S-EXPRESS** Rhythm King LEFT 21 ......**1**	13 wks
23 Jul 88	● **SUPERFLY GUY** Rhythm King LEFT 28 ......**5**	9 wks
18 Feb 89	● **HEY MUSIC LOVER** Rhythm King LEFT 30 ......**6**	10 wks
16 Sep 89	**MANTRA FOR A STATE OF MIND** Rhythm King LEFT 35 ......**21**	8 wks
15 Sep 90	**NOTHING TO LOSE** Rhythm King SEXY 01 ......**32**	4 wks
30 May 92	**FIND 'EM, FOOL 'EM, FORGET 'EM** Rhythm King 6580137 ......**43**	2 wks

SABRES - *See Denny SEYTON and the SABRES*

SABRES OF PARADISE UK, male instrumental group — 8 wks

2 Oct 93	**SMOKEBELCH II** Sabres Of Paradise PT 009CD **55**	3 wks
9 Apr 94	**THEME** Sabres Of Paradise PT 014CD **56**	3 wks
17 Sep 94	**WILMOT** Warp WAP 50CD **36**	2 wks

SABRINA Italy, female vocalist — 22 wks

6 Feb 88	**BOYS (SUMMERTIME LOVE)** IBIZA IBIZ 1 ......**60**	3 wks
11 Jun 88	● **BOYS (SUMMERTIME LOVE) (re-entry)** IBIZA IBIZ 1..**3**	11 wks
1 Oct 88	**ALL OF ME** PWL PWL 19 ......**25**	7 wks
1 Jul 89	**LIKE A YO-YO** Videogram DCUP 1......**72**	1 wk

SAD CAFE UK, male vocal / instrumental group — 44 wks

22 Sep 79	● **EVERY DAY HURTS** RCA PB 5180 ......**3**	12 wks
19 Jan 80	**STRANGE LITTLE GIRL** RCA PB 5202 ......**32**	5 wks
15 Mar 80	**MY OH MY** RCA SAD 3 ......**14**	11 wks
21 Jun 80	**NOTHING LEFT TOULOUSE** RCA SAD 4 ......**62**	4 wks
27 Sep 80	**LA-DI-DA** RCA SAD 5......**41**	6 wks
20 Dec 80	**I'M IN LOVE AGAIN** RCA SAD 6 ......**40**	6 wks

SADE UK, female / male vocal / instrumental group — 63 wks

25 Feb 84	● **YOUR LOVE IS KING** Epic A 4137 ......**6**	11 wks
19 May 84	**YOUR LOVE IS KING (re-entry)** Epic A 4137 ......**75**	1 wk
26 May 84	**WHEN AM I GONNA MAKE A LIVING** Epic A 4437.**36**	5 wks
15 Sep 84	**SMOOTH OPERATOR** Epic A 4655 ......**19**	10 wks
12 Oct 85	**THE SWEETEST TABOO** Epic A 6609 ......**31**	5 wks

11 Jan 86	**IS IT A CRIME** Epic A 6742	**49**	3 wks
2 Apr 88	**LOVE IS STRONGER THAN PRIDE** Epic SADE 1	**44**	3 wks
4 Jun 88	**PARADISE** Epic SADE 2	**29**	7 wks
10 Oct 92	**NO ORDINARY LOVE** Epic 6583567	**26**	3 wks
28 Nov 92	**FEEL NO PAIN** Epic 6588297	**56**	2 wks
8 May 93	**KISS OF LIFE** Epic 6591162	**44**	3 wks
5 Jun 93	**NO ORDINARY LOVE (re-entry)** Epic 6583562	**14**	8 wks
31 Jul 93	**CHERISH THE DAY** Epic 6594812	**53**	2 wks

Staff Sergeant Barry SADLER US, male vocalist   **8 wks**

| 24 Mar 66 | **BALLAD OF THE GREEN BERETS** RCA 1506 .... | **24** | 8 wks |

SAFFRON UK, female vocalist   **2 wks**

| 16 Jan 93 | **CIRCLES** WEA SAFF 9CD .... | **60** | 2 wks |

SAFFRONS - See CINDY and the SAFFRONS

Mike SAGAR UK, male vocalist   **5 wks**

| 8 Dec 60 | **DEEP FEELING** HMV POP 819 .... | **44** | 5 wks |

SAGAT US, male rapper   **6 wks**

| 4 Dec 93 | **FUNK DAT** ffrr FCD 224 .... | **25** | 5 wks |
| 3 Dec 94 | **LUVSTUFF** ffrr FCD 250 .... | **71** | 1 wk |

Carole Bayer SAGER US, female vocalist   **9 wks**

| 28 May 77 | ● **YOU'RE MOVING OUT TODAY** Elektra K 12257 .... | **6** | 9 wks |

Bally SAGOO India, female vocalist   **1 wk**

| 3 Sep 94 | **CHURA LIYA** Columbia 6607092 .... | **64** | 1 wk |

SAILOR UK, male vocal / instrumental group   **24 wks**

6 Dec 75	● **GLASS OF CHAMPAGNE** Epic EPC 3770	**2**	12 wks
27 Mar 76	● **GIRLS GIRLS GIRLS** Epic EPC 3858	**7**	8 wks
19 Feb 77	**ONE DRINK TOO MANY** Epic EPC 4804	**35**	4 wks

ST. ANDREWS CHORALE UK, church choir   **5 wks**

| 14 Feb 76 | **CLOUD 99** Decca F 13617 .... | **31** | 5 wks |

ST. CECILIA UK, male vocal / instrumental group   **17 wks**

| 19 Jun 71 | **LEAP UP AND DOWN (WAVE YOUR KNICKERS IN THE AIR)** Polydor 2058 104 .... | **12** | 17 wks |

SAINT ETIENNE
UK, male / female vocal / instrumental group   **34 wks**

18 May 91	**NOTHING CAN STOP US / SPEEDWELL** Heavenly HVN 009	**54**	3 wks
7 Sep 91	**ONLY LOVE CAN BREAK YOUR HEART / FILTHY** Heavenly HVN 12	**39**	4 wks
16 May 92	**JOIN OUR CLUB / PEOPLE GET REAL** Heavenly HVN 15	**21**	3 wks
17 Oct 92	**AVENUE** Heavenly HVN 2312	**40**	2 wks
13 Feb 93	**YOU'RE IN A BAD WAY** Heavenly HVN 25CD	**12**	5 wks
22 May 93	**HOBART PAVING / WHO DO YOU THINK YOU ARE** Heavenly HVN 29CD	**23**	5 wks
18 Dec 93	**I WAS BORN ON CHRISTMAS DAY** Heavenly HVN 36CD	**37**	5 wks
19 Feb 94	**PALE MOVIE** Heavenly HVN 37CD	**28**	3 wks
28 May 94	**LIKE A MOTORWAY** Heavenly HVN 40CD	**47**	2 wks
1 Oct 94	**HUG MY SOUL** Heavenly HVN 42CD	**32**	2 wks

See also Various Artists (EPs & LPs) - The Fred EP.

Barry ST. JOHN UK, female vocalist   **1 wk**

| 9 Dec 65 | **COME AWAY MELINDA** Columbia DB 7783 .... | **47** | 1 wk |

ST. JOHN'S COLLEGE SCHOOL CHOIR and the Band of the GRENADIER GUARDS
UK, school choir and military band   **3 wks**

| 3 May 86 | **THE QUEEN'S BIRTHDAY SONG** Columbia Q1 .... | **40** | 3 wks |

ST. LOUIS UNION UK, male vocal / instrumental group   **10 wks**

| 13 Jan 66 | **GIRL** Decca F 12318 .... | **11** | 10 wks |

Crispian ST. PETERS UK, male vocalist   **31 wks**

6 Jan 66	● **YOU WERE ON MY MIND** Decca F 12287	**2**	14 wks
31 Mar 66	● **PIED PIPER** Decca F 12359	**5**	13 wks
15 Sep 66	**CHANGES** Decca F 12480	**49**	1 wk
29 Sep 66	**CHANGES (re-entry)** Decca F 12480	**47**	3 wks

ST. PHILIPS CHOIR UK, choir   **4 wks**

| 12 Dec 87 | **SING FOR EVER** BBC RESL 222 .... | **49** | 4 wks |

ST. THOMAS MORE SCHOOL CHOIR - See Scott FITZGERALD

ST. WINIFRED'S SCHOOL CHOIR
UK, school choir   **11 wks**

| 22 Nov 80 | ★ **THERE'S NO ONE QUITE LIKE GRANDMA** MFP FP 900 .... | **1** | 11 wks |

Buffy SAINTE-MARIE Canada, female vocalist   **29 wks**

17 Jul 71	● **SOLDIER BLUE** RCA 2081	**7**	18 wks
18 Mar 72	**I'M GONNA BE A COUNTRY GIRL AGAIN** Vanguard VRS 35143	**34**	5 wks
8 Feb 92	**THE BIG ONES GET AWAY** Ensign ENY 650	**39**	5 wks
4 Jul 92	**FALLEN ANGELS** Ensign ENY 655	**57**	1 wk

SAINTS Australia, male vocal / instrumental group   **4 wks**

| 16 Jul 77 | **THIS PERFECT DAY** Harvest HAR 5130 .... | **34** | 4 wks |

Kyu SAKAMOTO Japan, male vocalist   **13 wks**

| 27 Jun 63 | ● **SUKIYAKI** HMV POP 1171 .... | **6** | 13 wks |

Riuichi SAKAMOTO - See David SYLVIAN

SAKKARIN - See Jonathan KING

SALFORD JETS UK, male vocal / instrumental group   **2 wks**

| 31 May 80 | **WHO YOU LOOKING AT** RCA PB 5239 .... | **72** | 2 wks |

SALSOUL ORCHESTRA - See CHARO and the SALSOUL ORCHESTRA

SALT-N-PEPA US, female rap duo   **110 wks**

26 Mar 88	**PUSH IT / I AM DOWN** ffrr FFR 2	**41**	6 wks
25 Jun 88	● **PUSH IT / TRAMP** Champion CHAMP 51 & ffrr FFR 2 ..	**2**	13 wks
3 Sep 88	**SHAKE YOUR THANG (IT'S YOUR THING)** ffrr FFR 11 [1]	**22**	8 wks
12 Nov 88	● **TWIST AND SHOUT** ffrr FFR 16	**4**	9 wks
14 Apr 90	**EXPRESSION** ffrr F 127	**40**	6 wks
25 May 91	● **DO YOU WANT ME** ffrr F 151	**5**	12 wks
31 Aug 91	● **LET'S TALK ABOUT SEX** ffrr F 162 [2]	**2**	13 wks

30 Nov 91	YOU SHOWED ME *ffrr F 174*	...............................**15**	9 wks
28 Mar 92	EXPRESSION (re-issue) *ffrr F 182*	.................**23**	6 wks
3 Oct 92	START ME UP *ffrr F 196*	...........................**39**	3 wks
9 Oct 93	SHOOP *ffrr FCD 219*	...............................**29**	3 wks
19 Mar 94	● WHATTA MAN *ffrr FCD 222* [3]	......................**7**	10 wks
28 May 94	SHOOP (re-mix) *ffrr FCD 234*	....................**13**	8 wks
12 Nov 94	NONE OF YOUR BUSINESS *ffrr FCD 244*	.......**19**	4 wks

[1] Salt-N-Pepa featuring E.U. [2] Salt-N-Pepa featuring Psychotropic [3] Salt-N-Pepa with En Vogue

I Am Down only listed from 2 April 88. The disc re-entered on 25 June when it was made available on Champion with a different flip side. Sales for both discs were amalgamated.

SAM and DAVE US, male vocal duo   39 wks

16 Mar 67	SOOTHE ME *Stax 601 004*	........................**48**	2 wks
13 Apr 67	SOOTHE ME (re-entry) *Stax 601 004*	.........**35**	6 wks
1 Nov 67	SOUL MAN *Stax 601 023*	...........................**24**	14 wks
13 Mar 68	I THANK YOU *Stax 601 030*	.....................**34**	9 wks
29 Jan 69	SOUL SISTER BROWN SUGAR *Atlantic 584 237*	......**15**	8 wks

See also Lou Reed.

SAM THE SHAM and the PHARAOHS
US, male vocal / instrumental group   **18 wks**

24 Jun 65	WOOLY BULLY *MGM 1269*	....................**11**	15 wks
4 Aug 66	LIL' RED RIDING HOOD *MGM 1315*	.................**48**	1 wk
18 Aug 66	LIL' RED RIDING HOOD (re-entry) *MGM 1315*	........**46**	2 wks

Richie SAMBORA
US, male vocalist / instrumentalist - bass   **1 wk**

| 7 Sep 91 | BALLAD OF YOUTH *Mercury MER 350* | ....**59** | 1 wk |

Mike SAMMES SINGERS
UK, male / female vocal group   **38 wks**

| 15 Sep 66 | SOMEWHERE MY LOVE *HMV POP 1546* | ....**22** | 19 wks |
| 12 Jul 67 | SOMEWHERE MY LOVE (re-entry) *HMV POP 1546* | ..**14** | 19 wks |

Dave SAMPSON UK, male vocalist   6 wks

| 19 May 60 | SWEET DREAMS *Columbia DB 4449* | ....**48** | 1 wk |
| 2 Jun 60 | SWEET DREAMS (re-entry) *Columbia DB 4449* | ....**29** | 5 wks |

SAMSON UK, male vocal / instrumental group   6 wks

4 Jul 81	RIDING WITH THE ANGELS *RCA 67*	...............**55**	3 wks
24 Jul 82	LOSING MY GRIP *Polydor POSP 471*	...................**63**	2 wks
5 Mar 83	RED SKIES *Polydor POSP 554*	...............................**65**	1 wk

SAN JOSÉ featuring Rodriguez ARGENTINA *UK, male instrumental group*   **8 wks**

| 17 Jun 78 | ARGENTINE MELODY (CANCION DE ARGENTINA) *MCA 369* | ....**14** | 8 wks |

Rodriguez Argentina is Rod Argent. See also Argent; Silsoe.

SAN REMO STRINGS US, orchestra   8 wks

| 18 Dec 71 | FESTIVAL TIME *Tamla Motown TMG 795* | ....**39** | 8 wks |

Chris SANDFORD UK, male vocalist   9 wks

| 12 Dec 63 | NOT TOO LITTLE NOT TOO MUCH *Decca F 11778* | ....**17** | 9 wks |

SANDPIPERS US, male vocal group   33 wks

| 15 Sep 66 | ● GUANTANAMERA *Pye International 7N 25380* | ....**7** | 17 wks |

5 Jun 68	QUANDO M'INNAMORO (A MAN WITHOUT LOVE) *A & M AMS 723*	...........................**33**	6 wks
26 Mar 69	KUMBAYA *A & M AMS 744*	.................................**39**	1 wk
9 Apr 69	KUMBAYA (re-entry) *A & M AMS 744*	...............**49**	1 wk
27 Nov 76	HANG ON SLOOPY *Satril SAT 114*	.....................**32**	8 wks

SANDRA Germany, female vocalist   8 wks

| 17 Dec 88 | EVERLASTING LOVE *Siren SRN 85* | ....**45** | 8 wks |

Jodie SANDS US, female vocalist   10 wks

| 17 Oct 58 | SOMEDAY *HMV POP 533* | ....**14** | 10 wks |

Tommy SANDS US, male vocalist   7 wks

| 4 Aug 60 | OLD OAKEN BUCKET *Capitol CL 15143* | ....**25** | 7 wks |

Samantha SANG Australia, female vocalist   13 wks

| 4 Feb 78 | EMOTION *Private Stock PVT 128* | ....**11** | 13 wks |

SANTA CLAUS and the CHRISTMAS TREES
UK, male vocal / instrumental group   **10 wks**

| 11 Dec 82 | SINGALONG-A-SANTA *Polydor IVY 1* | ....**19** | 5 wks |
| 10 Dec 83 | SINGALONG-A-SANTA AGAIN *Polydor IVY 2* | ....**39** | 5 wks |

SANTA ESMERALDA and Leroy GOMEZ
US / France, male / female vocal / instrumental group   **5 wks**

| 12 Nov 77 | DON'T LET ME BE MISUNDERSTOOD *Philips 6042 325* | ....**41** | 5 wks |

SANTANA US, male vocal / instrumental group   25 wks

28 Sep 74	SAMBA PA TI *CBS 2561*	...............................**27**	7 wks
15 Oct 77	SHE'S NOT THERE *CBS 5671*	...........................**11**	12 wks
25 Nov 78	WELL ALL RIGHT *CBS 6755*	...........................**53**	3 wks
22 Mar 80	ALL I EVER WANTED *CBS 8160*	......................**57**	3 wks

SANTO and JOHNNY
US, male instrumental duo - steel and electric guitars   **5 wks**

| 16 Oct 59 | SLEEP WALK *Pye International 7N 25037* | ....**22** | 4 wks |
| 31 Mar 60 | TEARDROP *Parlophone R 4619* | ....**50** | 1 wk |

Mike SARNE UK, male vocalist   43 wks

10 May 62	★ COME OUTSIDE *Parlophone R 4902* [1]	.................**1**	19 wks
30 Aug 62	WILL I WHAT *Parlophone R 4932* [2]	.................**18**	10 wks
10 Jan 63	JUST FOR KICKS *Parlophone R 4974*	.................**22**	7 wks
28 Mar 63	CODE OF LOVE *Parlophone R 5010*	.........................**29**	7 wks

[1] Mike Sarne with Wendy Richard [2] Mike Sarne with Billie Davis

Joy SARNEY UK, female vocalist   6 wks

| 7 May 77 | NAUGHTY NAUGHTY NAUGHTY *Alaska ALA 2005* | ..**26** | 6 wks |

SARR BAND
Italy / UK / France, male / female vocal / instrumental group   **1 wk**

| 16 Sep 78 | MAGIC MANDRAKE *Calendar Day 111* | ....**68** | 1 wk |

Peter SARSTEDT UK, male vocalist   25 wks

| 5 Feb 69 | ★ WHERE DO YOU GO TO MY LOVELY *United Artists UP 2262* | ....**1** | 16 wks |
| 4 Jun 69 | ● FROZEN ORANGE JUICE *United Artists UP 35021* | ....**10** | 9 wks |

Robin SARSTEDT UK, male vocalist — **9 wks**

8 May 76	● **MY RESISTANCE IS LOW** Decca F 13624	3	9 wks

SASHA UK, male producer — **8 wks**

31 Jul 93	**TOGETHER** ffrr FCD 212 [1]	57	1 wk
19 Feb 94	**HIGHER GROUND** Deconstruction 74321189002 [2]	19	3 wks
27 Aug 94	**MAGIC** Deconstruction 74321221862 [2]	32	4 wks

[1] Danny Campbell and Sasha [2] Sasha with Sam Mollison

Joe SATRIANI US, male / vocalist / instrumentalist - guitar — **1 wk**

13 Feb 93	**THE SATCH EP** Relativity 6589532	53	1 wk

Tracks on The Satch EP: The Extremist / Banana Mango / Summer Song / Crazy.

SATURDAY NIGHT BAND
US, male vocal / instrumental group — **9 wks**

1 Jul 78	**COME ON DANCE DANCE** CBS 6367	16	9 wks

Kevin SAUNDERSON - See INNER CITY

Edna SAVAGE UK, female vocalist — **1 wk**

13 Jan 56	**ARRIVEDERCI DARLING** Parlophone R 4097	19	1 wk

Telly SAVALAS US, male vocalist — **12 wks**

22 Feb 75	★ **IF** MCA 174	1	9 wks
31 May 75	**YOU'VE LOST THAT LOVIN' FEELING** MCA 189	47	3 wks

SAVANNA US, male vocalist / instrumentalist - guitar — **4 wks**

10 Oct 81	**I CAN'T TURN AWAY** R & B RBS 203	61	4 wks

SAVUKA - See Johnny CLEGG and SAVUKA

SAW DOCTORS Ireland, male vocal / instrumental group — **3 wks**

12 Nov 94	**SMALL BIT OF LOVE** Shamtown SAW 001CD	24	3 wks

SAXON UK, male vocal / instrumental group — **61 wks**

22 Mar 80	**WHEELS OF STEEL** Carrere CAR 143	20	11 wks
21 Jun 80	**747 (STRANGERS IN THE NIGHT)** Carrere CAR 151	13	9 wks
28 Jun 80	**BACKS TO THE WALL** Carrere HM 6	64	2 wks
28 Jun 80	**BIG TEASER / RAINBOW THEME** Carrere HM 5	66	2 wks
29 Nov 80	**STRONG ARM OF THE LAW** Carrere CAR 170	63	3 wks
11 Apr 81	**AND THE BANDS PLAYED ON** Carrere CAR 180	12	8 wks
18 Jul 81	**NEVER SURRENDER** Carrere CAR 204	18	6 wks
31 Oct 81	**PRINCESS OF THE NIGHT** Carrere CAR 208	57	3 wks
23 Apr 83	**POWER AND THE GLORY** Carrere SAXON 1	32	5 wks
30 Jul 83	**NIGHTMARE** Carrere CAR 284	50	3 wks
31 Aug 85	**BACK ON THE STREETS** Parlophone R 6103	75	1 wk
29 Mar 86	**ROCK 'N' ROLL GYPSY** Parlophone R 6112	71	1 wk
30 Aug 86	**WAITING FOR THE NIGHT** EMI EMI 5575	66	2 wks
5 Mar 88	**RIDE LIKE THE WIND** EMI EM 43	52	4 wks
30 Apr 88	**I CAN'T WAIT ANYMORE** EMI EM 54	71	1 wk

Al SAXON UK, male vocalist — **10 wks**

16 Jan 59	**YOU'RE THE TOP CHA** Fontana H 164	17	4 wks
28 Aug 59	**ONLY SIXTEEN** Fontana H 205	24	3 wks
22 Dec 60	**BLUE-EYED BOY** Fontana H 278	39	2 wks
7 Sep 61	**THERE I'VE SAID IT AGAIN** Piccadilly 7N 35011	48	1 wk

Leo SAYER UK, male vocalist — **148 wks**

15 Dec 73	● **THE SHOW MUST GO ON** Chrysalis CHS 2023	2	13 wks
15 Jun 74	● **ONE MAN BAND** Chrysalis CHS 2045	6	9 wks
14 Sep 74	● **LONG TALL GLASSES** Chrysalis CHS 2052	4	9 wks
30 Aug 75	● **MOONLIGHTING** Chrysalis CHS 2076	2	8 wks
30 Oct 76	● **YOU MAKE ME FEEL LIKE DANCING** Chrysalis CHS 2119	2	12 wks
29 Jan 77	★ **WHEN I NEED YOU** Chrysalis CHS 2127	1	13 wks
9 Apr 77	● **HOW MUCH LOVE** Chrysalis CHS 2140	10	8 wks
10 Sep 77	**THUNDER IN MY HEART** Chrysalis CHS 2163	22	8 wks
16 Sep 78	● **I CAN'T STOP LOVIN' YOU (THOUGH I TRY)** Chrysalis CHS 2240	6	11 wks
25 Nov 78	**RAINING IN MY HEART** Chrysalis CHS 2277	21	10 wks
5 Jul 80	● **MORE THAN I CAN SAY** Chrysalis CHS 2442	2	11 wks
13 Mar 82	● **HAVE YOU EVER BEEN IN LOVE** Chrysalis CHS 2596	10	9 wks
19 Jun 82	**HEART (STOP BEATING IN TIME)** Chrysalis CHS 2616	22	10 wks
12 Mar 83	**ORCHARD ROAD** Chrysalis CHS 2677	16	8 wks
15 Oct 83	**TILL YOU COME BACK TO ME** Chrysalis LEO 01	51	3 wks
8 Feb 86	**UNCHAINED MELODY** Chrysalis LEO 3	54	4 wks
13 Feb 93	**WHEN I NEED YOU (re-issue)** Chrysalis CDCHS 3926	65	2 wks

Alexei SAYLE UK, male vocalist — **8 wks**

25 Feb 84	**'ULLO JOHN GOT A NEW MOTOR?** Island IS 162	15	8 wks

SCAFFOLD UK, male vocal group — **62 wks**

22 Nov 67	● **THANK U VERY MUCH** Parlophone R 5643	4	12 wks
27 Mar 68	**DO YOU REMEMBER** Parlophone R 5679	34	5 wks
6 Nov 68	★ **LILY THE PINK** Parlophone R 5734	1	24 wks
1 Nov 69	**GIN GAN GOOLIE** Parlophone R 5812	38	11 wks
24 Jan 70	**GIN GAN GOOLIE (re-entry)** Parlophone R 5812	50	1 wk
1 Jun 74	● **LIVERPOOL LOU** Warner Bros. K 16400	7	9 wks

Boz SCAGGS US, male vocalist — **31 wks**

30 Oct 76	**LOWDOWN** CBS 4563	28	4 wks
22 Jan 77	● **WHAT CAN I SAY** CBS 4869	10	10 wks
14 May 77	**LIDO SHUFFLE** CBS 5136	13	9 wks
10 Dec 77	**HOLLYWOOD** CBS 5836	33	8 wks

SCARLET FANTASTIC
UK, male / female vocal / instrumental group — **12 wks**

3 Oct 87	**NO MEMORY** Arista RIS 36	24	10 wks
23 Jan 88	**PLUG ME IN (TO THE CENTRAL LOVE LINE)** Arista 109693	67	2 wks

SCARLET PARTY UK, male vocal / instrumental group — **5 wks**

16 Oct 82	**101 DAM-NATIONS** Parlophone R 6058	44	5 wks

Michael SCHENKER GROUP
Germany / UK, male vocal / instrumental group — **9 wks**

13 Sep 80	**ARMED AND READY** Chrysalis CHS 2455	53	3 wks
8 Nov 80	**CRY FOR THE NATIONS** Chrysalis CHS 2471	56	3 wks
11 Sep 82	**DANCER** Chrysalis CHS 2636	52	3 wks

Lalo SCHIFRIN US, orchestra — **9 wks**

9 Oct 76	**JAWS** CTI CTSP 005	14	9 wks

Peter SCHILLING Germany, male vocalist — **6 wks**

5 May 84	**MAJOR TOM (COMING HOME)** PSP/WEA X 9438	42	5 wks
16 Jun 84	**MAJOR TOM (COMING HOME) (re-entry)** PSP/WEA X 9438	73	1 wk

SCIENTIST UK, male instrumentalist — 13 wks

6 Oct 90	THE EXORCIST Kickin KICK 1	62	3 wks
1 Dec 90	THE EXORCIST (re-mix) Kickin KICK 1TR	46	3 wks
15 Dec 90	THE BEE Kickin KICK 3S	52	3 wks
26 Jan 91	THE BEE (re-entry) Kickin KICK 3S	47	3 wks
11 May 91	SPIRAL SYMPHONY Kickin KICK 5	74	1 wk

Phillip SCOFIELD UK, male vocalist — 6 wks

5 Dec 92	CLOSE EVERY DOOR Really Useful RUR 11	27	6 wks

SCORPIONS Germany, male vocal/instrumental group — 35 wks

26 May 79	IS THERE ANYBODY THERE / ANOTHER PIECE OF MEAT Harvest HAR 5185	39	4 wks
25 Aug 79	LOVEDRIVE Harvest HAR 5188	69	2 wks
31 May 80	MAKE IT REAL Harvest HAR 5206	72	2 wks
20 Sep 80	THE ZOO Harvest HAR 5212	75	1 wk
3 Apr 82	NO ONE LIKE YOU Harvest HAR 5219	65	3 wks
1 May 82	NO ONE LIKE YOU (re-entry) Harvest HAR 5219	64	1 wk
17 Jul 82	CAN'T LIVE WITHOUT YOU Harvest HAR 5221	63	2 wks
4 Jun 88	RHYTHM OF LOVE Harvest HAR 5240	59	2 wks
18 Feb 89	PASSION RULES THE GAME Harvest 5242	74	1 wk
1 Jun 91	WIND OF CHANGE Vertigo VER 54	53	3 wks
28 Sep 91	● WIND OF CHANGE (re-issue) Vertigo VER 58	2	9 wks
30 Nov 91	SEND ME AN ANGEL Vertigo VER 60	27	3 wks
28 Dec 91	SEND ME AN ANGEL (re-entry) Vertigo VER 60	68	2 wks

SCOTLAND WORLD CUP SQUAD
UK, male football team vocalists — 22 wks

22 Jun 74	EASY EASY Polydor 2058 452	20	4 wks
27 May 78	● OLE OLA (MULHER BRASILEIRA) Riva 15 [1]	4	6 wks
1 May 82	● WE HAVE A DREAM WEA K 19145	5	9 wks
9 Jun 90	SAY IT WITH PRIDE RCA PB 43791	45	3 wks

[1] Rod Stewart featuring the Scottish World Cup Football Squad

Jack SCOTT Canada, male vocalist — 28 wks

10 Oct 58	● MY TRUE LOVE London HLU 8626	9	10 wks
25 Sep 59	THE WAY I WALK London HLL 8912	30	1 wk
10 Mar 60	WHAT IN THE WORLD'S COME OVER YOU Top Rank JAR 280	11	15 wks
2 Jun 60	BURNING BRIDGES Top Rank JAR 375	32	2 wks

Linda SCOTT US, female vocalist — 14 wks

18 May 61	● I'VE TOLD EVERY LITTLE STAR Columbia DB 4638	7	13 wks
14 Sep 61	DON'T BET MONEY HONEY Columbia DB 4692	50	1 wk

Millie SCOTT US, female vocalist — 11 wks

12 Apr 86	PRISONER OF LOVE Fourth & Broadway BRW 45	52	4 wks
23 Aug 86	AUTOMATIC Fourth & Broadway BRW 51	56	3 wks
21 Feb 87	EV'RY LITTLE BIT Fourth & Broadway BRW 58	63	4 wks

Simon SCOTT UK, male vocalist — 8 wks

13 Aug 64	MOVE IT BABY Parlophone R 5164	37	8 wks

Tony SCOTT US, male vocalist — 6 wks

15 Apr 89	THAT'S HOW I'M LIVING / THE CHIEF Champion CHAMP 97	48	4 wks
10 Feb 90	GET INTO IT / THAT'S HOW I'M LIVING (re-issue) Champion CHAMP 232	63	2 wks

The Chief was only listed from 22 Apr 89.

SCOTTISH RUGBY TEAM with Ronnie BROWNE UK, male rugby team vocalists — 1 wk

2 Jun 90	FLOWER OF SCOTLAND Greentrax STRAX 1001	73	1 wk

SCREAMING BLUE MESSIAHS
UK, male vocal/instrumental group — 6 wks

16 Jan 88	I WANNA BE A FLINTSTONE WEA YZ 166	28	6 wks

SCREAMING TREES
US, male vocal/instrumental group — 2 wks

6 Mar 93	NEARLY LOST YOU Epic 6582372	50	1 wk
1 May 93	DOLLAR BILL Epic 6591792	52	1 wk

SCRITTI POLITTI UK, male vocal/instrumental group — 77 wks

21 Nov 81	THE SWEETEST GIRL Rough Trade RT 091	64	3 wks
22 May 82	FAITHLESS Rough Trade RT 101	56	4 wks
7 Aug 82	ASYLUMS IN JERUSALEM / JACQUES DERRIDA Rough Trade RT 111	43	5 wks
10 Mar 84	● WOOD BEEZ (PRAY LIKE ARETHA FRANKLIN) Virgin VS 657	10	12 wks
9 Jun 84	ABSOLUTE Virgin VS 680	17	9 wks
17 Nov 84	HYPNOTIZE Virgin VS 725	68	2 wks
11 May 85	● THE WORD GIRL Virgin VS 747 [1]	6	12 wks
7 Sep 85	PERFECT WAY Virgin VS 780	48	5 wks
7 May 88	OH PATTI (DON'T FEEL SORRY FOR LOVERBOY) Virgin VS 1006	13	9 wks
27 Aug 88	FIRST BOY IN THIS TOWN (LOVE SICK) Virgin VS 1082	63	3 wks
12 Nov 88	BOOM! THERE SHE WAS Virgin VS 1143 [2]	55	3 wks
16 Mar 91	SHE'S A WOMAN Virgin VS 1333 [3]	20	7 wks
3 Aug 91	TAKE ME IN YOUR ARMS AND LOVE ME Virgin VS 1346	47	3 wks

[1] Scritti Politti featuring Ranking Ann [2] Scritti Politti featuring Roger [3] Scritti Politti featuring Shabba Ranks

Sweetie Irie is credited on the sleeve of Take Me In Your Arms And Love Me.

Earl SCRUGGS - See Lester FLATT and Earl SCRUGGS

SEA LEVEL US, male instrumental group — 4 wks

17 Feb 79	FIFTY-FOUR Capricorn POSP 28	63	4 wks

SEAL UK, male vocalist — 49 wks

8 Dec 90	● CRAZY ZTT ZANG 8	2	15 wks
4 May 91	FUTURE LOVE EP ZTT ZANG 11	12	6 wks
20 Jul 91	THE BEGINNING ZTT ZANG 21	24	6 wks
16 Nov 91	● KILLER (EP) ZTT ZANG 23	8	8 wks
29 Feb 92	VIOLET ZTT ZANG 27	39	2 wks
21 May 94	PRAYER FOR THE DYING ZTT ZANG 51CD	14	5 wks
30 Jul 94	KISS FROM A ROSE ZTT ZANG 52CD1	20	5 wks
5 Nov 94	NEWBORN FRIEND ZTT ZANG 58CD	45	2 wks

Tracks on Future Love EP: Future Love Paradise / A Minor Groove / Violet.
Tracks on Killer (EP): Killer / Hey Joe / Come See What Love Has Done. See also Adamski.

SEARCHERS UK, male vocal/instrumental group — 128 wks

27 Jun 63	★ SWEETS FOR MY SWEET Pye 7N 15533	1	16 wks
10 Oct 63	SWEET NOTHINS Philips BF 1274	48	2 wks
24 Oct 63	● SUGAR AND SPICE Pye 7N 15566	2	13 wks
16 Jan 64	★ NEEDLES AND PINS Pye 7N 15594	1	15 wks
16 Apr 64	★ DON'T THROW YOUR LOVE AWAY Pye 7N 15630	1	11 wks

16 Jul 64	SOMEDAY WE'RE GONNA LOVE AGAIN		
	Pye 7N 15670	11	8 wks
17 Sep 64 ●	WHEN YOU WALK IN THE ROOM Pye 7N 15694	3	12 wks
3 Dec 64	WHAT HAVE THEY DONE TO THE RAIN		
	Pye 7N 15739	13	11 wks
4 Mar 65 ●	GOODBYE MY LOVE Pye 7N 15794	4	11 wks
8 Jul 65	HE'S GOT NO LOVE Pye 7N 15878	12	10 wks
14 Oct 65	WHEN I GET HOME Pye 7N 15950	35	3 wks
16 Dec 65	TAKE ME FOR WHAT I'M WORTH Pye 7N 15992	20	8 wks
21 Apr 66	TAKE IT OR LEAVE IT Pye 7N 17094	31	6 wks
13 Oct 66	HAVE YOU EVER LOVED SOMEBODY		
	Pye 7N 17170	48	2 wks

SEASHELLS UK, female vocal group — 5 wks

| 9 Sep 72 | MAYBE I KNOW CBS 8218 | 32 | 5 wks |

Jon SECADA US, male vocalist — 35 wks

18 Jul 92 ●	JUST ANOTHER DAY SBK SBK 35	5	15 wks
31 Oct 92	DO YOU BELIEVE IN US SBK SBK 37	30	4 wks
6 Feb 93	ANGEL SBK CDSBK 39	23	5 wks
17 Jul 93	DO YOU REALLY WANT ME SBK CDSBK 41	30	4 wks
16 Oct 93	I'M FREE SBK CDSBK 44	50	2 wks
14 May 94	IF YOU GO SBK CDSBK 51	39	4 wks
2 Jul 94	IF YOU GO (re-entry) SBK CDSBK 51	71	1 wk

SECCHI featuring Orlando JOHNSON
Italy/US, male vocal/instrumental duo — 3 wks

| 4 May 91 | I SAY YEAH Epic 6568467 | 46 | 3 wks |

Harry SECOMBE UK, male vocalist — 35 wks

9 Dec 55	ON WITH THE MOTLEY Philips PB 523	16	3 wks
3 Oct 63	IF I RULED THE WORLD Philips BF 1261	44	2 wks
21 Nov 63	IF I RULED THE WORLD (re-entry) Philips BF 1261	18	15 wks
23 Feb 67 ●	THIS IS MY SONG Philips BF 1539	2	15 wks

SECOND CITY SOUND UK, male instrumental group — 8 wks

| 20 Jan 66 | TCHAIKOVSKY ONE Decca F 12310 | 22 | 7 wks |
| 2 Apr 69 | DREAM OF OLWEN Major Minor MM 600 | 43 | 1 wk |

SECOND IMAGE UK, male vocal/instrumental group — 11 wks

24 Jul 82	STAR Polydor POSP 457	60	2 wks
2 Apr 83	BETTER TAKE TIME Polydor POSP 565	67	2 wks
26 Nov 83	DON'T YOU MCA 848	68	2 wks
11 Aug 84	SING AND SHOUT MCA MCA 882	53	3 wks
2 Feb 85	STARTING AGAIN MCA 936	65	2 wks

SECOND PHASE US, male producer - Joey Beltram — 2 wks

| 21 Sep 91 | MENTASM R & S RSUK 2 | 48 | 2 wks |

SECRET AFFAIR UK, male vocal/instrumental group — 34 wks

1 Sep 79	TIME FOR ACTION I-Spy SEE 1	13	10 wks
10 Nov 79	LET YOUR HEART DANCE I-Spy SEE 3	32	6 wks
8 Mar 80	MY WORLD I-Spy SEE 5	16	9 wks
23 Aug 80	SOUND OF CONFUSION I-Spy SEE 8	45	5 wks
17 Oct 81	DO YOU KNOW I-Spy SEE 10	57	4 wks

SECRET LIFE UK, male vocal group — 8 wks

12 Dec 92	AS ALWAYS Cowboy 7RODEO 9	45	4 wks
7 Aug 93	LOVE SO STRONG Cowboy RODEO 18CD	38	2 wks
7 May 94	SHE HOLDS THE KEY Pulse 8 CDLOSE 58	63	1 wk
29 Oct 94	I WANT YOU Pulse 8 CDLOSE 71	70	1 wk

SECRETARY OF ENTERTAINMENT - See RAZE

Neil SEDAKA US, male vocalist — 190 wks

24 Apr 59 ●	I GO APE RCA 1115	9	13 wks
13 Nov 59 ●	OH CAROL RCA 1152	3	17 wks
14 Apr 60 ●	STAIRWAY TO HEAVEN RCA 1178	8	15 wks
1 Sep 60	YOU MEAN EVERYTHING TO ME RCA 1198	45	3 wks
2 Feb 61 ●	CALENDAR GIRL RCA 1220	8	14 wks
18 May 61 ●	LITTLE DEVIL RCA 1236	9	12 wks
21 Dec 61 ●	HAPPY BIRTHDAY SWEET SIXTEEN RCA 1266	3	18 wks
19 Apr 62	KING OF CLOWNS RCA 1282	23	11 wks
19 Jul 62 ●	BREAKING UP IS HARD TO DO RCA 1298	7	16 wks
22 Nov 62	NEXT DOOR TO AN ANGEL RCA 1319	29	4 wks
30 May 63	LET'S GO STEADY AGAIN RCA 1343	42	1 wk
13 Jun 63	LET'S GO STEADY AGAIN (re-entry) RCA 1343	43	2 wks
7 Oct 72	OH CAROL / BREAKING UP IS HARD TO DO /		
	LITTLE DEVIL (re-issue) RCA Maximillion 2259	19	14 wks
4 Nov 72	BEAUTIFUL YOU RCA 2269	43	3 wks
24 Feb 73	THAT'S WHEN THE MUSIC TAKES ME RCA 2310	18	10 wks
2 Jun 73	STANDING ON THE INSIDE MGM 2006 267	26	9 wks
25 Aug 73	OUR LAST SONG TOGETHER MGM 2006 307	31	8 wks
9 Feb 74	A LITTLE LOVIN' Polydor 2058 434	34	6 wks
22 Jun 74	LAUGHTER IN THE RAIN Polydor 2058 494	15	9 wks
22 Mar 75	THE QUEEN OF 1964 Polydor 2058 546	35	5 wks

SEDUCTION US, female vocal group — 1 wk

| 21 Apr 90 | HEARTBEAT Breakout USA 685 | 75 | 1 wk |

SEEKERS Australia/Sri Lanka, male/female vocal group — 120 wks

7 Jan 65 ★	I'LL NEVER FIND ANOTHER YOU		
	Columbia DB 7431	1	23 wks
15 Apr 65 ●	A WORLD OF OUR OWN Columbia DB 7532	3	18 wks
28 Oct 65 ★	THE CARNIVAL IS OVER Columbia DB 7711	1	17 wks
24 Mar 66	SOMEDAY ONE DAY Columbia DB 7867	11	11 wks
8 Sep 66 ●	WALK WITH ME Columbia DB 8000	10	12 wks
24 Nov 66	MORNINGTOWN RIDE Columbia DB 8060	2	15 wks
23 Feb 67	GEORGY GIRL Columbia DB 8134	3	11 wks
20 Sep 67	WHEN WILL THE GOOD APPLES FALL		
	Columbia DB 8273	11	12 wks
13 Dec 67	EMERALD CITY Columbia DB 8313	50	1 wk

Bob SEGER and the SILVER BULLET BAND
US, male vocal/instrumental group — 21 wks

30 Sep 78	HOLLYWOOD NIGHTS Capitol CL 16004	42	6 wks
3 Feb 79	WE'VE GOT TONITE Capitol CL 16028	41	6 wks
24 Oct 81	HOLLYWOOD NIGHTS Capitol CL 223	49	3 wks
6 Feb 82	WE'VE GOT TONITE Capitol CL 235	60	4 wks
9 Apr 83	EVEN NOW Capitol CL 284	73	2 wks

Capitol CL 223 and CL 235 were live versions of earlier studio hits.

SEIKO and Donnie WAHLBERG
Japan/US, female/male vocal duo — 5 wks

| 18 Aug 90 | THE RIGHT COMBINATION Epic 656203 7 | 44 | 5 wks |

SELECTER UK, male/female vocal/instrumental group — 28 wks

13 Oct 79 ●	ON MY RADIO 2 Tone CHSTT 4	8	9 wks
2 Feb 80	THREE MINUTE HERO 2 Tone CHS TT 8	16	6 wks
29 Mar 80	MISSING WORDS 2 Tone CHS TT 10	23	8 wks
23 Aug 80	THE WHISPER Chrysalis CHSS 1	36	5 wks

See also Various Artists (EPs & LPs) - The Two Tone EP.

Peter SELLERS UK, male vocalist — 39 wks

2 Aug 57	ANY OLD IRON Parlophone R 4337	21	3 wks
6 Sep 57	ANY OLD IRON (re-entry) Parlophone R 4337	17	8 wks
10 Nov 60 ●	GOODNESS GRACIOUS ME Parlophone R 4702 [1]	4	14 wks
12 Jan 61	BANGERS AND MASH Parlophone R 4724 [1]	22	5 wks
23 Dec 65	A HARD DAY'S NIGHT Parlophone R 5393	14	7 wks

| 27 Nov 93 | **A HARD DAY'S NIGHT** (re-issue) *EMI CDEMS 293* ..**52** | 2 wks |

[1] Peter Sellers and Sophia Loren

Michael SEMBELLO *US, male vocalist*   **6 wks**

| 20 Aug 83 | **MANIAC** *Casablanca CAN 1017* ....**43** | 6 wks |

SEMPRINI *UK, orchestra*   **8 wks**

| 16 Mar 61 | **THEME FROM 'EXODUS'** *HMV POP 842* ....**25** | 8 wks |

SENSELESS THINGS
UK, male vocal / instrumental group   **18 wks**

22 Jun 91	**EVERYBODY'S GONE** *Epic 6569807* **73**	1 wk
28 Sep 91	**GOT IT AT THE DELMAR** *Epic 6574497* **50**	3 wks
11 Jan 92	**EASY TO SMILE** *Epic 6576957* **18**	4 wks
11 Apr 92	**HOLD IT DOWN** *Epic 6579267* **19**	4 wks
5 Dec 92	**HOMOPHOBIC ASSHOLE** *Epic 6588337* **52**	2 wks
13 Feb 93	**PRIMARY INSTINCT** *Epic 6589402* **41**	2 wks
12 Jun 93	**TOO MUCH KISSING** *Epic 6592502* **69**	1 wk
5 Nov 94	**CHRISTINE KEELER** *Epic 6609572* **56**	1 wk

SENSER *UK, male / female vocal / instrumental group*   **4 wks**

25 Sep 93	**THE KEY** *Ultimate TOPP 019CD* **47**	1 wk
19 Mar 94	**SWITCH** *Ultimate TOPP 022CD* **39**	2 wks
23 Jul 94	**AGE OF PANIC** *Ultimate TOPP 027CD* **52**	1 wk

SEPULTURA *Brazil, male vocal / instrumental group*   **6 wks**

2 Oct 93	**TERRITORY** *Roadrunner RR 23823* **66**	2 wks
26 Feb 94	**REFUSE-RESIST** *Roadrunner RR 23773* **51**	2 wks
4 Jun 94	**SLAVE NEW WORLD** *Roadrunner RR 23745* **46**	2 wks

SERIOUS INTENTION
US, male vocal / instrumental group   **6 wks**

| 16 Nov 85 | **YOU DON'T KNOW (OH-OH-OH)** *Important TAN 8* ..**75** | 1 wk |
| 5 Apr 86 | **SERIOUS** *Pow Wow LON 93* ....**51** | 5 wks |

SERIOUS ROPE
UK, male / female vocal / instrumental group   **3 wks**

| 22 May 93 | **HAPPINESS** *Rumour RUMACD 64* [1] ....**54** | 2 wks |
| 1 Oct 94 | **HAPPINESS – YOU MAKE ME HAPPY** (re-mix) *Mercury MERCD 407* ....**70** | 1 wk |

[1] Serious Rope presents Sharon Dee Clarke

SET THE TONE *UK, male vocal / instrumental group*   **4 wks**

| 22 Jan 83 | **DANCE SUCKER** *Island WIP 6836*.............**62** | 2 wks |
| 26 Mar 83 | **RAP YOUR LOVE** *Island IS 110* ....**67** | 2 wks |

SETTLERS *UK, male / female vocal / instrumental group*   **5 wks**

| 16 Oct 71 | **THE LIGHTNING TREE** *York SYK 505* ....**36** | 5 wks |

Taja SEVELLE *US, female vocalist*   **13 wks**

| 20 Feb 88 | ● **LOVE IS CONTAGIOUS** *Paisley Park W 8257* ......**7** | 9 wks |
| 14 May 88 | **WOULDN'T YOU LOVE TO LOVE ME** *Paisley Park W 8127* ....**59** | 4 wks |

SEVEN GRAND HOUSING AUTHORITY
UK, male producer - Terence Parker   **1 wk**

| 23 Oct 93 | **THE QUESTION** *Olympic ELYCD 010*..........**70** | 1 wk |

7669 *US, female rap group*   **1 wk**

| 18 Jun 94 | **JOY** *Motown TMGCD 1429* ....**60** | 1 wk |

7TH HEAVEN *UK, male vocal group*   **5 wks**

| 14 Sep 85 | **HOT FUN** *Mercury MER 199* ....**47** | 5 wks |

SEVERINE *France, female vocalist*   **11 wks**

| 24 Apr 71 | ● **UN BANC, UN ARBRE, UNE RUE** *Philips 6009 135* ......**9** | 11 wks |

David SEVILLE *US, male vocalist*   **6 wks**

| 23 May 58 | **WITCH DOCTOR** *London HLU 8619* ....**11** | 6 wks |

See also Chipmunks; Alfi and Harry.

Janette SEWELL - *See DOUBLE TROUBLE*

SEX PISTOLS *UK, male vocal / instrumental group*   **85 wks**

18 Dec 76	**ANARCHY IN THE U.K.** *EMI 2566* **38**	4 wks
4 Jun 77	● **GOD SAVE THE QUEEN** *Virgin VS 181*.........**2**	9 wks
9 Jul 77	● **PRETTY VACANT** *Virgin VS 184* **6**	8 wks
22 Oct 77	● **HOLIDAYS IN THE SUN** *Virgin VS 191* **8**	6 wks
8 Jul 78	● **NO ONE IS INNOCENT/MY WAY** *Virgin VS 220* [1] ..**7**	10 wks
3 Mar 79	● **SOMETHING ELSE / FRIGGIN' IN THE RIGGIN'** *Virgin VS 240* **3**	12 wks
7 Apr 79	● **SILLY THING** *Virgin VS 256* **6**	8 wks
30 Jun 79	● **C'MON EVERYBODY** *Virgin VS 272* **3**	9 wks
13 Oct 79	**THE GREAT ROCK 'N' ROLL SWINDLE** *Virgin VS 290* **21**	6 wks
14 Jun 80	**(I'M NOT YOUR) STEPPING STONE** *Virgin VS 339* ..**21**	8 wks
3 Oct 92	**ANARCHY IN THE UK** (re-issue) *Virgin VS 1431* **33**	3 wks
5 Dec 92	**PRETTY VACANT** (re-issue) *Virgin VS 1448* **56**	2 wks

[1] Sex Pistols, punk prayer by Ronald Biggs

The listed flip side of Silly Thing was Who Killed Bambi by Ten Pole Tudor. The listed flip side of The Great Rock 'n' Roll Swindle was Rock Around The Clock, also by Ten Pole Tudor.

SEX-O-LETTES - *See DISCO TEX and the SEX-O-LETTES*

Denny SEYTON and the SABRES
UK, male vocal / instrumental group   **1 wk**

| 17 Sep 64 | **THE WAY YOU LOOK TONIGHT** *Mercury MF 824* ....**48** | 1 wk |

S.F.X. *UK, male instrumental / production duo*   **3 wks**

| 15 May 93 | **LEMMINGS** *Parlophone CDR 6343*............**51** | 3 wks |

SHADES OF RHYTHM
UK, male instrumental / production group   **24 wks**

2 Feb 91	**HOMICIDE / EXORCIST** *ZTT ZANG 13* **53**	3 wks
13 Apr 91	**SWEET SENSATION** *ZTT ZANG 18* **54**	4 wks
20 Jul 91	**THE SOUND OF EDEN** *ZTT ZANG 22* **35**	5 wks
30 Nov 91	**EXTACY** *ZTT ZANG 24* **16**	7 wks
20 Feb 93	**SWEET REVIVAL (KEEP IT COMIN')** *ZTT ZANG 40CD* **61**	1 wk
11 Sep 93	**SOUND OF EDEN** (re-issue) *ZTT ZANG 44CD*..........**37**	3 wks
5 Nov 94	**THE WANDERING DRAGON** *Public Demand PPDCD 5* **55**	1 wk

SHADOWS *UK, male instrumental / vocal group*   **359 wks**

21 Jul 60	★ **APACHE** *Columbia DB 4484* **1**	21 wks
10 Nov 60	● **MAN OF MYSTERY / THE STRANGER** *Columbia DB 4530* **5**	15 wks
9 Feb 61	● **F. B. I.** *Columbia DB 4580* **6**	19 wks

11 May 61 ● FRIGHTENED CITY Columbia DB 4637	3	20 wks
7 Sep 61 ★ KON-TIKI Columbia DB 4698	1	10 wks
16 Nov 61 ● THE SAVAGE Columbia DB 4726	10	8 wks
23 Nov 61 KON-TIKI (re-entry) Columbia DB 4698	37	2 wks
1 Mar 62 ★ WONDERFUL LAND Columbia DB 4790	1	19 wks
2 Aug 62 ● GUITAR TANGO Columbia DB 4870	4	15 wks
13 Dec 62 ★ DANCE ON! Columbia DB 4948	1	15 wks
7 Mar 63 ★ FOOT TAPPER Columbia DB 4984	1	16 wks
6 Jun 63 ● ATLANTIS Columbia DB 7047	2	17 wks
19 Sep 63 ● SHINDIG Columbia DB 7106	6	12 wks
5 Dec 63 GERONIMO Columbia DB 7163	11	12 wks
5 Mar 64 THEME FOR YOUNG LOVERS Columbia DB 7231	12	10 wks
7 May 64 ● THE RISE AND FALL OF FLINGEL BUNT Columbia DB 7261	5	14 wks
3 Sep 64 RHYTHM AND GREENS Columbia DB 7342	22	7 wks
3 Dec 64 GENIE WITH THE LIGHT BROWN LAMP Columbia DB 7416	17	10 wks
11 Feb 65 MARY ANNE Columbia DB 7476	17	10 wks
10 Jun 65 STINGRAY Columbia DB 7588	19	7 wks
5 Aug 65 ● DON'T MAKE MY BABY BLUE Columbia DB 7650	10	10 wks
25 Nov 65 WAR LORD Columbia DB 7769	18	9 wks
17 Mar 66 I MET A GIRL Columbia DB 7853	22	5 wks
7 Jul 66 A PLACE IN THE SUN Columbia DB 7952	24	6 wks
3 Nov 66 THE DREAMS I DREAM Columbia DB 8034	42	6 wks
13 Apr 67 MAROC 7 Columbia DB 8170	24	8 wks
8 Mar 75 LET ME BE THE ONE EMI 2269	12	9 wks
16 Dec 78 ● DON'T CRY FOR ME ARGENTINA EMI 2890	5	14 wks
28 Apr 79 ● THEME FROM THE DEER HUNTER (CAVATINA) EMI 2939	9	14 wks
26 Jan 80 RIDERS IN THE SKY EMI 5027	12	12 wks
23 Aug 80 EQUINOXE (PART V) Polydor POSP 148	50	3 wks
2 May 81 THE THIRD MAN Polydor POSP 255	44	4 wks

All the above hits were instrumentals except for Mary Anne, Don't Make My Baby Blue, I Met A Girl, The Dream I Dream and Let Me Be The One. See also Cliff Richard.

SHAFT UK, male instrumental / production duo　　9 wks

21 Dec 91 ● ROOBARB AND CUSTARD Ffrreedom TAB 100	7	8 wks
25 Jul 92 MONKEY Ffrreedom TAB 114	61	1 wk

SHAG - See Jonathan KING

SHAGGY Jamaica, male vocalist　　22 wks

6 Feb 93 ★ OH CAROLINA Greensleeves GRECD 361	1	19 wks
10 Jul 93 SOON BE DONE Greensleeves GRECD 380	46	3 wks

SHAI US, male vocal group　　6 wks

19 Dec 92 IF I EVER FALL IN LOVE MCA MCS 1727	36	6 wks

SHAKATAK UK, male / female vocal / instrumental group　　85 wks

8 Nov 80 FEELS LIKE THE RIGHT TIME Polydor POSP 188	41	5 wks
7 Mar 81 LIVING IN THE U.K. Polydor POSP 230	52	4 wks
25 Jul 81 BRAZILIAN DAWN Polydor POSP 282	48	3 wks
21 Nov 81 EASIER SAID THAN DONE Polydor POSP 375	12	17 wks
3 Apr 82 ● NIGHT BIRDS Polydor POSP 407	9	8 wks
19 Jun 82 STREETWALKIN' Polydor POSP 452	38	6 wks
4 Sep 82 INVITATIONS Polydor POSP 502	24	7 wks
6 Nov 82 STRANGER Polydor POSP 530	43	3 wks
4 Jun 83 DARK IS THE NIGHT Polydor POSP 595	15	8 wks
27 Aug 83 IF YOU COULD SEE ME NOW Polydor POSP 635	49	4 wks
7 Jul 84 ● DOWN ON THE STREET Polydor POSP 688	9	11 wks
15 Sep 84 DON'T BLAME IT ON LOVE Polydor POSP 699	55	3 wks
16 Nov 85 DAY BY DAY Polydor POSP 770 [1]	53	3 wks
24 Oct 87 MR. MANIC AND SISTER COOL Polydor MANIC 1	56	3 wks

[1] Shakatak with Al Jarreau

SHAKESPEARS SISTER
UK / US, female vocal / instrumental duo　　**49 wks**

29 Jul 89 ● YOU'RE HISTORY ffrr F 112	7	9 wks
14 Oct 89 RUN SILENT ffrr F 119	54	3 wks
10 Mar 90 DIRTY MIND ffrr F 128	71	1 wk
12 Oct 91 GOODBYE CRUEL WORLD London LON 309	59	2 wks
25 Jan 92 ★ STAY London LON 314	1	16 wks
16 May 92 ● I DON'T CARE London LON 318	7	7 wks
18 Jul 92 GOODBYE CRUEL WORLD (re-issue) London LON 322	32	4 wks
7 Nov 92 HELLO (TURN YOUR RADIO ON) London LON 330	14	6 wks
27 Feb 93 MY 16TH APOLOGY (EP) London LONCD 337	61	1 wk

Tracks on My 16th Apology (EP): My 16th Apology / Catwoman / Dirty Mind / Hot Love.

SHAKY and BONNIE - See Shakin' STEVENS; Bonnie TYLER

SHALAMAR US, male / female vocal group　　134 wks

14 May 77 UPTOWN FESTIVAL Soul Train FB 0885	30	5 wks
9 Dec 78 TAKE THAT TO THE BANK RCA FB 1379	20	12 wks
24 Nov 79 THE SECOND TIME AROUND Solar FB 1709	45	9 wks
9 Feb 80 RIGHT IN THE SOCKET Solar SO2	44	6 wks
30 Aug 80 I OWE YOU ONE Solar SO 11	13	10 wks
28 Mar 81 MAKE THAT MOVE Solar SO 17	30	10 wks
27 Mar 82 ● I CAN MAKE YOU FEEL GOOD Solar K 12599	7	11 wks
12 Jun 82 ● A NIGHT TO REMEMBER Solar K 13162	5	12 wks
4 Sep 82 ● THERE IT IS Solar K 13194	5	10 wks
27 Nov 82 FRIENDS Solar CHUM 1	12	10 wks
11 Jun 83 ● DEAD GIVEAWAY Solar E 9819	8	10 wks
13 Aug 83 DISAPPEARING ACT Solar E 9807	18	8 wks
15 Oct 83 OVER AND OVER Solar E 9792	23	6 wks
24 Mar 84 DANCING IN THE SHEETS CBS A 4171	41	3 wks
31 Mar 84 DEADLINE USA MCA MCA 866	52	3 wks
24 Nov 84 AMNESIA Solar/MCA SHAL 1	61	2 wks
2 Feb 85 MY GIRL LOVES ME MCA SHAL 2	45	3 wks
26 Apr 86 A NIGHT TO REMEMBER (re-mix) MCA SHAL 3	52	4 wks

SHAM 69 UK, male vocal / instrumental group　　53 wks

13 May 78 ANGELS WITH DIRTY FACES Polydor 2059 023	19	10 wks
29 Jul 78 IF THE KIDS ARE UNITED Polydor 2059 050	9	9 wks
14 Oct 78 ● HURRY UP HARRY Polydor POSP 7	10	8 wks
24 Mar 79 QUESTIONS AND ANSWERS Polydor POSP 27	18	9 wks
4 Aug 79 ● HERSHAM BOYS Polydor POSP 64	6	9 wks
27 Oct 79 YOU'RE A BETTER MAN THAN I Polydor POSP 82	49	5 wks
12 Apr 80 TELL THE CHILDREN Polydor POSP 136	45	3 wks

SHAMEN UK, male / female vocal / instrumental group　　66 wks

7 Apr 90 PRO-GEN One Little Indian 36 TP7	55	4 wks
22 Sep 90 MAKE IT MINE One Little Indian 46 TP7	42	5 wks
6 Apr 91 HYPERREAL One Little Indian 48 TP7	29	5 wks
27 Jul 91 ● MOVE ANY MOUNTAIN (re-mix) One Little Indian 52 TP7	4	10 wks
18 Jul 92 ● LSI One Little Indian 68 TP7	6	8 wks
5 Sep 92 ★ EBENEEZER GOODE One Little Indian 78 TP7	1	10 wks
7 Nov 92 ● BOSS DRUM One Little Indian 88 TP7	4	7 wks
7 Nov 92 BOSS DRUM (re-mix) One Little Indian 88 TP12	58	1 wk
19 Dec 92 ● PHOREVER PEOPLE One Little Indian 98 TP7	5	10 wks
6 Mar 93 RE: EVOLUTION One Little Indian 118 TP7CD [1]	18	2 wks
6 Nov 93 THE SOS EP One Little Indian 108 TP7CD	14	4 wks

[1] Shamen with Terence McKenna

Move Any Mountain is a re-mix of Pro-Gen. Tracks on SOS EP: Comin' On / Make It Mine / Possible Worlds. Make It Mine on the EP is a re-mix of their second hit. Group were male only duo for first four hits.

SHAMPOO UK, female vocal duo — **16 wks**

30 Jul 94	**TROUBLE** Food CDFOOD 51	.....**11**	12 wks
15 Oct 94	**VIVA LA MEGABABES** Food CDFOOD 54	.....**27**	4 wks

Jimmy SHAND UK, male dance band — **2 wks**

23 Dec 55	**BLUEBELL POLKA** Parlophone F 3436	.....**20**	2 wks

Paul SHANE and the YELLOWCOATS
UK, male vocalist with male / female vocal group — **5 wks**

16 May 81	**HI DE HI (HOLIDAY ROCK)** EMI 5180	.....**36**	5 wks

SHANGRI-LAS US, female vocal group — **48 wks**

8 Oct 64	**REMEMBER (WALKIN' IN THE SAND)** Red Bird RB 10008	.....**14**	13 wks
14 Jan 65	**LEADER OF THE PACK** Red Bird RB 10014	.....**11**	9 wks
14 Oct 72	● **LEADER OF THE PACK (re-issue)** Kama Sutra 2013 024	.....**3**	14 wks
5 Jun 76	● **LEADER OF THE PACK (2nd re-issue)** Charly CS 1009	.....**7**	11 wks
12 Jun 76	● **LEADER OF THE PACK (3rd re-issue)** Contempo CS 9032	.....**7**	10 wks

From 19 Jun 76 until 14 Aug 76, the last week of the disc's chart run, the Charly and Contempo releases of Leader Of The Pack were bracketed together on the chart.

SHANICE US, female vocalist — **20 wks**

23 Nov 91	**I LOVE YOUR SMILE** Motown ZB 44907	.....**55**	4 wks
22 Feb 92	● **I LOVE YOUR SMILE (re-mix)** Motown TMG 1401	..**2**	10 wks
14 Nov 92	**LOVIN' YOU** Motown TMG 1409	.....**54**	1 wk
16 Jan 93	**SAVING FOREVER FOR YOU** Giant W 0148CD	.....**42**	3 wks
13 Aug 94	**I LIKE** Motown TMGCD 1427	.....**49**	2 wks

SHANNON US, female vocalist — **36 wks**

19 Nov 83	**LET THE MUSIC PLAY** Club LET 1	.....**51**	3 wks
28 Jan 84	**LET THE MUSIC PLAY (re-entry)** Club LET 1	.....**14**	12 wks
7 Apr 84	**GIVE ME TONIGHT** Club JAB 1	.....**24**	7 wks
30 Jun 84	**SWEET SOMEBODY** Club JAB 3	.....**25**	8 wks
20 Jul 85	**STRONGER TOGETHER** Club JAB 15	.....**46**	6 wks

Del SHANNON US, male vocalist — **147 wks**

27 Apr 61	★ **RUNAWAY** London HLX 9317	.....**1**	22 wks
14 Sep 61	● **HATS OFF TO LARRY** London HLX 9402	.....**6**	12 wks
7 Dec 61	● **SO LONG BABY** London HLX 9462	.....**10**	11 wks
15 Mar 62	● **HEY LITTLE GIRL** London HLX 9515	.....**2**	15 wks
6 Sep 62	**CRY MYSELF TO SLEEP** London HLX 9587	.....**29**	6 wks
11 Oct 62	● **SWISS MAID** London HLX 9609	.....**2**	17 wks
17 Jan 63	● **LITTLE TOWN FLIRT** London HLX 9653	.....**4**	13 wks
25 Apr 63	● **TWO KINDS OF TEARDROPS** London HLX 9710	.....**5**	13 wks
22 Aug 63	**TWO SILHOUETTES** London HLX 9761	.....**23**	8 wks
24 Oct 63	**SUE'S GOTTA BE MINE** London HLU 9800	.....**21**	8 wks
12 Mar 64	**MARY JANE** Stateside SS 269	.....**35**	5 wks
30 Jul 64	**HANDY MAN** Stateside SS 317	.....**36**	4 wks
14 Jan 65	● **KEEP SEARCHIN' (WE'LL FOLLOW THE SUN)** Stateside SS 368	.....**3**	11 wks
18 Mar 65	**STRANGER IN TOWN** Stateside SS 395	.....**40**	2 wks

Roxanne SHANTE US, female rapper — **10 wks**

1 Aug 87	**HAVE A NICE DAY** Breakout USA 612	.....**58**	3 wks
4 Jun 88	**GO ON GIRL** Breakout USA 633	.....**55**	3 wks
29 Oct 88	**SHARP AS A KNIFE** Club JAB 73 **1**	.....**45**	3 wks
14 Apr 90	**GO ON GIRL (re-mix)** Breakout USA 689	.....**74**	1 wk

1 Brandon Cooke featuring Roxanne Shante

Helen SHAPIRO UK, female vocalist — **119 wks**

23 Mar 61	● **DON'T TREAT ME LIKE A CHILD** Columbia DB 4589	..**3**	20 wks
29 Jun 61	★ **YOU DON'T KNOW** Columbia DB 4670	.....**1**	23 wks
28 Sep 61	★ **WALKIN' BACK TO HAPPINESS** Columbia DB 4715	..**1**	19 wks
15 Feb 62	● **TELL ME WHAT HE SAID** Columbia DB 4782	.....**2**	15 wks
3 May 62	**LET'S TALK ABOUT LOVE** Columbia DB 4824	.....**23**	7 wks
12 Jul 62	● **LITTLE MISS LONELY** Columbia DB 4869	.....**8**	11 wks
18 Oct 62	**KEEP AWAY FROM OTHER GIRLS** Columbia DB 4908	.....**40**	6 wks
7 Feb 63	**QUEEN FOR TONIGHT** Columbia DB 4966	.....**33**	5 wks
25 Apr 63	**WOE IS ME** Columbia DB 7026	.....**35**	6 wks
24 Oct 63	**LOOK WHO IT IS** Columbia DB 7130	.....**47**	3 wks
23 Jan 64	**FEVER** Columbia DB 7190	.....**38**	4 wks

Feargal SHARKEY UK, male vocalist — **58 wks**

13 Oct 84	**LISTEN TO YOUR FATHER** Zarjazz JAZZ 1	.....**23**	7 wks
29 Jun 85	**LOVING YOU** Virgin VS 770	.....**26**	10 wks
12 Oct 85	★ **A GOOD HEART** Virgin VS 808	.....**1**	16 wks
4 Jan 86	● **YOU LITTLE THIEF** Virgin VS 840	.....**5**	9 wks
5 Apr 86	**SOMEONE TO SOMEBODY** Virgin VS 828	.....**64**	3 wks
16 Jan 88	**MORE LOVE** Virgin VS 992	.....**44**	5 wks
16 Mar 91	**I'VE GOT NEWS FOR YOU** Virgin VS 1294	.....**12**	8 wks

SHARONETTES UK, female vocal group — **8 wks**

26 Apr 75	**PAPA OOM MOW MOW** Black Magic BM 102	.....**26**	5 wks
12 Jul 75	**GOING TO A GO-GO** Black Magic BM 104	.....**46**	3 wks

Debbie SHARP - *See DREAM FREQUENCY*

Dee Dee SHARP US, female vocalist — **2 wks**

25 Apr 63	**DO THE BIRD** Cameo Parkway C 244	.....**46**	2 wks

Barrie K. SHARPE - *See See Diana BROWN and Barrie K. SHARPE.*

Rocky SHARPE and the REPLAYS
UK, male / female vocal group — **41 wks**

16 Dec 78	**RAMA LAMA DING DONG** Chiswick CHIS 104	.....**17**	10 wks
24 Mar 79	**IMAGINATION** Chiswick CHIS 110	.....**39**	6 wks
25 Aug 79	**LOVE WILL MAKE YOU FAIL IN SCHOOL** Chiswick CHIS 114 **1**	.....**60**	4 wks
9 Feb 80	**MARTIAN HOP** Chiswick CHIS 121 **1**	.....**55**	4 wks
17 Apr 82	**SHOUT SHOUT (KNOCK YOURSELF OUT)** Chiswick DICE 3	.....**19**	9 wks
7 Aug 82	**CLAP YOUR HANDS** RAK 345	.....**54**	3 wks
26 Feb 83	**IF YOU WANNA BE HAPPY** Polydor POSP 560	.....**46**	5 wks

1 Rocky Sharpe and the Replays featuring the Top Liners

SHARPE and NUMAN - *See Gary NUMAN*

Mark SHAW UK, male vocalist — **1 wk**

17 Nov 90	**LOVE SO BRIGHT** EMI EM 161	.....**54**	1 wk

Sandie SHAW UK, female vocalist — **165 wks**

8 Oct 64	★ **(THERE'S) ALWAYS SOMETHING THERE TO REMIND ME** Pye 7N 15704	.....**1**	11 wks
10 Dec 64	● **GIRL DON'T COME** Pye 7N 15743	.....**3**	12 wks
18 Feb 65	● **I'LL STOP AT NOTHING** Pye 7N 15783	.....**4**	11 wks
13 May 65	★ **LONG LIVE LOVE** Pye 7N 15841	.....**1**	14 wks
23 Sep 65	● **MESSAGE UNDERSTOOD** Pye 7N 15940	.....**6**	10 wks
18 Nov 65	**HOW CAN YOU TELL** Pye 7N 15987	.....**21**	9 wks
27 Jan 66	● **TOMORROW** Pye 7N 17036	.....**9**	9 wks
19 May 66	**NOTHING COMES EASY** Pye 7N 17086	.....**14**	9 wks
8 Sep 66	**RUN** Pye 7N 17163	.....**32**	5 wks
24 Nov 66	**THINK SOMETIMES ABOUT ME** Pye 7N 17212	.....**32**	4 wks

19 Jan 67	I DON'T NEED ANYTHING Pye 7N 17239	50	1 wk
16 Mar 67	★ PUPPET ON A STRING Pye 7N 17272	1	18 wks
12 Jul 67	TONIGHT IN TOKYO Pye 7N 17346	21	6 wks
4 Oct 67	YOU'VE NOT CHANGED Pye 7N 17378	18	12 wks
7 Feb 68	TODAY Pye 7N 17441	27	7 wks
12 Feb 69	● MONSIEUR DUPONT Pye 7N 17675	6	15 wks
14 May 69	THINK IT ALL OVER Pye 7N 17726	42	4 wks
21 Apr 84	HAND IN GLOVE Rough Trade RT 130	27	5 wks
14 Jun 86	ARE YOU READY TO BE HEARTBROKEN Polydor POSP 793	68	1 wk
12 Nov 94	NOTHING LESS THAN BRILLIANT Virgin VSCDT 1521	66	2 wks

See also Various Artists (EPs & LPs) - Gimme Shelter (EP).

Winifred SHAW US, female vocalist — 4 wks

| 14 Aug 76 | LULLABY OF BROADWAY United Artists UP 36131 | 42 | 4 wks |

SHE ROCKERS UK, female vocal duo — 2 wks

| 13 Jan 90 | JAM IT JAM Jive JIVE 233 | 58 | 2 wks |

George SHEARING UK, male instrumentalist - piano — 15 wks

| 19 Jul 62 | LET THERE BE LOVE Capitol CL 15257 [1] | 11 | 14 wks |
| 4 Oct 62 | BAUBLES BANGLES AND BEADS Capitol CL 15269 | 49 | 1 wk |

[1] Nat 'King' Cole with George Shearing

Gary SHEARSTON Australia, male vocalist — 8 wks

| 5 Oct 74 | ● I GET A KICK OUT OF YOU Charisma CB 234 | 7 | 8 wks |

SHED SEVEN UK, male vocal / instrumental group — 9 wks

25 Jun 94	DOLPHIN Polydor YORCD 2	28	4 wks
27 Aug 94	SPEAKEASY Polydor YORCD 3	24	3 wks
12 Nov 94	OCEAN PIE Polydor YORCD 4	33	2 wks

SHEEP ON DRUGS UK, male vocal / instrumental duo — 5 wks

27 Mar 93	15 MINUTES OF FAME Transglobal CID 564	44	2 wks
30 Oct 93	FROM A TO H AND BACK AGAIN Transglobal CID 575	40	2 wks
14 May 94	LET THE GOOD TIMES ROLL Transglobal CID 576	56	1 wk

SHEER BRONZE featuring Lisa MILLETT
UK, male / female vocal / instrumental duo — 1 wk

| 3 Sep 94 | WALKIN' ON Go.Beat GODCD 115 | 63 | 1 wk |

SHEER ELEGANCE UK, male vocal group — 23 wks

20 Dec 75	MILKY WAY Pye International 7N 25697	18	10 wks
3 Apr 76	● LIFE IS TOO SHORT GIRL Pye International 7N 25703	9	9 wks
24 Jul 76	IT'S TEMPTATION Pye International 7N 25715	41	4 wks

SHEILA and B. DEVOTION - See Sheila B. DEVOTION

Doug SHELDON UK, male vocalist — 15 wks

9 Nov 61	RUNAROUND SUE Decca F 11398	36	3 wks
4 Jan 62	YOUR MA SAID YOU CRIED IN YOUR SLEEP LAST NIGHT Decca F 11416	29	6 wks
7 Feb 63	I SAW LINDA YESTERDAY Decca F 11564	36	6 wks

Pete SHELLEY UK, male vocalist — 1 wk

| 12 Mar 83 | TELEPHONE OPERATOR Genetic XX1 | 66 | 1 wk |

Peter SHELLEY UK, male vocalist — 20 wks

| 14 Sep 74 | ● GEE BABY Magnet MAG 12 | 4 | 10 wks |
| 22 Mar 75 | ● LOVE ME LOVE MY DOG Magnet MAG 22 | 3 | 10 wks |

Anne SHELTON UK, female vocalist — 31 wks

16 Dec 55	ARRIVEDERCI DARLING HMV POP 146	17	4 wks
13 Apr 56	SEVEN DAYS Philips PB 567	20	4 wks
24 Aug 56	★ LAY DOWN YOUR ARMS Philips PB 616	1	14 wks
20 Nov 59	VILLAGE OF ST. BERNADETTE Philips PB 969	27	1 wk
26 Jan 61	● SAILOR Philips PB 1096	10	8 wks

SHEPHERD SISTERS US, female vocal group — 6 wks

| 15 Nov 57 | ALONE HMV POP 411 | 14 | 5 wks |
| 3 Jan 58 | ALONE (re-entry) HMV POP 411 | 22 | 1 wk |

SHERBET Australia, male vocal / instrumental group — 10 wks

| 25 Sep 76 | ● HOWZAT Epic EPC 4574 | 4 | 10 wks |

Tony SHERIDAN - See BEATLES

Allan SHERMAN US, male vocalist — 10 wks

| 12 Sep 63 | HELLO MUDDAH HELLO FADDAH Warner Bros. WB 106 | 14 | 10 wks |

Bobby SHERMAN US, male vocalist — 4 wks

| 31 Oct 70 | JULIE DO YA LOVE ME CBS 5144 | 28 | 4 wks |

SHERRICK US, male vocalist — 10 wks

| 1 Aug 87 | JUST CALL Warner Bros. W 8380 | 23 | 8 wks |
| 21 Nov 87 | LET'S BE LOVERS TONIGHT Warner Bros. W 8146 | 63 | 2 wks |

Pluto SHERVINGTON Jamaica, male vocalist — 20 wks

7 Feb 76	● DAT Opal Pal 5	6	8 wks
10 Apr 76	RAM GOAT LIVER Trojan TR 7978	43	4 wks
6 Mar 82	YOUR HONOUR KR KR 4 [1]	19	8 wks

[1] Pluto

Holly SHERWOOD US, female vocalist — 7 wks

| 5 Feb 72 | DAY BY DAY Bell 1182 | 29 | 7 wks |

Tony SHEVETON UK, male vocalist — 1 wk

| 13 Feb 64 | MILLION DRUMS Oriole CB 1895 | 49 | 1 wk |

SHINEHEAD Jamaica, male vocalist — 6 wks

| 3 Apr 93 | JAMAICAN IN NEW YORK Elektra EKR 161CD | 30 | 5 wks |
| 26 Jun 93 | LET 'EM IN Elektra EKR 168CD | 70 | 1 wk |

SHIRELLES US, female vocal group — 29 wks

9 Feb 61	● WILL YOU LOVE ME TOMORROW Top Rank JAR 540	4	15 wks
31 May 62	SOLDIER BOY HMV POP 1019	23	9 wks
23 May 63	FOOLISH LITTLE GIRL Stateside SS 181	38	5 wks

SHIRLEY and COMPANY
US, female vocalist and male vocal / instrumental backing group — 9 wks

| 8 Feb 75 | ● SHAME SHAME SHAME All Platinum 6146 301 | 6 | 9 wks |

SHO NUFF US, male vocal / instrumental group — **4 wks**

| 24 May 80 | **IT'S ALRIGHT** Ensign ENY 37 | **53** | 4 wks |

Michelle SHOCKED US, female vocalist — **10 wks**

8 Oct 88	**ANCHORAGE** Cooking Vinyl LON 193	**60**	4 wks
14 Jan 89	**IF LOVE WAS A TRAIN** Cooking Vinyl LON 212	**63**	3 wks
11 Mar 89	**WHEN I GROW UP** Cooking Vinyl LON 219	**67**	3 wks

SHOCKING BLUE
Holland, male / female vocal / instrumental group — **14 wks**

| 17 Jan 70 ● | **VENUS** Penny Farthing PEN 702 | **8** | 11 wks |
| 25 Apr 70 | **MIGHTY JOE** Penny Farthing PEN 713 | **43** | 3 wks |

Troy SHONDELL US, male vocalist — **11 wks**

| 2 Nov 61 | **THIS TIME** London HLG 9432 | **22** | 11 wks |

SHONDELLS - See Tommy JAMES and the SHONDELLS

SHOOTING PARTY UK, male vocal duo — **2 wks**

| 31 Mar 90 | **LET'S HANG ON** Lisson DOLE 15 | **66** | 2 wks |

SHOWADDYWADDY
UK, male vocal / instrumental group — **209 wks**

18 May 74 ●	**HEY ROCK AND ROLL** Bell 1357	**2**	14 wks
17 Aug 74	**ROCK 'N' ROLL LADY** Bell 1374	**15**	9 wks
30 Nov 74	**HEY MR. CHRISTMAS** Bell 1387	**13**	8 wks
22 Feb 75	**SWEET MUSIC** Bell 1403	**14**	9 wks
17 May 75 ●	**THREE STEPS TO HEAVEN** Bell 1426	**2**	11 wks
6 Sep 75 ●	**HEARTBEAT** Bell 1450	**7**	7 wks
15 Nov 75	**HEAVENLY** Bell 1460	**34**	6 wks
29 May 76	**TROCADERO** Bell 1476	**32**	3 wks
6 Nov 76 ★	**UNDER THE MOON OF LOVE** Bell 1495	**1**	15 wks
5 Mar 77 ●	**WHEN** Arista 91	**3**	11 wks
23 Jul 77 ●	**YOU GOT WHAT IT TAKES** Arista 126	**2**	10 wks
5 Nov 77 ●	**DANCIN' PARTY** Arista 149	**4**	11 wks
25 Mar 78 ●	**I WONDER WHY** Arista 174	**2**	11 wks
24 Jun 78 ●	**A LITTLE BIT OF SOAP** Arista 191	**5**	12 wks
4 Nov 78 ●	**PRETTY LITTLE ANGEL EYES** Arista ARIST 222	**5**	12 wks
31 Mar 79	**REMEMBER THEN** Arista 247	**17**	8 wks
28 Jul 79	**SWEET LITTLE ROCK 'N' ROLLER** Arista 278	**15**	9 wks
10 Nov 79	**A NIGHT AT DADDY GEE'S** Arista 314	**39**	5 wks
27 Sep 80	**WHY DO LOVERS BREAK EACH OTHER'S HEARTS** Arista ARIST 359	**22**	10 wks
29 Nov 80	**BLUE MOON** Arista ARIST 379	**32**	9 wks
13 Jun 81	**MULTIPLICATION** Arista ARIST 416	**39**	4 wks
28 Nov 81	**FOOTSTEPS** Bell BELL 1499	**31**	9 wks
28 Aug 82	**WHO PUT THE BOMP (IN THE BOMP-A-BOMP-A-BOMP)** RCA 236	**37**	6 wks

SHOWDOWN US, male vocal / instrumental group — **3 wks**

| 17 Dec 77 | **KEEP DOIN' IT** State STAT 63 | **41** | 3 wks |

SHOWDOWN - See Garry LEE and SHOWDOWN

SHOWSTOPPERS US, male vocal group — **25 wks**

13 Mar 68	**AIN'T NOTHING BUT A HOUSEPARTY** Beacon 3-100	**11**	15 wks
13 Nov 68	**EENY MEENY** MGM 1436	**33**	7 wks
30 Jan 71	**AIN'T NOTHING BUT A HOUSEPARTY (re-issue)** Beacon BEA 100	**43**	1 wk
13 Feb 71	**AIN'T NOTHING BUT A HOUSEPARTY (re-entry of re-issue)** Beacon BEA 100	**33**	1 wk
27 Feb 71	**AIN'T NOTHING BUT A HOUSEPARTY (2nd re-entry of re-issue)** Beacon BEA 100	**36**	1 wk

SHRIEKBACK UK, male vocal / instrumental group — **4 wks**

| 28 Jul 84 | **HAND ON MY HEART** Arista SHRK 1 | **52** | 4 wks |

SHUT UP AND DANCE
UK, male vocal / production group — **10 wks**

21 Apr 90	**£20 TO GET IN** Shut Up And Dance SUAD 3	**56**	3 wks
28 Jul 90	**LAMBORGHINI** Shut Up And Dance SUAD 4	**55**	2 wks
8 Feb 92	**AUTOBIOGRAPHY OF A CRACKHEAD / THE GREEN MAN** Shut Up And Dance SUAD 21	**43**	2 wks
30 May 92 ●	**RAVING I'M RAVING** Shut Up And Dance SUAD 30S [1]	**2**	2 wks
15 Aug 92	**THE ART OF MOVING BUTTS** Shut Up And Dance SUAD 34S [2]	**69**	1 wk

[1] Shut Up And Dance featuring Peter Bouncer [2] Shut Up And Dance featuring Erin

SHY UK, male vocal / instrumental group — **3 wks**

| 19 Apr 80 | **GIRL (IT'S ALL I HAVE)** Gallery GA 1 | **60** | 3 wks |

SHY FX - See UK APACHI with SHY FX

Labi SIFFRE UK, male vocalist — **44 wks**

27 Nov 71	**IT MUST BE LOVE** Pye International 7N 25572	**14**	12 wks
25 Mar 72	**CRYING LAUGHING LOVING LYING** Pye International 7N 25576	**11**	9 wks
29 Jul 72	**WATCH ME** Pye International 7N 25586	**29**	6 wks
4 Apr 87 ●	**(SOMETHING INSIDE) SO STRONG** China WOK 12	**4**	13 wks
21 Nov 87	**NOTHIN'S GONNA CHANGE** China WOK 16	**52**	4 wks

SIGUE SIGUE SPUTNIK
UK, male vocal / instrumental group — **20 wks**

1 Mar 86 ●	**LOVE MISSILE F1-11** Parlophone SSS 1	**3**	9 wks
7 Jun 86	**TWENTY-FIRST CENTURY BOY** Parlophone SSS 2	**20**	5 wks
19 Nov 88	**SUCCESS** Parlophone SSS 3	**31**	3 wks
1 Apr 89	**DANCERAMA** Parlophone SSS 5	**50**	2 wks
20 May 89	**ALBINONI VS STAR WARS** Parlophone SSS 4	**75**	1 wk

SILENCERS UK, male vocal / instrumental group — **7 wks**

25 Jun 88	**PAINTED MOON** RCA HUSH 1	**57**	4 wks
27 May 89	**SCOTTISH RAIN** RCA PB 42701	**71**	2 wks
15 May 93	**I CAN FEEL IT** RCA 74321147112	**62**	1 wk

SILENT UNDERDOG
UK, male instrumentalist - Paul Hardcastle — **1 wk**

| 16 Feb 85 | **PAPA'S GOT A BRAND NEW PIGBAG** Kaz KAZ 50 | **73** | 1 wk |

SILJE Norway, female vocalist — **6 wks**

| 15 Dec 90 | **TELL ME WHERE YOU'RE GOING** EMI EM 159 | **55** | 6 wks |

SILK US, male vocal group — **10 wks**

24 Apr 93	**FREAK ME** Elektra EKR 165CD	**46**	5 wks
5 Jun 93	**GIRL U FOR ME** Elektra EKR 167CD	**67**	2 wks
9 Oct 93	**BABY IT'S YOU** Elektra EKR 173CD	**44**	2 wks
26 Feb 94	**FREAK ME (re-entry)** Elektra EKR 165CD	**72**	1 wk

SILKIE UK, male / female vocal / instrumental group — **6 wks**

| 23 Sep 65 | **YOU'VE GOT TO HIDE YOUR LOVE AWAY** Fontana TF 603 | **28** | 6 wks |

SILSOE UK, male instrumentalist - keyboards   4 wks

21 Jun 86   **AZTEC GOLD** CBS A 7231 ....**48** 4 wks

Aztec Gold was the ITV theme to the 1986 World Cup Finals and was performed by Rod Argent under the title Silsoe. See also Argent; San José featuring Rodriquez Argentina.

SILVER BULLET UK, male vocal / instrumental duo   20 wks

2 Sep 89	**BRING FORTH THE GUILLOTINE** Tam Tam TTT 013 ..**70**	1 wk
9 Dec 89	**20 SECONDS TO COMPLY** Tam Tam 7TTT 019 ......**11**	10 wks
3 Mar 90	**BRING FORTH THE GUILLOTINE (re-entry)**	
	Tam Tam TTT 013 ....**45**	5 wks
13 Apr 91	**UNDERCOVER ANARCHIST** Parlophone R 6284 ......**33**	4 wks

SILVER BULLET BAND - *See Bob SEGER and the SILVER BULLET BAND*

SILVER CITY UK, male / female vocal / instrumental duo   1 wk

30 Oct 93   **LOVE INFINITY** Silver City GFJMCD 1 ....**62** 1 wk

SILVER CONVENTION
Germany / US, female vocal group   35 wks

5 Apr 75	**SAVE ME** Magnet MAG 26 ....**30**	7 wks
15 Nov 75	**FLY ROBIN FLY** Magnet MAG 43 ....**28**	8 wks
3 Apr 76	● **GET UP AND BOOGIE** Magnet MAG 55 ....**7**	11 wks
19 Jun 76	**TIGER BABY / NO NO JOE** Magnet MAG 69 ....**41**	4 wks
29 Jan 77	**EVERYBODY'S TALKIN' 'BOUT LOVE**	
	Magnet MAG 81...**25**	5 wks

Dooley SILVERSPOON US, male vocalist   3 wks

31 Jan 76   **LET ME BE THE NUMBER ONE** Seville SEV 1020 ......**44** 3 wks

Harry SIMEONE CHORALE US, choir   14 wks

13 Feb 59	**LITTLE DRUMMER BOY** Top Rank JAR 101 ....**13**	7 wks
22 Dec 60	**ONWARD CHRISTIAN SOLDIERS** Ember EMBS 118..**35**	1 wk
5 Jan 61	**ONWARD CHRISTIAN SOLDIERS (re-entry)**	
	Ember EMBS 118 ....**38**	1 wk
21 Dec 61	**ONWARD CHRISTIAN SOLDIERS (2nd re-entry)**	
	Ember EMBS 118...**36**	3 wks
20 Dec 62	**ONWARD CHRISTIAN SOLDIERS (re-issue)**	
	Ember EMBS 144...**38**	2 wks

Gene SIMMONS US, male vocalist   4 wks

27 Jan 79   **RADIOACTIVE** Casablanca CAN 134 ....**41** 4 wks

Carly SIMON US, female vocalist   76 wks

16 Dec 72	● **YOU'RE SO VAIN** Elektra K 12077 ....**3**	15 wks
31 Mar 73	**THE RIGHT THING TO DO** Elektra K 12095 ....**17**	9 wks
16 Mar 74	**MOCKINGBIRD** Elektra K 12134 [1] **34**	5 wks
6 Aug 77	● **NOBODY DOES IT BETTER** Elektra K 12261 ....**7**	12 wks
21 Aug 82	● **WHY** WEA K 79300 ....**10**	13 wks
24 Jan 87	● **COMING AROUND AGAIN** Arista ARIST 687 ....**10**	12 wks
10 Jun 89	**WHY (re-issue)** WEA U 7501 ....**56**	5 wks
20 Apr 91	**YOU'RE SO VAIN (re-issue)** Elektra EKR 123.........**41**	5 wks

[1] Carly Simon and James Taylor

See also Will Powers.

Joe SIMON US, male vocalist   10 wks

16 Jun 73   **STEP BY STEP** Mojo 2093 030 ....**14** 10 wks

Paul SIMON US, male vocalist   83 wks

19 Feb 72   ● **MOTHER AND CHILD REUNION** CBS 7793 ....**5** 12 wks

29 Apr 72	**ME AND JULIO DOWN BY THE SCHOOLYARD**	
	CBS 7964 ....**15**	9 wks
16 Jun 73	● **TAKE ME TO THE MARDI GRAS** CBS 1578 ....**7**	11 wks
22 Sep 73	**LOVES ME LIKE A ROCK** CBS 1700 ....**39**	5 wks
10 Jan 76	**50 WAYS TO LEAVE YOUR LOVER** CBS 3887..........**23**	6 wks
3 Dec 77	**SLIP SLIDIN' AWAY** CBS 5770 ....**36**	5 wks
6 Sep 80	**LATE IN THE EVENING** Warner Bros. K 17666 ....**58**	4 wks
13 Sep 86	● **YOU CAN CALL ME AL** Warner Bros. W 8667 ....**4**	13 wks
13 Dec 86	**THE BOY IN THE BUBBLE** Warner Bros. W 8509 ....**26**	8 wks
6 Oct 90	**THE OBVIOUS CHILD** Warner Bros. W 9549 ....**15**	10 wks

See also Simon and Garfunkel.

Ronni SIMON UK, male vocalist   1 wk

13 Aug 94   **B GOOD 2 ME** Network NWKCD 80..................**73** 1 wk

Tito SIMON Jamaica, male vocalist   4 wks

8 Feb 75   **THIS MONDAY MORNING FEELING**
                Horse HOSS 57 ....**45** 4 wks

SIMON and GARFUNKEL US, male vocal duo   87 wks

24 Mar 66	● **HOMEWARD BOUND** CBS 202045 ....**9**	12 wks
16 Jun 66	**I AM A ROCK** CBS 202303 ....**17**	10 wks
10 Jul 68	● **MRS. ROBINSON** CBS 3443 ....**4**	12 wks
8 Jan 69	● **MRS. ROBINSON (EP)** CBS EP 6400 ....**9**	5 wks
30 Apr 69	● **THE BOXER** CBS 4162 ....**6**	14 wks
21 Feb 70	★ **BRIDGE OVER TROUBLED WATER** CBS 4790 ....**1**	19 wks
15 Aug 70	**BRIDGE OVER TROUBLED WATER (re-entry)**	
	CBS 4790 ....**45**	1 wk
7 Oct 72	**AMERICA** CBS 8336 ....**25**	7 wks
7 Dec 91	**A HAZY SHADE OF WINTER / SILENT NIGHT -**	
	SEVEN O'CLOCK NEWS Columbia 6576537 ....**30**	6 wks
15 Feb 92	**THE BOXER (re-issue)** Columbia 6578067 ....**75**	1 wk

Tracks on Mrs. Robinson (EP): Mrs. Robinson / Scarborough Fair - Canticle / Sounds of Silence / April Come She Will. This EP would have stayed more than five weeks on chart had a decision to exclude EPs from chart in Feb 69 not been taken. See also Paul Simon; Art Garfunkel.

SIMONE US, female vocalist   1 wk

23 Nov 91   **MY FAMILY DEPENDS ON ME**
                Strictly Rhythm A 8678 ....**75** 1 wk

Nina SIMONE US, female vocalist   46 wks

5 Aug 65	**I PUT A SPELL ON YOU** Philips BF 1415 ....**49**	1 wk
16 Oct 68	● **AIN'T GOT NO - I GOT LIFE / DO WHAT**	
	YOU GOTTA DO RCA 1743 ....**2**	18 wks
15 Jan 69	● **TO LOVE SOMEBODY** RCA 1779 ....**5**	9 wks
15 Jan 69	**I PUT A SPELL ON YOU (re-issue)** Philips BF 1736 ..**28**	4 wks
31 Oct 87	● **MY BABY JUST CARES FOR ME** Charly CYZ 7112 ...**5**	11 wks
9 Jul 94	**FEELING GOOD** Mercury MERCD 403 ....**40**	3 wks

Do What You Gotta Do was only listed for the first eight weeks of the record's chart run. It peaked at position 7.

SIMPLE MINDS UK, male vocal / instrumental group   174 wks

12 May 79	**LIFE IN A DAY** Zoom ZUM 10..............................**62**	2 wks
23 May 81	**THE AMERICAN** Virgin VS 410 ....**59**	3 wks
15 Aug 81	**LOVE SONG** Virgin VS 434 ....**47**	4 wks
7 Nov 81	**SWEAT IN BULLET** Virgin VS 451 ....**52**	3 wks
10 Apr 82	**PROMISED YOU A MIRACLE** Virgin VS 488 ....**13**	11 wks
28 Aug 82	**GLITTERING PRIZE** Virgin VS 511 ....**16**	11 wks
13 Nov 82	**SOMEONE SOMEWHERE (IN SUMMERTIME)**	
	Virgin VS 538 ....**36**	5 wks
26 Nov 83	**WATERFRONT** Virgin VS 636 ....**13**	11 wks
28 Jan 84	**SPEED YOUR LOVE TO ME** Virgin VS 649.................**20**	4 wks
24 Mar 84	**UP ON THE CATWALK** Virgin VS 661 ....**27**	5 wks
20 Apr 85	● **DON'T YOU (FORGET ABOUT ME)** Virgin VS 749 ......**7**	11 wks
17 Aug 85	**DON'T YOU (FORGET ABOUT ME) (re-entry)**	
	Virgin VS 749 ....**61**	8 wks

12 Oct 85 ●	**ALIVE AND KICKING** *Virgin VS 817* **7**	9 wks
28 Dec 85	**DON'T YOU (FORGET ABOUT ME)** (2nd re-entry)	
	Virgin VS 749 ....**74**	1 wk
4 Jan 86	**ALIVE AND KICKING** (re-entry) *Virgin VS 817* **60**	2 wks
1 Feb 86 ●	**SANCTIFY YOURSELF** *Virgin SM 1* **10**	7 wks
15 Feb 86	**DON'T YOU (FORGET ABOUT ME)** (3rd re-entry)	
	Virgin VS 779 ....**62**	3 wks
15 Mar 86	**DON'T YOU (FORGET ABOUT ME)** (4th re-entry)	
	Virgin VS 779 ....**68**	1 wk
12 Apr 86 ●	**ALL THE THINGS SHE SAID** *Virgin VS 860* **9**	8 wks
14 Jun 86	**ALL THE THINGS SHE SAID** (re-entry)	
	Virgin VS 860 ....**73**	1 wk
15 Nov 86	**GHOSTDANCING** *Virgin VS 907* **13**	6 wks
3 Jan 87	**GHOSTDANCING** (re-entry) *Virgin VS 907* **68**	2 wks
20 Jun 87	**PROMISED YOU A MIRACLE** *Virgin SM 2* **19**	7 wks
18 Feb 89 ★	**BELFAST CHILD** *Virgin SMX 3*.................**1**	11 wks
22 Apr 89	**THIS IS YOUR LAND** *Virgin SMX4* **13**	4 wks
29 Jul 89	**KICK IT IN** *Virgin SM 5* **15**	5 wks
9 Dec 89	**THE AMSTERDAM EP** *Virgin SMX 6* **18**	6 wks
23 Mar 91 ●	**LET THERE BE LOVE** *Virgin VS 1332* **6**	7 wks
25 May 91	**SEE THE LIGHTS** *Virgin VS 1343* **20**	4 wks
31 Aug 91	**STAND BY LOVE** *Virgin VS 1358* **13**	4 wks
26 Oct 91	**REAL LIFE** *Virgin VS 1382* **34**	3 wks
10 Oct 92 ●	**LOVE SONG / ALIVE AND KICKING** (re-issue)	
	Virgin VS 1440 ....**6**	6 wks

The 1987 version of Promised You A Miracle was a live recording. Tracks on The Amsterdam EP: Let It All Come Down / Jerusalem / Sign Of The Times.

SIMPLICIOUS *US, male vocal group* **9 wks**

29 Sep 84	**LET HER FEEL IT** *Fourth & Broadway BRW 13*...........**65**	3 wks
2 Feb 85	**LET HER FEEL IT** (re-issue)	
	Fourth & Broadway BRW 18 ....**34**	6 wks

The re-issue of Let Her Feel It was listed with Personality by Eugene Wilde.

SIMPLY RED *UK, male vocal / instrumental group* **139 wks**

15 Jun 85	**MONEY'S TOO TIGHT (TO MENTION)**	
	Elektra EKR 9 ....**13**	12 wks
21 Sep 85	**COME TO MY AID** *Elektra EKR 19* **66**	2 wks
16 Nov 85	**HOLDING BACK THE YEARS** *Elektra EKR 29* **51**	4 wks
8 Mar 86	**JERICHO** *WEA YZ 63* **53**	3 wks
17 May 86 ●	**HOLDING BACK THE YEARS** (re-issue) *WEA YZ 70* ..**2**	13 wks
9 Aug 86	**OPEN UP THE RED BOX** *WEA YZ 75* **61**	4 wks
14 Feb 87	**THE RIGHT THING** *WEA YZ 103* **11**	10 wks
23 May 87	**INFIDELITY** *Elektra YZ 114* **31**	5 wks
28 Nov 87	**EV'RY TIME WE SAY GOODBYE** *Elektra YZ 161* ...**11**	9 wks
12 Mar 88	**I WON'T FEEL BAD** *Elektra YZ 172* **68**	2 wks
28 Jan 89	**IT'S ONLY LOVE** *Elektra YZ 349* **13**	8 wks
8 Apr 89 ●	**IF YOU DON'T KNOW ME BY NOW** *Elektra YZ 377* ..**2**	10 wks
8 Jul 89	**A NEW FLAME** *WEA YZ 404* **17**	8 wks
28 Oct 89	**YOU'VE GOT IT** *Elektra YZ 424* **46**	3 wks
21 Sep 91	**SOMETHING GOT ME STARTED** *East West YZ 614* ..**11**	8 wks
30 Nov 91 ●	**STARS** *East West YZ 626* **8**	10 wks
8 Feb 92 ●	**FOR YOUR BABIES** *East West YZ 642* **9**	8 wks
2 May 92	**THRILL ME** *East West YZ 671* **33**	5 wks
25 Jul 92	**YOUR MIRROR** *East West YZ 689* **17**	4 wks
21 Nov 92	**MONTREUX EP** *East West YZ 716* **11**	10 wks

Tracks on Montreux EP: Drowning In My Own Tears / Granma's Hands / Lady Godiva's Room / Love For Sale.

Paul SIMPSON - *See ADEVA*

SIMPSONS *US, male / female cartoon group* **19 wks**

26 Jan 91 ★	**DO THE BARTMAN** *Geffen GEF 87* **1**	12 wks
6 Apr 91 ●	**DEEP DEEP TROUBLE** *Geffen GEF 88* ☐1 ....**7**	7 wks

☐1 Simpsons featuring Bart and Homer

W/Cdr. A.E. SIMS - *See Central Band of the ROYAL AIR FORCE, conductor W/Cdr. A.E. SIMS, O.B.E*

Joyce SIMS *US, female vocalist* **35 wks**

19 Apr 86	**ALL AND ALL** *London LON 94* **16**	10 wks
13 Jun 87	**LIFETIME LOVE** *London LON 137* **34**	6 wks
9 Jan 88 ●	**COME INTO MY LIFE** *London LON 161* **7**	9 wks
23 Apr 88	**WALK AWAY** *London LON 176* **24**	6 wks
17 Jun 89	**LOOKING FOR A LOVE** *ffrr F 109* **39**	4 wks

Kym SIMS *US, female vocalist* **22 wks**

7 Dec 91 ●	**TOO BLIND TO SEE IT** *Atco B 8667* **5**	12 wks
28 Mar 92	**TAKE MY ADVICE** *Atco B 8591* **13**	7 wks
27 Jun 92	**A LITTLE BIT MORE** *Atco B 8528* **30**	3 wks

Frank SINATRA *US, male vocalist* **439 wks**

9 Jul 54	**YOUNG AT HEART** *Capitol CL 14064* **12**	1 wk
16 Jul 54 ★	**THREE COINS IN THE FOUNTAIN** *Capitol CL 14120*....**1**	19 wks
10 Jun 55	**YOU MY LOVE** *Capitol CL 14240* **13**	3 wks
22 Jul 55	**YOU MY LOVE** (re-entry) *Capitol CL 14240*.................**17**	2 wks
5 Aug 55 ●	**LEARNIN' THE BLUES** *Capitol CL 14296* **2**	13 wks
12 Aug 55	**YOU MY LOVE** (2nd re-entry) *Capitol CL 14240*.....**17**	2 wks
2 Sep 55	**NOT AS A STRANGER** *Capitol CL 14326* **18**	1 wk
13 Jan 56 ●	**LOVE AND MARRIAGE** *Capitol CL 14503* **3**	8 wks
20 Jan 56 ●	**THE TENDER TRAP** *Capitol CL 14511* **2**	9 wks
15 Jun 56	**SONGS FOR SWINGING LOVERS** (LP)	
	Capitol LCT 6106 ....**12**	8 wks
22 Nov 57	**ALL THE WAY** *Capitol CL 14800* **29**	1 wk
29 Nov 57	**CHICAGO** *Capitol CL 14800* **25**	1 wk
6 Dec 57	**ALL THE WAY** (re-entry) / **CHICAGO**	
	Capitol CL 14800 ....**21**	1 wk
13 Dec 57 ●	**ALL THE WAY** *Capitol CL 14800* **3**	17 wks
7 Feb 58	**WITCHCRAFT** *Capitol CL 14819* **12**	8 wks
14 Nov 58	**MR. SUCCESS** *Capitol CL 14956* **29**	1 wk
12 Dec 58	**MR. SUCCESS** (re-entry) *Capitol CL 14956* **25**	2 wks
2 Jan 59	**MR. SUCCESS** (2nd re-entry) *Capitol CL 14956* **26**	1 wk
10 Apr 59	**FRENCH FOREIGN LEGION** *Capitol CL 14997*.................**18**	5 wks
15 May 59	**COME DANCE WITH ME** (LP) *Capitol LCT 6179* **30**	1 wk
28 Aug 59	**HIGH HOPES** *Capitol CL 15052* **28**	1 wk
11 Sep 59 ●	**HIGH HOPES** (re-entry) *Capitol CL 15052*.................**6**	13 wks
10 Mar 60	**HIGH HOPES** (2nd re-entry) *Capitol CL 15052* **42**	1 wk
7 Apr 60	**IT'S NICE TO GO TRAV'LING** *Capitol CL 15116* **48**	2 wks
16 Jun 60	**RIVER STAY 'WAY FROM MY DOOR**	
	Capitol CL 15135 ....**18**	9 wks
8 Sep 60	**NICE 'N EASY** *Capitol CL 15150* **15**	12 wks
24 Nov 60	**OL' MACDONALD** *Capitol CL 15168* **11**	8 wks
20 Apr 61	**MY BLUE HEAVEN** *Capitol CL 15193* **33**	7 wks
28 Sep 61	**GRANADA** *Reprise R 20010* **15**	8 wks
23 Nov 61	**THE COFFEE SONG** *Reprise R 20035* **39**	3 wks
5 Apr 62	**EVERYBODY'S TWISTING** *Reprise R 20063* **22**	12 wks
13 Dec 62	**ME AND MY SHADOW** *Reprise R 20128* ☐1 ....**20**	7 wks
7 Feb 63	**ME AND MY SHADOW** (re-entry)	
	Reprise R 20128 ☐1 ....**47**	2 wks
7 Mar 63	**MY KIND OF GIRL** *Reprise R 20148* ☐2 ....**35**	6 wks
24 Sep 64	**HELLO DOLLY** *Reprise R 20351* ☐2 ....**47**	1 wk
12 May 66 ★	**STRANGERS IN THE NIGHT** *Reprise R 23052* **1**	20 wks
29 Sep 66	**SUMMER WIND** *Reprise RS 20509* **36**	5 wks
15 Dec 66	**THAT'S LIFE** *Reprise RS 20531* **46**	5 wks
23 Mar 67 ★	**SOMETHIN' STUPID** *Reprise R 23166* ☐3 ....**1**	18 wks
23 Aug 67	**THE WORLD WE KNEW** *Reprise RS 20610* **33**	11 wks
2 Apr 69 ●	**MY WAY** *Reprise RS 20817* **5**	42 wks
4 Oct 69 ●	**LOVE'S BEEN GOOD TO ME** *Reprise RS 20852*.................**8**	18 wks
31 Jan 70	**MY WAY** (re-entry) *Reprise RS 20817*.................**49**	1 wk
28 Feb 70	**MY WAY** (2nd re-entry) *Reprise RS 20817*.................**30**	5 wks
11 Apr 70	**MY WAY** (3rd re-entry) *Reprise RS 20817*.................**33**	9 wks
27 Jun 70	**MY WAY** (4th re-entry) *Reprise RS 20817*.................**28**	21 wks
28 Nov 70	**MY WAY** (5th re-entry) *Reprise RS 20817*.................**18**	16 wks
6 Mar 71	**I WILL DRINK THE WINE** *Reprise RS 23487*.................**16**	12 wks
27 Mar 71	**MY WAY** (6th re-entry) *Reprise RS 20817*.................**22**	19 wks
4 Sep 71	**MY WAY** (7th re-entry) *Reprise RS 20817*.................**39**	8 wks
1 Jan 72	**MY WAY** (8th re-entry) *Reprise RS 20817*.................**50**	1 wk
20 Dec 75	**I BELIEVE I'M GONNA LOVE YOU**	
	Reprise K 14400 ....**34**	7 wks
9 Aug 80	**THEME FROM NEW YORK, NEW YORK**	
	Reprise K 14502 ....**59**	4 wks

SLADE pose in February 1975, unaware that their next release will break their string of consecutive top ten hits. (LFI)

TOP 35

DIANA ROSS sings at Wembley Arena in July 1994, her unmatched stretch of consecutive years on chart still in progress. (Steve Gillett)

TOP 8

The only one of the all-time top ten chart acts who was also a star before the chart began, **FRANK SINATRA** sings into a National Broadcasting Company radio microphone. (LFI)

TOP 4

22 Feb 86 ●	THEME FROM NEW YORK, NEW YORK (re-entry)		
	Reprise K 14502 4	10 wks
4 Dec 93 ●	I'VE GOT YOU UNDER MY SKIN *Island CID 578* [4] ..4	9 wks
16 Apr 94	MY WAY (re-issue) *Reprise W 0163CD* 45	2 wks

[1] Frank Sinatra and Sammy Davis Jr [2] Frank Sinatra with Count Basie [3] Nancy Sinatra and Frank Sinatra [4] Frank Sinatra with Bono

Tracks on Songs For Swinging Lovers LP: You Make Me Feel So Young / It Happened In Monterey / You're Getting To Be A Habit With Me / You Brought A New Kind Of Love To Me / Too Marvellous For Words / Old Devil Moon / Pennies From Heaven / Love Is Here To Stay / I've Got You Under My Skin / I Thought About You / We'll Be Together Again / Making Whoopee / Swingin' Down The Lane / Anything Goes / How About You. Tracks on Come Dance With Me LP: Something's Gotta Give / Just In Time / Dancing In The Dark / Too Close For Comfort / I Could Have Danced All Night / Saturday Night Is The Loneliest Night Of The Week / Day In Day Out / Cheek To Cheek / Baubles Bangles And Beads / The Song Is You / The Last Dance. All The Way and Chicago, Capitol CL 14800, were at first billed separately, then together for one week, then All The Way on its own. I've Got You Under My Skin was the listed B-side of Stay (Faraway So Close) *by U2.*

See also U2.

Nancy SINATRA *US, female vocalist* **99 wks**

27 Jan 66 ★	THESE BOOTS ARE MADE FOR WALKING		
	Reprise R 20432 1	14 wks
28 Apr 66	HOW DOES THAT GRAB YOU DARLIN'		
	Reprise R 20461 19	8 wks
19 Jan 67 ●	SUGAR TOWN *Reprise RS 20527* 8	10 wks
23 Mar 67 ★	SOMETHIN' STUPID *Reprise RS 23166* [1] 1	18 wks
5 Jul 67	YOU ONLY LIVE TWICE / JACKSON		
	Reprise RS 20595 [2] 11	19 wks
8 Nov 67	LADYBIRD *Reprise RS 20629* [3] 47	1 wk
29 Nov 69	HIGHWAY SONG *Reprise RS 20869* 21	10 wks
21 Aug 71 ●	DID YOU EVER *Reprise K 14093* [4] 2	19 wks

[1] Nancy Sinatra and Frank Sinatra [2] Nancy Sinatra/Nancy Sinatra and Lee Hazlewood [3] Nancy Sinatra and Lee Hazlewood [4] Nancy and Lee

Jackson listed with You Only Live Twice *from 12 Jul 67.*

SINCLAIR *UK, male vocalist* **8 wks**

21 Aug 93	AIN'T NO CASANOVA *Dome CDDOME 1004* 28	5 wks
26 Feb 94	(I WANNA KNOW) WHY *Dome CDDOME 1009* 58	2 wks
6 Aug 94	DON'T LIE *Dome CDDOME 1010* 70	1 wk

SINE *US, disco aggregation* **9 wks**

10 Jun 78	JUST LET ME DO MY THING *CBS 6351* 33	9 wks

SINFONIA OF LONDON - *See Peter AUTY and the SINFONIA OF LONDON*

SINGING CORNER - *See DONOVAN*

SINGING DOGS *Denmark, canine vocal group* **4 wks**

25 Nov 55	THE SINGING DOGS (MEDLEY) *Nixa N 15009* 13	4 wks

Medley songs: Pat-a-Cake / Three Blind Mice / Jingle Bells / Oh Susanna.

SINGING NUN (Soeur Sourire)
Belgium, female vocalist **14 wks**

5 Dec 63 ●	DOMINIQUE *Philips BF 1293* 7	14 wks

SINGING SHEEP *UK, computerized sheep noises* **5 wks**

18 Dec 82	BAA BAA BLACK SHEEP *Sheep BAA 1* 42	5 wks

Maxine SINGLETON *US, female vocalist* **3 wks**

2 Apr 83	YOU CAN'T RUN FROM LOVE *Creole CR 50* 57	3 wks

SINITTA *US, female vocalist* **104 wks**

8 Mar 86	SO MACHO / CRUISING *Fanfare FAN 7* 47	11 wks
28 Jun 86 ●	SO MACHO / CRUISING (re-entry) *Fanfare FAN 7* 2	17 wks
11 Oct 86	FEELS LIKE THE FIRST TIME *Fanfare FAN 8* 45	5 wks
25 Jul 87	TOY BOY *Fanfare FAN 12* 4	14 wks
12 Dec 87	G.T.O *Fanfare FAN 14* 15	9 wks
19 Mar 88 ●	CROSS MY BROKEN HEART *Fanfare FAN 15* 6	9 wks
24 Sep 88	I DON'T BELIEVE IN MIRACLES *Fanfare FAN 16* 22	8 wks
3 Jun 89 ●	RIGHT BACK WHERE WE STARTED FROM		
	Fanfare FAN 18 4	10 wks
7 Oct 89	LOVE ON A MOUNTAIN TOP *Fanfare FAN 21* 20	6 wks
21 Apr 90	HITCHIN' A RIDE *Fanfare FAN 24* 24	6 wks
22 Sep 90	LOVE AND AFFECTION *Fanfare FAN 31* 62	3 wks
4 Jul 92	SHAME SHAME SHAME *Arista 74321100327* 28	4 wks
17 Apr 93	THE SUPREME EP *Arista 74321139592* 49	2 wks

Tracks on The Supreme EP: Where Did Our Love Go / Stop! In The Name Of Love / You Can't Hurry Love / Remember Me.

SIOUXSIE and the BANSHEES
UK, female / male vocal / instrumental group **146 wks**

26 Aug 78 ●	HONG KONG GARDEN *Polydor 2059 052* 7	10 wks
31 Mar 79	THE STAIRCASE (MYSTERY) *Polydor POSP 9* 24	8 wks
7 Jul 79	PLAYGROUND TWIST *Polydor POSP 59* 28	6 wks
29 Sep 79	MITTAGEISEN (METAL POSTCARD)		
	Polydor 2059 151 47	3 wks
15 Mar 80	HAPPY HOUSE *Polydor POSP 117* 17	8 wks
7 Jun 80	CHRISTINE *Polydor 2059 249* 22	8 wks
6 Dec 80	ISRAEL *Polydor POSP 205* 41	8 wks
30 May 81	SPELLBOUND *Polydor POSP 273* 22	8 wks
1 Aug 81	ARABIAN KNIGHTS *Polydor POSP 309* 32	7 wks
29 May 82	FIRE WORKS *Polydor POSPG 450* 22	6 wks
9 Oct 82	SLOWDIVE *Polydor POSP 510* 41	4 wks
4 Dec 82	MELT / IL EST NE LE DIVIN ENFANT		
	Polydor POSP 539 49	5 wks
1 Oct 83 ●	DEAR PRUDENCE *Wonderland SHE 4* 3	8 wks
24 Mar 84	SWIMMING HORSES *Wonderland SHE 6* 28	4 wks
2 Jun 84	DAZZLE *Wonderland SHE 7* 33	3 wks
27 Oct 84	THE THORN EP *Wonderland SHEEP 8* 47	3 wks
26 Oct 85	CITIES IN DUST *Wonderland SHE 9* 21	6 wks
8 Mar 86	CANDYMAN *Wonderland SHE 10* 34	5 wks
17 Jan 87	THIS WHEEL'S ON FIRE *Wonderland SHE 11* 14	6 wks
28 Mar 87	THE PASSENGER *Wonderland SHE 12* 41	6 wks
25 Jul 87	SONG FROM THE EDGE OF THE WORLD		
	Wonderland SHE 13 59	3 wks
30 Jul 88	PEEK-A-BOO *Wonderland SHE 14* 16	6 wks
8 Oct 88	THE KILLING JAR *Wonderland SHE 15* 41	3 wks
3 Dec 88	THE LAST BEAT OF MY HEART		
	Wonderland SHE 16 44	1 wk
25 May 91	KISS THEM FOR ME *Wonderland SHE 19* 32	4 wks
13 Jul 91	SHADOWTIME *Wonderland SHE 20* 57	1 wk
25 Jul 92	FACE TO FACE *Wonderland SHE 21* 21	4 wks
20 Aug 94	INTERLUDE *Parlophone CDR 6365* [1] 25	2 wks

[1] Morrissey and Siouxsie

Tracks on The Thorn EP: Overground / Voices / Placebo Effect / Red Over White.

SIR DOUGLAS QUINTET
US, male vocal / instrumental group **10 wks**

17 Jun 65	SHE'S ABOUT A MOVER *London HLU 9964* 15	10 wks

SIR MIX-A-LOT *US, male rapper* **2 wks**

8 Aug 92	BABY GOT BACK *Def American DEFA 20* 56	2 wks

SIRRON - *See PLUS ONE featuring SIRRON*

SISTER BLISS with COLETTE
UK / US, female vocal duo　　　　　　　　　　　**4 wks**

15 Oct 94	**CANTGETAMAN CANTGETAJOB (LIFE'S A BITCH)**			
	Go.Beat GODCD 124	31	4 wks

SISTER SLEDGE *US, female vocal group*　　　**111 wks**

21 Jun 75	**MAMA NEVER TOLD ME** *Atlantic K 10619*	20	6 wks
17 Mar 79 ●	**HE'S THE GREATEST DANCER**		
	Atlantic/Cotillion K 11257	6	11 wks
26 May 79 ●	**WE ARE FAMILY** *Atlantic/Cotillion K 11293*	8	10 wks
11 Aug 79	**LOST IN MUSIC** *Atlantic/Cotillion K 11337*	17	10 wks
19 Jan 80	**GOT TO LOVE SOMEBODY**		
	Atlantic/Cotillion K 11404	34	4 wks
28 Feb 81	**ALL AMERICAN GIRLS** *Atlantic K 11656*	41	5 wks
26 May 84	**THINKING OF YOU** *Cotillion/Atlantic B 9744*	11	13 wks
8 Sep 84	**LOST IN MUSIC (re-mix)** *Cotillion/Atlantic B 9718*	4	12 wks
17 Nov 84	**WE ARE FAMILY (re-mix)** *Cotillion/Atlantic B 9692*	33	4 wks
1 Jun 85 ★	**FRANKIE** *Atlantic A 9547*	1	16 wks
31 Aug 85	**DANCING ON THE JAGGED EDGE** *Atlantic A 9520*	50	3 wks
23 Jan 93 ●	**WE ARE FAMILY (2nd re-mix)** *Atlantic A 4508CD*	5	8 wks
13 Mar 93	**LOST IN MUSIC (2nd re-mix)** *Atlantic A 4509CD*	14	5 wks
12 Jun 93	**THINKING OF YOU (re-mix)** *Atlantic A 4515CD*	17	4 wks

SISTERS OF MERCY
UK, male vocalist Andrew Eldritch and backing musicians　　**40 wks**

16 Jun 84	**BODY AND SOUL / TRAIN**		
	Merciful Release MR 029	46	3 wks
20 Oct 84	**WALK AWAY** *Merciful Release MR 033*	45	3 wks
9 Mar 85	**NO TIME TO CRY** *Merciful Release MR 035*	63	2 wks
3 Oct 87 ●	**THIS CORROSION** *Merciful Release MR 39*	7	6 wks
27 Feb 88	**DOMINION** *Merciful Release MR 43*	13	6 wks
18 Jun 88	**LUCRETIA MY REFLECTION**		
	Merciful Release MR 45	20	4 wks
13 Oct 90	**MORE** *Merciful Release MR 47*	14	4 wks
22 Dec 90	**DOCTOR JEEP** *Merciful Release MR 51*	37	4 wks
2 May 92 ●	**TEMPLE OF LOVE** *Merciful Release MR 53*	3	5 wks
28 Aug 93	**UNDER THE GUN** *Merciful Release MR 59CDX*	19	3 wks

SIVUCA *Brazil, male vocalist*　　　　　　　　**3 wks**

28 Jul 84	**AIN'T NO SUNSHINE** *London LON 51*	56	3 wks

SKATALITES *Jamaica, male instrumental group*　　**6 wks**

20 Apr 67	**GUNS OF NAVARONE** *Island WI 168*	36	6 wks

Peter SKELLERN *UK, male vocalist*　　　　**24 wks**

23 Sep 72 ●	**YOU'RE A LADY** *Decca F 13333*	3	11 wks
29 Mar 75	**HOLD ON TO LOVE** *Decca F 13568*	14	9 wks
28 Oct 78	**LOVE IS THE SWEETEST THING**		
	Mercury 6008 603 [1]	60	4 wks

[1] Peter Skellern featuring Grimethorpe Colliery Band

SKID ROW *US, male / female vocal / instrumental group*　**25 wks**

18 Nov 89	**YOUTH GONE WILD** *Atlantic A 8935*	42	3 wks
3 Feb 90	**18 AND LIFE** *Atlantic A 8883*	12	6 wks
31 Mar 90	**I REMEMBER YOU** *East West A 8836*	36	4 wks
15 Jun 91	**MONKEY BUSINESS** *Atlantic A 7673*	19	3 wks
14 Sep 91	**SLAVE TO THE GRIND** *Atlantic A 7603*	43	2 wks
23 Nov 91	**WASTED TIME** *Atlantic A 7570*	20	3 wks
29 Aug 92	**YOUTH GONE WILD (re-issue)** *Atlantic A 7444*	22	4 wks

SKIDS *UK, male vocal / instrumental group*　　**60 wks**

23 Sep 78	**SWEET SUBURBIA** *Virgin VS 227*	70	1 wk
7 Oct 78	**SWEET SUBURBIA (re-entry)** *Virgin VS 227*	71	2 wks
4 Nov 78	**THE SAINTS ARE COMING** *Virgin VS 232*	48	3 wks

---

17 Feb 79 ●	**INTO THE VALLEY** *Virgin VS 241*	10	11 wks
26 May 79	**MASQUERADE** *Virgin VS 262*	14	9 wks
29 Sep 79	**CHARADE** *Virgin VS 288*	31	6 wks
24 Nov 79	**WORKING FOR THE YANKEE DOLLAR**		
	Virgin VS 306	20	11 wks
1 Mar 80	**ANIMATION** *Virgin VS 323*	56	3 wks
16 Aug 80	**CIRCUS GAMES** *Virgin VS 359*	32	7 wks
18 Oct 80	**GOODBYE CIVILIAN** *Virgin VS 373*	52	4 wks
6 Dec 80	**WOMEN IN WINTER** *Virgin VSK 101*	49	3 wks

SKIN *UK / Germany, male vocal / instrumental group*　　**13 wks**

25 Dec 93	**THE SKIN UP EP** *Parlophone CDR 6363*	67	2 wks
12 Mar 94	**HOUSE OF LOVE** *Parlophone CDR 6374*	45	2 wks
30 Apr 94	**MONEY / UNBELIEVEABLE** *Parlophone CDRS 6381*	18	3 wks
23 Jul 94	**TOWER OF STRENGTH** *Parlophone CDRS 6387*	19	3 wks
15 Oct 94	**LOOK BUT DON'T TOUCH (EP)**		
	Parlophone CDRS 6391	33	3 wks

Tracks on The Skin Up EP: Look But Don't Touch / Shine Your Light / Monkey. Tracks on Look But Don't Touch (EP): Look But Don't Touch / Should I Stay Or Should I Go / Pump It Up / Monkey. The first and last tracks on this EP are, of course, re-issues of two tracks from The Skin Up EP.

SKIN UP *UK, male producer*　　　　　　　**9 wks**

7 Sep 91	**IVORY** *Love EVOL 4*	48	3 wks
14 Mar 92	**A JUICY RED APPLE** *Love EVOL 11*	32	4 wks
18 Jul 92	**ACCELERATE** *Love EVOL 17*	45	2 wks

SKIPWORTH and TURNER *US, male vocal duo*　**12 wks**

27 Apr 85	**THINKING ABOUT YOUR LOVE**		
	Fourth & Broadway BRW 23	24	10 wks
21 Jan 89	**MAKE IT LAST** *Fourth & Broadway BRW 118*	60	2 wks

SKY *UK / Australia, male instrumental group*　　**11 wks**

5 Apr 80 ●	**TOCCATA** *Ariola ARO 300*	5	11 wks

SKYHOOKS *Australia, male vocal / instrumental group*　**1 wk**

9 Jun 79	**WOMEN IN UNIFORM** *United Artists UP 36508*	73	1 wk

SLADE *UK, male vocal / instrumental group*　　**276 wks**

19 Jun 71	**GET DOWN AND GET WITH IT** *Polydor 2058 112*	16	14 wks
30 Oct 71 ★	**COZ I LUV YOU** *Polydor 2058 155*	1	15 wks
5 Feb 72 ●	**LOOK WOT YOU DUN** *Polydor 2058 195*	4	10 wks
3 Jun 72 ★	**TAKE ME BAK 'OME** *Polydor 2058 231*	1	13 wks
2 Sep 72 ★	**MAMA WEER ALL CRAZEE NOW** *Polydor 2058 274*	1	10 wks
25 Nov 72 ●	**GUDBUY T'JANE** *Polydor 2058 312*	2	13 wks
3 Mar 73 ★	**CUM ON FEEL THE NOIZE** *Polydor 2058 339*	1	12 wks
30 Jun 73 ★	**SKWEEZE ME PLEEZE ME** *Polydor 2058 377*	1	10 wks
6 Oct 73 ●	**MY FREND STAN** *Polydor 2058 407*	2	8 wks
15 Dec 73	**MERRY XMAS EVERYBODY** *Polydor 2058 422*	1	9 wks
6 Apr 74 ●	**EVERYDAY** *Polydor 2058 453*	3	7 wks
6 Jul 74 ●	**BANGIN' MAN** *Polydor 2058 492*	3	7 wks
19 Oct 74 ●	**FAR FAR AWAY** *Polydor 2058 522*	2	6 wks
15 Feb 75	**HOW DOES IT FEEL** *Polydor 2058 547*	15	7 wks
17 May 75 ●	**THANKS FOR THE MEMORY (WHAM BAM THANK YOU MAM)** *Polydor 2058 585*	7	7 wks
22 Nov 75	**IN FOR A PENNY** *Polydor 2058 663*	11	8 wks
7 Feb 76	**LET'S CALL IT QUITS** *Polydor 2058 690*	11	7 wks
5 Feb 77	**GYPSY ROAD HOG** *Barn 2014 105*	48	2 wks
29 Oct 77	**MY BABY LEFT ME - THAT'S ALL RIGHT (MEDLEY)**		
	Barn 2014 114	32	4 wks
18 Oct 80	**SLADE ALIVE AT READING '80 EP**		
	Cheapskate CHEAP 5	44	5 wks
27 Dec 80	**MERRY XMAS EVERYBODY**		
	Cheapskate CHEAP 11 [1]	70	2 wks
31 Jan 81 ●	**WE'LL BRING THE HOUSE DOWN**		
	Cheapskate CHEAP 16	10	9 wks

4 Apr 81	WHEELS AIN'T COMING DOWN		
	Cheapskate CHEAP 21 ....**60**	3 wks
19 Sep 81	LOCK UP YOUR DAUGHTERS RCA 124 ......**29**	8 wks
19 Dec 81	MERRY XMAS EVERYBODY (re-entry)	
	Polydor 2058 422 ....**32**	4 wks
27 Mar 82	RUBY RED RCA 191 ....**51**	3 wks
27 Nov 82	(AND NOW - THE WALTZ) C'EST LA VIE RCA 291....**50**	6 wks
25 Dec 82	MERRY XMAS EVERYBODY (2nd re-entry)	
	Polydor 2058 422 ....**67**	3 wks
19 Nov 83	● MY OH MY RCA 373 ....**2**	11 wks
10 Dec 83	MERRY XMAS EVERYBODY (3rd re-entry)	
	Polydor 2058 422 ....**20**	5 wks
4 Feb 84	● RUN RUN AWAY RCA 385 ....**7**	10 wks
17 Nov 84	ALL JOIN HANDS RCA 455 ....**15**	9 wks
15 Dec 84	MERRY XMAS EVERYBODY (4th re-entry)	
	Polydor 2058 422 ....**47**	4 wks
26 Jan 85	7 YEAR BITCH RCA 475 ....**60**	3 wks
23 Mar 85	MYZSTERIOUS MIZTER JONES RCA PB 40027 ......**50**	5 wks
30 Nov 85	DO YOU BELIEVE IN MIRACLES RCA PB 40449....**54**	6 wks
21 Dec 85	MERRY XMAS EVERYBODY (re-issue)	
	Polydor POSP 780 ....**48**	3 wks
27 Dec 86	MERRY XMAS EVERYBODY (re-entry of re-issue)	
	Polydor POSP 780 ....**71**	1 wk
21 Feb 87	STILL THE SAME RCA PB 41137 ....**73**	2 wks
19 Oct 91	RADIO WALL OF SOUND Polydor PO 180 ......**21**	5 wks

1 Slade and the Reading Choir

Tracks on Slade Alive At Reading Alive '80 EP: When I'm Dancin' I Ain't Fightin' / Born To Be Wild / Somethin' Else / Pistol Packin' Mama / Keep A Rollin'.

SLAMM UK, male vocal / instrumental group · **4 wks**

17 Jul 93	ENERGIZE PWL International PWCD 266 ......**57**	2 wks
23 Oct 93	VIRGINIA PLAIN PWL International PWCD 274 ......**60**	1 wk
22 Oct 94	THAT'S WHERE MY MIND GOES	
	PWL International PWCD 310 ....**68**	1 wk

SLAUGHTER US, male vocal / instrumental group · **2 wks**

29 Sep 90	UP ALL NIGHT Chrysalis CHS 3556 ....**62**	1 wk
2 Feb 91	FLY TO THE ANGELS Chrysalis CHS 3634.....**55**	1 wk

SLAVE US, male vocal / instrumental group · **3 wks**

8 Mar 80	JUST A TOUCH OF LOVE	
	Atlantic / Cotillion K 11442 ....**64**	3 wks

SLAYER US, male vocal / instrumental group · **2 wks**

13 Jun 87	CRIMINALLY INSANE Def Jam LON 133 ......**64**	1 wk
26 Oct 91	SEASONS IN THE ABYSS Def American DEFA 9 ......**51**	1 wk

Kathy SLEDGE US, female vocalist · **2 wks**

16 May 92	TAKE ME BACK TO LOVE AGAIN Epic 6579837 ......**62**	2 wks

Percy SLEDGE US, male vocalist · **34 wks**

12 May 66	● WHEN A MAN LOVES A WOMAN Atlantic 584 001 ..**4**	17 wks
4 Aug 66	WARM AND TENDER LOVE Atlantic 584 034 ......**34**	7 wks
14 Feb 87	● WHEN A MAN LOVES A WOMAN (re-issue)	
	Atlantic YZ 96 ....**2**	10 wks

SLEEPER UK, male / female vocal / instrumental group · **1 wk**

21 May 94	DELICIOUS Indolent SLEEP 003CD **75**	1 wk

SLICK US, male / female vocal / instrumental group · **15 wks**

16 Jun 79	SPACE BASS Fantasy FTC 176 ....**16**	10 wks
15 Sep 79	SEXY CREAM Fantasy FTC 182 ....**47**	5 wks

Grace SLICK US, female vocalist · **4 wks**

24 May 80	DREAMS RCA PB 9534 ....**50**	4 wks

SLIK UK, male vocal / instrumental group · **18 wks**

17 Jan 76	★ FOREVER AND EVER Bell 1464 ....**1**	9 wks
8 May 76	REQUIEM Bell 1478 ....**24**	9 wks

SLIM CHANCE - See Ronnie LANE and SLIM CHANCE

SLIPSTREEM UK, male vocal group · **7 wks**

19 Dec 92	WE ARE RAVING - THE ANTHEM	
	Boogie Food 7BF 1 ....**18**	7 wks

SLITS UK, female vocal / instrumental group · **3 wks**

13 Oct 79	TYPICAL GIRLS / I HEARD IT THROUGH	
	THE GRAPEVINE Island WIP 6505 ....**60**	3 wks

P.F. SLOAN US, male vocalist · **3 wks**

4 Nov 65	SINS OF THE FAMILY RCA 1482 ....**38**	3 wks

SLO-MOSHUN UK, male instrumental / production duo · **4 wks**

5 Feb 94	BELLS OF NY Six6 SIXCD 108 ....**29**	3 wks
30 Jul 94	HELP MY FRIEND Six6 SIXCD 117 ....**52**	1 wk

SLOWDIVE UK, male / female vocal / instrumental group · **2 wks**

15 Jun 91	CATCH THE BREEZE / SHINE Creation CRE 112 ......**52**	1 wk
29 May 93	OUTSIDE YOUR ROOM (EP) Creation CRESCD 119 ..**69**	1 wk

Tracks on Outside Your Room (EP): Outside Your Room / Alison / So Tired / Souvlaki Space Station.

SL2 UK, male instrumental / production duo · **23 wks**

2 Nov 91	DJS TAKE CONTROL / WAY IN MY BRAIN	
	XL XLS 24 ....**11**	5 wks
4 Jan 92	DJS TAKE CONTROL / WAY IN MY BRAIN	
	(re-entry) XL XLS 24 ....**71**	1 wk
18 Apr 92	● ON A RAGGA TIP XL XLS 29 ....**2**	11 wks
19 Dec 92	WAY IN MY BRAIN (re-issue) XL XLS 36 ....**26**	6 wks

SLY and the FAMILY STONE
US, male / female vocal / instrumental group · **42 wks**

10 Jul 68	● DANCE TO THE MUSIC Direction 58 3568 ......**7**	14 wks
2 Oct 68	M'LADY Direction 58 3707 ....**32**	7 wks
19 Mar 69	EVERYDAY PEOPLE Direction 58 3938 ....**36**	1 wk
9 Apr 69	EVERYDAY PEOPLE (re-entry) Direction 58 3938....**37**	4 wks
8 Jan 72	FAMILY AFFAIR Epic EPC 7632 ....**15**	8 wks
15 Apr 72	RUNNIN' AWAY Epic EPC 7810 ....**17**	8 wks

SLY FOX US, male vocal / instrumental duo · **16 wks**

31 May 86	● LET'S GO ALL THE WAY Capitol CL 403 ....**3**	16 wks

SLY and ROBBIE
Jamaica, male vocal / instrumental duo · **15 wks**

4 Apr 87	BOOPS (HERE TO GO) Fourth & Broadway BRW 61..**12**	11 wks
25 Jul 87	FIRE Fourth & Broadway BRW 71 ....**60**	4 wks

Heather SMALL - See M PEOPLE

SMALL ADS UK, male vocal/instrumental group — **3 wks**

18 Apr 81	**SMALL ADS** Bronze BRO 115	**63**	3 wks

SMALL FACES UK, male vocal/instrumental group — **137 wks**

2 Sep 65	**WHATCHA GONNA DO ABOUT IT?** Decca F 12208	**14**	12 wks
10 Feb 66	● **SHA LA LA LA LEE** Decca F 12317	**3**	11 wks
12 May 66	● **HEY GIRL** Decca F 12393	**10**	9 wks
11 Aug 66	★ **ALL OR NOTHING** Decca F 12470	**1**	12 wks
17 Nov 66	● **MY MIND'S EYE** Decca F 12500	**4**	11 wks
9 Mar 67	**I CAN'T MAKE IT** Decca F 12565	**26**	7 wks
8 Jun 67	**HERE COME THE NICE** Immediate IM 050	**12**	10 wks
9 Aug 67	● **ITCHYCOO PARK** Immediate IM 057	**3**	14 wks
6 Dec 67	● **TIN SOLDIER** Immediate IM 062	**9**	12 wks
17 Apr 68	● **LAZY SUNDAY** Immediate IM 064	**2**	11 wks
10 Jul 68	**UNIVERSAL** Immediate IM 069	**16**	11 wks
19 Mar 69	**AFTERGLOW OF YOUR LOVE** Immediate IM 077	**36**	1 wk
13 Dec 75	● **ITCHYCOO PARK (re-issue)** Immediate IMS 102	**9**	11 wks
20 Mar 76	**LAZY SUNDAY (re-issue)** Immediate IMS 106	**39**	5 wks

SMART E'S UK, male instrumental/production group — **9 wks**

11 Jul 92	● **SESAME'S TREET** Suburban Base SUBBASE 12S	**2**	9 wks

S*M*A*S*H UK, male vocal/instrumental group — **1 wk**

6 Aug 94	**(I WANT TO) KILL SOMEBODY** Hi-Rise FLATSCD 5	**26**	1 wk

SMASHING PUMPKINS
US, male/female vocal/instrumental group — **8 wks**

5 Sep 92	**I AM ONE** Hut HUTT 18	**73**	1 wk
3 Jul 93	**CHERUB ROCK** Hut HUTCD 31	**31**	2 wks
25 Sep 93	**TODAY** Hut HUTCD 37	**44**	2 wks
5 Mar 94	**DISARM** Hut HUTCD 43	**11**	3 wks

SMEAR CAMPAIGN - See MR. BEAN and SMEAR CAMPAIGN featuring Bruce DICKINSON

SMELLS LIKE HEAVEN
Italy, male producer - Fabi Paras — **1 wk**

10 Jul 93	**LONDRES STRUTT** Deconstruction 74321154312	**57**	1 wk

Anne Marie SMITH - See FARGETTA and Anne Marie SMITH

'Fast' Eddie SMITH - See DJ 'FAST' EDDIE

Hurricane SMITH UK, male vocalist — **35 wks**

12 Jun 71	● **DON'T LET IT DIE** Columbia DB 8785	**2**	12 wks
29 Apr 72	● **OH BABE WHAT WOULD YOU SAY?** Columbia DB 8878	**4**	16 wks
2 Sep 72	**WHO WAS IT** Columbia DB 8916	**23**	7 wks

Jimmy SMITH US, male instrumentalist - organ — **3 wks**

28 Apr 66	**GOT MY MOJO WORKING** Verve VS 536	**48**	2 wks
19 May 66	**GOT MY MOJO WORKING (re-entry)** Verve VS 536	**48**	1 wk

Keely SMITH US, female vocalist — **10 wks**

18 Mar 65	**YOU'RE BREAKIN' MY HEART** Reprise R 20346	**14**	10 wks

Mandy SMITH UK, female vocalist — **2 wks**

20 May 89	**DON'T YOU WANT ME BABY** PWL PWL 37	**59**	2 wks

Mark E. SMITH - See INSPIRAL CARPETS

Mel SMITH UK, male vocalist — **10 wks**

5 Dec 87	● **ROCKIN' AROUND THE CHRISTMAS TREE** 10 TEN 2 [1]	**3**	7 wks
21 Dec 91	**ANOTHER BLOOMING CHRISTMAS** Epic 6576877	**59**	3 wks

[1] Mel and Kim

Muriel SMITH UK, female vocalist — **17 wks**

15 May 53	● **HOLD ME THRILL ME KISS ME** Philips PB 122	**3**	17 wks

O.C. SMITH US, male vocalist — **23 wks**

29 May 68	● **SON OF HICKORY HOLLER'S TRAMP** CBS 3343	**2**	15 wks
26 Mar 77	**TOGETHER** Caribou CRB 4910	**25**	8 wks

Rex SMITH - See Rachel SWEET

Richard Jon SMITH South Africa, male vocalist — **2 wks**

16 Jul 83	**SHE'S THE MASTER OF THE GAME** Jive JIVE 38	**63**	2 wks

Whistling Jack SMITH UK, male whistler — **12 wks**

2 Mar 67	● **I WAS KAISER BILL'S BATMAN** Deram DM 112	**5**	12 wks

Patti SMITH GROUP
US, female vocalist, male instrumental backing group — **16 wks**

29 Apr 78	● **BECAUSE THE NIGHT** Arista 181	**5**	12 wks
19 Aug 78	**PRIVILEGE (SET ME FREE)** Arista 197	**72**	1 wk
2 Jun 79	**FREDERICK** Arista 264	**63**	3 wks

SMITHS UK, male vocal/instrumental group — **104 wks**

12 Nov 83	**THIS CHARMING MAN** Rough Trade RT 136	**25**	12 wks
28 Jan 84	**WHAT DIFFERENCE DOES IT MAKE** Rough Trade RT 146	**12**	9 wks
2 Jun 84	● **HEAVEN KNOWS I'M MISERABLE NOW** Rough Trade RT 156	**10**	8 wks
1 Sep 84	**WILLIAM, IT WAS REALLY NOTHING** Rough Trade RT 166	**17**	6 wks
9 Feb 85	**HOW SOON IS NOW?** Rough Trade RT 176	**24**	6 wks
30 Mar 85	**SHAKESPEARE'S SISTER** Rough Trade RT 181	**26**	4 wks
13 Jul 85	**THAT JOKE ISN'T FUNNY ANYMORE** Rough Trade RT 186	**49**	3 wks
5 Oct 85	**THE BOY WITH THE THORN IN HIS SIDE** Rough Trade RT 191	**23**	5 wks
31 May 86	**BIG MOUTH STRIKES AGAIN** Rough Trade RT 192	**26**	4 wks
2 Aug 86	**PANIC** Rough Trade RT 193	**11**	8 wks
1 Nov 86	**ASK** Rough Trade RT 194	**14**	5 wks
7 Feb 87	**SHOPLIFTERS OF THE WORLD UNITE** Rough Trade RT 195	**12**	4 wks
25 Apr 87	● **SHEILA TAKE A BOW** Rough Trade RT 196	**10**	5 wks
22 Aug 87	**GIRLFRIEND IN A COMA** Rough Trade RT 197	**13**	5 wks
14 Nov 87	**I STARTED SOMETHING I COULDN'T FINISH** Rough Trade RT 198	**23**	4 wks
19 Dec 87	**LAST NIGHT I DREAMT THAT SOMEBODY LOVED ME** Rough Trade RT 200	**30**	4 wks
15 Aug 92	● **THIS CHARMING MAN (re-issue)** WEA YZ 0001	**8**	5 wks
12 Sep 92	**HOW SOON IS NOW (re-issue)** WEA YZ 0002	**16**	4 wks
24 Oct 92	**THERE IS A LIGHT THAT NEVER GOES OUT** WEA YZ 0003	**25**	3 wks

SMOKE UK, male vocal/instrumental group — **3 wks**

9 Mar 67	**MY FRIEND JACK** Columbia DB 8115	**45**	3 wks

SMOKIE UK, male vocal/instrumental group — 106 wks

Date	Title	Pos	Wks
19 Jul 75	● IF YOU THINK YOU KNOW HOW TO LOVE ME RAK 206 [1]	3	9 wks
4 Oct 75	● DON'T PLAY YOUR ROCK 'N ROLL TO ME RAK 217 [1]	8	7 wks
31 Jan 76	SOMETHING'S BEEN MAKING ME BLUE RAK 227	17	8 wks
25 Sep 76	I'LL MEET YOU AT MIDNIGHT RAK 241	11	9 wks
4 Dec 76	● LIVING NEXT DOOR TO ALICE RAK 244	5	11 wks
19 Mar 77	LAY BACK IN THE ARMS OF SOMEONE RAK 251	12	9 wks
16 Jul 77	● IT'S YOUR LIFE RAK 260	5	9 wks
15 Oct 77	● NEEDLES AND PINS RAK 263	10	9 wks
28 Jan 78	FOR A FEW DOLLARS MORE RAK 267	17	6 wks
20 May 78	● OH CAROL RAK 276	5	13 wks
23 Sep 78	MEXICAN GIRL RAK 283	19	9 wks
19 Apr 80	TAKE GOOD CARE OF MY BABY RAK 309	34	7 wks

[1] Smokey

Joe SMOOTH US, male vocalist — 4 wks

Date	Title	Pos	Wks
4 Feb 89	PROMISED LAND DJ International DJIN 6	56	4 wks

SMOOTH TOUCH US, male instrumental/production duo — 1 wk

Date	Title	Pos	Wks
2 Apr 94	HOUSE OF LOVE (IN MY HOUSE) Six6 SIXCD 112	58	1 wk

SMURFS - See FATHER ABRAHAM and the SMURFS

Patty SMYTH - See Don HENLEY

SNAP
US/Germany, male/female vocal/instrumental group — 104 wks

Date	Title	Pos	Wks
24 Mar 90	★ THE POWER Arista 113133	1	15 wks
16 Jun 90	● OOOPS UP Arista 113296	5	12 wks
22 Sep 90	● CULT OF SNAP Arista 113596	8	7 wks
8 Dec 90	● MARY HAD A LITTLE BOY Arista 113831	8	10 wks
30 Mar 91	● SNAP MEGAMIX Arista 114169	10	6 wks
21 Dec 91	THE COLOUR OF LOVE Arista 114678	54	3 wks
4 Jul 92	★ RHYTHM IS A DANCER Arista 115309	1	19 wks
9 Jan 93	● EXTERMINATE! Arista 74321106962 [1]	2	11 wks
12 Jun 93	● DO YOU SEE THE LIGHT (LOOKING FOR) Arista 74321147622 [1]	10	8 wks
17 Sep 94	● WELCOME TO TOMORROW Arista 74321223852 [2]	6	13 wks

[1] Snap featuring Niki Harris [2] Snap featuring Summer

SNIFF 'N' THE TEARS
UK, male vocal/instrumental group — 5 wks

Date	Title	Pos	Wks
23 Jun 79	DRIVER'S SEAT Chiswick CHIS 105	42	5 wks

SNOOP DOGGY DOGG US, male rapper — 14 wks

Date	Title	Pos	Wks
4 Dec 93	WHAT'S MY NAME? Death Row A 8337CD	20	8 wks
12 Feb 94	GIN AND JUICE Death Row A 8316CD	39	3 wks
20 Aug 94	DOGGY DOGG WORLD Death Row A 8289CD	32	3 wks

SNOW Canada, male rapper — 18 wks

Date	Title	Pos	Wks
13 Mar 93	● INFORMER East West America A 8436CD	2	15 wks
5 Jun 93	GIRL I'VE BEEN HURT East West America A 8417CD	48	2 wks
4 Sep 93	UHH IN YOU Atlantic A 8378CD	67	1 wk

Phoebe SNOW US, female vocalist — 7 wks

Date	Title	Pos	Wks
6 Jan 79	EVERY NIGHT CBS 6842	37	7 wks

SNOWMAN - See Peter AUTY

British Hit Singles Part One: Alphabetically by Artist

Date of chart entry/Title & catalogue no./Peak position reached/Weeks on chart

★ Number One   ● Top Ten   † still on chart at 31 Dec 1994

□ = credited to act billed in footnote

SNOWMEN UK, male vocal/instrumental group — 12 wks

Date	Title	Pos	Wks
12 Dec 81	HOKEY COKEY Stiff ODB 1	18	8 wks
18 Dec 82	XMAS PARTY Solid STOP 006	44	4 wks

SO UK, male vocal/instrumental group — 3 wks

Date	Title	Pos	Wks
13 Feb 88	ARE YOU SURE Parlophone R 6173	62	3 wks

Gino SOCCIO Canada, male instrumentalist - keyboards — 5 wks

Date	Title	Pos	Wks
28 Apr 79	DANCER Warner Bros. K 17357	46	5 wks

SOEUR SOURIRE - See SINGING NUN

SOFT CELL UK, male vocal/instrumental duo — 107 wks

Date	Title	Pos	Wks
1 Aug 81	★ TAINTED LOVE Some Bizzare BZS 2	1	16 wks
14 Nov 81	● BED SITTER Some Bizzare BZS 6	4	12 wks
9 Jan 82	TAINTED LOVE (re-entry) Some Bizzare BZS 2	43	10 wks
6 Feb 82	● SAY HELLO WAVE GOODBYE Some Bizzare BZS 7	3	9 wks
29 May 82	● TORCH Some Bizzare BZS 9	2	9 wks
24 Jul 82	TAINTED LOVE (2nd re-entry) Some Bizzare BZS 2	50	4 wks
21 Aug 82	● WHAT Some Bizzare BZS 11	3	8 wks
4 Dec 82	WHERE THE HEART IS Some Bizzare BZS 16	21	7 wks
5 Mar 83	NUMBERS/BARRIERS Some Bizzare BZS 17	25	4 wks
24 Sep 83	SOUL INSIDE Some Bizzare BZS 20	16	5 wks
25 Feb 84	DOWN IN THE SUBWAY Some Bizzare BZS 22	24	6 wks
9 Feb 85	TAINTED LOVE (3rd re-entry) Some Bizzare BZS 2	43	6 wks
23 Mar 91	SAY HELLO WAVE GOODBYE '91 [1] Mercury SOFT 1	38	3 wks
18 May 91	● TAINTED LOVE (re-issue) [1] Mercury SOFT 2	5	8 wks

[1] Soft Cell/Marc Almond

SOHO UK, male/female vocal/instrumental group — 11 wks

Date	Title	Pos	Wks
5 May 90	HIPPY CHICK Savage 7SAV 106	67	1 wk
19 Jan 91	● HIPPY CHICK (re-entry) Savage 7SAV 106	8	8 wks
9 Nov 91	BORN TO BE ALIVE MCA MCS 1578 [1]	51	2 wks

[1] Adamski featuring Soho

The listed flip side of Born To Be Alive was Never Goin' Down by Adamski featuring Jimi Polo.

SOLO UK, male producer - Stuart Crichton — 4 wks

Date	Title	Pos	Wks
20 Jul 91	RAINBOW (SAMPLE FREE) Reverb RVBT 003	59	2 wks
18 Jan 92	COME ON! Reverb RVBT 008	75	1 wk
11 Sep 93	COME ON! (re-mix) Stoatin' STOAT 003CD	63	1 wk

Sal SOLO UK, male vocalist — 13 wks

Date	Title	Pos	Wks
15 Dec 84	SAN DAMIANO (HEART AND SOUL) MCA MCA 930	15	10 wks
6 Apr 85	MUSIC AND YOU MCA MCA 946 [1]	52	3 wks

[1] Sal Solo with the London Community Gospel Choir

Belouis SOME UK, male vocalist — 26 wks

Date	Title	Pos	Wks
27 Apr 85	IMAGINATION Parlophone R 6097	50	7 wks
18 Jan 86	IMAGINATION (re-issue) Parlophone R 1986	17	10 wks
12 Apr 86	SOME PEOPLE Parlophone R 6130	33	7 wks
16 May 87	LET IT BE WITH YOU Parlophone R 6154	53	2 wks

Jimmy SOMERVILLE
UK, male vocalist **36 wks**

11 Nov 89	COMMENT TE DIRE ADIEU *London LON 241* [1] **14**	9 wks
13 Jan 90	● YOU MAKE ME FEEL (MIGHTY REAL)	
	London LON 249................**5**	8 wks
17 Mar 90	READ MY LIPS (ENOUGH IS ENOUGH)	
	London LON 254 ....**26**	6 wks
3 Nov 90	● TO LOVE SOMEBODY *London LON 281* **8**	11 wks
10 Aug 91	RUN FROM LOVE *London LON 301* **52**	2 wks

[1] Jimmy Somerville featuring June Miles-Kingston

See also Bronski Beat: *Various Artists (EPs & LPs) - Gimme Shelter (EP).*

SONIA
UK, female vocalist **78 wks**

24 Jun 89	★ YOU'LL NEVER STOP ME LOVING YOU	
	Chrysalis CHS 3385 ....**1**	13 wks
7 Oct 89	CAN'T FORGET YOU *Chrysalis CHS 3419* **17**	6 wks
9 Dec 89	● LISTEN TO YOUR HEART *Chrysalis CHS 3465* **10**	10 wks
7 Apr 90	COUNTING EVERY MINUTE *Chrysalis CHS 3492*........**16**	7 wks
23 Jun 90	YOU'VE GOT A FRIEND *Jive CHILD 90* [1] **14**	6 wks
25 Aug 90	END OF THE WORLD *Chrysalis/PWL CHS 3557* **18**	7 wks
1 Jun 91	● ONLY FOOLS (NEVER FALL IN LOVE) *IQ ZB 44613* ..**10**	8 wks
31 Aug 91	BE YOUNG BE FOOLISH BE HAPPY *IQ ZB 44935*.....**22**	5 wks
16 Nov 91	YOU TO ME ARE EVERYTHING *IQ ZB 45121* **13**	5 wks
12 Sep 92	BOOGIE NIGHTS *Arista 74321113467* **30**	3 wks
1 May 93	BETTER THE DEVIL YOU KNOW	
	Arista 74321146872 ....**15**	7 wks
30 Jul 94	HOPELESSLY DEVOTED TO YOU	
	Cockney COCCD 2 ....**61**	1 wk

[1] Big Fun and Sonia

SONIC SOLUTION
UK, male producer – Steve Cop **1 wk**

| 4 Apr 92 | BEATSTIME *R & S RSUK 11* ....**59** | 1 wk |

SONIC SURFERS
Holland, male instrumental / production duo **2 wks**

| 20 Mar 93 | TAKE ME UP *A & M AMCD 210* [1] ....**61** | 1 wk |
| 30 Jul 94 | DON'T GIVE IT UP *Brilliant CDBRIL 6*................**54** | 1 wk |

[1] Sonic Surfers featuring Jocelyn Brown

SONIC THE HEDGEHOG – *See HWA featuring SONIC THE HEDGEHOG*

SONIC YOUTH
US, male / female vocal / instrumental group **13 wks**

11 Jul 92	100% *DGC DGCS 11*................**28**	4 wks
7 Nov 92	YOUTH AGAINST FASCISM *Geffen GFS 26* **52**	2 wks
3 Apr 93	SUGAR KANE *Geffen GFSTD 37* **26**	3 wks
7 May 94	BULL IN THE HEATHER *Geffen GFSTD 72* **24**	2 wks
10 Sep 94	SUPERSTAR *A & M 5807932* **45**	2 wks

The listed flip side of Superstar was Yesterday Once More by Redd Kross.

SONNY
US, male vocalist **11 wks**

| 19 Aug 65 | ● LAUGH AT ME *Atlantic AT 4038*................**9** | 11 wks |

See also Sonny and Cher.

SONNY and CHER
US, male / female vocal duo **78 wks**

12 Aug 65	★ I GOT YOU BABE *Atlantic AT 4035* **1**	12 wks
16 Sep 65	BABY DON'T GO *Reprise R 20309* **11**	9 wks
21 Oct 65	BUT YOU'RE MINE *Atlantic AT 4047* **17**	8 wks
17 Feb 66	WHAT NOW MY LOVE *Atlantic AT 4069* **13**	11 wks
30 Jun 66	HAVE I STAYED TOO LONG *Atlantic 584 018*........**42**	3 wks
8 Sep 66	● LITTLE MAN *Atlantic 584 040* **4**	10 wks
17 Nov 66	LIVING FOR YOU *Atlantic 584 057* **44**	4 wks
2 Feb 67	THE BEAT GOES ON *Atlantic 584 078* **29**	8 wks
15 Jan 72	● ALL I EVER NEED IS YOU *MCA MU 1145* **8**	12 wks

| 22 May 93 | I GOT YOU BABE (re-issue) *Epic 6592402* ....**66** | 1 wk |

See also Sonny; Cher.

SON'Z OF A LOOP DA LOOP ERA
UK, male producer - Danny Breaks **4 wks**

| 15 Feb 92 | FAR OUT *Suburban Base SUBBASE 008* ....**36** | 3 wks |
| 17 Oct 92 | PEACE + LOVEISM *Suburban Base SUBBASE 14*........**60** | 1 wk |

See also *Various Artists (EPs & LPs) - Subplates Volume 1 EP.*

SORROWS
UK, male vocal / instrumental group **8 wks**

| 16 Sep 65 | TAKE A HEART *Piccadilly 7N 35260* ....**21** | 8 wks |

S.O.S. BAND
US, male / female vocal / instrumental group **46 wks**

19 Jul 80	TAKE YOUR TIME (DO IT RIGHT) PART 1	
	Tabu TBU 8564 ....**51**	4 wks
26 Feb 83	GROOVIN' (THAT'S WHAT WE'RE DOIN')	
	Tabu TBU A3120 ....**72**	1 wk
7 Apr 84	JUST BE GOOD TO ME *Tabu A 3626* **13**	11 wks
4 Aug 84	JUST THE WAY YOU LIKE IT *Tabu A 4621* **32**	7 wks
13 Oct 84	WEEKEND GIRL *Tabu A 4785* **51**	5 wks
29 Mar 86	THE FINEST *Tabu A 6997* **17**	10 wks
5 Jul 86	BORROWED LOVE *Tabu A 7241* **50**	5 wks
2 May 87	NO LIES *Tabu 650444 7* **64**	3 wks

Jimmy SOUL
US, male vocalist **5 wks**

11 Jul 63	IF YOU WANNA BE HAPPY *Stateside SS 178* **39**	2 wks
15 Jun 91	IF YOU WANNA BE HAPPY (re-issue)	
	Epic 6569647 ....**68**	3 wks

David SOUL
US, male vocalist **56 wks**

18 Dec 76	★ DON'T GIVE UP ON US *Private Stock PVT 84* **1**	16 wks
26 Mar 77	● GOING IN WITH MY EYES OPEN	
	Private Stock PVT 99 ....**2**	8 wks
27 Aug 77	★ SILVER LADY *Private Stock PVT 115* **1**	14 wks
17 Dec 77	● LET'S HAVE A QUIET NIGHT IN	
	Private Stock PVT 130 ....**8**	9 wks
27 May 78	IT SURE BRINGS OUT THE LOVE IN YOUR EYES	
	Private Stock PVT 137 ....**12**	9 wks

SOUL ASYLUM
US, male vocal / instrumental group **29 wks**

19 Jun 93	RUNAWAY TRAIN *Columbia 6593902* **37**	8 wks
4 Sep 93	SOMEBODY TO SHOVE *Columbia 6596492* **34**	3 wks
13 Nov 93	● RUNAWAY TRAIN (re-entry) *Columbia 6593902*.......**7**	11 wks
22 Jan 94	BLACK GOLD *Columbia 6598442* **26**	4 wks
26 Mar 94	SOMEBODY TO SHOVE (re-issue)	
	Columbia 6602245 ....**32**	3 wks

SOUL BROTHERS
UK, male vocal / instrumental group **3 wks**

| 22 Apr 65 | I KEEP RINGING MY BABY *Decca F 12116*................**42** | 3 wks |

SOUL CITY ORCHESTRA
UK / Holland, instrumental / production group **1 wk**

| 11 Dec 93 | IT'S JURASSIC *London JURCD 1*................**70** | 1 wk |

SOUL CITY SYMPHONY - *See Van McCOY*

SOUL FAMILY SENSATION
UK, male / female vocal / instrumental group **4 wks**

| 11 May 91 | I DON'T EVEN KNOW IF I SHOULD CALL | |
| | YOU BABY *One Little Indian 47 TP7* ....**49** | 4 wks |

SOUL SONIC FORCE - *See Afrika BAMBAATAA*

SOUL II SOUL UK, male producer - Jazzie B   **74 wks**

21 May 88	**FAIRPLAY** *10 TEN 228* [1]	....................**63**	3 wks
17 Sep 88	**FEEL FREE** *10 TEN 236* [2]	....................**64**	2 wks
18 Mar 89	● **KEEP ON MOVING** *10 TEN 263* [3]	.......**5**	12 wks
10 Jun 89	★ **BACK TO LIFE (HOWEVER DO YOU WANT ME)** *10 TEN 265* [3]	.........**1**	14 wks
9 Dec 89	● **GET A LIFE** *10 TEN 284*	....................**3**	13 wks
5 May 90	● **A DREAM'S A DREAM** *10 TEN 300*	...**6**	6 wks
24 Nov 90	**MISSING YOU** *10 TEN 345* [4]	...........**22**	7 wks
4 Apr 92	● **JOY** *Ten TEN 350*	....................**4**	7 wks
13 Jun 92	**MOVE ME NO MOUNTAIN** *Ten TEN 400* [5]	**31**	4 wks
26 Sep 92	**JUST RIGHT** *Ten TEN 410*	...........**38**	2 wks
6 Nov 93	**WISH** *Virgin VSCDG 1480*	...........**24**	4 wks

[1] Soul II Soul featuring Rose Windross [2] Soul II Soul featuring Do'reen
[3] Soul II Soul featuring Caron Wheeler [4] Soul II Soul featuring Kym Mazelle
[5] Soul II Soul, lead vocals Kofi

S.O.U.L. S.Y.S.T.E.M. introducing Michelle VISAGE US, male/female vocal/instrumental group   **5 wks**

| 16 Jan 93 | **IT'S GONNA BE A LOVELY DAY** *Arista 74321125692* | ....**17** | 5 wks |

SOULED OUT Italy/US/UK, male/female vocal/instrumental group   **1 wk**

| 9 May 92 | **IN MY LIFE** *Columbia 6578367* | ....**75** | 1 wk |

SOUND 9418 - See Jonathan KING

SOUND FACTORY Sweden, male vocal/instrumental duo   **1 wk**

| 5 Jun 93 | **2 THE RHYTHM** *Logic 74321149422* | ....**72** | 1 wk |

SOUND OF ONE US, male/female vocal/instrumental duo   **1 wk**

| 20 Nov 93 | **AS I AM** *Cooltempo CDCOOL 280* | ......**65** | 1 wk |

SOUNDGARDEN US, male vocal/instrumental group   **15 wks**

11 Apr 92	**JESUS CHRIST POSE** *A & M AM 862*	....**30**	3 wks
20 Jun 92	**RUSTY CAGE** *A & M AM 874*	...........**41**	1 wk
21 Nov 92	**OUTSHINED** *A & M AM 0102*	...........**50**	1 wk
26 Feb 94	**SPOONMAN** *A & M 5805392*	...........**20**	3 wks
30 Apr 94	**THE DAY I TRIED TO LIVE** *A & M 5805952*	**42**	2 wks
20 Aug 94	**BLACK HOLE SUN** *A & M 5807532*	.......**12**	5 wks

SOUNDS INCORPORATED UK, male instrumental group   **11 wks**

| 23 Apr 64 | **THE SPARTANS** *Columbia DB 7239* | ....**30** | 6 wks |
| 30 Jul 64 | **SPANISH HARLEM** *Columbia DB 7321* | ...**35** | 5 wks |

SOUNDS NICE UK, male instrumental group   **11 wks**

| 6 Sep 69 | **LOVE AT FIRST SIGHT (JE T'AIME ... MOI NON PLUS)** *Parlophone R 5797* | ....**18** | 11 wks |

Has credit: Tim Mycroft on organ.

SOUNDS OF BLACKNESS US, male/female gospel choir   **25 wks**

22 Jun 91	**OPTIMISTIC** *Perspective PERSS 786*	....**45**	4 wks
28 Sep 91	**THE PRESSURE PART 1** *Perspective PERSS 816*	...**71**	1 wk
15 Feb 92	**OPTIMISTIC** (re-issue) *Perspective PERSS 849*	**28**	4 wks
25 Apr 92	**THE PRESSURE PART 1** (re-issue) *Perspective PERSS 867*	...........**49**	2 wks
8 May 93	**I'M GOING ALL THE WAY** *Perspective 5874252*	**27**	3 wks

26 Mar 94	**I BELIEVE** *A & M 5874512*	...........**17**	4 wks
2 Jul 94	**GLORYLAND** *Mercury MERCD 404* [1]	...**36**	4 wks
20 Aug 94	**EVERYTHING IS GONNA BE ALRIGHT** *A & M 5874672*	...........**29**	3 wks

[1] Daryl Hall and the Sounds Of Blackness

SOUNDS ORCHESTRAL UK, orchestra   **18 wks**

| 3 Dec 64 | ● **CAST YOUR FATE TO THE WIND** *Piccadilly 7N 35206* | ....**5** | 16 wks |
| 8 Jul 65 | **MOONGLOW** *Piccadilly 7N 35248* | ....**43** | 2 wks |

SOUNDSOURCE Sweden/UK, male instrumental/production group   **1 wk**

| 11 Jan 92 | **TAKE ME UP** *ffrr FX 177* | ....**62** | 1 wk |

SOUP DRAGONS UK, male vocal/instrumental group   **23 wks**

20 Jun 87	**CAN'T TAKE NO MORE** *Raw TV RTV 3*	...**65**	1 wk
5 Sep 87	**SOFT AS YOUR FACE** *Raw TV RTV 4*	...**66**	2 wks
14 Jul 90	● **I'M FREE** *Raw TV RTV 9* [1]	...........**5**	12 wks
20 Oct 90	**MOTHER UNIVERSE** *Big Life BLR 30*	...**26**	5 wks
11 Apr 92	**DIVINE THING** *Big Life BLR 68*	.......**53**	3 wks

[1] Soup Dragons featuring Junior Reid

SOURCE UK, male producer - John Truelove   **12 wks**

| 2 Feb 91 | ● **YOU GOT THE LOVE** *Truelove TLOVE 7001* [1] | ....**4** | 11 wks |
| 26 Dec 92 | **ROCK THE HOUSE** *React 12REACT 12* [2] | ...**63** | 1 wk |

[1] Source featuring Candi Staton [2] Source featuring Nicole

Joe SOUTH US, male vocalist   **11 wks**

| 5 Mar 69 | ● **GAMES PEOPLE PLAY** *Capitol CL 15579* | **6** | 11 wks |

Jeri SOUTHERN US, female vocalist   **3 wks**

| 21 Jun 57 | **FIRE DOWN BELOW** *Brunswick 05665* | ...**22** | 3 wks |

SOUTHLANDERS UK, male vocal group   **10 wks**

| 22 Nov 57 | **ALONE** *Decca F 10946* | ....**17** | 10 wks |

SOVEREIGN COLLECTION UK, orchestra   **6 wks**

| 3 Apr 71 | **MOZART 40** *Capitol CL 15676* | ....**27** | 6 wks |

Red SOVINE US, male vocalist   **8 wks**

| 13 Jun 81 | ● **TEDDY BEAR** *Starday SD 142* | ....**4** | 8 wks |

Bob B. SOXX and the BLUE JEANS US, male/female vocal group   **2 wks**

| 31 Jan 63 | **ZIP-A-DEE-DOO-DAH** *London HLU 9646* | **45** | 2 wks |

SPACE France, male instrumental group   **12 wks**

| 13 Aug 77 | ● **MAGIC FLY** *Pye International 7N 25746* | ...**2** | 12 wks |

SPACE MONKEY UK, male producer - Paul Goodchild   **4 wks**

| 8 Oct 83 | **CAN'T STOP RUNNING** *Innervision A 3742* | **53** | 4 wks |

SPAGNA Italy, female vocalist   **23 wks**

25 Jul 87	● **CALL ME** *CBS 650279 7*	...........**2**	12 wks
17 Oct 87	**EASY LADY** *CBS 651169 7*	...........**62**	3 wks
20 Aug 88	**EVERY GIRL AND BOY** *CBS SPAG 1*	...**23**	8 wks

SPANDAU BALLET
UK, male vocal / instrumental group   **159 wks**

15 Nov 80	● TO CUT A LONG STORY SHORT		
	Reformation CHS 2473....................**5**	11 wks
24 Jan 81	THE FREEZE *Reformation CHS 2486*.......**17**	8 wks
4 Apr 81	● MUSCLEBOUND / GLOW *Reformation CHS 2509*......**10**	10 wks
18 Jul 81	● CHANT NO. 1 (I DON'T NEED THIS PRESSURE ON)		
	Reformation CHS 2528....................**3**	10 wks
14 Nov 81	PAINT ME DOWN *Chrysalis CHS 2560* **30**	5 wks
30 Jan 82	SHE LOVED LIKE DIAMOND *Chrysalis CHS 2585*....**49**	4 wks
10 Apr 82	● INSTINCTION *Chrysalis CHS 2602* **10**	11 wks
2 Oct 82	● LIFELINE *Chrysalis CHS 2642* **7**	9 wks
12 Feb 83	COMMUNICATION *Reformation CHS 2662* **12**	10 wks
23 Apr 83	★ TRUE *Reformation SPAN 1* **1**	12 wks
13 Aug 83	● GOLD *Reformation SPAN 2* **2**	9 wks
9 Jun 84	● ONLY WHEN YOU LEAVE *Reformation SPAN 3* **3**	9 wks
18 Aug 84	ONLY WHEN YOU LEAVE (re-entry)		
	Reformation SPAN 3 ....**74**	1 wk
25 Aug 84	● I'LL FLY FOR YOU *Reformation SPAN 4*....**9**	9 wks
20 Oct 84	HIGHLY STRUNG *Reformation SPAN 5* **15**	5 wks
8 Dec 84	ROUND AND ROUND *Reformation SPAN 6* **18**	8 wks
26 Jul 86	FIGHT FOR OURSELVES *Reformation A 7264*..........**15**	7 wks
8 Nov 86	● THROUGH THE BARRICADES *Reformation SPANS 1* ..**6**	10 wks
14 Feb 87	HOW MANY LIES *Reformation SPANS 2* **34**	4 wks
3 Sep 88	RAW *CBS SPANS 3* **47**	3 wks
26 Aug 89	BE FREE WITH YOUR LOVE *CBS SPANS 4* **42**	4 wks

SPARKS
US, male vocal / instrumental duo   **73 wks**

4 May 74	● THIS TOWN AIN'T BIG ENOUGH FOR BOTH OF US		
	Island WIP 6193 ....**2**	10 wks
20 Jul 74	● AMATEUR HOUR *Island WIP 6203* **7**	9 wks
19 Oct 74	NEVER TURN YOUR BACK ON MOTHER EARTH		
	Island WIP 6211 ....**13**	7 wks
18 Jan 75	SOMETHING FOR THE GIRL WITH EVERYTHING		
	Island WIP 6221 ....**17**	7 wks
19 Jul 75	GET IN THE SWING *Island WIP 6236* **27**	7 wks
4 Oct 75	LOOKS LOOKS LOOKS *Island WIP 6249* **26**	4 wks
21 Apr 79	THE NUMBER ONE SONG IN HEAVEN		
	Virgin VS 244 ....**14**	12 wks
21 Jul 79	● BEAT THE CLOCK *Virgin VS 270*...........**10**	9 wks
27 Oct 79	TRYOUTS FOR THE HUMAN RACE *Virgin VS 289* **45**	5 wks
29 Oct 94	WHEN DO I GET TO SING 'MY WAY'		
	Logic 74321234472.....................**38**	3 wks

Group were a UK / US group for first six hits.

SPEAR OF DESTINY
UK, male vocal / instrumental group   **43 wks**

21 May 83	THE WHEEL *Epic A 3372* **59**	5 wks
21 Jan 84	PRISONER OF LOVE *Epic A 4068* **59**	3 wks
14 Apr 84	LIBERATOR *Epic A 4310* **67**	2 wks
15 Jun 85	ALL MY LOVE (ASK NOTHING) *Epic A 6333* **61**	3 wks
10 Aug 85	COME BACK *Epic 6445* **55**	3 wks
7 Feb 87	STRANGERS IN OUR TOWN *10 TEN 148*....**49**	4 wks
4 Apr 87	NEVER TAKE ME ALIVE *10 TEN 162* **14**	11 wks
25 Jul 87	WAS THAT YOU *10 TEN 173* **55**	4 wks
3 Oct 87	THE TRAVELLER *10 TEN 189* **44**	3 wks
24 Sep 88	SO IN LOVE WITH YOU *Virgin VS 1123* **36**	5 wks

SPEARHEAD *US, male vocal / instrumental group*   **1 wk**

| 17 Dec 94 | OF COURSE YOU CAN *Capitol CDCL 733* .....**74** | 1 wk |

Billie Jo SPEARS *US, female vocalist*   **40 wks**

12 Jul 75	● BLANKET ON THE GROUND		
	United Artists UP 35805 ....**6**	13 wks
17 Jul 76	● WHAT I'VE GOT IN MIND *United Artists UP 36118* **4**	13 wks
11 Dec 76	SING ME AN OLD FASHIONED SONG		
	United Artists UP 36179 ....**34**	9 wks
21 Jul 79	I WILL SURVIVE *United Artists UP 601* **47**	5 wks

SPECIALS *UK, male vocal / instrumental group*   **100 wks**

28 Jul 79	● GANGSTERS *2 Tone CHS TT 1* [1] **6**	12 wks
27 Oct 79	● A MESSAGE TO YOU RUDY / NITE CLUB		
	2 Tone CHS TT 5 [2] **10**	14 wks
26 Jan 80	★ THE SPECIAL A.K.A. LIVE! EP *2 Tone CHS TT 7* [1] ...**1**	10 wks
24 May 80	● RAT RACE / RUDE BOYS OUTA JAIL		
	2 Tone CHS TT 11 ....**5**	9 wks
20 Sep 80	● STEREOTYPE / INTERNATIONAL JET SET		
	2 Tone CHS TT 13 ....**6**	8 wks
13 Dec 80	● DO NOTHING / MAGGIE'S FARM *2 Tone CHS TT 16* ..**4**	11 wks
20 Jun 81	★ GHOST TOWN *2 Tone CHS TT 17* **1**	14 wks
23 Jan 82	THE BOILER *2 Tone CHS TT 18* [3] **35**	5 wks
3 Sep 83	RACIST FRIEND *2 Tone CHS TT 25* [1] **60**	3 wks
17 Mar 84	● NELSON MANDELA *2 Tone CHS TT 26* [1] **9**	10 wks
8 Sep 84	WHAT I LIKE MOST ABOUT YOU IS		
	YOUR GIRLFRIEND *2 Tone CHS TT 27* [1] **51**	4 wks

[1] Special A.K.A. [2] Specials (featuring Rico +) [3] Rhoda with the Special A.K.A.

Tracks on The Special A.K.A. Live! EP: Too Much Too Young / Guns Of Navarone / Long Shot Kick De Bucket / Liquidator / Skinhead Moonstomp. Maggie's Farm only listed with Do Nothing from 10 Jan 81. Group were male / female for last four hits. See also Various Artists (EPs & LPs) - The Two Tone EP.

SPECTRUM *UK, male instrumental / production group*   **1 wk**

| 26 Sep 92 | TRUE LOVE WILL FIND YOU IN THE END | | |
| | *Silvertone ORE 44*.....................**70** | 1 wk |

Chris SPEDDING
UK, male vocalist / instrumentalist - guitar   **8 wks**

| 23 Aug 75 | MOTOR BIKING *RAK 210* ....**14** | 8 wks |

Johnnie SPENCE *UK, orchestra*   **15 wks**

| 1 Mar 62 | THEME FROM DR. KILDARE *Parlophone R 4872*......**15** | 15 wks |

Don SPENCER *UK, male vocalist*   **12 wks**

| 21 Mar 63 | FIREBALL *HMV POP 1087* ....**32** | 11 wks |
| 13 Jun 63 | FIREBALL (re-entry) *HMV POP 1087*.........**49** | 1 wk |

Tracie SPENCER *US, female vocalist*   **2 wks**

| 4 May 91 | THIS HOUSE *Capitol CL 612* ....**65** | 2 wks |

SPIDER *UK, male vocal / instrumental group*   **5 wks**

| 5 Mar 83 | WHY D'YA LIE TO ME *RCA 313* ....**65** | 2 wks |
| 10 Mar 84 | HERE WE GO ROCK 'N' ROLL *A & M AM 180* ....**57** | 3 wks |

SPIN DOCTORS *US, male vocal / instrumental group*   **27 wks**

15 May 93	● TWO PRINCES *Epic 6591452* **3**	15 wks
14 Aug 93	LITTLE MISS CAN'T BE WRONG *Epic 6584892*........**23**	5 wks
9 Oct 93	JIMMY OLSEN'S BLUES *Epic 6597582* **40**	2 wks
4 Dec 93	WHAT TIME IS IT *Epic 6599552* **56**	1 wk
25 Jun 94	CLEOPATRA'S CAT *Epic 6604192* **29**	2 wks
30 Jul 94	YOU LET YOUR HEART GO TOO FAST		
	Epic 6606612 ....**66**	1 wk
29 Oct 94	MARY JANE *Epic 6609772* **55**	1 wk

SPINAL TAP *US/UK, male vocal / instrumental group*   **3 wks**

| 28 Mar 92 | BITCH SCHOOL *MCA MCS 1624* ....**35** | 2 wks |
| 2 May 92 | THE MAJESTY OF ROCK *MCA MCS 1629* ....**61** | 1 wk |

SPINNERS - *See DETROIT SPINNERS*

SPIRAL TRIBE
UK, male / female vocal / instrumental group　**2 wks**

29 Aug 92	**BREACH THE PEACE (EP)** Butterfly BLRT 79............**66**	1 wk
21 Nov 92	**FORWARD THE REVOLUTION** Butterfly BLRT 85 ......**70**	1 wk

Tracks on Breach The Peace (EP): *Breach The Peace / Do Et / Seven / 25 Minute Warning.*

SPIRITS *UK, male / female vocal duo*　**3 wks**

19 Nov 94	**DON'T BRING ME DOWN** MCA MCSTD 2018 ....**31**	3 wks

SPIRITUAL COWBOYS - See Dave STEWART

SPIRITUALIZED *UK, male vocal / instrumental group*　**4 wks**

30 Jun 90	**ANYWAY YOU WANT ME / STEP INTO THE BREEZE** Dedicated ZB 43783 ....**75**	1 wk
17 Aug 91	**RUN** Dedicated SPIRIT 002 ....**59**	1 wk
25 Jul 92	**MEDICATION** Dedicated SPIRIT 005T **55**	1 wk
23 Oct 93	**ELECTRIC MAINLINE** Dedicated SPIRIT 007CD **49**	1 wk

SPITTING IMAGE *UK, male / female puppets*　**18 wks**

10 May 86	★ **THE CHICKEN SONG** Virgin SPIT 1 ....**1**	10 wks
26 Jul 86	**THE CHICKEN SONG (re-entry)** Virgin SPIT 1 ....**67**	1 wk
6 Dec 86	**SANTA CLAUS IS ON THE DOLE / FIRST ATHEIST TABERNACLE CHOIR** Virgin VS 921 ....**22**	7 wks

SPLINTER *UK, male vocal / instrumental duo*　**10 wks**

2 Nov 74	**COSTAFINE TOWN** Dark Horse AMS 7135.........**17**	10 wks

SPLIT ENZ
New Zealand / UK, male vocal / instrumental group　**15 wks**

16 Aug 80	**I GOT YOU** A & M AMS 7546 ....**12**	11 wks
23 May 81	**HISTORY NEVER REPEATS** A & M AMS 8128 ....**63**	4 wks

A SPLIT SECOND
Belgium / Italy, male instrumental / production group　**1 wk**

14 Dec 91	**FLESH** ffrr FX 178.................................**68**	1 wk

SPLODGENESSABOUNDS
UK, male vocal / instrumental group　**17 wks**

14 Jun 80	● **SIMON TEMPLAR / TWO PINTS OF LAGER AND A PACKET OF CRISPS PLEASE** Deram BUM 1..**7**	8 wks
6 Sep 80	**TWO LITTLE BOYS / HORSE** Deram ROLF 1.............**26**	7 wks
13 Jun 81	**COWPUNK MEDLUM** Deram BUM 3 ....**69**	2 wks

SPOOKY *UK, male vocal / instrumental duo*　**1 wk**

13 Mar 93	**SCHMOO** Guerilla GRRR 45CD **72**	1 wk

SPOTNICKS *Sweden, male instrumental group*　**37 wks**

14 Jun 62	**ORANGE BLOSSOM SPECIAL** Oriole CB 1724 ....**29**	10 wks
6 Sep 62	**ROCKET MAN** Oriole CB 1755 ....**38**	9 wks
31 Jan 63	**HAVA NAGILA** Oriole CB 1790.....................**13**	12 wks
25 Apr 63	**JUST LISTEN TO MY HEART** Oriole CB 1818.............**36**	6 wks

Dusty SPRINGFIELD *UK, female vocalist*　**207 wks**

21 Nov 63	● **I ONLY WANT TO BE WITH YOU** Philips BF 1292 ......**4**	18 wks
20 Feb 64	**STAY AWHILE** Philips BF 1313 ....**13**	10 wks
2 Jul 64	● **I JUST DON'T KNOW WHAT TO DO WITH MYSELF** Philips BF 1348 ....**3**	12 wks
22 Oct 64	● **LOSING YOU** Philips BF 1369 ....**9**	13 wks

18 Feb 65	**YOUR HURTIN' KIND OF LOVE** Philips BF 1396 ......**37**	4 wks
1 Jul 65	● **IN THE MIDDLE OF NOWHERE** Philips BF 1418 ....**8**	10 wks
16 Sep 65	● **SOME OF YOUR LOVIN'** Philips BF 1430 ....**8**	12 wks
27 Jan 66	**LITTLE BY LITTLE** Philips BF 1466 ....**17**	9 wks
31 Mar 66	★ **YOU DON'T HAVE TO SAY YOU LOVE ME** Philips BF 1482 ....**1**	13 wks
7 Jul 66	● **GOING BACK** Philips BF 1502 ....**10**	10 wks
15 Sep 66	● **ALL I SEE IS YOU** Philips BF 1510 ....**9**	12 wks
23 Feb 67	**I'LL TRY ANYTHING** Philips BF 1553 ....**13**	9 wks
25 May 67	**GIVE ME TIME** Philips BF 1577 ....**24**	6 wks
10 Jul 68	● **I CLOSE MY EYES AND COUNT TO TEN** Philips BF 1682 ....**4**	12 wks
4 Dec 68	● **SON OF A PREACHER MAN** Philips BF 1730............**9**	9 wks
20 Sep 69	**AM I THE SAME GIRL** Philips BF 1811............**43**	3 wks
18 Oct 69	**AM I THE SAME GIRL (re-entry)** Philips BF 1811 ......**46**	1 wk
19 Sep 70	**HOW CAN I BE SURE** Philips 6006 045 ....**36**	4 wks
20 Oct 79	**BABY BLUE** Mercury DUSTY 4 ....**61**	5 wks
22 Aug 87	● **WHAT HAVE I DONE TO DESERVE THIS** Parlophone R 6163 [1] **2**	9 wks
25 Feb 89	**NOTHING HAS BEEN PROVED** Parlophone R 6207 ..**16**	7 wks
2 Dec 89	**IN PRIVATE** Parlophone R 6234 ....**14**	10 wks
26 May 90	**REPUTATION** Parlophone R 6253 ....**38**	6 wks
24 Nov 90	**ARRESTED BY YOU** Parlophone R 6266 ....**70**	2 wks
30 Oct 93	**HEART AND SOUL** Columbia 6598562 [2] **75**	1 wk

[1] Pet Shop Boys and Dusty Springfield [2] Cilla Black with Dusty Springfield

See also Springfields.

Rick SPRINGFIELD *Australia, male vocalist*　**13 wks**

14 Jan 84	**HUMAN TOUCH / SOULS** RCA RICK 1 ....**23**	7 wks
24 Mar 84	**JESSIE'S GIRL** RCA RICK 2 ....**43**	6 wks

Souls only listed from 11 Feb 84. It peaked at position 24.

SPRINGFIELDS
UK, male / female vocal / instrumental group　**66 wks**

31 Aug 61	**BREAKAWAY** Philips BF 1168 ....**31**	8 wks
16 Nov 61	**BAMBINO** Philips BF 1178 ....**16**	11 wks
13 Dec 62	● **ISLAND OF DREAMS** Philips 326557 BF **5**	26 wks
28 Mar 63	● **SAY I WON'T BE THERE** Philips 326577 BF **5**	15 wks
25 Jul 63	**COME ON HOME** Philips BF 1263.................**31**	6 wks

Bruce SPRINGSTEEN *US, male vocalist*　**132 wks**

22 Nov 80	**HUNGRY HEART** CBS 9309 ....**44**	4 wks
13 Jun 81	**THE RIVER** CBS A 1179 ....**35**	6 wks
26 May 84	**DANCING IN THE DARK** CBS A 4436 ....**28**	7 wks
6 Oct 84	**COVER ME** CBS 4662 ....**38**	5 wks
12 Jan 85	● **DANCING IN THE DARK (re-entry)** CBS A 4436 ....**4**	16 wks
23 Mar 85	**COVER ME (re-entry)** CBS A 4662.................**16**	8 wks
15 Jun 85	● **I'M ON FIRE / BORN IN THE USA** CBS A 6342 ....**5**	12 wks
3 Aug 85	**GLORY DAYS** CBS A 6375 ....**17**	6 wks
14 Dec 85	● **SANTA CLAUS IS COMIN' TO TOWN / MY HOMETOWN** CBS A 6773 ....**9**	5 wks
29 Nov 86	**WAR** CBS 650193 7............................**18**	7 wks
7 Feb 87	**FIRE** CBS 650381 7 ....**54**	2 wks
23 May 87	**BORN TO RUN** CBS BRUCE 2 ....**16**	4 wks
3 Oct 87	**BRILLIANT DISGUISE** CBS 651141 7 ....**20**	5 wks
12 Dec 87	**TUNNEL OF LOVE** CBS 651295 7 ....**45**	4 wks
18 Jun 88	**TOUGHER THAN THE REST** CBS BRUCE 3 ....**13**	8 wks
24 Sep 88	**SPARE PARTS** CBS BRUCE 4 ....**32**	3 wks
21 Mar 92	**HUMAN TOUCH** Columbia 6578727............**11**	5 wks
23 May 92	**BETTER DAYS** Columbia 6578907 ....**34**	3 wks
25 Jul 92	**57 CHANNELS (AND NOTHIN' ON)** Columbia 6581387 ....**32**	4 wks
24 Oct 92	**LEAP OF FAITH** Columbia 6583697 ....**46**	2 wks
10 Apr 93	**LUCKY TOWN (LIVE)** Columbia 6592282 ....**48**	3 wks
19 Mar 94	● **STREETS OF PHILADELPHIA** Columbia 6600652 ....**2**	12 wks

SPRINGWATER *UK, male instrumentalist - Phil Cordell*　**12 wks**

23 Oct 71	● **I WILL RETURN** Polydor 2058 141 ....**5**	12 wks

SPYRO GYRA US, male instrumental group   **10 wks**

21 Jul 79	**MORNING DANCE** Infinity INF 111	**17**	10 wks

SQUADRONAIRES - See Joan REGAN

SQUEEZE UK, male vocal / instrumental group   **114 wks**

8 Apr 78	**TAKE ME I'M YOURS** A & M AMS 7335	**19**	9 wks
10 Jun 78	**BANG BANG** A & M AMS 7360	**49**	5 wks
18 Nov 78	**GOODBYE GIRL** A & M AMS 7398	**63**	2 wks
24 Mar 79	● **COOL FOR CATS** A & M AMS 7426	**2**	11 wks
2 Jun 79	● **UP THE JUNCTION** A & M AMS 7444	**2**	11 wks
8 Sep 79	**SLAP AND TICKLE** A & M AMS 7466	**24**	8 wks
1 Mar 80	**ANOTHER NAIL IN MY HEART** A & M AMS 7507	**17**	9 wks
10 May 80	**PULLING MUSSELS (FROM THE SHELL)** A & M AMS 7523	**44**	6 wks
16 May 81	**IS THAT LOVE** A & M AMS 8129	**35**	8 wks
25 Jul 81	**TEMPTED** A & M AMS 8147	**41**	5 wks
10 Oct 81	● **LABELLED WITH LOVE** A & M AMS 8166	**4**	10 wks
24 Apr 82	**BLACK COFFEE IN BED** A & M AMS 8219	**51**	4 wks
23 Oct 82	**ANNIE GET YOUR GUN** A & M AMS 8259	**43**	4 wks
15 Jun 85	**LAST TIME FOREVER** A & M AM 255	**45**	5 wks
8 Aug 87	**HOURGLASS** A & M AM 400	**16**	10 wks
17 Oct 87	**TRUST ME TO OPEN MY MOUTH** A & M AM 412	**72**	1 wk
25 Apr 92	**COOL FOR CATS (re-issue)** A & M AM 860	**62**	2 wks
24 Jul 93	**THIRD RAIL** A & M 5803372	**39**	3 wks
11 Sep 93	**SOME FANTASTIC PLACE** A & M 5803792	**73**	1 wk

Billy SQUIER US, male vocalist   **3 wks**

3 Oct 81	**THE STROKE** Capitol CL 214	**52**	3 wks

Dorothy SQUIRES UK, female vocalist   **56 wks**

5 Jun 53	**I'M WALKING BEHIND YOU** Polygon P 1068	**12**	1 wk
24 Aug 61	**SAY IT WITH FLOWERS** Columbia DB 4665 [1]	**23**	10 wks
20 Sep 69	**FOR ONCE IN MY LIFE** President PT 267	**24**	10 wks
20 Dec 69	**FOR ONCE IN MY LIFE (re-entry)** President PT 267	**48**	1 wk
21 Feb 70	**TILL** President PT 281	**25**	10 wks
9 May 70	**TILL (re-entry)** President PT 281	**48**	1 wk
8 Aug 70	**MY WAY** President PT 305	**25**	5 wks
19 Sep 70	**MY WAY (re-entry)** President PT 305	**34**	8 wks
28 Nov 70	**MY WAY (2nd re-entry)** President PT 305	**25**	10 wks

[1] Dorothy Squires and Russ Conway

STABBS
Finland / US / Cameroon, male instrumental / production group   **1 wk**

24 Dec 94	**JOY AND HAPPINESS** Hi-Life HICD 3	**65**	1 wk

Jim STAFFORD US, male vocalist   **16 wks**

27 Apr 74	**SPIDERS AND SNAKES** MGM 2006 374	**14**	8 wks
6 Jul 74	**MY GIRL BILL** MGM 2006 423	**20**	8 wks

Jo STAFFORD US, female vocalist   **28 wks**

14 Nov 52	★ **YOU BELONG TO ME** Columbia DB 3152	**1**	19 wks
19 Dec 52	**JAMBALAYA** Columbia DB 3169	**11**	2 wks
7 May 54	● **MAKE LOVE TO ME** Philips PB 233	**8**	1 wk
9 Dec 55	**SUDDENLY THERE'S A VALLEY** Philips PB 509	**12**	5 wks
3 Feb 56	**SUDDENLY THERE'S A VALLEY (re-entry)** Philips PB 509	**19**	1 wk

Terry STAFFORD US, male vocalist   **9 wks**

7 May 64	**SUSPICION** London HLU 9871	**31**	9 wks

STAIFFI and his MUSTAFAS
France, male vocal / instrumental group   **1 wk**

28 Jul 60	**MUSTAFA** Pye International 7N 25057	**43**	1 wk

STAKKA BO Sweden, male producer   **12 wks**

25 Sep 93	**HERE WE GO** Polydor PZCD 280	**13**	8 wks
18 Dec 93	**DOWN THE DRAIN** Polydor PZCD 301	**64**	4 wks

Frank STALLONE US, male vocalist   **2 wks**

22 Oct 83	**FAR FROM OVER** RSO 95	**68**	2 wks

STAMFORD BRIDGE UK, male vocal group   **1 wk**

16 May 70	**CHELSEA** Penny Farthing PEN 715	**47**	1 wk

STAN UK, male vocal / instrumental duo   **3 wks**

31 Jul 93	**SUNTAN** Hug CDBUM 1	**40**	3 wks

Lisa STANSFIELD UK, female vocalst   **109 wks**

25 Mar 89	**PEOPLE HOLD ON** Ahead Of Our Time CCUT 5 [1]	**11**	9 wks
12 Aug 89	**THIS IS THE RIGHT TIME** Arista 112512	**13**	8 wks
28 Oct 89	★ **ALL AROUND THE WORLD** Arista 112693	**1**	14 wks
10 Feb 90	● **LIVE TOGETHER** Arista 112914	**10**	6 wks
12 May 90	**WHAT DID I DO TO YOU (EP)** Arista 113168	**25**	4 wks
19 Oct 91	● **CHANGE** Arista 114820	**10**	7 wks
21 Dec 91	**ALL WOMAN** Arista 115000	**20**	8 wks
14 Mar 92	**TIME TO MAKE YOU MINE** Arista 115113	**14**	8 wks
6 Jun 92	**SET YOUR LOVING FREE** Arista 74321100587	**28**	4 wks
19 Dec 92	● **SOMEDAY (I'M COMING BACK)** Arista 74321123567	**10**	9 wks
1 May 93	★ **FIVE LIVE EP** Parlophone CDRS 6340 [2]	**1**	11 wks
5 Jun 93	● **IN ALL THE RIGHT PLACES** MCA MCSTD 1780	**8**	11 wks
24 Jul 93	**FIVE LIVE EP (re-entry)** Parlophone CDRS 6340 [2]	**74**	1 wk
23 Oct 93	**SO NATURAL** Arista 74321169132	**15**	5 wks
11 Dec 93	**LITTLE BIT OF HEAVEN** Arista 74321178202	**32**	4 wks

[1] Coldcut featuring Lisa Stansfield [2] George Michael and Queen with Lisa Stansfield

Tracks on What Did I Do To You (EP): What Did I Do To You / My Apple Heart / Lay Me Down / Something's Happenin'. Tracks on Five Live EP: Somebody To Love / These Are The Days Of Our Lives / Calling You / Papa Was A Rolling Stone - Killer (medley). Lisa Stansfield appears only on the second track.

Viv STANSHALL - See Mike OLDFIELD

STAPLE SINGERS US, male / female vocal group   **14 wks**

10 Jun 72	**I'LL TAKE YOU THERE** Stax 2025 110	**30**	8 wks
8 Jun 74	**IF YOU'RE READY (COME GO WITH ME)** Stax 2025 224	**34**	6 wks

Cyril STAPLETON UK, orchestra   **27 wks**

27 May 55	**ELEPHANT TANGO** Decca F 10488	**20**	2 wks
1 Jul 55	**ELEPHANT TANGO (re-entry)** Decca F 10488	**20**	1 wk
22 Jul 55	**ELEPHANT TANGO (2nd re-entry)** Decca F 10488	**19**	1 wk
23 Sep 55	● **BLUE STAR (THE MEDIC THEME)** Decca F 10559 [1]	**2**	12 wks
6 Apr 56	**THE ITALIAN THEME** Decca F 10703	**18**	2 wks
1 Jun 56	**THE HAPPY WHISTLER** Decca F 10735 [2]	**22**	4 wks
19 Jul 57	**FORGOTTEN DREAMS** Decca F 10912	**27**	5 wks

[1] Cyril Stapleton Orchestra featuring Julie Dawn [2] Cyril Stapleton Orchestra featuring Desmond Lane, penny whistle

STARDUST
Sweden, male / female vocal / instrumental group   **3 wks**

8 Oct 77	**ARIANA** Satril SAT 120	**42**	3 wks

Alvin STARDUST UK, male vocalist   **119 wks**

3 Nov 73	● **MY COO-CA-CHOO** Magnet MAG 1	**2**	21 wks
16 Feb 74	★ **JEALOUS MIND** Magnet MAG 5	**1**	11 wks

4 May 74	● RED DRESS *Magnet MAG 8* **7**	8 wks
31 Aug 74	● YOU YOU YOU *Magnet MAG 13* **6**	10 wks
30 Nov 74	TELL ME WHY *Magnet MAG 19*........................**16**	8 wks
1 Feb 75	GOOD LOVE CAN NEVER DIE *Magnet MAG 21* **11**	9 wks
12 Jul 75	SWEET CHEATIN' RITA *Magnet MAG 32* **37**	4 wks
5 Sep 81	● PRETEND *Stiff BUY 124* **4**	10 wks
21 Nov 81	A WONDERFUL TIME UP THERE *Stiff BUY 132* **56**	8 wks
5 May 84	● I FEEL LIKE BUDDY HOLLY *Chrysalis CHS 2784* ...**7**	11 wks
27 Oct 84	● I WON'T RUN AWAY *Chrysalis CHS 2829* **7**	13 wks
15 Dec 84	SO NEAR TO CHRISTMAS *Chrysalis CHS 2835* **29**	4 wks
23 Mar 85	GOT A LITTLE HEARTACHE *Chrysalis CHS 2856* ...**55**	2 wks

Alvin started his career as Shane Fenton. See also Shane Fenton and the Fentones.

STARGARD *US, female vocal group* **14 wks**

28 Jan 78	THEME FROM 'WHICH WAY IS UP' *MCA 346* **19**	7 wks
15 Apr 78	LOVE IS SO EASY *MCA 354* **45**	1 wk
9 Sep 78	WHAT YOU WAITING FOR *MCA 382* **39**	6 wks

STARGAZERS *UK, male vocal/instrumental group* **53 wks**

13 Feb 53	BROKEN WINGS *Decca F 10047* **11**	1 wk
27 Feb 53	★ BROKEN WINGS (re-entry) *Decca F 10047* **1**	11 wks
19 Feb 54	★ I SEE THE MOON *Decca F 10213* **1**	15 wks
9 Apr 54	HAPPY WANDERER *Decca F 10259* **12**	1 wk
4 Mar 55	SOMEBODY *Decca F 10437* **20**	1 wk
3 Jun 55	CRAZY OTTO RAG *Decca F 10523* **18**	3 wks
9 Sep 55	● CLOSE THE DOOR *Decca F 10594* **6**	9 wks
11 Nov 55	● TWENTY TINY FINGERS *Decca F 10626* **4**	11 wks
22 Jun 56	HOT DIGGITY *Decca F 10731* **28**	1 wk

See also Dickie Valentine.

STARGAZERS *UK, male vocal/instrumental group* **3 wks**

| 6 Feb 82 | GROOVE BABY GROOVE (EP) *Epic EPC A 1924* ....**56** | 3 wks |

Tracks on Groove Baby Groove EP: Groove Baby Groove/Jump Around/ La Rock 'N' Roll (Quelques Uns A La Lune)/Red Light Green Light.

STARJETS *UK, male vocal/instrumental group* **5 wks**

| 8 Sep 79 | WAR STORIES *Epic EPC 7770* ....**51** | 5 wks |

STARLAND VOCAL BAND
US, male/female vocal group **10 wks**

| 7 Aug 76 | AFTERNOON DELIGHT *RCA 2716* ....**18** | 10 wks |

STARLIGHT *Italy, male instrumental/production group* **11 wks**

| 19 Aug 89 | ● NUMERO UNO *Citybeat CBE 742* ....**9** | 11 wks |

STARLITERS - *See Joey DEE and the STARLITERS*

Edwin STARR *US, male vocalist* **70 wks**

12 May 66	STOP HER ON SIGHT (SOS) *Polydor BM 56 702*........**35**	8 wks
18 Aug 66	HEADLINE NEWS *Polydor 56 717* **39**	3 wks
11 Dec 68	STOP HER ON SIGHT (SOS)/HEADLINE NEWS (re-issue) *Polydor 56 753*..........................**11**	11 wks
13 Sep 69	25 MILES *Tamla Motown TMG 672* **36**	6 wks
24 Oct 70	● WAR *Tamla Motown TMG 754* **3**	12 wks
20 Feb 71	STOP THE WAR NOW *Tamla Motown TMG 764* **33**	1 wk
27 Jan 79	● CONTACT *20th Century BTC 2396* **6**	12 wks
26 May 79	● H.A.P.P.Y. RADIO *RCA TC 2408* **9**	11 wks
1 Jun 85	IT AIN'T FAIR *Hippodrome HIP 101* **56**	4 wks
30 Oct 93	WAR *Weekend CDWEEK 103* [1] **69**	2 wks

[1] Edwin Starr and Shadow

Headline News *not listed with SOS from 22 Jan 69 to 19 Feb 69. It peaked at position 16. War in '93 was a re-recording and was listed with the flip side* Wild Thing *by the Troggs and Wolf.*

Freddie STARR *UK, male vocalist* **14 wks**

| 23 Feb 74 | ● IT'S YOU *Tiffany 6121 501* ....**9** | 10 wks |
| 20 Dec 75 | WHITE CHRISTMAS *Thunderbird THE 102* ....**41** | 4 wks |

Kay STARR *US, female vocalist* **58 wks**

5 Dec 52	★ COMES A-LONG A-LOVE *Capitol CL 13808* **1**	16 wks
24 Apr 53	● SIDE BY SIDE *Capitol CL 13871* **7**	14 wks
19 Mar 54	● CHANGING PARTNERS *Capitol CL 14050* **4**	14 wks
15 Oct 54	AM I A TOY OR A TREASURE *Capitol CL 14151* ...**17**	3 wks
12 Nov 54	AM I A TOY OR A TREASURE (re-entry) *Capitol CL 14151* **20**	1 wk
17 Feb 56	★ ROCK AND ROLL WALTZ *HMV POP 168* **1**	20 wks

Ringo STARR *UK, male vocalist* **56 wks**

17 Apr 71	● IT DON'T COME EASY *Apple R 5898*....................**4**	11 wks
1 Apr 72	● BACK OFF BOOGALOO *Apple R 5944* **2**	10 wks
27 Oct 73	● PHOTOGRAPH *Apple R 5992* **8**	13 wks
23 Feb 74	● YOU'RE SIXTEEN *Apple R 5995* **4**	10 wks
30 Nov 74	ONLY YOU *Apple R 6000* **28**	11 wks
6 Jun 92	WEIGHT OF THE WORLD *Private Music 115392* **74**	1 wk

STARSHIP *US, female/male vocal/instrumental group* **41 wks**

26 Jan 80	JANE *Grunt FB 1750* [1] **21**	9 wks
16 Nov 85	WE BUILT THIS CITY *RCA PB 49929* **12**	12 wks
8 Feb 86	SARA *RCA FB 49893* **66**	3 wks
11 Apr 87	★ NOTHING'S GONNA STOP US NOW *Grunt FB 49757*..**1**	17 wks

[1] Jefferson Starship

STARSOUND *Holland, producer Jaap Eggermont with male/female session singers* **37 wks**

18 Apr 81	● STARS ON 45 *CBS A 1102* **2**	14 wks
4 Jul 81	● STARS ON 45 VOL.2 *CBS A 1407* **2**	10 wks
19 Sep 81	STARS ON 45 VOL.3 *CBS A 1521* **17**	6 wks
27 Feb 82	STARS ON STEVIE *CBS A 2041* **14**	7 wks

STARTRAX *UK, male/female session group* **8 wks**

| 1 Aug 81 | STARTRAX CLUB DISCO *Picksy KSY 1001* ....**18** | 8 wks |

STARTURN ON 45 (PINTS) *UK, male vocal group* **9 wks**

| 24 Oct 81 | STARTURN ON 45 (PINTS) *V Tone V TONE 003* ....**45** | 4 wks |
| 30 Apr 88 | PUMP UP THE BITTER *Pacific DRINK 1* ....**12** | 5 wks |

STARVATION *Multi-national, male/female vocal/ instrumental charity assembly* **6 wks**

| 9 Mar 85 | STARVATION/TAM-TAM POUR L'ETHIOPE *Zarjazz JAZZ 3* ....**33** | 6 wks |

STATLER BROTHERS *US, male vocal group* **4 wks**

| 24 Feb 66 | FLOWERS ON THE WALL *CBS 201976* ....**38** | 4 wks |

Candi STATON *US, female vocalist* **58 wks**

29 May 76	● YOUNG HEARTS RUN FREE *Warner Bros. K 16730* **2**	13 wks
18 Sep 76	DESTINY *Warner Bros. K 16806* **41**	3 wks
23 Jul 77	● NIGHTS ON BROADWAY *Warner Bros. K 16972* **6**	12 wks
3 Jun 78	HONEST I DO LOVE YOU *Warner Bros. K 17164* **48**	5 wks
24 Apr 82	SUSPICIOUS MINDS *Sugarhill SH 112* **31**	9 wks
31 May 86	YOUNG HEARTS RUN FREE (re-mix) *Warner Bros. W 8680* **47**	5 wks
2 Feb 91	● YOU GOT THE LOVE *Truelove TLOVE 7001* [1] **4**	11 wks

[1] Source featuring Candi Staton

STATUS IV US, male vocal group — **3 wks**

Date	Title	Pos	Weeks
9 Jul 83	**YOU AIN'T REALLY DOWN** TMT TMT 4	**56**	3 wks

STATUS QUO UK, male vocal/instrumental group — **399 wks**

Date	Title	Pos	Weeks
24 Jan 68	● **PICTURES OF MATCHSTICK MEN** Pye 7N 17449	**7**	12 wks
21 Aug 68	● **ICE IN THE SUN** Pye 7N 17581	**8**	12 wks
28 May 69	**ARE YOU GROWING TIRED OF MY LOVE** Pye 7N 17728	**46**	2 wks
18 Jun 69	**ARE YOU GROWING TIRED OF MY LOVE (re-entry)** Pye 7N 17728	**50**	1 wk
2 May 70	**DOWN THE DUSTPIPE** Pye 7N 17907	**12**	17 wks
7 Nov 70	**IN MY CHAIR** Pye 7N 17998	**21**	14 wks
13 Jan 73	● **PAPER PLANE** Vertigo 6059 071	**8**	11 wks
14 Apr 73	**MEAN GIRL** Pye 7N 45229	**20**	11 wks
8 Sep 73	● **CAROLINE** Vertigo 6059 085	**5**	13 wks
4 May 74	● **BREAK THE RULES** Vertigo 6059 101	**8**	8 wks
7 Dec 74	★ **DOWN DOWN** Vertigo 6059 114	**1**	12 wks
17 May 75	● **ROLL OVER LAY DOWN** Vertigo QUO 13	**9**	8 wks
14 Feb 76	● **RAIN** Vertigo 6059 133	**7**	7 wks
10 Jul 76	**MYSTERY SONG** Vertigo 6059 146	**11**	9 wks
11 Dec 76	● **WILD SIDE OF LIFE** Vertigo 6059 153	**9**	12 wks
8 Oct 77	● **ROCKIN' ALL OVER THE WORLD** Vertigo 6059 184	**3**	16 wks
2 Sep 78	**AGAIN AND AGAIN** Vertigo QUO 1	**13**	9 wks
25 Nov 78	**ACCIDENT PRONE** Vertigo QUO 2	**36**	8 wks
22 Sep 79	● **WHATEVER YOU WANT** Vertigo 6059 242	**4**	9 wks
24 Nov 79	**LIVING ON AN ISLAND** Vertigo 6059 248	**16**	10 wks
11 Oct 80	● **WHAT YOU'RE PROPOSING** Vertigo QUO 3	**2**	11 wks
6 Dec 80	**LIES/DON'T DRIVE MY CAR** Vertigo QUO 4	**11**	10 wks
28 Feb 81	● **SOMETHING 'BOUT YOU BABY I LIKE** Vertigo QUO 5	**9**	7 wks
28 Nov 81	● **ROCK 'N' ROLL** Vertigo QUO 6	**8**	11 wks
27 Mar 82	● **DEAR JOHN** Vertigo QUO 7	**10**	8 wks
12 Jun 82	**SHE DON'T FOOL ME** Vertigo QUO 8	**36**	5 wks
30 Oct 82	**CAROLINE (LIVE AT THE N.E.C.)** Vertigo QUO 10	**13**	7 wks
10 Sep 83	● **OL' RAG BLUES** Vertigo QUO 11	**9**	8 wks
5 Nov 83	**A MESS OF THE BLUES** Vertigo QUO 12	**15**	6 wks
10 Dec 83	● **MARGUERITA TIME** Vertigo QUO 14	**3**	11 wks
19 May 84	**GOING DOWN TOWN TONIGHT** Vertigo QUO 15	**20**	6 wks
27 Oct 84	● **THE WANDERER** Vertigo QUO 16	**7**	11 wks
17 May 86	● **ROLLIN' HOME** Vertigo QUO 18	**9**	6 wks
26 Jul 86	**RED SKY** Vertigo QUO 19	**19**	8 wks
4 Oct 86	● **IN THE ARMY NOW** Vertigo QUO 20	**2**	14 wks
6 Dec 86	**DREAMIN'** Vertigo QUO 21	**15**	8 wks
26 Mar 88	**AIN'T COMPLAINING** Vertigo QUO 22	**19**	6 wks
21 May 88	**WHO GETS THE LOVE** Vertigo QUO 23	**34**	4 wks
20 Aug 88	**RUNNING ALL OVER THE WORLD** Vertigo QUAID 1	**17**	6 wks
3 Dec 88	● **BURNING BRIDGES (ON AND OFF AND ON AGAIN)** Vertigo QUO 25	**5**	10 wks
28 Oct 89	**NOT AT ALL** Vertigo QUO 26	**50**	2 wks
29 Sep 90	● **THE ANNIVERSARY WALTZ - PART 1** Vertigo QUO 28	**2**	9 wks
15 Dec 90	**THE ANNIVERSARY WALTZ - PART 2** Vertigo QUO 29	**16**	7 wks
7 Sep 91	**CAN'T GIVE YOU MORE** Vertigo QUO 30	**37**	3 wks
18 Jan 92	**ROCK 'TIL YOU DROP** Vertigo QUO 32	**38**	3 wks
10 Oct 92	**ROADHOUSE MEDLEY (ANNIVERSARY WALTZ PART 25)** Polydor QUO 33	**21**	4 wks
6 Aug 94	**I DIDN'T MEAN IT** Polydor QUOCD 34	**21**	4 wks
22 Oct 94	**SHERRI DON'T FAIL ME NOW** Polydor QUOCD 35	**38**	2 wks
3 Dec 94	**RESTLESS** Polydor QUOCD 36	**39**	2 wks

Don't Drive My Car listed from 20 Dec 80 only. Running All Over The World is a re-recorded version of Rockin' All Over The World, with a slightly changed lyric, released to promote the Race Against Time of 28 Aug 88.

STAXX UK, male/female vocal/instrumental group — **6 wks**

Date	Title	Pos	Weeks
2 Oct 93	**JOY** Champion CHAMPCD 303	**25**	6 wks

STEALER'S WHEEL
UK, male vocal/instrumental group — **22 wks**

Date	Title	Pos	Weeks
26 May 73	● **STUCK IN THE MIDDLE WITH YOU** A & M AMS 7036	**8**	10 wks
1 Sep 73	**EVERYTHING'L TURN OUT FINE** A & M AMS 7079	**33**	6 wks
26 Jan 74	**STAR** A & M AMS 7094	**25**	6 wks

STEAM US, male vocal group — **14 wks**

Date	Title	Pos	Weeks
31 Jan 70	● **NA NA HEY HEY KISS HIM GOODBYE** Fontana TF 1058	**9**	14 wks

Anthony STEEL and the RADIO REVELLERS
UK, male vocalist/male instrumental group — **6 wks**

Date	Title	Pos	Weeks
10 Sep 54	**WEST OF ZANZIBAR** Polygon P 1114	**11**	6 wks

STEEL PULSE UK, male vocal/instrumental group — **12 wks**

Date	Title	Pos	Weeks
1 Apr 78	**KU KLUX KLAN** Island WIP 6428	**41**	4 wks
8 Jul 78	**PRODIGAL SON** Island WIP 6449	**35**	6 wks
23 Jun 79	**SOUND SYSTEM** Island WIP 6490	**71**	2 wks

Tommy STEELE UK, male vocalist — **145 wks**

Date	Title	Pos	Weeks
26 Oct 56	**ROCK WITH THE CAVEMAN** Decca F 10795 [1]	**13**	4 wks
30 Nov 56	**ROCK WITH THE CAVEMAN (re-entry)** Decca F 10795 [1]	**23**	1 wk
14 Dec 56	★ **SINGING THE BLUES** Decca F 10819 [1]	**1**	13 wks
15 Feb 57	**KNEE DEEP IN THE BLUES** Decca F 10849 [1]	**15**	9 wks
19 Apr 57	**SINGING THE BLUES (re-entry)** Decca F 10819 [1]	**24**	1 wk
3 May 57	**BUTTERFINGERS** Decca F 10877 [1]	**25**	1 wk
17 May 57	● **BUTTERFINGERS (re-entry)** Decca F 10877 [1]	**8**	17 wks
17 May 57	**SINGING THE BLUES (2nd re-entry)** Decca F 10819 [1]	**29**	1 wk
16 Aug 57	● **WATER WATER/HANDFUL OF SONGS** Decca F 10923 [1]	**5**	16 wks
30 Aug 57	**SHIRALEE** Decca F 10896 [1]	**11**	4 wks
22 Nov 57	**HEY YOU** Decca F 10941 [1]	**28**	1 wk
13 Dec 57	**WATER WATER/HANDFUL OF SONGS (re-entry)** Decca F 10923 [1]	**28**	1 wk
7 Mar 58	● **NAIROBI** Decca F 10991	**3**	11 wks
25 Apr 58	**HAPPY GUITAR** Decca F 10976	**20**	5 wks
18 Jul 58	**THE ONLY MAN ON THE ISLAND** Decca F 11041	**16**	8 wks
14 Nov 58	● **COME ON LET'S GO** Decca F 11072	**10**	13 wks
14 Aug 59	**TALLAHASSEE LASSIE** Decca F 11152	**16**	4 wks
28 Aug 59	**GIVE GIVE GIVE** Decca F 11152	**28**	2 wks
25 Sep 59	**TALLAHASSEE LASSIE (re-entry)** Decca F 11152	**25**	1 wk
4 Dec 59	● **LITTLE WHITE BULL** Decca F 11177	**6**	12 wks
10 Mar 60	**LITTLE WHITE BULL (re-entry)** Decca F 11177	**30**	5 wks
23 Jun 60	● **WHAT A MOUTH** Decca F 11245	**5**	11 wks
29 Dec 60	**MUST BE SANTA** Decca F 11299	**40**	1 wk
17 Aug 61	**WRITING ON THE WALL** Decca F 11372	**30**	5 wks

[1] Tommy Steele and the Steelmen

Handful Of Songs listed together with Water Water from week of 23 Aug 57. See also Various Artists (EPs & LPs) - All Star Hit Parade No.2.

STEELEYE SPAN
UK, male/female vocal/instrumental group — **18 wks**

Date	Title	Pos	Weeks
8 Dec 73	**GAUDETE** Chrysalis CHS 2007	**14**	9 wks
15 Nov 75	● **ALL AROUND MY HAT** Chrysalis CHS 2078	**5**	9 wks

STEELY DAN US, male vocal/instrumental group — **21 wks**

Date	Title	Pos	Weeks
30 Aug 75	**DO IT AGAIN** ABC 4075	**39**	4 wks
11 Dec 76	**HAITIAN DIVORCE** ABC 4152	**17**	9 wks
29 Jul 78	**FM (NO STATIC AT ALL)** MCA 374	**49**	4 wks
2 Sep 78	**FM (NO STATIC AT ALL) (re-entry)** MCA 374	**75**	1 wk
10 Mar 79	**RIKKI DON'T LOSE THAT NUMBER** ABC 4241	**58**	3 wks

Jim STEINMAN US, male vocalist   **9 wks**

4 Jul 81	**ROCK 'N' ROLL DREAMS COME THROUGH**		
	Epic EPC A 1236 [1] **52**	7 wks
23 Jun 84	**TONIGHT IS WHAT IT MEANS TO BE YOUNG**		
	MCA MCA 889 [2] **67**	2 wks

[1] Jim Steinman, vocals by Rory Dodd [2] Jim Steinman and Fire Inc.

STEINSKI and MASS MEDIA
US, male producer and rapper   **2 wks**

| 31 Jan 87 | **WE'LL BE RIGHT BACK** Fourth & Broadway BRW 59**63** | 2 wks |

Mike STEIPHENSON - See BURUNDI STEIPHENSON BLACK

Doreen STEPHENS - See Billy COTTON and his BAND

Ritchie STEPHENS - See MAD COBRA featuring Ritchie STEPHENS

Martin STEPHENSON and the DAINTEES
UK, male vocal / instrumental group   **7 wks**

8 Nov 86	**BOAT TO BOLIVIA** Kitchenware SL 27 ....**70**	2 wks
17 Jan 87	**TROUBLE TOWN** Kitchenware SK 13 [1] **58**	3 wks
27 Jun 92	**BIG SKY NEW LIGHT** Kitchenware SK 57 ....**71**	2 wks

[1] Daintees

STEPPENWOLF
US / Canada, male vocal / instrumental group   **9 wks**

| 11 Jun 69 | **BORN TO BE WILD** Stateside SS 8017 ....**30** | 7 wks |
| 9 Aug 69 | **BORN TO BE WILD (re-entry)** Stateside SS 8017 .....**50** | 2 wks |

STEREO MC'S UK, male rap group   **31 wks**

29 Sep 90	**ELEVATE MY MIND** Fourth & Broadway BRW 186....**74**	1 wk
9 Mar 91	**LOST IN MUSIC** Fourth & Broadway BRW 198 ....**46**	3 wks
26 Sep 92	**CONNECTED** Fourth & Broadway BRW 262...............**18**	6 wks
5 Dec 92	**STEP IT UP** Fourth & Broadway BRW 266 ....**12**	12 wks
20 Feb 93	**GROUND LEVEL** Fourth & Broadway BRCD 268 ....**19**	5 wks
29 May 93	**CREATION** Fourth & Broadway BRCD 276 ....**19**	4 wks

STEREOLAB
UK / France, male / female vocal / instrumental group   **4 wks**

8 Jan 94	**JENNY ONDIOLINE / FRENCH DISKO**		
	Duophonic UHF DUHFD 01 ....**75**	1 wk
30 Jul 94	**PING PONG** Duophonic UHF DUHFCD 04 ....**45**	2 wks
12 Nov 94	**WOW AND FLUTTER** Duophonic UHF DUHFCD 07....**70**	1 wk

STETASONIC US, male rap group   **2 wks**

| 24 Sep 88 | **TALKIN' ALL THAT JAZZ** Breakout USA 640.............**73** | 2 wks |

STEVE and EYDIE - See Steve LAWRENCE; Eydie GORMÉ

April STEVENS - See Nino TEMPO and April STEVENS

Cat STEVENS UK, male vocalist   **96 wks**

20 Oct 66	**I LOVE MY DOG** Deram DM 102 ....**28**	7 wks
12 Jan 67	● **MATTHEW AND SON** Deram DM 110 ....**2**	10 wks
30 Mar 67	● **I'M GONNA GET ME A GUN** Deram DM 118 ....**6**	10 wks
2 Aug 67	**A BAD NIGHT** Deram DM 140 ....**20**	8 wks
20 Dec 67	**KITTY** Deram DM 156 ....**47**	1 wk
27 Jun 70	● **LADY D'ARBANVILLE** Island WIP 6086 ....**8**	13 wks
28 Aug 71	**MOON SHADOW** Island WIP 6092 ....**22**	11 wks
1 Jan 72	● **MORNING HAS BROKEN** Island WIP 6121 ....**9**	13 wks
9 Dec 72	**CAN'T KEEP IT IN** Island WIP 6152 ....**13**	12 wks
24 Aug 74	**ANOTHER SATURDAY NIGHT** Island WIP 6206 ....**19**	8 wks
2 Jul 77	**(REMEMBER THE DAYS OF THE)**		
	OLD SCHOOL YARD Island WIP 6387 ....**44**	3 wks

Connie STEVENS US, female vocalist   **20 wks**

5 May 60	● **SIXTEEN REASONS** Warner Bros. WB 3......................**9**	11 wks
5 May 60	**KOOKIE KOOKIE (LEND ME YOUR COMB)**		
	Warner Bros. WB 5 [1] **27**	8 wks
4 Aug 60	**SIXTEEN REASONS (re-entry)** Warner Bros. WB 3 ..**45**	1 wk

[1] Edward Byrnes and Connie Stevens

Ray STEVENS US, male vocalist   **64 wks**

16 May 70	● **EVERYTHING IS BEAUTIFUL** CBS 4953 ....**6**	16 wks
13 Mar 71	● **BRIDGET THE MIDGET (THE QUEEN OF THE BLUES)**		
	CBS 7070 ....**2**	14 wks
25 Mar 72	**TURN YOUR RADIO ON** CBS 7634 ....**33**	4 wks
25 May 74	★ **THE STREAK** Janus 6146 201 ....**1**	12 wks
21 Jun 75	● **MISTY** Janus 6146 204 ....**2**	10 wks
27 Sep 75	**INDIAN LOVE CALL** Janus 6146 205 ....**34**	4 wks
5 Mar 77	**IN THE MOOD** Warner Bros. K 16875 ....**31**	4 wks

In The Mood features Ray Stevens not as a conventional vocalist, but as a group of chickens.

Ricky STEVENS UK, male vocalist   **7 wks**

| 14 Dec 61 | **I CRIED FOR YOU** Columbia DB 4739 ....**34** | 7 wks |

Shakin' STEVENS UK, male vocalist   **277 wks**

16 Feb 80	**HOT DOG** Epic EPC 8090 ....**24**	9 wks
16 Aug 80	**MARIE MARIE** Epic EPC 8725 ....**19**	10 wks
28 Feb 81	★ **THIS OLE HOUSE** Epic EPC 9555 ....**1**	17 wks
2 May 81	● **YOU DRIVE ME CRAZY** Epic A 1165 ....**2**	12 wks
25 Jul 81	● **GREEN DOOR** Epic A 1354 ....**1**	12 wks
10 Oct 81	● **IT'S RAINING** Epic A 1643 ....**10**	9 wks
16 Jan 82	★ **OH JULIE** Epic EPC A 1742 ....**1**	10 wks
24 Apr 82	● **SHIRLEY** Epic EPC A 2087 ....**6**	6 wks
21 Aug 82	**GIVE ME YOUR HEART TONIGHT** Epic EPC A 2656 ..**11**	10 wks
16 Oct 82	● **I'LL BE SATISFIED** Epic EPC A 2846 ....**10**	8 wks
11 Dec 82	● **THE SHAKIN' STEVENS EP** Epic SHAKY 1 ....**2**	7 wks
23 Jul 83	**IT'S LATE** Epic A 3565 ....**11**	7 wks
5 Nov 83	● **CRY JUST A LITTLE BIT** Epic A 3774 ....**3**	12 wks
7 Jan 84	● **A ROCKIN' GOOD WAY** Epic A 4071 [1] **5**	9 wks
24 Mar 84	● **A LOVE WORTH WAITING FOR** Epic A 4291 ....**2**	10 wks
15 Sep 84	● **A LETTER TO YOU** Epic A 4677 ....**10**	8 wks
24 Nov 84	● **TEARDROPS** Epic A 4882.........................**5**	9 wks
2 Mar 85	**BREAKING UP MY HEART** Epic A 6072 ....**14**	7 wks
12 Oct 85	**LIPSTICK POWDER AND PAINT** Epic A 6610 ....**11**	9 wks
7 Dec 85	★ **MERRY CHRISTMAS EVERYONE** Epic A 6769 ....**1**	8 wks
8 Feb 86	**TURNING AWAY** Epic A 6819 ....**15**	7 wks
1 Nov 86	● **BECAUSE I LOVE YOU** Epic SHAKY 2 ....**14**	10 wks
20 Dec 86	**MERRY CHRISTMAS EVERYONE (re-entry)**		
	Epic A 6769 ....**58**	3 wks
27 Jun 87	**A LITTLE BOOGIE WOOGIE (IN THE BACK**		
	OF MY MIND) Epic SHAKY 3 ....**12**	10 wks
19 Sep 87	**COME SEE ABOUT ME** Epic SHAKY 4 ....**24**	6 wks
28 Nov 87	● **WHAT DO YOU WANT TO MAKE THOSE EYES**		
	AT ME FOR Epic SHAKY 5 ....**5**	8 wks
23 Jul 88	**FEEL THE NEED IN ME** Epic SHAKY 6 ....**26**	5 wks
15 Oct 88	**HOW MANY TEARS CAN YOU HIDE**		
	Epic SHAKY 7 ....**47**	4 wks
10 Dec 88	**TRUE LOVE** Epic SHAKY 8 ....**23**	6 wks
18 Feb 89	**JEZEBEL** Epic SHAKY 9 ....**58**	2 wks
13 May 89	**LOVE ATTACK** Epic SHAKY 10 ....**28**	4 wks
24 Feb 90	**I MIGHT** Epic SHAKY 11 ....**18**	6 wks
12 May 90	**YES I DO** Epic SHAKY 12 ....**60**	2 wks
18 Aug 90	**PINK CHAMPAGNE** Epic SHAKY 13 ....**59**	2 wks
13 Oct 90	**MY CUTIE CUTIE** Epic SHAKY 14 ....**75**	1 wk
15 Dec 90	**THE BEST CHRISTMAS OF THEM ALL**		
	Epic SHAKY 15 ....**19**	4 wks
7 Dec 91	**I'LL BE HOME THIS CHRISTMAS** Epic 6576507 .....**34**	5 wks
10 Oct 92	**RADIO** Epic 6584367 [2] **37**	3 wks

[1] Shaky and Bonnie [2] Shaky featuring Roger Taylor

Tracks on The Shakin' Stevens EP: Blue Christmas / Que Sera Sera / Josephine / Lawdy Miss Clawdy.

If **ROD STEWART** had succeeded in professional football as he once hoped, the chart would have been deprived of his 50 hits. (LFI)

STATUS QUO play flat out rock 'n' roll. (LFI)

RED SOVINE died at the age of 61, a year before he made his British chart debut.

Red Sovine

SHAKIN' STEVENS is the only artist to have had hits with three different "Christmas" titles. (Allan Ballard)

STEVENSON'S ROCKET
UK, male vocal / instrumental group **5 wks**

29 Nov 75	**ALRIGHT BABY** Magnet MAG 47	**37**	2 wks
20 Dec 75	**ALRIGHT BABY (re-entry)** Magnet MAG 47	**45**	3 wks

Al STEWART
UK, male vocalist **6 wks**

29 Jan 77	**YEAR OF THE CAT** RCA 2771	**31**	6 wks

Amii STEWART
US, female vocalist **61 wks**

7 Apr 79	● **KNOCK ON WOOD** Atlantic/Hansa K 11214	**6**	12 wks
16 Jun 79	● **LIGHT MY FIRE / 137 DISCO HEAVEN (MEDLEY)** Atlantic/Hansa K 11278	**5**	11 wks
3 Nov 79	**JEALOUSY** Atlantic/Hansa K 11386	**58**	3 wks
19 Jan 80	**THE LETTER / PARADISE BIRD** Atlantic/Hansa K 11424	**39**	4 wks
19 Jul 80	**MY GUY - MY GIRL (MEDLEY)** Atlantic/Hansa K 11550 [1]	**39**	5 wks
29 Dec 84	**FRIENDS** RCA 471	**12**	11 wks
17 Aug 85	● **KNOCK ON WOOD / LIGHT MY FIRE (re-mix)** Sedition EDIT 3303	**7**	12 wks
25 Jan 86	**MY GUY - MY GIRL (MEDLEY)** Sedition EDIT 3310 [2]	**63**	3 wks

[1] Amii Stewart and Johnny Bristol [2] Amii Stewart and Deon Estus

Andy STEWART
UK, male vocalist **67 wks**

15 Dec 60	**DONALD WHERE'S YOUR TROOSERS** Top Rank JAR 427	**37**	1 wk
12 Jan 61	**A SCOTTISH SOLDIER** Top Rank JAR 512	**19**	38 wks
1 Jun 61	**THE BATTLE'S O'ER** Top Rank JAR 565	**28**	13 wks
12 Oct 61	**A SCOTTISH SOLDIER (re-entry)** Top Rank JAR 512	**43**	2 wks
12 Aug 65	**DR. FINLAY** HMV POP 1454	**50**	1 wk
26 Aug 65	**DR. FINLAY (re-entry)** HMV POP 1454	**43**	4 wks
9 Dec 89	● **DONALD WHERE'S YOUR TROOSERS (re-issue)** Stone SON 2353	**4**	8 wks

Billy STEWART
US, male vocalist **2 wks**

8 Sep 66	**SUMMERTIME** Chess CRS 8040	**39**	2 wks

Dave STEWART
UK, male instrumentalist - keyboards **30 wks**

14 Mar 81	**WHAT BECOMES OF THE BROKEN HEARTED** Stiff BROKEN 1 [1]	**13**	10 wks
19 Sep 81	★ **IT'S MY PARTY** Broken BROKEN 2 [2]	**1**	13 wks
13 Aug 83	**BUSY DOING NOTHING** Broken BROKEN 5 [2]	**49**	4 wks
14 Jun 86	**THE LOCOMOTION** Broken BROKEN 8 [2]	**70**	3 wks

[1] Dave Stewart. Guest vocals: Colin Blunstone [2] Dave Stewart with Barbara Gaskin

Dave STEWART
UK, male vocalist / instrumentalist - guitar **19 wks**

24 Feb 90	● **LILY WAS HERE** RCA ZB 43045 [1]	**6**	12 wks
18 Aug 90	**JACK TALKING** RCA PB 43907 [2]	**69**	2 wks
3 Sep 94	**HEART OF STONE** East West YZ 845CD	**36**	5 wks

[1] David A. Stewart featuring Candy Dulfer [2] Dave Stewart and the Spiritual Cowboys

Jermaine STEWART
US, male vocalist **42 wks**

9 Aug 86	● **WE DON'T HAVE TO...** 10 TEN 96	**2**	14 wks
1 Nov 86	**JODY** 10 TEN 143	**50**	4 wks
16 Jan 88	● **SAY IT AGAIN** 10 TEN 188	**7**	12 wks
2 Apr 88	**GET LUCKY** Siren SRN 82	**13**	9 wks
24 Sep 88	**DON'T TALK DIRTY TO ME** Siren SRN 86	**61**	3 wks

John STEWART
US, male vocalist **6 wks**

30 Jun 79	**GOLD** RSO 35	**43**	6 wks

Rod STEWART
UK, male vocalist **437 wks**

4 Sep 71	**REASON TO BELIEVE** Mercury 6052 097	**19**	2 wks
18 Sep 71	★ **MAGGIE MAY** Mercury 6052 097	**1**	19 wks
12 Aug 72	★ **YOU WEAR IT WELL** Mercury 6052 171	**1**	12 wks
18 Nov 72	● **ANGEL / WHAT MADE MILWAUKEE FAMOUS (HAS MADE A LOSER OUT OF ME)** Mercury 6052 198	**4**	11 wks
5 May 73	**I'VE BEEN DRINKING** RAK RR 4 [1]	**27**	6 wks
8 Sep 73	**OH NO NOT MY BABY** Mercury 6052 371	**6**	9 wks
5 Oct 74	● **FAREWELL – BRING IT ON HOME TO ME / YOU SEND ME** Mercury 6167 033	**7**	7 wks
16 Aug 75	★ **SAILING** Warner Bros. K 16600	**1**	11 wks
15 Nov 75	● **THIS OLD HEART OF MINE** Riva 1	**4**	9 wks
5 Jun 76	● **TONIGHT'S THE NIGHT** Riva 3	**5**	9 wks
21 Aug 76	● **THE KILLING OF GEORGIE** Riva 4	**2**	10 wks
4 Sep 76	● **SAILING (re-entry)** Warner Bros. K 16600	**3**	20 wks
20 Nov 76	**GET BACK** Riva 6	**11**	9 wks
4 Dec 76	**MAGGIE MAY (re-entry)** Mercury 6160 006	**31**	7 wks
23 Apr 77	★ **I DON'T WANT TO TALK ABOUT IT / FIRST CUT IS THE DEEPEST** Riva 7	**1**	13 wks
15 Oct 77	● **YOU'RE IN MY HEART** Riva 11	**3**	10 wks
28 Jan 78	● **HOTLEGS / I WAS ONLY JOKING** Riva 10	**5**	8 wks
27 May 78	● **OLE OLA (MULHER BRASILEIRA)** Riva 15 [2]	**4**	6 wks
18 Nov 78	★ **DA YA THINK I'M SEXY?** Riva 17	**1**	13 wks
3 Feb 79	**AIN'T LOVE A BITCH** Riva 18	**11**	8 wks
5 May 79	**BLONDES (HAVE MORE FUN)** Riva 19	**63**	3 wks
31 May 80	**IF LOVING YOU IS WRONG (I DON'T WANT TO BE RIGHT)** Riva 23	**23**	9 wks
8 Nov 80	**PASSION** Riva 26	**17**	10 wks
20 Dec 80	**MY GIRL** Riva 28	**32**	7 wks
17 Oct 81	● **TONIGHT I'M YOURS (DON'T HURT ME)** Riva 33	**8**	13 wks
12 Dec 81	**YOUNG TURKS** Riva 34	**11**	9 wks
27 Feb 82	**HOW LONG** Riva 35	**41**	4 wks
4 Jun 83	★ **BABY JANE** Warner Bros. W 9608	**1**	14 wks
27 Aug 83	● **WHAT AM I GONNA DO** Warner Bros. W 9564	**3**	8 wks
10 Dec 83	**SWEET SURRENDER** Warner Bros. W 9440	**23**	9 wks
26 May 84	**INFATUATION** Warner Bros. W 9256	**27**	7 wks
28 Jul 84	**SOME GUYS HAVE ALL THE LUCK** Warner Bros. W 9204	**15**	10 wks
24 May 86	**LOVE TOUCH** Warner Bros. W 8668	**27**	5 wks
5 Jul 86	**LOVE TOUCH (re-entry)** Warner Bros. W 8668	**69**	3 wks
12 Jul 86	● **EVERY BEAT OF MY HEART** Warner Bros. W 8625	**2**	9 wks
20 Sep 86	**ANOTHER HEARTACHE** Warner Bros. W 8631	**54**	2 wks
28 Mar 87	**SAILING (2nd re-entry)** Warner Bros. K 16600	**41**	3 wks
28 May 88	**LOST IN YOU** Warner Bros. W 7927	**21**	6 wks
13 Aug 88	**FOREVER YOUNG** Warner Bros. W 7796	**57**	3 wks
6 May 89	**MY HEART CAN'T TELL YOU NO** Warner Bros. W 7729	**49**	4 wks
11 Nov 89	**THIS OLD HEART OF MINE** Warner Bros. W 2686 [3]	**51**	3 wks
13 Jan 90	● **DOWNTOWN TRAIN** Warner Bros. W 2647	**10**	12 wks
24 Nov 90	● **IT TAKES TWO** Warner Bros. ROD 1 [4]	**5**	8 wks
16 Mar 91	● **RHYTHM OF MY HEART** Warner Bros. W 0017	**3**	11 wks
15 Jun 91	● **THE MOTOWN SONG** Warner Bros. W 0030	**10**	8 wks
7 Sep 91	**BROKEN ARROW** Warner Bros. W 0059	**54**	3 wks
7 Mar 92	**PEOPLE GET READY** Epic 6577567 [1]	**49**	3 wks
18 Apr 92	**YOUR SONG / BROKEN ARROW (re-issue)** Warner Bros. W 0104	**41**	4 wks
5 Dec 92	● **TOM TRAUBERT'S BLUES (WALTZING MATILDA)** Warner Bros. W 0144	**6**	9 wks
20 Feb 93	**RUBY TUESDAY** Warner Bros. W 0158CD	**11**	6 wks
17 Apr 93	**SHOTGUN WEDDING** Warner Bros. W 0171CD	**21**	4 wks
26 Jun 93	● **HAVE I TOLD YOU LATELY** Warner Bros. W 0185CD	**5**	9 wks
21 Aug 93	**REASON TO BELIEVE** Warner Bros. W 0198CD1	**51**	3 wks
18 Dec 93	**PEOPLE GET READY** Warner Bros. W 0226CD1	**45**	4 wks
15 Jan 94	● **ALL FOR LOVE** A & M 5804772 [5]	**2**	13 wks

[1] Jeff Beck and Rod Stewart [2] Rod Stewart featuring the Scottish World Cup Football Squad [3] Rod Stewart featuring Ronald Isley [4] Rod Stewart and Tina Turner [5] Bryan Adams, Rod Stewart and Sting

Reason To Believe and People Get Ready in '93 were re-recordings. Reason To Believe additionally credits Ronnie Wood on the sleeve. See also Faces; Glass Tiger; Python Lee Jackson.

STEX UK, male vocal group — **2 wks**

19 Jan 91	**STILL FEEL THE RAIN** Some Bizzare SBZ 7002	**63**	2 wks

STIFF LITTLE FINGERS
UK, male vocal / instrumental group — **39 wks**

29 Sep 79	**STRAW DOGS** Chrysalis CHS 2368	**44**	4 wks
16 Feb 80	**AT THE EDGE** Chrysalis CHS 2406	**15**	9 wks
24 May 80	**NOBODY'S HERO / TIN SOLDIERS** Chrysalis CHS 2424	**36**	5 wks
2 Aug 80	**BACK TO FRONT** Chrysalis CHS 2447	**49**	4 wks
28 Mar 81	**JUST FADE AWAY** Chrysalis CHS 2510	**47**	6 wks
30 May 81	**SILVER LINING** Chrysalis CHS 2517	**68**	3 wks
23 Jan 82	**LISTEN EP** Chrysalis CHS 2580	**33**	6 wks
18 Sep 82	**BITS OF KIDS** Chrysalis CHS 2637	**73**	2 wks

Tracks on Listen EP: That's When Your Blood Bumps / Two Guitars Clash / Listen / Sad-Eyed People.

Curtis STIGERS US, male vocalist — **30 wks**

18 Jan 92	● **I WONDER WHY** Arista 114716	**5**	10 wks
28 Mar 92	● **YOU'RE ALL THAT MATTERS TO ME** Arista 115273	**6**	12 wks
11 Jul 92	**SLEEPING WITH THE LIGHTS ON** Arista 74321102307	**53**	4 wks
17 Oct 92	**NEVER SAW A MIRACLE** Arista 74321117257	**34**	4 wks

Stephen STILLS US, male vocalist — **4 wks**

13 Mar 71	**LOVE THE ONE YOU'RE WITH** Atlantic 2091 046	**37**	4 wks

See also Crosby Stills Nash and Young.

STILTSKIN UK, male vocal / instrumental group — **15 wks**

7 May 94	★ **INSIDE** White Water LEV 1CD	**1**	13 wks
24 Sep 94	**FOOTSTEPS** White Water WWRD 2	**34**	2 wks

STING UK, male vocalist — **111 wks**

14 Aug 82	**SPREAD A LITTLE HAPPINESS** A & M AMS 8217	**16**	8 wks
8 Jun 85	**IF YOU LOVE SOMEBODY SET THEM FREE** A & M AM 258	**26**	7 wks
24 Aug 85	**LOVE IS THE SEVENTH WAVE** A & M AM 272	**41**	5 wks
19 Oct 85	**FORTRESS AROUND YOUR HEART** A & M AM 286	**49**	3 wks
7 Dec 85	**RUSSIANS** A & M AM 292	**12**	11 wks
15 Feb 86	**MOON OVER BOURBON STREET** A & M AM 305	**44**	4 wks
1 Mar 86	**RUSSIANS (re-entry)** A & M AM 292	**71**	1 wk
7 Nov 87	**WE'LL BE TOGETHER** A & M AM 410	**41**	4 wks
20 Feb 88	**ENGLISHMAN IN NEW YORK** A & M AM 431	**51**	3 wks
9 Apr 88	**FRAGILE** A & M AM 439	**70**	2 wks
11 Aug 90	**ENGLISHMAN IN NEW YORK (re-mix)** A & M AM 580	**15**	7 wks
12 Jan 91	**ALL THIS TIME** A & M AM 713	**22**	4 wks
9 Mar 91	**MAD ABOUT YOU** A & M AM 721	**56**	2 wks
4 May 91	**THE SOUL CAGES** A & M AM 759	**57**	1 wk
29 Aug 92	**IT'S PROBABLY ME** A & M AM 883 [1]	**30**	5 wks
13 Feb 93	**IF I EVER LOSE MY FAITH IN YOU** A & M AMCD 0172	**14**	6 wks
24 Apr 93	**SEVEN DAYS** A & M 5802232	**25**	4 wks
19 Jun 93	**FIELDS OF GOLD** A & M 5803012	**16**	6 wks
4 Sep 93	**SHAPE OF MY HEART** A & M 5803532	**57**	1 wk
20 Nov 93	**DEMOLITION MAN** A & M 5804512	**21**	4 wks
15 Jan 94	● **ALL FOR LOVE** A & M 5804772 [2]	**2**	13 wks
26 Feb 94	**NOTHING 'BOUT ME** A & M 5805292	**32**	3 wks
29 Oct 94	**WHEN WE DANCE** A & M 5808612	**9**	7 wks

[1] Sting with Eric Clapton [2] Bryan Adams, Rod Stewart and Sting

STINGERS - See B. BUMBLE and the STINGERS

Catherine STOCK UK, female vocalist — **6 wks**

18 Oct 86	**TO HAVE AND TO HOLD** Sierra FED 29	**17**	6 wks

STOCK AITKEN WATERMAN UK, male producers — **36 wks**

25 Jul 87	**ROADBLOCK** Breakout USA 611	**13**	9 wks
24 Oct 87	● **MR. SLEAZE** London NANA 14	**3**	10 wks
12 Dec 87	**PACKJAMMED (WITH THE PARTY POSSE)** Breakout USA 620	**41**	6 wks
21 May 88	**ALL THE WAY** MCA GOAL 1 [1]	**64**	2 wks
3 Dec 88	**SS PAPARAZZI** PWL PWL 22	**68**	2 wks
20 May 89	★ **FERRY 'CROSS THE MERSEY** PWL PWL 41 [2]	**1**	7 wks

[1] England Football Team with the 'sound' of Stock Aitken and Waterman
[2] Christians, Holly Johnson, Paul McCartney, Gerry Marsden and Stock Aitken Waterman

The listed flip side of Mr. Sleaze was Love In The First Degree by Bananarama.

Rhet STOLLER UK, male instrumentalist - guitar — **8 wks**

12 Jan 61	**CHARIOT** Decca F 11302	**26**	8 wks

Morris STOLOFF US, orchestra — **11 wks**

1 Jun 56	● **MOONGLOW / THEME FROM PICNIC** Brunswick 05553	**7**	11 wks

R & J STONE UK / US, male / female vocal duo — **9 wks**

10 Jan 76	● **WE DO IT** RCA 2616	**5**	9 wks

STONE ROSES UK, male vocal / instrumental group — **62 wks**

29 Jul 89	**SHE BANGS THE DRUMS** Silvertone ORE 6	**36**	3 wks
25 Nov 89	● **WHAT THE WORLD IS WAITING FOR / FOOL'S GOLD** Silvertone ORE 13	**8**	14 wks
6 Jan 90	**SALLY CINNAMON** Revolver REV 36	**75**	1 wk
20 Jan 90	**SALLY CINNAMON (re-entry)** Revolver REV 36	**46**	4 wks
3 Mar 90	● **ELEPHANT STONE** Silvertone ORE 1	**8**	6 wks
17 Mar 90	**MADE OF STONE** Silvertone ORE 2	**20**	4 wks
31 Mar 90	**SHE BANGS THE DRUMS (re-entry)** Silvertone ORE 6	**34**	3 wks
14 Jul 90	● **ONE LOVE** Silvertone ORE 17	**4**	7 wks
15 Sep 90	**WHAT THE WORLD IS WAITING FOR / FOOL'S GOLD (re-entry)** Silvertone ORE 13	**22**	5 wks
14 Sep 91	**I WANNA BE ADORED** Silvertone ORE 31	**20**	3 wks
11 Jan 92	**WATERFALL** Silvertone ORE 35	**27**	4 wks
11 Apr 92	**I AM THE RESURRECTION** Silvertone ORE 40	**33**	2 wks
30 May 92	**FOOL'S GOLD (re-mix)** Silvertone ORET 13	**73**	1 wk
3 Dec 94	● **LOVE SPREADS** Geffen GFSTD 84	**2†**	5 wks

STONE TEMPLE PILOTS
US, male vocal / instrumental group — **11 wks**

27 Mar 93	**SEX TYPE THING** Atlantic A 5769CD	**60**	2 wks
4 Sep 93	**PLUSH** Atlantic A 7349CD	**23**	4 wks
27 Nov 93	**SEX TYPE THING (re-issue)** Atlantic A 7293CD	**55**	2 wks
20 Aug 94	**VASOLINE** Atlantic A 5650CD	**48**	2 wks
10 Dec 94	**INTERSTATE LOVE SONG** Atlantic A 7192CD	**53**	1 wk

STONEBRIDGE McGUINNESS
UK, male vocal / instrumental duo — **2 wks**

14 Jul 79	**OO-EEH BABY** RCA PB 5163	**54**	2 wks

STONEFREE UK, male vocalist — **1 wk**

23 May 87	**CAN'T SAY GOODBYE** Ensign ENY 607	**73**	1 wk

STONKERS - See HALE and PACE and the STONKERS

STOP THE VIOLENCE
US, male / female rap charity ensemble — **1 wk**

18 Feb 89	**SELF DESTRUCTION** Jive BDPST 1	**75**	1 wk

Axel STORDAHL - *See June HUTTON and Axel STORDAHL*

STORM
UK, male/female vocal/instrumental group **10 wks**

17 Nov 79	**IT'S MY HOUSE** Scope SC 10	36	10 wks

Danny STORM
UK, male vocalist **4 wks**

12 Apr 62	**HONEST I DO** Piccadilly 7N 35025	42	4 wks

Rebecca STORM
UK, female vocalist **13 wks**

13 Jul 85	**THE SHOW (THEME FROM 'CONNIE')** Towerbell TVP 3	22	13 wks

STORYVILLE JAZZ BAND - *See Bob WALLIS and his STORYVILLE JAZZ BAND*

Izzy STRADLIN'
US, male vocalist/instrumentalist - guitar **2 wks**

26 Sep 92	**PRESSURE DROP** Geffen GFS 25	45	2 wks

Nick STRAKER BAND
UK, male vocal/instrumental group **15 wks**

2 Aug 80	**A WALK IN THE PARK** CBS 8525	20	12 wks
15 Nov 80	**LEAVING ON THE MIDNIGHT TRAIN** CBS 9088	61	3 wks

Peter STRAKER and the HANDS OF DR.TELENY
UK, male vocalist and male vocal/instrumental group **4 wks**

19 Feb 72	**THE SPIRIT IS WILLING** RCA 2163	40	4 wks

STRANGE BEHAVIOUR - *See Jane KENNAWAY and STRANGE BEHAVIOUR*

STRANGLERS
UK, male vocal/instrumental group **194 wks**

19 Feb 77	**(GET A) GRIP (ON YOURSELF)** United Artists UP 36211	44	4 wks
21 May 77	● **PEACHES/GO BUDDY GO** United Artists UP 36248	8	14 wks
30 Jul 77	● **SOMETHING BETTER CHANGE/STRAIGHTEN OUT** United Artists UP 36277	9	8 wks
24 Sep 77	● **NO MORE HEROES** United Artists UP 36300	8	9 wks
4 Feb 78	**FIVE MINUTES** United Artists UP 36350	11	9 wks
6 May 78	**NICE 'N SLEAZY** United Artists UP 36379	18	8 wks
12 Aug 78	**WALK ON BY** United Artists UP 36429	21	8 wks
18 Aug 79	**DUCHESS** United Artists BP 308	14	9 wks
20 Oct 79	**NUCLEAR DEVICE (THE WIZARD OF AUS)** United Artists BP 318	36	4 wks
1 Dec 79	**DON'T BRING HARRY (EP)** United Artists STR 1	41	3 wks
22 Mar 80	**BEAR CAGE** United Artists BP 344	36	5 wks
7 Jun 80	**WHO WANTS THE WORLD** United Artists BPX 355	39	4 wks
31 Jan 81	**THROWN AWAY** Liberty BP 383	42	4 wks
14 Nov 81	**LET ME INTRODUCE YOU TO THE FAMILY** United Artists BP 405	42	3 wks
9 Jan 82	● **GOLDEN BROWN** Liberty BP 407	2	12 wks
24 Apr 82	**LA FOLIE** Liberty BP 410	47	3 wks
24 Jul 82	● **STRANGE LITTLE GIRL** Liberty BP 412	7	9 wks
8 Jan 83	● **EUROPEAN FEMALE** Epic EPC A 2893	9	6 wks
26 Feb 83	**MIDNIGHT SUMMER DREAM** Epic EPC A 3167	35	4 wks
6 Aug 83	**PARADISE** Epic A 3387	48	3 wks
6 Oct 84	**SKIN DEEP** Epic A 4738	15	7 wks
1 Dec 84	**NO MERCY** Epic A 4921	37	7 wks
16 Feb 85	**LET ME DOWN EASY** Epic A 6045	48	4 wks
23 Aug 86	**NICE IN NICE** Epic 650057	30	5 wks
18 Oct 86	**ALWAYS THE SUN** Epic SOLAR 1	30	5 wks
13 Dec 86	**BIG IN AMERICA** Epic HUGE 1	48	6 wks
7 Mar 87	**SHAKIN' LIKE A LEAF** Epic SHEIK 1	58	4 wks
9 Jan 88	● **ALL DAY AND ALL OF THE NIGHT** Epic VICE 1	7	7 wks
28 Jan 89	**GRIP '89 (GET A) GRIP (ON YOURSELF) (re-mix)** EMI EM 84	33	3 wks
17 Feb 90	**96 TEARS** Epic TEARS 1	17	6 wks
21 Apr 90	**SWEET SMELL OF SUCCESS** Epic TEARS 2	65	2 wks
5 Jan 91	**ALWAYS THE SUN (re-mix)** Epic 6564307	29	5 wks
30 Mar 91	**GOLDEN BROWN (re-mix)** Epic 6567617	68	2 wks
22 Aug 92	**HEAVEN OR HELL** Psycho WOK 2025	46	2 wks

Go Buddy Go *credited with Peaches from 11 Jun 77.* Straighten Out *credited with* Something Better Change *from 13 Aug 77. Tracks on* Don't Bring Harry (EP): *Don't Bring Harry/ Wired/ Crabs (Live)/ In The Shadows (Live).*

STRAWBERRY SWITCHBLADE
UK, female vocal duo **26 wks**

17 Nov 84	● **SINCE YESTERDAY** Korova KOW 38	5	17 wks
23 Mar 85	**LET HER GO** Korova KOW 39	59	5 wks
21 Sep 85	**JOLENE** Korova KOW 42	53	4 wks

STRAWBS
UK, male vocal/instrumental group **27 wks**

28 Oct 72	**LAY DOWN** A & M AMS 7035	12	13 wks
27 Jan 73	● **PART OF THE UNION** A & M AMS 7047	2	11 wks
6 Oct 73	**SHINE ON SILVER SUN** A & M AMS 7082	34	3 wks

STRAY CATS
US, male vocal/instrumental group **49 wks**

29 Nov 80	● **RUNAWAY BOYS** Arista SCAT 1	9	10 wks
7 Feb 81	● **ROCK THIS TOWN** Arista SCAT 2	9	8 wks
25 Apr 81	**STRAY CAT STRUT** Arista SCAT 3	11	10 wks
20 Jun 81	**THE RACE IS ON** Swansong SSK 19425 [1]	34	6 wks
7 Nov 81	**YOU DON'T BELIEVE ME** Arista SCAT 4	57	3 wks
6 Aug 83	**(SHE'S) SEXY AND 17** Arista SCAT 6	29	9 wks
4 Mar 89	**BRING IT BACK AGAIN** EMI USA MT 62	64	3 wks

[1] Dave Edmunds and the Stray Cats

STRAY MOB - *See MC SKAT KAT and the STRAY MOB*

STREETBAND
UK, male vocal/instrumental group **6 wks**

4 Nov 78	**TOAST/HOLD ON** Logo GO 325	18	6 wks

Barbra STREISAND
US, female vocalist **130 wks**

20 Jan 66	**SECOND HAND ROSE** CBS 202025	14	13 wks
30 Jan 71	**STONEY END** CBS 5321	46	1 wk
13 Feb 71	**STONEY END (re-entry)** CBS 5321	27	10 wks
30 Mar 74	**THE WAY WE WERE** CBS 1915	31	6 wks
9 Apr 77	● **LOVE THEME FROM 'A STAR IS BORN' (EVERGREEN)** CBS 4855	3	19 wks
25 Nov 78	● **YOU DON'T BRING ME FLOWERS** CBS 6803 [1]	5	12 wks
3 Nov 79	● **NO MORE TEARS (ENOUGH IS ENOUGH)** Casablanca CAN 174I CBS 8000 [2]	3	13 wks
4 Oct 80	★ **WOMAN IN LOVE** CBS 8966	1	16 wks
6 Dec 80	**GUILTY** CBS 9315 [3]	34	10 wks
30 Jan 82	**COMIN' IN AND OUT OF YOUR LIFE** CBS A 1789	66	3 wks
20 Mar 82	**MEMORY** CBS A 1903	34	6 wks
5 Nov 88	**TILL I LOVED YOU (LOVE THEME FROM 'GOYA')** CBS BARB 2 [4]	16	7 wks
7 Mar 92	**PLACES THAT BELONG TO YOU** Columbia 6577947	17	5 wks
5 Jun 93	**WITH ONE LOOK** Columbia 6593422	30	3 wks
5 Jan 94	**THE MUSIC OF THE NIGHT** Columbia 6597382 [5]	54	3 wks
30 Apr 94	**AS IF WE NEVER SAID GOODBYE** Columbia 6603572	20	3 wks

[1] Barbra and Neil [2] Donna Summer and Barbra Streisand [3] Barbra Streisand and Barry Gibb [4] Barbra Streisand and Don Johnson [5] Barbra Streisand (duet with Michael Crawford)

Neil *was Neil Diamond.* No More Tears (Enough Is Enough) *was released simultaneously on two different labels, a 7-inch single on Casablanca and a 12-inch on CBS.*

STRESS UK, male vocal/instrumental group — **1 wk**

13 Oct 90	BEAUTIFUL PEOPLE *Eternal YZ 495*	74	1 wk

STRETCH UK, male vocal/instrumental group — **9 wks**

8 Nov 75	WHY DID YOU DO IT *Anchor ANC 1021*	16	9 wks

STRIKE
UK/Australia, male/female vocal/instrumental group — **2 wks**

24 Dec 94	U SURE DO *Fresh FRSHD 19*	31†	2 wks

STRIKERS US, male vocal/instrumental group — **5 wks**

6 Jun 81	BODY MUSIC *Epic EPC A 1290*	45	5 wks

STRING-A-LONGS US, male instrumental group — **16 wks**

23 Feb 61	● WHEELS *London HLU 9278*	8	16 wks

STRINGS OF LOVE
Italy, male/female vocal/instrumental group — **2 wks**

3 Mar 90	NOTHING HAS BEEN PROVED *Breakout USA 688*	59	2 wks

Joe STRUMMER UK, male vocalist — **1 wk**

2 Aug 86	LOVE KILLS *CBS A 7244*	69	1 wk

Chad STUART and Jeremy CLYDE
UK, male vocal duo — **7 wks**

28 Nov 63	YESTERDAY'S GONE *Ember EMB S 180*	37	7 wks

STUMP UK, male vocal/instrumental group — **1 wk**

13 Aug 88	CHARLTON HESTON *Ensign ENY 614*	72	1 wk

STUTZ BEARCATS and the Denis KING ORCHESTRA UK, male/female vocal group with orchestra — **6 wks**

24 Apr 82	THE SONG THAT I SING (THEME FROM 'WE'LL MEET AGAIN') *Multi-Media Tapes MMT 6*	36	6 wks

STYLE COUNCIL UK, male vocal/instrumental duo — **103 wks**

19 Mar 83	● SPEAK LIKE A CHILD *Polydor TSC 1*	4	8 wks
28 May 83	MONEY GO ROUND (PART 1) *Polydor TSC 2*	11	6 wks
13 Aug 83	● LONG HOT SUMMER/PARIS MATCH *Polydor TSC 3*	3	9 wks
20 Aug 83	MONEY GO ROUND (PART 1) (re-entry) *Polydor TSC 2*	74	1 wk
19 Nov 83	● SOLID BOND IN YOUR HEART *Polydor TSC 4*	11	8 wks
18 Feb 84	● MY EVER CHANGING MOODS *Polydor TSC 5*	5	7 wks
26 May 84	● GROOVIN' (YOU'RE THE BEST THING)/BIG BOSS GROOVE *Polydor TSC 6*	5	8 wks
13 Oct 84	● SHOUT TO THE TOP *Polydor TSC 7*	7	8 wks
11 May 85	● WALLS COME TUMBLING DOWN! *Polydor TSC 8*	6	7 wks
6 Jul 85	COME TO MILTON KEYNES *Polydor TSC 9*	23	5 wks
28 Sep 85	THE LODGERS *Polydor TSC 10*	13	6 wks
5 Apr 86	HAVE YOU EVER HAD IT BLUE *Polydor CINE 1*	14	6 wks
17 Jan 87	● IT DIDN'T MATTER *Polydor TSC 12*	9	5 wks
14 Mar 87	WAITING *Polydor TSC 13*	52	3 wks
31 Oct 87	WANTED *Polydor TSC 14*	20	4 wks
28 May 88	LIFE AT A TOP PEOPLE'S HEALTH FARM *Polydor TSC 15*	28	3 wks
23 Jul 88	HOW SHE THREW IT ALL AWAY (EP) *Polydor TSC 16*	41	2 wks
18 Feb 89	PROMISED LAND *Polydor TSC 17*	27	5 wks
27 May 89	LONG HOT SUMMER 89 (re-mix) *Polydor LHS 1*	48	2 wks

Paris Match *was listed with* Long Hot Summer *from 3 Sep 83. It peaked at position 7. Tracks on* How She Threw It All Away (EP): How She Threw It All Away/Love The First Time/Long Hot Summer/I Do Like To Be B-Side The A-Side. *The version of* Long Hot Summer *on the EP is a re-recording of their third hit.*

STYLISTICS US, male vocal group — **143 wks**

24 Jun 72	BETCHA BY GOLLY WOW *Avco 6105 011*	13	12 wks
4 Nov 72	● I'M STONE IN LOVE WITH YOU *Avco 6105 015*	9	10 wks
17 Mar 73	BREAK UP TO MAKE UP *Avco 6105 020*	34	5 wks
30 Jun 73	PEEK-A-BOO *Avco 6105 023*	35	6 wks
19 Jan 74	● ROCKIN' ROLL BABY *Avco 6105 026*	6	9 wks
13 Jul 74	● YOU MAKE ME FEEL BRAND NEW *Avco 6105 028*	2	14 wks
19 Oct 74	● LET'S PUT IT ALL TOGETHER *Avco 6105 032*	9	9 wks
25 Jan 75	STAR ON A TV SHOW *Avco 6105 035*	12	8 wks
10 May 75	● SING BABY SING *Avco 6105 036*	3	10 wks
26 Jul 75	★ CAN'T GIVE YOU ANYTHING (BUT MY LOVE) *Avco 6105 039*	1	11 wks
15 Nov 75	● NA NA IS THE SADDEST WORD *Avco 6105 041*	5	10 wks
14 Feb 76	● FUNKY WEEKEND *Avco 6105 044*	10	7 wks
24 Apr 76	● CAN'T HELP FALLING IN LOVE *Avco 6105 050*	4	7 wks
7 Aug 76	● 16 BARS *H & L 6105 059*	7	9 wks
27 Nov 76	YOU'LL NEVER GET TO HEAVEN (EP) *H & L STYL 001*	24	9 wks
26 Mar 77	7000 DOLLARS AND YOU *H & L 6105 073*	24	7 wks

Tracks on You'll Never Get To Heaven EP: You'll Never Get To Heaven/Country Living/You Are Beautiful/The Miracle.

STYX US, male vocal/instrumental group — **18 wks**

5 Jan 80	● BABE *A & M AMS 7489*	6	10 wks
24 Jan 81	THE BEST OF TIMES *A & M AMS 8102*	42	5 wks
18 Jun 83	DON'T LET IT END *A & M AM 120*	56	3 wks

SUB SUB UK, male instrumental/production group — **12 wks**

10 Apr 93	● AIN'T NO LOVE (AIN'T NO USE) *Rob's CDROB 9* [1]	3	11 wks
19 Feb 94	RESPECT *Rob's CDROB 19*	49	1 wk

[1] Sub Sub featuring Melanie Williams

SUBLIMINAL CUTS
Holland, male vocal/instrumental group — **1 wk**

15 Oct 94	LE VOIE LE SOLEIL *XL XLS 53CD*	69	1 wk

SUBSONIC 2 UK, male rap duo — **3 wks**

13 Jul 91	THE UNSUNG HEROES OF HIP HOP *Unity 6577947*	63	3 wks

SUBTERRANIA featuring Ann CONSUELO
Sweden, male/female vocal/instrumental duo — **1 wk**

5 Jun 93	DO IT FOR LOVE *Champion CHAMPCD 297*	68	1 wk

SUEDE UK, male vocal/instrumental group — **28 wks**

23 May 92	THE DROWNERS/TO THE BIRDS *Nude NUD 1S*	49	2 wks
26 Sep 92	METAL MICKEY *Nude NUD 3S*	17	3 wks
6 Mar 93	● ANIMAL NITRATE *Nude NUD 4CD*	7	7 wks
29 May 93	SO YOUNG *Nude NUD 5CD*	22	3 wks
26 Feb 94	● STAY TOGETHER *Nude NUD 9CD*	3	6 wks
24 Sep 94	WE ARE THE PIGS *Nude NUD 10CD*	18	3 wks
19 Nov 94	THE WILD ONES *Nude NUD 11CD1*	18	4 wks

SUENO LATINO featuring Carolina DAMAS
Italy, male production duo and female vocalist — **5 wks**

23 Sep 89	SUENO LATINO *BCM BCM 323*	47	5 wks

SUGAR US, male vocal / instrumental group — **7 wks**

31 Oct 92	**A GOOD IDEA** Creation CRE 143	65	1 wk
30 Jan 93	**IF I CAN'T CHANGE YOUR MIND** Creation CRESCD 149	30	2 wks
21 Aug 93	**TILTED** Creation CRECD 156	48	1 wk
3 Sep 94	**YOUR FAVORITE THING** Creation CRESCD 186	40	2 wks
29 Oct 94	**BELIEVE WHAT YOU'RE SAYING** Creation CRESCD 193	73	1 wk

SUGAR CANE US, male / female vocal group — **5 wks**

30 Sep 78	**MONTEGO BAY** Ariola Hansa AHA 524	54	5 wks

SUGARCUBES
Iceland, female / male vocal / instrumental group — **22 wks**

14 Nov 87	**BIRTHDAY** One Little Indian TP 7	65	3 wks
30 Jan 88	**COLD SWEAT** One Little Indian 7TP 9	56	4 wks
16 Apr 88	**DEUS** One Little Indian 7TP 10	51	3 wks
3 Sep 88	**BIRTHDAY** One Little Indian 7TP 11	65	3 wks
16 Sep 89	**REGINA** One Little Indian 26TP7	55	2 wks
11 Jan 92	**HIT** One Little Indian 62 TP7	17	6 wks
3 Oct 92	**BIRTHDAY (re-mix)** One Little Indian 104 TP12	64	1 wk

7TP 11 is a re-recording of their first hit.

SUGARHILL GANG US, male rap group — **16 wks**

1 Dec 79	● **RAPPER'S DELIGHT** Sugarhill SHL 101	3	11 wks
11 Sep 82	**THE LOVER IN YOU** Sugarhill SH 116	54	3 wks
25 Nov 89	**RAPPER'S DELIGHT (re-mix)** Sugarhill SHRD 0007	58	2 wks

SULTANA Italy, male instrumental / production group — **1 wk**

26 Mar 94	**TE AMO** Union City UCRD 28	57	1 wk

SULTANS OF PING
Ireland, male vocal / instrumental group — **12 wks**

8 Feb 92	**WHERE'S ME JUMPER** Divine ATHY 01 [1]	67	2 wks
9 May 92	**STUPID KID** Divine ATHY 02 [1]	67	1 wk
10 Oct 92	**VERONICA** Divine ATHY 03 [1]	69	1 wk
9 Jan 93	**YOU TALK TOO MUCH** Rhythm King 6588872 [1]	26	3 wks
11 Sep 93	**TEENAGE PUNKS** Epic 6595792	49	2 wks
30 Oct 93	**MICHIKO** Epic 6598222	43	2 wks
19 Feb 94	**WAKE UP AND SCRATCH ME** Epic 6601122	50	1 wk

[1] Sultans Of Ping FC

SUMMER - See SNAP

Donna SUMMER US, female vocalist — **287 wks**

17 Jan 76	● **LOVE TO LOVE YOU BABY** GTO GT 17	4	9 wks
29 May 76	**COULD IT BE MAGIC** GTO GT 60	40	7 wks
25 Dec 76	**WINTER MELODY** GTO GT 76	27	6 wks
9 Jul 77	★ **I FEEL LOVE** GTO GT 100	1	11 wks
20 Aug 77	● **DEEP DOWN INSIDE (THEME FROM 'THE DEEP')** Casablanca CAN 111	5	10 wks
24 Sep 77	**I REMEMBER YESTERDAY** GTO GT 107	14	7 wks
3 Dec 77	● **LOVE'S UNKIND** GTO GT 113	3	13 wks
10 Dec 77	● **I LOVE YOU** Casablanca CAN 114	10	9 wks
25 Feb 78	**RUMOUR HAS IT** Casablanca CAN 122	19	8 wks
22 Apr 78	**BACK IN LOVE AGAIN** GTO GT 117	29	7 wks
10 Jun 78	**LAST DANCE** Casablanca TGIF 2	70	1 wk
24 Jun 78	**LAST DANCE (re-entry)** Casablanca TGIF 2	51	8 wks
14 Oct 78	● **MACARTHUR PARK** Casablanca CAN 131	5	10 wks
17 Feb 79	**HEAVEN KNOWS** Casablanca CAN 141	34	8 wks
12 May 79	**HOT STUFF** Casablanca CAN 151	11	10 wks
7 Jul 79	**BAD GIRLS** Casablanca CAN 155	14	10 wks
1 Sep 79	**DIM ALL THE LIGHTS** Casablanca CAN 162	29	9 wks
3 Nov 79	● **NO MORE TEARS (ENOUGH IS ENOUGH)** Casablanca CAN 174/ CBS 8000 [1]	3	13 wks
16 Feb 80	**ON THE RADIO** Casablanca NB 2236	32	6 wks
21 Jun 80	**SUNSET PEOPLE** Casablanca CAN 198	46	5 wks
27 Sep 80	**THE WANDERER** Warner Bros./Geffen K 79810	48	6 wks
17 Jan 81	**COLD LOVE** Geffen K 79183	44	3 wks
10 Jul 82	**LOVE IS IN CONTROL (FINGER ON THE TRIGGER)** Warner Bros. K 79302	18	11 wks
6 Nov 82	**STATE OF INDEPENDENCE** Warner Bros. K 79344	14	11 wks
4 Dec 82	**I FEEL LOVE (re-mix)** Casablanca FEEL 7	21	10 wks
5 Mar 83	**THE WOMAN IN ME** Warner Bros. U 9983	62	2 wks
18 Jun 83	**SHE WORKS HARD FOR THE MONEY** Mercury DONNA 1	25	8 wks
24 Sep 83	**UNCONDITIONAL LOVE** Mercury DONNA 2	14	12 wks
21 Jan 84	**STOP LOOK AND LISTEN** Mercury DONNA 3	57	2 wks
24 Oct 87	**DINNER WITH GERSHWIN** Warner Bros. U 8237	13	11 wks
23 Jan 88	**ALL SYSTEMS GO** WEA U 8122	54	3 wks
25 Feb 89	● **THIS TIME I KNOW IT'S FOR REAL** Warner Bros. U 7780	3	14 wks
27 May 89	● **I DON'T WANNA GET HURT** Warner Bros. U 7567	7	9 wks
26 Aug 89	**LOVE'S ABOUT TO CHANGE MY HEART** Warner Bros. U 7494	20	6 wks
25 Nov 89	**WHEN LOVE TAKES OVER YOU** WEA U 7361	72	1 wk
17 Nov 90	**STATE OF INDEPENDENCE (re-issue)** Warner Bros. U 2857	45	3 wks
12 Jan 91	**BREAKAWAY** Warner Bros. U 3308	49	4 wks
30 Nov 91	**WORK THAT MAGIC** Warner Bros. U 5937	74	1 wk
12 Nov 94	**MELODY OF LOVE (WANNA BE LOVED)** Mercury MERCD 418	21	3 wks

[1] Donna Summer and Barbra Streisand

No More Tears (Enough Is Enough) was released simultaneously on two different labels, a 7-inch single on Casablanca and 12-inch on CBS. Unconditional Love features the additional vocals of Musical Youth.

Mark SUMMERS UK, male producer — **6 wks**

26 Jan 91	**SUMMER'S MAGIC** Fourth & Broadway BRW 205	27	6 wks

SUNDANCE - See DJ 'FAST' EDDIE

SUNDAYS UK, male / female vocal / instrumental group — **7 wks**

11 Feb 89	**CAN'T BE SURE** Rough Trade RT 218	45	5 wks
3 Oct 92	**GOODBYE** Parlophone R 6319	27	2 wks

SUNDRAGON UK, male vocal / instrumental duo — **1 wk**

21 Feb 68	**GREEN TAMBOURINE** MGM 1380	50	1 wk

SUNFIRE US, male vocal / instrumental group — **11 wks**

12 Mar 83	**YOUNG, FREE AND SINGLE** Warner Bros. W 9897	20	11 wks

SUNNY UK, female vocalist — **10 wks**

30 Mar 74	● **DOCTOR'S ORDERS** CBS 2068	7	10 wks

SUNSCREEM
UK, female / male vocal / instrumental group — **23 wks**

29 Feb 92	**PRESSURE** Sony S2 6578017	60	2 wks
18 Jul 92	**LOVE U MORE** Sony S2 6581727	23	6 wks
17 Oct 92	**PERFECT MOTION** Sony S2 6584057	18	5 wks
9 Jan 93	**BROKEN ENGLISH** Sony S2 6589032	13	5 wks
27 Mar 93	**PRESSURE US (re-mix)** Sony S2 6591102	19	5 wks

SUNSHINE BAND - See KC and the SUNSHINE BAND

SUPERCAT Jamaica, male / female vocal duo — **1 wk**

1 Aug 92	**IT FE DONE** Columbia 6582737	66	1 wk

SUPERGRASS UK, male vocal / instrumental group — **2 wks**

29 Oct 94	**CAUGHT BY THE FUZZ** Parlophone CDR 6396 ....**43**	2 wks

SUPERTRAMP UK / US, male vocal / instrumental group — **52 wks**

15 Feb 75	**DREAMER** A & M AMS 7132.................**13**	10 wks
25 Jun 77	**GIVE A LITTLE BIT** A & M AMS 7293 ....**29**	7 wks
31 Mar 79	● **THE LOGICAL SONG** A & M AMS 7427 ....**7**	11 wks
30 Jun 79	**BREAKFAST IN AMERICA** A & M AMS 7451......**9**	10 wks
27 Oct 79	**GOODBYE STRANGER** A & M AMS 7481 ....**57**	3 wks
30 Oct 82	**IT'S RAINING AGAIN** A & M AMS 8255 [1] **26**	11 wks

[1] Supertramp featuring vocals by Roger Hodgson

SUPREMES US, female vocal group — **306 wks**

3 Sep 64	● **WHERE DID OUR LOVE GO** Stateside SS 327 ....**3**	14 wks
22 Oct 64	★ **BABY LOVE** Stateside SS 350 ....**1**	15 wks
21 Jan 65	**COME SEE ABOUT ME** Stateside SS 376 ......**27**	6 wks
25 Mar 65	● **STOP IN THE NAME OF LOVE** Tamla Motown TMG 501 ....**7**	12 wks
10 Jun 65	**BACK IN MY ARMS AGAIN** Tamla Motown TMG 516 ....**40**	5 wks
9 Dec 65	**I HEAR A SYMPHONY** Tamla Motown TMG 543 ......**50**	1 wk
23 Dec 65	**I HEAR A SYMPHONY (re-entry)** Tamla Motown TMG 543 ....**39**	4 wks
8 Sep 66	● **YOU CAN'T HURRY LOVE** Tamla Motown TMG 575 ..**3**	12 wks
1 Dec 66	● **YOU KEEP ME HANGIN' ON** Tamla Motown TMG 585 ....**8**	10 wks
2 Mar 67	**LOVE IS HERE AND NOW YOU'RE GONE** Tamla Motown TMG 597 ....**17**	10 wks
11 May 67	● **THE HAPPENING** Tamla Motown TMG 607 ....**6**	12 wks
30 Aug 67	● **REFLECTIONS** Tamla Motown TMG 616 [1] **5**	14 wks
29 Nov 67	**IN AND OUT OF LOVE** Tamla Motown TMG 632 [1] **13**	13 wks
10 Apr 68	**FOREVER CAME TODAY** Tamla Motown TMG 650 [1] **28**	8 wks
3 Jul 68	**SOME THINGS YOU NEVER GET USED TO** Tamla Motown TMG 662 [1] **34**	6 wks
20 Nov 68	**LOVE CHILD** Tamla Motown TMG 677 [1] **15**	14 wks
29 Jan 69	● **I'M GONNA MAKE YOU LOVE ME** Tamla Motown TMG 685 [2] **3**	11 wks
23 Apr 69	**I'M GONNA MAKE YOU LOVE ME (re-entry)** Tamla Motown TMG 685 [2] **49**	1 wk
23 Apr 69	**I'M LIVING IN SHAME** Tamla Motown TMG 695 [1] **14**	9 wks
2 Jul 69	**I'M LIVING IN SHAME (re-entry)** Tamla Motown TMG 695 [1] **50**	1 wk
16 Jul 69	**NO MATTER WHAT SIGN YOU ARE** Tamla Motown TMG 704 [1] **37**	7 wks
20 Sep 69	**I SECOND THAT EMOTION** Tamla Motown TMG 709 [2] **18**	8 wks
13 Dec 69	**SOMEDAY WE'LL BE TOGETHER** Tamla Motown TMG 721 [1] **13**	13 wks
21 Mar 70	**WHY (MUST WE FALL IN LOVE)** Tamla Motown TMG 730 [2] **31**	7 wks
2 May 70	● **UP THE LADDER TO THE ROOF** Tamla Motown TMG 735 ....**6**	15 wks
16 Jan 71	● **STONED LOVE** Tamla Motown TMG 760 ....**3**	13 wks
26 Jun 71	**RIVER DEEP MOUNTAIN HIGH** Tamla Motown TMG 777 [3] **11**	10 wks
21 Aug 71	● **NATHAN JONES** Tamla Motown TMG 782 ....**5**	11 wks
20 Nov 71	**YOU GOTTA HAVE LOVE IN YOUR HEART** Tamla Motown TMG 793 [3] **25**	10 wks
4 Mar 72	● **FLOY JOY** Tamla Motown TMG 804 ....**9**	10 wks
15 Jul 72	● **AUTOMATICALLY SUNSHINE** Tamla Motown TMG 821 ....**10**	9 wks
21 Apr 73	**BAD WEATHER** Tamla Motown TMG 847 ....**37**	4 wks
24 Aug 74	**BABY LOVE (re-issue)** Tamla Motown TMG 915 [1] **12**	10 wks
18 Feb 89	**STOP! IN THE NAME OF LOVE (re-issue)** Motown ZB 41963 [1] **62**	1 wk

[1] Diana Ross and the Supremes [2] Diana Ross and the Supremes and the Temptations [3] Supremes and the Four Tops

Al B. SURE! US, male vocalist — **13 wks**

16 Apr 88	**NITE AND DAY** Uptown W 8192 ....**44**	5 wks
30 Jul 88	**OFF ON YOUR OWN (GIRL)** Uptown W 7870..........**70**	2 wks
10 Jun 89	**IF I'M NOT YOUR LOVER** Warner Bros. W 2908....**54**	3 wks
31 Mar 90	**SECRET GARDEN** Qwest W 9992 [1] **67**	1 wk
12 Jun 93	**BLACK TIE WHITE NOISE** Arista 74321148682 [2] **36**	2 wks

[1] Quincy Jones featuring Al B. Sure!, James Ingram, El DeBarge and Barry White [2] David Bowie featuring Al B. Sure!

SURFACE US, male vocal / instrumental duo — **14 wks**

23 Jul 83	**FALLING IN LOVE** Salsoul SAL 104.............**67**	3 wks
23 Jun 84	**WHEN YOUR 'EX' WANTS YOU BACK** Salsoul SAL 106.............**52**	4 wks
28 Feb 87	**HAPPY** CBS 650393 7.............**56**	5 wks
12 Jan 91	**THE FIRST TIME** Columbia 6564767.............**60**	2 wks

SURFACE NOISE UK, male instrumental group — **11 wks**

31 May 80	**THE SCRATCH** WEA K 18291 ....**26**	8 wks
30 Aug 80	**DANCIN' ON A WIRE** Groove GP102 ....**59**	3 wks

SURFARIS US, male instrumental group — **14 wks**

25 Jul 63	● **WIPE OUT** London HLD 9751 ....**5**	14 wks

SURPRISE SISTERS UK, female vocal group — **3 wks**

13 Mar 76	**LA BOOGA ROOGA** Good Earth GD 1 ....**38**	3 wks

SURVIVOR US, male vocal / instrumental group — **26 wks**

31 Jul 82	★ **EYE OF THE TIGER** Scotti Brothers SCT A 2411 ....**1**	15 wks
1 Feb 86	● **BURNING HEART** Scotti Brothers A 6708.............**5**	11 wks

SUTHERLAND BROTHERS and QUIVER
UK, male vocal / instrumental group — **20 wks**

3 Apr 76	● **ARMS OF MARY** CBS 4001 ....**5**	12 wks
20 Nov 76	**SECRETS** CBS 4668.............**35**	4 wks
2 Jun 79	**EASY COME EASY GO** CBS 7121 [1] **50**	4 wks

[1] Sutherland Brothers

Pat SUZUKI US, female vocalist — **1 wk**

14 Apr 60	**I ENJOY BEING A GIRL** RCA 1171 ....**49**	1 wk

Billy SWAN US, male vocalist — **13 wks**

14 Dec 74	● **I CAN HELP** Monument MNT 2752.............**6**	9 wks
24 May 75	**DON'T BE CRUEL** Monument MNT 3244.............**42**	4 wks

SWAN LAKE US, male vocalist / multi-instrumentalist — **4 wks**

17 Sep 88	**IN THE NAME OF LOVE** Champion CHAMP 86.........**53**	4 wks

SWANS WAY
UK, male / female vocal / instrumental group — **12 wks**

4 Feb 84	**SOUL TRAIN** Exit EXT 3 ....**20**	7 wks
26 May 84	**ILLUMINATIONS** Balgier PH 5 ....**57**	5 wks

Patrick SWAYZE featuring Wendy FRASER
US, male / female vocal duo — **11 wks**

26 Mar 88	**SHE'S LIKE THE WIND** RCA PB 49565 ....**17**	11 wks

The original hitmaking line-up of the **SUPREMES** consisted of (left to right) Diana Ross, Florence Ballard and Mary Wilson. (LFI)

DONNA SUMMER was number one on the Billboard Hot 100 once in 1978 and three times in 1979. (LFI)

TAKE THAT took four consecutive releases straight to number one.
(Philip Ollerenshaw/LFI)

Keith SWEAT US, male vocalist — **14 wks**

20 Feb 88	**I WANT HER** Vintertainment EKR 68	**26**	10 wks
14 May 88	**SOMETHING JUST AIN'T RIGHT**		
	Vintertainment EKR 72	**55**	3 wks
14 May 94	**HOW DO YOU LIKE IT** Elektra EKR 185CD	**71**	1 wk

Michelle SWEENEY US, female vocalist — **1 wk**

29 Oct 94	**THIS TIME** Big Beat A 8229CD	**57**	1 wk

SWEET UK, male vocal / instrumental group — **159 wks**

13 Mar 71	**FUNNY FUNNY** RCA 2051	**13**	14 wks
12 Jun 71	● **CO-CO** RCA 2087	**2**	15 wks
16 Oct 71	**ALEXANDER GRAHAM BELL** RCA 2121	**33**	5 wks
5 Feb 72	**POPPA JOE** RCA 2164	**11**	12 wks
10 Jun 72	● **LITTLE WILLY** RCA 2225	**4**	14 wks
9 Sep 72	● **WIG-WAM BAM** RCA 2260	**4**	13 wks
13 Jan 73	★ **BLOCKBUSTER** RCA 2305	**1**	15 wks
5 May 73	● **HELL RAISER** RCA 2357	**2**	11 wks
22 Sep 73	● **BALLROOM BLITZ** RCA 2403	**2**	9 wks
19 Jan 74	● **TEENAGE RAMPAGE** RCA LPBO 5004	**2**	8 wks
13 Jul 74	● **THE SIX TEENS** RCA LPBO 5037	**9**	7 wks
9 Nov 74	**TURN IT DOWN** RCA 2480	**41**	2 wks
15 Mar 75	● **FOX ON THE RUN** RCA 2524	**2**	10 wks
12 Jul 75	**ACTION** RCA 2578	**15**	6 wks
24 Jan 76	**LIES IN YOUR EYES** RCA 2641	**35**	4 wks
28 Jan 78	● **LOVE IS LIKE OXYGEN** Polydor POSP 1	**9**	9 wks
26 Jan 85	**IT'S IT'S THE SWEET MIX** Anagram ANA 28	**45**	5 wks

It's It's The Sweet Mix *is a medley of the following songs: Blockbuster / Fox On The Run / Teenage Rampage / Hell Raiser / Ballroom Blitz.*

Rachel SWEET US, female vocalist — **15 wks**

9 Dec 78	**B-A-B-Y** Stiff BUY 39	**35**	8 wks
22 Aug 81	**EVERLASTING LOVE** CBS A 1405 [1]	**35**	7 wks

[1] Rex Smith and Rachel Sweet

SWEET DREAMS UK, male / female vocal duo — **12 wks**

20 Jul 74	● **HONEY HONEY** Bradley's BRAD 7408	**10**	12 wks

SWEET DREAMS UK, male / female vocal group — **7 wks**

9 Apr 83	**I'M NEVER GIVING UP** Ariola ARO 333	**21**	7 wks

SWEET PEOPLE France, male vocal / instrumental group — **10 wks**

4 Oct 80	● **ET LES OISEAUX CHANTAIENT (AND THE BIRDS WERE SINGING)** Polydor POSP 179	**4**	8 wks
29 Aug 87	**ET LES OISEAUX CHANTAIENT (AND THE BIRDS WERE SINGING) (re-entry)** Polydor POSP 179	**73**	2 wks

SWEET SENSATION UK, male vocal group — **17 wks**

14 Sep 74	★ **SAD SWEET DREAMER** Pye 7N 45385	**1**	10 wks
18 Jan 75	**PURELY BY COINCIDENCE** Pye 7N 45421	**11**	7 wks

SWEET TEE US, female rapper — **8 wks**

16 Jan 88	**IT'S LIKE THAT Y'ALL / I GOT DA FEELIN'** Cooltempo COOL 160	**31**	6 wks
13 Aug 94	**THE FEELING** Deep Distraxion OILYCD 029 [1]	**32**	2 wks

[1] Tin Tin Out featuring Sweet Tee

Sally SWEETLAND - See Eddie FISHER

SWERVEDRIVER UK, male vocal / instrumental group — **3 wks**

10 Aug 91	**SANDBLASTED EP** Creation CRE 102	**67**	1 wk

30 May 92	**NEVER LOSE THAT FEELING** Creation CRE 120	**62**	1 wk
14 Aug 93	**DUEL** Creation CRESCD 136	**60**	1 wk

Tracks on Sandblasted EP: Sandblaster / Flawed / Out / Laze It Up.

SWIMMING WITH SHARKS Germany, female vocal duo — **3 wks**

7 May 88	**CARELESS LOVE** WEA YZ 173	**63**	3 wks

SWING KIDS - See K7

SWING OUT SISTER UK, male / female vocal / instrumental group — **55 wks**

25 Oct 86	● **BREAKOUT** Mercury SWING 2	**4**	14 wks
10 Jan 87	● **SURRENDER** Mercury SWING 3	**7**	8 wks
18 Apr 87	**TWILIGHT WORLD** Mercury SWING 4	**32**	6 wks
11 Jul 87	**FOOLED BY A SMILE** Mercury SWING 5	**43**	4 wks
8 Apr 89	**YOU ON MY MIND** Fontana SWING 6	**28**	9 wks
8 Jul 89	**WHERE IN THE WORLD** Fontana SWING 7	**47**	4 wks
11 Apr 92	**AM I THE SAME GIRL** Fontana SWING 9	**21**	6 wks
20 Jun 92	**NOTGONNACHANGE** Fontana SWING 10	**49**	2 wks
27 Aug 94	**LA LA (MEANS I LOVE YOU)** Fontana SWIDD 11	**37**	2 wks

SWINGING BLUE JEANS UK, male vocal / instrumental group — **57 wks**

20 Jun 63	**IT'S TOO LATE NOW** HMV POP 1170	**30**	6 wks
8 Aug 63	**IT'S TOO LATE NOW (re-entry)** HMV POP 1170	**46**	3 wks
12 Dec 63	● **HIPPY HIPPY SHAKE** HMV POP 1242	**2**	17 wks
19 Mar 64	**GOOD GOLLY MISS MOLLY** HMV POP 1273	**11**	10 wks
4 Jun 64	● **YOU'RE NO GOOD** HMV POP 1304	**3**	13 wks
20 Jan 66	**DON'T MAKE ME OVER** HMV POP 1501	**31**	8 wks

SWITCH US, male vocal / instrumental group — **3 wks**

10 Nov 84	**KEEPING SECRETS** Total Experience XE 502	**61**	3 wks

S.W.V. US, female vocal group — **29 wks**

1 May 93	**I'M SO INTO YOU** RCA 74321144972	**17**	6 wks
26 Jun 93	**WEAK** RCA 74321153352	**33**	3 wks
28 Aug 93	● **RIGHT HERE** RCA 74321160482	**3**	12 wks
26 Feb 94	**DOWNTOWN** RCA 74321189012	**19**	5 wks
11 Jun 94	**ANYTHING** RCA 74321212212	**24**	3 wks

SYBIL US, female vocalist — **66 wks**

1 Nov 86	**FALLING IN LOVE** Champion CHAMP 22	**68**	3 wks
25 Apr 87	**LET YOURSELF GO** Champion CHAMP 42	**32**	6 wks
29 Aug 87	**MY LOVE IS GUARANTEED** Champion CHAMP 55	**42**	5 wks
22 Jul 89	**DON'T MAKE ME OVER** Champion CHAMP 213	**59**	5 wks
14 Oct 89	**DON'T MAKE ME OVER (re-entry)** Champion CHAMP 213	**19**	6 wks
27 Jan 90	● **WALK ON BY** PWL PWL 48	**6**	9 wks
21 Apr 90	**CRAZY FOR YOU** PWL PWL 53	**71**	1 wk
16 Jan 93	● **THE LOVE I LOST** PWL Sanctuary PWCD 253 [1]	**3**	13 wks
20 Mar 93	● **WHEN I'M GOOD AND READY** PWL International PWCD 260	**5**	13 wks
26 Jun 93	**BEYOND YOUR WILDEST DREAMS** PWL International PWCD 265	**41**	2 wks
11 Sep 93	**STRONGER TOGETHER** PWL International PWCD 269	**41**	2 wks
11 Dec 93	**MY LOVE IS GUARANTEED** PWL International PWCD 227	**48**	1 wk

[1] West End featuring Sybil

SYLVESTER US, male vocalist — **45 wks**

19 Aug 78	● **YOU MAKE ME FEEL (MIGHTY REAL)** Fantasy FTC 160	**8**	15 wks
18 Nov 78	**DANCE (DISCO HEAT)** Fantasy FTC 163	**29**	12 wks

31 Mar 79	**I (WHO HAVE NOTHING)** Fantasy FTC 171	**46**	5 wks
7 Jul 79	**STARS** Fantasy FTC 177	**47**	3 wks
11 Sep 82	**DO YOU WANNA FUNK** London LON 13 [1]	**32**	8 wks
3 Sep 83	**BAND OF GOLD** London LON 33	**67**	2 wks

[1] Sylvester with Patrick Cowley

SYLVIA US, female vocalist — 11 wks

| 23 Jun 73 | **PILLOW TALK** London HL 10415 | **14** | 11 wks |

SYLVIA Sweden, female vocalist — 33 wks

10 Aug 74	● **Y VIVA ESPANA** Sonet SON 2037	**4**	19 wks
4 Jan 75	**Y VIVA ESPANA (re-entry)** Sonet SON 2037	**35**	9 wks
26 Apr 75	**HASTA LA VISTA** Sonet SON 2055	**38**	5 wks

David SYLVIAN UK, male vocalist — 34 wks

7 Aug 82	**BAMBOO HOUSES / BAMBOO MUSIC** Virgin VS 510 [1]	**30**	4 wks
2 Jul 83	**FORBIDDEN COLOURS** Virgin VS 601 [2]	**16**	8 wks
2 Jun 84	**RED GUITAR** Virgin VS 633	**17**	5 wks
18 Aug 84	**THE INK IN THE WELL** Virgin VS 700	**36**	3 wks
3 Nov 84	**PULLING PUNCHES** Virgin VS 717	**56**	2 wks
14 Dec 85	**WORDS WITH THE SHAMAN** Virgin VS 835	**72**	1 wk
9 Aug 86	**TAKING THE VEIL** Virgin VS 815	**53**	3 wks
17 Jan 87	**BUOY** Virgin VS 910 [3]	**63**	2 wks
10 Oct 87	**LET THE HAPPINESS IN** Virgin VS 1001	**66**	1 wk
13 Jun 92	**HEARTBEAT (TAINAI KAIKI II) RETURNING TO THE WOMB** Virgin America VUS 57 [4]	**58**	3 wks
28 Aug 93	**JEAN THE BIRDMAN** Virgin VSCDG 1462 [5]	**68**	2 wks

[1] Sylvian Sakamoto [2] David Sylvian and Riuichi Sakamoto [3] Mick Karn featuring David Sylvian [4] David Sylvian and Riuichi Sakamoto featuring Ingrid Chavez [5] David Sylvian and Robert Fripp

SYMARIP UK, male vocal / instrumental group — 3 wks

| 2 Feb 80 | **SKINHEAD MOONSTOMP** Trojan TRO 9062 | **54** | 3 wks |

SYMBOLS UK, male vocal / instrumental group — 15 wks

| 2 Aug 67 | **BYE BYE BABY** President PT 144 | **44** | 3 wks |
| 3 Jan 68 | **BEST PART OF BREAKING UP** President PT 173 | **25** | 12 wks |

SYREETA US, female vocalist — 30 wks

21 Sep 74	**SPINNIN' AND SPINNIN'** Tamla Motown TMG 912	**49**	3 wks
1 Feb 75	**YOUR KISS IS SWEET** Tamla Motown TMG 933	**12**	8 wks
12 Jul 75	**HARMOUR LOVE** Tamla Motown TMG 954	**32**	4 wks
15 Dec 79	● **WITH YOU I'M BORN AGAIN** Motown TMG 1159 [1]	**2**	11 wks
8 Mar 80	**IT WILL COME IN TIME** Motown TMG 1175 [1]	**47**	4 wks

[1] Billy Preston and Syreeta

SYSTEM US, male vocal / instrumental duo — 2 wks

| 9 Jun 84 | **I WANNA MAKE YOU FEEL GOOD** Polydor POSP 685 | **73** | 2 wks |

SYSTEM 7
UK / France, male / female vocal / instrumental duo — 2 wks

| 13 Feb 93 | **7:7 EXPANSION** Butterfly BFLD 2 | **39** | 1 wk |
| 17 Jul 93 | **SINBAD QUEST** Butterfly BFLD 8 | **74** | 1 wk |

T

TACK HEAD US, male rapper — 3 wks

| 30 Jun 90 | **DANGEROUS SEX** SBK SBK 7014 | **48** | 3 wks |

TAFFY UK, female vocalist — 14 wks

| 10 Jan 87 | ● **I LOVE MY RADIO (MY DEE JAY'S RADIO)** Transglobal TYPE 1 | **6** | 10 wks |
| 18 Jul 87 | **STEP BY STEP** Transglobal TYPE 5 | **59** | 4 wks |

TAG TEAM US, male rap duo — 8 wks

8 Jan 94	**WHOOMP! (THERE IT IS)** Club Tools SHXCD 1	**34**	5 wks
29 Jan 94	**ADDAMS FAMILY (WHOOMP!)** Atlas PZCD 305	**53**	1 wk
10 Sep 94	**WHOOMP! (THERE IT IS) (re-mix)** Club Tools SHXR 1	**48**	2 wks

TAKE THAT UK, male vocal group — 119 wks

23 Nov 91	**PROMISES** RCA PB 45085	**38**	2 wks
8 Feb 92	**ONCE YOU'VE TASTED LOVE** RCA PB 45257	**47**	3 wks
6 Jun 92	● **IT ONLY TAKES A MINUTE** RCA 74321101007	**7**	8 wks
15 Aug 92	**I FOUND HEAVEN** RCA 74321108137	**15**	6 wks
10 Oct 92	● **A MILLION LOVE SONGS** RCA 74321116307	**7**	9 wks
12 Dec 92	● **COULD IT BE MAGIC** RCA 74321123137	**3**	12 wks
20 Feb 93	● **WHY CAN'T I WAKE UP WITH YOU** RCA 74321133102	**2**	10 wks
17 Jul 93	★ **PRAY** RCA 74321154502	**1**	11 wks
9 Oct 93	★ **RELIGHT MY FIRE** RCA 74321167722 [1]	**1**	14 wks
18 Dec 93	★ **BABE** RCA 74321182122	**1**	10 wks
9 Apr 94	★ **EVERYTHING CHANGES** RCA 74321167732	**1**	10 wks
9 Jul 94	● **LOVE AIN'T HERE ANYMORE** RCA 74321214832	**3**	10 wks
15 Oct 94	★ **SURE** RCA 74321236622	**1†**	12 wks
15 Oct 94	**LOVE AIN'T HERE ANYMORE (re-entry)** RCA 74321214832	**55**	2 wks

[1] Take That featuring Lulu

Billy TALBOT - *See Ian McNABB*

TALK TALK UK, male vocal / instrumental group — 73 wks

24 Apr 82	**TALK TALK** EMI 5284	**52**	4 wks
24 Jul 82	**TODAY** EMI 5314	**14**	13 wks
13 Nov 82	**TALK TALK (re-mix)** EMI 5352	**23**	10 wks
19 Mar 83	**MY FOOLISH FRIEND** EMI 5373	**57**	3 wks
14 Jan 84	**IT'S MY LIFE** EMI 5443	**46**	5 wks
7 Apr 84	**SUCH A SHAME** EMI 5433	**49**	6 wks
11 Aug 84	**DUM DUM GIRL** EMI 5480	**74**	1 wk
18 Jan 86	**LIFE'S WHAT YOU MAKE IT** EMI EMI 5540	**16**	9 wks
15 Mar 86	**LIVING IN ANOTHER WORLD** EMI EMI 5551	**48**	4 wks
17 May 86	**GIVE IT UP** Parlophone R 6131	**59**	3 wks
19 May 90	**IT'S MY LIFE (re-issue)** Parlophone R 6254	**13**	9 wks
1 Sep 90	**LIFE'S WHAT YOU MAKE IT (re-issue)** Parlophone R 6264	**23**	6 wks

TALKING HEADS
US / UK, male / female vocal / instrumental group — 54 wks

7 Feb 81	**ONCE IN A LIFETIME** Sire SIR 4048	**14**	10 wks
9 May 81	**HOUSES IN MOTION** Sire SIR 4050	**50**	3 wks
21 Jan 84	**THIS MUST BE THE PLACE** Sire W 9451	**51**	3 wks
3 Nov 84	**SLIPPERY PEOPLE** EMI 5504	**68**	2 wks
12 Oct 85	● **ROAD TO NOWHERE** EMI EMI 5530	**6**	16 wks
8 Feb 86	**AND SHE WAS** EMI EMI 5543	**17**	8 wks
6 Sep 86	**WILD WILD LIFE** EMI EMI 5567	**43**	4 wks
16 May 87	**RADIO HEAD** EMI EM 1	**52**	2 wks
13 Aug 88	**BLIND** EMI EM 68	**59**	3 wks
10 Oct 92	**LIFETIME PILING UP** EMI EM 250	**50**	3 wks

TAMS US, male vocal group — 31 wks

14 Feb 70	**BE YOUNG BE FOOLISH BE HAPPY** Stateside SS 2123	**32**	7 wks
31 Jul 71	★ **HEY GIRL BE DON'T BOTHER ME** Probe PRO 532	**1**	17 wks
21 Nov 87	**THERE AIN'T NOTHING LIKE SHAGGIN'** Virgin VS 1029	**21**	7 wks

Norma TANEGA *US, female vocalist*   **8 wks**

7 Apr 66   **WALKING MY CAT NAMED DOG** *Stateside SS 496* ..**22**   8 wks

The Children of TANSLEY SCHOOL
UK, children's choir   **4 wks**

28 Mar 81   **MY MUM IS ONE IN A MILLION** *EMI 5151* ....**27**   4 wks

Jimmy TARBUCK *UK, male vocalist*   **2 wks**

16 Nov 85   **AGAIN** *Safari SAFE 68* ....**74**   1 wk
30 Nov 85   **AGAIN (re-entry)** *Safari SAFE 68*................**68**   1 wk

Bill TARMEY *UK, male vocalist*   **9 wks**

3 Apr 93   **ONE VOICE** *Arista 74321140852*................**16**   4 wks
19 Feb 94   **WIND BENEATH MY WINGS** *EMI CDEM 304* ....**40**   3 wks
19 Nov 94   **IOU** *EMI CDEM 361* ....**55**   2 wks

TARRIERS *US, male vocal / instrumental group*   **6 wks**

14 Dec 56   **CINDY OH CINDY** *London HLN 8340* [1] ....**26**   1 wk
1 Mar 57   **BANANA BOAT SONG** *Columbia DB 3891* ....**15**   5 wks

[1] Vince Martin and the Tarriers

A TASTE OF HONEY *US, female vocal duo*   **19 wks**

17 Jun 78 ● **BOOGIE OOGIE OOGIE** *Capitol CL 15988* ....**3**   16 wks
18 May 85   **BOOGIE OOGIE OOGIE (re-mix)** *Capitol CL 357* ......**59**   3 wks

TAVARES *US, male vocal group*   **77 wks**

10 Jul 76 ● **HEAVEN MUST BE MISSING AN ANGEL**
       Capitol CL 15876 ....**4**   11 wks
9 Oct 76 ● **DON'T TAKE AWAY THE MUSIC** *Capitol CL 15886* ....**4**   10 wks
5 Feb 77   **MIGHTY POWER OF LOVE** *Capitol CL 15905* ....**25**   6 wks
9 Apr 77 ● **WHODUNIT** *Capitol CL 15914* ....**5**   10 wks
2 Jul 77   **ONE STEP AWAY** *Capitol CL 15930* ....**16**   7 wks
18 Mar 78   **THE GHOST OF LOVE** *Capitol CL 15968*.....................**29**   6 wks
6 May 78 ● **MORE THAN A WOMAN** *Capitol CL 15977*.............**7**   11 wks
12 Aug 78   **SLOW TRAIN TO PARADISE** *Capitol CL 15996* ....**62**   3 wks
22 Feb 86   **HEAVEN MUST BE MISSING AN ANGEL (re-issue)**
       Capitol TAV 1 ....**12**   9 wks
3 May 86   **IT ONLY TAKES A MINUTE** *Capitol TAV 2* ....**46**   4 wks

TAXMAN - *See KICKING BACK with TAXMAN*

Andy TAYLOR *UK, male vocalist*   **2 wks**

20 Oct 90   **LOLA** *A & M AM 596* ....**60**   2 wks

Dina TAYLOR - *See BBG*

Felice TAYLOR *US, female vocalist*   **13 wks**

25 Oct 67   **I FEEL LOVE COMIN' ON** *President PT 155*...............**11**   13 wks

James TAYLOR *US, male vocalist*   **23 wks**

21 Nov 70   **FIRE AND RAIN** *Warner Bros. WB 6104* ....**42**   3 wks
28 Aug 71 ● **YOU'VE GOT A FRIEND** *Warner Bros. WB 16085* ....**4**   15 wks
16 Mar 74   **MOCKINGBIRD** *Elektra K 12134* [1] ....**34**   5 wks

[1] Carly Simon and James Taylor

John TAYLOR *UK, male vocalist*   **4 wks**

15 Mar 86   **I DO WHAT I DO...THEME FOR '9 ½ WEEKS'**
       Parlophone R 6125 ....**42**   4 wks

Johnnie TAYLOR *US, male vocalist*   **7 wks**

24 Apr 76   **DISCO LADY** *CBS 4044* ....**25**   7 wks

J.T. TAYLOR *US, male vocalist*   **5 wks**

24 Aug 91   **LONG HOT SUMMER NIGHT** *MCA MCS 1567*...........**63**   2 wks
30 Nov 91   **FEEL THE NEED** *MCA MCS 1592* ....**57**   1 wk
18 Apr 92   **FOLLOW ME** *MCA MCS 1617* ....**59**   2 wks

R. Dean TAYLOR *Canada, male vocalist*   **48 wks**

19 Jun 68   **GOTTA SEE JANE** *Tamla Motown TMG 656* ....**17**   12 wks
3 Apr 71 ● **INDIANA WANTS ME** *Tamla Motown TMG 763*........**2**   15 wks
11 May 74 ● **THERE'S A GHOST IN MY HOUSE**
       Tamla Motown TMG 896 ....**3**   12 wks
31 Aug 74   **WINDOW SHOPPING** *Polydor 2058 502* ....**36**   5 wks
21 Sep 74   **GOTTA SEE JANE (re-issue)**
       Tamla Motown TMG 918 ....**41**   4 wks

Roger TAYLOR *UK, male vocalist*   **15 wks**

18 Apr 81   **FUTURE MANAGEMENT** *EMI 5157* ....**49**   4 wks
16 Jun 84   **MAN ON FIRE** *EMI 5478* ....**66**   2 wks
10 Oct 92   **RADIO** *Epic 6584367* [1] ....**37**   3 wks
14 May 94   **NAZIS** *Parlophone CDR 6379* ....**22**   2 wks
1 Oct 94   **FOREIGN SAND** *Parlophone CDR 6389* [2] ....**26**   2 wks
26 Nov 94   **HAPPINESS** *Parlophone CDR 6399*........................**32**   2 wks

[1] Shaky featuring Roger Taylor [2] Roger Taylor and Yoshiki

TC *Italy, male instrumental / production duo*   **5 wks**

14 Mar 92   **BERRY** *Union City UCRT 1* [1] ....**73**   1 wk
21 Nov 92   **FUNKY GUITAR** *Union City UCRT 13* [2] ....**40**   2 wks
10 Jul 93   **HARMONY** *Union City UCRD 20* [3] ....**51**   2 wks

[1] TC 1991 [2] TC 1992 [3] TC 1993

T-CONNECTION *US, male vocal / instrumental group*   **27 wks**

18 Jun 77   **DO WHAT YOU WANNA DO** *TK XC 9109* ....**11**   8 wks
14 Jan 78   **ON FIRE** *TK TKR 6006* ....**16**   5 wks
10 Jun 78   **LET YOURSELF GO** *TK TKR 6024* ....**52**   3 wks
24 Feb 79   **AT MIDNIGHT** *TK TKR 7517* ....**53**   5 wks
5 May 79   **SATURDAY NIGHT** *TK TKR 7536* ....**41**   6 wks

T-COY - *See VARIOUS ARTISTS (EPs & LPs) - The Further Adventures Of North EP.*

Kiri TE KANAWA *New Zealand, female vocalist*   **11 wks**

28 Sep 91 ● **WORLD IN UNION** *Columbia 6574817*........................**4**   11 wks

TEACH-IN *Holland, male / female vocal / instrumental group*   **7 wks**

12 Apr 75   **DING-A-DONG** *Polydor 2058 570*........................**13**   7 wks

TEAM *UK, male vocal / instrumental group*   **5 wks**

1 Jun 85   **WICKI WACKY HOUSE PARTY** *EMI 5519* ....**55**   5 wks

TEARDROP EXPLODES
UK, male vocal / instrumental group   **50 wks**

27 Sep 80   **WHEN I DREAM** *Mercury TEAR 1*........................**47**   6 wks
31 Jan 81 ● **REWARD** *Vertigo TEAR 2* ....**6**   13 wks
2 May 81   **TREASON (IT'S JUST A STORY)** *Mercury TEAR 3* ......**18**   8 wks
29 Aug 81   **PASSIONATE FRIEND** *Zoo TEAR 5* ....**25**   10 wks
21 Nov 81   **COLOURS FLY AWAY** *Mercury TEAR 6* ....**54**   3 wks
19 Jun 82   **TINY CHILDREN** *Mercury TEAR 7* ....**44**   7 wks
19 Mar 83   **YOU DISAPPEAR FROM VIEW** *Mercury TEAR 8* ......**41**   3 wks

TEARS FOR FEARS UK, male vocal / instrumental duo 139 wks

2 Oct 82	● MAD WORLD Mercury IDEA 3 3	16 wks
5 Feb 83	● CHANGE Mercury IDEA 4 4	9 wks
30 Apr 83	● PALE SHELTER Mercury IDEA 5.....................5	8 wks
3 Dec 83	THE WAY YOU ARE Mercury IDEA 6 24	8 wks
18 Aug 84	MOTHER'S TALK Mercury IDEA 7 14	8 wks
1 Dec 84	● SHOUT Mercury IDEA 8 4	16 wks
30 Mar 85	● EVERYBODY WANTS TO RULE THE WORLD	
	Mercury IDEA 9...2	14 wks
22 Jun 85	HEAD OVER HEELS Mercury IDEA 10 12	9 wks
31 Aug 85	SUFFER THE CHILDREN Mercury IDEA 1.....52	4 wks
7 Sep 85	PALE SHELTER (re-issue) Mercury IDEA 2 73	2 wks
12 Oct 85	I BELIEVE (A SOULFUL RE-RECORDING)	
	Mercury IDEA 11..23	4 wks
22 Feb 86	EVERYBODY WANTS TO RULE THE WORLD	
	(re-entry) Mercury IDEA 9 73	1 wk
31 May 86	● EVERYBODY WANTS TO RUN THE WORLD	
	Mercury RACE 1...5	6 wks
19 Jul 86	EVERYBODY WANTS TO RUN THE WORLD	
	(re-entry) Mercury RACE 1 73	1 wk
2 Sep 89	● SOWING THE SEEDS OF LOVE Fontana IDEA 12 5	9 wks
18 Nov 89	WOMAN IN CHAINS Fontana IDEA 13 26	8 wks
3 Mar 90	ADVICE FOR THE YOUNG AT HEART	
	Fontana IDEA 14.......................................36	4 wks
22 Feb 92	LAID SO LOW (TEARS ROLL DOWN)	
	Fontana IDEA 17..17	5 wks
25 Apr 92	WOMAN IN CHAINS (re-issue)	
	Fontana IDEA 16 [1] 57	1 wk
29 May 93	BREAK IT DOWN AGAIN Mercury IDECD 18 20	5 wks
31 Jul 93	COLD Mercury IDECD 19 72	1 wk

[1] Tears For Fears featuring Oleta Adams

Mercury RACE 1 was a slightly changed version of Mercury IDEA 9, released to promote the Race Against Time of 15 May 1986. Oleta Adams is given no label credit on the original release of Woman In Chains. From '92 Tears For Fears were essentially a male vocalist / multi-instrumentalist - Roland Orzabal.

TECHNICIAN 2 UK, male instrumental / production group 1 wk

| 14 Nov 92 | PLAYING WITH THE BOY MCA MCS 1710.................70 | 1 wk |

TECHNO TWINS UK, male / female vocal duo 2 wks

| 16 Jan 82 | FALLING IN LOVE AGAIN PRT 7P 224..........75 | 1 wk |
| 30 Jan 82 | FALLING IN LOVE AGAIN (re-entry) PRT 7P 224 ....70 | 1 wk |

TECHNOTRONIC Belgium, male producer - Jo Bogaert 64 wks

2 Sep 89	● PUMP UP THE JAM Swanyard SYR 4 [1] 2	15 wks
3 Feb 90	● GET UP (BEFORE THE NIGHT IS OVER)	
	Swanyard SYR 8 [2] 2	10 wks
7 Apr 90	THIS BEAT IS TECHNOTRONIC Swanyard SYR 9 [3] 14	7 wks
14 Jul 90	● ROCKIN' OVER THE BEAT Swanyard SYR 14 [2] 9	9 wks
6 Oct 90	● MEGAMIX Swanyard SYR 19 6	8 wks
15 Dec 90	TURN IT UP Swanyard SYD 9 [4] 42	4 wks
25 May 91	MOVE THAT BODY ARS 6568377 [5] 12	7 wks
3 Aug 91	WORK ARS 6573317 [5] 40	4 wks

[1] Technotronic featuring Felly [2] Technotronic featuring Ya Kid K [3] Technotronic featuring MC Eric [4] Technotronic featuring Melissa and Einstein [5] Technotronic featuring Reggie

See also Hi-Tek 3 featuring Ya Kid K.

TEDDY BEARS US, male / female vocal group 17 wks

19 Dec 58	● TO KNOW HIM IS TO LOVE HIM London HLN 8733 ..2	16 wks
14 Apr 79	TO KNOW HIM IS TO LOVE HIM (re-issue)	
	Lightning LIG 9015.....................................66	1 wk

To Know Him Is To Love Him re-issue was coupled with Endless Sleep by Jody Reynolds as a double A-side.

T-EMPO UK, male / female vocal / instrumental group 3 wks

| 7 May 94 | SATURDAY NIGHT SUNDAY MORNING | |
| | ffrr FCD 232 ....19 | 3 wks |

TEENAGE FANCLUB
UK, male vocal / instrumental group 9 wks

24 Aug 91	STAR SIGN Creation CRE 105 44	2 wks
2 Nov 91	THE CONCEPT Creation CRE 111 51	1 wk
8 Feb 92	WHAT YOU DO TO ME (EP) Creation CRE 115 31	2 wks
26 Jun 93	RADIO Creation CRESCD 130 31	2 wks
2 Oct 93	NORMAN 3 Creation CRESCD 142 50	1 wk
2 Apr 94	FALLIN' Epic 6602622 [1] 59	1 wk

[1] Teenage Fanclub and De La Soul

Tracks on What You Do To Me (EP): What You Do To Me / B-Side / Life's A Gas / Filler.

TEENAGERS - See Frankie LYMON and the TEENAGERS

TEKNO TOO UK, male instrumental / production duo 2 wks

| 13 Jul 91 | JET-STAR D-Zone DANCE 012 ....56 | 2 wks |

TELEVISION US, male vocal / instrumental group 10 wks

16 Apr 77	MARQUEE MOON Elektra K 12252 30	4 wks
30 Jul 77	PROVE IT Elektra K 12262 25	4 wks
22 Apr 78	FOXHOLE Elektra K 12287 36	2 wks

TELEX Belgium, male vocal / instrumental duo 7 wks

| 21 Jul 79 | ROCK AROUND THE CLOCK Sire SIR 4020 ....34 | 7 wks |

Sylvia TELLA - See BLOW MONKEYS

TEMPERANCE SEVEN
UK, male vocal / instrumental band 45 wks

30 Mar 61	★ YOU'RE DRIVING ME CRAZY Parlophone R 4757......1	16 wks
15 Jun 61	● PASADENA Parlophone R 4781 4	17 wks
28 Sep 61	HARD HEARTED HANNAH / CHILI BOM BOM	
	Parlophone R 4823...................................28	4 wks
7 Dec 61	CHARLESTON Parlophone R 4851 22	8 wks

Chili Bom Bom only listed with Hard Hearted Hannah for the weeks of 12 and 19 Oct 61.

TEMPLE OF THE DOG
US, male vocal / instrumental group 2 wks

| 24 Oct 92 | HUNGER STRIKE A & M AM 0091 ....51 | 2 wks |

Nino TEMPO and April STEVENS
US, male / female vocal duo 19 wks

| 7 Nov 63 | DEEP PURPLE London HLK 9782 ....17 | 11 wks |
| 16 Jan 64 | WHISPERING London HLK 9829................20 | 8 wks |

TEMPTATIONS US, male vocal group 203 wks

18 Mar 65	MY GIRL Stateside SS 378 43	1 wk
1 Apr 65	IT'S GROWING Tamla Motown TMG 504 49	1 wk
15 Apr 65	IT'S GROWING (re-entry)	
	Tamla Motown TMG 504 45	1 wk
14 Jul 66	AIN'T TOO PROUD TO BEG	
	Tamla Motown TMG 565 21	11 wks
6 Oct 66	BEAUTY IS ONLY SKIN DEEP	
	Tamla Motown TMG 578 18	10 wks
15 Dec 66	(I KNOW) I'M LOSING YOU	
	Tamla Motown TMG 587 19	9 wks

6 Sep 67	**YOU'RE MY EVERYING**		
	Tamla Motown TMG 620 ....**26**	15 wks
6 Mar 68	**I WISH IT WOULD RAIN** *Tamla Motown TMG 641* ...**45**	1 wk
12 Jun 68	**I COULD NEVER LOVE ANOTHER**		
	Tamla Motown TMG 658 ....**47**	1 wk
29 Jan 69	● **I'M GONNA MAKE YOU LOVE ME**		
	Tamla Motown TMG 685 [1] **3**	11 wks
5 Mar 69	● **GET READY** *Tamla Motown TMG 688* **10**	9 wks
23 Apr 69	**I'M GONNA MAKE YOU LOVE ME (re-entry)**		
	Tamla Motown TMG 685 [1] **49**	1 wk
23 Aug 69	**CLOUD NINE** *Tamla Motown TMG 707* **15**	10 wks
20 Sep 69	**I SECOND THAT EMOTION**		
	Tamla Motown TMG 709 [1] **18**	8 wks
17 Jan 70	**I CAN'T GET NEXT TO YOU**		
	Tamla Motown TMG 722 ....**13**	9 wks
21 Mar 70	**WHY (MUST WE FALL IN LOVE)**		
	Tamla Motown TMG 730 [1] **31**	7 wks
13 Jun 70	**PSYCHEDELIC SHACK** *Tamla Motown TMG 741*.........**33**	7 wks
19 Sep 70	● **BALL OF CONFUSION** *Tamla Motown TMG 749*.........**7**	12 wks
19 Dec 70	**BALL OF CONFUSION (re-entry)**		
	Tamla Motown TMG 749 ....**48**	3 wks
22 May 71	● **JUST MY IMAGINATION (RUNNING**		
	AWAY WITH ME) *Tamla Motown TMG 773* **8**	16 wks
5 Feb 72	**SUPERSTAR (REMEMBER HOW YOU GOT**		
	WHERE YOU ARE) *Tamla Motown TMG 800* **32**	5 wks
15 Apr 72	**TAKE A LOOK AROUND** *Tamla Motown TMG 808* ..**13**	10 wks
13 Jan 73	**PAPA WAS A ROLLIN' STONE**		
	Tamla Motown TMG 839 ....**14**	8 wks
29 Sep 73	**LAW OF THE LAND** *Tamla Motown TMG 866*...........**41**	4 wks
12 Jun 82	**STANDING ON THE TOP (PART 1)**		
	Motown TMG 1263 [2] **53**	3 wks
17 Nov 84	**TREAT HER LIKE A LADY** *Motown TMG 1365* **12**	10 wks
15 Aug 87	**PAPA WAS A ROLLIN' STONE (re-mix)**		
	Motown ZB 41431 ....**31**	6 wks
6 Feb 88	**LOOK WHAT YOU STARTED** *Motown ZB 41733*.........**63**	2 wks
21 Oct 89	**ALL I WANT FROM YOU** *Motown ZB 43233*...........**71**	1 wk
15 Feb 92	● **MY GIRL (re-issue)** *Epic 6576767* **2**	10 wks
22 Feb 92	**THE JONES'** *Motown TMG 1403* **69**	1 wk

[1] Diana Ross and the Supremes and the Temptations [2] Temptations featuring Rick James

10 C.C. *UK, male vocal / instrumental group*   **131 wks**

23 Sep 72	● **DONNA** *UK 6* **2**	13 wks
19 May 73	★ **RUBBER BULLETS** *UK 36* **1**	15 wks
25 Aug 73	● **THE DEAN AND I** *UK 48* **10**	8 wks
15 Jun 74	● **WALL STREET SHUFFLE** *UK 69* **10**	10 wks
14 Sep 74	**SILLY LOVE** *UK* **24**	7 wks
5 Apr 75	● **LIFE IS A MINESTRONE** *Mercury 6008 010*...**7**	8 wks
31 May 75	★ **I'M NOT IN LOVE** *Mercury 6008 014* **1**	11 wks
29 Nov 75	● **ART FOR ART'S SAKE** *Mercury 6008 017* **5**	10 wks
20 Mar 76	● **I'M MANDY FLY ME** *Mercury 6008 019* **6**	9 wks
11 Dec 76	● **THINGS WE DO FOR LOVE** *Mercury 6008 022* ..**6**	11 wks
16 Apr 77	● **GOOD MORNING JUDGE** *Mercury 6008 025* **5**	12 wks
12 Aug 78	★ **DREADLOCK HOLIDAY** *Mercury 6008 035* **1**	13 wks
7 Aug 82	**RUN AWAY** *Mercury MER 113* **50**	4 wks

From Things We Do For Love *10 C.C. were a male vocal / instrumental duo.*

TEN CITY *US, male vocal / instrumental group*   **21 wks**

21 Jan 89	● **THAT'S THE WAY LOVE IS** *Atlantic A 8963*...........**8**	10 wks
8 Apr 89	**DEVOTION** *Atlantic A 8916*....................**29**	4 wks
22 Jul 89	**WHERE DO WE GO** *Atlantic A 8864* **60**	1 wk
27 Oct 90	**WHATEVER MAKES YOU HAPPY** *Atlantic A 7819*....**60**	2 wks
15 Aug 92	**ONLY TIME WILL TELL / MY PEACE OF HEAVEN**		
	East West America A 8516 ....**63**	2 wks
11 Sep 93	**FANTASY** *Columbia 6595042* **45**	2 wks

TEN POLE TUDOR *UK, male vocal / instrumental group*   **40 wks**

7 Apr 79	● **WHO KILLED BAMBI** *Virgin VS 256* **6**	8 wks
13 Oct 79	**ROCK AROUND THE CLOCK** *Virgin VS 290*...............**21**	6 wks
25 Apr 81	● **SWORDS OF A THOUSAND MEN** *Stiff BUY 109* **6**	12 wks

1 Aug 81	**WUNDERBAR** *Stiff BUY 120* **16**	9 wks
14 Nov 81	**THROWING MY BABY OUT WITH THE BATHWATER**		
	Stiff BUY 129 ....**49**	5 wks

The listed flip side of Who Killed Bambi was Silly Thing by the Sex Pistols. The listed flip side of Rock Around The Clock was The Great Rock 'n' Roll Swindle also by the Sex Pistols.

TEN SHARP *Holland, male vocal / instrumental duo*   **15 wks**

21 Mar 92	● **YOU** *Columbia 6566647*....................**10**	13 wks
20 Jun 92	**AIN'T MY BEATING HEART** *Columbia 6580947* **63**	2 wks

10,000 MANIACS
US, female / male vocal / instrumental group   **7 wks**

12 Sep 92	**THESE ARE DAYS** *Elektra EKR 156* **58**	3 wks
10 Apr 93	**CANDY EVERYBODY WANTS** *Elektra EKR 160CD1*..**47**	3 wks
23 Oct 93	**BECAUSE THE NIGHT** *Elektra EKR 175CD* **65**	1 wk

TEN YEARS AFTER
UK, male vocal / instrumental group   **18 wks**

6 Jun 70	● **LOVE LIKE A MAN** *Deram DM 299* **10**	18 wks

TENNESSEE THREE - *See Johnny* CASH

TENOR FLY - *See* REBEL MC

TERMINATERS - *See* ARNEE *and the* TERMINATERS

Tammi TERRELL - *See Marvin* GAYE

TERRORIZE *UK, male producer - Shaun Imrei*   **6 wks**

2 May 92	**IT'S JUST A FEELING** *Hamster STER 1* **52**	3 wks
22 Aug 92	**FEEL THE RHYTHM** *Hamster 12STER 2* **69**	1 wk
14 Nov 92	**IT'S JUST A FEELING (re-issue)** *Hamster STER 8*......**47**	2 wks

TERRORVISION *UK, male vocal / instrumental group*   **23 wks**

19 Jun 93	**AMERICAN TV** *Total Vegas CDVEGAS 3* **63**	1 wk
30 Oct 93	**NEW POLICY ONE** *Total Vegas CDVEGAS 4* **42**	2 wks
8 Jan 94	**MY HOUSE** *Total Vegas CDVEGAS 5* **29**	4 wks
9 Apr 94	**OBLIVION** *Total Vegas CDVEGASS 6*................**21**	5 wks
25 Jun 94	**MIDDLEMAN** *Total Vegas CDVEGAS 7* **25**	4 wks
3 Sep 94	**PRETEND BEST FRIEND** *Total Vegas CDVEGASS 8* **25**	3 wks
29 Oct 94	**ALICE WHAT'S THE MATTER**		
	Total Vegas CDVEGAS 9 ....**24**	4 wks

Helen TERRY *UK, female vocalist*   **6 wks**

12 May 84	**LOVE LIES LOST** *Virgin VS 678* **34**	6 wks

Tony TERRY *US, male vocalist*   **6 wks**

27 Feb 88	**LOVEY DOVEY** *Epic TONY 2*....................**44**	6 wks

Todd TERRY PROJECT *US, male producer*   **3 wks**

12 Nov 88	**WEEKEND** *Sleeping Bag SBUK 1T* **56**	3 wks

TESLA *US, male vocal / instrumental group*   **1 wk**

27 Apr 91	**SIGNS** *Geffen GFS 3* **70**	1 wk

Joe TEX *US, male vocalist*   **11 wks**

23 Apr 77	● **AIN'T GONNA BUMP NO MORE (WITH NO**		
	BIG FAT WOMAN) *Epic EPC 5035*...........**2**	11 wks

TEXAS *UK, male / female vocal / instrumental group*   **40 wks**

4 Feb 89	● **I DON'T WANT A LOVER** *Mercury TEX 1* **8**	11 wks
6 May 89	**THRILL HAS GONE** *Mercury TEX 2* **60**	3 wks

5 Aug 89	**EVERYDAY NOW** Mercury TEX 3	......................**44**	5 wks
2 Dec 89	**PRAYER FOR YOU** Mercury TEX 4	......................**73**	1 wk
7 Sep 91	**WHY BELIEVE IN YOU** Mercury TEX 5	......................**66**	1 wk
26 Oct 91	**IN MY HEART** Mercury TEX 6	......................**74**	1 wk
8 Feb 92	**ALONE WITH YOU** Mercury TEX 7	......................**32**	4 wks
25 Apr 92	**TIRED OF BEING ALONE** Mercury TEX 8	......................**19**	6 wks
11 Sep 93	**SO CALLED FRIEND** Vertigo TEXCD 9	......................**30**	3 wks
30 Oct 93	**YOU OWE IT ALL TO ME** Vertigo TEXCD 10	......................**39**	3 wks
12 Feb 94	**SO IN LOVE WITH YOU** Vertigo TEXCD 11	......................**28**	2 wks

THAT PETROL EMOTION
UK, male vocal / instrumental group   **24 wks**

11 Apr 87	**BIG DECISION** Polydor TPE 1	......................**43**	7 wks
11 Jul 87	**DANCE** Polydor TPE 2	......................**64**	2 wks
17 Oct 87	**GENIUS MOVE** Virgin VS 1002	......................**65**	2 wks
31 Mar 90	**ABANDON** Virgin VS 1242	......................**73**	1 wk
1 Sep 90	**HEY VENUS** Virgin VS 1290	......................**49**	4 wks
9 Feb 91	**TINGLE** Virgin VS 1312	......................**49**	4 wks
27 Apr 91	**SENSITIZE** Virgin VS 1261	......................**55**	4 wks

The THE
UK, male vocalist – Matt Johnson and backing musicians   **50 wks**

4 Dec 82	**UNCERTAIN SMILE** Epic EPC A 2787	......................**68**	3 wks
17 Sep 83	**THIS IS THE DAY** Epic A 3710	......................**71**	3 wks
9 Aug 86	**HEARTLAND** Some Bizzare TRUTH 2	......................**29**	10 wks
25 Oct 86	**INFECTED** Some Bizzare TRUTH 3	......................**48**	5 wks
24 Jan 87	**SLOW TRAIN TO DAWN** Some Bizzare TENSE 1	......................**64**	2 wks
23 May 87	**SWEET BIRD OF TRUTH** Epic TENSE 2	......................**55**	2 wks
1 Apr 89	**THE BEAT(EN) GENERATION** Epic EMU 8	......................**18**	5 wks
22 Jul 89	**GRAVITATE TO ME** Epic EMU 9	......................**63**	3 wks
7 Oct 89	**ARMAGEDDON DAYS ARE HERE (AGAIN)** Epic EMU 10	......................**70**	1 wk
2 Mar 91	**SHADES OF BLUE EP** Epic 6557968	......................**54**	1 wk
16 Jan 93	**DOGS OF LUST** Epic 6584572	......................**25**	4 wks
17 Apr 93	**SLOW EMOTION REPLAY** Epic 6590772	......................**35**	3 wks
19 Jun 93	**LOVE IS STRONGER THAN DEATH** Epic 6593712	......................**39**	3 wks
15 Jan 94	**DIS-INFECTED EP** Epic 6598112	......................**17**	4 wks

Tracks on Shades Of Blue EP: Jealous Of Youth / Another Boy Drowning
(Live) / Solitude / Dolphins. Tracks on Dis-Infected EP: That Was The Day /
Dis-Infected / Helpline Operator / Dogs Of Lust. That Was The Day and
Dis-Infected on the EP are re-recordings of earlier hits, Dogs Of Lust is a
re-mix.

THEATRE OF HATE
UK, male vocal / instrumental group   **9 wks**

23 Jan 82	**DO YOU BELIEVE IN THE WESTWORLD** Burning Rome BRR 2	......................**40**	7 wks
29 May 82	**THE HOP** Burning Rome BRR 3	......................**70**	2 wks

THEM
UK, male vocal / instrumental group   **23 wks**

7 Jan 65	● **BABY PLEASE DON'T GO** Decca F 12018	......................**10**	9 wks
25 Mar 65	● **HERE COMES THE NIGHT** Decca F 12094	......................**2**	12 wks
9 Feb 91	**BABY PLEASE DON'T GO (re-issue)** London LON 292	......................**65**	2 wks

THEN JERICO
UK, male vocal / instrumental group   **36 wks**

31 Jan 87	**LET HER FALL** London LON 97	......................**65**	3 wks
25 Jul 87	**THE MOTIVE (LIVING WITHOUT YOU)** London LON 145	......................**18**	12 wks
24 Oct 87	**MUSCLE DEEP** London LON 156	......................**48**	4 wks
28 Jan 89	**BIG AREA** London LON 204	......................**13**	7 wks
8 Apr 89	**WHAT DOES IT TAKE** London LON 223	......................**33**	4 wks
12 Aug 89	**SUGAR BOX** London LON 235	......................**22**	6 wks

THERAPY?
UK, male vocal / instrumental group   **21 wks**

31 Oct 92	**TEETHGRINDER** A & M AM 0097	......................**30**	2 wks
20 Mar 93	● **SHORTSHARPSHOCK EP** A & M AMCD 208	......................**9**	4 wks
12 Jun 93	**FACE THE STRANGE EP** A & M 5803052	......................**18**	3 wks

28 Aug 93	**OPAL MANTRA** A & M 5803612	......................**14**	3 wks
29 Jan 94	**NOWHERE** A & M 5805052	......................**18**	4 wks
12 Mar 94	**TRIGGER INSIDE** A & M 5805352	......................**22**	3 wks
11 Jun 94	**DIE LAUGHING** A & M 5805892	......................**29**	2 wks

Tracks on Shortsharpshock EP: Screamager / Auto Surgery / Totally
Random Man / Accelerator. Tracks on Face The Strange EP: Turn /
Speedball / Bloody Blue / Neckfreak.

THESE ANIMAL MEN
UK, male vocal / instrumental group   **1 wk**

24 Sep 94	**THIS IS THE SOUND OF YOUTH** Hi-Rise FLATSCD 7	..**72**	1 wk

THEY MIGHT BE GIANTS
US, male vocal / instrumental duo   **13 wks**

3 Mar 90	● **BIRDHOUSE IN YOUR SOUL** Elektra EKR 104	......................**6**	11 wks
2 Jun 90	**ISTANBUL (NOT CONSTANTINOPLE)** Elektra EKR 110	......................**61**	2 wks

THIN LIZZY
Ireland, male vocal / instrumental group   **128 wks**

20 Jan 73	● **WHISKEY IN THE JAR** Decca F 13355	......................**6**	12 wks
29 May 76	● **THE BOYS ARE BACK IN TOWN** Vertigo 6059 139	....**8**	10 wks
14 Aug 76	**JAILBREAK** Vertigo 6059 150	......................**31**	4 wks
15 Jan 77	**DON'T BELIEVE A WORD** Vertigo LIZZY 001	...........**12**	7 wks
13 Aug 77	**DANCIN' IN THE MOONLIGHT (IT'S CAUGHT ME IN THE SPOTLIGHT)** Vertigo 6059 177	......................**14**	8 wks
13 May 78	**ROSALIE - COWGIRLS' SONG (MEDLEY)** Vertigo LIZZY 2	......................**20**	13 wks
3 Mar 79	● **WAITING FOR AN ALIBI** Vertigo LIZZY 003	......................**9**	8 wks
16 Jun 79	**DO ANYTHING YOU WANT TO** Vertigo LIZZY 004	..**14**	9 wks
20 Oct 79	**SARAH** Vertigo LIZZY 5	......................**24**	13 wks
24 May 80	**CHINATOWN** Vertigo LIZZY 6	......................**21**	7 wks
27 Sep 80	● **KILLER ON THE LOOSE** Vertigo LIZZY 7	......................**10**	7 wks
2 May 81	**KILLERS LIVE EP** Vertigo LIZZY 8	......................**19**	7 wks
8 Aug 81	**TROUBLE BOYS** Vertigo LIZZY 9	......................**53**	4 wks
6 Mar 82	**HOLLYWOOD (DOWN ON YOUR LUCK)** Vertigo LIZZY 10	......................**53**	3 wks
12 Feb 83	**COLD SWEAT** Vertigo LIZZY 11	......................**27**	5 wks
7 May 83	**THUNDER AND LIGHTNING** Vertigo LIZZY 12	......................**39**	2 wks
6 Aug 83	**THE SUN GOES DOWN** Vertigo LIZZY 13	......................**52**	3 wks
26 Jan 91	**DEDICATION** Vertigo LIZZY 14	......................**35**	3 wks
23 Mar 91	**THE BOYS ARE BACK IN TOWN (re-issue)** Vertigo LIZZY 15	......................**63**	1 wk

Tracks on Killers Live EP: Bad Reputation / Are You Ready / Dear Miss
Lonely Hearts.

3RD BASS
US, male rap group   **5 wks**

10 Feb 90	**THE GAS FACE** Def Jam 655627 0	......................**71**	1 wk
7 Apr 90	**BROOKLYN-QUEENS** Def Jam 655830 7	......................**61**	2 wks
22 Jun 91	**POP GOES THE WEASEL** Def Jam 6569547	......................**64**	2 wks

THIRD WORLD
Jamaica, male vocal / instrumental group   **53 wks**

23 Sep 78	● **NOW THAT WE'VE FOUND LOVE** Island WIP 6457	..**10**	9 wks
6 Jan 79	**COOL MEDITATION** Island WIP 6469	......................**17**	10 wks
16 Jun 79	**TALK TO ME** Island WIP 6496	......................**56**	5 wks
6 Jun 81	● **DANCING ON THE FLOOR (HOOKED ON LOVE)** CBS A 1214	......................**10**	15 wks
17 Apr 82	**TRY JAH LOVE** CBS A 2063	......................**47**	6 wks
9 Mar 85	**NOW THAT WE'VE FOUND LOVE (re-issue)** Island IS 219	......................**22**	8 wks

THIRST
UK, male vocal / instrumental group   **2 wks**

6 Jul 91	**THE ENEMY WITHIN** Ten TEN 379	......................**61**	2 wks

THIS ISLAND EARTH
UK, male / female vocal / instrumental group   **5 wks**

5 Jan 85	**SEE THAT GLOW** Magnet MAG 266	......................**47**	5 wks

THIS MORTAL COIL
UK, male / female vocal / instrumental group   **3 wks**

| 22 Oct 83 | **SONG TO THE SIREN** *4AD AD 310* ....**66** | 2 wks |
| 12 Nov 83 | **SONG TO THE SIREN (re-entry)** *4AD AD 310* ....**75** | 1 wk |

THIS WAY UP *UK, male vocal / instrumental duo*   **2 wks**

| 22 Aug 87 | **TELL ME WHY** *Virgin VS 954* ....**72** | 2 wks |

THIS YEAR'S BLONDE
UK, male / female vocal / instrumental group   **8 wks**

| 10 Oct 81 | **PLATINUM POP** *Creole CR 19* ....**46** | 5 wks |
| 14 Nov 87 | **WHO'S THAT MIX** *Debut DEBT 3034* ....**62** | 3 wks |

B.J. THOMAS *US, male vocalist*   **4 wks**

| 21 Feb 70 | **RAINDROPS KEEP FALLING ON MY HEAD** *Wand WN1* ....**38** | 3 wks |
| 2 May 70 | **RAINDROPS KEEP FALLING ON MY HEAD (re-entry)** *Wand WN1* ....**49** | 1 wk |

Carla THOMAS - *See Otis REDDING*

Evelyn THOMAS *US, female vocalist*   **29 wks**

24 Jan 76	**WEAK SPOT** *20th Century BTC 1014* **26**	7 wks
17 Apr 76	**DOOMSDAY** *20th Century BTC 1017* **41**	1 wk
1 May 76	**DOOMSDAY (re-entry)** *20th Century BTC 1017* **45**	1 wk
21 Apr 84	● **HIGH ENERGY** *Record Shack SOHO 18* **5**	17 wks
25 Aug 84	**MASQUERADE** *Record Shack SOHO 25* **60**	3 wks

Jamo THOMAS *US, male vocalist*   **2 wks**

| 26 Feb 69 | **I SPY FOR THE FBI** *Polydor 56755* ....**48** | 1 wk |
| 12 Mar 69 | **I SPY FOR THE FBI (re-entry)** *Polydor 56755* ....**44** | 1 wk |

Kenny THOMAS *UK, male vocalist*   **51 wks**

26 Jan 91	**OUTSTANDING** *Cooltempo COOL 227* **12**	10 wks
1 Jun 91	● **THINKING ABOUT YOUR LOVE** *Cooltempo COOL 235* **4**	13 wks
5 Oct 91	**BEST OF YOU** *Cooltempo COOL 243* **11**	7 wks
30 Nov 91	**TENDER LOVE** *Cooltempo COOL 247* **26**	6 wks
10 Jul 93	**STAY** *Cooltempo CDCOOL 271* **22**	6 wks
4 Sep 93	**TRIPPIN' ON YOUR LOVE** *Cooltempo CDCOOL 277* **17**	5 wks
6 Nov 93	**PIECE BY PIECE** *Cooltempo CDCOOL 283* **36**	3 wks
14 May 94	**DESTINY** *Cooltempo CDCOOL 289* **59**	1 wk

Lillo THOMAS *US, male vocalist*   **10 wks**

27 Apr 85	**SETTLE DOWN** *Capitol CL 356* **66**	2 wks
21 Mar 87	**SEXY GIRL** *Capitol CL 445* **23**	5 wks
30 May 87	**I'M IN LOVE** *Capitol CL 450* **54**	3 wks

Mickey THOMAS - *See Elvin BISHOP*

Nicky THOMAS *Jamaica, male vocalist*   **14 wks**

| 13 Jun 70 | ● **LOVE OF THE COMMON PEOPLE** *Trojan TR 7750* ......**9** | 14 wks |

Rufus THOMAS *US, male vocalist*   **12 wks**

| 11 Apr 70 | **DO THE FUNKY CHICKEN** *Stax 144* ....**18** | 12 wks |

Tasha THOMAS *US, female vocalist*   **3 wks**

| 20 Jan 79 | **SHOOT ME (WITH YOUR LOVE)** *Atlantic LV 4* ....**59** | 3 wks |

Timmy THOMAS *US, male vocalist*   **20 wks**

24 Feb 73	**WHY CAN'T WE LIVE TOGETHER** *Mojo 2027 012* **12**	11 wks
28 Dec 85	**NEW YORK EYES** *Portrait A 6805* 1 ....**41**	7 wks
14 Jul 90	**WHY CAN'T WE LIVE TOGETHER (re-mix)** *TK TKR 1* **54**	2 wks

1 Nicole with Timmy Thomas

THOMAS and TAYLOR *US, male / female vocal duo*   **5 wks**

| 17 May 86 | **YOU CAN'T BLAME LOVE** *Cooltempo COOL 123* ....**53** | 5 wks |

Amanda THOMPSON - *See Lesley GARRETT and Amanda THOMPSON*

Carroll THOMPSON - *See MOVEMENT 98 featuring Carroll THOMPSON; Courtney PINE*

Chris THOMPSON *UK, male vocalist*   **5 wks**

| 27 Oct 79 | **IF YOU REMEMBER ME** *Planet K 12389* ....**42** | 5 wks |

Sue THOMPSON *US, female vocalist*   **9 wks**

2 Nov 61	**SAD MOVIES** *Polydor NH 66967* **46**	1 wk
16 Nov 61	**SAD MOVIES (re-entry)** *Polydor NH 66967* **48**	1 wk
21 Jan 65	**PAPER TIGER** *Hickory 1284* **50**	1 wk
11 Feb 65	**PAPER TIGER (re-entry)** *Hickory 1284* **30**	6 wks

THOMPSON TWINS
UK / New Zealand, male / female vocal / instrumental group   **110 wks**

6 Nov 82	**LIES** *Arista ARIST 486* **67**	3 wks
29 Jan 83	● **LOVE ON YOUR SIDE** *Arista ARIST 504* **9**	12 wks
16 Apr 83	● **WE ARE DETECTIVE** *Arista ARIST 526* **7**	9 wks
16 Jul 83	**WATCHING** *Arista TWINS 1* **33**	6 wks
19 Nov 83	● **HOLD ME NOW** *Arista TWINS 2* **4**	15 wks
4 Feb 84	● **DOCTOR DOCTOR** *Arista TWINS 3* **3**	10 wks
31 Mar 84	● **YOU TAKE ME UP** *Arista TWINS 4* **2**	9 wks
7 Jul 84	**SISTER OF MERCY** *Arista TWINS 5* **11**	8 wks
8 Sep 84	**SISTER OF MERCY (re-entry)** *Arista TWINS 5* **66**	1 wk
8 Dec 84	**LAY YOUR HANDS ON ME** *Arista TWINS 6* **13**	9 wks
31 Aug 85	**DON'T MESS WITH DOCTOR DREAM** *Arista TWINS 9* **15**	6 wks
19 Oct 85	**KING FOR A DAY** *Arista TWINS 7* **22**	6 wks
7 Dec 85	**REVOLUTION** *Arista TWINS 10* **56**	3 wks
4 Jan 86	**REVOLUTION (re-entry)** *Arista TWINS 10* **75**	1 wk
21 Mar 87	**GET THAT LOVE** *Arista TWINS 12* **68**	2 wks
11 Apr 87	**GET THAT LOVE (re-entry)** *Arista TWINS 12* **66**	1 wk
15 Oct 88	**IN THE NAME OF LOVE '88** *Arista 111808* **46**	3 wks
28 Sep 91	**COME INSIDE** *Warner Bros. W 0058* **56**	4 wks
25 Jan 92	**THE SAINT** *Warner Bros. W 0080* **53**	2 wks

David THORNE *US, male vocalist*   **8 wks**

| 24 Jan 63 | **ALLEY CAT SONG** *Stateside SS 141* ....**21** | 8 wks |

Ken THORNE *UK, orchestra*   **15 wks**

| 18 Jul 63 | ● **THEME FROM THE FILM 'THE LEGION'S LAST PATROL'** *HMV POP 1176* ....**4** | 15 wks |

THOSE 2 GIRLS *UK, female vocal duo*   **1 wk**

| 5 Nov 94 | **WANNA MAKE YOU GO...UUH!** *Final Vinyl 74321233782* ....**74** | 1 wk |

THOUSAND YARD STARE
UK, male vocal / instrumental group   **5 wks**

26 Oct 91	**SEASONSTREAM EP** *Stifled Aardvark AARD 5T* **65**	1 wk
8 Feb 92	**COMEUPPANCE** *Stifled Aardvark AARD 007* **37**	2 wks
11 Jul 92	**SPINDRIFT EP** *Stifled Aardvark AARDT 010* **58**	1 wk

8 May 93 **VERSION OF ME** *Polydor AARDC 012* ....**57** 1 wk

Tracks on Seasonstream EP: O-O AET / Village End / Keepsake / Worse For Wear. Tracks on Spindrift EP: Wideshire Two / Hand, Son / Happenstance / Mocca Pune.

THRASHING DOVES
UK, male vocal / instrumental group　　**3 wks**

24 Jan 87　**BEAUTIFUL IMBALANCE** *A & M TDOVE 1* ....**50** 3 wks

THREE DEGREES *US, female vocal group*　**111 wks**

13 Apr 74	**YEAR OF DECISION** *Philadelphia International PIR 2073* **13**	10 wks
27 Apr 74	**TSOP (THE SOUND OF PHILADELPHIA)** *Philadelphia International PIR 2289* [1] **22**	9 wks
13 Jul 74 ★	**WHEN WILL I SEE YOU AGAIN** *Philadelphia International PIR 2155* **1**	16 wks
2 Nov 74	**GET YOUR LOVE BACK** *Philadelphia International PIR 2737* **34**	4 wks
12 Apr 75 ●	**TAKE GOOD CARE OF YOURSELF** *Philadelphia International PIR 3177* **9**	9 wks
5 Jul 75	**LONG LOST LOVER** *Philadelphia International PIR 3352* **40**	4 wks
1 May 76	**TOAST OF LOVE** *Epic EPC 4215* **36**	4 wks
7 Oct 78	**GIVIN' UP GIVIN' IN** *Ariola ARO 130* **12**	10 wks
13 Jan 79 ●	**WOMAN IN LOVE** *Ariola ARO 141*.........**3**	11 wks
24 Mar 79	**THE RUNNER** *Ariola ARO 154* **10**	10 wks
23 Jun 79	**THE GOLDEN LADY** *Ariola ARO 170* **56**	3 wks
29 Sep 79	**JUMP THE GUN** *Ariola ARO 183* **48**	5 wks
24 Nov 79 ●	**MY SIMPLE HEART** *Ariola ARO 202* **9**	11 wks
5 Oct 85	**THE HEAVEN I NEED** *Supreme SUPE 102* **42**	5 wks

[1] MFSB featuring the Three Degrees

THREE DOG NIGHT
US, male vocal / instrumental group　　**23 wks**

8 Aug 70 ● **MAMA TOLD ME NOT TO COME** *Stateside SS 8052* ..**3** 14 wks
29 May 71　**JOY TO THE WORLD** *Probe PRO 523* ....**24** 9 wks

THREE GOOD REASONS
UK, male vocal / instrumental group　　**3 wks**

10 Mar 66　**NOWHERE MAN** *Mercury MF 899* ....**47** 3 wks

THREE KAYES - *See KAYE SISTERS*

THREE TONS OF JOY - *See Johnny OTIS SHOW*

THROWING MUSES
US, male / female vocal / instrumental group　　**5 wks**

9 Feb 91　**COUNTING BACKWARDS** *4AD AD 1001* ....**70** 2 wks
1 Aug 92　**FIREPILE (EP)** *4AD BAD 2012* ....**46** 1 wk
24 Dec 94　**BRIGHT YELLOW GUN** *4AD BAD 4018CD*.........**51†** 2 wks

Tracks on Firepile (EP): Firepile / Manic Depression / Snailhead / City Of The Dead.

T.H.S. - THE HORN SECTION
US, male / female vocal / instrumental group　　**3 wks**

18 Aug 84　**LADY SHINE (SHINE ON)** *Fourth & Broadway BRW 10* ....**54** 3 wks

Harry THUMANN
Germany, male instrumentalist - keyboards　　**6 wks**

21 Feb 81　**UNDERWATER** *Decca F 13901* ....**41** 6 wks

THUNDER
UK / US, male vocal / instrumental group　　**33 wks**

17 Feb 90　**DIRTY LOVE** *EMI EM 126* ....**32** 4 wks
12 May 90　**BACKSTREET SYMPHONY** *EMI EM 137* ....**25** 4 wks

14 Jul 90	**GIMME SOME LOVIN'** *EMI EM 148* **36**	3 wks
29 Sep 90	**SHE'S SO FINE** *EMI EM 158* **34**	3 wks
23 Feb 91	**LOVE WALKED IN** *EMI EM 175* **21**	4 wks
15 Aug 92	**LOW LIFE IN HIGH PLACES** *EMI EM 242*........**22**	5 wks
10 Oct 92	**EVERYBODY WANTS HER** *EMI EM 249*...........**36**	4 wks
13 Feb 93	**A BETTER MAN** *EMI CDBETTER 1* **18**	4 wks
19 Jun 93	**LIKE A SATELLITE (EP)** *EMI CDEM 272* **28**	2 wks

Tracks on Like A Satellite (EP): Like A Satellite / The Damage Is Done / Like A Satellite (Live) / Gimme Shelter. See also Various Artists (EPs & LPs) - Gimme Shelter (EP).

THUNDERBIRDS - *See Chris FARLOWE*

THUNDERCLAP NEWMAN
UK, male vocal / instrumental group　　**13 wks**

11 Jun 69 ★ **SOMETHING IN THE AIR** *Track 604-031* ....**1** 12 wks
27 Jun 70　**ACCIDENTS** *Track 2094 001* ....**46** 1 wk

THUNDERTHIGHS *UK, female vocal group*　**5 wks**

22 Jun 74　**CENTRAL PARK ARREST** *Philips 6006 386* ....**30** 5 wks

Bobby THURSTON *US, male vocalist*　**10 wks**

29 Mar 80 ● **CHECK OUT THE GROOVE** *Epic EPC 8348* ....**10** 10 wks

TIFFANY *US, female vocalist*　**45 wks**

16 Jan 88 ★	**I THINK WE'RE ALONE NOW** *MCA MCA 1211* **1**	13 wks
19 Mar 88 ●	**COULD'VE BEEN** *MCA TIFF 2* **4**	9 wks
4 Jun 88 ●	**I SAW HIM STANDING THERE** *MCA TIFF 3*.........**8**	7 wks
6 Aug 88	**FEELINGS OF FOREVER** *MCA TIFF 4* **52**	2 wks
12 Nov 88	**RADIO ROMANCE** *MCA TIFF 5*...........**13**	11 wks
11 Feb 89	**ALL THIS TIME** *MCA TIFF 6*...........**47**	3 wks

TIGERTAILZ *US, male vocal / instrumental group*　**2 wks**

24 Jun 89　**LOVE BOMB BABY** *Music For Nations KUT 132* ....**75** 1 wk
16 Feb 91　**HEAVEN** *Music For Nations KUT 137* ....**71** 1 wk

TIGHT FIT *UK, male / female vocal group*　**49 wks**

18 Jul 81 ●	**BACK TO THE SIXTIES** *Jive JIVE 002* **4**	11 wks
26 Sep 81	**BACK TO THE SIXTIES PART 2** *Jive JIVE 005* **33**	5 wks
23 Jan 82 ★	**THE LION SLEEPS TONIGHT** *Jive JIVE 9*.........**1**	15 wks
1 May 82 ●	**FANTASY ISLAND** *Jive JIVE 13* **5**	12 wks
31 Jul 82	**SECRET HEART** *Jive JIVE 20* **41**	6 wks

TIJUANA BRASS - *See Herb ALPERT*

TIK and TOK *UK, male vocal duo*　**2 wks**

8 Oct 83　**COOL RUNNING** *Survival SUR 016* ....**69** 2 wks

Tanita TIKARAM *UK, female vocalist*　**27 wks**

30 Jul 88 ●	**GOOD TRADITION** *WEA YZ 196*...........**10**	10 wks
22 Oct 88	**TWIST IN MY SOBRIETY** *WEA YZ 321*.........**22**	8 wks
14 Jan 89	**CATHEDRAL SONG** *WEA YZ 331* **48**	3 wks
18 Mar 89	**WORLD OUTSIDE YOUR WINDOW** *WEA YZ 363* **58**	2 wks
13 Jan 90	**WE ALMOST GOT IT TOGETHER** *WEA YZ 443* **52**	3 wks
9 Feb 91	**ONLY THE ONES WE LOVE** *East West YZ 558*...........**69**	1 wk

Johnny TILLOTSON *US, male vocalist*　**50 wks**

1 Dec 60 ★	**POETRY IN MOTION** *London HLA 9231* **1**	15 wks
2 Feb 61	**JIMMY'S GIRL** *London HLA 9275* **50**	1 wk
16 Feb 61	**JIMMY'S GIRL (re-entry)** *London HLA 9275* **43**	1 wk
12 Jul 62	**IT KEEPS RIGHT ON A HURTIN'** *London HLA 9550* ..**31**	10 wks
4 Oct 62	**SEND ME THE PILLOW YOU DREAM ON** *London HLA 9598*...........**21**	10 wks

27 Dec 62	**I CAN'T HELP IT** *London HLA 9642*	**42**	1 wk
10 Jan 63	**I CAN'T HELP IT (re-entry)** *London HLA 9642*	**47**	1 wk
24 Jan 63	**I CAN'T HELP IT (2nd re-entry)** *London HLA 9642*	**41**	4 wks
9 May 63	**OUT OF MY MIND** *London HLA 9695*	**34**	5 wks
14 Apr 79	**POETRY IN MOTION (re-issue)** *Lightning LIG 9016*	**67**	2 wks

TIMBUK 3 *US, male/female vocal/instrumental duo* **7 wks**

31 Jan 87	**THE FUTURE'S SO BRIGHT I GOTTA WEAR SHADES** *IRS IRM 126*	**21**	7 wks

TIME FREQUENCY
UK, male instrumental/production group **33 wks**

6 Jun 92	**REAL LOVE** *Jive JIVET 307*	**60**	1 wk
9 Jan 93	**NEW EMOTION** *Internal Affairs KGBCD 009*	**36**	6 wks
12 Jun 93	**THE ULTIMATE HIGH / THE POWER ZONE** *Internal Affairs KGBD 010*	**17**	11 wks
6 Nov 93	● **REAL LOVE (re-mix)** *Internal Affairs KGBCD 011*	**8**	6 wks
1 Jan 94	**REAL LOVE (re-entry of re-mix)** *Internal Affairs KGBCD 011*	**71**	2 wks
28 May 94	**SUCH A PHANTASY** *Internal Affairs KGBD 013*	**25**	4 wks
8 Oct 94	**DREAMSCAPE '94** *Internal Affairs KGBD 015*	**32**	3 wks

TIME UK *UK, male vocal/instrumental group* **3 wks**

8 Oct 83	**THE CABARET** *Red Bus/Aroadia TIM 123*	**63**	3 wks

TIME ZONE *UK/US, male vocal/instrumental duo* **9 wks**

19 Jan 85	**WORLD DESTRUCTION** *Virgin VS 743*	**44**	9 wks

TIMEBOX *UK, male vocal/instrumental group* **4 wks**

24 Jul 68	**BEGGIN'** *Deram DM 194*	**38**	4 wks

TIMELORDS *UK, male/female instrumental group* **9 wks**

4 Jun 88	★ **DOCTORIN' THE TARDIS** *KLF Communications KLF 003*	**1**	9 wks

TIMEX SOCIAL CLUB
US, male vocal/instrumental group **9 wks**

13 Sep 86	**RUMORS** *Cooltempo COOL 133*	**13**	9 wks

TIN MACHINE *US/UK, male vocal/instrumental group* **10 wks**

1 Jul 89	**UNDER THE GOD** *EMI-USA MT 68*	**51**	2 wks
9 Sep 89	**TIN MACHINE/MAGGIE'S FARM (LIVE)** *EMI-USA MT 73*	**48**	2 wks
24 Aug 91	**YOU BELONG IN ROCK 'N' ROLL** *London LON 305*	**33**	3 wks
2 Nov 91	**BABY UNIVERSAL** *London LON 310*	**48**	3 wks

TIN TIN OUT - *See SWEET TEE*

TINDERSTICKS *UK, male vocal/instrumental group* **1 wk**

5 Feb 94	**KATHLEEN (EP)** *This Way Up WAY 2833CD*	**61**	1 wk

Tracks on Kathleen (EP): Kathleen/Summat Moon/A Sweet Man/E-Type Joe.

TINGO TANGO *UK, male instrumental group* **2 wks**

21 Jul 90	**IT IS JAZZ** *Champion CHAMP 250*	**68**	2 wks

TINMAN *UK, male producer - Paul Dakeyne* **8 wks**

20 Aug 94	● **EIGHTEEN STRINGS** *ffrr FCD 242*	**9**	8 wks

TINY TIM *US, male vocalist* **1 wk**

5 Feb 69	**GREAT BALLS OF FIRE** *Reprise RS 20802*	**45**	1 wk

TITANIC *Norway/UK, male instrumental group* **12 wks**

25 Sep 71	● **SULTANA** *CBS 5365*	**5**	12 wks

TITIYO *Sweden, female vocalist* **6 wks**

3 Mar 90	**AFTER THE RAIN** *Arista 112722*	**60**	3 wks
6 Oct 90	**FLOWERS** *Arista 113212*	**71**	1 wk
5 Feb 94	**TELL ME I'M NOT DREAMING** *Arista 74321185622*	**45**	2 wks

Cara TIVEY - *See Billy BRAGG*

TLC *US, female vocal group* **10 wks**

20 Jun 92	**AIN'T 2 PROUD 2 BEG** *Arista 115265*	**13**	5 wks
22 Aug 92	**BABY-BABY-BABY** *LaFace 74321111297*	**55**	3 wks
24 Oct 92	**WHAT ABOUT YOUR FRIENDS** *LaFace 74321118177*	**59**	2 wks

T99 *Belgium, male instrumental/production group* **10 wks**

11 May 91	**ANASTHASIA** *XL XLS 19*	**14**	6 wks
19 Oct 91	**NOCTURNE** *Emphasis 6574097*	**33**	4 wks

TOADS - *See STAN FREBERG*

Art and Dotty TODD *US, male/female vocal duo* **7 wks**

13 Feb 53	● **BROKEN WINGS** *HMV B 10399*	**6**	7 wks

TOGETHER *UK, male vocal/instrumental group* **8 wks**

4 Aug 90	**HARDCORE UPROAR** *ffrr F 143*	**12**	8 wks

TOKENS *US, male vocal group* **12 wks**

21 Dec 61	**THE LION SLEEPS TONIGHT** *RCA 1263*	**11**	12 wks

TOL and TOL *Holland, male vocal/instrumental duo* **2 wks**

14 Apr 90	**ELENI** *Dover ROJ 5*	**73**	2 wks

TOM TOM CLUB
US, female/male vocal/instrumental group **20 wks**

20 Jun 81	● **WORDY RAPPINGHOOD** *Island WIP 6694*	**7**	9 wks
10 Oct 81	**GENIUS OF LOVE** *Island WIP 6735*	**65**	2 wks
7 Aug 82	**UNDER THE BOARDWALK** *Island WIP 6762*	**22**	9 wks

Satoshi TOMIIE - *See Frankie KNUCKLES*

TONGUE 'N' CHEEK
UK, male/female vocal/instrumental group **28 wks**

27 Feb 88	**NOBODY (CAN LOVE ME)** *Criminal BUS 6* ☐1	**59**	6 wks
25 Nov 89	**ENCORE** *Syncopate SY 33*	**41**	4 wks
14 Apr 90	**TOMORROW** *Syncopate SY 34*	**20**	7 wks
4 Aug 90	**NOBODY** *Syncopate SY 37*	**37**	5 wks
19 Jan 91	**FORGET ME NOTS** *Syncopate SY 39*	**26**	6 wks

☐1 Tongue In Cheek

TONIGHT UK, male vocal/instrumental group — 10 wks

| 28 Jan 78 | DRUMMER MAN Target TDS 1 | 14 | 8 wks |
| 20 May 78 | MONEY THAT'S YOUR PROBLEM Target TDS 2 | 66 | 2 wks |

TONY! TONI! TONÉ! US, male vocal group — 10 wks

30 Jun 90	OAKLAND STROKE Wing WING 7	50	5 wks
9 Mar 91	IT NEVER RAINS (IN SOUTHERN CALIFORNIA) Wing WING 10	69	2 wks
4 Sep 93	IF I HAD NO LOOT Polydor PZCD 292	44	3 wks

TOO TOUGH TEE - See DYNAMIX featuring TOO TOUGH TEE

TOP UK, male vocal/instrumental group — 2 wks

| 20 Jul 91 | NUMBER ONE DOMINATOR Island IS 496 | 67 | 2 wks |

TOP LINERS - See Rocky SHARPE and the REPLAYS

TOPOL Israel, male vocalist — 20 wks

| 20 Apr 67 | ● IF I WERE A RICH MAN CBS 202651 | 9 | 20 wks |

Mel TORMÉ US, male vocalist — 32 wks

27 Apr 56	MOUNTAIN GREENERY Vogue Coral Q 72150	15	11 wks
27 Jul 56	● MOUNTAIN GREENERY (re-entry) Vogue Coral Q 72150	4	13 wks
3 Jan 63	COMING HOME BABY London HLK 9643	13	8 wks

TORNADOS UK, male instrumental group — 59 wks

30 Aug 62	★ TELSTAR Decca F 11494	1	25 wks
10 Jan 63	● GLOBETROTTER Decca F 11562	5	11 wks
21 Mar 63	ROBOT Decca F 11606	17	12 wks
6 Jun 63	THE ICE CREAM MAN Decca F 11662	18	9 wks
10 Oct 63	DRAGONFLY Decca F 11745	41	2 wks

Mitchell TOROK US, male vocalist — 19 wks

28 Sep 56	● WHEN MEXICO GAVE UP THE RUMBA Brunswick 05586	6	17 wks
11 Jan 57	RED LIGHT GREEN LIGHT Brunswick 05626	29	1 wk
1 Feb 57	WHEN MEXICO GAVE UP THE RUMBA (re-entry) Brunswick 05586	30	1 wk

Peter TOSH Jamaica, male vocalist — 12 wks

| 21 Oct 78 | (YOU GOTTA WALK) DON'T LOOK BACK Rolling Stones 2859 | 43 | 7 wks |
| 2 Apr 83 | JOHNNY B. GOODE EMI RIC 115 | 48 | 5 wks |

TOTAL CONTRAST UK, male vocal/instrumental duo — 22 wks

3 Aug 85	TAKES A LITTLE TIME London LON 71	17	10 wks
19 Oct 85	HIT AND RUN London LON 76	41	5 wks
1 Mar 86	THE RIVER London LON 83	44	3 wks
10 May 86	WHAT YOU GONNA DO ABOUT IT London LON 95	63	4 wks

TOTO US, male vocal/instrumental group — 34 wks

10 Feb 79	HOLD THE LINE CBS 6784	14	11 wks
5 Feb 83	● AFRICA CBS A 2510	3	10 wks
9 Apr 83	ROSANNA CBS A 2079	12	8 wks
18 Jun 83	I WON'T HOLD YOU BACK CBS A 3392	37	5 wks

TOTO COELO UK, female vocal group — 14 wks

| 7 Aug 82 | ● I EAT CANNIBALS PART 1 Radialchoice TIC 10 | 8 | 10 wks |
| 13 Nov 82 | DRACULA'S TANGO / MUCHO MACHO Radialchoice TIC 11 | 54 | 4 wks |

TOTTENHAM HOTSPUR F.A. CUP FINAL SQUAD UK, male football team vocalists — 23 wks

9 May 81	● OSSIE'S DREAM (SPURS ARE ON THEIR WAY TO WEMBLEY) Rockney SHELF 1	5	8 wks
1 May 82	TOTTENHAM TOTTENHAM Rockney SHELF 2	19	7 wks
9 May 87	HOT SHOT TOTTENHAM! Rainbow RBR 16	18	5 wks
11 May 91	WHEN THE YEAR ENDS IN 1 A1 A 1324	44	3 wks

All hits feature the vocal and instrumental talents of Chas and Dave.

TOUCH OF SOUL UK, male/female vocal/instrumental group — 3 wks

| 19 May 90 | WE GOT THE LOVE Cooltempo COOL 204 | 46 | 3 wks |

TOURISTS UK, female/male vocal/instrumental group — 40 wks

9 Jun 79	BLIND AMONG THE FLOWERS Logo GO 350	52	5 wks
8 Sep 79	THE LONELIEST MAN IN THE WORLD Logo GO 360	32	7 wks
10 Nov 79	● I ONLY WANT TO BE WITH YOU Logo GO 370	4	14 wks
9 Feb 80	● SO GOOD TO BE BACK HOME AGAIN Logo TOUR 1	8	9 wks
18 Oct 80	DON'T SAY I TOLD YOU SO RCA TOUR 2	40	5 wks

Carol Lynn TOWNES US, female vocalist — 7 wks

| 4 Aug 84 | 99½ Polydor POSP 693 | 47 | 4 wks |
| 19 Jan 85 | BELIEVE IN THE BEAT Polydor POSP 720 | 56 | 3 wks |

Pete TOWNSHEND UK, male vocalist — 17 wks

5 Apr 80	ROUGH BOYS Atco K 11460	39	6 wks
21 Jun 80	LET MY LOVE OPEN YOUR DOOR Atco K 11486	46	6 wks
21 Aug 82	UNIFORMS (CORPS D'ESPRIT) Atco K 11751	48	5 wks

TOXIC TWO US, male instrumental/production duo — 6 wks

| 7 Mar 92 | RAVE GENERATOR PWL International PWL 223 | 13 | 6 wks |

TOY DOLLS UK, male vocal/instrumental group — 12 wks

| 1 Dec 84 | ● NELLIE THE ELEPHANT Volume VOL 11 | 4 | 12 wks |

TOYAH UK, female vocalist — 87 wks

14 Feb 81	● FOUR FROM TOYAH EP Safari TOY 1	4	14 wks
16 May 81	● I WANT TO BE FREE Safari SAFE 34	8	11 wks
3 Oct 81	● THUNDER IN THE MOUNTAINS Safari SAFE 38	4	9 wks
28 Nov 81	FOUR MORE FROM TOYAH EP Safari TOY 2	14	9 wks
22 May 82	BRAVE NEW WORLD Safari SAFE 45	21	8 wks
17 Jul 82	IEYA Safari SAFE 28	48	5 wks
9 Oct 82	BE LOUD BE PROUD (BE HEARD) Safari SAFE 52	30	7 wks
24 Sep 83	REBEL RUN Safari SAFE 56	24	5 wks
19 Nov 83	THE VOW Safari SAFE 58	50	5 wks
27 Apr 85	DON'T FALL IN LOVE (I SAID) Portrait A 6160	22	6 wks
29 Jun 85	SOUL PASSING THROUGH SOUL Portrait A 6359	57	3 wks
25 Apr 87	ECHO BEACH EG EGO 31	54	5 wks

Tracks on Four From Toyah EP: It's A Mystery / Revelations / War Boys / Angels And Demons. Tracks on Four More From Toyah EP: Good Morning Universe / Urban Tribesman / In The Fairground / The Furious Futures.

TOYS US, female vocal group — 17 wks

| 4 Nov 65 | ● A LOVER'S CONCERTO Stateside SS 460 | 5 | 13 wks |
| 27 Jan 66 | ATTACK Stateside SS 483 | 36 | 4 wks |

T'PAU UK, male/female vocal/instrumental group — 77 wks

| 8 Aug 87 | ● HEART AND SOUL Siren SRN 41 | 4 | 13 wks |

24 Oct 87	★ CHINA IN YOUR HAND Siren SRN 64	1	15 wks
30 Jan 88	● VALENTINE Siren SRN 69	9	8 wks
2 Apr 88	SEX TALK (LIVE) Siren SRN 80	23	7 wks
25 Jun 88	I WILL BE WITH YOU Siren SRN 87	14	6 wks
1 Oct 88	SECRET GARDEN Siren SRN 93	18	7 wks
3 Dec 88	ROAD TO OUR DREAM Siren SRN 100	42	6 wks
25 Mar 89	ONLY THE LONELY Siren SRN 107	28	6 wks
18 May 91	WHENEVER YOU NEED ME Siren SRN 140	16	6 wks
27 Jul 91	WALK ON AIR Siren SRN 142	62	2 wks
20 Feb 93	VALENTINE (re-issue) Virgin VALEG 1	53	1 wk

TRACIE UK, female vocalist — 24 wks

26 Mar 83	● THE HOUSE THAT JACK BUILT Respond KOB 701	9	8 wks
16 Jul 83	GIVE IT SOME EMOTION Respond KOB 704	24	9 wks
14 Apr 84	SOUL'S ON FIRE Respond KOB 708	73	2 wks
9 Jun 84	(I LOVE YOU) WHEN YOU SLEEP Respond KOB 710	59	3 wks
17 Aug 85	I CAN'T LEAVE YOU ALONE Respond SBS 1 [1]	60	2 wks

[1] Tracie Young

TRACY - See MASSIVO featuring TRACY

Jeanie TRACY US, female vocalist — 2 wks

11 Jun 94	IF THIS IS LOVE Pulse 8 CDLOSE 63	73	1 wk
5 Nov 94	DO YOU BELIEVE IN THE WONDER Pulse 8 CDLOSE 74	57	1 wk

TRAFFIC UK, male vocal/instrumental group — 40 wks

1 Jun 67	● PAPER SUN Island WIP 6002	5	10 wks
6 Sep 67	● HOLE IN MY SHOE Island WIP 6017	2	14 wks
29 Nov 67	● HERE WE GO ROUND THE MULBERRY BUSH Island WIP 6025	8	12 wks
6 Mar 68	NO FACE, NO NAME, NO NUMBER Island WIP 6030	40	4 wks

TRAMAINE US, female vocalist — 2 wks

5 Oct 85	FALL DOWN (SPIRIT OF LOVE) A & M AM 281	60	2 wks

TRAMMPS US, male vocal group — 55 wks

23 Nov 74	ZING WENT THE STRINGS OF MY HEART Buddah BDS 405	29	10 wks
1 Feb 75	SIXTY MINUTE MAN Buddah BDS 415	40	4 wks
11 Oct 75	● HOLD BACK THE NIGHT Buddah BDS 437	5	8 wks
13 Mar 76	THAT'S WHERE THE HAPPY PEOPLE GO Atlantic K 10703	35	8 wks
24 Jul 76	SOUL SEARCHIN' TIME Atlantic K 10797	42	3 wks
14 May 77	DISCO INFERNO Atlantic K 10914	16	7 wks
24 Jun 78	DISCO INFERNO (re-issue) Atlantic K 11135	47	10 wks
12 Dec 92	HOLD BACK THE NIGHT Network NWK 65 [1]	30	5 wks

[1] KWS featuring guest vocals from the Trammps

TRANSVISION VAMP
UK, female/male vocal/instrumantal group — 59 wks

16 Apr 88	TELL THAT GIRL TO SHUT UP MCA TVV 2	45	3 wks
25 Jun 88	● I WANT YOUR LOVE MCA TVV 3	5	13 wks
17 Sep 88	REVOLUTION BABY MCA TVV 4	30	5 wks
19 Nov 88	SISTER MOON MCA TVV 5	41	5 wks
1 Apr 89	● BABY I DON'T CARE MCA TVV 6	3	11 wks
10 Jun 89	THE ONLY ONE MCA TVV 7	15	6 wks
5 Aug 89	LANDSLIDE OF LOVE MCA TVV 8	14	5 wks
4 Nov 89	BORN TO BE SOLD MCA TVV 9	22	4 wks
13 Apr 91	(I JUST WANNA) B WITH U MCA TVV 10	30	4 wks
22 Jun 91	IF LOOKS COULD KILL MCA TVV 11	41	3 wks

TRANS-X Canada, female/male vocal/instrumental group — 9 wks

13 Jul 85	● LIVING ON VIDEO Boiling Point POSP 650	9	9 wks

TRASH UK, male vocal/instrumental group — 3 wks

25 Oct 69	GOLDEN SLUMBERS / CARRY THAT WEIGHT Apple 17	35	3 wks

TRASH CAN SINATRAS
UK, male vocal/instrumental group — 1 wk

24 Apr 93	HAYFEVER Go! Discs GODCD 98	61	1 wk

TRAVELING WILBURYS
UK/US, male vocal/instrumental group — 19 wks

29 Oct 88	HANDLE WITH CARE Wilbury W 7732	21	13 wks
11 Mar 89	END OF THE LINE Wilbury W 7637	52	4 wks
30 Jun 90	NOBODY'S CHILD Wilbury W 9773	44	2 wks

Randy TRAVIS US, male vocalist — 6 wks

21 May 88	FOREVER AND EVER, AMEN Warner Bros. W 8384	55	6 wks

John TRAVOLTA US, male vocalist — 81 wks

20 May 78	★ YOU'RE THE ONE THAT I WANT RSO 006 [1]	1	26 wks
16 Sep 78	★ SUMMER NIGHTS RSO 18 [1]	1	19 wks
7 Oct 78	● SANDY Polydor POSP 6	2	15 wks
2 Dec 78	GREASED LIGHTNIN' Polydor POSP 14	11	9 wks
22 Dec 90	GREASE MEGAMIX Polydor PO 114 [1]	3	10 wks
23 Mar 91	GREASE - THE DREAM MIX PWL/Polydor PO 136 [2]	47	2 wks

[1] John Travolta and Olivia Newton-John [2] Frankie Valli, John Travolta and Olivia Newton-John

TREMELOES UK, male vocal/instrumental group — 131 wks

2 Feb 67	● HERE COMES MY BABY CBS 202519	4	11 wks
27 Apr 67	★ SILENCE IS GOLDEN CBS 2723	1	15 wks
2 Aug 67	● EVEN THE BAD TIMES ARE GOOD CBS 2930	4	13 wks
8 Nov 67	BE MINE CBS 3043	39	2 wks
17 Jan 68	● SUDDENLY YOU LOVE ME CBS 3234	6	11 wks
8 May 68	HELULE HELULE CBS 2889	14	9 wks
18 Sep 68	● MY LITTLE LADY CBS 3480	6	12 wks
11 Dec 68	I SHALL BE RELEASED CBS 3873	29	5 wks
19 Mar 69	HELLO WORLD CBS 4065	14	8 wks
1 Nov 69	● (CALL ME) NUMBER ONE CBS 4582	2	14 wks
21 Mar 70	BY THE WAY CBS 4815	35	6 wks
12 Sep 70	● ME AND MY LIFE CBS 5139	4	18 wks
10 Jul 71	HELLO BUDDY CBS 7294	32	7 wks

See also Brian Poole and the Tremeloes.

Jackie TRENT UK, female vocalist — 17 wks

22 Apr 65	★ WHERE ARE YOU NOW (MY LOVE) Pye 7N 15776	1	11 wks
1 Jul 65	WHEN THE SUMMERTIME IS OVER Pye 7N 15865	39	2 wks
2 Apr 69	I'LL BE THERE Pye 7N 17693	38	4 wks

Ralph TRESVANT US, male vocalist — 21 wks

12 Jan 91	SENSITIVITY MCA MCS 1462	18	8 wks
15 Aug 92	● THE BEST THINGS IN LIFE ARE FREE Perspective PERSS 7400 [1]	2	13 wks

[1] Luther Vandross and Janet Jackson with special guests BBD and Ralph Tresvant

T. REX UK, male vocal/instrumental group — 235 wks

8 May 68	DEBORA Regal Zonophone RZ 3008 [1]	34	7 wks
4 Sep 68	ONE INCH ROCK Regal Zonophone RZ 3011 [1]	28	7 wks
9 Aug 69	KING OF THE RUMBLING SPIRES Regal Zonophone RZ 3022 [1]	44	1 wk

24 Oct 70	● RIDE A WHITE SWAN Fly BUG 1	2	20 wks
27 Feb 71	★ HOT LOVE Fly BUG 6	1	17 wks
10 Jul 71	★ GET IT ON Fly BUG 10	1	13 wks
13 Nov 71	● JEEPSTER Fly BUG 16	2	15 wks
29 Jan 72	★ TELEGRAM SAM T. Rex 101	1	12 wks
1 Apr 72	● DEBORA/ONE INCH ROCK (re-issue) Magnifly Echo 102 [1]	7	10 wks
13 May 72	★ METAL GURU EMI MARC 1	1	14 wks
16 Sep 72	● CHILDREN OF THE REVOLUTION EMI MARC 2	2	10 wks
9 Dec 72	● SOLID GOLD EASY ACTION EMI MARC 3	2	11 wks
10 Mar 73	● 20TH CENTURY BOY EMI MARC 4	3	9 wks
16 Jun 73	● THE GROOVER EMI MARC 5	4	9 wks
24 Nov 73	TRUCK ON (TYKE) EMI MARC 6	12	11 wks
9 Feb 74	TEENAGE DREAM EMI MARC 7 [2]	13	5 wks
13 Jul 74	LIGHT OF LOVE EMI MARC 8	22	5 wks
16 Nov 74	ZIP GUN BOOGIE EMI MARC 9	41	3 wks
12 Jul 75	NEW YORK CITY EMI MARC 10	15	8 wks
11 Oct 75	DREAMY LADY EMI MARC 11 [3]	30	5 wks
6 Mar 76	LONDON BOYS EMI MARC 13	40	3 wks
19 Jun 76	I LOVE TO BOOGIE EMI MARC 14	13	9 wks
2 Oct 76	LASER LOVE EMI MARC 15	41	4 wks
2 Apr 77	THE SOUL OF MY SUIT EMI MARC 16	42	3 wks
9 May 81	RETURN OF THE ELECTRIC WARRIOR EP Rarn MBSF 001 [4]	50	4 wks
19 Sep 81	YOU SCARE ME TO DEATH Cherry Red CHERRY 29 [4]	51	4 wks
27 Mar 82	TELEGRAM SAM (re-entry) T. Rex 101	69	2 wks
18 May 85	MEGAREX Marc On Wax TANX 1 [2]	72	2 wks
9 May 87	GET IT ON (re-mix) Marc On Wax MARC 10 [2]	54	4 wks
24 Aug 91	20TH CENTURY BOY (re-issue) Marc On Wax MARC 501 [2]	13	8 wks

[1] Tyrannosaurus Rex [2] Marc Bolan and T. Rex [3] T. Rex Disco Party [4] Marc Bolan

Tracks on Return Of The Electric Warrior EP: Sing Me A Song/Endless Sleep/The Lilac Hand Of Menthol Dan. Megarex is a medley of extracts from the following T. Rex hits: Truck On (Tyke)/The Groover/Telegram Sam/Shock Rock/Metal Guru/20th Century Boy/Children Of The Revolution/Hot Love.

TRIBAL HOUSE US, male vocal/instrumental group **2 wks**

3 Feb 90	MOTHERLAND-A-FRI-CA Cooltempo COOL 198	57	2 wks

Tony TRIBE Jamaica, male vocalist **2 wks**

16 Jul 69	RED RED WINE Downtown DT 419	50	1 wk
9 Aug 69	RED RED WINE (re-entry) Downtown DT 419	46	1 wk

A TRIBE CALLED QUEST US, male rap group **11 wks**

18 Aug 90	BONITA APPLEBUM Jive JIVE 256	47	3 wks
19 Jan 91	CAN I KICK IT Jive JIVE 265	15	7 wks
11 Jun 94	OH MY GOD Jive JIVECD 355	68	1 wk

TRIBE OF TOFFS UK, male vocal/instrumental group **5 wks**

24 Dec 88	JOHN KETTLEY (IS A WEATHERMAN) Completely Different DAFT 1	21	5 wks

TRICKY UK, male rapper **1 wk**

5 Feb 94	AFTERMATH Fourth & Broadway BRCD 288	69	1 wk

TRICKY DISCO UK, male vocal/instrumental group **10 wks**

28 Jul 90	TRICKY DISCO Warp WAP 7	14	8 wks
20 Apr 91	HOUSE FLY Warp 7WAP 11	55	2 wks

TRIFFIDS New Zealand, male vocal/instrumental group **1 wk**

6 Feb 88	A TRICK OF THE LIGHT Island IS 350	73	1 wk

TRINIDAD OIL COMPANY
Trinidad, male/female vocal/instrumental group **5 wks**

21 May 77	THE CALENDAR SONG Harvest HAR 5122	34	5 wks

TRINITY - See Julie DRISCOLL, Brian AUGER and the TRINITY

TRIO Germany, male vocal/instrumental group **10 wks**

3 Jul 82	● DA DA DA Mobile Suit Corporat CORP 5	2	10 wks

TRIUMPH Canada, male vocal/instrumental group **2 wks**

22 Nov 80	I LIVE FOR THE WEEKEND RCA 13	59	2 wks

TROGGS UK, male vocal/instrumental group **87 wks**

5 May 66	● WILD THING Fontana TF 689	2	12 wks
14 Jul 66	★ WITH A GIRL LIKE YOU Fontana TF 717	1	12 wks
29 Sep 66	● I CAN'T CONTROL MYSELF Page One POF 001	2	14 wks
15 Dec 66	● ANY WAY THAT YOU WANT ME Page One POF 010	8	10 wks
16 Feb 67	GIVE IT TO ME Page One POF 015	12	10 wks
1 Jun 67	NIGHT OF THE LONG GRASS Page One POF 022	17	6 wks
26 Jul 67	HI HI HAZEL Page One POF 030	42	3 wks
18 Oct 67	● LOVE IS ALL AROUND Page One POF 040	5	14 wks
28 Feb 68	LITTLE GIRL Page One POF 056	37	4 wks
30 Oct 93	WILD THING Weekend CDWEEK 103 [1]	69	2 wks

[1] Troggs and Wolf

Wild Thing in '93 is a re-recording and was listed with the flip side, War, by Edwin Starr and Shadow.

TRONIKHOUSE US, male producer - Kevin Saunderson **1 wk**

14 Mar 92	UP TEMPO KMS UK KMSUK 1	68	1 wk

TROUBADOURS DU ROI BAUDOUIN
Zaire, male/female vocal group **11 wks**

19 Mar 69	SANCTUS (MISSA LUBA) Philips BF 1732	28	6 wks
7 May 69	SANCTUS (MISSA LUBA) (re-entry) Philips BF 1732	37	5 wks

TROUBLE FUNK US, male vocal/instrumental group **3 wks**

27 Jun 87	WOMAN OF PRINCIPLE Fourth & Broadway BRW 70	65	3 wks

Doris TROY US, female vocalist **12 wks**

19 Nov 64	WHATCHA GONNA DO ABOUT IT Atlantic AT 4011	37	7 wks
21 Jan 65	WHATCHA GONNA DO ABOUT IT (re-entry) Atlantic AT 4011	38	5 wks

TRUCKIN' CO. - See Garnet MIMMS and TRUCKIN' CO.

Andrea TRUE CONNECTION
US, female vocalist, male instrumental backing group **16 wks**

17 Apr 76	● MORE MORE MORE Buddah BDS 442	5	10 wks
4 Mar 78	WHAT'S YOUR NAME WHAT'S YOUR NUMBER Buddah BDS 467	34	6 wks

TRUE FAITH with FINAL CUT
US, male/female vocal/instrumental group **4 wks**

2 Mar 91	TAKE ME AWAY Network NWK 20	51	4 wks

TRUE IMAGE - See Monie LOVE

TOP 46 50

Marc Bolan was the leader of T. REX long before anyone referred to 'dinosaur' rock acts. (LFI)

TINA TURNER sings with Mick Jagger at a sound check the day before Live Aid. (Kevin Mazur/LFI)

TOP 50 50

Ray Slijngaard of 2 UNLIMITED points to their World Music Award, held by partner Anita Dels. (David Fisher/LFI)

TRUSSEL US, male vocal / instrumental group · 4 wks

| 8 Mar 80 | LOVE INJECTION Elektra K 12412 | 43 | 4 wks |

TRUTH UK, male vocal duo · 6 wks

| 3 Feb 66 | GIRL Pye 7N 17035 | 27 | 6 wks |

TRUTH UK, male vocal / instrumental group · 16 wks

11 Jun 83	CONFUSION (HITS US EVERY TIME) Formation TRUTH 1	22	7 wks
27 Aug 83	A STEP IN THE RIGHT DIRECTION Formation TRUTH 2	32	7 wks
4 Feb 84	NO STONE UNTURNED Formation TRUTH 3	66	2 wks

TUBES US, male vocal / instrumental group · 18 wks

19 Nov 77	WHITE PUNKS ON DOPE A & M AMS 7323	28	4 wks
28 Apr 79	PRIME TIME A & M AMS 7423	34	10 wks
12 Sep 81	DON'T WANT TO WAIT ANYMORE Capitol CL 208	60	4 wks

TUBEWAY ARMY - See Gary NUMAN

Barbara TUCKER US, female vocalist · 5 wks

| 5 Mar 94 | BEAUTIFUL PEOPLE Positiva CDTIV 11 | 23 | 3 wks |
| 26 Nov 94 | I GET LIFTED Positiva CDTIV 23 | 33 | 2 wks |

Junior TUCKER UK, male vocalist · 2 wks

| 2 Jun 90 | DON'T TEST 10 TEN 299 | 54 | 2 wks |

Louise TUCKER Holland, female vocalist · 5 wks

| 9 Apr 83 | MIDNIGHT BLUE Ariola ARO 289 | 59 | 5 wks |

Tommy TUCKER US, male vocalist · 10 wks

| 26 Mar 64 | HI-HEEL SNEAKERS Pye 7N 25238 | 23 | 10 wks |

Claramae TURNER - See VARIOUS ARTISTS (EPs & LPs) - Carousel Soundtrack

Ike and Tina TURNER
US, male / female vocal instrumental duo · 44 wks

9 Jun 66	● RIVER DEEP MOUNTAIN HIGH London HL 10046	3	13 wks
28 Jul 66	TELL HER I'M NOT HOME Warner Bros. WB 5753	48	1 wk
27 Oct 66	A LOVE LIKE YOURS London HL 10083	16	10 wks
12 Feb 69	RIVER DEEP MOUNTAIN HIGH (re-issue) London HLU 10242	33	7 wks
8 Sep 73	● NUTBUSH CITY LIMITS United Artists UP 35582	4	13 wks

See also Tina Turner.

Ruby TURNER UK, female vocalist · 30 wks

25 Jan 86	IF YOU'RE READY (COME GO WITH ME) Jive JIVE 109 [1]	30	7 wks
29 Mar 86	I'M IN LOVE Jive JIVE 118	61	4 wks
13 Sep 86	BYE BABY Jive JIVE 126	52	3 wks
14 Mar 87	I'D RATHER GO BLIND Jive RTS 1	24	8 wks
16 May 87	I'M IN LOVE Jive RTS 2	57	2 wks
13 Jan 90	IT'S GONNA BE ALRIGHT Jive RTS 7	57	3 wks
5 Feb 94	STAY WITH ME BABY M & G MAGCD 53	39	3 wks

[1] Ruby Turner featuring Jonathan Butler

Sammy TURNER US, male vocalist · 2 wks

| 13 Nov 59 | ALWAYS London HLX 8963 | 26 | 2 wks |

Tina TURNER US, female vocalist · 183 wks

19 Nov 83	● LET'S STAY TOGETHER Capitol CL 316	6	13 wks
25 Feb 84	HELP Capitol CL 325	40	6 wks
16 Jun 84	● WHAT'S LOVE GOT TO DO WITH IT Capitol CL 334	3	16 wks
15 Sep 84	BETTER BE GOOD TO ME Capitol CL 338	45	5 wks
17 Nov 84	PRIVATE DANCER Capitol CL 343	26	9 wks
2 Mar 85	I CAN'T STAND THE RAIN Capitol CL 352	57	3 wks
20 Jul 85	● WE DON'T NEED ANOTHER HERO (THUNDERDOME) Capitol CL 364	3	12 wks
12 Oct 85	ONE OF THE LIVING Capitol CL 376	55	2 wks
2 Nov 85	IT'S ONLY LOVE A & M AM 285 [1]	29	6 wks
23 Aug 86	TYPICAL MALE Capitol CL 419	33	6 wks
8 Nov 86	TWO PEOPLE Capitol CL 430	43	4 wks
14 Mar 87	WHAT YOU GET IS WHAT YOU SEE Capitol CL 439	30	7 wks
13 Jun 87	BREAK EVERY RULE Capitol CL 452	43	3 wks
20 Jun 87	TEARING US APART Duck W 8299 [2]	56	3 wks
19 Mar 88	ADDICTED TO LOVE (LIVE) Capitol CL 484	71	2 wks
2 Sep 89	● THE BEST Capitol CL 543	5	12 wks
18 Nov 89	● I DON'T WANNA LOSE YOU Capitol CL 553	8	11 wks
17 Feb 90	STEAMY WINDOWS Capitol CL 560	13	6 wks
11 Aug 90	LOOK ME IN THE HEART Capitol CL 584	31	6 wks
13 Oct 90	BE TENDER WITH ME BABY Capitol CL 593	28	4 wks
24 Nov 90	● IT TAKES TWO Warner Bros. ROD 1 [3]	5	8 wks
21 Sep 91	NUTBUSH CITY LIMITS Capitol CL 630	23	5 wks
23 Nov 91	WAY OF THE WORLD Capitol CL 637	13	7 wks
15 Feb 92	LOVE THING Capitol CL 644	29	4 wks
6 Jun 92	I WANT YOU NEAR ME Capitol CL 659	22	4 wks
22 May 93	● I DON'T WANNA FIGHT Parlophone CDRS 6346	7	9 wks
28 Aug 93	DISCO INFERNO Parlophone CDR 6357	12	6 wks
30 Oct 93	WHY MUST WE WAIT UNTIL TONIGHT Parlophone CDR 6366	16	4 wks

[1] Bryan Adams and Tina Turner [2] Eric Clapton and Tina Turner [3] Rod Stewart and Tina Turner

See also Ike and Tina Turner.

TURNTABLE ORCHESTRA
US, male vocal / instrumental duo · 4 wks

| 21 Jan 89 | YOU'RE GONNA MISS ME Republic LIC 012 | 52 | 4 wks |

TURTLES US, male vocal / instrumental group · 39 wks

23 Mar 67	HAPPY TOGETHER London HL 10115	12	12 wks
15 Jun 67	● SHE'D RATHER BE WITH ME London HLU 10135	4	15 wks
30 Oct 68	● ELENORE London HL 10223	7	12 wks

TUXEDOS - See Bobby ANGELO and the TUXEDOS

TWEETS UK, male instrumental group · 34 wks

12 Sep 81	● THE BIRDIE SONG (BIRDIE DANCE) PRT 7P 219	2	23 wks
5 Dec 81	LET'S ALL SING LIKE THE BIRDIES SING PRT 7P 226	44	6 wks
18 Dec 82	THE BIRDIE SONG (BIRDIE DANCE) (re-entry) PRT 7P 219	46	5 wks

TWENTY FINGERS featuring GILLETTE
US, male / female vocal / instrumental group · 4 wks

| 26 Nov 94 | SHORT DICK MAN Multiply CDMULT 12 | 21 | 4 wks |

TWENTY 4 SEVEN - See CAPTAIN HOLLYWOOD PROJECT

TWICE AS MUCH UK, male vocal duo · 9 wks

| 16 Jun 66 | SITTIN' ON A FENCE Immediate IM 033 | 25 | 9 wks |

TWIGGY UK, female vocalist · 10 wks

| 14 Aug 76 | HERE I GO AGAIN Mercury 6007 100 | 17 | 10 wks |

TWIN HYPE US, male rap duo — **2 wks**

15 Jul 89	**DO IT TO THE CROWD** Profile PROF 255	65	2 wks

TWINKLE UK, female vocalist — **20 wks**

26 Nov 64	● **TERRY** Decca F 12013	4	15 wks
25 Feb 65	**GOLDEN LIGHTS** Decca F 12076	21	5 wks

TWISTED SISTER US, male vocal/instrumental group — **28 wks**

26 Mar 83	**I AM (I'M ME)** Atlantic A 9854	18	9 wks
28 May 83	**THE KIDS ARE BACK** Atlantic A 9827	32	6 wks
20 Aug 83	**YOU CAN'T STOP ROCK 'N' ROLL** Atlantic A 9792	43	4 wks
2 Jun 84	**WE'RE NOT GONNA TAKE IT** Atlantic A 9657	58	6 wks
18 Jan 86	**LEADER OF THE PACK** Atlantic A 9478	47	3 wks

Conway TWITTY US, male vocalist — **36 wks**

14 Nov 58	★ **IT'S ONLY MAKE BELIEVE** MGM 992	1	15 wks
27 Mar 59	**STORY OF MY LOVE** MGM 1003	30	1 wk
21 Aug 59	● **MONA LISA** MGM 1029	5	14 wks
21 Jul 60	**IS A BLUE BIRD BLUE** MGM 1082	43	3 wks
23 Feb 61	**C'EST SI BON** MGM 1118	40	3 wks

2 BAD MICE UK, male instrumental/production group — **3 wks**

15 Feb 92	**HOLD IT DOWN** Moving Shadow SHADOW 14	70	1 wk
8 Aug 92	**HOLD IT DOWN (re-entry)** Moving Shadow SHADOW 14	48	2 wks

TWO COWBOYS Italy, male instrumental/production duo — **11 wks**

9 Jul 94	● **EVERYBODY GONFI-GON** 3 Beat TABCD 221	7	11 wks

2 FOR JOY UK, male instrumental/production duo — **3 wks**

1 Dec 90	**IN A STATE** Mercury MER 333	61	1 wk
9 Nov 91	**LET THE BASS KICK** All Around The World GLOBE 102	67	2 wks

2 FUNKY 2 starring Katherine DION UK, male/female vocal/instrumental group — **2 wks**

6 Nov 93	**BROTHERS AND SISTERS** Logic 74321170772	56	2 wks

2 HOUSE US, male instrumental/production duo — **1 wk**

21 Mar 92	**GO TECHNO** Atlantic A 7519	65	1 wk

2 IN A ROOM US, male vocal duo — **13 wks**

18 Nov 89	**SOMEBODY IN THE HOUSE SAY YEAH!** Big Life BLR 12	66	1 wk
26 Jan 91	● **WIGGLE IT** SBK SBK 19	3	8 wks
6 Apr 91	**SHE'S GOT ME GOING CRAZY** SBK SBK 23	54	2 wks
22 Oct 94	**EL TRAGO (THE DRINK)** Positiva CDTIV 18	34	2 wks

2 IN A TENT UK, male instrumental/production duo — **3 wks**

17 Dec 94	**WHEN I'M CLEANING WINDOWS (TURNED OUT NICE AGAIN)** Love This SPONCD 1	25†	3 wks

Hit features the vocals of George Formby.

See also George Formby.

2 MAD UK, male vocal/instrumental duo — **4 wks**

9 Feb 91	**THINKING ABOUT YOUR BODY** Big Life BLR 37	43	4 wks

TWO MAN SOUND Belgium, male vocal/instrumental group — **7 wks**

20 Jan 79	**QUE TAL AMERICA** Miracle M 1	46	7 wks

TWO MEN, A DRUM MACHINE AND A TRUMPET UK, male instrumental duo — **17 wks**

9 Jan 88	**I'M TIRED OF GETTING PUSHED AROUND** London LON 141	18	8 wks
25 Jun 88	**HEAT IT UP** Jive JIVE 174 [1]	21	9 wks

[1] Wee Papa Girl Rappers featuring Two Men and a Drum Machine

TWO NATIONS UK, male vocal/instrumental group — **1 wk**

20 Jun 87	**THAT'S THE WAY IT FEELS** 10 TEN 168	74	1 wk

TWO PEOPLE UK, male vocal/instrumental group — **2 wks**

31 Jan 87	**HEAVEN** Polydor POSP 844	63	2 wks

2WO THIRD3 UK, male vocal/instrumental group — **13 wks**

19 Feb 94	**HEAR ME CALLING** Epic 6600642	48	3 wks
11 Jun 94	**EASE THE PRESSURE** Epic 6604782	45	2 wks
8 Oct 94	**I WANT THE WORLD** Epic 6608542	20	5 wks
17 Dec 94	**I WANT TO BE ALONE** Epic 6610852	29†	3 wks

2 UNLIMITED Holland, male/female vocal duo — **103 wks**

5 Oct 91	● **GET READY FOR THIS** PWL Continental PWL 206	2	15 wks
25 Jan 92	● **TWILIGHT ZONE** PWL Continental PWL 211	2	10 wks
2 May 92	● **WORKAHOLIC** PWL Continental PWL 228	4	7 wks
15 Aug 92	**THE MAGIC FRIEND** PWL Continental PWL 240	11	7 wks
30 Jan 93	★ **NO LIMIT** PWL Continental PWCD 256	1	16 wks
8 May 93	● **TRIBAL DANCE** PWL Continental PWCD 262	4	11 wks
4 Sep 93	● **FACES** PWL Continental PWCD 268	8	7 wks
20 Nov 93	**MAXIMUM OVERDRIVE** PWL Continental PWCD 276	15	8 wks
19 Feb 94	● **LET THE BEAT CONTROL YOUR BODY** PWL Continental PWCD 280	6	9 wks
21 May 94	● **THE REAL THING** PWL Continental PWCD 306	6	7 wks
1 Oct 94	**NO ONE** PWL Continental PWCD 314	17	6 wks

TYGERS OF PAN TANG UK, male vocal/instrumental group — **15 wks**

14 Feb 81	**HELLBOUND** MCA 672	48	3 wks
27 Mar 82	**LOVE POTION NO. 9** MCA 769	45	6 wks
10 Jul 82	**RENDEZVOUS** MCA 777	49	4 wks
11 Sep 82	**PARIS BY AIR** MCA 790	63	2 wks

Bonnie TYLER UK, female vocalist — **79 wks**

30 Oct 76	● **LOST IN FRANCE** RCA 2734	9	10 wks
19 Mar 77	**MORE THAN A LOVER** RCA PB 5008	27	6 wks
3 Dec 77	● **IT'S A HEARTACHE** RCA PB 5057	4	12 wks
30 Jun 79	**MARRIED MEN** RCA PB 5164	35	6 wks
19 Feb 83	★ **TOTAL ECLIPSE OF THE HEART** CBS TYLER 1	1	12 wks
7 May 83	**FASTER THAN THE SPEED OF NIGHT** CBS A 3338	43	4 wks
25 Jun 83	**HAVE YOU EVER SEEN THE RAIN** CBS A 3517	47	3 wks
7 Jan 84	● **A ROCKIN' GOOD WAY** Epic A 4071 [1]	5	9 wks
31 Aug 85	● **HOLDING OUT FOR A HERO** CBS A 4251	2	13 wks
14 Dec 85	**LOVING YOU'S A DIRTY JOB BUT SOMEBODY'S GOTTA DO IT** CBS A 6662 [2]	73	2 wks
28 Dec 91	**HOLDING OUT FOR A HERO (re-issue)** Total TYLER 10	69	2 wks

[1] Shaky and Bonnie [2] Bonnie Tyler, guest vocalist Todd Rundgren

TYMES US, male vocal group — **41 wks**

25 Jul 63	**SO MUCH IN LOVE** Cameo Parkway P 871	**21**	8 wks
15 Jan 69	**PEOPLE** Direction 58 3903	**16**	10 wks
21 Sep 74	**YOU LITTLE TRUST MAKER** RCA 2456	**18**	9 wks
21 Dec 74	★ **MS GRACE** RCA 2493	**1**	11 wks
17 Jan 76	**GOD'S GONNA PUNISH YOU** RCA 2626	**41**	3 wks

TYPICALLY TROPICAL
UK, male vocal / instrumental duo — **11 wks**

5 Jul 75	★ **BARBADOS** Gull GULS 14	**1**	11 wks

TYREE US, male producer — **10 wks**

25 Feb 89	**TURN UP THE BASS** ffrr FFR 24 [1]	**12**	7 wks
6 May 89	**HARDCORE HIP HOUSE** DJ International DJIN 11	**70**	2 wks
2 Dec 89	**MOVE YOUR BODY** CBS 655470 7 [2]	**72**	1 wk

[1] Tyree featuring Kool Rock Steady [2] Tyree featuring J.M.D.

TYRREL CORPORATION
UK, male vocal / instrumental duo — **6 wks**

14 Mar 92	**THE BOTTLE** Volante TYR 1	**71**	1 wk
15 Aug 92	**GOING HOME** Volante TYR 2	**58**	2 wks
10 Oct 92	**WAKING WITH A STRANGER / ONE DAY** Volante TYRS 3	**59**	1 wk
24 Sep 94	**YOU'RE NOT HERE** Cooltempo CDCOOL 292	**42**	2 wks

Judie TZUKE UK, female vocalist — **10 wks**

14 Jul 79	**STAY WITH ME TILL DAWN** Rocket XPRES 17	**16**	10 wks

UB40 UK, male vocal / instrumental group — **305 wks**

8 Mar 80	● **KING / FOOD FOR THOUGHT** Graduate GRAD 6	**4**	13 wks
14 Jun 80	● **MY WAY OF THINKING / I THINK IT'S GOING TO RAIN** Graduate GRAD 8	**6**	10 wks
1 Nov 80	● **THE EARTH DIES SCREAMING / DREAM A LIE** Graduate GRAD 10	**10**	12 wks
23 May 81	**DON'T LET IT PASS YOU BY / DON'T SLOW DOWN** DEP International DEP 1	**16**	9 wks
8 Aug 81	● **ONE IN TEN** DEP International DEP 2	**7**	10 wks
13 Feb 82	**I WON'T CLOSE MY EYES** DEP International DEP 3	**32**	6 wks
15 May 82	**LOVE IS ALL IS ALRIGHT** DEP International DEP 4	**29**	7 wks
28 Aug 82	**SO HERE I AM** DEP International DEP 5	**25**	9 wks
5 Feb 83	**I'VE GOT MINE** DEP International 7 DEP 6	**45**	4 wks
20 Aug 83	★ **RED RED WINE** DEP International 7 DEP 7	**1**	14 wks
15 Oct 83	● **PLEASE DON'T MAKE ME CRY** DEP International 7 DEP 8	**10**	8 wks
10 Dec 83	**MANY RIVERS TO CROSS** DEP International 7 DEP 9	**16**	8 wks
17 Mar 84	**CHERRY OH BABY** DEP International DEP 10	**12**	8 wks
22 Sep 84	● **IF IT HAPPENS AGAIN** DEP International DEP 11	**9**	8 wks
1 Dec 84	**RIDDLE ME** DEP International DEP 15	**59**	2 wks
3 Aug 85	★ **I GOT YOU BABE** DEP International DEP 20 [1]	**1**	13 wks
26 Oct 85	● **DON'T BREAK MY HEART** DEP International DEP 22	**3**	13 wks
12 Jul 86	● **SING OUR OWN SONG** DEP International DEP 23	**5**	9 wks
27 Sep 86	**ALL I WANT TO DO** DEP International DEP 24	**41**	4 wks
17 Jan 87	**RAT IN MI KITCHEN** DEP International DEP 25	**12**	7 wks
9 May 87	**WATCHDOGS** DEP International DEP 26	**39**	4 wks
10 Oct 87	**MAYBE TOMORROW** DEP International DEP 27	**14**	8 wks
27 Feb 88	**RECKLESS** EMI EM 41 [2]	**17**	8 wks
18 Jun 88	● **BREAKFAST IN BED** DEP International DEP 29 [1]	**6**	11 wks
20 Aug 88	**WHERE DID I GO WRONG** DEP International DEP 30	**26**	6 wks
17 Jun 89	**I WOULD DO FOR YOU** DEP International DEP 32	**45**	4 wks
18 Nov 89	● **HOMELY GIRL** DEP Internationl DEP 33	**6**	10 wks
27 Jan 90	**HERE I AM (COME AND TAKE ME)** DEP International DEP 34	**46**	3 wks
31 Mar 90	● **KINGSTON TOWN** DEP International DEP 35	**4**	12 wks
28 Jul 90	**WEAR YOU TO THE BALL** DEP International DEP 36	**35**	6 wks
3 Nov 90	● **I'LL BE YOUR BABY TONIGHT** EMI EM 167 [3]	**6**	10 wks
1 Dec 90	**IMPOSSIBLE LOVE** DEP International DEP 37	**47**	2 wks
2 Feb 91	**THE WAY YOU DO THE THINGS YOU DO** DEP International DEP 38	**49**	3 wks
12 Dec 92	**ONE IN TEN** ZTT ZANG 39 [4]	**17**	8 wks
22 May 93	★ **(I CAN'T HELP) FALLING IN LOVE WITH YOU** DEP International DEPDG 40	**1**	16 wks
21 Aug 93	● **HIGHER GROUND** DEP International DEPD 41	**8**	9 wks
11 Dec 93	**BRING ME YOUR CUP** DEP International DEPD 42	**24**	6 wks
2 Apr 94	**C'EST LA VIE** DEP International DEPD 43	**37**	3 wks
27 Aug 94	**REGGAE MUSIC** DEP International DEPDG 44	**28**	3 wks

[1] UB40 featuring Chrissie Hynde [2] Afrika Bambaataa with UB40 and Family [3] Robert Palmer and UB40 [4] 808 State vs UB40

UFO UK, male vocal / instrumental group — **31 wks**

5 Aug 78	**ONLY YOU CAN ROCK ME** Chrysalis CHS 2241	**50**	4 wks
27 Jan 79	**DOCTOR DOCTOR** Chrysalis CHS 2287	**35**	6 wks
31 Mar 79	**SHOOT SHOOT** Chrysalis CHS 2318	**48**	5 wks
12 Jan 80	**YOUNG BLOOD** Chrysalis CHS 2399	**36**	5 wks
17 Jan 81	**LONELY HEART** Chrysalis CHS 2482	**41**	5 wks
30 Jan 82	**LET IT RAIN** Chrysalis CHS 2576	**62**	3 wks
19 Mar 83	**WHEN IT'S TIME TO ROCK** Chrysalis CHS 2672	**70**	3 wks

U4EA featuring BERRI - See NEW ATLANTIC

UGLY KID JOE US, male vocal / instrumental group — **26 wks**

16 May 92	● **EVERYTHING ABOUT YOU** Mercury MER 367	**3**	9 wks
22 Aug 92	**NEIGHBOR** Mercury MER 374	**28**	4 wks
31 Oct 92	**SO DAMN COOL** Mercury MER 383	**44**	2 wks
13 Mar 93	● **CATS IN THE CRADLE** Mercury MERCD 385	**7**	9 wks
19 Jun 93	**BUSY BEE** Mercury MERCD 389	**39**	2 wks

UHF US, male instrumental / production group — **4 wks**

14 Dec 91	**UHF / EVERYTHING** XL XLS 25	**46**	4 wks

U.K. UK, male vocal / instrumental group — **2 wks**

30 Jun 79	**NOTHING TO LOSE** Polydor POSP 55	**67**	2 wks

U.K. APACHI with SHY FX
UK, male vocal / instrumental duo — **3 wks**

1 Oct 94	**ORIGINAL NUTTAH** Sound Of Underground SOUR 008CD	**39**	3 wks

U.K. MIXMASTERS UK, male producer - Nigel Wright **15 wks**

2 Feb 91	**THE NIGHT FEVER MEGAMIX** IQ ZB 44339 [1]	**23**	5 wks
27 Jul 91	**LUCKY 7 MEGAMIX** IQ ZB 44731	**43**	3 wks
7 Dec 91	**BARE NECESSITIES MEGAMIX** Connect ZB 35135	**14**	7 wks

[1] Mixmasters

U.K. PLAYERS UK, male vocal / instrumental group — **3 wks**

14 May 83	**LOVE'S GONNA GET YOU** RCA 326	**52**	3 wks

U.K. SUBS UK, male vocal / instrumental group — **39 wks**

23 Jun 79	**STRANGLEHOLD** Gem GEMS 5	**26**	8 wks

8 Sep 79	TOMORROW'S GIRLS Gem GEMS 10	28	6 wks
1 Dec 79	SHE'S NOT THERE / KICKS EP Gem GEMS 14	36	7 wks
8 Mar 80	WARHEAD Gem GEMS 23	30	4 wks
17 May 80	TEENAGE Gem GEMS 30	32	5 wks
25 Oct 80	PARTY IN PARIS Gem GEMS 42	37	4 wks
18 Apr 81	KEEP ON RUNNIN' (TILL YOU BURN) Gem GEMS 45	41	5 wks

Tracks on She's Not There / Kicks EP: She's Not There / Kicks / Victim / The Same Thing.

Tracey ULLMAN UK, female vocalist — 49 wks

19 Mar 83	● BREAKAWAY Stiff BUY 168	4	11 wks
24 Sep 83	● THEY DON'T KNOW Stiff BUY 180	2	11 wks
3 Dec 83	● MOVE OVER DARLING Stiff BUY 195	8	9 wks
3 Mar 84	MY GUY Stiff BUY 197	23	6 wks
28 Jul 84	SUNGLASSES Stiff BUY 205	18	9 wks
27 Oct 84	HELPLESS Stiff BUY 211	61	3 wks

ULTIMATE KAOS UK, male vocal group — 8 wks

| 22 Oct 94 | ● SOME GIRLS Wild Card CARDD 12 | 9 | 8 wks |

ULTRACYNIC UK, male / female vocal / instrumental group — 2 wks

| 29 Aug 92 | NOTHING IS FOREVER 380 PEW 2 | 50 | 2 wks |

ULTRA-SONIC UK, male instrumental / production duo — 1 wk

| 3 Sep 94 | OBSESSION Clubscene DCSRT 027 | 75 | 1 wk |

ULTRAMARINE UK, male instrumental duo — 3 wks

| 24 Jul 93 | KINGDOM blanco y negro NEG 65CD | 46 | 2 wks |
| 29 Jan 94 | BAREFOOT EP blanco y negro NEG 67CD | 61 | 1 wk |

Tracks on Barefoot EP: Hooter / The Badger / Urf / Happy Land.

ULTRAVOX UK / Canada, male vocal / instrumental group — 142 wks

5 Jul 80	SLEEPWALK Chrysalis CHS 2441	29	11 wks
18 Oct 80	PASSING STRANGERS Chrysalis CHS 2457	57	4 wks
17 Jan 81	● VIENNA Chrysalis CHS 2481	2	14 wks
28 Mar 81	SLOW MOTION Island WIP 6691	33	4 wks
6 Jun 81	● ALL STOOD STILL Chrysalis CHS 2522	8	10 wks
22 Aug 81	THE THIN WALL Chrysalis CHS 2540	14	8 wks
7 Nov 81	THE VOICE Chrysalis CHS 2559	16	12 wks
25 Sep 82	REAP THE WILD WIND Chrysalis CHS 2639	12	9 wks
27 Nov 82	HYMN Chrysalis CHS 2657	11	11 wks
19 Mar 83	VISIONS IN BLUE Chrysalis CHS 2676	15	6 wks
4 Jun 83	WE CAME TO DANCE Chrysalis VOX 1	18	7 wks
11 Feb 84	ONE SMALL DAY Chrysalis VOX 2	27	6 wks
19 May 84	● DANCING WITH TEARS IN MY EYES Chrysalis UV 1	3	10 wks
7 Jul 84	LAMENT Chrysalis UV 2	22	6 wks
4 Aug 84	DANCING WITH TEARS IN MY EYES (re-entry) Chrysalis UV 1	74	1 wk
25 Aug 84	LAMENT (re-entry) Chrysalis UV 2	73	1 wk
20 Oct 84	LOVE'S GREAT ADVENTURE Chrysalis UV 3	12	9 wks
27 Sep 86	SAME OLD STORY Chrysalis UV 4	31	4 wks
22 Nov 86	ALL FALL DOWN Chrysalis UV 5	30	5 wks
6 Feb 93	VIENNA (re-issue) Chrysalis CDCHSS 3936	13	4 wks

Piero UMILIANI Italy, orchestra and chorus — 8 wks

| 30 Apr 77 | ● MAH NA MAH NA EMI International INT 530 | 8 | 8 wks |

UNATION UK, male / female vocal / instrumental group — 3 wks

| 5 Jun 93 | HIGHER AND HIGHER MCA MCSTD 1773 | 42 | 2 wks |
| 7 Aug 93 | DO YOU BELIEVE IN LOVE MCA MCSTD 1796 | 75 | 1 wk |

UNCANNY ALLIANCE US, male / female vocal / instrumental duo — 5 wks

| 19 Dec 92 | I GOT MY EDUCATION A & M AM 0128 | 39 | 5 wks |

UNDERCOVER UK, male vocal / instrumental group — 29 wks

15 Aug 92	● BAKER STREET PWL International PWL 239	2	14 wks
14 Nov 92	● NEVER LET HER SLIP AWAY PWL International PWL 255	5	11 wks
6 Feb 93	I WANNA STAY WITH YOU PWL International PWCD 258	28	3 wks
14 Aug 93	LOVESICK PWL International PWCD 271 [1]	62	1 wk

[1] Undercover featuring John Matthews

UNDERTAKERS UK, male vocal / instrumental group — 1 wk

| 9 Apr 64 | JUST A LITTLE BIT Pye 7N 15607 | 49 | 1 wk |

UNDERTONES UK, male vocal / instrumental group — 67 wks

21 Oct 78	TEENAGE KICKS Sire SIR 4007	31	6 wks
3 Feb 79	GET OVER YOU Sire SIR 4010	57	4 wks
28 Apr 79	JIMMY JIMMY Sire SIR 4015	16	10 wks
21 Jul 79	HERE COMES THE SUMMER Sire SIR 4022	34	6 wks
20 Oct 79	YOU'VE GOT MY NUMBER (WHY DON'T YOU USE IT?) Sire SIR 4024	32	6 wks
5 Apr 80	● MY PERFECT COUSIN Sire SIR 4038	9	10 wks
5 Jul 80	WEDNESDAY WEEK Sire SIR 4042	11	9 wks
2 May 81	IT'S GOING TO HAPPEN! Ardeck AROS 8	18	9 wks
25 Jul 81	JULIE OCEAN Ardeck ARDS 9	41	5 wks
9 Jul 83	TEENAGE KICKS (re-issue) Ardeck ARDS 1	60	2 wks

UNDERWORLD UK, male instrumental group — 2 wks

| 18 Dec 93 | SPIKEE / DOGMAN GO Junior Boy's Own JBO 17CD | 63 | 1 wk |
| 25 Jun 94 | DARK AND LONG Junior Boy's Own JBO 19CDS | 57 | 1 wk |

UNDISPUTED TRUTH US, male / female vocal / instrumental group — 4 wks

| 22 Jan 77 | YOU + ME = LOVE Warner Bros. K 16804 | 43 | 4 wks |

U96 Germany, male producer - Alex Christiansen — 6 wks

| 29 Aug 92 | DAS BOOT M & G MAGS 28 | 18 | 5 wks |
| 4 Jun 94 | INSIDE YOUR DREAMS Logic 74321209722 | 44 | 1 wk |

UNION featuring the ENGLAND WORLD CUP SQUAD UK / Holland, male instrumental group with UK rugby team vocalists — 7 wks

| 12 Oct 91 | SWING LOW (RUN WITH THE BALL) Columbia 6575317 | 16 | 7 wks |

UNION GAP featuring Gary PUCKETT US, male vocal / instrumental group — 47 wks

17 Apr 68	★ YOUNG GIRL CBS 3365	1	17 wks
7 Aug 68	● LADY WILLPOWER CBS 3551	5	16 wks
28 Aug 68	WOMAN WOMAN CBS 3110 [1]	48	1 wk
15 Jun 74	● YOUNG GIRL CBS 8202 [1]	6	13 wks

[1] Gary Puckett and the Union Gap

UNIQUE US, male / female vocal / instrumental group — 7 wks

| 10 Sep 83 | WHAT I GOT IS WHAT YOU NEED Prelude A 3707 | 27 | 7 wks |

UNIQUE 3 UK, male rap / scratch group — 12 wks

| 4 Nov 89 | THE THEME 10 TEN 285 | 61 | 3 wks |
| 14 Apr 90 | MUSICAL MELODY / WEIGHT FOR THE BASS 10 TEN 298 | 29 | 5 wks |

| 10 Nov 90 | **RHYTHM TAKES CONTROL** 10 TEN 327 [1] ....41 | 3 wks |
| 16 Nov 91 | **NO MORE** 10 TEN 387 ....74 | 1 wk |

[1] Unique 3 featuring Karin

UNIT FOUR PLUS TWO
UK, male vocal / instrumental group **29 wks**

13 Feb 64	**GREEN FIELDS** Decca F 11821 48	2 wks
25 Feb 65	**CONCRETE AND CLAY** Decca F 12071 1	15 wks
13 May 65	**YOU'VE NEVER BEEN IN LOVE LIKE THIS BEFORE** Decca F 12144 14	11 wks
17 Mar 66	**BABY NEVER SAY GOODBYE** Decca F 12333...........49	1 wk

UNITED KINGDOM SYMPHONY *UK, orchestra* **4 wks**

| 27 Jul 85 | **SHADES (THEME FROM THE CROWN PAINT TELEVISION COMMERCIAL)** Food For Thought YUM 108 ....68 | 4 wks |

UNITONE - *See Laurel AITKEN and the UNITONE*

UNITONE ROCKERS featuring STEEL
UK, male vocal / instrumental group **1 wk**

| 26 Jun 93 | **CHILDREN OF THE REVOLUTION** The Hit Label HLC 4 ....60 | 1 wk |

UNITY *UK, male / female vocal / instrumental group* **2 wks**

| 31 Aug 91 | **UNITY** Cardiac CNY 6 ....64 | 2 wks |

UNTOUCHABLES *US, male vocal / instrumental group* **16 wks**

| 6 Apr 85 | **FREE YOURSELF** Stiff BUY 221 ....26 | 11 wks |
| 27 Jul 85 | **I SPY FOR THE FBI** Stiff BUY 227 ....59 | 5 wks |

Phil UPCHURCH COMBO
US, male instrumental group, Phil Upchurch bass guitar **2 wks**

| 5 May 66 | **YOU CAN'T SIT DOWN** Sue WI 4005 ....39 | 2 wks |

UPSETTERS *Jamaica, male instrumental group* **15 wks**

| 4 Oct 69 | ● **RETURN OF DJANGO / DOLLAR IN THE TEETH** Upsetter US 301 ....5 | 15 wks |

URBAN ALL STARS
UK, male / female vocal / instrumental group **2 wks**

| 27 Aug 88 | **IT BEGAN IN AFRICA** Urban URB 23 ....64 | 2 wks |

URBAN COOKIE COLLECTIVE
UK, male / female vocal / instrumental group **33 wks**

10 Jul 93	● **THE KEY THE SECRET** Pulse 8 CDLOSE 48 2	16 wks
13 Nov 93	● **FEELS LIKE HEAVEN** Pulse 8 CDLOSE 55 5	9 wks
19 Feb 94	**SAIL AWAY** Pulse 8 CDLOSE 56 18	4 wks
23 Apr 94	**HIGH ON A HAPPY VIBE** Pulse 8 CDLOSE 60 31	3 wks
15 Oct 94	**BRING IT ON HOME** Pulse 8 CDLOSE 73 56	1 wk

URBAN HYPE *UK, male production / instrumental group* **12 wks**

11 Jul 92	● **A TRIP TO TRUMPTON** Faze 2 FAZE 5 6	8 wks
17 Oct 92	**THE FEELING** Faze 2 FAZE 10 67	1 wk
9 Jan 93	**LIVING IN A FANTASY** Faze 2 CDFAZE 13 57	3 wks

URBAN SHAKEDOWN featuring Micky FINN
UK / Italy, male vocal / instrumental group **7 wks**

| 27 Jun 92 | **SOME JUSTICE** Urban Shakedown URBST 1 ....23 | 5 wks |
| 12 Sep 92 | **BASS SHAKE** Urban Shakedown URBST 2...........59 | 2 wks |

URBAN SOUL *US, male producer - Roland Clarke* **10 wks**

30 Mar 91	**ALRIGHT** Cooltempo COOL 231 60	4 wks
21 Sep 91	**ALRIGHT (re-mix)** Cooltempo COOL 244 43	3 wks
28 Mar 92	**ALWAYS** Cooltempo COOL 251 41	3 wks

URBAN SPECIES *UK, male vocal / instrumental group* **9 wks**

12 Feb 94	**SPIRITUAL LOVE** Talkin Loud TLKCD 45 35	4 wks
16 Apr 94	**BROTHER** Talkin Loud TLKCD 47 40	3 wks
20 Aug 94	**LISTEN** Talkin Loud TLKCD 50 [1] 47	2 wks

[1] Urban Species featuring MC Solaar

Midge URE *UK, male vocalist* **55 wks**

12 Jun 82	● **NO REGRETS** Chrysalis CHS 2618 9	10 wks
9 Jul 83	**AFTER A FASHION** Musicfest FEST 1 [1] 39	4 wks
14 Sep 85	★ **IF I WAS** Chrysalis URE 1 1	11 wks
16 Nov 85	**THAT CERTAIN SMILE** Chrysalis URE 2 28	4 wks
8 Feb 86	**WASTELANDS** Chrysalis URE 3 46	3 wks
7 Jun 86	**CALL OF THE WILD** Chrysalis URE 4 27	8 wks
20 Aug 88	**ANSWERS TO NOTHING** Chrysalis URE 5 49	4 wks
19 Nov 88	**DEAR GOD** Chrysalis URE 6 55	4 wks
17 Aug 91	**COLD COLD HEART** Arista 114555...............17	7 wks

[1] Midge Ure and Mick Karn

URGE OVERKILL *US, male vocal / instrumental group* **6 wks**

21 Aug 93	**SISTER HAVANA** Geffen GFSTD 51 67	1 wk
16 Oct 93	**POSITIVE BLEEDING** Geffen GFSTD 57 61	1 wk
19 Nov 94	**GIRL YOU'LL BE A WOMAN SOON** MCA MCSTD 2024 37	4 wks

US3 *UK, male instrumental / production duo* **13 wks**

10 Jul 93	**RIDDIM** Blue Note CDCL 686 [1] 34	6 wks
25 Sep 93	**CANTALOOP** Blue Note CDCL 696 [2] 23	5 wks
28 May 94	**I GOT IT GOIN' ON** Blue Note CDCL 708 [3] 52	2 wks

[1] Us3 featuring Tukka Yoot [2] Us3 featuring Rahsaan [3] Us3 featuring Kobie Powell and Rahsaan

USA FOR AFRICA *US, male / female vocal group* **9 wks**

| 13 Apr 85 | ★ **WE ARE THE WORLD** CBS USAID 1 ....1 | 9 wks |

USURA *Italy, male / female vocal / instrumental group* **12 wks**

| 23 Jan 93 | ● **OPEN YOUR MIND** Deconstruction 74321128042 ......7 | 9 wks |
| 10 Jul 93 | **SWEAT** Deconstruction 74321154602...............29 | 3 wks |

UTAH SAINTS *UK, male instrumental / production duo* **33 wks**

24 Aug 91	● **WHAT CAN YOU DO FOR ME** ffrr F 164 10	11 wks
6 Jun 92	● **SOMETHING GOOD** ffrr F 187 4	9 wks
8 May 93	● **BELIEVE IN ME** ffrr FCD 209 8	6 wks
17 Jul 93	**I WANT YOU** ffrr FCD 213 25	5 wks
25 Jun 94	**I STILL THINK OF YOU** ffrr FCD 225 32	2 wks

U2 *Ireland, male vocal / instrumental group* **153 wks**

8 Aug 81	**FIRE** Island WIP 6679 35	6 wks
17 Oct 81	**GLORIA** Island WIP 6733 55	4 wks
3 Apr 82	**A CELEBRATION** Island WIP 6770 47	4 wks
22 Jan 83	● **NEW YEARS DAY** Island IS 109 10	8 wks
2 Apr 83	**TWO HEARTS BEAT AS ONE** Island IS 109 18	5 wks
15 Sep 84	● **PRIDE (IN THE NAME OF LOVE)** Island IS 202 3	11 wks
4 May 85	● **THE UNFORGETTABLE FIRE** Island IS 220 6	6 wks
28 Mar 87	● **WITH OR WITHOUT YOU** Island IS 319 4	11 wks
6 Jun 87	● **I STILL HAVEN'T FOUND WHAT I'M LOOKING FOR** Island IS 328 6	11 wks
12 Sep 87	● **WHERE THE STREETS HAVE NO NAME** Island IS 340 4	6 wks

26 Dec 87	**IN GOD'S COUNTRY (IMPORT)** *Island 7-99385* **48**	4 wks
1 Oct 88	★ **DESIRE** *Island IS 400* **1**	8 wks
17 Dec 88	● **ANGEL OF HARLEM** *Island IS 402* **9**	6 wks
15 Apr 89	● **WHEN LOVE COMES TO TOWN** *Island IS 411* [1] **6**	7 wks
24 Jun 89	● **ALL I WANT IS YOU** *Island IS 422* **4**	6 wks
2 Nov 91	★ **THE FLY** *Island IS 500* **1**	5 wks
14 Dec 91	**MYSTERIOUS WAYS** *Island IS 509* **13**	7 wks
4 Jan 92	**THE FLY (re-entry)** *Island IS 500* **62**	1 wk
7 Mar 92	● **ONE** *Island IS 515* **7**	6 wks
20 Jun 92	**EVEN BETTER THAN THE REAL THING** *Island IS 525* **12**	7 wks
11 Jul 92	● **EVEN BETTER THAN THE REAL THING (re-mix)** *Island REAL U2* **8**	7 wks
5 Dec 92	**WHO'S GONNA RIDE YOUR WILD HORSES** *Island IS 550* **14**	8 wks
4 Dec 93	● **STAY (FARAWAY, SO CLOSE)** *Island CID 578* **4**	9 wks

[1] U2 featuring B.B. King

Stay (Faraway, So Close) was listed with I've Got You Under My Skin by Frank Sinatra with Bono, which was featured on many but not all formats.

VAGABONDS - *See Jimmy JAMES and the VAGABONDS*

Ricky VALANCE *UK, male vocalist* | **16 wks**

25 Aug 60	★ **TELL LAURA I LOVE HER** *Columbia DB 4493* **1**	16 wks

Ritchie VALENS *US, male vocalist* | **5 wks**

6 Mar 59	**DONNA** *London HL 8803* **29**	1 wk
1 Aug 87	**LA BAMBA** *RCA PB 41435* **49**	4 wks

Caterina VALENTE *France, female vocalist* | **14 wks**

19 Aug 55	● **THE BREEZE AND I** *Polydor BM 6002* **5**	14 wks

Dickie VALENTINE *UK, male vocalist* | **92 wks**

20 Feb 53	**BROKEN WINGS** *Decca F 9954* **12**	1 wk
13 Mar 53	● **ALL THE TIME AND EVERYWHERE** *Decca F 10038* **9**	3 wks
5 Jun 53	● **IN A GOLDEN COACH** *Decca F 10098* **7**	1 wk
5 Nov 54	**ENDLESS** *Decca F 10346* **19**	1 wk
17 Dec 54	● **MR. SANDMAN** *Decca F 10415* **5**	12 wks
17 Dec 54	★ **FINGER OF SUSPICION** *Decca F 10394* [1] **1**	15 wks
18 Feb 55	● **A BLOSSOM FELL** *Decca F 10430* **9**	9 wks
29 Apr 55	**A BLOSSOM FELL (re-entry)** *Decca F 10430* **18**	1 wk
3 Jun 55	● **I WONDER** *Decca F 10493* **4**	15 wks
25 Nov 55	★ **CHRISTMAS ALPHABET** *Decca F 10628* **1**	7 wks
16 Dec 55	**OLD PIANNA RAG** *Decca F 10645* **15**	5 wks
7 Dec 56	● **CHRISTMAS ISLAND** *Decca F 10798* **8**	5 wks
27 Dec 57	**SNOWBOUND FOR CHRISTMAS** *Decca F 10950* **28**	1 wk
13 Mar 59	**VENUS** *Pye Nixa 7N 15192* **28**	1 wk
3 Apr 59	**VENUS (re-entry)** *Pye Nixa 7N 15192* **25**	1 wk
17 Apr 59	**VENUS (2nd re-entry)** *Pye Nixa 7N 15192* **20**	4 wks
22 May 59	**VENUS (3rd re-entry)** *Pye Nixa 7N 15192* **25**	1 wk
19 Jun 59	**VENUS (4th re-entry)** *Pye Nixa 7N 15192* **28**	1 wk
23 Oct 59	**ONE MORE SUNRISE (MORGEN)** *Pye 7N 15221* **14**	8 wks

[1] Dickie Valentine with the Stargazers

See also Various Artists (EPs & LPs) - All Star Hit Parade.

VALENTINE BROTHERS *US, male vocal duo* | **1 wk**

23 Apr 83	**MONEY'S TOO TIGHT (TO MENTION)** *Energy NRG 1* **73**	1 wk

Joe VALINO *US, male vocalist* | **2 wks**

18 Jan 57	**GARDEN OF EDEN** *HMV POP 283* **23**	2 wks

Frankie VALLI *US, male vocalist* | **52 wks**

12 Dec 70	**YOU'RE READY NOW** *Philips 320226* **11**	13 wks
1 Feb 75	● **MY EYES ADORED YOU** *Private Stock PVT 1* **5**	11 wks
21 Jun 75	**SWEARIN' TO GOD** *Private Stock PVT 21* **31**	5 wks
17 Apr 76	**FALLEN ANGEL** *Private Stock PVT 51* **11**	7 wks
26 Aug 78	● **GREASE** *RSO 012* **3**	14 wks
23 Mar 91	**GREASE – THE DREAM MIX** [1] *PO 136* **47**	2 wks

[1] Frankie Vallit, John Travolta and Olivia Newton-John

See also Four Seasons.

David VAN DAY *UK, male vocalist* | **3 wks**

14 May 83	**YOUNG AMERICANS TALKING** *WEA DAY 1* **43**	3 wks

George VAN DUSEN *UK, male vocalist* | **4 wks**

17 Dec 88	**IT'S PARTY TIME AGAIN** *Bri-Tone 7BT 001* **43**	4 wks

Leroy VAN DYKE *US, male vocalist* | **20 wks**

4 Jan 62	● **WALK ON BY** *Mercury AMT 1166* **5**	17 wks
26 Apr 62	**BIG MAN IN A BIG HOUSE** *Mercury AMT 1173* **34**	3 wks

VAN HALEN
US / Holland, male vocal / instrumental group | **47 wks**

28 Jun 80	**RUNNIN' WITH THE DEVIL** *Warner Bros. HM 10* **52**	3 wks
4 Feb 84	● **JUMP** *Warner Bros. W 9384* **7**	13 wks
19 May 84	**PANAMA** *Warner Bros. W 9273* **61**	2 wks
5 Apr 86	● **WHY CAN'T THIS BE LOVE** *Warner Bros. W 8740* **8**	14 wks
12 Jul 86	**DREAMS** *Warner Bros. W 8642* **62**	2 wks
6 Aug 88	**WHEN IT'S LOVE** *Warner Bros. W 7816* **28**	7 wks
1 Apr 89	**FEELS SO GOOD** *Warner Bros. W 7565* **63**	1 wk
22 Jun 91	**POUNDCAKE** *Warner Bros. W 0045* **74**	1 wk
19 Oct 91	**TOP OF THE WORLD** *Warner Bros. W 0066* **63**	1 wk
27 Mar 93	**JUMP (LIVE)** *Warner Bros. W 0155CD* **26**	3 wks

VAN TWIST
Zaire / Belgium, male / female vocal / instrumental group | **2 wks**

16 Feb 85	**SHAFT** *Polydor POSP 729* **57**	2 wks

VANDELLAS - *See Martha REEVES and the VANDELLAS*

Luther VANDROSS *US, male vocalist* | **114 wks**

19 Feb 83	**NEVER TOO MUCH** *Epic EPC A 3101* **44**	6 wks
26 Jul 86	**GIVE ME THE REASON** *Epic A 7288* **60**	3 wks
21 Feb 87	**GIVE ME THE REASON (re-issue)** *Epic 650216 7* **71**	2 wks
28 Mar 87	**SEE ME** *Epic LUTH 1* **60**	4 wks
11 Jul 87	**I REALLY DIDN'T MEAN IT** *Epic LUTH 3* **16**	10 wks
5 Sep 87	**STOP TO LOVE** *Epic LUTH 2* **24**	7 wks
7 Nov 87	**SO AMAZING** *Epic LUTH 4* **28**	6 wks
23 Jan 88	**GIVE ME THE REASON (2nd re-issue)** *Epic LUTH 5* **26**	6 wks
16 Apr 88	**I GAVE IT UP (WHEN I FELL IN LOVE)** *Epic LUTH 6* **28**	5 wks
9 Jul 88	**THERE'S NOTHING BETTER THAN LOVE** *Epic LUTH 7* [1] **72**	1 wk
8 Oct 88	**ANY LOVE** *Epic LUTH 8* **31**	4 wks
4 Feb 89	**SHE WON'T TALK TO ME** *Epic LUTH 9* **34**	4 wks
22 Apr 89	**COME BACK** *Epic LUTH 10* **53**	3 wks
28 Oct 89	**NEVER TOO MUCH (re-mix)** *Epic LUTH 12* **13**	7 wks
6 Jan 90	**HERE AND NOW** *Epic LUTH 13* **43**	3 wks
27 Apr 91	**POWER OF LOVE - LOVE POWER** *Epic 6568227* **46**	5 wks
18 Jan 92	**THE RUSH** *Epic 6577237* **53**	3 wks
15 Aug 92	● **THE BEST THINGS IN LIFE ARE FREE** *Perspective PERSS 7400* [2] **2**	13 wks
22 May 93	**LITTLE MIRACLES (HAPPEN EVERY DAY)** *Epic 6590442* **28**	3 wks
18 Sep 93	**HEAVEN KNOWS** *Epic 6596522* **34**	3 wks
4 Dec 93	**LOVE IS ON THE WAY** *Epic 6599592* **38**	2 wks
17 Sep 94	● **ENDLESS LOVE** *Epic 6608062* [3] **3**	10 wks

26 Nov 94	**LOVE THE ONE YOU'RE WITH** *Epic 6610612* **31**	4 wks

1 Luther Vandross, duet with Gregory Hines 2 Luther Vandross and Janet Jackson with special guests BBD and Ralph Tresvant 3 Luther Vandross and Mariah Carey

VANGELIS *Greece, male instrumentalist - keyboards*   **25 wks**

9 May 81	**CHARIOTS OF FIRE - TITLES** *Polydor POSP 246* **12**	10 wks
11 Jul 81	**HEAVEN AND HELL, THIRD MOVEMENT (THEME FROM THE BBC-TV SERIES, THE COSMOS)** *BBC 1* **48**	6 wks
24 Apr 82	**CHARIOTS OF FIRE - TITLES (re-entry)** *Polydor POSP 246* **41**	7 wks
31 Oct 92	**CONQUEST OF PARADISE** *East West YZ 704* **60**	2 wks

See also Jon and Vangelis.

VANILLA FUDGE *US, male vocal / instrumental group*   **11 wks**

9 Aug 67	**YOU KEEP ME HANGIN' ON** *Atlantic 584 123* **18**	11 wks

VANILLA ICE *US, male rapper*   **32 wks**

24 Nov 90	★ **ICE ICE BABY** *SBK SBK 18* **1**	13 wks
2 Feb 91	● **PLAY THAT FUNKY MUSIC** *SBK SBK 20* **10**	6 wks
30 Mar 91	**I LOVE YOU** *SBK SBK 22* **45**	5 wks
29 Jun 91	**ROLLIN' IN MY 5.0** *SBK SBK 27* **27**	4 wks
10 Aug 91	**SATISFACTION** *SBK SBK 29*.............**22**	4 wks

VANITY FARE *UK, male vocal / instrumental group*   **34 wks**

28 Aug 68	**I LIVE FOR THE SUN** *Page One POF 075* **20**	9 wks
23 Jul 69	● **EARLY IN THE MORNING** *Page One POF 142*.............**8**	12 wks
27 Dec 69	**HITCHIN' A RIDE** *Page One POF 158* **16**	13 wks

Randy VANWARMER *US, male vocalist*   **11 wks**

4 Aug 79	● **JUST WHEN I NEEDED YOU MOST** *Bearsville WIP 6516* **8**	11 wks

VAPORS *UK, male vocal / instrumental group*   **23 wks**

9 Feb 80	● **TURNING JAPANESE** *United Artists BP 334* **3**	13 wks
5 Jul 80	**NEWS AT TEN** *United Artists BP 345* **44**	4 wks
11 Jul 81	**JIMMIE JONES** *Liberty BP 401* **44**	6 wks

VARDIS *UK, male vocal / instrumental group*   **4 wks**

27 Sep 80	**LET'S GO** *Logo VAR 1* **59**	4 wks

VARIOUS ARTISTS (EPs and LPs)   **35 wks**

15 Jun 56	**CAROUSEL - ORIGINAL SOUNDTRACK** (LP) *Capitol LCT 6105* **27**	1 wk
29 Jun 56	● **ALL STAR HIT PARADE** *Decca F 10752* **2**	9 wks
6 Jul 56	**CAROUSEL - ORIGINAL SOUNDTRACK** (LP) (re-entry)*Capitol LCT 6105* **26**	1 wk
26 Jul 57	**ALL STAR HIT PARADE NO. 2** *Decca F 10915*...........**15**	7 wks
9 Dec 89	**THE FOOD CHRISTMAS EP** *Food FOOD 23*..............**63**	1 wk
20 Jan 90	**THE FURTHER ADVENTURES OF NORTH EP** *Deconstruction PT 43372* **64**	2 wks
2 Nov 91	**THE APPLE EP** *Apple APP 1* **60**	1 wk
11 Jul 92	**FOURPLAY EP** *XL XLFP 1* **45**	2 wks
7 Nov 92	**THE FRED EP** *Heavenly HVN 19* **26**	3 wks
24 Apr 93	**GIMME SHELTER (EP)** *Food CDORDERA 1* **23**	4 wks

5 Jun 93	**SUBPLATES VOLUME 1 EP** *Suburban Base SUBBASE 24CD* **69**	1 wk
9 Oct 93	**THE TWO TONE EP** *2 Tone CHSTT 31* **30**	3 wks

Tracks and artists on Carousel are as follows: Carousel Waltz - Orchestra conducted by Alfred Newman; You're A Queer One Julie Jordan - Barbara Ruick and Shirley Jones; Mister Snow - Barbara Ruick; If I Loved You - Shirley Jones and Gordon MacRae; June Is Busting Out All Over - Claramae Turner; Soliloquy - Gordon MacRae; Blow High Blow Low - Cameron Mitchell; When The Children Are Asleep - Robert Rounseville and Barbara Ruick; This Was A Real Nice Clambake - Barbara Ruick, Claramae Turner, Robert Rounseville and Cameron Mitchell; Stonecutters Cut It On Stone (There's Nothing So Bad For A Woman) - Cameron Mitchell; What's The Use of Wonderin' - Shirley Jones; You'll Never Walk Alone - Claramae Turner; If I Loved You - Gordon MacRae; You'll Never Walk Alone - Shirley Jones. Tracks on All Star Hit Parade: Theme From the Threepenny Opera - Winifred Atwell; No Other Love - Dave King; My September Love - Joan Regan; A Tear Fell - Lita Roza; Out Of Town - Dickie Valentine; It's Almost Tomorrow - David Whitfield. Tracks on All Star Hit Parade No. 2: Around The World - Johnston Brothers; Puttin' On The Style - Billy Cotton; When I Fall In Love - Jimmy Young; A White Sport Coat - Max Bygraves; Freight Train - Beverley Sisters; Butterfly - Tommy Steele. Tracks on The Food Christmas EP: Like Princes Do - Crazyhead; I Don't Want That Kind Of Love - Jesus Jones; Info Freako - Diesel Park West. Tracks on The Further Adventures of North EP: Dream 17 - Annette; Carino 90 - T-Coy; The Way I Feel - Frequency 9; Stop This Thing - Dynasty Of Two featuring Rowetta. Tracks on The Apple EP: Those Were The Days - Mary Hopkin; That's The Way God Planned It - Billy Preston; Sour Milk Sea - Jackie Lomax; Come And Get It - Badfinger. Tracks on Fourplay EP: DJs Unite - DJs Unite; Alright - Glide; Be Free - Noise Factory; True Devotion - EQ. Tracks on The Fred EP: Deeply Dippy - Rockingbirds; Don't Talk Just Kiss - Flowered Up; I'm Too Sexy - Saint Etienne. Gimme Shelter (EP) was available on four formats, each featuring an interview with the featured artist plus the following artists performing versions of Gimme Shelter: (cassette) Jimmy Somerville and Voice Of The Beehive; Heaven 17; (12-inch) Blue Pearl, 808 State and Robert Owens; Pop Will Eat Itself vs Gary Clail; Ranking Roger and the Mighty Diamonds; (CD) Thunder; Little Angels; Hawkwind and Sam Fox; (2nd CD) Cud with Sandie Shaw; Kingmaker; New Model Army and Tom Jones. Tracks on Subplates Volume 1 EP: Style Warz - Son'z Of A Loop Da Loop Era; Funky Dope Track - A-Bass; The Chopper - DJ Hype; Look No Further - Run Tings. Tracks on the Two Tone EP: Gangsters - Special AKA; The Prince - Madness; On My Radio - Selecter; Tears Of A Clown - Beat.

VARIOUS ARTISTS (MONTAGES)   **31 wks**

17 May 80	**CALIBRE CUTS** *Calibre CAB 502* **75**	2 wks
25 Nov 89	**DEEP HEAT '89** *Deep Heat DEEP 10*...............**12**	11 wks
3 Mar 90	● **THE BRITS 1990** *RCA PB 43565*...............**2**	7 wks
28 Apr 90	**THE SIXTH SENSE** *Deep Heat DEEP 12* **49**	2 wks
10 Nov 90	**TIME TO MAKE THE FLOOR BURN** *Megabass MEGAX 1* **16**	9 wks

The following tracks are sampled:

Calibre Cuts: *Big Apples Rock - Black Ivory; Don't Hold Back - Chanson; The River Drive - Jupiter Beyond; Dancing In The Disco - LAX; Mellow Mellow Right On - Lowrell; Pata Pata - Osibisa; I Like It - Players Association; We Got The Funk - Positive Force; Holdin' On - Tony Rallo and the Midnight Band; Can You Feel The Force - Real Thing; Miami Heatwave - Seventh Avenue; Rappers Delight - Sugarhill Gang; Que Tal America - Two Man Sound; Remakes by session musicians: Ain't No Stoppin' Us Now, Bad Girls, We Are Family, Deep Heat '89 (credited to Latino Rave): Pump Up The Jam - Technotronic; Stakker Humanoid - Humanoid; A Day In The Life - Black Riot; Work It To The Bone - LNR; I Can Make U Dance - DJ 'Fast' Eddie; Voodoo Ray - A Guy Called Gerald; Numero Uno - Starlight; Bango (To The Batmobile) - Todd Terry; Break 4 Love - Raze; Don't Scandalize Mine - Sugar Bear*

The Brits 1990: *Street Tuff - Double Trouble and the Rebel MC; Voodoo Ray - A Guy Called Gerald; Theme From S Express - S Express; Hey DJ I Can't Dance To That Music You're Playing - Beatmasters; Eve Of The War - Jeff Wayne; Pacific State - 808 State; We Call It Acieed - D Mob; Got To Keep On - Cookie Crew*

The Sixth Sense (credited to Latino Rave): *Get Up - Technotronic; The Magic Number - De La Soul; G'Ding G'Ding (Do You Wanna Wanna) - Anna G; Show 'M The Bass - MC Miker G; Turn It Out (Go Base) - Rob Base; Eve Of The War (War Of The Worlds) - Project D; Moments In Love - 2 To The Power*

Time To Make The Floor Burn (credited to Megabass): *Do This My Way -*

Kid 'N' Play; Street Tuff - Double Trouble and the Rebel MC; Sex 4 Daze - Lake Eerie; Ride On Time - Black Box; Make My Body Rock - Jomanda; Don't Miss The Partyline - Bizz Nizz; Pump Pump It Up - Hypnotek; Big Fun - Inner City; Pump That Body - Mr Lee; Pump Up The Jam - Technotronic; This Beat Is Technotronic - Technotronic; Get Busy - Mr Lee; Touch Me - 49ers; Thunderbirds Are Go - FAB

Elaine VASSELL - See BEATMASTERS

Sven VÄTH   Germany, male producer   **5 wks**

24 Jul 93	L'ESPERANZA *Eye Q YZ 757*	**63**	2 wks
6 Nov 93	AN ACCIDENT IN PARADISE *Eye Q YZ 778CD*	**57**	2 wks
22 Oct 94	HARLEQUIN - THE BEAUTY AND THE BEAST *Eye Q YZ 857*	**72**	1 wk

Frankie VAUGHAN   UK, male vocalist   **232 wks**

29 Jan 54	ISTANBUL *HMV B 10599*	**11**	1 wk
28 Jan 55	HAPPY DAYS AND LONELY NIGHTS *HMV B 10783*	**12**	3 wks
22 Apr 55	TWEEDLE DEE *Philips PB 423*	**17**	1 wk
2 Dec 55	SEVENTEEN *Philips PB 511*	**18**	3 wks
3 Feb 56	MY BOY FLAT TOP *Philips PB 544*	**20**	2 wks
9 Nov 56	● GREEN DOOR *Philips PB 640*	**2**	15 wks
11 Jan 57	★ GARDEN OF EDEN *Philips PB 660*	**1**	13 wks
4 Oct 57	● MAN ON FIRE / WANDERIN' EYES *Philips PB 729*	**6**	12 wks
1 Nov 57	● GOTTA HAVE SOMETHING IN THE BANK FRANK *Philips PB 751* [1]	**8**	11 wks
20 Dec 57	● KISSES SWEETER THAN WINE *Philips PB 775*	**8**	11 wks
7 Mar 58	CAN'T GET ALONG WITHOUT YOU / WE ARE NOT ALONE *Philips PB 793*	**11**	6 wks
9 May 58	● KEWPIE DOLL *Philips PB 825*	**10**	12 wks
1 Aug 58	WONDERFUL THINGS *Philips PB 834*	**22**	3 wks
12 Sep 58	WONDERFUL THINGS (re-entry) *Philips PB 834*	**27**	3 wks
10 Oct 58	AM I WASTING MY TIME ON YOU *Philips PB 865*	**25**	2 wks
9 Jan 59	AM I WASTING MY TIME ON YOU (re-entry) *Philips PB 865*	**27**	2 wks
30 Jan 59	THAT'S MY DOLL *Philips PB 895*	**28**	2 wks
1 May 59	● COME SOFTLY TO ME *Philips PB 913* [1]	**9**	9 wks
24 Jul 59	● THE HEART OF A MAN *Philips PB 930*	**5**	14 wks
18 Sep 59	WALKIN' TALL *Philips PB 931*	**28**	1 wk
2 Oct 59	WALKIN' TALL (re-entry) *Philips PB 931*	**29**	1 wk
29 Jan 60	WHAT MORE DO YOU WANT *Philips PB 985*	**25**	2 wks
22 Sep 60	KOOKIE LITTLE PARADISE *Philips PB 1054*	**31**	5 wks
27 Oct 60	MILORD *Philips PB 1066*	**34**	6 wks
9 Nov 61	★ TOWER OF STRENGTH *Philips PB 1195*	**1**	13 wks
1 Feb 62	DON'T STOP TWIST *Philips 1219*	**22**	7 wks
27 Sep 62	HERCULES *Philips 326542 BF*	**42**	4 wks
24 Jan 63	● LOOP-DE-LOOP *Philips 326566 BF*	**5**	12 wks
20 Jun 63	HEY MAMA *Philips BF 1254*	**21**	9 wks
4 Jun 64	HELLO DOLLY *Philips BF 1339*	**18**	11 wks
11 Mar 65	SOMEONE MUST HAVE HURT YOU A LOT *Philips BF 1394*	**46**	1 wk
23 Aug 67	● THERE MUST BE A WAY *Columbia DB 8248*	**7**	21 wks
15 Nov 67	SO TIRED *Columbia DB 8298*	**21**	9 wks
28 Feb 68	NEVERTHELESS *Columbia DB 8354*	**29**	5 wks

[1] Frankie Vaughan and the Kaye Sisters

Malcolm VAUGHAN   UK, male vocalist   **106 wks**

1 Jul 55	● EVERY DAY OF MY LIFE *HMV B 10874*	**5**	16 wks
27 Jan 56	WITH YOUR LOVE *HMV POP 130*	**20**	1 wk
10 Feb 56	WITH YOUR LOVE (re-entry) *HMV POP 130*	**18**	1 wk
2 Mar 56	WITH YOUR LOVE (2nd re-entry) *HMV POP 130*	**20**	1 wk
26 Oct 56	ST. THERESE OF THE ROSES *HMV POP 250*	**27**	1 wk
16 Nov 56	● ST. THERESE OF THE ROSES (re-entry) *HMV POP 250*	**3**	19 wks
12 Apr 57	THE WORLD IS MINE *HMV POP 303*	**30**	1 wk
3 May 57	THE WORLD IS MINE (re-entry) *HMV POP 303*	**29**	2 wks
10 May 57	CHAPEL OF THE ROSES *HMV POP 325*	**13**	8 wks
31 May 57	THE WORLD IS MINE (2nd re-entry) *HMV POP 303*	**26**	1 wk
29 Nov 57	● MY SPECIAL ANGEL *HMV POP 419*	**3**	14 wks

21 Mar 58	TO BE LOVED *HMV POP 459* [1]	**14**	12 wks
17 Oct 58	● MORE THAN EVER (COME PRIMA) *HMV POP 538* [1]	**5**	14 wks
27 Feb 59	WAIT FOR ME / WILLINGLY *HMV POP 590*	**28**	1 wk
13 Mar 59	WAIT FOR ME (re-entry) *HMV POP 590*	**13**	14 wks

[1] Malcolm Vaughan with the Michael Sammes Singers

Norman VAUGHAN   UK, male vocalist   **5 wks**

17 May 62	SWINGING IN THE RAIN *Pye 7N 15438*	**34**	5 wks

Sarah VAUGHAN   US, female vocalist   **34 wks**

27 Sep 57	PASSING STRANGERS *Mercury MT 164* [1]	**22**	2 wks
11 Sep 59	● BROKEN HEARTED MELODY *Mercury AMT 1057*	**7**	13 wks
29 Dec 60	LET'S / SERENATA *Columbia DB 4542*	**37**	3 wks
2 Feb 61	LET'S / SERENATA (re-entry) *Columbia DB 4542*	**47**	1 wk
12 Mar 69	PASSING STRANGERS (re-issue) *Mercury MF 1082* [1]	**20**	15 wks

[1] Billy Eckstine and Sarah Vaughan

Billy VAUGHN   US, orchestra and chorus   **8 wks**

27 Jan 56	SHIFTING WHISPERING SANDS *London HLD 8205* [1]	**20**	1 wk
23 Mar 56	THEME FROM THE 'THREEPENNY OPERA' *London HLD 8238*	**12**	7 wks

[1] Billy Vaughn Orchestra and Chorus, narration by Ken Nordene

VDC - See BLAST featuring VDC

Bobby VEE   US, male vocalist   **134 wks**

19 Jan 61	● RUBBER BALL *London HLG 9255*	**4**	11 wks
13 Apr 61	● MORE THAN I CAN SAY / STAYING IN *London HLG 9316*	**4**	16 wks
3 Aug 61	● HOW MANY TEARS *London HLG 9389*	**10**	13 wks
26 Oct 61	● TAKE GOOD CARE OF MY BABY *London HLG 9438*	**3**	16 wks
21 Dec 61	● RUN TO HIM *London HLG 9470*	**6**	15 wks
8 Mar 62	PLEASE DON'T ASK ABOUT BARBARA *Liberty LIB 55419*	**29**	9 wks
7 Jun 62	● SHARING YOU *Liberty LIB 55451*	**10**	13 wks
27 Sep 62	A FOREVER KIND OF LOVE *Liberty LIB 10046*	**13**	19 wks
7 Feb 63	● THE NIGHT HAS A THOUSAND EYES *Liberty LIB 10069*	**3**	12 wks
20 Jun 63	BOBBY TOMORROW *Liberty LIB 55530*	**21**	10 wks

Staying In *listed with* More Than I Can Say *from 13 Apr to 4 May 61. It peaked at position 13.*

Louie VEGA and Marc ANTHONY
US, male vocal / instrumental duo   **2 wks**

5 Oct 91	RIDE ON THE RHYTHM *Atlantic A 7602* [1]	**71**	1 wk
23 May 92	RIDE ON THE RHYTHM (re-issue) *Atlantic A 7486*	**70**	1 wk

[1] Little Louie Vega and Marc Anthony

Suzanne VEGA   US, female vocalist   **51 wks**

18 Jan 86	SMALL BLUE THING *A & M AM 294*	**65**	3 wks
22 Mar 86	MARLENE ON THE WALL *A & M AM 309*	**21**	9 wks
7 Jun 86	LEFT OF CENTER *A & M AM 320* [1]	**32**	9 wks
23 May 87	LUKA *A & M VEGA 1*	**23**	8 wks
18 Jul 87	TOM'S DINER *A & M VEGA 2*	**58**	3 wks
19 May 90	BOOK OF DREAMS *A & M AM 559*	**66**	1 wk
28 Jul 90	TOM'S DINER *A & M AM 592* [2]	**2**	10 wks
22 Aug 92	IN LIVERPOOL *A & M AM 0029*	**52**	2 wks
24 Oct 92	99.9 °F *A & M AM 0085*	**46**	2 wks
19 Dec 92	BLOOD MAKES NOISE *A & M AM 0112*	**60**	3 wks
6 Mar 93	WHEN HEROES GO DOWN *A & M AMCD 0158*	**58**	1 wk

[1] Suzanne Vega featuring Joe Jackson [2] DNA featuring Suzanne Vega

The **VENTURES** became better known for their recording of the *Hawaii Five-O* television theme than for their early hits.

The same year Craig Douglas beat Gene McDaniels into the UK chart with 'A Hundred Pounds Of Clay', **FRANKIE VAUGHAN** trounced McDaniels' version of 'Tower Of Strength'. (LFI)

UB40 are the only act to register four consecutive double-sided hits.

JENNIFER WARNES was originally introduced to the music business as simply Jennifer. (REX)

Tata VEGA *US, female vocalist*   **4 wks**

26 May 79	**GET IT UP FOR LOVE / I JUST KEEP THINKING ABOUT YOU BABY** *Motown TMG 1140* **52**	4 wks

VEGAS *UK, male vocal / instrumental duo*   **10 wks**

19 Sep 92	**POSSESSED** *RCA 74321110437*.....................**32**	4 wks
28 Nov 92	**SHE** *RCA 74321124657*............................**43**	4 wks
3 Apr 93	**WALK INTO THE WIND** *RCA 74321122462* **65**	2 wks

Rosie VELA *US, female vocalist*   **7 wks**

17 Jan 87	**MAGIC SMILE** *A & M AM 369* **27**	7 wks

VELVELETTES *US, female vocal group*   **7 wks**

31 Jul 71	**THESE THINGS WILL KEEP ME LOVING YOU** *Tamla Motown TMG 780* **34**	7 wks

VELVET UNDERGROUND
UK / US, male / female vocal / instrumental group   **1 wk**

12 Mar 94	**VENUS IN FURS** *Sire W 0224CD* **71**	1 wk

VELVETS *US, male vocal group*   **2 wks**

11 May 61	**THAT LUCKY OLD SUN** *London HLU 9328* **46**	1 wk
17 Aug 61	**TONIGHT (COULD BE THE NIGHT)** *London HLU 9372*.........................**50**	1 wk

VENTURES *US, male instrumental group*   **31 wks**

8 Sep 60	● **WALK DON'T RUN** *Top Rank JAR 417* **8**	13 wks
1 Dec 60	● **PERFIDIA** *London HLG 9232* **4**	13 wks
9 Mar 61	**RAM-BUNK-SHUSH** *London HLG 9292* **45**	1 wk
11 May 61	**LULLABY OF THE LEAVES** *London HLG 9344*...........**43**	4 wks

Al VERLAINE - *See PING PING and Al VERLAINE*

VERNONS GIRLS *UK, female vocal group*   **31 wks**

17 May 62	**LOVER PLEASE** *Decca F 11450* **16**	9 wks
23 Aug 62	**LOVER PLEASE (re-entry) / YOU KNOW WHAT I MEAN** *Decca F 11450* **39**	7 wks
6 Sep 62	**LOCO-MOTION** *Decca F 11495* **47**	1 wk
18 Oct 62	**YOU KNOW WHAT I MEAN (re-entry)** *Decca F 11450* **37**	3 wks
15 Nov 62	**YOU KNOW WHAT I MEAN (2nd re-entry)** *Decca F 11450*......................**50**	1 wk
3 Jan 63	**FUNNY ALL OVER** *Decca F 11549* **31**	8 wks
18 Apr 63	**DO THE BIRD** *Decca F 11629*........................**50**	1 wk
2 May 63	**DO THE BIRD (re-entry)** *Decca F 11629* **44**	1 wk

You Know What I Mean *was not coupled with* Lover Please *on the chart of 23 Aug 62, but both sides of this record were listed for the following six weeks.*

VERUCA SALT *US, male vocal / instrumental group*   **2 wks**

2 Jul 94	**SEETHER** *Scared Hitless FRET 003CD* **61**	1 wk
3 Dec 94	**SEETHER (re-issue)** *Hi-Rise FLATSDG 12* **73**	1 wk

VERVE *UK, male vocal / instrumental group*   **2 wks**

4 Jul 92	**SHE'S A SUPERSTAR** *Hut HUT 16* **66**	1 wk
22 May 93	**BLUE** *Hut HUTCD 29* **69**	1 wk

VIBRATIONS - *See Tony JACKSON and the VIBRATIONS*

VIBRATORS *UK, male vocal / instrumental group*   **8 wks**

18 Mar 78	**AUTOMATIC LOVER** *Epic EPC 6137* **35**	5 wks
17 Jun 78	**JUDY SAYS (KNOCK YOU IN THE HEAD)** *Epic EPC 6393* **70**	3 wks

VICE SQUAD *UK, male / female vocal / instrumental group*   **1 wk**

13 Feb 82	**OUT OF REACH** *Zonophone Z 26* **68**	1 wk

VICIOUS PINK *UK, male / female vocal / instrumental duo*   **4 wks**

15 Sep 84	**CCCAN'T YOU SEE** *Parlophone R 6074* **67**	4 wks

Mike VICKERS - *See Kenny EVERETT*

Maria VIDAL *US, female vocalist*   **13 wks**

24 Aug 85	**BODY ROCK** *EMI America EA 189* **11**	13 wks

VIDEO KIDS *Holland, male / female vocal duo*   **1 wk**

5 Oct 85	**WOODPECKERS FROM SPACE** *Epic A 6504* **72**	1 wk

VIDEO SYMPHONIC *UK, orchestra*   **3 wks**

24 Oct 81	**THE FLAME TREES OF THIKA** *EMI EMI 5222* **42**	3 wks

VIENNA PHILHARMONIC ORCHESTRA
Austria, orchestra   **14 wks**

18 Dec 71	**THEME FROM 'THE ONEDIN LINE'** *Decca F 13259* **15**	14 wks

VIEW FROM THE HILL
UK, male / female vocal / instrumental group   **6 wks**

19 Jul 86	**NO CONVERSATION** *EMI EMI 5565* **58**	3 wks
21 Feb 87	**I'M NO REBEL** *EMI EM 5580* **59**	3 wks

VIKKI *UK, female vocalist*   **3 wks**

4 May 85	**LOVE IS...** *PRT 7P 326* **49**	3 wks

VILLAGE PEOPLE *US, male vocal / instrumental group*   **63 wks**

3 Dec 77	**SAN FRANCISCO (YOU'VE GOT ME)** *DJM DJS 10817* **45**	5 wks
25 Nov 78	★ **Y.M.C.A.** *Mercury 6007 192*...........**1**	16 wks
17 Mar 79	● **IN THE NAVY** *Mercury 6007 209* **2**	9 wks
16 Jun 79	**GO WEST** *Mercury 6007 221* **15**	8 wks
9 Aug 80	**CAN'T STOP THE MUSIC** *Mercury MER 16* **11**	11 wks
9 Feb 85	**SEX OVER THE PHONE** *Record Shack SOHO 34* **59**	5 wks
4 Dec 93	**Y.M.C.A. (re-mix)** *Bell 74321177182* **12**	7 wks
28 May 94	**IN THE NAVY (re-mix)** *Bell 74321198192*...........**36**	2 wks

V.I.M. *UK, male instrumental / production group*   **1 wk**

26 Jan 91	**MAGGIE'S LAST PARTY** *F2 BOZ 1* **68**	1 wk

Gene VINCENT *US, male vocalist*   **51 wks**

13 Jul 56	**BE BOP A LULA** *Capitol CL 14599* **30**	2 wks
24 Aug 56	**BE BOP A LULA (re-entry)** *Capitol CL 14599* **16**	3 wks
28 Sep 56	**BE BOP A LULA (2nd re-entry)** *Capitol CL 14599* **23**	2 wks
12 Oct 56	**RACE WITH THE DEVIL** *Capitol CL 14628* **28**	1 wk
19 Oct 56	**BLUE JEAN BOP** *Capitol CL 14637* **16**	5 wks
8 Jan 60	**WILD CAT** *Capitol CL 15099* **21**	3 wks
10 Mar 60	**MY HEART** *Capitol CL 15115* **16**	6 wks
10 Mar 60	**WILD CAT (re-entry)** *Capitol CL 15099* **39**	3 wks
28 Apr 60	**MY HEART (re-entry)** *Capitol CL 15115* **47**	1 wk

19 May 60	**MY HEART (2nd re-entry)** Capitol CL 15115	....**36**	1 wk
16 Jun 60	**PISTOL PACKIN' MAMA** Capitol CL 15136	...**15**	9 wks
1 Jun 61	**SHE SHE LITTLE SHEILA** Capitol CL 15202	..**22**	10 wks
17 Aug 61	**SHE SHE LITTLE SHEILA (re-entry)** Capitol CL 15202	...**44**	1 wk
31 Aug 61	**I'M GOING HOME** Capitol CL 15215	...**36**	4 wks

VINDALOO SUMMER SPECIAL
UK, male / female vocal / instrumental group **3 wks**

| 19 Jul 86 | **ROCKIN' WITH RITA (HEAD TO TOE)** Vindaloo UGH 13 | ....**56** | 3 wks |

Bobby VINTON *US, male vocalist* **29 wks**

2 Aug 62	**ROSES ARE RED** Columbia DB 4878	...**15**	8 wks
19 Dec 63	**THERE I'VE SAID IT AGAIN** Columbia DB 7179	...**34**	10 wks
29 Sep 90	● **BLUE VELVET** Epic 6505240	....**2**	10 wks
17 Nov 90	**ROSES ARE RED (MY LOVE) (re-issue)** Epic 6564677	...**71**	1 wk

VIOLINSKI *UK, male instrumental group* **9 wks**

| 17 Feb 79 | **CLOG DANCE** Jet 136 | ...**17** | 9 wks |

V.I.P.'S *UK, male vocal / instrumental group* **4 wks**

| 6 Sep 80 | **THE QUARTER MOON** Gem GEMS 39 | ...**55** | 4 wks |

VIPERS SKIFFLE GROUP
UK, male vocal / instrumental group **18 wks**

25 Jan 57	● **DON'T YOU ROCK ME DADDY-O** Parlophone R 4261	...**10**	9 wks
22 Mar 57	● **CUMBERLAND GAP** Parlophone R 4289	...**10**	6 wks
31 May 57	**STREAMLINE TRAIN** Parlophone R 4308	...**23**	3 wks

VISAGE *UK, male vocal / instrumental group* **56 wks**

20 Dec 80	● **FADE TO GREY** Polydor POSP 194	...**8**	15 wks
14 Mar 81	**MIND OF A TOY** Polydor POSP 236	...**13**	8 wks
11 Jul 81	**VISAGE** Polydor POSP 293	...**21**	7 wks
13 Mar 82	**DAMNED DON'T CRY** Polydor POSP 390	...**11**	8 wks
26 Jun 82	**NIGHT TRAIN** Polydor POSP 441	...**12**	10 wks
13 Nov 82	**PLEASURE BOYS** Polydor POSP 523	...**44**	3 wks
1 Sep 84	**LOVE GLOVE** Polydor POSP 691	...**54**	3 wks
28 Aug 93	**FADE TO GREY (re-mix)** Polydor PZCD 282	...**39**	2 wks

Michelle VISAGE - See S.O.U.L. S.Y.S.T.E.M. introducing Michelle VISAGE

VISCOUNTS *UK, male vocal group* **18 wks**

| 13 Oct 60 | **SHORT'NIN' BREAD** Pye 7N 15287 | ...**16** | 8 wks |
| 14 Sep 61 | **WHO PUT THE BOMP** Pye 7N 15379 | ...**21** | 10 wks |

VISION *UK, male vocal / instrumental group* **1 wk**

| 9 Jul 83 | **LOVE DANCE** MVM MVM 2886 | ...**74** | 1 wk |

VISIONMASTERS - See Kylie MINOGUE

VIXEN *US, female vocal / instrumental group* **21 wks**

3 Sep 88	**EDGE OF A BROKEN HEART** Manhattan MT 48	...**51**	4 wks
4 Mar 89	**CRYIN'** Manhattan MT 60	...**27**	4 wks
3 Jun 89	**LOVE MADE ME** EMI-USA MT 66	...**36**	4 wks
2 Sep 89	**EDGE OF A BROKEN HEART (re-entry)** EMI-USA MT 48	...**59**	2 wks
28 Jul 90	**HOW MUCH LOVE** EMI-USA MT 87	...**35**	3 wks

| 20 Oct 90 | **LOVE IS A KILLER** EMI-USA MT 91 | ...**41** | 2 wks |
| 16 Mar 91 | **NOT A MINUTE TOO SOON** EMI America MT 93 | ...**37** | 2 wks |

VOGGUE *Canada, female vocal duo* **6 wks**

| 18 Jul 81 | **DANCIN' THE NIGHT AWAY** Mercury MER 76 | ...**39** | 6 wks |

VOICE OF THE BEEHIVE
US / UK, male / female vocal / instrumental group **51 wks**

14 Nov 87	**I SAY NOTHING** London LON 151	...**45**	5 wks
5 Mar 88	**I WALK THE EARTH** London LON 169	...**42**	4 wks
14 May 88	**DON'T CALL ME BABY** London LON 175	...**15**	10 wks
23 Jul 88	**I SAY NOTHING (re-issue)** London LON 190	...**22**	6 wks
22 Oct 88	**I WALK THE EARTH (re-issue)** London LON 206	...**46**	4 wks
13 Jul 91	**MONSTERS AND ANGELS** London LON 302	...**17**	10 wks
28 Sep 91	**I THINK I LOVE YOU** London LON 308	...**25**	6 wks
11 Jan 92	**PERFECT PLACE** London LON 312	...**37**	6 wks

See also *Various Artists (EPs & LPs) - Gimme Shelter (EP)*.

Sterling VOID *UK, male vocalist* **3 wks**

| 4 Feb 89 | **RUNAWAY GIRL / IT'S ALRIGHT** ffrr FFR 21 | ...**53** | 3 wks |

VOLCANO
Norway / UK, male / female vocal / instrumental group **3 wks**

| 23 Jul 94 | **MORE TO LOVE** Deconstruction 74321221832 | ...**32** | 3 wks |

VOYAGE *UK / France, disco aggregation* **27 wks**

17 Jun 78	**FROM EAST TO WEST / SCOTS MACHINE** GTO GT 224	...**13**	13 wks
25 Nov 78	**SOUVENIRS** GTO GT 241	...**56**	7 wks
24 Mar 79	**LET'S FLY AWAY** GTO GT 245	...**38**	7 wks

Scots Machine credited from 24 Jun 78 until end of record's chart run.

VOYAGER *UK, male vocal / instrumental group* **8 wks**

| 26 May 79 | **HALFWAY HOTEL** Mountain VOY 001 | ...**33** | 8 wks |

Kristine W *US, female vocalist* **4 wks**

| 21 May 94 | **LOVE COME HOME** Triangle BLUESCD 001 [1] | ...**73** | 1 wk |
| 25 Jun 94 | **FEEL WHAT YOU WANT** Champion CHAMPCD 304 | ..**33** | 3 wks |

[1] Our Tribe with Frankë Pharoah and Kristine W

Adam WADE *US, male vocalist* **6 wks**

| 8 Jun 61 | **TAKE GOOD CARE OF HER** HMV POP 843 | ...**38** | 1 wk |
| 22 Jun 61 | **TAKE GOOD CARE OF HER (re-entry)** HMV POP 843 | ...**38** | 5 wks |

WAG YA TAIL *UK, male vocal / instrumental group* **1 wk**

| 3 Oct 92 | **XPAND YA MIND (EXPANSIONS)** PWL International PWL 238 | ...**49** | 1 wk |

WAH! *UK, male vocal / instrumental group* **26 wks**

| 25 Dec 82 | ● **THE STORY OF THE BLUES** Eternal JF 1 | ...**3** | 12 wks |
| 19 Mar 83 | **HOPE (I WISH YOU'D BELIEVE ME)** WEA X 9880 | ..**37** | 5 wks |

| 30 Jun 84 | **COME BACK** *Beggars Banquet BEG 111* [1] | ....**20** | 9 wks |

[1] Mighty Wah

Donnie WAHLBERG - *See SEIKO and Donnie WAHLBERG*

WAIKIKIS *Belgium, male instrumental group* **2 wks**

| 11 Mar 65 | **HAWAII TATTOO** *Pye International 7N 25286* | ....**41** | 2 wks |

WAILERS - *See Bob MARLEY and the WAILERS*

John WAITE *UK, male vocalist* **13 wks**

| 29 Sep 84 | ● **MISSING YOU** *EMI America EA 182* | ......**9** | 11 wks |
| 13 Feb 93 | **MISSING YOU (re-issue)** *Chrysalis CDCHS 3938* | ......**56** | 2 wks |

WAITRESSES *UK, female vocal group* **4 wks**

| 18 Dec 82 | **CHRISTMAS WRAPPING** *Ze/Island WIP 6821* | ....**45** | 4 wks |

Johnny WAKELIN *UK, male vocalist* **20 wks**

| 18 Jan 75 | ● **BLACK SUPERMAN (MUHAMMAD ALI)** *Pye 7N 45420* [1] | ......**7** | 10 wks |
| 24 Jul 76 | ● **IN ZAIRE** *Pye 7N 45595* | ......**4** | 10 wks |

[1] Johnny Wakelin and the Kinshasa Band

Narada Michael WALDEN
US, male vocalist/producer **28 wks**

23 Feb 80	**TONIGHT I'M ALL RIGHT** *Atlantic K 11437*	......**34**	9 wks
26 Apr 80	● **I SHOULDA LOVED YA** *Atlantic K 11413*	......**8**	9 wks
23 Apr 88	● **DIVINE EMOTIONS** *Reprise W 7967* [1]	......**8**	10 wks

[1] Narada

Gary WALKER *US, male vocalist* **12 wks**

| 24 Feb 66 | **YOU DON'T LOVE ME** *CBS 202036* | ....**26** | 6 wks |
| 26 May 66 | **TWINKIE LEE** *CBS 202081* | ......**26** | 6 wks |

See also Walker Brothers.

John WALKER *US, male vocalist* **6 wks**

| 5 Jul 67 | **ANNABELLA** *Philips BF 1593* | ......**48** | 1 wk |
| 19 Jul 67 | **ANNABELLA (re-entry)** *Philips BF 1593* | ......**24** | 5 wks |

See also Walker Brothers.

Junior WALKER and the ALL-STARS
US, male instrumental/vocal group **59 wks**

18 Aug 66	**HOW SWEET IT IS** *Tamla Motown TMG 571*	...........**22**	10 wks
2 Apr 69	**(I'M A) ROAD RUNNER** *Tamla Motown TMG 691*	....**12**	12 wks
18 Oct 69	**WHAT DOES IT TAKE (TO WIN YOUR LOVE)** *Tamla Motown TMG 712*	......**13**	12 wks
26 Aug 72	**WALK IN THE NIGHT** *Tamla Motown TMG 824*	......**16**	11 wks
27 Jan 73	**TAKE ME GIRL I'M READY** *Tamla Motown TMG 840*	......**16**	9 wks
30 Jun 73	**WAY BACK HOME** *Tamla Motown TMG 857*	...........**35**	5 wks

Scott WALKER *US, male vocalist* **30 wks**

6 Dec 67	**JACKIE** *Philips BF 1628*	......**22**	9 wks
1 May 68	● **JOANNA** *Philips BF 1662*	......**7**	11 wks
11 Jun 69	**LIGHTS OF CINCINATTI** *Philips BF 1793*	......**13**	10 wks

See also Walker Brothers.

WALKER BROTHERS *US, male vocal group* **93 wks**

| 29 Apr 65 | **LOVE HER** *Philips BF 1409* | ......**20** | 13 wks |

19 Aug 65	★ **MAKE IT EASY ON YOURSELF** *Philips BF 1428*	.........**1**	14 wks
2 Dec 65	● **MY SHIP IS COMING IN** *Philips BF 1454*	......**3**	12 wks
3 Mar 66	★ **THE SUN AIN'T GONNA SHINE ANYMORE** *Philips BF 1473*	......**1**	11 wks
14 Jul 66	**(BABY) YOU DON'T HAVE TO TELL ME** *Philips BF 1497*	......**13**	8 wks
22 Sep 66	**ANOTHER TEAR FALLS** *Philips BF 1514*	......**12**	8 wks
15 Dec 66	**DEADLIER THAN THE MALE** *Philips BF 1537*	......**34**	6 wks
9 Feb 67	**STAY WITH ME BABY** *Philips BF 1548*	......**26**	6 wks
18 May 67	**WALKING IN THE RAIN** *Philips BF 1576*	......**26**	6 wks
17 Jan 76	● **NO REGRETS** *GTO GT 42*	......**7**	9 wks

See also Gary Walker; John Walker; Scott Walker.

WALL OF SOUND featuring Gerald LETHAN
US, male vocal/instrumental group **1 wk**

| 31 Jul 93 | **CRITICAL (IF YOU ONLY KNEW)** *Positiva CDTIV 4* | ....**73** | 1 wk |

WALL OF VOODOO
US, male vocal/instrumental group **3 wks**

| 19 Mar 83 | **MEXICAN RADIO** *Illegal ILS 36* | ......**64** | 3 wks |

Jerry WALLACE *US, male vocalist* **1 wk**

| 23 Jun 60 | **YOU'RE SINGING OUR LOVE SONG TO SOMEBODY ELSE** *London HLH 9110* | ......**46** | 1 wk |

Bob WALLIS and his STORYVILLE JAZZ BAND
UK, male jazz band, Bob Wallis vocalist/instrumentalist - trumpet **7 wks**

| 6 Jul 61 | **I'M SHY MARY ELLEN I'M SHY** *Pye Jazz 7NJ 2043* | ..**44** | 2 wks |
| 4 Jan 62 | **COME ALONG PLEASE** *Pye Jazz 7NJ 2048* | ......**33** | 5 wks |

Joe WALSH *US, male vocalist* **15 wks**

| 16 Jul 77 | **ROCKY MOUNTAIN WAY EP** *ABC ABE 12002* | ......**39** | 4 wks |
| 8 Jul 78 | **LIFE'S BEEN GOOD** *Asylum K 13129* | ......**14** | 11 wks |

Tracks on Rocky Mountain Way EP: *Rocky Mountain Way/Turn To Stone/Meadows/Walk Away.*

Maureen WALSH - *See Maureen*

Sheila WALSH - *See Cliff RICHARD*

Steve WALSH *UK, male vocalist* **18 wks**

18 Jul 87	**I FOUND LOVIN'** *A1 A1 299*	......**74**	1 wk
29 Aug 87	● **I FOUND LOVIN' (re-entry)** *A1 A1 299*	......**9**	12 wks
12 Dec 87	**LET'S GET TOGETHER TONITE** *A1 A1 303*	......**74**	1 wk
30 Jul 88	**AIN'T NO STOPPING US NOW (PARTY FOR THE WORLD)** *A1 A1 304*	......**44**	4 wks

Trevor WALTERS *UK, male vocalist* **22 wks**

24 Oct 81	**LOVE ME TONIGHT** *Magnet MAG 198*	......**27**	8 wks
21 Jul 84	● **STUCK ON YOU** *Sanity IS 002*	......**9**	12 wks
1 Dec 84	**NEVER LET HER SLIP AWAY** *Polydor POSP 716*	......**73**	2 wks

WANG CHUNG *UK, male vocal/instrumental group* **12 wks**

| 28 Jan 84 | **DANCE HALL DAYS** *Geffen A 3837* | ......**21** | 12 wks |

Dexter WANSELL *US, male instrumentalist - keyboards* **3 wks**

| 20 May 78 | **ALL NIGHT LONG** *Philadelphia International PIR 6255* | ......**59** | 3 wks |

WAR *US/Canada/Denmark, male vocal/instrumental group* **32 wks**

| 24 Jan 76 | **LOW RIDER** *Island WIP 6267* | ......**12** | 7 wks |

26 Jun 76	ME AND BABY BROTHER Island WIP 6303	21	7 wks
14 Jan 78	GALAXY MCA 339	14	7 wks
15 Apr 78	HEY SENORITA MCA 359	40	2 wks
10 Apr 82	YOU GOT THE POWER RCA 201	58	4 wks
6 Apr 85	GROOVIN' Bluebird BR 16	43	5 wks

Anita WARD US, female vocalist — 11 wks

2 Jun 79	★ RING MY BELL TK TKR 7543	1	11 wks

Billy WARD US, male vocalist — 13 wks

13 Sep 57	STARDUST London HLU 8465	13	11 wks
29 Nov 57	DEEP PURPLE London HLU 8502	30	1 wk
3 Jan 58	STARDUST (re-entry) London HLU 8465	26	1 wk

Clifford T. WARD UK, male vocalist — 16 wks

30 Jun 73	● GAYE Charisma CB 205	8	11 wks
26 Jan 74	SCULLERY Charisma CB 221	37	5 wks

Michael WARD UK, male vocalist — 13 wks

29 Sep 73	LET THERE BE PEACE ON EARTH (LET IT BEGIN WITH ME) Philips 6006 340	15	10 wks
15 Dec 73	LET THERE BE PEACE ON EARTH (LET IT BEGIN WITH ME) (re-entry) Philips 6006 340	50	3 wks

WARD BROTHERS UK, male vocal/instrumental group — 8 wks

10 Jan 87	CROSS THAT BRIDGE Siren SIREN 37	32	8 wks

Justin WARFIELD - See BOMB THE BASS

WARM SOUNDS UK, male vocal duo — 6 wks

4 May 67	BIRDS AND BEES Deram DM 120	27	6 wks

Toni WARNE UK, female vocalist — 4 wks

25 Apr 87	BEN Mint CHEW 110	50	4 wks

Jennifer WARNES US, female vocalist — 37 wks

15 Jan 83	● UP WHERE WE BELONG Island WIP 6830 [1]	7	13 wks
25 Jul 87	FIRST WE TAKE MANHATTAN Cypress PB 49709	74	1 wk
31 Oct 87	● (I'VE HAD) THE TIME OF MY LIFE RCA PB 49625 [2]	6	12 wks
15 Dec 90	● (I'VE HAD) THE TIME OF MY LIFE (re-entry) RCA PB 49625 [2]	8	11 wks

[1] Joe Cocker and Jennifer Warnes [2] Bill Medley and Jennifer Warnes

WARRANT US, male vocal/instrumental group — 7 wks

17 Nov 90	CHERRY PIE CBS 6562587	59	2 wks
9 Mar 91	CHERRY PIE (re-issue) Columbia 6566867	35	5 wks

Ann WARREN - See Ruby MURRAY

Alysha WARREN UK, female vocalist — 1 wk

24 Sep 94	I'M SO IN LOVE Wild Card CARDD 10	61	1 wk

Dionne WARWICK US, female vocalist — 101 wks

13 Feb 64	ANYONE WHO HAD A HEART Pye International 7N 25234	42	3 wks
16 Apr 64	● WALK ON BY Pye International 7N 25241	9	14 wks
30 Jul 64	YOU'LL NEVER GET TO HEAVEN Pye International 7N 25256	20	8 wks
8 Oct 64	REACH OUT FOR ME Pye International 7N 25265	23	7 wks
1 Apr 65	YOU CAN HAVE HIM Pye International 7N 25290	37	5 wks
13 Mar 68	VALLEY OF THE DOLLS Pye International 7N 25445	28	8 wks
15 May 68	● DO YOU KNOW THE WAY TO SAN JOSÉ Pye International 7N 25457	8	10 wks
19 Oct 74	THEN CAME YOU Atlantic K 10495 [1]	29	6 wks
23 Oct 82	● HEARTBREAKER Arista ARIST 496	2	13 wks
11 Dec 82	● ALL THE LOVE IN THE WORLD Arista ARIST 507	10	10 wks
26 Feb 83	YOURS Arista ARIST 518	66	2 wks
28 May 83	I'LL NEVER LOVE THIS WAY AGAIN Arista ARIST 530	62	3 wks
9 Nov 85	THAT'S WHAT FRIENDS ARE FOR Arista ARIST 638 [2]	16	9 wks
15 Aug 87	LOVE POWER Arista RIS 27 [3]	63	3 wks

[1] Dionne Warwick and the Detroit Spinners [2] Dionne Warwick and Friends featuring Elton John, Stevie Wonder and Gladys Knight [3] Dionne Warwick and Jeffrey Osborne

WAS (NOT WAS) US, male vocal/instrumental duo — 58 wks

3 Mar 84	OUT COME THE FREAKS Ze/Geffen A 4178	41	5 wks
18 Jul 87	SPY IN THE HOUSE OF LOVE Fontana WAS 2	51	7 wks
3 Oct 87	● WALK THE DINOSAUR Fontana WAS 3	10	10 wks
6 Feb 88	SPY IN THE HOUSE OF LOVE (re-entry) Fontana WAS 2	21	8 wks
7 May 88	OUT COME THE FREAKS (AGAIN) Fontana WAS 4	44	3 wks
16 Jul 88	ANYTHING CAN HAPPEN Fontana WAS 5	67	3 wks
26 May 90	PAPA WAS A ROLLING STONE Fontana WAS 7	12	7 wks
11 Aug 90	HOW THE HEART BEHAVES Fontana WAS 8	53	3 wks
23 May 92	LISTEN LIKE THIEVES Fontana WAS 10	58	2 wks
11 Jul 92	● SHAKE YOUR HEAD Fontana WAS 11	4	9 wks
26 Sep 92	SOMEWHERE IN AMERICA (THERE'S A STREET NAMED AFTER MY DAD) Fontana WAS 12	57	1 wk

Fontana WAS 4 was a re-recorded version of their first hit. Shake Your Head features uncredited vocals by Ozzy Osbourne and Kim Basinger. See also Ozzy Osbourne.

Martha WASH US, female vocalist — 7 wks

28 Nov 92	CARRY ON RCA 74321125457	74	1 wk
6 Mar 93	GIVE IT TO YOU RCA 74321136562	37	4 wks
10 Jul 93	RUNAROUND/CARRY ON (re-mix) RCA 74321153702	49	2 wks

Dinah WASHINGTON US, female vocalist — 8 wks

30 Nov 61	SEPTEMBER IN THE RAIN Mercury AMT 1162	35	3 wks
18 Jan 62	SEPTEMBER IN THE RAIN (re-entry) Mercury AMT 1162	49	1 wk
4 Apr 92	MAD ABOUT THE BOY Mercury DINAH 1	41	4 wks

Geno WASHINGTON and the RAM JAM BAND
UK, male vocalist, male instrumental backing group — 20 wks

19 May 66	WATER Piccadilly 7N 35312	39	8 wks
21 Jul 66	HI HI HAZEL Piccadilly 7N 35329	45	3 wks
25 Aug 66	HI HI HAZEL (re-entry) Piccadilly 7N 35329	48	1 wk
6 Oct 66	QUE SERA SERA Piccadilly 7N 35346	43	3 wks
2 Feb 67	MICHAEL Piccadilly 7N 35359	39	5 wks

Grover WASHINGTON Jr.
US, male instrumentalist - saxophone — 7 wks

16 May 81	JUST THE TWO OF US Elektra K 12514	34	7 wks

Although uncredited, Bill Withers vocalises on Just The Two Of Us.

Keith WASHINGTON - See Kylie MINOGUE

Sarah WASHINGTON UK, female vocalist — 9 wks

14 Aug 93	I WILL ALWAYS LOVE YOU Almighty CDALMY 33	12	7 wks
27 Nov 93	CARELESS WHISPER Almighty CDALMY 43	45	2 wks

W.A.S.P. *US, male vocal / instrumental group* **38 wks**

31 May 86	WILD CHILD *Capitol CL 388*	71	2 wks
11 Oct 86	95 - NASTY *Capitol CL 432*	70	1 wk
29 Aug 87	SCREAM UNTIL YOU LIKE IT *Capitol CL 458*	32	5 wks
31 Oct 87	I DON'T NEED NO DOCTOR (LIVE) *Capitol CL 469*	31	5 wks
20 Feb 88	LIVE ANIMAL (F * * K LIKE A BEAST) *Music For Nations KUT 109*	61	3 wks
4 Mar 89	MEAN MAN *Capitol CL 521*	21	5 wks
27 May 89	THE REAL ME *Capitol CL 534*	23	5 wks
9 Sep 89	FOREVER FREE *Capitol CL 546*	25	5 wks
4 Apr 92	CHAINSAW CHARLIE (MURDERS IN THE NEW MORGUE) *Parlophone RS 6308*	17	2 wks
6 Jun 92	THE IDOL *Parlophone RPD 6314*	41	2 wks
31 Oct 92	I AM ONE *Parlophone 10RG 6324*	56	1 wk
23 Oct 93	SUNSET AND BABYLON *Capitol CDCL 698*	38	2 wks

WATERBOYS
UK / Ireland, male vocal / instrumental group **33 wks**

2 Nov 85	THE WHOLE OF THE MOON *Ensign ENY 520*	26	7 wks
14 Jan 89	FISHERMAN'S BLUES *Ensign ENY 621*	32	6 wks
1 Jul 89	AND A BANG ON THE EAR *Ensign ENY 624*	51	4 wks
6 Apr 91	● THE WHOLE OF THE MOON (re-issue) *Ensign ENY 642*	3	9 wks
8 Jun 91	FISHERMAN'S BLUES (re-issue) *Ensign ENY 645*	75	1 wk
15 May 93	THE RETURN OF PAN *Geffen GFSTD 42*	24	3 wks
24 Jul 93	GLASTONBURY SONG *Geffen GFSTD 49*	29	3 wks

WATERFRONT *UK, male vocal / instrumental duo* **19 wks**

15 Apr 89	BROKEN ARROW *Polydor WON 3*	63	2 wks
27 May 89	CRY *Polydor WON 1*	17	13 wks
9 Sep 89	NATURE OF LOVE *Polydor WON 2*	63	4 wks

Dennis WATERMAN *UK, male vocalist* **17 wks**

| 25 Oct 80 | ● I COULD BE SO GOOD FOR YOU *EMI 5009* [1] | 3 | 12 wks |
| 17 Dec 83 | WHAT ARE WE GONNA GET 'ER INDOORS *EMI MIN 101* [2] | 21 | 5 wks |

[1] Dennis Waterman with the Dennis Waterman Band [2] Dennis Waterman and George Cole

Crystal WATERS *US, female vocalist* **30 wks**

18 May 91	● GYPSY WOMAN (LA DA DEE) *A & M AM 772*	2	10 wks
7 Sep 91	MAKIN' HAPPY *A & M AM 790*	18	6 wks
11 Jan 92	MEGAMIX *A & M AM 843*	39	3 wks
3 Oct 92	GYPSY WOMAN (re-mix) *Epic 6584377*	35	2 wks
23 Apr 94	100% PURE LOVE *A & M 8586692*	15	7 wks
2 Jul 94	GHETTO DAY *A & M 8589592*	40	2 wks

The listed flip side of Gypsy Woman (re-mix) *was* Peace (re-mix) *by Sabrina Johnston.*

Muddy WATERS
US, male vocalist / instrumentalist - guitar **6 wks**

| 16 Jul 88 | MANNISH BOY *Epic MUD 1* | 51 | 6 wks |

Roger WATERS *UK, male vocalist / instrumentalist* **8 wks**

30 May 87	RADIO WAVES *Harvest EM 6*	74	1 wk
26 Dec 87	THE TIDE IS TURNING (AFTER LIVE AID) *Harvest EM 37*	54	4 wks
5 Sep 92	WHAT GOD WANTS PART 1 *Columbia 6581390*	35	3 wks

Michael WATFORD *US, male vocalist* **2 wks**

| 26 Feb 94 | SO INTO YOU *East West A 8309CD* | 53 | 2 wks |

Jody WATLEY *US, female vocalist* **34 wks**

9 May 87	LOOKING FOR A NEW LOVE *MCA MCA 1107*	13	11 wks
17 Oct 87	DON'T YOU WANT ME *MCA MCA 1198*	55	3 wks
8 Apr 89	REAL LOVE *MCA MCA 1324*	31	7 wks
12 Aug 89	FRIENDS *MCA MCA 1352* [1]	21	6 wks
10 Feb 90	EVERYTHING *MCA MCA 1395*	74	2 wks
11 Apr 92	I'M THE ONE YOU NEED *MCA MCS 1608*	50	3 wks
21 May 94	WHEN A MAN LOVES A WOMAN *MCA MCSTD 1964*	33	2 wks

[1] Jody Watley with Eric B. and Rakim

Johnny 'Guitar' WATSON
US, male vocalist, instrumentalist - guitar **8 wks**

| 28 Aug 76 | I NEED IT *DJM DJS 10694* | 35 | 5 wks |
| 23 Apr 77 | A REAL MOTHER FOR YA *DJM DJT 10762* | 44 | 3 wks |

WAVELENGTH *UK, male vocal group* **12 wks**

| 10 Jul 82 | HURRY HOME *Ariola ARO 281* | 17 | 12 wks |

WAX *US / UK, male vocal / instrumental duo* **16 wks**

| 12 Apr 86 | RIGHT BETWEEN THE EYES *RCA PB 40509* | 60 | 5 wks |
| 1 Aug 87 | BRIDGE TO YOUR HEART *RCA PB 41405* | 12 | 11 wks |

A WAY OF LIFE
US, male / female vocal / instrumental group **3 wks**

| 21 Apr 90 | TRIPPIN' ON YOUR LOVE *Eternal YZ 464* | 55 | 3 wks |

WAY OF THE WEST
UK, male vocal / instrumental group **5 wks**

| 25 Apr 81 | DON'T SAY THAT'S JUST FOR WHITE BOYS *Mercury MER 66* | 54 | 5 wks |

WAY OUT WEST *UK, male instrumental / production duo* **1 wk**

| 3 Dec 94 | AJARE *Deconstruction 74321243802* | 52 | 1 wk |

Jeff WAYNE *US, orchestra* **3 wks**

| 10 Jul 82 | MATADOR *CBS A 2493* | 57 | 3 wks |

See also Jeff Wayne's War Of The Worlds.

Jeff WAYNE'S WAR OF THE WORLDS
US / UK, male / female vocal / instrumental cast **18 wks**

| 9 Sep 78 | EVE OF THE WAR *CBS 6496* | 36 | 8 wks |
| 25 Nov 89 | ● EVE OF THE WAR (re-mix) *CBS 6551267* | 3 | 10 wks |

See also Jeff Wayne.

WEATHER GIRLS *US, female vocal duo* **14 wks**

| 27 Aug 83 | IT'S RAINING MEN *CBS A 2924* | 73 | 3 wks |
| 3 Mar 84 | ● IT'S RAINING MEN (re-entry) *CBS A 2924* | 2 | 11 wks |

WEATHER PROPHETS
UK, male vocal / instrumental group **2 wks**

| 28 Mar 87 | SHE COMES FROM THE RAIN *Elevation ACID 1* | 62 | 2 wks |

WEATHERMEN - *See Jonathan KING*

Marti WEBB *UK, female vocalist* **42 wks**

9 Feb 80	● TAKE THAT LOOK OFF YOUR FACE *Polydor POSP 100*	3	12 wks
19 Apr 80	TELL ME ON A SUNDAY *Polydor POSP 111*	67	2 wks
20 Sep 80	YOUR EARS SHOULD BE BURNING NOW *Polydor POSP 166*	61	4 wks
8 Jun 85	● BEN *Starblend STAR 6*	5	11 wks

| 20 Sep 86 | **ALWAYS THERE** BBC RESL 190 .... | **13** | 12 wks |
| 6 Jun 87 | **I CAN'T LET GO** Rainbow RBR 12 .... | **65** | 1 wk |

Always There features the Simon May Orchestra. See also Simon May.

Joan WEBER US, female vocalist   **1 wk**

| 18 Feb 55 | **LET ME GO LOVER** Philips PB 389 .... | **16** | 1 wk |

WEDDING PRESENT
UK, male vocal/instrumental group   **36 wks**

5 Mar 88	**NOBODY'S TWISTING YOUR ARM** Reception REC 009	**46**	2 wks
1 Oct 88	**WHY ARE YOU BEING SO REASONABLE NOW** Reception REC 011	**42**	2 wks
7 Oct 89	**KENNEDY** RCA PB 43117	**33**	3 wks
17 Feb 90	**BRASSNECK** RCA PB 43403	**24**	3 wks
29 Sep 90	**3 SONGS EP** RCA PB 44021	**25**	4 wks
11 May 91	**DALLIANCE** RCA PB 44495	**29**	3 wks
27 Jul 91	**LOVENEST** RCA PT 44750	**58**	1 wk
18 Jan 92	**BLUE EYES** RCA PB 45185	**26**	2 wks
15 Feb 92	**GO-GO DANCER** RCA PB 45183	**20**	1 wk
14 Mar 92	**THREE** RCA PB 45181	**14**	2 wks
18 Apr 92	**SILVER SHORTS** RCA PB 45311	**14**	1 wk
16 May 92	● **COME PLAY WITH ME** RCA PB 45313	**10**	2 wks
13 Jun 92	**CALIFORNIA** RCA PB 45315	**16**	1 wk
18 Jul 92	**FLYING SAUCER** RCA 74321101157	**22**	1 wk
15 Aug 92	**BOING!** RCA 74321101177	**19**	1 wk
19 Sep 92	**LOVE SLAVE** RCA 743211101167	**17**	1 wk
17 Oct 92	**STICKY** RCA 74321116917	**17**	1 wk
14 Nov 92	**THE QUEEN OF OUTER SPACE** RCA 74321116927 ....**23**		1 wk
19 Dec 92	**NO CHRISTMAS** RCA 74321116937	**25**	1 wk
10 Sep 94	**YEAH YEAH YEAH YEAH YEAH** Island CID 585....	**51**	2 wks
26 Nov 94	**IT'S A GAS** Island CID 591	**71**	1 wk

Tracks on 3 Songs EP: Corduroy/Crawl/Make Me Smile (Come Up And See Me).

Fred WEDLOCK UK, male vocalist   **10 wks**

| 31 Jan 81 | ● **OLDEST SWINGER IN TOWN** Rocket XPRES 46 ....**6** | | 10 wks |

WEE PAPA GIRL RAPPERS UK, female vocal duo   **27 wks**

12 Mar 88	**FAITH** Jive JIVE 164	**60**	4 wks
25 Jun 88	**HEAT IT UP** Jive JIVE 174 [1]	**21**	9 wks
1 Oct 88	**WEE RULE** Jive JIVE 185	**6**	9 wks
24 Dec 88	**SOULMATE** Jive JIVE 193	**45**	4 wks
25 Mar 89	**BLOW THE HOUSE DOWN** Jive JIVE 197	**65**	1 wk

[1] Wee Papa Girl Rappers featuring Two Men And A Drum Machine

Bert WEEDON UK, male instrumentalist - guitar   **38 wks**

15 May 59	● **GUITAR BOOGIE SHUFFLE** Top Rank JAR 117 ....**10**		9 wks
20 Nov 59	**NASHVILLE BOOGIE** Top Rank JAR 221	**29**	2 wks
10 Mar 60	**BIG BEAT BOOGIE** Top Rank JAR 300	**37**	3 wks
7 Apr 60	**BIG BEAT BOOGIE (re-entry)** Top Rank JAR 300 ......**49**		1 wk
9 Jun 60	**TWELFTH STREET RAG** Top Rank JAR 360	**47**	2 wks
28 Jul 60	**APACHE** Top Rank JAR 415	**44**	1 wk
11 Aug 60	**APACHE (re-entry)** Top Rank JAR 415	**24**	3 wks
27 Oct 60	**SORRY ROBBIE** Top Rank JAR 517	**28**	11 wks
2 Feb 61	**GINCHY** Top Rank JAR 537	**35**	5 wks
4 May 61	**MR. GUITAR** Top Rank JAR 559	**47**	1 wk

WEEKEND
Multi-national, male/female vocal/instrumental group   **5 wks**

| 14 Dec 85 | **CHRISTMAS MEDLEY / AULD LANG SYNE** Lifestyle XY 1 .... | **47** | 5 wks |

Frank WEIR UK, orchestra   **4 wks**

| 15 Sep 60 | **CARIBBEAN HONEYMOON** Oriole CB 1559 .... | **42** | 4 wks |

See also Vera Lynn.

Eric WEISSBERG - See 'DELIVERANCE' SOUNDTRACK

Paul WELLER UK, male vocalist   **27 wks**

18 May 91	**INTO TOMORROW** Freedom High FHP 1 [1]	**36**	3 wks
10 Oct 92	**ABOVE THE CLOUDS** Go! Discs GOD 91	**47**	2 wks
17 Jul 93	**SUNFLOWER** Go! Discs GODCD 102	**16**	5 wks
15 Aug 92	**UH HUH OH YEH** Go! Discs GOD 86	**18**	5 wks
4 Sep 93	**WILD WOOD** Go! Discs GODCD 104	**14**	3 wks
13 Nov 93	**THE WEAVER (EP)** Go! Discs GODCD 107	**18**	3 wks
9 Apr 94	**HUNG UP** Go! Discs GODCD 111	**11**	3 wks
5 Nov 94	**OUT OF THE SINKING** Go! Discs GODCD 121	**20**	3 wks

[1] Paul Weller Movement

Tracks on The Weaver (EP): The Weaver/There Is No Time/Another New Day/Ohio.

Brandi WELLS US, female vocalist   **1 wk**

| 20 Feb 82 | **WATCH OUT** Virgin VS 479 .... | **74** | 1 wk |

Houston WELLS UK, male vocalist   **10 wks**

| 1 Aug 63 | **ONLY THE HEARTACHES** Parlophone R 5031 .... | **22** | 10 wks |

Mary WELLS US, female vocalist   **25 wks**

21 May 64	● **MY GUY** Stateside SS 288	**5**	14 wks
30 Jul 64	**ONCE UPON A TIME** Stateside SS 316 [1]	**50**	1 wk
8 Jul 72	**MY GUY (re-issue)** Tamla Motown TMG 820.............	**14**	10 wks

[1] Marvin Gaye and Mary Wells

Terri WELLS US, female vocalist   **9 wks**

| 2 Jul 83 | **YOU MAKE IT HEAVEN** Phillyworld PWS 111............. | **53** | 2 wks |
| 5 May 84 | **I'LL BE AROUND** Phillyworld LON 48 .... | **17** | 7 wks |

Alex WELSH UK, male instrumentalist - trumpet   **4 wks**

| 10 Aug 61 | **TANSY** Columbia DB 4686............. | **45** | 4 wks |

WENDY and LISA US, female vocal duo   **31 wks**

5 Sep 87	**WATERFALL** Virgin VS 999	**66**	4 wks
16 Jan 88	**SIDE SHOW** Virgin VS 1012	**49**	5 wks
18 Feb 89	**ARE YOU MY BABY** Virgin VS 1156	**70**	3 wks
29 Apr 89	**LOLLY LOLLY** Virgin VS 1175	**64**	3 wks
8 Jul 89	**SATISFACTION** Virgin VS 1194	**27**	8 wks
18 Nov 89	**WATERFALL (re-mix)** Virgin VS 1223	**69**	2 wks
30 Jun 90	**STRUNG OUT** Virgin VS 1272	**44**	5 wks
10 Nov 90	**RAINBOW LAKE** Virgin VS 1280.............	**70**	1 wk

Dodie WEST UK, female vocalist   **4 wks**

| 14 Jan 65 | **GOING OUT OF MY HEAD** Decca F 12046 .... | **39** | 4 wks |

Keith WEST UK, male vocalist   **18 wks**

| 9 Aug 67 | ● **EXCERPT FROM A TEENAGE OPERA** Parlophone R 5623 .... | **2** | 15 wks |
| 22 Nov 67 | **SAM** Parlophone R 5651 .... | **38** | 3 wks |

Kit WEST - See DEGREES OF MOTION featuring BITI

WEST END - See SYBIL

WEST HAM UNITED CUP SQUAD
UK, male football team vocalists   **2 wks**

| 10 May 75 | **I'M FOREVER BLOWING BUBBLES** Pye 7N 45470 ....**31** | 2 wks |

WEST STREET MOB *US, male vocal group*　　　**3 wks**

8 Oct 83	**BREAK DANCIN' - ELECTRIC BOOGIE**		
	Sugarhill SH 128 ....**71**		1 wk
22 Oct 83	**BREAK DANCIN' - ELECTRIC BOOGIE (re-entry)**		
	Sugarhill SH 128 ....**64**		2 wks

WESTBAM *Germany, male producer*　　　**3 wks**

9 Jul 94	**CELEBRATION GENERATION** *Low Spirit PQCD 5* **48**		2 wks
19 Nov 94	**BAM BAM BAM** *Low Spirit PZCD 329* **57**		1 wk

Kim WESTON - *See Marvin GAYE*

WESTWORLD
UK/US, male/female vocal/instrumental group　　　**23 wks**

21 Feb 87	**SONIC BOOM BOY** *RCA BOOM 1* **11**		7 wks
2 May 87	**BA-NA-NA-BAM-BOO** *RCA BOOM 2* **37**		5 wks
25 Jul 87	**WHERE THE ACTION IS** *RCA BOOM 3* **54**		4 wks
17 Oct 87	**SILVERMAC** *RCA BOOM 4* **42**		5 wks
15 Oct 88	**EVERYTHING GOOD IS BAD** *RCA PB 42243* **72**		2 wks

WET WET WET *UK, male vocal/instrumental group*　　　**150 wks**

11 Apr 87	● **WISHING I WAS LUCKY** *Precious JEWEL 3* **6**		14 wks
25 Jul 87	● **SWEET LITTLE MYSTERY** *Precious JEWEL 4* **5**		12 wks
5 Dec 87	● **ANGEL EYES (HOME AND AWAY)** *Precious JEWEL 6*.**5**		12 wks
19 Mar 88	**TEMPTATION** *Precious JEWEL 7* **12**		8 wks
14 May 88	★ **WITH A LITTLE HELP FROM MY FRIENDS**		
	Childline CHILD 1 ......**1**		11 wks
30 Sep 89	● **SWEET SURRENDER** *Precious JEWEL 9* **6**		8 wks
9 Dec 89	**BROKE AWAY** *Precious JEWEL 10* **19**		7 wks
10 Mar 90	**HOLD BACK THE RIVER** *Precious JEWEL 11* **31**		4 wks
11 Aug 90	**STAY WITH ME HEARTACHE / I FEEL FINE**		
	Precious JEWEL 13 ......**30**		4 wks
14 Sep 91	**MAKE IT TONIGHT** *Precious JEWEL 15* **37**		3 wks
2 Nov 91	**PUT THE LIGHT ON** *Precious JEWEL 16* **56**		2 wks
4 Jan 92	★ **GOODNIGHT GIRL** *Precious JEWEL 17* **1**		11 wks
21 Mar 92	**MORE THAN LOVE** *Precious JEWEL 18* **19**		5 wks
11 Jul 92	**LIP SERVICE (EP)** *Precious JEWEL 19* **15**		5 wks
8 May 93	**BLUE FOR YOU / THIS TIME (LIVE)**		
	Precious JWLCD 20 ......**38**		2 wks
6 Nov 93	**SHED A TEAR** *Precious JWLCD 21* **22**		5 wks
8 Jan 94	**COLD COLD HEART** *Precious JWLCD 22* **23**		4 wks
21 May 94	★ **LOVE IS ALL AROUND** *Precious JWLCD 23* ......**1†**		33 wks

The listed A-side with With A Little Help From My Friends *was* She's
Leaving Home *by Billy Bragg with Cara Tivey. Tracks on Lip Service (EP):*
Lip Service / High On The Happy Side / Lip Service (Live) / More Than Love
(Live).

WE'VE GOT A FUZZBOX AND WE'RE
GONNA USE IT *UK, female vocal/instrumental group*　　　**39 wks**

26 Apr 86	**XX SEX / RULES AND REGULATIONS**		
	Vindaloo UGH 11 ......**41**		7 wks
15 Nov 86	**LOVE IS THE SLUG** *Vindaloo UGH 14* **31**		4 wks
7 Feb 87	**WHAT'S THE POINT** *Vindaloo YZ 101* **51**		2 wks
25 Feb 89	**INTERNATIONAL RESCUE** *WEA YZ 347* **11**		10 wks
20 May 89	**PINK SUNSHINE** *WEA YZ 401* **14**		10 wks
5 Aug 89	**SELF!** *WEA YZ 408* **24**		6 wks

WHALE *Sweden, male/female vocal/instrumental group*　　　**2 wks**

19 Mar 94	**HOBO HUMPIN' SLOBO BABE**		
	East West YZ 798CD **46**		2 wks

WHALERS - *See Hal PAGE and the WHALERS*

WHAM! *UK, male vocal duo*　　　**137 wks**

16 Oct 82	● **YOUNG GUNS (GO FOR IT)** *Innervision IVL A2766* **3**		17 wks

---

15 Jan 83	● **WHAM RAP** *Innervision IVL A2442* **8**		11 wks
14 May 83	● **BAD BOYS** *Innervision A 3143* **2**		14 wks
30 Jul 83	● **CLUB TROPICANA** *Innervision A 3613* **4**		11 wks
3 Dec 83	**CLUB FANTASTIC MEGAMIX** *Innervision A 3586* **15**		8 wks
26 May 84	★ **WAKE ME UP BEFORE YOU GO GO** *Epic A 4440* **1**		16 wks
13 Oct 84	★ **FREEDOM** *Epic A 4743* **1**		14 wks
15 Dec 84	● **LAST CHRISTMAS / EVERYTHING SHE WANTS**		
	Epic A 4949 ......**2**		13 wks
23 Nov 85	★ **I'M YOUR MAN** *Epic A 6716* **1**		12 wks
14 Dec 85	● **LAST CHRISTMAS (re-issue)** *Epic WHAM 1* **6**		7 wks
21 Jun 86	★ **THE EDGE OF HEAVEN / WHERE DID**		
	YOUR HEART GO *Epic FIN 1* **1**		10 wks
20 Dec 86	**LAST CHRISTMAS (2nd re-issue)** *Epic 650269 7* **45**		4 wks

*Where Did Your Heart Go only listed from 2 August 86. It peaked at posi-
tion 28.*

WHATNAUTS - *See MOMENTS*

Caron WHEELER *UK, female vocalist*　　　**42 wks**

18 Mar 89	● **KEEP ON MOVING** *10 TEN 263* [1] **5**		12 wks
10 Jun 89	★ **BACK TO LIFE (HOWEVER DO YOU WANT ME)**		
	10 TEN 265 [1] **1**		14 wks
8 Sep 90	**LIVIN' IN THE LIGHT** *RCA PB 43939* **14**		6 wks
10 Nov 90	**UK BLAK** *RCA PB 43719* **40**		4 wks
8 Feb 91	**DON'T QUIT** *RCA PB 44259* **53**		3 wks
7 Nov 92	**I ADORE YOU** *Perspective PERSS 7407* **59**		2 wks
11 Sep 93	**BEACH OF THE WAR GODDESS** *EMI CDEM 282* **75**		1 wk

[1] *Soul II Soul featuring Caron Wheeler*

Bill WHELAN featuring ANUNA and the RTE
CONCERT ORCHESTRA *Ireland, male composer, male/
female choir and orchestra*　　　**3 wks**

17 Dec 94	**RIVERDANCE** *Son RTEBUACD 1* ......**15†**		3 wks

WHEN IN ROME *UK, male vocal/instrumental group*　　　**3 wks**

28 Jan 89	**THE PROMISE** *10 TEN 244* **58**		3 wks

WHIGFIELD *Denmark, female vocalist*　　　**20 wks**

17 Sep 94	★ **SATURDAY NIGHT** *Systematic SYSCD 3* ......**1†**		16 wks
10 Dec 94	● **ANOTHER DAY** *Systematic SYSCD 4* ......**10†**		4 wks

Nancy WHISKEY - *See Charles McDEVITT SKIFFLE GROUP featuring
Nancy WHISKEY*

WHISPERS *US, male vocal group*　　　**52 wks**

2 Feb 80	● **AND THE BEAT GOES ON** *Solar SO 1* **2**		12 wks
10 May 80	**LADY** *Solar SO 4* **55**		3 wks
12 Jul 80	**MY GIRL** *Solar SO 8* **26**		6 wks
14 Mar 81	● **IT'S A LOVE THING** *Solar SO 16* **9**		11 wks
13 Jun 81	**I CAN MAKE IT BETTER** *Solar SO 19* **44**		5 wks
19 Jan 85	**CONTAGIOUS** *MCA MCA 937* **56**		3 wks
28 Mar 87	**AND THE BEAT GOES ON (re-issue)**		
	Solar MCA 1126 ......**45**		4 wks
23 May 87	**ROCK STEADY** *Solar MCA 1152* **38**		6 wks
15 Aug 87	**SPECIAL F/X** *Solar MCA 1178* **69**		2 wks

WHISTLE *US, male rap group*　　　**8 wks**

1 Mar 86	● **(NOTHIN' SERIOUS) JUST BUGGIN'**		
	Champion CHAMP 12 ......**7**		8 wks

Barry WHITE *US, male vocalist*　　　**127 wks**

9 Jun 73	**I'M GONNA LOVE YOU JUST A LITTLE**		
	BIT MORE BABY *Pye International 7N 25610* **23**		7 wks

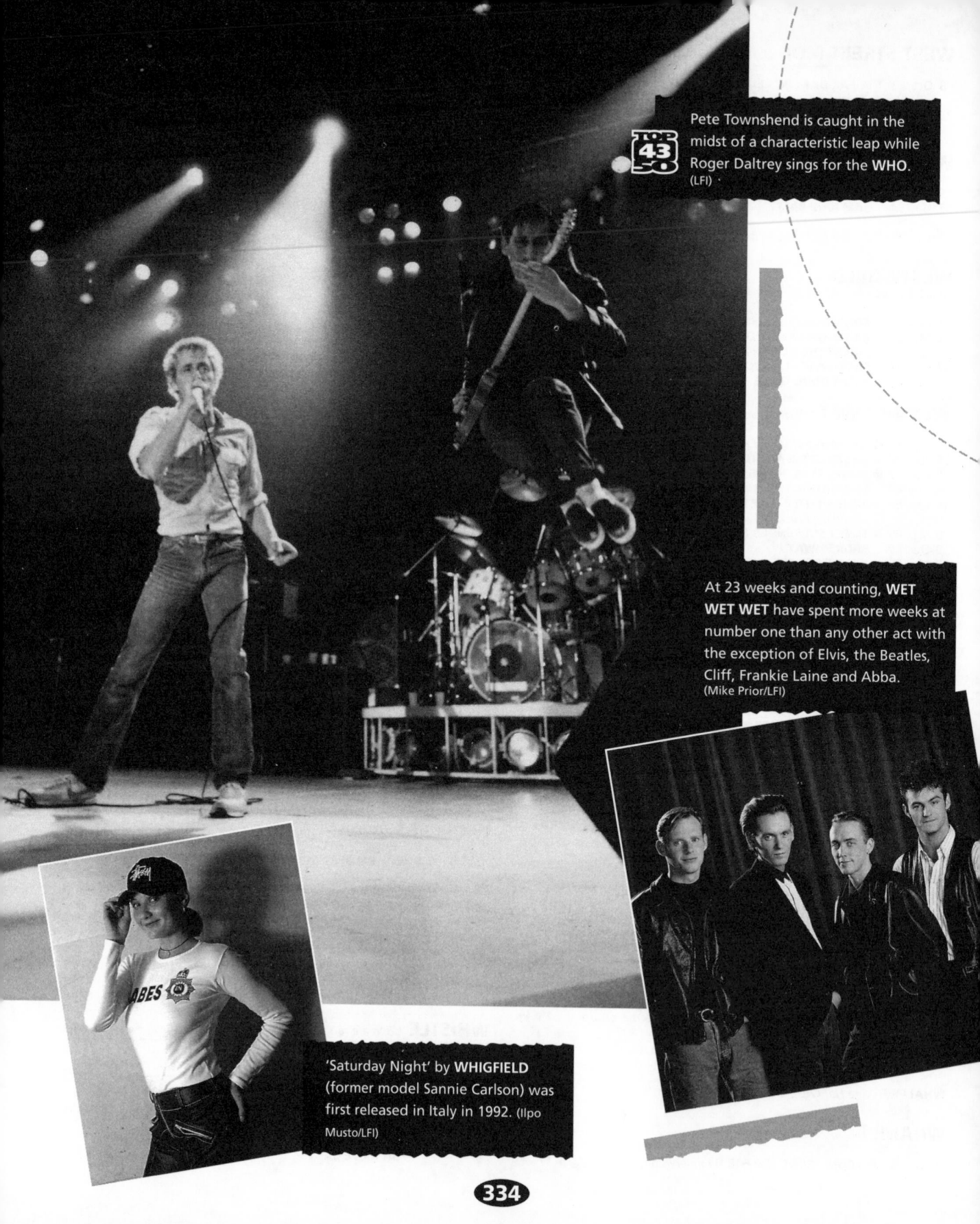

Pete Townshend is caught in the midst of a characteristic leap while Roger Daltrey sings for the **WHO**. (LFI)

At 23 weeks and counting, **WET WET WET** have spent more weeks at number one than any other act with the exception of Elvis, the Beatles, Cliff, Frankie Laine and Abba. (Mike Prior/LFI)

'Saturday Night' by **WHIGFIELD** (former model Sannie Carlson) was first released in Italy in 1992. (Ilpo Musto/LFI)

26 Jan 74	NEVER NEVER GONNA GIVE YA UP		
	Pye International 7N 25633 ....**14**	11 wks
17 Aug 74 ●	CAN'T GET ENOUGH OF YOUR LOVE BABE		
	Pye International 7N 25661 ....**8**	12 wks
2 Nov 74 ★	YOU'RE THE FIRST THE LAST MY EVERYTHING		
	20th Century BTC 2133 ....**1**	14 wks
8 Mar 75 ●	WHAT AM I GONNA DO WITH YOU		
	20th Century BTC 2177 ....**5**	8 wks
24 May 75	I'LL DO ANYTHING YOU WANT ME TO		
	20th Century BTC 2208 ....**20**	6 wks
27 Dec 75 ●	LET THE MUSIC PLAY *20th Century BTC 2265* **9**	8 wks
6 Mar 76 ●	YOU SEE THE TROUBLE WITH ME		
	20th Century BTC 2277 ....**2**	10 wks
21 Aug 76	BABY WE BETTER TRY AND GET IT TOGETHER		
	20th Century BTC 2298 ....**15**	7 wks
13 Nov 76	DON'T MAKE ME WAIT TOO LONG		
	20th Century BTC 2309 ....**17**	8 wks
5 Mar 77	I'M QUALIFIED TO SATISFY		
	20th Century BTC 2328 ....**37**	5 wks
15 Oct 77	IT'S ECSTASY WHEN YOU LAY DOWN NEXT TO ME		
	20th Century BTC 2350 ....**40**	3 wks
16 Dec 78	JUST THE WAY YOU ARE *20th Century BTC 2380* **12**	12 wks
24 Mar 79	SHA LA LA MEANS I LOVE YOU		
	20th Century BTC 1041 ....**55**	6 wks
7 Nov 87	SHO' YOU RIGHT *Breakout USA 614* **14**	7 wks
16 Jan 88	NEVER NEVER GONNA GIVE YOU UP (re-mix)		
	Club JAB 59 ....**63**	2 wks
31 Mar 90	SECRET GARDEN *Qwest W 9992* [1] **67**	1 wk

[1] Quincy Jones featuring Al B. Sure!, James Ingram, El DeBarge and Barry White

Chris WHITE *UK, male vocalist* — 4 wks

| 20 Mar 76 | SPANISH WINE *Charisma CB 272* ....**37** | 4 wks |

Karyn WHITE *US, female vocalist* — 38 wks

5 Nov 88	THE WAY YOU LOVE ME *Warner Bros. W 7773* **42**	5 wks
18 Feb 89	SECRET RENDEZVOUS *Warner Bros. W 7562* **52**	3 wks
10 Jun 89	SUPERWOMAN *Warner Bros. W 2920* **11**	13 wks
9 Sep 89	SECRET RENDEZVOUS (re-issue)		
	Warner Bros. W 2855 ....**22**	9 wks
17 Aug 91	ROMANTIC *Warner Bros. W 0028* **23**	5 wks
18 Jan 92	THE WAY I FEEL ABOUT YOU		
	Warner Bros. W 0073 ....**65**	2 wks
24 Sep 94	HUNGAH *Warner Bros. W 0264CD* **69**	1 wk

Snowy WHITE
UK, male vocalist / instrumentalist - guitar — 12 wks

24 Dec 83 ●	BIRD OF PARADISE *Towerbell TOW 42* **6**	10 wks
28 Dec 85	FOR YOU *R4 FOR 3* **65**	1 wk
18 Jan 86	FOR YOU (re-entry) *R4 FOR 3* **72**	1 wk

Tam WHITE *UK, male vocalist* — 4 wks

| 15 Mar 75 | WHAT IN THE WORLD'S COME OVER YOU | | |
| | *RAK 193* ....**36** | 4 wks |

Tony Joe WHITE *US, male vocalist* — 10 wks

| 6 Jun 70 | GROUPIE GIRL *Monument MON 1043* ....**22** | 10 wks |

WHITE and TORCH *UK, male vocal / instrumental duo* — 4 wks

| 2 Oct 82 | PARADE *Chrysalis CHS 2641* ....**54** | 4 wks |

WHITE PLAINS *UK, male vocal group* — 56 wks

7 Feb 70 ●	MY BABY LOVES LOVIN' *Deram DM 280* **9**	11 wks
18 Apr 70	I'VE GOT YOU ON MY MIND *Deram DM 291* **17**	11 wks
24 Oct 70 ●	JULIE DO YA LOVE ME *Deram DM 315* **8**	14 wks
12 Jun 71	WHEN YOU ARE A KING *Deram DM 333* **13**	11 wks
17 Feb 73	STEP INTO A DREAM *Deram DM 371* **21**	9 wks

WHITEOUT *UK, male vocal / instrumental group* — 1 wk

| 24 Sep 94 | DETROIT *Silvertone ORECD 66* ....**73** | 1 wk |

WHITESNAKE *UK, male vocal / instrumental group* — 111 wks

24 Jun 78	SNAKE BITE EP *EMI International INEP 751* [1] **61**	3 wks
10 Nov 79	LONG WAY FROM HOME *United Artists BP 324* [1] **55**	2 wks
26 Apr 80	FOOL FOR YOUR LOVING *United Artists BP 352* **13**	9 wks
12 Jul 80	READY AN' WILLING (SWEET SATISFACTION)		
	United Artists BP 363 ....**43**	4 wks
22 Nov 80	AIN'T NO LOVE IN THE HEART OF THE CITY		
	Sunburst/Liberty BP 381 ....**51**	4 wks
11 Apr 81	DON'T BREAK MY HEART AGAIN *Liberty BP 395* **17**	9 wks
6 Jun 81	WOULD I LIE TO YOU *Liberty BP 399* **37**	6 wks
6 Nov 82	HERE I GO AGAIN / BLOODY LUXURY		
	Liberty BP 416 ....**34**	10 wks
13 Aug 83	GUILTY OF LOVE *Liberty BP 420* **31**	5 wks
14 Jan 84	GIVE ME MORE TIME *Liberty BP 422* **29**	4 wks
28 Apr 84	STANDING IN THE SHADOW *Liberty BP 423* **62**	2 wks
9 Feb 85	LOVE AIN'T NO STRANGER *Liberty BP 424* **44**	4 wks
28 Mar 87	STILL OF THE NIGHT *EMI EMI 5606* **16**	8 wks
6 Jun 87 ●	IS THIS LOVE *EMI EM 3* **9**	11 wks
31 Oct 87 ●	HERE I GO AGAIN (re-mix) *EMI EM 35* **9**	11 wks
6 Feb 88	GIVE ME ALL YOUR LOVE *EMI EM 23* **18**	6 wks
2 Dec 89	FOOL FOR YOUR LOVING *EMI EM 123* **43**	2 wks
10 Mar 90	THE DEEPER THE LOVE *EMI EM 128* **35**	3 wks
25 Aug 90	NOW YOU'RE GONE *EMI EM 150* **31**	4 wks
6 Aug 94	IS THIS LOVE (re-issue) / SWEET LADY LUCK		
	EMI CDEM 329 ....**25**	4 wks

[1] David Coverdale's Whitesnake

Tracks on Snake Bite EP: *Bloody Mary / Steal Away / Ain't No Love In The Heart Of The City / Come On. EM 123 is a re-recording of their third hit.*

David WHITFIELD *UK, male vocalist* — 181 wks

2 Oct 53 ●	BRIDGE OF SIGHS *Decca F 10129* **9**	1 wk
16 Oct 53 ★	ANSWER ME *Decca F 10192* **1**	13 wks
11 Dec 53	RAGS TO RICHES *Decca F 10207* **12**	1 wk
8 Jan 54 ●	RAGS TO RICHES (re-entry) *Decca F 10207* **3**	10 wks
29 Jan 54	ANSWER ME (re-entry) *Decca F 10192* **12**	1 wk
19 Feb 54 ●	THE BOOK *Decca F 10242* **5**	12 wks
28 May 54 ●	THE BOOK (re-entry) *Decca F 10242* **10**	3 wks
18 Jun 54 ★	CARA MIA *Decca F 10327* [1] **1**	25 wks
12 Nov 54 ●	SANTO NATALE *Decca F 10399* **2**	10 wks
11 Feb 55 ●	BEYOND THE STARS *Decca F 10458* [1] **8**	9 wks
27 May 55	MAMA *Decca F 10515* **20**	1 wk
24 Jun 55	MAMA (re-entry) *Decca F 10515* **19**	2 wks
8 Jul 55 ●	EV'RYWHERE *Decca F 10515* **3**	20 wks
29 Jul 55	MAMA (2nd re-entry) *Decca F 10515* **12**	8 wks
25 Nov 55 ●	WHEN YOU LOSE THE ONE YOU LOVE		
	Decca F 10627 [1] **7**	11 wks
2 Mar 56	MY SEPTEMBER LOVE *Decca F 10690* **19**	2 wks
23 Mar 56	MY SEPTEMBER LOVE (re-entry) *Decca F 10690* **18**	1 wk
6 Apr 56 ●	MY SEPTEMBER LOVE (2nd re-entry)		
	Decca F 10690 ....**3**	20 wks
24 Aug 56	MY SON JOHN *Decca F 10769* **22**	4 wks
31 Aug 56	MY UNFINISHED SYMPHONY *Decca F 10769* **29**	1 wk
7 Sep 56	MY SEPTEMBER LOVE (3rd re-entry)		
	Decca F 10690 ....**25**	1 wk
25 Jan 57 ●	ADORATION WALTZ *Decca F 10833* **9**	11 wks
5 Apr 57	I'LL FIND YOU *Decca F 10864* **28**	2 wks
7 Jun 57	I'LL FIND YOU (re-entry) *Decca F 10864* **27**	2 wks
14 Feb 58	CRY MY HEART *Decca F 10978* **22**	3 wks
16 May 58	ON THE STREET WHERE YOU LIVE *Decca F 11018* ..**16**	14 wks
8 Aug 58	THE RIGHT TO LOVE *Decca F 11039* **30**	1 wk
24 Nov 60	I BELIEVE *Decca F 11289* **49**	1 wk

[1] David Whitfield with chorus and Mantovani and his orchestra

See also Various Artists (EPs & LPs) - All-Star Hit Parade; Mantovani.

Slim WHITMAN *US, male vocalist* — 75 wks

| 15 Jul 55 ★ | ROSE MARIE *London HL 8061* ....**1** | 19 wks |

29 Jul 55	●	**INDIAN LOVE CALL** *London L 1149*	7	12 wks
23 Sep 55		**CHINA DOLL** *London L 1149*	15	2 wks
9 Mar 56		**TUMBLING TUMBLEWEEDS** *London HLU 8230*	19	2 wks
13 Apr 56		**I'M A FOOL** *London HLU 8252*	16	3 wks
11 May 56		**I'M A FOOL (re-entry)** *London HLU 8252*	29	1 wk
22 Jun 56		**SERENADE** *London HLU 8287*	24	3 wks
27 Jul 56	●	**SERENADE (re-entry)** *London HLU 8287*	8	12 wks
12 Apr 57	●	**I'LL TAKE YOU HOME AGAIN KATHLEEN** *London HLP 8403*	7	13 wks
5 Oct 74		**HAPPY ANNIVERSARY** *United Artists UP 35728*	14	10 wks

Roger WHITTAKER *Kenya, male vocalist* **85 wks**

8 Nov 69		**DURHAM TOWN (THE LEAVIN')** *Columbia DB 8613*	12	18 wks
11 Apr 70	●	**I DON'T BELIEVE IN IF ANYMORE** *Columbia DB 8664*	8	18 wks
10 Oct 70		**NEW WORLD IN THE MORNING** *Columbia DB 8718*	17	14 wks
3 Apr 71		**WHY** *Columbia DB 8752*	47	1 wk
2 Oct 71		**MAMMY BLUE** *Columbia DB 8822*	31	10 wks
26 Jul 75	●	**THE LAST FAREWELL** *EMI 2294*	2	14 wks
8 Nov 86		**THE SKYE BOAT SONG** *Tembo TML 119* [1]	10	10 wks

[1] Roger Whittaker and Des O'Connor

WHO *UK, male vocal/instrumental group* **245 wks**

18 Feb 65	●	**I CAN'T EXPLAIN** *Brunswick 05926*	8	13 wks
27 May 65	●	**ANYWAY ANYHOW ANYWHERE** *Brunswick 05935*	10	12 wks
4 Nov 65	●	**MY GENERATION** *Brunswick 05944*	2	13 wks
10 Mar 66	●	**SUBSTITUTE** *Reaction 591 001*	5	13 wks
24 Mar 66		**A LEGAL MATTER** *Brunswick 05956*	32	6 wks
1 Sep 66	●	**I'M A BOY** *Reaction 591 004*	2	13 wks
1 Sep 66		**THE KIDS ARE ALRIGHT** *Brunswick 05965*	41	2 wks
22 Sep 66		**THE KIDS ARE ALRIGHT (re-entry)** *Brunswick 05965*	48	1 wk
15 Dec 66	●	**HAPPY JACK** *Reaction 591 010*	3	11 wks
27 Apr 67	●	**PICTURES OF LILY** *Track 604 002*	4	10 wks
26 Jul 67		**THE LAST TIME/UNDER MY THUMB** *Track 604 006*	44	3 wks
18 Oct 67	●	**I CAN SEE FOR MILES** *Track 604 011*	10	12 wks
19 Jun 68		**DOGS** *Track 604 023*	25	5 wks
23 Oct 68		**MAGIC BUS** *Track 604 024*	26	6 wks
19 Mar 69	●	**PINBALL WIZARD** *Track 604 027*	4	13 wks
4 Apr 70		**THE SEEKER** *Track 604 036*	19	11 wks
8 Aug 70		**SUMMERTIME BLUES** *Track 2094 002*	38	4 wks
10 Jul 71	●	**WON'T GET FOOLED AGAIN** *Track 2094 009*	9	12 wks
23 Oct 71		**LET'S SEE ACTION** *Track 2094 012*	16	12 wks
24 Jun 72	●	**JOIN TOGETHER** *Track 2094 102*	9	9 wks
13 Jan 73		**RELAY** *Track 2094 106*	21	5 wks
13 Oct 73		**5:15** *Track 2094 115*	20	6 wks
24 Jan 76	●	**SQUEEZE BOX** *Polydor 2121 275*	10	9 wks
30 Oct 76	●	**SUBSTITUTE (re-issue)** *Polydor 2058 803*	7	7 wks
22 Jul 78		**WHO ARE YOU** *Polydor WHO 1*	18	12 wks
28 Apr 79		**LONG LIVE ROCK** *Polydor WHO 2*	48	5 wks
7 Mar 81	●	**YOU BETTER YOU BET** *Polydor WHO 004*	9	8 wks
9 May 81		**DON'T LET GO THE COAT** *Polydor WHO 005*	47	4 wks
2 Oct 82		**ATHENA** *Polydor WHO 6*	40	4 wks
26 Nov 83		**READY STEADY WHO EP** *Polydor WHO 7*	58	2 wks
20 Feb 88		**MY GENERATION (re-issue)** *Polydor POSP 907*	68	2 wks

Tracks on Ready Steady Who EP: Disguises / Circles / Batman / Bucket 'T' / Barbara Ann. See also High Numbers.

WHODINI *US, male rap/scratch duo* **10 wks**

25 Dec 82		**MAGIC'S WAND** *Jive JIVE 28*	47	6 wks
17 Mar 84		**MAGIC'S WAND (THE WHODINI ELECTRIC EP)** *Jive JIVE 61*	63	4 wks

Tracks on The Whodini Electric EP: Jive Magic Wand / Nasty Lady / Rap Machine / The Haunted House of Rock.

WHOOLIGANZ *US, male rap duo* **2 wks**

13 Aug 94		**PUT YOUR HANDZ UP** *Positiva CDTIV 17*	53	2 wks

WHYCLIFFE *UK, male vocalist* **2 wks**

20 Nov 93		**HEAVEN** *MCA MCSTD 1944*	56	1 wk
2 Apr 94		**ONE MORE TIME** *MCA MCSTD 1955*	72	1 wk

Jane WIEDLIN *US, female vocalist* **14 wks**

6 Aug 88		**RUSH HOUR** *Manhattan MT 36*	12	11 wks
29 Oct 88		**INSIDE A DREAM** *Manhattan MT 55*	64	3 wks

WIGAN'S CHOSEN FEW *US, instrumental track plus UK crowd vocal* **11 wks**

18 Jan 75	●	**FOOTSEE** *Pye Disco Demand DDS 111*	9	11 wks

WIGAN'S OVATION *UK, male vocal/instrumental group* **19 wks**

15 Mar 75		**SKIING IN THE SNOW** *Spark SRL 1122*	12	10 wks
28 Jun 75		**PER-SO-NAL-LY** *Spark SRL 1129*	38	6 wks
29 Nov 75		**SUPER LOVE** *Spark SRL 1133*	41	3 wks

Jack WILD *UK, male vocalist* **2 wks**

2 May 70		**SOME BEAUTIFUL** *Capitol CL 15635*	46	2 wks

WILD CHERRY *US, male vocal/instrumental group* **11 wks**

9 Oct 76	●	**PLAY THAT FUNKY MUSIC** *Epic EPC 4593*	7	11 wks

WILD PAIR - See Paula ABDUL

WILD WEEKEND *UK, male vocal/instrumental group* **2 wks**

29 Apr 89		**BREAKIN' UP** *Parlophone R 6204*	74	1 wk
5 May 90		**WHO'S AFRAID OF THE BIG BAD LOVE** *Parlophone R 6249*	70	1 wk

Eugene WILDE *US, male vocalist* **15 wks**

13 Oct 84		**GOTTA GET YOU HOME TONIGHT** *Fourth & Broadway BRW 15*	18	9 wks
2 Feb 85		**PERSONALITY** *Fourth & Broadway BRW 18*	34	6 wks

Personality was coupled with Let Her Feel It by Simplicious.

Kim WILDE *UK, female vocalist* **191 wks**

21 Feb 81	●	**KIDS IN AMERICA** *RAK 327*	2	13 wks
9 May 81	●	**CHEQUERED LOVE** *RAK 330*	4	9 wks
1 Aug 81		**WATER ON GLASS/BOYS** *RAK 334*	11	8 wks
14 Nov 81		**CAMBODIA** *RAK 336*	12	12 wks
17 Apr 82		**VIEW FROM A BRIDGE** *RAK 342*	16	7 wks
16 Oct 82		**CHILD COME AWAY** *RAK 352*	43	4 wks
30 Jul 83		**LOVE BLONDE** *RAK 360*	23	8 wks
12 Nov 83		**DANCING IN THE DARK** *RAK 365*	67	2 wks
13 Oct 84		**THE SECOND TIME** *MCA KIM 1*	29	6 wks
8 Dec 84		**THE TOUCH** *MCA KIM 2*	56	3 wks
27 Apr 85		**RAGE TO LOVE** *MCA KIM 3*	19	8 wks
25 Oct 86	●	**YOU KEEP ME HANGIN' ON** *MCA KIM 4*	2	14 wks
4 Apr 87	●	**ANOTHER STEP CLOSER TO YOU** *MCA KIM 5* [1]	6	11 wks
8 Aug 87		**SAY YOU REALLY WANT ME** *MCA KIM 6*	29	5 wks
5 Dec 87	●	**ROCKIN' AROUND THE CHRISTMAS TREE** *10 TEN 2* [2]	3	7 wks
14 May 88		**HEY MISTER HEARTACHE** *MCA KIM 7*	31	5 wks
16 Jul 88	●	**YOU CAME** *MCA KIM 8*	3	11 wks
1 Oct 88	●	**NEVER TRUST A STRANGER** *MCA KIM 9*	7	9 wks
3 Dec 88	●	**FOUR LETTER WORD** *MCA KIM 10*	6	12 wks
4 Mar 89		**LOVE IN THE NATURAL WAY** *MCA KIM 11*	32	6 wks
14 Apr 90		**IT'S HERE** *MCA KIM 12*	42	4 wks
16 Jun 90		**TIME** *MCA KIM 13*	71	3 wks
15 Dec 90		**I CAN'T SAY GOODBYE** *MCA KIM 14*	51	3 wks

2 May 92	**LOVE IS HOLY** *MCA KIM 15*	**16**	6 wks
27 Jun 92	**HEART OVER MIND** *MCA KIM 16*	**34**	3 wks
12 Sep 92	**WHO DO YOU THINK YOU ARE** *MCA KIM 17* ...	**49**	3 wks
10 Jul 93	**IF I CAN'T HAVE YOU** *MCA KIMTD 18*	**12**	8 wks
13 Nov 93	**IN MY LIFE** *MCA KIMTD 19*	**54**	1 wk

1 Kim Wilde and Junior 2 Mel and Kim

Mel is Mel Smith.

Marty WILDE *UK, male vocalist* — **117 wks**

11 Jul 58	● **ENDLESS SLEEP** *Philips PB 835*	**4**	14 wks
6 Mar 59	● **DONNA** *Philips PB 902*	**3**	16 wks
5 Jun 59	● **A TEENAGER IN LOVE** *Philips PB 926*	**2**	17 wks
3 Jul 59	**DONNA (re-entry)** *Philips PB 902*	**25**	2 wks
25 Sep 59	● **SEA OF LOVE** *Philips PB 959*	**3**	12 wks
11 Dec 59	● **BAD BOY** *Philips PB 972*	**7**	8 wks
10 Mar 60	**JOHNNY ROCCO** *Philips PB 1002*	**30**	4 wks
19 May 60	**THE FIGHT** *Philips PB 1022*	**47**	1 wk
22 Dec 60	**LITTLE GIRL** *Philips PB 1078*	**16**	9 wks
26 Jan 61	● **RUBBER BALL** *Philips PB 1101*	**9**	9 wks
27 Jul 61	**HIDE AND SEEK** *Philips PB 1161*	**47**	2 wks
9 Nov 61	**TOMORROW'S CLOWN** *Philips PB 1191*	**33**	5 wks
24 May 62	**JEZEBEL** *Philips PB 1240*	**19**	11 wks
25 Oct 62	**EVER SINCE YOU SAID GOODBYE** *Philips 326546 BF*	**31**	7 wks

Matthew WILDER *US, male vocalist* — **11 wks**

21 Jan 84	● **BREAK MY STRIDE** *Epic A 3908*	**4**	11 wks

WILDHEARTS *UK, male vocal / instrumental group* — **7 wks**

20 Nov 93	**TV TAN** *Bronze YZ 784CD*	**53**	2 wks
19 Feb 94	**CAFFEINE BOMB** *Bronze YZ 794CD*	**31**	3 wks
9 Jul 94	**SUCKERPUNCH** *Bronz YZ 828CD*	**38**	2 wks

Sue WILKINSON *UK, female vocalist* — **8 wks**

2 Aug 80	**YOU GOTTA BE A HUSTLER IF YOU WANNA GET ON** *Cheapskate CHEAP 2*	**25**	8 wks

WILL TO POWER
US, male / female vocal / instrumental duo — **18 wks**

7 Jan 89	● **BABY I LOVE YOUR WAY - FREEBIRD** *Epic 653094 7*	**6**	9 wks
22 Dec 90	**I'M NOT IN LOVE** *Epic 6565377*	**29**	9 wks

Alyson WILLIAMS *US, female vocalist* — **28 wks**

4 Mar 89	**SLEEP TALK** *Def Jam 654656 7*	**17**	9 wks
6 May 89	**MY LOVE IS SO RAW** *Def Jam 654898 7* 1 ...	**34**	5 wks
19 Aug 89	**I NEED YOUR LOVIN'** *Def Jam 655143 7*	**8**	11 wks
18 Nov 89	**I SECOND THAT EMOTION** *Def Jam 655456 7* ..	**44**	3 wks

1 Alyson Williams featuring Nikki D

Andy WILLIAMS *US, male vocalist* — **228 wks**

19 Apr 57	★ **BUTTERFLY** *London HLA 8399*	**1**	15 wks
21 Jun 57	**I LIKE YOUR KIND OF LOVE** *London HLA 8437*	**16**	10 wks
30 Aug 57	**BUTTERFLY (re-entry)** *London HLA 8399* ...	**29**	1 wk
14 Jun 62	**STRANGER ON THE SHORE** *CBS AAG 103*	**30**	10 wks
21 Mar 63	● **CAN'T GET USED TO LOSING YOU** *CBS AAG 138*	**2**	18 wks
27 Feb 64	**A FOOL NEVER LEARNS** *CBS AAG 182*	**40**	4 wks
16 Sep 65	● **ALMOST THERE** *CBS 201813*	**2**	17 wks
24 Feb 66	**MAY EACH DAY** *CBS 202042*	**19**	8 wks
22 Sep 66	**IN THE ARMS OF LOVE** *CBS 202300*	**33**	7 wks
4 May 67	**MUSIC TO WATCH GIRLS BY** *CBS 2675*	**33**	6 wks
2 Aug 67	**MORE AND MORE** *CBS 2886*	**45**	1 wk
13 Mar 68	● **CAN'T TAKE MY EYES OFF YOU** *CBS 3298* ..	**5**	18 wks
7 May 69	**HAPPY HEART** *CBS 4062*	**47**	1 wk
21 May 69	**HAPPY HEART (re-entry)** *CBS 4062*	**19**	9 wks
14 Mar 70	● **CAN'T HELP FALLING IN LOVE** *CBS 4818* ..	**3**	17 wks
1 Aug 70	**IT'S SO EASY** *CBS 5113*	**13**	13 wks
7 Nov 70	**IT'S SO EASY (re-entry)** *CBS 5113*	**49**	1 wk
21 Nov 70	● **HOME LOVIN' MAN** *CBS 5267*	**7**	12 wks
20 Mar 71	● **(WHERE DO I BEGIN) LOVE STORY** *CBS 7020*	**4**	17 wks
24 Jul 71	**(WHERE DO I BEGIN) LOVE STORY (re-entry)** *CBS 7020*	**49**	1 wk
5 Aug 72	**LOVE THEME FROM THE GODFATHER** *CBS 8166* ..	**50**	1 wk
2 Sep 72	**LOVE THEME FROM THE GODFATHER (re-entry)** *CBS 8166*	**44**	3 wks
30 Sep 72	**LOVE THEME FROM THE GODFATHER (2nd re-entry)** *CBS 8166*	**42**	5 wks
8 Dec 73	● **SOLITAIRE** *CBS 1824*	**4**	18 wks
18 May 74	**GETTING OVER YOU** *CBS 2181*	**35**	5 wks
31 May 75	**YOU LAY SO EASY ON MY MIND** *CBS 3167*	**32**	7 wks
6 Mar 76	**THE OTHER SIDE OF ME** *CBS 3903*	**42**	3 wks

Andy and David WILLIAMS *US, male vocal duo* — **5 wks**

24 Mar 73	**I DON'T KNOW WHY** *MCA MUS 1183*	**37**	5 wks

Do not see Andy Williams. This Andy is the nephew of the other Andy.

Billy WILLIAMS *US, male vocalist* — **9 wks**

2 Aug 57	**I'M GONNA SIT RIGHT DOWN AND WRITE MYSELF A LETTER** *Vogue Coral Q 72266*	**22**	8 wks
18 Oct 57	**I'M GONNA SIT RIGHT DOWN AND WRITE MYSELF A LETTER (re-entry)** *Vogue Coral Q 72266*	**28**	1 wk

Danny WILLIAMS *UK, male vocalist* — **74 wks**

25 May 61	**WE WILL NEVER BE AS YOUNG AS THIS AGAIN** *HMV POP 839*	**44**	3 wks
6 Jul 61	**THE MIRACLE OF YOU** *HMV POP 885*	**41**	8 wks
2 Nov 61	★ **MOON RIVER** *HMV POP 932*	**1**	19 wks
18 Jan 62	**JEANNIE** *HMV POP 968*	**14**	14 wks
12 Apr 62	● **WONDERFUL WORLD OF THE YOUNG** *HMV POP 1002*	**8**	13 wks
5 Jul 62	**TEARS** *HMV POP 1035*	**22**	7 wks
28 Feb 63	**MY OWN TRUE LOVE** *HMV POP 1112*	**45**	3 wks
30 Jul 77	**DANCIN' EASY** *Ensign ENY 3*	**30**	7 wks

Deniece WILLIAMS *US, female vocalist* — **59 wks**

2 Apr 77	★ **FREE** *CBS 4978*	**1**	10 wks
30 Jul 77	● **THAT'S WHAT FRIENDS ARE FOR** *CBS 5432* .	**8**	11 wks
12 Nov 77	**BABY BABY MY LOVE'S ALL FOR YOU** *CBS 5779*	**32**	5 wks
25 Mar 78	● **TOO MUCH TOO LITTLE TOO LATE** *CBS 6164* 1	**3**	14 wks
29 Jul 78	**YOU'RE ALL I NEED TO GET BY** *CBS 6483* 1 .	**45**	6 wks
5 May 84	● **LET'S HEAR IT FOR THE BOY** *CBS A 4319* .	**2**	12 wks
4 Aug 84	**LET'S HEAR IT FOR THE BOY (re-entry)** *CBS A 4319*	**75**	1 wk

1 Johnny Mathis and Deniece Williams

Diana WILLIAMS *US, female vocalist* — **3 wks**

25 Jul 81	**TEDDY BEAR'S LAST RIDE** *Capitol CL 207* ..	**54**	3 wks

Don WILLIAMS *US, male vocalist* — **16 wks**

19 Jun 76	**I RECALL A GYPSY WOMAN** *ABC 4098*	**13**	10 wks
23 Oct 76	**YOU'RE MY BEST FRIEND** *ABC 4144*	**35**	6 wks

Freedom WILLIAMS *US, male rapper* — **31 wks**

15 Dec 90	● **GONNA MAKE YOU SWEAT (EVERYBODY DANCE NOW)** *CBS 6564540* 1	**3**	12 wks
30 Mar 91	**HERE WE GO** *Columbia 6567537* 1	**20**	7 wks
6 Jul 91	● **THINGS THAT MAKE YOU GO HMMM...** *Columbia 6566907* 1	**4**	11 wks
5 Jun 93	**VOICE OF FREEDOM** *Columbia 6593342*	**62**	1 wk

1 C & C Music Factory (featuring Freedom Williams)

Geoffrey WILLIAMS UK, male vocalist — 5 wks

11 Apr 92	IT'S NOT A LOVE THING EMI EM 228	63	2 wks
22 Aug 92	SUMMER BREEZE EMI EM 245	56	3 wks

Iris WILLIAMS UK, female vocalist — 8 wks

27 Oct 79	HE WAS BEAUTIFUL (CAVATINA) (THE THEME FROM 'THE DEER HUNTER') Columbia DB 9070	18	8 wks

John WILLIAMS UK, male instrumentalist - guitar — 11 wks

19 May 79	CAVATINA Cube BUG 80	13	11 wks

John WILLIAMS US, orchestra leader with US, orchestra — 12 wks

18 Dec 82	THEME FROM 'E.T.' (THE EXTRA-TERRESTRIAL) MCA 800	17	10 wks
14 Aug 93	THEME FROM JURASSIC PARK MCA MCSTD 1927	45	2 wks

Kenny WILLIAMS US, male vocalist — 7 wks

19 Nov 77	(YOU'RE) FABULOUS BABE Decca FR 13731	35	7 wks

Larry WILLIAMS US, male vocalist — 18 wks

20 Sep 57	SHORT FAT FANNY London HLN 8472	21	8 wks
17 Jan 58	BONY MORONIE London HLU 8532	11	10 wks

Lenny WILLIAMS US, male vocalist — 7 wks

5 Nov 77	SHOO DOO FU FU OOH ABC 4194	38	4 wks
16 Sep 78	YOU GOT ME BURNING ABC 4228	67	3 wks

Mark WILLIAMS - See Karen BODDINGTON and Mark WILLIAMS

Mason WILLIAMS US, male instrumentalist - guitar — 13 wks

28 Aug 68	● CLASSICAL GAS Warner Bros. WB 7190	9	13 wks

Maurice WILLIAMS and the ZODIACS
US, male vocal group — 9 wks

5 Jan 61	STAY Top Rank JAR 526	14	9 wks

Melanie WILLIAMS UK, female vocalist — 17 wks

10 Apr 93	● AIN'T NO LOVE (AIN'T NO USE) Rob's CDROB 9 [1]	3	11 wks
9 Apr 94	ALL CRIED OUT Columbia 6601872	60	2 wks
11 Jun 94	EVERYDAY THANG Columbia 6604712	38	3 wks
17 Sep 94	NOT ENOUGH Columbia 6607752	65	1 wk

[1] Sub Sub featuring Melanie Williams

Vanessa WILLIAMS US, female vocalist — 16 wks

20 Aug 88	THE RIGHT STUFF Wing WING 3	71	1 wk
25 Mar 89	DREAMIN' Wing WING 4	74	2 wks
19 Aug 89	THE RIGHT STUFF (re-mix) Wing WINR 3	62	2 wks
21 Mar 92	● SAVE THE BEST FOR LAST Polydor PO 192	3	11 wks

Vesta WILLIAMS US, female vocalist — 13 wks

20 Dec 86	ONCE BITTEN TWICE SHY A & M AM 362	14	13 wks

Wendell WILLIAMS US, male rapper — 6 wks

6 Oct 90	EVERYBODY (RAP) Deconstruction PB 44701 [1]	30	4 wks
18 May 91	SO GROOVY Deconstruction PB 44567	74	2 wks

[1] Criminal Element Orchestra and Wendell Williams

WILLING SINNERS - See Marc ALMOND

Bruce WILLIS US, male vocalist — 30 wks

7 Mar 87	● RESPECT YOURSELF Motown ZB 41117	7	10 wks
30 May 87	● UNDER THE BOARDWALK Motown ZB 41349	2	15 wks
12 Sep 87	SECRET AGENT MAN - JAMES BOND IS BACK Motown ZB 41437	43	4 wks
23 Jan 88	COMIN' RIGHT UP Motown ZB 41453	73	1 wk

Chill WILLS - See LAUREL and HARDY with the AVALON BOYS featuring Chill WILLS

Viola WILLS US, female vocalist — 16 wks

6 Oct 79	● GONNA GET ALONG WITHOUT YOU NOW Ariola/Hansa AHA 546	8	10 wks
15 Mar 86	BOTH SIDES NOW / DARE TO DREAM Streetwave KHAN 66	35	6 wks

Al WILSON US, male vocalist — 5 wks

23 Aug 75	THE SNAKE Bell 1436	41	5 wks

Dooley WILSON US, male vocalist — 9 wks

3 Dec 77	AS TIME GOES BY United Artists UP 36331	15	9 wks

Disc has credit 'with the voices of Humphrey Bogart and Ingrid Bergman'.

Jackie WILSON US, male vocalist — 97 wks

15 Nov 57	● REET PETITE Coral Q 72290	6	14 wks
14 Mar 58	TO BE LOVED Coral Q 72306	27	1 wk
28 Mar 58	TO BE LOVED (re-entry) Coral Q 72306	23	6 wks
16 May 58	TO BE LOVED (2nd re-entry) Coral Q 72306	23	6 wks
15 Sep 60	ALL MY LOVE Coral Q 72407	33	6 wks
3 Nov 60	ALL MY LOVE (re-entry) Coral Q 72407	47	1 wk
22 Dec 60	ALONE AT LAST Coral Q 72412	50	1 wk
14 May 69	(YOUR LOVE KEEPS LIFTING ME) HIGHER AND HIGHER MCA BAG 2	11	11 wks
29 Jul 72	● I GET THE SWEETEST FEELING MCA MU 1160	9	13 wks
3 May 75	I GET THE SWEETEST FEELING / HIGHER AND HIGHER (re-issue) Brunswick BR 18	25	8 wks
29 Nov 86	★ REET PETITE (re-issue) SMP SKM 3	1	17 wks
28 Feb 87	● I GET THE SWEETEST FEELING (2nd re-issue) SMP SKM 1	3	11 wks
4 Jul 87	HIGHER AND HIGHER (2nd re-issue) SMP SKM 10	15	7 wks

Higher and Higher was not listed together with I Get The Sweetest Feeling on Brunswick until 17 May 75.

Mari WILSON UK, female vocalist — 34 wks

6 Mar 82	BEAT THE BEAT Compact PINK 2	59	3 wks
8 May 82	BABY IT'S TRUE Compact PINK 3	42	6 wks
11 Sep 82	● JUST WHAT I ALWAYS WANTED Compact PINK 4	8	10 wks
13 Nov 82	(BEWARE) BOYFRIEND Compact PINK 5	51	4 wks
19 Mar 83	CRY ME A RIVER Compact PINK 6	27	7 wks
11 Jun 83	WONDERFUL Compact PINK 7	47	4 wks

Meri WILSON US, female vocalist — 10 wks

27 Aug 77	● TELEPHONE MAN Pye International 7N 25747	6	10 wks

Mike 'Hitman' WILSON US, male producer — 1 wk

22 Sep 90	ANOTHER SLEEPLESS NIGHT Arista 113506	74	1 wk

Precious WILSON - See ERUPTION; MESSIAH

WILSON PHILLIPS US, female vocal group — 33 wks

26 May 90 ● HOLD ON SBK SBK 6	6	12 wks
18 Aug 90 RELEASE ME SBK SBK 11	36	5 wks
10 Nov 90 IMPULSIVE SBK SBK 16	42	3 wks
11 May 91 YOU'RE IN LOVE SBK SBK 25	29	5 wks
23 May 92 YOU WON'T SEE ME CRY SBK SBK 34	18	5 wks
22 Aug 92 GIVE IT UP SBK SBK 36	36	3 wks

Chris WILTSHIRE - See CLASS ACTION featuring Chris WILTSHIRE

WIN UK, male vocal / instrumental group — 3 wks

4 Apr 87 SUPER POPOID GROOVE Swamplands LON 128	63	3 wks

WINANS US, male vocal group — 1 wk

30 Nov 85 LET MY PEOPLE GO (PART 1) Qwest W 8874	71	1 wk

WINDJAMMER US, male vocal / instrumental group — 12 wks

30 Jun 84 TOSSING AND TURNING MCA MCA 897	18	12 wks

Rose WINDROSS - See SOUL II SOUL

WING AND A PRAYER FIFE AND DRUM CORPS
US, male / female vocal / instrumental group — 7 wks

24 Jan 76 BABY FACE Atlantic K 10705	12	7 wks

WINGER US, male vocal / instrumental group — 3 wks

19 Jan 91 MILES AWAY Atlantic A 7802	56	3 wks

Pete WINGFIELD UK, male vocalist — 7 wks

28 Jun 75 ● EIGHTEEN WITH A BULLET Island WIP 6231	7	7 wks

WINGS - See Paul McCARTNEY

Edgar WINTER GROUP US, male instrumental group — 9 wks

26 May 73 FRANKENSTEIN Epic EPC 1440	18	9 wks

Ruby WINTERS US, female vocalist — 35 wks

5 Nov 77 ● I WILL Creole CR 141	4	13 wks
29 Apr 78 COME TO ME Creole CR 153	11	12 wks
26 Aug 78 I WON'T MENTION IT AGAIN Creole CR 160	45	5 wks
16 Jun 79 BABY LAY DOWN Creole CR 171	43	5 wks

Steve WINWOOD UK, male vocalist — 33 wks

17 Jan 81 WHILE YOU SEE A CHANCE Island WIP 6655	45	5 wks
9 Oct 82 VALERIE Island WIP 6818	51	4 wks
28 Jun 86 HIGHER LOVE Island IS 288	13	9 wks
13 Sep 86 FREEDOM OVERSPILL Island IS 294	69	1 wk
24 Jan 87 BACK IN THE HIGH LIFE AGAIN Island IS 303	53	2 wks
19 Sep 87 VALERIE (re-issue) Island IS 336	19	8 wks
11 Jun 88 ROLL WITH IT Virgin VS 1085	53	4 wks

WIRE UK, male vocal / instrumental group — 4 wks

27 Jan 79 OUTDOOR MINER Harvest HAR 5172	51	3 wks
13 May 89 EARDRUM BUZZ Mute MUTE 87	68	1 wk

Norman WISDOM UK, male vocalist — 20 wks

19 Feb 54 ● DON'T LAUGH AT ME Columbia DB 3133	3	15 wks
15 Mar 57 WISDOM OF A FOOL Columbia DB 3903	13	5 wks

Bill WITHERS US, male vocalist — 29 wks

12 Aug 72 LEAN ON ME A & M AMS 7004	18	9 wks
14 Jan 78 ● LOVELY DAY CBS 5773	7	8 wks
25 May 85 OH YEAH! CBS A 6154	60	3 wks
10 Sep 88 ● LOVELY DAY (re-mix) CBS 653001 7	4	9 wks

See also Grover Washington Jr.

WIZZARD UK, male vocal / instrumental group — 77 wks

9 Dec 72 ● BALL PARK INCIDENT Harvest HAR 5062	6	12 wks
21 Apr 73 ★ SEE MY BABY JIVE Harvest HAR 5070	1	17 wks
1 Sep 73 ★ ANGEL FINGERS Harvest HAR 5076	1	10 wks
8 Dec 73 ● I WISH IT COULD BE CHRISTMAS EVERYDAY Harvest HAR 5079 [1]	4	9 wks
27 Apr 74 ● ROCK 'N' ROLL WINTER Warner Bros. K 16357	6	7 wks
10 Aug 74 THIS IS THE STORY OF MY LOVE (BABY) Warner Bros. K 16434	34	4 wks
21 Dec 74 ● ARE YOU READY TO ROCK Warner Bros. K 16497	8	10 wks
19 Dec 81 I WISH IT COULD BE CHRISTMAS EVERYDAY (re-issue) Harvest HAR 5173 [1]	41	4 wks
15 Dec 84 I WISH IT COULD BE CHRISTMAS EVERYDAY (re-entry of re-issue) Harvest HAR 5173 [1]	23	4 wks

[1] Wizzard featuring vocal backing by the Suedettes plus the Stockland Green Bilateral School First Year Choir with additional noises by Miss Snob and Class 3C

Jah WOBBLE'S INVADERS OF THE HEART
UK, male vocalist / multi-instrumentalist — 10 wks

1 Feb 92 VISIONS OF YOU Oval OVAL 103	35	5 wks
30 Apr 94 BECOMING MORE LIKE GOD Island CID 571	36	2 wks
25 Jun 94 THE SUN DOES RISE Island CID 587	41	3 wks

First hit features the uncredited vocals of Sinead O'Connor.

Terry WOGAN Ireland, male vocalist — 5 wks

7 Jan 78 FLORAL DANCE Philips 6006 592	21	5 wks

WOLFSBANE US, male vocal / instrumental group — 1 wk

5 Oct 91 EZY Def American DEFA 11	68	1 wk

Bobby WOMACK US, male vocalist — 20 wks

16 Jun 84 TELL ME WHY Motown TMG 1339	60	3 wks
5 Oct 85 I WISH HE DIDN'T TRUST ME SO MUCH MCA MCA 994	64	2 wks
26 Sep 87 SO THE STORY GOES Chrysalis LIB 3 [1]	34	8 wks
7 Nov 87 LIVING IN A BOX MCA MCA 1210	70	2 wks
3 Apr 93 I'M BACK FOR MORE Dome CDDOME 1002 [2]	27	5 wks

[1] Living In A Box featuring Bobby Womack [2] Lulu and Bobby Womack

See also Wilton Felder.

WOMACK and WOMACK
US, male / female vocal duo — 51 wks

28 Apr 84 LOVE WARS Elektra E 9799	14	10 wks
30 Jun 84 BABY I'M SCARED OF YOU Elektra E 9733	72	2 wks
6 Dec 86 SOUL LOVE - SOUL MAN Manhattan MT 16	58	6 wks
6 Aug 88 TEARDROPS Fourth & Broadway BRW 101	3	17 wks
12 Nov 88 LIFE'S JUST A BALLGAME Fourth & Broadway BRW 116	32	5 wks
25 Feb 89 CELEBRATE THE WORLD Fourth & Broadway BRW 125	19	8 wks
5 Feb 94 SECRET STAR Warner Bros. W 0222CD [1]	46	3 wks

[1] House Of Zekkariyas AKA Womack and Womack

WOMBLES
UK, male vocalist, arranger and producer - Mike Batt — 87 wks

26 Jan 74 ● THE WOMBLING SONG CBS 1794	4	23 wks

6 Apr 74	● REMEMBER YOU'RE A WOMBLE *CBS 2241*	3	16 wks
22 Jun 74	● BANANA ROCK *CBS 2465*	9	13 wks
12 Oct 74	MINUETTO ALLEGRETTO *CBS 2710*	16	9 wks
7 Dec 74	● WOMBLING MERRY CHRISTMAS *CBS 2842*	2	8 wks
10 May 75	WOMBLING WHITE TIE AND TAILS *CBS 3266*	22	7 wks
9 Aug 75	SUPER WOMBLE *CBS 3480*	20	6 wks
13 Dec 75	LET'S WOMBLE TO THE PARTY TONIGHT *CBS 3794*	34	5 wks

Stevie WONDER
US, male vocalist / multi-instrumentalist — **404 wks**

3 Feb 66	UPTIGHT *Tamla Motown TMG 545*	14	10 wks
18 Aug 66	BLOWIN' IN THE WIND *Tamla Motown TMG 570*	36	5 wks
5 Jan 67	A PLACE IN THE SUN *Tamla Motown TMG 588*	20	5 wks
26 Jul 67	● I WAS MADE TO LOVE HER *Tamla Motown TMG 613*	5	15 wks
25 Oct 67	I'M WONDERING *Tamla Motown TMG 626*	22	8 wks
8 May 68	SHOO BE DOO BE DOO DA DAY *Tamla Motown TMG 653*	46	4 wks
18 Dec 68	● FOR ONCE IN MY LIFE *Tamla Motown TMG 679*	3	13 wks
19 Mar 69	I DON'T KNOW WHY *Tamla Motown TMG 690*	14	10 wks
9 Jul 69	I DON'T KNOW WHY (re-entry) *Tamla Motown TMG 690*	43	1 wk
16 Jul 69	● MY CHERIE AMOUR *Tamla Motown TMG 690*	4	15 wks
15 Nov 69	● YESTER-ME YESTER-YOU YESTERDAY *Tamla Motown TMG 717*	2	13 wks
28 Mar 70	● NEVER HAD A DREAM COME TRUE *Tamla Motown TMG 731*	6	12 wks
18 Jul 70	SIGNED SEALED DELIVERED I'M YOURS *Tamla Motown TMG 744*	15	9 wks
26 Sep 70	SIGNED SEALED DELIVERED I'M YOURS (re-entry) *Tamla Motown TMG 744*	49	1 wk
21 Nov 70	HEAVEN HELP US ALL *Tamla Motown TMG 757*	29	11 wks
15 May 71	WE CAN WORK IT OUT *Tamla Motown TMG 772*	27	7 wks
22 Jan 72	IF YOU REALLY LOVE ME *Tamla Motown TMG 798*	20	7 wks
3 Feb 73	SUPERSTITION *Tamla Motown TMG 841*	11	9 wks
19 May 73	● YOU ARE THE SUNSHINE OF MY LIFE *Tamla Motown TMG 852*	7	11 wks
13 Oct 73	HIGHER GROUND *Tamla Motown TMG 869*	29	5 wks
12 Jan 74	LIVING FOR THE CITY *Tamla Motown TMG 881*	15	9 wks
13 Apr 74	● HE'S MISSTRA KNOW IT ALL *Tamla Motown TMG 892*	10	9 wks
19 Oct 74	YOU HAVEN'T DONE NOTHIN' *Tamla Motown TMG 921*	30	5 wks
11 Jan 75	BOOGIE ON REGGAE WOMAN *Tamla Motown TMG 928*	12	8 wks
18 Dec 76	● I WISH *Tamla Motown TMG 1054*	5	10 wks
9 Apr 77	● SIR DUKE *Motown TMG 1068*	2	9 wks
10 Sep 77	ANOTHER STAR *Motown TMG 1083*	29	5 wks
24 Feb 79	POPS WE LOVE YOU *Motown TMG 1136* [1]	66	5 wks
24 Nov 79	SEND ONE YOUR LOVE *Motown TMG 1149*	52	3 wks
26 Jan 80	BLACK ORCHID *Motown TMG 1173*	63	3 wks
29 Mar 80	OUTSIDE MY WINDOW *Motown TMG 1179*	52	4 wks
13 Sep 80	● MASTERBLASTER (JAMMIN') *Motown TMG 1204*	2	10 wks
27 Dec 80	● I AIN'T GONNA STAND FOR IT *Motown TMG 1215*	10	10 wks
7 Mar 81	● LATELY *Motown TMG 1226*	3	13 wks
25 Jul 81	● HAPPY BIRTHDAY *Motown TMG 1235*	2	11 wks
23 Jan 82	THAT GIRL *Motown TMG 1254*	39	6 wks
10 Apr 82	★ EBONY AND IVORY *Parlophone R 6054* [2]	1	10 wks
5 Jun 82	DO I DO *Motown TMG 1269*	10	7 wks
25 Sep 82	RIBBON IN THE SKY *Motown TMG 1280*	45	4 wks
25 Aug 84	★ I JUST CALLED TO SAY I LOVE YOU *Motown TMG 1349*	1	24 wks
1 Dec 84	LOVE LIGHT IN FLIGHT *Motown TMG 1364*	44	5 wks
29 Dec 84	DON'T DRIVE DRUNK *Motown TMG 1372*	71	1 wk
12 Jan 85	DON'T DRIVE DRUNK (re-entry) *Motown TMG 1372*	62	2 wks
7 Sep 85	● PART-TIME LOVER *Motown ZB 40351*	3	12 wks
9 Nov 85	THAT'S WHAT FRIENDS ARE FOR *Arista ARIST 638* [3]	16	9 wks
23 Nov 85	GO HOME *Motown ZB 40501*	67	2 wks
28 Dec 85	I JUST CALLED TO SAY I LOVE YOU (re-entry) *Motown TMG 1349*	64	2 wks
8 Mar 86	OVERJOYED *Motown ZB 40567*	17	8 wks
17 Jan 87	STRANGER ON THE SHORE OF LOVE *Motown WOND 2*	55	3 wks
31 Oct 87	SKELETONS *Motown ZB 41439*	59	3 wks
28 May 88	GET IT *Motown ZB 41883* [4]	37	4 wks
6 Aug 88	● MY LOVE *CBS JULIO 2* [5]	5	11 wks
20 May 89	FREE *Motown ZB 42855*	49	5 wks
12 Oct 91	FUN DAY *Motown ZB 44957*	63	1 wk

[1] Diana Ross, Marvin Gaye, Smokey Robinson and Stevie Wonder [2] Paul McCartney with Stevie Wonder [3] Dionne Warwick and Friends featuring Elton John, Gladys Knight and Stevie Wonder [4] Stevie Wonder and Michael Jackson [5] Julio Iglesias featuring Stevie Wonder

WONDER DOGS *UK, canine vocal group* — **7 wks**

21 Aug 82	RUFF MIX *Flip FLIP 001*	31	7 wks

WONDER STUFF *UK, male vocal / instrumental group* — **66 wks**

30 Apr 88	GIVE GIVE GIVE ME MORE MORE MORE *Polydor GONE 3*	72	2 wks
16 Jul 88	A WISH AWAY *Polydor GONE 4*	43	5 wks
24 Sep 88	IT'S YER MONEY I'M AFTER BABY *Polydor GONE 5*	40	3 wks
11 Mar 89	WHO WANTS TO BE THE DISCO KING *Far Out GONE 6*	28	3 wks
23 Sep 89	DON'T LET ME DOWN GENTLY *Polydor GONE 7*	19	4 wks
11 Nov 89	GOLDEN GREEN / GET TOGETHER *Polydor GONE 8*	33	3 wks
12 May 90	CIRCLESQUARE *Polydor GONE 10*	20	4 wks
13 Apr 91	● THE SIZE OF A COW *Polydor GONE 11*	5	7 wks
25 May 91	CAUGHT IN MY SHADOW *Polydor GONE 12*	18	3 wks
7 Sep 91	SLEEP ALONE *Polydor GONE 13*	43	2 wks
26 Oct 91	★ DIZZY *Sense SIGH 712* [1]	1	12 wks
25 Jan 92	● WELCOME TO THE CHEAP SEATS (EP) *Polydor GONE 14*	8	5 wks
25 Sep 93	● ON THE ROPES (EP) *Polydor GONCD 15*	10	4 wks
27 Nov 93	FULL OF LIFE (HAPPY NOW) *Polydor GONCD 16*	28	3 wks
26 Mar 94	HOT LOVE NOW *Polydor GONCD 17*	19	3 wks
10 Sep 94	UNBEARABLE *Polydor GONCD 18*	16	3 wks

[1] Vic Reeves and the Wonder Stuff

Tracks on Welcome To The Cheap Seats (EP): *Welcome To The Cheap Seats / Me, My Mom, My Dad And My Brother / Will The Circle Be Unbroken / That's Entertainment. Tracks on* On The Ropes (EP): *On The Ropes / Professional Disturber Of The Peace / Hank And John.*

WONDRESS - *See* MANTRONIX

Brenton WOOD *US, male vocalist* — **14 wks**

27 Dec 67	● GIMME LITTLE SIGN *Liberty LBF 15021*	8	14 wks

Roy WOOD *UK, male vocalist / multi-instrumentalist* — **39 wks**

11 Aug 73	DEAR ELAINE *Harvest HAR 5074*	18	8 wks
1 Dec 73	● FOREVER *Harvest HAR 5078*	8	13 wks
15 Jun 74	GOING DOWN THE ROAD *Harvest HAR 5083*	13	7 wks
31 May 75	OH WHAT A SHAME *Jet 754*	13	7 wks
22 Nov 86	WATERLOO *IRS IRM 125* [1]	45	4 wks

[1] Doctor and the Medics featuring Roy Wood

WOODENTOPS *UK, male vocal / instrumental group* — **1 wk**

11 Oct 86	EVERYDAY LIVING *Rough Trade RT 178*	72	1 wk

Edward WOODWARD *UK, male vocalist* — **2 wks**

16 Jan 71	THE WAY YOU LOOK TONIGHT *DJM DJS 232*	50	1 wk
30 Jan 71	THE WAY YOU LOOK TONIGHT (re-entry) *DJM DJS 232*	42	1 wk

STEVIE WONDER is embraced by Barbra Streisand and admired by ASCAP President Morton Gould and Lionel Richie at the 1986 ASCAP Awards Dinner. (LFI)

MARTY WILDE poses with his family, the children labelled for future reference books such as this.

KIM WILDE shares a photo with Rick Astley in 1987, the same year she joined Junior and Mel Smith for top ten duets.

Sheb WOOLEY US, male vocalist — **8 wks**

| 20 Jun 58 | **PURPLE PEOPLE EATER** MGM 981 | **12** | 8 wks |

WORKING WEEK
UK, male/female vocal/instrumental group — **2 wks**

| 9 Jun 84 | **VENCEREMOS - WE WILL WIN** Virgin VS 684 | **64** | 2 wks |

WORLD - See LIL' LOUIS

WORLD OF TWIST UK, male vocal/instrumental group — **12 wks**

24 Nov 90	**THE STORM** Circa YR 55	**42**	3 wks
5 Jan 91	**THE STORM (re-entry)** Circa YR 55	**74**	2 wks
23 Mar 91	**SONS OF THE STAGE** Circa YR 62	**47**	3 wks
12 Oct 91	**SWEETS** Circa YR 72	**58**	2 wks
22 Feb 92	**SHE'S A RAINBOW** Circa YR 82	**62**	2 wks

WORLD PARTY
Ireland/UK, male vocal/instrumental group — **27 wks**

14 Feb 87	**SHIP OF FOOLS** Ensign ENY 606	**42**	6 wks
16 Jun 90	**MESSAGE IN THE BOX** Ensign ENY 631	**39**	6 wks
15 Sep 90	**WAY DOWN NOW** Ensign ENY 634	**66**	2 wks
18 May 91	**THANK YOU WORLD** Ensign ENY 643	**68**	1 wk
10 Apr 93	**IS IT LIKE TODAY** Ensign CDENY 658	**19**	6 wks
10 Jul 93	**GIVE IT ALL AWAY** Ensign CDENY 659	**43**	3 wks
2 Oct 93	**ALL I GAVE** Ensign CDENYS 660	**37**	3 wks

WORLD PREMIERE US, male vocal/instrumental group — **4 wks**

| 28 Jan 84 | **SHARE THE NIGHT** Epic A 4133 | **64** | 4 wks |

WORLD WARRIOR UK, male producer - Simon Harris — **1 wk**

| 16 Apr 94 | **STREET FIGHTER II** Living Beat LBECD 27 | **70** | 1 wk |

See also Simon Harris

WORLD'S FAMOUS SUPREME TEAM
US, male vocal/scratch group — **18 wks**

4 Dec 82	● **BUFFALO GALS** Charisma MALC 1 [1]	**9**	12 wks
25 Feb 84	**HEY DJ** Charisma TEAM 1	**52**	5 wks
8 Dec 90	**OPERAA HOUSE** Virgin VS 1273 [2]	**75**	1 wk

[1] Malcolm McLaren and the World's Famous Supreme Team [2] World's Famous Supreme Team Show

WORLDS APART UK, male vocal group — **17 wks**

27 Mar 93	**HEAVEN MUST BE MISSING AN ANGEL** Arista 74321139362	**29**	3 wks
3 Jul 93	**WONDERFUL WORLD** Arista 74321153402	**51**	1 wk
25 Sep 93	**EVERLASTING LOVE** Bell 74321164802	**20**	4 wks
26 Mar 94	**COULD IT BE I'M FALLING IN LOVE** Bell 74321189952	**15**	6 wks
4 Jun 94	**BEGGIN' TO BE WRITTEN** Bell 74321211982	**29**	3 wks

WRECKX-N-EFFECT US, male vocal group — **18 wks**

13 Jan 90	**JUICY** Motown ZB 43295 [1]	**29**	7 wks
5 Dec 92	**RUMP SHAKER** MCA MCS 1725	**24**	7 wks
7 May 94	**WRECKX SHOP** MCA MCSTD 1969	**26**	2 wks
13 Aug 94	**RUMP SHAKER (re-issue)** MCA MCSTD 1989	**40**	2 wks

[1] Wrecks-N-Effect

Betty WRIGHT US, female vocalist — **23 wks**

| 25 Jan 75 | **SHOORAH SHOORAH** RCA 2491 | **27** | 7 wks |
| 19 Apr 75 | **WHERE IS THE LOVE** RCA 2548 | **25** | 7 wks |

| 8 Feb 86 | **PAIN** Cooltempo COOL 117 | **42** | 6 wks |
| 9 Sep 89 | **KEEP LOVE NEW** Sure Delight SD 11 | **71** | 3 wks |

Ian WRIGHT UK, male vocalist — **2 wks**

| 28 Aug 93 | **DO THE RIGHT THING** M & G MAGCD 45 | **43** | 2 wks |

Ruby WRIGHT UK, female vocalist — **15 wks**

16 Apr 54	● **BIMBO** Parlophone R 3816	**7**	4 wks
21 May 54	**BIMBO (re-entry)** Parlophone R 3816	**12**	1 wk
22 May 59	**THREE STARS** Parlophone R 4556	**19**	10 wks

Three Stars is narrated by Dick Pike.

Steve WRIGHT UK, male vocalist — **10 wks**

27 Nov 82	**I'M ALRIGHT** RCA 296 [1]	**40**	6 wks
15 Oct 83	**GET SOME THERAPY** RCA RCA 362 [2]	**75**	1 wk
1 Dec 84	**THE GAY CAVALIEROS (THE STORY SO FAR)** MCA 925	**61**	3 wks

[1] Young Steve and the Afternoon Boys [2] Steve Wright and the Sisters of Soul

WURZELS UK, male vocal/instrumental group — **28 wks**

2 Feb 67	**DRINK UP THY ZIDER** Columbia DB 8081 [1]	**45**	1 wk
15 May 76	★ **COMBINE HARVESTER (BRAND NEW KEY)** EMI 2450	**1**	13 wks
11 Sep 76	● **I AM A CIDER DRINKER (PALOMA BLANCA)** EMI 2520	**3**	9 wks
25 Jun 77	**FARMER BILL'S COWMAN (I WAS KAISER BILL'S BATMAN)** EMI 2637	**32**	5 wks

[1] Adge Cutler and the Wurzels.

WWF SUPERSTARS US/UK, male wrestling vocalists — **15 wks**

12 Dec 92	● **SLAM JAM** Arista 74321124887	**4**	8 wks
13 Feb 93	**SLAM JAM (re-entry)** Arista 74321124887	**75**	1 wk
3 Apr 93	**WRESTLEMANIA** Arista 74321136832	**14**	5 wks
10 Jul 93	**USA** Arista 74321153092	**71**	1 wk

Robert WYATT UK, male vocalist — **11 wks**

| 28 Sep 74 | **I'M A BELIEVER** Virgin VS 114 | **29** | 5 wks |
| 7 May 83 | **SHIPBUILDING** Rough Trade RT 115 | **35** | 6 wks |

Michael WYCOFF US, male vocalist — **2 wks**

| 23 Jul 83 | **(DO YOU REALLY LOVE ME) TELL ME LOVE** RCA 348 | **60** | 2 wks |

Pete WYLIE UK, male vocalist — **18 wks**

3 May 86	**SINFUL** Eternal MDM 7	**13**	10 wks
13 Sep 86	**DIAMOND GIRL** Eternal MDM 12	**57**	3 wks
13 Apr 91	**SINFUL!** Siren SRN 138 [1]	**28**	5 wks

[1] Pete Wylie with the Farm

Bill WYMAN UK, male vocalist — **13 wks**

| 25 Jul 81 | **(SI SI) JE SUIS UN ROCK STAR** A & M AMS 8144 | **14** | 9 wks |
| 20 Mar 82 | **A NEW FASHION** A & M AMS 8209 | **37** | 4 wks |

Jane WYMAN - See Bing CROSBY

Tammy WYNETTE US, female vocalist — **35 wks**

| 26 Apr 75 | ★ **STAND BY YOUR MAN** Epic EPC 7137 | **1** | 12 wks |
| 28 Jun 75 | **D. I. V. O. R. C. E.** Epic EPC 3361 | **12** | 7 wks |

12 Jun 76	I DON'T WANNA PLAY HOUSE *Epic EPC 4091* **37**	4 wks
7 Dec 91 ●	JUSTIFIED AND ANCIENT	
	KLF Communications KLF 099 [1] **2**	12 wks

[1] KLF, guest vocals: Tammy Wynette

Mark WYNTER *UK, male vocalist* **80 wks**

25 Aug 60	IMAGE OF A GIRL *Decca F 11263* **11**	10 wks
10 Nov 60	KICKING UP THE LEAVES *Decca F 11279* **24**	10 wks
9 Mar 61	DREAM GIRL *Decca F 11323* **27**	5 wks
8 Jun 61	EXCLUSIVELY YOURS *Decca F 11354* **32**	7 wks
4 Oct 62 ●	VENUS IN BLUE JEANS *Pye 7N 15466* **4**	15 wks
13 Dec 62 ●	GO AWAY LITTLE GIRL *Pye 7N 15492* **6**	11 wks
6 Jun 63	SHY GIRL *Pye 7N 15525* **28**	6 wks
14 Nov 63	IT'S ALMOST TOMORROW *Pye 7N 15577*.........**12**	12 wks
9 Apr 64	ONLY YOU *Pye 7N 15626* **38**	4 wks

Malcolm X *US, male orator* **4 wks**

| 7 Apr 84 | NO SELL OUT *Tommy Boy IS 165* ....**60** | 4 wks |

Hit features credit: 'Music by Keith Le Blanc'.

Miss X *UK, female vocalist - Joyce Blair* **6 wks**

| 1 Aug 63 | CHRISTINE *Ember S 175* ....**37** | 6 wks |

XAVIER *US, male vocal / instrumental group* **3 wks**

| 20 Mar 82 | WORK THAT SUCKER TO DEATH / LOVE | |
| | IS THE ONE *Liberty UP 651* ....**53** | 3 wks |

XPANSIONS *UK, male producer - Ritchie Malone* **16 wks**

6 Oct 90	ELEVATION *Optimism 113683* **49**	5 wks
23 Feb 91 ●	MOVE YOUR BODY (re-mix) *Arista 113 683* **7**	9 wks
15 Jun 91	WHAT YOU WANT *Arista 114 246* [1] **55**	2 wks

[1] Xpansions featuring Dale Joyner

Move Your Body is a re-mix of Elevation.

X-PRESS 2 *UK, male instrumental / production group* **5 wks**

5 Jun 93	LONDON X-PRESS *Junior Boy's Own JBO 12* **59**	1 wk
16 Oct 93	SAY WHAT! *Junior Boy's Own JBO 16CD*...........**32**	2 wks
30 Jul 94	ROCK 2 HOUSE / HIP HOUSIN'	
	Junior Boy's Own JBO 21CD [1] **55**	2 wks

[1] X-Press 2 featuring Lo-Pro

X-RAY SPEX *UK, male / female vocal / instrumental group* **32 wks**

29 Apr 78	THE DAY THE WORLD TURNED DAY-GLO	
	EMI International INT 553 ....**23**	7 wks
22 Jul 78	IDENTITY *EMI International INT 563* **24**	10 wks
4 Nov 78	GERM FREE ADOLESCENCE	
	EMI International INT 573 ....**19**	11 wks
21 Apr 79	HIGHLY INFLAMMABLE *EMI International INT 583*..**45**	4 wks

XSCAPE *US, female vocal group* **4 wks**

| 20 Nov 93 | JUST KICKIN' IT *Columbia 6598622*..................**49** | 2 wks |
| 5 Nov 94 | JUST KICKIN' IT (re-issue) *Columbia 6608642*......**54** | 2 wks |

XTC *UK, male vocal / instrumental group* **70 wks**

12 May 79	LIFE BEGINS AT THE HOP *Virgin VS 259*..............**54**	4 wks
22 Sep 79	MAKING PLANS FOR NIGEL *Virgin VS 282* **17**	11 wks
6 Sep 80	GENERALS AND MAJORS / DON'T LOSE	
	YOUR TEMPER *Virgin VS 365*....................**32**	8 wks
18 Oct 80	TOWERS OF LONDON *Virgin VS 372* **31**	5 wks
24 Jan 81	SGT ROCK (IS GOING TO HELP ME) *Virgin VS 384* ..**16**	9 wks
23 Jan 82 ●	SENSES WORKING OVERTIME *Virgin VS 462* **10**	9 wks
27 Mar 82	BALL AND CHAIN *Virgin VS 482* **58**	4 wks
15 Oct 83	LOVE ON A FARMBOY'S WAGES *Virgin VS 613* **50**	4 wks
29 Sep 84	ALL YOU PRETTY GIRLS *Virgin VS 709* **55**	5 wks
28 Jan 89	MAYOR OF SIMPLETON *Virgin VS 1158* **46**	5 wks
4 Apr 92	THE DISAPPOINTED *Virgin VS 1404* **33**	5 wks
13 Jun 92	THE BALLAD OF PETER PUMPKINHEAD	
	Virgin VS 1415 ....**71**	1 wk

Y & T *US, male vocal / instrumental group* **4 wks**

| 13 Aug 83 | MEAN STREAK *A & M AM 135* ....**41** | 4 wks |

YA KID K - *See HI-TEK 3 featuring YA KID K; TECHNOTRONIC*

Weird Al YANKOVIC *US, male vocalist* **8 wks**

| 7 Apr 84 | EAT IT *Scotti Brothers/Epic A 4257* ....**36** | 7 wks |
| 4 Jul 92 | SMELLS LIKE NIRVANA *Scotti Brothers PO 219*........**58** | 1 wk |

YARBROUGH and PEOPLES
US, male / female vocal / instrumental duo **20 wks**

27 Dec 80 ●	DON'T STOP THE MUSIC *Mercury MER 53* **7**	12 wks
5 May 84	DON'T WASTE YOUR TIME	
	Total Experience XE 501 ....**60**	3 wks
11 Jan 86	GUILTY *Total Experience FB 49905* **53**	3 wks
5 Jul 86	I WOULDN'T LIE *Total Experience FB 49841* **61**	2 wks

YARDBIRDS *UK, male vocal / instrumental group* **62 wks**

12 Nov 64	GOOD MORNING LITTLE SCHOOLGIRL	
	Columbia DB 7391 ....**44**	4 wks
18 Mar 65 ●	FOR YOUR LOVE *Columbia DB 7499* **3**	12 wks
17 Jun 65 ●	HEART FULL OF SOUL *Columbia DB 7594*................**2**	13 wks
14 Oct 65 ●	EVIL HEARTED YOU / STILL I'M SAD	
	Columbia DB 7706 ....**3**	10 wks
3 Mar 66 ●	SHAPES OF THINGS *Columbia DB 7848* **3**	9 wks
2 Jun 66 ●	OVER UNDER SIDEWAYS DOWN	
	Columbia DB 7928 ....**10**	9 wks
27 Oct 66	HAPPENINGS TEN YEARS TIME AGO	
	Columbia DB 8024 ....**43**	5 wks

YAZOO *UK, female / male vocal / instrumental duo* **53 wks**

17 Apr 82 ●	ONLY YOU *Mute MUTE 020* **2**	14 wks
17 Jul 82 ●	DON'T GO *Mute YAZ 001* **3**	11 wks
20 Nov 82	THE OTHER SIDE OF LOVE *Mute YAZ 002* **13**	9 wks
21 May 83 ●	NOBODY'S DIARY *Mute YAZ 003* **3**	11 wks
8 Dec 90	SITUATION *Mute YAZ 4* **14**	8 wks

YAZZ *UK, female vocalist* **67 wks**

20 Feb 88 ●	DOCTORIN' THE HOUSE	
	Ahead Of Our Time CCUT 27 [1] **6**	9 wks
23 Jul 88 ★	THE ONLY WAY IS UP *Big Life BLR 4* [2] **1**	15 wks
29 Oct 88 ●	STAND UP FOR YOUR LOVE RIGHTS *Big Life BLR 5* ..**2**	12 wks
4 Feb 89 ●	FINE TIME *Big Life BLR 6*...........................**9**	8 wks
29 Apr 89	WHERE HAS ALL THE LOVE GONE *Big Life BLR 8*....**16**	6 wks
23 Jun 90	TREAT ME GOOD *Big Life BLR 24* **20**	5 wks

28 Mar 92	**ONE TRUE WOMAN** *Polydor PO 198*		**60**	2 wks
31 Jul 93	**HOW LONG** *Polydor PZCD 252* **3**		**31**	5 wks
2 Apr 94	**HAVE MERCY** *Polydor PZCD 309*		**42**	3 wks
9 Jul 94	**EVERYBODY'S GOT TO LEARN SOMETIME** *Polydor PZCD 316*		**56**	2 wks

1 Coldcut featuring Yazz and the Plastic Population **2** Yazz and the Plastic Population **3** Yazz and Aswad

YELL! *UK, male vocal duo* **8 wks**

20 Jan 90	● **INSTANT REPLAY** *Fanfare FAN 22*		**10**	8 wks

YELLO *Switzerland, male vocal / instrumental duo* **42 wks**

25 Jun 83	**I LOVE YOU** *Stiff BUY 176*		**41**	4 wks
26 Nov 83	**LOST AGAIN** *Stiff BUY 191*		**73**	1 wk
9 Aug 86	**GOLDRUSH** *Mercury MER 218*		**54**	3 wks
22 Aug 87	**THE RHYTHM DIVINE** *Mercury MER 253* **1**		**54**	2 wks
27 Aug 88	● **THE RACE** *Mercury YELLO 1*		**7**	11 wks
17 Dec 88	**TIED UP** *Mercury YELLO 2*		**60**	5 wks
25 Mar 89	**OF COURSE I'M LYING** *Mercury YELLO 3*		**23**	8 wks
22 Jul 89	**BLAZING SADDLES** *Mercury YELLO 4*		**47**	2 wks
8 Jun 91	**RUBBERBANDMAN** *Mercury YELLO 5*		**58**	2 wks
5 Sep 92	**JUNGLE BILL** *Mercury MER 376*		**61**	2 wks
7 Nov 92	**THE RACE (re-issue)** *Mercury MER 382*		**55**	1 wk
15 Oct 94	**HOW HOW** *Mercury MERCD 414*		**59**	1 wk

1 Yello featuring Shirley Bassey

YELLOW DOG *US / UK, male vocal / instrumental group* **13 wks**

4 Feb 78	● **JUST ONE MORE NIGHT** *Virgin VS 195*		**8**	9 wks
22 Jul 78	**WAIT UNTIL MIDNIGHT** *Virgin VS 217*		**54**	4 wks

YELLOW MAGIC ORCHESTRA
Japan, male instrumental group **11 wks**

14 Jun 80	**COMPUTER GAME (THEME FROM 'THE INVADERS')** *A & M AMS 7502*		**17**	11 wks

YELLOWCOATS - *See Paul SHANE and the YELLOWCOATS*

YES *UK / South Africa, male vocal / instrumental group* **31 wks**

17 Sep 77	● **WONDEROUS STORIES** *Atlantic K 10999*		**7**	9 wks
26 Nov 77	**GOING FOR THE ONE** *Atlantic K 11047*		**24**	4 wks
9 Sep 78	**DON'T KILL THE WHALE** *Atlantic K 11184*		**36**	4 wks
12 Nov 83	**OWNER OF A LONELY HEART** *Acto B 9817*		**28**	9 wks
31 Mar 84	**LEAVE IT** *Acto B 9787*		**56**	4 wks
3 Oct 87	**LOVE WILL FIND A WAY** *Atco A 9449*		**73**	1 wk

Group were UK only for first three hits.

Melissa YIANNAKOU - *See DESIYA featuring Melissa YIANNAKOU*

YIN and YAN *UK, male vocal duo* **5 wks**

29 Mar 75	**IF** *EMI 2282*		**25**	5 wks

Y?N-VEE *US, female vocal group* **1 wk**

17 Dec 94	**CHOCOLATE** *RAL RALCD 2*		**65**	1 wk

Tukka YOOT - *See US3*

YOSHIKI - *See Roger TAYLOR*

YOTHU YINDI *Australia, male vocal / instrumental group* **1 wk**

15 Feb 92	**TREATY** *Hollywood HWD 116*		**72**	1 wk

Faron YOUNG *US, male vocalist* **23 wks**

15 Jul 72	● **IT'S FOUR IN THE MORNING** *Mercury 6052 140*		**3**	23 wks

Jimmy YOUNG *UK, male vocalist* **88 wks**

9 Jan 53	**FAITH CAN MOVE MOUNTAINS** *Decca F 9986*		**11**	1 wk
21 Aug 53	● **ETERNALLY** *Decca F 10130*		**8**	9 wks
6 May 55	★ **UNCHAINED MELODY** *Decca F 10502*		**1**	19 wks
16 Sep 55	★ **THE MAN FROM LARAMIE** *Decca F 10597*		**1**	12 wks
23 Dec 55	**SOMEONE ON YOUR MIND** *Decca F 10640*		**13**	5 wks
16 Mar 56	● **CHAIN GANG** *Decca F 10694*		**9**	6 wks
8 Jun 56	**WAYWARD WIND** *Decca F 10736*		**27**	1 wk
22 Jun 56	**RICH MAN POOR MAN** *Decca F 10736*		**25**	1 wk
28 Sep 56	● **MORE** *Decca F 10774*		**4**	17 wks
3 May 57	**ROUND AND ROUND** *Decca F 10875*		**30**	1 wk
10 Oct 63	**MISS YOU** *Columbia DB 7119*		**15**	13 wks
26 Mar 64	**UNCHAINED MELODY** *Columbia DB 7234*		**43**	3 wks

The versions of Unchained Melody *on Decca and on Columbia are different recordings.* Round and Round *is with the Michael Sammes Singers. See also Various Artists (EPs & LPs) - All Star Hit Parade No.2.*

John Paul YOUNG *Australia, male vocalist* **16 wks**

29 Apr 78	● **LOVE IS IN THE AIR** *Ariola ARO 117*		**5**	13 wks
14 Nov 92	**LOVE IS IN THE AIR (re-mix)** *Columbia 6587697*		**49**	3 wks

Karen YOUNG *UK, female vocalist* **21 wks**

6 Sep 69	● **NOBODY'S CHILD** *Major Minor MM 625*		**6**	21 wks

Karen YOUNG *US, female vocalist* **8 wks**

19 Aug 78	**HOT SHOT** *Atlantic K 11180*		**34**	7 wks
24 Feb 79	**HOT SHOT (re-issue)** *Atlantic LV 8*		**75**	1 wk

Neil YOUNG *Canada, male vocalist* **22 wks**

11 Mar 72	● **HEART OF GOLD** *Reprise K 14140*		**10**	11 wks
6 Jan 79	**FOUR STRONG WINDS** *Reprise K 14493*		**57**	4 wks
27 Feb 93	**HARVEST MOON** *Reprise W 0139CD*		**36**	3 wks
17 Jul 93	**THE NEEDLE AND THE DAMAGE DONE** *Reprise W 0191CD*		**75**	1 wk
30 Oct 93	**LONG MAY YOU RUN (LIVE)** *Reprise W 0207CD*		**71**	1 wk
9 Apr 94	**PHILADELPHIA** *Reprise W 0242CD*		**62**	2 wks

See also Crosby, Stills, Nash and Young.

Paul YOUNG *UK, male vocalist* **132 wks**

18 Jun 83	★ **WHEREVER I LAY MY HAT (THAT'S MY HOME)** *CBS A 3371*		**1**	15 wks
10 Sep 83	● **COME BACK AND STAY** *CBS A 3636*		**4**	9 wks
19 Nov 83	● **LOVE OF THE COMMON PEOPLE** *CBS A 3585*		**2**	13 wks
13 Oct 84	● **I'M GONNA TEAR YOUR PLAYHOUSE DOWN** *CBS A 4786*		**9**	7 wks
8 Dec 84	● **EVERYTHING MUST CHANGE** *CBS A 4972*		**9**	11 wks
9 Mar 85	● **EVERY TIME YOU GO AWAY** *CBS A 6300*		**4**	11 wks
22 Jun 85	**TOMB OF MEMORIES** *CBS A 6321*		**16**	7 wks
17 Aug 85	**TOMB OF MEMORIES (re-entry)** *CBS A 6321*		**74**	1 wk
4 Oct 86	**WONDERLAND** *CBS YOUNG 1*		**24**	5 wks
29 Nov 86	**SOME PEOPLE** *CBS YOUNG 2*		**56**	3 wks
7 Feb 87	**WHY DOES A MAN HAVE TO BE STRONG** *CBS YOUNG 3*		**63**	2 wks
12 May 90	**SOFTLY WHISPERING I LOVE YOU** *CBS YOUNG 4*		**21**	6 wks
7 Jul 90	**OH GIRL** *CBS YOUNG 5*		**25**	6 wks
6 Oct 90	**HEAVEN CAN WAIT** *CBS YOUNG 6*		**71**	2 wks
12 Jan 91	**CALLING YOU** *CBS YOUNG 7*		**57**	2 wks
30 Mar 91	● **SENZA UNA DONNA (WITHOUT A WOMAN)** *London LON 294* **1**		**4**	12 wks
10 Aug 91	**BOTH SIDES NOW** *MCA MCS 1546* **2**		**74**	1 wk
26 Oct 91	**DON'T DREAM IT'S OVER** *Columbia 6574117*		**20**	5 wks

British Hit Singles Part One: Alphabetically by Artist
Date of chart entry/Title & catalogue no./Peak position reached/Weeks on chart
★ Number One ● Top Ten † still on chart at 31 Dec 1994
□ = credited to act billed in footnote

25 Sep 93	**NOW I KNOW WHAT MADE OTIS BLUE**		
	Columbia 6596412	**14**	7 wks
27 Nov 93	**HOPE IN A HOPELESS WORLD** Columbia 6598652	**42**	3 wks
23 Apr 94	**IT WILL BE YOU** Columbia 6602812	**34**	4 wks

1 Zucchero and Paul Young 2 Clannad and Paul Young

Retta YOUNG *US, female vocalist*   **7 wks**

| 24 May 75 | **SENDING OUT AN S. O. S.** All Platinum 6146 305 | **28** | 7 wks |

Tracie YOUNG - *See TRACIE*

Leon YOUNG STRING CHORALE - *See Mr Acker BILK*

YOUNG and COMPANY
US, male / female vocal / instrumental group   **12 wks**

| 1 Nov 80 | **I LIKE (WHAT YOU'RE DOING TO ME)** | | |
| | Excalibur EXC 501 | **20** | 12 wks |

YOUNG BLACK TEENAGERS *US, male rap group*   **3 wks**

| 9 Apr 94 | **TAP THE BOTTLE** MCA MCSTD 1967 | **39** | 3 wks |

YOUNG AND MOODY BAND
UK, male vocal / instrumental group   **4 wks**

| 10 Oct 81 | **DON'T DO THAT** Bronze BRO 130 | **63** | 4 wks |

YOUNG DISCIPLES
UK / US, male / female vocal / instrumental group   **17 wks**

13 Oct 90	**GET YOURSELF TOGETHER** Talkin Loud TLK 2	**68**	1 wk
23 Feb 91	**APPARENTLY NOTHIN'** Talkin Loud TLK 5	**46**	4 wks
3 Aug 91	**APPARENTLY NOTHIN'** (re-entry)		
	Talkin Loud TLK 5	**13**	7 wks
5 Oct 91	**GET YOURSELF TOGETHER** (re-issue)		
	Talkin Loud TLK 15	**65**	2 wks
5 Sep 92	**YOUNG DISCIPLES EP** Talkin Loud TLK 18	**48**	3 wks

Tracks on Young Disciples EP: Move On / Freedom / All I Have In Me / Move On (re-mix).

YOUNG IDEA *UK, male vocal duo*   **6 wks**

| 29 Jun 67 | ● **WITH A LITTLE HELP FROM MY FRIENDS** | | |
| | Columbia DB 8205 | **10** | 6 wks |

YOUNG MC *US, male rapper*   **7 wks**

15 Jul 89	**BUST A MOVE** Delicious Vinyl BRW 137	**73**	2 wks
17 Feb 90	**PRINCIPAL'S OFFICE** Delicious Vinyl BRW 161	**54**	3 wks
17 Aug 91	**THAT'S THE WAY LOVE GOES** Capitol CL 623	**65**	2 wks

YOUNG ONES - *See Cliff RICHARD*

YOUNG RASCALS *US, male vocal / instrumental group* **17 wks**

| 25 May 67 | ● **GROOVIN'** Atlantic 584 111 | **8** | 13 wks |
| 16 Aug 67 | **A GIRL LIKE YOU** Atlantic 584 128 | **37** | 4 wks |

Sydney YOUNGBLOOD *US, male vocalist*   **31 wks**

| 26 Aug 89 | ● **IF ONLY I COULD** Circa YR 34 | **3** | 14 wks |
| 9 Dec 89 | **SIT AND WAIT** Circa YR 40 | **16** | 8 wks |

31 Mar 90	**I'D RATHER GO BLIND** Circa YR 43	**44**	5 wks
29 Jun 91	**HOOKED ON YOU** Circa YR 65	**72**	2 wks
20 Mar 93	**ANYTHING** RCA 74321138672	**48**	2 wks

Helmut ZACHARIAS *Germany, orchestra*   **11 wks**

| 29 Oct 64 | ● **TOKYO MELODY** Polydor YNH 52341 | **9** | 11 wks |

Pia ZADORA *US, female vocalist*   **6 wks**

27 Oct 84	**WHEN THE RAIN BEGINS TO FALL**		
	Arista ARIST 584 1	**68**	2 wks
12 Nov 88	**DANCE OUT OF MY HEAD**		
	Epic 652886 1 2	**65**	4 wks

1 Jermaine Jackson and Pia Zadora 2 Pia

Michael ZAGER BAND
US, male / female vocal / instrumental group   **12 wks**

| 1 Apr 78 | ● **LET'S ALL CHANT** Private Stock PVT 143 | **8** | 12 wks |

ZAGER and EVANS *US, male vocal duo*   **13 wks**

| 9 Aug 69 | ★ **IN THE YEAR 2525 (EXORDIUM AND TERMINUS)** | | |
| | RCA 1860 | **1** | 13 wks |

Georghe ZAMFIR
Romania, male instrumentalist - pipes   **9 wks**

| 21 Aug 76 | ● **(LIGHT OF EXPERIENCE) DOINA DE JALE** | | |
| | Epic EPC 4310 | **4** | 9 wks |

Tommy ZANG *US, male vocalist*   **1 wk**

| 16 Feb 61 | **HEY GOOD LOOKING** Polydor NH 66957 | **45** | 1 wk |

ZAPP *US, male vocal / instrumental group*   **6 wks**

25 Jan 86	**IT DOESN'T REALLY MATTER**		
	Warner Bros. W 8879	**57**	3 wks
24 May 86	**COMPUTER LOVE (PART 1)** Warner Bros. W 8805	**64**	3 wks

Francesco ZAPPALA *Italy, male producer*   **3 wks**

| 10 Aug 91 | **WE GOTTA DO IT** Fourth & Broadway BRW 225 1 | **57** | 2 wks |
| 2 May 92 | **NO WAY OUT** PWL Continental PWL 230 | **69** | 1 wk |

1 DJ Professor featuring Francesco Zappala

Lena ZAVARONI *UK, female vocalist*   **14 wks**

| 9 Feb 74 | ● **MA HE'S MAKING EYES AT ME** Philips 6006 367 | **10** | 11 wks |
| 1 Jun 74 | ● **PERSONALITY** Philips 6006 391 | **33** | 3 wks |

ZEPHYRS *UK, male vocal / instrumental group*   **1 wk**

| 18 Mar 65 | **SHE'S LOST YOU** Columbia DB 7481 | **48** | 1 wk |

ZERO B *UK, male instrumentalist - keyboards*   **6 wks**

| 22 Feb 92 | **THE EP** Ffrreedom TAB 102 | **32** | 4 wks |
| 24 Jul 93 | **RECONNECTION EP** Internal LIECD 6 | **54** | 2 wks |

Tracks on The EP: Lock Up / Spinning Wheel / Module / Eclipse. Tracks on Reconnection EP: Lock Up / Lock Up (re-mix) / Ou Est Le Spoon / Love To Be In Love. All three versions of Lock Up are different mixes of the same track.

ZERO ZERO
UK, male instrumental / production duo **1 wk**

10 Aug 91	**ZEROXED** *Kickin KICK 9*	**71**	1 wk

ZHANE
US, female vocal duo **9 wks**

11 Sep 93	**HEY MR. DJ** *Epic 6596102*	**26**	3 wks
4 Dec 93	**HEY MR. DJ (re-entry)** *Epic 6596102*	**50**	2 wks
19 Mar 94	**GROOVE THANG** *Motown TMGCD 1423*..........	**34**	3 wks
20 Aug 94	**VIBE** *Motown TMGCD 1430*	**67**	1 wk

ZIG and ZAG
Ireland, male puppet duo **2 wks**

24 Dec 94	● **THEM GIRLS THEM GIRLS** *RCA 74321251042*	**8†**	2 wks

ZIGZAG JIVE FLUTES - *See ELIAS and his ZIGZAG JIVE FLUTES*

ZODIACS - *See Maurice WILLIAMS and the ZODIACS*

ZOE
UK, female vocalist **22 wks**

10 Nov 90	**SUNSHINE ON A RAINY DAY** *M & G MAGS 6*	**53**	5 wks
24 Aug 91	● **SUNSHINE ON A RAINY DAY (re-mix)**		
	M & G MAGS 14	**4**	11 wks
2 Nov 91	**LIGHTNING** *M & G MAGS 18*	**37**	4 wks
29 Feb 92	**HOLY DAYS** *M & G MAGS 21*	**72**	2 wks

ZOMBIES
UK, male vocal / instrumental group **16 wks**

13 Aug 64	**SHE'S NOT THERE** *Decca F 11940*	**12**	11 wks
11 Feb 65	**TELL HER NO** *Decca F 12072*..................	**42**	5 wks

ZOO EXPERIENCE featuring DESTRY
UK / US, male / female vocal / instrumental group **1 wk**

22 Aug 92	**LOVE'S GOTTA HOLD ON ME**		
	Cooltempo COOL 261	**66**	1 wk

ZUCCHERO
Italy, male vocalist / instrumentalist - guitar, Adelmo Fornaciari **24 wks**

30 Mar 91	● **SENZA UNA DONNA (WITHOUT A WOMAN)**		
	London LON 294 [1]	**4**	12 wks
18 Jan 92	**DIAMANTE** *London LON 313* [2]	**44**	7 wks
24 Oct 92	**MISERERE** *London LON 329* [3]	**15**	5 wks

[1] Zucchero and Paul Young [2] Zucchero with Randy Crawford [3] Zucchero with Luciano Pavarotti

ZZ TOP
US, male vocal / instrumental group **91 wks**

3 Sep 83	**GIMME ALL YOUR LOVIN'**		
	Warner Bros. W 9693	**61**	3 wks
26 Nov 83	**SHARP DRESSED MAN** *Warner Bros. W 9576*	**53**	3 wks
31 Mar 84	**TV DINNERS** *Warner Bros. W 9334*	**67**	3 wks
6 Oct 84	● **GIMME ALL YOUR LOVIN' (re-entry)**		
	Warner Bros. W 9693	**10**	15 wks
15 Dec 84	**SHARP DRESSED MAN (re-entry)**		
	Warner Bros. W 9576	**22**	10 wks
23 Feb 85	**LEGS** *Warner Bros. W 9272*	**16**	7 wks
13 Jul 85	**SUMMER HOLIDAY** (EP) *Warner Bros. W 8946*.........	**51**	5 wks
19 Oct 85	**SLEEPING BAG** *Warner Bros. W 2001*	**27**	5 wks
15 Feb 86	**STAGES** *Warner Bros. W 2002*	**43**	3 wks
19 Apr 86	**ROUGH BOY** *Warner Bros. W 2003*	**23**	9 wks
4 Oct 86	**VELCRO FLY** *Warner Bros. W 8650*.........	**54**	3 wks
21 Jul 90	**DOUBLEBACK** *Warner Bros. W 9812*	**29**	6 wks
13 Apr 91	**MY HEAD'S IN MISSISSIPPI**		
	Warner Bros. W 0009	**37**	5 wks
11 Apr 92	● **VIVA LAS VEGAS** *Warner Bros. W 0098*	**10**	7 wks
20 Jun 92	**ROUGH BOY (re-issue)** *Warner Bros. W 0111*	**49**	3 wks
29 Jan 94	**PINCUSHION** *RCA 74321184732*	**15**	3 wks
7 May 94	**BREAKAWAY** *RCA 74321192282*	**60**	1 wk

Tracks on Summer Holiday EP: Tush / Got Me Under Pressure / Beer Drinkers and Hell Raisers / I'm Bad, I'm Nationwide.

Different songs/tunes with the same title (e.g. 'Zoom' which has been a hit title for both the Commodores and Fat Larry's Band) are indicated by [A], [B] etc. Where there is no letter in brackets after the title, all hit recordings are of just one song. Individual titles of songs or tunes on EP, LP, medley or megamix singles which made the chart are not included here, with the obvious exception of titles that are actually part of the overall title of the hit in question.

The recording act named alongside each song title is the act that is billed on the record, but is not necessarily the act under whose name all the information about the title can be found in Part One. So, for example 'Zing A Little Zong' is credited correctly in Part Two to Bing Crosby and Jane Wyman, but in Part One is to be found in the list of Bing Crosby hits, with a footnote indicating the fact that it was a duet with Jane Wyman. We have also simplified some act names in Part Two in the interests of saving space. For example 'Happy Xmas (War Is Over)' is credited here to John Lennon, but if you look up John Lennon in Part One, you will discover the actual credit for that hit was 'John and Yoko, the Plastic Ono Band with the Harlem Community Choir'.

The year of chart entry column contains the year in which each disc made its very first appearance on the chart. Subsequent

WHITNEY HOUSTON

appearances are only listed here if they signify a period of success *totally* separate from the disc's first impact. So, for example, 'Bohemian Rhapsody' by Queen is listed as having been a hit in 1975 and 1991, but Cliff Richard's original version of 'Living Doll', which re-entered the charts for one brief week in 1960 after topping the charts in 1959, is shown only as a hit in 1959.

349

362

382

389

All the chart achievements you need to know about are here. Which record took over from 'Hey Jude' at the top of the chart? Who has had more consecutive top ten hits than Cliff Richard? From which chart position did 'Happy Talk' leap to the top? How long did 'Tainted Love' stay on the charts? Did anybody spend more time on the charts in 1994 than Take That? Who was the first woman to debut at number one? Who has a hit record span of over 42 years?

The answer to all these questions, as well as several even more significant, are to be found in this section. Nothing here proves that anybody produces better or worse music than anybody else, or that any particular record is more enjoyable to listen to than any other. All we are doing is listing the facts; we leave the opinions to you.

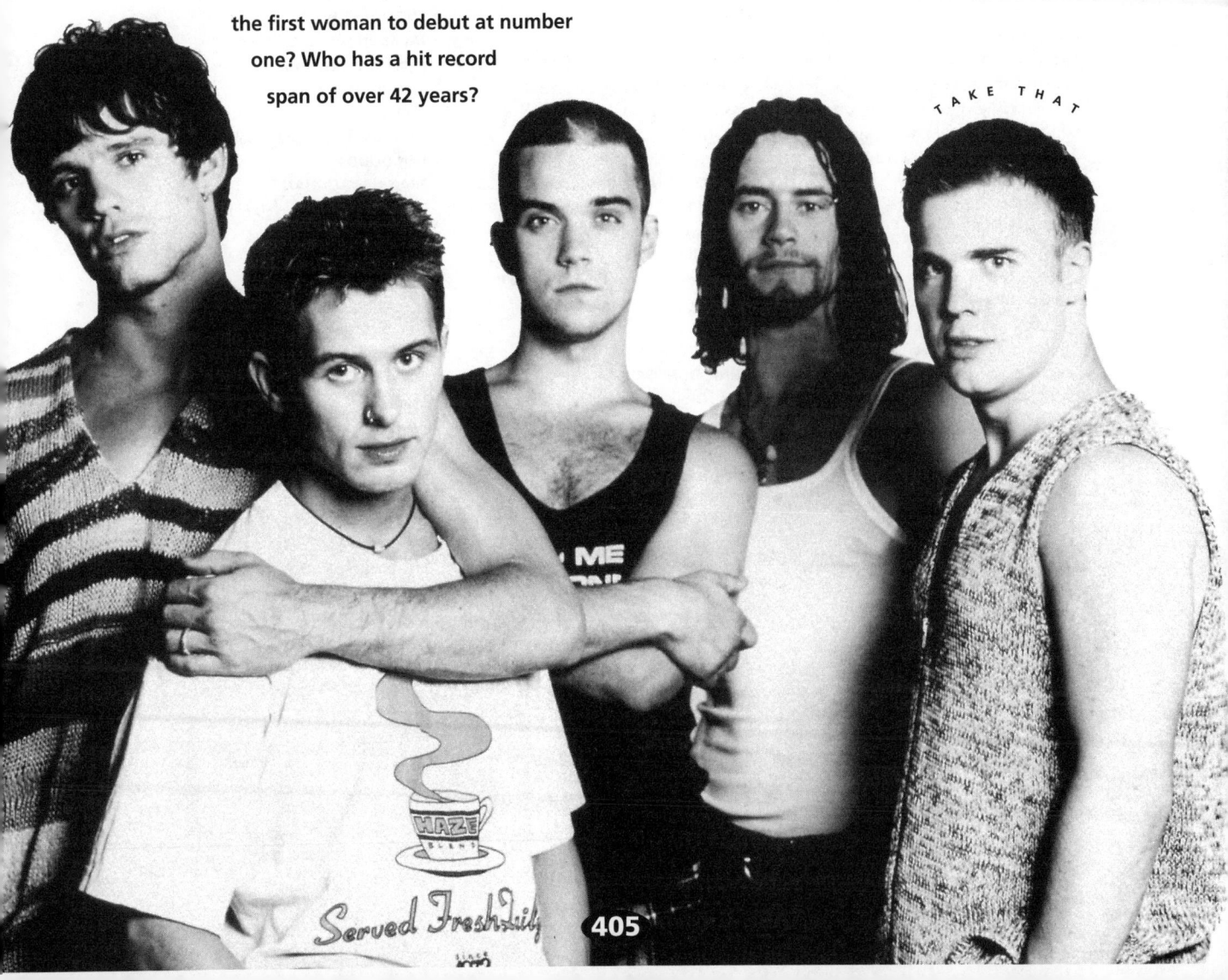

TAKE THAT

This table lists the 269 recording acts that have spent 100 weeks or more on the British singles charts from 14 November 1952 up to the end of December 1994. It is of course possible for an act to be credited with two chart weeks in the same week if that act has two or more records on the chart at once. Double-sided hits, EPs and double singles only count as one hit each week, as do the handful of albums which have hit the singles chart over the years.

Weeks

Act	Weeks
ELVIS PRESLEY	1145
CLIFF RICHARD	1100

(including 16 with Sarah Brightman, 13 with Phil Everly, 11 with Young Ones, 8 with Elton John, 7 with Olivia Newton-John, 6 with Van Morrison and 2 with Sheila Walsh)

ELTON JOHN	508

(includes 24 with Kiki Dee, 10 with George Michael, 9 with Dionne Warwick and Friends, 8 with Cliff Richard, 7 with RuPaul, 5 with Millie Jackson, 4 with Eric Clapton, 4 with Marcella Detroit, 4 with John Lennon, 3 with Aretha Franklin and 3 with Jennifer Rush)

FRANK SINATRA	439

(includes 18 with Nancy Sinatra, 9 with Sammy Davis Jr. and 9 with Bono)

ROD STEWART	437

(includes 13 with Bryan Adams and Sting, 9 with Jeff Beck and 8 with Tina Turner. + 46 with Faces)

BEATLES	434

(includes 23 with Billy Preston and 1 with Tony Sheridan)

DAVID BOWIE	418

(includes 12 with Mick Jagger, 11 with Queen, 8 with Bing Crosby, 7 with Pat Metheny and 2 with Al B. Sure!)

DIANA ROSS	415

(includes 20 with Marvin Gaye, 12 with Lionel Richie, 8 with Julio Iglesias, 5 with Marvin Gaye, Smokey Robinson and Stevie Wonder and 4 with Michael Jackson. + 197 as a Supreme, 27 with Supremes and Temptations)

STEVIE WONDER	404

(includes 11 with Julio Iglesias, 10 with Paul McCartney, 9 with Dionne Warwick and Friends, 5 with Diana Ross, Smokey Robinson and Marvin Gaye and 4 with Michael Jackson)

STATUS QUO	399
PAUL McCARTNEY/WINGS	397

(includes 25 with Michael Jackson, 10 with Stevie Wonder and 7 with Christians, Holly Johnson, Paul McCartney, Gerry Marsden and Stock Aitken Waterman)

MICHAEL JACKSON	382

(includes 25 with Paul McCartney, 4 with Diana Ross and 4 with Stevie Wonder. + 235 as a Jackson)

MADONNA	382
SHADOWS	359

(+ 404 backing Cliff Richard)

QUEEN	357

(includes 12 with George Michael and Lisa Stansfield and 11 with David Bowie)

TOM JONES	356

(includes 7 with Art Of Noise)

ROLLING STONES	352
ROY ORBISON	345

(includes 6 weeks with k.d. lang)

EVERLY BROTHERS	337

(Phil Everly 6 more solo and 13 with Cliff Richard)

BEE GEES	322
JIM REEVES	322
LONNIE DONEGAN	321
FOUR TOPS	318

(includes 20 with Supremes)

HOLLIES	318
SHIRLEY BASSEY	315

(includes 2 with Yello)

SUPREMES	306

(includes 27 with Temptations and 20 with Four Tops)

UB40	305

(includes 8 with Afrika Bambaataa and Family, 9 with Robert Palmer and 8 with 808 State)

PAT BOONE	296
PERRY COMO	294
DONNA SUMMER	287

(includes 13 with Barbra Streisand)

BILLY FURY	281
FRANKIE LAINE	281

(includes 16 with Jimmy Boyd, 16 with Four Lads, 8 with Doris Day and 4 with Johnnie Ray)

BEACH BOYS	277

(includes 12 with Fat Boys)

SHAKIN' STEVENS	277

(includes 9 with Bonnie Tyler)

SLADE	276
HOT CHOCOLATE	272
PRINCE	269

(includes 5 with Sheena Easton)

MADNESS	258
ELECTRIC LIGHT ORCHESTRA	255

(includes 11 with Olivia Newton-John)

ABBA	252
ADAM FAITH	251
PETULA CLARK	247
WHO	245

(+ 4 as High Numbers)

CONNIE FRANCIS	241
NAT 'KING' COLE	237
ENGELBERT HUMPERDINCK	235
JACKSON FIVE/JACKSONS	235

(113 as Jackson Five and 122 as Jacksons)

T. REX	235

(includes 8 billed as Marc Bolan)

KEN DODD	233
FRANKIE VAUGHAN	232

(includes 20 with Kaye Sisters)

ANDY WILLIAMS	228
FLEETWOOD MAC	223
OLIVIA NEWTON-JOHN	221

(includes 57 with John Travolta, 11 with Electric Light Orchestra, and 7 with Cliff Richard)

MANFRED MANN	217

(includes 41 as Manfred Mann's Earth Band)

KINKS	213
GENE PITNEY	212

(includes 12 with Marc Almond)

HERMAN'S HERMITS	211
BRENDA LEE	210
SHOWADDYWADDY	209
DEPECHE MODE	208
DURAN DURAN	207
KOOL AND THE GANG	207
DUSTY SPRINGFIELD	207

(includes 9 with Pet Shop Boys and 1 with Cilla Black. + 66 as a Springfield)

PHIL COLLINS	204

(includes 13 with Marilyn Martin, 12 with Philip Bailey and 3 with David Crosby)

WHITNEY HOUSTON	204

(includes 5 with Teddy Pendergrass, 5 with Aretha Franklin and 5 with Bobby Brown)

9 with Delaney and Bonnie and Friends, 5 with Sting, 4 with Elton John and 3 with Tina Turner)

HUMAN LEAGUE	131
10 C.C.	131
TREMELOES	131

(+ 90 with Brian Poole)

RAY CHARLES	130

(includes 7 with Quincy Jones)

MARMALADE	130
BARBRA STREISAND	130

(includes 13 with Donna Summer, 12 with Neil Diamond, 10 with Barry Gibb, 7 with Don Johnson and 3 with Michael Crawford)

ANTHONY NEWLEY	129
DOLLAR	128
RONNIE HILTON	128
JONATHAN KING	128

(67 as Jonathan King and 61 more under pseudonyms: Sakkarin (14), Shag (13), One Hundred Ton And A Feather (9), Weathermen (9), Bubblerock (5), Father Abraphart and the Smurps (4), 53rd And 3rd (4) and Sound 9418 [3])

SEARCHERS	128
THIN LIZZY	128
KARL DENVER	127

(includes 3 with Happy Mondays)

MATT MONRO	127
PRETENDERS	127
BARRY WHITE	127
BELINDA CARLISLE	126
ROXETTE	126
BON JOVI	125
EARTH WIND AND FIRE	125

(includes 13 with Emotions)

ROBERT PALMER	124

(includes 10 with UB40)

OTIS REDDING	124

(includes 16 with Carla Thomas)

BOOMTOWN RATS	123
AC/DC	122
MEAT LOAF	122

(includes 6 with John Parr)

SUZI QUATRO	122

(includes 8 with Chris Norman)

MARIAH CAREY	121

(includes 10 with Luther Vandross)

COMMODORES	121
NEIL DIAMOND	121

(includes 12 with Barbra Streisand)

SEEKERS	120
DIRE STRAITS	119
HELEN SHAPIRO	119
ALVIN STARDUST	119

(+ 28 as Shane Fenton)

TAKE THAT	119

(includes 14 weeks with Lulu)

DONNY OSMOND	118

(+ 37 with Marie Osmond. +91 as an Osmond)

CHRIS REA	118
WINIFRED ATWELL	117

(includes 6 with Frank Chacksfield. + 9 as one of the artists on All Star Hit Parade)

DARTS	117
DES O'CONNOR	117

(includes 10 with Roger Whittaker)

MARTY WILDE	117
INXS	116

(includes 8 with Jimmy Barnes)

GEORGIE FAME	115

(includes 10 with Alan Price)

GERRY AND THE PACEMAKERS	114

(Gerry Marsden +7 with Christians, Holly Johnson, Paul McCartney, Gerry Marsden and Stock Aitken Waterman)

MOODY BLUES	114
REAL THING	114
SQUEEZE	114
LUTHER VANDROSS	114

(includes 13 with Janet Jackson, 10 with Mariah Carey and 1 with Gregory Hines)

BAY CITY ROLLERS	113
CHUBBY CHECKER	112

(includes 4 with Bobby Rydell and 11 with Fat Boys)

CRAIG DOUGLAS	112
PETER GABRIEL	112

(includes 11 with Kate Bush and 7 with Youssou N'Dour)

BAD MANNERS	111
DEACON BLUE	111
SISTER SLEDGE	111
STING	111

(includes 13 with Bryan Adams and Rod Stewart and 5 with Eric Clapton)

THREE DEGREES	111

(includes 9 with MFSB)

WHITESNAKE	111
ALMA COGAN	110
MOVE	110
RUBY MURRAY	110
MIKE OLDFIELD	110

(includes 38 with Maggie Reilly, 6 with Aled Jones, Anita Hegerland and Barry Palmer)

ROSE ROYCE	110
SALT-N-PEPA	110

(includes 13 with Psychotropic, 10 with En Vogue and 8 with E.U.)

THOMPSON TWINS	110
DAVID CASSIDY	109

(+ 53 with Partridge Family)

DAWN	109

(Tony Orlando +11 solo)

FATS DOMINO	109

KENNY ROGERS	109

(includes 51 with New Edition, 15 with Dolly Parton and 7 with Sheena Easton)

LISA STANSFIELD	109

(includes 12 with Queen and George Michael and 9 with Coldcut)

ISLEY BROTHERS	108
LITTLE RICHARD	108
R.E.M.	107
SOFT CELL	107

(includes 11 with Marc Almond)

HERB ALPERT	106
BILLY IDOL	106
JOHNNY NASH	106
ALEXANDER O'NEAL	106

(includes 20 with Cherelle)

JIMMY RUFFIN	106
SMOKIE	106
MALCOLM VAUGHAN	106
EDDIE FISHER	105
IMAGINATION	105
ALISON MOYET	105
MARC ALMOND	104

(includes 12 with Gene Pitney, 12 with Bronski Beat, 11 with Soft Cell, 5 with Willing Sinners and 3 as Marc and the Mambas)

ALICE COOPER	104
DR. HOOK	104
KC AND THE SUNSHINE BAND	104
SINITTA	104
SMITHS	104
SNAP	104

(includes 19 with Niki Harris and 13 with Summer)

CULTURE CLUB	103
SHEENA EASTON	103

(includes 14 with Prince and 7 with Kenny Rogers)

HOWARD JONES	103
STYLE COUNCIL	103
2 UNLIMITED	103
JAMES BROWN	101

(includes 5 with Afrika Bambaataa, 4 with Full Force and 1 with Dakeyne)

GUNS N' ROSES	101
MARILLION	101
MONKEES	101
GARY MOORE	101

(includes 10 with Phil Lynott, 3 with Albert King and 3 with B.B. King)

DIONNE WARWICK	101

(includes 9 with Friends, 6 with Detroit Spinners and 3 with Jeffrey Osborne)

BIG COUNTRY	100
DONOVAN	100

(includes 9 with Jeff Beck Group and 1 with Singing Corner Meets Donovan)

SPECIALS	100

(includes 5 with Rhoda)

TERRY HALL   179

(4 solo, 78 with Specials, 50 with Fun Boy Three, 20 with Bananarama, 18 with Colourfield and 9 with Vegas)

PAUL SIMON   170

(83 solo and 87 with Simon and Garfunkel)

ALAN PRICE   166

(78 solo, 78 as an Animal and 10 with Fame and Price Together)

EDDY GRANT   163

(94 solo, 69 as an Equal)

JIMMY SOMERVILLE   162

(36 solo, 76 with Communards, 38 with Bronski Beat and 12 with Bronski Beat ' and Marc Almond)

JOHN LYDON   159

(9 as featured vocalist with Time Zone, 84 with Sex Pistols, 5 with Leftfield Lydon and 61 as leader of Public Image Ltd.)

MIDGE URE   154

(51 solo, 4 with Mick Karn, 56 as part of Visage, 18 as part of Slik, 5 as a Rich Kid and 20 as a leader of Band Aid. This does not include his 138 weeks with Ultravox listed above)

STEVE WINWOOD   144

(33 solo, 71 with Spencer Davis Group and 40 with Traffic)

FEARGAL SHARKEY   135

(58 solo, 67 with Undertones and 10 with Assembly)

BOBBY BROWN   127

(85 solo, 9 with Glenn Medeiros, 5 with Whitney Houston and 28 with New Edition)

ART GARFUNKEL   124

(37 solo, 87 with Simon and Garfunkel)

SCOTT WALKER   123

(30 solo, 93 with Walker Brothers)

DAVID SYLVIAN   116

(15 solo, 81 with Japan, 15 with Sylvian Sakamoto, 2 with Mick Karn, 2 with Robert Fripp and 1 with Rain Tree Crow)

BILL MEDLEY   115

(6 solo, 23 with Jennifer Warnes and 86 as a Righteous Brother)

SMOKEY ROBINSON   112

(29 solo, 71 with Miracles, 7 with Four Tops and 5 with Diana Ross, Marvin Gaye and Stevie Wonder)

B.E.F.   109

(Ian Craig Marsh and Martyn Ware have been on the charts for 5 weeks as B.E.F. featuring Lalah Hathaway, 79 as part of Heaven 17 and 25 as part of Human League)

DAVE EDMUNDS   107

(87 solo, 14 with Love Sculpture and 6 with Stray Cats)

DARYL HALL   107

(19 solo, 84 with Hall and Oates and 4 with Sounds Of Blackness)

GARY WALKER   105

(12 solo and 93 as a Walker Brother)

DAVID GRANT   104

(38 solo, 45 with Linx and 21 with Jaki Graham)

MICHAEL McDONALD   104

(45 solo, 45 with Doobie Brothers and 14 uncredited with Warren G and Nate Dogg)

DICKIE VALENTINE   101

(92 solo and 9 with All Star Hit Parade)

MOST WEEKS ON CHART
1 9 9 3

50	WHITNEY HOUSTON
42	TAKE THAT
40	2 UNLIMITED
38	LISA STANSFIELD
34	M PEOPLE
33	UB40
31	SYBIL
30	DINA CARROLL
	EAST 17
	MICHAEL JACKSON

In 1993, Whitney Houston carried on from her 1992 triumph with the biggest-selling single in Britain ever recorded by a woman, 'I Will Always Love You', by enjoying more weeks on the British charts during the year than any other artist. She thus became the third American female vocalist, after Donna Summer and Madonna, to be British singles chart champion. Four of the top ten acts were female vocalists, Lisa Stansfield owing her success partly to her participation in the Queen/George Michael 'Five Live' EP. Only Take That (fourth in 1992, second in 1993) and Michael Jackson (number one in 1992, number seven in 1993) survived from the previous year's top ten chart acts. Five of the top six acts had at least one chart-topping single during the year, the odd one out being M People.

MOST WEEKS ON CHART
1 9 9 4

45	MARIAH CAREY
44	TAKE THAT
39	REEL 2 REAL featuring THE MAD STUNTMAN
37	WET WET WET
36	D:REAM
	EAST 17
	ELTON JOHN
35	ETERNAL
30	ACE OF BASE
	LET LOOSE

Mariah Carey followed Whitney Houston to become the fourth American woman to be our singles chart champion, although she only pipped Take That by one week, thanks to the ten weeks she racked up in duet with Luther Vandross. Take That were second for a second successive year: their decision not to release a Christmas single was certainly the reason they did not take final chart honours for the year.

In a good 12 months for British acts, Elton John came back to this chart for the first time since 1983, becoming one of the three acts (along with Michael Jackson and Cliff Richard) to have featured in the annual top ten in three different decades. Ace Of Base became the third Swedish act, after Abba and Roxette, to make the top ten, but apart from Take That, only East 17, the year end chart-topping act, remained in the top ten for a second consecutive year.

The acts who spent the most time on the charts in each year are:

Year	Act	Weeks
1952	**Vera Lynn**	10
1953	**Frankie Laine**	84
1954	**Frankie Laine**	67
1955	**Ruby Murray**	80
1956	**Bill Haley and his Comets**	110
1957	**Elvis Presley**	108
1958	**Elvis Presley**	70
1959	**Russ Conway**	79
1960	**Cliff Richard**	78
1961	**Elvis Presley**	88
1962	**Chubby Checker**	73
1963	**Beatles**	68
1964	**Jim Reeves**	73
1965	**Seekers**	51
1966	**Dave Dee, Dozy, Beaky, Mick and Tich**	50
1967	**Engelbert Humperdinck**	97
1968	**Tom Jones**	58
1969	**Marvin Gaye**	60
1970	**Elvis Presley**	59
1971	**Elvis Presley**	66
1972	**T. Rex**	58
1973	**David Bowie**	55
1974	**Wombles**	65
1975	**Mud**	45
1976	**Rod Stewart**	48
1977	**Elvis Presley**	51
1978	**John Travolta**	60
1979	**Donna Summer**	46
1980	**Madness**	46
1981	**Adam and the Ants**	91
1982	**Soft Cell**	49
1983	**Michael Jackson**	60
1984	**Frankie Goes To Hollywood**	68
1985	**Madonna**	84
1986	**Madonna**	59
1987	**Madonna**	41
1988	**Kylie Minogue**	54
1989	**Bobby Brown**	52
1990	**New Kids On The Block**	56
1991	**R.E.M.**	36
1992	**Michael Jackson**	38
1993	**Whitney Houston**	50
1994	**Mariah Carey**	45

(Frankie Laine's **1953** total includes 16 weeks in duet with Jimmy Boyd and two with Doris Day. Chubby Checker's **1962** total includes three weeks in duet with Bobby Rydell. The Beatles' **1963** total includes one week backing Tony Sheridan. Marvin Gaye's **1969** total includes 29 weeks in duet with Tammi Terrell. John Travolta's **1978** total includes 42 weeks in duet with Olivia Newton-John. Donna Summer's **1979** total includes nine weeks in duet with Barbra Streisand. Michael Jackson's **1983** total includes 14 weeks in duet with Paul McCartney. Kylie Minogue's **1988** total includes four weeks in duet with Jason Donovan. Mariah Carey's **1994** total includes ten weeks in duet with Luther Vandross.)

Elvis Presley has been chart champion six times, over a span of 21 years. 1986 was the first year since the King's chart debut in 1956 in which he did not hit the British singles chart at all. Two other people, Frankie Laine and Michael Jackson, have been chart champions twice, and Madonna has been chart queen in three consecutive years, a feat that not even Elvis achieved.

Vera Lynn has scored the fewest chart weeks in total of any year's champion - only 46 in her entire chart career. The other chart champions who have not scored a total of 100 weeks are John Travolta (81 weeks), Wombles (87 weeks), New Kids On The Block (90 weeks) and Bobby Brown (99 weeks).

R.E.M.'s total of 36 weeks in 1991 was the lowest needed to take the title in a complete year. Russ Conway (1959) is the only instrumentalist to have been chart champion.

VERA LYNN

110	Bill Haley and his Comets	1956
108	Elvis Presley	1957
97	Engelbert Humperdinck	1967
91	Adam and the Ants	1981
88	Elvis Presley	1961
84	Frankie Laine	1953
84	Pat Boone	1957
84	Madonna	1985
80	Ruby Murray	1955
79	Russ Conway	1959
78	Cliff Richard	1960
77	Adam Faith	1960
73	Chubby Checker	1962
73	Jim Reeves	1964
72	Beatles	1964
71	Mr. Acker Bilk	1962
70	Bachelors	1964
70	Elvis Presley	1958

Frankie Laine's 1953 total includes 16 weeks in duet with Jimmy Boyd and two weeks in duet with Doris Day. Chubby Checker's 1962 total includes three weeks in duet with Bobby Rydell.

. . . .

MOST HITS

Double-sided hits, double singles, EPs and albums only count as one hit each time. Re-issues and re-entries do not count as new hits, nor do re-mixes if the same vocal track is used. We follow the philosophy that if the named act on the label has not gone into the studio to make a new record, then there is no new hit. Re-recordings of the same song by the same act do count as two hits.

A record is a hit if it makes the charts, even if for only one week at number 75.

115 **CLIFF RICHARD** (includes 2 with Phil Everly, 1 with Olivia Newton-John, 1 with Sheila Walsh, 1 with Young Ones, 1 with Elton John, 1 with Van Morrison and 1 with Sarah Brightman)

109 **ELVIS PRESLEY**

66 **ELTON JOHN** (includes 2 with Kiki Dee, 1 with Millie Jackson, 1 with John Lennon, 1 with Cliff Richard, 1 with Aretha Franklin , 1 with George Michael, 1 with Eric Clapton, 1 with Dionne Warwick and Friends, 1 with Jennifer Rush, 1 with RuPaul and 1 with Marcella Detroit)

54 **DIANA ROSS** (includes 2 with Marvin Gaye, 1 with Michael Jackson, 1 with Marvin Gaye, Smokey Robinson and Stevie Wonder, 1 with Lionel Richie and 1 with Julio Iglesias. + 18 with Supremes and 2 with Supremes & Temptations)

53 **DAVID BOWIE** (includes 1 with Queen, 1 with Bing Crosby, 1 with Pat Metheny, 1 with Al B. Sure! and 1 with Mick Jagger. + 4 as part of Tin Machine)

50 **ROD STEWART** (includes 2 with Jeff Beck, 1 with Tina Turner. + 5 with Faces, 1 with Python Lee Jackson, 1 with Glass Tiger and 1 with Bryan Adams and Sting)

49 **STEVIE WONDER** (includes 1 with Paul McCartney, 1 with Diana Ross, Marvin Gaye and Smokey Robinson, 1 with Michael Jackson, 1 with Dionne Warwick and Friends and 1 with Julio Iglesias)

48 **STATUS QUO**

47 **PAUL McCARTNEY/WINGS** (includes 21 as Wings, 2 with Michael Jackson, 1 with Stevie Wonder and 1 with Christians, Holly Johnson, Gerry Marsden and Stock Aitken Waterman)

42 **QUEEN** (includes 1 with David Bowie and 1 with George Michael and Lisa Stansfield)

41 **MICHAEL JACKSON** (includes 2 with Paul McCartney, 1 with Diana Ross and 1 with Stevie Wonder. +25 as a Jackson)

41 **ROLLING STONES**

39 **PRINCE** (includes 1 with Sheena Easton)

39 **UB40** (includes 1 with Afrika Bambaataa and Family, 1 with 808 State and 1 with Robert Palmer)

37 **SHAKIN' STEVENS** (includes 1 with Shaky and Bonnie)

36 **FRANK SINATRA** (includes 1 with Sammy Davis Jr., 1 with Nancy Sinatra and 1 with Bono)

36 **DONNA SUMMER** (includes 1 with Barbra Streisand)

35 **MADONNA**

34 **TOM JONES** (includes 1 with Art Of Noise)

34 **SLADE**

33 **BEE GEES**

33 **ROY ORBISON** (includes 1 with k.d. lang)

32 **ELVIS COSTELLO** (includes 2 as the Imposter)

32 **GARY NUMAN** (includes 3 with Sharpe and Numan and 2 with Radio Heart)

31 **SHADOWS** (+ 30 with Cliff Richard)

31 **STRANGLERS**

31 **FRANKIE VAUGHAN** (includes 2 with Kaye Sisters)

30 **NAT 'KING' COLE** (includes 1 with George Shearing)

30 **DEPECHE MODE**

30 **LONNIE DONEGAN**

30 **HOLLIES**

30 **HOT CHOCOLATE**

29 **BEACH BOYS** (includes 1 with Fat Boys)

29 **BEATLES** (includes 1 with Tony Sheridan and 1 with Billy Preston)

29 **ELECTRIC LIGHT ORCHESTRA** (includes 1 with Olivia Newton-John)

29 **EVERLY BROTHERS** (Phil Everly + 1 solo and 2 with Cliff Richard)

29 **FOUR TOPS** (includes 2 with Supremes)

29 **BILLY FURY**

29 **LEVEL 42**

29 **CHRIS REA**

29 **SUPREMES** (includes 3 with Temptations and 2 with Four Tops)

28 **SIOUXSIE AND THE BANSHEES** (1 with Morrissey, Siouxsie and Budgie + 3 as the Creatures)

28 **TINA TURNER** (includes 1 with Rod Stewart, 1 with Bryan Adams and 1 with Eric Clapton. +4 with Ike Turner)

28 **WHO** (+ 1 as High Numbers)

28 **KIM WILDE** (includes 1 with Junior and 1 with Mel Smith [Mel and Kim])

27 **SHIRLEY BASSEY** (includes one with Yello)

27 **PETULA CLARK**

27 **ARETHA FRANKLIN** (includes 1 with George Benson, 1 with Eurythmics, 1 with George Michael, 1 with Elton John and 1 with Whitney Houston)

27 **FRANKIE LAINE** (includes 1 with Jimmy Boyd, 1 with Doris Day and 1 with Johnnie Ray)

27 **ORCHESTRAL MANOEUVRES IN THE DARK**

26 **BANANARAMA** (includes 2 with Fun Boy Three and 1 with La Na Nee Nee Noo Noo)

26 **PAT BOONE**

26 **KATE BUSH** (includes 1 with Peter Gabriel and 1 with Larry Adler)

26 **IRON MAIDEN**

26 **JACKSON FIVE/JACKSONS** (11 as Jackson Five and 15 as Jacksons)

26 **JIM REEVES**

26 **TEMPTATIONS** (includes 3 with Supremes)

26 **T. REX** (includes 2 credited to Marc Bolan)

25 **ABBA**

25 **DURAN DURAN**

25 **DAVID ESSEX** (includes 1 with Catherine Zeta Jones)

25 **MADNESS**

24 **AC/DC**

24 **PHIL COLLINS** (includes 1 with Marilyn Martin, 1 with Philip Bailey and 1 with David Crosby)

24 **GLORIA ESTEFAN** (includes 2 as Miami Sound Machine)

24 **EURYTHMICS** (includes 1 with Aretha Franklin)

24 **ADAM FAITH**

24 **FLEETWOOD MAC**

24 **GLADYS KNIGHT AND THE PIPS** (includes 1 with Johnny Mathis and 1 with Dionne Warwick and Friends)

24 **PET SHOP BOYS** (includes 1 with Dusty Springfield and 1 with Absolutely Fabulous)

24 **SIMPLE MINDS**

24 **DUSTY SPRINGFIELD** (includes 1 with Cilla Black and 1 with Pet Shop Boys. + 5 as a Springfield)

23 **PERRY COMO**

23 **CONNIE FRANCIS**

23 **MARVIN GAYE** (includes 6 with Tammi Terrell, 2 with Diana Ross, 1 with Kim Weston, 1 with Mary Wells and 1 with Diana Ross, Smokey Robinson and Stevie Wonder)

23 **LULU** (includes 1 with Bobby Womack and 1 with Take That)

23 **NEW ORDER** (includes 1 as part of Englandneworder and 2 as Joy Division, more or less)

23 **OLIVIA NEWTON-JOHN** (includes 4 with John Travolta, 1 with Electric Light Orchestra and 1 with Cliff Richard)

23 **ROBERT PALMER** (includes 1 with UB40)

23 **SHOWADDYWADDY**

22 **DAVE CLARK FIVE**

22 **CURE**

22 **DUANE EDDY** (includes 1 with Art Of Noise)

22 **KINKS**

22 **BRENDA LEE**

22 **MANFRED MANN** (17 as Manfred Mann, 5 as Manfred Mann's Earth Band)

22 **KYLIE MINOGUE** (includes 1 with Jason Donovan, 1 with Keith Washington and 1 with Visionmasters with Tony King)

22 **GENE PITNEY** (includes 1 with Marc Almond)

21 **MARC ALMOND** (includes 1 as Marc and the Mambas, 1 with Bronski Beat, 1 with Gene Pitney and 2 as Soft Cell/Marc Almond. + 9 with Soft Cell)

21 **GEORGE BENSON** (includes 1 with Aretha Franklin and 1 with Patti Austin)

21 **CILLA BLACK** (includes 1 with Dusty Springfield)

21 **CHER** (includes 1 with Beavis and Butt-Head. +9 with Sonny and 1 uncredited with Meat Loaf)

21 **ERASURE**

21 **BRYAN FERRY** (+16 with Roxy Music)

21 **FIVE STAR**

21 **GENESIS**

21 **GARY GLITTER**

21 **WHITNEY HOUSTON** (includes 1 with Teddy Pendergrass, 1 with Bobby Brown and 1 with Aretha Franklin)

21 **INXS** (includes 1 with Jimmy Barnes)

21 **JANET JACKSON** (includes 1 with Luther Vandross)

21 **KOOL AND THE GANG**

21 **MARILLION**

21 **STING** (includes 1 with Eric Clapton, 1 with Rod Stewart and Bryan Adams. +16 with Police)

21 **U2** (includes 1 with B.B. King)

21 **WEDDING PRESENT**

21 **ANDY WILLIAMS**

20 **ADAM AND THE ANTS/ADAM ANT**

20 **BIG COUNTRY**

20 **BUCKS FIZZ**

20 **RUSS CONWAY** (includes 1 with Dorothy Squires)

20 **DEACON BLUE**

20 **FATS DOMINO**

20 **PETER GABRIEL** (includes 1 with Kate Bush, 1 with Youssou N'Dour. + 1 with Genesis)

20 **HERMAN'S HERMITS**

20 **BILLY JOEL**

20 **SANDIE SHAW**

20 **SPANDAU BALLET**

20 **BRUCE SPRINGSTEEN**

20 **LUTHER VANDROSS** (includes 1 with Gregory Hines, 1 with Janet Jackson and 1 with Mariah Carey)

20 **PAUL YOUNG** (includes 1 with Zucchero and 1 with Clannad. + 1 with Street Band)

other acts that have clocked up 20 hits or more under more than one name are:

45 **PAUL WELLER** (9 solo, 18 with Jam, 17 with Style Council and 1 with Council Collective)

37 **MIDGE URE** (8 solo, 17 with Ultravox, 7 with Visage, 2 as part of Slik, 1 as a Rich Kid and 1 with Mick Karn. +1 as a leader of Band Aid)

34 **MORRISSEY** (16 solo, 1 with Siouxsie and 17 as a Smith)

31 **LIONEL RICHIE** (16 solo, 13 with the Commodores, 1 with Diana Ross and 1 as a leader of USA For Africa)

29 **ERIC CLAPTON** (15 solo, 7 with Cream, 2 with the Yardbirds, 1 with Elton John, 1 with Delaney and Bonnie and Friends and 1 with Tina Turner)

29 **TERRY HALL** (3 solo, 11 with Specials, 8 with Fun Boy Three, 4 with Colour Field and 3 with Vegas)

28 **GEORGE MICHAEL** (14 solo, 10 with Wham!, 1 with Elton John, 1 with Aretha Franklin,1 with Queen and Lisa Stansfield and 1 with Boogie Box High)

25 **DONNY OSMOND** (11 solo, 10 as an Osmond, 4 as half of Donny and Marie)

24 **BOY GEORGE** (9 solo, 10 with Culture Club, 4 as Jesus Loves You, 1 with PM Dawn)

24 **DEBORAH HARRY** (9 solo, 1 with Iggy Pop and 14 with Blondie)

24 **JOHN LYDON** (1 as Leftfield Lydon, 12 with Public Image Ltd.,10 with Sex Pistols and 1 with Time Zone)

24 **ROY WOOD** (4 solo, 10 with Move, 7 with Wizzard, 1 with Electric Light Orchestra, 1 with Doctor and the Medics and 1 with Jive Bunny)

23 **DAVID SYLVIAN** (6 solo, 12 with Japan, 3 with Sylvian Sakamoto, 1 with Robert Fripp and 1 with Mick Karn)

23 **JODY WATLEY** (6 solo and 17 with Shalamar)

22 **BUDDY HOLLY** (18 solo and 4 as a Cricket)

22 **PHIL LYNOTT** (3 solo, 18 with Thin Lizzy and 1 with Gary Moore)

22 **GARY MOORE** (17 solo, 1 with Phil Lynott, 1 with B.B. King, and at least 3 with Thin Lizzy)

22 **FRANKIE VALLI** (5 solo and 17 with Four Seasons)

21 **BELINDA CARLISLE** (19 solo and 2 with Go-Gos)

21 **FISH** (8 solo, 1 with Tony Banks and 12 with Marillion)

21 **DARYL HALL** (4 solo, 1 with Sounds Of Blackness and 16 with John Oates)

21 **BILLY IDOL** (15 solo and 6 with Generation X)

21 **TREMELOES** (13 as a group. +8 backing Brian Poole)

20 **JON BON JOVI** (2 solo and 18 with Bon Jovi)

20 **BOB GELDOF** (4 solo, 14 with Boomtown Rats, 1 with Band Aid and 1 with USA For Africa)

20 **ALISON MOYET** (15 solo and 5 with Yazoo)

20 **STEVE WINWOOD** (6 solo, 10 with Spencer Davis Group and 4 with Traffic)

MOST HITS IN ONE CALENDAR YEAR

ELVIS PRESLEY

During 1992, **Wedding Present** released 12 singles, all of which hit the top 30 and eight of which made the top 20. Only one, their May release 'Come Play With Me', hit the top ten, and none of them spent more than two weeks on the chart. Five of their singles were top 20 hits which spent only one week on the chart. No other act has ever had more than ten new hit singles in one calendar year.

In 1957, **Elvis Presley** actually charted with 16 different titles, but these involved only ten new hit singles during the year. Four titles were on the chart in the first week of the year, having hit the chart originally during 1956. Two of these titles, 'Blue Moon' at number 22 and 'I Don't Care If The Sun Don't Shine' at number 30, were on HMV POP 272. Of the ten new hits he enjoyed in 1957, two were double-sided, giving the King 12 more chart placings during the year.

In 1983, **Jam** enjoyed 14 chart entries, but these included one hit hanging over from 1982 and 13 re-issues of old hits. Nine of the re-entries came in the same chart, for the week ending 22 January 1983, which is a record for chart entries in one week. On 3 September 1977, **Elvis Presley** scored eight simultaneous chart entries, all re-issues. He had a further three new hits that year, giving him a total of 11 hits.

MOST TOP TEN HITS

The same rules apply as for the MOST HITS list, except that a disc must have made the top ten for at least one week to qualify.

63 **CLIFF RICHARD** (includes 1 with Phil Everly, 1 with Young Ones and 1 with Sarah Brightman)

55 **ELVIS PRESLEY**

33 **MADONNA**

29 **MICHAEL JACKSON** (includes 2 with Paul McCartney. + 11 as a Jackson)

25 **BEATLES**

25 **ROD STEWART** (includes 1 with Tina Turner, 1 with Bryan Adams and Sting, 3 with Faces and 1 with Python Lee Jackson)

24 **PAUL McCARTNEY/WINGS** (includes 12 as Wings, and 2 with Michael Jackson, 1 with Stevie Wonder and 1 with Christians, Holly Johnson, Gerry Marsden and Stock Aitken Waterman)

23 **DAVID BOWIE** (includes 1 with Queen, 1 with Bing Crosby and 1 with Mick Jagger)

22 **ELTON JOHN** (includes 2 with Kiki Dee, 1 with George Michael and 1 with RuPaul)

22 **STATUS QUO**

21 **QUEEN** (includes 1 with David Bowie and 1 with George Michael and Lisa Stansfield)

21 **ROLLING STONES**

19 **ABBA**

19 **FRANKIE LAINE** (includes 1 with Jimmy Boyd and 1 with Doris Day)

18 **STEVIE WONDER** (includes 1 with Paul McCartney and 1 with Julio Iglesias)

17 **BEE GEES**

17 **LONNIE DONEGAN**

17 **HOLLIES**

17 **DIANA ROSS** (includes 1 with Marvin Gaye and 1 with Lionel Richie. + 7 with Supremes and 1 with Supremes and Temptations)

16 **MANFRED MANN** (includes 3 as Manfred Mann's Earth Band)

16 **KYLIE MINOGUE** (includes 1 with Jason Donovan)

16 **SHADOWS** (+ 25 backing Cliff Richard)

16 **SLADE**

16 **UB40** (includes 1 with Robert Palmer)

15 **ELECTRIC LIGHT ORCHESTRA** (includes 1 with Olivia Newton-John)

15 **ERASURE**

15 **TOM JONES** (includes 1 with Art Of Noise)

15 **MADNESS**

15 **PET SHOP BOYS** (includes 1 with Dusty Springfield and 1 as Absolutely Fabulous)

15 **SHAKIN' STEVENS** (includes 1 with Bonnie Tyler)

14 **PRINCE**

14 **U2**

13 **BEACH BOYS** (includes 1 with Fat Boys)

13 **NAT 'KING' COLE**

13 **PERRY COMO**

13 **DURAN DURAN**

13 **EVERLY BROTHERS** (Phil Everly + 1 with Cliff Richard)

13 **KINKS**

13 **SUPREMES** (includes 1 with Temptations)

13 **WHO**

12 **SHIRLEY BASSEY**

12 **GARY GLITTER** (+ 1 with Timelords)

12 **HOT CHOCOLATE**

12 **GUY MITCHELL**

12 **ROY ORBISON**

12 **FRANK SINATRA** (includes 1 with Nancy Sinatra and 1 with Bono)

11 **WINIFRED ATWELL** (+ 1 as part of All Star Hit Parade)

11 **CILLA BLACK**

11 **PAT BOONE**

11 **PETULA CLARK**

11 **ADAM FAITH**

11 **FOUR TOPS**

11 **BILLY FURY**

11 **GUNS N' ROSES**

11 **WHITNEY HOUSTON**

11 **JACKSON FIVE/JACKSONS** (6 as Jackson Five and 5 as Jacksons)

11 **MUD**

11 **GENE PITNEY** (includes 1 with Marc Almond)

11 **DUSTY SPRINGFIELD** (includes 1 with Pet Shop Boys. + 2 with Springfields)

11 **T. REX**

11 **10 C.C.** (+ 1 as Hotlegs, more or less)

11 **FRANKIE VAUGHAN** (includes 2 with Kaye Sisters)

11 **DAVID WHITFIELD** (+ 1 as part of All Star Hit Parade)

10 **ADAM AND THE ANTS/ADAM ANT**

10 **BANANARAMA** (includes 1 with Fun Boy Three and 1 with La Na Nee Nee Noo Noo)

10 **BAY CITY ROLLERS**

10 **BLONDIE**

10 **BONEY M**

10 **DORIS DAY** (includes 2 with Frankie Laine and 1 with Johnnie Ray)

10 **JASON DONOVAN** (includes 1 with Kylie Minogue)

10 **DAVID ESSEX**

10 **CONNIE FRANCIS**

10 **HERMAN'S HERMITS**

10 **IRON MAIDEN**

10 **OLIVIA NEWTON-JOHN** (includes 3 with John Travolta and 1 with ELO)

10 **POLICE**

10 **JOHNNIE RAY** (includes 1 with Doris Day)

10 **ROXY MUSIC**

10 **LEO SAYER**

10 **SHOWADDYWADDY**

10 **SPANDAU BALLET**

10 **STYLISTICS**

10 **SWEET**

10 **TAKE THAT**

also strongly represented on top ten hits are:

20 **GEORGE MICHAEL** (7 solo, 9 as part of Wham!, 1 with Aretha Franklin, 1 with Elton John, 1 with Queen and Lisa Stansfield and 1 as part of Boogie Box High)

19 **PHIL COLLINS** (9 solo, 8 as part of Genesis, 1 with Marilyn Martin and 1 with Philip Bailey)

15 **ROY WOOD** (1 solo, 7 with Move, 6 with Wizzard and 1 with Electric Light Orchestra)

14 **ANNIE LENNOX** (3 solo, 8 as part of Eurythmics, 2 as a Tourist and 1 as a Eurythmic with Aretha Franklin)

13 **DONNY OSMOND** (6 solo, 5 as one of the Osmonds and 2 with Marie Osmond)

12 **LIONEL RICHIE** (7 solo, 4 as a Commodore and 1 with Diana Ross)

12 **DAVE STEWART** (1 with Candy Dulfer, 8 as part of the Eurythmics, 2 as a Tourist and 1 as a Eurythmic with Aretha Franklin)

11 **CHER** (7 solo, 3 with Sonny and Cher and 1 uncredited with Meat Loaf)

32	**MADONNA**
26	**CLIFF RICHARD** (with the Shadows for 11 consecutive)
24	**BEATLES** (first 24 releases)
23	**ELVIS PRESLEY** (first 23 RCA releases)
19	**ROLLING STONES**
18	**ABBA**
13	**KYLIE MINOGUE** (first 13 hits, including 1 with Jason Donovan)
12	**SHADOWS** (first 12 hits), **SLADE**
11	**GARY GLITTER** (first 11 hits), **FRANKIE LAINE, GUY MITCHELL** (first 11 hits), **T. REX**
10	**BAY CITY ROLLERS** (first 10 hits), **DURAN DURAN, DAVID WHITFIELD**

At the start of Elvis Presley's run of 23 consecutive top ten hits, three old HMV releases appeared on the chart, one of which, 'Paralysed', reached the top ten. Three EPs by Elvis also hit the charts without reaching the top ten during the five and a half years in which every Elvis single hit the Top Ten, with 20 of the 23 reaching the top three.

'Holiday' by Madonna reappeared in the top ten twice during her run of 27 top ten hits with consecutive releases. As it was first a top ten hit before the release of 'Lucky Star', her first

single to fail to hit the upper reaches, it does not count as one of her consecutive top ten hits. Her re-mixed version of 'Crazy For You', which also hit the top ten, does not count as an extra hit. The run ended with her final single of 1994, 'Take A Bow', which peaked at number 16.

Kylie Minogue's record of 13 consecutive top ten hits with her first 13 releases (including one in duet with Jason Donovan) represents the best start to a chart career by any act ever. The Beatles' first 24 releases all eventually hit the top ten but their first single, 'Love Me Do' only did so as a re-issue 20 years on.

Between May 1959 and December 1963, the Shadows released 30 singles, either solo or backing Cliff Richard, all of which hit the top ten.

The Rolling Stones' run of 19 consecutive top ten hits began on 12 March 1964, with 'Not Fade Away', and finished on July 21 1978 when 'Miss You/Far Away Eyes' dropped out of the top ten. This is the longest time span for a run of top ten hits with consecutive releases, none of which were re-mixes or re-issues.

At the end of 1994, the longest active string of consecutive top ten hits was by Take That, with nine.

ROLLING STONES

This list continues to grow rapidly as more and more records make the top 75 for a shorter and shorter time, which means, statistically, that the average chart peak must be getting lower. The full list of those acts that have had at least ten hits to the end of 1994, without ever reaching the top ten is:

ACT	HITS	HIGHEST PLACING
AC/DC	24	12 - Heatseeker, 1988
ALARM	16	17 - 68 Guns, 1983
MISSION	15	11 - Wasteland, 1987
SAXON	15	12 - And The Bands Played On, 1981
CULT	14	11 - Lil' Devil, 1987
INSPIRAL CARPETS	14	12 - Dragging Me Down, 1992
NEW MODEL ARMY	14	25 - Here Comes The War, 1993
The THE	14	17 - Dis-infected EP, 1994
LLOYD COLE	13	17 - Lost Weekend, 1985
JUDAS PRIEST	13	12 - Living After Midnight, 1980
		12 - Breaking The Law, 1980
KILLING JOKE	13	16 - Love Like Blood, 1985
PUBLIC ENEMY	13	18 - Don't Believe The Hype, 1988
		18 - Welcome To The Terrordome, 1990
		18 - Give It Up, 1994
AEROSMITH	12	13 - Love In An Elevator, 1989
JULIAN COPE	12	19 - World Shut Your Mouth, 1986
FALL	12	30 - There's A Ghost In My House, 1987
LITTLE ANGELS	12	12 - Womankind, 1993
LOOSE ENDS	12	13 - Hanging On A String (Contemplating), 1985
		13 - Don't Be A Fool, 1990
RUSH	12	13 - Spirit Of Radio, 1980
W.A.S.P.	12	17 - Chainsaw Charlie (Murders In The New Morgue), 1992
ADEVA	11	17 - Respect, 1989
		17 - Warning, 1989
		17 - I Thank You, 1989
NICK HEYWARD	11	11 - Take That Situation, 1983
TOM PETTY	11	28 - I Won't Back Down, 1989
POISON	11	13 - Every Rose Has Its Thorn, 1989
		13 - Your Mama Don't Dance, 1989
DAVID SYLVIAN	11	16 - Forbidden Colours, 1983
ANTHRAX	10	14 - Bring The Noise, 1991
MONIE LOVE	10	12 - It's A Shame (My Sister), 1990
ST. ETIENNE	10	12 - You're In A Bad Way, 1993
SPEAR OF DESTINY	10	14 - Never Take Me Alive, 1987

Julian Cope, David Sylvian and Nick Heyward have been involved in top ten hits as members of The Teardrop Explodes, Japan and Haircut 100 respectively. Bjork has enjoyed five solo hits, one with 808 State and six as lead singer of the Sugarcubes, a total of 12 hits, without hitting the top ten. Clash had 19 hits without hitting the top ten before the re-release of their 16th hit, 'Should I Stay Or Should I Go', went all the way to number one. Sting's 19th single was his top ten hit with Bryan Adams and Rod Stewart, 'All For Love'. Two singles later, he enjoyed his first solo top ten hit. Chris Rea's 18th hit was his first, and to date only, top ten hit. Fats Domino had 18 hits after his only top ten hit. Elvis Costello has charted 21 times since his last top ten hit at the end of 1981, 19 times under his own name and twice as The Imposter. Since Gary Numan's last top ten appearance in June 1982, he has clocked up 23 more hits - 18 solo hits, three hits with Bill Sharpe and two with Radio Heart. The highest position any of these hits reached was 17 by 'Change Your Mind'. Luther Vandross has had 18 solo hits without ever straying above position 13, but has reached number two in duet with Janet Jackson in 1992, and number three with Mariah Carey in 1994.

That Petrol Emotion currently holds the record for most hits without reaching the top 40. They have had seven chart hits, but their highest position is number 43, which was the peak of their first chart hit, 'Big Decision', in 1987.

AC/DC

This table shows which acts had to wait for the longest time between chart hits. The definition of a 'hit' is the same as in other lists in this section, i.e. re-issues and re-entries do not count as new hits.

For that reason the Righteous Brothers, for example, do not feature in this list, as they have had no new hits since 1966. The gap is calculated between the last day of one chart run and the first day of the chart run of the next hit.

The 39 acts who have waited patiently for over 15 years between hits are:

PEREZ PRADO	36 years 27 days	(7 Nov 58 to 4 Dec 94)
COASTERS	34 years 113 days	(11 Dec 59 to 3 Apr 94)
DINAH WASHINGTON	30 years 71 days	(24 Jan 62 to 4 Apr 92)
EARTHA KITT	28 years 170 days	(16 Jun 55 to 3 Dec 83)
RITCHIE VALENS	28 years 142 days	(12 Mar 59 to 1 Aug 87)
JOHN LEE HOOKER	28 years 66 days	(19 Aug 64 to 24 Oct 92)
PATSY CLINE	27 years 340 days	(2 Jan 63 to 8 Dec 90)
BOBBY VINTON	26 years 215 days	(27 Feb 64 to 29 Sep 90)
FRANK IFIELD	24 years 288 days	(22 Feb 67 to 7 Dec 91)
JIMMY CLIFF	23 years 140 days	(24 Oct 70 to 13 Mar 94)
ROLF HARRIS	22 years 232 days	(20 Jun 70 to 7 Feb 93)
CHELSEA F.C.	21 years 359 days	(14 May 72 to 8 May 94)
ARSENAL F.C.	21 years 324 days	(19 Jun 71 to 9 May 93)
GLENN MILLER	21 years 312 days	(18 Mar 54 to 24 Jan 76)
LEEDS UNITED FC	19 years 293 days	(7 Jul 72 to 25 Apr 92)
BUFFY SAINTE-MARIE	19 years 293 days	(21 April 72 to 8 Feb 92)
GARY 'U.S.' BONDS	19 years 223 days	(18 Oct 61 to 30 May 81)
CILLA BLACK	19 years 190 days	(16 Mar 74 to 12 Sep 93)
ROY ORBISON	19 years 19 days	(26 Dec 69 to 14 Jan 89)
SIMON & GARFUNKEL	19 years 13 days	(24 Nov 72 to 7 Dec 91)
NINA SIMONE	18 years 262 days	(11 Feb 69 to 31 Oct 87)
WILSON PICKETT	18 years 255 days	(11 Mar 69 to 21 Nov 87)
PAUL EVANS	18 years 254 days	(6 Apr 60 to 16 Dec 78)
KENNY LYNCH	18 years 16 days	(4 Aug 65 to 20 Aug 83)
BING CROSBY	17 years 338 days	(5 Sep 57 to 9 Aug 75)
WILLIAM BELL	17 years 284 days	(16 Jul 68 to 26 Apr 86)
RINGO STARR	17 years 113 days	(14 Feb 75 to 6 Jun 92)
MONKEES	17 years 109 days	(1 Jul 69 to 18 Oct 86)
JOE COCKER	17 years 92 days	(14 Aug 70 to 14 Nov 87)
SLIM WHITMAN	17 years 86 days	(11 Jul 57 to 5 Oct 74)
MIKE BERRY	17 years 73 days	(22 May 63 to 2 Aug 80)
DOROTHY SQUIRES	16 years 101 days	(11 Jun 53 to 20 Sep 69)
EVERLY BROTHERS	16 years 96 days	(18 Jun 68 to 22 Sep 84)
BORIS GARDINER	16 years 87 days	(1 May 70 to 26 Jul 86)
DEE CLARK	16 years 3 days	(8 Oct 59 to 11 Oct 75)
TAMS	15 years 360 days	(26 Nov 71 to 21 Nov 87)
BILLY FURY	15 years 349 days	(21 Sep 66 to 4 Sep 82)
MAX BYGRAVES	15 years 325 days	(18 Jan 74 to 9 Dec 89)
JOHNNY TILLOTSON	15 years 306 days	(12 Jun 63 to 14 Apr 79)

(**William Bell** hit the charts with Judy Clay in late 1968 and early 1969. **Dorothy Squires** had a hit with Russ Conway in 1961. In 1983 both **Phil Everly** and **Joe Cocker** had top ten hits, with Cliff Richard and Jennifer Warnes respectively. **Roy Orbison** charted as a member of the Traveling Wilburys in 1988. **Glenn Miller** and **Johnny Tillotson's** reappearances were both as a result of a re-issue of a hit, coupled with tracks that had not previously hit the chart, thus counting the re-issue as a new hit.)

Of these acts, the top five to come back with newly recorded material are Eartha Kitt, John Lee Hooker, Jimmy Cliff, Rolf Harris and Chelsea F.C.

There was a gap of 33 years and 87 days between appearances of the **Chipmunks'** name in the charts, but their comeback hit was not only with Billy Ray Cyrus, but also it came over 20 years after the death of the creator of the Chipmunks, Ross Bagdasarian, better known as David Seville. The 1992 Chipmunks were the creation of Seville's son, Ross Bagdasarian Jr. There was a gap of 28 years and 339 days between **Nat 'King' Cole's** consecutive new hits 'Dear Lonely Hearts' and 'The Christmas Song', but the re-issue of 'When I Fall In Love' had given him a hit four years before 'The Christmas Song' charted, thus disqualifying him from this table. Similarly, **Louis Armstrong** was absent from the chart with new hits for 26 years 104 days between 'Sunshine Of Love' and 'We Have All The Time In The World', but the re-issue of 'What A Wonderful World' hit the charts in the interim. Some acts have returned in a slightly different format. After 25 years and 329 days off the chart, **Karl Denver** reappeared in June 1990 with Happy Mondays. **The Troggs** came back in 1993, 25 years and 217 days since their previous chart appearance, with a re-recording of 'Wild Thing', with the Gladiator, Wolf. **Donovan** made his comeback with Singing Corner on 1 December

PEREZ PRADO

1990, 21 years and 307 days since his final solo chart hit, and 21 years and 83 days since his duet with Jeff Beck lapsed into chart oblivion. **Ray Charles** charted as vocalist with Quincy Jones 21 years and 261 days after his final solo hit dropped off the chart. For **P.P. Arnold** there was a chart hiatus of exactly 20 years between her last solo hit and her appearance on the Beatmasters hit, 'Burn It Up' in 1988. **Crosby Stills and Nash** spent 19 years and 269 days in the chart wilderness before Crosby Stills Nash and Young had their first UK chart hit in January 1989. **Jeff Beck and Rod Stewart** had consecutive hits as a duet 18 years and 266 days apart, but both partners hit the charts in the interim. **Elton John and Kiki Dee** were absent as a duo from the charts for 17 years and 43 days, but both had plenty of solo hits in the interim. There was a gap of 15 years and 304 days between **Des O'Connor's** last solo appearance and his re-emergence late in 1986 in partnership with Roger Whittaker. **Tammy Wynette** enjoyed her final solo chart hit 15 years and 151 days before re-emerging on KLF's 'Justified And Ancient' at the end of 1991.

39 other acts have been off the chart for over ten years between hits. They are:

SPARKS (14 years 333 days), Sandie SHAW (14/315), Trini LOPEZ (14/223), Danny WILLIAMS (14/132), Dionne WARWICK (14/92), Mick JAGGER (14/60), Robin GIBB (13/349), CHER (13/271), Mr. Acker BILK (13/167), INNER CIRCLE (13/152), FRANKIE MILLER (13/28), DION (13/27), CHAIRMEN OF THE BOARD (13/20), LITTLE RICHARD (12/345), Murray HEAD (12/280), Donny OSMOND (12/253), Marianne FAITHFULL (12/247), EXCITERS (12/219), Billy PRESTON (12/105), Duncan BROWNE (12/84), PINK FLOYD (12/79), DOORS (12/70), Paul ANKA (12/37), Tony OSBORNE SOUND (11/339), Henry MANCINI (11/314), Johnny MATHIS (11/290), ENGLAND WORLD CUP SQUAD (11/232), Duane EDDY (11/185), Millie JACKSON (11/107), Robert JOHN (11/61), Gene CHANDLER (10/216), INCOGNITO (10/206), Dobie GRAY (10/166), Linda RONSTADT (10/158), Betty WRIGHT (10/146), CHAKACHAS (10/130), BOOKER T. & THE M.G.'s (10/80), Wayne GIBSON (10/68) and Charlie DRAKE (10/12).

(**Dionne Warwick, Mick Jagger, Robin Gibb, Billy Preston, Donny Osmond** and **Linda Ronstadt** all appeared on the charts as part of groups during their solo absences. Linda Ronstadt's comeback hit featured the uncredited vocals of Aaron Neville).

Barry Blue was absent from the charts for 14 years and 278 days before reappearing under the guise of Cry Sisco! **The Trammps** disappeared for 14 years and 96 days before re-emerging in partnership with KWS in 1992. **Gene Pitney** missed 14 years and 39 days of chart action before hitting again with Marc Almond in 1989. **Shirley Bassey** had been absent from the chart for 14 years and 33 days when she reappeared with Yello. **Al Green's** chart duet with Annie Lennox came 13 years and 215 days after his last hit fell off the chart. **Cozy Powell** came back in duet with Brian May, 13 years and 208 days after his final solo hit disappeared. **Timmy Thomas** went missing from the charts for 12 years and 231 days between his last solo hit and his duet with Nicole. **Lindisfarne** spent 12 years and 7 days out of chart sight before coming back with Gazza on 10 November 1990. **Pete Waterman** hit the charts as 14–18 11 years and 239 days before he became one third of Stock Aitken Waterman and hit the charts again. **Scott Fitzgerald's** solo chart debut came 10 years and 44 days after his hit duet with Yvonne Keeley. **Roger Whittaker** had a gap of 11 years and 9 days between his last solo chart appearance and his hit with Des O'Connor. **Duane Eddy** not only had a gap of 11 years and 185 days between solo chart hits, he then had to wait a further 10 years and 310 days after his last solo hit before re-emerging with Art Of Noise and a re-make of his first top ten hit, 'Peter Gunn Theme'. **Dolly Parton** was absent for 10 years and 3 days before she came back in a duet with James Ingram. **Roy Wood's** name was out of the chart for 11 years and 127 days before his comeback with Dr. and the Medics, although he had a re-issued hit as leader of Wizzard in the interim. There was a gap of 11 years and 59 days between **Shane Fenton's** final day on the charts and **Alvin Stardust's** first appearance.

THE COASTERS

Since 13 May 1978, when the top 75 was first published, 24 acts have clocked up a chart career consisting of only one week at number 75. They are:

ADICTS	Bad Boy	14 May 83
ANGELWITCH	Sweet Danger	7 Jun 80
APPLES	Eye Wonder	23 Mar 91
BABY JUNE	Hey! What's Your Name	15 Aug 92
D'BORA	Dream About You	14 Sep 91
DAYTON	The Sound Of Music	10 Dec 83
DTOX	Shattered Glass	21 Nov 92
THULI DUMAKUDE	The Funeral	2 Jan 88
EXPOSE	I'll Never Get Over You (Getting Over Me)	28 Aug 93
GEORGE FENTON and JONAS GWANGWA	Cry Freedom	2 Jan 88
GOOD GIRLS	Just Call Me	24 Jul 93
GRAND PRIX	Keep On Believing	27 Feb 82
HEARTBEAT COUNTRY	Heartbeat	31 Dec 94
ANTHONY HOPKINS	Distant Star	27 Dec 86
LOST	Techno Funk	22 Jun 91
MICHAEL LOVESMITH	Ain't Nothin' Like It	5 Oct 85
MC DUKE	I'm Riffin' (English Rasta)	11 Mar 89
PRETTY BOY FLOYD	Rock And Roll (Is Gonna Set The Night On Fire)	10 Mar 90
CHERYL PEPSII RILEY	Thanks For My Child	28 Jan 89
SEDUCTION	Heartbeat	21 Apr 90
SIMONE	My Family Depends On Me	23 Nov 91
SLEEPER*	Delicious	21 May 94
SOULED OUT	In My Life	9 May 92
ULTRA-SONIC	Obsession	3 Sep 94

*Sleeper hit the singles chart again in early 1995 with 'Inbetweener'.

Adicts and Grand Prix have also hit the album charts, with marginally more success. Thuli Dumakude's hit was the flip side of the George Fenton and Jonas Gwangwa record, both tracks from the soundtrack of the film, Cry Freedom.

There are seven other acts who have spent only one week at number 75 in this particular combination, but they have had hits under other guises.

CILLA BLACK and DUSTY SPRINGFIELD	Heart And Soul	30 Oct 93

(both have had number one solo hits)

JOHNNY CLEGG and SAVUKA	Scatterlings Of Africa	16 May 87

(Clegg also hit as part of Juluka)

NIKKI D	Daddy's Little Girl	30 Mar 91

(has hit with Alyson Williams)

DEJA	Serious	29 Aug 87

(Deja were Starlena Young and Curt Jones, who had hits as members of both Aurra and Slave)

FISH and TONY BANKS	Short Cut To Somewhere	18 Oct 86

(both have had solo hits, as well as with Marillion and Genesis respectively)

MELISSA MANCHESTER and AL JARREAU	The Music Of Goodbye	5 Apr 86

(Jarreau has had 5 solo hits)

STOP THE VIOLENCE	Self Destruction	18 Feb 89

(charity ensemble consisting of several chart acts)

The Ruthless Rap Assassins are the only act to the end of 1994 whose chart career has consisted of two singles, both of which peaked at number 75 for one week. Robert Owens' only chart hit, 'I'll Be Your Friend', peaked at number 75 for two weeks in December 1991.

From 10 March 1960 to 6 May 1978, when only a top 50 was published, nine acts managed a chart career that consisted of only one week at number 50. They were Angels, Chaquito, Jimmy Clanton, Cookies, Tim Hardin, Tony Hatch, Moontrekkers, Hal Page and the Whalers and Sundragon.

Marvin Gaye and Mary Wells also spent only one week at number 50, but they both had much bigger solo successes.

Keith Relf, lead vocalist of the hitmaking Yardbirds, also spent just one week at number 50 as a soloist.

BILL MAYNARD, a.k.a. *Heartbeat Country* (Yorkshire Television).

Fifteen of the top 20 acts (actually 21, as there is a tie for 20th place), listed according to the number of weeks they have spent on the UK singles chart, featured on the charts of 1993 and 1994. Although three of the top 20 acts are dead, opportunities for further chart life with re-issues and rediscovered recordings means that the top of the all-time list remains very active. Nobody has dropped out of the top 20, although the Bee Gees have eased in to the bottom slot equal with Jim Reeves, and the Hollies and UB40 are within striking distance.

Cliff Richard is closing the gap on Elvis Presley at the very top, but it is Rod Stewart and Madonna who have made the biggest moves in the past two years. Rod has climbed from ninth to fifth, overtaking the Beatles, David Bowie, Stevie Wonder and Status Quo. Madonna has leapt from 19th to 12th equal, but is still some way behind Diana Ross, the top woman on the list. Madonna still ranks way ahead of the rest in percentage of top ten hits, but the Beatles have a higher percentage of number one hits - 58.6% of all their releases, official and unofficial, hit the very top.

There is no completely satisfactory way of ranking chart careers, and this table which gives precedence to the number of weeks spent on the chart has attracted criticism, especially from Abba and Police fans. However, we feel that longevity is a major achievement in popular music, and the feature of Status Quo's career, for example, which sets them apart from other bands is that they just keep on going. If you don't want to put Tom Jones on a higher pedestal than Roy Orbison, you can always refer to the Most Number One Hits table.

Act/Country		Chart Span	Wks	Hits	Top 10 Hits	No. 1s	Ave Wks/Hit	% of Top 10 Hits
Elvis Presley	USA	56-92	1145	109	55	17	10.5	50.5%
Cliff Richard	UK	58-94	1100	115	63	13	9.6	54.8%
Elton John	UK	71-94	508	66	22	3	7.7	33.3%
Frank Sinatra	USA	54-94	439	36	12	3	12.2	33.3%
Rod Stewart	UK	71-94	437	50	25	6	8.7	50.0%
Beatles	UK	62-92	434	29	25	17	15.0	86.2%
David Bowie	UK	69-93	418	53	23	5	7.9	43.4%
Diana Ross	USA	70-94	415	54	17	2	7.7	31.5%
Stevie Wonder	USA	66-91	404	49	18	2	8.2	36.7%
Status Quo	UK	68-94	399	48	22	1	8.3	45.8%
Paul McCartney	UK	71-93	397	47	24	3	8.4	51.1%
Madonna	USA	84-94	382	35	33	7	10.9	94.3%
Michael Jackson	USA	72-94	382	41	29	4	9.3	70.7%
Shadows	UK	60-81	359	31	16	5	11.6	51.6%
Queen	UK	74-93	357	42	21	5	8.5	50.0%
Tom Jones	UK	65-94	356	34	15	2	10.5	44.1%
Roy Orbison	USA	60-93	352	33	12	3	10.7	36.4%
Rolling Stones	UK	63-91	340	38	21	8	8.9	55.3%
Everly Brothers	USA	57-84	337	29	13	4	11.6	44.8%
Bee Gees	UK	67-94	322	33	17	5	9.8	51.5%
Jim Reeves	USA	60-72	322	26	6	1	12.4	23.1%

• •

By category, and again ranking the acts according to the number of weeks they have spent on the singles charts, the top acts are:

1. MALE VOCALISTS

	Overall	UK acts	USA acts
1.	Elvis Presley	Cliff Richard	Elvis Presley
2.	Cliff Richard	Elton John	Frank Sinatra
3.	Elton John	Rod Stewart	Stevie Wonder
4.	Frank Sinatra	David Bowie	Michael Jackson
5.	Rod Stewart	Paul McCartney	Roy Orbison

2. FEMALE VOCALISTS

	Overall	UK acts	USA acts
1.	Diana Ross	Shirley Bassey	Diana Ross
2.	Madonna	Petula Clark	Madonna
3.	Shirley Bassey	Olivia Newton-John	Donna Summer
4.	Donna Summer	Dusty Springfield	Connie Francis
5.	Petula Clark	Cilla Black	Brenda Lee

3. GROUPS

	Overall	UK acts	USA acts
1.	Beatles	Beatles	Everly Brothers
2.	Status Quo	Status Quo	Four Tops
3.	Shadows	Shadows	Supremes
4.	Queen	Queen	Beach Boys
5.	Rolling Stones	Rolling Stones	Jackson 5/Jacksons

4. INSTRUMENTALISTS

	Overall	UK acts	USA acts
1.	Shadows	Shadows	Duane Eddy
2.	Duane Eddy	Russ Conway	Herb Alpert
3.	Russ Conway	Acker Bilk	Johnny & the Hurricanes
4.	Acker Bilk	Kenny Ball	Booker T & M.G.'s
5.	Kenny Ball	Winifred Atwell	Sandy Nelson

5. OTHER NATIONALITIES

1. Abba
2. Kylie Minogue
3. Boney M
4. U2
5. Jason Donovan, Bob Marley

From these charts, it can be seen that America supplies the successful women and Britain the successful groups. After Duane Eddy and Herb Alpert, hit-making American instrumentalists are few and far between.

DATE DISC HIT THE TOP   NUMBER OF WEEKS AT NUMBER ONE

1950s

1 9 5 2 (Top Twelve - NME Chart)

14 Nov	HERE IN MY HEART Al Martino	9

1 9 5 3

16 Jan	YOU BELONG TO ME Jo Stafford	1
23 Jan	COMES A-LONG A-LOVE Kay Starr	1
30 Jan	OUTSIDE OF HEAVEN Eddie Fisher	1
6 Feb	DON'T LET THE STARS GET IN YOUR EYES Perry Como	5
13 Mar	SHE WEARS RED FEATHERS Guy Mitchell	4
10 Apr	BROKEN WINGS The Stargazers	1
17 Apr	(HOW MUCH IS) THAT DOGGIE IN THE WINDOW Lita Roza	1
24 Apr	I BELIEVE Frankie Laine	9
26 Jun	I'M WALKING BEHIND YOU Eddie Fisher featuring Sally Sweetland	1
3 Jul	I BELIEVE Frankie Laine	6
14 Aug	MOULIN ROUGE Mantovani	1
21 Aug	I BELIEVE Frankie Laine	3
11 Sep	LOOK AT THAT GIRL Guy Mitchell	6
23 Oct	HEY JOE Frankie Laine	2
6 Nov	ANSWER ME David Whitfield	1
13 Nov	ANSWER ME Frankie Laine	8
	(ANSWER ME by David Whitfield returned to number one for one week to share the top spot with Frankie Laine's version on 11 Dec 1953)	

1 9 5 4

8 Jan	OH MEIN PAPA Eddie Calvert	9
12 Mar	I SEE THE MOON Stargazers	5
16 Apr	SECRET LOVE Doris Day	1
23 Apr	I SEE THE MOON Stargazers	1
30 Apr	SUCH A NIGHT Johnnie Ray	1
7 May	SECRET LOVE Doris Day	8
2 Jul	CARA MIA David Whitfield, with chorus and Mantovani and his orchestra	10
10 Sep	LITTLE THINGS MEAN A LOT Kitty Kallen	1
17 Sep	THREE COINS IN THE FOUNTAIN Frank Sinatra	3

Top Twenty began 1 Oct 1954

8 Oct	HOLD MY HAND Don Cornell	4
5 Nov	MY SON MY SON Vera Lynn	2
19 Nov	HOLD MY HAND Don Cornell	1
26 Nov	THIS OLE HOUSE Rosemary Clooney	1
3 Dec	LET'S HAVE ANOTHER PARTY Winifred Atwell	5

1 9 5 5

7 Jan	FINGER OF SUSPICION Dickie Valentine	1
14 Jan	MAMBO ITALIANO Rosemary Clooney	1
21 Jan	FINGER OF SUSPICION Dickie Valentine	2
4 Feb	MAMBO ITALIANO Rosemary Clooney	2
18 Feb	SOFTLY SOFTLY Ruby Murray	3
11 Mar	GIVE ME YOUR WORD Tennessee Ernie Ford	7
29 Apr	CHERRY PINK AND APPLE BLOSSOM WHITE Perez Prado	2
13 May	STRANGER IN PARADISE Tony Bennett	2
27 May	CHERRY PINK AND APPLE BLOSSOM WHITE Eddie Calvert	4
24 Jun	UNCHAINED MELODY Jimmy Young	3
15 Jul	DREAMBOAT Alma Cogan	2
29 Jul	ROSE MARIE Slim Whitman	11
14 Oct	THE MAN FROM LARAMIE Jimmy Young	4
11 Nov	HERNANDO'S HIDEAWAY Johnston Brothers	2
25 Nov	ROCK AROUND THE CLOCK Bill Haley and his Comets	3
16 Dec	CHRISTMAS ALPHABET Dickie Valentine	3

1 9 5 6

6 Jan	ROCK AROUND THE CLOCK Bill Haley and his Comets	2
20 Jan	SIXTEEN TONS Tennessee Ernie Ford	4
17 Feb	MEMORIES ARE MADE OF THIS Dean Martin	4
16 Mar	IT'S ALMOST TOMORROW Dreamweavers	2
30 Mar	ROCK AND ROLL WALTZ Kay Starr with the Hugo Winterhalter Orchestra	1
6 Apr	IT'S ALMOST TOMORROW Dreamweavers	1

Top Thirty began 13 April 1956

13 Apr	POOR PEOPLE OF PARIS Winifred Atwell	3
4 May	NO OTHER LOVE Ronnie Hilton	6
15 Jun	I'LL BE HOME Pat Boone	5
20 Jul	WHY DO FOOLS FALL IN LOVE Teenagers featuring Frankie Lymon	3
10 Aug	WHATEVER WILL BE WILL BE Doris Day	6
21 Sep	LAY DOWN YOUR ARMS Anne Shelton	4
19 Oct	A WOMAN IN LOVE Frankie Laine	4
16 Nov	JUST WALKIN' IN THE RAIN Johnnie Ray	7

1 9 5 7

4 Jan	SINGING THE BLUES Guy Mitchell	1
11 Jan	SINGING THE BLUES Tommy Steele and the Steelmen	1
18 Jan	SINGING THE BLUES Guy Mitchell	1
25 Jan	THE GARDEN OF EDEN Frankie Vaughan	4
	(SINGING THE BLUES by Guy Mitchell returned to number one for one week to share the top spot with GARDEN OF EDEN by Frankie Vaughan on 1 Feb 1957)	
22 Feb	YOUNG LOVE Tab Hunter	7
12 Apr	CUMBERLAND GAP Lonnie Donegan	5
17 May	ROCK-A-BILLY Guy Mitchell	1
24 May	BUTTERFLY Andy Williams	2
7 Jun	YES TONIGHT JOSEPHINE Johnnie Ray	3
28 Jun	GAMBLIN' MAN/PUTTING ON THE STYLE Lonnie Donegan	2

12 Jul	ALL SHOOK UP Elvis Presley	7
30 Aug	DIANA Paul Anka	9
1 Nov	THAT'LL BE THE DAY Crickets	3
22 Nov	MARY'S BOY CHILD Harry Belafonte	7

1 9 5 8

10 Jan	GREAT BALLS OF FIRE Jerry Lee Lewis	2
24 Jan	JAILHOUSE ROCK Elvis Presley	3
14 Feb	THE STORY OF MY LIFE Michael Holliday	2
28 Feb	MAGIC MOMENTS Perry Como	8
25 Apr	WHOLE LOTTA WOMAN Marvin Rainwater	3
16 May	WHO'S SORRY NOW Connie Francis	6
27 Jun	ON THE STREET WHERE YOU LIVE Vic Damone	2
	(On 4 Jul 1958 ON THE STREET WHERE YOU LIVE by Vic Damone and ALL I HAVE TO DO IS DREAM/CLAUDETTE by the Everly Brothers shared the top spot)	
4 Jul	ALL I HAVE TO DO IS DREAM/CLAUDETTE Everly Brothers	7
22 Aug	WHEN Kalin Twins	5
26 Sept	CAROLINA MOON/STUPID CUPID Connie Francis	6
7 Nov	IT'S ALL IN THE GAME Tommy Edwards	3
28 Nov	HOOTS MON Lord Rockingham's XI	3
19 Dec	IT'S ONLY MAKE BELIEVE Conway Twitty	5

1 9 5 9

23 Jan	THE DAY THE RAINS CAME Jane Morgan	1
30 Jan	ONE NIGHT/I GOT STUNG Elvis Presley	3
20 Feb	AS I LOVE YOU Shirley Bassey	4
20 Mar	SMOKE GETS IN YOUR EYES Platters	1
27 Mar	SIDE SADDLE Russ Conway	4
24 Apr	IT DOESN'T MATTER ANYMORE Buddy Holly	3
15 May	A FOOL SUCH AS I/I NEED YOUR LOVE TONIGHT Elvis Presley	5
19 Jun	ROULETTE Russ Conway	2
3 Jul	DREAM LOVER Bobby Darin	4
31 Jul	LIVING DOLL Cliff Richard and the Drifters	6
11 Sep	ONLY SIXTEEN Craig Douglas	4
9 Oct	HERE COMES SUMMER Jerry Keller	1
16 Oct	MACK THE KNIFE Bobby Darin	2
30 Oct	TRAVELLIN' LIGHT Cliff Richard and the Shadows	5
4 Dec	WHAT DO YOU WANT Adam Faith	3
	(On 18 Dec 1959 WHAT DO YOU WANT by Adam Faith and WHAT DO YOU WANT TO MAKE THOSE EYES AT ME FOR by Emile Ford and the Checkmates shared the top spot)	
18 Dec	WHAT DO YOU WANT TO MAKE THOSE EYES AT ME FOR Emile Ford And The Checkmates	6

1960s

1 9 6 0

| 29 Jan | STARRY EYED Michael Holliday | 1 |
| 5 Feb | WHY Anthony Newley | 4 |

Record Retailer, **now** *Music Week*, **began publication of a Top Fifty on 10 Mar 1960. From this point on their charts are used. The final** *New Musical Express* **chart used is that of 26 Feb 1960, as the chart published in** *Record Retailer* **on 10 Mar 1960 was dated 5 Mar and clearly corresponded with the** *NME* **chart of 4 Mar 1960.**

10 Mar	POOR ME Adam Faith	1
17 Mar	RUNNING BEAR Johnny Preston	2
31 Mar	MY OLD MAN'S A DUSTMAN Lonnie Donegan	4
28 Apr	DO YOU MIND Anthony Newley	1
5 May	CATHY'S CLOWN Everly Brothers	7
23 Jun	THREE STEPS TO HEAVEN Eddie Cochran	2
7 Jul	GOOD TIMIN' Jimmy Jones	3
28 Jul	PLEASE DON'T TEASE Cliff Richard and the Shadows	2
4 Aug	SHAKIN' ALL OVER Johnny Kidd and the Pirates	1
11 Aug	PLEASE DON'T TEASE Cliff Richard and the Shadows	2
25 Aug	APACHE Shadows	5
29 Sep	TELL LAURA I LOVE HER Ricky Valance	3
20 Oct	ONLY THE LONELY Roy Orbison	2
3 Nov	IT'S NOW OR NEVER Elvis Presley	8
29 Dec	I LOVE YOU Cliff Richard and the Shadows	2

1 9 6 1

12 Jan	POETRY IN MOTION Johnny Tillotson	2
26 Jan	ARE YOU LONESOME TONIGHT Elvis Presley	4
23 Feb	SAILOR Petula Clark	1
2 Mar	WALK RIGHT BACK/EBONY EYES Everly Brothers	3
23 Mar	WOODEN HEART Elvis Presley	6
4 May	BLUE MOON Marcels	2
18 May	ON THE REBOUND Floyd Cramer	1
25 May	YOU'RE DRIVING ME CRAZY Temperance Seven	1
1 Jun	SURRENDER Elvis Presley	4
29 Jun	RUNAWAY Del Shannon	3
20 Jul	TEMPTATION Everly Brothers	2
3 Aug	WELL I ASK YOU Eden Kane	1
10 Aug	YOU DON'T KNOW Helen Shapiro	3
31 Aug	JOHNNY REMEMBER ME John Leyton	3
21 Sep	REACH FOR THE STARS/CLIMB EV'RY MOUNTAIN Shirley Bassey	1
28 Sep	JOHNNY REMEMBER ME John Leyton	1
5 Oct	KON-TIKI Shadows	1
12 Oct	MICHAEL Highwaymen	1
19 Oct	WALKIN' BACK TO HAPPINESS Helen Shapiro	3
9 Nov	LITTLE SISTER/HIS LATEST FLAME Elvis Presley	4
7 Dec	TOWER OF STRENGTH Frankie Vaughan	3
28 Dec	MOON RIVER Danny Williams	2

1 9 6 2

11 Jan	THE YOUNG ONES Cliff Richard and the Shadows	6
22 Feb	ROCK-A-HULA BABY/CAN'T HELP FALLING IN LOVE Elvis Presley	4
22 Mar	WONDERFUL LAND Shadows	8
17 May	NUT ROCKER B. Bumble and the Stingers	1
24 May	GOOD LUCK CHARM Elvis Presley	5
28 Jun	COME OUTSIDE Mike Sarne with Wendy Richard	2

12 Jul	I CAN'T STOP LOVING YOU Ray Charles	2
26 Jul	I REMEMBER YOU Frank Ifield	7
13 Sep	SHE'S NOT YOU Elvis Presley	3
4 Oct	TELSTAR Tornados	5
8 Nov	LOVESICK BLUES Frank Ifield	5
13 Dec	RETURN TO SENDER Elvis Presley	3

1 9 6 3

3 Jan	THE NEXT TIME/BACHELOR BOY Cliff Richard and the Shadows	3
	(BACHELOR BOY listed from 10 Jan 63 only)	
24 Jan	DANCE ON! Shadows	1
31 Jan	DIAMONDS Jet Harris and Tony Meehan	3
21 Feb	WAYWARD WIND Frank Ifield	3
14 Mar	SUMMER HOLIDAY Cliff Richard and the Shadows	2
28 Mar	FOOT TAPPER Shadows	1
4 Apr	SUMMER HOLIDAY Cliff Richard and the Shadows	1
11 Apr	HOW DO YOU DO IT Gerry and the Pacemakers	3
2 May	FROM ME TO YOU Beatles	7
20 Jun	I LIKE IT Gerry and the Pacemakers	4
18 Jul	CONFESSIN' Frank Ifield	2
1 Aug	(YOU'RE THE) DEVIL IN DISGUISE Elvis Presley	1
8 Aug	SWEETS FOR MY SWEET Searchers	2
22 Aug	BAD TO ME Billy J. Kramer and the Dakotas	3
12 Sep	SHE LOVES YOU Beatles	4
10 Oct	DO YOU LOVE ME Brian Poole and the Tremeloes	3
31 Oct	YOU'LL NEVER WALK ALONE Gerry and the Pacemakers	4
28 Nov	SHE LOVES YOU Beatles	2
12 Dec	I WANT TO HOLD YOUR HAND Beatles	5

1 9 6 4

16 Jan	GLAD ALL OVER Dave Clark Five	2
30 Jan	NEEDLES AND PINS Searchers	3
20 Feb	DIANE Bachelors	1
27 Feb	ANYONE WHO HAD A HEART Cilla Black	3
19 Mar	LITTLE CHILDREN Billy J. Kramer and the Dakotas	2
2 Apr	CAN'T BUY ME LOVE Beatles	3
23 Apr	WORLD WITHOUT LOVE Peter and Gordon	2
7 May	DON'T THROW YOUR LOVE AWAY Searchers	2
21 May	JULIET Four Pennies	1
28 May	YOU'RE MY WORLD Cilla Black	4
25 Jun	IT'S OVER Roy Orbison	2
9 Jul	HOUSE OF THE RISING SUN Animals	1
16 Jul	IT'S ALL OVER NOW Rolling Stones	1
23 Jul	HARD DAY'S NIGHT Beatles	3
13 Aug	DO WAH DIDDY DIDDY Manfred Mann	2
27 Aug	HAVE I THE RIGHT Honeycombs	2
10 Sep	YOU REALLY GOT ME Kinks	2
24 Sep	I'M INTO SOMETHING GOOD Herman's Hermits	2
8 Oct	OH PRETTY WOMAN Roy Orbison	2
22 Oct	(THERE'S) ALWAYS SOMETHING THERE TO REMIND ME Sandie Shaw	3
12 Nov	OH PRETTY WOMAN Roy Orbison	1
19 Nov	BABY LOVE Supremes	2
3 Dec	LITTLE RED ROOSTER Rolling Stones	1
10 Dec	I FEEL FINE Beatles	5

1 9 6 5

14 Jan	YEH YEH Georgie Fame and the Blue Flames	2
28 Jan	GO NOW Moody Blues	1
4 Feb	YOU'VE LOST THAT LOVIN' FEELIN' Righteous Brothers	2
18 Feb	TIRED OF WAITING FOR YOU Kinks	1
25 Feb	I'LL NEVER FIND ANOTHER YOU Seekers	2
11 Mar	IT'S NOT UNUSUAL Tom Jones	1
18 Mar	THE LAST TIME Rolling Stones	3
8 Apr	CONCRETE AND CLAY Unit Four Plus Two	1
15 Apr	THE MINUTE YOU'RE GONE Cliff Richard	1
22 Apr	TICKET TO RIDE Beatles	3
13 May	KING OF THE ROAD Roger Miller	1
20 May	WHERE ARE YOU NOW (MY LOVE) Jackie Trent	1
27 May	LONG LIVE LOVE Sandie Shaw	3
1 Jul	CRYING IN THE CHAPEL Elvis Presley	1
24 Jun	I'M ALIVE Hollies	1
17 Jun	CRYING IN THE CHAPEL Elvis Presley	1
8 Jul	I'M ALIVE Hollies	2
22 Jul	MR. TAMBOURINE MAN Byrds	2
5 Aug	HELP! Beatles	3
26 Aug	I GOT YOU BABE Sonny and Cher	2
9 Sep	(I CAN'T GET NO) SATISFACTION Rolling Stones	2
23 Sep	MAKE IT EASY ON YOURSELF Walker Brothers	1
30 Sep	TEARS Ken Dodd	5
4 Nov	GET OFF OF MY CLOUD Rolling Stones	3
25 Nov	THE CARNIVAL IS OVER Seekers	3
16 Dec	DAY TRIPPER/WE CAN WORK IT OUT Beatles	5

1 9 6 6

20 Jan	KEEP ON RUNNING Spencer Davis Group	1
27 Jan	MICHELLE Overlanders	3
17 Feb	THESE BOOTS ARE MADE FOR WALKIN' Nancy Sinatra	4
17 Mar	THE SUN AIN'T GONNA SHINE ANYMORE Walker Brothers	4
14 Apr	SOMEBODY HELP ME Spencer Davis Group	2
28 Apr	YOU DON'T HAVE TO SAY YOU LOVE ME Dusty Springfield	1
5 May	PRETTY FLAMINGO Manfred Mann	3
26 May	PAINT IT, BLACK Rolling Stones	1
2 Jun	STRANGERS IN THE NIGHT Frank Sinatra	3
23 Jun	PAPERBACK WRITER Beatles	2
7 Jul	SUNNY AFTERNOON Kinks	2
21 Jul	GET AWAY Georgie Fame and the Blue Flames	1
28 Jul	OUT OF TIME Chris Farlowe and the Thunderbirds	1
4 Aug	WITH A GIRL LIKE YOU Troggs	2
18 Aug	YELLOW SUBMARINE/ELEANOR RIGBY Beatles	4
15 Sep	ALL OR NOTHING Small Faces	1
22 Sep	DISTANT DRUMS Jim Reeves	5
27 Oct	REACH OUT I'LL BE THERE Four Tops	3
17 Nov	GOOD VIBRATIONS Beach Boys	2
1 Dec	GREEN GREEN GRASS OF HOME Tom Jones	7

1 9 6 7

| 19 Jan | I'M A BELIEVER Monkees | 4 |
| 16 Feb | THIS IS MY SONG Petula Clark | 2 |

2 Mar   RELEASE ME Engelbert Humperdinck 6
13 Apr   SOMETHING STUPID Nancy Sinatra and Frank Sinatra 2
27 Apr   PUPPET ON A STRING Sandie Shaw 3
18 May   SILENCE IS GOLDEN Tremeloes 3
8 Jun   WHITER SHADE OF PALE Procol Harum 6
19 Jul   ALL YOU NEED IS LOVE Beatles 3
9 Aug   SAN FRANCISCO (BE SURE TO WEAR SOME
          FLOWERS IN YOUR HAIR) Scott McKenzie 4
6 Sep   THE LAST WALTZ Engelbert Humperdinck 5
11 Oct   MASSACHUSETTS Bee Gees 4
8 Nov   BABY NOW THAT I'VE FOUND YOU Foundations . . . 2
22 Nov   LET THE HEARTACHES BEGIN Long John Baldry 2
6 Dec   HELLO GOODBYE Beatles 7

1 9 6 8

24 Jan   BALLAD OF BONNIE AND CLYDE Georgie Fame 1
31 Jan   EVERLASTING LOVE Love Affair 2
14 Feb   MIGHTY QUINN Manfred Mann 2
28 Feb   CINDERELLA ROCKEFELLA Esther and Abi Ofarim . . . 3
20 Mar   THE LEGEND OF XANADU Dave Dee, Dozy, Beaky,
          Mick and Tich 1
27 Mar   LADY MADONNA Beatles 2
10 Apr   CONGRATULATIONS Cliff Richard 2
24 Apr   WHAT A WONDERFUL WORLD/CABARET
          Louis Armstrong 4
22 May   YOUNG GIRL Union Gap featuring Gary Puckett 4
19 Jun   JUMPING JACK FLASH Rolling Stones 2
3 Jul   BABY COME BACK Equals 3
24 Jul   I PRETEND Des O'Connor 1
31 Jul   MONY MONY Tommy James and the Shondells 2
14 Aug   FIRE Crazy World of Arthur Brown 1
21 Aug   MONY MONY Tommy James and the Shondells 1
28 Aug   DO IT AGAIN Beach Boys 1
4 Sep   I'VE GOTTA GET A MESSAGE TO YOU Bee Gees 1
11 Sep   HEY JUDE Beatles 2
25 Sep   THOSE WERE THE DAYS Mary Hopkin 6
6 Nov   WITH A LITTLE HELP FROM MY FRIENDS Joe Cocker . 1
13 Nov   THE GOOD THE BAD AND THE UGLY
          Hugo Montenegro and his Orchestra and Chorus . 4
11 Dec   LILY THE PINK Scaffold 3

1 9 6 9

1 Jan   OB-LA-DI OB-LA-DA Marmalade 1
8 Jan   LILY THE PINK Scaffold 1
15 Jan   OB-LA-DI OB-LA-DA Marmalade 2
29 Jan   ALBATROSS Fleetwood Mac 1
5 Feb   BLACKBERRY WAY Move 1
12 Feb   (IF PARADISE IS) HALF AS NICE Amen Corner 2
26 Feb   WHERE DO YOU GO TO, MY LOVELY Peter Sarstedt . 4
26 Mar   I HEARD IT THROUGH THE GRAPEVINE Marvin Gaye 3
16 Apr   THE ISRAELITES Desmond Dekker and the Aces 1
23 Apr   GET BACK Beatles with Billy Preston 6
4 Jun   DIZZY Tommy Roe 1
11 Jun   THE BALLAD OF JOHN AND YOKO Beatles 3
2 Jul   SOMETHING IN THE AIR Thunderclap Newman 3
23 Jul   HONKY TONK WOMEN Rolling Stones 5

30 Aug   IN THE YEAR 2525 (EXORDIUM AND TERMINUS)
          Zager and Evans 3
20 Sep   BAD MOON RISING Creedence Clearwater Revival . . .3
11 Oct   JE T'AIME....MOI NON PLUS Jane Birkin
          and Serge Gainsbourg 1
18 Oct   I'LL NEVER FALL IN LOVE AGAIN Bobbie Gentry 1
25 Oct   SUGAR SUGAR Archies 8
20 Dec   TWO LITTLE BOYS Rolf Harris 6

1970s

1 9 7 0

31 Jan   LOVE GROWS (WHERE MY ROSEMARY GOES)
          Edison Lighthouse 5
7 Mar   WAND'RIN' STAR Lee Marvin 3
28 Mar   BRIDGE OVER TROUBLED WATER
          Simon and Garfunkel 3
18 Apr   ALL KINDS OF EVERYTHING Dana 2
2 May   SPIRIT IN THE SKY Norman Greenbaum 2
16 May   BACK HOME England World Cup Squad 3
6 Jun   YELLOW RIVER Christie 1
13 Jun   IN THE SUMMERTIME Mungo Jerry 7
1 Aug   THE WONDER OF YOU Elvis Presley 6
12 Sep   TEARS OF A CLOWN Smokey Robinson and
          the Miracles 1
19 Sep   BAND OF GOLD Freda Payne 6
31 Oct   WOODSTOCK Matthews' Southern Comfort 3
21 Nov   VOODOO CHILE Jimi Hendrix Experience 1
28 Nov   I HEAR YOU KNOCKIN' Dave Edmunds 6

1 9 7 1

9 Jan   GRANDAD Clive Dunn 3
30 Jan   MY SWEET LORD George Harrison 5
6 Mar   BABY JUMP Mungo Jerry 2
20 Mar   HOT LOVE T. Rex 6
1 May   DOUBLE BARREL Dave and Ansil Collins 2
15 May   KNOCK THREE TIMES Dawn 5
19 Jun   CHIRPY CHIRPY CHEEP CHEEP Middle of the Road . . 5
24 Jul   GET IT ON T. Rex 4
21 Aug   I'M STILL WAITING Diana Ross 4
18 Sep   HEY GIRL DON'T BOTHER ME Tams 3
9 Oct   MAGGIE MAY Rod Stewart 5
13 Nov   COZ I LUV YOU Slade 4
11 Dec   ERNIE (THE FASTEST MILKMAN IN THE WEST)
          Benny Hill 4

1 9 7 2

8 Jan   I'D LIKE TO TEACH THE WORLD TO SING
          (IN PERFECT HARMONY) New Seekers 4
5 Feb   TELEGRAM SAM T. Rex 2
19 Feb   SON OF MY FATHER Chicory Tip 3
11 Mar   WITHOUT YOU Nilsson 5
15 Apr   AMAZING GRACE The Pipes and Drums and
          Military Band of the Royal Scots Dragoon Guards . 5

424

20 May	METAL GURU T. Rex	4
17 Jun	VINCENT Don McLean	2
1 Jul	TAKE ME BAK 'OME Slade	1
8 Jul	PUPPY LOVE Donny Osmond	5
12 Aug	SCHOOL'S OUT Alice Cooper	3
2 Sep	YOU WEAR IT WELL Rod Stewart	1
9 Sep	MAMA WEER ALL CRAZEE NOW Slade	3
30 Sep	HOW CAN I BE SURE David Cassidy	2
14 Oct	MOULDY OLD DOUGH Lieutenant Pigeon	4
11 Nov	CLAIR Gilbert O'Sullivan	2
25 Nov	MY DING-A-LING Chuck Berry	4
23 Dec	LONG HAIRED LOVER FROM LIVERPOOL Little Jimmy Osmond	5

1 9 7 3

27 Jan	BLOCKBUSTER Sweet	5
3 Mar	CUM ON FEEL THE NOIZE Slade	4
31 Mar	TWELFTH OF NEVER Donny Osmond	1
7 Apr	GET DOWN Gilbert O'Sullivan	2
21 Apr	TIE A YELLOW RIBBON ROUND THE OLD OAK TREE Dawn featuring Tony Orlando	4
19 May	SEE MY BABY JIVE Wizzard	4
16 Jun	CAN THE CAN Suzi Quatro	1
23 Jun	RUBBER BULLETS 10 C.C.	1
30 Jun	SKWEEZE ME PLEEZE ME Slade	3
21 Jul	WELCOME HOME Peters and Lee	1
28 Jul	I'M THE LEADER OF THE GANG (I AM) Gary Glitter	4
25 Aug	YOUNG LOVE Donny Osmond	4
22 Sep	ANGEL FINGERS Wizzard	1
29 Sep	EYE LEVEL Simon Park Orchestra	4
27 Oct	DAYDREAMER/THE PUPPY SONG David Cassidy	3
17 Nov	I LOVE YOU LOVE ME LOVE Gary Glitter	4
15 Dec	MERRY XMAS EVERYBODY Slade	5

1 9 7 4

19 Jan	YOU WON'T FIND ANOTHER FOOL LIKE ME New Seekers	1
26 Jan	TIGER FEET Mud	4
23 Feb	DEVIL GATE DRIVE Suzi Quatro	2
9 Mar	JEALOUS MIND Alvin Stardust	1
16 Mar	BILLY DON'T BE A HERO Paper Lace	3
6 Apr	SEASONS IN THE SUN Terry Jacks	4
4 May	WATERLOO Abba	2
18 May	SUGAR BABY LOVE Rubettes	4
15 Jun	THE STREAK Ray Stevens	1
22 Jun	ALWAYS YOURS Gary Glitter	1
29 Jun	SHE Charles Aznavour	4
27 Jul	ROCK YOUR BABY George McCrae	3
17 Aug	WHEN WILL I SEE YOU AGAIN Three Degrees	2
31 Aug	LOVE ME FOR A REASON Osmonds	3
21 Sept	KUNG FU FIGHTING Carl Douglas	3
12 Oct	ANNIE'S SONG John Denver	1
19 Oct	SAD SWEET DREAMER Sweet Sensation	1
26 Oct	EVERYTHING I OWN Ken Boothe	3
16 Nov	GONNA MAKE YOU A STAR David Essex	3

7 Dec	YOU'RE THE FIRST THE LAST MY EVERYTHING Barry White	2
21 Dec	LONELY THIS CHRISTMAS Mud	4

1 9 7 5

18 Jan	DOWN DOWN Status Quo	1
25 Jan	MS. GRACE Tymes	1
1 Feb	JANUARY Pilot	3
22 Feb	MAKE ME SMILE (COME UP AND SEE ME) Steve Harley and Cockney Rebel	2
8 Mar	IF Telly Savalas	2
22 Mar	BYE BYE BABY Bay City Rollers	6
3 May	OH BOY Mud	2
17 May	STAND BY YOUR MAN Tammy Wynette	3
7 Jun	WHISPERING GRASS Windsor Davies and Don Estelle	3
28 Jun	I'M NOT IN LOVE 10 C.C.	2
12 Jul	TEARS ON MY PILLOW Johnny Nash	1
19 Jul	GIVE A LITTLE LOVE Bay City Rollers	3
9 Aug	BARBADOS Typically Tropical	1
16 Aug	CAN'T GIVE YOU ANYTHING (BUT MY LOVE) Stylistics	3
6 Sep	SAILING Rod Stewart	4
4 Oct	HOLD ME CLOSE David Essex	3
25 Oct	I ONLY HAVE EYES FOR YOU Art Garfunkel	2
8 Nov	SPACE ODDITY David Bowie	2
22 Nov	D.I.V.O.R.C.E. Billy Connolly	1
29 Nov	BOHEMIAN RHAPSODY Queen	9

1 9 7 6

31 Jan	MAMMA MIA Abba	2
14 Feb	FOREVER AND EVER Slik	1
21 Feb	DECEMBER '63 (OH WHAT A NIGHT) Four Seasons	2
6 Mar	I LOVE TO LOVE (BUT MY BABY LOVES TO DANCE) Tina Charles	3
27 Mar	SAVE YOUR KISSES FOR ME Brotherhood Of Man	6
8 May	FERNANDO Abba	4
5 Jun	NO CHARGE J.J. Barrie	1
12 Jun	COMBINE HARVESTER (BRAND NEW KEY) Wurzels	2
26 Jun	YOU TO ME ARE EVERYTHING Real Thing	3
17 Jul	THE ROUSSOS PHENOMENON (EP) Demis Roussos	1
24 Jul	DON'T GO BREAKING MY HEART Elton John and Kiki Dee	6
4 Sep	DANCING QUEEN Abba	6
11 Oct	MISSISSIPPI Pussycat	4
13 Nov	IF YOU LEAVE ME NOW Chicago	3
4 Dec	UNDER THE MOON OF LOVE Showaddywaddy	3
25 Dec	WHEN A CHILD IS BORN (SOLEADO) Johnny Mathis	3

1 9 7 7

15 Jan	DON'T GIVE UP ON US David Soul	4
12 Feb	DON'T CRY FOR ME ARGENTINA Julie Covington	1
19 Feb	WHEN I NEED YOU Leo Sayer	3
12 Mar	CHANSON D'AMOUR Manhattan Transfer	3
2 Apr	KNOWING ME KNOWING YOU Abba	5
7 May	FREE Deniece Williams	2

21 May	I DON'T WANT TO TALK ABOUT IT/FIRST CUT IS THE DEEPEST Rod Stewart	4
18 Jun	LUCILLE Kenny Rogers	1
25 Jun	SHOW YOU THE WAY TO GO Jacksons	1
2 Jul	SO YOU WIN AGAIN Hot Chocolate	3
23 Jul	I FEEL LOVE Donna Summer	4
20 Aug	ANGELO Brotherhood Of Man	1
27 Aug	FLOAT ON Floaters	1
3 Sep	WAY DOWN Elvis Presley	5
8 Oct	SILVER LADY David Soul	3
29 Oct	YES SIR I CAN BOOGIE Baccara	1
5 Nov	NAME OF THE GAME Abba	4
3 Dec	MULL OF KINTYRE/GIRLS' SCHOOL Wings	9

1 9 7 8

4 Feb	UP TOWN TOP RANKING Althia and Donna	1
11 Feb	FIGARO Brotherhood Of Man	1
18 Feb	TAKE A CHANCE ON ME Abba	3
11 Mar	WUTHERING HEIGHTS Kate Bush	4
8 Apr	MATCHSTALK MEN AND MATCHSTALK CATS AND DOGS Brian and Michael	3
29 Apr	NIGHT FEVER Bee Gees	2

Top 75 began 6 May 1978

13 May	RIVERS OF BABYLON Boney M	5
17 Jun	YOU'RE THE ONE THAT I WANT John Travolta and Olivia Newton-John	9
19 Aug	THREE TIMES A LADY Commodores	5
23 Sep	DREADLOCK HOLIDAY 10 C.C.	1
30 Sep	SUMMER NIGHTS John Travolta and Olivia Newton-John	7
18 Nov	RAT TRAP Boomtown Rats	2
2 Dec	DA YA THINK I'M SEXY Rod Stewart	1
9 Dec	MARY'S BOY CHILD-OH MY LORD Boney M	4

1 9 7 9

6 Jan	Y.M.C.A. Village People	3
27 Jan	HIT ME WITH YOUR RHYTHM STICK Ian and the Blockheads	1
3 Feb	HEART OF GLASS Blondie	4
3 Mar	TRAGEDY Bee Gees	2
17 Mar	I WILL SURVIVE Gloria Gaynor	4
14 Apr	BRIGHT EYES Art Garfunkel	6
26 May	SUNDAY GIRL Blondie	3
16 Jun	RING MY BELL Anita Ward	2
30 Jun	ARE 'FRIENDS' ELECTRIC? Tubeway Army	4
28 Jul	I DON'T LIKE MONDAYS Boomtown Rats	4
25 Aug	WE DON'T TALK ANYMORE Cliff Richard	4
22 Sep	CARS Gary Numan	1
29 Sep	MESSAGE IN A BOTTLE Police	3
20 Oct	VIDEO KILLED THE RADIO STAR Buggles	1
27 Oct	ONE DAY AT A TIME Lena Martell	3
17 Nov	WHEN YOU'RE IN LOVE WITH A BEAUTIFUL WOMAN Dr Hook	3
8 Dec	WALKING ON THE MOON Police	1
15 Dec	ANOTHER BRICK IN THE WALL (PART II) Pink Floyd	5

1980s

1 9 8 0

19 Jan	BRASS IN POCKET Pretenders	2
2 Feb	THE SPECIAL AKA LIVE! (EP) Specials	2
16 Feb	COWARD OF THE COUNTY Kenny Rogers	2
1 Mar	ATOMIC Blondie	2
15 Mar	TOGETHER WE ARE BEAUTIFUL Fern Kinney	1
22 Mar	GOING UNDERGROUND/DREAMS OF CHILDREN Jam	3
12 Apr	WORKING MY WAY BACK TO YOU Detroit Spinners	2
26 Apr	CALL ME Blondie	1
3 May	GENO Dexy's Midnight Runners	2
17 May	WHAT'S ANOTHER YEAR Johnny Logan	2
31 May	THEME FROM M*A*S*H (SUICIDE IS PAINLESS) Mash	3
21 Jun	CRYING Don McLean	3
12 Jul	XANADU Olivia Newton-John and Electric Light Orchestra	2
26 Jul	USE IT UP AND WEAR IT OUT Odyssey	2
9 Aug	THE WINNER TAKES IT ALL Abba	2
23 Aug	ASHES TO ASHES David Bowie	2
6 Sep	START Jam	1
13 Sep	FEELS LIKE I'M IN LOVE Kelly Marie	2
27 Sep	DON'T STAND SO CLOSE TO ME Police	4
25 Oct	WOMAN IN LOVE Barbra Streisand	3
15 Nov	THE TIDE IS HIGH Blondie	2
29 Nov	SUPER TROUPER Abba	3
20 Dec	(JUST LIKE) STARTING OVER John Lennon	1
27 Dec	THERE'S NO-ONE QUITE LIKE GRANDMA St Winifred's School Choir	2

1 9 8 1

10 Jan	IMAGINE John Lennon	4
7 Feb	WOMAN John Lennon	2
21 Feb	SHADDAP YOU FACE Joe Dolce Music Theatre	3
14 Mar	JEALOUS GUY Roxy Music	2
28 Mar	THIS OLE HOUSE Shakin' Stevens	3
18 Apr	MAKING YOUR MIND UP Bucks Fizz	3
9 May	STAND AND DELIVER Adam and the Ants	5
13 Jun	BEING WITH YOU Smokey Robinson	2
27 Jun	ONE DAY IN YOUR LIFE Michael Jackson	2
11 Jul	GHOST TOWN Specials	3
1 Aug	GREEN DOOR Shakin' Stevens	4
29 Aug	JAPANESE BOY Aneka	1
5 Sep	TAINTED LOVE Soft Cell	2
19 Sep	PRINCE CHARMING Adam and the Ants	4
17 Oct	IT'S MY PARTY Dave Stewart with Barbara Gaskin	4
14 Nov	EVERY LITTLE THING SHE DOES IS MAGIC Police	1
21 Nov	UNDER PRESSURE Queen and David Bowie	2
5 Dec	BEGIN THE BEGUINE (VOLVER A EMPEZAR) Julio Iglesias	1
12 Dec	DON'T YOU WANT ME Human League	5

1 9 8 2

16 Jan	LAND OF MAKE BELIEVE Bucks Fizz	2
30 Jan	OH JULIE Shakin' Stevens	1
6 Feb	THE MODEL/COMPUTER LOVE Kraftwerk	1
13 Feb	A TOWN CALLED MALICE/PRECIOUS Jam	3
6 Mar	THE LION SLEEPS TONIGHT Tight Fit	3
27 Mar	SEVEN TEARS Goombay Dance Band	3
17 Apr	MY CAMERA NEVER LIES Bucks Fizz	1
24 Apr	EBONY AND IVORY Paul McCartney with Stevie Wonder	3
15 May	A LITTLE PEACE Nicole	2
29 May	HOUSE OF FUN Madness	2
12 Jun	GOODY TWO SHOES Adam Ant	2
26 Jun	I'VE NEVER BEEN TO ME Charlene	1
3 Jul	HAPPY TALK Captain Sensible	2
17 Jul	FAME Irene Cara	3
7 Aug	COME ON EILEEN Dexys Midnight Runners with the Emerald Express	4
4 Sep	EYE OF THE TIGER Survivor	4
2 Oct	PASS THE DUTCHIE Musical Youth	3
23 Oct	DO YOU REALLY WANT TO HURT ME Culture Club	3
13 Nov	I DON'T WANNA DANCE Eddy Grant	3
4 Dec	BEAT SURRENDER Jam	2
18 Dec	SAVE YOUR LOVE Renée and Renato	4

1 9 8 3

15 Jan	YOU CAN'T HURRY LOVE Phil Collins	2
29 Jan	DOWN UNDER Men At Work	3
19 Feb	TOO SHY Kajagoogoo	2
5 Mar	BILLIE JEAN Michael Jackson	1
12 Mar	TOTAL ECLIPSE OF THE HEART Bonnie Tyler	2
26 Mar	IS THERE SOMETHING I SHOULD KNOW Duran Duran	2
9 Apr	LET'S DANCE David Bowie	3
30 Apr	TRUE Spandau Ballet	4
28 May	CANDY GIRL New Edition	1
4 Jun	EVERY BREATH YOU TAKE Police	4
2 Jul	BABY JANE Rod Stewart	3
23 Jul	WHEREVER I LAY MY HAT (THAT'S MY HOME) Paul Young	3
13 Aug	GIVE IT UP KC and the Sunshine Band	3
3 Sep	RED RED WINE UB40	3
24 Sep	KARMA CHAMELEON Culture Club	6
5 Nov	UPTOWN GIRL Billy Joel	5
10 Dec	ONLY YOU Flying Pickets	5

1 9 8 4

14 Jan	PIPES OF PEACE Paul McCartney	2
28 Jan	RELAX Frankie Goes To Hollywood	5
3 Mar	99 RED BALLOONS Nena	3
24 Mar	HELLO Lionel Richie	6
5 May	THE REFLEX Duran Duran	4
2 Jun	WAKE ME UP BEFORE YOU GO GO Wham!	2
16 Jun	TWO TRIBES Frankie Goes To Hollywood	9
18 Aug	CARELESS WHISPER George Michael	3

8 Sep	I JUST CALLED TO SAY I LOVE YOU Stevie Wonder	6
20 Oct	FREEDOM Wham!	3
10 Nov	I FEEL FOR YOU Chaka Khan	3
1 Dec	I SHOULD HAVE KNOWN BETTER Jim Diamond	1
8 Dec	THE POWER OF LOVE Frankie Goes To Hollywood	1
15 Dec	DO THEY KNOW IT'S CHRISTMAS Band Aid	5

1 9 8 5

19 Jan	I WANT TO KNOW WHAT LOVE IS Foreigner	3
9 Feb	I KNOW HIM SO WELL Elaine Paige and Barbara Dickson	4
9 Mar	YOU SPIN ME ROUND (LIKE A RECORD) Dead Or Alive	2
23 Mar	EASY LOVER Philip Bailey (duet with Phil Collins)	4
20 Apr	WE ARE THE WORLD USA For Africa	2
4 May	MOVE CLOSER Phyllis Nelson	1
11 May	19 Paul Hardcastle	5
15 Jun	YOU'LL NEVER WALK ALONE Crowd	2
29 Jun	FRANKIE Sister Sledge	4
27 Jul	THERE MUST BE AN ANGEL (PLAYING WITH MY HEART) Eurythmics	1
3 Aug	INTO THE GROOVE Madonna	4
31 Aug	I GOT YOU BABE UB40, guest vocals by Chrissie Hynde	1
7 Sep	DANCING IN THE STREET David Bowie and Mick Jagger	4
5 Oct	IF I WAS Midge Ure	1
12 Oct	THE POWER OF LOVE Jennifer Rush	5
16 Nov	A GOOD HEART Feargal Sharkey	2
30 Nov	I'M YOUR MAN Wham!	2
14 Dec	SAVING ALL MY LOVE FOR YOU Whitney Houston	2
28 Dec	MERRY CHRISTMAS EVERYONE Shakin' Stevens	2

1 9 8 6

11 Jan	WEST END GIRLS Pet Shop Boys	2
25 Jan	THE SUN ALWAYS SHINES ON TV a-ha	2
8 Feb	WHEN THE GOING GETS TOUGH, THE TOUGH GET GOING Billy Ocean	4
8 Mar	CHAIN REACTION Diana Ross	3
29 Mar	LIVING DOLL Cliff Richard and the Young Ones	3
19 Apr	A DIFFERENT CORNER George Michael	3
10 May	ROCK ME AMADEUS Falco	1
17 May	THE CHICKEN SONG Spitting Image	3
7 Jun	SPIRIT IN THE SKY Doctor and the Medics	3
28 Jun	THE EDGE OF HEAVEN Wham!	2
12 Jul	PAPA DON'T PREACH Madonna	3
2 Aug	THE LADY IN RED Chris de Burgh	3
23 Aug	I WANT TO WAKE UP WITH YOU Boris Gardiner	3
13 Sep	DON'T LEAVE ME THIS WAY Communards	4
11 Oct	TRUE BLUE Madonna	1
18 Oct	EVERY LOSER WINS Nick Berry	3
8 Nov	TAKE MY BREATH AWAY Berlin	4
6 Dec	THE FINAL COUNT DOWN Europe	2
20 Dec	CARAVAN OF LOVE Housemartins	1
27 Dec	REET PETITE Jackie Wilson	4

1987

Date	Title	Weeks
24 Jan	JACK YOUR BODY Steve 'Silk' Hurley	2
7 Feb	I KNEW YOU WERE WAITING (FOR ME) Aretha Franklin and George Michael	2
21 Feb	STAND BY ME Ben E. King	3
14 Mar	EVERYTHING I OWN Boy George	2
28 Mar	RESPECTABLE Mel And Kim	1
4 Apr	LET IT BE Ferry Aid	3
25 Apr	LA ISLA BONITA Madonna	2
9 May	NOTHING'S GONNA STOP US NOW Starship	4
6 Jun	I WANNA DANCE WITH SOMEBODY (WHO LOVES ME) Whitney Houston	2
20 Jun	STAR TREKKIN' Firm	2
4 Jul	IT'S A SIN Pet Shop Boys	3
25 Jul	WHO'S THAT GIRL Madonna	1
1 Aug	LA BAMBA Los Lobos	2
15 Aug	I JUST CAN'T STOP LOVING YOU Michael Jackson with Siedah Garrett	2
29 Aug	NEVER GONNA GIVE YOU UP Rick Astley	5
3 Oct	PUMP UP THE VOLUME/ANITINA (THE FIRST TIME I SEE SHE DANCE) M/A/R/R/S	2
17 Oct	YOU WIN AGAIN Bee Gees	4
14 Nov	CHINA IN YOUR HAND T'Pau	5
19 Dec	ALWAYS ON MY MIND Pet Shop Boys	4

1988

Date	Title	Weeks
16 Jan	HEAVEN IS A PLACE ON EARTH Belinda Carlisle	2
30 Jan	I THINK WE'RE ALONE NOW Tiffany	3
20 Feb	I SHOULD BE SO LUCKY Kylie Minogue	5
26 Mar	DON'T TURN AROUND Aswad	2
9 Apr	HEART Pet Shop Boys	3
30 Apr	THEME FROM S EXPRESS S Express	2
14 May	PERFECT Fairground Attraction	1
21 May	WITH A LITTLE HELP FROM MY FRIENDS/SHE'S LEAVING HOME Wet Wet Wet/Billy Bragg with Cara Tivey	4
18 Jun	DOCTORIN' THE TARDIS Timelords	1
25 Jun	I OWE YOU NOTHING Bros	2
9 Jul	NOTHING'S GONNA CHANGE MY LOVE FOR YOU Glenn Medeiros	4
6 Aug	THE ONLY WAY IS UP Yazz and the Plastic Population	5
10 Sep	A GROOVY KIND OF LOVE Phil Collins	2
24 Sep	HE AIN'T HEAVY HE'S MY BROTHER Hollies	2
8 Oct	DESIRE U2	1
15 Oct	ONE MOMENT IN TIME Whitney Houston	2
29 Oct	ORINOCO FLOW Enya	3
19 Nov	FIRST TIME Robin Beck	3
10 Dec	MISTLETOE AND WINE Cliff Richard	4

1989

Date	Title	Weeks
7 Jan	ESPECIALLY FOR YOU Kylie Minogue and Jason Donovan	3
28 Jan	SOMETHING'S GOTTEN HOLD OF MY HEART Marc Almond with Gene Pitney	4
25 Feb	BELFAST CHILD Simple Minds	2
11 Mar	TOO MANY BROKEN HEARTS Jason Donovan	2
25 Mar	LIKE A PRAYER Madonna	3
15 Apr	ETERNAL FLAME Bangles	4
13 May	HAND ON YOUR HEART Kylie Minogue	1
20 May	FERRY 'CROSS THE MERSEY Christians, Holly Johnson, Paul McCartney, Gerry Marsden and Stock Aitken Waterman	3
10 Jun	SEALED WITH A KISS Jason Donovan	2
24 Jun	BACK TO LIFE (HOW EVER DO YOU WANT ME) Soul II Soul featuring Caron Wheeler	4
22 Jul	YOU'LL NEVER STOP ME LOVING YOU Sonia	2
5 Aug	SWING THE MOOD Jive Bunny And the Mastermixers	5
9 Sep	RIDE ON TIME Black Box	6
21 Oct	THAT'S WHAT I LIKE Jive Bunny and the Mastermixers	3
11 Nov	ALL AROUND THE WORLD Lisa Stansfield	2
25 Nov	YOU GOT IT (THE RIGHT STUFF) New Kids On The Block	3
16 Dec	LET'S PARTY Jive Bunny and the Mastermixers	1
23 Dec	DO THEY KNOW IT'S CHRISTMAS Band Aid II	3

1990s

1990

Date	Title	Weeks
13 Jan	HANGIN' TOUGH New Kids On The Block	2
27 Jan	TEARS ON MY PILLOW Kylie Minogue	1
3 Feb	NOTHING COMPARES 2 U Sinead O'Connor	4
3 Mar	DUB BE GOOD TO ME Beats International featuring Lindy Layton	4
31 Mar	THE POWER Snap	2
14 Apr	VOGUE Madonna	4
12 May	KILLER Adamski	4
9 Jun	WORLD IN MOTION Englandneworder	2
23 Jun	SACRIFICE/HEALING HANDS Elton John	5
28 Jul	TURTLE POWER Partners In Kryme	4
25 Aug	ITSY BITSY TEENY WEENY YELLOW POLKA DOT BIKINI Bombalurina	3
15 Sep	THE JOKER Steve Miller Band	2
29 Sep	SHOW ME HEAVEN Maria McKee	4
27 Oct	A LITTLE TIME The Beautiful South	1
3 Nov	UNCHAINED MELODY Righteous Brothers	4
1 Dec	ICE ICE BABY Vanilla Ice	4
29 Dec	SAVIOUR'S DAY Cliff Richard	1

1991

Date	Title	Weeks
5 Jan	BRING YOUR DAUGHTER...TO THE SLAUGHTER Iron Maiden	2
19 Jan	SADNESS PART 1 Enigma	1
26 Jan	INNUENDO Queen	1
2 Feb	3 AM ETERNAL KLF featuring Children of the Revolution	2
16 Feb	DO THE BARTMAN Simpsons	3

STAY ANOTHER DAY

EAST 17

After 714 number one hits in 42 years, only 16 acts have achieved as many as five number one hits. Another 13 have topped the charts four times, and 25 have enjoyed three number ones.

Artist

17	**BEATLES** (including 1 with Billy Preston)
	ELVIS PRESLEY
13	**CLIFF RICHARD** (including one with Young Ones)
9	**ABBA**
8	**ROLLING STONES**
7	**MADONNA**
6	**SLADE**
	ROD STEWART
5	**BEE GEES**
	BLONDIE
	DAVID BOWIE (including 1 with Queen and 1 with Mick Jagger)
	GEORGE MICHAEL (including 1 with Aretha Franklin and 1 with Elton John and 1 with Queen and Lisa Stansfield)
	POLICE
	QUEEN (including 1 with David Bowie and 1 with George Michael and Lisa Stansfield)
	SHADOWS (+ 7 with Cliff Richard)
	TAKE THAT (including 1 featuring Lulu)
4	**JASON DONOVAN** (including one with Kylie Minogue)
	EVERLY BROTHERS
	WHITNEY HOUSTON
	FRANK IFIELD
	MICHAEL JACKSON (+ 1 with Jacksons)
	JAM
	FRANKIE LAINE
	PAUL McCARTNEY (including 1 with Stevie Wonder and 1 with Christians, Holly Johnson, Gerry Marsden and Stock Aitken Waterman)
	KYLIE MINOGUE (including 1 with Jason Donovan)
	GUY MITCHELL
	PET SHOP BOYS
	SHAKIN' STEVENS
	T. REX
	WHAM!
3	**ADAM AND THE ANTS/ADAM ANT**
	BROTHERHOOD OF MAN
	BUCKS FIZZ
	PHIL COLLINS (including 1 with Philip Bailey)
	LONNIE DONEGAN
	GEORGIE FAME
	FRANKIE GOES TO HOLLYWOOD
	GERRY AND THE PACEMAKERS

GARY GLITTER
JIVE BUNNY AND THE MASTERMIXERS
ELTON JOHN (including 1 with Kiki Dee and 1 with George Michael)
KINKS
JOHN LENNON
MANFRED MANN
MUD
OLIVIA NEWTON-JOHN (2 with John Travolta and 1 with ELO)
ROY ORBISON
DONNY OSMOND (+1 with Osmonds)
JOHNNIE RAY
SANDIE SHAW
SEARCHERS
FRANK SINATRA (including 1 with Nancy Sinatra)
10 C.C.
UB40 (including 1 featuring Chrissie Hynde)
WET WET WET

Apart from those listed above, **Art Garfunkel** has had two solo number ones, and one more with Simon and Garfunkel. **Diana Ross** has had two solo number ones and one more with the Supremes. **Boy George** has headed the charts twice as lead singer with Culture Club, and once more as a soloist. **Midge Ure** first topped the charts as a member of Slik, and went on to co-write, produce and perform with Band Aid, before finally topping the charts as a soloist in 1985.

CLIFF RICHARD with the YOUNG ONES

MOST WEEKS AT NUMBER ONE
by artist

73	ELVIS PRESLEY
69	BEATLES
44	CLIFF RICHARD (including 3 weeks with Young Ones)
32	FRANKIE LAINE (1 week top equal)
31	ABBA
23	WET WET WET
20	QUEEN (including 2 weeks with David Bowie and 3 weeks with George Michael and Lisa Stansfield)
20	SLADE
19	EVERLY BROTHERS (1 week top equal)
18	MADONNA
18	ROLLING STONES (Mick Jagger 4 more weeks with David Bowie, total 22 weeks)
18	ROD STEWART
17	FRANK IFIELD
17	PAUL McCARTNEY (2 weeks solo, 9 weeks with Wings, 3 weeks with Stevie Wonder, and 3 weeks with Christians, Holly Johnson, Gerry Marsden and Stock Aitken Waterman)
16	BRYAN ADAMS
16	WHITNEY HOUSTON
16	SHADOWS (+ 29 weeks backing Cliff Richard, total 45 weeks. Hank Marvin 3 more weeks with Cliff and the Young Ones, total 48 weeks)
16	T. REX
16	JOHN TRAVOLTA AND OLIVIA NEWTON-JOHN (Olivia Newton-John 2 more weeks with Electric Light Orchestra, total 18 weeks)
15	DORIS DAY
15	FRANKIE GOES TO HOLLYWOOD (Holly Johnson 3 more weeks with Christians, Gerry Marsden, Paul McCartney and Stock Aitken Waterman, total 18 weeks)
14	GUY MITCHELL (1 week top equal)
13	BEE GEES
13	DAVID BOWIE (including 4 weeks with Mick Jagger and 2 weeks with Queen)
13	EDDIE CALVERT
13	PERRY COMO
13	ELTON JOHN (including 5 weeks with Kiki Dee and 2 weeks with George Michael)
13	GEORGE MICHAEL (including 3 weeks with Lisa Stansfield and Queen, 2 weeks with Aretha Franklin and 2 weeks with Elton John)
13	POLICE
12	BLONDIE
12	CONNIE FRANCIS
12	PET SHOP BOYS
12	DAVID WHITFIELD (1 week top equal)
11	ADAM AND THE ANTS/ADAM ANT
11	LONNIE DONEGAN
11	TENNESSEE ERNIE FORD
11	GERRY AND THE PACEMAKERS (Gerry Marsden 3 more weeks with Christians, Holly Johnson, Paul McCartney and Stock Aitken Waterman and 2 more weeks as lead vocalist with Crowd, total 16 weeks)
11	ENGELBERT HUMPERDINCK
11	JOHNNIE RAY
11	TAKE THAT
11	SLIM WHITMAN
10	KYLIE MINOGUE (including 3 weeks with Jason Donovan)
10	MUD
10	DONNY OSMOND (+ 3 weeks with Osmonds, total 13 weeks)
10	SHAKIN' STEVENS

Art Garfunkel has been number one for eight weeks, plus five weeks with Simon and Garfunkel. **Mantovani** has been number one for one week, plus ten more backing David Whitfield. **Lionel Richie** has had six weeks at number one, plus five more as one of the Commodores. **Boy George** has also been at the top for 11 weeks, two solo and nine with Culture Club.

MOST WEEKS AT NUMBER ONE
by an artist in one calendar year

27	FRANKIE LAINE (1 week top equal)	1953
18	ELVIS PRESLEY	1961
16	BRYAN ADAMS	1991
16	BEATLES	1963
16	JOHN TRAVOLTA & OLIVIA NEWTON-JOHN	1978
15	ELVIS PRESLEY	1962
15	FRANKIE GOES TO HOLLYWOOD	1984
15	WET WET WET	1994
12	CONNIE FRANCIS	1958
12	FRANK IFIELD	1962
12	BEATLES	1964
12	ABBA	1976

MOST WEEKS AT NUMBER ONE
by one disc, in total

18	I BELIEVE Frankie Laine	1953
16	(EVERYTHING I DO) I DO IT FOR YOU Bryan Adams	1991
15	LOVE IS ALL AROUND Wet Wet Wet	1994
14	BOHEMIAN RHAPSODY Queen	1975/6 and 1991/2
11	ROSE MARIE Slim Whitman	1955
10	CARA MIA David Whitfield	1954
10	I WILL ALWAYS LOVE YOU Whitney Houston	1993/94
9	HERE IN MY HEART Al Martino	1952/3
9	OH MEIN PAPA Eddie Calvert	1954
9	SECRET LOVE Doris Day	1954
9	DIANA Paul Anka	1957
9	MULL OF KINTYRE/GIRLS' SCHOOL Wings	1977/8
9	YOU'RE THE ONE THAT I WANT John Travolta and Olivia Newton-John	1978
9	TWO TRIBES Frankie Goes To Hollywood	1984

MOST WEEKS AT NUMBER ONE
by one disc – consecutive weeks

16	**(EVERYTHING I DO) I DO IT FOR YOU**	
	Bryan Adams	1991
15	**LOVE IS ALL AROUND** Wet Wet Wet	1994
11	**ROSE MARIE** Slim Whitman	1955
10	**CARA MIA** David Whitfield	1954
10	**I WILL ALWAYS LOVE YOU** Whitney Houston	1993/94
9	**HERE IN MY HEART** Al Martino	1952/3
9	**I BELIEVE** Frankie Laine	1953
9	**OH MEIN PAPA** Eddie Calvert	1954
9	**DIANA** Paul Anka	1957
9	**BOHEMIAN RHAPSODY** Queen	1975/6
9	**MULL OF KINTYRE/GIRLS' SCHOOL** Wings	1977/8
9	**YOU'RE THE ONE THAT I WANT** John Travolta	
	and Olivia Newton-John	1978
9	**TWO TRIBES** Frankie Goes To Hollywood	1984
8	**ANSWER ME** Frankie Laine (1 week top equal)	1953/4
8	**SECRET LOVE** Doris Day	1954
8	**MAGIC MOMENTS** Perry Como	1958
8	**IT'S NOW OR NEVER** Elvis Presley	1960
8	**WONDERFUL LAND** Shadows	1962
8	**SUGAR SUGAR** Archies	1969
8	**STAY** Shakespears Sister	1992

Between Stevie Wonder's 'I Just Called To Say I Love You' in 1984 and the 1989 Black Box number one, 'Ride On Time', there were 93 chart-toppers, none of which lasted for more than five weeks at the top.

MOST WEEKS AT NUMBER ONE
by one song

18 weeks	**I BELIEVE**	one version
16 weeks	**(EVERYTHING I DO) I DO IT FOR YOU**	one version
15 weeks	**LOVE IS ALL AROUND**	one version
14 weeks	**BOHEMIAN RHAPSODY**	one version
11 weeks	**MARY'S BOY CHILD**	two versions
11 weeks	**ROSE MARIE**	one version
11 weeks	**YOUNG LOVE**	two versions
10 weeks	**ANSWER ME**	two versions
10 weeks	**CARA MIA**	one version
10 weeks	**I WILL ALWAYS LOVE YOU**	one version

BRYAN ADAMS

MOST CONSECUTIVE NUMBER ONE HITS

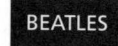

11 in a row:	**BEATLES** (from From Me To You through to Yellow Submarine/Eleanor Rigby, 1963 to 1966)
6 in a row:	**BEATLES** (from All You Need Is Love through to The Ballad Of John And Yoko, 1967 to 1969)
5 in a row:	**ELVIS PRESLEY** (from Little Sister/His Latest Flame through to Return To Sender, 1961 to 1962)
5 in a row:	**ROLLING STONES** (from It's All Over Now through to Get Off Of My Cloud, 1964 to 1965)
4 in a row:	**ELVIS PRESLEY** (from It's Now Or Never through to Surrender, 1960 to 1961) The first number one hat-trick.
4 in a row:	**T. REX** (from Hot Love through to Metal Guru, 1971 to 1972)

BEATLES

4 in a row: **TAKE THAT** (from Pray through to Everything Changes, 1993 to 1994)

3 in a row: **FRANK IFIELD** (I Remember You, Lovesick Blues and Wayward Wind, 1962 to 1963) The first hat-trick by a British artist.

3 in a row: **GERRY AND THE PACEMAKERS** (How Do You Do It, I Like It and You'll Never Walk Alone, 1963)

3 in a row: **ABBA** (Mamma Mia, Fernando and Dancing Queen, 1975 to 1976)

3 in a row: **ABBA** (Knowing Me Knowing You, The Name Of The Game and Take A Chance On Me, 1977 to 1978)

3 in a row: **POLICE** (Message In A Bottle, Walking On The Moon and Don't Stand So Close To Me, 1979 to 1980)

3 in a row: **BLONDIE** (Atomic, Call Me and The Tide Is High, 1980)

3 in a row: **JOHN LENNON** (Imagine, (Just Like) Starting Over and Woman, 1980) Either the fastest or slowest hat-trick depending on whether it started when Imagine first entered the chart in November 1975, or when (Just Like) Starting Over came in late in 1980.

3 in a row: **FRANKIE GOES TO HOLLYWOOD** (Relax, Two Tribes and The Power Of Love, 1984)

3 in a row: **JIVE BUNNY AND THE MASTERMIXERS** (Swing The Mood, That's What I Like and Let's Party, 1989).

Successive releases for the purpose of this table are successive official single releases. The Beatles' two runs of number ones were each interrupted by irregular releases. An old single with Tony Sheridan reached number 29 in the midst of their 11 number ones, and their double EP 'Magical Mystery Tour' made number two while 'Hello Goodbye' was becoming the second of their six chart-toppers on the trot. An album track, 'Jeepster', and an old recording, 'Debora/One Inch Rock' were released during T. Rex's run of number ones while the group were changing labels. An EP by Elvis, 'Follow That Dream', pottered about the lower reaches of the charts during Elvis's run of five consecutive number ones. During Police's hat-trick, one single on another label, one old single re-issued and a six-pack of singles hit the chart in an attempt to distract the compilers of this table. John Lennon's 'Imagine' was the first of the three singles of his hat-trick (his last single for five years) but the second of the three to reach the top. During his hat-trick, a flood of old Lennon hits swarmed back on to the chart.

All four of Take That's consecutive chart-toppers entered the charts at number one. The third hit of the hat-tricks by both Police and Jive Bunny and the Mastermixers came on to the chart at number one.

MOST NUMBER ONE HITS in a year

Four number ones in one year has been achieved twice, by Elvis Presley in 1961 and 1962. His chart-toppers in 1961 were 'Are You Lonesome Tonight' (Jan/Feb), 'Wooden Heart' (Mar/Apr), 'Surrender' (June) and 'Little Sister/His Latest Flame' (Nov/Dec). In 1962 they were 'Rock-A-Hula Baby/Can't Help Falling In Love' (Feb/Mar), 'Good Luck Charm' (May/Jun), 'She's Not You' (Sept) and 'Return To Sender' (Dec).

Three number ones in a year has been accomplished 13 times, as follows:

1953 **Frankie Laine** (I Believe, Hey Joe, Answer Me)

1963 **Gerry and the Pacemakers** (How Do You Do It, I Like It, You'll Never Walk Alone)

1963 **Beatles** (From Me To You, She Loves You, I Want To Hold Your Hand)

1964 **Beatles** (Can't Buy Me Love, A Hard Day's Night, I Feel Fine)

1965 **Beatles** (Ticket To Ride, Help!, Day Tripper/We Can Work It Out)

1965 **Rolling Stones** (The Last Time, (I Can't Get No) Satisfaction, Get Off Of My Cloud)

1973 **Slade** (Cum On Feel The Noize, Skweeze Me Pleeze Me, Merry Xmas Everybody)

1976 **Abba** (Mamma Mia, Fernando, Dancing Queen)

1980 **Blondie** (Atomic, Call Me, The Tide Is High)

1984 **Frankie Goes To Hollywood** (Relax, Two Tribes, The Power Of Love)

1989 **Jason Donovan** (Especially For You, Too Many Broken Hearts, Sealed With A Kiss)

1989 **Jive Bunny and the Mastermixers** (Swing The Mood, That's What I Like, Let's Party)

1993 **Take That** (Pray, Relight My Fire, Babe)

The most number one hits in total in any year is 24 in 1980. The longest-lived chart-topper of that year was 'Don't Stand So Close To Me' by the Police, which only lasted four weeks at the top.

The fewest new number one hits in a complete year is 11 in 1954. Three number ones that year each spent at least nine weeks at the top. There were only 12 new number ones in 1962 and 1992. In 1962 only eight different acts topped the charts.

Only 15 acts in the 42-year history of the chart have reached the top with each of their first two chart hits.

EDDIE CALVERT Oh Mein Papa; Cherry Pink and Apple Blossom White 1954, 55
ADAM FAITH What Do You Want; Poor Me 1959, 60
TENNESSEE ERNIE FORD Give Me Your Word; Sixteen Tons 1955, 56
FRANKIE GOES TO HOLLYWOOD Relax; Two Tribes 1984
ART GARFUNKEL I Only Have Eyes For You; Bright Eyes 1975, 79
GERRY AND THE PACEMAKERS How Do You Do It; I Like It 1963
JIVE BUNNY AND THE MASTERMIXERS Swing The Mood, That's What I Like 1989
GEORGE MICHAEL Careless Whisper; A Different Corner 1984, 86
MUNGO JERRY In The Summertime; Baby Jump 1970, 71
GARY NUMAN/TUBEWAY ARMY Are 'Friends' Electric?; Cars 1979
NEW KIDS ON THE BLOCK You Got It (The Right Stuff); Hangin' Tough 1989, 90
RIGHTEOUS BROTHERS You've Lost That Lovin' Feelin'; Unchained Melody 1965, 90
STARGAZERS Broken Wings; I See The Moon 1953, 54
ROD STEWART Maggie May; You Wear It Well 1971, 72
JOHN TRAVOLTA AND OLIVIA NEWTON-JOHN You're The One That I Want; Summer Nights 1978

Of these acts only Frankie Goes To Hollywood, Gerry and the Pacemakers, Jive Bunny, George Michael, Mungo Jerry, New Kids On The Block, the Righteous Brothers and John Travolta and Olivia Newton-John hit the top with their first two UK releases. For both the Righteous Brothers and New Kids On The Block, it took a re-issue to push one of their hits to the top. Band Aid and Band Aid II both hit number one with their only releases - the African famine relief singles, 'Do They Know It's Christmas'.

FIRST THREE HITS AT NUMBER ONE

Three acts, all British, have now achieved the feat of taking their first three hits to number one. They are **Gerry and the Pacemakers** in 1963, **Frankie Goes To Hollywood** in 1984 and **Jive Bunny and the Mastermixers** in 1989.

Gerry and the Pacemakers and Frankie Goes To Hollywood both came from Liverpool, both chose as their third single a pseudo-religious song, ('You'll Never Walk Alone' and 'The Power Of Love' respectively) and both took their fourth release to number two. Jive Bunny's fourth single peaked at number four. Gerry Marsden and Holly Johnson, the lead singers of Gerry and the Pacemakers and Frankie Goes To Hollywood subsequently combined with fellow Liverpudlians the Christians and Paul McCartney to create, along with producers Stock Aitken Waterman, yet another number one, 'Ferry Cross The Mersey'.

HOLLY JOHNSON

LAST HIT AT NUMBER ONE

Chart history shows that once an act has scored its first number one, it is far more likely to hit the top again than to have no more hits at all. Disappearing without trace chartwise, after a number one hit is fairly rare, and apart from the one-hit wonders, listed separately, only 12 acts have failed to follow up a number one. They are:

> **Charles Aznavour**
> **Firm**
> **Benny Hill**
> **Jam**
> **Tommy James and the Shondells**
> **Manchester United Football Club**
> **George Michael**
> **Steve Miller Band**
> **Queen**
> **Kay Starr**
> **Starship**
> **Wham!**

Both halves of Wham! have charted separately since the duo broke up, (Andrew Ridgeley with less force than George Michael) as have all three members of Jam since their demise. Paul Weller led Style Council to many hits, Bruce Foxton had three solo hits and Rick Buckler's Time UK nudged the charts once. Steve Miller's final UK hit was a re-issue of a track originally recorded before any of his other three UK hits, but it did not chart until 1990. Queen's last two hits were both number one hits, one being an EP with George Michael and Lisa Stansfield. Kay Starr uniquely holds the unlikely record of hitting number one with both her first and last British hit singles.

THE ONE-HIT WONDERS

Qualification: one number one hit, and nothing else - ever. 36 immortal acts now make up the list:

1954 **KITTY KALLEN** Little Things Mean A Lot
1956 **DREAMWEAVERS** It's Almost Tomorrow
1958 **KALIN TWINS** When
1959 **JERRY KELLER** Here Comes Summer
1960 **RICKY VALANCE** Tell Laura I Love Her
1962 **B. BUMBLE AND THE STINGERS** Nut Rocker
1966 **OVERLANDERS** Michelle
1968 **CRAZY WORLD OF ARTHUR BROWN** Fire
1969 **ZAGER AND EVANS** In The Year 2525
      JANE BIRKIN AND SERGE GAINSBOURG Je T'Aime...Moi Non Plus
      ARCHIES Sugar Sugar
1970 **LEE MARVIN** Wand'rin' Star
      NORMAN GREENBAUM Spirit In The Sky
      MATTHEWS' SOUTHERN COMFORT Woodstock
1971 **CLIVE DUNN** Grandad
1973 **SIMON PARK ORCHESTRA** Eye Level
1975 **TYPICALLY TROPICAL** Barbados
1976 **J.J. BARRIE** No Charge
1977 **FLOATERS** Float On
1978 **ALTHIA AND DONNA** Up Town Top Ranking
      BRIAN AND MICHAEL Matchstalk Men And Matchstalk Cats And Dogs
1979 **ANITA WARD** Ring My Bell
      LENA MARTELL One Day At A Time
1980 **FERN KINNEY** Together We Are Beautiful
      MASH Theme From M*A*S*H
      ST WINIFRED'S SCHOOL CHOIR There's No One Quite Like Grandma
1981 **JOE DOLCE MUSIC THEATRE** Shaddap You Face
1982 **CHARLENE** I've Never Been To Me
1985 **PHYLLIS NELSON** Move Closer
1987 **M/A/R/R/S** Pump Up The Volume
1988 **ROBIN BECK** First Time
1990 **PARTNERS IN KRYME** Turtle Power
1991 **HALE & PACE and the STONKERS** The Stonk
1993 **MR. BLOBBY** Mr. Blobby
1994 **DOOP** Doop
      PATO BANTON Baby Come Back

Apart from these acts, 22 other one-hit wonders exist, made up of acts who have had hits in other guises. They are

1967 **NANCY SINATRA AND FRANK SINATRA** Somethin' Stupid (both have had solo number one hits)

Baby D, East 17, Wet Wet Wet and Take That did not release a follow-up to their chart-topping 1994 hits before the end of the year, but we assume that by the time you read this book, they will all have made their way back into the charts.

1974 **JOHN DENVER** Annie's Song (has also hit with Placido Domingo)
1980 **OLIVIA NEWTON-JOHN AND ELECTRIC LIGHT ORCHESTRA** Xanadu (both have had solo hits)
1981 **QUEEN AND DAVID BOWIE** Under Pressure (both have had solo number one hits)
1982 **PAUL McCARTNEY WITH STEVIE WONDER** Ebony And Ivory (both have had solo number one hits)
1984 **BAND AID** Do They Know It's Christmas (a conglomeration of hit-makers)
1985 **ELAINE PAIGE AND BARBARA DICKSON** I Know Him So Well (both have had solo hits)
      USA FOR AFRICA We Are The World (another conglomeration of hit-makers)
      CROWD You'll Never Walk Alone (and another conglomeration)
      DAVID BOWIE AND MICK JAGGER Dancing In The Street (both have had solo hits)
1986 **CLIFF RICHARD AND THE YOUNG ONES WITH HANK MARVIN** Living Doll (Cliff and the Young Ones (a.k.a. Bad News) have both had solo hits, as has Hank Marvin)
1987 **STEVE 'SILK' HURLEY** Jack Your Body (Steve is one half of the duo J.M. Silk)
      ARETHA FRANKLIN AND GEORGE MICHAEL I Knew You Were Waiting For Me (both have had solo hits)
      FERRY AID Let It Be (Yet another conglomeration)
1988 **TIMELORDS** Doctorin' The Tardis (subsequently hit as The KLF)
1989 **KYLIE MINOGUE AND JASON DONOVAN** Especially For You (both have had solo number one hits)
      CHRISTIANS, HOLLY JOHNSON, PAUL McCARTNEY, GERRY MARSDEN AND STOCK AITKEN WATERMAN Ferry Cross The Mersey (Charity disc for the Hillsborough Disaster Fund)
      BAND AID II Do They Know It's Christmas? (The first case of two one-hit wonders reaching the top with the same song. Only Keren Woodward and Sarah Dallin of Bananarama appeared on both discs)
1990 **ENGLANDNEWORDER** World In Motion.. (a combination of New Order and the England World Cup Squad)
1991 **VIC REEVES AND THE WONDER STUFF** Dizzy (both acts have had separate hits)
      GEORGE MICHAEL AND ELTON JOHN Don't Let The Sun Go Down On Me (both have had solo number one hits, and number ones in other duets)
1993 **GEORGE MICHAEL AND QUEEN WITH LISA STANSFIELD** Five Live EP (all three acts have had separate number one hits)

Of all the acts that have enjoyed two or more number one hits, only nine acts have suffered through a gap of more than seven years between number ones, although two of them have, incredibly, done so twice. The Beatles crammed all of their 17 chart toppers into a period of six years and 54 days.

25 years 259 days	RIGHTEOUS BROTHERS	(11 Feb 65 to 28 Oct 90)
23 years 65 days	HOLLIES	(15 Jul 65 to 18 Sep 88)
14 years 363 days	QUEEN	(24 Jan 76 to 20 Jan 91)
14 years 172 days	DIANA ROSS	(11 Sep 71 to 2 Mar 86)
11 years 238 days	FRANK SINATRA	(1 Oct 54 to 27 May 66)
11 years 124 days	CLIFF RICHARD	(17 Apr 68 to 19 Aug 79)
9 years 231 days	BEE GEES	(4 Sep 68 to 23 Apr 78)
9 years 80 days	CLIFF RICHARD	(15 Sep 79 to 4 Dec 88)
8 years 215 days	BEE GEES	(10 Mar 79 to 11 Oct 87)
7 years 357 days	DON McLEAN	(24 Jun 72 to 15 Jun 80)
7 years 279 days	UB40	(31 Aug 85 to 6 Jun 93)

During **Cliff's** second hiatus, he took the top slot in March 1986 in association with the **Young Ones**. **Queen** hit the top with **David Bowie** in 1981, five years into their wait for a second chart-topper on their own.

Cher waited for 25 years and 239 days between dropping from number one in duet with her then husband Sonny in 1965 and reaching the top again on her own in 1992. There was a gap of 21 years and 200 days between 27 November 1963, the last day that **Gerry and the Pacemakers'** 'You'll Never Walk Alone' was at number one, and 15 June 1985, when the same song, with Gerry Marsden again on lead vocals, hit number one, this time by **the Crowd**.

20 years and 4 days after 'Back Home' by the **England World Cup Squad** dropped from number one, 'World In Motion...' by **Englandneworder** knocked Adamski off the top. None of the artists who appeared on the England World Cup Squad disc in 1970 survived the selectors' axe to be playing for England on the football field or in the recording studio in 1990.

16 years and 9 days elapsed between the last day of the final **Rolling Stones** number one, and **Mick Jagger's** reappearance at the top with David Bowie.

There was a gap of 14 years and 113 days between **Eddy Grant's** last day at number one as one of the **Equals** and his first day on top as a soloist.

Elton John's first solo number one hit, 'Sacrifice/Healing Hands, happened 13 years and 293 days after he and Kiki Dee dropped from number one with 'Don't Go Breaking My Heart'.

'Tears Of A Clown' by **Smokey Robinson** and the Miracles dropped from number one 10 years and 268 days before **Smokey Robinson's** solo hit 'Being With You' reached the summit.

Only five acts have scored number one hits over a period of more than 20 years. They are:

31 years 153 days	CLIFF RICHARD	(1959 to 1990)
25 years 286 days	RIGHTEOUS BROTHERS	(1965 to 1990)
23 years 105 days	HOLLIES	(1965 to 1988)
20 years 87 days	ELVIS PRESLEY	(1957 to 1977)
20 years 34 days	BEE GEES	(1967 to 1987)

Cher first hit number one as half of Sonny and Cher in August 1965, and dropped from the top after her solo number one in June 1991, almost 26 years later. **Diana Ross** first hit number one as lead singer for the Supremes in 1964 and dropped off the top for the final time as a soloist in 1986, over 21 years later.

Cliff Richard is the only act to have number one hits in five decades. In the 1950s he hit number one twice, in the 1960s seven times, in the 1970s once, in the 1980s once solo and once more with the Young Ones and Hank Marvin, and so far once in the 1990s. This record is unlikely ever to be equalled.

The only acts, apart from Cliff Richard, to have hit number one in three different decades are **Elvis Presley** (50s, 60s and 70s) and the **Bee Gees** (60s, 70s and 80s). **Queen** hit number one in the 70s and 90s, and also topped the charts in 1981 by teaming up with David Bowie.

Eight other acts (**Abba, Blondie, David Bowie, Don McLean, Police, Kenny Rogers, Diana Ross and Rod Stewart**) hit the top in the 70s and 80s, and so have a chance in the 90s to emulate Cliff, Elvis and the Gibb brothers.

Nine acts topped the charts in both the 50s and the 60s (**Shirley Bassey, Lonnie Donegan, Everly Brothers, Adam Faith, Michael Holliday, Elvis Presley, Cliff Richard, Frank Sinatra** and **Frankie**

Vaughan), but only three managed chart-toppers in the 60s and 70s - Elvis, Cliff and the Bee Gees.

The **Hollies** hit the top in the 60s and 80s, and the **Righteous Brothers** hit number one in the 60s and 90s.

Jason Donovan, Whitney Houston, Michael Jackson, Madonna, George Michael, Kylie Minogue, New Kids On The Block, Snap!, Lisa Stansfield, UB40 and **Wet Wet Wet** have already duplicated Cliff's feat of hitting number one in the 80s and 90s.

Cliff Richard's first week at the top came after 45 weeks on lower rungs. His final week at number one was his 1057th week on the chart, a span of 1012 chart weeks. **Elvis Presley's** first week at number one came after he had already clocked up 103 weeks on the British charts. His final week at number one 20 years later was his 1034th of chart action, a span of 931 chart weeks. No other act comes anywhere near these two in chart-topping longevity.

STRAIGHT IN AT NUMBER ONE

Thirty eight records, to the end of 1994, have hit the charts at number one. They are:

14 Nov 52	**HERE IN MY HEART** Al Martino
24 Jan 58	**JAILHOUSE ROCK** Elvis Presley
3 Nov 60	**IT'S NOW OR NEVER** Elvis Presley
11 Jan 62	**THE YOUNG ONES** Cliff Richard
23 Apr 69	**GET BACK** Beatles
3 Mar 73	**CUM ON FEEL THE NOIZE** Slade
30 Jun 73	**SKWEEZE ME PLEEZE ME** Slade
17 Nov 73	**I LOVE YOU LOVE ME LOVE** Gary Glitter
15 Dec 73	**MERRY XMAS EVERYBODY** Slade
22 Mar 80	**GOING UNDERGROUND/DREAMS OF CHILDREN** Jam
27 Sep 80	**DON'T STAND SO CLOSE TO ME** Police
9 May 81	**STAND AND DELIVER** Adam and the Ants
13 Feb 82	**A TOWN CALLED MALICE/PRECIOUS** Jam
4 Dec 82	**BEAT SURRENDER** Jam
26 Mar 83	**IS THERE SOMETHING I SHOULD KNOW?** Duran Duran
16 Jun 84	**TWO TRIBES** Frankie Goes To Hollywood
15 Dec 84	**DO THEY KNOW IT'S CHRISTMAS?** Band Aid
7 Sep 85	**DANCING IN THE STREET** David Bowie and Mick Jagger
4 Apr 87	**LET IT BE** Ferry Aid
20 May 89	**FERRY CROSS THE MERSEY** Christians, Holly Johnson, Paul McCartney, Gerry Marsden and Stock Aitken Waterman
10 Jun 89	**SEALED WITH A KISS** Jason Donovan
16 Dec 89	**LET'S PARTY** Jive Bunny and the Mastermixers
23 Dec 89	**DO THEY KNOW IT'S CHRISTMAS?** Band Aid II
5 Jan 91	**BRING YOUR DAUGHTER...TO THE SLAUGHTER** Iron Maiden
26 Jan 91	**INNUENDO** Queen
2 Nov 91	**THE FLY** U2
23 Nov 91	**BLACK OR WHITE** Michael Jackson
7 Dec 91	**DON'T LET THE SUN GO DOWN ON ME** George Michael & Elton John
21 Dec 91	**BOHEMIAN RHAPSODY/THESE ARE THE DAYS OF OUR LIVES** Queen
13 Jun 92	**ABBA-ESQUE EP** Erasure
1 May 93	**FIVE LIVE EP** George Michael, Queen and Lisa Stansfield
17 Jul 93	**PRAY** Take That
9 Oct 93	**RELIGHT MY FIRE** Take That featuring Lulu
18 Dec 93	**BABE** Take That
19 Feb 94	**WITHOUT YOU** Mariah Carey
9 Apr 94	**EVERYTHING CHANGES** Take That
17 Sep 94	**SATURDAY NIGHT** Whigfield
15 Oct 94	**SURE** Take That

Slade were the first act to enter the chart at number one with consecutive releases. **Take That** have entered the charts at number one five times in all, four times with consecutive releases.

In 1991, 'Black Or White', 'Don't Let The Sun Go Down On Me' and 'Bohemian Rhapsody/These Are The Days Of Our Lives' were consecutive number ones, the only time that three chart-toppers in a row have entered the charts at number one. The six instant number ones in 1991 easily beat the previous record of four in a year, set in 1973 and equalled in 1989 and 1994.

Gary Glitter's 'I Love You Love Me Love' and **Slade's** 'Merry Xmas Everybody' in 1973 were consecutive number ones, as were 'Ferry Cross The Mersey' and 'Sealed With A Kiss' in May and June 1989, and 'Saturday Night' and 'Sure' in 1994.

In December 1989 for the first time ever, new hits crashed in at number one in consecutive weeks.

Both **Police** and **Jive Bunny and the Mastermixers** completed a hat-trick of number ones by going straight to the top. **Take That** are the only act to score a hat-trick of singles, all of which came straight in at number one.

'Do They Know It's Christmas' is, of course, the only song to have gone straight to number one in two different versions.

BIGGEST JUMP TO NUMBER ONE

There have been 31 records, apart from those that came on to the chart at number one which are listed separately, which have jumped from outside the top ten straight to the top spot.

33 to 1	**HAPPY TALK** Captain Sensible	3 Jul 82
27 to 1	**SURRENDER** Elvis Presley	1 Jun 61
26 to 1	**PASS THE DUTCHIE** Musical Youth	2 Oct 82
22 to 1	**GREEN DOOR** Shakin' Stevens	1 Aug 81
21 to 1	**HEY JUDE** Beatles	11 Sep 68
21 to 1	**(JUST LIKE) STARTING OVER** John Lennon	20 Dec 80
19 to 1	**ARE YOU LONESOME TONIGHT?** Elvis Presley	26 Jan 61
19 to 1	**(IF PARADISE IS) HALF AS NICE** Amen Corner	12 Feb 69
19 to 1	**LOVE ME FOR A REASON** Osmonds	31 Aug 74
19 to 1	**STAND BY ME** Ben E. King	21 Feb 87
17 to 1	**GET OFF OF MY CLOUD** Rolling Stones	4 Nov 65
16 to 1	**I HEAR YOU KNOCKIN'** Dave Edmunds	28 Nov 70
16 to 1	**CHIRPY CHIRPY CHEEP CHEEP** Middle Of The Road	19 Jun 71
16 to 1	**YOUNG LOVE** Donny Osmond	25 Aug 73
16 to 1	**DANCING QUEEN** Abba	4 Sep 76
15 to 1	**I DON'T LIKE MONDAYS** Boomtown Rats	28 Jul 79
15 to 1	**THE SPECIAL AKA LIVE EP** Specials	2 Feb 80
14 to 1	**EYE LEVEL** Simon Park Orchestra	29 Sep 73
13 to 1	**IN THE SUMMERTIME** Mungo Jerry	13 Jun 70
13 to 1	**STAR TREKKIN'** Firm	20 Jun 87
12 to 1	**LOVE GROWS (WHERE MY ROSEMARY GOES)** Edison Lighthouse	31 Jan 70
12 to 1	**THE POWER** Snap	31 Mar 90
11 to 1	**(THERE'S) ALWAYS SOMETHING THERE TO REMIND ME** Sandie Shaw	22 Oct 64
11 to 1	**TICKET TO RIDE** Beatles	22 Apr 65
11 to 1	**MICHELLE** Overlanders	27 Jan 66
11 to 1	**LADY MADONNA** Beatles	20 Mar 68
11 to 1	**SUGAR SUGAR** Archies	25 Oct 69
11 to 1	**SHE** Charles Aznavour	29 Jun 74
11 to 1	**SUMMER NIGHTS** John Travolta and Olivia Newton-John	30 Sep 78
11 to 1	**THE CHICKEN SONG** Spitting Image	17 May 86
11 to 1	**NOTHING'S GONNA CHANGE MY LOVE FOR YOU** Glenn Medeiros	9 Jul 88

The biggest jump within the chart is a leap of 62 places from 66 to 4 on 11 Oct 86 by **Nick Berry's** 'Every Loser Wins'. Two other number one hits have climbed over 50 places in one week on their way to the top - the **Firm's** 'Star Trekkin' which leapt from 74 to 13 to 1, a leap of 61 places followed by a leap of 12 places, and the **Flying Pickets'** 'Only You' , which jumped 51 places on 3 Dec 83. The lowest initial entry by a record that went on to hit the top is 74 by 'Star Trekkin', on 6 Jun 87, beating the previous record-holder, **Charlene's** 'I've Never Been To Me' by one place. Charlene entered the chart at number 73 on 15 May 82.

BIGGEST FALLS FROM NUMBER ONE

Only 24 records have fallen out of the top five directly from the very top:

1 to 12	**MARY'S BOY CHILD** Harry Belafonte	10 Jan 58
1 to 10	**ONLY YOU** Flying Pickets	14 Jan 84
1 to 9	**CHRISTMAS ALPHABET** Dickie Valentine	6 Jan 56
1 to 9	**YOU'RE DRIVING ME CRAZY** Temperance Seven	1 Jun 61
1 to 9	**THESE BOOTS ARE MADE FOR WALKIN'** Nancy Sinatra	17 Mar 66
1 to 9	**BRING YOUR DAUGHTER... TO THE SLAUGHTER** Iron Maiden	19 Jan 91
1 to 8	**HELLO GOODBYE** Beatles	24 Jan 68
1 to 8	**LONELY THIS CHRISTMAS** Mud	18 Jan 75
1 to 7	**WAYWARD WIND** Frank Ifield	14 Mar 63
1 to 7	**YOUNG LOVE** Donny Osmond	22 Sep 73
1 to 7	**KNOWING ME KNOWING YOU** Abba	7 May 77
1 to 6	**HERE IN MY HEART** Al Martino	16 Jan 53
1 to 6	**ROCK AROUND THE CLOCK** Bill Haley and his Comets	20 Jan 56
1 to 6	**CATHY'S CLOWN** Everly Brothers	23 Jun 60
1 to 6	**SUMMER HOLIDAY** Cliff Richard and the Shadows	11 Apr 63
1 to 6	**SUGAR BABY LOVE** Rubettes	15 Jun 74
1 to 6	**YOU TO ME ARE EVERYTHING** Real Thing	17 Jul 76
1 to 6	**BRIGHT EYES** Art Garfunkel	26 May 79
1 to 6	**THERE'S NO ONE QUITE LIKE GRANDMA** St Winifred's School Choir	10 Jan 81
1 to 6	**IT'S MY PARTY** Dave Stewart with Barbara Gaskin	14 Nov 81
1 to 6	**LET'S DANCE** David Bowie	30 Apr 83
1 to 6	**YOU SPIN ME ROUND (LIKE A RECORD)** Dead Or Alive	23 Mar 85
1 to 6	**A DIFFERENT CORNER** George Michael	10 May 86
1 to 6	**BELFAST CHILD** Simple Minds	11 Mar 89

At the end of 1988, three consecutive chart-toppers dropped from number one to number five. They were 'Orinoco Flow' by **Enya** on 19 November, 'First Time' by **Robin Beck** on 10 December, and 'Mistletoe And Wine' by **Cliff Richard** on 7 January 1989.

Queen's second number one, 'Innuendo', is the only record ever to top the charts, but spend only two weeks in the top ten. It entered the chart at number one, then fell to number two and then to number 12.

On 30 May 1992 **Shut Up And Dance** hit the chart at number two with a rave version of Marc Cohn's 'Walking In Memphis', under the title 'Raving I'm Raving' . The next week it fell to number 15, and a week later it had disappeared completely.

If an artist is ever going to have a number one hit, it usually happens within a year or two of that artist's first hit. About half of all the acts who have hit the very top did so with their first chart hit. There are 23 acts whose first number one came more than ten years after their chart debut. They are:

29 years	42 days	**JACKIE WILSON**	(15 Nov 57 to 27 Dec 86)
26 years	19 days	**BEN E. KING**	(2 Feb 61 to 21 Feb 87)
25 years	259 days	**CHER**	(19 Aug 65 to 4 May 91)
19 years	151 days	**ELTON JOHN**	(23 Jan 71 to 23 Jun 90)
18 years	218 days	**STEVIE WONDER**	(3 Feb 66 to 8 Sep 84)
18 years	216 days	**JOHNNY MATHIS**	(23 May 58 to 25 Dec 76)
18 years	13 days	**MANCHESTER UNITED F.C.**	(8 May 76 to 21 May 94)
16 years	218 days	**BORIS GARDINER**	(17 Jan 70 to 23 Aug 86)
15 years	157 days	**CHUCK BERRY**	(21 Jun 57 to 25 Nov 72)
15 years	156 days	**MEAT LOAF**	(20 May 78 to 23 Oct 93)
15 years	127 days	**LOUIS ARMSTRONG**	(19 Dec 52 to 24 Apr 68)
14 years	279 days	**BARBRA STREISAND**	(20 Jan 66 to 25 Oct 80)
14 years	94 days	**PRINCE**	(19 Jan 80 to 23 Apr 94)
13 years	341 days	**CLASH**	(2 Apr 77 to 9 Mar 91)
13 years	327 days	**STEVE MILLER BAND**	(23 Oct 76 to 15 Sep 90)
13 years	140 days	**FOUR SEASONS**	(4 Oct 62 to 21 Feb 76)
12 years	321 days	**PAUL McCARTNEY**	(27 Feb 71 to 14 Jan 84)
12 years	260 days	**PINK FLOYD**	(30 Mar 67 to 15 Dec 79)
11 years	164 days	**JOHN LENNON**	(9 Jul 69 to 20 Dec 80)
10 years	314 days	**IRON MAIDEN**	(23 Feb 80 to 5 Jan 91)
10 years	298 days	**BENNY HILL**	(16 Feb 61 to 11 Dec 71)
10 years	22 days	**BLUEBELLS**	(12 Mar 83 to 3 Apr 93)
10 years	8 days	**SISTER SLEDGE**	(21 Jun 75 to 29 Jun 85)

LOUIS ARMSTRONG (EMI)

Of these acts, **Cher, Elton John, Stevie Wonder, Paul McCartney** and **John Lennon** had featured on number ones before their solo successes. John Lennon is the only act on this list to achieve more than one solo number one. His first number one was the first of a hat-trick. Stevie Wonder's first week at number one was his 301st of solo chart action, but Elton John's was his 371st week, the longest wait in chart terms for a number one. It was a re-issue of his 45th and 46th solo hits, the most hits ever achieved by any act before their first number one. Cher, who hit number one in duet with her then husband Sonny in only their third week of chart action, had less luck as a soloist. Hers is the longest wait of all those who finally hit the top with a newly-recorded song. The number one hits by Jackie Wilson, Ben E. King, Clash, the Steve Miller Band and the Bluebells were re-issues of old recordings.

Before **Louis Armstrong** became the first act to take more than ten years to hit the top, in 1968, the slowest ascent of the charts was by **Petula Clark**, who took 6 years 257 days from her chart debut on 11 June 1954 until she first topped the charts on 23 February 1961.

Lulu has never had a solo number one, but there was a gap of 29 years and 148 days from her first week on the charts on 14 May 1964 until she topped the charts with Take That on 9 October 1993. **Gene Pitney** has never had a solo number one, but there was a gap of 27 years and 311 days from his first week on the charts on 23 March 1961 until he topped the charts with Marc Almond on 28 January 1989.

Fourteen recordings have taken longer than 200 days to hit the top after their first appearance on the chart:

29 years	42 days	**REET PETITE** - Jackie Wilson (15 Nov 57 to 27 Dec 86)
25 years	244 days	**STAND BY ME** - Ben E. King (22 Jun 61 to 21 Feb 87)
25 years	83 days	**UNCHAINED MELODY** - Righteous Brothers (12 Aug 65 to 3 Nov 90)
18 years	356 days	**HE AIN'T HEAVY, HE'S MY BROTHER** - Hollies (4 Oct 69 to 24 Sep 88)
8 years	284 days	**YOUNG AT HEART** - Bluebells (23 Jun 84 to 3 Apr 93)
8 years	166 days	**SHOULD I STAY OR SHOULD I GO** - Clash (25 Sep 82 to 9 Mar 91)
7 years	327 days	**LIVING ON MY OWN** - Freddie Mercury (21 Sep 85 to 14 Aug 93)
6 years	63 days	**SPACE ODDITY** - David Bowie (6 Sep 69 to 8 Nov 75)
5 years	70 days	**IMAGINE** - John Lennon (1 Nov 75 to 10 Jan 81)
	322 days	**ROCK AROUND THE CLOCK** - Bill Haley and his Comets (7 Jan 55 to 25 Nov 55)
	308 days	**EYE LEVEL** - Simon Park Orchestra (25 Nov 72 to 29 Sep 73)
	301 days	**HEALING HANDS** - Elton John (26 Aug 89 to 23 Jun 90)
	231 days	**SACRIFICE** - Elton John (4 Nov 89 to 23 Jun 90)
	210 days	**THE MODEL/COMPUTER LOVE** - Kraftwerk (11 Jul 81 to 6 Feb 82)

All these records dropped off the charts between their original chart entry and their chart-topping reappearances. The slowest climb to number one by any record that stayed on the chart all the time is 16 weeks (112 days) by 'The Power Of Love' by **Jennifer Rush**, from 29 Jun 85 to 12 Oct 85. The previous record of 15 weeks (105 days) had been set only seven months earlier by **Dead Or Alive's** 'You Spin Me Round (Like a Record)',which took from 1 Dec 84 to 9 Mar 85 to climb to number one.

Whigfield's chart debut in September 1994 provided the only instance of an artist hitting the number one spot in their first ever week on the chart, with the obvious exception of Al Martino in the first chart of all. The 15 acts who have hit the top within two weeks are:

0 days	AL MARTINO	(14 Nov 52)
0 days	WHIGFIELD	(17 Sep 94)
7 days	EDISON LIGHTHOUSE	(24 to 31 Jan 70)
7 days	MUNGO JERRY	(6 to 13 Jun 70)
7 days	DAVE EDMUNDS	(21 to 28 Nov 70)
7 days	NICOLE	(8 to 15 May 82)
7 days	MUSICAL YOUTH	(25 Sep to 3 Oct 82)
7 days	SPITTING IMAGE	(10 to 17 May 86)
7 days	SNAP	(24 to 31 Mar 90)
7 days	PARTNERS IN KRYME	(21 to 28 Jul 90)
7 days	VANILLA ICE	(24 Nov to 1 Dec 90)
7 days	GABRIELLE	(19 to 26 Jun 93)
7 days	MR. BLOBBY	(4 to 11 Dec 93)
7 days	DOOP	(12 Mar to 19 Mar 94)
7 days	STILTSKIN	(7 May to 14 May 94)

Of these acts, only **Mungo Jerry** and **Snap** have topped the charts again, and only **Snap** have racked up a total of more than 100 weeks on the charts.

Other first-time chart acts, who had already been in the charts under another name who have also had rapid climbs to the top:

0 days	BAND AID (1984)
0 days	DAVID BOWIE AND MICK JAGGER (1985)
0 days	FERRY AID (1987)
0 days	CHRISTIANS, HOLLY JOHNSON, PAUL McCARTNEY, GERRY MARSDEN AND STOCK AITKEN WATERMAN (1989)
0 days	BAND AID II (1989)
0 days	GEORGE MICHAEL AND ELTON JOHN (1991)
0 days	GEORGE MICHAEL AND QUEEN WITH LISA STANSFIELD (1993)
7 days	GEORGE HARRISON (1971)
7 days	QUEEN AND DAVID BOWIE (1981)
7 days	CAPTAIN SENSIBLE (1982)
7 days	USA FOR AFRICA (1985)
7 days	CLIFF RICHARD AND THE YOUNG ONES (1986)
7 days	ARETHA FRANKLIN AND GEORGE MICHAEL (1987)
7 days	BOY GEORGE (1987)
7 days	ENGLANDNEWORDER (1990)

Vanilla Ice made his chart debut at number three in November 1990, the highest position achieved by a totally new chart act since the first week of the charts 38 years earlier. In May 1991, this record was matched by **Crystal Waters**, and in July 1992 by **Smart E's**. In June 1993, **Gabrielle** broke this record by coming in at number two, and in September 1994 **Whigfield** finally achieved the ultimate quick start by coming in at number one with her first hit. Apart from the top five acts in the first chart of all (Al Martino, Jo Stafford, Nat 'King' Cole, Bing Crosby and Guy Mitchell) the only acts to have spent their first week of chart action in the top five are:

2 Jul 54	KITTY KALLEN	Little Things Mean A Lot	5
14 Jul 84	neil	Hole In My Shoe	5
20 Feb 88	BOMB THE BASS	Beat Dis	5
21 Jul 90	PARTNERS IN KRYME	Turtle Power	4
24 Nov 90	VANILLA ICE	Ice Ice Baby	3
18 May 91	CRYSTAL WATERS	Gypsy Woman (La Da Dee)	3
30 May 92	KRIS KROSS	Jump	4
11 Jul 92	SMART E'S	Sesame's Treet	3
12 Dec 92	WWF SUPERSTARS	Slam Jam	4
8 May 93	ACE OF BASE	All That She Wants	5
5 Jun 93	GREEN JELLY	Three Little Pigs	5
19 Jun 93	GABRIELLE	Dreams	2
4 Dec 93	MR. BLOBBY	Mr. Blobby	3
12 Mar 94	DOOP	Doop	3
23 Apr 94	CRASH TEST DUMMIES	Mmm Mmm Mmm Mmm	5
7 May 94	STILTSKIN	Inside	5
17 Sep 94	WHIGFIELD	Saturday Night	1
17 Dec 94	MIGHTY MORPHIN' POWER RANGERS	Power Rangers	3

There have been 12 records by combinations of previous chart acts which have also crashed straight into the top five. They are the seven discs which hit number one on their first week, listed above, and:

22 Mar 86	CLIFF RICHARD AND THE YOUNG ONES featuring HANK MARVIN	Living Doll	4
10 Dec 88	KYLIE MINOGUE AND JASON DONOVAN	Especially For You	2
2 Jun 90	ENGLANDNEWORDER	World In Motion...	2
9 Jul 94	BC-52S	Meet The Flintsones	5
17 Sep 94	LUTHER VANDROSS AND MARIAH CAREY	Endless Love	3

In the past few years, the record for the shortest chart life of a number one hit has been rewritten several times. Of the eighteen records which have topped the charts despite spending eight weeks or less on the chart, ten have done so since April 1987. The shortest-lived number ones of all time are:

5 wks **BRING YOUR DAUGHTER... TO THE SLAUGHTER**
..................................Iron Maiden

6 wks **LET'S PARTY** ....Jive Bunny and the Mastermixers
6 wks **DO THEY KNOW IT'S CHRISTMAS?** ....Band Aid II
6 wks **INNUENDO** ....Queen
6 wks **THE FLY** U2

7 wks **CHRISTMAS ALPHABET** ....Dickie Valentine
7 wks **LET IT BE** ....Ferry Aid
7 wks **FERRY CROSS THE MERSEY** ..Christians, Holly Johnson, Paul McCartney, Gerry Marsden and Stock Aitken Waterman
7 wks **THE STONK** ....Hale and Pace and the Stonkers

8 wks **HEY JOE** ....Frankie Laine
8 wks **LET'S HAVE ANOTHER PARTY.** ....Winifred Atwell
8 wks **LADY MADONNA.**........................Beatles
8 wks **MARY'S BOY CHILD - OH MY LORD** ....Boney M
8 wks **WHAT'S ANOTHER YEAR** ....Johnny Logan
8 wks **MY CAMERA NEVER LIES** ....Bucks Fizz
8 wks **HAPPY TALK** ....Captain Sensible
8 wks **DESIRE** U2
8 wks **TEARS ON MY PILLOW** ....Kylie Minogue

22 of the 115 acts that have been on the charts for 150 weeks or more have never had a number one hit. They are:

Wks	
281	**BILLY FURY**
245	**WHO**
234	**NAT 'KING' COLE**
210	**BRENDA LEE**
208	**DEPECHE MODE**
207	**KOOL AND THE GANG**
203	**TEMPTATIONS**
202	**BANANARAMA**
196	**DUANE EDDY**
194	**STRANGLERS**
193	**ORCHESTRAL MANOEUVRES IN THE DARK**
191	**KIM WILDE**
190	**NEIL SEDAKA**
187	**GLADYS KNIGHT AND THE PIPS**
183	**GENESIS**
183	**TINA TURNER**
177	**LEVEL 42**
176	**DRIFTERS**
173	**CARPENTERS**
171	**MR. ACKER BILK**
171	**GLORIA ESTEFAN**
167	**ELVIS COSTELLO**

There are very few acts that have hit the top ten ten times without enjoying even one brief week at the very top.

13 **NAT 'KING' COLE** (who has spent nine weeks at number two)
13 **WHO** (who had two number two hits)
11 **BILLY FURY** (who had only one number two hit, the aptly titled 'Jealousy')
11 **GUNS N' ROSES** (who have had one number two hit, the even more aptly titled 'Knockin On Heaven's Door')
10 **BANANARAMA** (who have had three number three hits, and an American number one)

Elvis Costello, with 32 hits, has had more hits than any act never to top the charts, but only three of those hits reached the top ten.

ELVIS COSTELLO

INSTRUMENTAL NUMBER ONE HITS

The only instrumentals to hit the very top of the charts have been:

THEME FROM 'MOULIN ROUGE' . . . . .Mantovani and his Orchestra, 1953

OH MEIN PAPA . . . . .Eddie Calvert, 1954

LET'S HAVE ANOTHER PARTY . . . . .Winifred Atwell, 1954

CHERRY PINK AND APPLE BLOSSOM WHITE . . . . . .Perez Prado, 1955

CHERRY PINK AND APPLE BLOSSOM WHITE . . . . . .Eddie Calvert, 1955

POOR PEOPLE OF PARIS (PAUVRE JEAN) . . . . .Winifred Atwell, 1956

HOOTS MON . . . . .Lord Rockingham's XI, 1958

SIDE SADDLE . . . . .Russ Conway, 1959

ROULETTE . . . . .Russ Conway, 1959

APACHE . . . . .Shadows, 1960

ON THE REBOUND . . . . .Floyd Cramer, 1961

KON-TIKI . . . . .Shadows, 1961

WONDERFUL LAND . . . . .Shadows, 1962

NUT ROCKER . . . . .B. Bumble and the Stingers, 1962

TELSTAR . . . . .Tornados, 1962

DANCE ON! . . . . .Shadows, 1963

DIAMONDS . . . . .Jet Harris and Tony Meehan, 1963

FOOT TAPPER . . . . .Shadows, 1963

THE GOOD THE BAD AND THE UGLY . . . . .Hugo Montenegro Orchestra, 1968

ALBATROSS . . . . .Fleetwood Mac, 1969

AMAZING GRACE . . . . .Royal Scots Dragoon Guards, 1972

MOULDY OLD DOUGH . . . . .Lieutenant Pigeon, 1972

EYE LEVEL . . . . .Simon Park Orchestra, 1973

DOOP . . . . .Doop, 1994

DOOP

HITS ON NINE DIFFERENT LABELS

Lulu, in a 30 year chart career, and **Tom Jones**, in a mere 29 years of chart action, have recorded hit singles on nine labels. No other performer approaches this total.

Lulu has had hits with Decca (1964-65), Columbia (1967-69), Atco (1969), Polydor (1974), Chelsea (1975), Alfa (1981), Jive (1986), Dôme (1993-94) and RCA (1993).

Tom Jones has had hits with Decca (1965-74 and 1988), EMI (1977), Epic (1987-88), China (1988), Jive (1989), Dover (1991), The Hit Label (1992), Childline (1993) and ZTT (1994).

Between March 1969 and January 1993, Lulu had eight consecutive hits on eight different labels. Tom Jones never had more than five consecutive hits on different labels. Both artists have had hits on Decca and Jive.

LULU

There has been a total of 577 records to the end of 1994 which have reached number two but failed to make that all important final climb to the very top. The 500th number two was 'Step By Step', by **New Kids On The Block**, which came straight on to the chart at number two on 16 June 1990, but failed to climb any higher. Over the past two years, there have been 29 records which peaked at number two, compared with 30 which went all the way to the top.

The acts whose chart climbs have most often peaked at number two are:

10	**CLIFF RICHARD**
9	**ELVIS PRESLEY**
7	**KYLIE MINOGUE**
6	**PAUL McCARTNEY/WINGS** (includes 1 with Michael Jackson)
6	**MADONNA**
5	**TOM JONES**
5	**QUEEN**
5	**SWEET**
4	**BEATLES, PAT BOONE, DAVID BOWIE, BROS, EVERLY BROTHERS, GARY GLITTER, HOLLIES, MICHAEL JACKSON** (includes 1 with Paul McCartney), **DEAN MARTIN, LEO SAYER, SHOWADDYWADDY, SLADE, T. REX, STEVIE WONDER**
3	**BEACH BOYS** (includes 1 with Fat Boys), **NAT 'KING' COLE, PHIL COLLINS, DARTS, DURAN DURAN, KINKS, FRANKIE LAINE, GUY MITCHELL, STATUS QUO, SHAKIN' STEVENS, ROD STEWART** (includes 1 with Bryan Adams and Sting)

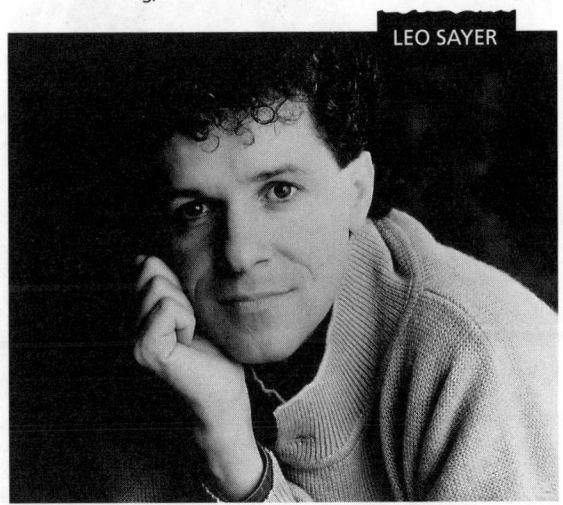

LEO SAYER

The record for being so near and yet so far is held by:

NAT 'KING' COLE	9 wks
FRANK CHACKSFIELD	8 wks
ALL-4-ONE	7 wks
DRIFTERS	7 wks
FATHER ABRAHAM AND THE SMURFS	6 wks
ALLISONS	6 wks
BRIGHOUSE AND RASTRICK BAND	6 wks
FREE	5 wks
OBERNKIRCHEN CHILDREN'S CHOIR	5 wks
SALT-N-PEPA	5 wks
SIMPLY RED	5 wks

Frank Chacksfield's 1953 recording of the theme from Charlie Chaplin's film *Limelight* spent a total of eight weeks at number two, between June and September of that year. However, the record was never at number two for more than three consecutive weeks. The most consecutive weeks at number two without hitting the top is seven, a record set in 1994 by **All-4-One** with 'I Swear', which could not overtake Wet Wet Wet's 15 week chart-topper, 'Love Is All Around'. Six consecutive weeks at number two has been achieved by 'The Floral Dance' by the **Brighouse And Rastrick Brass Band** (1977/78), 'The Smurf Song' by **Father Abraham and the Smurfs** (1978) and 'I'm Too Sexy' by **Right Said Fred** (1991). **Jo Stafford's** 'You Belong To Me' spent seven consecutive weeks at number two, and eight weeks in all, before taking over from Al Martino's 'Here In My Heart' as the second number one at the beginning of 1953.

Two recordings have reached number two on two totally separate occasions. 'Honey' by **Bobby Goldsboro** reached number two on 29 May 1968 for one week. It returned to number two as a re-issue on 26 April 1975, almost seven years later. **Madonna's** 'Crazy For You' hit number two for one week on 29 June 1985, and then a re-mixed version of the same record climbed back to the runner-up position for two weeks from 2 March 1991. **Fleetwood Mac's** 'Albatross', a number one hit when originally released, climbed to number two as a re-issue.

The longest titled songs to hit the top are:

45 letters   **SAN FRANCISCO (BE SURE TO WEAR SOME FLOWERS IN YOUR HAIR)** (Scott McKenzie, 1967)

43 letters   **I'D LIKE TO TEACH THE WORLD TO SING (IN PERFECT HARMONY)** (New Seekers, 1972)

39 letters   **ITSY BITSY TEENY WEENY YELLOW POLKA DOT BIKINI** (Bombalurina, 1990)

37 letters   **MATCHSTALK MEN AND MATCHSTALK CATS AND DOGS** (Brian and Michael, 1978)

37 letters   **WHEN THE GOING GETS TOUGH, THE TOUGH GET GOING** (Billy Ocean, 1986)

36 letters   **(THERE'S) ALWAYS SOMETHING THERE TO REMIND ME** (Sandie Shaw, 1964)

36 letters   **THERE MUST BE AN ANGEL (PLAYING WITH MY HEART)** (Eurythmics, 1985)

35 letters   **WHAT DO YOU WANT TO MAKE THOSE EYES AT ME FOR?** (Emile Ford and the Checkmates, 1959)

34 letters   **TIE A YELLOW RIBBON ROUND THE OLD OAK TREE** (Dawn featuring Tony Orlando, 1973)

34 letters   **WHEN YOU'RE IN LOVE WITH A BEAUTIFUL WOMAN** (Dr. Hook, 1979)

33 letters   **I'D DO ANYTHING FOR LOVE (BUT I WON'T DO THAT)** (Meat Loaf, 1993)

33 letters   **I WANNA DANCE WITH SOMEBODY (WHO LOVES ME)** (Whitney Houston, 1987)

Queen's double-sided 1991 chart-topper, 'Bohemian Rhapsody/These Are The Days Of Our Lives' is 41 letters long.

The longest title ever used for a hit single in Britain is the 20-word, 77-letter mega-title of the Pet Shop Boys' March 1991 top 10 hit, **Where The Streets Have No Name - Can't Take My Eyes Off You/How Do You Expect To Be Taken Seriously**. This, however, was three titles rolled into one double A-side, rather than a single song title.

The longest single song title to hit the charts is still the Carpenters' 1977 single which reached number nine, **Calling Occupants Of Interplanetary Craft (The Recognised Anthem Of World Contact Day)**. This contains 73 letters. It took over as the longest title from Winifred Atwell's 1954 instrumental, **Rachmaninoff's Eighteenth Variation On A Theme By Paganini (The Story Of Three Loves)** which only runs to 70 letters.

The longest hit title which is not a medley and which contains no brackets is the 60 letter 1981 hit for the Freshies, **I'm In Love With The Girl On A Certain Manchester Megastore Checkout Desk**. Meat Loaf gave them a good run for their money with his 52-letter 1994 hit, **Objects In The Rear View Mirror May Appear Closer Than They Are,** one letter longer than the Bellamy Brothers' 1979 epic **If I Said You Have A Beautiful Body Would You Hold It Against Me**.

'If I Love Ya Then I Need Ya, If I Need Ya Then I Want You Around', a 47-letter hit for Eartha Kitt in 1994 contains more words (17) in its title than any other unbracketed non-medley hit. **Mmm Mmm Mmm Mmm** by the Crash Test Dummies (1994) is the longest hit song title made up of only one letter repeated.

The longest word used in a hit single is Prince's original effort of 1986, **Anotherloverholenyohead**, a 23-letter word. This beats Tom Browne's 1982 word **Bebopafunkadiscolypso** by two letters.

CRASH TEST DUMMIES

The first ever one-letter hit title came on to the charts on 22 January 1994, and hung around for three weeks. It was called U, was recorded by New York songstress Loni Clark, and reached number 28. Before that, the nearest had been Ben E. King's US hit song which Shirley Bassey, Tom Jones and Sylvester covered, 'I (Who Have Nothing)', which has only one letter outside the brackets.

The shortest title for a number one hit, and the second shortest title for any hit, is 'If'. It has been used twice as a hit title, firstly by David Gates, who created a number one for Telly Savalas and a smaller hit for the comedy

LONI CLARK

duo Yin and Yan; and secondly by Janet Jackson and her co-writers for a number 14 hit in 1993.

There are five other two letter hit titles:

D.J. (David Bowie, 1979)

FX (A Guy Called Gerald, 1989)

GO (Scott Fitzgerald, 1988)

O.K? (Julie Covington, Rula Lenska, Charlotte Cornwell and Sue Jones-Davies, 1977)

T.V. (Flying Lizards 1980)

There are, of course, several titles that contain no letters at all, only numbers, like City Boy's '5-7-0-5', Paul Hardcastle's '19', four different hits called '1-2-3', Wilson Pickett's '634-5789' and Desmond Dekker's '007'. Prince, with '7' and '1999', is the only artist to hit twice with entirely numerical titles.

In deference to the extraordinary achievements of Manchester United, in topping the charts in Britain (and in Denmark) in 1994, and with apologies to Everton and Stoke fans because we inadvertently left out their team's great musical efforts in the previous edition, we print the up-to-date league table of footballing hits.

Of the 56 football chart hits, 11 are hits not related to any particular club, (six TV theme tunes, two soccer disaster charity discs, Don Fardon's ode to George Best, 'Belfast Boy', 'Goalie's Ball' on James' hit EP, 'Seven', and the Piglets' 'Johnny Reggae', which features the lyric, 'He's crazy about football and he looks me in the eye when he shoots'). Five more are by professional footballers, two by Paul 'Gazza' Gascoigne, one by Kevin Keegan, one by Ian Wright and one by Glenn and Chris, Hoddle and Waddle.

Sixteen football clubs (excluding St. Etienne, who are not named after the French club) have had a total of 40 chart hits between them. Fourteen are English league clubs and the others are the England and Scotland national squads. The clear football song champions are England, followed by Scotland, but Manchester United win the title as the most successful League club in chart terms. If we added in Gazza's two hits and Glenn and Chris's hit to the Tottenham Hotspur list, as all were made while the players were on Tottenham's books, then Spurs are the chart leaders.

TEAM	No. of hits	No. 1 hits	Top 10 hits	Weeks on chart
England	5	2	3	46
Scotland	5	0	3	30
Manchester United	5	1	2	28
Tottenham Hotspur	5	0	1	35
Liverpool	4	0	1	16
Chelsea	3	0	1	16
Leeds United	3	0	1	15
Arsenal	2	0	0	10
Nottingham Forest	1	0	0	6
Everton	1	0	0	5
West Ham United	1	0	0	2
Stoke City	1	0	0	2
Crystal Palace	1	0	0	2
Coventry City	1	0	0	2
Brighton & Hove Albion	1	0	0	2
Fulham	1	0	0	1

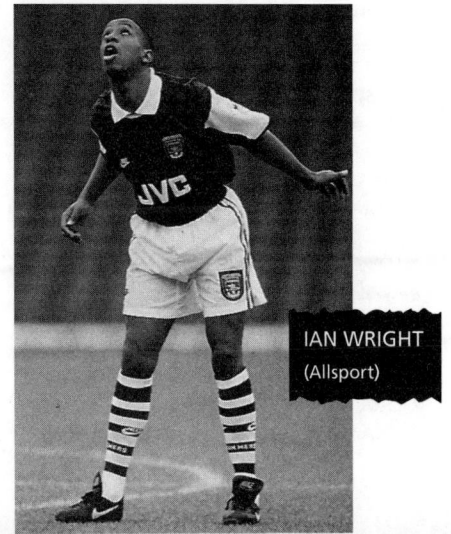

IAN WRIGHT
(Allsport)

The ten biggest league club hits are

	Title	Peak position	Wks	Year
Manchester United	Come On You Reds	1	15	1994
Liverpool	Anfield Rap	3	6	1988
Chelsea	Blue Is The Colour	5	12	1972
Tottenham H.	Ossie's Dream	5	8	1981
Leeds United	Leeds United	10	10	1972
Manchester United	We All Follow Man United	10	5	1985
Manchester United	Glory Glory Man United	13	5	1983
Tottenham H.	Nice One Cyril (Cockerel Chorus)	14	12	1973
Everton	Here We Go	14	5	1985
Liverpool	We Can Do It	15	4	1977

MOST WEEKS ON CHART
by recording

Total weeks on chart, regardless of the number of re-issues or re-entries. This list shows which recording has appeared on the singles charts for the most weeks. Re-recordings of the same song by the same artist do not count but re-mixes of the same track do.

Wks.	Chart Runs	
124	10	MY WAY Frank Sinatra
67	8	AMAZING GRACE Judy Collins
59	3	RELAX* Frankie Goes To Hollywood
57	8	ROCK AROUND THE CLOCK* Bill Haley and his Comets
56	1	RELEASE ME* Engelbert Humperdinck
55	1	STRANGER ON THE SHORE Mr Acker Bilk
49	4	BLUE MONDAY New Order
47	2	I LOVE YOU BECAUSE Jim Reeves
46	5	WHITE LINES (DON'T DON'T DO IT) Grandmaster Flash and Melle Mel
44	5	ALL RIGHT NOW Free
44	5	LET'S TWIST AGAIN Chubby Checker
44	5	TAINTED LOVE* Soft Cell
41	5	DECK OF CARDS Wink Martindale
40	1	RIVERS OF BABYLON* Boney M
40	2	A SCOTTISH SOLDIER Andy Stewart
40	2	TIE A YELLOW RIBBON ROUND THE OLD OAK TREE* Dawn
39	3	HE'LL HAVE TO GO Jim Reeves
38	2	SOMEWHERE MY LOVE Mike Sammes Singers
36	1	I BELIEVE* Frankie Laine
36	1	I PRETEND* Des O'Connor
36	2	THE POWER OF LOVE* Jennifer Rush
36	3	SHE LOVES YOU* Beatles
35	2	ALBATROSS* Fleetwood Mac
35	2	AND I LOVE YOU SO Perry Como
35	2	HOUND DOG Elvis Presley
35	4	LEADER OF THE PACK Shangri-Las
34	1	CHIRPY CHIRPY CHEEP CHEEP* Middle Of The Road
34	2	WHAT A WONDERFUL WORLD* Louis Armstrong
34	3	HEARTBREAK HOTEL Elvis Presley
34	3	JE T'AIME...MOI NON PLUS* Jane Birkin and Serge Gainsbourg
34	3	NIGHTS IN WHITE SATIN Moody Blues
34	3	SAILING* Rod Stewart
34	4	YOU'VE LOST THAT LOVIN' FEELIN'* Righteous Brothers
33	1	LOVE IS ALL AROUND* Wet Wet Wet
32	2	LET'S DANCE Chris Montez
32	3	I GET THE SWEETEST FEELING Jackie Wilson
32	3	WITHOUT YOU* Nilsson
32	5	JAILHOUSE ROCK* Elvis Presley
31	1	GHOSTBUSTERS Ray Parker Jr.
31	2	BOHEMIAN RHAPSODY* Queen
31	2	REET PETITE* Jackie Wilson
31	5	HAPPY CHRISTMAS (WAR IS OVER) John Lennon
30	1	AGADOO Black Lace
30	1	AS LONG AS HE NEEDS ME Shirley Bassey
30	1	JUST LOVING YOU Anita Harris
30	1	SIDE SADDLE* Russ Conway
30	1	THEME FROM A SUMMER PLACE Percy Faith
30	2	BREAKING UP IS HARD TO DO Neil Sedaka
30	2	OH CAROL Neil Sedaka
30	2	PARANOID Black Sabbath
30	2	TRUE LOVE Bing Crosby and Grace Kelly
30	2	YOUNG GIRL* Union Gap featuring Gary Puckett
30	3	TAKE MY BREATH AWAY* Berlin

'Love Is All Around' was still on the charts at the end of 1994.

Only 24 of the 53 records that have spent 30 or more weeks on the chart have reached number one (marked by an asterisk *). Five of the records, those by **Wink Martindale, Mike Sammes Singers, Jane Birkin and Serge Gainsbourg, Percy Faith** and **Bing Crosby and Grace Kelly**, were the only hits by those artists.

'Leader Of The Pack' by the **Shangri-Las** holds the unique distinction of having been a hit on four different labels, Red Bird, Kama Sutra, Charly and Contempo.

MOST CONSECUTIVE WEEKS ON CHART

56	**RELEASE ME** Engelbert Humperdinck
55	**STRANGER ON THE SHORE** Mr. Acker Bilk
48	**RELAX** Frankie Goes To Hollywood
42	**MY WAY** Frank Sinatra
40	**RIVERS OF BABYLON** Boney M
39	**I LOVE YOU BECAUSE** Jim Reeves
39	**TIE A YELLOW RIBBON ROUND THE OLD OAK TREE** Dawn
38	**A SCOTTISH SOLDIER** Andy Stewart
38	**WHITE LINES (DON'T DON'T DO IT)** Grandmaster Flash and Melle Mel
36	**I BELIEVE** Frankie Laine
36	**I PRETEND** Des O'Connor

34	**CHIRPY CHIRPY CHEEP CHEEP** Middle Of The Road
33	**LOVE IS ALL AROUND** Wet Wet Wet
32	**AMAZING GRACE** Judy Collins
32	**THE POWER OF LOVE** Jennifer Rush
31	**AND I LOVE YOU SO** Perry Como
31	**GHOSTBUSTERS** Ray Parker Jr.
31	**SHE LOVES YOU** Beatles
30	**AGADOO** Black Lace
30	**AS LONG AS HE NEEDS ME** Shirley Bassey
30	**HE'LL HAVE TO GO** Jim Reeves
30	**JUST LOVING YOU** Anita Harris
30	**SIDE SADDLE** Russ Conway
30	**THEME FROM A SUMMER PLACE** Percy Faith

'Love Is All Around' was still on the charts at the end of 1994.

MOST WEEKS ON CHART
by a song in all its recorded versions

This list shows the most successful songs chartwise from 1952 to 1990. Only complete recordings of the song count - parts of songs in medley discs are not included.

Weeks		Chart Versions
165	**MY WAY**	4, all vocal
94	**AMAZING GRACE**	2, one vocal, one instrumental
79	**UNCHAINED MELODY**	7, 6 vocal, 1 instrumental
70	**ROCK AROUND THE CLOCK**	3, all vocal
68	**CAN'T HELP FALLING IN LOVE**	5, all vocal
65	**STRANGER ON THE SHORE**	2, one vocal, one instrumental
62	**THEME FROM 'THE THREEPENNY OPERA'/ MACK THE KNIFE**	6, all vocal
62	**ONLY YOU**	5, all vocal
59	**RELAX**	1, vocal
58	**JE T'AIME...MOI NON PLUS/ LOVE AT FIRST SIGHT**	4, 3 vocal, 1 instrumental
56	**DECK OF CARDS**	2, both vocal
56	**RELEASE ME**	1, vocal
56	**TRUE LOVE**	5, 4 vocal, 1 instrumental
54	**I BELIEVE**	3, all vocal
51	**IT'S ONLY MAKE BELIEVE**	4, all vocal
50	**LET'S TWIST AGAIN**	2, both vocal
	WHEN I FALL IN LOVE	3, all vocal

'Blue Monday' has spent 49 weeks on the chart by New Order, while the derivative 1992 hit, 'How Does It Feel' by Electroset, spent a further three weeks on the chart. 'My Girl', written by Smokey Robinson, has spent 43 weeks on the chart in three different versions, and a further eight weeks on the chart in two versions of a medley with another Robinson song, 'My Guy'. It also earned two weeks of chart action in a medley with 'The Way You Do The Things You Do', under the title 'A Night At The Apollo Live!' by Hall and Oates, featuring David Ruffin and Eddie Kendrick.

'Let Me Go Lover', written by Jennie Lou Carson, 'It's Only Make Believe', written by Conway Twitty and Jack Nance, 'Can't Help Falling In Love', written by Hugo Peretti, Luigi Creatore and George David Weiss and 'Unchained Melody', written by Alex North and Hy Zaret, are the only songs in British chart history to have been top ten hits in four different versions.

'White Christmas', written by Irving Berlin, has been a hit in eight different versions - by Pat Boone, Max Bygraves, Bing Crosby, Darts, Jim Davidson, Keith Harris and Orville, Mantovani and Freddie Starr. 'Unchained Melody' has been a hit in seven different versions.

'Stranger in Paradise' (written by Robert Wright and George Forrest, based on a theme by Aleksandr Borodin) and 'Theme

From The Threepenny Opera (Mack The Knife)' (written by Kurt Weill and Bertholt Brecht, English lyrics by Marc Blitzstein) have hit the charts in six versions each. A further instrumental version of the 'Theme From The Threepenny Opera', by Winifred Atwell, hit the chart as one track on the All Star Hit Parade in 1956.

The most commonly used title for a hit single is 'Tonight'. There have been 11 different hit songs called 'Tonight', by Shirley Bassey, Boomtown Rats, David Bowie, Def Leppard, Zaine Griff, Steve Harvey, Kool and the Gang, Modettes, Move, New Kids On The Block and the Rubettes. The biggest hit version was by Kool and the Gang, who took it to number two. New Kids On The Block are the only other act to take this title into the top ten, climbing to number three in 1990.

NUMBER ONE IN TWO DIFFERENT VERSIONS

Eighteen songs have been taken to number one in two different versions, as follows:

ANSWER ME
David Whitfield . . . . .6 Nov 53 for 1 wk
. . . . .and 11 Dec 53 for 1 wk
Frankie Laine .13 Nov 53 for 8 wks
(on 11 Dec 53, these two versions were placed top equal)

BABY COME BACK
Equals . . . . .3 Jul 68 for 3 wks
Pato Banton . . . . .29 Oct 94 for 4 wks

CAN'T HELP FALLING IN LOVE
Elvis Presley . . . . .22 Feb 62 for 4 wks
UB40 . . . . .12 Jun 93 for 2 wks
UB40's version was titled '(I Can't Help) Falling In Love With You'

CHERRY PINK AND APPLE BLOSSOM WHITE
Perez Prado . . . . .29 Apr 55 for 2 wks
Eddie Calvert . . . . .27 May 55 for 4 wks

DIZZY
Tommy Roe . . . . .4 Jun 69 for 1 wk
Vic Reeves and the Wonder Stuff . . . . .9 Nov 91 for 2 wks

DO THEY KNOW IT'S CHRISTMAS
Band Aid . . . . .15 Dec 84 for 5 wks
Band Aid II . . . . .23 Dec 89 for 3 wks

EVERYTHING I OWN
Ken Boothe . . . . .26 Oct 74 for 3 wks
Boy George . . . . .14 Mar 87 for 2 wks

I GOT YOU BABE
Sonny and Cher . . . . .26 Aug 65 for 2 wks
UB40 with Chrissie Hynde . . . . .31 Aug 85 for 1 wk

LIVING DOLL
Cliff Richard and the Drifters . . . . .31 Jul 59 for 6 wks
Cliff Richard and the Young Ones . . . . .29 Mar 86 for 3 wks

MARY'S BOY CHILD
Harry Belafonte .22 Nov 57 for 7 wks
Boney M . . . . .9 Dec 78 for 4 wks
Boney M's version was in a medley with 'Oh My Lord'

SINGING THE BLUES
Guy Mitchell . . . . .4 Jan 57 for 1 wk, 18 Jan 57 for 1 wk and
. . . . .1 Feb 57 for 1 wk
Tommy Steele . . . . .11 Jan 57 for 1 wk

SPIRIT IN THE SKY
Norman Greenbaum . . . . .2 May 70 for 2 wks
Doctor and the Medics . . . . .7 Jun 86 for 3 wks

THIS OLE HOUSE
Rosemary Clooney . . . . .26 Nov 54 for 1 wk
Shakin' Stevens .28 Nov 81 for 3 wks

UNCHAINED MELODY
Jimmy Young . . . . .24 Jun 55 for 3 wks
Righteous Brothers . . . . .3 Nov 90 for 4 wks

WITH A LITTLE HELP FROM MY FRIENDS
Joe Cocker . . . . .6 Nov 68 for 1 wk
Wet Wet Wet . . . . .21 May 88 for 4 wks

WITHOUT YOU
Nilsson . . . . .11 Mar 72 for 5 wks
Mariah Carey . . . . .19 Feb 94 for 4 wks

YOU'LL NEVER WALK ALONE
Gerry and the Pacemakers . . . . .31 Oct 63 for 4 wks
Crowd . . . . .15 Jun 85 for 2 wks

YOUNG LOVE
Tab Hunter . . . . .22 Feb 57 for 7 wks
Donny Osmond .25 Aug 73 for 4 wks

Take A Chance On Me, a chart-topper for Abba, also featured as one track on Erasure's number one hit EP, Abba-esque. Both **Killer**, a number one for Adamski, and **These Are The Days Of Our Lives**, a number one for Queen, featured on Five Live EP, performed by George Michael, Lisa Stansfield and Queen.

Four titles have been used twice for different songs at number one - **Forever And Ever** (Slik and Demis Roussos, both 1976), **The Power Of Love** (Frankie Goes To Hollywood in 1984 and Jennifer Rush in 1985), **Tears On My Pillow** (Johnny Nash in 1975 and Kylie Minogue in 1990), and **Woman In Love** (Frankie Laine in 1956 and Barbra Streisand in 1980).

Vanilla Ice's **Ice Ice Baby**, a 1990 number one, sampled heavily from Queen and David Bowie's 1981 number one, **Under Pressure**. Jive Bunny's three number ones were mixes featuring brief extracts of several chart-toppers.

The Eurovision Song Contest began in 1956, so the 40th contest takes place in 1995. The full list of winners, their British chart placings, British Eurovision entries and their success in the contest and in the charts is as follows:

Year	Winner	Artist/Country	UK Entry/Position
(Figures in brackets indicate highest placing in UK charts)			
1956	Refrains	Lys Assia **Switzerland**	No entry
1957	Net Als Toen	Corry Brokken **Netherlands**	All Patricia Bredin/7th
1958	Dors, Mon Amour	André Claveau **France**	No entry
1959	Een Beetje	Teddy Scholten **Netherlands**	Sing Little Birdie (12 Pearl Carr & Teddy Johnson/2nd
1960	Tom Pillibi (33)	Jacqueline Boyer **France**	Looking High High High (20) Bryan Johnson/2nd
1961	Nous Les Amoureux	Jean Claude Pascal **Luxembourg**	Are You Sure (2) Allisons/2nd
1962	Un Premier Amour	Isabelle Aubret **France**	Ring A Ding Girl (46) Ronnie Carroll/4th
1963	Dansevise	Grethe & Jørgen Ingmann **Denmark**	Say Wonderful Things (6) Ronnie Carroll/4th
1964	Non Ho L'Eta Per Amarti (17)	Gigliola Cinquetti **Italy**	I Love The Little Things Matt Monro/2nd
1965	Poupée de Cire, Poupée de Son	France Gall **Luxembourg**	I Belong (36) Kathy Kirby/2nd
1966	Merci Cheri	Udo Jurgens **Austria**	A Man Without Love (30) Kenneth McKellar/9th
1967	Puppet On a String (1)	Sandie Shaw **U.K.**	Puppet On a String (1) Sandie Shaw/1st
1968	La La La (35)	Massiel **Spain**	Congratulations (1) Cliff Richard/2nd
1969	Boom Bang-A-Bang (2)	Lulu **U.K.**	Boom Bang-A-Bang (2) Lulu/1st equal
	Un Jour, Un Enfant	Frida Boccara **France**	
	Vivo Cantando	Salome **Spain**	
	De Troubadour	Lennie Kuhr **Netherlands**	
1970	All Kinds Of Everything (1)	Dana **Ireland**	Knock Knock Who's There (2) Mary Hopkin/2nd
1971	Un Banc, Un Arbre, Une Rue (9)	Severine **Monaco**	Jack In The Box (4) Clodagh Rodgers/4th
1972	Après Toi	Vicky Leandros **Luxembourg**	Beg Steal Or Borrow (2) New Seekers/2nd
	(Come What May) (2)		
1973	Tu Te Reconnaitras	Anne-Marie David **Luxembourg**	Power To All Our Friends (4) Cliff Richard/3rd
	(Wonderful Dream) (13)		
1974	Waterloo (1)	Abba **Sweden**	Long Live Love (11) Olivia Newton-John/4th
1975	Ding-A-Dong (13)	Teach-In **Netherlands**	Let Me Be The One (12) Shadows/2nd

ABBA

1976	Save Your Kisses For Me (1) . . . . .Brotherhood Of Man **U.K.**
1977	L'Oiseau Et L'Enfant (42) . . . . .Marie Myriam **France**
1978	A Ba Ni Bi (20) . . . . .Izhar Cohen & Alphabeta **Israel**
1979	Hallelujah (5) . . . . .Milk & Honey **Israel**
1980	What's Another Year (1) . . . . .Johnny Logan **Ireland**
1981	Making Your Mind Up (1) . . . . .Bucks Fizz **U.K.**
1982	Ein Bisschen Frieden . . . . .Nicole **W. Germany** (A Little Peace) (1)
1983	Si La Vie Est Cadeau . . . . .Corinna Hermes **Luxembourg**
1984	Diggy-Loo Diggi-Ley (46) . . . . .Herreys **Sweden**
1985	La Det Swinge . . . . .Bobbysocks **Norway** (Let It Swing) (44)
1986	J'Aime La Vie . . . . .Sandra Kim **Belgium**
1987	Hold Me Now (2) . . . . .Johnny Logan **Ireland**
1988	Ne Partez Sans Moi . . . . .Celine Dion **Switzerland**
1989	Rock Me Riva **Yugoslavia**
1990	Insieme: 1992 . . . . .Toto Cotugno **Italy**
1991	Fangad Av En Stormvind . . . . .Carola **Sweden**
1992	Why Me? (59) . . . . .Linda Martin **Ireland**
1993	In Your Eyes (24) . . . . .Niamh Kavanagh **Ireland**
1994	Rock'n'Roll Kids . . . . .Paul Harrington & Charlie McGettigan **Ireland**

Save Your Kisses For Me (1)
Brotherhood Of Man/1st
Rock Bottom (19)
Lynsey de Paul & Mike
Moran/2nd
Bad Old Days (13)
Co-Co/11th
Mary Ann (42)
Black Lace/7th
Love Enough For Two (48)
Prima Donna/3rd
Making Your Mind Up (1)
Bucks Fizz/1st
One Step Further (2)
Bardo/7th
I'm Never Giving Up (21)
Sweet Dreams/6th
Love Games (11)
Belle & the Devotions/7th
Love Is.. (49)
Vikki/4th
Runner In The Night
Ryder/7th
Only The Light
Rikki/13th
Go (52)
Scott Fitzgerald/2nd
Why Do I Always Get It Wrong
(73)
Live Report/2nd
Give A Little Love Back To
The World (33) Emma/6th
A Message To Your Heart (30)
Samantha Janus/10th
One Step Out Of Time (20)
Michael Ball/2nd
Better The Devil You Know (15)
Sonia/2nd
Lonely Symphony (25)
Frances Ruffelle/10th

With six wins in total, including three in succession from 1992 to 1994, Ireland would seem to have a virtual monopoly on the Eurovision Song Contest. However, if we take a closer look at the results over the first 39 years of the contest, using the current scoring system of 12 points for first place, ten for second place, eight for third, seven for fourth and so on down to one point for tenth place, the resulting table shows UK with a commanding lead. Ireland would need to win for each of the next nine years, with UK coming nowhere, to overhaul our tally of 273 points. France, the surprise second place nation, has in recent years shown a remarkable reluctance to take part at all, but even they would need to finish in the top two places for each of the next five years, while UK misses out altogether, to overtake us.

	Country	Wins	2nd	3rd	Total	
1	United Kingdom	4	14	2	273	
2	France	5	4	7	223	
3	Ireland	6	3	1	175	
4	W. Germany	1	4	4	160	
5	Switzerland	2	3	3	156	
6	Italy	2	1	4	147	
7	Luxembourg	5	-	2	142	
8	Sweden	3	1	2	124	
9	Netherlands	4	-	1	112	
10	Spain	2	3	1	107	
11	Monaco	1	1	3	97	
12	Belgium	1	1	-	94	
13	Israel	2	2	1	90	
14	Denmark	1	-	3	85	
15	Austria	1	-	-	71	
16	Norway	1	-	1	60	
17	Yugoslavia	1	-	-	58	
18	Finland	-	-	-	31	Best: 6th
19	Greece	-	-	-	26	Best: 5th
20	Malta	-	-	1	22	

BROTHERHOOD OF MAN

The biggest victory ever recorded was by UK in 1976, when Brotherhood Of Man won 164 points for their rendition of Save Your Kisses For Me, including six top scores of 12 points. This represented 80.4% of the maximum possible that year.

North To Alaska

Seattle

Grand
Coolie Dam

Rocky Mountain Way

Atomic City

Black Hills Of Dakota

Let's Go To San Francisco
San Francisco (Be Sure To Wear Some Flowers In Your Hair)
I left my heart in San Francisco

Do You Know The Way To San José

California Dreamin'
California Girls
California Man
Hotel California

Las Vegas
Viva Las Vegas

Ventura
Highway
Last Train
To San Fernando
San Bernadino
Hollywood Nights
MacArthur Park
From New York To L.A.

Wichita Lineman

Twenty Four Hours From Tulsa

Arizona Sky

Is this the way to Amarillo ?

Red River Rock

San Miguel

El Paso

Yellow Rose Of Texas

Texas

San Antonio

Christine

a i love america born in the
ove america calling a
g in america
the king and queen of ameri
ca hello a
america calling
merica i love america
america kids
merica living in an
breakfast in
m america calling ar
erica born in the
erica hello america i love
usa the king
merica letter from am

What Made Milwaukee Famous
(Has Made A Loser Out Of Me)

Must Be Madison

Detroit City

Chicago

Kansas City

Walkin' To Missouri

Banks Of The Ohio

Kentucky Rain

Last Train
To Clarksville

Tennessee Wig Walk

Cumberland Gap

Mississippi

Nashville Cats
Nashville
Jackson

My Head's In Mississippi

All The Way From Memphis
Memphis Tennessee
Graceland

Alabama Song

Alabama Jubilee

Way Down Yonder In New Orleans
Battle Of New Orleans
Witch Queen Of New Orleans
Walking To New Orleans

alveston

The Boston Tea Party

Massachusetts

Amityville (The House On The Hill)

Buffalo Gals

Woodstock

Spanish Harlem
Brooklyn-Queens
Central Park Attack
Theme From New York, New York
Boy From New York City

Bristol Stomp

Philadelphia Freedom
Streets Of Philadelphia
Philadelphia

Delaware

Indiana Wants Me

Carolina Moon

Charleston

The Devil Went Down To Georgia
Rainy Night In Georgia
Georgia On My Mind

Tallahassee Lassie

Miami Vice
Theme

Key
Largo

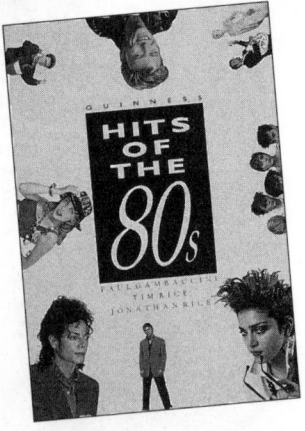

HIT MUSIC MAGAZINE

For the true fan of the UK music charts comes *Hit Music Magazine!*

The definitive companion to the weekly music charts

Designed as the perfect complement to the UK music charts, Hit Music offers a level of detail and analysis for the charts not available anywhere before. Not only are the top 200 singles and albums charts listed (as used by BBC Radio 1 FM and Top of the Pops) but much, much more!

Detailed analysis of all new entries in the singles and albums charts: producer, publisher, writer, line-up, first/last/biggest hit, album, contact number, background facts & information about each artist.

* *Every top 40 hit this year, listed by artist including its peak position*
* *The hits showing the greatest sales gains*
* *The top 10 singles and albums in America*
* *The British acts bubbling under*
* *Top 30 artists and hits of the year to date*
* *The records most likely to be in next week's chart*
* *No. 1 singles from around the world*
* *British Phonographic Industry sales awards*
* *Weekly genre charts: The Rock Chart, broadcast by Radio 1 and the Dance Chart, broadcast by Kiss-FM*
* *The Top 100 Airplay Chart*

Annual UK price is £120 (inc. p+p)

For further information and subscription details on this magazine contact:
Louise Jefferson, Hit Music, 8th Floor, Ludgate House, 245 Blackfriars Road, London SE1 9UR

The Authors

PAUL GAMBACCINI

The Frank Bruno of broadcasting, PAUL GAMBACCINI ducks and dives and somehow manages to stay in the ring. Since the publication of the previous edition of this book Paul became the last survivor of the original breakfast television team, continuing his film reviews on GMTV. He managed to slip away after his final Radio 1 documentary in December 1993 without any of the "I quit - You're fired" palaver that plagued his peers. He continued to present the Classic Countdown on Classic FM, where *Gorecki: Symphony No. 3* became the "My Way" of the chart. During 1994 Paul re-read Jack Kirby's entire 102-issue (plus six annuals) run on *Fantastic Four* as a tribute to the great man.

JONATHAN RICE

Jonathan Rice has spent 1993 and 1994 writing books (*Curiosities of Golf*, *Gordon Brittas: Sharing The Dream, Keeping Up Appearances* as well as several Guinness titles), completing his collection of number one hit singles, and getting very wet indeed watching Fulham FC. He also won £10 on the National Lottery, but he has not let the prize money go to his head. He is the same brilliant, charming and unassuming man he has always been, only £10 richer.

TIM RICE

Tim Rice's most recent work includes lyrics for the Disney animated feature film *The Lion King*, with music by Elton John. Two songs, 'Can You Feel The Love Tonight' and 'Circle Of Life' became hit singles but unfortunately failed to make the top ten in Great Britain. Almost everywhere else around the world they did much better.